T... ...OK OF

TH... ...CAN
CONGRESS

THE
OXFORD
HANDBOOKS
OF
AMERICAN
POLITICS

GENERAL EDITOR: GEORGE C. EDWARDS III

The Oxford Handbooks of American Politics is a set of reference books offering authoritative and engaging critical overviews of the state of scholarship on American politics.

Each volume focuses on a particular aspect of the field. The project is under the General Editorship of George C. Edwards III, and distinguished specialists in their respective fields edit each volume. The *Handbooks* aim not just to report on the discipline, but also to shape it as scholars critically assess the current state of scholarship on a topic and propose directions in which it needs to move. The series is an indispensable reference for anyone working in American politics.

THE OXFORD HANDBOOK OF

THE AMERICAN CONGRESS

Edited by

ERIC SCHICKLER

and

FRANCES E. LEE

OXFORD
UNIVERSITY PRESS

OXFORD
UNIVERSITY PRESS

Great Clarendon Street, Oxford, OX2 6DP,
United Kingdom

Oxford University Press is a department of the University of Oxford.
It furthers the University's objective of excellence in research, scholarship,
and education by publishing worldwide. Oxford is a registered trade mark of
Oxford University Press in the UK and in certain other countries

© The several contributors 2011

The moral rights of the authors have been asserted

First published 2011
First published in paperback 2013

Impression: 1

British Library Cataloguing in Publication Data

Data available

Library of Congress Cataloging in Publication Data

Data available

ISBN 978–0–19–955994–7 (Hbk.)
ISBN 978–0–19–965052–1 (Pbk.)

Printed in Great Britain by
Ashford Colour Press Ltd., Gosport, Hampshire

Contents

PART VI   POLITICS AND POLICYMAKING

PART VII   CONGRESSIONAL DEVELOPMENT

PART VIII   CONGRESS AND THE CONSTITUTIONAL SYSTEM

PART IX   REFLECTIONS

ABOUT THE CONTRIBUTORS

E. Scott Adler is associate professor of political science at the University of Colorado, Boulder.

Stephen Ansolabehere is professor of government at Harvard University.

Michael A. Bailey is Colonel William J. Walsh Professor of American Government in the Department of Government at Georgetown University.

Ross K. Baker is professor of political science at Rutgers University.

William Bendix is a Ph.D. candidate in political science at the University of British Columbia.

Richard Bensel is professor of government at Cornell University.

Sarah Binder is a senior fellow in governance studies at the Brookings Institution and is professor of political science at George Washington University.

Abby Blass is a Ph.D. candidate in government at the University of Texas, Austin.

David W. Brady is professor of political science and Bowen H. and Janice Arthur McCoy Professor in Leadership Values at Stanford University and Deputy Director and Davies Family Senior Fellow at the Hoover Institution.

Jamie L. Carson is associate professor of political science at the University of Georgia.

Gary W. Cox is professor of political science at Stanford University.

Douglas Dion is associate professor of political science at the University of Iowa.

C. Lawrence Evans is Newton Family Professor of Government at the College of William and Mary.

Diana Evans is professor of political science at Trinity College, Hartford, Connecticut.

Morris P. Fiorina is the Wendt Family Professor of Political Science and a Senior Fellow of the Hoover Institution at Stanford University.

Linda L. Fowler is professor of government and Frank J. Reagan '09 Chair in Policy Studies at Dartmouth College.

John B. Gilmour is associate director of the Thomas Jefferson Program in Public Policy Program and a professor of government at the College of William and Mary.

John D. Griffin is associate professor of political science at the University of Notre Dame.

Patrick Hickey is a Ph.D. candidate in government at the University of Texas, Austin.

Jeffery A. Jenkins is associate professor of politics at the University of Virginia.

Philip Edward Jones is assistant professor of political science and international relations at the University of Delaware.

Ira Katznelson is Ruggles Professor of Political Science and History at Columbia University.

Robin Kolodny is associate professor of political science at Temple University.

Frances E. Lee is professor of political science at the University of Maryland.

Beth L. Leech is associate professor of political science at Rutgers University.

Nolan McCarty is Susan Dod Brown Professor of Politics and Public Affairs in the Woodrow Wilson School and Department of Politics at Princeton University.

Mathew D. McCubbins is the Provost Professor of Business, Law and Political Economy at the University of Southern California.

Michael P. McDonald is assistant professor of government and politics in the Public and International Affairs Department at George Mason University.

Forrest Maltzman is professor of political science at the George Washington University.

David R. Mayhew is Sterling Professor of Political Science at Yale University.

Bruce I. Oppenheimer is professor of political science at Vanderbilt University.

Barry Pump is a Ph.D. candidate in the department of political science at the University of Washington, Seattle.

Paul J. Quirk is Phil Lind Chair in U.S. Politics and Representation at the University of British Columbia.

Jason M. Roberts is associate professor of political science at the University of North Carolina-Chapel Hill.

Stella M. Rouse is assistant professor of government and politics at University of Maryland-College Park.

Brian F. Schaffner is associate professor of political science at the University of Massachusetts, Amherst.

Eric Schickler is the Jeffrey and Ashley McDermott Chair in Political Science at the University of California, Berkeley.

Wendy J. Schiller is associate professor of political science and public policy at Brown University.

Charles R. Shipan is the J. Ira and Nicki Harris Professor of Social Science and Professor of Public Policy at the University of Michigan.

Randall W. Strahan is professor of political science at Emory University.

Tracy Sulkin is associate professor of political science at the University of Illinois at Urbana-Champaign.

Michele L. Swers is associate professor of government at Georgetown University.

Sean Theriault is associate professor of government at the University of Texas, Austin.

Craig Volden is professor of political science at the Ohio State University.

Gregory J. Wawro is associate professor of political science at Columbia University.

John D. Wilkerson is associate professor of political science at the University of Washington, Seattle.

Alan E. Wiseman is associate professor of political science and law at Vanderbilt University.

B. Dan Wood is professor of political science, Cornerstone Fellow and Director of the American Politics Program at Texas A&M University.

PART I

INTRODUCTION

CHAPTER 1

INTRODUCTION

ERIC SCHICKLER
FRANCES E. LEE

No legislature in the world has a greater influence over its nation's public affairs than the U.S. Congress. This remains true, despite a weakening of legislatures relative to executives both in the U.S. and around the world. Article I of the Constitution places Congress at the center of American government, giving it chief responsibility for lawmaking and designing it as the most representative branch of the national government. Over time, the Congress may not have turned out to be the increasingly dominant "impetuous vortex" that James Madison described in *Federalist* 48, but it continues to stand as an autonomous and highly consequential institution in American politics. Made up of representatives and senators whose political fortunes are to a considerable extent separate from both presidents and political parties, Congress is a site of independent legislative entrepreneurship, confrontation with presidents, investigation of public concerns, deliberation on policy and administration, and from time to time, decisive action.

The Congress's centrality in the U.S. system of government has placed research on Congress at the heart of scholarship on American politics. Since the emergence of political science as an academic discipline in the late nineteenth century, generations of American government scholars working in a wide range of methodological traditions have sought to understand Congress, both as a lawmaking body and as a representative institution.

The purpose of this volume is to take stock of this impressive, extensive, and diverse literature, identifying areas of accomplishment and promising directions for future work. We have commissioned thirty-seven chapters by leading scholars in the field. Each chapter critically engages the scholarship on a particular aspect of congressional politics. Beyond simply bringing readers up to speed on the current state of the literature, the chapters offer critical analysis of how each area of inquiry has progressed—or failed to progress—in recent decades. The chapters identify the major questions posed by each line of research and assess the answers that have been offered. The goal is not simply to tell us where we have been as a field, but to set an agenda for research on Congress for the next decade.

"Congress" means "coming together." In that sense, this volume offers a congress of its own. Like legislative assemblies, it capitalizes on division of labor and diversity of voice. It brings together accomplished scholars writing in areas of expertise able to provide authoritative treatment of key concerns. But it also benefits from multiplicity of perspective, representing scholars working within different methodological traditions. The book also seeks to achieve a balance between the enduring and the timely. In addition to broad-ranging chapters on basic questions, it also offers chapters focused on narrower topics of special contemporary importance, including partisan polarization; supermajority procedures in the U.S. Senate; and congressional war powers.

ORGANIZATION

Chapters two to six of this volume examine different approaches to the study of Congress. While most scholars employ a combination of approaches, we believe that it is crucial to assess the distinctive contributions, strengths, and weaknesses of each of the major methodological traditions. Arguably the two most prominent approaches have been behavioral studies and formal models. Indeed, one could well argue that congressional scholarship has been a key site for both the behavioral "revolution" and the rise of rational choice. The chapters by Bruce I. Oppenheimer ("Behavioral Approaches to the Study of Congress") and by Craig Volden and Alan E. Wiseman ("Formal Approaches to the Study of Congress") consider behavioral and formal analyses of Congress, with particular attention both to what has been learned from studies in these traditions and to how such studies can be advanced going forward. Both formal and behavioral studies frequently rely upon measures of legislators' preferences. The chapter by Nolan McCarty assesses the vast literature on estimating these preferences. McCarty's chapter identifies the key assumptions made in constructing measures of member ideal points and assesses the uses (and abuses) of these measures in scholarly work. While behavioral and formal approaches have been especially prominent in recent decades, interviews and direct observation have also figured prominently as approaches to the study of Congress. Ross K. Baker's chapter surveys the many challenges involved in observational research, while also testifying to its unique value and continued utility. While observational approaches have become less common in recent years, there has been a revival of historical work on Congress since the 1980s. Ira Katznelson's chapter traces the promise inherent in this historical turn and what he sees as missed opportunities—thus far—in linking the study of congressional history to broader themes in American political development.

The "electoral connection" rests at the foundation of Congress's place in the American political system. We commissioned four chapters that consider aspects of congressional elections. Jamie L. Carson and Jason M. Roberts review the literature on House and Senate elections, covering such issues as incumbency advantage, candidate emergence, and partisan tides in election outcomes. While the literature on congressional campaigns has been slower to develop than that on election outcomes and incumbency, Tracy Sulkin's chapter demonstrates that considerable progress has been made in recent years on such topics as how candidates choose positions and issues in campaigns, the type and quality of information provided to voters, and the relationship between campaigning and governing. We also include chapters examining what is known about the processes and effects of two key aspects of the electoral system: Michael P. McDonald offers a careful look at basic and cutting-edge issues in congressional redistricting, and Robin Kolodny navigates the difficult waters of campaign finance.

A departure in this volume from past efforts to take stock of the Congress literature is an extended examination of "representation and responsiveness." More specifically, we commissioned a series of chapters designed to tap into the diverse meanings of representation. These include *descriptive representation*: Michele L. Swers and Stella M. Rouse examine the extent to which Congress "looks like America" and what this means for congressional politics and policymaking. A chapter on *bicameral representation* examines the effects of representing two different types of constituencies in two different chambers. Stephen Ansolabehere and Philip Edward Jones take stock of *dyadic representation*: they examine the strong connections—ties forged in both policy agreement and personal relationships—that link individual lawmakers to their constituencies. We include a chapter on *allocative representation*, because constituents consider their members' ability to bring home a fair share of government largesse an important aspect of representation, albeit one perennially decried by presidents and the nation's editorial pages. Diana Evans synthesizes the extensive literature on pork barrel politics in Congress, examining what scholars have learned about who gets what, why, and with what effects on legislative coalitions and electoral outcomes. David W. Brady focuses on *collective representation*, the aggregate responsiveness of Congress to national public opinion. Finally, John D. Griffin traces the factors that drive the *public's evaluations of Congress*, highlighting the extent to which public dissatisfaction with Congress stems from sources beyond discontent with the policies it enacts.

A crucial question is how the 535 members of Congress organize themselves and their institution once they arrive in Washington. Part V brings together six chapters on congressional institutions and procedures. Political parties and committees have long been the two cornerstones of congressional organization; the chapters by Randall W. Strahan and C. Lawrence Evans review the extensive bodies of work that have shaped our understanding of these core features. We also include more specialized chapters on important features of legislative organization. Gregory J. Wawro takes on one of the most publicly salient—and politically important—recent developments: the increased frequency of obstruction in the Senate and the development of what has been called the "supermajority Senate," in which sixty votes are required to approve most major policy initiatives. Gary W. Cox and Mathew D. McCubbins provide a synthetic account of a core problem faced by any legislature: how to allocate plenary time, given the shortage of time relative to proposals that could potentially command support. They place the U.S. Congress in a comparative perspective, while underscoring important House–Senate differences. A recurrent theme in legislative studies has been efforts to reform the way Congress operates. E. Scott Adler's chapter reviews the scholarship on congressional reform drives and calls for scholars to apply their empirical and theoretical insights to the complex business of evaluating and recommending legislative reforms. Part V on congressional organization concludes with John B. Gilmour's chapter on the budget process, a subject that has been a particular focus of reformers over the years—and one that has come to occupy an increasing share of Congress's attention.

The main reason to care about congressional organization is that it shapes the way Congress makes policy, and, at least potentially, policy outcomes themselves. Six chapters focus on important facets of politics and policymaking. The dramatic increase in party polarization since the 1980s has marked a major transformation in congressional politics, with consequences reverberating throughout the political system. Brian F. Schaffner reviews the growing literature on the return of high levels of party polarization to Capitol Hill. Paul J. Quirk and William Bendix examine the processes, quality, and effectiveness of congressional deliberation. Sean Theriault, Patrick Hickey, and Abby Blass turn to how members make their most public decisions as they cast roll-call votes. Beth L. Leech synthesizes the literature on lobbying, highlighting how research regularly calls into question conventional wisdom on lobbyists' influence. John D. Wilkerson and Barry Pump focus on legislative entrepreneurship and coalition-building. A major question underlying each of these chapters is how the various features of the policymaking process impact Congress's ability to fulfill its lawmaking responsibilities. Sarah Binder's chapter, which concludes this part, tackles the "macro" question of explaining legislative productivity and gridlock.

Dramatic changes in congressional politics and policymaking in recent decades have coincided with renewed attention to the development of congressional institutions. We commissioned chapters on the development of three basic institutions: elections, party leadership, and the committee system. Wendy J. Schiller sheds light on how the politics and processes of congressional elections evolved over time and lays down an ambitious research agenda for extending scholarship in this area. Jeffery A. Jenkins sets in historical context the relatively powerful, institutionalized party leadership of the contemporary era, tracing what is known and still needs to be uncovered about its evolution over time. One of the central questions in historical work on Congress has been how the House came to adopt a system of majority rule that greatly limits the minority's ability to obstruct business, while the Senate grants very substantial protections to the minority. Douglas Dion's chapter analyzes the key issues involved in understanding how the House and the Senate have balanced—or failed to balance—majority rule against minority rights.

A major promise of historical scholarship on Congress is to relate the legislative branch's evolving structure and processes to broad themes in American political development, such as the transformation in the role of the national government and the building of national administrative capacity. Richard Bensel's chapter on "Sectionalism and Congressional Development" illuminates regional conflict—specifically, an enduring divergence between a wealthy, capital-rich, technologically advanced "core" and a largely rural "periphery"—as a key driver of institutional development in Congress. He makes the important point that, when sectional conflicts cut across the parties, autonomous congressional institutions, such as standing committees, become more powerful; but when sectional conflicts overlap with partisan divisions, party conflict in Congress escalates and committees are weakened.

One of the clear implications to emerge from the literature on congressional development is that one cannot take for granted that Congress will maintain its place in the constitutional system. We include three chapters that focus on Congress's relationship with the other branches. B. Dan Wood's chapter on "Congress and the Executive Branch: Delegation and Presidential Dominance" and Linda L. Fowler's chapter on "Congressional War Powers" each point to the many challenges faced by the legislative branch as it confronts an executive branch that enjoys numerous advantages in battles for influence. By contrast, the chapter by Michael A. Bailey, Forrest Maltzman, and Charles R. Shipan highlights the complex, interdependent relationship between the legislative and judicial branches. Even as judicial policymaking has expanded, Congress has many tools to respond to and to shape the federal bench, which belies any simple claim that power has migrated from Congress to the courts.

The volume concludes with reflections from two distinguished scholars who have played leading roles in shaping the Congress literature—and in the study of American politics more generally. Morris P. Fiorina's chapter traces the rise of rational choice-based approaches to the study of Congress in the 1970s and 1980s, highlighting the ease with which this intellectual transition occurred. In contrast to some scholarly communities that became embroiled in pitched battles between competing theoretical approaches, Fiorina argues that basic rational choice concepts gained rapid acceptance in the study of Congress, in part due to the willingness of the field's leading scholars to draw upon new methodological tools.

This methodological openness is personified by Richard F. Fenno, perhaps the most influential Congress scholar of the twentieth century. While Fenno's early work was heavily influenced by sociological concepts such as "role," "norm," and "socialization," his classic *Congressmen in Committees* (1973) was a turning point in the incorporation of rational choice concepts, embracing as it did an analysis that takes its starting point from the individual member's goals. Fenno's subsequent work was exemplary of what can be learned through interview-based and observational approaches that may seem, on the surface, distant from rational choice modeling. Nevertheless, Fenno continued to draw upon rational choice's signature focus on the incentives and aspirations of individuals. Fiorina also highlights the continuing vibrancy of debates within the rational choice tradition. Rather than giving rise to a homogenization of perspective, rational choice-oriented scholars continue to engage in lively disputes on such questions as the nature of party power in Congress and the function of committees. In short, Fiorina's chapter underscores the progress that congressional scholarship has made, a theme that also emerges from many of the chapters in this volume. New theoretical approaches and empirical tools have enabled each new generation of congressional scholars to build upon and move beyond the insights offered by earlier generations.

David R. Mayhew's chapter suggests that there is considerable continuity in the ways in which Congress scholars have approached this institution, even as their theoretical lenses have changed. In particular, from Woodrow Wilson's *Congressional Government* (1885) to leading works in rational choice of the past decade, scholars make claims that involve both "highlighting" and what Mayhew calls "localism." That is, scholars highlight particular aspects of legislative politics, putting them in sharp relief by pushing aside other important features, which complicate the picture being drawn. Theoretical accounts also exhibit temporal localism, in that they tend to fit current conditions but falter when applied to other periods. Mayhew's chapter contends that political scientists have succeeded in capturing basic truths about congressional politics, but each of these truths is more time-bound than is generally acknowledged. Mayhew depicts a field of study that has advanced, but in fits and starts, and with a persistent blind spot when it comes to grappling theoretically with change. Mayhew also raises the possibility that theoretical traditions can get bogged down—a state in which "highlighting builds on highlighting"—rather than engaging with new realities. Instead, fresh research may be needed to speak to the contemporary Congress, especially to current public concerns about an institution perceived as consisting of "mediocre slackers given to nastiness, pork-barreling, corruption, extremism, broken processes, [and] lapdog behavior toward presidents of their own party" (Mayhew, p. 890).

The Fiorina and Mayhew chapters encapsulate crucial perspectives, which we urge readers to keep in mind as they reflect on the contributions collected in this volume. The two chapters concur that the Congress field has benefited from theoretical and empirical innovation. The next generation of scholars will build upon a far more extensive knowledge base and theoretical infrastructure than was available in the past, while confronting the many unanswered questions and undertaking the promising research agendas laid out in the substantive chapters in this volume. The two chapters, however, do give rise to somewhat different assessments of the field's current trajectory. While Fiorina conveys considerable optimism about the current state of the field, Mayhew suggests that "a new behavioral revolution steeped in on-site experience" might be in order, given what he sees as a disconnect between current Congress scholarship and the contemporary realities of Capitol Hill (p. 890). The chapters in this volume should allow readers to measure the progress that has been made and to assess whether current theoretical and empirical approaches have indeed fallen into a "rut" that requires more dramatic rethinking and new theoretical departures.

PART II

STUDYING THE CONGRESS

....

CHAPTER 2

BEHAVIORAL APPROACHES TO THE STUDY OF CONGRESS

....

BRUCE I. OPPENHEIMER

As a graduate student at the University of Wisconsin preparing for my Ph.D. comprehensive examinations nearly forty years ago, I had the great good fortune to read a then recently published volume *Congress: Two Decades of Analysis*, co-authored by Ralph K. Huitt and Robert L. Peabody (1969). Not only did it contain six of Huitt's most important articles on Congress, including four classics that had previously appeared in the APSR, but it also opened with Bob Peabody's insightful essay "Research on Congress: A Coming of Age" (1969). In it Peabody analyzed and evaluated the research on Congress in the post-World War II era, as the sub-field made the transition from largely traditional and reformist writings to more systematic behavioral and empirical social science. For my immediate purpose, pulling together what at the time seemed like an extensive literature and being able to draw upon it to answer a potential exam question, Peabody's essay was invaluable. More importantly, however, the essay provided thoughtful perspectives on how far the behavioral study of Congress had come in little more than two decades, why enormous strides had been made, what still needed to be done—and some thoughts on how the goals he set forth could be achieved in the decades ahead. As I began work on this chapter, I recalled the Peabody essay, reread it, and again found it a tool that could extricate me from a difficult challenge. How could I make sense of the behavioral research on

Congress that had been enriched with an additional four decades of scholarly activity? Thankfully, Bob Peabody provided a foundation, an organizational structure, and a set of expectations. (Have we reached the goals he posited?)

So Bob Peabody's essay will serve as the starting point for this chapter. In briefly summarizing it, I will establish a benchmark from which we can begin to evaluate the progress that the behavioral study of Congress has brought to our understanding of the workings of the institution over the past four decades: the actions of its members, individually and collectively; the changes that have occurred in its organizational structure, rules, and procedures; and the role that political parties and party leaders play in influencing decisions, among other things. My analysis will not be exhaustive. Instead, I will focus on particular topics that, I find, illustrate both the strengths and shortcomings of the congressional research enterprise. (Some of those topics will be the major themes of other chapters in this volume.) Those topics include: the decline in the study of committees; the linking of the study of process to its policy consequences; the progress in parsing out the influence of constituency, party, and ideology on member behavior; the growing attention to institutional change and, with it, the movement away from cross-sectional to over-time analysis; the dominant focus of research on the House of Representatives and its members and the insufficient attention paid to the Senate until recently; and the increasing reliance on a limited range of empirical measures and methodological approaches.

The examination of these topics, taken together, hopefully provides a sufficiently representative overview that will allow me to draw appropriate conclusions about the state of behavioral research on Congress—how it has evolved, whether it asks and answers important questions, in what direction it is headed, and whether course corrections are needed. My perspective will not be uncritical, although there is much about which the community of congressional scholars can be justly proud. If this chapter results in a serious attempt to address our shortcomings as a scholarly community, I will consider that a bonus.

PEABODY REVISITED

Bob Peabody's analysis of the state of the literature on congressional behavior is both analytical and prescriptive. After discussing the value and shortcomings of the "traditional, legalistic, and reformist" studies that dominated the congressional literature from Woodrow Wilson's writing of *Congressional Government* (1885) until the mid-twentieth century, some of which continued to appear well into the 1960s (Burns 1963; Bolling 1965; Davidson, Kovenock, and O'Leary 1966), Peabody examines the evolution of behavioral–empirical studies, beginning with the qualitative phase and through the quantitative one (Peabody 1969, 3). Peabody credits early works of Stephen Bailey (1950), Bertram Gross (1953), Ralph Huitt (1961), and Lewis Anthony

Dexter (1957) as path-breaking in moving the study of Congress beyond "formal and legal descriptions," to focus on attitudes and behaviors of members and staff (Peabody 1969, 10). To that list one should also add Donald Matthews' highly influential volume *U.S. Senators and Their World* (1960). In addition to asking different types of questions, these researchers also integrated the theories and approaches of other social sciences, in order to develop a more systematic understanding of Congress and its members. Importantly, they moved the scholarly study of Congress out of the university library, observing behavior on Capitol Hill and interviewing the participants, not just reading the formal record and journalists' accounts of what transpired.

Peabody notes other substantive areas where the qualitative arm of behavioral research on Congress had begun to flourish: the two most fruitful were the study of committees and the study of parties and party leadership. In a series of cross-sectional (or limited time period) studies of individual committees—Jones on Agriculture (1961), Fenno on Appropriations (1962) and on Education and Labor (1963), Robinson (1963) and Cummings and Peabody (1963) on Rules, Manley on Ways and Means (1965), among others—often initially in articles and then in major books that followed, the study of congressional committees exploded. Despite the focus on single committees and on limited time frames, these studies engaged a range of sociologically-based social science theories, including systems, role, group, and exchange, to develop hypotheses, guide analysis, and structure findings. They allowed consumers of this research to start theorizing about variation across committees. Given that this research was undertaken at the apex of the Era of Committee Government, the fact that so many scholars gravitated around the study of committees is hardly surprising.

The second major path, although less frequently chosen, focused on parties and party leaders. Clearly, Ralph K. Huitt's article "Democratic Party Leadership in the Senate" (1961) provided a context and a stimulus for additional work. Even the reputed master of the Senate, Lyndon Johnson, was seen to be constrained by the senators' responsiveness to their constituencies and by the attachments to somewhat autonomous committees requiring the Senate leader to help "individual senators to maximize their effectiveness" and to structure policy alternatives in a way that a maximum number of senators could support (Peabody 1969, 15). Together with the companion studies of majority (Ripley 1969a) and minority (Jones 1970) party leadership in Congress, as well as with Froman and Ripley's work on the Democratic whip system in the House (1965) and with the study of leadership contests (Polsby 1963; Peabody 1966, 1967), the literature presented what, in comparison to the earlier, traditional writing, was a far more complete picture and analysis of the workings of parties, leaders, and party organizations.

The analysis of hard data and the use of systematic interview schedules was included in several of these and related studies. What clearly separates them from previous work, however, is the engagement of political scientists with a level of access to the congressional process and to members of Congress through participant observation and elite unstructured, but not unscientific, interviewing that had been absent in earlier work.

Although qualitative analysis dominated the early behavioral study of Congress, Peabody gives equal attention to quantitative studies, which also began to thrive. Just as in the urban politics literature of that period, there was a parallel concern with questions of power and influence. Beginning with an article by Shapley and Shubik in 1954, scholars focused on power and coalition formation. In a form of analysis that is a precursor to Krehbiel's (1998) contemporary work, Shapley and Shubik calculate the differential power of members and "observe the relative positions of the straight-party pivotal men in the House and Senate, the President, and also the 2/3-majority pivotal men in the House and Senate" (1954, 789). Riker and Niemi (1962) later refined this work in a study of roll calls during the 86th Congress.

Certainly, no quantitative article of the period has had the long-term impact of the Miller and Stokes classic piece on constituency influence on member roll-call behavior (1963). By examining the paths and level of congruence between constituency attitudes and member votes on three policy dimensions, Miller and Stokes provided a groundbreaking perspective on why constituency influence on member behavior varies across policy and on how it is mediated through member perception of constituent attitudes and the member's own policy preferences.

Receiving equal attention from Peabody as the Miller–Stokes article, although surprisingly not having its lasting influence, is Raymond Wolfinger and Joan Heifetz's (1965) analysis of the limits of the Democratic presidents' influence on the behavior of the party's members, and especially of the countervailing influence of southern conservatives. The authors test two competing theories, offering to explain the difficulties Democratic presidents faced in garnering support from their own party members in Congress: the "textbook theory" and the "insiders' theory." The former argues that the lack of electoral competition in the South results in southern members having seniority advantages and disproportionate institutional control. The latter places much of the responsibility for the regional differential in congressional influence on the northern Democrats, who, it is argued, leave the House to run for other political positions rather than reaping the benefits of congressional seniority. Wolfinger and Heifetz gather and analyze data and find qualified support for the textbook theory, while rejecting most of the assumptions of the insiders' theory.

Peabody also devotes a section of his essay to the development of more sophisticated approaches to the analysis of roll-call behavior. He acknowledges that the study of roll calls dates back at least as far as A. Lawrence Lowell's (1902) piece, and that work by Stuart Rice (1928) in the 1920s established measures of party cohesion and likeness well before the behavioral movement of the post-World War II era. It was not until V. O. Key, in *Southern Politics in State and Nation* (1949), reawakened interest in these measures by examining the cohesion of southern Democrats, Republicans, and all Democrats in Congress that political scientists renewed their attention to the use of roll-call analysis. Subsequent major books by Julius Turner (1951) and David Truman (1959) provide more in-depth analysis of the competing influence of party and constituency on roll-call voting. This was part of an effort to engage in a more systematic and scientific analysis of behavior. Casting roll calls, after all, was clear behavioral activity. The behavior was measurable and highly reliable. Replication, a scientific canon, was easy.

The next step was to aggregate and analyze roll calls in a meaningful way. Peabody credits Duncan MacRae, Jr. (1958) and David Mayhew (1966) with important efforts in creating and analyzing roll calls across a range of policy dimensions. Both employed substantive policy dimensions rather than a single underlying ideological one and found variation at the level of constituency responsiveness and party line voting across dimensions.

In his evaluation of the roll-call studies, Peabody also discusses the general short-comings of relying on roll-call votes alone, especially in an institutional setting where the most important decisions were usually made in a less public setting, not on the floor. Peabody does not mention problems researchers faced in that era when they wanted to make roll-call vote score comparisons over time and across chambers. Many scholars undoubtedly made these comparisons, although they were well aware of the limitations of the data for making comparisons across congresses. It was several decades before Poole and Rosenthal (1991) would create the NOMINATE data, allowing for valid over-time comparisons.

Although he separates studies into those that are primarily qualitative in their approach and those that are primarily quantitative, Peabody notes that many congressional scholars employed an integrative approach and let technique be guided by the specific research question. In particular, he cites three major studies of the period: Matthews' book on the Senate (1960); Fenno's *The Power of the Purse* (1966); and Bauer, Pool, and Dexter's decade of research that led to the publication of *American Business and Public Policy* (1963). Importantly, these scholars and others set a tone for the behavioral study of Congress that has continued until the present day. There has been a consistent tolerance for a wide range of research approaches in an inclusive scholarly community. In the 1950s and 1960s, that open attitude was a catalyst for the growth in the number of investigators and in the quantity and breadth of research on Congress. Research on Congress clearly outstripped the study of other American political institutions. The leadership in the study of courts and of the presidency, by contrast, was far more protective of traditional approaches and resisted the theoretical and methodological innovations of new generations of scholars who, by comparison, received a more welcoming reception into the study of Congress. In another chapter in this volume, Mo Fiorina concurs with this perspective, although his primary focus is on the acceptance of formal approaches to the study of Congress.

All of this did not happen by accident. Three critical factors made the advancement of the behavioral study of Congress smoother: the APSA Study of Congress Project; the APSA Congressional Fellowship Program; and the afore-mentioned attitude of well-established congressional scholars. Beginning in 1953, the APSA began placing political scientists and journalists in congressional offices, where they served in staff capacities for a year. Although it is difficult to measure the direct effect of the program on the resulting change in the nature of congressional scholarship, the program has clearly had a major influence on the course of research by providing researchers both with first-hand experience, as participant observers, and with access to those involved in decision-making. In addition, it has undoubtedly served to attract young scholars of political institutions to the study of Congress.

Less well known to the present-day congressional research community is the impact of the Study of Congress Project on the course of behavioral research. Begun in 1964 under Huitt's leadership, it initially engaged twenty-five political scientists in a meeting designed to discuss the direction of research on Congress. Peabody quotes Huitt's initial working paper, which challenges those gathered to build on the "descriptive and prescriptive work" of earlier scholars and to develop a more complete analysis of "Congress, its subsystems, and its relations with its environment" (as quoted in Huitt and Peabody 1969, 68). By the end of 1964, fourteen projects were underway under the auspices of the Study of Congress, and others were added in the next year. Many of these studies were later published as part of the Little, Brown Study of Congress series. Not only did the Study of Congress project jumpstart behavioral study of the institution, but it imposed direction on the collective enterprise. The landscape was divided up in a way intended to maximize coverage and to foster complementarity across the various studies. Yet these constraints did not seem to stifle innovation.

The influence that Huitt, Dick Fenno, and others had in making the study of Congress inclusive rather than exclusive and in establishing a tolerance for a limitless range of methodological approaches should not be underestimated. Although the resources available through the Congressional Fellows Program and through the Study of Congress were important incentives attracting new generations of scholars to study Congress, it was equally important that the only ticket for admission was for a researcher to have something to contribute. This did not mean that the work was viewed uncritically, but rather that the first concern was whether there was something to be learned from a given piece of research. Fortunately, this spirit persists.

Peabody's optimistic analysis of what congressional scholars had achieved in two decades concluded with expectations for the future of research. Although he recognized that there would be a reward for a continuation of established work, he acknowledged that future progress in the study of Congress depended on the capacity to develop theory at various levels. At the lowest level there was a need to "convert isolated facts into working hypotheses and, ultimately, into tested generalizations" (1969, 70). Second, he argued that there was a need to understand variation across members, committees, leaders, and chambers in the form of middle-level theory, as opposed to relying on a series of separate behavioral descriptions. Finally, he held out hope for the development of a "general, or overarching, theory of congressional behavior" (1969, 71). Such a theory would not only understand the behavior of internal congressional actors but would also include others in the governing system and stretch over time and cross-nationally. Peabody correctly believed that a good deal of low-level generalization was already underway and some middle-level theory was proceeding, but he argued that the last goal could best be achieved if "a team of congressional scholars should undertake a comprehensive, long-range, well-organized, and well-financed study of Congress and national public policy-making" (1969, 72).

Without the financing and coordinated direction to the research enterprise, Peabody argued we would come to rely on "a continued proliferation of individual studies" that would not do the job. He feared that individuals without sufficient time and resources would be "like the proverbial blind men examining the elephant: each of us feels and understands only a part. The relationship of the part to the whole is almost impossible for any one scholar to capture" (1969, 73).

The fact that Peabody briefly acknowledged the need to understand Congress over time also reveals much about the first two decades of the behavior study of Congress. With few exceptions (Polsby 1968; Cooper 1971; Young 1966), the historical research on Congress upon which congressional scholars relied was from an earlier period and very traditional in approach, employing a modest amount of archival material and drawing largely on secondary and tertiary sources. One of the unanticipated consequences and excesses of the behavioral revolution in the study of Congress was a disdain for historical institutional research. Most scholars were rejecting historical work out of hand, as a return to a more traditional (and rejected) approach to the study of political institutions and/or as a task to be left to historians. They did not appreciate how historical analysis could contribute to a behavioral understanding of the contemporary Congress and to an understanding of institutional stability and change.

The vision that Peabody and others shared for a well-funded, carefully coordinated enterprise to direct the scholarly study of Congress did not come to fruition. Instead we have spent forty years as independent entrepreneurs in—at best—a loosely coop-erative marketplace engaged in the behavioral study of Congress and legislatures more broadly. And, although we certainly have not fulfilled the challenge that Peabody set forth, we need to acknowledge what we, as congressional scholars, have been able to achieve. I will argue that we have done better in understanding member behavior and institutional workings than Peabody's blind men did, and we have a better sense of the whole and not just of the parts, even if a fully encompassing behavioral theory of Congress is still well out of reach.

COMMITTEES

The study of committees continued to flourish in the years immediately follow-ing the Peabody essay. Rohde and Schepsle (1973), for example, gained access to committee assignment requests and provided important theoretical understanding and empirical tests of this pathway to influence in the House. More critically, two major studies that for the first time examined variations across committees were published. Dick Fenno's classic, *Congressmen in Committees* (1973), provided the theo-retical underpinnings for analyzing variation across committees that had been lacking previously. His concepts of member goals, environmental constraints, and strategic premises established frameworks that congressional scholars quickly adopted. And, as he applied them to empirical findings about six House committees, Fenno gave us important initial steps to generalization and a broader theory of member behavior in committee selection and in the collective behavior of members on committees. Through no fault of Fenno's, congressional scholars have largely focused only on the process implications of this work and have given relatively little attention to the implications for committee decisions that Fenno discusses in the last chapter. Often one feels that many have just taken away the three goals that members seek in committee assignments (reelection, good public policy, and influence within the House), and have not fully appreciated the broader theoretical contributions of the book. At the most elementary level, variation in the mix of member goals in different committees, conditioned as it is by a variety of environmental constraints and strategic premises, affects the influence particular committees have over public policy and, in turn, how effectively Congress competes with other institutional players for policy dominance. In addition, although the book primarily focuses on House committees, Fenno does provide a chapter that examines variation across Senate committees and offers important conclusions about differences between House and Senate committees.

In his book on Senate committees, *Who Makes the Laws?* (1972), David Price develops a different approach from Fenno's in analyzing variation across committees. He focuses on how three Senate committees vary in the way they perform six different policy functions (instigation and publicizing, formulation, information gathering, interest aggregation, mobilization, and modification) and gives considerable attention to the level of centralization versus pluralism in committee decision-making, as well as to the role of different committee chairs. In the end, he applies the findings about behavioral variation to the influence that each committee has over the different stages in the passage of major pieces of legislation. Perhaps because Senate committees are not as important to the parent institution as House committees are, Price's book proved less influential than Fenno's in defining the conceptual framework to which congressional scholarship on committees subsequently adhered. It remains, however, the major study of Senate behavior to appear between Matthews (1960) and Sinclair (1989).

Both Fenno and Price provide a level of generalization that was lacking from earlier single committee studies, offer conceptual richness that was previously missing, and suggest the tools for grasping variation across committees. The one thing that was still absent, however, was a grasp of behavioral variation across time. These studies, as well as the earlier ones on single committees, were all undertaken during the Era of Committee Government. Although there was variation across committee, there was limited variation in the role of the committee system as a whole. In general, committees and committee chairs were strong. Seniority played a critical role. Committees tended to be autonomous of the parent chamber. Parties, party organizations, and party leaders were comparatively weak. And most scholars and observers assumed that these parameters would persist.

By the mid-1970s, however, these accepted principles for describing and analyzing the Congress in the post-World War II period were no longer fully accurate. And a new generation of APSA Congressional Fellows began informing colleagues about the changes that were occurring and about their behavioral manifestations (Ornstein 1975; Rohde and Ornstein 1977; Dodd and Oppenheimer 1977; Smith and Deering 1984). In their descriptions of the changes and analysis of their impact, these scholars and their contributors examined, among other things, the impact of the election of committee chairs, the Subcommittee Bill of Rights, the new budget committees and process, the use of multiple referrals, and the change in the committee assignment process. In addition, others (Rudder 1977; Oppenheimer 1977) updated earlier work on key House committees, documenting significant changes from conventional wisdom. They found that committees' internal distribution of authority and responsiveness to the majority party leadership, as well as the roles they played, were very different from the accounts drawn by the single committee studies of only a few years earlier.

The importance of this new wave of work on committees was threefold. First, it updated the descriptive and analytical findings about how Congress and its committees worked. The Era of Committee Government would become a thing of the past within a few years. Second, it led many scholars to question whether the strong prior focus on institutional stability and unchanging incentives influencing member behavior was a mistake. Instead, congressional scholars needed to focus more on institutional change and its impact on member behavior. Third, it gradually turned congressional research away from the study of committees (first, to the study of subcommittee government, and then to the growing influence of parties and party leaders) as the locus of decision-making in Congress. In addition, it should be noted that the research on change in Congress focused almost exclusively on the House of Representatives, because the changes came first to the House and were seemingly of greater magnitude than those in the Senate, and because committees were more central to the operation of the House and to the differential influence of its members.

Especially as the power of parties and party leaders continued to grow in the three-plus decades following the revolution of the 1970s, there was a marked decline in the attention that congressional scholars paid to committees. With certain notable exceptions—including an important research interchange over whether or not committees were composed of preference outliers who biased outcomes and the nature of the collective action problems that committees were able to address (Hall 1987; Krehbiel 1990, for example) and more recent work that grapples with conditions that facilitate and hinder committee change (Adler 2002; Aldrich and Rohde 2000)—what is most notable is the relative absence of work on committees. Clearly, Larry Evans addresses this void more fully in another chapter in this volume. Although committees may be less important to the workings of Congress and have less bearing on the success, influence, and loyalties of members, they remain important. Yet, with few exceptions (Evans 2001; Strahan 1990), we lack the richness of understanding of their workings that the single committee studies of the 1960s provided. Furthermore, we do not have a sense of variation in operation and influence across committees that Fenno, Price, and, later, Smith and Deering provided.

If congressional scholars veered away from the study of congressional committees, increasingly their attention focused on the growing influence of parties and party leaders and on the new resources they possessed to influence the legislative agendas. Recent scholarship has put forward competing theories to explain the seeming increases in party voting and party cohesion.

What many of those engaged in the study of the "revolution" that was occurring in Congress in the 1970s did not immediately appreciate was that Congress is always changing, albeit to greater or lesser degrees. This became more apparent in the decades following the end of the Era of Committee Government. Importantly, the situation also provided an impetus to study the development of Congress and the behavior of members over longer historical periods.

PARTIES AND PARTY LEADERS

Congressional researchers analyzing the changes that were occurring in the 1970s perceived the decline in the influence of committees as redistributing influence in two different directions. The first involved the devolution of influence from committees and committee chairs to subcommittees and individual members. Initially, this seemed to be the stronger thrust of the changes that were occurring. The second direction was the revitalization of the party caucuses and a centralization of power in party organizations and party leaders. By the late 1970s, the shortcomings of subcommittee government in meeting collective action problems and the growing capacities of party leaders had become apparent. Party leaders had begun to exploit more fully the additional authority they had received over such things as committee assignments, the selection of committee chairs, sway with the Rules Committee, multiple referral of bills, and use of the budget process, among other things. These developments made it clear that influence and decision-making had become more centralized and that any near-term return to committee government was highly unlikely. As this transpired, the work of congressional scholars shifted as well.

Interestingly, this work came on the heels of some very fine research (Brady, Cooper, and Hurley 1979), which showed the long-term decline of party voting in Congress. Throughout the early 1970s, that was certainly an accurate conclusion. However, as research began to appear analyzing the growing power of party and party leaders, especially in the House, in the aftermath of the Subcommittee Bill of Rights, others began to document the electoral and constituency-based changes that strengthened the hand of party leaders. The gradual movement of conservative southerners into the Republican Party in the aftermath of the Voting Rights Act was changing the ideological composition of the two parties in Congress. The most notable impact was a closing of the split between southern and northern Democrats in Congress, which had existed since 1937, and the declining significance of the conservative coalition. In his book *Parties and Leaders in the Postreform House*, David Rohde (1990) pulls together both the internal and the external changes that resulted in the growing strength of parties and party leaders in the House and introduces the concept of "conditional party government"—a theory that would receive further development in subsequent work he and John Aldrich undertook. Not only does Rohde analyze how changes in the leadership and party powers within the House and in the composition of the Democratic membership affected the levels of party voting and party cohesion, but he also discusses the polarizing effect of the Reagan presidency in cementing moderate, and even some fairly conservative, Democratic members to their party in the years following the 1982 election.

Additional richness in documenting the changes that had occurred and the way in which the Democratic party leadership was using the new tools in its possession is provided by Barbara Sinclair (1995), partly on the basis of her role as a participant observer in 1978–79, and again in 1987–88, in the office of Jim Wright (D-Texas), first as Majority Leader and then as Speaker. Couching her analysis in a principal agent approach, Sinclair is able to link the growing strength of party leadership with the greater ideological homogeneity of Democratic House members and their districts. Members are willing to grant parties and leaders more authority when they know that the leadership will not use it in a manner that will cause them electoral difficulties. Leaders are then able to use these new powers to resolve collective action problems, holding the party membership together in order to enact partisan priority legislation. When the party's members and the constituencies they represent are ideologically diverse, by contrast, members resist giving power to the leadership, lest their party leaders force them to support legislation that will make them electorally vulnerable and go against their own personal policy preferences. The costs simply outweigh the benefits. As important as the theory underpinning Sinclair's analysis is, the documenting of all the efforts that majority party leadership undertakes in terms of communication, agenda structuring, and constructing majorities on the floor offers a perspective that goes beyond a simple spatial approach, to an understanding of the influence that party and party leaders play in affecting outcomes.

In *The Logic of Congressional Action* (1990), Douglas Arnold contributed both theory and case analysis to our understanding of the important role party or coalition leaders play in structuring legislation so that their members can support it. He argues, for example, that leaders win the support of members by making it so that the benefits of legislation occur in the near term, while the costs are moved into the future—a procedure that enables members to avoid short-term electoral accountability for those costs.

Although arguing that the strength of parties and party leaders in the House had been of longer duration than Rohde or Sinclair claimed, Cox and McCubbins provided another major angle on their importance of understanding collective behavior in members (1993). They view the collective action problem as ensuring the distribution of federal largesse, and they see the party leaders' decision to vote together as the indicator of a party position on legislation.

These perspectives, however, did not go unchallenged. In Chapters 1 and 8 of *Pivotal Politics*, Keith Krehbiel (1998) argues that there are both theoretical and empirical shortcomings to the work of those who find increased influence of parties and party leaders in Congress. He tests the predictions of a unidimensional, ideologically-based spatial approach against those based on partisan theories and finds that the former produces superior performance. Krehbiel concludes: "to the extent that lawmaking outcomes in the United States are not approximate legislative-median outcomes, the explanation seems not to be found in a theory of party strength in legislatures" (1998, 185). Krehbiel's analysis clearly stimulated a wide array of research, some supporting and others challenging his arguments. Some deal with agenda-setting, others with rule changes, and yet others with arguments over dimensions. One problem underlying many of these efforts is an assumption that the voting behavior of members is an accurate indication of their underlying ideological preference, when in fact roll-call votes are preferences that have already been subjected to the influence of party and party leaders. More importantly, despite the intensity, quantity, and quality of the scholarly debate about the relative importance of party and party leaders in affecting member decisions and outcomes, I question whether the debate over the competing influence of party, ideology, and constituency factors over member behavior has been much advanced, even while it has been refined. We may have a better theory and measurement, more stringent tests, and better conceptualizations; but are we any closer to answering the questions about the relative influence of competing factors in affecting the behavior of members, either as individuals or collectively? At times, I am uncertain whether we have advanced knowledge much beyond that available in the works of Julius Turner (1951) and David Truman (1959). Thus I share in part Steve Smith's conclusions in *Party Influence in Congress* (2007), where he takes to task many of those involved in the ongoing debate and argues that the search for direct party effects is likely to remain frustrating. In the end he concludes: "political science has not done a very good job in sorting through the conceptual issues. In fact, I think some recent literature has muddled them" (Smith 2007, 216).

Perhaps, instead of struggling to specify the relative importance of party, ideology, and constituency for member behavior, we need to be asking different questions. I suggest two here. First, under what conditions are party, ideology, and constituency likely to play a smaller and a larger role in member behavior? Second, does the relative influence of these factors vary depending on the types of decisions being made? Narrowly, research attempting to answer these questions might examine the types of roll-call votes on the floor (procedural, amendments, final passage), or of floor votes versus committee votes. More broadly, it may involve analysis of a range of behaviors that have policy consequences—committee and subcommittee preferences, choices about issues on which to focus time and resources, and so on. The main lesson is that we need to start shedding more light and less heat on a central question in the study of Congress. Sean Theriault takes steps in this direction (2008; see also his chapter on roll-call voting in the present volume). Most recently, Frances Lee's book *Beyond Ideology: Politics, Principles, and Partisanship in the U.S. Senate* (2009) contrasts ideologically-based partisan conflict in the Senate with partisan conflict that arises from other sources, especially from presidential agendas.

STABILITY AND CHANGE

In contrast with the seemingly endless debate over the relative influence of party and party leaders, congressional scholars have made far greater strides in the analysis of institutional change and its implications for member behavior since Peabody's evaluation. With few exceptions, the behavioral study of Congress in the 1950s and the 1960s focused only on narrow time slices. As I mentioned previously, there was an underlying assumption that Congress, and perhaps political institutions generally, were subject only to incremental changes. For many scholars in the 1960s, the modern Congress began at the end of World War II, although it was assumed to be relatively unchanged in the Era of Committee Government, which began in the years following the revolt against Speaker Cannon. So it was natural that most research focused on the analysis of the features of the institution that fostered its stability and on how change was effectively resisted or short-lived. Mistrust of historical work as being linked to the more traditional study of Congress meant that few scholars embarked on research that did not focus on the modern Congress.

There were some notable exceptions. Clearly, Nelson Polsby's seminal piece on "The Institutionalization of the U.S. House of Representatives" (1968) demonstrates how much could be learned by examining member behavior over long periods of time. For example, it sensitized scholars to the way in which context affects the incentives of members either to stay or to leave office and to the impact that increasing length of service has on the institution (the selection of leaders, the growth in internal complexity, and the development of a seniority system, among other things). But, once institutionalized, the workings of the House and the behavior of its members were seen as relatively unchanging. Joe Cooper's (1971) research, most notably (but not limited to) his study of the development of the committee system, provided valuable insights into the importance of broader social and political context on the behavior of members and into the establishment and alteration of institutional structures. And most American institutions graduate students in my cohort found James Young's (1966) engaging analysis of Washington political life in the early nineteenth century on the syllabus in their Congress classes. We did need to know that Congress had a history, and we need to know something about its development. But it was now a mature and stable institution. Our job was to describe, study, and analyze an institution that was no longer changing very much. In the aftermath of the Reorganization Act of 1946, the modern Congress came into existence and would endure.

Thus, what occurred to the workings of Congress in the early 1970s and what a new generation of APSA Congressional Fellows began to report in their research came as a shock to many, and some dismissed it as an aberration. In two collections, *Congress in Change* (Ornstein 1975) and the first edition of *Congress Reconsidered* (Dodd and Oppenheimer 1977), congressional researchers were informing their colleagues and students that much of the accepted knowledge of Congress was no longer accurate. From the impact of the election of committee chairs to the new budget process to the subcommittee bill of rights to changes in the Ways and Means Committee and the Rules Committee to the use of multiple referrals, the War Powers Act, and the legislative veto, a seemingly new landscape was being created to which members and party leaders were having to adapt.

Initially, many of those engaged in writing about this groundswell of change assumed that they were dealing with an exceptional and brief period of major institutional change, perhaps akin in magnitude to the one that occurred in 1910. Thus the expectation was that some new stable era would replace the Era of Committee Government and that it might take a few years for things to settle. From a personal perspective I can attest to the fact that, when Larry Dodd and I collaborated on the initial volume of *Congress Reconsidered*, we did not anticipate that there would be a need for subsequent editions or, if there were subsequent editions, that they would entail a greater number of new than of revised articles. But then the power of parties and party leaders continued to increase, the conservative coalition for all practical purposes disappeared, increasingly large numbers of women and minorities were being elected, the amending of the budget process gave reconciliation real importance, the seemingly permanent Democratic majorities were displaced in a Republican revolution, the speakership briefly became as powerful as it had been in the era of the tzars, committee chairs were term-limited, and so on. At some point we, and others who had written about the changes of the 1970s, came to realize that Congress is a political institution in a constant state of change, which is sometimes more rapid and of greater magnitude than at other times. If anything, the period from the end of World War II until 1970 was exceptional because of its relative stability. (And a careful analysis would reveal that a great deal of change occurred within the Era of Committee Government.) Far more importantly than to provide a rationale for new editions of *Congress Reconsidered*, the realization that Congress was much less stable than had previously been thought had profound effects on the behavioral research on the institution and its members. Cross-sectional or limited time research was largely discarded and replaced by time series and broader historical scholarship. Instead of studying particular rule changes or reform efforts at a particular time, the newer literature took a longer-term perspective and tried to generalize about the conditions under which changes would occur (Binder 1997; Schickler 2001). Analysis of historical data has resulted in the rejection of long-accepted wisdom about such things as the development of floor leadership (Smith and Gamm 2005), the use of the filibuster (Oppenheimer 1981; Binder and Smith 1997; Wawro and Schickler 2006; Koger 2010), or the reelection behavior of members (Carson, Engstrom, and Roberts 2007). Rarely does published work focus on activity in a single Congress or in a limited time range. Instead there is an effort to generalize more broadly, understand variation over time, develop grander theory, and analyze the long-term development of the institution.

In undertaking these types of analysis, we have been fortunate to have some guidance from scholars who have more experience in historical research on Congress. Earlier pieces, such as Cooper and Brady's (1981) study of the power of speakers, make us aware of the dangers of drawing comparisons without substantial grounding in context. And there is a healthy debate between those who see members as shaping institutional change in order to meet their strategic goals and those who recognize the importance of context and path dependence.

For all the advantages we reap from the focus on longer time periods—in terms of understanding the sources of variance, building broader generalizations, and contributing to the overall development of a theory of Congress (goals consistent with Peabody's view of the proper direction of congressional research)—something has been lost in the neglect of cross-sectional work. Perhaps we have now a deficit by comparison with the rich descriptive and analytic research on contemporary Congresses, committees, leaders, and issues, which was so prevalent and useful in the 1950s and 1960s. Do we have a firm grasp on how committee assignments are now made, on how committee chairs are selected, on which committees are more successful on the chamber floors and why, on the relative distribution of influence within committees, on how party leaders use the resources available to them to hold their membership together, and an understanding of how contemporary features of the legislative process affect the capacity of Congress to influence major contemporary issues of public policy? Or is research that addresses these questions of legislative behavior now less valued because it does not contribute to a grand theory of Congress or give us a broad perspective of variation over time? Perhaps an analogy with literature could make my point more clearly. If everyone is trying to write the great American novel, is there anyone left to author great short stories?

RESEARCH ON THE SENATE

For a variety of reasons, much of the research on congressional behavior until recent years has focused on the House of Representatives and its members. Political scientists found House members more accessible than senators. The larger House membership meant a large N when doing statistical tests, allowing for the inclusion of more independent variables and increasing the likelihood of uncovering statistically significant findings. It was a well-accepted fact among congressional scholars that committees were more important in the House than in the Senate, both in terms of the influence of individual members and in terms of focus in decision-making. To the degree that congressional research concentrated on committees, it only made sense that scholars would gravitate around the House rather than around the Senate. Finally, the all-encompassing nature of Matthews' seminal book on the Senate may have served as a barrier that few scholars were willing to challenge. With rare exceptions, such as the previously discussed book by Price on Senate committees and Fenno's residual coverage of the Senate, both in *The Power of the Purse* (1966) and in *Congressmen in Committees* (1973), the Senate remained largely untouched for nearly a quarter of a century. Instead, findings about the House were often assumed to apply to the Senate, although some research on the House featured occasional caveats about generalizing to the other chamber. And the dramatic changes that occurred in the House in the 1970s often had more muted counterparts in the Senate. Perhaps the one major exception was committee jurisdictional reform, where the enactment of the Stevenson committee reforms stood in sharp contrast to the House's failure to adopt most of the recommendations of the Bolling committee (Davidson and Oleszek 1977; Davidson 1981).

With the publication of Barbara Sinclair's *The Transformation of the U.S. Senate* (1989), there began a gradual recognition of how the House-dominated literature offered a skewed and incomplete view of Congress. Sinclair demonstrated, through a series of empirical tests, that the centerpiece of Matthews' analysis of the Senate of the 1950s, the concept of folkways, no longer held. Her analysis documented a marked decline in apprenticeship, specialization, reciprocity, comity, and institutional loyalty. Sinclair argued that the folkways frustrated the goals of the large number of liberal Democrats, whose ranks swelled following the 1958 election. Over time, folkways were replaced with a behavioral norm of individualism, which altered both the behavior of individual senators and the overall workings of the institution. In addition, Dick Fenno's series of books on five senators and his study of a more comparative character, *Senators on the Campaign Trail* (1996), provided a perspective on the linkage between running for the Senate and governing and on the wide variation across senators and state contexts. Subsequent studies by Lee and Oppenheimer (1999) and by Schiller (2000) focused on the important attributes of the Senate that were not present in the House and on the individual and collective effects of those features. The former study analyzed the implications of the apportionment basis of the Senate for a range of behavioral differences across senators on the basis of the populations of their states, including representational contact, competitiveness of elections, campaign financing, committee choices, and strategic opportunities, as well as the effect of apportionment of policy outcomes. Schiller examined the consequences of dual representation in the same geographic constituencies by same state senators, as each tries to establish an individual identity and opportunities for conflict and cooperation. A series of conferences, one at Vanderbilt and the other, in two stages, at Duke and the University of Minnesota, led to the publication of two edited volumes (Oppenheimer 2002; Monroe, Roberts, and Rohde 2008). The former includes a range of articles that contrast findings on the Senate with conventional wisdom on the Senate largely on the basis of House research, while the latter includes research that focuses on the impact of parties in the Senate.

In addition, there has been a rich, largely Senate-based vein of research on the role of the filibuster (Binder and Smith 1997; Wawro and Schickler 2006; and Koger 2010), which has provided excellent historical analysis of the development and changes in the frequency of filibusters and their impact. In addition, Koger includes a broader analysis of a range of delaying tactics, the circumstances under which they are used, and a contrast of filibuster frequency over time in the House and the Senate. Seemingly, over the past decade or so, congressional scholars have recognized that the Senate is not just the House with fewer members, longer terms, and generally more populous constituencies to represent. And the strategic behavior of senators is not just a mirror of those engaged in by House members.

There still remain serious gaps in our knowledge about the Senate. This is especially true in the area of party leadership. Although there is a good deal of literature on the structure and workings of parties and party leadership in the House, including material on leadership selection, fund raising, committee assignment practices, and the whip systems, there is very little comparable work on Senate party leadership. This gap may be due to the fact that studying Senate party leadership focuses largely on the study of individual floor leaders rather than of organizational structures. There is nothing, in the contemporary setting, comparable to Huitt's study of Lyndon Johnson as a majority leader. Perhaps a lack of access to Senate leaders explains the absence of scholarship (Sellers 2010 is a partial exception). Preferably we might benefit from a comparative study of leadership behavior and strategy over time. Indeed, in the more personal environment of the Senate, the behavior and skills of individual party leaders may have a greater impact than corresponding features of House party leaders, who can draw on a great array of procedural controls and resources.

If our knowledge of party leadership in the Senate is limited and often anecdotal, then our understanding of the workings—bargaining, negotiating, strategizing—between House and Senate leaders is, for all purposes, non-existent. We have a sense, especially in periods when the same party controls both chambers, that the Speaker and the Senate Majority Leader will interact frequently, deciding, among other things, in which chamber a bill should be considered first, which house should take tough votes on an issue, how to use the agenda in one chamber as a bargaining chip to move the agenda in another chamber, whether to use a conference committee or to pursue other bargaining strategies to accommodate differences between House and Senate versions of legislation, and what priority to give to different pieces of legislation. These behaviors on the part of party leaders may be crucial, but there is scant reporting and nothing in the way of systematic research. Because these behaviors are not readily observable, should we assume instead that either they do not occur or, if they do, they are of little consequence? Could we develop unobtrusive measures—such as simulations, game theoretic and formal models, or measures derived from archival materials (such as oral histories)—to get some grasp on the nature of leadership bargaining across chambers? Or, if we are trying to understand the 2009–10 struggle over health care legislation, should we naively assume that Nancy Pelosi and Harry Reid simply worked in separate orbits when it came to strategizing over what provisions to include in the final bill, for example? It is disappointing to observe that, for most congressional scholars, our knowledge of working relationships between House and Senate leaders is limited to stories of cooperation between Sam Rayburn and Lyndon Johnson in the 1950s (Sundquist 1968). An overarching behavioral understanding of Congress without significant empirical work on bicameral leadership interaction is as incomplete as gumbo without Tabasco. Not only is a key ingredient missing, but the end product is flat.

Reliance on NOMINATE scores

One of the most important contributions to the behavioral study of Congress in recent decades has been Keith Poole and Howard Rosenthal's (1991, 1997) development of NOMINATE scores. Despite some methodological shortcomings that I will not discuss here (the reader should examine Nolan McCarty's chapter in this volume for a discussion of such issues), these scores are far superior to anything that was previously available to measure roll-call behavior. Regardless of whether one interprets the first dimension of NOMINATE scores as a liberal–conservative ideological indicator or as an indicator of partisan attachment (or a mixture of the two), these score are so far superior to the voting scores that congressional scholars had relied upon before that one is almost willing to overlook the flaws. (See McCarty's chapter for a discussion of the weaknesses of these other measures as well).

The most important advance made by Poole and Rosenthal is that NOMINATE scores make possible some meaningful comparisons over time, at least within broad political eras. So, although the initial assumption is that members will not change their underlying preferences and that their scores are likely to remain the same, when scores do change it is assumed that those changes are real. And it is possible to compare collectivities of members over time—in terms of their means and medians, in order to address questions (such as whether parties are more polarized), and in terms of standard deviations, in order to test for changes in party cohesiveness, for example. Moreover, Keith Poole and his assistants have provided extraordinary service to those using the NOMINATE data. It is hard to imagine that anyone could be as professionally generous with his time and resources. Although not without problems, the advantages of NOMINATE scores far outweigh many of the methodological shortcomings. And many of the problems arise from inappropriate applications, not from the scores themselves.

NOMINATE scores are undoubtedly superior to anything previously available in providing an overall measure of roll-call behavior, but I fear that researchers have become overly dependent on them as measures of both individual and aggregate

behavior, almost to the point of addiction. The ease of access and the general acceptance of NOMINATE data as valid and reliable measures of behavior have meant that
scholars are less likely to develop or use other indicators of member behavior or to
employ other methodological approaches to measure behavior. I wonder, for example, if even those who focus on roll-call votes have fewer incentives to develop other
measures. Are scholars so accepting of the existence of a single underlying dimension that they have abandoned efforts to develop secondary or other dimensions?
Certainly, earlier work by Clausen (1973) and by Sinclair (1982) made a strong case
for variation when one examined various substantive policies. There is the additional
problem that the placement of issues on the underlying first NOMINATE dimension
is dictated by the roll-call outcome itself, not predicated on where one might place
the issue on that dimension prior to the vote. Any vote that divides Republicans from
Democrats will scale on the first dimension, regardless of whether it relates to matters
of ideological dispute between liberals and conservatives. In her recent book, Frances
Lee (2009) finds that presidential cue-giving has a polarizing effect on the Senate
parties, dividing the parties on issues that do not bear any obvious relationships to
ideological questions about the role and scope of government. Others (Katznelson
and Lapinski 2006) also challenge the over-reliance on a single dimension and argue
for the inclusion of substantive dimensions like those that Clausen and Sinclair
employed in their earlier work.

  Beyond this, I have become increasingly concerned that roll-call behavior and
the availability of NOMINATE scores has reduced the incentives for congressional
scholars to examine other behaviors and to employ a broader range of methodological
approaches. I am amazed at how few research efforts are directed at other behaviors
in which members engage: decisions to move faster or to slow down the progress
of given pieces of legislation, leadership behavior in managing an entire legislative
agenda rather than an individual bill, participation in post-committee/pre-floor
substantive adjustments to the contents of bills, congressional oversight activities,
decisions over what legislation to introduce, and activity in incubating legislation
are just a few examples where either our knowledge is partial and outdated or non-
existent. Some scholars do rely on relatively easily acquired behavioral measures,
like bill introductions and co-sponsorship, although I question whether these are
indicators of great importance. To examine more complex behaviors is not an easy
undertaking, and likely involves many of the techniques first introduced by the
scholars engaged in the Study of Congress project and by their contemporaries:
observation (participant and otherwise), elite interviewing, and more generally soak
and poke approaches. And this cannot be limited to studying members in their
constituencies. To develop a more sophisticated understanding of a broader range
of congressional behaviors requires that legislative researchers spend more time
studying Congress, where it works, instead of drawing conclusions based solely on
the analysis of roll calls and other data available for downloading onto their office
computers. This is not a recommendation that scholars should limit themselves to
one or the other. Rather it is a belief that the best research requires a multi-method

approach—hardly a new idea. But I am amazed at how little scholarly publication of the past decade or more provides any indication of an inside Washington component. One might have hoped that more scholars would have followed the methodological path that Rick Hall carved with his excellent book on committee participation (1993). Although published seventeen years ago, it remains notable for both the quality of the research and Hall's willingness to delve into more complex behaviors.

Are there other reasons for this shift away from studying a broader range of member and leader behaviors and the dearth of Washington-based approaches other than the availability of NOMINATE data? Of course there are. Access to members certainly has not become any easier. With greater attention to their districts, a more family-friendly schedule, and a tendency not to have a primary residence in the Washington, DC area, the time members spend in Washington and have available to meet with congressional research scholars has diminished. Increased security measures in and around the Capitol restrict some of the casual access that scholars had prior to September 11, 2001. In addition, members are undoubtedly more wary that anything they say, even when a researcher guarantees it, will not be used with attribution. (But the relative costs of doing observation and elite interviewing have always been high, a subject discussed in more detail by Ross Baker in his contribution to this volume.) Finally, I suspect academic researchers had better House and Senate access during the sustained period of Democratic party control than from 1995 to 2007, when Republicans were in the majority. The partisan leanings of congressional scholars are likely tilted toward the Democrats, with—I suspect—more political science APSA fellows electing to spend their year in Democratic rather than in Republican offices—a definite handicap when the Republicans were in the majority. More speculatively, my impression has been that Republican House members, senators, and their staffs are generally less trusting of academic researchers than their Democratic counterparts are.

What has happened is that we now have a broadly accepted measure of behavior that is accessible at a minimal cost in terms of time and effort, while the costs involved in soak and poke methodologies on Capitol Hill have risen, and the benefits have declined. Yet there are perspectives that one can only obtain by using the latter. Perhaps one example will illustrate some of what is to be gained. During the course of research on the impact of the Senate's apportionment scheme, I undertook a series of interviews with senators, former senators, and lobbyists (among others). Often those interviews amounted to getting the interviewees' reactions to the data analysis that had already been completed. It never failed to be the case that those interviews served as a basis for verifying the prior empirical work, uncovering errors in the way we were interpreting the data, raising questions that we had not previously considered, and adding nuance to the overall findings. One of the many things that struck me during the course of those interviews is how insensitive the interviewees generally were to the magnitude of Senate malapportionment. Despite this, many suggested new perspectives that we had not previously entertained.

CONCLUSION

It is clear that the behavioral revolution enabled the congressional research community to make great strides in the study of Congress and of its members in the four decades since Peabody wrote his essay. In moving from isolated facts to tested hypotheses and generalizations, in developing a better grasp of variation across members, committees, party leaders, and chambers (and doing it over time, as well), in positing and articulating broader theories of Congress as an institution and of legislatures in general, and in putting those theories to the test, we have developed a far more complete and sophisticated understanding of the institution. As I have discussed in this chapter, though, we should not be too quick to pat ourselves on the back. There are shortcomings in the research, and some questions seem to be no closer to having accepted answers than they were in 1969. Undoubtedly, however, the study of congressional behavior has advanced, in part because a far larger number of well-trained, committed scholars has been involved in that effort since Peabody wrote. And because there has continued to be an inclusive environment, new scholars using a mixture of new and tried approaches have produced findings that have challenged conventional wisdom and added substantially to knowledge.

Compared with the early years of the behavioral study of Congress, however, the scholarly inquiry of the past forty years has been less planned and less centrally directed. A free marketplace for research has yielded sizeable returns. It supported a competitive environment, in which scholarly entry is open. No single scholar could claim ownership of a particular topic. In that sense, it is quite unlike the more planned approach at the heart of the Study of Congress, which provided a more central direction for dividing up the scope of the scholarly inquiry and other forms of support for a more defined group of congressional scholars. Peabody's concern that, without financing and without a coordinated direction of future congressional research— perhaps a larger Study of Congress project—the result would be considerably short of optimal, with an excess of narrow research projects, overlap, and duplication has fortunately not proved to be grounded. Nevertheless, when I read yet one more manuscript that rehashes or tweaks previous findings on a topic that has received more attention than it warrants, I sometimes think that greater central direction is needed in the study of congressional behavior. The formal controls that are in place, such as peer review of manuscripts and of NSF proposals, may not be sufficient to ensure that the individual energies of a talented and ambitious group of scholars are optimally employed. Small conferences on selected topics including congressional history, congressional parties, Senate research, and bicameralism have provided a catalyst for research on important, and sometimes neglected, topics. Perhaps books like this one will further efforts to set priorities for future behavioral research on Congress. I will leave it to others to assess whether these measures are sufficient to guide the future course of research or to decide whether some modern-day equivalent to the early meetings of the Study of Congress group is appropriate. And, if organized, could congressional scholars agree on topics that require attention, would they commit to undertaking research with a goal of addressing gaps in coverage, and would they seek funding to support those endeavors?

REFERENCES

ADLER, E. S. 2002. *Why Congressional Reforms Fail*. Chicago: University of Chicago Press.

ALDRICH, J. H., and ROHDE, D. W. 2000. The Republican Revolution and the House Appropriations Committee. *Journal of Politics*, 62: 1–33.

ARNOLD, R. D. 1990. *The Logic of Congressional Action*. New Haven: Yale University Press.

BAILEY, S. K. 1950. *Congress Makes a Law*. New York: Columbia University Press.

BAUER, R. A., SOLA POOL, I. DE, and DEXTER, L. A. 1963. *American Business and Public Policy: The Politics of Foreign Trade*. New York: Atherton Press.

BINDER, S. A. 1997. *Minority Rights, Majority Rule*. New York: Cambridge University Press.

——and SMITH, S. S. 1997. *Politics or Principle: Filibustering in the United States Senate*. Washington, DC: The Brookings Institution.

BOLLING, R. 1965. *House out of Order*. New York: Dutton.

BRADY, D. W., COOPER, J., and HURLEY, P. A. 1979. The Decline in Party in the U.S. House of Representatives. *Journal of Politics*, 4: 381–407.

BURNS, J. M. 1963. *The Deadlock of Democracy: Four Party Politics in America*. Englewood Cliffs, NJ: Prentice-Hall.

CARSON, J. L., ENGSTROM, E. J., and ROBERTS, J. M. 2007. Candidate Quality, the Personal Vote, and the Incumbency Advantage in Congress. *American Political Science Review*, 101: 289–301.

CLAUSEN, A. R. 1973. *How Congressmen Decide: A Policy Focus*. New York: St. Martin's Press.

COOPER, J. 1971. *The Origins of the Standing Committees and the Development of the Modern House*. Houston: Rice University Studies.

——and BRADY, D. W. 1981. Institutional Context and Leadership Style. *American Political Science Review*, 75: 411–25.

COX, G. W., and MCCUBBINS, M. D. 1993. *Legislative Leviathan: Party Government in the House*. Berkeley: University of California Press.

CUMMINGS, JR., M. C., and PEABODY, R. L. 1963. The Decision to Enlarge the Committee on Rules: An Analysis of the 1961 Vote, pp. 167–94 in *New Perspectives on the House of Representatives*, ed. R. L. Peabody and N. W. Polsby. Chicago: Rand McNally.

DAVIDSON, R. H. 1981. Two Avenues of Change: House and Senate Committee Reorganization. pp. 107–36 in *Congress Reconsidered*, ed. L. C. Dodd and B. I. Oppenheimer. 2nd edn. Washington: CQ Press.

——KOVENOCK, D. M., and O'LEARY, M. K. 1966.*Congress in Crisis: Politics and Congressional Reform*. Belmont, CA: Wadsworth.

——and OLESZEK, W. J. 1977. *Congress against Itself*. Bloomington, Indiana: Indiana University Press.

DEXTER, L. A. 1957. The Representative and His District. *Human Organization*, 16: 2–13.

DODD, L. C., and OPPENHEIMER, B. I. 1977. *Congress Reconsidered*. New York: Praeger.

EVANS, C. LAWRENCE. 2001. *Leadership in Congress*. Ann Arbor: University of Michigan Press.

FENNO, JR., R. F. 1962. The House Appropriations Committee as a Political System: The Problem of Integration. *American Political Science Review*, 56: 310–24.

——1963. The House of Representatives and Federal Aid to Education, pp. 195–235 in *New Perspectives on the House of Representatives*, ed. R. L. Peabody and N. W. Polsby. Chicago: Rand McNally.

——1966. *The Power of the Purse: Appropriations Politics in Congress.* Boston: Little, Brown & Co.

——1973. *Congressmen in Committees.* Boston: Little, Brown & Co.

——1996. *Senators on the Campaign Trail: The Politics of Representation.* Norman: University of Oklahoma Press.

FROMAN, JR., L. A. and RIPLEY, R. B. 1965. Conditions for Party Leadership: The Case of the House Democrats. *American Political Science Review*, 59: 52–63.

GROSS, B. M. 1953. *The Legislative Struggle: A Study in Social Combat.* New York: McGraw-Hill.

JONES, C. O. 1961. Representation in Congress: The Case of the House Agriculture Committee. *American Political Science Review*, 55: 358–67.

——1970. *Minority Party Leadership in Congress.* Boston: Little, Brown.

HALL, RICHARD L. 1987. Participation and Purpose in Committee Decision Making. *American Political Science Review*, 81: 105–27.

——1993. *Participation in Committee.* New Haven: Yale University Press.

HUITT, R. K. 1961. Democratic Party Leadership in the Senate. *American Political Science Review*, 55: 333–44.

HUITT, R. K., and PEABODY, R. L. 1969. *Congress: Two Decades of Analysis.* New York: Harper and Row.

KATZNELSON, I., and LAPINSKI, J. 2006. The Substance of Representation: Studying Policy Content and Legislative Behavior, pp. 96–128 in *The Macropolitics of Congress*, ed. E. Scott Adler and J. Lapinski. Princeton: Princeton University Press.

KOGER, G. 2010. *Filibustering: A Political History of Obstruction in the U.S. House and Senate.* Chicago: University of Chicago Press.

KREHBIEL, K. 1990. *Information and Legislative Organization.* Ann Arbor: University of Michigan Press.

——1998. *Pivotal Politics: A Theory of U.S. Lawmaking.* Chicago: University of Chicago Press.

KEY, V. O. 1949. *Southern Politics in State and Nation.* New York: Knopf.

LEE, F. E. 2009. *Beyond Ideology: Politics, Principles and Partisanship in the U.S. Senate.* Chicago: University of Chicago Press.

——and OPPENHEIMER, B. I. 1999. *Sizing up the Senate: The Unequal Consequences of Equal Representation.* Chicago: The University of Chicago Press.

LOWELL, A. L. 1902. The Influence of Party upon Legislation in England and America, pp. 319–542 in *Annual Report of the American Historical Association for 1901*, vol. I. Washington: Government Printing Office.

MANLEY, J. F. 1965. The House Committee on Ways and Means: Conflict Management in a Congressional Committee. *American Political Science Review*, 59: 927–39.

MATTHEWS, D. 1960. *U.S. Senators and Their World.* Chapel Hill, NC: University of North Carolina Press.

MACRAE, JR., D. 1958. *Dimensions of Congressional Voting: A Statistical Study of the House of Representatives in the Eighty-First Congress.* Berkeley: University of California Press.

MAYHEW, D. R. 1966. *Party Loyalty Among Congressmen: The Difference Between Democrats and Republicans, 1947–1962.* Cambridge, MA: Harvard University Press.

MILLER, W. E., and STOKES, D. E. 1963. Constituency Influence in Congress. *American Political Science Review*, 57: 45–56.

MONROE, N. W., ROBERTS, J. M., and ROHDE, D. W. 2008. *Why Not Parties? Party Effects in the United States Senate.* Chicago: University of Chicago Press.

OPPENHEIMER, BRUCE I. 1977. The Rules Committee: New Arm of Leadership in a Decentralized House, pp. 96–116 in *Congress Reconsidered*, ed. L. C. Dodd and B. I. Oppenheimer. New York: Praeger.

OPPENHEIMER, BRUCE I. 1985. Changing Time Constraints on Congress: Historical Perspectives on the Use of Cloture, pp. 393–413 in *Congress Reconsidered*, ed. L. C. Dodd and B. I. Oppenheimer. 3rd edn. Washington: CQ Press.

—— 2002. *U.S. Senate Exceptionalism*. Columbus: Ohio State University Press.

ORNSTEIN, N. J. 1975. *Congress in Change: Evolution and Reform*. New York: Praeger.

PEABODY, R. L. 1966. *The Ford-Halleck Minority Leadership Contest, 1965*. New York: McGraw-Hill.

—— 1967. Party Leadership Change in the House of Representatives. *American Political Science Review*, 61: 675–93.

—— 1969. Research on Congress: A Coming of Age, pp. 3-73 in *Congress: Two Decades of Analysis*, ed. R. K. Huitt and R. L. Peabody. New York: Harper and Row.

POLSBY, N. W. 1963. Two Strategies for Influence: Choosing a Majority Leader, 1962, pp. 237–70 in *New Perspectives on the House of Representatives*, ed. R. L. Peabody and N. W. Polsby. Chicago: Rand McNally.

—— 1968. The Institutionalization of the U.S. House of Representatives. *American Political Science Review*, 62: 144–68.

POOLE, K. T., and ROSENTHAL, H. 1991. Patterns of Congressional Voting. *American Journal of Political Science*, 35: 228–78.

—— —— 1997. *Congress: A Political–Economic History of Roll Call Voting*. New York: Oxford University Press.

PRICE, D. E. 1972. *Who Makes the Laws?* Cambridge, MA: Schenkman.

RICE, S. 1928. *Quantitative Methods in Politics*. New York: Knopf.

RIKER, W. H., and NIEMI, D. 1962. Stability of Coalitions on Roll Calls in the House of Representatives. *American Political Science Review*, 56: 58–65.

RIPLEY, R. B. 1969a. *Majority Party Leadership in Congress*. Boston: Little, Brown.

—— 1969b. *Power in the Senate*. New York: St. Martin's Press.

ROBINSON, J. A. 1963. *The House Rules Committee*. Indianapolis: Bobbs-Merrill.

ROHDE, D. W. 1991. *Parties and Leaders in the Postreform House*. Chicago: University of Chicago Press.

—— and SCHEPSLE, K. A. 1973. Democratic Committee Assignments in the U.S. House of Representatives. *American Political Science Review*, 67: 889–905.

—— and N. J. ORNSTEIN. 1977. Shifting Forces, Changing Rules and Political Outcomes: The Impact of Congressional Change on Four House Committees, pp. 186–269 in *New Perspectives on the House of Representatives*, ed. R. L. Peabody and N. W. Polsby. 3rd edn. Chicago: Rand McNally.

RUDDER, C. E. 1977. Committee Reform and the Revenue Process, pp. 117–39 in *Congress Reconsidered*, ed. L. C. Dodd and B. I. Oppenheimer. New York: Praeger.

SCHICKLER, E. 2001. *Disjointed Pluralism: Institutional Innovation and the Development of the U.S. Congress*. Princeton: Princeton University Press.

SCHILLER, W. J. 2000. *Partners and Rivals: Representation in U.S. Senate Delegations*. Princeton, NJ: Princeton University Press.

SELLERS, P. J. 2010. *Cycles of Spin: Strategic Communication in the U.S. Congress*. New York: Cambridge University Press.

SHAPLEY, L. D., and SHUBIK, M. 1954. A Method for Evaluating the Distribution of Power in a Committee System. *American Political Science Review*, 48: 787–92.

SINCLAIR, B. 1982. *Congressional Realignment, 1925–1978*. Austin: University of Texas Press.

—— 1989. *The Transformation of the U.S. Senate*. Baltimore: Johns Hopkins University Press.

—— 1995. *Legislators, Leaders, and Lawmaking: The U.S. House of Representatives in the Postreform Era*. Baltimore: Johns Hopkins University Press.

SMITH, S. S. 2007. *Party Influence in Congress.* New York: Cambridge University Press.

—— and DEERING, C. 1984. *Committees in Congress.* Washington: CQ Press.

—— and GAMM, G. 2005. The Dynamics of Party Government in Congress, pp. 181–206 in *Congress Reconsidered*, ed. L. C. Dodd and B. I. Oppenheimer. 8th edn. Washington: CQ Press.

STRAHAN, R. 1990. *New Ways and Means: Reform and Change in a Congressional Committee.* Chapel Hill: University of North Carolina Press.

SUNDQUIST, J. L. 1968. *Politics and Policy.* Washington: Brookings.

THERIAULT, S. 2008. *Party Polarization in Congress.* New York: Cambridge University Press.

TRUMAN, D. 1959. *The Congressional Party: A Case Study.* New York: John Wiley & Sons.

TURNER, J. 1951. *Party and Constituency: Pressures on Congress.* Baltimore: The Johns Hopkins Press.

WAWRO, G. J., and SCHICKLER, E. 2006. *Filibuster: Obstruction and Lawmaking in the U.S. Senate.* Princeton: Princeton University Press.

WILSON, W. 1885. *Congressional Government.* Baltimore: Johns Hopkins University Press.

WOLFINGER, R. E., and HEIFETZ, J. 1965. Safe Seats, Seniority, and Power in Congress. *American Political Science Review*, 59: 337–49.

YOUNG, J. S. 1966. *The Washington Community, 1800–1828.* New York: Columbia University Press.

CHAPTER 3

FORMAL APPROACHES TO THE STUDY OF CONGRESS

CRAIG VOLDEN
ALAN E. WISEMAN[*]

OVER the past half century one of the most notable developments in the study of the American Congress has been the incorporation and expansion of rational choice approaches and formal models to enhance our understanding of legislative policymaking, of internal congressional politics, and of external interactions between Congress and its broader environment. While formal models have been developed to analyze a wide range of topics in congressional studies, they have been adopted inconsistently and have had varying impacts across substantive sub-fields. We believe that much of the promise of formal approaches lies in their ability to cut straight to the heart of strategic decision-making, offering (sometimes counterintuitive) explanations of broad empirical patterns.

  * The authors thank the formal theory lunchtime workshop participants in the Ohio State Department of Political Science, who provided valuable insights during the early stages of this project, and Scott Ashworth, David Austen-Smith, Dave Baron, Jon Bendor, Gary Cox, Daniel Diermeier, John Ferejohn, Mo Fiorina, Sean Gailmard, Keith Krehbiel, Frances Lee, Neil Malhotra, Nolan McCarty, Adam Meirowitz, Gary Miller, William Minozzi, Bill Niskanen, John Patty, Dave Primo, Eric Schickler, Ken Shepsle, Chuck Shipan, Ken Shotts, and Mike Ting for helpful comments on an earlier draft.

Yet such promise is limited when formalization is incompletely exercised or when formal modelers do not make their findings readily accessible to a broad audience.

To help overcome these limitations, we take on five main tasks in this chapter. First, we define what constitutes a complete formal model, thus laying the groundwork for understanding the potential contributions of formal approaches. Second, we survey examples of how formal models have been used to study the internal politics of Congress (with a specific focus on distributive politics and coalition formation) and the external relations between Congress and other institutions (specifically examining congressional–bureaucratic relations). Third, we draw upon the development of formal models in these two areas, to identify lessons about how techniques of formal modeling can be used to overcome scholarly roadblocks commonly found throughout the study of Congress (as well as throughout political science more broadly). Fourth, we apply these lessons learned to suggest paths forward in the contentious debates regarding parties in Congress. We conclude by identifying other substantive areas ripe for further scholarly exploration via formal approaches.

A complete formal model

Congressional scholars rooted in the rational choice tradition tend to assume that members of Congress are goal-directed and take certain actions to enhance their chances of achieving those goals. Such approaches, while still controversial to some, are commonplace in the study of Congress today. However, much less work has explicitly analyzed clearly articulated formal theories of Congress and congressional policymaking. For the purposes of our discussion below, we begin by defining a *complete formal model* as a mathematical (i.e. formal) characterization of politics (i.e. model) that specifies actors, structure, outcomes, preferences, and decision criteria. These last five elements, needed to make a formal model *complete*, are detailed as follows:

(a) *Actors.* A complete formal model specifies the relevant actors for the topic being studied. Actors in models of Congress, for example, may include individual legislators, committees, parties, voters, lobbyists, bureaucrats, and presidents, as well as the Congress as a whole, treated as a single actor.

(b) *Structure.* A complete formal model identifies how the actors interact. Model structure therefore can capture such considerations as the sequence of events that actors confront and the range of actions that are available to them. The foundation for such structure might be found within codified rules (e.g. the Standing Rules of the House of Representatives) or within less codified settings, such as behind-the-scenes coalition formation processes; or model structure may have little real-world foundation whatsoever.

(c) *Outcomes*. A complete formal model specifies the outcomes that occur when the actors interact within the structure of the model. Outcomes in models of Congress include such wide-ranging results as a policy choice on a left–right unidimensional space or in a multidimensional space, division of a budget, appointment of a judge, or reelection of an incumbent member of Congress.

(d) *Preferences*. A complete formal model specifies the preferences of the actors over such outcomes. Actors might be motivated, for example, by the desire to be reelected; they could have spatial policy preferences and receive much less utility as outcomes diverge from their ideal points; or they could care about directing spending to their districts. Yet it may be costly to engage in the fundraising, information gathering, and coalition building that help achieve these beneficial results.

(e) *Decision criteria*. A complete formal model articulates the criteria that underlie actors' decisions. More specifically, a complete formal model includes assumptions about such concerns as actors' cognitive constraints (e.g. whether they optimize or satisfice when making choices), the solution concept employed (e.g. Nash equilibrium, perfect Bayesian equilibrium, or the core), and the actors' beliefs about the structure of interactions and the preferences of other actors. The default (and often unstated) assumptions in most contemporary formal models of Congress are that all actors are fully rational and fully informed about the model structure and the preferences of other actors. Yet this need not be the case.

These five elements should sound familiar to students of non-cooperative game theory, far and away the most common formal approach used to study Congress. Under such an approach, the game structure specifies the possible actions available to players and the order of play. The set of possible actions players can take each time they are faced with a decision defines their strategy set. And the commonly used Nash equilibrium concept then generates a coherent description about how the game is played, wherein all players' strategies are matched in such a way that no player can unilaterally reach a more preferred outcome by changing her own strategy alone. Thus a game-theoretic equilibrium characterizes the strategies that actors (element *a*) take within the model structure (element *b*) to help bring about the outcomes (element *c*) that they prefer (element *d*), while they are constrained by their decision-making abilities and beliefs (element *e*) and by the strategic choices of other actors. While these five elements of a complete formal model are thus immediately relevant in non-cooperative game theory, with minor modifications they also apply broadly to other formal approaches, such as cooperative game theory, social choice theory, bounded rationality models, and agent-based models.[1]

---

[1]   In cooperative game theory, for example, the model structure typically allows players to make binding agreements before and during the play of the game, and outcomes are sought that satisfy a number of normatively attractive axioms. In social choice theory, scholars are interested in how individual preferences map into collective choices over outcomes. Without relying on a specific *game structure*, social choice theorists do not typically focus on actor strategies and actions, but still tend to be interested in *model structure*, because changes in such features as the dimensions of the policy space or

Models that are incomplete in any of these elements cannot be solved mathematically so that we may derive formal principles about the workings of Congress. For example, if the possible outcomes in a strategic situation are not specified, it is impossible to know what ends actors are pursuing. If actor preferences are not specified, we cannot determine what actions they will take. Or, if their decision criteria are unspecified, we cannot discern how actors will behave in the face of complex decisions or limited information. In other words, a model without these elements relies on other (often implicit) assumptions to justify its conclusions.

As we allude above, a substantial body of literature in the rational choice tradition specifies the relevant actors and their preferences, while leaving the other crucial elements (structure, outcomes, and decision criteria) unstated. Hence, many such studies make arguments about congressional politics and policymaking (i.e. claims regarding strategic behavior and the resultant outcomes), but in so doing they rely on fundamentally unstated assumptions that, upon closer inspection, may be inconsistent with their stated premises.

We argue neither that all studies of Congress should contain complete formal models nor that all complete formal models help advance a better understanding of Congress. Rather, we define a complete formal model to clarify which types of studies we review here, and to set the stage for a clearer view of how such formal models have been used (and can be used better in the future) to study the internal workings of Congress and its important role in the American separation of powers system.

The internal workings of Congress

Formal approaches to studying the internal workings of Congress have addressed such topics as the roles of committees, rules, leaders, and bicameralism in producing policy outcomes, to name just a few areas of scholarship. Rather than recount the contributions in all of these areas, we focus here on the contributions of formal modeling in the area of coalition formation and distributive politics. We chose this area to comment upon because of its importance and because it is well suited to show the benefits of formal approaches as well as the challenges that must be overcome in adopting such approaches.

some members' veto powers lead to different model conclusions. Models of bounded rationality feature decision criteria in which actors are cognitively constrained. Rather than reasoning through all actions and their implications, these actors may rely on heuristics or simplifications, such as continuing to take an action that has worked relatively well in the past. Such models are solved either analytically or computationally, the latter being often referred to as "agent-based modeling." In most of these approaches, actors' beliefs are irrelevant (because everyone is fully informed) or are treated in special ways, for instance as following Bayes' Theorem in non-cooperative game theory, or as being cognitively limited under bounded rationality approaches. For some of the tradeoffs across these approaches, see Krehbiel (1988) and Diermeier and Krehbiel (2003), who ultimately advocate in favor of non-cooperative game theory.

Before turning to the specifics of coalition formation in the realm of distributive politics, a brief aside regarding the historical development of formal approaches in political science is worthwhile. Early work applying mathematical tools to the study of political strategy sought a high level of generality. In the area of legislative politics, social choice scholars, in particular, investigated what collective outcomes resulted from the consideration only of actors' policy preferences and of the aggregation rules that governed the collective decision. In so doing, they hoped to achieve general understandings of politics without being limited to the description of any one particular institutional setting. While yielding a variety of useful insights, these approaches were seen as reaching an impasse when scholars discovered that many such general models did not typically generate significant limitations over which policies were likely to emerge (e.g. Plott 1967; McKelvey 1976; McKelvey and Schofield 1987).[2]

Although such general social choice approaches continue to offer helpful answers to political science questions, such as identifying the existence of equilibria under broad modeling assumptions, the vast majority of formal modelers in political science have turned toward the incorporation of specific institutional structures within their (largely game-theoretic) models. The benefit of general models, where they can be used successfully, is that they do not limit our understanding to, say, one subcommittee's decision-making processes. On the other hand, to the extent that specific legislative rules and interactions matter for political behavior and policy outcomes, fully and properly characterizing those structures is essential to understanding legislative behavior.

Early formal work

This over-time trend from the general to the specific can be seen in the formal models constructed to study most areas of congressional politics. In the area of coalition formation for the division of budgets across legislative districts (commonly referred to as distributive politics), classic general studies, such as those of Riker (1962) and Buchanan and Tullock (1962), actually referred to Congress very little, as congressional politics was just one of the many broad political phenomena these scholars intended to address. These early theoretical treatments made several arguments that still resonate in the contemporary scholarly literature, including the ideas that supermajority voting rules generically protect the rights of minorities, that coalition formation can be difficult, and that adding superfluous members to coalitions is costly (and thus leads to the prediction of minimum winning coalitions).

---

[2] In more technical terms, social choice scholars were exploring the difficulty in obtaining a "nonempty core" in multidimensional settings, among other concerns. Austen-Smith and Banks (1999) offer an excellent overview and formalization of the findings of this vast literature.

Building upon these arguments, a body of scholarship emerged nearly 20 years later that imposed more explicit structure on these early authors' theoretical foundations; and, in being more explicit about actors, their preferences, their decision criteria, and model structures, this next generation of scholarship began to identify the limits and additional implications of these early scholarly arguments. Among the foundational works in this second "generation" of scholarship was a series of articles by Weingast (1979), Shepsle and Weingast (1981), and Weingast, Shepsle, and Johnsen (1981). Weingast (1979) analyzes the conditions under which legislators would collectively prefer to form universal coalitions around distributive projects instead of the minimum winning coalitions suggested by Riker. Similar to earlier works, Weingast's assumes that projects can be characterized by district-specific benefits with costs that are evenly dispersed across all districts through broad-based taxes. Yet Weingast argues that, if given the choice, legislators would prefer to commit *ex ante* to forming universalistic coalitions, whereby all members of the legislature receive some project benefits. Because an individual legislator does not know whether she will be included in any particular minimum-winning coalition, she would prefer to remove all uncertainty and increase her *ex ante* utility by pre-committing to a "norm of universalism." While Weingast notes (1979, 253) that legislators would still have short-term incentives to propose minimal-winning coalitions, he suggests potential mechanisms that the chamber might adopt to support a universalistic norm, including punishing members who deviate from this desirable practice.

Shepsle and Weingast (1981) build directly on Weingast (1979) to identify how this norm of universalism can be obtained even when project costs unambiguously exceed project benefits—that is, for the classic case of pork barrel politics. Related to this point, Weingast, Shepsle, and Johnsen (1981) establish a relationship between legislature size and the scope of distributive policy inefficiency. Denoted as "the Law of $1/n$," the result states that, if each district's share of aggregate taxes is decreasing in the number of districts, then projects should become more inefficient as the legislature increases in size (1981, 654). In other words, because a legislator's district receives all the benefits from a particular project but pays only $1/n$ of the costs, the district receives a net benefit for projects that cost up to n times as much as their benefits. Under the norm of universalism, such highly inefficient bills are nevertheless included in the universalistic coalition.

Questions and concerns

These last three works thus offer interesting insights into the size and nature of coalitions as well as into the level of inefficiency found in distributive politics. Yet, in terms of our definition of a complete formal model, these models fall short. They all clearly specify the relevant actors (individual legislators) and their preferences (more district spending, fewer taxes) over outcomes (budget divisions across districts). That said, all three of these papers lack a formal statement of the model's structure, and details regarding aspects of actors' decision criteria are somewhat ambiguous.

Specifically, rather than a process by which bills and proposals are placed on an agenda and voted upon, it appears that these models rely on an assumption that all legislators can merely add their own pet projects to the pork barrel and the norm of universalism will ensure that all pass. Agenda-setting, voting, and the specific mechanisms through which such a norm would be obtained and enforced are all left unspecified.[3]

Such lack of specificity in model structure was particularly troubling given the social choice findings at this point in time regarding the lack of a "core" of collectively preferred policies in a multidimensional policy space (see McKelvey 1976; McKelvey and Schofield 1987). More specifically, for any status quo policy, a majority can be found that prefers a different policy under almost all circumstances (Plott 1967). Because distributive politics clearly contains multiple dimensions (each legislative district being a separate dimension of spending), models that did not confront this result, but instead assumed the existence of an equilibrium through a norm of universalism (without explicitly modeling voting and amendment procedures), were not completely satisfying theoretically.

Moreover, on the empirical side of scholarship, the theoretical claims of universalism were confronted by a problematic reality, as qualitative accounts were backed up by quantitative evidence that federal outlays were far from universalistic (e.g. Bickers and Stein 1994; Stein and Bickers 1995). Thus the early work, while provocative, faced skepticism both theoretically and empirically. Many questions remained regarding the nature of coalition formation, coalition sizes, and budgetary efficiency. Unfortunately, on theoretical grounds, there seemed little way forward to overcome the general lack of equilibrium inherent in multidimensional distributive policymaking.

Overcoming obstacles

The seminal breakthrough in this area was Baron and Ferejohn's (1989) work on "bargaining in legislatures," analyzing how a legislature divides a budget, stylized as a single dollar, into particularistic projects by majority rule. Similarly to what one finds in Weingast, Shepsle, and Weingast (as well as in others), projects are particularistic in that they only provide benefits to the legislators (districts) that receive them. Unlike in these earlier works, however, the agenda formation process, possible amendments, and voting mechanisms are all fully specified, thus producing a complete formal model of distributive politics. One technical breakthrough of Baron and Ferejohn came in their explicit assumption that the legislature is governed by a recognition rule, in that proposals cannot be made unless a legislator is recognized, each member having a specific probability of recognition.

In their baseline closed-rule model (1989, 1183–4), Baron and Ferejohn assume that the game begins with a randomly recognized legislator making a policy proposal to

---

[3] This point is raised and addressed by Niou and Ordeshook (1985), who derive universalism in a specific game-theoretic model based on constituency motivations.

divide the dollar. After the proposal is made, it is subject to an up-or-down vote and, if it obtains at least a minimal majority of "yes" votes, the allocation ensues as defined by the proposal. If, however, the proposal fails, another round of recognition occurs, where a randomly chosen legislator makes another proposal that is subject to the same terms of debate and agreement. The model allows for discounting across proposal periods, so if a proposal fails, the size of the resource available for distribution effectively shrinks before the next proposal is made.

Whereas without a clear bargaining structure little could be said formally about how governmental resources are distributed, the structure of this complete formal model generated clear equilibrium predictions.[4] In the model's equilibrium, the dollar is divided in the first period among a minimal majority of legislators, and all coalition partners (other than the proposer) receive exactly the amount of resources necessary to make them indifferent between accepting the proposal and rejecting it (and thus moving to the next round of bargaining). The model's structure also allows the *politics* (agenda-setting, amending, voting) of distributive policymaking to be examined explicitly, rather than hidden behind assumed norms of behavior. Substantively, the Baron and Ferejohn results illustrate how proposal power (which diminishes with open voting rules and rises in coalition partner impatience), coalition size (which rises above minimum winning when amendments are possible), and variance in budgetary divisions depend on key parameters of the model.

Beyond these substantive points, it is not an overstatement to say that the technology deployed in their analysis revolutionized the field of formal legislative studies, as it was readily portable into numerous subsequent works.[5] Baron (1991), for example, builds on the Baron–Ferejohn structure to model legislative bargaining over particularistic goods with explicitly derived distributive taxation, which allows him directly to engage the works of Weingast (1979), Shepsle and Weingast (1981), and Weingast, Shepsle, and Johnsen (1981) so as to identify when universalism might be obtained, and when legislatures (such as Congress) might engage in efficient (or inefficient) policymaking. McCarty (2000) adds a presidential veto to the Baron–Ferejohn model, with implications for divided government and electoral rules. Ansolabehere, Snyder, and Ting (2003) build upon Baron–Ferejohn technology to analyze legislative bargaining in bicameral settings (analogous to policymaking in the House and the Senate) and demonstrate conditions under which malapportionment and supermajoritarian rules can induce unequal divisions of expenditures across

---

[4] Because proposals could continue endlessly in this model (until one of them passes), the Baron–Ferejohn model is a type of infinitely repeated game. A commonly understood result, or folk theorem, associated with infinitely repeated games of this sort is that they tend to contain an infinite number of equilibria, depending on the nature of the "punishments" associated with deviating from equilibrium behavior. Another technological innovation that Baron and Ferejohn employ is a stationary equilibrium refinement, wherein the same proposal is made in all instances of players confronting identical game structures moving forward from the point of their proposal, which allows the authors to focus on a single equilibrium to their game.

[5] Moreover, the Baron–Ferejohn results have proven to be quite robust to variations in fundamental assumptions (e.g. Kalandrakis 2006).

legislative districts. Volden and Wiseman (2007) use the Baron–Ferejohn technology to analyze legislative policymaking over district-specific particularistic projects and collective goods, and identify (among other things) why institutional reforms aimed at curtailing particularistic incentives may actually induce greater levels of particularistic spending.

The Baron–Ferejohn approach, and the development of other similarly complete formal models with explicit proposal and voting structures, allowed scholars to revisit the classic "Law of $1/n$" and coalition size debates, which had seen a clash between theoretical and empirical findings. Primo and Snyder (2008), for example, demonstrate that, for a wide range of taxation and distribution assumptions, the "Law of $1/n$" does not hold; and in fact the opposite result can be easily obtained. Chen and Malhotra (2007) incorporate a Baron–Ferejohn bargaining protocol into a model of bicameral legislative policymaking. This allows them to establish a relationship between the number of members in a legislature's upper chamber (n), the ratio between the number of members in the lower and upper chambers (k), and the amount and inefficiency of legislative spending. This resultant "Law of k/n" states that total legislative spending decreases in the ratio of lower-to-upper chamber seats. Chen and Malhotra continue to find that total legislative spending increases in the number of seats (now in a legislature's upper chamber); and they illustrate that both of these results more cleanly match the empirical literature (and their own analysis) than the classic "Law of $1/n$" does.

Regarding coalition sizes, complete formal models with explicit proposal and voting stages offered insights into when one might expect to find universalistic coalitions, minimum-winning coalitions, and all sizes in between. Carrubba and Volden (2000), for example, develop a formal theory of logrolling where a legislature votes over packages of particularistic projects that have distributive costs. One of the more novel contributions of their theory is that they embed their model of legislative logrolls in a broader model of endogenous rule choice, thus creating a "metagame" that allows them to characterize the chamber's *ex ante* choice of voting rules (e.g. minimum majority versus supermajority versus unanimity), given the *ex post* incentives of legislators to renege on logrolls after their own bills have been passed. Taking a different approach, Snyder (1991) and Groseclose and Snyder (1996) analyze how non-policy-relevant factors, such as favors or campaign contributions, might be used by interested actors (whom they label "vote-buyers") to influence coalition formation, coalition sizes, and policy outcomes.[6] Embedding their models in a spatial setting where legislators have preferences over a one-dimensional policy space in addition to distributive, non-policy relevant "bribes," these authors characterize how the presence of one vote-buyer (Snyder 1991) or two competing vote-buyers (Groseclose and Snyder 1996) can lead to the passage of legislation that would normally not have

---

[6] An interesting extension to the vote-buying literature is developed by Dal Bó (2007) and by Snyder and Ting (2005), who analyze the dynamics of coalition formation when vote-buyers are able to make offers that are conditional on whether voters are pivotal in determining the outcome. The primary finding of these models is that vote-buyers can generally obtain their most preferred outcomes at almost no cost.

sufficient support within the chamber, and can potentially result in supermajoritarian coalitions designed to withstand attacks from the opposing side.

Lessons learned

The distributive politics and coalition formation literature has been unambiguously successful at expanding our insights about how legislators interact with each other to produce public policy outcomes. In considering the evolution of this literature over the last fifty years, certain lessons emerge that might explain this success. We highlight four such lessons here, in the hope that they can be fruitfully applied in the future to other areas of research.

First, the development of the distributive politics literature clearly demonstrates the virtues of *specifying a complete formal model*, which includes an explicit model structure. By making explicit assumptions about the sequence of play and the range of actors' choices and information, scholars have succeeded in moving beyond the foundational works in this literature, to identify the scope (and limits) of earlier works as well as the breadth of their own models' findings.

Second, the distributive politics literature has advanced as the result of *cumulative model building*. The scientific enterprise features early work setting the stage for subsequent inquiry. Foundational contributions that identify important phenomena and ask key questions (e.g. Shepsle–Weingast) can set the scholarly community on a productive course of discovery. In addition, however, the literature on distributive politics has clearly benefited from cumulative theoretical advancements, wherein later scholars build upon foundational models (e.g. Baron–Ferejohn) that help them gain leverage on different substantive and theoretical matters.

Third, scholars studying distributive politics have made substantial efforts to *account for empirical findings* with their models. Empirical stylized facts are crucial in helping formal modelers make realistic assumptions about actors, their preferences, and the structure of their interactions. Moreover, empirical implications of model results have never before been as subject to deep scrutiny and sophisticated testing as they are today. Successful theoretical contributions to our understanding of coalition formation, for example, resulted from taking seriously the empirical evidence that neither universal nor minimum winning coalitions are especially prevalent in Congress or other legislatures. Moreover, because legislative models are abstract, they can often be applied outside of Congress to legislative bodies in the U.S. or around the world. Tests of these theories in diverse settings can help advance both theoretical and empirical research.

Fourth, distributive politics theorists have successfully developed and employed *metagames* to study broad questions of institutional choice. Model variants with differing institutional structures not only allow scholars to determine how politics plays out in different settings, but also to explore why particular institutions may be chosen in the first place. Baron (1991), for example, was able to discern when open or closed rules are preferred. Carrubba and Volden (2000) identify optimal voting rules (such as majority rule in the House, or a sixty-vote cloture rule in the Senate). Similarly, Diermeier and Myerson (1999) build upon vote-buying foundations to identify how legislatures organize themselves to respond to external veto points in a separation of powers system.[7]

CONGRESS AND EXTERNAL ACTORS

Just as there has been a vast formal literature on the internal workings of Congress, so too scholars have extensively studied the relations between Congress and external actors. Interactions between Congress and the president, Congress and the judiciary, Congress and interest groups, voters and elected politicians, or states and the federal government have all received formal treatments. We once again choose depth over breadth in limiting our examination here to the interaction between Congress and the federal bureaucracy.

Early formal work

The body of scholarship that focuses on the interactions between Congress and the bureaucracy finds much of its early inspiration in the foundational work of Niskanen (1971), who treats agencies as budget maximizers and analyzes congressional control of agencies through the appropriations process.[8] The actors in Niskanen's model consist of the Congress and a representative agency. The model's structure is adapted from a microeconomic model of monopoly production, wherein the agency submits a budget request to Congress, and Congress approves or vetoes the request. Outcomes in the model include a budget for the agency and policy outputs. Regarding preferences, the agency wants as large a budget as possible, while Congress cares about agency outputs and the efficiency of agency services. In terms of decision criteria, Congress's preferences are common knowledge, while the agency's production function (i.e. how their budget maps into policy outputs) is known only to the agency and cannot be discerned by Congress on the basis of the agency's proposal. This complete formal model produced the equilibrium result that the agency is able to amass sizable budgetary slack because of Congress's notable informational disadvantage and its limited role in merely accepting or rejecting the agency's proposal.

---

[7] Related to this final lesson, however, is the third lesson above: the need for scholars to consider the insights from their theories in light of empirical evidence and the historical record. This point is particularly relevant to questions regarding institutional choice, where institutions arguably facilitate different goals at different points in time; and the theoretical justification for these institutions' creation may be somewhat unrelated to why they are sustained (and vice versa).

[8] Niskanen (2001) discusses the evolution of his thinking about bureaucracy over subsequent decades.

As instructive as this parsimonious model was, it was seen as lacking much of the politics surrounding congressional delegation to (and control of) the bureaucracy. Most notably, Miller and Moe (1983) build a complete formal model using the Niskanen structure, but also incorporating several other actors, including high- and low-demanding committees, private-sector counterparts to the agency, and competing agencies within government. They argue (and thus adopt the assumptions) that Congress: (a) has an active role in deciding the agency's budget, (b) has its own informational advantages, and (c) can engage in different types of oversight. "Demand-revealing" oversight occurs when the function characterizing Congress's demand for the agency's goods is publicly known, whereas "demand-concealing" oversight occurs when its demand function is private information. In their equilibrium analysis, Miller and Moe illustrate how demand-concealing oversight counterbalances some of the bureaucratic biases of Niskanen's model. They also show how agency competition and the privatization of tasks enhance governmental efficiency.

Banks (1989) varies Niskanen's model in a different way, giving the legislature the opportunity to uncover the agency's private information.[9] In the "closed procedure" version of Banks' model (which is similar to Niskanen's), the legislature can simply accept or reject the agency's budgetary proposal. In the "open procedure" version of the model, however, the legislature can accept, reject, engage in a costly audit to learn the agency's production function, and/or make a counterproposal to the agency. Analyzing Congress–agency budget negotiations within this framework allows Banks to identify how auditing tools might curtail an agency's agenda-setting power in the budget process, and how these tools influence the ultimate size of the budgetary request and outcome.

Building upon this modeling framework, Banks and Weingast (1992) establish relationships among auditing costs, agency design, and legislator–constituent interactions. More specifically, because higher auditing costs necessarily imply a greater informational advantage for the agency, Banks and Weingast argue that legislatures (e.g. Congress) have an incentive to ensure that agencies with high auditing costs have strong ties to external stakeholders who will inform legislators if the agency engages in inefficient policymaking. As such, constituency correspondence with legislators can serve as a substitute to agency auditing; and strategic legislators will structure agencies in such a way as to ensure that they can obtain sufficient information.[10]

Questions and concerns

While such models advanced and refined the "agency as budget maximizer" view, many congressional researchers questioned whether this approach was based on an

[9] In the two decades between the works of Niskanen and Banks, game theory advanced to include "models of incomplete information." Banks was therefore able to incorporate the ability of Congress to (at least partially) discern the nature of the agency's production function based on the information contained in the agency's budget request.

[10] Bendor, Taylor, and Van Gaalen (1985, 1987) engage similar information and monitoring topics, formulating models that yield further insights regarding the design of agencies and the utilization of legislative tools.

overly limited notion of legislative–bureaucratic relations. For example, while it had been understood since the writings of Max Weber that bureaucratic information and expertise was an important source of political influence, it was not clear that this asymmetric information was mainly over budgets and the production function for the provision of governmental services. Alternatively, perhaps, bureaucratic expertise could involve agencies bringing about better policy outcomes themselves. In particular, scholars started to confront whether bureaucrats had their own substantive policy preferences (rather than preferring simple budget maximization), whether those preferences differed from those of Congress, and whether bureaucratic information and discretion therefore led to policy outcomes that diverged significantly from those desired in a representative democracy. The well-honed tools in hand to engage congressional–bureaucratic budgetary relations seemed inadequately designed to tackle this set of concerns.[11]

McCubbins, Noll, and Weingast (1987, 1989) forcefully raised and confronted the idea that bureaucratic agencies had policy preferences apart from those of Congress and of the president, and had the ability to move policy away from the preferred outcomes of elected politicians and thus perhaps away from the desires of the American people. These authors (commonly referred to, collectively, as "McNollgast") followed aspects of the early social choice tradition in trying to ascertain what patterns could generally be revealed about the policy decisions that emerged from interactions among the president, the Congress, and a substantive policy agency, broadly construed. These three actors were each assumed to have preferences over policy outcomes in a (potentially multidimensional) policy space. Yet, falling short of our definition of a complete formal model, the model in the McNollgast works did not specify the structure and order of interactions among the actors. In terms of decision criteria and beliefs, all actors in the McNollgast setting are assumed to know each other's ideal points and the exact relationship between the policies that are chosen and the final policies that are implemented.[12]

While no equilibrium generally exists under a majority rule in such a multidimensional policy space (Plott 1967), the veto role of actors in the McNollgast models generates a set of stable equilibrium policies. The main take-away point from these models, then, was that, because various administrative procedures can influence the location of an agency's ideal point as well as which actors are involved in which decisions, the design of institutions and administrative procedures can systematically influence public policies. Hence the models demonstrate why Congress devotes

[11]   This is not to say that all formal scholarship through this era assumed that agencies care only about budgets, or that all subsequent work focused on spatial policy preferences, or that these have been the only two relevant perspectives. A wide body of work has analyzed other considerations that might motivate Congress and agencies (e.g. Fiorina's 1977 discussion of blame avoidance); but the dominant body of formal–theoretic work has considered one or the other of these two perspectives as driving congressional–bureaucratic interactions.

[12]   While McCubbins, Noll, and Weingast (1989, 440) suggest that their theory could accommodate uncertainty over actors' preferences and over policy outcomes, their analysis never explicitly accounts for these possibilities.

significant attention to questions of structure and process in the design and oversight of agencies.

While ambitious and general in scope, the McNollgast work raised many questions that their model was unable to address without a detailed structure of the interactions among key actors. First, to be consistent with the expertise and informational advantage of bureaucrats, how do these policy dynamics play out in an uncertain environment? Second, what are the tools and relative powers of Congress and of the president vis-à-vis an agency in attempting to influence policy outputs? Third, how might administrative procedures influence policy outcomes beyond simply shaping agency preferences?[13]

Overcoming obstacles

Such questions could be answered neither in the Niskanen setting, which is focused on budgets, nor in the McNollgast setting, which lacks explicit model structure. And yet the tools to answer such questions were already available in the formal theory literature. What scholars had yet to discern, however, was how to import the relevant modeling techniques appropriately into the study of legislative–bureaucratic relations and to make them accessible to a broader audience. Epstein and O'Halloran helped overcome these hurdles with respect to delegation to the bureaucracy in a series of insightful works (e.g. 1994, 1996, 1999). Piece by piece, they systematically identify how uncertainty (regarding the mapping between chosen policies and realized policy outcomes) influences the degree of discretion given to agencies.[14] Across the variants of their main model, the common actors include a congressional median voter and an executive agency, whose preferences are defined over a unidimensional policy space. Specifically, actors' preferences are represented by quadratic loss utility functions over the final policy outcome, X, thus characterizing risk-averse policymakers. Most significantly, regarding information and decision criteria, Epstein and O'Halloran incorporate a technical innovation in that they define an outcome (X) to be a function of the policy chosen (p) and of the state of nature (ω), where $X = p + \omega$, with ω representing a disconnection between the written policy and its true effect. This "policy shock" is unknown to Congress but revealed to the agency via bureaucratic expertise. Although the $X = p + \omega$ technology to model policy uncertainty was borrowed from Gilligan and Krehbiel's (1987, 1989) work on legislative signaling games (which, in turn, was borrowed from Crawford and Sobel 1982), the importation of this technology allowed scholars to focus on the policy preferences and expertise of agencies within a well-structured model of legislative–bureaucratic relations.

[13] Many of these broad points are engaged in Moe's (1989) seminal work on the politics of bureaucratic structure, in which he argues (albeit not with a formal model) that, because agencies create policy, political conflicts over policy necessarily imply that decisions about agency structures are politicized. As a result, this conflict among political interests ensures that agencies are not designed to be effective.

[14] See Holmstrom (1984) and Martin (1997) for similar approaches exploring delegation to more fully informed bureaucrats.

The baseline model structure is a sequence of events that begins with Congress setting a policy and a level of agency discretion (d) that defines the extent of policy modifications that can be made by the agency. After discretion is established, the agency learns the state of the world (ω) and modifies the congressional policy within its bounds of discretion. Model variants include a possible legislative veto of the agency's proposal and the possibility of relying on a partially informed congressional committee rather than an executive agency. Equilibrium results characterize the policy choice, the optimal level of legislative delegation, and the relations between legislative delegation, increased uncertainty, and variations in the actors' ideal points across periods (e.g. "coalitional drift," 1994: 712–15). The Epstein–O'Halloran modeling framework also facilitates comparative institutional analysis, such as identifying when a legislature and agency will strictly prefer the existence of a legislative veto or will prefer internal information gathering instead of bureaucratic discretion.

Epstein and O'Halloran's modeling framework, and their technological advancement of incorporating policy uncertainty via $X = p + \omega$, in particular, provided scholars with a new tool to engage numerous questions. Gailmard (2002), for example, uses the Epstein–O'Halloran approach to analyze how legislative delegation relates to the legislature's ability to undertake costly agency investigations, as well an agency's ability to engage in costly "subversion" activities whereby it proposes policies that are outside of its bounds of discretion, thus incurring a penalty. Volden (2002) builds upon the Epstein–O'Halloran framework to analyze how the possibility of a presidential veto yields the maintenance of high bureaucratic discretion to executive agencies and the increased reliance of independent agencies under divided government.

After a decade of scholars relying heavily on the Epstein–O'Halloran approach, Bendor and Meirowitz (2004) sought to reevaluate this research program. Their concern was that the additive policy shock and the specific risk-averse preferences, along with other canonical model assumptions, were so frequently used in combination with one another that scholars were unable to discern which assumptions were critical to which theoretical results. To address such concerns, Bendor and Meirowitz consider a much broader family of models that represent the delegation relationship between a principal (e.g. Congress) and an agent (e.g. a bureaucratic agency) and establish a series of general results about their interactions. In so doing, they parse out the necessity and importance of earlier modeling assumptions, showing that few results of this literature hinge on risk aversion but that many are dependent on the fixed and additive policy shock. They loosen such assumptions and derive a broad set of additional results, which involve such considerations as costs of specialization, monitoring, and multiple principals.

While yielding a large and fairly robust set of findings, the Epstein–O'Halloran models, like all formal approaches, faced the usual tradeoff between model complexity and tractability. For scholars who were less concerned about the role of uncertainty and expertise, the Epstein–O'Halloran approach was too constraining, as adding further relevant actors and strategic interactions often resulted in a level of complexity that did not give way to clear and understandable solutions and predictions about political behavior. Many scholars were therefore attracted to the alternative approach of Ferejohn and Shipan (1990), who present a spatial model that builds upon the classic median voter findings of Black (1948). The actors in their model consist of a congressional committee, an agency, the House median voter, a court, and a president. All actors' preferences are defined over a unidimensional policy outcome space; and all actors make rational decisions under complete and perfect information. In other words, all actors know each other's preferences and the full range of possible actions, with no uncertainty over available policy choices or how outcomes follow from those choices.

With respect to model structure, Ferejohn and Shipan begin with a preliminary model in which an agency proposes a policy, and then a congressional committee either proposes to change the agency proposal or engages in "gatekeeping," whereby no changes to the agency proposal can be considered. If the committee makes a policy proposal, the proposal is considered by the entire House, subject to an open amendment procedure. Building upon this foundation, Ferejohn and Shipan incorporate other actors including the courts, which may strike down an agency proposal through statutory review, and the president, who may veto the new congressional policy. Analysis of the model reveals the scope of congressional influence over bureaucratic policymaking in a separation of powers system, by characterizing the role each actor has in bringing about (or stopping) specific policy changes. The key permutations of the model involve the spatial ordering of actors and the temporal order in which they make policy decisions.

The simplicity and flexibility of Ferejohn and Shipan's model has facilitated numerous extensions. Steunenberg (1992), for example, builds upon a Ferejohn–Shipan framework to analyze when agency policymaking (i.e. that of Ferejohn and Shipan's model) will be more desirable to the legislature than "statutory policymaking," wherein a committee proposes legislation that is subsequently subject to House and presidential approval. Huxtable (1994) builds directly upon Ferejohn–Shipan, examining how their results are affected by the addition of a Rules Committee. More recently, Shipan (2004) analyzes a Ferejohn–Shipan model in a bicameral setting, to study the scope of congressional control over the Food and Drug Administration. In these (and many other) works, refinements to the Ferejohn–Shipan model have allowed scholars to identify how specific institutional assumptions, either involving actors or the sequence of actions, yield various equilibrium policy proposals and outcomes.

With the Epstein-O'Halloran and Ferejohn–Shipan approaches in hand, the scholarly literature has dramatically expanded in recent years, explicitly to consider the roles of different actors within and outside of Congress. In doing so, the literature has been able to return to questions from the foundational works of McNollgast and Niskanen, among others. Ting (2002), for example, revisits the McNollgast questions about agency design and control with a model that identifies when Congress would choose to assign multiple tasks to one, rather than several, agencies. Gailmard (2009) bridges the two relatively distinct camps of budget-focused and preference-focused actors and illustrates how, even if scholars are currently placing less emphasis on certain types of analytical approaches (such as the Niskanen type of assumption that bureaucrats are budget-motivated), the insights from earlier literatures can inform contemporary scholarship in a variety of interesting ways.[15]

Lessons learned

Similar to the distributive politics and coalition formation literature, formal models of congressional interactions with the bureaucracy have notably evolved over the past forty years, and have expanded our understanding of the fundamental nature of legislative delegation, bureaucratic control, and the implementation of law. Once again, relevant lessons can be drawn about how obstacles have been overcome to bring about new insights. Many such lessons in the congressional–bureaucratic relations literature reinforce those above, such as the need for complete formal models and the benefits of cumulative model building, seen clearly in both the Epstein–O'Halloran and in the Ferejohn–Shipan approaches. Beyond those points, we highlight three additional lessons.

First, scholars of congressional–bureaucratic interactions have made several gains by *building useful technologies or by borrowing them* from other fields. More specifically, the congressional–bureaucratic politics literature was clearly advanced by Epstein and O'Halloran's incorporation of the $X = p + \omega$ technology to model policy uncertainty, and by the clarity of the Ferejohn and Shipan spatial modeling approach. In both cases, the authors relied on well-understood technologies from other fields and sub-fields, but offered important contributions by appropriately applying them to a new substantive topic of interest. Bringing in models that did not capture compelling aspects of the relations between Congress and bureaucratic agencies would not have resulted in the same level of cumulative scholarly insight.

Second, a consideration of this literature also highlights the virtues of substantively appropriate *simplification*. Simultaneously considering the joint impacts of a multi-member Congress, of a hierarchical judiciary, of a diverse agency, and of other actors on the policymaking process can be analytically intractable, unless scholars are willing to make certain simplifying assumptions. Ferejohn and Shipan (1990) and the scholarship that they inspired rely on completely informed actors, and thus remain silent on issues of information and uncertainty. Yet such analytical simplification allows

---

[15] Several other studies of congressional–bureaucratic relations have relied on the insights and approaches of Epstein–O'Halloran and Ferejohn–Shipan, although not building on their modeling technologies directly. For example, Bawn (1995, 1997) focuses on the roles of different legislative coalitions and internal actors of Congress, such as committee chairs, to characterize how their positions and preferences map into choices about bureaucratic discretion and control. Huber and Shipan (2002) model the interactions between a legislature and a bureaucratic agency, where the legislature sets an initial level of bureaucratic discretion, and the agency decides what (if any) policy to implement in light of non-statutory factors, such as constituent feedback, which can lead to legislative sanctions. Boehmke, Gailmard, and Patty (2006) analyze how both bureaucratic agencies and interest groups can serve as competing sources of relevant information for Congress. More recently, Wiseman (2009) engages the topic of contemporary executive clearance, developing a model in which agency policies are subject to *ex post* oversight by an executive with divergent preferences both from the agency and from Congress.

the broad incorporation of numerous actors and institutions, while still retaining a parsimonious model that yields new and interesting theoretical insights.

Third, scholars in this field have been very willing to *refine and reassess* their modeling choices. As the congressional–bureaucratic politics literature evolved, scholars made specific modeling choices, which had a substantive and technological impact on subsequent work. While modelers have aggressively refined existing models and pushed them in new directions, this sub-field is also notable in that scholars (e.g. Bendor and Meirowitz 2004) have been cognizant of how initial modeling choices influence the subsequent literature. By reassessing the findings of canonical models and by modifying their assumptions, the breadth of these contributions can be better understood and new directions can be taken.

PARTIES IN CONGRESS

Having surveyed the literature on the internal workings and external relations of Congress in two specific settings, we have uncovered a series of lessons about the benefits of formal approaches. In this section we rely on those lessons to offer suggestions for the further development of formal approaches to the study of parties in Congress. In so doing, we seek to illustrate how important (and often contentious) areas of scholarly inquiry may benefit from the use of formal approaches. Once again, we characterize early contributions as well as the questions and concerns raised by such works. Here, however, we then examine how the lessons learned from the previous sections can be applied to help answer the questions and overcome the obstacles faced within this literature.

Early formal work

While scholars have long considered the role of parties in Congress, formal theoretic work began systematically to address congressional parties in the late 1980s and early 1990s. This scholarship corresponded, understandably enough, to a time when parties seemed to be gaining prominence in Congress. While several studies that developed during this period paved the way for contemporary research, we highlight three, in particular, that helped to set the agenda for subsequent decades.

One approach was developed by David Rohde (1991), who articulated the theory of "conditional party government," which holds that, when parties face relatively little intra-party heterogeneity but relatively substantial inter-party heterogeneity, members of the majority party empower their leaders to control the legislative agenda and to induce majority party-favorable policy outcomes. A second, complementary perspective was advanced by John Aldrich (1995), who argued that strong parties help solve numerous social choice problems (see Arrow 1951; Plott 1967; and McK-elvey 1976) that make policymaking unpredictable and problematic for the average reelection-seeking member of Congress. A third perspective was offered by Gary Cox and Mathew McCubbins (1993), who argued that the role of parties in legislatures was something analogous to the role of Thomas Hobbes's *Leviathan*. Because reelection-seeking legislators, left to their own devices, would pursue selfish goals culminating in sub-optimal (and possibly electorally destructive) policy outcomes, members of Congress are willing to sacrifice some of their individual autonomy to a party (to a legislative leviathan, so to speak). By structuring the legislative agenda, by promoting some policies over others, and by instilling party discipline in a way that facilitates an electorally valuable party brand name, the majority party thus advances the interests of its members.

Questions and concerns

While all three of these works formalized their ideas to some degree, none offered a complete formal model as delineated above. All three, for example, specified the relevant actors and their preferences (to varying degrees), yet explicit discussions of the models' structures and of the actors' decision criteria were vague or nonex-istent. As a result, the claims regarding the theories' predictions (e.g. the actions of majority party leaders) did not clearly follow from the theories' postulates, and key strategic details were left unspecified (e.g. what specific powers were ceded to leaders or what mechanisms were used to enforce party discipline). While such lingering issues might prove troublesome from an epistemological viewpoint, these scholars' arguments stimulated numerous debates and questions that were ripe for empirical and theoretical pursuits.

A central point of inquiry (and a source of much frustration) quickly emerged under the rubric of the "parties vs. preferences debate." This rubric featured the claim that congressional politics (and policy) are merely byproducts of legislators' preferences independent of party affiliation (conservatives tend to be Republicans, while Democrats tend to be liberal), rather than the result of strong partisan activities and pressures (e.g. Krehbiel 1993). In this view, members would be torn between acting in favor of their electorally induced preferences and pursuing their party's goals. Why, then, would they choose to delegate parliamentary authority to party leaders whose choices might ultimately harm their electoral prospects?

Moving beyond this broad debate, other questions emerged as scholars sought to understand the relative influences of parties in the electoral and legislative arenas, as well as to uncover the proper analytical unit within political parties. For example, what specific steps might parties take to move policy outcomes away from what would occur in the absence of such partisan activities? Furthermore, would it be appropriate (and worthwhile) to think of a party as a sometimes divided collection of voters, activists, and officeholders, and/or to think of leaders as being responsive to a majority (or even a supermajority) of party members?

Overcoming obstacles with lessons learned

As the parties-in-Congress literature stood a decade ago, scholars were unsure about how to separate parties from preferences, how to isolate the substantive actions of parties, and even how to characterize a party and say what constituted it. Over the past ten years, however, some progress has been made as formal approaches have begun to address many of these topics. Moreover, in looking ahead, one would imagine that, if formal approaches to the study of Congress are to have much value, these sorts of issues should be (at least partially) resolved through the adoption of such approaches. In this sub-section, then, we take the seven lessons learned from the distributive politics and from congressional–bureaucratic relations literatures and apply them to the questions and concerns faced by the parties-in-Congress literature. In so doing, we hope to illustrate how formal approaches can be (and have been) used to further our understanding of Congress.

Lesson I: Specify a complete formal model, including explicit model structure

While the foundational works of Rohde, Aldrich, and Cox and McCubbins generated significant scholarly interest, the relatively vague theoretical structures in these authors' works left many of their results ambiguous, and thus open to debate and misinterpretation. The imposed clarity of complete formal models could help resolve scholarly confusion over how, when, and why parties matter. Indeed, over the past decade, scholars have started to formalize the arguments found in these earlier foundational works. For example, Cox and McCubbins (2002, 2005) build on their earlier work, having a complete formal model of partisan agenda-setting in Congress. In their model, the majority party median (in a one-dimensional policy space) decides what policies are sent to the floor for consideration under an open amendment rule. In equilibrium, the majority party exerts negative agenda power whenever the status quo is closer to the party median than the floor median position is, and is thus never "rolled" by losing a floor vote. Responding to Cox and McCubbins's theoretical claims and empirical tests, Krehbiel (2007) develops a formal model of probabilistic voting in Congress that seeks to establish a reasonable null hypothesis regarding roll rates without majority party influence. Also illustrating the power of formalization, Patty (2008) obtains Aldrich–Rohde-style conditional party government results by modeling party strength as a bond which is determined endogenously by majority party members, and which is effectively sacrificed by members if they vote against the party.

Lesson II: Build or borrow useful technologies

While a wide body of qualitative and quantitative literature addresses the multiple dimensions of congressional politics and policymaking, most of the formal theoretical work on parties to date has not advanced beyond a one-dimensional policy space (implicitly building on Black 1948). The status of this sub-field stands in contrast to that of the broader collection of multidimensional models that have made in-roads in studies of distributive politics and legislative–bureaucratic relations. Beyond the spatial setting, insights and technologies from other fields and sub-fields could be appropriately applied to the study of parties in Congress. For example, models from industrial organization (within economics) and from "the theory of the firm" could be imported to study parties' internal organization and their production of public policies.[16] Similarly, while scholars consistently suggest that parties solve collective action problems (e.g. "party cartel" arguments), these models typically only rely on a prisoners' dilemma setting rather than building upon the technologies used, in order to study market cartels and other collective action problems within the field of industrial organization.[17] Alternatively, scholars might seek to adopt approaches from other fields of legislative studies and apply them to studying parties in Congress. For example, Austen-Smith and Banks (1988) develop a formal model of elections and subsequent legislative policymaking in a parliamentary democracy that speaks to the role of parties both in the electoral and in the legislative arena. Such concerns are clearly relevant to scholarship on the U.S. Congress; yet similar congressional models that simultaneously incorporate elections, legislative politics, and policy choice have yet to be developed and solved.[18]

Lesson III: Build models cumulatively

In considering the body of formal–theoretic work on parties in Congress, one clear weakness, compared to the two sub-fields discussed above, is its relative failure to engage constructively in cumulative scholarship. As suggested above, the field has not advanced very far beyond Black's basic spatial model of legislative policymaking. That said, there are a couple of notable exceptions to this general trend that exemplify the virtues of cumulative model-building. Krehbiel's (1996) pivotal politics theory represents a constructive hybrid between Black (1948) and Romer and Rosenthal's (1978) agenda-setter model, which allows him to speak to the role of political parties in producing (or inhibiting) legislation. Building directly upon Krehbiel, Chiou and Rothenberg (2003) incorporate additional actors into their model, in order to engage more explicitly the potential roles of parties in legislative policymaking under different assumptions about the scope and tools of partisan influence. Among other benefits, such cumulative work helps ensure clarity, in that all scholars building upon

---

[16] Weingast and Marshall (1988) explore possible ties between industrial organization and legislative organization.

[17] An extensive body of scholarship analyzes these topics in firm and market scenarios. Tirole (1988) provides a broad overview of theoretical scholarship on industrial organization, while Roberts (2004) provides a more recent, non-technical overview of research analyzing firm organization and strategies. An interesting distinction between economic models and models of politics involves the ability to transfer utility from one actor to another in economics (via money and incentive-based contracts), which is much more limited across the institutions of government.

[18] Fruitful work in this vein includes Snyder and Ting (2002), who develop a formal model of partisan affiliation in the electoral arena with implications for legislative policymaking. Unlike the work of Austen-Smith and Banks, however, theirs does not explicitly model legislative interactions that occur after the election. In an alternative approach, Groseclose and McCarty (2001) include the voting public as an audience in the blame game of high-level bargaining between Congress and the president.

similar model structures will tend to use the same terms with similar actors and common modeling assumptions.

Lesson IV: Simplify when appropriate

While the body of scholarship that develops complete formal models of parties in Congress is relatively small, as it grows and becomes more cumulative, the lessons of simplification will become more valuable. Some such benefits are already apparent. Krehbiel and Meirowitz (2002), for example, adopt a simple stylized version of the motion to recommit to illustrate how minority rights and majority power vary depending on the order of moves by (and preference divergence among) the model's main actors. Cox and McCubbins's (2002, 2005) negative agenda-setting model significantly simplifies and clarifies their earlier works (from an analytical perspective) and, in doing so, allows them to incorporate additional actors into their model of the policymaking process (e.g. committees) and to provide the motivation for well-explicated empirical hypotheses.

Lesson V: Account for empirical findings

The literature on coalition formation in Congress showed a healthy interchange between initial models, empirical examinations, further model developments, and subsequent tests of those models' new hypotheses. Down this path of scientific progress, the parties-in-Congress literature has not developed as far as it might. Without question, scholars (e.g. Clinton 2007; Krehbiel 1993, 1999; McCarty, Poole, and Rosenthal 2001; Snyder and Groseclose 2000; Wiseman and Wright 2008) have empirically investigated the theoretical postulates of Aldrich, Rohde, and Cox and McCubbins, to identify the presence (or absence) of party effects in legislative organization, policymaking, and politics. While a robust empirical debate ensued, there has been much less theoretical scholarship that explicitly engages these challenging empirical findings. Hence, to some degree scholars have been talking past each other, with empirical analyses identifying support and limitations of partisan theories, and little effort has been made to refine explicit theories that can account for these regularities and suggest new directions for empirical research.

Lesson VI: Use metagames to study institutional choice

As shown in our examples above, cumulative model building can give way to the production of metagames that allow scholars to study institutional choice. Models of legislative–bureaucratic relations can then be used to study why Congress establishes bureaucratic agencies in the first place; and models of coalition formation under different voting rules can be used to study the initial selection of such rules. Given the limited cumulative model building around parties in Congress, this is still an area ripe for investigation. Promising early work in this area includes Volden and Bergman (2006), who add a first-stage party cohesion decision to Krehbiel's (1996) pivotal politics model, to explore when party members have an incentive to empower their leaders to impose discipline on party members.[19] Among other findings, such a model produces many of the hypotheses arising from the conditional party government theory.

Lesson VII: Reassess modeling choices

Perhaps the lesson of reassessing modeling choices would be more aptly applied were there a larger set of formal models of parties to draw upon. However, even among the models advanced to date, there are many assumptions that could be examined and reassessed, on the basis of our definition of a complete formal model:

- Who are the relevant *actors* that constitute a party? Is it sufficient and appropriate simply to model a party as a monolith (e.g. as the median party member in Congress), or should scholars model the party as the whole of the party's members in Congress, or perhaps as a collection of political elites both inside and outside of the chamber? Should scholars treat parties differently across the House and Senate chambers? Should scholars consider majority and minority parties to be analytically distinct from one another?

- What model *structure* characterizes the relevant interactions between parties and other key actors? Does a party attempt to exert influence in committees or during votes on the floor? How do parties facilitate relations between the House and the Senate or between Congress and the president? Are interactions among these actors, or between parties and their members, best modeled as repeated events?

- What are the relevant *outcomes* over which parties and their members have *preferences*? Do parties mainly seek to obtain and maintain majority status or do they simply wish to protect incumbent members? When do policy goals trump electoral goals, such that parties at the peak of their power adopt policies that may differ from what average Americans desire?

- How might *decision criteria* regarding the optimizing or satisficing behavior of parties or the uncertainty about future interactions between parties, their members, and the electorate influence party activities and legislator actions?

CONCLUSIONS AND FUTURE DIRECTIONS

In considering the impact of formal approaches to the study of the U.S. Congress, we have sought to define a complete formal model, to draw lessons from sub-fields that have used such models in order to achieve significant theoretical advancements in recent years, and to illustrate how those lessons could be fruitfully applied to

---

[19] Bawn (1998) also uses a series of formal models to examine the incentives of party leaders.

advance scholarship in somewhat less theoretically developed areas of inquiry. We do not argue that distributive and coalitional politics or congressional–bureaucratic relations are the main areas of successful formal modeling of Congress, nor that the parties-in-Congress area faces the greatest need of reform. Indeed, we believe that the lessons drawn above could be applied to advance formal modeling enterprises broadly, both within and beyond the study of Congress. We conclude therefore not with a reiteration of our arguments but with a brief survey of exciting areas for future theoretical work on Congress, ordered so as to match, roughly, topics from this *Handbook*, with significant formal contributions highlighted that may well serve as starting points upon which to build these sub-fields further, in light of the lessons suggested here.

Capacity and ability of members

All too frequently, models of Congress treat all legislators identically, varying only in their preferences in a policy space or in the districts to which they would like spending to be directed. Models that allow for the possibility that members of Congress differ in their capacity to understand politics and form coalitions, to see the linkages between written laws and on-the-ground policy outcomes, or to shepherd more effectively their preferred legislation through the policy process would capture a much fuller view of congressional politics. One building block along these lines might be the model of Denzau and Munger (1986), wherein the varied abilities of members influence legislative organization as well as how legislators interact with each other in distributive policymaking, bureaucratic oversight, and partisan politics. An alternative approach might capture varying levels of competence through different probabilities of recognition across members, in a Baron and Ferejohn (1989) type of bargaining model.

Elections

As we develop more sophisticated models of congressional politics, it is important not to lose focus on the fact that Congress is best understood in the broader context of American democracy. Among other considerations, this means that scholars should examine how electoral mechanisms and incentives influence legislators' careers and choices. Ashworth (2005), consistently with the point immediately above, assumes that legislators vary in their abilities, and that they choose how to allocate their efforts between policy work and constituency service over time. Voters retain their member depending on their assessments of his or her ability. Among other findings, Ashworth's analysis explains why more junior members of Congress might devote more effort to constituency service than do senior legislators; and his model also has implications for legislative organization.

Deliberation

Despite the inclusion of decision criteria among the main elements in our definition of a complete formal model, we have given little attention to the cognitive limits of congressional actors or to the formation of their beliefs. This is a function of the sparse theoretical coverage of these topics in the study of Congress. Despite models of how pivotal legislators make choices based on the information at hand, very little scholarship has explicitly analyzed how groups of legislators arrive at collective decisions on the basis of the sharing of information. The broad subject of deliberation in Congress is clearly worthy of study, but has yet to overcome many of the obstacles confronted in the areas of study that we explore in-depth above. Austen-Smith and Riker (1987), however, offer a foundational study upon which further theories of deliberation could be advanced.[20] In their model, legislators possess private information about the effects of proposed policies, choosing what information to reveal to their colleagues during the debate process. Equilibrium results identify when legislators have incentives to withhold information, as well as when legislative debate makes final decisions deviate from the collective preferences of members.

Congressional development

As Congress has evolved over its more than 220 years of history, members have experimented with a wide range of innovative internal structures and parliamentary practices. Given such broad historical development, it would be constructive to think systematically about which institutional structures are most beneficial to Congress and its members at any given point in time. Although vastly important, formal theoretical scholarship in this area has been piecemeal at best. Some highlights in the area of congressional committees, upon which further developments could be based, include Gilligan and Krehbiel's (1987) analysis of information and expertise, Denzau and Mackay's (1983) work on restrictive rules and agenda-setting, and Crombez, Groseclose, and Krehbiel's (2006) study of gatekeeping.

Congress and the private sector

In considering interactions between Congress and external actors, surprisingly little formal work has been conducted on the relationship between Congress and business interests. While complete formal models exist that consider the interactions between Congress and lobbyists (e.g. Austen-Smith and Wright 1992), less work focuses on how private (corporate) interests influence the content of legislation and the enforcement of existing laws. Encouraging signs of an emerging formal literature in this area have appeared, however, in Gordon and Hafer's (2005, 2007) studies of the

---

[20]   Landa and Meirowitz (2009) offer a useful review and discussion of game-theoretic approaches to the study of deliberation more generally.

relationship between corporate campaign contributions and regulatory oversight, and in David Baron's research program (e.g. 1999, 2001, 2006) on integrated governmental and non-governmental lobbying strategies by private interests. Both of these approaches present foundations upon which much more work could be built.

Congress in the Separation of Powers System

Finally, although the literature on congressional–presidential and congressional–judicial relations is nowhere as sparsely developed as many of the above topics, the richness of these inter-branch relations merits far more theoretical attention than it has received in the past.[21] Here the building blocks are far more numerous and well established. For example, Canes-Wrone (2006) and Cameron (2000) offer excellent models, which seriously engage the relationship between Congress and the president in policy formation and execution. Similarly, Rohde and Shepsle's (2007) and Krehbiel's (2007) recent work on Supreme Court confirmations illustrate how even partial characterizations of congressional–judicial relations yield interesting and important insights.[22]

The consideration of these and numerous other sub-fields in congressional studies suggests many areas that are deserving of theoretical investigation. We hope that this chapter, and the lessons offered here, will prove helpful to future scholars, regardless of what substantive areas they choose to pursue.

References

Aldrich, J. H. 1995. Why Parties? *The Origin and Transformation of Party Politics in America.* Chicago, IL: University of Chicago Press.

Ansolabehere, S., Snyder, Jr., J. M., and Ting, M. M. 2003. Bargaining in Bicameral Legislatures: When and Why Does Malapportionment Matter? *American Political Science Review,* 97(3): 471–81.

Arrow, K. J. 1951. *Social Choice and Individual Values.* New York: Wiley.

Ashworth, S. 2005. Reputational Dynamics and Political Careers. *Journal of Law, Economics, and Organization,* 21(2): 441–66.

Austen-Smith, D., and Banks, J. S. 1988. Elections, Coalitions, and Legislative Outcomes. *American Political Science Review,* 82(2): 405–22.

———— 1999. *Positive Political Theory I: Collective Preference.* Ann Arbor: University of Michigan Press.

——and Riker, W. H. 1987. Asymmetric Information and the Coherence of Legislation. *American Political Science Review,* 81(3): 897–918.

---

[21] Similarly, the important role of Congress within American federalism deserves a far more robust theoretical treatment than it has received to date.

[22] These works build upon the model and empirical examinations of Moraski and Shipan (1999).

——and WRIGHT, J. T. 1992. Competitive Lobbying for a Legislator's Vote. *Social Choice and Welfare*, 9(3): 229–57.

BANKS, J. S. 1989. Agency Budgets, Cost Information, and Auditing. *American Journal of Political Science*, 33(3): 670–99.

——and WEINGAST, B. R. 1992. The Political Control of Bureaucracies under Asymmetric Information. *American Journal of Political Science*, 36(2): 509–24.

BARON, D. P. 1991. Majoritarian Incentives, Pork Barrel Programs, and Procedural Control. *American Journal of Political Science*, 35(1): 57–90.

——1999. Integrated Market and Nonmarket Strategy in Client and Interest Group Politics. *Business and Politics*, 1(1): 7–34.

——2001. Theories of Strategic Nonmarket Participation: Majority Rule and Executive Institutions. *Journal of Economics and Management Strategy*, 10(1): 47–89.

——2006. Competitive Lobbying and Supermajorities in a Majority-Rule Institution. *Scandinavian Journal of Economics*, 108(4): 607–42.

——and FEREJOHN, J. A. 1989. Bargaining in Legislatures. *American Political Science Review*, 83(4): 1181–206.

BAWN, K. 1995. Political Control Versus Expertise: Congressional Choices about Administrative Procedures. *American Political Science Review*, 89(1): 62–73.

——1997. Choosing Strategies to Control the Bureaucracy: Statutory Constraints, Oversight, and the Committee System. *Journal of Law, Economics, and Organization*, 13(1): 101–26.

——1998. Congressional Party Leadership: Utilitarian Versus Majoritarian Incentives. *Legislative Studies Quarterly*, 23(2): 219–243.

BENDOR, J., and MEIROWITZ, A. 2004. Spatial Models of Delegation. *American Political Science Review*, 98(2): 293–310.

——TAYLOR, S., and VAN GAALEN, R. 1985. Bureaucratic Expertise Versus Legislative Authority: A Model of Deception and Monitoring in Budgeting. *American Political Science Review*, 79(4): 1041–60.

——————1987. Politicians, Bureaucrats, and Asymmetric Information. *American Journal of Political Science*, 31(4): 796–828.

BICKERS, K. N., and STEIN, R. M. 1994. Congressional Elections and the Pork Barrel. *Journal of Politics*, 65(2): 377–99.

BLACK, D. 1948. On the Rationale of Group Decision-Making. *Journal of Political Economy*, 56(1): 23–34.

BOEHMKE, F. J., GAILMARD, S., and WIGGS PATTY, J. 2006. Whose Ear to Bend? Information Sources and Venue Choice in Policy-Making. *Quarterly Journal of Political Science*, 1(2): 139–69.

BUCHANAN, J. M., and TULLOCK, G. 1962. *The Calculus of Consent*. Ann Arbor: University of Michigan Press.

CAMERON, C. M. 2000. *Veto Bargaining: Presidents and the Politics of Negative Power*. New York: Cambridge University Press.

CANES-WRONE, B. 2006. *Who Leads Whom? Presidents, Policy and the Public*. Chicago: University of Chicago Press.

CARRUBBA, C. J., and VOLDEN, C. 2000. Coalitional Politics and Logrolling in Legislative Institutions. *American Journal of Political Science*, 44(2): 255–71.

CHEN, J., and MALHOTRA, N. 2007. The Law of k/n: The Effect of Chamber Size on Government Spending in Bicameral Legislatures. *American Political Science Review*, 101(4): 657–76.

CHIOU, FANG-YI, and ROTHENBERG, L. S. 2003. When Pivotal Politics Meets Partisan Politics. *American Journal of Political Science*, 47(3): 503–22.

CLINTON, J. 2007. Lawmaking and Roll Calls. *Journal of Politics*, 69(2): 455–67.

COX, G. W., and MCCUBBINS, M. D. 1993. *Legislative Leviathan: Party Government in the House.* Berkeley: University of California Press.

—————2002. Agenda Power in the U.S. House of Representatives, pp. 107–45 in *Party, Process and Political Change in Congress*, ed. D. W. Brady and M. D. McCubbins. Stanford, CA: Stanford University Press.

—————2005. *Setting the Agenda: Responsible Party Government in the U.S. House of Representatives.* New York: Cambridge University Press.

CRAWFORD, V. P., and SOBEL, J. 1982. Strategic Information Transmission. *Econometrica*, 50(6): 1431–51.

CROMBEZ, C., GROSECLOSE, T., and KREHBIEL, K. 2006. Gatekeeping. *Journal of Politics*, 68(2): 322–34.

DAL BÓ, E. 2007. Bribing Voters. *American Journal of Political Science*, 51(4): 789–803.

DENZAU, A. T. and MACKAY, R. J. 1983. Gatekeeping and Monopoly Power of Committees: An Analysis of Sincere and Sophisticated Behavior. *American Journal of Political Science*, 27(4): 740–61.

——and MUNGER, M. C. 1986. Legislators and Interest Groups: How Unorganized Interests Get Represented. *American Political Science Review*, 80(1): 89–106.

DIERMEIER, D., and KREHBIEL, K. 2003. Institutionalism as a Methodology. *Journal of Theoretical Politics*, 15(2): 123–44.

——and MYERSON, R. B. 1999. Bicameralism and Its Consequences for the Internal Organization of Legislatures. *American Economic Review*, 89(5): 1182–96.

EPSTEIN, DAVID, and O'HALLORAN, SHARYN. 1994. Administrative Procedures, Information, and Agency Discretion. *American Journal of Political Science*, 38(3): 697–722.

—————1996. Divided Government and the Design of Administrative Procedures: A Formal Model and Empirical Test. *Journal of Politics*, 58(2): 373–97.

—————1999. *Delegating Powers: A Transaction Cost Politics Approach to Policy Making under Separate Powers.* Cambridge: Cambridge University Press.

FEREJOHN, J., and SHIPAN, C. 1990. Congressional Influence on Bureaucracy. *Journal of Law, Economics, and Organization*, 6(Special Issue): 1–20.

FIORINA, M. P. 1977. *Congress: Keystone of the Washington Establishment.* New Haven: Yale University Press.

GAILMARD, S. 2002. Expertise, Subversion and Bureaucratic Discretion. *Journal of Law, Economics, and Organization*, 18(2): 536–55.

——2009. Discretion Rather than Rules: Choice of Instruments to Control Bureaucratic Policy Making. *Political Analysis*, 17(1): 25–44.

GILLIGAN, T. W., and KREHBIEL, K. 1987. Collective Decision-Making and Standing Committees: An Informational Rationale for Restrictive Amendment Procedures. *Journal of Law, Economics, and Organization*, 3(2): 145–93.

—————1989. Asymmetric Information and Legislative Rules with a Heterogeneous Committee. *American Journal of Political Science*, 33(2): 459–90.

GORDON, S. C., and HAFER, C. 2005. Flexing Muscle: Corporate Political Expenditures as Signals to the Bureaucracy. *American Political Science Review*, 99(2): 245–61.

—————2007. Corporate Influence and the Regulatory Mandate. *Journal of Politics*, 69(2): 300–19.

GROSECLOSE, T., and MCCARTY, N. 2001. The Politics of Blame: Bargaining before an Audience. *American Journal of Political Science*, 45(1): 100–19.

——and SNYDER, JR., J. M. 1996. Buying Supermajorities. *American Political Science Review*, 90(2): 303–15.

HOLMSTROM, B. 1984. On the Theory of Delegation, pp. 115-41 in *Bayesian Models in Economic Theory*, ed. M. Boyer and R. E. Kihlstrom. New York: McGraw-Hill.

HUBER, J. D., and SHIPAN, C. R. 2002. *Deliberate Discretion? The Institutional Foundations of Bureaucratic Autonomy*. New York: Cambridge University Press.

HUXTABLE, P. A. 1994. Incorporating the Rules Committee: An Extension of the Ferejohn/Shipan Model. *Journal of Law, Economics, and Organization*, 10(1): 160–7.

KALANDRAKIS, T. 2006. Proposal Rights and Political Power. *American Journal of Political Science*, 50(2): 441–8.

KREHBIEL, K. 1988. Spatial Models of Legislative Choice. *Legislative Studies Quarterly*, 13(3): 259–319.

—— 1993. Where's the Party? *British Journal of Political Science*, 23(2): 235–66.

—— 1996. Institutional and Partisan Sources of Gridlock: A Theory of Divided and Unified Government. *Journal of Theoretical Politics*, 8(1): 7–40.

—— 1999. The Party Effect from A to Z and Beyond. *Journal of Politics*, 61(3): 832–40.

—— 2007. Partisan Roll Rates in a Nonpartisan Legislature. *Journal of Law, Economics, and Organization*, 23(1): 1–23.

—— 2007. Supreme Court Appointments as a Move-the-Median Game. *American Journal of Political Science*, 51(2): 231–40.

—— and MEIROWITZ, A. 2002. Minority Rights and Majority Power: Theoretical Consequences of the Motion to Recommit. *Legislative Studies Quarterly*, 27(2): 191–217.

LANDA, D., and MEIROWITZ, A. 2009. Game Theory, Information, and Deliberative Democracy. *American Journal of Political Science*, 53(2): 427–44.

MARTIN, E. M. 1997. An Informational Theory of the Legislative Veto. *Journal of Law, Economics, and Organization*, 13(2): 319–43.

MAYHEW, D. R. 1974. *Congress: The Electoral Connection*. New Haven: Yale University Press.

McCARTY, N. M. 2000. Presidential Pork: Executive Veto Power and Distributive Politics. *American Political Science Review*, 94(1): 117–29.

—— POOLE, K., and ROSENTHAL, H. 2001. The Hunt for Party Discipline in Congress. *American Political Science Review*, 95(3): 673–87.

McCUBBINS, M. D., NOLL, R. G., and WEINGAST, B. R. 1987. Administrative Procedures as Instruments of Political Control. *Journal of Law, Economics, and Organization*, 3(2): 243–77.

—— —— —— 1989. Structure and Process, Politics and Policy: Administrate Arrangements and the Political Control of Agencies. *Virginia Law Review*, 75(2): 431–82.

McKELVEY, R. D. 1976. Intransitivities in Multi-Dimensional Voting Models and Some Implications for Agenda Control. *Journal of Economic Theory*, 12(3): 472–82.

—— and NORMAN SCHOFIELD. 1987. Generalized Symmetry Conditions at a Core Point. *Econometrica*, 55(4): 923–33.

MILLER, G. J., and MOE, T. M. 1983. Bureaucrats, Legislators and the Size of Government. *American Political Science Review*, 77(2): 297–322.

MOE, T. M. 1989. The Politics of Bureaucratic Structure, pp. 267–329 in *Can the Government Govern?*, ed. John E. Chubb and Paul E. Peterson. Washington, DC: Brookings Institution Press.

MORASKI, B. J., and C. R. SHIPAN. 1999. The Politics of Supreme Court Nominations: A Theory of Institutional Constraints and Choices. *American Journal of Political Science*, 43(4): 1069–95.

NIOU, E. M. S., and ORDESHOOK, P. C. 1985. Universalism in Congress. *American Journal of Political Science*, 29(2): 246–58.

NISKANEN, W. A. 1971. *Bureaucracy and Representative Government*. Chicago: Aldine-Atherton.

—— 2001. Bureaucracy, pp. 258–70 in *Elgar Companion to Public Choice*, ed. W. F. Shughart, II and L. Razzolini. Cheltenham, UK: Edward Elgar.

PATTY, J. W. 2008. Equilibrium Party Government. *American Journal of Political Science*, 52(3): 636–55.

PLOTT, C. 1967. A Notion of Equilibrium and its Possibility Under Majority Rule. *American Economic Review*, 57(4): 146–60.

PRIMO, D. M., and SNYDER, JR., J. M. 2008. Distributive Politics and the Law of 1/n. *Journal of Politics*, 70(2): 477–86.

RIKER, W. H. 1962. *The Theory of Political Coalitions*. New Haven: Yale University Press.

ROBERTS, J. 2004. *The Modern Firm: Organizational Design for Performance and Growth*. New York: Oxford University Press.

ROHDE, D. W. 1991. *Parties and Leaders in the Postreform House*. Chicago: University of Chicago Press.

—— and SHEPSLE, K. A. 2007. Advising and Consenting in the 60-Vote Senate: Strategic Appointments to the Supreme Court. *Journal of Politics*, 69(3): 664–77.

ROMER, T., and ROSENTHAL, H. 1978. Political Resource Allocation, Controlled Agendas, and the Status Quo. *Public Choice*, 33(4): 27–43.

SHEPSLE, K. A., and WEINGAST, B. R. 1981. Political Preferences for the Pork Barrel: A Generalization. *American Journal of Political Science*, 25(1): 96–111.

SHIPAN, C. R. 2004. Regulatory Regimes, Agency Actions, and the Conditional Nature of Congressional Influence. *American Political Science Review*, 98(3): 467–80.

STEUNENBERG, B. 1992. Congress, Bureaucracy, and Regulatory Policy-Making. *Journal of Law, Economics, and Organization*, 8(3): 673–94.

—— 1991. On Buying Legislatures. *Economics and Politics*, 3(2): 93–109.

—— and GROSECLOSE, T. 2000. Estimating Party Influence in Congressional Roll-Call Voting. *American Journal of Political Science*, 44(2): 193–211.

—— and TING, M. M. 2002. An Informational Rationale for Political Parties. *American Journal of Political Science*, 46(1): 90–110.

—— —— 2005. Why Roll Calls? A Model of Position-Taking in Legislative Voting and Elections. *Journal of Law, Economics, and Organization*, 21(1): 153–78.

STEIN, R. M., and BICKERS, K. 1995. *Perpetuating the Pork Barrel: Policy Subsystems and American Democracy*. New York: Cambridge University Press.

TING, M. M. 2002. A Theory of Jurisdictional Assignments in Bureaucracies. *American Journal of Political Science*, 46(2): 364–78.

TIROLE, J. 1988. *The Theory of Industrial Organization*. Cambridge, MA: MIT Press.

VOLDEN, C. 2002. A Formal Model of the Politics of Delegation in a Separation of Powers System. *American Journal of Political Science*, 46(1): 111–33.

—— and BERGMAN, ELIZABETH. 2006. How Strong Should Our Party Be? Party Member Preferences Over Party Cohesion. *Legislative Studies Quarterly*, 31(1): 71–104.

—— and WISEMAN, A. E. 2007. Bargaining in Legislatures over Particularistic and Collective Goods. *American Political Science Review*, 101(1): 79–92.

WEINGAST, B. R. 1979. A Rational Choice Perspective on Congressional Norms. *American Journal of Political Science*, 23(2): 245–62.

—— and MARSHALL, W. 1988. The Industrial Organization of Congress. *Journal of Political Economy*, 96(1): 132–63.

—— SHEPSLE, K. A., and JOHNSEN, C. 1981. The Political Economy of Benefits and Costs: A Neoclassical Approach to Distributive Politics. *Journal of Political Economy*, 89(4): 642–64.

WISEMAN, A. E. 2009. Delegation and Positive-Sum Bureaucracies. *Journal of Politics*, 71(3): 998–1014.

—— and WRIGHT, J. R. 2008. The Legislative Median and Partisan Policy. *Journal of Theoretical Politics*, 20(1): 5–29.

CHAPTER 4

....

MEASURING LEGISLATIVE PREFERENCES

....

NOLAN McCARTY

INTRODUCTION

....

INNOVATION in the estimation of spatial models of roll-call voting has been one of the most important developments in the study of Congress and other legislative and judicial institutions. The seminal contributions of Poole and Rosenthal (1991, 1997) launched a massive literature marked by sustained methodological innovation and new applications. Alternative estimators of ideal points have been developed by Heckman and Snyder (1997), Londregan (2000a), Martin and Quinn (2002), Clinton, Jackman, and Rivers (2004), and Poole (2000). The scope of application has expanded greatly from the original work on the U.S. Congress. Spatial mappings and ideal points have now been estimated for all fifty state legislatures (Wright and Schaffner 2002; Shor and McCarty 2010), the Supreme Court (e.g. Martin and Quinn 2002; Bailey and Chang 2001; Bailey 2007), U.S. presidents (e.g. McCarty and Poole 1995; Bailey and Chang 2001; Bailey 2007), a large number of non-U.S. legislatures (e.g. Londregan 2000b; Morgenstern 2004), the European Parliament (e.g. Hix, Noury, and Roland 2006), and the U.N. General Assembly (Voeten 2000).

The popularity of ideal point estimation results in large part from its very close link to theoretical work on legislative politics and collective decision-making. Many of the models and paradigms of contemporary legislative decision-making are based on spatial representations of preferences.[1] Consequently, ideal point estimates are key ingredients for much of the empirical work on legislatures, and increasingly on courts and executives.[2] This has contributed to a much tighter link between theory and empirics in these subfields of political science.[3]

The goal of this chapter is to provide a general, less technical overview of the literature on ideal point estimation. So attention is paid to the concerns of the end-user; the empirical researcher who wishes to use ideal point estimates in applications. In order to highlight the advantages and disadvantages of using ideal point estimates in applied work, I make explicit comparisons to the primary alternative: interest group ratings. My main argument is that the choice of legislative preference measures often involves substantial tradeoffs that hinge on seemingly subtle modeling choices and identification strategies. While these variations may or may not affect the results of particular applications, it is very important for the applied researcher to understand the nature of these tradeoffs to avoid incorrect inferences and interpretations.

THE SPATIAL MODEL

Although there is a longer tradition of using factor or cluster analysis to extract ideological or position scales from roll-call voting data, I concentrate exclusively on those models that are generated explicitly from the spatial model of voting.[4] The spatial model assumes that policy alternatives can be represented as points in a geometric space—a line, plane, or hyperplane.[5] Legislators have preferences defined over these alternatives.[6] In almost all the statistical applications of the spatial model, researchers assume these preferences satisfy two properties:

- Single-peakedness: When alternatives are arranged spatially, the legislator cannot have two policies that they rank higher than all adjacent alternatives. In other words, for all policies but one, there is a nearby policy that is better. Consequently, the legislator's most preferred outcome is a single point. We call this point the legislator's *ideal point*.

---

[1] A non-exhaustive sampling of a vast literature includes Gilligan and Krehbiel (1987), Krehbiel (1998), Cameron (2000), and Cox and McCubbins (2005).

[2] A sample of such work includes Cox and McCubbins (2005), McCarty and Poole (1995), Clinton (2007), Cameron (2000), Clinton and Meirowitz (2003).

[3] This is not to say that there is no slippage between statistical and theoretical spatial models. I return to the issue of the congruence between empirical and theoretical work below.

[4] My scope is limited both for space reasons and a desire to focus on the link between empirical and theoretical work. See Poole (2005, 8–11) for a discussion of this earlier work.

[5] For a slightly more technical introduction to the spatial model, see McCarty and Meirowitz (2006, 21–4).

[6] I refer to the voter throughout the chapter as a legislator even though ideal points of executives, judges, and regulators have also been estimated using these techniques.

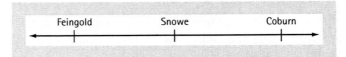

Fig. 4.1. Ideal points of three Senators

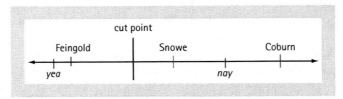

Fig. 4.2. Cut point of a roll-call vote

- Symmetry: If x and y are alternatives represented by two points equal distance from a legislator's ideal point, the legislator is indifferent between the two.

To make these ideas concrete, consider Figure 4.1 that introduces a simple motivating example that I use throughout the chapter. The example assumes that policies can be represented as points on a single line and that Senators Russell Feingold, Olympia Snowe, and Tom Coburn have ideal points.

Figure 4.2 places two voting alternatives, *yea* and *nay*, on the line along with the ideal points of the senators. Under the assumption that preferences are symmetric, the model predicts that in any binary comparison each senator prefers the policy closest to his or her ideal point. Given the simple pairwise comparison of *yea* and *nay*, it seems natural to assume that each senator would vote for the closest outcome. This assumption is known as *sincere voting*.[7] Clearly, Feingold is closer to *yea* than to *nay* and so is predicted to vote for it. Alternatively, Snowe and Coburn would support the *nay* alternative. More generally, knowing the spatial positions of the alternatives allows us to distinguish precisely between the ideal points of supporters and opponents.

A second useful fact is that given our assumption of symmetric preferences, each roll call can be characterized by a *cut point* or *cut line* that divides the ideal points of supporters from those of opponents. When the space of ideal points and alternatives is unidimensional as is the case in Figures 4.1 and 4.2, the cut line is simply a point. This point falls exactly half-way between the position of the *yea* and *nay* outcomes. This cut point is represented in Figure 4.2 where clearly all senators with ideal points to the left support the motion and all those to the right oppose it.

Consequently, if voting is based solely on the spatial preferences of legislators and there is no random component to vote choice, we can represent all voting coalitions in terms of ideal points and cut lines. This property turns out to be a crucial one for models of ideal point estimation. But it is important to remember that this

---

[7] In more complex settings, where legislators vote over a sequence of proposals to reach a final outcome, sincere voting may not be a reasonable assumption.

convenience comes at the cost of the somewhat restrictive assumptions of symmetry and single-peakedness. To see why the assumption of symmetry is important, assume that Coburn's preferences in Figure 4.2 are asymmetric in that he prefers alternatives d units to the left of his ideal point to those d units to the right. This would make it possible to identify combinations of *yea* and *nay* outcomes for which Feingold and Coburn vote together against Snowe. Such a coalition structure cannot be represented by a single cut point. Similarly, if Coburn's preferences had two peaks the cut point condition could be violated. If he had a second preference peak between Feingold and Snowe, it would be easy to generate a roll call with a Feingold–Coburn versus Snowe outcome.

Before turning to the statistical models that have been developed to estimate legislative ideal points (and cut lines), it is instructive to consider the primary alternative to ideal point estimates: interest group ratings. The properties of these measures help clarify the potentials and the pitfalls of ideal point measures.

INTEREST GROUP RATINGS

Interest group ratings of legislators have been compiled by a very diverse set of organizations, most notably the Americans for Democratic Action, the American Conservative Union, and the League of Conservation Voters. Many of the ratings go back a long time. Though precise details differ, interest group ratings are generally constructed in the following way:

1. An interest group identifies a set of roll calls that are important to the group's legislative agenda.[8]
2. The group identifies the position on the roll call that supports the group's agenda.
3. A rating is computed by dividing the number of votes in support of the group's agenda by the total number of votes identified by the group.[9]

For example, suppose a group chooses twenty votes. A legislator who votes favorably eighteen times gets a 90 percent rating and one who supports the group five times gets a 25 percent rating.

It is easy to see how an interest group rating might be used as an estimate of a legislator's ideal point on the dimension defined by the group's agenda.[10] Assume

---

[8] Usually the roll calls are selected after the votes have taken place, but on some occasions a group will announce that an upcoming vote will be included in their rating.

[9] Some groups treat abstention and absences as votes against the group's position.

[10] For expositional purposes, I assume throughout this section that legislators engage in *perfect spatial voting* in that behavior is determined solely by spatial preferences and without any random component. All the issues would continue to arise with probabilistic spatial voting.

that a group chooses p roll calls and that the cut points are $c_1 \leq c_2 \leq \ldots \leq c_{p-1} \leq c_p$.[11] Furthermore, assume that the group has an ideal point greater than c_p. If all legislators vote in perfect accordance with their spatial preferences, all legislators with ideal points greater than c_p vote with the group p out of p times and get a 100 percent rating. Conversely, legislators with ideal points less than c_1 never support the group. In general, we can infer (under the assumption of perfect voting) that a legislator with a rating of $\frac{i}{p}$ has an ideal point between c_j and c_{j+1}. Unfortunately, we know only that $c_{j+1} > c_j$ and cannot observe c_j directly. Thus, interest group ratings provide only the ordinal ranking of ideal points. The upshot of this is that we have no way of knowing whether the distance between a 40 percent and a 50 percent rating is the same as the distance between a 50 percent and a 60 percent rating. This is a point ignored by almost all empirical work that uses interest group based measures.

Clearly, interest group ratings have many advantages. First, the scores directly relate to the policy concerns of the groups that compile them. League of Conservation Voters scores are based on environmental votes; the National Right to Life committee chooses votes on abortion, euthanasia, and stem cells. Second, groups often focus on important votes, whereas many of the statistical estimators discussed below use all or almost all votes. The expertise of the interest group in identifying key amendment or procedural votes adds value to their measures.[12] Finally, interest group ratings are easy to understand: Senator x supported group y's position p percent of the time.

But there are many ways in which interest group ratings perform poorly as estimates of legislator ideal points. I discuss each not to criticize interest group ratings, but because some of the issues reappear in ideal point estimation (albeit in a less transparent way).

Lumpiness

The first concern with interest group ratings as measures of preferences is that they are "lumpy" in that they take on only a small number of distinct values. If p votes are used to construct a rating, then the rating takes on only $p + 1$ different values: $0, 100/p, 200/p, \ldots$, and 100. In many cases, this entails a significant loss of information about legislative preferences. If two members vote identically on the twenty votes selected by a group, they receive the same interest group score regardless of how consistent their voting behavior is on all of the other votes. So legislators with very different true positions may achieve the same score. Lumpiness also exacerbates problems of measurement error (beyond those caused by the small sample of votes used). Because scores can only take on a small set of values, small deviations from pure spatial voting can lead to large changes in voting score. Suppose an interest group has chosen ten votes that generate the cut points in Figure 4.3 below. The figure illustrates the interest group rating for each legislator located between adjacent cut

[11] Note that the indexing is arbitrary so this string of inequalities is without any loss of generality. Ruling out $c_i = c_{i+1}$ is for simplicity, but I shall return to it shortly.

[12] The concept of 'importance' may not be clear in some cases, however. Groups may often include votes that represent purely symbolic support of their position.

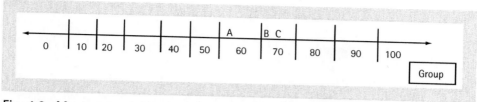

Fig. 4.3. Measurement error in interest group ratings

points. The interest group rating for legislator A is 60 percent and it is 70 percent for legislators B and C. But suppose there was some small idiosyncratic factor that caused B to vote against the group on vote 7. Then B would have a 60 percent rating which is the same as A despite the fact that legislator B is located much closer to C who still scores 70 percent. Obviously, part of the problem is that the interest group has selected too few votes. If the group selected enough votes such that there were cut lines between A and B and between B and C the problem would be ameliorated somewhat. But no interest group chooses enough roll calls to distinguish 435 House members and 100 senators. But even if one did select enough votes, the interest group rating would still only reflect the order of the ideal points.

Artificial extremism

A second problem with interest group ratings concerns the relationship between the distributions of interest group ratings and ideal points. This problem was first identified by Snyder (1992). He provides a much more formal analysis of the problem, but it can be illustrated easily with a couple of figures. In Figure 4.4, there are five legislators and roll call cut points separate each of them. Consequently, each legislator gets a distinct score so that the distribution of ratings more or less matches the distribution of ideal points. But consider Figure 4.5. The difference is that now the cut points are concentrated in the middle of the spectrum.

Now legislators 1 and 2 have perfect 100 percent ratings and legislators 4 and 5 have 0 percent ratings. So it appears that the legislature is extremely polarized. But this is simply an artifact of the group having selected votes where the cutting lines are concentrated in the middle.

In generalizing this argument, Snyder proves that if the variance of the distribution of cut points is smaller than the variance of ideal points, the distribution of ideal points will be bimodal even if preferences are unimodal. Ultimately, the severity of this problem depends on the selection criteria that interest groups use. But it seems entirely plausible that groups are more interested in a rough division of the legislature into friends and enemies than in creating fine-grained measures of preferences for political science research.[13]

---

[13] In 2008, 20 percent of senators and 17 percent of House members recieved either a 100 percent or a 0 percent rating from the Americans for Democratic Action. The total number of 100 percent ratings would have been larger but for the practice of counting abstentions and missed votes as votes against the group.

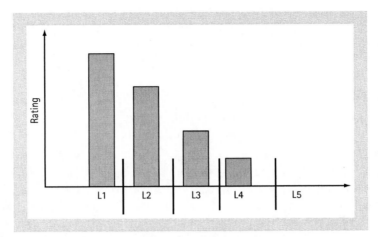

Fig. 4.4. Interest group ratings with uniform cut points

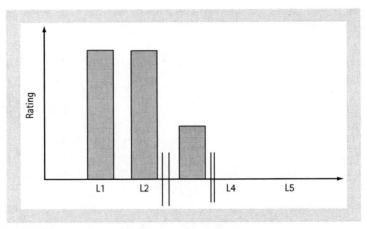

Fig. 4.5. Artificial extremism in interest group ratings

Comparisons over time and across legislatures

Often, researchers would like to compare the voting records of two legislators serving at different points in time or in different legislative bodies. Interest group ratings have been used for this purpose under the supposition that groups will maintain consistent standards for evaluation. Unfortunately, the supposition is invalid. The key to comparing ideal points of different legislators is the ability to observe how they vote on a common set of roll calls. If legislator *A* is voting over apples (Granny Smith versus McIntosh) and legislator *B* is voting over oranges (Navel versus Clementine), there is no way to compare their positions. This problem has both temporal and cross-sectional dimensions.

It should be clear from the discussion above that comparability of interest group ratings requires that the distribution of cut points be the same across time or across legislatures. Of course, this is an impossibly stringent condition likely never to be satisfied. Consequently, obtaining a rating of 60 percent in time t may be quite different from obtaining a rating of 60 percent at time $t + 1$. A score of 75 percent in the House is not the same as a score of 75 percent in the Senate.

Because variation in the distribution of cut points is inevitable, temporal and longitudinal comparisons of interest group ratings require strong assumptions to adjust scores into a common metric. For example, Groseclose, Levitt, and Snyder (1999) assume that each legislator's average latent Americans for Democratic Action score remains constant over time and upon moving from the House to the Senate. Similar problems persist in models of ideal point estimation. But, as I discuss below, ideal point models provide additional leverage for dealing with these problems.

Folding and dimensionality

Properly interpreting interest group ratings as (ordinal) measures of ideal points requires two additional assumptions. The first is that the interest group's ideal point is not 'interior' to the set of legislator ideal points.[14] The second is that the interest group's agenda covers only a single dimension.

The importance of the requirement that the interest group occupy an extreme position on its issue agenda is straightforward. If a moderate interest group compiles a rating, legislators occupying distinct positions to the group's left and its right will obtain the same score. Thus, rankings will not correlate with ideal points. A related problem concerns ratings from a group concerned with multiple policy areas where legislative preferences are not perfectly correlated. Suppose a group is concerned with liberalism on both social and economic issues. If the number of selected votes is the same across dimensions, a 50 percent rating would be obtained by a legislator supporting the group 50 percent on each issue and one supporting 100 percent on one issue and 0 percent on the other. Clearly, interest group ratings would not accurately reflect ideal points on either dimension.

IDEAL POINT ESTIMATION

The preceding discussion highlights many of the difficulties in using interest group ratings as measures of legislative preferences. Most of these problems, however, are not unique and resurface in the statistical models discussed below. Because there are

---

[14] See Poole and Rosenthal (1997; ch. 8) for a more extended discussion.

no free lunches, the improvements afforded always come at some cost. Either we must make strong assumptions about behavior or we must allow the models to perform less well in some other aspect. Because it ultimately falls to the end-user to decide which measures to use, understanding the underlying assumptions and tradeoffs is crucial.

The basic logic

The underlying assumption of the spatial model is that each legislator votes *yea* or *nay* depending on which outcome location is closer to his or her ideal point. Of course the legislator may make mistakes and depart from what would usually be expected, as a result of pressures from campaign contributors, constituents, courage of conviction, or just plain randomness. But if we assume that legislators generally vote on the basis of their spatial preferences and that errors are infrequent, we can estimate the ideal points of the members of Congress directly from the hundreds or thousands of roll-call choices made by each legislator.

To understand better how this is done, consider the following three senator example. Suppose we observed only the following roll-call voting patterns from Senators Feingold, Snowe, and Coburn.

Vote	Feingold	Snowe	Coburn
1	YEA	NAY	NAY
2	YEA	YEA	NAY
3	NAY	YEA	YEA
4	NAY	NAY	YEA
5	YEA	YEA	YEA
6	NAY	NAY	NAY

Notice that all of these voting patterns can be explained by a simple model where all senators are assigned an ideal point on a left–right scale and every roll call is given a cut point that divides the senators who vote *yea* from those who vote *nay*. For example, if we assign ideal points such that Feingold<Snowe<Coburn, vote 1 can be perfectly explained by a cut point between Feingold and Snowe, and vote 2 can be explained by a cut point between Snowe and Coburn. In fact, all six votes can be explained in this way. Note that a scale with Coburn<Snowe<Feingold works just as well. But, a single cut point cannot rationalize votes 1–4 if the ideal points are ordered Snowe<Feingold<Coburn, Snowe<Coburn<Feingold, Coburn<Feingold<Snowe, or Feingold<Coburn<Snowe. Therefore none of these orderings is consistent with a one-dimensional spatial model. It is worth emphasizing that the data contained in the table is incapable (without further modeling assumptions) of producing a cardinal preference scale. Just like interest group ratings, it is impossible to know whether Coburn is closer to Snowe than Snowe is to Feingold.

As the two orderings of ideal points work equally well, which one should we choose? Given that Feingold espouses liberal (left wing) views and Coburn is known for his conservative (right wing) views, Feingold<Snowe<Coburn seems like a logical choice. Alternatively, one may look at the substance of the votes. If votes 1, 3, and 5 are liberal initiatives and 2, 4, and 6 are conservative proposals, the Feingold<Snowe<Coburn ordering also seems natural. But it is important to remember that there is no information contained in the matrix of roll calls itself to make this determination. It is purely an interpretive exercise conducted by the researcher.

An issue that recurs throughout the literature on ideal point estimation concerns unanimous votes like 5 and 6. Clearly, any ordering of legislators and any designation of cut points exterior to the range of ideal points can rationalize these votes. So in the sense of classical statistics, they are uninformative and would therefore play no role in the estimation of a spatial model.[15]

Probabilistic voting

The real world is rarely so well behaved as to generate the nice patterns of votes 1–6. What if we observe that Coburn and Feingold occasionally vote together against Snowe, as in votes 7 and 8 below? Clearly, such votes cannot be explained by the ordering Feingold<Snowe<Coburn.

Vote	Feingold	Snowe	Coburn
7	YEA	NAY	YEA
8	NAY	YEA	NAY

If there are only a few votes like 7 and 8, it is reasonable to conclude that they may be generated by more or less random factors outside the model. To account for such random or *stochastic* behavior, estimators for spatial models assume that voting is probabilistic. There are many ways to generate probabilistic voting in a spatial context. One might assume for example that legislator ideal points are stochastic: Coburn might vote with Feingold against Snowe if his ideal point receives a sufficiently larger liberal shock than Snowe's does. Alternatively, one might assume that the voting alternatives are perceived differently by different legislators: Coburn might vote *yea* with Feingold against Snowe if he believes that the *yea* is more conservative than Snowe perceives it to be. Despite these logically coherent alternatives, the literature on ideal point estimation has converged on the random utility model. In the random utility model, a legislator i with ideal point x_i is assumed to evaluate alternative z_j according to some utility function $U(x_i, z_j)$ plus some error tern ε_{ij}. In such a framework, we might observe vote 7 if the underlying preferences predict vote 1 but

---

[15] Such votes may be informative in the Bayesian models I discuss below if one assumes informative priors about the distributions of ideal points and roll-call outcomes.

Senator Coburn receives a large positive shock in favor of the *yea* outcome. Of course, such an outcome can be rationalized in many other ways. A shock to Snowe's utility could lead a vote 5 to be observed as vote 7. So identification of the ideal points and bill locations is sensitive to both the specification of the utility function U and the distribution of the error terms.[16] Within the range of modeling assumptions found in the literature, the differences in estimates are usually small.

One of the payoffs to a probabilistic specification is that cardinal ideal point measures can be obtained whereas the deterministic analysis above produced only an ordinal ranking of ideal points. In the random utility framework, the frequency of the deviant votes provides additional information about cardinal values of the ideal points. Suppose we assume that small shocks to the utility functions are more frequent than large shocks. Then, if there are few votes pitting Coburn and Feingold against Snowe, the random utility models place Coburn and Feingold far apart, to mimic the improbability that random events lead them to vote together. Alternatively, if the Coburn–Feingold coalition were common, the models place them closer together, consistent with the idea that small random events can lead to such a voting pattern. But clearly, if we assume that large shocks are more common than small shocks, the logic would be reversed. So estimates of nominal ideal points are somewhat sensitive to the specification of random process.[17]

Multiple dimensions

Sometimes there are so many votes like 7 and 8 that it becomes unreasonable to maintain that they are simply the result of random utility shocks. An alternative is to assume that a Coburn–Feingold coalition forms because there exists some other policy dimension on which they are closer together than they are to Snowe. We can accommodate such behavior by estimating ideal points on a second dimension. In this example, a second dimension in which Coburn and Feingold share a position distinct from Snowe's, explains votes 7 and 8. In fact, both dimensions combined explain all the votes. Obviously, in a richer example with 100 senators rather than three, two dimensions cannot explain all the votes, but adding a second dimension adds explanatory power. So the primary question about whether to estimate a one, two, or more dimensional model is one of whether the higher dimensions can both explain substantially more behavior and can be interpreted substantively. Otherwise, the higher dimensions may simply be fitting noise.

---

[16] See Kalandrakis (forthcoming) for a disussion of the importance of various parametric assumptions for obtaining ideal points from roll-call data.

[17] This problem is not unique to ideal point estimation. It is generic to the estimation of discrete choice models. For example, in a probit or logit model, the predicted probabilities are identified purely from the form of the distribution function. Post-estimation analysis tends to support the assumption that the error process is unimodal around zero as most deviations from the prediction of the spatial model cluster around the cut point. See Poole and Rosenthal (1997, 33).

ESTIMATION

How exactly are ideal points estimated? For a clearer presentation, I focus on the case of a one-dimensional model. The generalization to multiple dimensions is fairly straightforward, but I will indicate where it is not.

As discussed above, the common framework is a random utility model where the utilities of voting for a particular outcome are based on a deterministic utility function over the location of the outcome and a random component. Formally, let x_i be legislator i's ideal point, y_j be the spatial location associated with the *yea* outcome on vote j and n_j be the location of the *nay* outcome. Moreover, let ε_j^y and ε_j^n be random shocks to the utilities of *yea* and *nay*, respectively. Therefore, the utilities for voting *yea* and *nay* can be written as

$$U(x_i, y_j) + \varepsilon_j^y$$

$$U(x_i, n_j) + \varepsilon_j^n$$

where it is assumed that U is decreasing in the distance between the ideal point and the location of the alternative. It is further assumed that the utility functions are Bernoulli functions that satisfy the axioms of the von Neuman–Morgernstern theorem.[18] A consequence of these assumptions is that we can rescale the x_i, y_j, and n_j without affecting voting behavior. Specifically, estimates of ideal points and bill locations are identified only up to a linear transformation.[19] This issue generates problems similar to those associated with comparing interest group ratings across chambers or years. Without common legislators or common votes, the ideal point estimates of different chambers differ by unobserved scale factors. I discuss below several attempts to work around this problem.

Given a specification of utility functions, the behavioral assumption is that each legislator votes for the outcome that generates the highest utility.[20] Specifying a functional form for the random shocks allows the derivation of choice probabilities and the likelihood function of the observed votes which can be used for maximum likelihood or Bayesian estimation.[21]

A complication arises in that except under fairly restrictive modeling choices, the likelihood function will be extremely non-linear in its parameters. So typically

---

[18] See McCarty and Meirowitz (2006, 36–7).

[19] Formally, $x_i' = a + \beta x_i$, $y_j' = a + \beta y_j$ and $n_j' = a + \beta n_j$ produce identical behavior as x_i, y_j, and n_j.

[20] This assumption is not innocuous. It rules out some forms of strategic voting. But if legislators vote on a binary agenda, we can reinterpret y_j and n_j as the sophisticated equivalents of a *yea* and *nay* vote (see Ordeshook 1986).

[21] Formally, the model predicts that legislator i votes *yea* on roll call j if and only if

$$U(x_i, y_j) + \varepsilon_j^y \geq U(x_i, n_j) + \varepsilon_j^n$$

$$U(x_i, y_j) - U(x_i, n_j) \geq \varepsilon_j^n - \varepsilon_j^y$$

estimating ideal point models will either involve alternating procedures (e.g. Poole and Rosenthal 1997) or Bayesian simulation (e.g. Clinton, Jackman, and Rivers 2004; Martin and Quinn 2002).

NOMINATE

The seminal contribution to estimating legislator ideal points from a probabilistic spatial voting model is Poole and Daniels (1985) NOMINATE model.[22] The earliest static version of the model implements a probabilistic voting model by assuming that the utility of alternative z for a legislator with ideal point x is

$$U(x, z) = \beta \exp\left[-\frac{(x - z)^2}{2}\right]$$

and that the random shocks are distributed according to the Type I extreme value distribution. The parameter β represents the 'signal-to-noise' ratio or weight on the deterministic portion of the utility function.[23]

The utility function employed by NOMINATE has the same shape as the density of the normal distribution and is therefore bell-shaped. For convenience in estimation, Poole and Rosenthal transform the model so that the roll-call parameters y and n are replaced by a cut point parameter $m = \frac{y+n}{2}$ and a distance parameter $d = \frac{y-n}{2}$.

Although Poole and Rosenthal selected this functional form to facilitate the estimation of the *yea* and *nay* outcome positions,[24] it has important substantive consequences. This exponential form implies that a legislator will be roughly indifferent between two alternatives that are located very far from her ideal point (in the tails, the utilities converge to zero). This is quite different from the implications of the quadratic utility function $U(x, z) = -(x - z)^2$ used in much of the applied theoretical literature and later models of ideal point estimation. With quadratic utility functions, the difference in utilities between two alternatives grows at an increasing

---

Let F be the cumulative distribution function of $\varepsilon_j^n - \varepsilon_j^y$, then the probabilities of voting *yea* and *nay* are simply

$$\Pr\{yea\} = F(U(x_i, y_j) - U(x_i, n_j))$$

$$\Pr\{nay\} = 1 - F(U(x_i, y_j) - U(x_i, n_j))$$

[22] The term NOMINATE is derived from *NOMINAl Three-step Estimation.*
[23] Under these assumptions, $\varepsilon_j^n - \varepsilon_j^y$ is distributed logistically and

$$\Pr\{yea\} = \frac{\exp\left[U(x_i, y_j)\right]}{\exp\left[U(x_i, y_j)\right] + \exp\left[U(x_i, n_j)\right]}$$

[24] See Poole and Rosenthal (1991, n 6).

rate as the alternatives move away from the ideal point.[25] As a substantive conjecture about behavior, the exponential assumption seems more reasonable. Who would perceive bigger differences between Fabian socialism and communism? A free-market conservative or a communist? The communist seems the better bet. Clearly, however, it is unsettling that the identification of y and n depend on the choice of function. But while estimates of d are less than robust, the cut point m is estimated precisely.

Poole and Rosenthal (1997) extend this static model to a dynamic one (D-NOMINATE) and estimate the ideal points of almost all legislators serving between 1789 and 1986 and the parameters associated with almost every roll call.[26] In estimating the dynamic model, Poole and Rosenthal confront the same comparability problem that I discussed above in the context of interest group ratings. Their main leverage for establishing comparability is that many members of Congress serve multiple terms and that Congress never turns over all at once. So there are many overlapping cohorts of legislators. These overlapping cohorts can be used to facilitate comparability. For example, the fact that Kay Bailey Hutchison served with both Phil Gramm and John Cornyn as Senators from Texas allows us to compare Gramm and Cornyn even though they never served together. This would be accomplished most directly if we assume that Hutchison's ideal point was fixed throughout her career. But that assumption is much stronger than what is required. Instead, Poole and Rosenthal assume that each legislator's ideal point moves as a polynomial function of time served, though they find that a linear trend for each legislator is sufficient.

Despite the fact that D-NOMINATE produces a scale on which Ted Kennedy can be compared to John Kennedy and to Harry Truman, some caution is obviously warranted in making too much of those comparisons. Although the model can constrain the movements of legislators over time, the substance of the policy agenda is free to move. Being liberal in 1939 meant something different than liberal in 1959 or in 2009. So one has to interpret NOMINATE scores in different eras relative to the policy agendas and debates of each.[27]

---

[25] Carroll, Lewis, et al. (forthcoming) show that within the empirically relevant range of roll-call locations, the difference in choice probabilities generated by these two utility functions is quite small.

[26] Obviously, estimating a legislator's ideal point requires a reasonable sample of roll calls. Poole and Rosenthal decided only to include those legislators who voted at least twenty-five times. Recall from the discussion above, unanimous votes are not informative in that they are consistent with an infinite number of cut points (any that are exterior to the set of ideal points). When voting is probabilistic, near unanimous roll calls are not very informative either. So Poole and Rosenthal include only roll calls where at least 2.5 percent of legislators vote on the minority side.

[27] In an attempt to overcome this problem, Bailey (2007) exploits the fact that Supreme Court justices, presidents, and legislators often opine about old Supreme Court decisions. If one assumes that these statements are good predictors of how these actors would have voted on those cases, justices, presidents, and legislators can be estimated on a common scale with a fixed policy context. For example, if Justice Scalia says he supports the decision in Brown, we are to infer that he would have voted for it and we can use that information to rank his preferences along with those who were on the court in 1953. But this is a very strong assumption. Perhaps Scalia supports Brown because it is settled law or the social costs of reversal are high, or it is just bad politics now to say otherwise. Thus, it would be difficult to infer from his contemporary statements how he would have voted.

Perhaps the most important substantive finding of their dynamic analysis is that legislative voting is very well explained by low dimension spatial models. With the exception of two eras (the so-called 'Era of Good Feeling' and the period leading up to the Civil War) a single dimension explains the bulk of legislative voting decisions. Across all congresses the single dimension spatial model correctly predicts 83 percent of the vote choices. Of course, unlike the case of interest group ratings, labeling that dimension is somewhat subjective. Poole and Rosenthal argue that the first dimension primarily reflects disagreements about the role of the federal government especially in economic matters. But the content of this debate changed dramatically over time from internal improvements, to bimetallism, to the income tax, and so on.

Overall, a two-dimensional version of the D-NOMINATE model explains 87 percent of voting choices, just 4 percent more than the one-dimensional model. There are periods in which a second dimension increases explanatory power substantially. The most sustained appearance of a second dimension runs from the end of Word War II through the 1960s where racial and civil rights issues formed cleavages within the Democratic Party that differed from conflicts on the economic dimension.

Newer flavors

Subsequent to their work using D-NOMINATE, Poole and Rosenthal have refined their models in a variety of directions. D-NOMINATE assumes that legislators place equal weight on each policy dimension. Consequently, the importance of a dimension is reflected in the variation of ideal points and bill locations along that dimension. The variation of ideal points increases with the salience of the dimension. An alternative approach is to fix the variation of ideal points and bill locations and allow the weight that legislators place on each dimension to vary. W-NOMINATE implements just such an alternative. Additionally, W-NOMINATE contains several technical innovations that optimize it for use on desktop computers (D-NOMINATE was originally estimated on a supercomputer).

Subsequently, McCarty, Poole, and Rosenthal (1997) developed a dynamic version of W-NOMINATE. In addition to distinct weights for each dimension, DW-NOMINATE differs from D-NOMINATE in that the stochastic component of the utility function is based on the normal distribution rather than the Type II extreme value.

While D- and DW-NOMINATE address the intertemporal comparability problem by restricting the movement of legislators over time, the sets of scores for the House and Senate are not comparable. In order to address this issue, Poole (1998) developed a model that uses members who serve in both chambers to transform DW-NOMINATE scores into a common scaling for both chambers. He has dubbed these results 'common space NOMINATE.' Finally, Poole (2001) developed a related model based on quadratic utilities and normal error distributions. This is often referred to as the QN model.

ESTIMATION ISSUES

All of the standard ideal point models have to confront a number of practical issues that emerge in estimation. Although some of these issues may seem a little subtle or arcane, it is in how these issues are handled that distinguishes the primary approaches to ideal point estimation. Consequently, the applied researcher should be familiar with these issues and the consequences of different means of addressing them.

Scale choice

As I discussed above, the scale of ideal points is latent and identified only up to a linear transformation. Consequently, any estimation procedure needs to make some assumptions to pin down the scale. For example, in one dimension, NOMINATE assumes that the leftmost legislator is located at -1 and the rightmost is located at 1. Not only does this assumption help pin down the scale, but it alleviates the following problem. Suppose a legislator was so conservative that she voted in the conservative direction on every single roll call. Independent of any other ideal point location, her ideal point could be 1, 10, or 100 with very little impact on the likelihood of the estimate. Constraining her ideal point to be no higher than 1 and constraining the gap between her and the nearest legislator alleviates what Poole and Rosenthal dub the "sag" problem—an appeal to the image of extreme legislators' positions spreading out like an old waistband.

The estimates of some roll-call parameters must also be constrained for identification reasons. Consider the cut point of the roll call $m = \frac{y+n}{2}$. Suppose that there is a near unanimous roll call in favor of a liberal proposal. Then any $m > 1$ might be a reasonable estimate of this parameter. Consequently, m is constrained to a location between -1 and 1. Problems also arise with the distance parameter $d = \frac{y-n}{2}$. Suppose that on some roll call every legislator flips a fair coin. Very different values of d can produce the appropriate likelihood function. When $d = 0$, the alternatives are the same so that legislators flip coins. When $d = \infty$ (and m is between -1 and 1), both alternatives are so bad that a legislator is indifferent and flips a coin. Given this problem, d is constrained so that at least one of the bill locations (y or n) lies on the unit interval.[28]

A final issue in the selection of the scale concerns the variance of the random utility shocks. Whether NOMINATE is estimated with a logit function (as in D-) or a probit function (as in DW-), the assumed variance of the shocks is fixed—one roll call has just as much randomness as another. The parameter β, however, controls for the weight placed on the deterministic part of the utility function so that the effects of the variance are scaled by $\frac{1}{\beta}$. Without β to control the effects of variance, the estimates of the distance parameter d would be distorted in trying to account for it. To see this,

---

[28] These constraints together imply that $|\min(m + d, m - d)| < 1$.

compare two roll calls that differ only in the variance of the error terms. In the noisier roll call, the choice probabilities should all be closer to .5. One way to achieve this is to move the estimate of d closer to zero (i.e. make y and n more similar). Consequently, our confidence in estimates of d (and therefore y and z) depends on β capturing all of the effects of the variance of the stochastic term. Since d is imprecisely estimated, the *yea* and *nay* outcome coordinates will be as well. Therefore, use of the outcome coordinates is not recommended without adjusting for the level of noise in the roll call (see McCarty and Poole 1995). This problem has limited the applicability of ideal point models for studying policy change.

Sample size

The number of parameters per dimension for the NOMINATE models is $p + 2q$ where p is the number of legislators and q is the number of roll calls. Of course, for any typical legislature this will be a very large number of parameters. Fortunately, the sample of vote choices is pq and is consequently larger than the number of parameters so long as $p > \frac{2q}{q-1}$. However, because one cannot increase the sample size without increasing the number of parameters, it is impossible to guarantee that the parameter estimates converge to their true values as the sample size goes to infinity, that is, the estimates are inconsistent.[29] Therefore, Poole and Rosenthal conducted numerous Monte Carlo studies to establish that NOMINATE does a reasonable job at recovering the underlying parameters in finite samples.

Heckman and Snyder (1997) propose an alternative model that does consistent estimates of ideal points, but not bill locations. In addition to the assumption of quadratic preferences, the Heckman–Snyder estimator requires that $\varepsilon_y - \varepsilon_n$ be distributed uniformly. They demonstrate that under these assumptions ideal points can be estimated using factor analysis.[30] When implementing the model, they find that their results for one or two dimensions are almost identical to NOMINATE apart from some differences in the extremes of the ideal point distribution. This suggests that the consequences of the inconsistency of NOMINATE are small.[31]

Both the asymptotic results of Heckman and Snyder and the Monte Carlo work of Poole and Rosenthal suggest that it is important for both p and q to be large. The following example from Londregan (2000a, 2000b) helps illustrate why. Consider a situation with only three legislators: 1, 2, and 3. On a particular roll call, they vote as shown in Figure 4.6. Note that both cut points m' and m'' are consistent with the observed voting pattern. The precise estimate of m (and therefore y and n) will depend entirely on the functional form of the random component of the utilities. Consequently, m is also likely to be estimated with large amounts of error. Of course,

---

[29]   This is known as the incidental parameters problem.

[30]   While Heckman and Snyder's estimates of bill locations are inconsistent, the linearity of the model prevents this inconsistency from feeding back into the estimates of ideal points.

[31]   The primary differences between Poole–Rosenthal and Heckman–Snyder concern the dimensionality of the policy space. I take this issue up below.

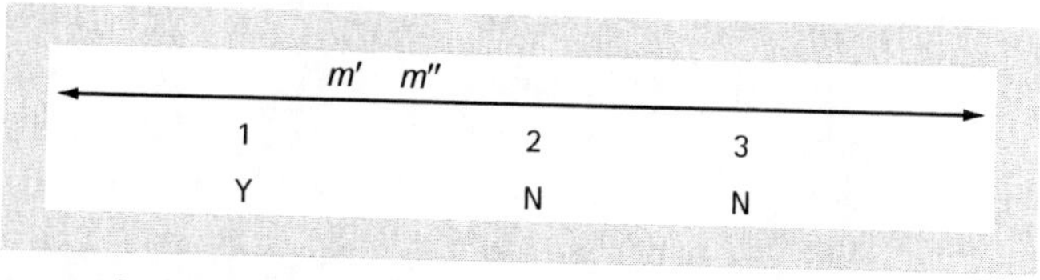

Fig. 4.6. The granularity problem

if we are only interested in the ideal points this may be tolerable. But remember that the quality of the estimates of the ideal points will depend on the quality of the estimates of m. So the ideal points will be estimated poorly as well.

Unfortunately, many of the institutions for which we would like ideal point estimates, such as courts and regulatory boards, are quite small. So how should researchers approach such applications?

An obvious choice is to simply accept that the problem exists and go ahead and run NOMINATE or Heckman–Snyder. The downside, of course, is that the estimates will not be precise.[32] Doing better than that requires an accurate diagnosis of the problem. At the root of the problem is that roll-call voting data contains precious little information necessary to generate cardinal estimates. As I discussed above, cardinality requires making assumptions about the random process that generates voting errors. When there are few legislators, the reliance on parametric assumptions rises disproportionately. The real problem is that roll-call data by itself is inadequate. More data about legislative preferences or proposals can help ameliorate this problem.

First consider observable covariates about preferences. Let's say we have an observed variable w. Something like region, value-added from manufacturing, or district partisanship that we believe is plausibly related to legislative policy preferences. Then we could model each ideal point as $x_i = a_{1i} + a_{2i}w_i$. The inclusion of w_i helps pin down the scale and locate ideal points. This in turn improves the estimation of roll-call cut points, which improves ideal point estimation, and so on.

Information about proposals can also be useful. The best application of this insight is Krehbiel and Rivers's (1988) work on the minimum wage. Because minimum wage proposals are denominated in dollars, y and n (and therefore m) are observed directly. Given the observed cut points, one only has to estimate the ideal points on the scale defined by dollars.

The difficulty of both approaches relates to the availability of auxiliary data. Numerous potential covariates exist for preferences. The trick is generating a parsimonious specification. Moreover, many scholars are interested in an unobserved component (ideology?) of legislative preferences, so preference covariates can never

---

[32] In the case of the earlier versions of NOMINATE, this problem is confounded by the fact that its iterative maximum likelihood procedure underestimates the uncertainty associated with its estimates. Estimation of the covariance matrix in the Heckman–Snyder model is computationally prohibitive. More recently, Lewis and Poole (2004) have implemented bootstrapping procedures to better recover the uncertainty in parameter estimates. The Bayesian procedures described below deal with estimation uncertainty directly.

eliminate the problem. One encounters the opposite problem when it comes to modeling proposals with observable variables. Many legislative proposals cannot be quantified like budgets and wage floors can be. Londregan (2000a, 2000b) takes an approach that makes fewer demands in terms of observable data. Rather than attempt to measure preferences and proposals, he models the proposal-making process. In general, such an approach would involve assuming that legislator i's optimal proposal can be related to the other parameters of the model. Such assumptions can be used to pin down some of the model's parameters. Londregan assumes that legislators always propose their own ideal point.[33] Of course, the accuracy of the estimates depends on the validity of the proposal function.

A similar approach is employed by Clinton and Meirowitz (2003, 2004). They leverage the fact that along an agenda sequence, one of two things must be true. If a new proposal is adopted at time $t - 1$, it becomes the status quo at time t. If the new proposal fails at time $t - 1$, then the status quo from $t - 1$ becomes the status quo at time t. Imposing these constraints helps pin down the proposal parameters.

It is important to note, however, that all these approaches simply shift the weight of one set of parametric assumptions—the stochastic process—to another set—modeling choices about covariates, proposal making, or agendas. The only alternative to this tradeoff is to give up on the ability to generate cardinal ideal points and settle for extracting the ordinal information from the roll-call data. Such is the approach of Poole's (2000) Optimal Classification (OC) algorithm. As I demonstrated above, when legislative voting is in perfect accord with spatial preferences, it is possible to rank order the ideal points of legislators on the issue dimension. But of course, the distances between any two legislators is unidentified without voting errors and assumptions about the distribution of the shocks that generate those errors. In the presence of voting error, Poole's algorithm makes no assumptions about the process generating those errors. It simply tries to order the legislators in such a way as to minimize the number of errors. For large legislatures, the OC estimates correlate very highly with the ranking of NOMINATE ideal points. For smaller bodies the correlations are much lower, reflecting the importance of parametric assumptions in pinning down cardinal estimates. But even in large legislatures, OC and NOMI-NATE sometimes produce substantively important differences. Suppose a legislator is a "maverick" like John McCain or Russ Feingold and makes large voting errors. Parametric models like NOMINATE penalize such errors harshly. Consequently, the model will move legislators to more moderate positions in order to minimize the large errors. In OC, an error is an error, no matter how large. Without the extra penalty, OC will weigh Feingold's predictably liberal votes and McCain's predictably conservative votes relatively more than their "mavericky" votes. So Feingold is more likely to be identified as a liberal and McCain as a conservative in OC than in NOMINATE.

---

[33] Londregan's model departs from the standard model by assuming that some legislators make "better" proposals than others. This valence effect is equivalent to assuming that the distribution of ε_y varies across legislators.

BAYESIAN ESTIMATION

Since the year 2000, there has been tremendous progress in applying Bayesian Item Response Theory (IRT) to the task of estimating spatial models of roll-call voting. IRT was originally developed in the context of educational testing to facilitate the estimation of test-takers' ability when the quality and difficulty of an examination is unknown. Beginning in the 1990s, scholars began applying Bayesian estimation techniques such as Markov Chain Monte Carlo (MCMC) and Gibbs sampling (Albert 1992; Albert and Chib 1993).[34]

To justify the use of the Bayesian IRT, scholars (Jackman 2001; Clinton, Jackman, and Rivers 2004; Martin and Quinn 2002) assume that legislator preferences are quadratic. Together with the assumption that voting errors are normally distributed, this implies that the probability of a *yea* outcome is simply $\Phi(a_{j0} + a_{j1}x_i)$ where $a_{j0} = n_j^2 - y_j^2$, $a_{j1} = 2(y_j - n_j)$, and Φ is the normal distribution function. This probability is analogous to the probability of a correct answer in educational testing. In IRT, x_i represents the student's ability. Assuming $a_1 > 0$, higher ability students are more likely to answer questions correctly. The parameter a_{j0} represents difficulty of the test item; easy questions have higher values of a_{j0}. Finally, a_{j1} is known as the discrimination parameter as it determines the marginal impact of student ability on the probability of a correct answer. If a_{j1} is close to zero, good and bad students get the correct answer at roughly equal probabilities as the item fails to discriminate on ability.

These interpretations extend (albeit imperfectly) to the ideal point context. The difficulty parameter a_{j0} is the difference between the distances from 0 for the two alternatives. When $y_j^2 < n_j^2$, the likelihood of voting *yea* is higher, holding the ideal point constant. The discrimination parameter a_{j1} plays two roles. First, it defines the polarity of the roll call so that when $a_{j1} > 0$, the *yea* outcome is the conservative outcome and legislators with higher values of x_i are more likely to support it. Second, by reflecting the difference between the two alternatives, the absolute value of a_{j1} controls how well the roll call discriminates between liberal and conservative legislators.[35]

Perhaps the most direct benefit of the Bayesian approach is that uncertainty in the estimated parameters is easily measured and summarized. The magnitude of this advantage, however, may have narrowed with the advent of the parametric bootstrap for computing the standard errors of NOMINATE parameters.

The Bayesian model provides some distinct computational advantages and disadvantages. A major advantage is that it is much more straightforward to use covariates and other information to model ideal points and proposal parameters. For example, Clinton, Jackman, and Rivers (2004) incorporate party membership directly into

---

[34] Carroll et al. (forthcoming) provide a very comprehensive survey of the differences between W-NOMINATE and the Bayesian model in the case of a single dimension.

[35] The cut point and distance parameters can be easily recovered from the IRT parameters as $m = -\frac{a_0}{a_1}$ and $d = \frac{a_1}{2}$.

the model to estimate distinct cut points for each party.[36] Because the likelihood function of NOMINATE is already highly non-linear and non-concave, estimating more complex models is often infeasible. The primary disadvantage, however, is that even the simplest IRT model can be very time consuming to estimate when compared to NOMINATE or Heckman–Snyder.

Identification of the Bayesian model can be achieved either by the imposition of prior distributions on the parameters or through constraints like those used in NOMINATE. Early implementations such as Jackman (2001) assume prior distribution that is normal with mean 0 and unit variance. But because this is an assumption about the population from which ideal points are drawn, rather than the sample of legislators, it does not fully anchor the scale and leads to an overstatement of estimation uncertainty (see Lewis and Poole 2004). So later models such as Clinton, Jackman, and Rivers (2004) identify the scale by setting one legislator to −1 and another to +1 a priori. In estimating their dynamic model of Supreme Court voting, Martin and Quinn (2002) assume informative priors for several justices (in their first term) to pin down the scale.

In the end, it appears that differences in estimates between NOMINATE and the Bayesian models are quite small. As the extensive Monte Carlo analysis of Carroll, Lewis, et al. (forthcoming) concludes, subtle differences are created by the different functional form assumptions as well as procedural choice in the handling of identification restrictions. But with the development of the Poole's QN model and MCMC versions of NOMINATE (Carroll, Lewis, et al. 2009), the differences are likely to get smaller and the choice between estimators will become one of convenience and taste.

MODEL EVALUATION

While in principle one could apply any measure of fit appropriate for a maximum likelihood or Bayesian estimator, much of the literature, beginning with Poole and Rosenthal, focuses on measures of predictive or "classification" success. Such measures are straightforward. They reflect the percentage of cases where the vote choice with the higher estimated likelihood corresponds to the observed vote. The primary virtue of classification measures is that they are intuitive and easy to interpret. A second advantage of classification success is that it is straightforward to compare very different models. Not only does it allow comparisons between different parametric models like NOMINATE, Heckman–Snyder, and the Bayesian model, it can also compare them against non-parametric alternatives like Optimal Classification.[37]

---

[36] See also McCarty, Poole, and Rosenthal (2000).

[37] Of course, because OC maximizes classification success, it will generally outperform on this criterion the alternatives based on maximum likelihood.

Classification success has a number of drawbacks as well. The first is that it can be artificially inflated if there are a large number of lopsided votes. Suppose for example that the average margin on a roll-call vote is 65 percent. Then a 65 percent classification success can be generated by a naive model that predicts that all legislators vote for the winning alternative. If for some reason winning margins increase, the baseline classification rate will rise even if the ideal point model has no additional explanatory power. For this reason, scholars beginning with Poole and Rosenthal have often focused on a measure called proportional reduction in error (PRE). Intuitively, the PRE specifies how much better the spatial model performs than a 'majority' model that assumes that every legislator votes for the more popular alternative. Formally,

$$PRE = \frac{Majority\ Errors\ -\ Model\ Errors}{Majority\ Errors}$$

where *Majority Errors* are the number of votes against the majority position and *Model Errors* are the number of incorrect predictions of the spatial model. A second concern is that both classification success and the PRE weigh mistakes close to the cut line just as heavily as big mistakes. To penalize mistakes according to their magnitude generally requires the use of likelihood-based measures. Poole and Rosenthal propose the use of the geometric mean probability (GMP) which is computed as the anti-log of the average log-likelihood. Unfortunately, such measures are more difficult to compare across estimators.

Finally, classification measures do not easily lend themselves to formal statistical inference the way that other methods such as the Wald statistic and likelihood-ratio test do. This issue has been the most prominent in the debate over the dimensionality of roll-call voting. On the basis of classification analysis, Poole and Rosenthal conclude that congressional voting in the United States is largely one-dimensional. With the exception of a few definable eras, the classification success of a two-dimensional model is generally no more that two percentage points higher than a one-dimensional model. But efforts to apply formal statistical inference to the question of dimensionality generally reject the unidimensional model in favor of higher-dimensional alternatives (see Heckman and Snyder 1997 and Jackman 2001). These different findings present something of a conundrum to applied researchers. Clearly formal statistical tests are preferable to ad hoc rules of thumb.[38] But substantive significance and parsimony are also important considerations. Given these competing considerations, this debate will likely continue.

---

[38] There are reasons to be wary of the statistical tests that have thus far been proposed. First, testing a two-dimensional model versus a one-dimensional model involves one restricted parameter per legislator and two per roll call. So tests can be sensitive to the penalties imposed for additional parameters (see Jackman 2001). Second, the tests have been carried out under the assumption that unobserved errors are independent across legislators. Higher-dimensional models may simply be fitting cross-legislator correlations that do not constitute substantively important dimensions.

INTERPRETATION

In the end, the key problem for legislative scholars is figuring out exactly what the ideal point estimates mean. Technically, ideal points are simply a low dimension representation of all the considerations that go into roll-call voting. But what are the political, psychological, and strategic factors that create the types of coalition structures that are so easily represented in one or two dimensions? Drawing on the ideas of Phillip Converse (1964), Poole and Rosenthal have explained low dimensionality in terms of *belief constraint*. This is the notion that political elites share beliefs about which issue opinions go together. Support for tax cuts is correlated with support for deregulation which is correlated with higher defense spending because elites believe that those issues are related. But constraint is really little more than a description of the phenomena, not an explanation. There is no logical underpinning for the issue configurations that define left and right. Why exactly should a pro-life position predict support for tax cuts? Moreover, these configurations have changed over time. Protectionism used to be the province of the conservative. Ideal point estimation and dimensional analysis can identify when such changes occur, but it has more limited value in explaining why.

One of the more contentious debates surrounding the interpretation of ideal points is the argument about the role of ideology. The argument that ideal points reflect ideological preferences is based on several empirical findings. The first is that ideal point estimates are quite stable for politicians throughout their career. Of course, there are a few prominent examples of politicians whose positions did change; such as the right to left movements of Wayne Morse, or the left to right movements of Richard Schweiker or the right to left to right movements of John McCain. A very small number of politicians like William Proxmire have been nothing if not erratic. But for the most part, legislators' ideal points only move significantly if they switch parties (and of course party switching is quite rare).[39] Even a member whose constituency changes quite dramatically, either by elevation to the Senate or through major redistricting, rarely changes positions in a significant way. In a very careful study, the assumption that legislators maintain the same ideological position throughout their careers performs just as well statistically as the assumption that legislators are able to change positions in each biennial term.[40]

The second piece of evidence in favor of an ideological interpretation is that the behavior of legislators deviates in large and systematic ways from the preferences of their average or median constituent. This finding persists even when we do not worry about the mismeasurement of constituency interests or preferences. For example, senators from the same state do not vote identically. Most obviously, senators from the same state but different parties, such as Bill Nelson and Mel Martinez of Florida,

---

[39] See McCarty, Poole, and Rosenthal (2001).
[40] See Poole (2007).

pursue very different policy goals. The difference is picked up in their polarized ideal point estimates. If the two senators are from the same party, they are, of course, more similar. Even here, however, there are differences. Consider California Democrats Diane Feinstein and Barbara Boxer. They not only represent the same state but were first elected by exactly the same electorate on the same day in 1992. In the most recent Senate term, Boxer has a DW-NOMINATE score of -0.601 making her the third most liberal member of the U.S. Senate. Conversely, Dianne Feinstein's ideal point is just -0.384 making her the 37th most liberal. Moreover, there is nothing unusual about this California duo. Four other states have pairs of senators from the same party whose NOMINATE scores differ at least as much.

House districts, being single-member, do not allow the same natural experiment that is possible for the Senate. It is possible, however, to compare the voting behavior of a member to his or her successor. The same-party replacements of House members can have ideal points that are very different from those of their predecessors. True, a relatively liberal Democrat is likely to be replaced by another liberal Democrat, but the variation in the scores of the same-party replacements is very large. It is about half as large as the total variation of positions within the party.[41] In other words, the ideal point of the outgoing incumbent is at best a crude predictor of the position of the new member even if they are in the same party.

While the evidence is strong that ideal points reflect ideology to some degree, clearly ideal point estimates may also reflect any number of other influences such as constituent interests, interest group pressure, or partisan strategies. A large body of literature trys to parse these components but there is currently little methodological or substantive agreement.[42]

Another important issue for the end-user concerns how to interpret ideal points in multiple dimensions. Perhaps because ideal point producers like to name their dimensions—economic, social, race, and so on—end-users often mistakenly infer that the ideal point coordinate from the social dimension is the best predictor of abortion votes and the coordinate from the race dimension is the best predictor of civil rights votes. This confusion arises because the estimated dimensions are orthogonal by design. But few substantive issues are completely uncorrelated from all others. Consequently, it is not the coordinates from specific dimensions that are best predictors, but rather the projection of the ideal point vector (the coordinates from all dimensions) onto a line that is perpendicular to the cut line. To illustrate, consider Figure 4.7 which represents Senate ideal points and voting on the 1964 Civil Rights Act. Clearly, the positions on the first dimension are inadequate to explain this vote, as they predict that many southern Democrats would actually support the bill. But the second dimension alone does not do so well either. It would considerably overpredict the number of Republicans who voted for the bill. Instead, multi-dimensionality

---

[41] See Poole and Romer (1993).

[42] A sampling of some of this work includes Glazer and Robbins (1985), Kalt and Zupan (1990), Levitt (1996), Rothenberg and Sanders (2000), Snyder and Ting (2003), Lee, Moretti, and Butler (2004), and McCarty, Poole, and Rosenthal (2006).

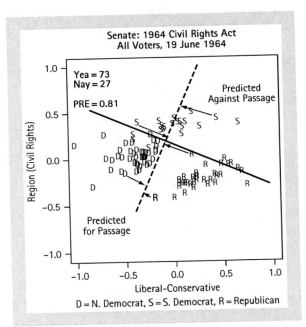

Fig. 4.7. The spatial mapping of the Senate vote on the 1964 Civil Rights Act

is reflected in the fact that the cut line for the bill deviates considerably from the vertical line one would expect for a first-dimension vote (yet it also is not horizontal as would be expected by a purely second-dimension vote). But we can generate a single measure reflecting civil rights voting. First, we choose a line perpendicular to the cut line such as the dotted line in the figure. Then we project the ideal points onto the perpendicular line. In other words, we move each ideal point to its closest point on the perpendicular line. The projection is illustrated by the arrows in the figure. Note that the new positions do as good a job representing the vote as the two-dimensional configuration. Any senator with a projection below the intersection is predicted to support the measure and any one with a point above it is predicted to oppose it. Consequently, the projection represents the substantive civil rights dimension.[43]

In practice, however, it will usually be unnecessary to compute this projection. If one wants simply to estimate a regression model of a vote on NOMINATE scores, including the coordinate for each dimension is usually sufficient. The coefficient on the second-dimension coordinate would be properly interpreted as the effect of the second-dimension holding positions on the first-dimension constant. If one, however, wants a single summary measure of positions on a substantive issue, computing the projection is the appropriate way to proceed.

---

[43] If one wants to use more than one vote in constructing the measure, one would project to a line perpendicular to the average cut line of the votes.

DIRECTIONS FOR THE FUTURE

Clearly ideal point estimation has become a large and influential literature with a broad impact on the study of institutions in the United States and the world. Certainly there remain open questions about the implementation and interpretation of the basic spatial model. But I suspect much of the efforts moving forward will involve estimating more complex and theoretically-driven models of legislative behavior. In particular, work on strategic voting and logrolling has been limited. Although the basic model can accommodate simple forms of strategic voting, richer models of strategic voting, such as those under incomplete information, are just now being considered. Similarly, logrolling and vote trading are inconsistent with the independence assumptions underlying the basic model. How vote trading affects ideal point estimation and confounds the evaluation of dimensionality clearly needs further work. The use of scaling models to detect vote trading and other forms of legislator coordination may also be another important avenue for work. Finally, it seems that the real potential of Bayesian MCMC has yet to be reached in this area. Its ability to estimate hierarchical models of ideal points and alternatives with additional sources of data is far from exhausted.

While such technical advances will be welcome, even more work is yet to be done in terms of interpreting the implications of ideal point estimates for our understanding of politics. Obviously, issues as to whether ideal points are reflections of member ideology, party pressure, or constituency interest are far from resolved. Moreover, very little is known about the dynamics of how issues map (or not) into the major dimensions of conflict over time. Progress on this front will entail significantly more attention to methodological challenges of estimating policy outcomes in addition to ideal points.

REFERENCES

ALBERT, J. 1992. Bayesian Estimation of Normal Ogive Item Response Curves Using Gibbs Sampling. *Journal of Educational Statistics*, 17: 251–69.

—— and CHI, S. 1993. Bayesian Analysis of Binary and Polychotomous Response Data. *Journal of the American Statistical Association*, 88: 669–79.

BAILEY, M., and CHANG, K. 2001. Comparing Presidents, Senators, and Publications Justices: Inter-institutional Preference Estimation. *Journal of Law, Economics and Organization*, 17(2): 477–506.

—— 2007. Comparable Preference Estimates across Time and Institutions for the Court, Congress and Presidency. *American Journal of Political Science*, 51(3): 433–48.

CAMERON, C. M. 2000. *Veto Bargaining: Presidents and the politics of Negative Power*. New York: Cambridge University Press.

CARROLL, R., LEWIS, J. B., LO, J., POOLE, K. T., and ROSENTHAL, H. 2009. The Structure of Utility in Spatial Models of Voting. Presented at the Fourth Annual Conference on Empirical Legal Studies, Los Angeles.

———— ———— ———— ———— ———— n.d. Comparing NOMINATE and IDEAL: Points of Difference and Monte Carlo Tests. Forthcoming. *Legislative Studies Quarterly.*

CLINTON, J. D. 2007. Lawmaking and Roll Calls, *Journal of Politics*, 69: 457–69.

—— JACKMAN, S. D., and RIVERS, D. 2004. The Statistical Analysis of Roll Call Data: A Unified Approach. *American Political Science Review*, 98: 355–70.

—— and MEIROWITZ, A. H. 2003. Integrating Voting Theory and Roll Call Analysis: A Framework. *Political Analysis*, 11: 381–96.

—— ———— 2004. Testing Accounts of Legislative Strategic Voting. *American Journal of Political Science*, 48: 675–89.

COX, G. W., and McCUBBINS, M. D. 2005. *Setting the Agenda: Responsible Party Government in the U.S. House of Representatives.* New York: Cambridge University Press.

GILLIGAN, T. W., and KREHBIEL, K. 1987. Collective Decisionmaking and Standing Committees: An Informational Rationale for Retrictive Amendment Procedures. *Journal of Law, Economics, and Organizations*, 3(2): 287–335.

GLAZER, A., and ROBBINS, M. 1985. Congressional Responsiveness to Constituency Change. *American Journal of Political Science*, 29: 259–72.

GROSECLOSE, T., LEVITT, S. D., and SNYDER, JR., J. M. 1999. Comparing Interest Group Scores across Time and Chambers: Adjusted ADA Scores for the U.S. Congress. *American Political Science Review*, 93(1): 33–50.

HECKMAN, J., and SNYDER, J. 1997. Linear Probability Models of the Demand for Attributes with an Empirical Application to Estimating the Preferences of Legislators. *Rand Journal of Economics*, 28: S142–89.

HIX, S., NOURY, A., and ROLAND, G. 2006. *Democratic Politics in the European Parliament.* Cambridge: Cambridge University Press.

JACKMAN, S. 2001. Multidimensional Analysis of Roll Call Data via Bayesian Simulation: Identification, Estimation, Inference and Model Checking. *Political Analysis*, 9: 227–41.

KALANDRAKIS, T. n.d. Rationalizable Voting. Forthcoming. *Theoretical Economics.*

KREHBIEL, K., and RIVERS, D. 1988. The Analysis of Committee Power: An Application to Senate Voting on the Minimum Wage. *American Journal of Political Science*, 32(4): 1151–74.

—— 1989. *Informational and Legislative Organization.* Ann Arbor: University of Michigan Press.

—— 1998. *Pivotal Politics: A Theory of U.S. Lawmaking.* Chicago: University of Chicago Press.

LEE, D. S., MORETTI, E., and BUTLER, M. 2004. Do Voters Affect or Elect Policies: Evidence from the U.S. House. *Quarterly Journal of Economics*, 119(3): 807–59.

LEVITT, S. 1996. How Do Senators Vote? Disentangling the Role of Voter Preferences, Party Affiliation, and Senator Ideology. *American Political Science Review*, 83(3): 425–41.

LONDREGAN, J. 2000a. Estimating Legislators' Preferred Points. *Political Analysis*, 8(1): 35–56.

—— 2000b. *Legislative Institutions and Ideology in Chile.* New York: Cambridge University Press.

MARTIN, A., and QUINN, K. 2002. Dynamic Ideal Point Estimation via Markov Chain Monte Carlo for the U.S. Supreme Court, 1953–1999. *Political Analysis*, 10(2): 134–53.

McCARTY, N., and MEIROWITZ, A. 2006. *Political Game Theory: An Introduction.* New York: Cambridge University Press.

——and POOLE, K. T. 1995. Veto Power and Legislation: An Empirical Analysis of Executive-Legislative Bargaining from 1961–1986. *Journal of Law, Economics, & Organization,* 11(2): 282–312.

——— and ROSENTHAL, H. 1997. *Income Redistribution and the Realignment of American Politics.* Washington DC: AEI Press.

——— 2001. The Hunt for Party Discipline in Congress. *American Political Science Review,* 95: 673–87.

——— 2006. *Polarized America: The Dance of Ideology and Unequal Riches.* Cambridge, MA: MIT Press.

MORGENSTERN, S. 2004. *Patterns of Legislative Politics: Roll Call Voting in the Latin America and the United States.* Cambridge: Cambridge University Press.

KALT, J. P., and ZUPAN, M. A. 1990. The Apparent Ideological Behavior of Legislators: Testing for Principal-Agent Slack in Political Institutions. *Journal of Law and Economics,* 33: 103–31.

LONDREGAN, J. B. 2000a. Estimating Legislators' Preferred Points. *Political Analysis,* 8(1): 35–56.

—— 2000b. *Legislative Institutions and Ideology in Chile.* New York: Cambridge University Press.

LOTT, JR., J. R., and BRONARS, S. G. 1993. Time Series Evidence on Shirking in the U.S. House of Representatives. *Public Choice,* 74: 461–84.

LEWIS, J. B., and POOLE, K. T. 2004. Measuring Bias and Uncertainty in Ideal Point Estimates via the Parametric Bootstrap. *Political Analysis,* 12: 105–27.

ORDESHOOK, P. C. 1986. *Game Theory and Political Theory.* New York: Cambridge University Press.

PHILLIP, C. 1964. The Nature of Belief Systems in the Mass Public, pp. 206–61 in *Ideology and Discontent,* ed. D. Apter. New York: Free Press, 206–61.

POOLE, K. T., and ROSENTHAL, H. 1985. A Spatial Model for Legisaltive Roll Call Analysis. *American Journal of Political Science,* 29: 357–84.

—— 1998. Recovering a Basic Space From a Set of Issue Scales. *American Journal of Political Science,* 42(3): 954–93.

—— 2000. Non-parametric Unfolding of Binary Choice Data. *Political Analysis,* 8(3): 211–37.

—— 2001. The Geometry of Multidimensional Quadratic Utility in Models of Parliamentary Roll Call Voting. *Political Analysis,* 9, 211–26.

—— 2005. *Spatial Models of Parliamentary Voting.* New York: Cambridge University Press.

—— 2007. Changing Minds? Not in Congress. *Public Choice,* 131: 435–51.

—— and DANIELS, R. S. 1985. Ideology, Party, and Voting in the U.S. Congress, 1959–1980. *American Political Science Review,* 79(2): 373–99.

—— and ROSENTHAL, H. 1991. Patterns of Congressional Voting. *American Journal of Political Science,* 35: 228–78.

—— and ROMER, T. 1993. Ideology, Shirking, and Representation. *Public Choice,* 77: 185–96.

—— and ROSENTHAL, H. 1997. *Congress: A Political Economic History of Rollcall Voting.* New York: Oxford University Press.

ROTHENBERG, L. S., and SANDERS, M. S. 2000. Severing the Electoral Connection: Shirking in the Contemporary Congress. *American Journal of Political Science,* 44: 316–25.

SHOR, B., and McCARTY, N. 2010. The Ideological Mapping of the American States. Typescript, University of Chicago.

SNYDER, JR., J. M., 1992. Artificial Extremism in Interest Groups Ratings. *Legislative Studies Quarterly*, 17: 319–45.

SNYDER, J., and TING, M. 2003. Party Labels, Roll-Call Votes, and Elections. *Political Analysis*, 11(4): 419–44.

VOETEN, E. 2000. Clashes in the Assembly, *International Organization*, 54(2): 185–215.

WRIGHT, G. C., and SCHAFFNER, B. F. 2002. The Influence of Party: Evidence from the State Legislatures. *American Political Science Review*, 96(2): 367–79.

....

CHAPTER 5

TOUCHING THE BONES: INTERVIEWING AND DIRECT OBSERVATIONAL STUDIES OF CONGRESS

....

ROSS K. BAKER

It is fifty years since the publication of Donald R. Matthews's *U.S. Senators and Their World* (1960). Since that time, the approach to the study of Congress pioneered by Matthews, one relying importantly on interviews with senators, has constituted a small minority of all congressional studies. Yet those who have emulated Matthews's approach have contributed a disproportionate amount to our understanding of Congress. But the paucity of interview-based work also speaks eloquently of the difficulty of conducting this type of research. Later in this chapter, I will dwell on some of the practical problems of interviewing members of Congress and why these interviews form a distinct, elite category. First, however, it is important to review the contributions of the most influential of the works relying significantly on interview materials. It should be noted at the outset that few of the most important works rest solely on interviews. Most are augmented by other kinds of data, ranging from roll-call votes to the volume and content of constituent mail. Donald Matthews's study is a good place to start not only because of its pioneering status but also because its most celebrated findings initiated decades of debate among congressional scholars. The ensuing discussion will not touch on every interview-based study of Congress; it will rather focus on what seems a representative group.

At the heart of *U.S. Senators and Their World* are Matthews's observations about the role of norms and folkways in the upper chamber. Remarkably, for all the discussion and debate they occasioned, these observations constitute but a small portion of the book. Matthews was able to cull from his interviews evidence of six folkways that governed and constrained the behavior of senators. The first of these, *apprenticeship*, or serving a kind of tutelary period in which the newcomer is seen but not heard, was on its way to oblivion by the time Matthews noted it. The other five—*legislative work, specialization, courtesy, reciprocity, institutional patriotism*—still operated, with varying degrees of vitality. The debate over the ensuing decades with the decline of the old conservative leadership of the body, the rise of candidate-centered campaigns, the broadening of committee assignments, and increasingly individualistic behavior led some scholars to proclaim the decline and fall of folkways.

Matthews himself, writing forty-one years after *U.S. Senators and Their Worlds*, lamented that, "while the study of the Senate is thriving, the institution itself seems to be in some trouble. Does a highly partisan, highly individualistic, easily deadlocked and poorly representative institution have a future?" (Matthews 2001, 169). Matthews' verdict on the contemporary Senate comports with the scarceness of any significant mention of norms and folkways in today's scholarly literature. But it kicked off a lively discussion, which lasted into the late 1980s.

Next in seniority among the major interview-based studies is John W. Kingdon's *Congressmen's Voting Decisions* (1973), which drew on fieldwork conducted in the late 1960s. Focused on the House, Kingdon examined the various factors that contribute to the ultimate decision of House members on how to vote on a bill. Kingdon chose to interview members of the House of Representatives rather than the Senate, "in the belief that access to the former would be somewhat easier to obtain" (Kingdon 1973, 15). This was a prudent decision that any scholar would be tempted to make, because, as we shall see, the Senate offers an unusually imposing barrier to researchers. These are not insuperable barriers, but the process of conducting interviews would be far less efficient and the process more elongated.

For Kingdon, the unit of analysis was not the House member but the *decision*. Kingdon's contribution to our understanding of how members arrive at decisions to support or oppose legislation is what he characterized as "the consensus mode of decision." Using a series of filters, members arrive at a decision by making an initial judgment on whether or not the vote is controversial. If they see no obvious danger signals, to use Kingdon's term, they "vote with the environment."

If the vote is more problematic, there is a series of questions a member poses to pick up voting cues. These come from a variety of sources: the constituency, relevant interest groups, the state delegation, the position taken by the president, and the member's own appraisal of whether the measure accords with his or her own conception of good public policy. Rather surprising was Kingdon's conclusion that the influence of congressional staff was much more limited than he had anticipated. But Kingdon speculated that staff influence on senators' decisions was likely to be greater than with House members. On a broader level, we are indebted to Kingdon for his shrewd understanding of the importance of agenda-setting in the policy process. This, perhaps, is the most lasting contribution of *Congressmen's Voting Decisions.*

The appearance of Barbara Sinclair's *The Transformation of the U.S. Senate* (1989) marked both the continuation and also, in a sense, the *coda* to discussion of Senate norms. On the basis of her interviews with senior staff members of eighteen senators, Sinclair found that many of the most important norms described by Matthews had lost much of their vitality. In particular, "the norms of specialization, legislative work, reciprocity, and institutional patriotism became defunct or drastically changed their form" (Sinclair 1989, 209).

Sinclair also noted that, although the Senate had become an effective forum for the articulation of interests and agenda-setting, decision-making had become more problematic. Changes in the institution since Matthews wrote have promoted the advancement of individual senators' goals at the expense of collective action.

Two years after the appearance of Sinclair's work, C. Lawrence Evans published *Leadership in Committee* (1991), a study consisting of three components, one of which was interviews with a total of twenty-one senators and 100 Senate staff members who participated or closely observed the work of four committees. Evans managed to interview the chairmen and ranking minority members of four target committees: Commerce, Labor (now Health, Education, Labor, and Pensions Committee), Judiciary, and Environment and Public Works. Given the legendary difficulties of academics in gaining access to senators for interviews, Evans' accomplishment was prodigious.

Evans concluded that each Senate committee operates under constraints imposed by the policy environment in which it functions. Not surprisingly, on committees whose jurisdictions touched on the most controversial areas of pubic policy or where the ideological distance between the chairman and ranking minority members was greatest, leadership was the most tentative. Evans's conclusion squared nicely with what we know about the distinctive place committees occupy in the policy domains of Washington, and it contributed to the understanding that some committees, by reason of their jurisdiction, are necessarily more bipartisan than others. This would have been more evident had Evans examined the Appropriations Committee; but, even without it, his conclusion that Judiciary faced a much more fraught environment than Commerce would be accepted by anyone familiar with the Senate. The relatively cooperative leadership relationship on Environment and Public Works was not only a product of the less contentious nature of environmental policy in the 1980s, but also of the narrowness of the ideological distance between Democrat Lloyd Bentsen and Republican Robert Staffford. One could hardly imagine such a relationship between the contemporary leaders, Chairman Barbara Boxer and ranking Republican James

Inhofe, in the context of a widening gap between Democrats and Republicans on such topics as climate change legislation.

Evans's work, which relied so significantly on interviews of senators and staff, was followed seven years later by Richard L. Hall's enormously influential *Participation in Congress* (1996). Taking issue with the work of formal theorists, Hall brings down the analysis of the policymaking process to the behavior of individual members and their differential rates of participation.

Participation by a member is more likely if he or she has some constituency-related interest in a piece of legislation, is a member of a committee that has jurisdiction over it, or has a personal interest in the policy area. Those familiar with Richard F. Fenno's earliest works, *The Power of the Purse* (1966) and *Congressmen in Committees* (1973), will recognize the pattern of mixed member motivations in such things as choice of committee assignment and voting decisions. Hall provides the same kind of lens, through which the decision to get involved with a bill can be discerned, together with the levels of involvement. Hall offers a highly differentiated view of the various entry-points for participation-subcommittee, full committee, and floor action.

Roughly contemporaneous with Hall's work is a quite different study undertaken by Bruce I. Oppenheimer and Frances E. Lee: *Sizing up the Senate* (1999), which draws upon (among other sources) interviews with "senators, former senators, lobbyists, Senate staffers, and other political consultants with some Senate experience" (9). As is usually the case with Senate interviews, the sample of interviewees is not random but, also typically, the authors strive to get equal numbers of Democrats and Republicans. Significantly, Oppenheimer and Lee withheld interviewing until the latter stages of their research, which relied on multiple sources of data, including data on federal outlays, Federal Election Commission figures, and archival material. They use the interviews, in effect, as a kind of quality check on the other materials.

They deal with one of the most intriguing, elusive and, to many critics, vexing features of the United States Senate: its constitutionally hallowed deviation from the one-person-one-vote principle, an anomaly very much commented upon by the media during the discussions among half a dozen members of the Finance Committee during the national health insurance debate in the summer of 2009. The participants— Max Baucus (D-Mt.), Jeff Bingaman (D-N.M.), Kent Conrad (D-N.D.), Olympia Snowe (R-Maine), Mike Enzi (R-Wyo.), and Chuck Grassley (R-Ia.)—collectively represented only about 2.5 percent of the U.S. population. Oppenheimer and Lee cast a broad net, with findings ranging from the superior access to members of Congress of small-state citizens to the greater margins of victory of small-state senators, to important distributive discrepancies in terms of federal money. Some of these questions could obviously be answered through the use of the National Election Study or U.S. Census Bureau data, but other concerns could only be investigated through the subjective testimony of personal interviews.

In 2004, Nelson Polsby's *How Congress Evolves* appeared. While not presenting new interview material, it featured an appendix on methods and sources which sums up elegantly the joys and pitfalls of interview-based and observational studies of Congress. Sensible and practical, and written with Polsby's characteristic felicity of prose, the book describes Polsby's "quasi-anthropological" approach to studying Congress, which emphasizes the use of multiple sources and types of data to augment the interview and observational material.

In all of these examples of research on Congress dating back half a century, which employed interviews, each interview was typically a single event at a given hour on a specific day. In some cases there were return visits, but none involved sustained contact with members of Congress. None of these researchers was, in current parlance, "embedded" with members. The sole exception to that was the work of the pre-eminent scholar of Congress in the last fifty years, Richard F. Fenno, Jr., in *Home Style* (2003). The fact that no other political scientist has attempted a study on the scale of Fenno's multi-year feat of shadowing members of Congress as they traveled from Washington to present themselves to their constituents on home territory is eloquent testimony to the uniqueness of this attempt. Even more, it is a study whose findings have stood the test of time. Some of the most universally accepted formulations regarding the House member–constituency nexus come from Fenno's work. But, if his work is widely admired, why, in the words of John R. Hibbing (2003) is *Homestyle*, "a remarkably uninfluential book"?

The answer to why Fenno is universally praised but never emulated can be found in the fifty-page appendix to *Homestyle* entitled "Notes on Method: Participant Observation." In this essay, which many people consider the most brilliant part of the book, Fenno, with refreshing candor, describes the techniques, challenges, and pitfalls of his approach to understanding the peculiar chemistry of member–constituent relationships away from Washington, DC.

CAUTIONARY TALES

Few graduate students in political science, upon reading this epilogue, would be tempted to follow in Fenno's path, at least not as a dissertation project. He confesses early on that "participant observation seems less likely to be used to test an existing hypothesis than to formulate hypotheses for testing by others or to uncover some relationship that strikes others as worth hypothesizing about and testing" (Fenno 2003).

Now, if that were not enough to dissuade eager Ph.D. candidates earnestly seeking hypotheses to test, he confesses subsequently that his collection of House members was in no technical sense a sample and, furthermore, was unrepresentatively Republican, given the partisan balance in the House at that time. Then, with the bravado only to be found in scholars at the top of their game, he airily reports that "the decision to stop at eighteen (members) was arbitrary, occasioned not by the thought that the 'sample' was complete, but the thought that it was about time to stop running around and to begin to communicate what I was finding" (Fenno 2003, 351).

As Fenno's essay unfolds, he posts a "proceed at your own risk" placard as he details the obstacles that would have to be surmounted to replicate his approach. To reinforce the point about his own research and, in general, research that deals with small numbers of cases, he stresses that "it is the 'small n' that makes this type of research unamenable to statistical analysis" (Fenno 2003, 255). He then adds that this kind of research is both costly and hard to finance and is further constrained by the necessity to conform it to a teaching schedule. How utterly discouraging!

Fenno is not alone in lamenting the obstacles in conducting interviews with members of Congress. Goldstein (2002) confesses that, even in research projects less ambitious than Fenno's,

getting the interview is more art than science and, with a few exceptions, political scientists are not particularly well known for our skill at the art of "cold calling." Even the most charming political scientists may find it difficult to pick up the phone and call the offices of power-ful and busy government officials or lobbyists and navigate through busy receptionists and schedulers.   (Goldstein 2002)

Having issued these caveats, Goldstein embarks on a discussion of the challenges of sampling a population of elites and cites the work of Baumgartner and colleagues, which is based on interviews with Washington lobbyists, as a model for how to surmount the sampling challenge; but two paragraphs later he drops the other shoe. "Of course," he writes, "picking a good sample is of little use if you cannot get sample units to speak with you" (Goldstein 2002, 671). This melancholy observation begs an interesting question: is interviewing members of Congress a unique challenge? Are there, in the universe of elites, those whose characteristics are singular and who dwell in a loftier realm, which requires special approaches and distinctive caveats? Do elected officials—members of Congress in particular—form a discrete category of elites?

Elites and hyper-elites

There is a question of differential access that sets members of Congress apart from other elites. In my own experience, it is far easier to secure an appointment, either in person or by phone, with an influential lobbyist, a reporter from a major national medium, or a business executive than it is with a member of Congress, and most particularly with U.S. senators.

Now it is arguably easier to get interview time with a low-ranking House member than with the head of a peak interest group in Washington; but, between those extremes, it is the member of Congress who would seem not only more likely to be strapped for time than the lobbyist, but also warier of the questions of an inquiring academic. One big difference between members of Congress and other non-elective elites is access.

THE INQUIRING STRANGER VERSUS THE PALACE GUARD

Around each member of Congress—and this is especially the case with U.S. senators—there is a protective cordon of staff members, alert to any situation that might imperil their boss politically or, more commonly, to demand his or her precious time. But there is another obstacle that one encounters on Capitol Hill and almost nowhere else: a kind of wariness of strangers that often borders on xenophobia. My own experience on Capitol Hill has convinced me that the staff reaction to such a person as an inquiring stranger in a congressional office is akin to the reaction of human antibodies to an invading pathogen. The question is not solely "is this person worthy of five minutes of my boss's time," but also "what possible damage can this person inflict on my boss?" Even with the solidest recommendations, the inquiring stranger is an object of suspicion, even dread.

In terms of access problems, then, I would submit that congressional elites are in a class of their own and require extraordinary reassurances that no harm will come to the House member or senator from an inquisitive scholar. But I have discovered that, once I received my "letters of transit" in the form of recommendations from trusted individuals, interviews with members of Congress are gratifyingly candid, remarkably rich, and even revelatory, and this richness often grows as the seniority and electoral security of the interviewee increases. Congressional elites, I believe, are a distinct class of elites, who pose a more formidable problem for access but who yield interviews of matchless value.

"EMBEDDEDNESS" AS AN ACCESS STRATEGY

I had no idea what aspect of Congress I wanted to investigate when I applied to my university for my first sabbatical leave. Being an experiential learner by nature, I needed to "touch the bones" before I could decide what to study. This was critical in my case in view of the fact that I had not concentrated in graduate school on American government, to say nothing of legislative politics. My university's then generous sabbatical leave policy gave me a full year off at full salary. This enabled me to present myself as a free good to a congressional office for a calendar year, an offer which, I thought, no sensible member of Congress would refuse.

I could not have been more mistaken; for, despite a *curriculum vitae* that demonstrated that I could write—a skill always in short supply on the Hill—I found the prevalent attitude to be "thanks, but no, thanks." Even if I were able to overcome this resistance, I would incur substantial transaction costs in order to gain access to a congressional office, with only a hope that I would find a subject worthy of investigation.

Getting in the front door was the first problem, and that involved invoking the help of people who would vouch for me. Academic references opened a few doors, but I was eventually able to enlist some people I knew at *The Washington Post* to attest to my *bona fides*. Aberbach and Rockman (2002) advise that "[i]t helps to have the imprimatur of a major and respected research house like the Brookings Institution." A thumbs-up from either of those Washington fixtures would be of immeasurable help in breaking down the wall of suspicion. In my case, with the help of the *Post*, I was invited to join the staff of a senator who had recently returned to the Senate after having decided not to seek the 1976 Democratic nomination.

There is, in congressional offices, a prevalent concern that a visiting scholar invited to be part of the senator's official family might be tempted to write a "kiss and tell" book. Interviewing with a Democratic Senate chief of staff, I was told that several years before they had hosted an anthropologist who, on returning to his university, wrote a book in which he divulged information that embarrassed the senator. While accepting that a journalist might pose a more obvious risk, it seems that academics fall under a similar discrimination.

The question, often posed to me in innocent, wrapping over, thinly disguised suspicion, was "what do you intend to do with your experiences?" and it compelled me to offer assurances that no sensitive inside information would be divulged once I was safely back on campus.

This suspicion was puzzling in light of the fact that it was obvious—to me, at least—that it would be in my self-interest to be discreet inasmuch as I would surely want to return to the Hill on future sabbaticals and I would not want to poison the well. Only after an extended period, but unfortunately just prior to my departure from my first Senate office, was my *bona fides* finally accepted.

In spite of the disappointments of my first Senate experience, it proved valuable in providing me with credentials for the next one. I now had an entry on my CV that said: "Senate Staff." Accordingly, I was more marketable and found myself as the chief speech writer for a senator who was seeking the Democratic presidential nomination in 1976. In those days, there were few restrictions on using Senate staff to conduct what was essentially presidential campaign activity. The distance that had existed between me and my previous host shrunk dramatically as I traveled with the senator to primary election states, working on his speeches and remarks. But my exhilaration at the proximity was tempered by the fact that I was now on the road most of the time and removed from the business of the Senate, the ostensible target of my research agenda. Other than returning to Washington for votes that might be important for his presidential ambitions, we were either in Iowa or New Hampshire.

My second host was forced to suspend his campaign after successive defeats in New Hampshire and Massachusetts and, as is typical with senators who aspire unsuccessfully for a presidential nomination, he returned to a Senate that had moved on without him. He also had little need for a speech writer, so I migrated to my third Senate host—another Senate Democrat, who was a late entrant to the 1976 contest.

The transition was very smooth, as I could now boast service with two Senate colleagues; but, again, I found myself part of a primary election campaign rather than engrossed in the business of observing a senator in action or Senate business. But this experience drew me closer to the senator than I had been with two previous hosts.

THE PAYOFF OF EMBEDDEDNESS

On the face of it, my year spent with three senators was a failure or, at best, a partial success, since so little of it was spent observing a senator involved in the work of the institution. But incurring the opportunity and transaction costs involved in a year of observation that offered only limited exposure to seeing senators interacting with their colleagues turned out to be a profitable gamble. I was now a known quantity in the minds of my former Capitol Hill colleagues. After I had the time and distance to formulate a project, I could use the trust that I had earned to get access to the people I needed for my work.

This false confidence caused me to assume that I was now an "insider." It followed, then, that I would have no difficulty in securing the interviews I wanted in order to formulate an ambitious research agenda, based on some hypotheses I had developed in the course of my time on the Hill. It was my intention to conduct in-person interviews in Washington, DC with incumbent U.S. senators to test my major hypothesis that, in the modern Senate, personal relations between and among senators would have little influence on their official behavior.

I had planned to interview a representative sample of senators, with a balance between Democrats and Republicans that corresponded to the then current balance in the chamber, and also with a balance between levels of seniority that would give me some sense of how the influence of friendship might have changed over time. "Drawing a sample of members of Congress [is] quite straightforward," as Aberbach and Rockman (2002) point out. "Lists of members are easily accessible and drawing them at random ... [is] a simple process." But, like Richard Fenno, I quickly discovered that there is no correlation between such variables as access, partisanship, or seniority.

NEGATIVE EXTERNALITIES

Two hundred miles separated my home from Washington, DC; so travel was a necessity. I was fortunate that my town was an Amtrak stop on the Eastern Corridor, but rail tickets were relatively expensive, which meant arranging multiple interviews for each visit. Consolidating several interviews over a period of two days made sense, but often involved stays in Washington's notoriously expensive hotels.

Anyone who has made an appointment with a member of Congress has quickly learned that all such arrangements are provisional. Unless the interview is timed for a congressional recess, in which case the member or senator is likely to be back in the constituency, the fickleness of the legislative process often leads to cancellations. This is especially true of appointments with senators.

The House of Representatives, with its highly structured legislative process, built on the majority party's control over the agenda and the extensive whip network, presents the researcher with fewer unpleasant surprises. As you ascend the ladder of seniority and influence, the House member does come more to resemble the senator in terms of responsibilities and claims on his or her time. At least one reason why a vastly greater volume of political science research focuses on the House is that interview-based research is likely to be less hindered by scheduling problems. In the Senate, especially in the period close to adjournment, when the likelihood of filibusters increases, the interview is apt to be postponed, interrupted by quorum calls, or preempted by meetings with individuals more important than political scientists. More than once, I have invested in a train ticket and a steep hotel bill only to return home empty-handed.

I also encountered a scheduling problem that, I assumed, was restricted to American politicians—until encountering the work of Rivera and her colleagues (2002), who conducted interviews in post-Soviet Russia and China and reported

a penchant for day-to-day scheduling without much advance notice. As a matter of fact, when requesting an appointment for the following week, respondents frequently told us that it was too far in advance to plan and requested that we can call back on the day we wished to speak to them.   (Rivera, Kozyreva, and Sarovskii 2002)

The unpredictability of the Senate schedule often forced me to make last-minute arrangements on the advice of schedulers, but that did not insure that there would not be last-minute cancellations.

Middlemen and graybeards

A solid personal relationship with a member of Congress is the surest element in amassing a suitable number of interviews. It is remarkable how effective it is to have a member vouch for you. This reduces substantially the wariness of members, especially if the member recommending you stands high in the estimation of his or her colleagues. I was able, in 1984, to secure interviews with virtually all members of the House Democratic Steering and Policy Committee who had voted to remove Representative Phil Gramm of Texas from the Budget Committee because of the advocacy of the chairman of the Democratic Caucus in whose office I had spent one year (see Baker 1985).

To secure the support of a senator or House member willing to make your case to colleagues proved enormously helpful; but, as I became more familiar with the pattern of interpersonal interactions among incumbent senators, it became clear that I would need to take a longitudinal approach to ascertain the nature of changes over time in the importance and impact of these relationships. I quickly discovered sources of interviewees who could provide me with the longer view: former members of Congress.

There is an organization, the United States Association of Former Members of Congress, that maintains a list of ex-members and their contact information. This list is especially helpful in reaching former House members; but former senators are more elusive, and it is necessary to turn to the Office of the Senate Historian, who can provide current data on ex-senators. Thirty years ago, it was more common for retirees and defeated senators to return home rather than to remain in Washington and, typically, to embark on a career of lobbying.

The abundance of former senators was exceeded only by their agreeable willingness to be interviewed and by the richness of their responses. While these ex-legislators no longer have a vote, they do have opinions, especially those who are actively lobbying. They also share a trait that becomes obvious to the interviewer: they wish to set straight the historical record.

With regard to interviewing former members of Congress, some of them whose service dates back many years, Seldon cautions: "A common finding is that the older the witness, and the more distant the events under discussion, the less valuable the evidence." He reports that "David Marquand, in his interviews for his biography of Ramsay McDonald, "found memories amazingly short and amazingly fallible" (1998, 6).

I found the memories of former members anything but short and, while certainly not infallible, usually lucid, especially on the matters that I wanted to discuss. While serving members of Congress may attempt to spin the interviewer on contemporary matters, the congressional graybeards often want to set the record straight (as they see it) and look upon the interviewer as a kind of recording angel, to insure that their version is the one entered.

I found it amusing, and revealing, that many of my interviewees referred to me as an historian despite the fact that I had introduced myself as a political scientist. I am inclined to think that they regard historians somehow as the keepers of the canon. Some, especially the older ones, seem to regard political science as a lesser discipline and find the term "political science" presumptuous. I confess that I ceased arguing strenuously against being labeled an historian, since it seemed to confer advantage in interviewing.

The problem with the older members and senators was less failure of memory or muddled recollection, but rather a tendency to look upon the time of their service as a kind of Homeric Age, populated by nobler politicians. I found that particularly ironic, in light of the fact that so many of them were contemporaries of Senator Joseph R. McCarthy, during what was certainly one of the nastier periods in the history of Congress.

To tape or not to tape

Berry makes an implicit case for recording interviews if the interviewee consents. As he puts it: "If you're taking notes rather than recording the interview, the challenge ... becomes even more daunting. How can you make a clear-headed decision about your next question when you're listening, trying to make sense of the answer, and taking notes all at the same time?" (Berry 2002, 682). Without skill at shorthand (or even at being an efficient cursive writer), I opted for recording the interviews.

I anticipated that I would get some resistance from interviewees who might prefer to be paraphrased rather than quoted directly, but my guarantee that the interview would not be for attribution enabled me to get all interviews on tape. The principal virtues of taped interviews are not only that they are *verbatim,* but that they capture inflection and emphasis. In transcribing the interviews, these tonal features can be noted parenthetically.

My first impulse was to transcribe interviews personally from tape; but, without a foot-pedal operated tape-machine the tedium of pressing the "play" and "pause" became oppressive, so I hired a transcriber. This created problems of its own. The transcriber was unfamiliar with politics and the names of political figures, so I would have to treat every transcript as a very rough draft. In the extreme case, I would listen to an entire taped interview while making corrections on a transcript riddled with errors. The transcriber's unfamiliarity with the subject matter also resulted in many gaps in the transcription. In spite of the tedium involved, I ultimately found it simply more efficient to do the transcription myself.

Identified sources vs. Senator X

I approached the interviews with the incumbent and former United States senators for *Friend and Foe in the U.S. Senate* (Baker 1980) being convinced of the virtue of not identifying my interviewees by name. The virtues of neither identifying them nor attributing responses to them by name seemed self-evident. Non-attribution would yield more candid responses and would also give me a picture of interpersonal relationships uncontaminated by the public reputation of the interviewee.

Having decided not to identify the senators by name, I ran immediately into the problem of whether to include the names of colleagues referred to in the interviews by the interviewees. Using actual names might enable a reader to figure out the identity of the interviewee. Fenno used pseudonyms throughout *Home Style*, but I decided to take the risk and use the actual names of the colleagues referred to by the interviewees, feeling that it would make for a more interesting study.

CAUTIOUS SCHOLARS, CANDID POLITICIANS

Throughout my interviews with members of Congress I was consistently surprised by the fact that I was invariably more cautious than the interviewee in reporting statements that might be considered controversial, or even impolitic. When an interviewee expressed such statements, I would inquire whether he or she wanted me to turn off the recorder. Invariably they would say, usually with the wave of a hand, "Oh go right ahead and use it."

Because both individuals involved are now dead, I can illustrate this phenomenon through an interview I conducted with Senator Frank Moss (D-UT, 1959–77) in regard to his state's other senator, Wallace Bennett (R-UT, 1951–74, and father of Senator Robert Bennett, 1993–2011).

Q: Senator Bennett was the senior senator when you arrived?
A: Yes, he was Utah's senior senator.
Q: And he was a Republican.
A: Yes.
Q: Was he of particular help in getting you to learn the ropes of the Senate?
A:: Well, no, he was not. I think it was in his nature. He's sort of a austere kind of man. I don't think he was capable of being warm and friendly at any place—either among his own Republican peers or with me.

I asked Moss if he wanted me to delete those comments and he said, "No, that's how I felt about him. Everyone in the Senate knew it. It was no secret."

An exception to this general rule was Senator Claiborne Pell (D-RI, 1960–96):

Q: Senator Pastore was the senior senator when you arrived?
A: That's correct.
Q: Could you tell me if senator Pastore was particularly helpful to you in learning the Senate ropes?
A: I don't like to pinpoint any particular senator—incidentally, is this for publication or what?

TRUSTING YOUR SOURCES

Anthony Seldon, the distinguished British historian and the biographer of Prime Minister Tony Blair, has stated categorically: "There is broad agreement that the least satisfactory of interviewees is current or retired politicians, who often have pathological difficulties distinguishing the truth, so set have their minds become by long experience of partisan thought." (1988, 10)

Perhaps it is the fact that the subject matter of my own investigations has been less susceptible to blatantly dishonest or tendentious responses, but I have never had cause to question the veracity of any of my interviewees. There have undoubtedly been instances of emphasis, nuance, or shading that might have led me to erroneous conclusions, but in interviewing senators who had previously served in the House of Representatives about their views on the differences between the chambers (see Baker 1989), or in interviewing senators discussing the effect of personal likes and dislikes or their political behavior (Baker 1980), I found that there seemed little incentive for interviewees to dissemble.

The area of inquiry that seemed to offer the greatest likelihood that the interviewee would try to put one over on me was my examinations of relationships between same-state senators. Here a combination of the well-known Senate gossip network and the renowned skill of journalists to sniff out conflict gave me the quality control that I needed. So, if Senator Frank Lautenberg (D-NJ) had told me that he and his New Jersey colleague, Robert Torricelli, worked harmoniously together, the comment could be immediately discounted on the basis of what was generally known about the relationship.

This method of quality control is recommended by John P. Dean and William F. Whyte, who subject interviewee testimony to the test of: "*implausibility*. If an account strongly strains our credulity and does not seem at all plausible, then we are justified in suspecting distortion" (Dean and Whyte 1970, 126).

There are, however, other checks on the veracity of the interviewees' responses, simply by comparing the response of one interviewee to those of others to the same question. While this method is certainly not foolproof, it often works quite well. Dean and Whyte advance it as the major way in which they detect distortion and correct for it. They concede: "We have little opportunity in field research for anything that resembles direct cross examination, but we can certainly *cross-check* the accounts given us by different informants for discrepancies and try to clear these up by asking for further clarification" (Dean and Whyte 1970, 127–8).

In the course of interviewing the members of the House Democratic Steering and Policy Committee on the Committee's decision to remove Representative Phil Gramm from the Budget Committee in 1983—not merely for actively supporting the Reagan budget cuts but for colluding with the White House on budget-cutting strategy—the responses of the various members of the committee were remarkably uniform. A number of conservative "Boll Weevil" Democrats had supported Reagan's budget cuts and tax increases in 1981, yet only Gramm was formally punished by the caucus.

I had hypothesized that the sanctioning of Gramm was purely an expression of party discipline at a time when defections from the party on major legislation, and even party-switching, had become a problem for House Democrats.

When asked why the caucus sanctioned Gramm and not the others, a border-state Democrat said:

What Phil did affects working relationships within the system ... it was sure as hell against the people and their working relationships within the system ... The fact that nobody trusts Gramm anymore is not the real damage. That reflects on him as an individual. It's what happens to the working relationships within the system that really concerned folks around here.   (Baker 1985, 327)

Another border-state Democrat echoed the views of this colleague that damage to trust among colleagues was Gramm's transgression:

We didn't discipline Phil Gramm for being against us on the budget. There were others who did that . . . What we disciplined him for was for a basic human indiscretion that a professional in any career . . . can't yield to if he's going to be effective in the long run, and that is if you huddle with a group of people to work out a deal, you don't take that deal to the other side and use it against the people you've been dealing with.   (Baker 1985, 327)

A western Democrat said much the same thing: "It has nothing to do with party . . . It was the fact that this is simply not the way to play the game of politics. Anybody out there on the street understands that, and it's certainly not the way we operate here" (Baker 1985, 328).

The quality check on the veracity of each single interview was the other responses to the same question. The congruent responses were critical in understanding that the caucus was remarkably tolerant of those Democrats who sided with Reagan, including one (Representative Kent Hance (D-TX)) who co-sponsored the Reagan budget along with Budget Committee chairman Barber Conable (R-NY). It appeared, then, that what was in operation was not so much an enforcement of party discipline as much as the enforcement of the norm of trust (see Asher 1973).

Seldon follows up his dismissive treatment of the trustworthiness of politicians with a fragrant bouquet he tosses to bureaucrats: "Civil servants tend to be dispassionate creatures by nature and profession: cat-like, they observe action, storing the information in mental boxes that yield a rich harvest to those who take the trouble to prise them open" (Seldon 1988, 10).

Perhaps the British civil servants to whom Seldon refers are men and women more thoroughly immunized to partisan feelings than their American counterparts, but I would be skeptical of such a claim.

I am tempted to wonder whether Seldon's belief in the superior veracity of civil servants might have something to do with the fact that they are more accessible than members of Parliament. Aberbach and Rockman tipped me off to this possibility in the following passage:

[B]ureaucratic elites are little studied by political scientists, so response rates were very high (over 90% for career civil servants). They were lower for members of Congress in the high seventies in the first round of our study (1970–71) and lower when we tried a second round in 1986–87.   (Aberbach and Rockman 2002, 673)

I hesitate to think that the very availability of a class of interviewees may make them more attractive to the researcher. But, like anyone who is always in danger of falling in love with members of Congress as interviewees because, as a population, they are so interesting, I would naturally favor interviewing them rather than civil servants.

THE BLAND LEADING THE BLIND

While I felt reassured with the safeguards against out-and-out deception on the part of my interviewees, there was another problem that verged on untruthfulness but was not stemming from an active effort to deceive: bland, innocuous responses. Posing the initial question about a senator's friendships tended to produce one typical response: an endless recitation of names. Typical of this response was that of Senator John Sparkman (D-AL, 1946–78). My first question always inquired about which of a senator's senior colleagues had been especially helpful in teaching him or her the ropes. Sparkman's response was: "I think all senators are helpful ... I always had fine cooperation from the *official* leadership of the Senate and I always found very fine cooperation with lots of senators."

I was obviously disappointed by this Pollyanna view of the U.S. Senate and prodded Sparkman to single out a few especially close friends. Only a short time before, I had interviewed Frank Moss (see above), who had identified his senior colleague Wallace Bennett as having a most unfriendly and unhelpful disposition, so I was amused when Sparkman, on being prodded to give names, said: "I worked with a fellow across the aisle when I was chairman of the Senate Banking Committee. I can't recall his name. Utah. Wallace Bennett, a very fine fellow to work with."

A similarly uninspiring initial response came from Leverett Saltonstoll (R-MA, 1945–67), who replied in this way to the question about the senators with whom he felt closest: "I always had a friendly feeling with all. I always say that if you don't like people, you'd better stay out of politics. I don't know of any Republican or Democrat in the United States Senate that I didn't get along with." But then, in an unguarded moment, Saltonstall added: "Although, there were some that I hated ... Well... What I mean is that I found that I had urgent business to do in my office when they started to speak."

THE DELIGHTS OF OPEN-ENDEDNESS

A half century ago, Charles Morrissey conducted interviews for the oral histories of the Truman and Kennedy administrations and approached the officials who served these two presidents with a very simple methodology:

One of the things we emphasized was to let the interviewee talk. It's his show. Let him run with the ball ... He would take off ... [and] I would sit and listen. There's a value to this because he's volunteering what's foremost in his recollections.   (Morrissey 1970, 111)

Morrissey goes on to report that, "in phrasing our questions, we found it most important to leave them open-ended, that is not to indicate in the phrasing of the question the answer you expect to get" (Morrissey 1970, 111).

Berry admired the interviewing skills of his mentor, Robert Peabody, who counseled him that

the best interviewer is not the one who writes the best questions. Rather, excellent interviewers are excellent conversationalists. They make interviews seem like good talk among old friends. He didn't carry a printed set of questions in front of him to consult as the interview progressed; yet he always knew where he was going and never lost control of the discussion. He gave his subjects a lot of license to roam but would occasionally corral them if the discussion went too far astray.   (Berry 2002, 679)

Morrissey characterizes the interplay between interviewer and interviewee as "two reflective men trying to find out how things happen, but the less informed and experienced one (the interviewer) deferring to the wiser one and learning from him" (Morrissey 1970, 56).

These sensible guidelines suggest that the interviewer should not become too enamored of his or her list of questions and strive doggedly to follow them in the order in which they are written down. It is well to bring a flexible approach to elite interviewing. Members of Congress will talk about what members of Congress will talk about, and it is counterproductive to try to muscle them back to the topic that you want addressed. Just get out of the way, wait them out and gently nudge them back in the preferred direction. I rarely left an interview thinking that that the interviewee has been totally unresponsive or provided only useless digression.

HOUSE CALLS VS. THE DISEMBODIED VOICE

At the time when I first decided to base my research, in large measure, on personal interviews, it did not occur to me to do them in any way other than in person. For my first interview-based book, *Friend and Foe in the U.S. Senate*, all interviews were on the home court of the interviewee. The kind of research I wanted to conduct was just not susceptible to the use of a questionnaire, and I felt that phone interviews would deprive me of useful observations on facial expressions and body language as well as of noting interesting and useful features of the senators' own milieu.

This course of action committed me to multiple trips to Washington, DC, to interview the incumbents, and even many of the former senators who elected to stay in the nation's capital after their terms in the Senate. But, as I decided to consider longitudinally the changes in patterns and effects of personal relationships, tracking down retirees outside of Washington became necessary.

My field interviews with the former senators turned out to be the most enjoyable, if not necessarily the most valuable ones. Visiting former Senator Margaret Chase Smith (R-ME, 1949–73) at her home in Skowkegan, Maine filled in a picture of her that could probably not have been assembled elsewhere. Enormously proud of her independence and with a reputation of being both starchy and sensitive, Smith I believe was more at ease with me, even expansive, in her own element. The same applied to former Senator John O. Pastore (D-RI, 1950–76) in his memento-filled office at the Turk's Head Building in Providence, RI and to Joseph S. Clark (D-PA, 1957–69) in his comfortable living-room in Chestnut Hill, Philadelphia.

The Senate offices of incumbents were, from the perspective of ambience, not as interesting, because most feature the standard array of political trophies and are often less personal. But, out of those who do expose their personalities through office artifacts, these objects are great ice-breakers—for instance the barber's chair in the office of Senator Chuck Hagel (R-NE, 1996–2008), which came from his father's shop, or the portrait of the crepuscular Andrew Jackson, which hangs over the desk of Senator Harry Reid, the currently Majority Leader—a reminder to Reid of the transience of power and of the brevity of life.

But interviews by phone do offer some considerable advantages. First, you don't need to travel, with the attendant cost in time and money. Second, I found that it was, on the whole, easier to get a phone appointment than one in person. I also found that phone interviews were less subject to cancellation. Phone interviews were simply more efficient and, if you don't mind the tradeoff of intimacy for convenience and efficiency, the phone is a most useful instrument. I have not, however, tried to interview by email. That would be entirely too denatured to suit me.

MOMENTS OF REVELATION: THE GOOD STUFF YOU CAN'T USE

One incalculable advantage of in-person interviews over phone interviews is that there occurs every so often a moment in which a member of Congress will reveal himself or herself in an unexpected way. These dramatic moments may have little to do with the subject-matter of your interview, and may not even result from any probing or leading questions that you have posed. But, quite adventitiously, the interviewee may present to you the human being that is often so well-concealed beneath the armored exterior of the politician. And, while these revelatory moments may never appear in your publications because of their deeply personal nature or their irrelevance to the subject under investigation, they stand out as eloquent testimony to the fact that elites can sometimes act in very non-elite ways.

House and Senate (1989) was a project in which I interviewed U.S. senators who had previously served in the House in order to gain their bicameral perspective. Before I conducted these interviews, in the dark days before Google, I would usually consult the biographical material in *The Almanac of American Politics* and *CQ Politics in America*, or microfilmed editions of *The New York Times* and *Washington Post*.

In a few cases, the interviewee had written a campaign biography, perhaps in preparation for a presidential run, and this would provide additional information. One of my interviewees had written a brief book about his House career that also contained a considerable amount of personal information, and I read it in preparation for the interview, which was scheduled to take place in his office.

A last-minute scheduling change had me waiting for him off the Senate floor, while he and his colleagues were involved with the impeachment trial of federal Judge Alcee Hastings. Standing in the corner of the senators' reception room, with my tape recorder thrust up under his chin, in the hope of getting his responses above the hubbub around us, I collected his impressions as a newcomer to the Senate.

At the end of the interview, after I had thanked him, I recalled a passage in his book in which he spoke feelingly about the hope that his daughter would not suffer long-lasting damage from the divorce he had been involved in at the time. I asked him about his daughter and told him that I, too, was going through a divorce and was concerned about its effects on my own daughters. The mood of the conversation changed dramatically; he began a long, sad story about the rift with his daughter that had not yet healed, and proceeded to give me advice on the basis of his own experience. He then described how difficult it was to manage the relationship with his daughter when he was dealing with the problems of his aged parents who, in his words, "were living in a one-bedroom apartment, hating each other and waiting to die." It was more than I wanted to hear.

Another interview, this one in a member's office, also found me on the receiving end of a confession. This interview was of a House member who was presiding over the chamber when the House voted to expel Representative Ozzie Myers (D-PA, 1976–80). I had watched the C–SPAN clip of the expulsion vote and noticed that, as he read out the expulsion order, the presiding officer, my interviewee, seemed moved to tears. I remarked on that and suggested that he must have been overcome with pity for Myers. He shook his head.

It had nothing to do with Myers. What I was thinking was that Myers was being expelled from the House but he had his whole life in front of him with many years to repair his life. My son died of a drug overdose and will never have that chance.

If these rare moments in the course of my interviews taught me anything, it is to guard against the mortal enemy of the interviewer who takes on elites, and especially on members of Congress: excessive awe. If you tell yourself that the people you are interviewing walk in the footsteps of Daniel Webster, you will be dysfunctionally deferential. A decent respect for the person and office will be sufficient to gain the confidence of the interviewee. Taking a quick reading on the personality of the politician will tell you about the person's formality or relaxation. There is no handbook, schematic or wiring diagram for the good interview. And, as is the case with so many other things, luck helps.

Another caution is in order here: because the process of securing interviews, as we have seen, is so arduous, there is a strong temptation to waste nothing. This should be resisted, lest what is central to evaluating your hypotheses gets buried in a morass of amusing but extraneous anecdotes. Members of Congress can be engaging story-tellers, but it is critical to exert discipline on the raw material.

For me, the temptation was particularly strong when I was able to score an interview with a senior member who was known to be leery of giving interviews to academics. It is important to remind yourself that what is rare is not necessarily valuable. The shrewd observation of a junior member may be more illuminating than the weary platitudes of a committee chairman.

REFERENCES

ABERBACH, J. D., and ROCKMAN, B. A. 2002. Conducting and Coding Elite Interviews. *PS: Political Science and Politics*, 35 (December): 673–6.

ASHER, H. 1973. The Learning of Legislative Norms. *American Political Science Review*, 67: 499–513.

BAKER, R. K. 1980. *Friend and Foe in the U.S. Senate*. New York: The Free Press.

——1985. Party and Institutional Sanctions in the U.S. House: The Case of Congressman Gramm. *Legislative Studies Quarterly*, 10(3), 315–37.

——1989. *House and Senate*. New York: W.W. Norton.

——2000. Constitutional Cohabitation, pp. 15–31 in *Esteemed Colleagues: Civility and Deliberation in the U.S. Senate*, B. A. Loomis. Washington, DC: The Brookings Institution.

BERRY, J. M. 2002. Validity and Reliability Issues in Elite Interviewing. *PS: Political Science and Politics*, 35 (December): 679–82.

DEAN, J. P., and FOOTE WHYTE, W. 1970. What Kind of Truth Do You Get? *Elite and Specialized Interviewing*, ed. L. A. Dexter. Evanston, IL: Northwestern University Press.

EVANS, C. L. 1991. *Leadership in Committee: A Comparative Analysis of Leadership Behavior in the U.S. Senate*. University of Michigan Press.

FENNO, JR., R. F. 1966. *The Power of the Purse: Appropriations Politics in Congress*. Little, Brown.

——1973. *Congressmen in Committees*. Little, Brown.

——2003. *Home Style: House Members in Their Districts*. New York: Longman.

GOLDSTEIN, K. 2002. Getting in the Door: Sampling and Completing Elite Interviews. *PS: Political Science and Politics*, 35 (December): 669–72.

HIBBING, J. R. 2003. Foreword in *Home Style*, R. F. Fenno, Jr. New York: Longman.

KINGDON, J. W. 1973. *Congressmen's Voting Decisions*. University of Michigan Press.

MATTHEWS, D. 1960. *U.S. Senators and Their World*. University of North Carolina Press.

——2001. Reflections on Forty Years of the Senate, pp. 167–9 in *The Contentious Senate*, ed. C. C. Campbell and N. C. Rae. Lanham, MD: Rowman and Littlefield.

MORRISSEY, C. 1970. On Oral History Interviewing, *Elite and Specialized Interviewing*, L. A. Dexter. Evanston, IL: Northwestern University Press.

OPPENHEIMER, B. I., and LEE, F. E. 1999. *Sizing up the Senate: The Unequal Consequences of Equal Representation*. Chicago: University of Chicago Press.

POLSBY, N. W. 2004. *How Congress Evolves*. Oxford: Oxford University Press.

RIESMAN, D. 1964. *Abundance for What? And Other Essays*. New York: Doubleday.

RIVERA, S. W., KOZYREVA, P. M., and SAROVSKII, E. G. 2002. Interviewing Political Elites: Lessons from Russia. *PS: Political Science and Politics*, 35 (December): 683–8.

SELDON, A., ed. 1988. *Contemporary History*. New York: Basil Blackwell.

SINCLAIR, B. 1989. *The Transformation of the U.S. Senate*. Baltimore: Johns Hopkins Press.

CHAPTER 6

HISTORICAL APPROACHES TO THE STUDY OF CONGRESS: TOWARD A CONGRESSIONAL VANTAGE ON AMERICAN POLITICAL DEVELOPMENT

IRA KATZNELSON*

* I particularly want to thank Quinn Mulroy for her research assistance, Frances Lee and Eric Schickler for their editorial suggestions, and Richard Bensel, Wendy Schiller, Charles Stewart, Richard Valelly, and Gregory Wawro for their counsel about recent scholarship.

A beckoning opportunity remains to be fully grasped. The sub-field of American political development (APD) will remain incomplete without a sufficiently robust congressional focus. Reciprocally, historical approaches to Congress risk fragmented and dispersed research programs in the absence of closer ties to the central intellectual problems that have shaped the progress of APD.

Six years after Heinz Eulau identified what at best was an "uneasy partnership between history and political science" in the study of Congress, Keith Whittington lamented how scholars within this intellectual community had "never fully integrated Congress, as they have other important institutions such as the bureaucracy, the presidency, political parties and the courts" (Eulau 1993; Whittington 1999, 44).[1] Shortly thereafter, a "state of the discipline" survey concluded that, notwithstanding Keith Poole and Howard Rosenthal's massive and comprehensive analysis of roll-call votes across the full sweep of American history, "most scholarship on the Congress has remained ahistorical" (Poole and Rosenthal 1997; Gamm and Huber 2002). Over the course of the past decade, by contrast, there has been a jump in the degree of attention paid to Congress by political scientists who identify closely with APD, a dramatic growth in historical work by mainstream congressional scholars, and increasingly active exchanges among members of both groups.[2] With mutual learning and engagement underway, and with some significant aspects of convergent views about preferences and historical situations expressed by historical and rational choice institutionalists (Katznelson and Weingast 2005), no time since the creation of APD has been as auspicious for the achievement of congressional scholarship that can move ahead with that orientation's central aims, and, in turn, for APD to inform further advances in congressional studies that take a long view.

Presently, there is something of a mismatch. While scholars who focus primarily on Congress have been turning to historical sources and subjects, the study of Congress within APD remains patchy, despite the manifest significance of political representation as a particularly important aspect of the American system on the basis of a separation of powers and an uncommonly autonomous role for the national legislature. Of the 107 substantive articles to have appeared in the sub-field's flagship journal, *Studies in American Political Development*, between 2001 and the first half of 2010, just ten, some 9 percent, concerned Congress and its role. The sub-field has yet sufficiently to integrate into its many powerful efforts to understand the key qualities of America's broadly liberal pattern of state formation open and contingent investigations that concern when, how, and with respect to what features of the

---

[1] Just four years later, Whittington co-authored a programmatic article that lamented the relative importance of congressional studies within the discipline. Written with Daniel Carpenter, it regretted how congressional studies had come to dominate mainstream American politics in what they described as an exaggerated model of congressional dominance (Whittington and Carpenter 2003). As leading students, within APD, of executive agencies and the courts, they resisted the degree of attention paid to Congress in the larger profession. But their complaint, I believe, had less to do with Congress as a subject for inquiry than with the way congressional investigations, though deepening in method and analytical capacity, had largely eschewed the kind of work that APD had been developing.
[2] Especially valuable has been the series of annual Congress and History meetings that first met in 2000, and now gather each spring.

American experience Congress has been a central pivot in American politics and governance.

This chapter assesses the status of historical approaches to the study of Congress, with particular attention to the intersection of Congress and APD. It looks back to missed chances. More importantly, it looks to how advantageous substantive and methodological conditions created during the past decade might be seized to achieve the goal John Lapinski and I put forward a half-decade ago: to make the "study of Congress as an institution and as a site for discussion, behavior, and choice about public policy a more constitutive part of APD." The secondary place of Congress within APD, we argued, had proved "paradoxical and expensive: paradoxical because political representation, as a concept and as an institutional practice, offers a rich site to probe both temporality and the qualities of political liberalism in the United States; expensive because Congress has been a constitutive part of the American state, especially in its role in the policy process" (Katznelson and Lapinski 2006a, 243, 245). Achieving such an ambition by building a closer relationship between APD and studies of Congress is important beyond the confines of that sub-field; for, without the kind of thematic integration APD potentially offers, historical studies of Congress risk being scattered and insufficiently focused, better in their parts than as a coherent vantage from which to understand the trajectories of American politics.

ABORTED BEGINNINGS

I start with missed chances, though not simply as an elegy for what might have been. Working against the grain, important initiatives to remedy the neglect of history by most students of Congress were undertaken for some two decades, starting in the mid-1960s—well before APD was self-consciously launched to promote the imbrication of history and political science. By the end of the 1980s, however, this work had suffered two blows. APD failed to exploit the rich opportunities this body of scholarship offered. At most, Congress played a peripheral role in the agenda-setting volumes by Stephen Skowronek (*Building a New American State*, 1982), Theda Skocpol (*Protecting Soldiers and Mothers*, 1992), and Rogers Smith (*Civic Ideals*, 1997). Moreover, it soon was superseded by powerful scientific impulses that elided historical topics and methods.

Published in 1966, David Mayhew's first book called on political scientists to harness congressional analysis in order to probe and understand America's past. *Party Loyalty among Congressmen* opened with an account of disciplinary transformations. It observed how "political science has changed more in the last half century than the Congress itself. The profession has been converted from a subdivision of history into a subdivision of sociology, and it is fast becoming a subdivision of mathematics" (Mayhew 1966, 1). Studies concerned with the character of congressional representation, he noted, had moved away from the "comparative and historical approach" in A. Lawrence Lowell's "The Influence of Party Upon Legislation in England and America," a work that had pioneered the use of quantitative data to contrast each country's long-term trends (Lowell 1901). Instead, the field had come to be marked either by large-N behavioral research searching for timeless propositions, as represented by David Truman's *The Congressional Party: A Case Study*, which focused intensively on political behavior in the 81st Congress (Truman 1959), or, more recently, by deductive modeling of the type found in R. Duncan Luce and Arnold Rogow's "A Game Theory Analysis of Congressional Power Distributions for a Stable Two Party System" (Luce and Rogow 1956). While appreciating the new rigor represented by both types of scholarship, Mayhew ruefully took note of how post-war behavioral and game theoretic work, in contradistinction to early and some mid-twentieth-century scholarship, was showing little interest in history or policy questions. "In many recent discussions of legislative voting," he wrote, "a concern with methodological refinement has been accompanied by a diminishing interest in the study of historical events." He keenly regretted that "in the latest works applying mathematics to legislative voting, the detachment of political science from history is almost complete" (Mayhew 1966, 4–5).

Mayhew's book—a study of partisan differences in Congress between 1947 and 1962, with respect to agrarian, urban, labor, and western regional policy matters—pushed back. Describing his study "as a historical essay," Mayhew underscored how it systematically addressed what had happened "in a given historical period. No corollary conclusions are drawn about congressional behavior in any other era of history" (Mayhew 1966, 4). In this respect, he identified with a particular tradition within congressional studies, seeking to join hands with more senior and eminent "political scientists of a historical bent [who] have used congressional voting data to shed light on particular historical problems." Like historians "concerned with the unique," these colleagues, including his teacher V.O. Key, Jr., had described and analyzed vexing matters in proper-name history. In addition to the ground-breaking work of Lowell, Mayhew cited Key's *Southern Politics in State and Nation* (1949) for its quest to comprehend the one-party South in Congress, Julius Turner's *Party and Constituency* (1951) for the way it marshaled evidence from the 67th to the 78th Congress to grasp the nature of shifting party alignments during that period, and Robert Dahl's *Congress and Foreign Policy* (1950) for its use of roll-call data in order better to understand how a country that not long before had been a provincial backwater had come to command the globe (Mayhew 1966, 2). What also joined these works was a fascination with large questions in American history and a passion for utilizing both qualitative and quantitative techniques to make the process and outputs of congressional lawmaking central to the discovery of persuasive answers.

Mayhew, of course, could not have anticipated how his dissertation-based initiative would be the first in a robust set of efforts to understand Congress as an historical institution and to map the institution's effects on partisanship and policy, and thus on how American democratic politics and state-making had proceeded in time.

For the history of Congress as an institution, the period's landmark contribution was Nelson Polsby's (1968) article on the institutionalization of the House, which traced how it became well-bounded and internally complex, and how it came to follow universalistic rather than particularistic criteria and rules. There quickly followed a detailed exposition about the growth of the seniority system in the House (Polsby, Gallaher, and Rundquist 1969), and other comparative and longitudinal studies of institutional development, with a particular focus on parties, on leadership, and on the distinctive role played by the committee system (Nelson 1974, 1977).

Especially impressive were two partially overlapping large data-set research programs, rife with historical interest and temporal inventiveness, which followed. The first, principally conducted by David Brady and Joseph Cooper, powerfully combined a historical imagination with quantitative research. In part, this program was concerned with the history of Congress, as, for example, in Cooper's *The Origins of the Standing Committees and the Development of the Modern House* (1970) or in Cooper and Brady's (1981a) exploration of how leadership styles in the House changed from the days of Speaker Cannon to Speaker Rayburn. But this work also examined how key processes that concerned parties, politics, and policies were shaped and altered by the historical contexts in which they were embedded, causally understood. The goal, as Brady and Cooper put it in a review essay critiquing the absence of genuinely diachronic studies, was to discover "the ways in which environmental factors—both fixed and variable—shape the operations and performance of Congress" (Cooper and Brady 1981b, 988). Writing in a tone of skepticism regarding conventional wisdom about such issues as electoral realignment and party coalitions, this array of books and articles offered a significant contribution to political history, albeit one that historians and historically-oriented political scientists often found difficult to apprehend because of its by then standard mode of behavioral presentation—which seemed to be, far more than it was, a long way from historical monographs and narrative history (Brady 1973; Brady 1978; Brady and Bullock 1980; Brady and Stewart 1982; Brady and Sinclair 1984; Brady 1985; Brady 1988; also see Collie 1988a, 1988b, 1989).

This also proved to be the case with a second historical program, which focused on the substance of representation. Organized by a five-dimensional classification of congressional roll calls developed by Aage Clausen, this body of research got a jump start from an influential *American Political Science Review* article by Clausen and his student, future Vice President Richard B. Cheney, which sought to show how "a policy orientation leading to subjective divisions of items into policy domains provides the basis for comparative and longitudinal studies" (Clausen and Cheney 1970, 152). It was soon followed by Clausen's book-length demonstration of the vitality of such a substantive approach to studies of Congress in *How Congressmen Decide: A Policy Focus* (1973). This orientation to classification generated a slew of historical studies, especially those by Barbara Deckard Sinclair, on the transformation of the political agenda, party cohesion, and regional fragmentation in Congress during the first three-quarters of the twentieth century, with a particular focus on the New

Deal and Fair Deal (Sinclair 1977a, 1977b, 1978, 1982). This substantive orientation treated public policy subjects both as independent and as dependent variables. It asked how the subjects of political engagement could serve to shape the politics of voting blocs and of political coalitions in the legislature by altering the relevant party and constituency pressures across issue areas. With public policy being not just the cause but also the outcome of lawmaking, this research was oriented to real-world puzzles that concerned how America had been made and remade by congressional decisions and non-decisions.

Notwithstanding how the Brady–Cooper and Clausen–Sinclair initiatives advanced a historical agenda joining behavioral assessment, substantive classification, and temporal sensibilities to produce an inviting way to treat lawmaking as policymaking, and thus as statemaking, this wide-ranging and vigorous enterprise lost steam within the discipline, the initiative moving toward more parsimonious theoretical—and less historical—efforts. Not without irony, the most important catalyst for this development was the brilliant and simple framework David Mayhew offered in *Congress: The Electoral Connection* (1974). Famously, that tightly argued book powerfully influenced the subsequent organization of congressional studies by positing a single, dominant, and seemingly timeless purposive motive—an interest in getting reelected—that could make sense of legislative behavior, of the weakness of parties, of the role of distributive politics, and of the decentralized and specialized committee system, among other topics. With this provocation, the scientific study of Congress took flight, but at a price. Policy and proper-name history, indeed any conception of the public interest, dropped out.

Earlier, in 1966, Mayhew also could not have anticipated how, over the course of the subsequent two decades, a loosely coupled group of political scientists, sharing his articulated concerns, would develop APD in an effort to investigate the American experience and the character of its polity in time. Drawing on an array of assets—including, among others, nineteenth- and twentieth-century social theory, approaches to the state by political sociologists and students of comparative politics, and scholarship in political theory on the Western liberal tradition—APD developed into a broad quest to understand the largest features of the country's political regime and the qualities of its political culture, the complex and uneven applications of its liberal and republican commitments regarding matters of race, class, and gender, and the characteristics of particular eras, including transitional ones, in terms of shifting patterns of governance and political participation. To bring American history into sharp focus, APD developed a conceptual tool kit and probed questions of temporality and sequence by examining such processes and mechanisms as policy feedback, policy selection, and institutional intercurrence (Katznelson 1993; Pierson 2000, 2004; Orren and Skowronek 2002, 2004).

With APD sharing Mayhew's early skepticism about ahistorical scholarship and his persistent doubts about the timelessness of motives and the constancy of behavior, models, and generalization across time, the aspiration for a more historical political science devoted to American politics took flight—but with Congress serving as a curious and costly omission. The methods, goals, patterns of inference, and short time horizons of most congressional studies helped prod APD's founders to identify other topics and to pursue different directions. With the primary focus in Congress mainstream literature being "on the internal dynamics of congressional institutions" and not "linked to the major transformations in the scale of the national government or the powers of the other branches," as Polsby and Schickler wrote in a thoughtful overview (2002, 355), the sub-field quickly developed in contradistinction to the non- or anti-historical trends in American politics that Mayhew initially resisted and then projected.

Notwithstanding some noteworthy congressional writings during the early phase of APD, most notably Richard Bensel's *Sectionalism in American Political Development* (1984), as well as a concurrent turn to history by sympathetic scholars just to the side of APD (Stewart 1989; Hansen 1991), Whittington's summary judgment about a sub-field silence rang true in 1999, in part because APD failed to integrate the Brady–Cooper and Clausen–Sinclair research programs within its ken. Perhaps their "normal science" methods, expository style, and publication sites made such scholarship seem more distant than it actually was.[3] By not engaging with this work, or for that matter with Mayhew's prior historical work on partisanship, APD let pass an early opportunity to place Congress inside its most important concerns. Just as APD burst out—a fact signified by the 1986 appearance of *Studies in American Political Development*—it neglected the most vibrant turn to history among leading Congress scholars of the day. Thus a considerable chance was lost by promoters of the new initiative—a chance to build on these achievements and to turn them in the direction of the big historical and institutional questions that other Congress scholars had abandoned and would, in the main, continue to ignore.

APD remains confined to these beginnings, but much has also changed. It is now possible to recoup and advance. Though the main currents of APD, as the pages of *Studies in American Political Development* reveal, are still largely elsewhere, the Congress field rediscovered a strong taste for historical research, and a stream of APD books on Congress has appeared, authored by, among others, Richard Bensel (1990, 2000), Elaine Swift (1996), Elizabeth Sanders (1999), Eric Schickler (2001), Jasmine Farrier (2004), and Gregory Wawro and Schickler (2006). Here I should like to review promising features in recent scholarship and take note of still incomplete possibilities that are underway. But I also wish to caution that there are no guarantees that the solipsisms characteristic of a divided discipline (Almond 1990) will not triumph, or that encouraging intellectual promises will be redeemed. So I will conclude with suggestions, both substantive and methodological, about how a vibrant congressional vantage for APD might presently proceed.

---

[3] Importantly, David Brady was one of the founding presidents of the Politics and History Section of the American Political Science Association in 1987–1999, an intellectual venue where APD has thrived.

RETURN TO HISTORY

Once again, it was David Mayhew who helped establish, or at least began, an important trend—this time, the active return of political scientists, both within and outside APD, to historical subjects about Congress. By so doing, he and they have sought to accomplish what Heinz Eulau once thought to be impossible: testing theories and empirical propositions with historical evidence, and offering interpretations of historical developments by way of systematic theories and empirical research.[4] Put differently, this growing and heterogeneous body of historical congressional scholarship is at ease with efforts to climb up and down a ladder of abstraction, whose bottom rungs designate proper-name historical persons, places, and events, which either are objects of explanation or means with which to assess models and propositions about institutions, mechanisms, and processes.

This particular kind of return to history was strongly signaled by the publication of Mayhew's *America's Congress* in 2000, a book that rests on a heroic coding effort across two centuries of American history, geared to identify and measure the agency of named members of Congress (not role categories) who pursued projects and actions, "operating in the public sphere with consequence." Arguing that the agency of particular politicians over long periods of time had become "recessive . . . in contemporary political science," and noting that "I do not see any need in this book to cling to the theoretical purism of the electoral incentive," he investigated what he called "actions," including "legislating, investigating, impeaching, taking public stands, intruding into foreign policy, and . . . staging opposition to presidential administrations" by members of the House and Senate over the full course of American history, on the basis of a systematic and coded classification of the past, undertaken in an "exploration of the territory rather than a causal analysis" (Mayhew 2000, ix, x, xii, 17, 28). Among its merits, this work links types of scholarship that usually have been kept apart—work on Congress as an institution, and work on the ways Congress is affected by, and in turn shapes, the wider environment in which it is located.

America's Congress fits awkwardly with mainstream congressional studies in how it abjures models and generalizations, names names, cares about policy substance, and explicitly links a systematic study to big issues in political theory, including the status of the public sphere. It also fits awkwardly with APD, by virtue of the central role it accords to Congress and to its member actors, both of whom had come to play a secondary role within the sub-field. But it effectively prodded both groups to think anew about the scope of research, types of exposition, and the systematic engagement with historical materials.

What has followed is, in many respects, quite remarkable. Both sets of issues with which Mayhew was concerned—the institutional development of Congress and its significance for the content and contours of America's past and present—have attracted many inventive and thoughtful efforts, which have done far more to advance

---

[4] "I doubt that this formulation is acceptable to historians of any ilk" (Eulau 1993, 584).

our understanding of these matters than the scholarship accomplished by political historians—among whom Congress, although with significant exceptions (Silbey 1991; Zelizer 2000, 2004, 2006; Frydl 2009), is an almost completely avoided subject.

Consider how much more we know today about the history of Congress as a formal organization and as a site for the process of lawmaking, whose rules and patterns of action have changed over time. From the second half of the 1990s, historical considerations of congressional development took flight. A pioneering work, Sarah Binder's (1997) comparative analysis chronicled majority party influence in the House as distinct from a more robust role of the minority party in the Senate. Especially important and comprehensive was Schickler's *Disjointed Pluralism* (2001). This sweeping first book, which grew out of a dissertation written under Mayhew's supervision at Yale,[5] comprehensively surveys four periods of congressional reform and battles about congressional power (1890–1910, 1919–32, 1937–52, and 1970–89). Focused on shifts to rules, committees, and leadership patterns that have accrued over time to produce a complex composite and layered institutional result, the book draws on and advances more than one type of theory to construct a multidimensional causal argument that is at once historical and attuned to particularity and to identifiable mechanisms, like path dependence, in order to account for reform efforts, coalitions, and the dynamics of change and institutional accrual. Eschewing parsimony for an approach that offers a configuration of causal elements—including the ebb and flow of party power, the bases of personal power in the legislature, and the interest of members in the capacity of Congress vis-à-vis that of the executive branch—the book advances our understanding of how institutional arrangements connect authority structures and interests so as to affect the course of lawmaking.

In the decade since the publication of Mayhew, Binder, and Schickler's volumes, a host of other important projects in institutional history have been launched. Some of the most significant ones are in process. Charles Stewart and Wendy Schiller are pursuing the history of the indirect election of U.S. senators by state legislatures between 1871 and 1913; Jeffrey Jenkins and Stewart are working on the rise of party government in the House of Representatives; Gerald Gamm and Steven Smith are probing the development of Senate party leadership in the nineteenth and twentieth centuries; Daniel Carpenter has been investigating the place of citizen petitions in legislative affairs; and Tony Madonna is examining shifts in institutional practices, including the decline of the voice vote from 1807 to 1990, the emergence of a formal parliamentarian in the 1920s, and the changing role of the Vice President as the Senate's presiding officer. These and other colleagues who aim to enrich our analytical understanding of the history of Congress can now draw on an abounding literature, which has taken up the challenge first projected by Polsby's classic article on institutionalization and further developed in his more recent *longue durée* account of how the House of Representatives has changed over time (Polsby 2005).

---

[5] *Disjointed Pluralism* was published in the APD book series, Princeton Studies in American Politics: Historical, International, and Comparative Perspectives, edited by Ira Katznelson, Martin Shefter, and Theda Skocpol.

The enlargement of this domain has been particularly notable during the past half-decade; research has focused on how the creation and transformation of congressional rules and institutional mechanisms has profoundly affected the productivity and content of lawmaking. Among this cornucopia, a number of key contributions stand out. Moving beyond the more contemporary emphases and beyond the emphases on policy that are found in significant earlier work (Binder and Smith 1996), and at the same time building on prior linkages that connect strategic and historical analysis of the treatment of intense minorities in the legislature (Dion 2001), two major studies have substantially enhanced our understanding of legislative obstruction. Wawro and Schickler (2006) produced a deep consideration of how the Senate's actions have been shaped by the changing normative and practical role played by parliamentary obstruction. Greg Koger's (2010) account further distinguishes patterns of obstruction in the House as well as in the Senate before 1901, and chronicles the subsequent institutionalization and expansion of the filibuster in the Senate. Institutional themes that we have come to know a good deal more about also include the nature of congressional floor debate before the Civil War (Wirls 2007a), the question of whether member behavior changes during lame-duck sessions as distinct from regular ones (Jenkins and Nokken 2008) the origins of special procedural rights accorded to home state senators (Binder 2007), the impact on representation of the 17th Amendment, mandating the direct election of senators (Lapinski 2000; Schiller 2006; Gailmard and Jenkins 2009), the changing history of congressional investigations (Schickler 2008; Parker and Dull 2009), patterns of effective policy and partisan entrepreneurship by congressional leaders (Strahan 2007; Champagne, Harris, et al. 2009), agenda control as a key source of party power (Cox and McCubbins 2005; Gailmard and Jenkins 2007; Schickler and Pearson 2009), and the history of congressional elections, including a focus on contested elections, electoral laws, and patterns of redistricting (Engstrom 2006; Engstrom and Kernell 2005; Carson and Roberts 2005; Carson, Engstrom, and Roberts 2006; Jenkins 2004, 2005; James 2007).

What stands out in this multifaceted body of work is a commitment to understand the origins and impact of institutions and the difference made by such arrangements, small and large, in affecting how Congress conducts its business. Such analytical histories are located at some distance from more traditional institutional analyses, which characterized the first phase of modern political science; for these draw both on behavioral and on strategic methods to search for meanings and to explore effects. Though not all the scholars who have produced such institutional and historical work identify with APD, they have been carrying out one of the central features of that subfield: the privileging of institutional development in time.

Side by side with this scholarship on the changing Congress over the long term, there has been an efflorescence of research and writing geared toward better understanding the variety of relationships that link Congress to the wider society and polity. Focused on aggregate patterns of lawmaking, on particular items or types of legislation, and on the impact of these outputs in shaping, and reshaping, the

American national state, a subject that has been yet another central preoccupation of APD, this content-rich work has been heterogeneous in scope and approach.

Four overlapping types can be distinguished. First are accounts of very particular historical episodes that treat the subject of how specific historical developments reordered key institutional features of American political life, and how these changes affected congressional representation. Among the growing number of such studies we can find considerations of the relationships linking social movements and roll-call voting under the impact of Populist mobilization (Hirano 2008), how the development of security and trade policies in the late 1940s at the outset of the Cold War affected the ties between public opinion and roll-call behavior (Bailey 2003), the activism of African Americans with respect to South African apartheid (Tillery 2006), and factors that affected the constituency bases of congressional political parties from just before the Civil War to just before World War I (Jenkins, Schickler, and Carson 2004).

Second are rigorous searches, based on large data-sets and innovative methods to identify and evaluate what members of Congress have produced as lawmakers, not just as roll-call voters. In the recent past, there have been a series of impressive and original attempts to gauge legislative accomplishment by way of methodological creativity brought to bear on freshly organized evidence. Working in this mode and utilizing a data-set containing every public statute enacted between 1877 and 1994, Joshua Clinton and John Lapinski have offered new ways to measure the performance of Congress as a legislature, to measure the significance of legislation systematically, and to get inside the process of lawmaking, which cannot be reduced to calculating roll-call behavior—since most laws pass without recorded votes on the floor (Clinton and Lapinski 2006, 2007, 2008). Working with the full span of the history of the Congress, a parallel program by Tobin Grant and Nathan Kelly likewise has been developing methodologies for measuring legislative productivity and for creating an index of major legislation (Grant and Kelly 2008).

Third are efforts to utilize congressional evidence, systematically deployed, better to account for central puzzles in American political history. An example concerns the fate of the American labor movement, which declined from a robust and growing position, taking in a third of the labor force by 1954, to a declining force in the country's economic and political life. Farhang and Katznelson (2005) argue that these long-term changes were profoundly shaped by congressional decisions about the legal framework for union organization, and that these labor law outcomes depended on the choices taken by southern representatives who increasingly came to view organized labor in the 1940s as a threat to their region's system of racial segregation. More broadly, an enormous amount of progress has been made in charting how southern preferences as well as attempts to grapple with southern patterns of politics and society have shaped congressional rules and behavior. Currently active research programs have illuminated the ante-bellum status of slavery within Congress, especially the gag rule (Meinke 2007; Wirls 2007b), how reactions to southern arrangements were instrumental in shaping key congressional rules and procedures, including the Reed Rules that remade the House (Valelly 2009), the ways southern power has been deployed to alter the substantive content of significant legislation (Katznelson 2005), the long-term history of efforts aimed at broadening black civil rights (Jenkins, Peck, and Weaver 2010), and the mid-twentieth-century party shift on civil rights, with Democrats supplanting Republicans as the supporters of racial liberalism (Feinstein and Schickler 2008; Pearson and Schickler 2009; Schickler, Pearson, and Feinstein forthcoming).

Fourth are works concerned with the idea and practice of political representation that span political theory and empirical studies. Once taken for granted by the literature on Congress, this complex site at the heart of any liberal polity has been generating increasing attention ever since the publication of Bernard Manin's deeply historical analysis in *The Principles of Representative Government* (1997), which highlighted what he underscored as the aristocratic features of representation. By contrast, Nadia Urbinati's equally historical *Representative Democracy: Principles and Genealogy* (2006) stresses its democratic aspects. Examining the field of tension defined by these positions and drawing on their conflicting positions, other scholars have looked to create new typologies of representation (Andeweg and Thomassen 2005; Rehfeld 2005, 2006, 2009) and to bring empirical evidence and logical reasoning to bear on the clash between elitist and democratic views of representation (Mansbridge 2003; Ferejohn and Rosenbluth 2010). Yet again, it has been Mayhew who insists, as his chapter in this volume underscores, that systematic and theoretical approaches to the study of Congress must be more deeply historical and thus more modest in their specification of the scope of their claims situated both in time and space (Mayhew 2011). What he calls the "catechism of sharpness" that has made congressional studies less vague and more elegant loses power, he argues, unless sufficient attention is paid to historical development and unless models and behavioral propositions are treated more as various logics of process than as accurate depictions of actual reality across moments, locations, and situations. Resisting timelessness, Mayhew deployed this sensibility in *Parties and Policies* (2008), a collection of his essays that neatly captures the recent rigorous and multifaceted analytical turn to substantive histories of events written in tandem with studies of the durable and the changing institutional features of Congress. While only a minority of the book's fourteen essays directly concern Congress—these include studies of congressional elections, policy waves in lawmaking, actions by members of the House and Senate, and supermajority rule in the Senate—"history supplies the empirical grist for all" (Mayhew 2008, 3).

MOVING FORWARD

Notwithstanding all this ferment and accomplishment, the place of Congress within APD and, in turn, the ways APD can particularly inform the historical turn in congressional studies remain to be determined. History as a grist is necessary but not sufficient for the incorporation into APD of the ways elected representatives make binding policy decisions, having been equipped by the mandates of their constituents and the legitimacy of their institution and its rules, and guided by their various commitments and normative desires. The fast-growing historical turn in congressional studies, both with respect to the history of Congress itself and to the ways it acts to create public statutes, pass resolutions, and ratify treaties, has opened prospects for a theoretically informed and empirically rich congressional vantage on American political development.

But these possibilities remain to be seized. For historical studies of Congress to cohere as a distinctive and compelling intellectual project, as well as to become a driving force within APD, more than a turn to the past is required. In the lack of integration by substantive research programs with sustained perspectives on institutional development, which can link various targeted studies, the historical impulse risks producing interesting but scattered substantive work, which offers an archive of heterogeneous factual information. In moving historical studies of Congress forward, APD thus possesses a yet unrealized, but potentially compelling, role. For APD can help promote frameworks for research that could prod scholars both within and to the side of the sub-field to take up compelling questions and deploy novel methods that promise to help advance the next phase of historical research. It can advance these aims by harnessing the diverse subjects and questions that have driven scholars of Congress to research endeavors that take up central historically situated puzzles of the kind that have motivated the creation and advancement of this style of work in political science, and by deploying approaches and methods that can make temporality a constitutive part of systematic political analysis.

APD, after all, has been committed as a disciplinary orientation to grapple with fundamental features and patterns of change in the American regime through the use of explicit conceptual categories and theory, and through systematic treatments of historical time. Like the larger domain of historical institutionalism of which it is a part, APD is "substantively focused and puzzle-driven." An overview by two leading practitioners summarized this orientation as "a coherent genre" that analyzes "organizational and institutional configurations where others look at particular settings in isolation; they pay attention to critical junctures and long-term processes where others look only at slices of time or short-term maneuvers"; and the authors focus on "the overarching contexts and interacting processes that shape and reshape states, politics, and public policymaking" (Pierson and Skowronek 2002, 697, 693).

Nestled within this broad orientation to the study of politics, APD has been especially concerned to understand how any particular institutional site connects to other institutions in a layered and strategic relationship, to larger historical trends, and to the course of state-making in a broadly liberal polity (Katznelson and Lapinski 2006a; Orren and Skowronek 2002, 2004). It strives to identify and ask the most important, difficult, and challenging historical questions about America's development. With the rich achievements and progress of the past decade, historical work on Congress offers building blocks for such efforts, but stops short of bringing Congress into APD either as a pivotal location that makes Congress more central to APD's main substantive concerns or in Congress-centered syntheses of the American experience.

There is a big opportunity waiting to be seized. No American institution is better documented than Congress in detail over time. Given the treasure trove of information available on congressional elections, roll-call voting, committee and floor debates, institutional development, and policymaking, opportunities beckon to advance APD with Congress at the center of its concerns. But promises are not redeemed just by wishing. To realize existing potentialities, systematic attention has to be paid to questions that bear on the status of historical evidence, methods of analysis, and especially the scope and hierarchy of questions to be probed. Unless integrated by self-conscious research programs that are motivated by these concerns, existing intellectual energy will fragment, perhaps even dissipate. How then, might the next chapter for a congressional vantage within, and informed by, APD advance?

I offer three sets of suggestions. The first concerns a return to themes central to the earlier historical turn that Mayhew pioneered in the mid-1960s. At its core was the emplacement of substance, studied with historical specificity, at the heart of congressional analysis. The second suggestion is the development of methods that are inherently more historical than current tools of analysis. Emplaced within such substantive and methodological turns, the third suggestion is a quest to probe more fully the contours and scope of political representation in America's liberal state.

The content of lawmaking was privileged in the 1960s and up until the early 1980s. As the first example, Mayhew's *Party Loyalty* used Rice likeness and cohesion scores to discern when members of the House followed the majority party position in distinct issue domains, each of which, it was clear, affected diverse constituencies differently, and thus evoked the solicitude of members differentially. Such an approach, especially when accompanied by non-arbitrary and more comprehensive selections of roll calls for examination, more nuanced means of policy classification, and a wider array of methods, promises to give content pride of place within congressional studies. Without privileging the substance of representation in this way, it will be difficult to harness the study of Congress for APD, whose central justification lies with a quest to understand the content of American state formation, and thus the nature of the country's regime over time.

Following the crest of attention to policy voting at specific historical moments, this valuable orientation became less fashionable, in part as a result of problems of specification and measurement; for the policy classifications that were deployed proved empirically too bulky and insufficiently grounded in theory. Furthermore, that literature lacked a sufficiently pointed specification of mechanisms that could account, as Theodore Lowi put the point, for when and how "a political relationship is determined by the type of policy at stake, so that for every policy there is likely to be a distinctive type of political relationship" (Lowi 1964, 688). Policy content is not a given as a motivating element, but only can be said to have such causal status when the substance under consideration interacts with key features of political representation, including personal preferences, constituency situations, and the party orientations of members under specific historical circumstances. Together, these factors shape how legislators order their preferences, and how they talk and behave with regard to specific issues (Katznelson and Lapinski 2006a, 245, 252; Katznelson and Lapinski 2006b; Lapinski 2008). Furthermore, it is important, as Frances Lee has emphasized (2009), to distinguish carefully issues that produce partisan voting due to ideology and issues that produce partisan voting due to particular political circumstances, such as contests about the parties' reputation for competence or struggles for power that have little to do with ideological differences.

Tracing these matters and making such distinctions are problems quite central to APD. Scholars working in this orientation long have understood that politics in liberal democracies never is politics in general, but always concerns distinct subjects that bear on relationships defining ties between the modern state, the economy, society, and the international arena that determine the content and boundaries of stateness in America. At stake in lawmaking in each area of policy is whether, and how, the federal government has governed, with what instruments, and with what degrees and implements of inducement, regulation, and coercion. These are APD's largest concerns that can be directly informed by reviving the aborted lineage of inquiry that asked whether and how the substance of policy shapes behavior within distinctive historical contexts. A committed effort to reopen this substantive focus can open "fresh opportunities to probe long-standing vexing historical issues about the content and character of the political regime in the United States" (Katznelson and Lapinski 2006b, 121).

Such a quest demands methodological inventiveness. To this end, Lapinski and I have devoted considerable attention to creating a new three-tiered, theoretically informed policy classification that underpins a large-scale data set of congressional roll calls (Katznelson and Lapinski 2006b). Concurrently, Gregory Wawro and I have begun to explore alternatives to standard regression models that treat parameters as non-varying over long stretches of history. Rather than treat history simply as data, with the implicit assumption of an equivalence among facts and particulars found in various periods and contexts, it is important to find methods that can advance considerations of temporality (the importance of the sequence of events), periodicity (the clustering of events along the dimension of time), specificity (the uniqueness of events in historical time), and context (the larger environments within which events take place) in historical studies of Congress. Parameter variation within multilevel modeling offers a potential solution, for it can permit the effects of explanatory variables to change over time, and thus it can strike a balance between incorporating historical complexity and imposing the kind of structure that is required in order to reveal underlying causal mechanisms and processes.

Irrespective of method, the most fundamental feature of an engagement of APD with Congress is the emplacement of political representation at the heart of inquiry about America's polity in order to illuminate the distinctive qualities of the national state and the role political ideas about institutions and process have played in its development. Every democratic founding, Richard Bensel has stressed, starts with a legislature. There, representatives weigh and dispose alternatives and treat decisions as legitimate, if also as provisional (Bensel 2007). Composed of members and leaders acting within determinate rules, legislators are both agents of their constituents and autonomous deliberating principals. Writing about political representation in his *Second Treatise*, John Locke assertively claimed, in what has become a classic proposition, that "the Legislative" is the "Supream Power of any Common-wealth," that because it makes laws

promulgated and known to the People, and not by Extemporary Decrees ... the *first and fundamental positive* Law of all Commonwealths, *is the establishing of the Legislative Power* ... This *Legislative* is not only *the supream power* of the Common-wealth, but sacred and unalterable in the hands where the Community have once placed it.   (Locke 1960, 353, 255, 356)

Within the United States, congressional representation has been at the heart of the regime in just this way. The lawmaking it has produced has defined the character of the country's national state, as well as the meaning, and limits, of its liberal and republican traditions. But representation has not proceeded without distortions and limits. Any Congress-centered account thus must reckon not only with patterns of inclusion and incorporation, but with the boundaries of exclusion, in terms of who has gained access to the terms of citizenship offered by the process of representation, and by identifying which issues fall within, and which outside, the scope of effective legislative consideration.

These questions have multiple aspects. These include rules for membership, for instance immigration arrangements, and patterns of incorporation of ethnic and racial minorities in American political life. The longest-standing and most vexing of these matters has pivoted on race, particularly on the place of African Americans in the polity and on the role played by the South, with its historical and legal commitment until the mid-1960s to white supremacy as the foundation for its political order. Southern regionalism also, as noted, concerns the limits placed in different eras on the substantive scope of political representation (Key 1949; Katznelson 2005). To study these topics, Lapinski and I are examining the extent to which southern members of the House and Senate acted as if they were members of a distinctive nation during the era spanning the end of Reconstruction in 1877 and the passage of the Voting Rights Act in 1965.

Another important, and understudied, institutional candidate for the limits of representation is the changing role of Congress with regard to war and peace (Katznelson and Shefter 2002). In the early republic, Congress played a robust role in defining the contours of what Secretary of War John Calhoun called an expansible military, an armed force that could grow during periods of war but quickly demobilize in order to protect citizen rights in a liberal political order. By contrast, ever since the 1940s, military questions have affected congressional representation and its limits in a new way, which has raised fundamental questions about the scope of congressional capacity.

During World War II, some leading scholars considered how total warfare and the growth of enduring challenges to national security threatened to erode the traditional distinction between commonplace political moments and unusual times of crisis, when ordinary politics might have to be suspended, if reluctantly and temporarily

(Lasswell 1941; Riesman 1942). They ruminated about the price that would be exacted for democracy if wartime emergencies were to become permanent. These apprehensions bore directly on the standing of the legislature. At an earlier moment, an authoritarian strand of criticism had evaluated parliamentary government as inherently inadequate to govern under modern conditions (Schmitt 1923). The breakdown of the majority of the globe's democracies in the heyday of Fascism, Stalinism, and other forms of authoritarianism and dictatorship was instigated by parties and movements that shared this diagnosis.

After the war, fierce democrats like Robert Dahl and C. Wright Mills insisted that, unless realistic and empirical understandings could be fashioned, liberal democracy would remain vulnerable to such unfriendly assaults. Dahl cautioned in 1953 that atomic energy is but "one of a growing class of situations for which the traditional democratic processes are rather unsuitable and for which traditional theories of democracy provide no rational answer" (Dahl 1953, 6). Shortly thereafter, Mills characterized American politics as divided between subjects and policy disputes that are settled in Congress in a process marked by interest group pressure and negotiation, and policy matters reserved for decision-making undertaken outside the legislative sphere, by a smaller, more insulated, elite (Mills 1956). A congressional research agenda suggested by these charged claims about Congress and national security—an agenda tailor-made for APD, which brings us back to the challenge of discerning how variation to the content of policy issues can affect the basic contours and character of the legislative process—never took off within political science, but is needed now more than ever.

In all, the conclusion Lapinski and I offered a half-decade ago still holds. "A generation ago," we then wrote, "APD and congressional studies missed the opportunity to join forces on the terrain of policy to advance our understanding of liberalism and the state. This chance need not, and certainly should not, be missed again" (Katznelson and Lapinski 2005, 253).

REFERENCES

ALMOND, G. A. 1990. *A Discipline Divided: Schools and Sects in Political Science*. Newbury Park, CA: Sage Publications.

ANDEWEG, R. B., and THOMASSEN, J. J. A. 2005. Modes of Political Representation: Toward a New Typology. *Legislative Studies Quarterly*, 30 (November): 507–28.

BAILEY, M. A. 2003. The Politics of the Difficult: Congress, Public Opinion, and Early Cold War Aid and Trade Policies. *Legislative Studies Quarterly*, 28 (May): 147–77.

BENSEL, R. 1984. *Sectionalism and American Political Development, 1880–1980*. Madison: University of Wisconsin Press.

——1990. *Yankee Leviathan: The Origins of Central State Authority in America, 1859–1877*. New York: Cambridge University Press.

——2000. *The Political Economy of American Industrialization, 1877–1900*. New York: Cambridge University Press.

BENSEL, R. 2007. 'States Out of Nature': The Legislative Founding of Democracies. Unpublished paper presented to the Congress and History Conference, Princeton University.

BINDER, S. A. 1997. *Minority Rights, Majority Rule: Partisanship and the Development of Congress.* Cambridge: Cambridge University Press.

——2007. Where Do Institutions Come From? Exploring the Origins of the Senate Blue Slip. *Studies in American Political Development*, 21 (Spring): 1–14.

——and SMITH, S. S. 1996. *Politics or Principle? Filibustering in the United States Senate.* Washington, D.C: The Brookings Institution.

BRADY, D. W. 1973. *Congressional Voting in a Partisan Era: A Study of the McKinley Houses and a Comparison to the Modern House of Representatives.* Lawrence: University of Kansas Press.

——1978. Critical Elections, Congressional Parties and Clusters of Policy Changes. *British Journal of Political Science*, 8 (January): 79–99.

——1985. A Reevaluation of Realignments in American Politics: Evidence from the House of Representatives. *American Political Science Review*, 79 (March): 28–49.

——1988. *Critical Elections and Congressional Policymaking.* Stanford: Stanford University Press.

——and BULLOCK, III, C. S. 1980. Is There a Conservative Coalition in the House? *Journal of Politics*, 42 (May): 549–59.

——and SINCLAIR, B. 1984. Building Majorities for Policy Changes in the House of Representatives. *Journal of Politics*, 46 (November): 1033–60.

——and STEWART, JR., J. 1982. Congressional Party Realignment and Transformations of Public Policy in Three Realignment Eras. *American Journal of Political Science*, 26 (May): 333–60.

CARSON, J. L., and ROBERTS, J. M. 2005. Strategic Politicians and U.S. House Elections, 1874–1914. *Journal of Politics*, 67 (May): 474–96.

——ENGSTROM, E. J., and ROBERTS, J. M. 2006. Redistricting, Candidate Entry, and the Politics of Nineteenth-Century U.S. House Elections. *American Journal of Political Science*, 50 (April): 283–93.

CHAMPAGNE, A., HARRIS, D. B., RIDDLESBERGER, J. W., AND NELSON, G. 2009. *The Austin–Boston Connection: Decades of House Democratic Leadership, 1937–1989.* University Station: Texas A&M University Press.

CLAUSEN, A. R. 1973. *How Congressmen Decide: A Policy Focus.* New York: St. Martin's Press.

——and CHENEY, R. B. 1970. A Comparative Analysis of Senate House Voting on Economic and Welfare Policy, 1953–1964. *American Political Science Review*, 64 (March): 138–52.

CLINTON, J. D., and LAPINSKI, J. 2006. Measuring Legislative Accomplishment, 1877–1994. *American Journal of Political Science*, 50 (January): 232–49.

————2007. Measuring Significant Legislation, 1877–1948, pp. 361–78 in *Party, Process, and Political Change in Congress, Volume 2: Further New Perspectives on the History of Congress*, ed. D. W. Brady and M. D. McCubbins. Stanford: Stanford University Press.

————2008. Laws and Roll Calls in the U.S. Congress, 1891–1994. *Legislative Studies Quarterly*, 33 (November): 511–41.

COLLIE, M. P. 1988a. The Rise of Coalition Politics: Voting in the U.S. House, 1933–1980. *Legislative Studies Quarterly*, 13 (August): 321–42.

——1988b. Universalism and the Parties in the U.S. House of Representatives. *American Journal of Political Science*, 32 (November): 865–83.

——1989. Electoral Patterns and Voting Alignments in the U.S. House, 1886–1986. *Legislative Studies Quarterly*, 14 (February): 107–27.

Cooper, J. 1970. *The Origins of the Standing Committees and the Development of the Modern House.* Houston: William Marsh Rice University Press.

——and Brady, D. W. 1981a. Institutional Context and Leadership Style: The House from Cannon to Rayburn. *American Political Science Review*, 74 (June): 411–25.

——1981b. Toward a Diachronic Analysis of Congress. *American Political Science Review*, 4 (December): 988–1006.

Cox, G. W., and McCubbins, M. D. 2005. *Setting the Agenda: Responsible Party Government in the U.S. House of Representatives*. Cambridge: Cambridge University Press.

Dahl, R. A. 1950. *Congress and Foreign Policy*. New York: Harcourt Brace.

——1953. Atomic Energy and the Democratic Process. In *The Impact of Atomic Energy. The Annals of the American Academy of Political and Social Science*, ed. R. A. Dahl. 290 (November).

Dion, G. D. 2001. *Turning the Legislative Thumbscrew: Minority Rights and Procedural Change in Legislative Politics*. Ann Arbor: University of Michigan Press.

Engstrom, E. J. 2006. Stacking the States, Stacking the House: The Partisan Consequences of Congressional Redistricting in the 19th Century. *American Political Science Review*, 100 (August): 419–27.

——and Kernell, S. 2005. Manufactured Responsiveness: The Impact of State Electoral Laws on Unified Party Control of the Presidency and House of Representatives, 1840–1940. *American Journal of Political Science*, 49 (July): 531–49.

Eulau, H. 1993. The Congress as a Research Arena: An Uneasy Partnership between History and Political Science: A Review Essay. *Legislative Studies Quarterly*, 18 (November): 569–92.

Farrier, J. 2004. *Passing the Buck: Congress, the Budget and Deficits*. Lexington: University of Kentucky.

Farhang, S., and Katznelson, I. 2005. The Southern Imposition: Congress and Labor in the New Deal and Fair Deal. *Studies in American Political Development*, 19 (Spring): 1–29.

Feinstein, B. D., and Schickler, E. 2008. Platforms and Partners: The Civil Rights Realignment Reconsidered. *Studies in American Political Development*, 22 (Spring): 1–30.

Ferejohn, J. and Rosenbluth, F. 2010. Electoral Representation and the Aristocratiz Thesis, pp. 271–304 in *Political Representation*. I. Shapiro, S. C. Stokes, E. J. Woods, and A. S. Kirshner. Cambridge: Cambridge University Press.

Frydl, K. J. 2009. *The G.I. Bill*. Cambridge: Cambridge University Press.

Gailmard, S., and Jenkins, J. A. 2007. Negative Agenda Control in the Senate and House: Fingerprints of Majority Party Power. *Journal of Politics*, 69 (August): 689–700.

————Agency Problems, Electoral Institutions, and the 17th Amendment. *American Journal of Political Science*, 53 (April): 324–42.

Gamm, G., and Huber, J. 2002. Legislatures as Political Institutions: Beyond the Contemporary Congress, pp. 313–41 in *Political Science: State of the Discipline*, ed. I. Katznelson and H. Milner. New York: W.W. Norton & Company.

Grant, J. T., and Kelly, N. J. 2008. Legislative Productivity of the U.S. Congress, 1787–2004. *Political Analysis*, 16 (Summer): 303–23.

Hansen, J. M. 1991. *Gaining Access: Congress and the Farm Lobby, 1919–1981*. Chicago: University of Chicago Press.

Hirano, S. 2008. Third Parties, Elections, and Roll-Call Votes: The Populist Party and the Late Nineteenth-Century U.S. Congress. *Legislative Studies Quarterly*, 33 (February): 131–60.

James, S. C. 2007. Timing and Sequence in Congressional Elections: Interstate Contagion and America's Nineteenth-Century Scheduling Regime. *Studies in American Political Development*, 21 (Fall): 181–202.

Jenkins, J. A. 2004. Partisanship and Contested Election Cases in the House of Representatives, 1789–2002. *Studies in American Political Development*, 18 (Fall): 112–35.

JENKINS, J. A. 2005. Partisanship and Contested Election Cases in the Senate, 1789–2002. *Studies in American Political Development*, 19 (Spring): 53–74.

—— and NOKKEN, T. P. 2008. Legislative Shirking in the Pre-Twentieth Amendment Era: Presidential Influence, Party Power, and Lame Duck Sessions of Congress, 1877–1933. *Studies in American Political Development*, 22 (Spring): 111–40.

—— PECK, J., and WEAVER, V. M. 2010. Between Reconstructions: Congressional Action on Civil Rights, 1891–1940. *Studies in American Political Development*, 24 (April): 57–89.

—— SCHICKLER, E., and CARSON, J. L. 2004. Constituency Cleavages and Congressional Parties: Measuring Homogeneity and Polarization, 1857–1913. *Social Science History*, 28 (Winter): 537–73.

LASSWELL, H. D. 1941. The Garrison State. *American Journal of Sociology*, 46 (January): 455–68.

LOCKE, J. 1960. *Two Treatises of Government*, ed. J. Laslett. Cambridge: Cambridge University Press.

LOWELL, A. L. 1901. The Influence of Party Upon Legislation in England and America. *Annual Report of the American Historical Association for 1901*. Washington, DC: American Historical Association.

KATZNELSON, I. 1993. The State to the Rescue? Political Science and History Reconnect. *Social Research*, 59 (Winter): 719–37.

—— 2002. Flexible Capacity: The Military and Early American Statebuilding, pp. 82–110 in *Shaped by War and Trade: International Influences on American Political Development*, ed. I. Katznelson and M. Shefter. Princeton: Princeton University Press.

—— 2005. *When Affirmative Action Was White: An Untold History of Racial Inequality in Twentieth-Century America*. New York: W.W. Norton.

—— and J. S. LAPINSKI. 2006a. At the Crossroads: Congress and American Political Development. *Perspectives on Politics*, 4 (June): 243–60.

—— —— 2006b. The Substance of Representation: Studying Policy Content and Legislative Behavior, pp. 96–126 in *The Macropolitics of Congress*, ed. E. S. Adler and J. S. Lapinski. Princeton: Princeton University Press.

—— and SHEFTER, M. 2002. *Shaped by War and Trade: International Influences on American Political Development*. Princeton: Princeton University Press.

—— and WEINGAST, B., eds. 2005. *Preferences and Situations: Points of Intersection Between Historical and Rational Choice Institutionalism*. New York: Russell Sage.

KEY, JR., V. O. 1949. *Southern Politics in State and Nation*. New York: Alfred A. Knopf.

KOGER, G. 2010. *Filibustering: A Political History of Obstruction in the House and Senate*. Chicago: University of Chicago Press.

LAPINSKI, J. S. 2000. Representation and Reform: A Congress Centered Approach to American Political Development. Ph.D. Thesis. Department of Political Science, Columbia University.

—— 2008. Policy Substance and Performance in American Lawmaking. *American Journal of Political Science*, 52 (April): 1–17.

LEE, F. E. 2009. *Beyond Ideology: Politics, Principles, and Partisanship in the U.S. Senate*. Chicago: University of Chicago Press.

LOWI, T. J. 1964. American Business, Public Policy, Case Studies, and Political Theory. *World Politics*, 16 (July): 577–715.

LUCE, R. D., and ROGOW, A. A. 1956. A Game Theory Analysis of Congressional Power Distributions for a Stable Two Party System. *American Behavioral Scientist*, 95 (April): 83–95.

MANIN, B. 1997. *Principles of Representative Government*. Cambridge: Cambridge University Press.

MANSBRIDGE, J. 2003. Rethinking Representation. *American Political Science Review*, 97 (November): 515–28.

MAYHEW, D. R. 1966. *Party Loyalty Among Congressmen: The Difference between Democrats and Republicans, 1947–1962*. Cambridge: Harvard University Press.

—— 1974. *Congress: The Electoral Connection*. New Haven: Yale University Press.

—— 2000. *America's Congress: Actions in the Public Sphere, James Madison to Newt Gingrich*. New Haven: Yale University Press.

—— 2008. *Parties and Policies: How the American Government Works*. New Haven: Yale University Press.

—— 2011. Theorizing About Congress, pp. 875–93 in *The Oxford Handbook of the American Congress*, ed. E. Schickler and F. E. Lee. New York: Oxford University Press.

MEINKE, S. R. 2007. Slavery, Partisanship, and Procedure in the U.S. House: The Gag Rule, 1836–1845. *Legislative Studies Quarterly*, 32 (February): 33–57.

MILLS, C. W. 1956. *The Power Elite*. New York: Oxford University Press.

NELSON, G. 1974. Assessing the Congressional Committee System: Contributions from a Comparative Perspective. *Annals of the American Academy of Political and Social Science*, 411 (January): 120–32.

—— 1977. Partisan Patterns of House Leadership Change, 1787–1987. *American Political Science Review*, 71 (September): 918–39.

ORREN, K., and SKOWRONEK, S. 2002. The Study of American Political Development, pp. 722–54 in *Political Science: State of the Discipline*, ed. I. Katznelson and H. Milner. New York: W.W. Norton & Company.

—— 2004. *The Search for American Political Development*. New York: Cambridge University Press.

PARKER, D. C. W., and DULL, M. 2009. Divided We Quarrel: The Politics of Congressional Investigations, 1947–2004. *Legislative Studies Quarterly*, 34 (August): 319–45.

PEARSON, K., and SCHICKLER, E. 2009. Discharge Petitions, Agenda Control, and the Congressional Committee System, 1929–1976. *Journal of Politics*, 71 (October): 1238–56.

PIERSON, P. 2000. Increasing Returns, Path Dependence, and the Study of Politics. *American Political Science Review*, 94(2): 251–67.

—— 2004. *Politics in Time: History, Institutions, and Social Analysis*. Princeton: Princeton University Press.

—— and SKOCPOL, T. 2002. Historical Institutionalism in Contemporary Political Science, pp. 693–721 in *Political Science: State of the Discipline*, ed. I. Katznelson and H. Milner. New York: W.W. Norton & Company.

POLSBY, N. W. 1968. The Institutionalization of the U.S. House of Representatives. *American Political Science Review*, 62 (March): 144–68.

—— 2005. *How Congress Evolves: Social Bases of Institutional Change*. New York: Oxford University Press.

—— and SCHICKLER, E. 2002. Landmarks in the Study of Congress since 1945. *Annual Review of Political Science*, 5: 333–67.

—— GALLAHER, M., and RUNDQUIST, B. S. 1969. The Growth of Seniority in the House of Representatives. *American Political Science Review*, 63 (September): 787–807.

POOLE, K. T., and ROSENTHAL, H. 1997. *Congress: A Political–Economic History of Roll Call Voting*. New York: Oxford University Press.

REHFELD, A. 2005. *The Concept of Constituency: Political Representation, Democratic Legitimacy and Institutional Design*. Cambridge: Cambridge University Press.

—— 2006. Toward a General Theory of Political Representation. *Journal of Politics*, 68(February): 1–21.

—— 2009. Representation Rethought: On Trustees, Delegates and Gyroscopes in the Study of Political Representation and Democracy. *American Political Science Review*, 103 (May): 214–30.

RIESMAN, D. 1942. Civil Liberties in a Period of Transition, pp. 33–96 in *Public Policy*, ed. C. Friedrich and E. Mason. Cambridge, MA: Harvard University Press.

SANDERS, E. 1999. *Roots of Reform: Farmers, Workers and the American State*. Chicago: University of Chicago Press.

SCHICKLER, E. 2001. *Disjointed Pluralism: Institutional Innovation and the Development of the U.S. Congress*. Princeton, NJ: Princeton University Press.

—— 2008. Entrepreneurial Defenses of Congressional Power, pp. 293–315 in *Formative Acts: American Politics in the Making*, ed. S. Skowronek and M. Glassman. Philadelphia: University of Pennsylvania Press.

—— and PEARSON, K. 2009. Agenda Control, Majority Party Power, and the House Committee on Rules, 1937–52. *Legislative Studies Quarterly*, 34 (November): 455–91.

—— —— and FEINSTEIN, B. Forthcoming. Shifting Partisan Coalitions: Support for Civil Rights in Congress from 1933–1972. *Journal of Politics*.

SCHILLER, W. J. 2006. Building Careers and Courting Constituents: U.S. Senate Representation, 1889–1924. *Studies in American Political Development*, 20 (Fall): 185–97.

SCHMITT, C. 1923. *Die geistesgeschichtliche Lage des heutigen Parlamentarismus*. Berlin: Dunker & Humblot.

SILBEY, J., ed. 1991. *The Congress of the United States, 1789–1989*, 9 vols. Brooklyn: Carlson Publishing.

SINCLAIR, B. D. 1977a. Determinants of Aggregate Party Cohesion in the U.S. House of Representatives, 1901–1956. *Legislative Studies Quarterly*, 2 (May): 155–75.

—— 1977b. Party Realignment and the Transformation of the Political Agenda: The House of Representatives, 1925–1938. *American Political Science Review*, 71 (September): 940–53.

—— 1978. From Party Voting to Regional Fragmentation: The House of Representatives, 1933–1956. *American Politics Quarterly*, 8 (April): 125–46.

—— 1982. *Congressional Realignment, 1925–1978*. Austin: University of Texas Press.

SKOCPOL, T. 1992. *Protecting Soldiers and Mothers: The Political Origins of Social Policy in the United States*. Cambridge: Harvard University Press.

SKOWRONEK, S. 1982. *Building a New American State: The Expansion of National Administrative Capacities, 1877–1920*. Cambridge: Cambridge University Press.

SMITH, R. M. 1997. *Civic Ideals: Conflicting Visions of Citizenship in US History*. New Haven: Yale University Press.

STEWART, C. 1989. *Budget Reform Politics: The Design of the Appropriations Process in the House of Representatives, 1865–1921*. Cambridge: Cambridge University Press.

STRAHAN, R. 2007. *Leading Representatives: The Agency of Leaders in the Politics of the U.S. House*. Baltimore: Johns Hopkins University Press.

SWIFT, E. K. 1996. *The Making of an American Senate: Reconstitutive Change in Congress, 1787–1841*. Ann Arbor: University of Michigan Press.

TILLERY, A. B. 2006. Foreign Policy Activism and Power in the House of Representatives: Black Members of Congress and South Africa, 1968–1986. *Studies in American Political Development*, 20 (Spring): 88–103.

TRUMAN, D. E. 1959. *The Congressional Party: A Case Study*. New York: John Wiley and Sons.

TURNER, J. 1951. *Party and Constituency: Pressures on Congress*. Baltimore: Johns Hopkins University Press.

URBINATI, N. 2006. *Representative Democracy: Principles and Genealogy*. Chicago: University of Chicago Press.

VALELLY, R. M. 2009. The Reed Rules and Republican Party Building: A New Look. *Studies in American Political Development*, 23 (October): 115–42.

WAWRO, G. J., and SCHICKLER, E. 2006. *Filibuster: Obstruction and Lawmaking in the U.S. Senate*. Princeton: Princeton University Press.

WHITTINGTON, K. E. 1999. What's the Point of APD? *Clio*, 9(2): 5, 43–5.

—— and CARPENTER, D. P. 2003. Executive Power in American Institutional Development. *Perspectives on Politics*, 1 (September): 495–513.

WIRLS, D. 2007a. The 'Golden Age' Senate and Floor Debate in the Antebellum Congress. *Legislative Studies Quarterly*, 32 (May): 193–222.

—— 2007b. 'The Only Mode of Avoiding Everlasting Debate': The Overlooked Senate Gag Rule for Antislavery Petitions. *Journal of the Early Republic*, 27 (Spring): 115–38.

ZELIZER, J. E. 2000. *Taxing America: Wilbur D. Mills, Congress, and the State, 1945–1975*. Cambridge: Cambridge University Press.

—— ed. 2004. *The American Congress: The Building of Democracy*. Boston: Houghton Mifflin Harcourt.

—— 2006. *On Capitol Hill: The Struggle to Reform Congress and its Consequences, 1948–2000*. Cambridge: Cambridge University Press.

PART III

ELECTIONS

CHAPTER 7

....

HOUSE AND SENATE ELECTIONS

....

JAMIE L. CARSON*

JASON M. ROBERTS

RESEARCH on U.S. congressional elections, and House elections in particular, has made remarkable progress in the past four decades. Starting with Mayhew's (1974a) observation that members of Congress are "single-minded seekers of reelection," students of congressional politics have spent countless hours investigating a wide variety of puzzles generated by elections to the House and Senate. A considerable amount of attention has focused on questions ranging from the sources of the incumbency advantage in Congress to why voter turnout is so much lower in mid-term elections. Although much has been learned in the past few decades from this research on congressional elections, there are still a number of unanswered questions that, in our view, have received insufficient attention to date. This is unfortunate, as elections go to the very heart of accountability and representation, and an insufficient understanding of how they are conducted—as well as of their direct and indirect effects—limits our ability to generalize from them.

This chapter seeks to assess the state of research on U.S. House and Senate elections, most notably by examining a few central themes that have permeated the literature on congressional elections since the early 1970s. Prior to that time, congressional elections were rarely mentioned in research on Congress, which instead was largely focused on congressional institutions. However, that changed quite dramatically approximately forty years ago, when Mayhew (1974b) first noticed the decline in

* We thank Mike Crespin, Carrie Eaves, Frances Lee, Anthony Madonna, and Eric Schickler for helpful comments.

incumbent marginality in his research examining House elections from 1956 to 1972. In light of the exponential growth in the amount of scholarship on congressional elections during the past few decades, it would be impossible to focus on all facets of this research in a single chapter. Instead, we seek to examine what we have determined to be some of the more important questions in the field to provide the necessary context in evaluating where we are in answering them. From there, we conclude by discussing the implications for research on House and Senate elections in terms of where we should go from here.

THE ELECTORAL CONNECTION

Since it was first published in 1974, David Mayhew's book, *Congress: The Electoral Connection*, has had a profound impact on the way congressional scholars have analyzed both legislative behavior and congressional organization.[1] In his book, Mayhew offers a theoretically rich, coherent, and provocative argument as to why members of Congress—House members in particular—behave the way they do. In attempting to build a general theory of congressional organization and behavior, Mayhew begins with a very simple assumption: members of Congress are "single-minded seekers of reelection" (1974a, 5). He explains that this assumption is largely motivated by his observations of legislators while working on Capitol Hill. Moreover, he explains that an emphasis on the reelection motivation is attractive for a number of reasons. First, he contends that it fits political reality well. Additionally, "it puts the spotlight directly on men rather than on parties and pressure groups, which in the past have often entered discussions of American politics as analytic phantoms" (6). Mayhew also believes that politics is best studied as a struggle between individuals to gain and maintain power. Finally, and perhaps most importantly to Mayhew, "the reelection quest establishes an accountability relationship with an electorate, and any serious thinking about democratic theory has to give a central place to the question of accountability" (6).

Mayhew contends that it is one thing to assume that legislators are single-minded seekers of reelection, but quite another to assume that they are in a position to necessarily achieve this goal. Indeed, Mayhew argues that members can and must constantly engage in three types of activities related to reelection. The first activity is *advertising*, in which legislators attempt to disseminate their name among constituents to create a favorable image (with little or no issue content) among the electorate (49). This is known as creating a brand name that constituents can identify with. Second, members engage in what Mayhew refers to as *credit claiming*, a practice

---

[1] Although Mayhew (1974a) focuses exclusively on the modern era in his discussion, recent evidence (see e.g. Bianco, Spence, and Wilkerson 1996; Carson and Engstrom 2005) suggests that his argument may extend back to earlier political eras as well.

whereby legislators try to convince constituents that they are responsible for causing something positive to occur.[2] Whether it involves providing distributive benefits or casework, voters become accustomed to the variety of services that legislators can provide on their behalf, thus increasing their chances of getting reelected. Finally, Mayhew argues that representatives engage in *position taking*, defined as a public statement on a subject of potential interest to the public (position taking can be in the form of speech, press release, or even a roll-call vote). Here the position is the political commodity; members act more as speakers than as doers.

In numerous ways, the distinctions between advertising, credit claiming, and position taking have proven invaluable for scholars seeking to build upon Mayhew's analysis, especially with regard to the electoral implications of member behavior. In exploring issues associated with the incumbency advantage, for instance, scholars such as Cover and Brumberg (1982) have explored whether incumbents received electoral benefits from increasing their levels of name recognition. Additionally, Fiorina (1977), Bickers and Stein (1997), Alvarez and Saving (1997), Sellers (1997), Lee (1998, 2003), and Bovitz (2002) have investigated credit claiming in order to seek a better understanding of the electoral rewards that accrue to members for providing distributive benefits to their constituents.[3] Finally, Erikson (1971), Wright (1978), Arnold (1990), Jacobson (1993), Jones (2003), and Bovitz and Carson (2006), among others, have explored both the electoral calculus and the implications of position-taking for members of Congress.

Successive generations of scholars have been heavily influenced by Mayhew's work, as many of his ideas have been extended or reevaluated in light of recent events transpiring in the political arena. Despite the extensive literature that has developed in response to Mayhew's portrayal of Congress, in certain respects it has restricted the way in which scholars have analyzed institutional changes and legislative behavior. Although we agree that Mayhew's thought experiment about members acting as "single-minded" seekers of reelection explains a large amount of congressional behavior, the single-goal theories of politics that have emanated from it have been limiting. Assuming that members are primarily reelection seekers diverted attention from the complexity of congressional politics. Armed with Mayhew's statement that parties lacked theoretical importance in explaining congressional activity, legislative scholars largely ignored the resurgence of political parties in the U.S. House for nearly two decades (but see Rohde 1991). To this day, the literature on the role of parties in the U.S. House suffers from early attempts to develop theories and explanations of behavior that emanate from a reelection only motivation (Smith 2007).

---

[2] The notion of credit claiming is central to Mayhew's argument concerning the importance of committees in the congressional arena. As Mayhew claims, members serving on constituency-oriented committees can use the influence of their positions to procure pork barrel projects for their district, thereby fostering an opportunity to accept the credit for these particularized benefits.

[3] Mayhew's notion of credit claiming has also extended into the debate in the congressional organization literature regarding the relevance of the distributive perspective with respect to committee outliers. This perspective is often contrasted with the partisan theory advanced by Aldrich and Rohde (2000) and Cox and McCubbins (2005, 2007) and with the informational perspective advanced by Krehbiel (1991).

It is also the case that the single-goal form of research has led to a disproportionate focus on House elections at the expense of Senate elections. Though the regularity of House elections, combined with the large number of cases, makes House elections an easier target of research, it is also true that institutional features of the House make it fit the single-goal reelection narrative better than the Senate does.[4] The six-year term undoubtedly frees senators from constantly being in campaign mode; thus other goals—such as public policy and institutional influence—may play a larger role in their activities (on this point, see especially Fenno 1978). Unfortunately, students of legislative behavior have only recently begun focusing on these types of trends in research on the U.S. Senate (see, e.g., Lee 1998; Lee and Oppenheimer 1999; Monroe, Roberts, and Rohde 2008).

One notable exception to the House-centric research on the electoral connection is more recent investigations into how the adoption of direct election in 1913 affected both the Senate as an institution and the type of representation among senators. For several decades, conventional wisdom suggested that passage of the 17th Amendment had little or no impact on the Senate institution. More recently, however, scholars have found evidence that adoption of direct election affected the composition of the Senate chamber (Crook and Hibbing 1997), changes in voting patterns among senators (Bernhard and Sala 2006), and representational styles (Schiller 2006; Gailmard and Jenkins 2009). Additionally, Meinke (2008) suggests that direct election intensified existing electoral incentives in the upper chamber, leading to increased patterns of bill sponsorship and participation by senators.

THE INCUMBENCY ADVANTAGE

In the congressional elections literature, no single subject has drawn the attention of scholars more than trying to explain and measure the advantages accruing to incumbent members of Congress. Beginning with the work of scholars first recognizing the apparent advantages of incumbency (see Erikson 1971; Mayhew 1974b; Ferejohn 1977; Cover 1977; Fiorina 1977), a variety of explanations were offered to account for the high rates at which incumbent legislators get reelected in the contemporary era. Initially, the incumbency effect was attributed to a wide range of institutional features such as legislative casework (Fiorina 1977), legislative activism (Johannes and McAdams 1981), advertising (Cover and Brumberg 1982), replacement among members (Born 1979; Alford and Hibbing 1981), and redistricting (Erikson 1972;

---

[4] Although Mayhew (1974) appears to focus principally on the House in his discussion of the electoral connection, occasionally he does single out the Senate when elaborating on a specific aspect of his argument. This is certainly the case in conjunction with position taking (67), an activity Mayhew believes has become far more common among candidates running for elected office (179). For more recent evidence of this behavior, see Jones (2003).

Cover 1977).[5] Some scholars believe that the advantage can be explained by legislators' personal home styles in their districts (Fenno 1978), rational entry and exit decisions by strategic candidates (Jacobson and Kernell 1981; Krasno 1994; Cox and Katz 1996), a growing 'personal' vote (Cain, Ferejohn, and Fiorina 1987), and a greater emphasis on television appearances in a candidate-centered electoral era (Prior 2007).[6] Still others place greater emphasis on the role of donations and money in contributing to the incumbency advantage, especially in terms of the increasing costs of House and Senate campaigns (Abramowitz 1989, 1991) and on the growing disparity between incumbents and challengers in terms of their fundraising capabilities (i.e. the "strategic money" thesis as discussed by Jacobson and Kernell 1981).[7]

In their critique of the existing scholarly literature on the incumbency advantage, Gelman and King (1990) rigorously show that the most commonly used measures of the incumbency advantage—such as sophomore surge and retirement slump—produce biased and/or inconsistent estimates of the advantage.[8] As a result, Gelman and King develop a technique that, they argue, corrects for most of the inherent problems in measuring the incumbency advantage, especially those that rely on traditional measures such as the retirement slump or the sophomore surge. As such, they find evidence of a vote-denominated incumbency advantage as early as the beginning of the twentieth century, and evidence of a large increase in the advantage accruing to incumbents in the mid-1960s.

In drawing upon this new estimation technique established by Gelman and King (1990), Cox and Katz (1996) re-examine why the incumbency advantage grew so sharply in the mid-1960s. Their model of the incumbency advantage is a refined version of the Gelman–King model that allows them to account for the differences in candidate quality between the political parties and for the possibility that incumbents "scare off" high-quality challengers, who might otherwise reduce their margins of victory. While they consider alternative explanations for the growth in the incumbency advantage, they ultimately conclude that the dramatic growth was driven almost entirely by an increase in the quality effect (i.e. the advantage that incumbent legislators received from not facing an experienced challenger).[9] In discussing the

---

[5] Critics of congressional redistricting as a possible explanation for the incumbency advantage quickly pointed out that, since incumbent senators were also reelected at very high rates, redistricting could not be a contributing factor, given that state boundaries do not change every ten years. On this point, see especially Tufte (1973).

[6] See also Jacobson (1987) for a discussion suggesting that incumbents are no safer than they had been in the past. For a critique of this argument, see Bauer and Hibbing (1989) and Ansolabehere, Brady, and Fiorina (1992).

[7] For a more recent discussion of the extent to which incumbents outraise challengers, see Herrnson (2007). He also elaborates on the logic by which access-oriented contributions go to incumbents rather than to challengers.

[8] Although Erikson (1971) was among the first to note that traditional measures of the incumbency advantage such as the retirement slump or the sophomore surge could result in biased estimates, Gelman and King (1990) formally demonstrated the nature of this bias in their work.

[9] For an alternative explanation for the increase in the incumbency advantage, see Levitt and Wolfram (1997). For evidence demonstrating that redistricting can be used to estimate incumbents' personal vote by treating redistricted voters as a control group, see also Ansolabehere, Snyder, and Stewart (2000) and Desposato and Petrocik (2003).

implications of their findings, they noted that the challenge for future scholars was to discover why the quality effect had steadily increased over time.

In more recent work, Cox and Katz (2002) provide one of the most comprehensive accounts of the incumbency advantage in the literature to date. Unlike in other treatments of this subject, Cox and Katz find that the regularity of redistricting that resulted from the Supreme Court decision in *Wesberry* v *Sanders* (1964) drove the large 1960s increase in the incumbency advantage. They find convincing evidence that the combination of liberal-leaning judges and Democratically controlled state legislatures drew new district boundaries, which efficiently spread Democratic voters across districts in a way that maximized the share of seats Democrats could expect to control in the House. At the same time, this also created extremely safe seats for the remaining Republican members.[10]

In terms of the incumbency advantage, Cox and Katz offer two distinct conclusions, one short-term and the other long-term. For the former, they hold that the mid-1960s redistricting created a larger incumbency advantage for Republicans, which explains the explosive growth of the incumbency advantage in the 1960s. In terms of the latter, they maintain that the regularity of redistricting following *Wesberry* created an electoral environment whereby quality challengers and incumbents avoided facing each other as much as possible. In particular, Cox and Katz attribute this decline in the candidate "collision rate" to the strategic entry and exit decisions of incumbents and experienced challengers. These challengers recognize the difficulty inherent in defeating a sitting incumbent, so they wait until she decides not to seek reelection before they decide to run. Likewise, incumbents are apt readers of the proverbial tea-leaves, often opting for retirement when their odds of winning reelection are reduced by scandal, poor fund raising, or the emergence of a high-quality challenger to run against them.

In another innovative analysis of the incumbency advantage, Ansolabehere, Snyder, and Stewart (2000) offer valuable insights into the sources of such advantages, which incumbents retain over non-incumbents. In their study, they employ the quasi-experiment associated with congressional redistricting in the U.S. to determine the extent to which the advantage incumbents enjoy stems from a personal vote (the vote incumbents receive as a result of the "homestyle" legislators maintain with their constituents). More specifically, they compare legislative vote percentages in the old and new territory within redrawn congressional districts controlling for the political inclinations of both sets of voters. All else being equal, they hold that incumbents should do better within the counties of the district that they have represented before, since voters are already familiar with them and their policies, which positively shapes their personal vote (2000, 18). As expected, the authors find that a significant portion of the advantage incumbents retain stems from a legislator's personal vote as opposed to other factors such as candidate quality and an incumbent's ability to

---

[10]   This is analogous to Jacobson's (2009) work showing that Republican voters are more efficiently distributed across congressional districts than Democrat voters.

scare off experienced challengers. Indeed, Ansolabehere, Snyder, and Stewart conclude that the personal vote comprises anywhere from one-half to two-thirds of the overall incumbency advantage on average. This finding was important in that it demonstrated a personal vote for members of the House long before television, easy travel, large staffs, and the widespread use of the franking privilege. In doing so, this paper convincingly demonstrated that these factors could not have been the necessary conditions for the apparent modern-day growth in the incumbency advantage.

In some ways, research on the incumbency advantage in Congress is like the Energizer Bunny—it just keeps going and going. As early as 1982, Doug Arnold declared that scholarship on the incumbency advantage was an "overtilled" field of American politics. Despite this pronouncement, work on the incumbency advantage has continued unabated. Why has this proven to be the case? We believe there are several plausible reasons for this trend. First, the incumbency advantage is an important theoretical concept. The idea that incumbent office-holders have an advantage over their would-be challengers runs afoul of many tenets of democratic theory. From a normative perspective, elections are supposed to be fair and reflect the will of the voters, thus determining why incumbents apparently do so well at the polls is inherently important. If incumbent legislators are gaining an electoral advantage due to the rules of the game being skewed in their favor, then this would be especially problematic and would require some form of change. However, if legislators are securing high rates of reelection as a result of being exemplary representatives, then we should applaud them and the voters.

Second, since congressional elections occur every two years, new data in the form of electoral outcomes are constantly being generated. As such, our election data-sets become even richer, and we are in a position to develop more accurate measurements of advantages that appear to be accruing to incumbents. Moreover, events occur in subsequent elections that allow critical tests of concepts related to incumbency. The House banking scandal in the early 1990s, for instance, is a prominent example, which allowed legislative scholars to examine how charges of corruption affected a member's reelection chances (Groseclose and Krehbiel 1994; Jacobson and Dimock 1994). The first two years of the Clinton presidency also provided an opportunity to examine the effects of voting against the view of one's congressional district and the impact such behavior had on members' electoral fortunes (Canes-Wrone, Brady, and Cogan 2002).

Finally, research on the incumbency advantage continues to develop new insights and interpretations, often leading us to reevaluate existing explanations for this advantage. In their analysis of state and federal offices from 1942 to 2000, Ansolabehere and Snyder (2002) show that the incumbency advantage increased for other offices at about the same time as it did for House elections, which undermines redistricting as a potential explanation for why incumbents are more likely to get reelected. Through their use of a regression discontinuity design, Friedman and Holden (2009) demonstrate that, contrary to conventional wisdom, changes in redistricting have actually reduced the likelihood that incumbents will be reelected over time. Lee (2008) employs a similar estimation technique in his analysis of House elections to illustrate the difference between having an incumbent *party* advantage and having an incumbent *legislator* advantage in congressional races. Furthermore, recent historical work by Carson, Engstrom, and Roberts (2007) suggests that the incumbency advantage and the personal vote are not simply modern phenomena, but actually extend as far back as the late nineteenth century.

One additional argument pertaining to the potential advantages accruing to incumbents merits attention. A recent book by Jeffrey Stonecash (2008) makes the stunning claim that much of the apparent growth in the incumbency advantage is actually an illusion. Stonecash maintains that most of the increase in incumbent vote margins is an artifact of how uncontested elections are treated by analysts. Most scholars have omitted uncontested elections when studying the incumbency advantage, but included elections that are contested, yet not very close. Stonecash (2008) argues that, around the late 1960s, the number of uncontested races declined sharply, to be replaced by races in which the incumbent won handily. This change, he maintains, explains much of the increase in incumbent vote margins over time in contrast to many of the existing explanations popular today.

Stonecash's book demonstrates that the progress of science is not always linear. If we buy his argument that the incumbency advantage has not really grown in the past fifty years, then we have come full circle as a scholarly community. Stonecash's point about non-contested seats is well taken; nevertheless, a number of his other arguments are likely to be disputed by students of elections and congressional politics. For example, Stonecash finds fault with scholars using open seat elections as a reference point in determining how large the incumbency advantage is in incumbent held seats, or whether there is such an advantage. Yet we think that the analytical leverage provided by open seats is the key to making accurate empirical inferences about the incumbency advantage. Similarly, his claims about the role of realignment in the growth of the incumbency advantage are undermined by the growing literature that discounts much of the conventional wisdom regarding electoral realignment (Mayhew 2004).

Despite the wealth of articles and books on the incumbency advantage, we think this field is far from overtilled and we expect to see many new works on this theme in the future. Although much of the work to date has focused on House elections, the findings are often equally applicable to Senate elections as well. That being said, we would like to see more work explicitly examining the differences between House and Senate incumbent reelection rates over time, especially since Senate elections have traditionally been somewhat more competitive than House races (Krasno 1994). Additionally, and perhaps most importantly, we believe that research examining *multiple* explanations for the incumbency advantage (as opposed to yet another study arguing that one *single* factor is almost entirely responsible for this increase) is poised to make the largest contributions to the study of congressional elections in the coming years.

STRATEGIC POLITICIANS AND CANDIDATE COMPETITION

Over time, research on candidate competition in congressional elections has come to the conclusion that focusing on the incumbent side of the equation can only tell us so much about electoral outcomes. Beginning with the work by Hinckley (1980a), but especially with Jacobson and Kernell's (1981) important work on the role of strategic politicians, students of congressional politics began to stop putting so much emphasis on what congressional incumbents were doing right, and to focus instead on what challengers were doing wrong or not at all. In this and much of the subsequent research on congressional elections, attention has begun to shift exclusively away from the incumbent, to include also the challenger in the explanation of electoral outcomes. According to Hinckley (1980a), variation in electoral success is as much explained by the quality of the challenger as it is by any advantages inherent to incumbents. In many ways, this argument represented an important step in the congressional elections literature, as scholars since then have regularly examined the effect of challenger quality on election outcomes.[11]

Scholars interested in the subject of candidate competition in congressional elections have spent considerable energy examining the issue in question and have approached the topic from a variety of perspectives. While several early studies redirected attention away from an exclusive emphasis on the incumbent to focus on the role of the challenger in explaining election outcomes (see e.g. Mann 1978; Mann and Wolfinger 1980; Hinckley 1980a, 1980b), Kazee (1980, 1983) was among the first to study various conditions under which candidates chose to emerge in House races.[12] Drawing upon interviews with individual candidates, Kazee (1980) found that many candidates ran for Congress simply for the experience or joy of running for office. In his subsequent work, Kazee (1983) confirmed that incumbency regularly served as an effective deterrent to potential challengers from emerging in congressional races.

In their now classic study of challenger emergence in congressional elections, Jacobson and Kernell (1981) examine whether political candidates exhibit strategic behavior in deciding whether or not to seek office. Through an examination of aggregate patterns of candidates' career decisions, the authors speculate as to the underlying motivations for the politicians' behavior. As their theory is premised on rational calculations, they argue that experienced candidates (those who have previously run for, and won, an elected office) are more likely to run for the House when national and partisan conditions are more favorable in terms of their likelihood of success.

---

[11] To be fair, Hinckley was not the first congressional scholar to discuss the impact of challenger quality on election outcomes. Indeed both Erikson (1971) and Jacobson (1978) mention it as a potential variable in explaining electoral outcomes. However, we believe she was the first to explore it systematically in the context of a given election.

[12] For a general discussion of ambition theory that examines the motivations for individuals to choose to run for office or to make a career out of politics, see Fowler and McClure (1989); Rohde (1979); and Schlesinger (1966).

Jacobson and Kernell (1981) test their theory of strategic behavior on data from the 1974, 1980, and 1982 congressional elections and find convincing evidence in support of their hypotheses concerning strategic politicians. Not only do they conclude that experienced challengers wait until circumstances are optimal before they decide to run, they also find that strategic politicians play a pivotal role in determining both the results of district-level elections and the overall partisan composition of Congress.[13]

Jacobson (1989) offers additional support for the strategic politicians theory by testing it with congressional elections data from 1946 to 1986. Through his examination of elections data during this forty-year period, he finds that experienced challengers do not emerge randomly. Rather, their likelihood of running varies with their perceived chance of winning (1989, 775). Indeed, Jacobson concludes that a greater proportion of experienced or quality candidates emerge when prospects appear favorable to their party. As a result, he argues that strategic decisions by congressional candidates, based on factors such as likelihood of victory, value of the seat, and opportunity costs, both reflect and enhance national partisan tides. In support of his contention that experienced politicians act strategically, he recognizes that quality challengers are more likely to emerge when a seat is uncontested, and they rely increasingly on an incumbent's prior margin of victory as an important cue in deciding whether or not to run (778).

In an attempt to further discern challengers' motivations in running for Congress, Banks and Kiewiet (1989) examine an interesting puzzle regarding the behavior of non-experienced or weak candidates who emerge to challenge incumbents. While they agree with Jacobson and Kernell (1981) concerning the deterrent effects of incumbency with respect to the emergence of experienced challengers, they seek to understand why incumbency does not have the same effect on weak challengers; as they point out, nearly all incumbents are challenged from one election to the next, usually by candidates lacking electoral or political experience. Through their analysis of congressional primary data from 1980 to 1984, Banks and Kiewiet conclude that weak challengers run against incumbents for the same reason that strong challengers are more likely to run in open seat contests—to maximize their probability of getting elected to Congress (1989, 1002).[14] Even though their chances of defeat in the fall election are high, political amateurs recognize that running against an incumbent affords them the best opportunity to win their party's nomination, especially since more experienced challengers are likely to stay out of the race in the absence of favorable national or partisan conditions.

---

[13] For critiques and extensions of the Jacobson–Kernell strategic politicians hypothesis in the context of House races, see Bianco (1984); Bond, Covington, and Fleisher (1985); and Born (1986). For more recent evidence confirming the hypothesis in the context of both House and Senate elections, see Carson (2005).

[14] For an alternative perspective regarding political amateurs' motivation for running for Congress, see Canon (1990, 1993). In brief, Canon argues that amateurs would be better off running in open seat contests, since they actually do *not* maximize their chances of winning by running against incumbents. Canon (1993: 1130–8) adds that to fully understand why inexperienced candidates challenge 'safe' incumbents, it is necessary for scholars to distinguish between experience-seeking amateurs and ambitious amateurs.

To date, the literature on the role of candidate quality in House elections has generated a number of good insights. Jacobson's and Kernell's measure of challenger quality is parsimonious, fairly easy to find (for most candidates), and a reliable predictor of electoral success. Despite numerous attempts to develop more detailed codings of challenger quality (see Bond, Covington, and Fleisher 1985; Krasno and Green 1988), the simple dichotomy has typically proven just as reliable a predictor of a competitive House election. There are no doubt a few candidates each year who go on to be successful without having held previous office (by this measure, Hillary Clinton was a "non-quality" Senate candidate; on this point, see also Canon 1993), and there are some previous office holders who are incapable of mounting a competitive campaign for a House seat. Nevertheless, for all the reasons mentioned above, we believe that trying to come up with yet another alternative measure of candidate quality represents an area where further research is clearly unwarranted.

In contrast to research on strategic politicians in the House, very little attention has been given to the same phenomenon in the Senate, and nothing much has been offered in the way of cross-chamber comparisons, either (but see Carson 2005). The one notable exception has been Lublin's (1994) article, which examines the impact of strategic politicians in Senate elections from 1952 to 1990. On the basis of his analysis of these election years, Lublin finds that, among all the quality challengers running in Senate races, U.S. House members gain a much higher percentage of the vote than other elected officials. Moreover, he finds that, like their counterparts running in House races, potential Senate challengers take into account economic, local, and national conditions when deciding whether or not to emerge. Furthermore, Lublin maintains that, even when incumbent senators do not lose to quality challengers, they are often weakened in the long run, since "past margins of victory relate directly to future electoral prospects. A small victory margin further endangers an incumbent's reelection indirectly by spurring strong challengers in the future" (1994, 239).

To understand the impact of strategic politicians further, we would like to see more work exploring the initial decision to seek elected office. It is fairly clear why experienced candidates wait until conditions are ideal until they decide to run for elected office, since running and losing could affect their career prospects adversely. At the same time, it could be the case that many more House and Senate elections would actually become competitive if a significantly higher proportion of experienced candidates decided to emerge. To date, the innovative work by Maisel and Stone (1997) and Stone and Maisel (2003) has gone a long way toward filling this void in the literature by way of their challenger emergence project. In particular, they have shown that a greater number of potential quality challengers choose not to emerge because they do not want to give up their current elected position or they believe the economic or political costs of running are too high (on this point, see also Maestas, et al. 2006).[15] We believe that additional studies building upon this research agenda would

---

[15] For evidence of why a greater proportion of women decide not to run for office, see Lawless and Fox (2005).

be especially beneficial in helping to better understand the factors promoting greater democratic accountability and competition in both House and Senate elections.

MONEY IN CONGRESSIONAL ELECTIONS

As a result of Jacobson and Kernell's (1981) pathbreaking study, congressional scholars have regularly begun controlling for challenger quality in models explaining election outcomes. Even before this important work became widely known, however, Jacobson (1978, 1980) had made an earlier theoretical discovery in his analysis of the effects of campaign spending in congressional elections. In examining the independent effects of both incumbent and challenger spending on electoral outcomes, Jacobson came up with a rather counterintuitive finding. While Jacobson found that increased spending by a challenger increased both levels of name recognition and the challenger's chances of winning, he found the opposite effect for incumbents. Indeed, the more money spent by an incumbent, the worse he or she did.

Jacobson contends that, although surprising at first, this anomaly can best be understood in terms of the quality of the challenger and of the perceived closeness of the race. Incumbents who run against a quality challenger in an election often have to raise and spend additional money in their campaign; but additional spending does not yield much in the way of further advantages since incumbents often start off with relatively high levels of name recognition. Moreover, high-quality or experienced candidates are usually adept at raising money themselves, which makes it more challenging for an incumbent to defeat them. Incumbents who perceive themselves to be in electoral danger can, and do, typically raise and spend more money than incumbents who perceive themselves to be relatively safe in a particular election. Therefore, on average, incumbents who win by a large electoral margin spend relatively small amounts of money when compared to incumbents in close races. Thus, Jacobson concludes that increased spending can definitely help the challenger, but it is almost always associated with lower vote shares for the incumbent.

Given Jacobson's rather counterintuitive findings regarding the effects of challenger and incumbent spending, subsequent research has attempted to offer alternative perspectives on the role of money in congressional elections. Green and Krasno (1988), for instance, reexamine the 1978 House elections, arguing that Jacobson's findings are subject to three specific forms of model misspecification. In particular, they claim that his failure to control for challenger quality, include interaction effects, and adequately deal with the issue of reciprocal causation leads to a variety of erroneous conclusions. More specifically, Green and Krasno rely on the lagged value of incumbent spending as an instrument for the endogenous spending levels. When these biases are corrected, the marginal effect of incumbent spending is found to be substantial and, under certain circumstances, on par with the effect of challenger spending (Green and

Krasno 1988, 884). Moreover, they conclude that the quality of the challenger appears to be an important predictor of the overall vote, especially when large sums of money are spent in the race against the incumbent.[16]

Other students of elections seeking to build upon Green and Krasno's (1988) critique of Jacobson's findings have searched for alternative and presumably better instruments for dealing with the endogenous nature of campaign spending in congressional elections. Abramowitz (1991), for instance, includes a measure predicting the closeness of the election and finds that challenger spending continues to outmatch spending by the incumbent, which is consistent with Jacobson's original conclusion. Kenny and McBurnett (1992) find similar evidence for challenger spending using a lag of contributions and a research design that employs a dynamic model (but see Ansolabehere and Gerber 1994). Alternatively, Erikson and Palfrey (1998) estimate simultaneous equations to identify three separate equations they seek to estimate. They find that incumbent spending matters a great deal in House elections and is actually a major source of the incumbency advantage. Moreover, they conclude that incumbent spending has an enduring effect on incumbent success, which is one of the main reasons why challengers have such a difficult time gaining traction in races contested by incumbents.

Extending research on campaign spending in the House, Gerber (1998) analyzes Senate elections from 1974 through to 1992, in an attempt to gain additional leverage on the debate over spending effects. One of Gerber's principal criticisms of the prior literature is that many of the instruments that have been used for challenger or incumbent spending have been inappropriate, since they may themselves be endogenous. Recognizing that both challenger and incumbent spending are related to the expected closeness of the election, Gerber relies upon levels of candidate wealth as his instruments. In his analysis of Senate races, he finds roughly equivalent marginal effects of incumbent and challenger spending on candidate vote share. Beyond acknowledging the potential policy consequences of his results for campaign finance reform, Gerber also takes issue with prior research on campaign spending—especially with respect to Jacobson's somewhat controversial findings about spending effects in congressional races.

Given the complications associated with evaluating the independent effects of money in congressional elections, Goldstein and Freedman (2000) pursue an alternative estimation strategy for evaluating these effects in the context of Senate races. More specifically, they rely on a new data-set targeting political advertising during the 1996 Senate elections, which they merged with the 1996 National Election Study in order to develop a unique measure of political advertising. With this measure, they find that both incumbent and challenger advertising had an independent effect on individual vote choice during the election. Goldstein and Freedman argue that,

---

[16] See also Thomas (1989) for a critique of Jacobson's conclusions about the effects of incumbent spending in congressional races. For a response to Green and Krasno's (1988) critique, see Jacobson (1990). Green and Krasno (1990) follow up with a rebuttal immediately after Jacobson's response.

since a substantial amount of campaign spending goes to political advertising, their approach offers a cleaner measure of campaign effects in Senate races.

In another innovative analysis of campaign spending effects, Moon (2006) considers a possible explanation as to why incumbent spending is less effective than challenger spending in congressional elections. In particular, Moon maintains that the overall efficiency of incumbent spending depends on the marginality of individual seats (i.e. spending by "safe" incumbents is much less effective than spending by marginal incumbents, given the disparity in the number of swing voters). Through an analysis of U.S. Senate elections from 1974 to 2000, Moon demonstrates that, while safe incumbent spending is much less effective than spending by challengers, spending by marginal incumbents is not. Additionally, Moon argues that the reason why this finding has not previously been identified in research on spending effects in congressional elections is due to not disaggregating marginal and safe races.

Regardless of the divergent findings discussed above, nearly everyone agrees that money clearly shapes election outcomes and is a critical component of electoral success. Furthermore, there is little doubt that congressional elections, like presidential elections, have become much more expensive in recent decades. Growing disparities in spending patterns by incumbents and challengers raise obvious concerns about representation and democratic accountability in the context of House and Senate elections. As noted earlier, some scholars view the lack of financial competitiveness in congressional races as a major component of the incumbency advantage and of the decline in relative levels of electoral competition during the post-World War II era (see, e.g., Abramowitz 1989, 1991; Jacobson and Kernell 1981). In light of existing disagreements in the elections literature concerning the evaluation of spending effects in congressional races, we hope to see additional, innovative studies, which attempt to resolve this debate in order to evaluate better both how and why electoral competition may be affected.

In a related discussion of the role of money in elections, students of congressional politics often believe that incumbents accumulate large sums of money in their war chests in an attempt to "scare off" potential challengers from running in a given election (Epstein and Zemsky 1995; Jacobson 1990, 2009). Indeed, using a variety of different measures, a number of scholars have found that the amount of money raised by an incumbent does serve as a potential deterrent to candidate entry in congressional races (see Box-Steffensmeier 1996; Carson 2003; Goidel and Gross 1994; Goldenberg, Traugott, and Baumgartner 1986; Hersch and McDougall 1994). Nevertheless, not everyone who studies congressional elections agrees with this conclusion about the deterrent effect of money. Several different students of legislative politics (see Krasno and Green 1988; Epstein and Zemsky 1995; Milyo 1998; Ansolabehere and Snyder 2000; Goodliffe 2001) have all found that the amount of money raised by an incumbent does *not* serve as an effective deterrent to challenger entry in House races. In his follow-up analysis of the deterrent effect of incumbent war chests in Senate elections, Goodliffe (2007) finds similar evidence in the upper chamber.

In light of the aforementioned controversy over the deterrent effects of incumbent war chests on candidate entry decisions, we believe additional research is necessary in an attempt to try to resolve this debate. Although both sides present compelling arguments for their findings, it is theoretically unclear why large war chests would not deter strong challengers from running against incumbents. From the perspective of rational choice theory, this argument has a certain intuitive appeal. If we assume that legislators are rational actors and we know that they dislike raising large sums of money, it is unclear why they would continue to repeat this cycle each election, if money had little or no measurable impact on strategic challenger entry. On the other hand, if we assume that legislators do not habitually squander their limited time or scarce resources, then it seems reasonable to conclude that they are making rational calculations when raising money for their reelection campaigns, since this seems like a prudent thing to do. After all, raising money may not necessarily deter challengers, but it will most certainly help incumbents fund their campaign, should a strong challenger emerge.

Surge and decline

In addition to focusing on individual elections and patterns in electoral outcomes, some students of congressional politics have sought to explore more general patterns of aggregate seat change, especially those that occur during mid-term congressional elections. V.O. Key (1958, 615) was among the first to recognize the mid-term loss phenomenon in congressional elections when he wrote: "The president's party, whether it basks in public favor or is declining in public esteem, ordinarily loses House strength at mid-term—a pattern that, save for one exception, has prevailed since the Civil War." Two years later, Angus Campbell (1960) proposed a general theory of "surge and decline" that examines how many congressional seats the party of the president loses at the mid-term election. According to the theory, the more seats the party of the president picks up during a presidential election, the more seats are at risk during a mid-term election. Without the president on the national ballot at the mid-term, individual congressional candidates become more vulnerable to local conditions and also potentially suffer if the economy or national conditions have declined in the months preceding the election. Thus the number of seats the president's party loses at the mid-term (the decline) is a function of the number of seats gained in the previous presidential election (the surge).[17]

Building on the work of Angus Campbell (1960), several scholars have offered various offshoots of the surge and decline theory to account for why the party of the president tends to lose seats during mid-term elections. Tufte (1975), for instance,

[17] For more recent extensions of Angus Campbell's work on surge and decline, see Campbell (1991, 1997). For a specific extension to Senate races, see Abramowitz and Segal (1986). The arguments presented in this context are not all that dissimilar from work examining presidential coat-tails in House and Senate races (see e.g. Ferejohn and Calvert 1984; Campbell and Sumners 1990).

frames the loss of seats in terms of the referenda theory of mid-term elections. In particular, he states:

Because there are no other targets available at the midterm, it is not unreasonable to expect that some voters opposed to the president might take out their dissatisfaction with the incumbent's administration on the congressional candidates of the president's party.   (Tufte 1975, 813)

Following up on this work, Kernell (1977) offers a slightly different perspective on the referenda theory, which places a greater amount of emphasis on negative evaluations. Most notably, Kernell maintains that negative impressions about the current administration (especially those pertaining to economic considerations) tend to be much more salient to voters than positive ones, which leads to greater bias against the members of the president's party in Congress. Kernell's findings are similar to those reported by Erikson (1988) in his analysis of mid-term loss and fit remarkably well with the retrospective voting model discussed by Fiorina (1981).

Oppenheimer, Waterman, and Stimson (1986) offer a different version of the referenda theory—what they term the *exposure thesis*—to account for the loss of seats at the mid-term by the president's party. In short, their theory evaluates the extent to which a party's pre-election seat holdings exceed or fall below that party's normal share of seats. On the bass of their analysis of House elections since 1938, Oppenheimer and colleagues determine that the average number of seats held by the Democrats during this period was 254. When the number of Democratic seats falls below 254, the party is considered to be underexposed and is most likely to pick up additional seats in the upcoming election. In contrast, increases beyond 254 seats would leave the party overexposed and at greater risk of losing seats in the next mid-term election. Despite the accuracy of the exposure thesis in predicting seat loss from 1938 to 1984, its explanatory power has been undermined to a certain extent in more recent elections.[18]

On the whole, research on surge and decline and the referenda theories of mid-term loss have held up remarkably well over time. If one updates Key's earlier quotation about mid-term loss, the president's party has lost House seats in all but three mid-term elections since the Civil War. Somewhat interestingly, two recent mid-term elections—in 1998 and 2002—have challenged the conventional view associated with surge and decline theory, as the president's party actually gained a few additional seats in each of these mid-term elections. Whether these recent elections are simply anomalies or harbingers of aggregate electoral change is as yet unclear.[19] For now, those scholars interested in predicting aggregate outcomes in congressional elections would be best served by offering greater comparisons of seat loss in *both* House and Senate races, since this is an area that definitely could use additional research.

---

[18] Waterman, Oppenheimer, and Stimson (1991) extend their analysis of the exposure thesis to an earlier era (1896–1928) in their follow-up work. For an application of the exposure thesis to both the House and Senate, see Waterman (1990).

[19] For a recent analysis that considers seat change in light of these two mid-term elections, see Finocchiaro (2003).

IMPLICATIONS FOR FUTURE RESEARCH

In her discussion of the state of legislative elections research in the mid-1990s, Ragsdale (1994) is critical of a lack both of theoretical and of comparative focus in this context, especially as it pertains to questions concerning voters' choices and legislative decisions.[20] Although some progress along these lines has occurred during the past fifteen years, we recognize that there is still room for improvement in the literature. In terms of specific suggestions for where we think the literature should go in the next ten years, we offer several additional ideas in the remainder of this chapter—beyond those discussed in the preceding pages. To be clear, we do not believe the following suggestions are exhaustive in terms of where the research should go next. Rather, they should be viewed as a starting point for research and for scholars interested in making additional contributions to our understanding of House and Senate elections.

Our first suggestion for future work on congressional elections is to encourage scholars working in this area to recognize that congressional elections did not begin in 1946. Most individuals who study elections naturally rely upon Gary Jacobson's House elections data extending back to World War II, but an unfortunate consequence of this reliance is that almost all research on elections has focused exclusively on the modern era. In fact, and until recently, most of our knowledge about nineteenth- and early twentieth-century elections was based largely on anecdotal or historical accounts from that period. Moreover, almost no one thought it worthwhile to examine House elections prior to 1946, given the enormous costs associated with collecting data from earlier periods. Nevertheless, as more of these historical data have become available (see Dubin 1998; Carson, Engstrom, and Roberts 2007), it is much easier to analyze House elections in a comparative context by examining changes across time.

On a related point, we would like to see additional research focusing on Senate elections over a greater period of history. Surprisingly little research has focused on Senate races outside of the modern era, for instance. Lublin's (1994) analysis of the impact of strategic politicians in the Senate only considers elections extending back to 1952. Although Highton (2000) examines Senate elections from 1920 to 1994, his focus is more limited on the influence of certain variables on predicting election outcomes. As noted earlier, several recent studies have examined how the adoption of direct election in 1913 influenced the institution of the Senate as well as the behavior of its members (see Bernhard and Sala 2006; Gailmard and Jenkins 2009; Meinke 2008; Schiller 2006). Nevertheless, this line of research represents only a drop in the bucket in terms of the types of research questions that are awaiting to be addressed in the context of the Senate.

Analyzing House and Senate elections over a longer time span offers us a number of distinct advantages in terms of understanding congressional elections. First, extending the study of elections further back in time offers us the opportunity to generate

---

[20] See also Squire (1995) for a summary of the state of congressional elections research in the mid-1990s.

more dynamic theories of elections and of legislative behavior. For instance, take analyses seeking to better understand the mid-term loss phenomenon. As is generally known, the president's party almost always suffers a loss of seats in the House during a mid-term election. Two recent exceptions to this rule occurred in 1998 and 2002, as noted previously, where the party of the president actually picked up seats at the mid-term. If we wanted to study these unique elections in a larger historical context, we would have to go back to 1934, since this was the last time such an event occurred at a mid-term. By turning to the past, we can begin to search for alternative explanations that may account for this rather unusual electoral phenomenon.

A second advantage of studying House and Senate elections across time is that it can lead to greater generalizability, which stems from increased variation in outcomes. Consider again the preceding example concerning instances when the president's party actually gained seats during a mid-term election. With only three instances of this occurrence since the Civil War, it could prove challenging to try to derive a reasonable explanation for this phenomenon. However, if we extend our analysis back in time to include all mid-term elections during the nineteenth century, we have a much larger sample of elections to draw upon. This, in turn, has the added benefit of increasing the accuracy of our theoretical explanation, since there presumably will be much more variation across election outcomes during the past 200+ years.

A third advantage of studying congressional elections across time is greater institutional variation. The Australian or secret ballot gained regular usage in the United States beginning in the mid-1890s; thus it is impossible to discern the full effect of this change using data from 1946 to the present. Similarly, the direct primary system of choosing congressional candidates emerged in the early decades of the twentieth century and replaced the system by which House candidates were selected by party bosses. To truly capture the effects of these and other institutional changes on elections and election outcomes, scholars should employ data that pre-date and post-date the changes they seek to study.

One final advantage of studying congressional elections across time is that this gives us the chance to correct historical inaccuracies in the conventional wisdom. Consider, for instance, our understanding of strategic politicians. Most observers of contemporary politics would argue that the impact of experienced candidates should be greatest in the modern era of candidate-centered elections. However, Carson and Roberts (2005) find that, regardless of the era, candidates with prior electoral experience were more likely to run for office when national and local conditions favored their candidacies. Similarly, incumbents during the late nineteenth century responded to changes in their district boundaries brought on by redistricting, running in favorable districts, and bailing out when they were given an unfriendly congressional district (on this point, see Carson, Engstrom, and Roberts 2006; Engstrom 2006).

Furthermore, recent evidence suggests the presence of an incumbency advantage as far back as the late nineteenth century, well before the onset of careerism (Ansolabehere, Snyder, and Stewart 2000; Carson, Engstrom, and Roberts 2007).

While we would argue that finding that there was an incumbency advantage in the nineteenth century is interesting in and of itself, this type of research presents new contexts for understanding research by employing historical data. For example, given that we know there was an incumbency advantage in Congress as early as the 1870s, we can definitively claim that factors such as the Australian ballot, direct primary, frequent travel, large staff support, court-ordered redistricting and the rise of television are not *necessary* conditions for an incumbency advantage to exist. As each of these examples illustrates, our understanding of both modern and historical elections can change considerably when these phenomena are analyzed in a broader, historical context.

Beyond examining past elections, we would also encourage students of House and Senate elections to place more emphasis on congressional primary elections. For the past few decades, and with very few exceptions, nearly all the research on congressional elections has focused exclusively on the general election stage.[21] Although this emphasis has helped us understand general election outcomes to a much greater extent, it has also failed to illuminate a number of potentially interesting puzzles and questions about primaries that remain unaddressed. For instance, under what conditions will candidates decide to emerge in congressional primaries? Are state legislators more likely to be successful in these types of races than other experienced candidates are? If so, why might this be the case? Is greater familiarity with voters in statewide constituencies a significant advantage for state legislative candidates who decide to pursue higher office? What role are national party organizations playing in encouraging and deterring candidates from running in primaries?

In addition to the above questions concerning congressional primaries, we also know very little about the effects of primaries on general election outcomes. To what extent are general election outcomes significantly influenced by what occurs at the earlier primary stage of the electoral process? Are otherwise strong or experienced candidates deterred from emerging in congressional primaries by incumbent's war chests or by national party leaders? If so, what are the implications for electoral accountability and representation? How difficult is it for House and Senate candidates to raise sufficient sums of money to wage a competitive primary campaign, in comparison to what is necessary to win during the general election? Where do candidates running in congressional primaries obtain a majority of their campaign funds from? How do positions taken in primary campaigns translate into general election positions and positions taken within the chamber? We believe that addressing these and a variety of related questions will go a long way in illuminating a number of previously unexplored puzzles in the context of congressional elections research.

A third avenue for making an independent contribution with respect to our understanding of House and Senate elections is to focus more carefully on interactions between congressional behavior, campaigns, and election outcomes. To date, most

---

[21] For a few notable exceptions of research examining congressional primaries, see Ansolabehere, Hansen, et al. (2007); Banks and Kiewiet (1989); Fox and Lawless (2005); Galderisi, Ezra, and Lyons (2001); and Maisel and Stone (2003).

research on congressional elections bypasses the details of congressional actions (exceptions being aggregate voting statistics and interest group ratings) and election campaigns (other than the quality of the candidate emerging and how much money is spent) in favor of what happens when voters go to the polls on Election Day (but see Sellers 1998). This is unfortunate, however, as it overlooks a variety of important factors that might actually shape election outcomes and behavior inside the beltway. Most followers of congressional elections are familiar with anecdotal accounts of a vote or a scandal by a legislator causing them electoral harm, but what is missing is the mechanism by which the harm occurs. Are some incumbents better at explaining away controversial votes or behavior? Are some challengers better at exploiting these issues than others? Are some electorates more or less responsive to campaign messages? Additional case studies and analyses focusing on these specific questions would be a welcome addition to the literature on elections to the U.S. House and Senate.

On a related point, consider again the role of candidate quality in elections. We know that experienced candidates are more likely to defeat incumbents than are non-quality candidates or political amateurs. Are these candidates more likely to win because they have greater name recognition than political amateurs, or are they simply better at the art of electioneering? While some might contend that it is actually a combination of both factors that determines victory in congressional races, we simply do not know if each of these related explanations *independently* contributes to electoral success. Indeed, it could be the case that a candidate's connection with voters is far more valuable than electioneering in determining who wins an election, especially if both candidates running for a particular seat in Congress have roughly the same financial resources. Nevertheless, without greater attention to what candidates actually do during the campaign, we cannot sufficiently answer this question.

Furthermore, we would like to see additional research investigating how candidates utilize money in congressional campaigns and where those funds come from. Beyond focusing on the effects of challenger and incumbent spending in determining election outcomes (see Jacobson 1980, 1990), we know considerably less about candidates' allocation strategies as well as the effects of such strategies on their congressional campaigns. At the same time, only limited attention has been given to identifying sources of candidates' campaign funds. Larson (2004) was among the first to analyze incumbent contributions to congressional campaign committees. More recently, Cann (2008) has focused on member-to-member contributions as well as the increasing role of leadership PACs in influencing election outcomes. Additionally, Gimpel, Lee, and Kaminski (2006) and Gimpel, Lee, and Pearson-Merkowitz (2008) have begun examining the geographic component of campaign contributions, particularly as it relates to interdistrict funding flows in House races. More research on fundraising in this vein would help fill a noticeable gap in the congressional campaigns literature.

We believe that future work that examines elections across *both* the House and Senate would be especially valuable as well. For too long, research on Congress has focused almost exclusively on the House with little or no attention paid to the Senate. Although this has begun to change in recent years, there is still an overwhelming amount of work focusing on House rather than Senate races (for two notable exceptions, see Gronke 2000; Krasno 1994). By analyzing elections across both chambers, we can gain a better understanding of how differences in lengths of terms, chamber rules and procedures, and individual legislator goals can directly impact election outcomes. Moreover, more cross-chamber comparisons can further illustrate how legislative outcomes in a bicameral context may be influenced directly or indirectly by the underlying electoral context in individual races.

An additional area in need of more development in the congressional campaigns literature involves the linkage between campaigns and legislative representation. Sulkin (2005) and Sulkin and Swigger (2008) have made an important contribution along these lines in their work on issue politics, agendas, and campaign advertisements, but more research is necessary. For instance, to what extent do candidates shape their campaign message in terms of the quality of the challenger they face in an election? Do legislators seek to offset controversial positions with more positive campaign messages? How effective are candidates' communication strategies in reaching out to potential voters? Addressing these and other related questions will help raise awareness of an area of congressional elections research that has largely been overlooked to date.

One final area where additional research could significantly enhance our understanding of congressional elections is in terms of analyzing voter behavior and turnout in elections. The recent development of the Cooperative Congressional Elections Study (CCES) across a large number of universities is an important step in better understanding voter behavior across individual states and congressional districts. Through individual-level surveys conducted via this study, we can seek to systematically examine why turnout varies so dramatically across districts and states, whether voters feel as though they influence policy outcomes, and how representation is viewed by individual voters. With such a large sample of voters spread out across the country, analyses that employ these individual-level surveys should be more accurate and generalizable in terms of the conclusions they draw about voter attitudes and behavior.

We believe that greater attention to legislator–constituency linkages as perceived by the voter will help us address a number of research questions that have been largely overlooked. For instance, how do different styles of representation affect voters' perceptions of incumbents? Do voters regularly punish legislators for behavior that is perceived to be too ideological or too partisan?[22] Are newly elected legislators constrained by the "homestyle" of the previous House member, as Fenno (1978) suggests, or do they have the opportunity to establish their own unique style of representation? When and under what conditions will legislators be perceived as being out of touch with their constituents? After an incumbent's congressional district is redrawn, how do legislators adapt to their new constituencies consisting of a mix of "old" and "new" voters? Greater attention to these types of questions, as

---

[22] For an extended discussion of this particular question in the context of House races over time, see Carson, Koger, Lebo, and Young (2010).

well as to others, will serve to further enrich our understanding of House and Senate elections for many years to come.

REFERENCES

ABRAMOWITZ, A. I. 1988. Explaining Senate Election Outcomes. *American Political Science Review*, 82: 385–403.

——1989. Campaign Spending in U.S. Senate Elections. *Legislative Studies Quarterly*, 14: 487–507.

——1991. Incumbency, Campaign Spending, and the Decline of Competition in U.S. House Elections. *The Journal of Politics*, 53: 34–56.

——and Segal, J. 1986. Determinants of the Outcomes of U.S. Senate Elections. *The Journal of Politics*, 48 (May): 433–9.

ALDRICH, J. H., and ROHDE, D. W. 2000. The Consequences of Party Organization in the House: The Role of Majority and Minority Parties in Conditional Party Government, pp. 31–72 in *Polarized Politics: Congress and the President in a Partisan Era*, ed. J. Bond and R. Fleisher. Washington, DC: CQ Press.

ALFORD, J. R., and HIBBING, J. H. 1981. Increased Incumbency Advantage in the House. *The Journal of Politics*, 43: 1042–61.

ALVAREZ, R. M., and SAVING, J. L. 1997. Deficits, Democrats, and Distributive Benefits: Congressional Elections and the Pork Barrel in the 1980s. *Political Research Quarterly*, 50(4): 809–31.

ANSOLABEHERE, S., BRADY, D., and FIORINA, M. 1992. The Vanishing Marginals and Electoral Responsiveness. *British Journal of Political Science*, 22: 21–38.

——and GERBER, A. 1994. The Mismeasure of Campaign Spending: Evidence from the 1990 U.S. House Elections. *Journal of Politics*, 56 (November): 1106–18.

——HANSEN, J. M., HIRANO, S., and SNYDER, JR., J. M. 2007. The Incumbency Advantage in U.S. Primary Elections. *Electoral Studies*, 26: 660–8.

——and SNYDER, J. M. 2000. Campaign War Chests in Congressional Elections. *Business and Politics*, 2: 9–33.

————2002. The Incumbency Advantage in U.S. Elections: An Analysis of State and Federal Offices, 1942–2000. *Election Law Journal: Rules, Politics, and Policy*, 1 (September): 315–38.

——SNYDER, JR., J. M., and STEWART, III, C. 2000. Old Voters, New Voters, and the Personal Vote: Using Redistricting to Measure the Incumbency Advantage. *American Journal of Political Science*, 44: 17–34.

ARNOLD, R. D. 1982. Overtilled and Undertilled Fields in American Politics. *Political Science Quarterly*, 97(1): 91–103.

——1990. *The Logic of Congressional Action*. New Haven: Yale University Press.

BANKS, J. S., and KIEWIET, D. R. 1989. Explaining Patterns of Candidate Competition in Congressional Elections. *American Journal of Political Science*, 33: 997–1015.

BAUER, M., and HIBBING, J. R. 1989. Which Incumbents Lose in House Elections: A Response to Jacobson's 'The Marginals Never Vanished.' *American Journal of Political Science*, 33: 262–71.

BERNHARD, W., and SALA, B. R. 2006. The Remaking of an American Senate: The 17th Amendment and Ideological Responsiveness. *Journal of Politics*, 68: 345–57.

BIANCO, W. T. 1984. Strategic Decisions on Candidacy in U.S. Congressional Districts. *Legislative Studies Quarterly*, 9: 351–64.

—— SPENCE, D. B., and WILKERSON, J. D. 1996. The Electoral Connection in the Early Congress: The Case of the Compensation Act of 1816. *American Journal of Political Science*, 40: 145–71.

BICKERS, K. N., and STEIN, R. M. 1997. *Perpetuating the Pork Barrel: Policy Subsystems and American Democracy*. New York: Cambridge University Press.

BOND, J. R., COVINGTON, C., and FLEISHER, R. 1985. Explaining Challenger Quality in Congressional Elections. *The Journal of Politics*, 47: 510–29.

BORN, R. 1979. Generational Replacement and the Growth of Incumbent Reelection Margins in the U.S. House. *American Political Science Review*, 73: 811–17.

—— 1986. Strategic Politicians and Unresponsive Voters. *American Political Science Review*, 80: 599–612.

BOVITZ, G. L. 2002. Electoral Consequences of Porkbusting in the U.S. House of Representatives. *Political Science Quarterly*, 117 (Autumn): 455–77.

—— and CARSON, J. L. 2006. Position-Taking and Electoral Accountability in the U.S. House of Representatives. *Political Research Quarterly*, 59(2): 297–312.

BOX-STEFFENSMEIER, J. M. 1996. A Dynamic Analysis of the Role of War Chests in Campaign Strategy. *American Journal of Political Science*, 40: 352–71.

CAIN, B., JOHN FEREJOHN, J., and FIORINA, M. P. 1987. *The Personal Vote*. Cambridge, MA: Harvard University Press.

CAMPBELL, A. 1960. Surge and Decline: A Study of Electoral Change. *Public Opinion Quarterly*, 24(3): 397–418.

CAMPBELL, J. E. 1991. The Presidential Surge and Its Midterm Decline in Congressional Elections, 1868–1988. *Journal of Politics*, 53 (May): 477–87.

—— 1997. *The Presidential Pulse of Congressional Elections*, 2nd edn. Lexington: The University Press of Kentucky.

—— and SUMNERS, J. A. 1990. Presidential Coattails in Senate Elections. *American Political Science Review*, 84 (June): 513–24.

CANES-WRONE, B., BRADY, D. W., and COGAN, J. F. 2002. Out of Step, Out of Office: Electoral Accountability and House Members' Voting. *American Political Science Review*, 96: 127–40.

CANN, D. M. 2008. *Sharing the Wealth: Member Contributions and the Exchange Theory of Party Influence in the U.S. House of Representatives*. Albany: State University of New York Press.

CANON, D. T. 1990. *Actors, Athletes, and Astronauts: Political Amateurs in the United States Congress*. Chicago: University of Chicago Press.

—— 1993. Sacrificial Lambs or Strategic Politicians? Political Amateurs in U.S. House Elections. *American Journal of Political Science*, 37: 1119–41.

CARSON, J. L. 2003. Strategic Interaction and Candidate Competition in U.S. House Elections: Empirical Applications of Probit and Strategic Probit Models. *Political Analysis*, 11(4): 368–80.

—— 2005. Strategy, Selection, and Candidate Competition in U.S. House and Senate Elections. *Journal of Politics*, 67(1): 1–28.

—— and ENGSTROM, E. J. 2005. Assessing the Electoral Connection: Evidence from the Early United States. *American Journal of Political Science*, 49(4): 746–57.

—— —— and ROBERTS, J. M. 2006. Redistricting, Candidate Entry, and the Politics of Nineteenth Century U.S. House Elections. *American Journal of Political Science*, 50(2): 283–93.

—— —— —— 2007. Candidate Quality, the Personal Vote, and the Incumbency Advantage in Congress. *American Political Science Review*, 101(2): 289–301.

CARSON, J. L., KOGER, G., LEBO, M., and YOUNG, E. 2010. The Electoral Costs of Party Loyalty in Congress. *American Journal of Political Science*, 54(3): 598–616.

—— and ROBERTS, J. M. 2005. Strategic Politicians and U.S. House Elections, 1874–1914. *Journal of Politics*, 67(2): 474–96.

COVER, A. D. 1977. One Good Term Deserves Another: The Advantage of Incumbency in Congressional Elections. *American Journal of Political Science*, 21: 523–41.

—— and BRUMBERG, B. S. 1982. Baby Books and Ballots: The Impact of Congressional Mail on Constituency Opinion. *American Political Science Review*, 76: 347–59.

COX, G. W., and KATZ, J. N. 1996. Why Did the Incumbency Advantage in U.S. House Elections Grow? *American Journal of Political Science*, 40: 478–97.

———— 2002. *Elbridge Gerry's Salamander: The Electoral Consequences of the Reapportionment Revolution*. New York: Cambridge University Press.

—— and McCUBBINS, M. D. 2005. *Setting the Agenda: Responsible Party Government in the U.S. House of Representatives*. New York: Cambridge University Press.

—— 2007. *Legislative Leviathan: Party Government in the House*, 2nd edn. New York: Cambridge University Press.

CROOK, S. B., and HIBBING, J. R. 1997. A Not-So-Distant Mirror: The 17th Amendment and Institutional Change. *American Political Science Review*, 91: 845–54.

DESPOSATO, S. W., and PETROCIK, J. R. 2003. The Variable Incumbency Advantage: New Voters, Redistricting, and the Personal Vote. *American Journal of Political Science*, 47: 18–32.

DUBIN, M. J. 1998. *United States Congressional Elections, 1788-1997: The Official Results of the Elections of the 1st through 105th Congresses*. North Carolina: McFarland and Company.

ENGSTROM, E. J. 2006. Stacking the States, Stacking the House: The Politics of Congressional Redistricting in the 19th Century. *American Political Science Review*, 100 (August): 419–28.

EPSTEIN, D., and ZEMSKY, P. 1995. Money Talks: Deterring Quality Challengers in Congressional Elections. *American Political Science Review*, 89: 295–308.

ERIKSON, R. S. 1971. The Advantage of Incumbency in Congressional Elections. *Polity*, 3: 395–405.

—— 1972. Malapportionment, Gerrymandering, and Party Fortunes. *American Political Science Review*, 66: 1234–45.

—— 1988. The Puzzle of Midterm Loss. *Journal of Politics*, 50: 1011–29.

—— and PALFREY, T. R. 1998. Campaign Spending and Incumbency: An Alternative Simultaneous Equations Approach. *Journal of Politics*, 60 (May): 355–73.

FENNO, R. F. 1978. *Home Style: House Members in their Districts*. New York: HarperCollins.

FEREJOHN, J. A. 1977. On the Decline of Competition in Congressional Elections. *American Political Science Review*, 71: 166–76.

—— and CALVERT, R. L. 1984. Presidential Coattails in Historical Perspective. *American Journal of Political Science*, 28 (February): 127–46.

FINOCCHIARO, C. J. 2003. An Institutional View of Congressional Elections: The Impact of Congressional Image on Seat Change in the House. *Political Research Quarterly*, 56 (March): 59–65.

FIORINA, M. P. 1977. The Case of the Vanishing Marginals: The Bureaucracy Did It. *American Political Science Review*, 71: 177–81.

—— 1981. *Retrospective Voting in American National Elections*. New Haven: Yale University Press.

FOWLER, L. L., and McCLURE, R. D. 1989. *Political Ambition: Who Decides to Run for Congress*. New Haven: Yale University Press.

FOX, R. L., and LAWLESS, J. L. 2005. To Run or Not to Run for Office: Explaining Nascent Political Ambition. *American Journal of Political Science*, 49: 642–59.

FRIEDMAN, J N., and HOLDEN, R. T. 2009. The Rising Incumbent Reelection Rate: What's Gerrymandering Got to Do With It? *Journal of Politics*, 71(2): 593–611.

GAILMARD, S., and JENKINS, J. A. 2009. Agency Problems, the 17th Amendment, and Representation in the Senate. *American Journal of Political Science*, 53 (April): 324–42.

GALDERISI, P. F., EZRA, M., and LYONS, M. 2001. *Congressional Primaries and the Politics of Representation*. New York: Rowman and Littlefield Publishers.

GELMAN, A., and KING, G. 1990. Estimating Incumbency Advantage without Bias. *American Journal of Political Science*, 34: 1142–64.

GERBER, A. 1998. Estimating the Effect of Campaign Spending on Senate Election Outcomes Using Instrumental Variables. *American Political Science Review*, 92 (June): 401–11.

GIMPEL, J. G., LEE, F. E., and KAMINSKI, J. 2006. The Political Geography of Campaign Contributions in American Politics. *Journal of Politics*, 68: 626–39.

——— and PEARSON-MERKOWITZ, S. 2008. The Check is in the Mail: Interdistrict Funding Flows in Congressional Elections. *American Journal of Political Science*, 52: 373–94.

GOIDEL, R. K., and GROSS, D. A. 1994. A Systems Approach to Campaign Finance in U.S. House Elections. *American Politics Quarterly*, 22: 125–53.

GOLDENBERG, E. N., TRAUGOTT, M. W., and BAUMGARTNER, F. R. 1986. Preemptive and Reactive Spending in U.S. House Races. *Political Behavior*, 8: 3–20.

GOLDSTEIN, K., and FREEDMAN, P. 2000. New Evidence for New Arguments: Money and Advertising in the 1996 Senate Elections. *Journal of Politics*, 64 (November): 1087–108.

GOODLIFFE, J. 2001. The Effect of War Chests on Challenger Entry in U.S. House Elections. *American Journal of Political Science*, 45 (November): 830–44.

—— 2007. Campaign War Chests and Challenger Quality in Senate Elections. *Legislative Studies Quarterly*, 32 (February): 135–56.

GREEN, D. P., and KRASNO, J. S. 1988. Salvation for the Spendthrift Incumbent: Reestimating the Effects of Campaign Spending in House Elections. *American Journal of Political Science*, 32 (November): 884–907.

——— 1990. Rebuttal to Jacobson's "New Evidence for Old Arguments." *American Journal of Political Science*, 34 (May): 363–72.

GRONKE, P. 2000. *The Electorate, the Campaign, and the Office: A Unified Approach to Senate and House Elections*. Ann Arbor: University of Michigan Press.

GROSECLOSE, T., and KREHBIEL, K. 1994. Golden Parachutes, Rubber Checks, and Strategic Retirements from the 102d House. *American Journal of Political Science*, 38: 75–99.

HERRNSON, P. S. 2007. *Congressional Elections: Campaigning at Home and in Washington*. Washington, DC: CQ Press.

HERSCH, P. L., and McDOUGALL, G. S. 1994. Campaign War Chests as a Barrier to Entry in Congressional Races. *Economic Inquiry*, 32: 630–41.

HIGHTON, B. 2000. Senate Elections in the United States, 1920–94. *British Journal of Political Science*, 30: 483–506.

HINCKLEY, B. 1980a. House Re-elections and Senate Defeats: The Role of the Challenger. *British Journal of Political Science*, 10: 441–60.

—— 1980b. The American Voter in Congressional Elections. *American Political Science Review*, 74: 641–50.

JACOBSON, G. C. 1978. The Effects of Campaign Spending in Congressional Elections. *American Political Science Review*, 72 (June): 469–91.

—— 1980. *Money in Congressional Elections*. New Haven: Yale University Press.

—— 1987. The Marginals Never Vanished: Incumbency and Competition in Elections to the U.S. House of Representatives, 1952–1982. *American Journal of Political Science*, 31: 126–41.

JACOBSON, G. C. 1989. Strategic Politicians and the Dynamics of U.S. House Elections, 1946–1986. *American Political Science Review*, 83 (September): 773–93.

——1990. The Effects of Campaign Spending in House Elections: New Evidence for Old Arguments. *American Journal of Political Science*, 34: 334–62.

——1993. Deficit-Cutting Politics and Congressional Elections. *Political Science Quarterly*, 108 (Autumn): 375–402.

——2009. *The Politics of Congressional Elections*, 7th edn. New York: Longman.

——and DIMOCK, M. A. 1994. Checking Out: The Effects of Bank Overdrafts on the 1992 House Elections. *American Journal of Political Science*, 38: 601–24.

——and KERNELL, S. 1981. *Strategy and Choice in Congressional Elections*. New Haven: Yale University Press.

JOHANNES, J. R., and McADAMS, J. C. 1981. The Congressional Incumbency Effect: Is It Casework, Policy Compatibility, or Something Else? *American Journal of Political Science*, 25: 520–42.

JONES, D. R. 2003. Position Taking and Position Avoidance in the U.S. Senate. *The Journal of Politics*, 65 (August): 851–63.

KAZEE, T. A. 1980. The Decision to Run for the U.S. Congress: Challenger Attitudes in the 1970s. *Legislative Studies Quarterly*, 5: 79–100.

——1983. The Deterrent Effect of Incumbency on Recruiting Challengers in U.S. House Elections. *Legislative Studies Quarterly*, 8: 469–80.

KENNY, C., and McBURNETT, M. 1992. A Dynamic Model of the Effect of Campaign Spending on Congressional Vote Choice. *American Journal of Political Science*, 36 (November): 923–37.

KERNELL, S. 1977. Presidential Popularity and Negative Voting: An Alternative Explanation of the Midterm Congressional Decline of the President's Party. *American Political Science Review*, 71 (March): 44–66.

KEY, V. O. 1958. *Politics, Parties, and Pressure Groups*. New York: Thomas Y. Crowell.

KRASNO, J. S. 1994. *Challengers, Competition, and Reelection: Comparing Senate and House Elections*. New Haven: Yale University Press.

——and GREEN, D. P. 1988. Preempting Quality Challengers in House Elections. *Journal of Politics*, 50: 920–36.

KREHBIEL, K. 1991. *Information and Legislative Organization*. Ann Arbor: University of Michigan Press.

LARSON, B. A. 2004. Incumbent Contributions to the Congressional Campaign Committees, 1990–2000. *Political Research Quarterly*, 57 (March): 155–61.

LAWLESS, J. L., and FOX, R. L. 2005. *It Takes a Candidate: Why Women Don't Run for Office*. New York: Cambridge University Press.

LEE, D. S. 2008. Randomized Experiments from Non-Random Selection in U.S. House Elections. *Journal of Econometrics*, 142: 675–97.

LEE, F. E. 1998. Representation and Public Policy: The Consequences of Senate Apportionment for the Geographic Distribution of Federal Funds. *The Journal of Politics*, 60 (February): 34–62.

——2003. Geographic Politics in the U.S. House of Representatives: Coalition Building and Distribution of Benefits. *American Journal of Political Science*, 47 (October): 714–28.

——and OPPENHEIMER, B. I. 1999. *Sizing up the Senate: The Unequal Consequences of Equal Representation*. Chicago: University of Chicago Press.

LEVITT, S. D., and WOLFRAM, C. D. 1997. Decomposing the Sources of Incumbency Advantage in the U.S. House. *Legislative Studies Quarterly*, 22: 45–60.

LUBLIN, D. I. 1994. Quality, Not Quantity: Strategic Politicians in U.S. Senate Elections, 1952–1990. *The Journal of Politics*, 56: 228–41.

MAESTAS, C. D., FULTON, S. A., MAISEL, L. S., and STONE, W. J. 2006. When to Risk It? Institutions, Ambition, and the Decision to Run for the U.S. House. *American Political Science Review*, 100 (May): 195–208.

MAISEL, L. S., and STONE, W. J. 1997. Determinants of Candidate Emergence in U.S. House Elections: An Exploratory Study. *Legislative Studies Quarterly*, 22: 79–96.

———— 2003. The Not-So-Simple Calculus of Winning: Potential U.S. House Candidates' Nomination and General Election Prospects. *Journal of Politics*, 65 (November): 951–77.

MANN, T. E. 1978. *Unsafe at Any Margin: Interpreting Congressional Elections*. Washington, DC: American Enterprise Institute.

——and WOLFINGER, R. E. 1980. Candidates and Parties in Congressional Elections. *American Political Science Review*, 74: 617–32.

MAYHEW, D. R. 1974a. *Congress: The Electoral Connection*. New Haven: Yale University Press.

——1974b. Congressional Elections: The Case of the Vanishing Marginals. *Polity*, 6: 295–317.

——2004. *Electoral Realignments: A Critique of an American Genre*. New Haven: Yale University Press.

MEINKE, S. R. 2008. Institutional Change and the Electoral Connection in the Senate: Revisiting the Effects of Direct Election. *Political Research Quarterly*, 61 (September): 445–57.

MILYO, J. 1998. *The Electoral Effects of Campaign Spending in House Elections*. Los Angeles: Citizens' Research Foundation.

MONROE, N. W., ROBERTS, J. M., and ROHDE, D. W. 2008. *Why Not Parties? Party Effects in the United States Senate*. Chicago: University of Chicago Press.

MOON, W. 2006. The Paradox of Less Effective Incumbent Spending: Theory and Tests. *British Journal of Political Science*, 36(4): 705–21.

OPPENHEIMER, B. I., WATERMAN, R. W., and STIMSON, J. A. 1986. Interpreting U.S. Congressional Elections: The Exposure Thesis. *Legislative Studies Quarterly*, 11 (May): 227–47.

PRIOR, M. 2007. *Post-Broadcast Democracy: How Media Choice Increases Inequality in Political Involvement and Polarizes Elections*. New York: Cambridge University Press.

RAGSDALE, L. 1994. Old Approaches and New Challenges in Legislative Election Research. *Legislative Studies Quarterly*, 19(4): 537–82.

ROHDE, D. W. 1979. Risk Bearing and Progressive Ambition: The Case of Members of the United States House of Representatives. *American Journal of Political Science*, 23: 1–26.

——1991. *Parties and Leaders in the Postreform House*. Chicago: University of Chicago Press.

SCHAFFNER, B. F. 2005. Priming Gender: Campaigning on Women's Issues in U.S. Senate Elections. *American Journal of Political Science*, 49 (October): 803–17.

SCHILLER, W. J. 2006. Building Careers and Courting Constituents: U.S. Senate Representation 1889–1924. *Studies in American Political Development*, 20 (October): 185–97.

SCHLESINGER, J. A. 1966. *Ambition and Politics: Political Careers in the United States*. Chicago: Rand McNally.

SELLERS, P. J. 1997. Fiscal Consistency and Federal District Spending in Congressional Elections. *American Journal of Political Science*, 41 (July): 1024–41.

——1998. Strategy and Background in Congressional Campaigns. *American Political Science Review*, 92: 159–71.

SMITH, S. S. 2007. *Party Influence in Congress*. New York: Cambridge University Press.

SQUIRE, P. 1989. Challengers in U.S. Senate Elections. *Legislative Studies Quarterly*, 14: 531–47.

——1991. Preemptive Fund-Raising and Challenger Profile in Senate Elections. *Journal of Politics*, 53: 1150–64.

——1992. Challenger Quality and Voting Behavior in U.S. Senate Elections. *Legislative Studies Quarterly*, 17: 247–63.

SQUIRE, P. 1995. Candidates, Money, and Voters: Assessing the State of Congressional Elections Research. *Political Research Quarterly*, 48(4): 891–917.

STONE, W. J., and MAISEL, L. S. 2003. The Not-so-Simple Calculus of Winning: Potential U.S. Candidates' Nomination and General Election Prospects. *Journal of Politics*, 65: 951–77.

STONECASH, J. M. 2008. *Reassessing the Incumbency Effect*. New York: Cambridge University Press.

SULKIN, T. 2005. *Issue Politics in Congress*. New York: Cambridge University Press.

—— and SWIGGER, N. 2008. Is There Truth in Advertising? Campaign Ad Images as Signals about Legislative Behavior. *Journal of Politics*, 70 (February): 232–44.

THOMAS, S. 1989. Do Incumbent Campaign Expenditures Matter? *Journal of Politics*, 51 (November): 965–75.

TUFTE, E. R. 1973. The Relationship between Seats and Votes in Two-Party Systems. *American Political Science Review*, 67 (June): 540–54.

—— 1975. Determinants of the Outcomes of Midterm Congressional Elections. *American Political Science Review*, 69 (September): 812–26.

WATERMAN, R. W. 1990. Comparing Senate and House Electoral Outcomes: The Exposure Thesis. *Legislative Studies Quarterly*, 15 (February): 99–114.

—— OPPENHEIMER, B. I., and STIMSON, J. A. 1991. Sequence and Equilibrium in Congressional Elections: An Integrated Approach. *Journal of Politics*, 53: 373–93.

WESTLYE, M. C. 1983. Competitiveness of Senate Seats and Voting Behavior in Senate Elections. *American Journal of Political Science*, 27: 253–83.

WRIGHT, JR., G. C. 1978. Candidates' Policy Positions and Voting in U.S. Congressional Elections. *Legislative Studies Quarterly*, 3 (August): 445–64.

CHAPTER 8

....

CONGRESSIONAL
CAMPAIGNS

....

TRACY SULKIN

CONGRESSIONAL campaigns are central to democratic governance. They are, as Fenno argues, "the *place* where our representative form of government begins and ends" (1996, 9) and serve as the central institutional mechanism for interaction between legislators and their constituents. Moreover, given representatives' and senators' focus on reelection, they take seriously what happens on the campaign trail, even if their races are not particularly competitive, and these campaign experiences shape and are shaped by their behavior as policymakers in Congress.

Accordingly, legislative scholars have long been interested in the dynamics of congressional campaigns. Compared to other topics in the field, though, campaigns remain relatively undertilled as a research area. Thus, while we know a great deal about legislators as casters of roll-call votes, much about them as members of committees, and an increasing amount about them as introducers and cosponsors of legislation, we know less about their activities as campaigners. Fortunately, the past decade or so has brought increased attention to the subject, with the promise of more to come. Continued research on representatives' and senators' campaign behavior and experiences is valuable because of the insight it can lend into a number of important normative questions about the quality of campaigns and the health of the democratic process. For example, do congressional campaigns provide voters with the information they need to know to make good choices? Do incumbents and quality challengers run better campaigns than their less experienced peers? Are candidates sincere in their appeals, or are campaign messages just "cheap talk"?

Less obviously, but equally importantly, the study of campaigns contributes to a richer and more nuanced view of legislators' behavior in Washington, DC. Legislators' campaign choices offer perspective on their strategies and priorities, help to explain the content and volume of their activity in office, and provide us with a broader conception of representation and a more precise understanding of the electoral connection. To realize these benefits fully will require that work on the electoral and legislative arenas, areas of inquiry that have often proceeded along largely separate lines, be united. What is needed is more focus on campaigns, particularly the activities of candidates, and more exploration of the relationships between campaigns and governance. In this chapter I focus on what legislative scholars know about these topics and I highlight areas that are ripe for further research.

IS CAMPAIGNS REALLY AN UNDERTILLED FIELD?

At first glance, a casual observer might reasonably contest my claim that congressional campaigns have been undertilled. After all, there is a voluminous literature on House and Senate elections (covered ably in other chapters of this volume), and Mayhew's (1974) "electoral connection" has been central to theorizing about Congress for almost four decades. However, I believe that the gap becomes clearer when we consider the following three propositions: first, that there are important distinctions between the study of *campaigns* and the study of *elections*; second, that much of what political scientists know about campaigns comes from presidential races and may not always travel equally well to congressional races; and, third, that the electoral connection, although broad in theory, has been applied in a fairly specific way, with much of the empirical work focusing on the causes and effects of electoral vulnerability, particularly as they relate to roll-call voting.

Campaigns vs. elections

Although "campaigns and elections" are often invoked in the same breath, the questions and units of analysis that motivate research on the two are actually quite different. In particular, the study of campaigns has focused primarily on the behavior of candidates, while the study of elections has targeted individual vote choice and aggregate outcomes. When we compare the volume of research on the two, it is clear that there has been more attention to the latter. As Fenno put it:

What is surprising to someone who follows the exploits of campaigning politicians is how little of our huge elections research effort has gone into the study of campaigns. An election is, after all, a two-sided business. Campaigning candidates are trying to influence the behavior of voters. But for most political scientists most of the time, the study of elections has meant only the study of voters and their voting behavior.   (Fenno 1996, 76)

In his analysis of the effects of Senate campaigns, Franklin echoes this point, arguing that:

The political nature of elections lies in the choices candidates make about strategy... As we have become adept at studying voters, it is ironic that we have virtually ignored the study of candidates. Yet it is in candidate behavior that politics intrudes into voting behavior. Without the candidates, there is only the psychology of vote choice and none of the politics.   (Franklin, 1991, 1201)

Why is this the case? What accounts for the relative dearth of attention to candidates? Given shifts in research focus in recent years, the above statements should probably be softened a bit. Traditionally, though, one explanation has been that data on voting behavior and election returns typically have been easier to come by than data on candidate behavior.[1] Another is that the analysis of elections has attracted scholars from a variety of sub-fields and research traditions. For instance, a fairly large proportion of political scientists who study congressional elections think about themselves first and foremost as scholars of mass political behavior, and so they approach House and Senate races as interesting and important contexts for understanding the political psychology and decision-making of ordinary citizens. Naturally, then, the questions of interest to them often differ from those of primary interest to congressional scholars.

However, legislative specialists' study of elections has also focused on voting, largely because of our interest in predicting and explaining electoral outcomes and the concomitant partisan composition of Congress. In his classic text on the subject, Jacobson argues: "The electoral politics of Congress may center largely on individual candidates and campaigns, but it is the collective results of congressional elections that shape the course of national politics" (2009, 157). As such, if our primary goal is to understand what produces the partisan divisions of power that animate policymaking in the House and Senate, targeting voters' decisions and aggregate election returns makes clear sense.

Should this be our only goal, though? As I discuss in more detail below, a sole focus on voting may limit our ability to understand fully both electoral politics and the dynamics of legislative behavior. And it may, at least occasionally, lead to inaccurate generalizations about the effects of campaigns and incomplete interpretations of election outcomes. For instance, when political scientists study campaign effects in the lab, we should aim to do so with experimental stimuli that approximate real-world congressional campaigns (i.e. an experimental study that assumes that candidates regularly offer specific positions on issues will not have as much external

---

[1] Data on the behavior of candidates—advertisements, speeches, direct mail, and the like—are often ephemeral and difficult to collect after a campaign ends. However, with recent advances like archives of campaign websites and the Wisconsin Advertising Project's collections of televised campaign advertisements (in easy to analyze storyboard form, with screenshots of the visuals and text of the audio), this is becoming less of a hurdle.

validity as one that presents most issue statements as relatively vague). Thus, nuanced investigations of how candidates actually behave also provide more insight into the effects of campaigns on voters.

Presidential vs. congressional races

A second, and related, issue is that much of what we do know about the behavior of candidates on the campaign trail comes from observations of presidential races. In determining whether these findings are likely to be applicable to House and Senate candidates, we need to consider differences in the context of these contests. One of the most fundamental differences is that competing presidential candidates are typically evenly matched (or nearly so) in resources, staff expertise, and access to strategic information about voters and their preferences, which is not the case in most congressional races (Burden and Wichowsky 2010; Shaw 2006). This variation has implications for presidential and congressional candidates' issue selection strategies, for their decisions about volume and tone of advertising, and for their interactions with their opponents.

To give just one example, while recent presidential nominees have produced dozens of unique television ads over the course of their campaigns, congressional candidates' efforts are much more limited. Although about 90 percent of Senate candidates air advertisements on television, only about 2/3 of House candidates do (Herrnson 2008),[2] and, in recent elections, the average winning House candidate aired only about four ads and the average winning Senate candidate about nine.[3] Thus ads may provide a good venue for exploring how presidential candidates respond in real time to their opponents' claims and criticisms, but the same is not true for the majority of congressional candidates, who run few ads, most of which are produced early in the campaign and therefore cannot be interpreted as responses to events that occur *during* the campaign.

The focus on presidential races in electoral studies may also have contributed to the relative lack of attention to the details of campaigns, since many of the conclusions that campaigns have "minimal effects" came from analyses of voting in presidential elections. As Shaw (2006) notes, in response to early studies (most notably Berelson, Lazarsfeld, and McPhee's *Voting*, published in 1954), which highlighted the lack of widespread direct persuasive effects of campaigns, scholars turned their attention to the role of non-campaign and non-candidate variables in explaining voting behavior (e.g. party identification and heuristics at the individual level; presidential approval and economic evaluations at the aggregate). Interestingly, though, even at the height

---

[2] The same basic finding holds for other types of advertising—Herrnson finds that almost 2/3 of House candidates and nearly all Senate candidates advertised on the radio, and 63% of House candidates and 80% of Senate candidates purchased newspaper ads (2008, 222–30).

[3] These figures come from my analyses of the advertisements of winning candidates in 1998, 2000, and 2002 (see Sulkin 2009). The ads were archived as part of the Wisconsin Advertising Project efforts. Losing candidates are less likely to run advertisements and, when they do advertise on television, they run fewer ads than their more successful peers.

of the (now passed) era of minimal effects for presidential elections, few scholars explicitly argued that the same held true for congressional races. Indeed, early studies of the effects of fundraising and spending (Jacobson 1978) and of the role of quality challengers (Jacobson and Kernell 1983) revealed that candidates and their campaigns could have strong effects on outcomes. Nonetheless, the focus on factors other than campaigns and their dynamics likely spilled over into the study of congressional elections.

Expanding the electoral connection

Finally, although the electoral connection has been central to research on legislative behavior and organization, work following on Mayhew (1974) has conceived of this linkage in a fairly narrow way, focusing primarily on vote shares. In particular, scholars have asked whether legislators who are electorally vulnerable vote differently from those who are safe (Deckard 1976; Fiorina 1973; Kuklinski 1977; Sullivan and Uslaner 1978), and whether voting records in office affect reelection prospects (see, for example, Ansolabehere, Snyder, and Stewart 2001; Bovitz and Carson 2006; Canes-Wrone, Brady, and Cogan 2002; Erikson 1971). More recently, analyses have been expanded to include activities other than voting, including introductions and cosponsorships (Kessler and Krehbiel 1996; Koger 2003; Schiller 1995; Wawro 2000), committee requests and behavior (Frisch and Kelly 2006; Hall 1996), and somewhat more intangible factors like involvement in scandals (Jacobson and Dimock 1994) or the expression of institutional loyalty (Lipinski, Bianco, and Work 2003). The general conclusion from these studies is the same as for voting—the relationship between vulnerability and governing activity (and vice versa) is, at best, mixed. Some studies find effects, but many reveal little connection between the two.

Scholars have been careful to note that a lack of discernible effects does *not* mean that legislators do not take electoral considerations into account when making decisions. Indeed, a large part of the explanation is likely that many legislators feel and behave as if they are vulnerable, even when they are objectively safe (Fenno 1978), so we do not actually observe the full range of behavior (i.e. how a legislator would act if he or she felt perfectly secure). Mayhew made the argument most colorfully, contending that we cannot know what would happen if a legislator deliberately set out to minimize the chances of reelection because "there is no congressman willing to make the experiment" (1974, 37). Along the same lines, legislators concerned about reprisal from their constituencies should be adept at anticipating and avoiding actions that might hurt them (Arnold 1990). Overall, this should mask the observed relationship between vote shares and activity.

In addition, vulnerability is not all, or even most, of the story about the linkages between electoral and legislative politics. I argue that a broader "campaign connection" exists between elections and governing. This point is not novel; a half-century ago, Matthews (1960, 68) noted: "It is difficult, really, to understand the senators, how they act and why, without considering what happens to them when they are running for office." In the intervening years, a number of scholars have argued that candidates' interpretations of the successes and failures of their campaigns should affect their subsequent behavior (Fenno 1996; Hershey 1984; Kingdon 1968). However, apart from a few studies of congressional promise-keeping (Ringquist and Dasse 2004; Sulkin 2009; Sullivan and O'Connor 1972), legislators' responses to policy critiques from their challengers (Sulkin 2005), and the relationships between campaign behavior and Hill styles (Fenno 1996, 2007), there has been little attention paid to the specific links between campaigning and policymaking. Put another way, although political scientists have devoted considerable effort to understanding campaign effects, our search for them typically ends when campaigns end—with voters on Election Day. Extending our focus to include the effects of campaigns on *winners* and their subsequent activity should therefore offer a more complete understanding of representation and of the electoral connection.

THREADS OF RESEARCH

It is clear that much remains to be learned about the dynamics of congressional campaigns. However, that campaigns have been undertilled does not mean that they have been ignored, or that the research that has been done has not been rigorous and influential. Indeed, work on congressional candidates and campaigns, as distinct from research that is solely about elections and voting, has focused on four major areas of inquiry, each with vibrant literatures: candidate emergence and challenger quality, position-taking and ideological placement, issue selection and campaign agendas, and advertising strategies and candidate interaction. Within these areas, there has also been a focus on explaining differences between types of candidates—incumbents vs. challengers, experienced vs. inexperienced candidates, men vs. women, etc. In what follows, I briefly summarize the development and trajectory of each of these literatures.[4]

Candidate emergence and challenger quality

By the mid-1970s, scholarly interest in the apparent decline of "marginal" seats in the House of Representatives led to a number of studies that sought to explain variation in competition across House (and, to a lesser extent, Senate) elections. The factor that quickly emerged as the most consistent predictor was the quality of the challenger (Jacobson 1978; Jacobson and Kernell 1983; see also Squire 1989, 1992; Westlye 1991). Incumbents who faced experienced, well-financed opponents fared worse and were

---

[4] On all of these topics, there are both formal and empirical literatures. In the interest of space, my review will focus primarily, although not solely, on the latter.

much more likely to lose their seats. In fact, challengers who had held office in the past were about four times as likely as their inexperienced peers to be successful in their bids for House seats (Jacobson 1990).

Under what conditions were these quality challengers most likely to emerge? Although incumbents embroiled in scandal or who diverged greatly from the interests of their constituents were (and are) more likely to face robust challenges, most studies found that the appearance of quality challengers seemed to be related less to the activity of the incumbent and more to aggregate conditions like national partisan tides or a larger pool of potential candidates (Bianco 1984; Bond, Covington, and Fleisher 1985; Lublin 1994; Squire 1989).[5]

Drawing on earlier work on political ambition (e.g. Schlesinger 1966), Jacobson and Kernell (1983) offered their "strategic politicians" theory to explain these patterns. They posited that quality challengers are savvy and want to maximize their chances of winning, so they enter races only when conditions are in their favor.[6] Thus, compared to lower-quality candidates, who may have motivations for running other than winning the election, their decisions are more sensitive to factors that affect the likelihood of their success, like the state of the economy and the popularity of the president. In election years where conditions are favorable to challengers overall (i.e. if there is rampant anti-incumbent sentiment) or to those from one party or the other, a stronger pool of challengers from one or both parties will emerge to contest races.

In addition to explaining variation in challenger quality from election to election, this argument also helped to resolve a puzzling disjuncture between individual and aggregate-level findings about voting in congressional elections. In short, congressional election outcomes are typically strongly correlated with aggregate factors like the health of the economy, but individual voters' views about the economy (or about their own economic situations) are not strong drivers of their voting decisions. To reconcile this, Jacobson and Kernell argued that voters react to the strength of the candidates when making their choices, and so they seem to be responding to national conditions even when they are not.

More nuanced explorations of the nature of challengers and their strategies followed. Canon (1990, 1993) demonstrated, for example, that not all amateurs are amateurish. Inexperienced challengers can still pose a threat to incumbents if they have other resources (e.g. celebrity) to draw on (see also Krasno and Green 1988), and amateurs who have serious ambitions about a political career in Congress behave more like experienced challengers than their solely "experience-seeking" colleagues. For instance, their decisions about when to run are a function of national political conditions, so they, too, appear to be strategic (see also Maisel and Stone 1997).

A major insight to come out of these investigations was that it is not necessarily prior elected office experience itself that matters in explaining why these challengers

---

[5] Research on congressional elections in the 1800s and early 1900s shows that a similar strategic politicians dynamic was at work then (see, for example, Carson, Engstrom, and Roberts 2006; Carson and Roberts 2005).

[6] This logic also applies to potential donors, who are less likely to contribute to challengers' campaigns when their chances of victory are remote.

do better. Instead, experience serves as a (quite often good, but sometimes noisy) proxy for a variety of factors that contribute to the strength of a challenge, including strategic resources (Krasno and Green 1988), personal qualities of the candidates (Stone, Maisel, and Maestas 2004), and seriousness of purpose (Maestas and Rugeley 2008). Thus, these results all suggest that local and candidate-level factors may be more important than originally thought.[7]

Other work on strategic politicians theory sought to disentangle still further the independent effects of challenger quality on electoral outcomes. Basinger and Ensley (2007) find, for instance, that, after taking into account the endogeneity inherent in the emergence of experienced challengers (i.e. they run when national tides are favorable), there is no direct effect (see also Born 1986). However, this does not mean that challenger experience is unimportant; instead, the authors hypothesize that experience serves as a signal to potential contributors, many of whom are located outside of the district, about the vulnerability of the incumbent.

Regardless of the nature of the aggregate effects, at the individual level, reelection-oriented House and Senate incumbents should be interested in trying to ward off strong challengers. Can they do so? Findings about pre-emptive fundraising in the form of "war chests" are mixed, with some studies showing that they help incumbents to deter quality challengers (Box-Steffensmeier 1996; Carson 2005) and others finding no effect (Goodliffe 2001, 2007; Krasno and Green 1988; Squire 1991). There is also little evidence that the amount of attention incumbents pay to their districts affects challenger emergence, or that, in line with the findings above about the influence of governing on vote shares, their volume of policy activities influences the behavior of potential challengers (Ragsdale and Cook 1987). However, the latter may be too blunt a measure to capture the effects of in-office behavior, since the *content* of an incumbent's activities is likely to matter more than their *volume*.

One promising area for future research, then, is to delve more deeply into the content of legislators' policymaking activity and candidates' campaign behavior, in order to determine how these interact to affect the dynamics of campaigns and electoral outcomes. For instance, in their study of the electoral consequences of the House banking scandal in the early 1990s, Jacobson and Dimock (1994) find that the effects of the objective indicators of involvement in the scandal (i.e. number and amount of overdrafts) on incumbents' prospects were conditional on the presence of a quality challenger. What produced this relationship? Was the effect indirect? Or were experienced challengers more likely to criticize incumbents for their role in the scandal, or perhaps to do so in a more effective way? More generally, while a number of studies have noted challengers' tendencies to highlight incumbents' weaknesses (Arnold 1990, 2004; Bailey 2001; Sulkin 2005), we have less understanding of how

---

[7] These findings are also in line with earlier, more qualitative work on patterns of competition and candidate ambition and emergence within districts (Fowler and McClure 1989; Kazee 1994). Recent research on the individual-level determinants of political ambition includes Maestas, Fulton, Maisel, and Stone 2006 and Fox and Lawless 2005. For a specific focus on gender and candidate emergence, see Lawless and Fox 2005 and Fulton, Maestas, Maisel, and Stone 2006.

they accomplish this and how the process might vary across challengers, both at the primary and the general election levels.

Position-taking in campaigns

The findings from the candidate emergence literature strongly support the claim that it matters who the candidates are, but they also suggest that what they do in their campaigns is important too. Although there are various decisions candidates must make and tactics they might adopt, the most studied dimension of candidate strategy has been their issue positions, usually operationalized as how they situate themselves ideologically. The simplest prediction, from a pure Downsian spatial model of candidate position-taking, is that there should be convergence to the median voter, either nationally or on a district-by-district or state-by-state basis. However, decades of empirical research show that substantial convergence is the exception, not the rule (e.g. Ansolabehere, Snyder, and Stewart 2001; Burden 2004; see also Grofman 2004 for a review of this literature). Instead, Democrats and Republicans in general tend to adopt different issue positions, as do those running against one another (such that the overall divergence is not a function of differences in districts or states).

What might account for this? The most likely culprits are the assumptions from median voter theory that voters select the candidate who is most proximate to them ideologically, and that candidates therefore need to converge to the median voter to win election or reelection. However, there are several reasons to expect that these assumptions do not always accurately capture real-world elections. First, congressional races are typically lopsided enough for incumbents to be able to win without moderating their positions (Burden 2004), and challengers who understand that their efforts are unlikely to result in a victory have little incentive to move to the middle. Instead, they may use their campaigns as a venue for "expressive campaigning," to articulate their own views and/or assist their party in other ways (Boatright 2004).

Second, voters may not actually evaluate candidates in the manner suggested by median voter theory, so candidates might not be punished for failure to converge. Indeed, there is a lively debate in the literature about whether classic "proximity" models (models where voters choose the candidate closest to them), "discounting" models (where voters prioritize policy outcomes over positions and so may sometimes choose candidates whose positions are farther from their own, but whom they believe to be more likely to bring about desirable outcomes), or "directional models" (where voters view issues as having two sides and select candidates who are on their side, even if their positions are further from their own ideal points) provide the most accurate depiction of voters' decision-making.[8]

A third possibility is that proximity models are correct, but that the institutional structure of elections means that the candidates' target is not necessarily the median voter in the district or in the state as a whole. For instance, the need to appeal to

---

[8] Tomz and Van Houweling (2008) provide an excellent review of these debates.

the base in primary elections may pull candidates away from the median (but see Ansolabehere, Snyder, and Stewart 2001, who find little evidence that primaries have this effect). More generally, when staking out positions, candidates and legislators may give more weight to the interests of important sub-constituencies rather than of the district or state median (Bishin 2009; Clinton 2006; Fiorina 1974; Miller and Stokes 1963).

Finally, a more practical consideration is that candidates who have staked out positions on issues through their roll-call votes or other activities in office cannot simply change those positions on the campaign trail without being attacked as flip-floppers or wafflers. And, even though the strictly reelection-oriented candidates and parties in Downs' model "never seek office as a means of carrying out particular policies; their only goal is to reap the rewards of holding office *per se*... parties formulate policies in order to win elections, rather than win elections in order to formulate policies" (1957, 28), most candidates and legislators have their own policy preferences, and these should affect the positions they express, particularly in an increasingly polarized system.

In interpreting this literature and its findings, one crucial point to remember is that, although it is framed as being about candidates and their positions, little of it focuses on actual campaign behavior. Instead, most scholars use one of Poole and Rosenthal's NOMINATE measures or other indicators based on roll-call voting or ideology in office. And, when campaign-based measures are used, they are usually aggregated in some manner. For example, part of Ansolabehere, Snyder, and Stewart's (2001) analysis uses Project Vote Smart's National Political Awareness Test (NPAT), where candidates were asked a large number of questions about their policy views. They then scale these responses and focus their analyses on the first dimension of the principal components analysis, which approximates NOMINATE and other ideological measures. Along the same lines, Burden (2004) surveys candidates, but his measure simply asks them to place themselves on a left–right ideological scale.

Such measures are certainly useful, and would be most valid if congressional candidates' campaigns focused on their liberalism or conservatism. Candidates' actual rhetoric, however, only rarely invokes their ideologies.[9] In addition, although their roll-call voting records may include positions on dozens of issues, only a subset of these are likely to be salient to their constituencies, and candidates typically have fairly focused agendas, so they highlight only a small handful of issues in their campaigns (Sides 2006; Sulkin 2009). This all suggests that the findings about position-taking might be different if we disaggregated the ideological indices to compare more and less salient issues, or to examine only those issues that actually came up in the campaign. For instance, because less salient issues should give candidates and legislators more leeway to express their own preferences or to appease high-demand sub-constituencies, candidates and legislators might position themselves differently on those issues than on others. Similarly, the choice to raise some issues and ignore others could be connected to their relative extremity vis-à-vis the constituency on

---

[9] However, it is not uncommon for candidates to criticize their opponents for being "too liberal" or "too conservative."

those issues. Of course, the analyses needed in order to answer these questions would present some difficulty in data collection, but, with the availability of more extensive archives of ads and websites, they are increasingly possible.

The value of focusing on campaign-specific behavior becomes even more apparent when we consider the disjuncture between the position-taking/ideological convergence literature and another literature, also on positions, that highlights the tendency of candidates to avoid taking them—at least of the type one usually thinks of (i.e. for or against the death penalty, or a particular tax plan or health care reform proposal). Stokes (1992) argued, for instance, that most campaigns are characterized not by positional issues where there are competing stances that can be arrayed along a left–right dimension, but by "valence politics," where candidates express support for consensual goals like a prosperous economy, or a strong national defense, or a government "in touch" with the needs of average Americans. Content analysis of House and Senate campaigns shows this to be the case; candidates often talk about issues in a general way, without staking out specific positions (Kahn and Kenney 1999; Sides 2006; Spiliotes and Vavreck 2002; Sulkin 2009; Vavreck 2001). Thus, they might claim that they are "champions for education" or "will make health care a priority" without linking these claims to particular policy solutions.

Candidates who avoid taking positions or who offer only ambiguous ones face the risk of being branded insincere and of losing support from those voters who prefer to know with certainty where candidates stand. The advantage, of course, is that, by being vague, candidates may be able to avoid alienating voters who do not agree with them. Shepsle (1972) highlighted the conditions under which there should be strategic advantages to ambiguity (see also Page 1976). Empirical tests of the effects of ambiguity have been more rare, but a recent experimental study by Tomz and Van Houweling (2009) finds evidence that, as predicted by Shepsle, ambiguity is not always harmful and may often help. Many voters respond positively to ambiguous claims, either because they do not mind risk or do not have strong policy preferences of their own, or because it enables them to project their own preferences onto their preferred candidate (96).

This discussion of the specificity of candidates' appeals raises a broader question, which lies just under the surface in all work on campaigns: how we should evaluate the strategies candidates adopt and the choices they make. Should the standard be whether they work (i.e. in the sense of producing an electoral pay-off)? Whether they accord with normative theorists' views of the ideal campaign? Whether voters themselves respond positively? Or some combination of these? For example, research has shown that the rhetoric candidates use when talking about issues is largely a function of the competitiveness of the election—the tighter the race, the more likely candidates are to offer specifics about their positions (Kahn and Kenney 1999; Sides 2006; Sulkin 2009). From the perspective of democratic theory, specific appeals are clearly better, because they contribute to the "information-rich" environment that is the prerequisite to substantive and deliberative campaigns (see Lipsitz 2004). On the other hand, voters themselves may not prefer such campaigns, finding them too demanding (Lipsitz, Trost, Grossman, and Sides 2005). In addition, there is little evidence to support the argument that specificity about an issue is a signal of a candidate's sincerity. In my work on promise keeping, I find that candidates who make appeals about an issue are more active on it in Congress than those who do not, but that specific and vague appeals serve as equally strong predictors of subsequent activity (Sulkin 2009). Thus, if we assume that, much of the time, voters care more about what issues their legislators will pursue than about the positions they will take on them, specific appeals are not necessarily more valuable from a representational perspective.

Issue selection and campaign agendas

Thus, although issue positions and ideology are central to candidate strategy, *what* candidates choose to talk about and *how* they do so are also important components. Indeed, rather than fights to win over the median voter, campaigns may be more accurately conceived of as heresthetical battles, where competing candidates maneuver to set the agenda in a way advantageous to them (Riker 1986, 1996). As Hammond and Humes explain: "Instead of the candidates trying to figure out what positions to take, then, political campaigns are turned into contests about what the issue dimensions of the campaign will be" (1993, 142).

It is common in some journalistic accounts of campaigns to interpret the lack of explicit position-taking as evidence that issues are unimportant to candidates and voters. Contrary to the popular wisdom, though, substantive issues occupy a central place in congressional campaigns. Over one half of House candidates make issues the *primary* focus of their campaign messages (Herrnson 2008), and very few candidates run campaigns that are completely devoid of substantive content. For instance, among the House and Senate winners included in the Wisconsin Advertising Project archives from 1998 to 2002, only about 1 percent ran television advertisements that contained no discussion at all of issues (Sides 2006; Sulkin 2009).

Understanding candidates' issue selection strategies is important because these choices offer insight into how candidates view campaigns and because winning candidates' agendas and those of their opponents both signal and shape future activity (Sulkin 2005; 2009; Sulkin and Swigger 2008). They also bear on broader normative issues; Riker, for example, argued that understanding the rhetorical content of campaigns helps address one of the fundamental questions of representative democracy—how it is that policies are "presented, discussed, and decided upon" (1996, 4).

How do candidates select their campaign themes? The basic argument in the literature on campaign agendas is that candidates choose to highlight issues that are likely to pay off for them. This should be most straightforward if they limit their choices to issues on which they hold some sort of advantage vis-à-vis their opponents. Raising issues on which the opponent holds the advantage will only increase the salience of dimensions on which they are weak and will hurt them electorally. This amounts to a simple priming effect; if voters prefer one's opponent on environmental issues, getting them to think more about the environment should increase the likelihood of their voting for the opponent (Ansolabehere and Iyengar 1994; Simon 2002).

From where should advantages on issues arise? Building on the work of Budge and Farlie (1983) and Petrocik (1996), most work on issue selection has highlighted the importance of partisan issue ownership. Petrocik argues that the parties have developed long-standing reputations for their handling of certain issues, on the basis of the demographic composition of their base constituencies and of their historical associations with certain issues and policies. Voters are thus more likely to respond favorably when candidates highlight issues that their party owns, as when a Democrat talks about the environment or a Republican emphasizes national defense. On the flip side, candidates should also be harmed when they "trespass" on the other party's issues.

Numerous studies have offered evidence that such strategies can work. Laboratory experiments on the effects of advertising have shown that candidates do indeed benefit when they highlight owned issues (Ansolabehere and Iyengar 1994; Iyengar and Valentino 2000; Simon 2002), and Abbe, et al.'s (2003) work on candidates and voters in the 1998 House races shows that voters are more likely to support a candidate when he or she runs on party-owned issues that the voters view as important.

However, when we switch the focus from the effects of an ownership strategy on individual attitudes to its effect on electoral outcomes, the relationships are much weaker. Candidates who highlight owned issues are no more or less likely to win than those who focus on performance issues (i.e. issues that are owned by neither party) or than those who trespass to talk about the other party's issues (Sides 2007). One possible reason for this is that perceptions of ownership are so ingrained in many voters' minds that candidates can do little through their actual behavior to change them. If this is the case, trespassing may not be harmful. For instance, Norpoth and Buchanan's (1992) study of the 1988 presidential campaign found that, although George Bush promised that he would be the "education president" and Michael Dukakis expressed support for increasing funding for defense, many voters believed it was Dukakis who made the education pledge and Bush who made the defense pledge.

More problematic, though, is that it turns out that there is only mixed evidence that candidates regularly adopt an issue ownership strategy. While there is a general tendency for Democrats and Republicans to differentiate their agendas, this is far from deterministic: many candidates cross lines to discuss issues owned by the other party (Kaplan, Park, and Ridout 2006; Sides 2006; Sulkin 2009). Why might candidates choose to trespass? As Downs hypothesized, they could do so to appear more moderate—"cast[ing] some policies into the other's territory in order to convince voters there that their net position is near them" (1957, 35). Another possibility is that candidates choose to "ride the wave" to focus on the issues that are most salient in a given election year and are receiving the most news coverage, regardless of whether or not their party owns them (Ansolabehere and Iyengar 1994; Brasher 2003; Sides 2007). Thus, if social security is high on the agenda, then all candidates may feel the need to address it, even though it has been a traditionally Democratic issue.

Another point to consider is that the parties' ownership advantages do not appear to be as permanent as early theoretical work might have suggested. Recent poll results show that many issues for which there were large partisan advantages in the 1980s no longer exhibit them.[10] Most notably, Republicans have lost the advantage on issues like taxes and crime, which were strongly in their category throughout much of the last half-century (Sides 2006; Sulkin, Moriarty, and Hefner 2007). This may be due in part to evolution in the ways these issues have been addressed by the parties. Sides (2006) argues, for example, that rather than thinking about issues being owned, it might be more fruitful to think about *dimensions* of issues as owned by one party or the other. For example, being "tough on crime" is a Republican theme, but gun control and school safety are Democratic themes. Thus, we could observe two competing candidates who both discuss crime, but highlight sub-themes on which they enjoy the advantage relative to their opponent (see also Holian 2004).

Finally, theoretical and experimental work on issue ownership seldom takes into account individual-level differences between candidates. For instance, in most contests, the Democrat may have the advantage over the Republican on health care, but if the Republican had been a physician and/or had taken a leadership role on health policy in the past, it would not be surprising to observe that candidate highlighting the issue. Indeed, empirical analyses of candidate's issue agendas have shown that a candidate's background is often a strong predictor of the issues they raise (Kaufmann 2004; Sellers 1998; Sides 2006; Sulkin 2009). As a result, ownership may be less about broad partisan differences and more about the specific histories and interests of candidates and their constituencies. For example, there is evidence that there may be a gender component at work, with men seen as better able to handle some issues and women as others; thus, men and women candidates may tend to highlight different issues (see Herrnson, Lay, and Stokes 2003; Kahn 1993). In turn, these choices about which issues to highlight can affect the gender gap in voting. Schaffner's (2006) work on voting in Senate elections showed that, when campaigns focus on "women's issues," women tend to vote Democratic more, but the voting behavior of men is not affected. Accordingly, candidates' issue selection strategies may influence election outcomes in a variety of ways, some straightforward and some more subtle.

Advertising strategies and interactions between candidates

This discussion of ownership and trespassing highlights the inherently dyadic nature of campaigns. After all, candidates do not make choices in a vacuum; most also face opponents who are also deciding which issues to discuss and which positions to take. Data constraints make it difficult to study the dynamics of the strategic interactions between candidates (i.e. how they anticipate and respond to one another's actions), but scholars have devoted considerable attention to two types of potential interaction—dialogue and negativity.

---

[10] The question asked to tap ownership is typically some variant of "Which party do you think is better able to handle [issue]?" Ownership differences are calculated by taking the percentage of respondents who think one party will do a better job and subtracting it from the percentage of respondents who think the other party is better able to handle it.

Dialogue, which has its roots in democratic theory about elections (see, for example, Kelley 1960), is usually defined as the extent to which candidates deliberate with one another about issues during the campaign. Such deliberation should be beneficial to voters, as it enables them to compare directly the views of competing candidates. A common lament, of course, is that, in real-world politics, dialogue is rare, and that candidates are instead more likely to "talk past one another." This point has been the subject of much scholarly debate, as there is a disjuncture between formal work that predicts that competing candidates should never discuss the same issues (e.g. Riker 1996; Simon 2002)[11] and empirical studies of candidates' issue emphases, which find that candidates often raise the same themes (Kaplan, Park, and Ridout 2006; Sigelman and Buell 2004).

A major difficulty in resolving these disagreements is that there has been little consensus about how dialogue should be measured. Some studies implicitly equate partisan trespassing with dialogue, but the two are not the same thing, since a trespassing candidate may be highlighting an issue that the opponent has not raised. For instance, taxes may be a Republican issue, but if the Republican in a race does not discuss it, then there can be no dialogue about it, even if the Democrat does. Along the same lines, Sigelman and Buell are critical of measures that consider only the relative balance of attention to an issue in a campaign, arguing that these capture "the extent to which a race featured even-handed expression of different positions on the issues, not the extent to which the competitors discussed the same issues" (2004, 7). They recommend a measure of "issue convergence," or the degree to which competing candidates' agendas overlap. Using this measure, they find that dialogue in presidential campaigns is common. Kaplan, Park, and Ridout (2006) apply this measure to Senate campaigns, finding more convergence than was predicted by many formal models, but considerably less than is found in presidential races.

Although measures of convergence probably more closely approximate theorists' conceptions of dialogue, they too are subject to criticism. In short, that competing candidates' agendas overlap does not necessarily mean that they directly engage with one another—for instance, by talking about the same dimensions of issues or by responding to each other's claims. In order to study this directly, we would need to delve more deeply into the specific content and timing of candidates' statements. Such nuanced analyses would also help to get at the causal story behind issue selection. For example, if we observe two candidates raising the same issue, did they decide simultaneously (perhaps by both responding to the same outside event), or is one drawing the other in?

Studying these questions does pose a number of challenges, mostly with data availability. News coverage is problematic, particularly for House races, because few receive sustained coverage (Arnold 2004) and because the content of the coverage that appears does not always correspond to the priorities of the candidates (Ridout and

---

[11] The argument here is that, on any issue one might consider, one candidate in the dyad will hold the advantage vis-à-vis the voters, so the other candidate will only be harmed by talking about it and raising its salience. Thus, if both candidates are behaving strategically, they should differentiate their agendas.

Mellen 2007). Fridkin and Kenney (2005) find, for example, that incumbents are typically much more successful than challengers at framing coverage, which could skew the observed relationships between the candidates. Relying on television advertising data presents similar problems, because it is spotty for House challengers and because we are most likely to see advertising for both candidates in races that are unusually competitive, so this kind of advertising does not provide for a representative sample of contests. And, as mentioned above, most House candidates produce and air few advertisements, so we must be careful when making inferences about temporality—that an ad is aired for the first time at a certain date does not mean it was produced then.

Resolving these issues and directly addressing questions about candidate interaction will likely require the collection of data from new and different sources. Candidate websites are one possibility, and have received increasing attention from scholars of campaign communication (see, for example, Druckman, Kifer, and Parkin 2009). Congressional candidates' websites tend to be more rudimentary than presidential candidates', although with each election they have become more advanced and more regularly updated. As such, they may provide a good venue for studying candidates' day-to-day or week-to-week responses to one another. Careful tracking of direct mail could do the same, as could more extended in-person observations of candidates on the campaign trail.

These data would also help to extend work on negativity in congressional campaigns. There is, of course, a huge literature on negative campaigning, but the bulk of it focuses on its effects on voters. A smaller literature highlights the factors explaining variation in negativity across candidates and races. Most notably, in their studies of Senate campaigns, Kahn and Kenney (1999, 2004) find that more competitive races are more negative (though closeness affects incumbents' tendency to go negative more so than non-incumbents), that criticisms do focus on character, but are more often about candidates' policy agendas or positions, and that there are important differences between male and female candidates, with women generally less likely than men to go on the attack (see also Herrnson and Lucas 2006).

Analyses of negativity in congressional campaigns have almost all been based on Senate races (see also Lau and Pomper 2004), so, while it seems likely that similar dynamics should hold in the House, we do not know for sure whether this is true. On average, House campaigns are less competitive than Senate campaigns, so it is likely that overall negativity will be lower. In addition, House candidates' ads are becoming more sophisticated, but until recently they did not approximate the types of negative advertisements we have become accustomed to in up-ballot races (e.g. "morphing" of one face into another). And, as was the case with dialogue, we do not yet have much insight into the back-and-forth interaction between candidates. Thus, although we know that negativity between competing candidates is correlated (i.e. if one campaign is negative, the other is more likely to be so), we do not know precisely how this arises (Lau and Pomper 2004). It might be that both candidates respond to a sense of competition by going negative, or they could adopt a tit for tat strategy, a trigger strategy, or something else. And, as with dialogue, it would be useful to understand whether incumbents or challengers are more successful at drawing the other candidate in.

FUTURE DIRECTIONS

Where does this leave us? One of the advantages of the fact that congressional campaigns have received comparatively little attention is that there are relatively few overtilled topics. However, it is probably safe to say that we now have some answers to basic questions about the emergence of challengers, the nature of position-taking and issue selection, and the prevalence of dialogue and negativity, and can now move the debates forward. For the reasons discussed above, more in-depth studies of candidates and their campaigns are important in and of themselves, but they are also useful for placing findings about voters and voting behavior in context. For instance, in experimental work on campaign effects, they can help to insure that the manipulations are realistic (i.e. that they approximate the ways in which congressional candidates actually criticize their opponents, offer positions, or adopt issue selection strategies). Linking data on candidate behavior with new district-level surveys of voters (like those done by the Congressional Elections Study and the Cooperative Congressional Elections Study) should also provide a better understanding of voters' responses to specific components of campaigns. In addition, congressional scholars might fruitfully draw more heavily on research on voter targeting, particularly on the field experiment studies being done by Gerber and Green and their colleagues (see, for example, Gerber, Green, and Green 2003; Green and Gerber 2008; Panagopoulos and Green 2008), to establish how the modes through which campaign messages are delivered (i.e. in person vs. mediated, radio vs. television, etc.) affect candidates' success.

In looking ahead to future work on House and Senate campaigns, there are four topics that seem particularly undertilled and worthy of further investigation. The first is candidate behavior in primary elections. The systematic study of primaries has been hampered by the fact that many candidates do not face primary challenges, and the presence or absence of a primary challenger seems to be a function both of the vulnerability of the incumbent and of the political culture of a district or state (some have more of a history of contested races). Nonetheless, it would be useful to understand whether congressional candidates' primary campaigns differ from their general election campaigns and, if so, how.[12] Does the need to appear consistent and to avoid charges of flip-flopping mean that their strategies are constant? Or, compared to what happens in the general election, are these candidates more likely to talk about

---

[12] An interesting wrinkle here is that the timing of primaries varies greatly—some states hold them as early as February of an election year, while others do not do so until September. Thus, we might expect that early primaries will be more distinct from general election campaigns than late primaries.

owned issues (to appeal to their base) or trespassed issues (since they are not yet facing an opponent of the opposite party)? Similarly, are they more or less likely to take positions? And what effects, if any, does primary campaign behavior have on general elections and their outcomes (Djupe and Peterson 2002)?

A second area ripe for additional research is candidates' behavior across time. With the exception of some work on the decision-making of repeat challengers (Squire and Smith 1984; Taylor and Boatright 2005), we have almost no longitudinal research on candidates and their strategies. For example, do candidates' position-taking and issue selection patterns change from election to election? Do they appear to learn? If their vote shares go down relative to the previous election, are they more likely to adopt a different strategy in the next campaign? How do progressively ambitious House incumbents running for the Senate change their strategies in those campaigns? An important contribution of such across-time studies of candidates' campaigns is that they will enable researchers to separate out the components of strategy that are relatively stable characteristics of candidates and those that are reactions to the political context.

Third, almost all work on advertising and candidate strategy has focused on the efforts of candidates. This was justifiable, since interest groups, 527s, and the like have been less involved in their own advertising efforts on behalf of congressional candidates (particularly for the House) than in presidential races. Recently, though, they have begun to assert themselves in a more direct way. Understanding the strategies these groups adopt is important. Perhaps of more interest to congressional scholars, though, is to examine how candidates alter their own strategies in response. If a group is running negative ads against a candidate's opponent, does that make the candidate more or less likely to do so him- or herself? Similarly, once in office, are winning candidates as responsive to a group's critiques of their policy record as they are to their challengers' critiques? Participation by outside groups also raises a number of questions about how successful candidates can be at controlling their own messages. In some cases, a group may help a candidate by reinforcing the points he or she wishes to make, but in other cases it may harm a candidate (even one it wishes to help) by making the message too diffuse or by being too negative in criticisms of the opponent, provoking a backlash. Candidates' management of these interactions is becoming an increasingly important component of modern congressional campaigns and so merits study from legislative scholars.

Finally, there is considerable leverage to be gained by uniting work on legislators' behavior as candidates with work on their behavior as policymakers. Although much of the scholarly and popular discussion of campaigns focuses on understanding their effects on vote choice, they also matter in another, often underappreciated, way— by serving as "a main point—perhaps *the* main point—of contact between elected officials and the populace over matters of public policy" (Riker 1996, 3). By linking the electoral and legislative arenas to explore how campaigns shape the content of lawmaking (and vice versa), congressional scholars can offer a unique contribution to the literature. In doing so, we can provide for a more in-depth understanding of legislative behavior and of the place of elections in the democratic process, heeding Fenno's call that: "The study of campaigns might be moved beyond the dominating focus on voters and beyond the dominant notion that campaigns are worth studying only to explain electoral outcomes" (Fenno 1996, 336).

References

ABBE, O., GOODLIFFE, J., HERRNSON, P., and PATTERSON, K. 2003. Agenda Setting in Congressional Elections: The Impact of Issues and Campaigns on Voting Behavior. *Political Research Quarterly*, 56(4): 419–30.

ANSOLABEHERE, S., and IYENGAR, S. 1994. Riding the Wave and Claiming Ownership over Issues: The Joint Effects of Advertising and News Coverage in Campaigns. *Public Opinion Quarterly*, 58(3): 335–57.

——SNYDER, JR., J. M., and STEWART, III, C. 2001. Candidate Positioning in U.S. House Elections. *American Journal of Political Science*, 45(1): 136–59.

ARNOLD, R. D. 1990. *The Logic of Congressional Action*. New Haven: Yale University Press.

——2004. *Congress, the Press, and Political Accountability*. Princeton, NJ: Princeton University Press.

BAILEY, M. 2001. Quiet Influence: The Representation of Diffuse Interests on Postwar Trade Policy. *Legislative Studies Quarterly*, 26(1): 45–80.

BASINGER, S., and ENSLEY, M. 2007. Candidates, Campaigns, or Partisan Conditions? Reevaluating Strategic-Politicians Theory. *Legislative Studies Quarterly*, 32(3): 361–94.

BERELSON, B., LAZARSFELD, P., and McPHEE, W. 1954. *Voting: A Study of Opinion Formation in a Presidential Campaign*. Chicago: University of Chicago Press.

BIANCO, W. 1984. Strategic Decisions on Candidacy in U.S. Congressional Districts. *Legislative Studies Quarterly*, 9(2): 351–64.

BISHIN, B. 2009. *Tyranny of the Minority: The Subconstituency Politics Theory of Representation*. Philadelphia: Temple University Press.

BOATRIGHT, R. G. 2004. *Expressive Politics: The Issue Strategies of Congressional Challengers*. Columbus: Ohio State University Press.

BOND, J., COVINGTON, C., and FLEISHER, R. 1985. Explaining Challenger Quality in Congressional Elections. *Journal of Politics*, 47(2): 510–29.

BORN, R. 1986. Strategic Politicians and Unresponsive Voters. *American Political Science Review*, 80(2): 599–612.

BOVITZ, G., and CARSON, J. 2006. Position-Taking and Electoral Accountability in the U.S. House of Representatives. *Political Research Quarterly*, 59(2): 297–312.

BOX-STEFFENSMEIER, J. 1996. A Dynamic Analysis of the Role of War Chests in Campaign Strategy. *American Journal of Political Science*, 4(2): 352–71.

BRASHER, H. 2003. Capitalizing on Contention: Issue Agendas in U.S. Senate Campaigns. *Political Communication*, 20(4): 453–71.

BUDGE, I., and FARLIE, D. 1983. Party Competition—Selective Emphasis or Direct Confrontation? An Alternative View with Data, pp. 267–306 in *Western European Party Systems*, ed. H. Daadler and P. Mair. Beverly Hills, CA: Sage.

BURDEN, B. 2004. Candidate Positioning in U.S. Congressional Elections. *British Journal of Political Science*, 34(2): 211–27.

BURDEN, B. and WICHOWSKY, A. 2010. The Possibilities of Congressional Elections, pp. 453–70 in *The Oxford Handbook of American Elections and Behavior*, ed. J. Leighley. Oxford: Oxford University Press.

CANES-WRONE, B., BRADY, D. W., and COGAN, J. F. 2002. Out of Step, Out of Office: Electoral Accountability and House Members' Voting. *American Political Science Review*, 96(1): 127–40.

CANON, D. T. 1990. *Actors, Athletes, and Astronauts: Political Amateurs in the United States Congress*. Chicago: University of Chicago Press.

—— 1993. Sacrificial Lambs or Strategic Politicians? Political Amateurs in U.S. House Elections. *American Journal of Political Science*, 37(4): 1119–41.

CARSON, J. 2005. Strategy, Selection, and Candidate Competition in U.S. House and Senate Elections. *Journal of Politics*, 67(1): 1–28.

—— ENGSTROM, E., and ROBERTS, J. 2006. Redistricting, Candidate Entry, and the Politics of Nineteenth Century House Elections. *American Journal of Political Science*, 50(2): 283–93.

—— and ROBERTS, J. 2005. Strategic Politicians and U.S. House Elections, 1874–1914. *Journal of Politics*, 67(2): 474–96.

CLINTON, J. 2006. Representation in Congress: Constituents and Roll Calls in the 106th House. *Journal of Politics*, 68(2): 397–409.

DECKARD, B. S. 1976. Electoral Marginality and Party Loyalty in House Roll Call Voting. *American Journal of Political Science*, 20(3): 469–81.

DJUPE, P., and PETERSON, D. A. M. 2002. The Impact of Negative Campaigning: Evidence from the 1998 Senatorial Primaries. *Political Research Quarterly*, 55(4): 845–60.

DOWNS, A. 1957. *An Economic Theory of Democracy*. New York: Harper.

DRUCKMAN, J., KIFER, M., and PARKIN, M. 2009. Campaign Communications in U.S. Congressional Elections. *American Political Science Review*, 103(3): 343–66.

ERIKSON, R. S. 1971. The Electoral Impact of Congressional Roll Call Voting. *American Political Science Review*, 65(4): 1018–32.

FENNO, R. F. 1978. *Home Style*. Boston: Little, Brown.

—— 1996. *Senators on the Campaign Trail: The Politics of Representation*. Norman: University of Oklahoma Press.

—— 2007. *Congressional Travels: Places, Connections, and Authenticity*. New York: Pearson Longman.

FIORINA, M. P. 1973. Electoral Margins, Constituency Influence, and Policy Moderation: A Critical Assessment. *American Politics Quarterly*, 1(4): 479–98.

—— 1974. *Representatives, Roll Calls, and Constituencies*. Boston: DC Heath.

FOWLER, L., and MCCLURE, R. 1989. *Political Ambition: Who Decides to Run for Congress*. New Haven: Yale University Press.

FOX, R. L., and LAWLESS, J. L. 2005. To Run or Not to Run for Office: Explaining Nascent Political Ambition. *American Journal of Political Science*, 49(3): 642–59.

FRANKLIN, C. H. 1991. Eschewing Obfuscation? Campaigns and the Perception of U.S. Senate Incumbents. *American Political Science Review*, 85(4): 1193–214.

FRIDKIN, K., and KENNEY, P. 2005. Campaign Frames: Can Candidates Influence Media Coverage? pp. 54–75 in *Framing American Politics*, ed. K. Callaghan and F. Schell. Pittsburgh: University of Pittsburgh Press.

FRISCH, S., and KELLY, S. 2006. *Committee Assignment Politics in the U.S. House of Representatives*. Norman: University of Oklahoma Press.

FULTON, S., MAESTAS, C., MAISEL, L. S., and STONE, W. 2006. The Sense of a Woman: Gender and Congressional Ambition. *Political Research Quarterly*, 59(2): 235–48.

GERBER, A. S., GREEN, D. P., and GREEN, M. N. 2003. The Effects of Partisan Direct Mail on Voter Turnout. *Electoral Studies*, 22(4): 563–79.

GOODLIFFE, J. 2001. The Effect of War Chests on Challenger Entry in U.S. House Elections. *American Journal of Political Science*, 45(4): 830–44.

—— 2007. Campaign War Chests and Challenger Quality in Senate Elections. *Legislative Studies Quarterly*, 32(1): 135–56.

GREEN, D., and GERBER, A. 2008. *Get out the Vote: How to Increase Voter Turnout*, 2nd edition. Washington, DC: Brookings Institution Press.

GROFMAN, B. 2004. Downs and Two-Party Convergence. *Annual Review of Political Science*, 7: 25–46.

HALL, R. L. 1996. *Participation in Congress*. New Haven: Yale University Press.

HAMMOND, T., and HUMES, B. 1993. The Spatial Model and Elections, pp. 141–59 in *Information, Participation, and Choice*, ed. B. Grofman. Ann Arbor: University of Michigan Press.

HERRNSON, P. S. 2008. *Congressional Elections*. 2nd edition. Washington, DC: CQ Press.

HERRNSON, P., LAY, C., and STOKES, A. 2003. Women Running 'as Women': Candidate Gender, Campaign Issues and Voter Targeting Strategies, *Journal of Politics*, 65(3): 244–55.

—— and LUCAS, J. 2006. The Fairer Sex? Gender and Negative Campaigning in U.S. Elections. *Political Research Quarterly*, 34(1): 69–94.

HERSHEY, M. R. 1984. *Running for Office: The Political Education of Campaigners*. Chatham, NJ: Chatham House Publishers.

HOLIAN, D. 2004. He's Stealing My Issues! Clinton's Crime Rhetoric and the Dynamics of Issue Ownership. *Political Behavior*, 26(2): 95–124.

IYENGAR, S., and VALENTINO, N. 2000. Who Says What? Source Credibility as a Mediator of Campaign Advertising, pp. 108–29 in *Elements of Reason*, ed. A. Lupia, M. D. McCubbins, and S. L. Popkin. New York: Cambridge University Press.

JACOBSON, G. C. 1978. The Effects of Campaign Spending in Congressional Elections. *American Political Science Review*, 72(2): 469–91.

—— 1990. *The Electoral Origins of Divided Government: Competition in U.S. House Elections, 1946–1988*. Boulder, CO: Westview Press.

—— 2009. *The Politics of Congressional Elections*. 7th edition. New York: Longman.

—— and DIMOCK, M. A. 1994. Checking Out: The Effects of Bank Overdrafts on the 1992 House Elections. *American Journal of Political Science*, 38(3): 601–24.

—— and KERNELL, S. 1983. *Strategy and Choice in Congressional Elections*. 2nd edition. New Haven: Yale University Press.

KAHN, K. F. 1993. Gender Differences in Campaign Messages: The Political Advertisements of Men and Women Candidates for U.S. Senate. *Political Research Quarterly*, 46(3): 481–502.

—— and KENNEY, P. 1999. *The Spectacle of U.S. Senate Campaigns*. Princeton: Princeton University Press.

——— 2004. *No Holds Barred: Negativity in U.S. Senate Campaigns*. Upper Saddle River, NJ: Prentice-Hall.

KAPLAN, N., PARK, D., and Ridout, T. 2006. Dialogue in American Political Campaigns? An Examination of Issue Convergence in Candidate Television Advertising. *American Journal of Political Science*, 50(3): 724–36.

KAUFMANN, K. 2004. Disaggregating and Reexamining Issue Ownership and Vote Choice. *Polity*, 36(2): 283–99.

KAZEE, T., ed. 1994. *Who Runs for Congress: Ambition, Context, and Candidate Emergence*. Washington, DC: Congressional Quarterly Press.

KELLEY, S. 1960. *Political Campaigning: Problems in Creating an Informed Electorate*. Washington, DC: Brookings Institution Press.

KESSLER, D., and KREHBIEL, K. 1996. Dynamics of Cosponsorship. *American Political Science Review*, 90(3): 555–66.

KINGDON, J. W. 1968. *Candidates for Office: Beliefs and Strategies*. New York: Random House.

KOGER, G. 2003. Position-Taking and Cosponsorship in the U.S. House. *Legislative Studies Quarterly*, 28(2): 225–46.

KRASNO, J. S., and GREEN, D. P. 1988. Preempting Quality Challengers in House Elections. *Journal of Politics*, 50(4): 920–36.

KUKLINSKI, J. H. 1977. District Competitiveness and Legislative Roll-Call Behavior: A Reassessment of the Marginality Hypothesis. *American Journal of Political Science*, 21(3): 627–38.

LAU, R. R., and POMPER, G. 2004. *Negative Campaigning: An Analysis of U.S. Senate Elections*. Lanham, MD: Rowman Littlefield.

LAWLESS, J., and FOX, R. 2005. *It Takes a Candidate: Why Women Don't Run for Office*. New York: Cambridge University Press.

LIPINSKI, D., BIANCO, W. T., and WORK, R. 2003. What Happens when House Members 'Run with Congress'? The Electoral Consequences of Institutional Loyalty. *Legislative Studies Quarterly*, 28(3): 413–29.

LIPSITZ, K. 2004. Democratic Theory and Political Campaigns. *Journal of Political Philosophy*, 12(2): 163–89.

—— TROST, C., GROSSMAN, M., and SIDES, J. 2005. What Voters Want from Political Campaign Communication. *Political Communication*, 22: 337–54.

LUBLIN, D. I. 1994. Quality, Not Quantity: Strategic Politicians in U.S. Senate Elections, 1952–1990. *Journal of Politics*, 56(1): 228–41.

MAESTAS, C., FULTON, S., MAISEL, L. S., and STONE, W. 2006. When to Risk It? Institutions, Ambitions, and the Decision to Run for the U.S. House. *American Political Science Review*, 100(2): 195–208.

—— and RUGELEY, C. 2008. Assessing the 'Experience Bonus' through Examining Strategic Entry, Candidate Quality, and Campaign Receipts in U.S. House Elections. *American Journal of Political Science*, 52(3): 520–35.

MAISEL, L. S., and STONE, W. 1997. Determinants of Candidate Emergence in U.S. House Elections: An Exploratory Study. *Legislative Studies Quarterly*, 22(1): 79–96.

MATTHEWS, D. R. 1960. *U.S. Senators and Their World*. Chapel Hill: University of North Carolina Press.

MAYHEW, D. R. 1974. *Congress: The Electoral Connection*. New Haven: Yale University Press.

MILLER, W. E., and STOKES, D. E. 1963. Constituency Influence in Congress. *American Political Science Review*, 57(1): 45–56.

NORPOTH, H., and BUCHANAN, B. 1992. Wanted: The Education President. Issue Trespassing by Political Candidates. *Public Opinion Quarterly*, 56(1): 87–99.

PAGE, B. 1976. The Theory of Political Ambiguity. *American Political Science Review*, 70(3): 742–52.

PANAGOPOULOS, C., and GREEN, D. 2008. Field Experiments Testing the Impact of Radio Advertisements on Electoral Competition. *American Journal of Political Science*, 52(1): 156–68.

PETROCIK, J. 1996. Issue Ownership in Presidential Elections, with a 1980 Case Study. *American Journal of Political Science*, 40(3): 825–50.

RAGSDALE, L., and COOK, T. E. 1987. Representatives' Actions and Challengers' Reactions: Limits to Candidate Connections in the House. *American Journal of Political Science*, 31(1): 45–81.

RIDOUT, T., and MELLEN, JR., R. 2007. Does the Media Agenda Reflect the Candidates' Agenda? *Harvard International Journal of Press/Politics*, 12(2): 44–62.

RIKER, W. 1986. *The Art of Political Manipulation*. New Haven: Yale University Press.

——1996. *The Strategy of Rhetoric: Campaigning for the American Constitution*. New Haven: Yale University Press.

RINGQUIST, E., and DASSE, C. 2004. Lies, Damned Lies, and Campaign Promises: Environmental Legislation in the 105th Congress. *Social Science Quarterly*, 85(2): 400–19.

SCHAFFNER, B. 2006. Priming Gender: Campaigning on Women's Issues in U.S. Senate Elections. *American Journal of Political Science*, 49(4): 803–17.

SCHILLER, W. J. 1995. Senators as Political Entrepreneurs: Using Bill Sponsorship to Shape Legislative Agendas. *American Journal of Political Science*, 39(1): 186–203.

SCHLESINGER, J. 1966. *Ambition and Politics: Political Careers in the United States*. Chicago: Rand-McNally.

SELLERS, P. J. 1998. Strategy and Background in Congressional Campaigns. *American Political Science Review*, 92(1): 159–71.

SHAW, D. 2006. *The Race to 270: The Electoral College and the Campaign Strategies of 2000 and 2004*. Chicago: University of Chicago Press.

SHEPSLE, K. 1972. The Strategy of Ambiguity: Uncertainty and Electoral Competition. *American Political Science Review*, 66(2): 555–68.

SIDES, J. 2006. The Origins of Campaign Agendas. *British Journal of Political Science*, 36(3): 407–36.

——2007. The Consequences of Campaign Agendas. *American Politics Research*, 35(4): 465–88.

SIGELMAN, L., and BUELL, E. 2004. Avoidance or Engagement? Issue Convergence in U.S. Presidential Campaigns, 1960–2000. *American Journal of Political Science*, 48(4): 650–61.

SIMON, A. F. 2002. *The Winning Message: Candidate Behavior, Campaign Discourse, and Democracy*. Cambridge: Cambridge University Press.

SPILIOTES, C., and VAVRECK, L. 2002. Campaign Advertising: Partisan Convergence or Divergence? *Journal of Politics*, 64(1): 249–61.

SQUIRE, P. 1989. Challengers in U.S. Senate Elections. *Legislative Studies Quarterly*, 14(4): 531–47.

——1991. Preemptive Fund-Raising and Challenger Profile in Senate Elections. *Journal of Politics*, 53(4): 1150–64.

——1992. Challenger Quality and Voting Behavior in U.S. Senate Elections. *Legislative Studies Quarterly*, 17(2): 247–63.

——and SMITH, E. R. A. N. 1984. Repeat Challengers in Congressional Elections. *American Politics Quarterly*, 12(1): 51–70.

STOKES, D. 1992. Valence Politics, pp. 141–64 in *Electoral Politics*, ed. D. Kavanagh. New York: Oxford University Press.

STONE, W., and MAISEL, L. S. 2003. The Not-So-Simple Calculus of Winning: Potential U.S. House Candidates' Nomination and General Election Chances. *Journal of Politics*, 65(4): 951–77.

——————and MAESTAS, C. 2004. Quality Counts: Extending the Strategic Politician Model of Incumbent Deterrence. *American Journal of Political Science*, 48(3): 479–96.

SULKIN, T. 2005. *Issue Politics in Congress*. New York: Cambridge University Press.

——2009. Campaign Appeals and Legislative Action. *Journal of Politics*, 71(3): 1093–108.

——MORIARTY, C., and HEFNER, V. 2007. Congressional Candidates' Issue Agendas On- and Off-Line. *Harvard International Journal of Press/Politics*, 12(2): 63–79.

SULKIN, T. and SWIGGER, N. 2008. Is There Truth in Advertising? Campaign Ad Images as Signals about Legislative Behavior. *Journal of Politics*, 70(1): 232–44.

SULLIVAN, J., and O'CONNOR, R. E. 1972. Electoral Choice and Popular Control of Public Policy: The Case of the 1966 House Elections. *American Political Science Review*, 66(4): 1256–68.

——and USLANER, E. 1978. Congressional Behavior and Electoral Marginality. *American Journal of Political Science*, 22(3): 536–53.

TAYLOR, A., and BOATRIGHT, R. 2005. The Personal and the Political in Repeat Congressional Candidacies. *Political Research Quarterly*, 58(4): 599–607.

TOMZ, M., and VAN HOUWELING, R. 2008. Candidate Positioning and Voter Choice. *American Political Science*, 102(3): 303–18.

——2009. The Electoral Implications of Candidate Ambiguity. *American Political Science Review*, 103(1): 83–98.

VAVRECK, L. 2001. The Reasoning Voter Meets the Strategic Candidate: Signals and Specificity in Campaign Advertising, 1998. *American Politics Research*, 29(5): 507–29.

WAWRO, G. 2000. *Legislative Entrepreneurship in the U.S. House of Representatives*. Ann Arbor: University of Michigan Press.

WESTLYE, M. C. 1991. *Senate Elections and Campaign Intensity*. Baltimore: Johns Hopkins University Press.

CHAPTER 9

CONGRESSIONAL REDISTRICTING

MICHAEL P. McDONALD

MEMBERS of the United States House of Representatives represent geographically defined constituencies known as districts. Redistricting is the redrawing of these districts' boundaries and may occur for legislative districts at all levels of government in countries around the world. An elaborate redistricting process exists for United States congressional districts, which reflects the nation's decentralization of power through its federal system of government. The fifty state governments are primarily responsible for drawing congressional districts within their borders, with modest—but important—federal oversight. The institutions and players vary across states. The political parties, incumbents, and minority voting rights groups that are key players in the process believe that the representational stakes are high. This confluence of varying institutions, highly motivated political actors, and observable effects has thus attracted numerous scholars to the study of redistricting.

REDISTRICTING MOTIVES

How votes are aggregated through any electoral system affects political outcomes. Single-member district systems tend to distort vote shares into seat shares more than other representational systems, to the detriment of non-geographically concentrated minor political parties (Duverger 1959; Lijphart 1999). Those who control redistricting can further manipulate these distortions to their advantage through a strategy known as gerrymandering. This pejorative term arises from an oddly shaped 1812 state legislative district enacted by Massachusetts Governor Elbridge Gerry, which a political cartoonist likened to a salamander, or a "Gerry-mander." Of course, gerrymandering occurred before it was given its modern name. For example, Patrick Henry proposed a Virginia redistricting plan designed to deny James Madison a congressional seat (Weber 1998). Gerrymandering has thus been used through the ages to affect the fortunes of political parties, the careers of incumbents, and the representation of racial and ethnic groups.

To understand the mechanics of partisan gerrymandering, consider first a single district in isolation. The electoral outcome in the district can be manipulated by placing more or fewer supporters of a political party within the district. Now consider a redistricting plan for an entire state or for another jurisdiction. In the theoretical extreme, it is possible for a political party that receives a quarter of the votes to win half of the seats, if it arranges its supporters such that they constitute a bare majority in half of the districts. In practice, the optimal partisan gerrymander is one that efficiently distributes partisans across districts such that a party expects to win elections in these districts by a comfortable margin in a typical election (Cain 1985; Owen and Grofman 1988), given reasonable geographical constraints (Musgrave 1977; Sherstyuk 1998). Optimal partisan gerrymandering may also require creating extremely safe districts for the opposition, so that their votes are wasted in seats that they win by an overwhelming margin. In this manner, it is even possible for a party that wins fewer votes to win more seats than its competitor, as happened in 1996 when Republicans won a majority of U.S. House seats, with approximately 280,000 fewer votes tallied across all congressional districts than the Democrats had.

The distribution of partisan supporters among districts may also be manipulated by varying the number of persons within districts, a practice known as malapportionment. Prior to the 1960s, state legislators—who often have primary authority to draw district lines—were loath to redistrict, since this upset connections between representatives and their constituents. Inaction created "creeping malapportionment" (Johnston 2002, 5), whereby fast-growing urban areas were incrementally afforded less representation than slow-growing rural areas. In the landmark case *Baker* v *Carr* 369 U.S. 186 (1962), the U.S. Supreme Court ruled that redistricting was not a political question outside the court's oversight and indicated that the courts would address malapportionment if the states did not—which it did for congressional districts in *Wesberry* v *Sanders* 376 U.S. 1 (1964). Redistricting must now occur in a timely manner, following a national decennial census, although state laws dictate whether states may redistrict more than once between censuses (Levitt and McDonald 2007).

The distribution of partisan supporters into districts is not solely determinative of election outcomes; it is just one of several inputs. Another important factor is the electoral advantage that incumbents tend to have over their challengers (e.g. Gelman and King 1990; Jacobson 2009). The power of incumbency can be diminished during redistricting through incumbent displacement (Cain 1985), for instance by pairing two incumbents from the same party into the same district. Another strategy is to shift dramatically a district's boundaries and thereby introduce new constituents into a district. These new, unfamiliar constituents—compared to continuing constituents within an incumbent's old and new district—tend to vote in congressional elections at lower rates (Hayes and McKee 2009), and they tend to vote for incumbents at lower rates (Ansolabehere, Snyder, and Stewart 2000; Desposato and Petrocik 2003). This latter dynamic explains another phenomenon, whereby strong candidates tend to emerge to challenge temporarily vulnerable incumbents in the election following a redistricting (Carson, Engstrom, and Roberts 2006; Hetherington, Larson, and Globetti 2003). Together, these studies suggest why, even though parties and incumbents attempt to reduce electoral competition by manipulating the partisanship of districts through redistricting (McDonald 2006a; compare Abramowitz, Alexander, and Gunning 2006), incumbents are often at greater electoral risk following redistricting (King 1989).

Redistricting can also be used to enhance incumbents' reelection chances by removing unfriendly voters from a district and by adding potential supporters. Redistricting thus presents an opportunity for a bipartisan logroll whereby incumbents of different parties are willing to trade territory containing each other's supporters to improve their collective reelection chances (Issacharoff 2002). In the post-2000 round of redistricting, nineteen incumbents situated in districts leaning towards the other party were placed into more compatible districts (Jacobson 2003; see also Cain 1985). When severe population shifts occur between states—causing a state to gain or lose congressional representation—or within states, district boundaries may dramatically change to achieve equal population of districts. In these circumstances, incumbent protection may be more defensive in nature.

If redistricting can affect partisan fortunes, it stands to reason that it can affect representation for any identifiable group, particularly racial and ethnic minorities. In 1965, the federal government enacted the Voting Rights Act (VRA) to protect minority voting rights. There is general agreement that the Voting Rights Act has been resoundingly successful at providing opportunities for minorities to elect thousands of minority preferred candidates to public office at all levels of government (Davidson and Grofman 1994). There is disagreement whether or not the so-called informal "65 percent rule" followed by the courts (Brace, Grofman, et al. 1988) is still the minimum minority population threshold needed to assure that a minority candidate of choice can be elected, and to what degree different minority communities form electoral coalitions (Cameron, Epstein, and O'Halloran 1996; Lublin 1999). Because minority–majority districts tend to be overwhelmingly Democratic—except for Cuban–American majority districts—they can be inefficient from a Democratic gerrymandering standpoint (Brace, Grofman, and Handley 1987; Lublin 1997), which may have contributed to Democratic losses in the 1994 mid-term elections (Grofman and Handley 1998). However, the presence of minority–majority districts may constrain Republican gerrymanders by forcing the creation of more Democratic seats than is optimal (Shotts 2001). There is also a substantive debate as to whether or not minority policy interests are furthered by the continued creation of minority–majority districts (Canon 1999; Epstein and O'Halloran 1999; Thernstrom and Thernstrom 1997). Robust debate on these issues will likely continue as the level of white crossover voting for minority candidates of choice evolves, the election of Barack Obama notwithstanding (Ansolabahere, Persily, and Stewart 2010).

REDISTRICTING INSTITUTIONS

Political actors attempt to achieve their various goals within U.S. states' redistricting institutions. In most countries that redistrict, a national commission is responsible for drawing lines. The commission may by the sole authority, or may serve an advisory role by submitting plans for legislative approval (Handley 2008). In accordance with Article I, Section 4 of the U.S. Constitution—which states: "The Times, Places and Manner of holding Elections for Senators and Representatives, shall be prescribed in each State by the Legislature thereof; but the Congress may at any time by law make or alter such regulations, except as to the places of choosing Senators"—each state is responsible for drawing their congressional districts, within any federally imposed regulation. The institutional structures vary among states, and can even vary for congressional and state legislative redistricting within the same state (Butler and Cain 1992; Levitt 2008; McDonald 2004). Among the states that have more than one congressional district, thirty-four states use the legislative process exclusively for congressional redistricting. These states' constitutions are often silent on the congressional redistricting process, so the legislative process is accepted by default. North Carolina's constitution grants the legislature sole authority, without the possibility of a governor's veto. Maryland's constitution requires that the governor propose plans to the legislature for approval.

There has been much interest in redistricting commissions, since such institutions are the norm in other countries. In the post-2000 census round of congressional redistricting, thirteen states used a commission at some stage. An advisory commission proposed plans to the legislature in Iowa, Maine, New York, Ohio, and Rhode Island. Indiana provides for a backup commission if the legislative process stalemates. Among these advisory and backup commissions, only Maine's advisory commission is described in the state's constitution. In all other states, these commissions exist by state law or by legislative resolution. Legislatures are not bound to use non-constitutional commissions for future redistricting, even if they exist under state law (see *O'Lear* v *Miller* No. 222 F. Supp. 2d 850, E.D.). Indeed, a typical state legislative chamber has a *de facto* advisory commission in the form of committees whose jurisdiction covers congressional redistricting; however, real plan-making power is often reserved to legislative leaders. Connecticut's constitution calls for an advisory commission and, in the event that it needs to be used, a separate backup commission. Arizona, California (as of 2010) Hawaii, Idaho, Montana, New Jersey, and Washington state constitutions invest a commission with sole congressional redistricting authority.

The courts play an important role at the end of the redistricting process. When the federal courts mandated that districts must have equal population, the courts became the reversionary point if a state fails to adopt a plan following a national census (Cox and Katz 2002). Courts may also intervene if there is a constitutional defect for redistricting criteria, which is discussed in more detail below. Some states require state Supreme Court review of a redistricting plan before it can become law, but only Idaho requires this review for congressional districts. States covered by Section 5 of the Voting Rights Act must have their plans approved by the Department of Justice or the District Court of DC to verify that minority representation is not degraded. Litigation results if no plan is approved.

Control of the redistricting process can be used to predict the type of redistricting plan that will be adopted (Cain and Campagna 1987; McDonald 2004). For those states that use the legislative process (or their two variants), when one party controls the process, a partisan gerrymander usually results. When control is divided, a bipartisan incumbent protection gerrymander compromise or court action will follow. Although one might consider courts neutral arbiters, they often adopt one of the plans proposed by the political parties (Butler and Cain 1992; McDonald 2006b), so expectations of the partisan character of the likely court to hear the case will influence bipartisan negotiations. These expectations may not be realized when other political considerations intrude. For example, in the post-2000 round of redistricting California Democrats—who controlled the state government—forged a bipartisan compromise when Republicans threatened to place a redistricting reform initiative on the ballot (Lawrence 2001).

Commissions' institutions also structure outcomes. When they have an uneven number of partisan-appointed members who adopt a plan on a majority vote, a partisan gerrymander is likely to result. If they adopt a plan on a super-majority vote, a bipartisan compromise will likely follow unless one party controls a super-majority on the commission. Where they begin with an equal number of partisan appointees who adopt a plan on a majority vote, commissioners either select a tie-breaking chairman by a supermajority vote, or have a tie-breaker appointed if they cannot agree to a tie-breaker or cannot adopt a plan. In the former case, a bipartisan compromise is structured in the selection of the tie-breaker by the commission. In the latter case, expectations of the appointing authority's—typically, the state Supreme Court's—preferred candidate will shape negotiations and usually lead to a partisan gerrymander. When an advisory commission is used, legislatures may adopt plans on majority or super-majority votes and the subsequent legislative action will dictate outcomes.

Typical research exploring redistricting effects correlates the kind of redistricting plan that is adopted with election outputs. Some scholars, typically in earlier studies, simply use partisan control of state government as their key independent variable (e.g. Abramowitz 1983; Born 1985; Erikson 1972). Although this measurement is "admirable for its simplicity, directness, and concreteness" (Niemi and Winsky 1992, 565), it is obviously deficient in commission states and where courts adopted plans, and may run afoul of instances where other political considerations confounded the expected outcome, such as in the case of California, described above. For this reason, a preferred measure scores the political character of the adopted plan (Basehart and

Comer 1991; Gelman and King 1994b; McDonald 2004). However, this measurement approach is susceptible to subjectivity. An expert opinion must be rendered on the basis of the circumstances of a plan's adoption and its predicted effects at the time of adoption, which borders on tautological reasoning for research agendas that correlate gerrymandering types and outcomes.

Another approach to study redistricting is to classify institutions along factors such as whether or not the legislature plays a role, or whether an "independent" commission produced a plan (Abramowitz, Alexander, and Gunning 2006). A problem with this approach is that commissions are typically not 'independent' from the legislature. Often, legislative leaders select commission members directly. Consider Washington's commission. Section 43 of the state constitution provides that legislative leaders of the two largest political parties in each legislative chamber select the commission's four members (a fifth non-voting chairman is selected by these four members). The commission adopts a congressional plan with approval from three out of four members, and the legislature may amend the adopted plan by a two-thirds vote. Washington's process is designed to produce a bipartisan compromise negotiated by representatives of the legislative leadership, not a plan free from political influence. While there are instances where state legislative politics intrude into congressional redistricting (e.g. McDonald 2004, 380), often state legislatures defer to the wishes of their congressional delegation (Cain 1984; Boatright 2004). The different plans that may be produced when members of Congress consult with a legislature or a commission are thus theoretically underdeveloped.

The notion that independent commissions may reduce political influence strays into normative debates about redistricting reform. Some argue that, since all redistricting plans inherently have political effects, the broad representative nature of a legislature makes it the best body to deliberate on thorny redistricting debates (e.g. Lowenstein and Steinberg 1985). Reformers argue that the potential for self-interested abuse is too great to allow individuals to draw their own districts, and they believe that this goal may be achieved by selecting impartial political actors as commissioners (McDonald 2007). The 1960 Alaska constitution (Article VI § 6) innovated this approach by requiring that "none [of the state legislative redistricting commissioners]...may be public employees or officials." Other states have adopted similar language, though sometimes a political operative—such as a lobbyist, a relative, or a retired staff member or elected official—may still be selected, so these prohibitions in practice have not limited political influence. Hawaii and Missouri (state legislature only) constitutions remove the potential conflict of interest of persons drawing their own districts by prohibiting commissioners from running for office in the districts they draw. (This prohibition vis-à-vis congressional redistricting may be unenforceable, since the U.S. Supreme Court ruled in *U.S. Term Limits, Inc.* v *Thornton*, 514 U.S. 779 (1995) that states cannot impose qualifications for congressional candidates in addition to those in the U.S. constitution.) These approaches were united in subsequent Idaho and Alaska reforms; furthermore, prospective Arizona and California commission members must abide by strict qualifications that attempt to disqualify those with a conflict of interest, and they are further vetted by a state administrative body before legislative leaders are allowed to select from the pool of potential candidates.

The reform of redistricting institutions raises the question as to why and under what conditions alternative redistricting institutions will be selected. There have been two waves of commission adoption. Prior to the early 1970s, and particularly immediately following *Baker v Carr*, commissions were adopted in order to ensure that a plan was produced in a timely and regular manner, so as to avoid malapportionment (Matsusaka 2006). Subsequently, commissions ostensibly designed to limit political influence by investing redistricting authority into a redistricting commission have been generally adopted through constitutional amendment ballot initiatives or referendums (excepting advisory commissions, which are usually adopted by statutes or legislative resolutions where the legislature retains a veto). These more recent redistricting commissions may be more "independent" in character, since they have elaborate structures to select commissioners, require transparency in the process, must follow strict criteria, and require public participation (McDonald 2007).

We may expect that a redistricting commission would be designed to achieve certain electoral goals, as is the case with electoral system choice, more broadly defined (March and Olsen 1996). Often a political party without redistricting control is likely to support a ballot initiative or a referendum. Recent Ohio experience is a prime example of the politics involved (McDonald 2008). Following the failure of a redistricting reform ballot initiative in 2005, legislative Democrats proposed a ballot referendum to reform the then Republican-controlled state legislative Apportionment Board, an act which requires state legislative approval. All the Democrats and no Republicans voted for the referendum. Since partisan control of the bicameral state legislature was divided, the referendum failed to be placed on the ballot. Following the 2006 elections, Democrats took control of the state offices that constitute a majority of the state legislative Apportionment Board, while the legislature remained divided. Republicans proposed the exact same referendum; and this time all Democrats voted against, and all Republicans voted for it, and it again failed to win legislative approval. When such initiatives or referendums do make it on the ballot, average voters know little about the arcane redistricting process (McDonald 2008). In this informational vacuum, voters tend to follow informational cues from party leaders to figure out who will be the likely winners and losers of redistricting reform and vote in accordance with their partisan attachments (Tolbert, Smith, and Green 2009). Despite the challenges to passing redistricting reform, states like Arizona (in 2000) and California (in 2008 and 2010) have been successful at adopting reform, and states that permit ballot initiative are more likely to have redistricting commissions (Matsusaka 2006, 161). While much has been made about high-profile California and Ohio redistricting reform failures in 2005, the politics of reform success are not as well understood.

REDISTRICTING CRITERIA

A theme woven through this narrative is that redistricting authorities are constrained in how districts may be drawn. The federal government has imposed some criteria through its oversight power granted in Article I, Section 4 of the U.S. Constitution.

These federal requirements may overlay state-imposed requirements. However, while all states have criteria for their state legislative districts, thirty-four states have no formal criteria for congressional districts (see Levitt 2008, 69; I include in this list states that may impose criteria if their state had more than one congressional district). Nearly all states with redistricting commissions have formal criteria to guide commissions' actions, which poses an identification problem for studies that wish to examine the effect of institutions and criteria on redistricting outcomes.

Criteria are used to constrain redistricting, and are therefore viewed as another means to reduce gerrymandering mischief. There are generally two types of criteria: those based on process and those based on outcomes (Cox 2004; McDonald 2007). Process-based criteria include equal population, contiguity, compactness, and respect for existing geographic or political boundaries. Since these criteria do not consider politics, they are often considered politically neutral and are labeled 'traditional redistricting principles.' However, they can, intentionally or unintentionally, have predictable political effects, or what Parker (1990) calls 'second-order bias.' In an example described by Parker, Hinds County, Mississippi Supervisorial districts were drawn on the basis of the seemingly neutral criterion that districts should have equal road mileage, since the county is responsible for maintaining county roads. This criterion meant that the county's five districts should have an equal balance of rural and urban areas, since county roads are longer than city roads. Jackson's minority communities were effectively divided among the five districts, and their voting strength was thereby diluted. Outcome-based criteria seek to meet political goals directly rather than hope that a set of criteria will fortuitously achieve such goals in a politically blind manner; they include the Voting Rights Act, political fairness, and competition.

Process-based redistricting criteria

Federal law currently mandates single-member congressional districts (Federal Code Title 2, Chapter 1 § 2c). As Martis (1982) details in his historical atlas of congressional districts, some states created multi-member at-large districts in the past. Over time, "the use of single-member districts became increasingly prevalent" (Butler and Cain 1992, 25). This notion was enshrined into federal law in 1842, but historical enforcement of this provision was virtually non-existent. Alabama was the last state to use multi-member at-large districts in 1960, when the state lost a seat to apportionment and the state legislature failed to reach compromise on a redistricting plan. While single-member districts are in use today, some states do have alternative electoral systems to traditional plurality-win, such as Louisiana's second-ballot system and New York's party cross-nominations (Cox 1997).

As mentioned above, the U.S. Supreme Court application of an equal population standard to districts is why redistricting occurs now with regular frequency following each decennial census, although state law determines if redistricting may occur more than once a decade (Levitt and McDonald 2007). At the time of application, the equal population requirement was anticipated to constrain gerrymandering by limiting the technique of malapportionment (White and Thomas 1964). In retrospect, the standard appears to have erased a pro-Republican electoral advantage outside the South, which was realized by malapportionment (Cox and Katz 2002; Erikson 1972); and it altered the distribution of federal money to over-represented counties (Ansolabehere, Gerber, and Snyder 2002), though inequities exist today because districts are not absolutely equally apportioned to states (Elis, Malhotra, and Meredith 2009). However, it was not a gerrymandering cure, as Gelman and King (1994b: 553) note: "population equality guarantees almost no form of fairness beyond numerical equality of population." Equal population is insufficient to limit gerrymandering techniques other than malapportionment. Indeed, to achieve a legal "safe harbor" from a constitutional challenge, a state's congressional plan needs to have the absolute minimum population deviation of one or zero persons between districts. By encouraging fine-tuning of districts at the city block level in order to attain absolute population equality, this requirement may unintentionally aid gerrymandering, such as by enabling the removal of potential primary and general election challengers to incumbents. Frequent redistricting may have further encouraged practice towards the perfection of gerrymandering techniques (Niemi and Winsky 1992, 566).

The U.S. constitution requires the apportionment of congressional districts to the states on the basis of total population, but there is no federal requirement that all people must be counted when districts' populations are equalized during redistricting. Indeed, the constitutions of Hawaii (Article IV § 4) and Kansas (Article 10 § 1) permit removing non-residents from the population counts for redistricting. Further adjustments to population for prisoners and non-citizens loom as emerging redistricting policy issues. Nearly all states disfranchise felony prisoners. These felons tend to have formerly lived in urban areas, but they are incarcerated in rural prisons. For redistricting purposes, these non-voters tend to buoy the populations of rural districts, whose representatives tend to favor tough sentencing requirements—perhaps to support their prison industry, or so the reform argument goes (Wagner 2006). The U.S. Supreme Court has supported Hawaii's use of voter registration as an approximation of the resident population for redistricting purposes and has more generally suggested that the voting-eligible population can be used; but lower courts have denied specific adjustments for non-citizens and minors (Reader 1994). These denials for citizenship and for minor adjustments have been rendered on the basis of representation, implying that representatives of districts with substantial non-citizen or minor populations can effectively represent these ineligible constituents. If states do make felon population adjustments, one might imagine that the inevitable legal arguments will center on representation. While one may assume that the policy preferences of prisoners and of the representatives of their prisons are at odds, there is no scholarly study confirming this hypothesis. Furthermore, a citizenship adjustment has not been heard at the U.S. Supreme Court level, and it has been years since such a case has been litigated, other than in a voting rights context, so this question may be ripe for a test case.

A reason why the issue of voting-eligible adjustment to population data has not been more prevalent in the past is that the necessary data to make such adjustments have generally not been available during redistricting; but this will change for the post-2010 redistricting round. The data used for redistricting are among the first data released by the Census Bureau. The PL94–171 file, named after the federal public law that mandates it, must be released by April 1 in the year following the decennial census. The PL94–171 file has total and voting-age population counts by racial and ethnic categories. These racial and ethnic data are necessary for racial bloc voting analyses to check compliance with the Voting Rights Act. There is no felony, citizenship, or any other data, as in the past the Census Bureau has not had enough time to process these additional data, which have been found typically on the census long form distributed to a sample of persons. As of 2005, the Census Bureau now conducts an annual American Community Survey (ACS), which is a large-sample, ongoing survey that is the replacement for the census long form. The ACS, with its rich array of demographic data, will now be available during redistricting. A caution for those wishing to make a voting-eligible adjustment or to examine demographic characteristics of districts is that the PL94–171 data are data aggregated at what is known as the 'block' level—essentially, a city block in urban areas—while the five-year ACS average is aggregated to higher levels of geography, which may still have a relatively large degree of uncertainty due to statistical sampling and other weighting issues. Still, it will be possible to estimate ACS data within alternative configurations of congressional districts created out of census blocks, and rolling five-year ACS data averages at the congressional district level may be a resource available to scholars in the future.

The aggregated nature of census data into census geography has ramifications for redistricting (Butler and Cain 1992, 42), so it is important to understand these data. In order to protect the confidentiality of respondents, census data are aggregated into geographic designations known as census geography. The smallest unit is the census block, and there are higher levels of aggregation, known as block groups and tracts. Political features may also be mapped into voting tabulation districts, which is the Census Bureau's generic name for wards and voting precincts; into census places, which may generally be thought of as cities, though there exist small census places that are not formal government entities; into election districts of various sorts; into counties; and into states. Congressional districts must have minimal population deviations that, almost always, can only be achieved by building districts out of census blocks. These blocks' boundaries are generally roads, rivers, and other visible features, and generally they respect political boundaries. The overlay of these boundaries permits disaggregation of election data into census blocks for evaluation of alternative districting scenarios. Census blocks can be split by a district line, but usually such splits occur in census blocks without population, since splitting a block that contains population may require justification if a redistricting plan is challenged for violating equal population.

A generally non-controversial requirement is that districts be contiguous, or con-nected. Contiguity invokes the concept that districts should define geographic areas that share common identities. From 1842 to 1929 (except for the period 1850–61), federal law required House districts to be contiguous (Altman 1998a). Although contiguity was dropped as a federal requirement in 1929, states generally respect contiguity or may have it explicitly stated in their state constitutions. Sometimes contiguity must be violated to connect islands, for example. However, there are examples where contiguity is stretched to an extreme. For example, in the 2000's decade, Ohio's 9th Congressional District is connected only by the Sandusky Bay Bridge, and New Jersey's 10th and 13th Congressional Districts apparently cross each other in Newark Bay. Altman (1998a) describes similar historical examples, including districts that touch only at a point. Although it is not a congressional district, Wisconsin's 61st Assembly district is simply not contiguous, as this Racine district includes a city park included in a city ward that is not contiguous to the city proper. Wisconsin's constitution requires that all districts be contiguous; so, to address this defect, the state passed a law declaring all wards contiguous (Wisconsin Code 5.15(2)(f)).

From 1901 to 1929, federal law required congressional districts to be compact. The 1901 congressional debate illuminates the difficulties of implementing a compactness standard that have plagued scholars and courts. When asked when a district is sufficiently compact, Representative Kluttz (D-NC) replied that compactness was intended "to prevent shoe-string districts" (quoted in Altman 1998a, 172); but no other definition was offered. It is perhaps not without irony, then, that the U.S. Supreme Court found North Carolina's 12th Congressional District used in the 1990s to violate compactness. This minority–majority district respected contiguity by tying together geographically dispersed African-American communities by following the I–85 median. In *Shaw v Reno* 509 U.S. 630 (1993), the U.S. Supreme Court found this district constitutionally impermissible, because racial considerations predominated over other criteria such as compactness; however, the court has ruled that compactness may be violated to protect incumbents (*Miller v Johnson*, 515 U.S. 900 (1995)). Perhaps the best example of violation of compactness committed in the 2000s' first decade in order to protect an incumbent is Illinois's 17th Congressional District, which cobbles together Democrats in Downstate Illinois by—at one point—cutting a block-wide path through Springfield, composed of strip malls and a golf course, in order to include a union area to the east, in Decatur.

The practical application of compactness as a reform goal is to prevent the intrusion of politics into the redistricting process. An intuition is that finger-like extensions and other non-compact shapes are evidence of gerrymandering. While these preceding examples are "shoe-string districts," a difficulty has been in devising a concrete measurement of compactness. There is thus considerable scholarly interest in formulating the best compactness measure, and to this end scholars have proposed over thirty different measures (Altman 1998b). Yet devising the best compactness measure is surprisingly difficult, as a measure will typically favor certain shapes over others, which may appear to be more compact upon visual inspection (Young 1988). Furthermore, most compactness measures are based on ideal shapes and not on practical application to districts drawn over census geography. For example, districts following straight-edged county boundaries will generally fare better on measures that minimize district perimeter lengths, while circular districts will fare poorly on these measures, since they are drawn out of census blocks, which do not have nicely rounded borders (McDonald 2009). One group of scholars thus recommends evaluating multiple compactness measures for all districts in a redistricting plan, rather than focusing on the application of one compactness measure to a single district (Niemi, Grofman, et al. 1990). And compactness is not, in itself, politically neutral, and thus it is not a cure for gerrymandering, as a geographically compact political party may be disadvantaged by compact districts (Altman 1998b; McDonald 2009; for a comparative perspective, see also Barkan, Densham, and Rushton 2006; Monroe and Rose 2002).

Another redistricting goal is to respect political subdivisions such as counties, cities, and even wards (i.e. voting precincts). This goal is rooted in the era prior to *Baker v Carr*, when congressional districts—except those in populous urban areas—were typically composed of whole counties (Martis 1982), and state legislative districts were apportioned to counties on the basis of their population. Respecting political subdivisions and communities of interest may further foster better linkages between constituents and their representatives (Engstrom 2005; Niemi, Powell, and Bicknell 1986). Winburn and Wagner (2010, 383) argue that "upholding county boundaries is effective protection against the negative effects of gerrymandering" (see also Winburn 2008). However, as in the case of the partisan consequences of compactness, respecting county boundaries may predictably disfavor a party concentrated within populous urban counties (McDonald 2009).

A seemingly related redistricting goal is to respect communities of interest. Yet a community of interest is not necessarily congruent with a political subdivision, as "these do not always coincide with other kinds of communities, such as ethnic and racial neighborhoods, topographical features, media markets, socioeconomic homogeneity, and the like" (Butler and Cain 1992, 70). The concept of communities of interest has grown in legal significance in reaction to U.S. Supreme Court voting rights decisions—discussed above—which find that race cannot predominate over a redistricting authority's decision-making, but community of interest may. Yet the concept is poorly defined; more scholarly work is needed to provide concrete definitions of what constitutes communities of interest.

Outcome-based redistricting criteria

Outcome-based criteria differ from process-based criteria in that achievement of a political goal is attempted. Once the political goal is established, the implementation of outcome-based criteria may be similar to that of process-based criteria, in that districts are drawn to achieve a specific target for districts' racial or political composition. It is necessarily an imprecise practice, because forecasts of future election outcomes are based on past census and election data: people may move, national or statewide swings may occur, incumbents may come and go, and scandals may erupt, among many other factors that affect election outcomes. However, the political and demographic composition of districts and the location of potential candidates' homes are election factors that a redistricting authority may influence. Thus, to paraphrase Butler and Cain (1992, 13), care should be taken to distinguish the claim that redistricting causes an election outcome from the claim that political actors seek to affect an election outcome. Yet the two are often confused when scholars conflate election outcomes with districts' characteristics.

A well-studied outcome-based criterion is the Voting Rights Act, which establishes important guidelines for fashioning districts where minority communities are able to elect a candidate of their choice. Section 2 of the Act establishes three conditions which, when considered within the totality of the circumstances, must be met to create such districts: these form the so-called Gingles test for the U.S. Supreme Court decision in *Thornburg v Gingles*, 478 US 30 (1986). First, a minority community must be large enough to draw a district around. Second, a minority community must be sufficiently compact. Third, there must be the presence of racially polarized voting, whereby whites only vote for white preferred candidates and minorities only vote for minority preferred candidates. Section 5 of the act requires certain jurisdictions covered by criteria established in Section 4 to submit their redistricting plans to the U.S. Department of Justice or District Court of DC for approval before they can take effect. These proposed plans cannot degrade or "retrogress" minority representation. Individual-level vote choices are typically unavailable for inspection, so statistical methods have been devised to estimate individual voting propensities from aggregate data—the so-called ecological inference problem (e.g. Goodman 1959; King 1997). From these estimates, target numbers of minority populations can be devised to elect a minority candidate of choice.

A redistricting authority may attempt to affect a partisan outcome by setting targets for the number of Democrats and Republicans within districts. One technique sets specific target values of aggregated election or registration data within alternative congressional districts (e.g. Kousser 1996). The choice of the best forecasting data is somewhat of an art. Since the objective is to estimate the partisan tendencies of districts, the best type of election data are those where partisanship is the primary voting determinant. For practitioners, these are typically statewide lower-ballot races where voters know little of candidates other than their party affiliation. There are no similar national data for those who study congressional districts. The only common election data across all congressional districts are those of the presidential election. To hold constant election-specific factors, the presidential election results preceding a redistricting are typically analyzed in the old and new districts (e.g. Cox and Katz 2002; Glazer, Grofman, and Robbins 1987; McDonald 2006a; compare Abramowitz, Alexander, and Gunning 2006). A further technique to gauge redistricting effects is to create a statistical model that estimates the relationship between a baseline measure of partisanship and other covariates like incumbency and legislative election results (e.g. Cain 1985; Gelman and King 1994a).

To constrain partisan or incumbent influence in redistricting, some states have imposed regulation. As discussed in McDonald (2007), Hawaii, Idaho, Iowa, and Washington require that districts shall not favor a person or faction. Arizona and Iowa forbid their redistricting authority access to election data and knowledge of where incumbents live (technically, a process-based regulation). Arizona, Washington, and Wisconsin (state legislative only in the 1980s) take a more affirmative approach, by requiring competitive districts. Theoretically, the application of competition without other constraints favors the minority political party within a jurisdiction (Niemi and Deegan 1978), which may explain why Democratic interests backed the ballot initiative that created the Arizona commission. The Arizona commission applied Gelman and King's (1994a) approach to measure the competitiveness balance of districts (McDonald 2006b).

Politicians clearly believe that redistricting is important, witnessed by the considerable amount of resources they expend on redistricting, yet scholarly research is divided on measureable effects. Tufte (1973) was among the first scholars to propose that redistricting affects the partisan bias and responsiveness of a state's electoral system (see also Mayhew 1971; Erikson 1972). Ferejohn (1977) later challenged this result; and conflicting findings have persisted in the literature since. Some scholars find partisan gerrymanders produce favorable outcomes for incumbents or political parties (Abramowitz 1983; Cain 1985; Gelman and King 1994b; Hirsch 2003; King 1989; Niemi and Abramowitz 1994; Niemi and Winsky 1992), while others find otherwise (e.g. Campagna and Grofman 1990; Glazer, Grofman, and Robbins 1987; Squire 1985). These conflicting results extend to whether redistricting results in fewer competitive districts (e.g. Swain, Borelli, and Reed 1998; Nolan, Poole, and Rosenthal 2009; McDonald 2006a) or not (Abramowitz, Alexander, and Gunning 2006).

The U.S. Supreme Court ruled, in *Davis v Bandemer* 478 U.S. 109 (1986), that partisan gerrymandering is impermissible. However, no redistricting plan has been overturned on federal grounds. In *League of United Latin American Citizens (LULAC) v Perry* 548 U. S. 399 (2006), the swing justice on this matter, Justice Kennedy, yet again refused to endorse a partisan gerrymandering standard among the many offered to him by plaintiffs and scholars who filed amicus briefs. Thus there is continued scholarly interest in devising a partisan gerrymandering test. One approach uses districts' partisanship—or more simply election results—to estimate the partisan bias and responsiveness of an electoral system (e.g. Campagna 1991; King and Browning 1987; Kendall and Stuart 1950; Tufte 1973). Partisan bias is the percentage of vote that a party needs in order to win half the seats (typically calculated by subtracting 50 percent from the necessary vote percentage) and responsiveness is the slope of the votes-to-seats line. Partisan bias may thus serve as a measure for partisan gerrymandering. Since the vote-to-seats line may be a curve, a more specific standard is partisan symmetry around 50 percent of seats, such that the two major parties win the same share of seats, given the same share of votes (Grofman and King 2007). This may generally be sufficient to detect gerrymandering, except in lopsided states, where the typical election result is not near 50 percent of the vote. Yet Justice Kennedy did not endorse this standard, articulated in a *LULAC* amicus brief co-authored by Grofman and King.

Another approach attempts to detect violations of criteria to establish the presence of gerrymandering. A computationally intensive approach builds upon automated redistricting, which was first proposed as a solution to gerrymandering in the 1960s (Vickrey 1961; Weaver and Hess 1963). Advocates proposed that programming a computer to optimize on some "neutral" criteria would prevent politics from entering into redistricting (despite the fact that these neutral criteria may have predictable political effects). These early automation attempts were discarded because they tended to produce shoe-string districts that did not make political sense, but they were the forerunners of today's geographic information systems (Altman, Mac Donald, and McDonald 2005). The redistricting optimization problem, even for a modestly sized jurisdiction, is a computationally intensive graph partitioning problem that current computing power is unable to guarantee finding the optimum of in billions of years (Altman 1997; Altman and McDonald 2009).

The difficulties in automated redistricting illuminate general problems with statistical analyses of redistricting outcomes (Altman and McDonald 2009). The distribution of any measure of feasible redistricting plans that one wishes to examine cannot be determined and thus cannot be shown to be normally distributed, which raises serious methodological questions for the many studies that use parametric statistical procedures to examine the relationship between redistricting processes and outcomes. To avoid such distributional assumptions, one could map out the full space of redistricting plans and compare this set of plans to the adopted plan on some characteristic of interest (Rossiter and Johnson 1981); however, even for a modestly sized jurisdiction, the number of permutations of feasible plans exceeds the number of quarks in the universe (Altman and McDonald 2009). Scholars have thus proposed approximating the feasible space through sampling, by 'randomly' generating redistricting plans (Engstrom and Wildgen 1977); but, as Knuth (1997) warns, programming a computer to do something randomly does not mean that an algorithm will produce a random sample. For example, a heuristic that creates districts by randomly adding adjacent census blocks until a target population is achieved will tend to generate compact districts (e.g. Cirincione, Darling, and O'Rourke 2000). In this example, the set of feasible redistricting plans will be those that are compact and of equal population. This may not be the correct formulation of the hypothesis one wishes to test. The plan in question may also attempt to achieve other goals, such as preservation of political boundaries. If these other goals are correlated with "gerrymandering," then this approach may find political manipulation, even if none occurred.

More generally, without knowing the set of feasible redistricting plans, it is difficult to know if a plan that was produced was the result of a gerrymander or a consequence of following redistricting criteria, as these are applied to a state. A further complication is that states' political composition interacts with redistricting criteria and with the size of the districts to be drawn in state-specific ways (Musgrave 1977; McDonald 2009). This holds of application of partisan symmetry (Grofman and King 2007) and of other proposed theoretical solutions to gerrymandering (e.g. Landau, Reid, and Yershov 2009), as it may be the case that a 'fair' plan simply does not exist, or it substantially violates other redistricting criteria. For these reasons, Altman and McDonald (2009) argue that the only methodologically sound way to test for the presence of gerrymandering is to compare an adopted plan against alternative plans on meaningful criteria. For example, if an adopted plan is the same in all respects to another plan on criteria a redistricting authority purportedly cared about, except that it contains one more minority–majority district, this revealed preference indicates that race was a factor in the creation of the additional district. Recognizing that a nearly infinite number of redistricting plans exists, the challenge is to identify the set of reasonably discoverable plans available for selection by a redistricting authority. An open and transparent redistricting process that allows public submissions may be one such way to measure this set.

As states have become familiar with the regulatory regime of the Voting Rights Act and as state criteria have proliferated, the legal focus has shifted away from the federal to the state courts (Cain, Mac Donald, and McDonald 2005). Scholarly interest in the various criteria that states impose, and additional criteria that have been packaged in reform proposals, will likely continue in the near term. These criteria, how they interact with one another, and how they are applied in different states and for different types of districts are not well understood by scholars, much less by those who are interested in reforming the redistricting process.

RELATED RESEARCH AGENDAS

Redistricting produces changes in constituencies. As such, it offers a natural experiment to study the effects of redistricting on other political phenomena, such as incumbency advantage, candidate emergence, voting behavior, and representative–constituency links. References to this scholarly research are peppered throughout the preceding discussion. To recapitulate these studies, scholars have found that the incumbency advantage is lower among new constituents than among continuing constituents (Ansolabehere, Snyder, and Stewart 2000; Desposato and Petrocik 2003) and that these new constituents vote in House races at comparably lower rates (Hayes and McKee 2009). The causal mechanics behind these phenomena are not well understood. Incumbents are typically involved in the decision to include these areas within their new districts; it would be irrational, for example, for an incumbent to trade a low participatory allied stronghold for a high participatory opposition stronghold. So it is likely that these studies are confounded by strategic redistricting decision-making.

Another line of research examines the effect of redistricting on the ideology of representatives. The partisan composition of a district is related to the ideological voting of its representative, a more conservative district being represented by a more conservative representative (e.g. Ansolabehere, Snyder, and Stewart 2001). Representatives shift their legislative behavior to conform with changes in the partisan composition—or ideology—of their district caused by redistricting (Hayes,

Hibbing, and Sulkin 2010; Crespin, forthcoming). It is possible that redistricting has thus contributed to ideological polarization. However, even if it were possible to create all perfectly partisan-balanced congressional districts, substantial interparty ideological differences would remain (McCarty, Poole, and Rosenthal 2009). There are some aspects that deserve more research. How do districts' constituencies affect members' roll-call voting independent of the internal pressures from leadership and from logroll deals? How do members use redistricting to create more ideologically consistent districts for themselves, as demonstrated by mismatched incumbents who were moved into districts more consistent with their party affiliation (Jacobson 2003)?

CONCLUSION

Redistricting provides an opportunity for politicians, reformers, and even scholars to participate in social engineering. There is no "perfect" electoral system that embodies all of a core set of basic principles that a society might care about (Arrow 1950). So, debates over any electoral reform, including the appropriate way to redistrict, ultimately devolve into debates about core beliefs. Should legislators be allowed to draw their own districts (Lowenstein and Steinberg 1985) or not (Issacharoff 2002)? Should redistricting be used to foster the creation of competitive districts (McDonald and Samples 2006) or not (Brunell 2008)? Does the Voting Rights Act foster better minority representation (Canon 1999) or not (Thernstrom and Thernstrom 1997)?

The general direction of policy is towards placing more constraints on redistricting, so these issues will continue to be relevant in the near future. The scholarly community can thus play a role in helping determine the validity of the reform claims so that informed decisions can be made. Hopefully, these studies will properly model the geographical and statutory constraints on redistricting. Heretofore, most scholars have simply assumed that states can be compared with one another, even though a Democratic gerrymander in Utah may be substantively different from one enacted in Massachusetts. This is also true for the application of other criteria, such as drawing districts respecting political boundaries: Utah is defined by counties and cities, while all of Massachusetts' geography is defined by townships. Scholars should also take seriously the endogenous relationship between outcomes and redistricting authorities' motives, as political actors are often keenly aware of the electoral consequences of changing districts' boundaries. And how these choices interact with constraints is not well understood; for example, an incumbent protection gerrymander following a state's loss of a congressional seat to apportionment may be more defensive in nature than one where a state's congressional delegation is static. The promise for redistricting scholars is that there is always another redistricting, and, as states increasingly use technology to increase the transparency of their processes, it is likely that more data will be available to fuel the continuing and active study of redistricting.

REFERENCES

ABRAMOWITZ, A. I. 1983. Partisan Redistricting and the 1982 Congressional Elections. *The Journal of Politics*, 45(3): 767–70.

—— ALEXANDER, B., and GUNNING, M. 2006. Incumbency, Redistricting, and the Decline of Competition in U.S. House Elections. *Journal of Politics*, 68(1): 75–88.

ALTMAN, M. 1997. Is Automation the Answer: The Computational Complexity of Automated Redistricting. *Rutgers Computer and Law Technology Journal*, 23(1): 81–141.

—— 1998a. Traditional Districting Principles, Judicial Myths vs. Reality. *Social Science History*, 22(2): 159–200.

—— 1998b. Modeling the Effect of Mandatory District Compactness on Partisan Gerrymanders, *Political Geography*, 17(8): 989–1012.

—— MacDONALD, K., and McDONALD, M. P. 2005. Pushbutton Gerrymanders? How Computing Has Changed Redistricting, pp. 51–66 in *Party Lines: Competition, Partisanship and Congressional Redistricting*, ed. Bruce Cain and Thomas Mann. Washington, DC: Brookings Press.

——————— 2009. BARD: Better Automated Redistricting. *Journal of Statistical, Software*, 31(3).

ANSOLABEHERE, S., JAMES, S., and STEWART, III, C. 2001. Candidate Positioning in U.S. House Elections. *American Journal of Political Science*, 45(1): 136–59.

—— GERBER, A., and SNYDER, J. 2002. Equal Votes, Equal Money: Court-Ordered Redistricting and Public Expenditures in the American States. *The American Political Science Review*, 96(4): 767–77.

—— PERSILY, N., and STEWART, III, C. 2010. Race, Region, and Vote Choice in the 2008 Election: Implications for the Future of the Voting Rights Act. *Harvard Law Review*, 123(6): 1368–436.

—— SNYDER, JR., J. M., and STEWART, III, C. 2000. Old Voters, New Voters, and the Personal Vote: Using Redistricting to Measure the Incumbency Advantage. *American Journal of Political Science*, 44(1): 17–34.

ARROW, K. J. 1950. A Difficulty in the Concept of Social Welfare. *Journal of Political Economy*, 58(4): 328–46.

AYRES, Q. W., and WHITEMAN, D. 1984. Congressional Reapportionment in the 1980s: Types and Determinants of Policy Outcomes. *Political Science Quarterly*, 99(2): 303–14.

BASEHART, H., and COMER, J. 1991. Partisan and Incumbent Effects in State Legislative Redistricting. *Legislative Studies Quarterly*, 16(1): 65–79.

BARKAN, J. D., DENSHAM, P. J., and RUSHTON, G. 2006. Space Matters: Designing Better Electoral Systems for Emerging Democracies. *American Journal of Political Science*, 50(4): 926–39.

BOATRIGHT, R. 2004. Static Ambition in a Changing World: Legislators' Preparations for and Responses to Redistricting. *State Politics and Policy Quarterly*, 4(4): 436–54.

BORN, R. 1985. Partisan Intentions and Election Day Realities in the Congressional Redistricting Process. *The American Political Science Review* 79(2): 305–19.

BRACE, K., GROFMAN, B., and HANDLEY, L. 1987. Does Redistricting Aimed to Help Blacks Necessarily Help Republicans? *Journal of Politics*, 49(1): 169–85.

——————— and Niemi, R. 1988. Minority Voting Equality: The 65 Percent Rule in Theory and Practice. *Law and Policy*, 10(1): 43–62.

BRUNELL, T. L. 2008. *Redistricting and Representation: Why Competitive Elections Are Bad for America*. New York: Routledge.

BUTLER, D., and CAIN, B. E. 1992. *Congressional Redistricting: Comparative and Theoretical Perspectives*. New York, NY: Macmillan.

CAIN, B. 1984. *The Reapportionment Puzzle*. Berkeley, CA: University of California Press.

——1985. Assessing the Partisan Effects of Redistricting. *The American Political Science Review*, 79(2): 320–33.

——MACDONALD, K., and MCDONALD, M. P. 2005. From Equality to Fairness: The Path of Political Reform Since Baker v Carr, pp. 6–30 in *Party Lines: Competition, Partisanship and Congressional Redistricting*, ed. Bruce Cain and Thomas Mann. Washington, DC: Brookings Press.

——and CAMPAGNA, J. 1987. Predicting Partisan Redistricting Disputes. *Legislative Studies Quarterly*, 12(2): 265–74.

CAMERON, C., EPSTEIN, D., and O'HALLORAN, S. 1996. Do Majority–Minority Districts Maximize Substantive Black Representation in Congress? *The American Political Science Review*, 90(4): 794–812.

CAMPAGNA, J. C. 1991. Bias and Responsiveness in the Seat-Vote Relationship. *Legislative Studies Quarterly*, 16(1): 81–9.

——and GROFMAN, B. 1990. Party Control and Partisan Bias in 1980s Congressional Redistricting. *The Journal of Politics*, 52(4): 1242–57.

CANON, D. 1999. *Race, Redistricting, and Representation: The Unintended Consequences of Black-Majority Districts*. Chicago: University of Chicago Press.

CARSON, J. L., ENGSTROM, E. J., and ROBERTS, J. M. 2006. Redistricting, Candidate Entry, and the Politics of Nineteenth-Century U.S. House Elections. *American Journal of Political Science* 50(2): 283–93.

CIRINCIONE, C., DARLING, T., and O'ROURKE, T. 2000. Assessing South Carolina's 1990's Congressional Districting. *Political Geography*, 19: 189–211.

COX, A. B. 2004. Partisan Fairness and Redistricting Politics. *New York University Law Review*, 70(3): 751–802.

COX, G. W. 1997. *Making Votes Count*. New York, NY: Cambridge University Press.

——and KATZ, J. N. 2002. *Elbridge Gerry's Salamander: The Electoral Consequences of the Reapportionment Revolution*. Cambridge, MA: Cambridge University Press.

CRESPIN, M. H. Forthcoming. Serving Two Masters. *Political Research Quarterly*.

DAVIDSON, C., and GROFMAN, B. eds. 1994. *Quiet Revolution in the South: The Impact of the Voting Rights Act 1965–1990*. Princeton, NJ: Princeton University Press.

DESPOSATO, S. W., and PETROCIK, J. R. 2003. The Variable Incumbency Advantage: New Voters, Redistricting, and the Personal Vote. *American Journal of Political Science*, 47(1): 18–32.

DUVERGER, M. 1959. *Political Parties: Their Organization and Activity in the Modern State*, 2nd edn. London: Methuen and Company.

ELIS, R., MALHOTRA, N., and MEREDITH, M. 2009. Apportionment Cycles as Natural Experiments. *Political Analysis*, 17(4): 358–76.

ENGSTROM, R. N. 2005. District Geography and Voters, pp. 65–86 in *Redistricting in the New Millennium*, ed. Peter F. Galderisis. Lanham, MD: Lexington.

——and WILDGEN, J. 1977. Pruning Thorns from the Thicket: An Empirical Test of the Existence of Racial Gerrymandering. *Legislative Studies Quarterly*, 4: 465–79.

EPSTEIN, D., and O'HALLORAN, S. 1999. Measuring the Electoral and Policy Impact of Majority–Minority Voting Districts. *American Journal of Political Science*, 43(2): 367–95.

ERIKSON, R. S. 1972. Malapportionment, Gerrymandering, and Party Fortunes in Congressional Elections. *The American Political Science Review* 66(4): 1234–45.

FEREJOHN, J. A. 1977. On the Decline of Competition in Congressional Elections. *The American Political Science Review*, 71(1): 166–76.

GELMAN, A., and KING, G. 1990. Estimating the Incumbency Advantage Without Bias. *American Journal of Political Science*, 34(4): 401–11.

—— 1994a. A Unified Method of Evaluating Electoral Systems and Redistricting Plans. *American Journal of Political Science*, 38(2): 514–54.

—— 1994b. Enhancing Democracy through Legislative Redistricting. *American Political Science Review*, 88(3): 541–59.

GLAZER, A., GROFMAN, B., and ROBBINS, M. 1987. Partisan and Incumbency Effects of 1970s Congressional Redistricting. *American Journal of Political Science*, 31(3): 680–707.

GOODMAN, L. 1959. Some Alternatives to Ecological Correlation. *The American Journal of Sociology*, 64(6): 610–25.

GROFMAN, B., and HANDLEY, L. 1998. Estimating the Impact of Voting-Rights-Act-Related Districting on Democratic Strength in the U.S. House of Representatives, pp. 51–66 in *Race and Redistricting in the 1990s*, ed. Bernard Grofman. New York, NY: Agathon Press.

—— and KING, G. 2007. The Future of Partisan Symmetry as a Judicial Test for Partisan Gerrymandering after LULAC v. Perry. *Election Law Journal: Rules, Politics, and Policy*, 6(1): 2–35.

HANDLEY, L. 2008. A Comparative Survey of Structures and Criteria for Boundary Delimination, pp. 265–84 in *Redistricting in Comparative Perspective*, ed. Lisa Handley and Bernard Grofman. Oxford, U.K.: Oxford University Press.

HAYES, D., and McKEE, S. C. 2009. "The Participatory Effects of Redistricting." *American Journal of Political Science*, 53(4): 1006–23.

HAYES, M., HIBBING, M. V., and SULKIN, T. 2010. Redistricting, Responsiveness, and Issue Attention. *Legislative Studies Quarterly*, 35(1): 91–115.

HETHERINGTON, M. J., LARSON, B. A., and GLOBETTI, S. 2003. The Redistricting Cycle and Strategic Candidate Decisions in U.S. House Races. *Journal of Politics*, 65(4): 1221–35.

HIRSCH, S. 2003. The United States House of Unrepresentatives: What Went Wrong in the Latest Round of Congressional Redistricting. *Election Law Journal*, 2(2): 179–216.

ISSACHAROFF, S. 2002. Gerrymandering and Political Cartels. *Harvard Law Review*, 116(2): 601–48.

JACOBSON, G. C. 2003. Terror, Terrain, and Turnout: Explaining the 2002 Midterm Elections. *Political Science Quarterly*, 118(1): 1–22.

—— 2009. *The Politics of Congressional Elections*, 7th edn. New York, NY: Longman.

JOHNSTON, R. J. 2002. Manipulating Maps and Winning Elections. *Political Geography*, 21(1): 1–31.

KENDALL, M.G., and STUART, A. 1950. The Law of Cubic Proportions in Electoral Results. *British Journal of Sociology*, 1(3): 183–96.

KING, G. 1989. Representation through Legislative Redistricting: A Stochastic Model. *American Journal of Political Science*, 33(4): 787–824.

—— 1997. *A Solution to the Ecological Inference Problem*. Princeton, NJ: Princeton University Press.

—— and BROWNING, R. X. 1987. Democratic Representation and Partisan Bias in Congressional Elections. *The American Political Science Review*, 81(4): 1251–73.

KNUTH, D. 1997. *The Art of Computer Programming: Seminumerical Algorithms*, 2nd edn. New York: Addison Wesley.

KOUSSER, J. M. 1996. Estimating the Partisan Consequences of Redistricting Plans—Simply. *Legislative Studies Quarterly*, 21(4): 521–41.

LANDAU, Z. O. R., and YERSHOV, I. 2009. A Fair Division Solution to the Problem of Redistricting. *Social Choice and Welfare*, 32(3): 479–92.

LAWRENCE, STEVE. 2001. Democrats May Not Seek Big Gains in House Delegation. *Associated Press State and Local Wire*, 14 August.

LIJPHART, A. 1999. *Patterns of Democracy: Government Forms and Performance in Thirty-Six Countries*. New Haven: Yale University Press.

LEVITT, J. 2008. *A Citizen's Guide to Redistricting*. New York: The Brennan Center for Justice at New York University School of Law.

——and McDONALD, M. P. 2007. Taking the 'Re' out of Redistricting: State Constitutional Provisions on Redistricting Timing. *Georgetown Law Review*, 95(4): 1247–86.

LOWENSTEIN, D., and STEINBERG, J. 1985. The Quest for Legislative Districting in the Public Interest: Elusive or Illusory? *UCLA Law Review*, 33(1): 1–75.

LUBLIN, D. 1997. *The Paradox of Representation*. Princeton: Princeton University Press.

——1999. Racial Redistricting and African–American Representation: A Critique of "Do Majority–Minority Districts Maximize Substantive Black Representation in Congress?" *The American Political Science Review*, 93(1): 183–6.

McCARTY, N., POOLE, K. T., and ROSENTHAL, H. 2009. Does Gerrymandering Cause Polarization? *American Journal of Political Science*, 53(3): 666–80.

McDONALD, M. P. 2004. A Comparative Analysis of U.S. State Redistricting Institutions. *State Politics and Policy Quarterly*, 4(4): 371–96.

——2006a. Drawing the Line on District Competition. *PS: Political Science and Politics*, 39(1): 91–4.

——2006b. Redistricting and District Competition, pp. 222–44 in *The Marketplace of Democracy*, ed. Michael P. McDonald and John Samples. Washington, DC: Brookings Press.

——2008. Legislative Redistricting, pp. 147–60 in *Democracy in the States: Experiments in Elections Reform*, ed. Bruce Cain, Todd Donovan, and Caroline Tolbert. Washington, DC: Brookings Press.

——2007. Regulating Redistricting. *PS: Political Science and Politics* 40(4): 675–9.

——2009. *Midwest Mapping Project*. Fairfax, VA: George Mason University Monograph.

——and SAMPLES, J. eds. 2006. *The Marketplace of Democracy: Electoral Competition and American Politics*. Washington, DC: Brookings Press.

MARCH, J., and OLSEN, J. P. 1996. Institutional Perspectives on Political Institutions. *Governance*, 9(3): 247–64.

MARTIS, K. C. 1982. *Historical Atlas of United States Congressional Districts, 1789–1983*. New York: Simon & Schuster.

MATSUSAKA, J. G. 2006. Direct Democracy and Electoral Reform, pp. 151–70 in *The Marketplace of Democracy*, ed. Michael P. McDonald and John Samples. Washington, DC: Brookings Press.

MAYHEW, D. 1971. Congressional Representation: Theory and Practice of Drawing the Districts, pp. 249–84 in *Reapportionment in the 1970s*, ed. Nelson W. Polsby. Berkeley: University of California Press.

MONROE, B. L., and ROSE, A. G. 2002. Electoral Systems and Unimagined Consequences: Partisan Effects of Districted Proportional Representation. *American Journal of Political Science*, 46(1): 67–89.

MUSGRAVE, P. 1977. *The General Theory of Gerrymandering*. Washington, DC: The Brookings Institution.

NIEMI, R. G., and ABRAMOWITZ, A. I. 1994. Partisan Redistricting and the 1992 Congressional Elections. *The Journal of Politics*, 56(3): 811–17.

NIEMI, R. G., and DEEGAN, J. 1978. A Theory of Political Districting. *The American Political Science Review*, 72(4): 1304–23.

—— Powell, L. W., and Bicknell, P. L. 1986. The Effects of Congruity between Community and District on Salience of U.S. House Candidates. *Legislative Studies Quarterly*, 11(2): 187–201.

—— Grofman, B., Carlucci, C., and Hofeller, T. 1990. Measuring Compactness and the Role of a Compactness Standard in a Test for Partisan and Racial Gerrymandering. *The Journal of Politics*, 52(4): 1155–81.

—— and Winsky, L. R. 1992. The Persistence of Partisan Redistricting Effects in Congressional Elections in the 1970s and 1980s. *The Journal of Politics*, 54(2): 565–72.

Owen, G., and Grofman, B. 1988. Optimal Partisan Gerrymandering. *Political Geography Quarterly*, 7(1): 5–22.

Parker, F. R. 1990. *Black Votes Count*. Chapel Hill, NC: University of North Carolina Press.

Reader, S. A. 1994. One Person, One Vote Revisited: Choosing a Population Basis to Form Political Districts. *Harvard Journal of Law and Public Policy*, 17: 521–65.

Rossiter, D., and Johnston, R. 1981. Program GROUP: The Identification of all Possible Solutions to a Constituency-Delimitation Problem. *Environment and Planning*, 13: 231–8.

Sherstyuk, K. 1998. How to Gerrymander: A Formal Analysis. *Public Choice*, 95: 27–49.

Shotts, K. W. 2001. The Effect of Majority–Minority Mandates on Partisan Gerrymandering. *American Journal of Political Science*, 45(1): 120–35.

Squire, P. 1985. Results of Partisan Redistricting in Seven U.S. States during the 1970s. *Legislative Studies Quarterly*, 10(2): 259–66.

Swain, J. W., Borrelli, S. A., and Reed, B. C. 1998. Partisan Consequences of the Post-1990 Redistricting for the U.S. House of Representatives. *Political Research Quarterly*, 51(4): 945–67.

Thernstrom, S., and Thernstrom, A. 1997. *America in Black and White: One Nation Indivisible*. New York, NY: Simon and Schuster.

Tobert, C. J., Smith, D. A., and Green, J. C. 2009. Strategic Voting and Legislative Redistricting Reform. *Political Research Quarterly*, 61(1): 92–109.

Tufte, E. R. 1973. The Relationship between Seats and Votes in Two-Party Systems. *The American Political Science Review*, 67(2): 540–54.

Vickrey, W. 1961. On the Prevention of Gerrymandering. *Political Science Quarterly*, 76(1): 105–10.

Wagner, P. 2006. Skewing Democracy: Where the Census Counts Prisoners, pp. 25–8 in *Poverty and Race in America: The Emerging Agenda*, ed. Chester Hartman. Lanham, MD: Lexington Books.

Weaver, J. B., and Hess, S. W. 1963. A Procedure for Nonpartisan Districting. *The Yale Law Journal*, 72(2): 228–308.

White, J. P., and Thomas, N. C. 1964. Urban and Rural Representation and State Legislative Apportionment. *The Western Political Quarterly*, 17(4): 724–41.

Webber, P. J. 1988. "Madison's Opposition to a Second Convention." *Polity*, 20(3): 489–517.

Winburn, J. 2008. *The Realities of Redistricting: Following the Rules and Limiting Gerrymandering in State Legislative Redistricting*. Lanham, MD: Lexington.

—— and Wagner, M. W. 2010. Carving Voters out: Redistricting's Influence on Political Information, Turnout, and Voting Behavior. *Political Research Quarterly*, 63(2): 373–86.

Young, H. P. 1988. Measuring the Compactness of Legislative Districts. *Legislative Studies Quarterly*, 13(1): 105–15.

CHAPTER 10

··

CAMPAIGN FINANCE IN CONGRESSIONAL ELECTIONS

··

ROBIN KOLODNY

CONGRESSIONAL campaign finance has understandably been linked to central questions around congressional elections. Does the candidate who spends the most always win? Which type of candidate raises funds most easily? Does the money spent on campaigns end up educating voters and enhancing democracy or hurting it? All of these are important questions about the role of money in elections. Indeed, Peverill Squire's 1995 review article on money in congressional elections devotes nearly the entire discussion to the effects of the overall amounts of monies raised on eventual election outcomes. That is, does challenger spending or incumbent spending matter most? While Squire points to an important debate, the implications of money-seeking behavior on the operation of the chamber are not discussed (Squire 1995). Similarly, Thomas Stratmann's literature review emphasizes the impact of spending on outcomes, highlighting how "scholars have noted that incumbents' vote shares and spending are simultaneously determined: while spending influences the vote share, the expected vote share may influence spending" (Stratmann 2005). Much of the literature in these previous reviews was written with the pre-1995 Congress in mind. Since the historic change in party control in the U.S. House of Representatives after the 1994 election, and since the rise of evenly balanced politics in congressional elections, the discussion of money in congressional elections still seems to be stuck on the matter of resources in individual races, rather than acknowledging that bona fide party competition at the congressional level has created a much different world.

As for the consequences of congressional campaign funds on the operation of Congress itself, much attention has been paid to trying to figure out if those who donate to members of Congress succeed in buying votes, or at least in influencing particular legislative outcomes. To a great extent, this literature has failed to establish a precise connection (e.g. a donation of $5,000 buys 0.75 amendments) between the two acts, acknowledging that the process of representation is more complicated than it seems at first.

The problem with these approaches is that they present a narrow and overly negative view of the effects of campaign finance on Congress. The politics of campaign finance seep into every aspect of congressional life, from elections to legislation, to media appearances, to constituency service, and to committee chair and leadership aspirations. Looking for the impact of money on election outcomes distracts us from answering other critical questions: What explains the current regulatory regime and why is there no public funding for congressional elections? Who donates to congressional candidates? What does the money buy? Is it all used for electioneering, and if not, what else is it used for? How is fundraising prowess rewarded in Congress? Does the current system pose a set of problems that needs to be fixed?

In this chapter I will discuss the evolution and current state of campaign finance regulation for Congress, the income side of campaign financing (about which a great deal is known and a great deal of causal conjecture prevails), the expenditure side of congressional campaign money (about which very little is known), and the implications congressional campaign fundraising has for legislative behavior and leadership ambition. Here I contend that most of the literature has focused too much on the potential "buying" of congressional votes by special interest groups and by wealthy donors and not enough on the structural context in which congressional campaign finance must exist. The inherent assumption in most congressional scholarship is that representatives ought to be conduits for the majority interest in their districts, undistorted by the economic interests of employers, employees, and investors who structure the political life of the represented districts. This is coupled with the idea that government-financed congressional campaigns would be an inappropriate use of taxpayer dollars. Instead, an entirely privately financed system of election campaigning ought somehow to accommodate the competing values of access to all groups and free speech rights for any individual or entity (Grant and Rudolph 2004). So much of the discussion, over time, has been about what is 'purchased'—interest group influence, party loyalty, special attention with the bureaucracy for individual donors—that we have failed to step back and look at the consequences of the system as a whole for issues of access and participation.

THE FEDERAL CAMPAIGN FINANCE SYSTEM

It is important to note that the divergence between the presidential and congressional campaign finance systems is no accident. Surprisingly little is understood about the rationale for the regulations on financing congressional elections, especially compared to presidential elections. Often, any understanding of money in politics is couched in the language of presidential elections, and those, of course, are the only races that run nationwide, which understandably makes the sums discussed vast. On the other hand, the resources needed for winning the presidency require so many contributors, especially under contribution limits, that it is hard to make the case that individual donors can have much direct effect on the presidential administration's decisions. Congress, however, is a different matter.

Great sums are spent in the aggregate in congressional elections, but the range can be extraordinarily large between individual campaigns. In addition, while there were campaign finance scandals in the 1960s and 1970s about presidential campaigning that were so outrageous that the country was willing to accept a dramatic solution such as public money to remedy them, no one felt strongly about applying these same measures to the Congress, especially not the lawmakers who set about writing the bills (La Raja 2008). As a result, in the 1970s, the Congress enacted sweeping campaign finance reforms, which limited contributions to all federal campaigns and included spending limits. These spending limits were set at levels far above any seen at that date for congressional races; but, for presidential campaigns, the limits were severely restrictive for contemporary campaign activities (Sundquist 1981). Congress took an active role when writing the Federal Election Campaign Act and amendments, to be sure that the independent regulatory agency, the Federal Election Commission (FEC), primarily oversaw presidential campaign finance report filings, trying instead to channel congressional campaign finance reporting through the House and Senate administrative offices. Brooks Jackson's account of the early problems with the FEC shows quite clearly that congressional leaders saw campaign finance as an area where Congress, not the executive branch, should dictate the terms of oversight (Jackson 1990).

When the landmark Supreme Court case challenging the constitutionality of FECA, *Buckley* v *Valeo,* was decided in 1976, the court made important changes to the law, but nothing substantial to the arrangement of public money for presidential campaigns and private money for congressional campaigns. The only major change for congressional candidates was the elimination of the campaign spending cap that FECA originally instituted. The reasoning went that spending limits were appropriate in the presidential system if candidates accepted public money, because they were receiving a "free" benefit and so should sacrifice freedom in exchange. It is important to underscore the voluntary nature of this system—presidential candidates are only bound by spending limits in the primary and the general elections if they accept public funds. All competitive presidential candidates accepted the public funds and spending limits until the 2000 presidential election, when George W. Bush declined matching funds and spending limits for the Republican presidential primary election campaign. In the aftermath of Watergate, presidential candidates had no qualms about taking public money to finance their general election campaigns. It was good for claiming to be beyond ethical reproach, and the money was enough to cover the contemporary costs of campaigns. Since the 2004 presidential election, however, we have seen the adequacy of public money for presidential campaigning wane and viable presidential candidates abandon the benefit of free money in favor of the freedom of spending where and how much they want. However, since there was never any public money in the congressional system, and hence no reward for abiding by limits, spending limits were inappropriate for congressional races in the court's opinion. No serious proponent of reform of the presidential public financing system believes that Congress could be included in such a reform (or expansion) of public financing.

From the 1970s to the present, the public has built up a perception, mostly due to inaccurate media coverage, that congressional campaigns are excessively expensive, which contributed to the hyperbole around the debate on what to do about the "rising" costs of campaigns. Ansolabehere, Snowberg, and Snyder found that newspapers reported the most expensive races, the "upper tail" as it were, as typical cases. Worse, the more educated a voter was, the more likely it was that their estimate of the cost of campaigns would be too high, which indicated that they read more of the misleading coverage than the less educated (Ansolabehere, Snowberg, and Snyder 2005). Also, these same voters grossly overestimated the amount of funds that political action committees (PACs) donated to these candidates, creating even more negativity towards Congress as an institution; as this furthered the belief that Congress was "owned" by special interests. Ironically, more disclosure about campaign costs may lead to less credible information.

Still, Congress has resisted the impulse to create a public financing system for itself up to the present day, and will likely never do so. While a few members of Congress who hate the act of fundraising might have liked to see public funds apply to them, most were content to have the luxury of raising as much as they needed to ward off potential strong challengers. Jay Goodliffe examined this problem most recently and concluded that the issue is incumbent uncertainty about the quality of their likely challenger in the upcoming election (Goodliffe 2001, 2004, 2005). Since the law allows incumbents to retain excess campaign funds for future elections, there is, in theory, no wastage of these funds, especially since the probability that congressional incumbents will run for reelection or other federal office is quite high. Therefore, it seems likely that incumbent members of Congress will engage in constant fundraising, regardless of proximity of the next election, to prepare themselves for the next potential "tough" matchup.

Political parties, collective action, and incumbent interests

And so the regulatory framework, where congressional candidates are subject to contribution limits and not overall fundraising or spending limits, continued throughout the remainder of the 1970s, 1980s, and into the 1990s. The 1994 election, when Republicans reclaimed a majority in the House after more than forty years in the minority, had a transformative effect on the conduct and composition of congressional campaign finance entities. Before 1994, the behavior of members of Congress looked highly individualistic and not at all collective—that is, the party dimension appeared to be absent. Incumbent members campaigned for themselves and acted as though majority party status for Democrats, especially in the House, was likely to be permanent. Therefore little concrete activity on the part of candidates (usually secure incumbents) for other candidates (especially challengers) happened, and what did take place was likely to occur through party leaders or through the political party campaign committees (Kolodny 1998). Unlike in most other national legislatures, political parties seem to be entirely absent from the congressional campaign finance narrative, and the candidate is king. As a result, an extensive literature emerged about the candidate-centered thesis. Paul Herrnson (1988), John Aldrich (1995) and many others argue that political parties controlled congressional campaigns until the mid-twentieth century, when candidates began to take charge. David Parker rejects this thesis by conducting a comprehensive review of when and how congressional candidates pursued their own resources, and he finds that personal pursuit of resources happened much earlier than is believed and was linked to the strength of state party organizations (Parker 2008). He argues that there is an interactive effect between the candidate's need to collect resources and the party organization's ability to deliver them. When the parties were weak resource providers, candidates stepped up their individual campaign efforts. When the parties were active resource providers, candidates had less need to establish individual campaign enterprises. Likewise, Ray La Raja (2008) contends that parties are not the passive actors in campaign politics they have been made out to be. Recently, Paul Herrnson has argued for a revised theory and definition of political party organization in campaign finance by showing how party-linked entities (including affiliated interest groups and party leadership PACs) perform tasks which complement the parties' mission (Herrnson 2009). While the return to competitive elections after 1994 certainly explains some of the change in the behavior of party actors and their members, Herrnson's revisionist view correctly suggests that the definitions we use have not kept up with the changed nature of the campaign finance environment since the 1970s.

As part of the new regulatory environment coming out of the 1970s, parties were explicitly limited with respect to their direct role in elections—at all levels. To this day, there is a deep suspicion, especially among jurists, that political parties are corrupt conduits and their role is simply to disguise contributions from large business or union interests to candidates. Consequently, the FECA significantly limited the amount of money political parties could donate to the candidates running under their banner and they likewise created the somewhat baffling category of 'coordinated expenditures' to limit the amount of funds parties could spend on behalf of congressional candidates with their knowledge and consent. The limit set in the original legislation is $10,000 per election, plus a cost of living adjustment (COLA). As this book goes to press, the 2010 election cycle limits are set at $43,700 per party committee (at the state and national levels each) for a de facto limit of $87,400. The limit on coordinated expenditures mattered very little initially, as the political party organizations were not in any position to maximize the spending allowed in all competitive races (La Raja 2008; Kolodny 1998; Herrnson 1988). Direct donations from political party committees to their endorsed or nominated candidates were capped at $5,000 per election per candidate, making the overall financial contribution allowed by the parties to their candidates very modest in the most competitive races. While the point of having congressional campaign committees is to pursue the collective goal of majority status, the law severely limited their ability to do so.

Yet so much of the literature on Congress tells us that political parties have an important role in structuring the nature of the body's business, its elections, and how the public perceives its conduct. In addition, it is through partisan channels that individuals and collective entities (the Hill committees, factional party groups, leadership PACs) raise funds to remain politically viable. However, the need for the parties to campaign for majority status in the chamber is sometimes at odds with the need for individual members to guarantee their own reelection. Gary Jacobson was the first to tackle the problem of the collective interests of the party not meshing with the individual interests of the candidates, particularly incumbents. Personal insecurities led incumbents to insist on a misallocation of resources—to them first, the candidates who needed it least—and if any were left over, to potentially successful challengers (Jacobson 1985).

A profound change in the nature of money in congressional elections happened after the 1994 mid-term congressional elections. This election ended the forty-year Democratic majority in the House of Representatives, which transformed the way members of Congress, party leaders, and the congressional campaign committees viewed preparation for election campaigns and campaign money. The 1994 election proved that national party appeals had some currency even in congressional elections and that the personal connection to one's district was no longer sufficient to guarantee a career in Congress. Two important developments followed: incumbents profession-alized their campaigns (especially with polls and increased television ads) and the political parties embarked upon a forceful redistribution of wealth among secure incumbents to insecure incumbents and promising challengers. Quickly, it became clear that, to secure an important committee or leadership position as part of your congressional career, a member would have to bestow considerable "dues" to their hill committee to pay for the benefits of majority status. Garret Glasgow measured the efficiency of party committee contributions, finding that the Democrats, with fewer resources, did a better job of allocating their monies toward the most competitive races than the Republicans did, and showing great improvement in party target-ing from Jacobson's earlier analysis (Glasgow 2002). The more ambitious members started establishing their own leadership PACs at a fast clip, furthering the adage of "doing good and doing well" (Cann 2008; Currinder 2009; Currinder 2003; Heberlig and Larson 2005; Heberlig 2003).

Enter soft money

Still, as a result of the FECA, all the congressional campaign committees became more adept at fundraising and pooling campaign resources (Kolodny 1998), but their activities as well as those of individual members of Congress remained modest by today's standards. But then, the political parties began to experiment with using "soft money" to assist candidates. Soft money referred to money donated to political parties in unlimited amounts, to promote party building through subsidizing fixed expenses such as office space, staff, and other overhead costs (La Raja 2008; Magleby 2003; Magleby 2000; Magleby and Monson 2004; Malbin 2003). Diana Dwyre explains how the early use of soft money was to help state parties institutionally, while extracting hard money donations out of the same state parties to compensate for the sponsorship of their programs. Such continual "spinning" of restricted soft money into usable hard money was how soft money first helped congressional candidates (Dwyre 1996). Starting with the 1996 presidential campaign, political parties experimented with using these funds to run "issue-advocacy" advertisements, ads that promoted or attacked particular candidates without explicitly asking for voters to vote for or against these individuals. Consequently, soft money, and the decisions of party leaders to spend a lot of it to help particular candidates, became an important strategic factor in the congressional campaigns of 1998, 2000, and 2002 (Magleby 2003; Magleby 2000; Magleby and Monson 2004).

Knowing that soft money was defining the campaign finance landscape, the scope of expertise in this area mushroomed in the late 1990s and early 2000s. In 1999, Michael Malbin founded the Campaign Finance Institute (CFI), a non-partisan think tank devoted to conducting academic studies of campaign finance to be of use to policymakers and academics alike. Although not confined to the congressional arena, CFI has brought much attention to particular congressional campaign finance matters such as the Senate's reluctance to speed up electronic filing of their own campaign finance reports, a study of the effects television advertising vouchers would have on congressional elections, and discussion of the appropriateness of limited coordinated expenditures between parties and congressional candidates (Campaign Finance Institute 2010). In 2002, the *Election Law Journal* was founded, featuring contributions from the growing numbers of legal scholars specializing in this area. The journal has some original research articles, but mostly contains book reviews of the latest academic research on legal issues regarding campaigns and summaries of recent relevant cases. Tom Mann wrote an account of the role the political science community had in providing research that informed reformers' understanding of the issues at hand and in engaging in the reform process themselves (Mann 2003).

David Magleby, Quin Monson, and Kelly Patterson ran a number of projects aimed at revealing how soft money, which was at one time poorly recorded, was spent in congressional campaigns by political parties and interest groups (Magleby 2003; Magleby 2000; Magleby and Monson 2004; Magleby, Monson, and Patterson 2007; Magleby and Patterson 2008). These studies—all of them run through Brigham Young University's (BYU) Center for the Study of Elections and Democracy (CSED)—highlighted a number of important realities about soft money. First, soft money issue advocacy campaigning by political parties and interest groups was concentrated in only the most competitive congressional races, ranging from about thirty-five to sixty per cycle, a considerable drop from even the 1980s when 100 or more races would be in contention. Second, the political parties would often match or exceed the total amount of expenditure spent by the candidate they were trying to assist on soft money issue advertising. Third, most of the money spent in this way was spent on television advertising, which was followed by direct mail and grassroots communications. When we consider that candidates have considerable overhead expenses to pay (such as office space and equipment) out of their overall expenditure, the amounts spent by the party soft money on campaign communications almost always exceeded the amount that campaigns could spend on their own communications efforts in competitive races. The use of soft money by political parties and interest groups was often a mixed blessing for the targeted candidates, though. As the laws strictly prohibited coordination, candidates had no control over the content of the appeals, limiting their ability to control the issue agenda discussed during the campaign, as well as the characterization of their opponent. This was especially problematic in a few cases, where soft money groups and political party organization made errors of fact in their ads—errors which reflected badly on the candidates they were supposed to help, as the media and the public were unaware of the legal distinctions between the campaign entities.

As a result, many members of Congress were ambivalent about soft money, even if the parties were fans of it. The impetus for the Bipartisan Campaign Finance Reform Act of 2002 (BCRA) was to close down this soft money loophole and, in compensation, to allow contribution limits to be both raised and indexed for inflation. Parties were here portrayed to be the bad actors, demonstrating their propensity to be "corrupt conduits" between wealthy donors seeking to "buy" policy outcomes and officeholders so seduced by the cash as to be ready to capitulate. The political complications of the BCRA itself are well documented in two books by Diana Dwyre and Victoria Farrar-Myers (Dwyre and Farrar-Myers 2001; Farrar-Myers and Dwyre 2007). They show first why BCRA initially failed to pass, and, second, how it eventually succeeded. Michael Malbin and the Campaign Finance Institute produced books that both predicted and evaluated BCRA's effects for a variety of political actors, with some particular focus on Congress (Malbin 2003, 2006). Moscardelli and Haspel explain the willingness of Democrats and of some Republicans to adopt a radical change like BCRA to be a function of party culture (more decentralized Democrats favoring outside group activity), as well as party ideology and perceived self-interest under the old regime (Moscardelli and Haspel 2007).

Another important change in the regulatory environment came from outside of the soft money debate. A Supreme Court case in 1996 (*Colorado Republican Federal Campaign Committee* v *Federal Election Commission*, 116 S.Ct.2309) decided that the political parties should have the ability to make hard money independent expenditures on behalf of their candidates in unlimited amounts, without the candidates' knowledge or consent (Corrado 1997). There was minimal experimentation with this new option in the late 1990s by the Hill committees. Independent expenditures were abandoned in favor of issue advocacy campaigning, ostensibly because of the ease of raising large soft money donations, compared to the relative difficulty of collecting much smaller hard money donations. But BCRA, by outlawing the collection of soft money, showed this perception about the scarcity of hard money to be false. Indeed, political parties not only compensated for the loss of soft money with hard, they far exceeded anyone's expectations (including their own) about the popularity parties would have with new donors not previously approached. Soft money had made the parties lazy in fundraising, even if it had not corrupted them (Malbin 2006). With soft money gone, the hard money option of independent expenditures gave congressional candidates reasons to pay attention to the political party organization and the collective interests of the party. Independent expenditures required hard money, some of it now raised with the help of incumbents. Likewise, some candidates' campaigns were likely to see not tens of thousands of dollars spent in their races, but millions.

While eliminating soft money, BCRA also increased the donation limits for individuals to candidates, political party committees, and overall per election cycle. In addition, these dollar limits were indexed for inflation, meaning that new limits are calculated by the FEC for each two-year cycle. Notably, BCRA does not index the contribution limits to PACs from individuals or from PACs to candidates. For 2010, individuals can give $2,400 per election (primary and general) to a candidate and $5,000 to a PAC. Before long, the two limits will meet, and eventually limits on donations to candidates will surpass donation limits to PACs. Consequently, BCRA privileges the link between candidates and individual donors, though, as we will see later, this does not necessarily widen the number of ties between candidates and individual donors but deepens them, as strong supporters will contribute at an increased level, whether those candidates truly need the funds for increased campaign communications or not. Challengers benefit from this emphasis as well, as they were never favored by the interest group community for campaign investment.

WHO DONATES TO CONGRESSIONAL CAMPAIGNS?

If, then, the system seems destined to stay in private hands, then just exactly who are the people who give money to congressional campaigns and why do they do it? Donations to congressional campaigns can be given by individual American citizens, political action committees (PACs), political parties, and the candidates themselves.

The democratic ideal seems to be that individuals, especially small donors, will give the bulk of monies that candidates need. Indeed, this has turned out to be the case. House candidates receive about 39 percent and Senate about 45 percent of their total direct campaign funds from individuals (Herrnson 2000). But what does it mean to get money from individuals? Again, the image is one of "average" people looking at the candidates, considering their issue positions, and making the donation in the purely idealistic wish to see their preferred policy positions enacted. Are individual citizens truly disinterested? The consensus seems to be that they are very interested indeed. Looking at the statement of employer requested by the FEC from individual donors, we know that donors are either employed by "interests" or may state that they are retired, self-employed, homemakers, or philanthropists. Since the FEC does not authenticate employment statements, it is impossible to know if a homemaker is married to a corporate CEO or if a philanthropist makes his or her donation from an inherited trust fund. In a comprehensive study of congressional donors, a team of academics found that donors in congressional races were motivated by material interests, ideological interests, and solidaristic interests. From previous literature, we would expect donors to be interested in the access that donations can buy in order to lobby on behalf of their material interests. However, a significant minority of donors said they gave to candidates whose views reflected theirs in a number of ideological causes (especially environment and social issues). Finally, some donors just wanted to go to a good cocktail party, picnic in their neighborhood, or to see and be seen (Francia, Green, Herrnson, Powell, and Wilcox 2003). While the social aspects of donating seem new to academics, some journalists have been more concerned about this "issue-less" motivation than about the "interested" ones (Birnbaum 2000).

Surprisingly, given the available (though user-unfriendly) data on donors since the 1970s, little research has been done about the motivations of donors in congressional campaigns. Michael Ensley explains that the literature divides into two major schools of thought: that of the quid pro quo motivation (PACs are assumed to want this) and that of the ideological motivation, to which individuals respond. Ensley looks to revisit a question earlier posed by James Snyder (Snyder 1990) about the importance of the match between candidate ideology and donor ideology by asking whether donors give to candidates with more extreme views and in races where the candidates differ greatly. He finds that, while ideology is clearly important, candidate divergence (in terms of policy distance) does not generate greater contributions (Ensley 2009). Ensley underscores the long-held belief that incumbents have significant non-policy advantages on the basis of their familiarity with constituents and reputations that allow them flexibility to pursue a wide range of policy positions and still fundraise effectively. The incumbency advantage explains the reverse side of donor desires—perhaps donors are not looking for candidates to influence with their investment as much as candidates are looking to persuade any supporter (no matter how tenuous) to become a donor. In one of the few studies of this relationship in congressional campaigns, Grant and Rudolph (2002) studied the role of solicitation in extracting contributions. They find that individuals who are asked to give money to campaigns are far more likely to do so than those who are not. While this may seem intuitively obvious, it illustrates that the relationship between donors and candidates is very much a two-way street. Donors looking to purchase access or influence will not wait for an invitation. Those who are interested predominantly in issues and social prestige will respond to a request, and it is this political interest, rather than high income, that determines whether or not a citizen becomes a donor.

Since the BCRA, and especially in the wake of the 2008 election, campaign finance watchers seem taken with the expansion of the small donor base in politics. Estimates of the proportion of the voting-age population donating to campaigns range from 10 to 14 percent for presidential races, and somewhere in the neighborhood of 2 to 3 percent for congressional races. Consequently, the only detailed surveys of small donors are in the presidential arena; yet these findings have great relevance here. In a report issued jointly by the Institute for Politics, Democracy and the Internet and the Campaign Finance Institute, donors to the 2004 presidential campaign were surveyed. These scholars asked what differences existed between those who donated $100 or less and those who donated $500 or more (two exclusive categories). Demographically, there is almost no difference in age between the small and large donors, but they do differ in income levels and level of education, the least educated donors giving the smallest amount (Graf, Reeher, et al. 2006). Also, small donors are more likely to be retired than large donors and are distributed at each end of the age spectrum (the youngest and oldest voters), although the median age for both groups was 57. Graf and colleagues found that small donors are not quite as elitist as large donors, but they are still wealthier and better educated than the general voting public.

One important aggregation of individuals is an interest group. Organized interests seek to influence policy in Congress. One obvious way they do this is by lobbying lawmakers during legislative sessions. Another way is to advocate the election of candidates who are friendly to your positions, or to encourage the defeat of those who are not. In the wake of the Buckley decision, much scholarly focus was addressed to the idea of political action committees (PACs), the overtly political arms of interest groups, and the reasons they wanted to give to congressional candidates. The PAC explosion became a popular topic as the number of PACs continued to grow. Whom did they give to? What was the result? While there was some discussion that PACs might actually be beneficial because they aided transparency, unlike the generic "individual" donations, and therefore helped disentangle members from their special interests, the great bulk of the literature assumed PAC influence to be negative (Cann 2008; Davis 1992; Grier and Munger 1993; Grier, Munger, and Roberts 1994; Rudolph 1999; Hojnacki and Kimball 2001). As discussed above and more below, political parties are a source of funds. Party organizations at the national, state, and local levels all can provide cash or in-kind contributions, which include important resources such as office space, staff, and other infrastructure items (e.g. utilities, office equipment, and transportation). Ostensibly, parties help candidates with the greatest chance of winning or losing, in other words those on the margins in highly competitive districts (this has been true since the 1994 election). During the soft money era, parties were accused of having inappropriate relationships with the donors who gave such vast sums (Apollonio and La Raja 2004). Such relationships were the chief motivation for the BCRA reforms.

Of course, free-speech rights guarantee that candidates can use their own money to fund their election campaigns if they desire. The law has changed over time, to allow more or less restrictions on this practice (i.e. whether candidates can loan themselves money that must be repaid, whether they can make unlimited donations to themselves, or whether their opponents get extra consideration in fundraising limits—aka BCRA's now defunct "millionaire's amendment"—in campaigns where candidates spent on themselves). Jennifer Steen has paid careful attention to the consequences of self-financed candidates on congressional elections themselves. Steen's analysis divides the problem into whether wealthy candidates have a chilling effect on competition, scaring away potential quality candidates (they do, but the effect is not as large as we may believe) and whether the wealthy candidates tend to succeed in "buying" the election (they don't; Steen 2006). The self-financed candidate problem is less prevalent than many believe, yet the idea of wealthy people paying for their own campaigns, as free-speech rights allow, seems undemocratic.

The existence of a wholly privately funded system has implications beyond the preferences of donors. What sorts of candidates are likely to emerge in an entrepreneurial system like this? While there has been work done in the literature on congressional candidate ambition and recruitment (Fowler and McClure 1989; Canon 1990; Kazee 1994), the fact that members of Congress must not only know wealthy people but know how to charm wealthy people to be serious candidates means that some able politicians will be excluded from service. Since the entire system forces candidates to be entrepreneurial in this way, the fundraising process has a deterring effect as well (Lawless and Fox 2005).

WHAT THE MONEY IS FOR

It seems obvious that congressional candidates need money to run their election campaigns. We commonly think of campaign expenses as meaning direct communication with voters. But long before the first commercial is aired or the first debate conducted, congressional candidates use campaign funds for a wide variety of additional functions. First, the size of a campaign fund signals to other candidates (prospective primary challengers and general election opponents) the potential for electoral success. Second, a great deal of money is expended for purposes other than direct campaign communications, especially since congressional candidates are discouraged from merging with local party organizations. Third, many electorally safe incumbents have a large discrepancy between what it costs to get reelected and what they can raise without much effort. Consequently, the use of excess campaign dollars to leverage leadership positions in Congress has very broad implications for the importance of campaign solicitation and for the nature of congressional business.

Signaling

Epstein and Zemsky argue that amassing "war chests" to deter significant challenges is a form of important signaling behavior on the part of incumbents. The transparency of reporting to the Federal Election Commission, which then quickly disseminates the information to the public, results in an "arms race" for funds between candidates that drives up the amount of money husbanded for congressional elections (Epstein and Zemsky 1995). This explains why fundraising is a constant feature of congressional life. Incumbent members of Congress raise money even when there is no campaign on the horizon. This again shows how members can end up spending more time visiting with their financial supporters than with the bulk of the constituents they represent (Francia, Green, et al. 2003). Herrnson has made an important distinction between campaigning for votes (at home) and campaigning in Washington (for resources, especially campaign donations) that is instructive for all candidates, but especially for challengers (Herrnson 2008). Since incumbents have a natural base in Washington from which to raise money, the challengers must prove their electoral potential very early on, through their ability to attract funders. If challengers can raise significant funds in the district, then they can persuade PACs and parties in Washington that further investment is worthwhile. Conversely, investment by interest groups and parties (including party leaders in Congress) helps persuade donors in the district of a candidate's electoral viability.

Campaign expenses

The data to study congressional campaign spending are very hard to come by. The literature on campaign effects uses aggregate campaign expenditures, or the total amount spent by a candidate during a campaign cycle, as an indicator of what campaigns cost, and therefore of what campaigning costs (Coleman and Manna 2000; Green and Krasno 1988; Jacobson 1990; Green and Krasno 1990). Ansolabehere and Gerber (1994) asked whether most models looking for campaign effects miss the mark because they use aggregate measures of campaign spending. They argue that this is problematic because total expenditures do not tell us how much was spent on actual campaigning (as opposed to overhead, personal travel, and as will be discussed below, contributions to other members/candidates and parties). The authors analyzed candidate spending in the 1990 mid-term election using data that coded spending in several broad categories: overhead, fundraising, polling, advertising, direct campaign activities, and donations. Their work confirmed previous negative results on incumbent spending (compared to challenger spending). In fact, they found that, as challengers spent more of their money on voter communications as a percentage, they tended to increase their vote share per dollar spent at a greater magnitude, while incumbents spending on communications tended to lose votes in the process (Ansolabehere and Gerber 1994). In a separate study of candidate spending in Senate elections, Gerber found that incumbent spending did indeed have a positive effect on vote share. When estimated with a TSLS method (rather than OLS),[1] which acknowledges the endogeneity of incumbent and challenger fundrais-

---

[1]   This stands for two-staged least squares (TSLS) and ordinary least squares (OLS), two different types of regression calculation.

ing, incumbent and challenger spending had about the same magnitude of effect. Since incumbents normally outspend challengers, they tended to reap the rewards electorally (Gerber 1998). While these analyses did show differences in how money was spent, very little other work exists, due to the difficulty of collecting data. Today, the FEC and repackaging websites such as the Center for Responsive Politics do report how candidates spend their money in broad categories, but the data are only available in recent election cycles, forcing those who would be interested in such disaggregation to go deep into the individual campaign filings of thousands of candidates.

Paul Herrnson, in his book *Congressional Elections*, includes a survey of congressional campaign managers and candidates, asking them to specify what percentage of their campaign budgets are spent on various types of campaign activities in both Senate and House elections (Herrnson 2008). This estimate is certainly an improvement over the lack of attention to the subject, but the recall involved in this data is not as good as having actual FEC reporting. Even more to the point, the study of campaign finance broadly, and of congressional campaign finance in particular, side-steps the question of who literally profits in this system. The legal set-up forces congressional candidates to operate their campaigns like small businesses, entirely separately from the party organizations, especially before a primary. This means that congressional campaigns must rent office space and office equipment and purchase stationary, office supplies, utilities, and labor. In addition, the campaigns must run fundraising and publicity events involving the purchase of food, the rental of venues, the production of bumper stickers, buttons, and lawn signs. Then, of course, there are the campaign ads and the direct mailing pieces. Campaigns purchase ad time, ad production, mailing pieces, and postage. Where races are extremely competitive, the political parties often get involved, purchasing advertising time, production, polls and mailing pieces as well. So, while we have tossed around the relationship between donors and representatives, we have not really considered the relationship between representatives/candidates and their vendors.

These relationships raise numerous ethical issues. Are relatives on the payroll? Are candidates, especially incumbents, receiving favorable deals on rental space for campaign headquarters or other campaign commodities—deals that amount to campaign contributions? Below we will discuss how campaign resources affect the policymaking process in Congress. But we seem not to have asked how the local campaign economy interacts with members' representational roles. What relationship is there between how much time members spend in the district and the distribution of campaign resources? What about the proportion of federal staff assigned to the district? Or about the number of district offices? So much congressional literature focuses on the importance of national variables that other explanations, such as the chance that a politician might have intensely place-oriented ambitions, are not considered. J. P. Monroe's argument that an elected official's district office is densely networked with other local officeholders' (such as state senator, state representative, county officials, members of the US House and Senate) all in the same geographic region (in this case, LA County) points to a different possibility for the ambitions and focus of members of Congress (Monroe 2001).

Non-campaign expenditures

In the aggregate analyses of spending, few scholars spend much time on how candidates transfer campaign funds to other candidates or to political party committees. In other words, virtually all studies of expenditures in the aggregate make the assumption that candidates spend all this money campaigning for themselves. While member-to-member transfers have been analyzed in the literature discussed in the next section, they are seldom referred to in the cost of campaigning. That is, scholars assume that all the money candidates spend is for the direct benefit of their electoral fortunes and therefore should be linked closely to competitiveness. Instead, it seems clear that an increasing proportion of incumbents plan for a certain portion of their campaign receipts to be spent on the campaigns of others in order to leverage power in the chamber for themselves, should they be reelected. Since transfers to candidates happen throughout the election cycle (especially in the case of special elections), these transfers can be made even if a member ends up with a competitive race. And, even if in the end they are not reelected, contributing to the well-being of the party will be remembered and potentially pay off, should the candidate decide to try a rematch or continue their career in politics in a different capacity (e.g. as a high-level staffer, lobbyist, or political consultant). In addition, political fundraising is the huge loophole in tough new regulations, which prohibit lobbyists paying for members' special perks. Organized interests can just contribute to a members' leadership PAC, and then that PAC hosts fundraising events and policy forums that include golf outings, fishing trips, dinners, sporting events, and so on, which the member and presumably lobbyist/donor, can enjoy (Kirkpatrick 2007).

IMPLICATIONS OF CAMPAIGN MONEY

As Squire's previous review of this literature explains, many political observers believe there is a relationship between campaign contributions, especially by interest groups, and the legislative behavior of congressmen (Squire 1995). The cynical view, researched in many different forms, was that campaign donations are given as "bribes" to congressman who might vote differently on legislation in the absence of such inappropriate influence. However, this relationship does not hold up well to close examination and probably never could be definitively proven anyway, given the complexity of appeals and constituency obligations of elected officials. A very important change in the discussion was fostered by Hall and Wayman (1990), who carefully demonstrate how PAC donations influence members' decisions on how to allocate their time and effort in the policy arena, but do not influence their votes. Using an impressive mix of quantitative and qualitative methods, Hall and Wayman reframe the way scholars understand the influence of money in politics, in terms of participation rather than of vote-buying. Beth Leech's chapter in this volume, "Lobbying and Interest Group Advocacy," discusses this literature further, assessing whether groups succeed by converting unfriendly members (they don't tend to) or by activating members already in favor of their position (a much more successful strategy).

Scholars next turned to the increasingly active role of the national political party organizations, especially the four Capitol Hill committees, and asked if the commitment of party resources was meant to influence partisan behavior in the policy process. First, attempts were made to assess how party support in congressional elections affected congressional party loyalty in the chamber. Kevin Leyden and Stephen Borelli first found mixed results, Republicans responding to coordinated spending by political parties with higher party unity, while Democrats seemed unaffected (Leyden and Borrelli 1990). David Cantor and Paul Herrnson found no relationship between party financial support and overall party unity scores, but did find increased loyalty among Democrats on key party votes who received not only cash, but a variety of campaign services from the party's congressional campaign committee (Cantor and Herrnson 1997). Richard Clucas found that party investment does not result in more partisan voting, but does have an effect on the legislative support that recipients give to the issues championed by the members of Congress who headed the campaign committees in the previous cycle, and thus assisted their election in a material way (Clucas 1997). But Damore and Hansford (1999) found that parties invest in candidates exclusively for campaign reasons, and not for the purpose of building stronger parties in terms of voting on bills. Tim Nokken found the same in his study of Senate contributions and coordinated expenditures, but he did find some evidence of ideological influence in independent expenditures. The latter finding may be easier to detect, due to the enormous variance in size of this spending category (Nokken 2003). Ultimately, the balance of the evidence suggests that the electoral imperatives of majority status trump ideological concerns. While some conforming behavior may occur, this is not a significant benefit of party investment.

The research agenda around what campaign money buys misses some fundamental questions about how campaign finance affects the internal operations of Congress. First, fundraising ability is now a critical tool to gain advancement in the party and committee leadership structures of the House and Senate. Second, the emphasis on fundraising affects how members spend their time while they are in Congress, and this in turn affects the nature of the policymaking process. Fortunately, in recent years there has been a series of studies looking at the consequences of members giving money to other members or to the party organization. This phenomenon barely existed before the 1990s, which shows how much the institutional environment of Congress and elections has changed. Once political parties began to spend significant amounts on congressional campaigns, they needed to have funds supplied to them, and they needed to decide where to spend the funds best. Parties turned to incumbent members to raise the funds, and some incumbents decided to redistribute campaign funds themselves in addition to, not instead of, collective party donations. What was the reward for this type of behavior? Consequently, what effect does such generosity have on the beneficiaries? Did they reward their donors with loyal policy support or personal support for leadership campaigns?

Several scholars have examined what happens when individual members decide to use their campaign fundraising abilities to distribute money to other candidates on their own. Eric Heberlig and Bruce Larson have conducted extensive research into members' donations to the party committees, members' donations to other candidates from their personal campaign accounts, and how this behaviour assists their own ambitions within Congress (Heberlig and Larson 2005, 2007; Heberlig 2003; Heberlig, Larson, et al. 2008; Heberlig, Hetherington, and Larson 2006; Larson 2004). Heberlig and Larson challenge us to examine fundamental ideas about what happens to campaign cash, and relate to them the idea that donors are unaware that their funds may be used for the election expenses of others. Marian Currinder examined leadership PAC contribution strategies from Members of Congress to other candidates for Congress (incumbent, challenger, or open seat). She found that those with the ambition to raise and spend money on behalf of others pursued the appropriate strategy either to help their party retain majority status by shoring up vulnerable incumbents, or to help their minority party become a majority by investing more in non-incumbent candidates. In addition, she finds that committee chairs and "extended" leadership position holders tend to invest more in incumbents than challengers in order to shore up support for their future leadership bids (Currinder 2003). Kristin Kanthak finds that, in the case of leadership PACs, a similar ideological position and likelihood of continued or future leadership support motivate this type of giving from members—and not a broader party strategy (Kanthak 2007). Raso examines leadership PACs, asking how the money is spent—for administrative expenses or for candidate contributions. He finds that members ambitious for leadership positions (in the majority party) or for the presidency have the greatest proportion of their funds devoted to others. While this seems intuitive, Raso's is the only study directly establishing the link (Raso 2008). Heberlig, Larson, et al. (2008) managed to obtain a rare data-set on incumbent fundraising for a major party committee dinner and compared it to incumbent donations to the party out of their personal campaign funds. They found that, when it came to raising money for the DC based gala, members turned to their "friends" in the lobbying community in Washington, where it seems that their policy ties matter more than the competitiveness of their individual campaigns or their party loyalty. Conversely, donations to the party from members' personal accounts depends much more on their level of party loyalty and on the race they expect to face next—the less competitive the race, the more is likely to be given to the party. This research suggests important new avenues for research concerning donor networks, the political parties, and the policy agenda.

Of great interest is the question of how the value of money in the chamber changes the currency of legislative exchange. Marian Currinder's *Money in the House* and Damon Cann's *Sharing the Wealth* deal with the implications of money transfers directly. While a generation ago the ability to forge compromise, garner expertise, and demonstrate moderation earned one a leadership position (Truman 1959; Peabody 1976), it seems clear that the ability to raise funds has supplanted those values and has become a central strategy for securing committee chairmanships and leadership positions (Cann 2008; Currinder 2009). For instance, since the 1994 elections, all incumbents have been assessed "dues" to pay to their relevant congressional campaign committee on a sliding scale commensurate with the prestige of their leadership or committee positions. The reaction to this development has been uniformly negative in the scholarly and practitioner community—but should it be? Raising money for other members means that you are by default concerned with the electoral fortunes of others and confronting the political party majority status collective action problem head on. Such reallocation of campaign funds by incumbents may, as a result, compound the voice of certain donors and organized interests, but this also has the result of drawing clearer lines between the political parties' positions and policy directions.

Understanding the internal dynamics of money inside Congress should also force us to reassess the idea that campaigns cost more than ever. We really do not know this to be true. We may find more dollars being collected, but many candidates do not spend their money to communicate with voters. If they send funds to party committees or other candidates, this tells us that they have ambitions within the chamber, not that they need to engage in more campaigning. As for the competitive districts where more and more money is spent on campaigning, it is unclear whether voters actually benefit from the increased communications, or whether they become over-saturated with messages. Future researchers should enter the study of congressional campaign finance with these broader questions in mind, perhaps trying to tie the strands of public opinion, donor behavior, and member behavior together.

The Citizens United decision and the future of corporate money

In January of 2010, the Supreme Court decided the case *Citizens United* v *FEC*. The decision gained national attention because of the court's bold declaration that corporations shared the same free speech rights as individuals in political campaigns. Therefore the long-standing requirement that corporations may only engage in overt campaign activity through the device of political action committees (PACs), whose donations were fully disclosed and held in a fund that was separate and segregated from the corporation's regular operating funds, is now eliminated. Starting with the 2010 election cycle, corporations can spend on independent campaign activity from their general operating funds. This means that there are no donation limits for corporate expenditures on independent campaigns, no disclosure requirements about the source of funds for these campaigns, and no disclosure requirements about the expenditure of funds. We may have no idea how much a corporation spends on politics and for what—information we have come to expect since the mid 1970s. If corporations choose to keep their PACs (and many will, as it is the only way still for them to donate to candidates directly), they will be one out of several options for corporate activity, not the only one. In addition, it is too early to know how the new regulatory environment will play out. Members of Congress have already introduced legislation to impose disclosure requirements and other limitations on corporate spending, which may well result in further litigation and uncertainty. The

Federal Election Commission has not yet issued bureaucratic rules in this area, nor had an opportunity to consider any compliance issues which may arise in the 2010 campaigns.

AVENUES FOR FUTURE RESEARCH

This review has tried to highlight what we do not know as much as what we do know. I also reveal some of the normative assumptions behind what is "good" or "appropriate" legislative behavior. Here I suggest future avenues for research.

The issue of access to and participation in the political system by citizens is a universal concern of scholars of democracy. In this context, is the nature of donor behavior as a form of participation meaningful? The donation itself is probably not the decisive act. It is all the behaviors that accompany the donation—requests for meetings, lobbying for particular legislation, or making a social appearance at a donor's party—that count. How can we study the relevance or irrelevance of donor demands on recipients? What representative and legislative actions are taken in response to donor considerations? Does a donor have to make an explicit request? Participant observation studies could reveal a great deal here, as could a study of district-based activities and the presence of donors. Mixed methods research would be particularly instructive.

The problem of public funding—the idea of public money for congressional campaign finance—is entirely far-fetched in the present climate. However, this chapter shows that we do not have a very good understanding of the reasons why. The literature has assumed that incumbents desire private financing because of their natural advantage vis-à-vis challengers to raise enough to scare off competition. The case of self-funded candidates calls that premise into question, as these candidates have an exceptionally high failure rate. But public financing would eliminate the asset of fundraising prowess as a consideration for leadership advancement and prestige committee assignments. Despite the sound-bite responses about members "hating" fundraising, perhaps some members find it easier to curry favor with donors than to carve out difficult policy compromises as a way to advance. Future research should look deeper at members' motives for maintaining the private system. After BCRA, we find that, for many members, it is now easier to raise money, not harder, and that more and more of the money is reshuffled among peers rather than used for campaign expenses. Is this all a net negative for the policy process? Perhaps not, as fundraising itself is an act of communication—explaining the needs of the party to donors while listening to the concerns of the major stakeholders in the political process. Which members are active with the party committees? What are their policy committee assignments? What relationship is there between fundraising activism and policy activism, or is this an inverse relationship?

Related to the issue of public versus private campaign finance is the question of party versus candidate campaign finance. We need more information on what happens when parties decide to get involved in particular races and what the consequences are. Certainly, there have been attempts to measure aggregate spending on election outcomes, but what sort of spending matters most? And how are members who win with party assistance socialized differently than those who win without it? We now have data since 1976 on how parties and candidates raise and spend their campaign money. While not all of the data are in analytically friendly formats, they are available. Starting in the 2008 cycle, more is available in user-friendly formats from a number of re-packaging sites. Also, no scholarly attention has been paid to the party staff members who perform these duties. What do they get from such familiarity with congressional campaigns? At least one former NRCC staffer, Tom Cole, got himself elected to Congress. Others now run important interest group PACs, political consulting firms, or have administrative roles in the legislative and executive branches. Network analysis can show us a great deal about the most influential actors in the party–candidate relationship.

We have very little information on the behavior and motivations of congressional donors. While we have good theorizing on donors who give to candidates for material and ideological reasons, we do not have a good framework for dealing with socially motivated donors. Those who literally want to throw and go to parties remind us of earlier discussions of the power elite and the distortion of agenda-setting and issue definitions. Future research should pay greater attention to the fundraising culture and its implications for member behavior at home and in Washington. For example, new members are coached to hold a fundraiser immediately after election and to plan their reelection campaigns virtually immediately. Some members keep campaign staff employed constantly (even during off years). How does the need to placate donors in a symbolic way influence the choice of district events to attend? Does it impact the time spent on the floor, giving accolades to constituents? These answers could yield important insights into the norms of congressional behavior that are informed by campaign finance.

The local context of campaign spending is crying out for study. Since federal laws force congressional candidates to run "enterprises" entirely separately from the state and local party organizations, does that mean that in practice incumbents have separate interactions with their local political structures? Here is where comparative case studies could be especially valuable—of congressional campaign staff, local party organization operatives, district staffers at the state and local level—and the networks that all of them may have with a local community of campaign vendors. Does information sharing occur even when the law states it should not happen? Do active donors—who may give to neighborhood candidates at many levels—perform an extra-institutional role between the disparate electoral actors? Does this system provide effective or distorted representation?

We have our work cut out for us. With 535 "enterprises" pursuing disparate goals in the collection and dissemination of campaign money, our study of congressional campaign finance will continue to yield important new insights.

References

ALDRICH, J. H. 1995. *Why Parties?: The Origin and Transformation of Political Parties in America.* Chicago: University of Chicago Press.

ANSOLABEHERE, S., and GERBER, A. 1994. The Mismeasure of Campaign Spending: Evidence from the 1990 U.S. House Elections. *Journal of Politics*, 56(4): 1106–18.

——SNOWBERG, E. C., and SNYDER, JR., J. M. 2005. Unrepresentative Information. *Public Opinion Quarterly*, 69(2): 213–31.

APOLLONIO, D. E., and LA RAJA, R. J. 2004. Who Gave Soft Money? The Effect of Interest Group Resources on Political Contributions. *Journal of Politics*, 66(4): 1134–54.

BIRNBAUM, J. H. 2000. *The Money Men: The Real Story of Fund-Raising's Influence on Political Power in America.* 1st edition. New York: Crown.

CAMPAIGN FINANCE INSTITUTE. 2010. Releases and Analyses. Available at: http://www.cfinst. org/pr/ (accessed January 6, 2010).

CANN, D. M. 2008. *Sharing the Wealth: Member Contributions and the Exchange Theory of Party Influence in the US House of Representatives.* Albany: State University of New York Press.

CANON, D. T. 1990. *Actors, Athletes, and Astronauts: Political Amateurs in the United States Congress.* Chicago: University of Chicago Press.

CANTOR, D. M., and HERRNSON, P. S. 1997. Party Campaign Activity and Party Unity in the U.S. House of Representatives. *Legislative Studies Quarterly*, 22(3): 393–415.

CLUCAS, R. A. 1997. Party Contributions and the Influence of Campaign Committee Chairs on Roll-Call Voting. *Legislative Studies Quarterly*, 22(2): 179–94.

COLEMAN, J. J., and MANNA, P. F. 2000. Congressional Campaign Spending and the Quality of Democracy. *The Journal of Politics*, 62(3): 757–89.

CORRADO, A., ed. 1997. *Campaign Finance Reform: A Sourcebook.* Washington, DC: Brookings Institution.

CURRINDER, M. 2009. *Money in the House: Campaign Funds and Congressional Party Politics.* Boulder, CO: Westview Press.

CURRINDER, M. L. 2003. Leadership PAC Contribution Strategies and House Member Ambitions. *Legislative Studies Quarterly*, 28(4): 551–77.

DAMORE, D. F., and HANSFORD, T. G. 1999. The Allocation of Party Controlled Campaign Resources in the House of Representatives, 1989–1996. *Political Research Quarterly*, 52(2): 371–85.

DAVIS, F. L. 1992. Sophistication in Corporate PAC Contributions. *American Politics Quarterly*, 20(4): 388–410.

DWYRE, D. 1996. Spinning Straw into Gold: Soft Money and US House Elections. *Legislative Studies Quarterly*, 21(3): 409–24.

——and FARRAR-MYERS, V., eds. 2001. *Legislative Labyrinth: Congress and Campaign Finance Reform.* Washington, DC: CQ Press.

ENSLEY, M. J. 2009. Individual Campaign Contributions and Candidate Ideology. *Public Choice*, 138(1/2): 221–38.

EPSTEIN, D., and ZEMSKY, P. 1995. Money Talks: Deterring Quality Challengers in Congressional Elections. *The American Political Science Review*, 89(2): 295–308.

FARRAR-MYERS, V. A., and DWYRE, D. 2007. *Limits and Loopholes: The Quest for Money, Free Speech, and Fair Elections.* Washington, DC: CQ Press.

FOWLER, L. L., and MCCLURE, R. D., eds. 1989. *Political Ambition: Who Decides to Run for Congress.* New Haven: Yale University Press.

FRANCIA, P. L., GREEN, J. C., HERRNSON, P. S., POWELL, L. W., and WILCOX, C., eds. 2003. *The Financiers of Congressional Elections: Investors, Ideologues, and Intimates.* New York, USA, and Chichester: Columbia University Press.

GERBER, A. 1998. Estimating the Effect of Campaign Spending on Senate Election Outcomes using Instrumental Variables. *The American Political Science Review*, 92(2): 401–11.

GLASGOW, G. 2002. The Efficiency of Congressional Campaign Committee Contributions in House Elections. *Party Politics*, 8(6): 657–72.

GOODLIFFE, J. 2001. The Effect of War Chests on Challenger Entry in US House Elections. *American Journal of Political Science*, 45(4): 830–44.

—— 2004. War Chests as Precautionary Savings. *Political Behavior*, 26(4): 289–315.

—— 2005. When do War Chests Deter? *Journal of Theoretical Politics*, 17(2): 249–77.

GRAF, J., REEHER, G., MALBIN, M. J., and PANAGOPOULOS, C. 2006. *Small Donors and Online Giving: A Study of Donors to the 2004 Presidential Campaigns*. Washington, DC: Institute for Politics, Democracy and the Internet and the Campaign Finance Institute. Available at: http://www.ipdi.org/UploadedFiles/Small%20Donors%20Report.pdf (accessed January 12, 2010).

GRANT, J. T., and RUDOLPH, T. J. 2002. To Give or Not to Give: Modeling Individuals' Contribution Decisions. *Political Behavior*, 24(1): 31–54.

—— —— eds. 2004. *Expression vs Equality: The Politics of Campaign Finance Reform*. Columbus, OH: Ohio State University Press.

GREEN, D. P., and KRASNO, J. S. 1988. Salvation for the Spendthrift Incumbent: Reestimating the Effects of Campaign Spending in House Elections. *American Journal of Political Science*, 32(4): 884–904.

—— —— 1990. Rebuttal to Jacobson's "New Evidence for Old Arguments." *American Journal of Political Science*, 34(2): 363–72.

GRIER, K. B., and MUNGER, M. C. 1993. Comparing Interest Group PAC Contributions to House and Senate Incumbents, 1980–1986. *Journal of Politics*, 55(3): 615–43.

—— —— and ROBERTS, B. E. 1994. The Determinants of Industry Political Activity, 1978–1986. *The American Political Science Review*, 88(4): 911–26.

HALL, R. L., and WAYMAN, F. W. 1990. Buying Time: Moneyed Interests and the Mobilization of Bias in Congressional Committees. *The American Political Science Review*, 84(3): 797–820.

HEBERLIG, E. S. 2003. Congressional Parties, Fundraising, and Committee Ambition. *Political Research Quarterly*, 56(2): 151–61.

—— and LARSON, B. A. 2005. Redistributing Campaign Funds by U.S. House Members: The Spiraling Costs of the Permanent Campaign. *Legislative Studies Quarterly*, 30(4): 597–622.

—— —— 2007. Party Fundraising, Descriptive Representation, and the Battle for Majority Control: Shifting Leadership Appointment Strategies in the US House of Representatives, 1990–2002. *Social Science Quarterly*, 88(2): 404–21.

—— HETHERINGTON, M., and LARSON, B. 2006. The Price of Leadership: Campaign Money and the Polarization of Congressional Parties. *Journal of Politics*, 68(4): 992–1005.

—— LARSON, B. A., SMITH, D. A., and SOLTIS, K. L. 2008. Look Who's Coming to Dinner: Direct Versus Brokered Member Campaign Contributions to the NRCC. *American Politics Research*, 36(3): 433–50.

HERRNSON, P. S. 1988. *Party Campaigning in the 1980s*. Cambridge, MA: Harvard University Press.

—— 2000. *Congressional Elections: Campaigning at Home and in Washington*, 3rd edition. Washington, DC: CQ Press.

—— 2008. *Congressional Elections: Campaigning at Home and in Washington*, 5th edition. Washington, DC: CQ Press.

—— 2009. The Roles of Party Organizations, Party-Connected Committees, and Party Allies in Elections. *Journal of Politics*, 71(4): 1207–24.

HOJNACKI, M., and KIMBALL, D. C. 2001. PAC Contributions and Lobbying Contracts in Congressional Committees. *Political Research Quarterly*, 54(1): 161–80.

JACKSON, B. 1990. *Broken Promise: Why the Federal Election Commission Failed*. New York: Priority Press.

JACOBSON, G. C. 1985. Party Organization and Distribution of Campaign Resources: Republicans and Democrats in 1982. *Political Science Quarterly*, 100(4): 603–25.

——1990. The Effects of Campaign Spending in House Elections: New Evidence for Old Arguments. *American Journal of Political Science*, 34(2): 334.

KANTHAK, K. 2007. Crystal Elephants and Committee Chairs: Campaign Contributions and Leadership Races in the US House of Representatives, 35(3): 389–406.

KAZEE, T. A., ed. 1994. *Who Runs for Congress? Ambition, Context, and Candidate Emergence*. Washington, DC: Congressional Quarterly.

KIRKPATRICK, D. D. 2007. Congress Finds Ways to Avoid Lobbyist Limits, *The New York Times*, February 11. Available at: *http://www.nytimes.com/2007/02/11/us/politics/11trips.html* (accessed January 20, 2009).

KOLODNY, R. 1998. *Pursuing Majorities: Congressional Campaign Committees in American Politics*. Norman: University of Oklahoma Press.

LA RAJA, R. J. 2008. *Small Change: Money, Political Parties, and Campaign Finance Reform*. Ann Arbor: University of Michigan Press.

LARSON, B. A. 2004. Incumbent Contributions to the Congressional Campaign Committees, 1990–2000. *Political Research Quarterly*, 57(1): 155–61.

LAWLESS, J. L., and FOX, R. L., eds. 2005. *It Takes a Candidate: Why Women Don't Run for Office*. Cambridge and New York: Cambridge University Press.

LEYDEN, K. M., and BORRELLI, S. A. 1990. Party Contributions and Party Unity: Can Loyalty be Bought? *The Western Political Quarterly*, 43(2): 343–65.

MAGLEBY, D. B., ed. 2000. *Outside Money: Soft Money and Issue Advocacy in the 1998 Congressional Elections*. Lanham, MD: Rowman & Littlefield Publishers.

——2003. *The Other Campaign: Soft Money and Issue Advocacy in the 2000 Congressional Elections*. Lanham, MD, and Oxford: Rowman & Littlefield.

——and PATTERSON, K. D., eds. 2008. *The Battle for Congress: Iraq, Scandal, and Campaign Finance in the 2006 Election*. Boulder, CO: Paradigm.

——and QUIN MONSON, J., eds. 2004. *The Last Hurrah? Soft Money and Issue Advocacy in the 2002 Congressional Elections*. Washington, DC: Brookings Institution Press.

————and PATTERSON, K. D., eds. 2007. *Electing Congress: New Rules for an Old Game*. Upper Saddle River, NJ: Pearson Prentice Hall.

MALBIN, M. J., ed. 2003. *Life After Reform: When the Bipartisan Campaign Reform Act Meets Politics*. Lanham, MD, and Oxford: Rowman & Littlefield.

——2006. *The Election After Reform: Money, Politics, and the Bipartisan Campaign Reform Act*. Lanham, MD: Rowman & Littlefield.

MANN, T. E. 2003. Linking Knowledge and Action: Political Science and Campaign Finance Reform. *Perspectives on Politics*, 1(1): 69–83.

MONROE, J. P. 2001. *The Political Party Matrix: The Persistence of Organization*. Albany: State University of New York Press.

MOSCARDELLI, V. G., and HASPEL, M. 2007. Campaign Finance Reform as Institutional Choice: Party Difference in the Vote to Ban Soft Money. *American Politics Research*, 35(1): 79–102.

NOKKEN, T. P. 2003. Ideological Congruence Versus Electoral Success: Distribution of Party Organization Contributions in Senate Elections, 1990–2000. *American Politics Research*, 31(1): 3–26.

PARKER, D. C. W. 2008. *The Power of Money in Congressional Campaigns, 1880–2006*. Norman: University of Oklahoma Press.

PEABODY, R. L. 1976. *Leadership in Congress: Stability, Succession and Change*. Boston: Little, Brown.

RASO, C. N. 2008. Leadership PAC Formation and Distribution Strategies in the United States Senate. *Journal of Political Marketing*, 7(1): 25–47.

RUDOLPH, T. J. 1999. Corporate and Labor PAC Contributions in House Elections: Measuring the Effects of Majority. *Journal of Politics*, 61(1): 195–206.

SNYDER, JR., J. M. 1990. Campaign Contributions as Investments: The U.S. House of Representatives, 1980–1986. *The Journal of Political Economy*, 98(6): 1195–227.

SQUIRE, P. 1995. Candidates, Money, and Voters. Assessing the State of Congressional Elections Research. *Political Research Quarterly*, 48(4): 891–917.

STEEN, J. A. 2006. *Self-Financed Candidates in Congressional Elections*. Ann Arbor: University of Michigan Press.

STRATMANN, T. 2005. Some Talk: Money in Politics. A (Partial) Review of the Literature. *Public Choice*, 124(1–2): 135–56.

SUNDQUIST, J. L. 1981. *The Decline and Resurgence of Congress*. Washington, DC: Brookings Institution.

TRUMAN, D. B. 1959. *The Congressional Party, a Case Study*. New York: Wiley.

PART IV

REPRESENTATION
AND
RESPONSIVENESS

DESCRIPTIVE REPRESENTATION: UNDERSTANDING THE IMPACT OF IDENTITY ON SUBSTANTIVE REPRESENTATION OF GROUP INTERESTS

MICHELE L. SWERS

STELLA M. ROUSE

WHEN Barack Obama took the oath of office as the nation's first African-American president in January 2009, he faced a very different Congress from that of the previous Democratic president, who presided over a Democratic House and Senate. Since Bill Clinton was elected president in 1992, Congress has experienced dramatic change in the demographic makeup of its membership. While Congress remains a largely white, male institution, the creation of majority–minority districts in the early 1990s resulted in the election of more African Americans and Hispanics to Congress. The 1992 election, dubbed the "Year of the Woman" by the national media, saw a dramatic increase in the number of women, particularly Democratic women, in Congress and this number has risen steadily over the years. The expansion of female and minority representation still continues, at a slow pace. The electoral advantage enjoyed by incumbents hinders the advancement of new groups into the institution. Moreover, to date, few minority legislators have been elected from districts that do not contain a high percentage of minority constituents. In fact, almost all of the minority legislators represent majority–minority districts (Lublin 1997; Clayton 2000). Furthermore, studies of political ambition demonstrate that women who have careers in professions that often lead to public office are less likely to express an interest in running for office than their male counterparts. Additionally, women are more likely to need the encouragement of party leaders or other opinion leaders before they decide to run for office (Lawless and Fox 2005). Research also shows that, once women are in office, they are more likely to be influenced by the effect of "career ceilings" (i.e. prolonged service in House without attaining leadership positions) as a determinant of whether or not they will seek reelection (Lawless and Theriault 2005). Literature on the congressional careers of minorities is quite sparse. Examining the career decisions of African Americans in the House of Representatives, Gerber (1996) finds that African-American legislators are significantly less likely than other Democrats to voluntarily exit from House service. He asserts that the long careers of African-American representatives bode well for their ability to attain political power in spite of their disproportionate numbers in Congress.

Although women and minorities remain underrepresented in Congress, individual legislators have achieved the seniority and political clout necessary to move into leadership positions. Thus Nancy Pelosi (D–CA) became Speaker of the House in the 110th Congress and James Clyburn an African American from South Carolina serves as Majority Whip. Several minority and female members have risen to chair influential committees in the 111th Congress, including Charles Rangel (D–NY) on Ways and Means and John Conyers (D–MI) on Judiciary. Silvestre Reyes (D–TX) in the House and Dianne Feinstein (D–CA) in the Senate lead the Select Committees on Intelligence.

The increasing presence and political power of women and minorities in Congress has led scholars to investigate whether the election of descriptive (women and minorities) representatives enhances the substantive representation of group interests. In this chapter we examine the theoretical expectations about the importance of descriptive representation and we evaluate the empirical evidence concerning the impact of gender, race, and ethnicity on the behavior of legislators. Finally, we identify important avenues for future research as the level of diversity in Congress continues to grow and more women and minorities enter the ranks of committee and party leadership.

THEORIES OF REPRESENTATION AND THE LINK BETWEEN DESCRIPTIVE AND SUBSTANTIVE REPRESENTATION

When the founders debated the Constitution, the quality of representation provided by the Congress was a major subject of contention. Anti-Federalists believed that Congress should be a microcosm reflecting society, while Federalists contended that groups have intertwined interests and the need to stand for frequent reelection would keep members loyal to all elements of their constituency (Storing 1981; Rossiter 1961). Today the debate continues as theorists weigh the importance of group representation against the negative consequences of dividing citizens based on demographic characteristics. The concern is that members of social groups are essentialized as having a specific set of shared interests and views that can only be represented by members of the group (Mansbridge 1999; Dovi 2002; Phillips 1991, 1995, 1998; Williams 1998).

In her classic work on representation, Pitkin (1967) makes a distinction between descriptive representatives, those who "stand for" a particular group because they share characteristics with the group such as race or gender, and substantive representatives, who "act for" a group by providing representation of the group's interests. Contemporary theorists debate whether the election of more descriptive representatives is a necessary or a sufficient condition for achieving the substantive representation of the interests of minority groups in society. Additionally, other scholars argue that descriptive representation may be neither strictly necessary nor sufficient for ensuring group representation, but it may still be beneficial, and thus it provides advantages that enhance the representation of group interests.

Theorists who advocate for the election of descriptive representatives identify a number of potential benefits. One set of arguments revolves around the enhancement of the connection between constituents and their representatives and the consequent increase in trust in government felt by underrepresented groups. The other major group of arguments in favor of descriptive representation focuses on the improvement of the quality of deliberation among legislators and on the impact on policy outputs (Mansbridge 1999; Dovi 2002; Williams 1998; Phillips 1991, 1995, 1998; Griffin and Newman 2008).

With regard to the relationship between legislators and their constituents, theorists argue that, in cases where there is a history of discrimination and mistrust, the election of a descriptive representative will improve communication between the minority group and government. As a result, constituents will feel more trust in their representatives and this will enhance the legitimacy of the government in the eyes of members of the underrepresented group. Moreover, the descriptive representatives will serve as role models for members of the underrepresented group, providing symbolic representation for group members and furthering a belief in their ability to rule in the eyes of both the minority and the majority (Phillips 1991, 1995, 1998; Mansbridge 1999; Dovi 2002).

Within the legislature, political theorists assert that the election of descriptive representatives will have important effects on the nature and quality of deliberation among legislators and the substantive representation of group interests in the content of policy outputs. On the basis of a history of shared experiences, descriptive representatives will bring new issues to the congressional agenda and will provide a different perspective on more established debates by delineating how those issues will differentially impact members of the underrepresented group. Descriptive representatives will be more likely to achieve inclusion of group interests in policy outcomes because of the moral authority they wield as members of the group and because of the vigorous advocacy they will bring to issues on the basis of their shared life experiences. The ability to bring divergent qualities to the representative arena increases the chances that a legislative body will achieve normative legitimacy (Mansbridge 1999; Williams 1998; Phillips 1991, 1995, 1998; Dovi 2002).

Of course a consensus does not exist on the relative costs and benefits of seeking to enhance descriptive representation. For example, Mansbridge (1999) argues that the benefits of descriptive representation vary by context; therefore, a descriptive representative is appropriate only under certain circumstances—specifically, when the benefits exceed the costs of such representation. In Mansbridge's view, the greatest cost of descriptive representation is that it reinforces tendencies toward "essentialism." This is the idea that members of a group have an "essential identity," shared only by members of that group. According to Mansbridge, the danger of "essentialism" is the assumption that members of a group are monolithic in their interests and that only those interests matter to the group. The empirical research on descriptive representation seeks to identify the conditions under which social identity influences legislative behavior.

DESCRIPTIVE REPRESENTATION AND THE CONSTITUENT–REPRESENTATIVE LINK

The expansion of representation resulting from the creation of majority–minority districts and the steady increase in the election of women and minorities since the early 1990s has allowed scholars systematically to test assertions about the potential impact of descriptive representation. Interviews with members of Congress demonstrate that minority and female members of Congress view racial minorities and women as a distinctive segment of their constituency; they feel a special responsibility to represent women and minority constituents, and they describe themselves as surrogate representatives of group members living outside their districts who do not have the benefit of a female or minority representative that understands their unique concerns (Reingold 1992; Carroll 2002; Hawkesworth 2003; Dodson, Carroll, et al. 1995; Dodson 2006; Swain 1993; Tate 2003). For example, in his qualitative study of black representatives, Fenno (2003) notes how Louis Stokes (D–OH) was well aware that his constituency encompassed much more than his district when he was first elected to Congress in 1968. Stokes commented on the significance of his election, which, along with that of two other newly elected African-American representatives, brought the total to nine black House members at that time:

The thrust of our elections was that many black people around America, who had formerly been unrepresented, now felt that the nine black members of the House owed them the obligation of also affording them representation in the House. It was in this context that each of the nine of us realized that in addition to representing our individual districts, we had to assume the onerous burden of acting as a congressmen-at-large for unrepresented people around America.   (Fenno 2003, 62)

This idea of surrogate representation led to the creation of the Congressional Black Caucus, of which Louis Stokes was a founding member. Scholars have emphasized the significance of group consciousness as the catalyst for the unity felt by members of the African-American community and the expectations they have of any descriptive representative (Dawson 1994; Tate 2003).

While the impact of descriptive representation on the motivations of legislators is clear, there is a limited number of studies that focus on whether the social identity of the representative influences the political views of their constituents. This line of research has produced mixed results. For example, on the one hand, Brunell, Anderson, and Cremona (2008) find that the election of a descriptive representative improves the attitudes of African-American voters toward their legislator. The authors also note that these voters' perceptions about the pervasiveness of African Americans in Congress enhance their opinion of Congress as an institution. On the other hand, scholars like Gay (2002) argue that the ability of blacks to identify racially with their representatives has little effect on how well they feel they are represented. Instead, blacks place more value on the policy preferences and policy responsiveness of their legislators. However, Gay does find that African-American constituents are more likely to contact an African-American representative, which may indicate at least a greater comfort level with a descriptive representative. Griffin and Flavin (2007) show that racial disparities exist at the level of the accountability placed on members of Congress; these disparities are based, in part, on differences between whites' and blacks' expectations of their representatives. The authors note that African Americans tend to be very loyal to descriptive representatives and that this loyalty is a disincentive to obtain information about the activities of their legislators or to be objective about their legislative behavior. With respect to ethnicity, Barreto (2007) finds that the presence of Latino candidates, regardless of their ideology or party affiliation, leads to greater Latino mobilization and participation. He shows that co-ethnicity serves as a strong heuristic for voter preferences, indicating that descriptive representation (i.e. the identity of the legislator) is important to Latinos.

With regard to women, there is currently very little empirical evidence that the political views of female constituents are dramatically affected by having a female representative. Burns, Schlozman, and Verba (2001) do find that the number of women candidates within a state and the presence of a female statewide officeholder improve feelings of political efficacy among women. Lawless (2004) found that women who were represented by women offered more positive evaluations of their representatives in Congress. However, these differences did not translate into increased feelings of political efficacy and trust in government, nor did they lead to increased levels of political interest or participation. Scholars should further investigate the impact that electing minorities and women may have on constituent opinion and political efficacy, particularly given the competitive presidential campaigns of Hillary Clinton and Barack Obama—as well as the presence of the first credible Hispanic presidential candidate, Bill Richardson—during the 2008 presidential election.

Furthermore, we should not expect descriptive representation to take the same forms and utilize the same mechanisms for all minority groups. Mansbridge (1999) points out that the history of mistrust and impaired communication between the majority and the minority has been the most severe on the issue of race. Mansbridge argues that African Americans must rely on descriptive representation in order to maximize the proportional numbers needed to accomplish important legislative goals such as deliberative synergy (i.e. the principle that more deliberation leads to better information), critical mass, dispersion of influence, and obtaining a wide range of policy views. The inability of blacks to benefit from these legislative qualities is reflected in the fact that the race gap (differences in public opinion and voting behavior between African Americans and whites) is the largest political gap in voting, larger than electoral gaps based on class or gender (Kaufmann, Petrocik, and Shaw 2008). Therefore, the importance of descriptive representation for constituent opinion regarding trust in government and political efficacy may be most pronounced for racial minorities.

DESCRIPTIVE REPRESENTATION AND SUBSTANTIVE REPRESENTATION OF GROUP INTERESTS

The vast majority of research on the impact of descriptive representation focuses on the question of whether electing descriptive representatives has a policy impact. Do these legislators bring issues of concern to their group to the policy agenda? Do they make these issues a priority and act as more vigorous advocates for the interests of their group? Do descriptive representatives bring different perspectives to policy debates and seek to illuminate the way proposals will impact their communities?

To address these questions, researchers must first define what we mean by group interests. Efforts to delineate the policy impact of women generally examine a set of women's issues related to the ever-changing relationship between the public and the private sphere (Sapiro 1981; Diamond and Hartsock 1981; Gelb and Palley 1996; Mansbridge 1999). Women's issues have been broadly defined as issues concerning women, children, and families. Studies focus on feminist issues such as the expansion of women's rights in the home, the workplace, and the political realm. Women's issues have also been defined so as to include the social welfare policies that underlie the gender gap and are traditionally considered to be women's interests, such as education and health care (Thomas 1994, 1997; Reingold 2000; Swers 2002; Dodson 2006).

Race scholars point to civil rights, poverty, crime, and unemployment as issues disproportionately important to African Americans (Whitby 1989; Kinder and Winter 2001; Whitby and Krause 2001; Tate 2003; Minta 2009). Haynie (2001) notes the homogeneity of African Americans (on the basis of shared culture, history, and values) in comparison to the state of other groups, as a characteristic that facilitates the identification of policy priorities for blacks.

Researchers note that Latinos are a much more heterogeneous group than African Americans. This heterogeneity has made it difficult to find a distinct set of policy issues to transcend the many sub-groups that fit under the label "Latino" (Bratton 2006). Beyond immigration and bilingual education, there is no consensus on which issues reflect Latino interests. Voter surveys demonstrate that Latinos prioritize issues such as education, crime, and health (Martinez-Ebers, Fraga, et al. 2000). These policies reflect "cross-cutting" issues that are important to multiple groups; they are not disproportionately identified with Latinos in the way in which civil rights concerns have been identified with African Americans. Indeed, there is a significant void in the literature on how Latino interests are defined and measured. Future research should focus on isolating the interests of Latino sub-groups rather than relying on an aggregate label. The difficulty of isolating an agreed upon set of group interests further highlights the danger of essentializing a group as sharing interests on a limited number of issues and with a common point of view. However, from an empirical standpoint, if policy differences exist, they are most likely to emerge on issues that are viewed as policies with a disproportionate impact on the minority group.

More recent work has begun to address the issue of relative group representation. Griffin and Newman (2008) examine the political influence of different groups in relation to one another. In particular, the authors emphasize the importance of looking at relative representation and equality, as it pertains to disparities in government response to majority, white interests, and minority group (African Americans and Latinos) demands. Griffin and Newman find "considerable inequality" of representation in American politics, noting that congressional votes and the content of legislation is largely more in line with the preferences of white Americans. However, the authors caution about the difficulty in grasping the meaning of political inequality. They argue that the assessment of political equality changes depending on what standards are applied, but that under certain circumstances descriptive representation does improve the relative representation of minorities, which leads to political parity.

VOTING BEHAVIOR AND REPRESENTATION OF MINORITY INTERESTS

Voting is the most frequent and public method by which members of Congress are forced to take a stand on policy that can be evaluated by voters in the next election. If descriptive representatives vote differently from members of the same party with similar constituency characteristics, this would be a clear indicator that these legislators have distinctive preferences and these preferences have potential consequences for policy outcomes.

The significance of voting behavior is especially pronounced in the literature on race and ethnicity. One major debate in the minority representation literature surrounds the effectiveness of majority–minority districts as an institutional tool to enhance the representation of minority interests. The argument for the creation and continued existence of majority–minority districts is that they provide minority groups with the best opportunity to achieve both descriptive and substantive representation (Davidson and Grofman 1994; Lublin 1997). However, some scholars argue that an unintended consequence of creating majority–minority districts has been the dilution of minorities in other districts for the purpose of concentrating them in smaller areas (Swain 1993; Cameron, Epstein, and O'Halloran 1996). Thus, packing minorities into single districts creates whiter and more conservative surrounding districts and significantly hurts the electoral prospects of white Democrats in those districts (Overby and Cosgrove 1996). In this respect, it is argued that majority–minority districts often promote descriptive representation at the expense of the broader substantive representation of minorities.

The creation of majority–minority districts was seen as a contributing factor to the election of a Republican majority in 1994 (Cameron, Epstein, and O'Halloran 1996). Scholars like Overby and Cosgrove (1996) argue that majority–minority districts have been a "mixed blessing"—allowing for the election of more black representatives, but at the same time diminishing the responsiveness of white representatives to the interests of African Americans in districts that had lost black constituents. This triggered a debate over whether the interests of racial minorities were better served by electing minority representatives and expanding the ranks of conservative, Republican representatives or by spreading the minority population across more districts, to elect more ideologically compatible white Democrats. Cameron, Epstein, and O'Halloran (1996) found that, in non-southern states, majority–minority districts do not enhance the substantive representation of African Americans; rather, black voters should be maximized by being distributed equally across districts, in order for as many Democrats as possible to be elected (i.e. giving up possible gains in descriptive representation in order to increase the substantive representation of group interests). Cameron, Epstein, and O'Halloran (1996) note, however, that in the South it makes more sense to have "concentrated" black districts, yet not to the point of creating majority–minority districts. They argue for the construction of southern districts that approximate 47 percent black voters, which would maximize black substantive representation while still providing a minority presence in other districts. Overall, the authors conclude that a tradeoff exists between the descriptive and the substantive representation of minorities and that these tradeoffs vary depending on regional and electoral context.

Other scholars contest the claim that the creation of majority–minority districts has led to a decrease in the substantive representation of minority voters. Shotts (2003) argues that, after racial redistricting in the South in the 1980s and 1990s, there was an increase in the election of legislators whose policy preferences were to the left rather than to the right of the median House member. To Shotts, this implies that the creation of majority–minority districts actually promoted liberal policy outcomes, despite a decline in the number of Democrats elected to Congress. However, Lublin and Voss (2003) dispute Shotts' findings; they contend that he fails to account for the sharp rightward shift of the House median member after the 1994 Republican takeover of Congress. Lublin and Voss argue that this omission leads to an incomplete and unrealistic account of the effects of majority–minority districts in southern states, where many moderate Democratic legislators were replaced by strong conservative Republicans. This debate over the actual consequences of racial redistricting calls for further research that considers, among other things, changes in party polarization and multiple shifts in congressional power.

The creation of majority–minority districts and the use of other institutional tools designed to maximize opportunities to elect minorities have raised questions about the link between descriptive and substantive representation. Some scholars are strong proponents of emphasizing substantive representation over descriptive representation, in part due to the "side effects" of majority–minority districts, as discussed above. In a study of African-American representation in Congress, Swain (1993) finds that party and not race is the strongest indicator of support for black interest legislation. Therefore, in similar manner to the arguments posited by Cameron, Epstein, and O'Halloran (1996), Swain states that the best way for African Americans to maximize substantive representation is to promote the election of more Democrats, regardless of race, rather than to focus on the narrow goal of increasing the number of blacks in Congress. However, in an analysis of DW–NOMINATE scores, McCarty, Poole, and Rosenthal (1997) argue that African-American legislators are different from other Democratic legislators, as these representatives anchor the liberal end of the ideological spectrum.

Other scholarship examines how well minority interests are represented by legislators elected form large minority districts. Gay (2007) compares the responsiveness of legislators from majority–white districts and legislators from majority–minority districts in California and finds that constituency preferences are just as likely to influence the policy positions of the former as they influence the policy choices of the latter. Gay concludes that, despite the usual criticisms of majority–minority districts—lack of electoral competition and low voter turnout—legislators from these districts do not eschew their role as representatives. Hutchings, McClerking, and Charles (2004) examine how and when black constituency size (i.e. district racial composition) affects a legislator's support for black interests. In particular, they look at the stability of support across varying districts and different legislative policies. They find that in the South, where there is more racial division, constituency size is a less consistent indicator of support for black policies among white Democrats (e.g. some legislators in the South with over 30 percent black constituents did not support legislation in the interest of blacks), while in the North the size of the black population reduces across-district variation in support for black interests among white Democrats. Among Republican legislators, the authors note that an increase in the size of a black constituency influences support for black legislation in the North, but not in the South.

To date, there are few studies that examine the legislative behavior of Latinos in Congress; the existing research has found an inconsistent link between descriptive and substantive representation. In one of the earliest studies on Latino representation, Welch and Hibbing (1984) looked at the effect of Latino constituencies and Latino representatives on roll-call voting. They found that Latino representatives and non-Latino representatives with a large Latino constituency exhibited a more liberal voting record than their non-Latino counterparts. Conversely, in a separate study conducted on the voting records of members of Congress, Hero and Tolbert (1995) maintain that there is no link between the descriptive and substantive representation of Latinos, despite an increase in the Latino population in the 1980s. Instead, they assert that Latinos receive "indirect" substantive representation through the policy agenda of the Democratic Party. Similarly, Santos and Huerta (2001) discern no ethnic influence on representation. Rather, they note that constituency (large Latino districts) and ideology are the strongest indicators of substantive representation of Latino interests. By contrast, using the same data as Hero and Tolbert (1995), Kerr and Miller (1997) arrive at a different conclusion. These scholars find not only that Latino House members exhibit a distinct voting behavior from non-Latino members, but that Latino legislators do indeed provide direct substantive representation to Latinos.

In a more recent piece on the representation of Latinos in Congress, Rocca, Sanchez, and Uscinski (2008) examine the effects of a representative's personal attributes on how she votes. They maintain that specific descriptive characteristics of Latino representatives (e.g. education, gender, generational status, nativity) influence voting behavior. The authors note that differences in descriptive attributes among Latinos help illustrate that Latino legislators are not a monolithic group and that a better understanding of the descriptive–substantive link must recognize within-group differences in representation. The work of Rocca et al. is one of the first to recognize the heterogeneity of Latino legislators and how this translates into distinctions in voting behavior and policy preferences. Future work should continue on this path of recognizing Latino sub-group differences.

Studies that seek to determine if women legislators are generally more liberal than male legislators have had varying results, depending on the time period and the measure of ideology utilized (Leader 1977; Frankovic 1977; Dolan 1997; Swers 1998, 2002; Schwindt-Bayer and Corbetta 2004; Frederick 2009, 2010). However, research does indicate that women vote more liberally on bills related to women's issues, particularly abortion (Dolan 1997; Swers 1998; Norton 1999; Tatalovich and Schier 1993; Frederick, 2010). The largest differences occur among Republicans, because taking a position in favor of reproductive rights involves going against the stance of the majority of the Republican Party. However, the dwindling of the ranks of moderate Republicans in recent years may eliminate the gender differences found in voting on abortion and other women's issues. Indeed, in an analysis of DW–NOMINATE scores over time, Frederick (2009) finds that the scores of Republican women have converged with the rest of the Republican caucus over time and that since the mid-2000s, Republican women are not distinctively more liberal than their male Republican colleagues.

The inconsistent results of the research on descriptive representation and voting behavior may partially stem from the fact that scholars rely mainly on interest group scores from groups such as the American Association of University Women (Dolan 1997; Swers 1998; Frederick 2010), the Leadership Conference on Civil Rights (Cameron, Epstein, and O'Halloran 1996; Swain 1993; Canon 1999), AFL–CIO Committee on Political Education (Swain 1993; Lublin 1997), the Southwest Voter Research Institute (Hero and Tolbert 1995; Kerr and Miller 1997), and the National Hispanic Leadership Agenda (Santos and Huerta 2001). The overall utility of interest group scores has been criticized on several fronts. First, many of the issues upon which the scores are based are not necessarily exclusive to one particular group (i.e. issues affect multiple groups similarly) and, second, these scores (and, more broadly, overall roll-call votes) measure only a binary vote choice (yea or nay) instead of a policy preference. The latter reason has lead scholars to look beyond the roll-call stage of the legislative process in order to assess quality of representation.

BEYOND VOTING BEHAVIOR: EXPLORING THE LINK BETWEEN DESCRIPTIVE AND SUBSTANTIVE REPRESENTATION THROUGHOUT THE LEGISLATIVE PROCESS

While roll-call voting is the most visible and parsimonious legislative activity, its usefulness as an indicator of the impact of descriptive representation is quite limited. Since roll-call votes occur at the end of the process, when the choices and policy options are already defined, we cannot determine through vote analyses if descriptive representatives are bringing new issues and different perspectives to the congressional agenda. In other words, roll-call voting is not the only way, or necessarily the best way to assess legislative effectiveness or the quality of representation. Since a large part of the potential impact of descriptive representation is to improve the deliberative process among legislators, we need measures that allow us to examine more closely whether descriptive representatives are more likely to prioritize issues related to group interests and whether they act as vigorous advocates for those issues with their colleagues, thereby translating descriptive representation into substantive representation. A broader approach to how minorities and women are substantively represented must include a more comprehensive examination of legislative activity.

Recent studies look beyond roll-call votes, to examine earlier stages of the legislative process and gage whether descriptive representatives have a distinctive influence on the definition of policy alternatives and on the debate over policy outcomes. Utilizing surveys of legislators' priorities and analyses of bill sponsorship, research on state legislatures demonstrated that women and minorities have distinctive policy priorities and are more likely to act as advocates for group interests (Haynie 2001; Bratton and Haynie 1999; Saint-Germain 1989; Thomas 1994; Dodson and Carroll 1991; Reingold 2000; Poggione 2004; Bratton 2006). State legislative studies have the advantage of being able to compare the influence of race, ethnicity, and gender in settings with different political cultures and institutional dynamics and varying levels of minority group representation. However, because of the complexity of gathering data across multiple state legislatures, these studies do not focus as much as they should on the impact of internal institutional norms, constituent influences, and the political opportunity structure.

At the congressional level, scholars have tried to determine whether the impact of race, ethnicity, and gender on legislators' policy activity persists after one has accounted for the major partisan, institutional, and constituency factors that influence legislative behavior. The evidence for a distinctive impact is most apparent at the agenda-setting stage. Agenda-setting provides legislators with a broad opportunity to define problems and establish policy alternatives (Kingdon 2005; Baumgartner and Jones 1993). For minorities, in particular, agenda-setting allows the representatives to exert individual rather than aggregate influence through their sponsorship and cosponsorship behavior. Therefore agenda-setting is the stage of the legislative process at which the link between descriptive and substantive representation may be most pronounced (Bratton and Haynie 1999; Swers 2002).

The literature on African-American legislators indicates strong links between descriptive and substantive representation at the agenda-setting stage and in committee deliberations. Thus, Canon (1999) finds that, in particular, black representatives who are willing to embrace and promote multiracial interests not only sponsor more legislation, but achieve greater success throughout the legislative process. Canon points out that blacks being elected from white majority districts will always be the exception rather than the rule. He argues that the creation of black majority districts should be embraced because they produce representatives who promote the common interests of multiple groups (what he refers to as the "politics of commonality") rather than the intended purpose of majority–minority districts, namely to produce representatives who would push for interests primarily important to African Americans (what Canon terms as the "politics of difference"). Canon refers to the election of these black legislators—those willing to embrace a "politics of commonality" that breaks down race barriers—as one of the "unintended consequences" of increases in minority descriptive representation. Haynie (2001) also argues that electing black legislators is crucial to achieving substantive representation of black interests. Through an examination of five state legislatures, Haynie finds that policies important to African Americans are more likely to be introduced and deliberated upon when black representatives are present. Haynie makes a strong connection between the race of a representative and the quality of representation African Americans receive (see also Bratton and Haynie 1999). At the committee stage, Gamble (2007) finds that African Americans in the House of Representatives are more likely than their white counterparts to participate actively in committee activities when black interest policies are being considered. Similarly, Minta (2009) notes that both African-American and Latino legislators are more likely to participate in oversight committee hearings dealing with minority interests such as enforcement of fair housing and other civil rights laws. Moreover, these minority legislators are more likely to focus their questions on minority interests.

In contrast to the literature on African Americans, there are few studies on Latino legislative behavior beyond roll-call voting. Comparing the sponsorship activity of Latino and non-Latino state legislators, Bratton (2006) finds that Latino legislators are more likely than non-Latino ones to sponsor "Latino interest" measures. In a study of Latinos in legislative leadership positions, Preuhs (2005) notes that these legislators use their leadership positions to block legislation that may negatively impact Latinos.

Studies of gender and representation have also highlighted the distinctive policy impact of female representatives. In a comprehensive study of gender differences in legislative activities including sponsorship, cosponsorship, and committee and floor behavior, Swers (2002) found that women were more likely to prioritize feminist and social welfare issues, even after accounting for members' party affiliation, constituency characteristics, and institutional position, including committee assignment and membership in the majority or minority party (see also Dodson 2006; Dodson et al. 1995; Norton 1995, 2002). Wolbrecht (2000, 2002) notes that women in Congress play a key role in bringing previously ignored women's concerns to the national agenda. In her longitudinal study of policymaking on women's issues, Wolbrecht found that women, particularly Democratic women, were the most likely to identify new issues related to women's rights and to bring new policy solutions to the agenda.

Recent work by Gerrity, Osborn, et al. (2007) and by MacDonald and O'Brien (forthcoming) holds constituency factors constant by comparing members who serve the same district over time. The authors found strong evidence for agenda-setting effects, as women introduced more bills related to women's issues than men representing the same district. However, Gerrity, Osborn, et al. (2007) found no differences in the frequency of floor speeches that members gave on women's issues.

As women continue to increase their numbers in Congress, there will be more opportunities to conduct studies of differences in policy priorities and behavior among members who represented the same district in Congress. However, the fact that the vast majority of African-American and Hispanic representatives represent majority–minority districts and are replaced with other minority legislators after they leave Congress makes this technique less useful for studying the effect of descriptive representation among racial minorities. The numerous studies of policy differences at various stages in the legislative process demonstrate that within the boundaries of what a constituency will accept legislators have significant latitude to decide which policies to champion, thus highlighting the importance of social identity and personal background as an influence on legislative behavior.

Descriptive representatives and vigorous advocacy for group interests

Case study and interview-based research demonstrate that minorities and women do act as vigorous advocates for the interests of their group. For example, in his descriptive account of the representation provided by four black legislators, Fenno (2003) notes the intensity by which black members of Congress advocate for the interests of the black community, particularly interests related to civil rights, poverty, and criminal justice. Fenno credits the strength of group consciousness within the black community for providing such policy consensus. Similarly, Fraga, Lopez, et al. (2007) discover in personal interviews that Latino state legislators also exhibit a commitment to the larger Latino community by supporting the policy priorities of other Latino legislators. These priorities include immigration, education, and healthcare. Although Latinos are much more heterogeneous than blacks in their policy interests and do not share a strong sense of group consciousness, the work of Fraga, Lopez, et al. demonstrates that Latino legislators are, nonetheless, willing to act collectively for the benefit of the broader Latino community.

With regard to women, Dodson (2006) found that women members were pivotal in placing issues such as domestic violence and women's health on the congressional agenda. Women lobbied their male colleagues to adopt these issues as priorities and played pivotal roles in the efforts to move bills through the legislative process on issues such as the Violence Against Women Act, or legislation designed to increase women's health research and to create an Office of Women's Health within the National Institutes of Health. (See also Swers 2002.) Studies of welfare reform indicate that Republican and Democratic women were instrumental in getting enhanced child support enforcement and greater childcare subsidies included in the final bill. Women of color were uniformly opposed to what they perceived as the punitive nature of the welfare reform and worked together to offer alternative legislation (Dodson 2006; Swers 2002; Hawkesworth 2003; Norton 2002; Johnson, Duerst-Lahti, and Norton 2007).

Analyses of floor debate indicate that women are more likely to speak about women's concerns and issues and they are more likely to invoke their authority as women and mothers (Shogan 2001; Cramer Walsh 2002; Levy, Tien, and Aved 2002). Additionally, in a study of the evolution of discourse on the frequently debated topic of abortion, Levy, Tien, and Aved (2001) find that female legislators have influenced the substance and style of their male colleagues' floor speeches. Understanding the ways in which women and minorities have influenced the legislative behavior of majority group legislators constitutes an important area for future research.

The greater levels and the intensity of activity on group-related concerns found in the research on descriptive representatives reflects both the policy preferences of legislators and the nature of the political opportunity structure in the legislative arena. Representatives are aided in their ability to build a legislative niche on these issues because of their perceived moral authority as members of the minority group. Furthermore, in an age of competitive elections and constant media attention, party leaders rely on women and minorities to champion the party's message on these issues with the public, in an effort to boost the party's image, and, in the case of both gender and ethnicity, to capitalize on the potential gap in voting, in which various groups of women and Latinos are seen as potential swing voting blocs (Swers 2002; Dodson 2006; Norton 2002; Alvarez and Garcia Bedolla 2003).

THE IMPORTANCE OF INSTITUTIONAL AND PARTISAN DYNAMICS

Empirical research has established that minorities and women do provide substantive representation of group interests in Congress. However, the impact of race and gender is not uniform across policy issues and the importance of identity as an influence on behavior is dependent on the nature of the political opportunity structure and on the legislator's position within the institutional context. With regard to issues, the strongest gender effects are found on feminist or women's rights issues rather than on social welfare issues. The ability and willingness of members to champion specific issues vary with changes in the political context. For example, Swers (2002) finds that women were more likely to sponsor social welfare bills when they were in the majority party and had access to the legislative agenda. However, there were no gender differences in sponsorship behavior on social welfare issues when women were in the minority. Moreover, moderate Republican women found it easier to champion feminist causes when they were in the minority party and were only expected to bring along their contingent of votes. As members of the majority, these Republican women risked alienating important party activists and in turn incurring the animosity of the party leaders and caucus members whom they relied on to advance other policy objectives and their own position within the institution (Swers 2002; Dodson 2006).

The changes in the strategic calculations that legislators make on the basis of the nature of the political environment argue for a continued focus on the influence of political context and institutional dynamics on the likelihood that descriptive representatives will pursue preferences on the basis of group membership. Among women, future work needs to focus more on the position of women within the Democratic and Republican caucuses. Party and ideology are two of the most important guides to congressional behavior. At the individual level, Democratic women are generally the most likely to bring women's issues to the legislative agenda and to spend political capital to pursue their inclusion in public policy (Swers 2002; Dodson 2006). Research demonstrates that moderate Republican women are actively engaged in pursuing legislation related to women's interests. Moderate Republican women drive differences in voting behavior on women's issues, as these women are taking positions that go against the majority in their party (Dolan 1997; Swers 1998, 2002; Dodson 2006).

In recent years, the ranks of moderate Republican women and moderate Republicans more generally have dwindled. Frederick (2010) notes a convergence in the DW–NOMINATE scores among Republican men and women as moderate Republican women from the Northeast have left Congress and are replaced by conservative women who hail from the South and the West, the current strongholds of the Republican Party (Frederick 2010; Elder 2008). Future research must examine whether and how conservative women engage women's issues. Do they perceive themselves as champions of women's interests and engage with those causes, for instance women's health, which can fit within their ideology? Do they deny the existence of women's issues, or do they engage with and champion these issues from a conservative or anti-feminist point of view? (See Swers and Larson (2005) for an analysis of Republican women's views on gender identity and women's issues.)

Beyond party affiliation and ideology, institutional factors such as seniority, committee position, and a member's relationship with and place within leadership all impact the ability of descriptive representatives to pursue group interests. Minorities and women who were elected in the early 1990s are now achieving enough seniority to gain access to more prestigious committees, such as Appropriations and Ways and Means, and to lay claim to subcommittee chairmanships and some full committee chairs. These changes call for new analyses of the impact of minorities and women on the agendas of congressional committees. Do subcommittees chaired by women and minorities hold more hearings on issues related to group interests? Do they draft more legislation on these issues? When committees include greater numbers of women and minorities, do these legislators join together to advocate for the inclusion of group interests in committee legislation?

Finally, the majority of research on descriptive representation focuses on the House of Representatives. Indeed, the increased representation for small states, which was built into the design of the Senate by the founding fathers, also inhibits the representation of racial and ethnic minorities and of minority group interests. Because more racial and ethnic minorities reside in large states including California, Texas, Illinois, and Florida than in small states like Montana and North and South Dakota, these minority groups have fewer opportunities to elect a descriptive representative, and their ability to translate their numbers into policy influence across senators is reduced (Dahl 1956; Lee and Oppenheimer 1999). Furthermore, Griffin (2006) found that, over time, there is an increasingly negative relationship between a state's voting weight in the Senate and the size of a state's African-American and Latino populations. Looking at representation of group interests, Griffin notes that there is no difference in the overall voting behavior of small- and large-state senators. However, in an analysis of LCCR (Leadership Conference on Civil Rights) voting scores, Griffin finds that senators who hail from states with greater voting weight in the Senate are more likely to oppose the policy positions of the LCCR. Thus the policy interests of racial minorities are clearly disadvantaged by the structure of the Senate (Griffin 2006).

While minorities continue to lag in their representation in the Senate, a similar proportion of women serves in the House and in the Senate. Further examination of descriptive representation in the Senate can shed light on how the influence of social identity varies with the nature of the institution. Thus the enhanced media profile of senators and the protection of minority rights provide senators with more opportunities to influence a range of policies in comparison to the opportunities House members, who are more constrained by such factors as the jurisdiction of their committees and the higher frequency of reelection. Scholars should examine whether the increased policy freedom enjoyed by senators leads women and minorities to act as more aggressive advocates for group interests. Alternatively, the need for senators to have policy proposals on all issues may diminish the distinctive importance of social identity (Swers 2007, 2008, forthcoming).

CRITICAL MASS AND INSTITUTIONAL INFLUENCE ON DESCRIPTIVE REPRESENTATION

The behavior of individuals within an institution is strongly conditioned by the makeup of its membership. Research in the disciplines of sociology and psychology reveals how institutions establish behavioral norms and how the relationship between the majority and minority groups influences individual actions. This work is quite relevant to the study of politics, in particular with respect to questions about institutional norms and their impact on individual legislative behavior. Furthermore, the insights from sociology and psychology highlight the need to examine the impact of the relative proportions of minority and majority group members. Do individual legislators exhibit a greater willingness to act on behalf of the substantive interests of the group when they constitute a larger proportion of the membership in the legislature? How does the presence of more minority group members influence the behavior of majority group members?

Race, gender, and institutional norms

With regard to institutional norms, scholars note that institutions reflect the preferences and norms of the dominant group. Therefore the standard operating procedures and accepted practices within Congress are both raced and gendered (Acker 1992; Kenney 1996; Duerst-Lahti 2002; Hawkesworth 2003; Rosenthal 1998, 2005). The need to adapt to and negotiate these standards sets up additional hurdles for gaining acceptance within the institution. Anecdotal and interview-based evidence from state legislative and congressional research indicates that women and minorities do report feeling that they have to work harder to prove themselves. Moreover, female and minority members are more likely to perceive the existence of these separate standards than are their majority group colleagues (Hawkesworth 2003; Thomas 1994; Kenney 1996). For example, Swers (2007) finds that staffers for female members felt that Democratic women senators had to work harder than ideologically similar male colleagues to prove themselves on defense issues to voters; and they believed they were taken less seriously by Pentagon officials. Additionally, an analysis of appearances on Sunday talk shows demonstrated that women needed to achieve leadership positions on defense-related committees and within the party before they were asked to talk about defense issues on these shows. By contrast, credentials did not play as significant a role in the appearances by male senators. While male senators who led important committees dominated the Sunday talk shows, other male senators who had not achieved leadership positions on foreign policy were also invited to speak on defense issues.

Hawkesworth (2003) finds that minority women serving in the Democratic controlled 103rd Congress and the Republican controlled 104th Congress felt marginalized by white male and female colleagues. Regardless of legislative setting or level of seniority, these minority women believed that their policy proposals were more likely to be ignored and their knowledge discounted by majority group members (see also Hedge, Button, and Spear 1996 and Smooth 2008 for evidence at the state level). Uncovering the gender and race-based norms within Congress is a very difficult task. Future research on the subject must be careful to account for other potential explanations, particularly ideology and partisanship. Moreover, it is very difficult to develop systematic measures of norms that will move us beyond subjective anecdotal and interview accounts.

Critical mass and legislative behavior

Understanding how the composition of the legislature as a whole influences the decision-making of individual legislators is another important question. Do legislators respond to chamber diversity when making decisions about policy interests and legislative agendas? Research at the state level has long focused on the impact of numbers, investigating whether the achievement of a "critical mass" makes it more likely that minorities and women will feel they can champion group interests without being stigmatized or marginalized (Thomas 1994; Kathlene 2005).

The majority of research that has focused on the "critical mass" debate is confined to the gender and politics literature. Thus, more work needs to be done on the impact of numbers on the behavior of ethnic and racial minorities. The critical mass research was based initially on the work of Rosabeth Moss Kanter (1977), who argued that token women in male dominated organizations (women who make up less than 15 percent of the organizational membership) feel pressure to conform, which is manifested in ways such as downplaying gender differences and work-related accomplishments. Kanter noted that minorities in these organizational settings try to obfuscate group differences, in an attempt to blend into the majority culture. Applied to the political setting, particularly legislative institutions, critical mass scholars have argued that it is necessary for women to achieve a certain percentage within a chamber (approaching 15 percent) in order to observe gender differences in the legislative priorities placed on issues important to women (Saint Germain 1989; Thomas 1991, 1994).

Early research on state legislatures found some evidence to support the idea that, as the proportion of women in the legislature rose, legislative activity on women's issues increased; however, there were no clear threshold effects (Saint Germain 1989; Thomas 1991, 1994). At the congressional level, MacDonald and O'Brien (forthcoming) examined sponsorship of feminist and social welfare bills from 1973 to 2002. They found that congresswomen sponsored more feminist and social welfare bills as the proportion of women in the House increased. However, other recent research contradicts critical mass theory by finding that women are more inclined to advocate for group interests when they are underrepresented in the legislature (Bratton 2005; Crowley 2004).

As a result of these contradictory findings, scholars have begun to question the usefulness of the critical mass concept (e.g. Bratton 2005; Childs and Krook 2006b; Beckwith 2007; Grey 2006). Researchers note that there are important differences between women as political actors and women in other institutional settings, such as corporations. Most importantly, women legislators must be responsive not only to colleagues but also to voters. To achieve reelection, legislators must develop a legislative niche and a record to promote to voters. If voters perceive women as more qualified to handle women's issues, then female legislators will be more active on these issues (Huddy and Terkildsen 1993; Dolan 2004; Crowley 2004). Moreover, status as a minority within a legislature may yield more of the media spotlight necessary to gain attention to one's proposals. Furthermore, as women become a greater presence within a legislative chamber, they may influence the behavior of men. If men become more willing to champion women's issues as the level of diversity within the chamber rises, then differences between the two groups will be minimized, as women approach a critical mass (Bratton 2005).

Finally, critical mass theory's focus on numbers ignores the importance of institutional position and the level of power a member wields within the institution. Thus scholars suggest that, instead of focusing on critical mass or on the need for women to achieve a particular proportion of membership, it is important to examine how members maximize their policy effectiveness and individual power within institutions (Grey 2006; Dahlerup 2006). Childs and Krook (2006b, 524) argue that the critical mass debate must be reframed from focusing on *when* women matter to "*how* the substantive representation of women occurs." They also point out that the diversity of women, as individuals rather than as a group, can provide a significant amount of legislative impact. Therefore, the focus should be on "critical actors" rather than on "critical mass," in order to understand policy effectiveness (Childs and Krook 2006b, 528).

CRITICAL MASS AND INSTITUTIONAL POWER IN CONGRESS

Taking into account the criticisms of critical mass theory and the findings from state legislative research, we argue for a renewed focus on how numbers combine with institutional position to affect the ability of descriptive representatives to influence policy. If numbers matter, when and how do they matter? It is likely that individual legislators look for a legislative niche to distinguish themselves to voters. Therefore the probability that any one woman or minority legislator will make these issues a part of their legislative agenda may be stronger when there are fewer members of the group in Congress. However, to achieve policy outcomes, legislators need to be able to form coalitions to convince other members to adopt their priorities. Thus we need to investigate whether and how women and minorities try to utilize their numbers to leverage their influence within Congress as a whole and within their party caucus.

The political culture of the Democratic Party emphasizes the importance of diversity (Evans 2005; Sanbonmatsu 2002; Wolbrecht 2000; Peters and Rosenthal 2010; Rosenthal 2008). All of the African-American members of Congress and the vast majority of the Hispanic members are Democrats. Since the 1992 election, the growth in the number of women in Congress has been almost entirely driven by the election of more Democratic women. Thus at the opening of the 111th Congress there were fifty-six Democratic women and only seventeen Republican women serving in the House of Representatives. Similarly, only four of the seventeen women serving in the U.S. Senate are Republicans (Center for the American Woman and Politics 2009). The concentration of women and minorities within the Democratic Party means that these groups have their greatest influence on policy when Democrats are in the majority and they have very little access to the agenda when Republicans are in the majority.

Scholars need to examine whether and how women and minorities leverage their numbers within the Democratic caucus to gain influence over the direction of policy. For example, scholars like Whitby (1989), Canon (1999), and Fenno (2003) demonstrate that African-American legislators have long-utilized the Congressional Black Caucus to pressure Democratic party leadership to adopt their legislative priorities, expand group membership on key committees, and move more African-American representatives into leadership positions on committees. Gertzog (2004) notes that because of the need to be bipartisan, the Congressional Caucus for Women's Issues never developed the power of the Congressional Black Caucus. However, women have used the caucus to craft legislation and build coalitions of support for individual legislator's bills.

Within the Democratic caucus, women have leveraged their numbers to demand a seat at the party leadership table and more influential committee seats. Indeed, when Nancy Pelosi (D–CA) was elected minority whip in the 107th Congress and later rose to the positions of party leader and Speaker in the 110th Congress, the Democratic women were an important part of her coalition (Rosenthal 2008; Peters and Rosenthal 2010; Swers and Larson 2005). In contrast to the situation of the Democrats, the smaller proportion of women in the Republican caucus, combined with a party culture that is less responsive to demands for increased diversity, limits the ability of Republican women to enhance their individual power or work together to advance group interests (Evans 2005; Swers and Larson 2005; Rosenthal 2008).

LEADERSHIP DIFFERENCES IN SUBSTANCE AND STYLE

The movement of more women and minorities into positions of leadership in the parties and committees offers an opportunity to examine differences in the substance and style of leadership. Studies of gender differences in leadership style in state legislatures note that female committee chairs were more likely to emphasize consensus building, compromise and open dialogue, while male chairs exhibit more hierarchical and competitive leadership styles (Kathlene 1994; Rosenthal 1998, 2005). While state legislatures vary in their level of professionalization and competitiveness, Congress is a highly competitive and professionalized setting. Therefore the norms of the institution and the set of skills necessary to gain election to Congress limit the likelihood that there will be significant differences in leadership style among men and women. However, gender, race, and ethnicity may affect the substance of representatives' leadership and their presentation of self. Thus scholars should examine whether female and minority chairs are more likely to include issues related to group concerns on the committee agenda and to include the differing perspectives of group members in committee deliberations on the range of issues under a committee's jurisdiction. For example, one could examine whether female and minority chairs schedule more hearings on group-related interests and whether they are more likely to seek testimony at hearings from interest group advocates of minority group interests such as women's organizations and civil rights groups.

At the level of party leadership, the advancement of Nancy Pelosi (D–CA) to Speaker of the House invites investigation of how gender impacts her leadership style. Early analyses describe her management style as that of a fierce partisan, in the mold of Newt Gingrich, rather than that of a consensus builder (Peters and Rosenthal 2010; Rosenthal 2008). However, gender has influenced Pelosi's decision-making. Women make up a key portion of her coalition of support and several Democratic women, particularly those from California, are among her closest advisors. Pelosi has taken more direct control of the committee appointment process than previous party leaders, and she has used her influence to place a premium on diversity in the committee assignment process, seeking representation for minorities, women, and conservative Democrats. In her public statements and her presentation of self, Pelosi emphasizes her interest in women and children. She constantly refers to herself as a mother and grandmother and asserts that these roles guide her political decision-making. The presentation of herself as a mother and grandmother also limits the ability of Republicans to paint her as a San Francisco liberal (Peters and Rosenthal 2010; Rosenthal 2008; Swers and Larson 2005).

DIVERSITY AND INTERSECTIONALITY

As minorities and women expand their numbers in Congress, the diversity of backgrounds, ideologies, and experiences within these groups expands. Future research needs to focus more on the diversity of opinion within and among minority groups rather than simply exploring similarities and differences across groups. The majority of research on racial minorities examines African-American legislators. We need to focus more in our studies on the impact of Latino representatives and on how they respond to the interests of Latino sub-groups. Scholarship to date has shown that Latinos vary in their opinions on a number of issues on the basis of their national origin, generational status, level of acculturation, and feelings of group consciousness (Sanchez 2006; Branton 2007; Rocca, Sanchez, and Skinks 2008). Future research into both the descriptive and substantive representation of Latinos needs to take into account variations in these characteristics.

We also need to investigate the impact of intersectionality to understand how race, gender, and ethnic identities influence the decision-making of, and interactions among, representatives. Do legislators experience conflict between the goals and values of their varying identities? How do these overlapping identities affect representatives' policy priorities and relationships within the institution? At the state level, Bratton, Haynie, and Reingold (2007) examine the agenda-setting behavior of African-American women in the lower chambers of ten state legislatures. The authors find that African-American women respond both to their gender and to their racial identities; African-American women sponsor more legislation in the interest of women and of blacks than other groups do. The authors also note an interesting "critical mass" effect whereby African-American women are less likely to sponsor women's interest bills in chambers that have a high proportion of women (see also Barrett 1995). Orey,

Smooth, et al. (2007), examining the one state legislature with the highest proportion of black representative (Mississippi), find that African-American women are more likely than any other group to introduce progressive legislation, including women's interest bills. Contrary to expectations, they also note that legislation introduced by African-American women is no less likely to be defeated than legislation passed by white males.

Fraga, Lopez, et al. (2007) look at the increasing role of Latina women in state legislatures. Using elite level interviews, the authors look at differences in policy priorities, legislative behavior, and policy success between Latinas and Latino men. They conclude that, although there are a number of representational similarities, several differences between the two groups emerged. Latinas place a greater emphasis than Latino males on representing the interests of multiple minority groups. As in the findings of the gender and race literature, Latinas are more likely than their male counterparts to introduce and successfully pass legislation dealing with a broad Latino agenda.

At the congressional level, Hawkesworth (2003) finds that African-American and Hispanic Democratic women were united in their opposition to welfare reform and used their floor time to speak against the stereotyping of welfare mothers as irresponsible, poor, minority women. By contrast, minority men and white women in the Democratic Party split their votes on the welfare reform bill. Thus minority women felt a responsibility to advocate for the interests of poor, minority women (see also Garcia Bedolla, Tate, and Wong 2005). Similarly, Dodson (2006) finds that, when Bill Clinton became president in 1992, abortion rights supporters hoped to achieve legislative victories after twelve years of Republican control of the presidency. She notes that white women focused their attention on the Freedom of Choice Act, a bill that would codify the right to abortion granted by *Roe* v *Wade*. By contrast, minority women were more committed to overturning the Hyde amendment, which prevents federal Medicaid dollars from being used to fund abortions. These minority women placed a priority on facilitating access to abortion services for their poor constituents rather than on codifying the abstract right (Dodson 2006; Dodson, Carroll et al. 1995). More work needs to be done on how the overlapping identities of race, gender, and/or ethnicity influence members' policy priorities and the type of coalitions they build to support their initiatives at the congressional level.

Moving beyond race and gender issues

The impact of descriptive representation on women's issues and civil rights concerns has been clearly established. Scholars need to focus more on the question of whether women and minorities bring a different perspective to issues outside of what is traditionally considered gender and race issues. Future research should look at deliberation within committees to examine whether women and minorities advocate for the interests of their group by addressing how a range of policies will differentially impact the group. For example, in an analysis of senators' legislative proposals on defense issues, Swers (2007, 2008) finds that women are more likely than their male partisan colleagues to focus on defense policies related to benefits for military personnel and veterans, such as health and education. These policies reflect the social welfare concerns that are traditionally associated with women. Moreover, women are also more likely to prioritize issues related to the needs of women who are serving in the military, from participation of women in combat to shining a spotlight on the incidence of sexual assault within the military (Swers, forthcoming). Additionally, Gamble (2007) shows that African Americans on legislative committees are more engaged and involved in the deliberative process when issues such as discrimination and crime are considered. Further examination of deliberation in committees and on the floor could highlight how the different perspective derived from shared experiences as a female and/or as a member of a racial or ethnic minority permeates legislative debates among members and impacts policy outcomes.

CONCLUSION

The integration of women and minorities into Congress and the state legislatures has spurred a plethora of research on the substantive and symbolic impact of electing descriptive representatives. While controversy persists over the need for and legitimacy of descriptive representation, the existing research does provide important insight into the influence of identity on legislative behavior. Research on gender and race (primarily on African Americans) indicates that the social identity of the legislator influences policy preferences and decision-making about what policy priorities to pursue and how much political capital to expend on these initiatives. Descriptive representatives have a particularly important impact at the agenda-setting stage, bringing new problems and policy solutions to the legislative arena. Moreover, descriptive representatives act as vigorous advocates for group interests, expending scarce resources of time, staff, and political capital in pursuit of group goals.

Having established that social identity does shape legislative behavior, scholars are now trying to delineate the circumstances in which gender, race, and ethnicity are most likely to influence representatives' decision-making. Future research will continue to examine how identity interacts with institutional norms, electoral incentives, and the political opportunity structure to influence members' policy choices and legislative activities. As women and racial and ethnic minorities continue to gain seniority in Congress and enter the party leadership structure, scholars will be able to examine more closely how identity impacts leadership style and whether these members leverage their leadership positions to advance group interests.

As the integration of women and minorities into Congress continues, the number of, and diversity among, minority group legislators will continue to grow. It is estimated that, by 2050, Latinos, already the largest minority group in the U.S., will triple in size and account for the majority of the country's population growth. By 2050, Latinos will make up 29 percent of the U.S. population, a 15 percent increase from 2005. In comparison, non-Hispanic whites, who currently account for 67 percent of the population will make up only 47 percent; while Asian Americans will increase from 5 percent to 9 percent, and African Americans will remain roughly the same at about 13 percent (Pew Research Center 2008). The changing dynamics of the U.S. population will provide more opportunities to test theories about the impact of descriptive representation on the substantive representation of group interests. Furthermore, as more women and minorities are elected, there will be greater ideological, partisan, and regional diversity within minority groups and more opportunities to investigate the influence of overlapping identities of race, ethnicity, and gender on legislative behavior.

REFERENCES

ACKER, J. 1992. Gendered Institution: From Sex Roles to Gendered Institutions. *Contemporary Sociology*, 21: 565–9.

ALVAREZ, M., and GARCIA BEDOLLA, L. 2003. The Foundations of Latino Voter Partisanship: Evidence from the 2000 Election. *Journal of Politics*, 65: 31–49.

BARRETO, M. A. 2007. Si se puede! Latino Candidates and the Mobilization of Latino Voters. *American Political Science Review*, 101: 425–41.

BARRETT, E. 1995. The Policy Priorities of African American Women in State Legislatures. *Legislative Studies Quarterly*, 20: 223–47.

BAUMGARTNER, F. R., and JONES, B. D. 1993. *Agendas and Instability in American Politics*. Chicago: University of Chicago Press.

BECKWITH, K. 2007. Numbers and Newness: The Descriptive and Substantive Representation of Women. *Canadian Journal of Political Science*, 40: 27–49.

BRANTON, R. 2007. Latino Attitudes Toward Various Areas of Public Policy: The Importance of Acculturation. *Political Research Quarterly*, 60: 293–303.

BRATTON, K. A. 2002. The Effect of Legislative Diversity on Agenda Setting: Evidence from Six State Legislatures. *American Politics Research*, 30: 115–42.

—— 2005. Critical Mass Theory Revisited: The Behavior and Success of Token Women in State Legislatures. *Politics and Gender*, 1: 97–125.

—— 2006. The Behavior and Success of Latino Legislators: Evidence from the States. *Social Science Quarterly*, 87: 1136–57.

—— and HAYNIE, K. L. 1999. Agenda-Setting and Legislative Success in State Legislatures: The Effects of Gender and Race. *Journal of Politics*, 61: 658–79.

—— —— and REINGOLD, B. 2007. Agenda Setting and African American Women in State Legislatures. *Journal of Women, Politics, and Policy*, 28: 71–96.

BRUNELL, T. L., ANDERSON, C. J., and CREMONA, R. K. 2008. Descriptive Representation, District Demography, and Attitudes toward Congress Among African Americans. *Legislative Studies Quarterly*, 33: 223–44.

BURNS, N., LEHMAN SCHLOZMAN, K., and VERBA, S. 2001. *The Private Roots of Public Action: Gender, Equality, and Political Participation*. Cambridge: Harvard University Press.

CAMERON, C., EPSTEIN, D., and O'HALLORAN, S. 1996. Do Majority–Minority Districts Maximize Substantive Black Representation in Congress? *The American Political Science Review*, 90: 794–812.

CANON, D. T. 1999. *Race, Redistricting and Representation: The Unintended Consequences of Black Majority Districts*. Chicago: University of Chicago Press.

CARROLL, S. 2002. Representing Women: Congresswomen's Perception of Their Representational Roles, pp. 50–68 in *Women Transforming Congress*, ed. C. S. Rosenthal. Norman: University of Oklahoma Press.

CENTER FOR THE AMERICAN WOMAN AND POLITICS. 2009. Fact Sheet: Women in the U.S. Congress 2009. New Brunswick: Center for American Women and Politics, Rutgers, The State University of New Jersey.

CHILDS, S., and KROOK, M. L. 2006a. Gender and Politics: The State of the Art. *Politics & Gender*, 26: 18–28.

————2006b. Should Feminists Give Up on Critical Mass? A Contingent Yes. *Politics & Gender*, 2: 522–30.

CLAYTON, D. M. 2000. *African Americans and the Politics of Congressional Redistricting*. New York: Garland Publishing.

CRAMER WALSH, K. 2002. Resonating to Be Heard: Gendered Debate on the Floor of the House, pp. 370–96 in *Women Transforming Congress*, ed. C. S. Rosenthal. Norman: University of Oklahoma Press.

CROWLEY, J. E. 2004. When Tokens Matter. *Legislative Studies Quarterly*, 29: 109–36.

DAHL, R. 1956. *A Preface to Democratic Theory*. Chicago: University of Chicago Press.

DAHLERUP, D. 2006. The Story of the Theory of Critical Mass. *Politics and Gender*, 2: 511–22.

DAVIDSON, C., and GROFMAN, B., eds. 1994. *Quiet Revolution in the South: The Impact of the Voting Rights Act 1965–1990*. Princeton: Princeton University Press.

DAWSON, M. 1994. *Behind the Mule: Race and Class in African American Voting*. Princeton: Princeton University Press.

DIAMOND, I., and HARTSOCK, N. 1981. Beyond Interests in Politics: A Comment on Virginia Sapiro's "When are Interests Interesting? The Problem of Political Representation of Women." *American Political Science Review*, 75: 717–21.

DODSON, D. L. 2006. *The Impact of Women in Congress*. New York: Oxford University Press.

————and CARROLL, S. 1991. *Reshaping the Agenda: Women in State Legislatures*. New Brunswick: Center for the American Woman and Politics, Rutgers, The State University of New Jersey.

————CARROLL, S. J., MANDEL, R. B., KLEEMAN, K. E., SCHREIBER, R., and LIEBOWITZ, D. 1995. *Voices, Views, Votes: The Impact of Women in the 103rd Congress*. New Brunswick: Center for the American Woman and Politics, Rutgers, The State University of New Jersey.

DOLAN, J. 1997. Support for Women's Interests in the 103rd Congress: The Distinct Impact of Congressional Women. *Women & Politics*, 18: 81–94.

DOLAN, K. 2004. *Voting for Women: How the Public Evaluates Women Candidates*. Boulder, CO: Westview Press.

DOVI, S. 2002. Preferable Descriptive Representatives: Or Will Just Any Women, Black, or Latino Do? *American Political Science Review*, 96: 745–54.

DUERST-LAHTI, G. 2002. Knowing Congress as a Gendered Institution: Manliness and the Implications of Women in Congress, pp. 20–49 in *Women Transforming Congress*, ed. C. S. Rosenthal. Norman: University of Oklahoma Press.

ELDER, L. 2008. Whither Republican Women: The Growing Partisan Gap among Women in Congress. *The Forum*, 6: Issue 1, Article 13.

EVANS, J. J. 2005. *Women, Partisanship, and the Congress*. New York: Palgrave MacMillan.

FENNO, R. F. 2003. *Going Home: Black Representatives and Their Constituents*. Chicago: University of Chicago Press.

FOX, R. L., and LAWLESS, J. L. 2005. To Run or Not to Run for Office: Explaining Nascent Political Ambition. *American Journal of Political Science*, 49: 642–59.

FRAGA, L. R., LOPEZ, L., MARTINEZ-EBERS, V., and RAMIREZ, R. 2007. Gender and Ethnicity: Patterns of Electoral Success and Legislative Advocacy among Latina and Latino State Officials in Four States. *Journal of Women, Politics, and Policy*, 28: 121–45.

FRANKOVIC, K. A. 1977. Sex and Voting in the U.S. House of Representatives 1961 to 1975. *American Politics Quarterly*, 5: 315–30.

FREDERICK, B. 2009. Are Female House Members still more Liberal in a Polarized Era? The Conditional Nature of the Relationship between Descriptive and Substantive Representation. *Congress and the Presidency*, 36: 181–202.

—— 2010. Gender and Patterns of Roll Call Voting in the U.S. Senate. *Congress and the Presidency*, 37: 103–24.

GAMBLE, K L. 2007. Black Political Representation: An Examination of Legislative Activity within U.S. House Committees. *Legislative Studies Quarterly*, 32: 421–46.

GARCIA BEDOLLA, L., TATE, K., and WONG, J. 2005. Indelible Effects: The Impact of Women of Color in the U.S. Congress, pp. 152–75 in *Women and Elective Office: Past, Present, and Future*, 2nd edition., ed. S. Thomas and C. Wilcox. New York: Oxford University Press.

GAY, C. 2002. Spirals of Trust? The Effect of Descriptive Representation on the Relationship Between Citizens and Their Government. *American Journal of Political Science*, 46: 717–33.

—— 2007. Legislating Without Constraints: The Effect of Minority Districting on Legislators' Responsiveness to Constituency Preferences. *Journal of Politics*, 69: 442–56.

GELB, J., and LIEF PALLEY, M. 1996. *Women and Public Policies: Reassessing Gender Politics*. Charlotsville, VA: University Press of Virginia.

GERBER, A. 1996. African Americans' Congressional Careers and the Democratic House Delegation. *Journal of Politics*, 58: 831–45.

GERRITY, J. C., OSBORN, T., and MOREHOUSE MENDEZ, J. 2007. Women and Representation: A Different View of the District. *Politics & Gender*, 3: 179–200.

GERTZOG, I. N. 2004. *Women and Power on Capitol Hill: Reconstructing the Congressional Women's Caucus*. Boulder: Lynn Rienner.

GREY, S. 2006. Numbers and Beyond: The Relevance of Critical Mass in Gender Research. *Politics & Gender*, 2: 492–502.

GRIFFIN, J. D. 2006. Senate Apportionment as a Source of Political Inequality. *Legislative Studies Quarterly*, 31: 405–32.

—— and FLAVIN, P. 2007. Racial Differences in Information, Expectations, and Accountability. *Journal of Politics*, 69: 220–36.

—— and NEWMAN, B. 2008. *Minority Report: Evaluating Political Equality in America*. Chicago: The University of Chicago Press.

HAWKESWORTH, M. 2003. Congressional Enactments of Race–Gender: Toward a Theory of Raced–Gendered Institutions. *American Political Science Review*, 97: 529–50.

HAYNIE, K. L. 2001. *African American Legislators in the American States*. New York: Columbia University Press.

HEDGE, D., BUTTON, J., and SPEAR, M. 1996. Accounting for the Quality of Black Legislative Life: The View From the States. *American Journal of Political Science*, 40: 82–98.

HERO, R. E., and TOLBERT, C. 1995. Latinos and Substantive Representation in the U.S. House of Representatives: Direct, Indirect, or Nonexistent? *American Journal of Political Science*, 39: 640–52.

HUDDY, L., and TERKILDSEN, N. 1993. The Consequences of Gender Stereotypes for Women Candidates at Different Levels and Types of Office. *Political Research Quarterly*, 46: 503–25.

HUTCHINGS, V. L., MCCLERKING, H. K., and CHARLES, G. U. 2004. Congressional Representation of Black Interests: Recognizing the Importance of Stability. *Journal of Politics*, 66: 450–68.

JOHNSON, C. M., DUERST-LAHTI, G., and NORTON, N. H. 2007. *Creating Gender: The Sexual Politics of Welfare Policy*. Boulder, CO: Lynne Rienner.

KANTER, R. M. 1977. Some Effects of Proportions on Group Life: Skewed Sex Ratios and Responses to Token Women. *American Journal of Sociology*, 82: 965–90.

KATHLENE, L. 1994. Power and Influence of State Legislative Policymaking: The Interaction of Gender and Position in Committee Hearing Debates. *American Political Science Review*, 88: 560–76.

——2005. In a Different Voice: Women and the Policy Process, pp. 213–29 in *Women and Elective Office: Past, Present, and Future*, ed. S. Thomas and C. Wilcox. New York: Oxford University Press.

KAUFMANN, K. M., PETROCIK, J. R., and SHAW, D. R. 2008. *Unconventional Wisdom: Facts and Myths About American Voters*. New York: Oxford University Press.

KENNEY, S. J. 1996. New Research on Gendered Political Institutions. *Political Research Quarterly*, 49: 445–66.

KERR, B., and MILLER, W. 1997. Latino Representation, It's Direct and Indirect. *American Journal of Political Science*, 41: 1066–71.

KINDER, D. R., and WINTER, N. 2001. Exploring the Racial Divide: Blacks, Whites, and Opinion on National Policy. *American Journal of Political Science*, 45: 439–56.

KINGDON, J. W. 2005. *Agendas, Alternatives, and Public Policies*, 2nd edition. New York: Longman.

LAWLESS, J. L. 2004. Politics of Presence: Women in the House and Symbolic Representation. *Political Research Quarterly*, 53: 81–99.

——and Fox, R. L. 2005. *It Takes a Candidate: Why Women Don't Run for Office*. New York: Cambridge University Press.

——and THERIAULT, S. M. 2005. Will She Stay or Will She Go? Career Ceilings and Women's Retirement from the U.S. Congress. *Legislative Studies Quarterly*, 30: 581–96.

LEADER, S. G. 1977. The Policy Impact of Elected Women Officials, pp. 265–84 in *The Impact of the Electoral Process*, ed. J. Cooper and L. Maisel. Beverly Hills: Sage Publications.

LEE, F. E., and OPPENHEIMER, B. L. 1999. *Sizing Up the Senate: The Unequal Consequences of Equal Representation*. Chicago: University of Chicago Press.

LEVY, D., TIEN, C., and AVED, R. 2002. Do Differences Matter? Women Members of Congress and the Hyde Amendment. *Women & Politics*, 23: 105–27.

LUBLIN, D. 1997. *The Paradox of Representation: Racial Gerrymandering and Minority Interests in Congress*. Princeton: University of Princeton Press.

——and VOSS, D. S. 2003. The Missing Middle: Why Median Voter Theory Can't Save Democrats from Singing the Boll-Weevil Blues. *Journal of Politics*, 65: 227–37.

MACDONALD, J. A., and O'BRIEN, E. E. Forthcoming. Quasi-Experimental Design, Constituency, and Advancing Women's Interests: 'Critically' Reexamining the Influence of Gender on Substantive Representation. *Political Research Quarterly*.

MANSBRIDGE, J. 1999. Should Blacks Represent Blacks and Women Represent Women? A Contingent 'Yes.' *Journal of Politics*, 61: 628–57.

MARTINEZ-EBERS, V., FRAGA, L., LOPEZ, L., and VEGA, A. 2000. Latino Interests in Education, Health and Criminal Justice Policy. *PS: Political Science and Politics*, 33: 547–54.

McCARTY, N., POOLE, K. T., and ROSENTHAL, H. 1997. *Income Redistribution and the Realignment of American Politics*. Washington, DC: AEI Press.

MINTA, M. D. 2009. Legislative Oversight and the Substantive Representation of Black and Latino Interests in Congress. *Legislative Studies Quarterly*, 34: 193–218.

NORTON, N. H. 1995. Women, It's Not Enough to Be Elected: Committee Position Makes a Difference, pp. 115–40 in *Gender Power, Leadership, and Governance*, ed. G. Duerst-Lahti and R. M. Kelly. Ann Arbor: University of Michigan Press.

——1999. Committee Influence over Controversial Policy: The Reproductive Policy Case. *Policy Studies Journal*, 27: 203–16.

——2002. Transforming Congress from the inside: Women in Committee, pp. 316–40 in *Women Transforming Congress*, ed. C. S. Rosenthal. Norman: University of Oklahoma Press.

OREY, B. D., SMOOTH, W., ADAMS, K. S., and HARRIS-CLARK, K. 2007. Race and Gender Matter: Refining Models of Legislative Policy Making in State Legislatures. *Journal of Women, Politics, and Policy*, 28: 97–119.

OVERBY, M. L., and COSGROVE, K. M. 1996. Unintended Consequences? Racial Redistricting and the Representation of Minority Interests. *Journal of Politics*, 58: 540–50.

PETERS, JR., R. M., and ROSENTHAL, C. S. 2010. *Speaker Nancy Pelosi and the New American Politics*. New York: Oxford University Press.

PEW RESEARCH CENTER. 2008. U.S. Population Projections: 2005–2050. *Social and Demographic Trends*. Washington, DC: Pew Hispanic Center.

PHILLIPS, A. 1991. *Engendering Democracy*. University Park: The Pennsylvania State University Press.

——1995. *The Politics of Presence*. Oxford: Oxford University Press.

——1998. Democracy and Representation: Or, Why Should it Matter Who our Representatives Are? pp. 224–40 in *Feminism and Politics*, ed. A. Phillips. New York: Oxford University Press.

PITKIN, H. F. 1967. *The Concept of Representation*. Berkley: University of California Press.

POGGIONE, S. 2004. Exploring Gender Differences in State Legislators' Policy Preferences. *Political Research Quarterly*, 57: 305–14.

PREUHS, R. R. 2005. Descriptive Representation, Legislative Leadership, and Direct Democracy: Latino Influence on English only Laws in the States, 1984–2002. *State Politics and Policy Quarterly*, 5: 203–24.

REINGOLD, B. 1992. Concepts of Representation among Female and Male State Legislators. *Legislative Studies Quarterly*, 17: 509–37.

——2000. *Representing Women: Sex Gender, and Legislative Behavior in Arizona and California*. Chapel Hill: The University of North Carolina Press.

ROCCA, M. S., SANCHEZ, G. R., and USCINSKI, J. 2008. Personal Attributes and Latino Voting Behavior in Congress. *Social Science Quarterly*, 89: 392–405.

ROSENTHAL, C. S. 1998. *When Women Lead: Integrative Leadership in State Legislatures*. New York: Oxford University Press.

——2005. Women Leading Legislatures: Getting There and Getting Things Done, pp. 197–212 in *Women in Elective Office: Past, Present, and Future*, ed. S. Thomas and C. Wilcox, 2nd edition. New York: Oxford University Press.

——2008. Climbing Higher: Opportunities and Obstacles Within the Party System, pp. 197–222 in *Legislative Women: Getting Elected, Getting Ahead*, ed. B. Reingold. Boulder: Lynne Reiner.

ROSSITER, C., ed. 1961. *The Federalist Papers: Alexander Hamilton, James Madison, John Jay.* New York: Mentor Book.

SAINT-GERMAIN, M. 1989. Does Their Difference Make a Difference? The Impact of Women on Public Policy in the Arizona Legislature. *Social Science Quarterly,* 70: 956–68.

SAPIRO, V. 1981. Research Frontier Essay: When Are Interests Interesting? The Problem of Political Representation of Women. *American Political Science Review,* 75: 701–16.

SANBONMATSU, K. 2002. *Gender Equality, Political Parties, and the Politics of Women's Place.* Ann Arbor: University of Michigan Press.

SANCHEZ, G. 2006. The Role of Group Consciousness in Latino Public Opinion. *Political Research Quarterly,* 59: 435–46.

SANTOS, A., and HUERTA, J. C. 2001. An Analysis of Descriptive and Substantive Latino Representation in Congress, pp. 57–75 in *Representation of Minority Groups in the U.S.: Implications for the Twenty-First Century,* ed. C. E. Menifield. Lanham, Maryland: Austin and Winfield Publishers.

SCHWINDT-BAYER, L. A., and CORBETTA, R. 2004. Gender Turnover and Roll-Call Voting in the U.S. House of Representatives. *Legislative Studies Quarterly,* 29: 215–29.

SHOGAN, C. 2001. Speaking out: An Analysis of Democratic and Republican Women-Invoked Rhetoric of the 105th Congress. *Women & Politics,* 23: 129–46.

SHOTTS, K. W. 2003. Does Racial Redistricting Cause Conservative Policy Outcomes? Policy Preferences of Southern Representatives in the 1980s and 1990s. *Journal of Politics,* 65: 216–26.

SMOOTH, W. 2008. Gender, Race, and the Exercise of Power and Influence, pp. 175–96 in *Legislative Women: Getting Elected, Getting Ahead,* ed. B. Reingold. Boulder, CO: Lynne Rienner.

SWAIN, C. M. 1993. *Black Faces, Black Interests: The Representation of African Americans in Congress.* Cambridge: Harvard University Press.

SWERS, M. L. 1998. Are Congresswomen More Likely to Vote for Women's Issue Bills Than Their Male Colleagues? *Legislative Studies Quarterly,* 23: 435–48.

—— 2002. *The Difference Women Make: The Policy Impact of Women in Congress.* Chicago: University of Chicago Press.

—— 2007. Building a Reputation on National Security: The Impact of Stereotypes Related to Gender and Military Experience. *Legislative Studies Quarterly,* 32: 559–96.

—— 2008. Policy Leadership Beyond 'Women's' Issues, pp. 117–34 in *Legislative Women: Getting Elected, Getting Ahead,* ed. B. Reingold. Boulder, CO: Lynne Rienner.

—— Forthcoming. *Making Policy in the New Senate Club: Women and Representation in the U.S. Senate.* Chicago: University of Chicago Press.

SWERS, M., and LARSON, C. 2005. Women and Congress: Do They Act as Advocates for Women's Issues? pp. 110–28 in *Women and Elective Office: Past, Present, and Future,* 2nd edition, ed. S. Thomas and C. Wilcox. New York: Oxford University Press.

TATALOVICH, R., and SCHIER, D. 1993. The Persistence of Ideological Cleavage in Voting on Abortion Legislation in the House of Representatives, 1973–1988. *American Politics Quarterly,* 21: 125–39.

TATE, K. 2003. *Black Faces in the Mirror: African Americans and Their Representatives in the U.S. Congress.* Princeton: Princeton University Press.

THOMAS, S. 1991. The Impact of Women on State Legislatures. *Journal of Politics,* 53: 958–76.

—— 1994. *How Women Legislate.* New York: Oxford University Press.

—— 1997. Why Gender Matters: The Perceptions of Women Officeholders. *Women and Politics,* 17: 27–53.

WELCH, S., and HIBBING, J. 1984. Hispanic Representation in the U.S. Congress. *Social Science Quarterly,* 65: 328–35.

WHITBY, K. J. 1989. Measuring Congressional Responsiveness to the Policy Interests of Black Constituents. *Social Science Quarterly*, 68: 367–77.

—— and KRAUSE, G. A. 2001. Race, Issue Heterogeneity, and Public Policy: The Republican Revolution in the 104th Congress and the Representation of African American Policy Interests. *British Journal of Political Science*, 31: 555–72.

WILLIAMS, M. 1998. *Voice, Trust, and Memory: Marginalized Groups and the Failings of Liberal Representation*. Princeton: Princeton University Press.

WOLBRECHT, C. 2000. *The Politics of Women's Rights: Parties, Positions, and Change*. Princeton: Princeton University Press.

—— 2002. Female Legislators and the Women's Rights Agenda, pp. 170–239 in *Women Transforming Congress*, ed. C. S. Rosenthal. Norman: University of Oklahoma Press.

....

BICAMERAL REPRESENTATION

....

FRANCES E. LEE[*]

In *Federalist* 51, James Madison justified the framers' decision to divide the national legislature into two branches as a means to disperse and check political power. To augment this check, the two chambers were then "render[ed] by different modes of election and different principles of action as little connected with each other" as possible (Hamilton, Jay, and Madison 1987, 320).

Reflecting on this institutional choice, Richard F. Fenno, Jr. (1982, vii) observed, "The division of our national legislature into two separate bodies was little debated in 1787, and it has been taken for granted ever since." Indeed, the case for bicameralism is so widely accepted in American politics that forty-nine of fifty state legislatures today also have two chambers. John Stuart Mill (1991, 249) was writing about continental politics, not America, when he observed, "of all topics relating to the theory of representative government, none have been the subject of more discussion ... than what is known as the question of the Two Chambers." In the U.S., bicameral institutions are, and have been for most of the country's history, broadly and tacitly accepted.

Like Americans generally, legislative scholars have tended to take bicameral institutions for granted. Nevertheless, there is a body of empirical and theoretical research bearing on the topic. The purpose of this chapter is to critically examine this work and suggest avenues for further investigation. After an examination of theories of bicameralism, the focus will be on two primary topics. First, the political and policy implications of dividing the legislature into two chambers will be examined. Second, those constitutional features that make the two chambers "as little connected with

* I am grateful to David Searle and the University of Maryland's Undergraduate Research Assistantship Program for research assistance on this chapter.

each other" as possible will be assessed. In other words, there is the fact of bicameralism itself and then the additional effects of constitutional provisions that render the two chambers so different from one another in their modes of election and basis of representation.

THE LOGIC OF BICAMERALISM

Although the constitutional convention was the site of much hard bargaining (Robertson 2005; Roche 1961), there was no controversy over the question of bicameralism itself. American government textbooks often discuss bicameralism in the context of the "Great Compromise" on congressional apportionment, but the framers' choice in favor of a bicameral Congress had nothing to do with the protracted negotiations over whether Senate representation should be based on population or allocated equally among the states (Lee and Oppenheimer 1999, 27–32). Instead, the delegates agreed to Madison's proposal that the "legislature ought to consist of two branches" soon after the convention began without any contention or even sustained discussion of the issue (Farrand 1937, I: 46). The bicameral Congress was adopted well before any question of representation was taken up.

As a basic principle of government, bicameralism enjoyed broad support during the founding era, just as it does today. In 1787 all the states except Pennsylvania and Georgia already had bicameral legislatures, and both those states would amend their constitutions to make their General Assemblies bicameral soon after. Nevertheless, the reasons bicameralism was favored by the Framers of the Constitution are quite different from the justifications offered for bicameralism today.

Support for bicameralism was part of the conventional wisdom of the founding era, which idealized the English constitution (Banning 1987; Wood 1969). The genius of the English system was thought to lie in the way that the interests of the "few" and the "many" were balanced in the House of Lords and the House of Commons. According to this logic, the role of the upper chamber was to check the excesses of the more democratic chamber. As a body directly responsible to the electorate, the delegates were concerned that the House of Representatives would "yield to the impulse of sudden and violent passions and ... be seduced by factious leaders into intemperate and pernicious resolutions" (Madison, Hamilton, and Jay 1987, 366). The framers did not view the creation of two chambers primarily as a way to ensure extended deliberation and additional review of legislative initiatives, as bicameralism is generally understood today. Instead, a Senate was instituted to check the popular branch's propensity to engage in precipitate, disproportionate, and ill-considered lawmaking. "No justification of the House as a check on the Senate was ever considered in debating the structure of Congress" (Binder 2003, 16).

The United States thus possesses a "working bicameralism directly inherited from the 16th century" (Huntington 1968, 116). But bicameral institutions have long outlasted the English theory of mixed government so esteemed by the framers (Binder 2003, 12–33). Rather than serving as a reactive body reviewing the work of the House, the early nineteenth-century Senate evolved into an independent, activist lawmaking body in its own right (Swift 1996). Neither chamber now serves as a primary agenda-setter, and the House continually responds to initiatives emerging from the Senate. In addition, political parties became institutionalized during the nineteenth century, giving rise to inter-chamber dynamics that the framers could not have anticipated. Divided party control of House and Senate magnifies the impact of bicameralism itself, as the party in control of each chamber exploits the legislative process for electoral position-taking.

Such changes in institutional theory and practice have not necessarily weakened support for bicameralism, either in the U.S. or elsewhere. Instead, modern bicameral theory just emphasizes different functions. Contemporary justifications for bicameralism center primarily on diversity of representation and rigorous, careful deliberation. Bicameralism is especially useful as a means of facilitating representation of regions or territories, in addition to representation on the basis of population. As such, it predominates among countries with federal structures (Lijphart 1999), though the U.S. Senate has evolved in ways that have made it more of a national policymaking institution than a federal chamber or states' house (Riker 1955). The need for differentiation of representation is often thought to recommend bicameralism for larger countries. Accordingly, the world's most populous countries tend to have bicameral institutions (Patterson and Mughan 1999). More than two-thirds of all advanced democracies today have bicameral legislatures (Norton 2004).

Formal theory offers further insight into the contemporary logic of bicameralism. One of the most famous and troubling findings in this body of research is McKelvey's (1976) chaos result: for settings in which more than two voters have preferences along two or more dimensions, there is no equilibrium. Under such a condition, simple majority rule will generally not converge on any policy proposal that could not then be defeated by another majority coalition, raising the prospect of endless cycles among alternatives. Theoretical models suggest that bicameral institutions can mitigate this problem. Bicameralism can bring about a "structure induced equilibrium" (Shepsle 1979) under some conditions where majority rule would otherwise be unstable.

Bicameralism can limit majority rule cycles by rendering majorities that form in only one chamber incapable of changing policy. Requiring the concurrence of two chambers with different preference distributions makes legislating more difficult and thereby engineers policy stability (Brennan and Hamlin 1992; Hammond and Miller 1987; Tsebelis and Money 1997). Policies that are blocked from change as a result of bicameral differences are referred to as "the bicameral core." These policies are "undominated," meaning no change from the status quo is possible, given the existing preference distribution in each chamber. As a result, most formal theory has found bicameral institutions to have a status quo bias (but see Rogers 2003 for an alternative argument).

Riker (1992) offers an unequivocally normative interpretation of such findings. He argues that unicameral legislatures promote majority tyranny because they permit out-of-equilibrium policies to be adopted, whereas bicameral institutions will force delay during majority rule cycles and will only allow policy change when politics is one-dimensional and thus capable of producing an equilibrium outcome. By contrast, Miller, Hammond, and Kile (1996, 99) contend that the policies protected within the bicameral core may be entirely arbitrary: "Every possible bicameral structure creates privileged minorities.... [S]ome interests are advantaged at the expense of other interests by having one bicameral partition rather than another." Along these lines, bicameralism engineered policy stability favoring slaveholders in the pre-Civil War era (Weingast 1998). The enhanced representation of slave states in the Senate guaranteed that, even if a national popular majority in the House of Representatives favored antislavery legislation, it could not be passed.

Although bicameralism is valued for different reasons today than in the founding era, it is important to note that the results of formal models do support Madison's contention that, for bicameralism to be effective, the two chambers need to be composed differently: "when legislators in the two chambers have preferences which are too similar, no bicameral core will exist" (Miller, Hammond, and Kile 2003, 98; see also Hammond, and Miller 1987). By extension, bicameralism should have more significant policy effects at some times than others, depending on the preference dissimilarity of the two chambers.

THE FACT OF TWO

Contemporary bicameral theory is intuitive. It is easy to see how two chambers rather than one can diversify representation and institutionalize additional veto points so as to make legislating more difficult. "Nearly half of the legislation passed in each chamber typically languishes unfinished in the other chamber at the end of each Congress" (Larocca 2010). Empirical work, moreover, reveals that the importance of bicameralism extends well beyond questions of policy stability and status quo bias. Research suggests that bicameralism also affects the distribution of power in Congress, internal congressional processes, and substantive policy outcomes.

Sarah Binder's (2003) research identifies bicameral differences as one of the most significant factors affecting the capacity of Congress to enact a legislative agenda. Previous work had tended to overlook the significance of bicameralism, focusing instead on the separation of powers between the executive and legislative branches as a key obstacle to national policymaking. But Binder (2003, 81) finds that "bicameralism is perhaps the most critical structural factor shaping the politics of gridlock." She constructs a measure of the divergence in House–Senate policy preferences for each Congress by calculating the average difference in the two chambers' support for identical legislative proposals (final passage of conference reports). Her analysis of legislative performance from the postwar period (1947–2000) concludes that higher levels of bicameral disagreement depress policymaking activity considerably more than the presence of divided party control between the executive and legislative branches of government. Differences in the distribution of policy preferences across the two chambers emerge as one of the most notable causes of policy stalemate.

The effects of bicameralism alone are amplified by the many institutional differences that have developed between the two chambers over time, including nonparallel committee jurisdictions (Larocca 2010) and dissimilar internal rules of procedure (Sinclair 2009a, 2009b). These institutional differences are not constitutionally required, but the U.S. Constitution permits each chamber of Congress to set its own rules. As a consequence, the procedural development of the House and Senate diverged down very different paths (Binder 1997). These rules differences create an additional source of interchamber conflict, one that compounds the importance of bicameralism itself.

Drawing on data from the early 1960s through 2008 Barbara Sinclair argues that bicameralism per se has only a modest depressing effect on the enactment of major legislation. Most major legislation that passed either House or Senate during this period went on to approval by both chambers: 89 percent of major measures passed one of the two chambers, and 74 percent passed both (Sinclair 2009b, 6). Once both House and Senate have approved related bills, the two chambers almost always then forge agreement on identical legislative language. "By the time legislation has made its way through both chambers, enough members have a stake in its success to induce the chambers to find a compromise" (Sinclair 2009b, 7–8).

The high levels of partisan conflict that have become the norm in both chambers since the 1990s appear to have affected the House and Senate differently. Senate rules require supermajority support to end debate; by contrast, a simple majority is all that is needed to halt debate and force a vote in the House. When the two parties strongly disagree and the majority party cannot muster sixty votes, Senate rules can thwart a majority party's attempts to legislate. Reflecting on the current status of Senate procedure, Rawls (2009, 52) writes, "If supported by 41 votes, [a Senate minority party's obstruction] is impenetrable, an absolute bar, a de facto legislative veto." No similar difficulty arises in the House, where the rules permit a unified majority party to enact its agenda without attracting any bipartisan support. Given that Senate majority parties almost never control sixty seats, partisan coalitions are considerably less likely to succeed in legislating in the Senate than in the House (Binder 2003, 97–105). Compared with the House, the Senate is thus less able to legislate on issues that sharply divide the parties.

Differences in the two chambers' rules, especially under conditions of party polarization, mean the two chambers may not check one another equally. Nonetheless, Binder (2003, 45) finds that throughout most of the postwar era, "neither the House nor Senate is disproportionately responsible for killing legislative measures." Similarly, Mayhew's (2010) analysis concludes that over the postwar period House and Senate were "near equal opportunity buriers of presidential initiatives." However, contemporary legislation is substantially more likely to clear the House than the Senate. "In the more recent Congresses legislation was much more likely to pass the House but fail in the Senate than the reverse" (Sinclair 2009a, 17; see also Binder 2003, 50). Mayhew (2010) also determines that after 1988 the president's legislative program was more likely to meet defeat in the Senate than in the House. In the highly partisan contemporary Congress, the Senate—not bicameralism itself—becomes the greater institutional obstacle to the passage of legislation.

Offering a precise account of the policy and political effects of bicameralism is not easy. The prevalence and permanence of bicameralism in the U.S. means that there is little variation across time and space for scholars to analyze. Furthermore, it is difficult to separate the effects of two chambers *per se* from all the other factors that make the House and Senate different. Given these difficulties, some scholars have attempted to study the effects of bicameralism using experimental methods (Bottom, Eavey, et al. 2000; Miller, Hammond, and Kile 1996). The benefit of experimental approaches is that they allow researchers to hold the distribution of legislators' preferences constant while varying institutional rules and vice versa. Results from such studies bolster findings from formal models, confirming that experimental subjects working through coalition-building problems tend to arrive at results consistent with formal theory. These studies find that bicameralism promotes policy stability favoring the status quo within the bicameral core.

The findings of formal theory and laboratory experiments both rest on the correspondence between the real world and the models or simulations. Rogers (2003) questions whether formal theory has adequately included all relevant features of the U.S. bicameral system, focusing on the use of a policy space of fixed dimensionality. In the strong bicameralism of the U.S., both chambers can originate as well as veto legislation and thereby introduce new dimensions of policy dispute into interchamber debate. Where both House and Senate can initiate as well as veto, Rogers argues, the effect of bicameralism on legislative productivity is theoretically indeterminate. The results of his analysis of the four U.S. states that have gone through cameral transitions afford no support for any inference that bicameralism by itself reduces the amount of legislation relative to unicameralism. There is still room for further theoretical and experimental work on bicameralism that strives for greater realism about legislative processes.

Investigation of bicameralism's effects should not end with research on legislative productivity, however. Although normative justifications for bicameralism often center on the value of policy stability, questions about the empirical effects of bicameralism should not be limited to status quo bias. Bicameralism also affects internal legislative procedures, as well as power relationships within the two chambers. It may also have substantive effects on public policy.

Different mechanisms for resolving bicameral disagreements distribute influence in Congress in varying ways (Krehbiel, Shepsle, and Weingast 1987). Generally speaking, the process of resolving differences between the chambers empowers the subset of members who conduct bicameral negotiations. Bicameral conferees put together large packages of policies, forcing members to cast up-or-down votes on a wide range of matters simultaneously (Krutz 2001). Measures that might never pass one or both chambers as a separate piece of legislation can be approved as part of a larger bicameral agreement. Members who broker bicameral accords may well insert favored policy provisions and thus enjoy enhanced influence over policy outcomes.

For Shepsle and Weingast (1987), the fact that conference committees are typically dominated by the chairs and members of the committees of jurisdiction is key to understanding the power of congressional committees. In representing their chamber's position during bicameral negotiations, committee members can refuse to agree to a conference settlement and thus wield an *ex post* veto over policies that depart too far from their preferences. Because it is well understood that committee members will play a central role in bicameral deal making, members not on the relevant committees who would like to propose floor amendments have an incentive to confer with committee members to devise amendments that will not provoke an *ex post* veto.

Bicameral assent can be achieved in ways other than conference committees. Regardless of the method used, however, only a small slice of the membership of House and Senate will usually be directly involved in the process. Since the late 1990s as senators have objected to motions to appoint conferees, congressional leaders have more frequently opted to pingpong bills between the chambers, rather than convene a conference committee. As Walter Oleszek (2008, 26) reports, "amendments pingponged between the houses are usually crafted in private by a relatively small number of members." Party leaders in House and Senate are central to this technique as they broker agreements via ad hoc meetings in their offices. Compared to a conference committee, this method makes the process less transparent and even more exclusive. The need to achieve bicameral assent on complex legislation can thus create another source of leverage for party and committee leaders.

Bicameral resolution of policy differences remains an understudied subject in legislative politics. In light of their importance for policy outcomes, internal processes, and legislative strategies, it is surprising how little attention scholars have devoted to bicameral interactions. Taking stock of the situation, Rohde (2002, 349) observed, "We just don't know a lot about conference committees." An early literature focused on the difficult question of "who wins?"—House or Senate—during conference negotiations (Ferejohn 1975; Strom and Rundquist 1977). Beyond this, little systematic work is available on the subject. Given the difficulty of collecting quantitative data in this area, scholarship unquestionably benefits from in-depth case study (Van Beek 1995). But relatively few works in this vein have appeared. An updating of Longley and Oleszek (1989) could illuminate the ways that the politics of bicameral resolution have changed since the 1980s, particularly in the more partisan 1990s and 2000s. Now that bicameral resolution happens more frequently without the conference process, if anything, we know even less than before.

Bicameralism may also predispose substantive policy in particular directions. Some work, for example, suggests that bicameralism may contribute to higher budget deficits (Heller 1997, 2001). An easy compromise when majorities in two chambers favor different programs is to increase expenditures to accommodate both sets of priorities. Bicameralism can thus lead to intercameral logrolls that raise overall spending, just as divided government is often hypothesized to incentivise interparty vote trades that undermine fiscal restraint (Cox and McCubbins 1991; McCubbins 1991). Findings from Heller's cross-national study support his hypothesis that deficits tend to be higher in bicameral systems than in unicameral systems. However, it is also possible that, by dividing power, bicameralism may afford political cover to legislators seeking to impose costs. Although logrolling can be an easy way to resolve disagreement, bicameralism obscures responsibility in ways that may allow policy entrepreneurs more freedom to push politically difficult policies. The substantive policy effects of bicameralism undoubtedly warrant additional scholarly attention.

CONSTITUTIONAL HOUSE–SENATE
DIFFERENCES

U.S. bicameralism takes on additional significance when one considers the profound differences between the House and Senate established by the Constitution. Under the Constitution, House members and senators represent very different constituencies and serve different terms of office in chambers of very different size. (See Baker 2001 for an extended investigation of these bicameral differences.) In particular, the apportionment of representatives is a foundational institutional choice that has innumerable downstream effects on representational relationships, on who will be elected, and on whose interests will be advantaged in policymaking (Kromkowski 2002). This was clearly well understood at the constitutional convention of 1787, where no issue aside from Senate apportionment was so controversial that it threatened to break up the convention before it finished its work.

The convention's lengthy and intractable dispute over Senate representation was eventually resolved in a way that grants some citizens and some political interests far more per capita representation in Congress than others. At the extremes, states vary enormously in population, with the most populous state (California) nearly seventy times the population of the least populous state (Wyoming). Furthermore, the departure from a population-based standard goes well beyond the wide range between the most and least populous states. Most Americans, in fact, have a very different amount of representational power in the Senate than they would have if the body were apportioned on the basis of population (Lee and Oppenheimer 1999, 10–12). Most states are overrepresented in the U.S. Senate relative to a population-based standard. Meanwhile, the bulk of the nation's residents are concentrated in a handful of states: more than a quarter of the nation's population resides in three states and elects only six senators. The forty senators from the twenty least populous states represent a mere 10 percent of the U.S. population. In light of these stark patterns, it is not surprising that the Senate is one of the most malapportioned legislatures in the democratic world by the standard of one person, one vote (Samuels and Snyder 2001). Because the smallest states typically grow slowly or even decline in population while the most populous states tend to have high growth rates, Senate malapportionment will only increase in coming decades.

House representation is relatively equal on a per capita basis throughout the country. The constitutional requirement to reapportion House representation after each decennial census, combined with court enforcement of this requirement (e.g. *Wesberry* v. *Sanders*, 1964), ensures that House representation generally reflects state population. However, the growing variation in the distribution of population across states creates difficulties for maintaining the House's population-based apportionment. Because every state is guaranteed at least one House member, and House members cannot be divided across states, "the House has become systematically malapportioned and is likely to become more so over time" (Ladewig and Jasinski 2008, 90).

Scholarship has not given sufficient attention to the consequences of these basic representational differences between House and Senate. Political scientists tend to focus on questions that remain live controversies. With respect to congressional representation, there has thus been far more scholarly attention to the effects of strict population apportionment standards and majority–minority districts in the House than to the Senate's extreme deviation from the one person, one vote standard. Although the settled status of Senate representation has rendered it a less prominent subject for study, it remains a key question for those seeking to understand U.S. bicameralism. Below I examine the effects of differences in House–Senate apportionment on policy outcomes; on interest, partisan and ideological representation; and on relationships between officeholders and constituents.

Policy outcomes

A sizeable and growing body of research shows that inequalities in representational power affect substantive policy outcomes. There is a notable bias in federal spending patterns stemming from the advantages small population states obtain from Senate representation. The pattern is both persistent and pervasive. It is evident in aggregate analyses across a variety of time periods, as well as across most individual types of distributive policy (Atlas, Gilligan, et al. 1995; Hoover and Pecorino 2005; Lee and Oppenheimer 1999). Controlling for states' funding needs, overrepresented states receive more federal dollars per capita than underrepresented states. The effect is most pronounced in the type of spending over which Congress retains the tightest control, programs in which funds are distributed according to statutory formula (Lee 1998). For example, Lauderdale's (2008, 248) analysis of federal transportation spending, one of the major non-discretionary distributive programs, concludes, "the existence of the Senate was worth over $200 per capita per year to the citizens of the smallest states, *on one bill*." Similarly, the distribution of earmarks also tends to exhibit a marked tilt toward small states (Balla, Lawrence, et al. 2002; Hauk and Wacziarg 2007).

Findings on the advantages constituencies gain from Senate overrepresentation are reinforced by a growing line of scholarship demonstrating similar effects in a variety of legislative settings. Elis, Malhotra, and Meredith (2009) treat the decennial reapportionment of the House as a natural experiment to isolate how changes in representational power affect distributive outcomes. States' relative House representation can shift quite dramatically as a result of reapportionment, especially given growing House malapportionment. Analyzing changes in states' shares of federal outlays before and after reapportionment, Elis, Malhotra, and Meredith (2009, 370) find that "a 10% increase in the number of [House] representatives causes a 0.67% increase in a state's share of federal outlays." To take the example of Utah, a state that came up only a little short of the population threshold for a fourth House seat after the 2000 redistricting, these authors estimate that the extra seat would have translated to an additional $100 per capita.

Ansolabehere, Gerber, and Snyder (2002) show that the 1960s court-ordered redistricting requiring strict equality of state legislative district population significantly altered the flow of state money from formerly overrepresented counties to formerly underrepresented counties. Scholars have also documented biases in distribution favoring overrepresented constituencies in Japan (2003), Germany (Pitlik, Schneider, and Strotmann 2006), Argentina (Porto and Sanguinetti 2001), and the European Union (Rodden 2002).

Recent theoretical work has improved understanding of precisely how overrepresented constituencies reap such distributive advantages. Lee (2000) theorizes that senators representing small population states enjoy advantages in the coalition building process because they represent states that need less federal money. Given that each senator's vote counts equally, coalition builders have incentives to reach out to small state senators as a less costly way to build winning coalitions. Improved coalitional efficiency enables policy entrepreneurs to prevail on policy outcomes while reserving additional funds for their own constituencies.

Ansolabehere, Snyder, and Ting (2003) develop a non-cooperative legislative bargaining model to ascertain the specific institutional mechanisms by which malapportionment translates into distributive inequities in bicameral systems. They find that malapportionment alone does not translate into distributive inequities unless the malapportioned chamber, like the U.S. Senate, has proposal power. The effects of malapportionment are then amplified by supermajority rules. When it is necessary to muster a supermajority, "the proposer may be forced to buy some small-state senators in order to clear the supermajority hurdle ... and small states are able to extract additional payments" (Ansolabehere, Snyder, and Ting 2003, 475). The effects of malapportionment are also magnified by "lumpy public expenditure programs," in which programs are not divisible to House districts: "Lumpy expenditure[s] ... make the marginal cost of the large-state senator higher than the marginal cost of a small-state senator. To buy a senator from a state with, say, three House members, a proposer must pay the price of all three House members .... Recognizing this, small states can command higher (per capita) prices for their membership in a coalition" (Ansolabehere, Snyder, and Ting 2003, 477). "Lumpy goods" are pervasive in the U.S. federal system. States are the federal government's most important administrative units, and most grant-in-aid money goes to state governments. House districts, by contrast, are merely electoral entities, not administrative units, and cannot directly receive intergovernmental grant money (Lee 2003). Biases resulting from Senate malapportionment are thus exacerbated by Senate procedures as well as by the dominant types of distributive goods available in the federal system.

The U.S. Constitution—under which "no State, without its Consent, shall be deprived of its equal Suffrage in the Senate" and "each State shall have at Least one Representative"—creates a bicameral system with marked representational inequalities. A wide range of research indicates that representational power has a significant influence on who gets what from government. Given the pervasiveness and the size of the effect, future research should consistently factor representational power into models of federal policymaking.

Interest representation

For any system of geographic representation, where constituency lines are drawn affects the representation of political interests. Legislative districting is so politically controversial because the construction of constituencies inevitably influences the access and influence that different groups have in the political system. In this sense, "all districting is gerrymandering" (Dixon 1968, 462). How the different representational systems in the two chambers of a bicameral legislature then interact is no less consequential. Any "particular bicameral partition [is] nonneutral" (Miller, Hammond, and Kile 1996, 99). Beyond the inevitable effects of combining two sets of different geographic constituencies in a bicameral legislature, the U.S. system advantages some interests over others because of the radical departure from the principle of one person, one vote that stems from the equal representation of states in the Senate.

James Madison, James Wilson, and other prominent delegates at the constitutional convention argued against state equality in the Senate by pointing out that the interests of large and small states were not opposed to one another. Indeed, it remains true that constituency size is not an important predictor of legislative roll-call votes. Sharp voting cleavages do not arise between the congressional representatives of large states and small states. Nevertheless, when the groups or political interests that predominate in large and small states are different, Senate representation disadvantages the interests concentrated in populous states and advantages those in less populous states.

Although Senate representation has received little attention compared with the amount of scholarship on the consequences of other electoral rules, a few studies shed light on the political interests advantaged and disadvantaged by equal state representation. When Dahl (1956, 118) briefly examined this issue, he found that Senate representation disadvantaged African Americans, sharecroppers, migrant workers, wage earners, and coal miners and advantaged the producers of wool, cotton, and silver. A range of recent work investigates the Senate's effects on the representation of racial and ethnic minorities in the U.S. Racial and ethnic minorities are concentrated in the most populous states, while the nation's least populous states tend to have less diverse populations (Baker and Dinkin 1997; Griffin 2006; Lee and Oppenheimer 1999; Malhotra and Raso 2007). Senate representation thus gives substantially less representational weight to African Americans, Latinos, and Asian Americans than does the House. Similarly, urban interests and labor unions are notably less prominent in the nation's least populous states than in its most populous states (Ross 1996). All these interests are thus systematically weaker in Senate constituencies than in House constituencies and in the nation as a whole.

One of the ironies of congressional representation is that the Senate—a body often celebrated for procedures that protect minority points of view—is constructed in such a way as to further disadvantage some important minority interests in the political process. Because small states tend to be significantly less racially and ethnically diverse than the nation as a whole, Senate representation dilutes the congressional representation of the nation's African-American, Latino, and Asian populations. Indeed, many of the nation's less populous states have populations that are more than 90 percent non-Hispanic white, as compared with an overall national population that is only 75 percent non-Hispanic white. Rather than enhancing the input of political minorities, Senate representation exaggerates the nation's majority when the body considers issues that affect the races differently (Griffin 2006; Griffin and Newman 2008).

Beyond issues related to racial cleavages, the Senate may well disadvantage other types of political minorities, as well. To the extent that populous states are systematically more politically diverse, encompassing interests and organizations that lack a presence in small population states, Senate representation disadvantages more political minorities in the U.S. than it advantages.

Further work investigating how important political interests are distributed across states is needed to assess the effects of Senate representation and to gain a better understanding of congressional politics more generally. Studies examining the congressional politics of trade, health care, energy, agriculture, transportation, and myriad other issues need to be more sensitive to whether key interests are concentrated in states with large or small populations and, if so, how these patterns affect House and Senate policy preferences and bicameral interactions. Thies (1998), for example, finds that important changes in U.S. farm policy were long delayed by the permanent rural overrepresentation in the Senate. Decline in the nation's farming population was reflected in adjustments in House priorities once court-ordered reapportionment ended rural overrepresentation in the House, but "the still-rural Senate used its veto to undermine House efforts to cut farm spending" (Thies 1998, 484). More attention to the political geography of interest representation in the House and Senate is needed to strengthen scholarly accounts of bicameral politics and policymaking.

Partisan and ideological representation

Just as the different bases of representation in the House and Senate advantage and disadvantage particular political interests, they can also affect the congressional balance between Democrats and Republicans, conservatives and liberals. Griffin (2006), for example, finds that liberals and Democratic-party identifiers are more likely to reside in large than in small states. At various points, scholars have documented a partisan or ideological tilt to House or Senate representation. In the early 2000s, Jacobson (2004) determined that Republican voters were distributed more efficiently across congressional districts than Democratic voters. Democratic voters tended to cluster together in lopsided congressional districts, especially in urban centers, and thus won fewer congressional seats than would be predicted based on the party's share of the two-party presidential vote.

Mayhew (2010) assesses the partisan skew of House and Senate representation throughout the postwar period. Comparing the two parties' national vote share with the median House district and state, Mayhew finds a consistent, but slight, Republican tilt. Generally speaking, however, the two parties performed about equally well across electoral units in the House, Senate, and electoral college. It is particularly striking that the partisan composition of the Senate tracks so closely to the national performance of the parties, given that chamber's wide departure from one person, one vote. But there is simply no close connection between a state's population and its partisan proclivity. Some large states (New York, California) lean toward Democrats, others toward the Republicans (Texas, Georgia). Both parties enjoy "rotten boroughs" in the Senate. The Republican Party's post-1980 Senate majorities clearly owe something to its superior performance in small-population states, but these advantages were not sizeable enough to generate widespread discontent among Democrats. The same party usually commands a majority in both House and Senate, and congressional majorities cannot be attributed to institutional biases in representation.

Differences between the bases of representation in the House and Senate can also affect the ability of ideological coalitions to prevail in national policymaking. Although the controversy has long faded from view, an earlier scholarly literature centered on the question, "Is the Senate more liberal than the House?" Between the 1940s and 1960s, it struck many observers as harder to push liberal initiatives—such as federal aid to education, public housing, and minimum wage legislation—through the House of Representatives than through the Senate (Froman 1963; Grofman, Griffin, and Glazer 1991; Kernell 1973). Mayhew (2010) reevaluates this debate, finding that the House was indeed a "conservative outlier" on important liberal initiatives during that era. Although frustrated liberals of that time period often attributed their difficulties to the hierarchy and veto points in that House's policy process, Mayhew finds little support for this explanation. Instead, he concludes that differences in House and Senate constituencies were probably more important. The House's rural bias before the reapportionment revolution contributed to the chamber's conservative tilt during this time period, especially in contrast to the radical farmer–labor tradition still lingering in some of the small states represented in the Senate.

This earlier debate on the relative ideological balance of the House and Senate offers a notable contrast to the present. Although differences between the House and Senate are consequential for national policymaking, complaints about partisan and ideological skew are notable more for their absence in the contemporary era. Recent reform proposals center more on the supermajority procedures in the Senate and that body's status quo bias than on any perceived deficiencies in its basis of representation. The wide divergence between House and Senate constituencies always raises the possibility for partisan and ideological bias in representation, but the current distribution of partisan and ideological strength across House and Senate constituencies broadly reflects the nation as a whole.

Representational relationships

The House was designed to maintain close connections between representatives and represented, while the Senate was expected to operate with more distance from democratic pressures. The Constitution promoted these differences in democratic responsiveness, in part, by requiring House members to stand for election every two years, while giving senators six-year terms of office. In other respects, however, changes since the Constitution was adopted have made representational relationships in the two chambers less different from one another. In her chapter on the development of congressional elections in this volume, Wendy Schiller examines the effects of the 17th Amendment to the Constitution, which made senators directly elected, just as House members are. Furthermore, the nation's growing population has affected both House and Senate. The average House district today has a population larger than the state of Virginia in 1790, the most populous state of the founding era. In addition, the population differences between large and small states in the contemporary Congress are many times greater than they were at the nation's founding (Lee and Oppenheimer 1999, 10–12).

It was well understood at the Constitution's framing that constituency size powerfully affects the bonds between legislators and their constituents. *Federalist* 60 was written to refute the claim that House districts were too large to permit an appropriate connection between members and their constituents. "Scarce any article, indeed, in the whole Constitution," Madison (1987, 335) observed, has been "assailed" "with more apparent force of argument" than the ratio of representation. With one House representative for every thirty thousand residents under the original Constitution, anti-Federalists charged that House members would be insufficiently acquainted with the local concerns of their constituents. In the contemporary Congress, the average House member represents almost 700,000 residents, and the average senator represents a state with over 6 million people. Averages, however, can be quite misleading. There is just as much variation in the "representational experience" (Oppenheimer 1996) within the Senate as between the two chambers.

Variation in constituency size has measurable effects on the connections between members of Congress and their constituencies. Representatives with more populous constituencies are necessarily more distant from their constituents. Residents of larger states are less likely to report having contact with their senators (Hibbing and Alford 1990; Krasno 1994; Lee and Oppenehimer 1999; Oppenheimer 1996). Increasing numbers of constituents also affects voters' perceptions of their representatives' personal accessibility. Recognizing the barriers of size, residents of more populous states are less likely than residents of small states to initiate contact with their senators and less likely to ask for help with a problem (Oppenheimer 1996). A senator like Max Baucus, D-Montana, "still takes all phone calls from constituents, unscreened" (*CQ's Politics in America* 2007, 598), while senators from large states obviously cannot permit nearly such open access. "Everybody in this town dreads dealing with those big state senators," reported one lobbyist (Lee and Oppenheimer 1999, 76), "they have a hundred different pressures on them. It's hard just getting them to focus on your issue.... Even getting an appointment is [tough]."

Not surprisingly, the closer, more personal relationships possible in smaller constituencies generate warmer ties between representatives and voters (Baker 2001). Average approval ratings tend to decline as senators' constituency size increases (Binder, Maltzman, and Siegelman 1998; Lee and Oppenheimer 1999). The wide variation in the size of contemporary House constituencies has enabled Frederick (2007, 2010) to establish that the same patterns are present for House members. These effects are meaningful for legislative representation in a growing nation where the average House district is projected to reach 836,000 residents by 2030 (Frederick 2010) and where eight senators already represent states of upwards of 18 million people while fourteen senators represent states the size of House districts.

A body of research indicates that the difference in term length also affects representational relationships in the House and Senate. A number of works indicate that senators engage in more intensive reelection-oriented activities in their final two years of office. Most senators do the bulk of their fundraising in the last two years of their terms, though senators representing populous states (who typically need far more campaign funds) must fundraise throughout their term (Lee and Oppenheimer 1999, 108–13). Shepsle, Van Houweling, et al. (2009) develop a model of the bicameral bargaining process that examines how the staggered terms of senators affects distributive politics. Testing the model with data from 1995 to 2004, they find a cyclical pattern in which Senate appropriators prioritize earmark funding for senators who are up for reelection at the end of the Congress; no such pattern is evident in the House, where earmarking activity remains a constant as all members come up for reelection every two years. Lazarus and Steigerwalt (2009) also find that senators in the last two years of their terms received more earmarked projects in 2008 appropriations bills, controlling for other factors that affected receipt of projects. Finally, there is some evidence that cross-pressured senators strategically moderate their voting records towards the end of their terms in order to improve their cross-party appeal (Bernstein, Wright, and Berkman 1988; Elling 1982; Thomas 1985; Wright and Berkman 1986).

Although the contemporary Senate has evolved far beyond anything that the Framers of the Constitution could have expected, constitutional differences between the two chambers continue to generate political differences between the House and

Senate. The high frequency of elections keeps House members more continuously attuned to constituency connections than Senators. Meanwhile, the enormous variation in Senate constituency size puts some senators under far greater constituency demands than others. These interchamber differences in incentives and constituency bonds create other potential sources of bicameral conflict.

FUTURE RESEARCH

"The United States has the most intricate lawmaking system in the world," (Jones 1994, 257). This intricacy is very much a byproduct of bicameralism. The House and Senate have both evolved into mature institutions with elaborate internal structures and procedures. A constitutional system creating two chambers—each having developed along its own trajectory over more than two centuries—adds enormous complexity to the legislative process. Beyond these institutional and procedural consequences, bicameralism also introduces a great deal of additional *political* complexity into the lawmaking process. The two chambers' differences in modes of election and bases of representation are a potent source of diverging interchamber policy preferences, legislative priorities, and political incentives.

There is room for much more scholarship on the consequences of U.S. bicameralism. New formal models of bicameralism are called for. Although recent work has produced improved models of distributive policymaking in a bicameral context (Ansolabehere, Snyder, and Ting 2003), pivotal politics models (e.g. Krehbiel 1998) require further elaboration to analyze bicameralism's effects on the legislative outcomes of spatial, left–right issues. New empirical work is also needed to uncover patterns in interchamber interactions. In particular, we need a much better understanding of how bicameral institutions affect the distribution of power in Congress. After the evolution of the "sixty-vote Senate" (see Gregory Wawro's chapter on this topic in this volume), one often hears practitioners suggest that the difficulty of running legislation through the Senate gauntlet gives that body enhanced leverage in interchamber negotiations. For example, during the December 2009 health care reform debate, Senator Kent Conrad, D-N.D., observed, "I think any bill is going to have to be very close to what the Senate has passed because we're still going to have to get 60 votes. Anybody who has watched this process can see how challenging it has been to get 60 votes."[1] An important question is whether Conrad's observation holds true generally. Does the Senate possess greater influence over bicameral negotiations since it has become a consistently supermajoritarian chamber?

Although there has been a great deal of scholarship on the relationship between bicameralism and status quo bias, more work is needed to uncover what sorts of

[1] Fox News Sunday, December 20, 2009.

policies are hindered or frustrated by bicameral processes. The empirical question remaining is less whether bicameralism results in the failure of legislative initiatives than what types of policy proposals or issue areas are most impeded. What policies lie within the contemporary bicameral core? Are there contemporary interests that enjoy the sort of advantages that slavery interests obtained from bicameral institutions in the antebellum era? Building on Rogers (2003), the ability of both chambers to initiate legislation may drive up overall legislative output in a bicameral system, even while some important policies are blocked from passage. More empirical work on the specific policy areas most impacted by bicameralism is needed.

Relatedly, understandings of American national politics would be greatly enhanced if we had a better picture of how important political interests are distributed across House and Senate constituencies. Systematic investigation is needed to identify the specific political interests that have better representation in the House than in the Senate and vice versa. Recent work on minority representation has established the extent to which Senate constituencies dilute minority representation in Congress, isolating one important place to look for systematic differences in House and Senate preferences and agendas. But one would like to know more about what other political interests have better representation in and access to one chamber than another. If one wants to know where and how bicameralism has substantive policy effects, it is necessary to identify where and how the two chambers differ in terms of the political interests they represent.

Bicameral institutions are a permanent fact about American national government, but they are no less important or interesting for their durability. Even as they endure, they are not fixed. The operations, functions, and policy effects of bicameralism change over time, as do their consequences for democratic government.

References

Ansolabehere, S., Gerber, A., and Snyder, J. 2002. Equal Votes, Equal Money: Court-Ordered Redistricting and Public Expenditures in the American States. *American Political Science Review*, 96: 767–77.

——Snyder, Jr., J. M., and Ting, M. M. 2003. Bargaining in Bicameral Legislatures: When and Why Does Malapportionment Matter? *American Political Science Review*, 97: 471–81.

Atlas, C. M., Gilligan, T. W., Hendershott, R. J., and Zupan, M. A. 1995. Slicing the Federal Government Net Spending Pie: Who Wins, Who Loses and Why. *American Economic Review*, 85: 624–9.

Baker, L. A., and Dinkin, S. 1997. The Senate: An Institution Whose Time Has Gone? *Journal of Law and Politics*, 65: 31–49.

Baker, R. K. 2001. *House and Senate*. New York: W. W. Norton & Company.

Balla, S. J., Lawrence, E. D., Maltzman, F., and Sigelman, L. 2002. Partisanship, Blame Avoidance, and the Distribution of Legislative Pork. *American Journal of Political Science*, 46: 515–25.

Banning, L. 1987. The Constitutional Convention, pp. 112–31 in *The Framing and Ratification of the Constitution*, ed. L. W. Levy and D. J. Mahoney.

BERNSTEIN, R. A., WRIGHT, JR., G. C., and BERKMAN, M. B. 1988. Do U.S. Senators Moderate Strategically? *American Political Science Review*, 82: 237–45.

BINDER, S. A. 1997. *Minority Rights, Majority Rule*. New York: Cambridge University Press.

——2003. *Stalemate: Causes and Consequences of Legislative Gridlock*. Washington, DC: Brookings Institution Press.

——MALTZMAN, F., and LEE SIEGELMAN, L. 1998. Accounting for Senators' Home State Reputations: Why Do Constituents Love a Bill Cohen So Much More Than an Al D'Amato? *Legislative Studies Quarterly*, 23: 545–60.

BOTTOM, W. P., EAVEY, C. L., MILLER, G. J., and VICTOR, J. N. 2000. The Institutional Effect on Majority Rule Instability: Bicameralism in Spatial Policy Decisions. *American Journal of Political Science*, 44: 523–49.

BRENNAN, G., and HAMLIN, A. 1992. Bicameralism and Majoritarian Equilibrium. *Public Choice*, 74: 169–79.

COX, G. W., and MCCUBBINS, M. D. 1991. Divided Control of Fiscal Policy, pp. 155–75 in *The Politics of Divided Government*, ed. G. W. Cox and S. Kernell. Boulder, CO: Westview Press.

DAHL, R. A. 1956. *A Preface to Democratic Theory*. Chicago: University of Chicago Press.

DIXON, JR., R. G. 1968. *Democratic Representation: Reapportionment in Law and Politics*. New York: Oxford University Press.

ELIS, R., MALHOTRA, N., and MEREDITH, M. 2009. Apportionment Cycles as Natural Experiments. *Political Analysis*, 17: 358–76.

ELLING, R. C. 1982. Ideological Change in the U.S. Senate: Time and Electoral Responsiveness. *Legislative Studies Quarterly*, 7: 75–92.

FARRAND, M. 1937. *The Records of the Federal Convention of 1787*. 3 vols. New Haven: Yale University Press.

FENNO, JR., R. F. 1982. *The United States Senate: A Bicameral Perspective*. Washington, DC: American Enterprise Institute for Public Policy Research.

FEREJOHN, J. A. 1975. Who Wins in Conference Committee? *Journal of Politics*, 37: 1033–46.

FREDERICK, B. 2007. Constituency Population and Representation in the U.S. House. *American Politics Research*, 36: 358–81.

——2010. *Congressional Representation and Constituents*. New York: Routledge.

FROMAN, JR., L. A. 1963. *Congressmen and Their Constituencies*. Chicago: Rand McNally.

GRIFFIN, J. D. 2006. Senate Apportionment as a Source of Political Inequality. *Legislative Studies Quarterly*, 31: 405–32.

——and NEWMAN, B. 2008. *Minority Report: Evaluating Political Equality in America*. Chicago: University of Chicago Press.

GROFMAN, B., GRIFFIN, R., and GLAZER, A. 1991. Is the Senate More Liberal Than the House?: Another Look. *Legislative Studies Quarterly*, 16: 281–95.

HAMILTON, A., JAY, J., and MADISON, J. 1987. *The Federalist Papers*, ed. I. Kramnick. New York: Penguin.

HAMMOND, T., and MILLER, G. 1987. The Core of the Constitution. *American Political Science Review*, 81: 1144–74.

HAUK, W. R., and WACZIARG, R. 2007. Small States, Big Pork. *Quarterly Journal of Political Science*, 2: 95–106.

HELLER, W. B. 1997. Bicameralism and Budget Deficits: The Effect of Parliamentary Structure on Government Spending. *Legislative Studies Quarterly*, 22: 485–516.

——2001. Political Denials: The Policy Effect of Intercameral Partisan Differences in Bicameral Parliamentary Systems. *The Journal of Law, Economics, and Organization*, 17: 34–61.

HIBBING, J. R., and ALFORD, J. R. 1990. Constituency Population and Representation in the U. S. Senate. *Legislative Studies Quarterly*, 15: 581–98.

Hoover, G. A., and Pecorino, P. 2005. The Political Determinants of Federal Expenditures at the State Level. *Public Choice*, 123: 95–113.

Horiuchi, Y., and Saito, J. 2003. Reapportionment and Redistribution: Consequences of Electoral Reform in Japan. *American Journal of Political Science*, 47: 669–82.

Huntington, S. P. 1968. *Political Order in Changing Societies*. New Haven: Yale University Press.

Jacobson, G. C. 2004. *The Politics of Congressional Elections*. New York: Pearson Longman.

Jones, C. O. 1994. *The Presidency in a Separated System*. Washington, DC: Brookings Institution Press.

Kernell, S. 1973. Is the Senate More Liberal than the House? *Journal of Politics*, 35: 332–66.

Koszczuk, J., and Angle, M. 2007. *CQ's Politics in America 2008: The 110th Congress*. Washington, DC: CQ Press.

Krasno, J. 1994. *Challengers, Competition and Reelection: Comparing Senate and House Elections*. New Haven: Yale University Press.

Krehbiel, K. 1998. *Pivotal Politics: A Theory of U.S. Lawmaking*. Chicago: University of Chicago Press.

——Shepsle, K. A., and Weingast, B. R. 1987. Why Are Congressional Committees Powerful? *American Political Science Review*, 81: 929–45.

Kromkowski, C. A. 2002. *Recreating the American Republic: Rules of Apportionment, Constitutional Change, and American Political Development, 1700–1870*. New York: Cambridge University Press.

Krutz, G. S. 2001. *Hitching a Ride: Omnibus Legislating in the U.S. Congress*. Columbus: Ohio State University Press.

Ladewig, J. W., and Jasinski, M. P. 2008. On the Causes and Consequences of and Remedies for Interstate Malapportionment of the U.S. House of Representatives. *Perspectives on Politics*, 6: 89–107.

Larocca, R. 2010. Committee Parallelism and Bicameral Agenda Coordination. *American Politics Research*, 38: 3–32.

Lazarus, J., and Steigerwalt, A. 2009. Different Houses: The Distribution of Earmarks in the U.S. House and Senate. *Legislative Studies Quarterly*, 34: 347–73.

Lee, F. E. 1998. Representation and Public Policy: The Consequences of Senate Apportionment for the Geographic Distribution of Federal Funds. *The Journal of Politics*, 60: 34–62.

——2000. Senate Representation and Coalition Building in Distributive Politics. *American Political Science Review*, 94: 59–72.

——2003. Geographic Politics in the U.S. House of Representatives: Coalition Building and Distribution of Benefits. *American Journal of Political Science*, 47: 713–27.

——and Oppenheimer, B. I. 1999. *Sizing Up The Senate: The Unequal Consequences of Equal Representation*. Chicago: University of Chicago Press.

Lijphart, A. 1999. *Patterns of Democracy*. New Haven: Yale University Press.

Longley, L. D., and Oleszek, W. 1989. *Bicameral Politics: Conference Committees in Congress*. New Haven: Yale University Press.

Madison, J., Hamilton, A., and Jay, J. 1987. *The Federalist Papers*. New York: Penguin Books.

Malhotra, N., and Raso, C. 2007. Racial Representation and U.S. Senate Apportionment. *Social Science Quarterly*, 88: 1038–48.

Mayhew, D. R. 2010. *Partisan Balance: The Presidency, the Senate, and the House*. Princeton, NJ: Princeton University Press.

McCubbins, M. D. 1991. Government on Lay-Away: Federal Spending and Deficits Under Divided Party Control, pp. 113–53 in *The Politics of Divided Government*, ed. G. W. Cox and S. Kernell. Boulder, CO: Westview Press.

McKelvey, R. D. 1976. Intransitivities in Multidimensional Voting Models. *Journal of Economic Theory*, 12: 472–82.

Mill, J. S. [1861] 1991. *Considerations on Representative Government*. Buffalo, NY: Prometheus Books.

Miller, G. J., Hammond, T. H., and Kile, C. 1996. Bicameralism and the Core: An Experimental Test. *Legislative Studies Quarterly*, 21: 83–103.

Norton, P. 2004. How Many Bicameral Legislatures Are There? *Journal of Legislative Studies*, 10: 1–9.

Oleszek, W. J. 2008. Whither the Role of Conference Committees?: An Analysis. CRS Report for Congress.

Oppenheimer, B. I. 1996. The Representational Experience: The Effect of State Population on Senator-Constituency Linkages. *American Journal of Political Science*, 40: 1280–99.

Patterson, S. C., and Mughan, A. 1999. Senates and the Theory of Bicameralism, pp. 1–31 in *Senates: Bicameralism in the Contemporary World*, ed. S. C. Patterson and A. Mughan. Columbus, OH: The Ohio State University Press.

Pitlik, H., Schneider, F., and Strotmann, H. 2006. Legislative Malapportionment and the Politicization of Germany's Intergovernmental Transfer System. *Public Finance Review*, 34: 637–62.

Porto, A., and Sanguinetti, P. 2001. Political Determinants of Intergovernmental Grants: Evidence from Argentina. *Economics and Politics*, 13: 237–56.

Rawls, W. L. 2009. *In Praise of Deadlock: How Partisan Struggle Makes Better Laws*. Washington, DC: Woodrow Wilson Center Press.

Riker, W. H. 1955. The Senate and American Federalism. *American Political Science Review*, 49: 452–69.

—— 1992. The Justification of Bicameralism. *International Political Science Review*, 13: 101–16.

Robertson, D. B. 2005. *The Constitution and America's Destiny*. New York: Cambridge University Press.

Roche, J. P. 1961. The Founding Fathers: A Reform Caucus in Action. *American Political Science Review*, 55: 799–816.

Rodden, J. 2002. Strength in Numbers? Representation and Redistribution in the European Union. *European Union Politics*, 3: 151–75.

Rogers, J. R. 2003. The Impact of Bicameralism on Legislative Production. *Legislative Studies Quarterly*, 28: 509–28.

Rohde, D. W. 2002. Seeing the House and Senate Together: Some Reflections on the Exceptional Senate, pp. 341–9 in *U.S. Senate Exceptionalism*, ed. B. I. Oppenheimer. Columbus, OH: The Ohio State University Press.

Ross, S. G. 1996. Urban Underrepresentation in the U.S. Senate. *Urban Affairs Review*, 31: 404–18.

Samuels, D., and Snyder, R. 2001. The Value of a Vote: Malapportionment in Comparative Perspective. *British Journal of Political Science*, 31: 651–71.

Shepsle, K. A. 1979. Institutional Arrangements and Equilibrium in Multidimensional Voting Models. *American Journal of Political Science*, 23: 27–59.

—— Van Houweling, R. P., Abrams, S. J., and Hanson, P. C. 2009. The Senate Electoral Cycle and Bicameral Appropriation Politics. *American Journal of Political Science*, 53: 343–59.

—— and Weingast, B. R. 1987. The Institutional Foundations of Committee Power. *American Political Science Review*, 81: 85–104.

Strom, G. S., and Rundquist, B. S. 1977. A Revised Theory of Winning in House-Senate Conferences. *American Political Science Review*, 71: 448–53.

SWIFT, E. K. 1996. *The Making of an American Senate: Reconstitutive Change in Congress, 1787–1841*. Ann Arbor: University of Michigan Press.

THEIS, M. F. 1998. When Will Pork Leave the Farm? Institutional Bias in Japan and the United States. *Legislative Studies Quarterly*, 23: 467–92.

THOMAS, M. 1985. Election Proximity and Senatorial Roll Call Voting. *American Journal of Political Science*, 29: 96–111.

TSEBELIS, G., and MONEY, J. 1997. *Bicameralism*. Cambridge: Cambridge University Press.

VAN BEEK, S. D. 1995. *Post-Passage Politics: Bicameral Resolution in Congress*. Pittsburgh: University of Pittsburgh Press.

WEINGAST, B. 1998. Political Stability and the Civil War: Institutions, Commitment, and American Democracy, pp. 148–93 in *Analytical Narratives*, ed. R. Bates, A. Greif, M. Levi, J. L. Rosenthal, and B. R. Weingast. Princeton: Princeton University Press.

WOOD, G. S. 1969. *The Creation of the American Republic, 1776–1787*. Chapel Hill: University of North Carolina Press.

WRIGHT, G. C., and BERKMAN, M. B. 1986. Candidates and Policy in United States Senate Elections. *American Political Science Review*, 80: 567–88.

CHAPTER 13

....

DYADIC REPRESENTATION

....

STEPHEN ANSOLABEHERE
PHILIP EDWARD JONES

CONGRESSIONAL representation occurs on two levels—local and national. Constituents select their representatives to Congress; the country as a whole elects the entire Congress. Our understanding of congressional elections and representation similarly operates on two levels—the relationship between an individual representative and his or her constituents and the relationship between national conditions and the politics of the legislature as a whole. This chapter considers the first of these levels. This is what is most often meant by representation in the United States. The often personal relationship between the individual representative and his or her constituency is perhaps the most distinctive aspect of the U.S. Congress and other elective office in America. Dyadic Representation, a term dating back at least to Miller and Stokes's (1963) "Constituency influence in Congress," refers to the connection between individual Members of Congress and their constituents.[1] This rather abstract term refers to a very basic feature of American political vocabulary. When Americans talk of Congress, they often refer to "my representative," the individual who represents the district in which they live.

The nexus between the individual legislator and her or his constituency has, of course, many forms and facets. Miller and Stokes viewed the dyadic relationship through the lens of public policy and legislative votes. Indeed, the classical view of representation is how well the sitting legislator acts as an agent for the constituency on legislative decisions—dyadic policy representation, to use Miller and

---

[1] See also Eulau, Wahlke, et al. (1959).

Stokes terminology. But representation involves much more. American politicians have taken on the roles of advocate, ombudsman, fixer, local celebrity, even friend for their constituents. Motivated by the need to win office on their own, as individuals, Members of Congress have developed innovative ways to appeal to their constituents, and, for their part, voters in the United States have come to evaluate their politicians not just on the basis of party, but also as individuals. That relationship, both personal and partisan, is what David Mayhew famously called "the electoral connection" and Richard Fenno described as the member's "homestyle."

The multiple inputs into that relationship have generated volumes of research. Mayhew discerned three inputs in developing a relationship between representative and constituents: policy agreement, casework, and advertising (campaigning). Extensive research on roll-call voting, on constituent relations, and on congressional campaigning has attempted to document the strategic behavior involved in each and the importance of each in congressional politics. Taken together, though, these all contribute to the connection between the individual legislator and her or his constituency. One of the central themes of this chapter is that the policy and non-policy forms of dyadic representation are difficult to disentangle. Below we introduce a simple analytical model to give guidance to empirical researchers about how these ideas operate at both the individual and aggregate level.

Dyadic representation is distinguished from *collective representation*. Collective representation occurs when a collective organization, rather than the individual legislator, is the basis for representation. Party government, in its purest form, is collective. Under this situation, politicians of a given party are entirely exchangeable. Voters choose a Democrat or Republican, and it doesn't matter who. Legislators may promise many policies but they always answer to their party's call. Inside the legislature, roll-call votes become irrelevant, as all members of the same party vote alike. And the electoral fates of the parties in the constituencies depend only on the balance among the competing parties in each district and national tides that rise or lower all candidates running under the same banner.

Even though Miller and Stokes expressed the relationship between representative and constituency as dyadic, they ultimately concluded that representation in America follows the collective form. They point out that constituents do not appear to know enough about their legislators' behavior in Congress to hold them accountable (Converse 1964; Miller and Stokes 1963; Stokes and Miller 1962). They further found very weak correlations between constituents' preferences on major policy domains (in their study race, welfare, and foreign policy) and their legislators' preferences in those same domains. Instead, Miller and Stokes found that party identities correlated much more strongly with approval of the legislator. These results lined up with the general conclusions of the authors of *The American Voter* that party dominates public opinion about political institutions and electoral choices.

Importantly, party attachments in this account lack the sort of policy content that one might typically ascribe to the labels Democrat or Republican. Party identification is just that, an identity. Developed in childhood and handed down from parent to child, party identities in this account are stable and unconnected to short-term considerations of policy. Rather, they are a form of social and psychological identity that structures perceptions of political choices, more than is shaped by or a response to the options offered. This is more akin to rooting for a team than making a reasoned policy choice. Party voting, by this account, is thus not the sort of dyadic policy representation envisioned by the classical notions of representation critiqued by Miller and Stokes and others.

The insight of Mayhew, Fenno, and others was that legislators act as individuals to gain the approval of their constituents and try to distinguish themselves, sometimes in quite subtle ways, from their party. Legislators must win office in order to pursue any personal political or ideological goals. That fact has led political scientists to characterize the modern Member of Congress as single-mindedly in pursuit of re-election. Although surely an oversimplification, the electoral motivation appears to capture much of what drives Members of Congress today and has shaped the nature of representation in America. The personal pursuit of office has led American legislators to cultivate personal ties with voters and represent the wishes of their constituents, even at the expense of the success of their party or President. And it has led Members of Congress to organize their legislature and legislative activities to facilitate the pursuit of reelection and the representation of individual districts. Party is extremely important both in Congress and in the electorate, but American legislators also spend much of their time and effort to cultivate the support of the people back home.

Representation in the United States, then, is at once collective and individualistic. The empirical picture that emerges from four decades of research shows that both party (collective) and policy (dyadic) representation exert strong pressures on legislators when they decide how to vote in Congress, and that the electorate is very responsive to both party images and the individual legislators' policy choices. The lengthy literature on roll-call voting in Congress has repeatedly documented that legislator's voting records are correlated with the ideological and partisan leanings of their constituencies (Erikson and Wright 1980; Erikson, Wright, and McIver 1993; Fiorina 1974; Jessee 2009). Analyses of roll-call voting have also shown that roll-call voting behavior is also influenced by party affiliation of the legislator as well as the constituents' policy preferences (see Ansolabehere, Snyder, and Stewart 2001a; Smith and Lawrence 2006) and also by the legislators' own personal policy preferences (Ansolabehere, Snyder, and Stewart 2001b; Sullivan and Uslaner 1978). Analyses of electoral returns document that politicians who are responsive to their constituents' policy leanings do better in elections than those who are out of step with their district (Ansolabehere, Snyder, and Stewart 2001a; Canes-Wrone, Brady, and Cogan 2002). It is difficult to untangle the extent to which these patterns result from dyadic policy representation, from party or from some other source in aggregate election returns and roll-call voting scores. However, the importance of both party and the constituency's policy preferences in shaping what Members of Congress do are undeniable.

The strong tie between individual representatives and their constituents in the United States surely depends on the context, and, in particular, distinctive features of American political institutions. Two such conditions deserve emphasis—district-based elections and presidential-congressional government structure.

Single-member districts, one of the primitives of American legislatures, facilitate such a connection. The selection of legislators from districts grounds politics in local geography. Members of the U.S. Congress represent communities and places. That is, of course, still possible in proportional representation systems, but the incentives to cultivate a tie between a politician and local community are weaker when politicians run on a national list and win a seat if their party wins a sufficient share of the vote nationwide. In proportional representation systems, it usually makes no sense to talk of dyadic policy representation, and it is impossible to separate party voting from policy representation.

The presidential–congressional government structure also shapes the incentives facing individual politicians in the United States. The fate of the government and the timing of the next election in the United States do not hinge on whether the legislator supports his or her party. In parliamentary systems, such as that of the United Kingdom, the government rises or falls with the discipline of the members of the parties. When the prime minister can no longer secure the support of a majority, the government fails and new elections are held. That is a powerful incentive to maintain party discipline—to keep the current majority in power and to avoid having to run for reelection. In the United States, the fate of the party in government and the electoral fate of the Members of Congress are not so clearly linked. An individual Member of Congress can make legislative decisions without risking the fate of his or her parties' presidential candidates or altering the date of the next election. Indeed, it is not uncommon for Members of the U.S. Congress to take a strong stand against their own party's president on critically important legislation in response to reactions to that legislation by constituents.

In most countries, dyadic representation takes the form solely of voting for the party; there is little room for a personal connection and little room for politicians to distinguish themselves ideologically from their parties' leadership in the parliament. Anthony King (1997) contrasts representatives in the United Kingdom, Canada, Japan, and Germany with those in the United States. He finds that representatives in most democracies place their fortunes and fates in the hands of their parties. In the United States, individual politicians have greater leeway within their parties. There is both the opportunity and expectation that Members of the United States Congress will represent their districts' interests and needs as well as, and often ahead of, their party. U.S. House Members, who by all appearances have much more secure jobs than their European counterparts, fret constantly about constituency service and their legislative record. American politicians must win in both the primary and general elections, and they run for reelection more often than their counterparts in Europe. They are, to use King's expression, constantly "running scared."

The remainder of this chapter examines the strength of dyadic relationship in the U.S. from macro-level election data and the ways that it is manifest in micro-level survey data. The basic lesson from consideration of these data is that the fit of the representative with the district is partly a product of selection by the electorate of the best person and partly attributable to effort by the sitting Member of Congress to stay in office. Much more is known and understood about the effectiveness of legislators' efforts on the electorate than is understood about the type of person that voters select, and empirical studies of election data reveal that selection is of equal importance to effort.

Macro observations

How important is dyadic representation? One way to address that question is to examine the extent to which congressional elections can be understood as the product of collective representation, especially choice of a party, or dyadic representation, choice of an individual politician. In aggregate election outcomes it is exceedingly difficult to sort out how much of the vote should be attributed to policy representation *per se*. We can, however, offer concrete measures of the relative importance of party and candidate, which offer insights as to the potential bounds of policy and non-policy forms of dyadic representation.

Two facts about American elections highlight the growing importance of candidates, and especially incumbent legislators, in U.S. elections. The first is the rise of split ticket voting; the second is the Incumbency Advantage.

Throughout the first half of the twentieth century U.S. elections exhibited an increasing tendency for voters to choose one party for president and another party for U.S. House or Senate. The adoption of the secret ballot and the office bloc ballot in the late nineteenth and early twentieth centuries afforded the opportunity for voters to break party ranks across offices—that is, to split their votes. Walter Dean Burnham (1965) estimated from aggregate data that split ticket voting in U.S. elections rose from just a few percent in 1900 to roughly 20 percent in the 1920s. In other words, nearly all voters cast straight party tickets in 1900, but just twenty years later one in five voters chose different parties for president and House. The cause of this change in voting behavior has been a central debate among political scientists since the 1960s. The fact, however, is not in dispute. Most American voters stick with their party, but, especially compared with other countries, a sizable proportion of the electorate, typically in the range of 20 percent, chooses politicians of different parties to represent them for president and House.[2]

Some time in the middle of the twentieth century arose a second, distinctive feature of U.S. elections: political scientists observed that House incumbents began to win reelection by increasingly larger vote margins. A House Member who won as an incumbent would receive a noticeably higher share of the vote compared with a House Member in a similar district who won in an open seat. A House Member who won by, say, 55 percent in an open seat race would win by 60 percent the following

[2] Campbell and Miller (1957); Moos (1952).

election (Erikson 1971). Over the first half of the twentieth century the incumbency effect appeared to be no more than 2 percentage points, and that a possible statistical artifact. By the 1960s, the incumbency effect had grown to 5 points or so, and in the 1980s it registered in excess of 10 percentage points and has remained at such a high level (Ansolabehere and Snyder 2002; Gelman and King 1990). As a result reelection rates of U.S. House Members, which have long exceeded 80 percent, inched up from the 1950s onward and reached an astounding 98 percent in the mid-1980s.

Although incumbency advantages often result in split tickets, the two phenomena are not equivalent. They have each followed different historical trajectories. Split-ticket voting emerged much earlier than the incumbency advantage. Studies of individual-level survey data reveal that someone who splits their ticket does not necessarily do so in favor of a congressional incumbent.[3] Incumbency effects surely explain some split-ticket voting, but not all. Instead, voters often deviate from the party line in order to pick a particularly qualified candidate in a particular office or to avoid someone they intensely dislike.

Nonetheless, ticket-splitting and incumbency point to one of the most salient features of U.S. elections: Americans vote for individual politicians as well as for parties. Such voting strategies create the conditions for the sort of dyadic representation exhibited in the U.S. Congress, and in many other elective offices in the United States. Because of the sort of ballots used in the United States and the multitude of offices up for election, American voters have the opportunity to vote for different parties for different offices. This creates an opportunity for individual politicians to pursue electoral strategies tailored to the needs and wishes of constituents and to develop a relationship between representative and constituent that goes beyond mere partisanship.

How much of the vote can be attributed to the dyadic relationship between constituents and politicians, especially those in office? A straightforward decomposition of the variance in the vote is highly instructive about the approximate magnitude of party- and candidate-oriented voting, and further instructive about the importance of office-holding.

Donald Stokes (1966) proposed the decomposition of variance as a way of describing the relative importance of national and local factors, and a method of measuring the partisan and other factors in election results. He took the sum of squared deviations of election returns in House contests from the overall mean and separated that total variation into (1) national variation over time (changes in the mean from year to year), (2) regional variation (largely the South versus the other regions), (3) state variation, and (4) district level variation, which he took to be the party normal vote in the district.

Ansolabehere and Snyder (2002) adapted that methodology to parse the variance in the vote in state and federal elections into the component accounted for by the district or state normal vote (party), national variation over time (the national party tide), the

---

[3] Much split-ticket voting appears to arise when individuals choose a presidential candidate that is not in line with the individual's partisan preferences.

incumbency effect, and the race specific (unexplained) component. In the 1940s and 1950s, party was by far the largest component of the vote. Since then, the two party components (district or state effects and national tides) have explained progressively smaller percentages of the overall variation in the vote across races and over time. The percentage of the vote accounted for by the presence of an incumbent running or not has grown and is now as important as party was sixty years ago. Specifically, the incumbency effect for nearly all offices during the 1940s and 1950s was in the range of 2 to 4 percentage points. By the 1980s it had grown to roughly 10 points for House, Senate, Governor and many other state offices. Interestingly, the idiosyncratic variation in the vote—which is specific to the match-up between two individual candidates—has also grown, and is now quite large. Both incumbency effects and split-ticket voting for other reasons can be accommodated in this decomposition, and each of these is found to be quite large.

This suggests that the dyadic relationship between representatives and constituents emerges for two reasons—selection of the "right type" of politician and reward to officeholders for the effort they exert. We will call these the "selection" effect and the "officeholder" effect.

Selection effects arise because voters attempt to choose the best candidate. In any contest, voters compare candidates not just on the basis of party, but also ideologies and values, social characteristics, and personalities. Jacobson (1978) introduced the argument that voters favor "high quality" candidates and demonstrated empirically that voters give more support to candidates with previous political experience and other advantageous characteristics. Candidates for the U.S. House who have held other offices, such as state legislative seats, are able to raise and spend more campaign money and win higher vote shares against incumbents compared with other sorts of challengers, and in open-seat elections experienced candidates have the best chances of winning, holding party constant. Experience is thought to indicate general political competence, charisma, and ideological agreement with the local electorate. The rather substantial literature on congressional elections has repeatedly found that challenger political experience, personal wealth, and occupation affect the division of the vote significantly.[4] The unexplained local variation in the vote from year to year reflects, in large part, variation in candidate quality, and the value that voters in the U.S. place on the selection of the right person to represent them.

Voters also reward politicians for performance in office, including voting on roll-call votes, addressing constituents' problems, and advocating for local interests. In the next section we will consider the micro-level (survey) evidence concerning the awareness and reaction of voters to representatives efforts and actions. Here our interest is in understanding the total effect of such activities and their relative importance as compared with the selection of the type of politician.

The incumbency effect, we have noted, has hovered in the range of 10 percentage points since the 1980s for most offices. That effect reflects both representatives' efforts

---

[4] See Canon (1990); Green and Krasno (1988); Jacobson (2004).

in office and the quality of the opposition they face in elections. How much does each contribute to the incumbency effect?

Two different estimation strategies reveal that the officeholder effect accounts for approximately half of the incumbency advantage. First, Levitt and Wolfram (1997) study repeat challenges. When the same two candidates face each other in repeated elections the qualities of the two candidates are held constant. Levitt and Wolfram consider all pairs of House elections in which the same two candidates faced each other and the first election was for an open seat and the second was incumbent contested. They measure the sophomore surge for each pair (the increase in vote share from the first to the second election in each pair). They estimate that sophomore surge for each pair is approximately half as large as the sophomore surge for all elections; hence, they conclude, candidate quality accounts for approximately half of the total incumbency advantage.

Second, Ansolabehere, Snyder, and Stewart (2000) examine the voting behavior of "old" and "new" voters. Specifically, they consider the rearrangement of areas that occurs with each decennial districting. Incumbents have some areas that they represented before redistricting—the old voters—and some areas that they did not represent—the new voters. In the first election after redistricting, the incumbent runs for reelection in two different types of constituencies—those the incumbent has represented and those that the incumbent has not represented. Importantly, the candidates running in these two types of constituencies are the same, and the difference between the incumbents' vote share among old voters and among new voters provides an estimate of the officeholder effect. Interestingly enough, the estimates of the officeholder effect from the contrast of old voters and new voters is almost exactly the same as the estimates of the officeholder effect from the repeat candidate method. Approximately half of the overall incumbency advantage can be attributed to the effort and activities of the officeholder, and half appears to be due to the quality of the challenger.

These estimates suggest that selection may be much more important than officeholder activities. Challenger quality appears to account for half of the incumbency effect, while officeholder effort and benefits account for the other half. In addition, idiosyncratic variation, usually attributed to unique characteristics of individual candidates, contributes a component of the variance of the vote as large as incumbency. We will return to this observation toward the end of the chapter.

One caution is in order. The relative importance of the electoral selection mechanism does not mean that what representatives do in office is relatively unimportant. On the contrary, elections select types of politicians who will do the voters' bidding. Elections select politicians in whom voters place a great deal of trust, and people with whom most voters already agree ideologically, and will thus vote the right way once in office. Expectations about such factors are already included in the votes received for winning politicians in open seat elections. When politicians do not fit their districts or when they do not provide sufficient constituent service, they run into electoral trouble (à la Canes-Wrone, Brady, and Cogan).

It may of course be the case that voters do not even care so much about what voters do, but instead pick the most attractive politician or the candidate with the right social profile. How much do legislators' actions affect their levels of public approval and electoral support?

MICRO CONNECTION

Study of individual constituents reveals further the extent to which people examine the policy preferences, personal characteristics, and constituency service of their representatives.

How is the relationship between representatives and constituents structured? We highlight three of the dimensions of representation—personal characteristics, personal connections, and policy congruence. In considering each dimension, a more nuanced picture of voters' relationship with their representative emerges.

In thinking about how individuals view their representatives the simple spatial model with a valence term provides useful guidance. In this model a voter's preferences over policy are described by the distance of any policy, X, from the voter's ideal policy, w, along a single dimension. Suppose that the legislator takes policy position x; then voter w's spatial utility is $-(x-w)^2$. So, the utility function is $u(x,v;w) = v - (x-w)^2$.[5] The valence term, v, allows the model to take into account features of the legislator that are unrelated to policy positions—such as personal characteristics, intelligence, charisma, competence, and so on. Valence terms may also take the form of economic evaluations or coattails, as in Alesina, Londregan, and Rosenthal (1993).

This formulation helps to clarify exactly what is meant by "policy congruence" or agreement and representation, how that relates to other forms of dyadic representation, and how it relates to voting. A constituent is congruent with or close to the representative if the ideological or policy distance (however that is measured) is small. If a legislator is somewhat liberal, conservative voters will say they disagree with their member or see a significant policy difference, so too might extremely liberal constituents. How close the constituent must feel in order to say they are "congruent" is a subjective matter. Furthermore, congruence is distinct from liking or approving, as non-policy considerations also matter. It is possible that a survey respondent says that he or she is represented well by the legislator, but for reasons unrelated to policy agreement. And many people may say that they are not well represented by their Members of Congress even though they are in complete agreement on policy matters.

The formulation is also helpful in sorting out different ways of measuring congruence. Two common approaches to measuring congruence are (1) ideological perceptions and (2) agreement on specific decisions. We consider each in turn.

[5] See Alesina, Londregan, and Rosenthal (1993); Ansolabehere and Snyder (2000); Groseclose (2001).

First, researchers may measure ideological congruence as the difference between the constituent's (or survey respondent's) own policy position or ideology and the constituent's perception of the representative's policy position or ideology. Surveys such as the American National Election Study and the Cooperative Congressional Study commonly ask respondents to place themselves on a Liberal–Conservative scale and also to place the candidates for office and their sitting representatives on that same scale. Surveys also include a wealth of questions about individual's positions on issues such as abortion, civil rights, military policy, and social spending. Unfortunately, few surveys include measures of what they think the legislators' position is on those items, or survey legislators. Exceptions include the 1958 ANES study and the Project Vote Smart candidate surveys. Assuming such measures exist one may calculate the difference between the constituent's self-placement on the scale and the constituent's placement of their representatives, along the lines of the formulation above.

Second, one may measure ideological or policy congruence by considering specific legislative decisions, or roll-call votes. Voters knows they would have voted on a piece of legislation if the proposed legislation is an improvement over the status quo. Assuming that voters learn how the legislator voted across a number of bills, they can assess the degree to which the voter and the legislator agree with each other. That is, on every bill voters observe whether they are closer to the bill or status quo and whether their Member of Congress is closer to the bill or status quo. That allows the voter to draw inferences about the degree of policy agreement and ideological proximity between the voter and the legislator. With functional form assumptions one may extract estimated ideal points for both the legislator and the constituent using this method and calculate the degree of agreement directly.

Such measures of ideological or policy distance are, in turn, used to measure the importance of policy congruence or representation. Specifically, one may perform a regression analysis in which the dependent variable is the constituent's approval of the legislator and the independent variables are policy or ideological agreement, party identification, and other factors that may take the form of the valence term, such as racial identity, constituency service, and candidate traits.

Whether the voter approves of the job the legislator is doing depends additionally on the valence term. Aggregate indicators of approval and aggregate election statistics, while indirectly informative, may, thus, be somewhat misleading about the origins of the incumbency advantage or the extent of policy agreement between legislator and constituents.

The model may be further extended to vote choice. A constituent chooses one candidate over the other on the basis of the utility differential between two candidates. Suppose the candidates' policy positions are x and y and the net valence advantage of candidate x is v. That is, v is the difference between the valence advantage of x and the valence advantage of y. Then the utility differential is: $u(x,v;w) - u(y,v;w) = v - (x - w)^2 + (y-w)^2$. The voter chooses candidate x if the differential is positive and candidate y if the differential is negative.

A few insights follow about approval and vote choice in the presence of policy and non-policy dyadic representation. First, approval and vote choice are quite distinct. A constituent who is very liberal may not approve of his or her representative because the representative does not reflect that person's policy preference very closely. Second, non-policy considerations can magnify or shrink the importance of policy considerations. If the valence difference between candidates is large, the relative weight of policy will be small. Third, valence advantages can create behavior that resembles directional voting, that is, moving "right" or "left." Suppose the left party is in office and the economy posts unusually strong performance. Voters will appear to vote "left," because all voters favor the left party somewhat more as a result of good economic voting. This would appear to be ideologically motivated directional voting, even though the source is a valence advantage. Finally, phenomenon such as the incumbency advantage can reflect policy and non-policy factors which cannot be distinguished in aggregate data. An incumbent might win because he or she is closer to the median than the challenger, or because he or she has done a lot of casework or some other form of non-dyadic representation, or both.

The quest to measure policy and non-policy components of constituent's evaluations of their representatives led congressional scholars to design the American National Election Study's 1978 Congressional Survey, which fostered careful study of the sources of the incumbency advantage and serves the foundation for more recent survey research efforts that target this subject. Most notably, the Cooperative Congressional Election Study, which began with the 2006 election, is designed around improving ways to measure policy representation.

Policy congruence

The classical notion of representation holds that voters judge their representatives on the basis of the legislative actions and decisions they have made. Voters choose to reelect legislators with whom they generally agree on important issues—that is, with whom there is a high degree of policy congruence.

The critique of this model arose out of the Michigan School's research and centered around the American public's apparent lack of democratic competence. In particular, Americans did not appear to care enough, know enough, or engage enough to even describe their participation as part of a "relationship" with their representatives. Miller's and Stokes's (1963) pioneering study found that many people could not identify the orientation of their representatives on questions of social welfare, racial integration, and foreign policy. And the one way in which the public's political information was organized—identification with the political parties—seemed to explicitly rule out much of a *dyadic* relationship. Voters identified as a Democrat or a Republican, but failed to differentiate between the parties and their own representatives (Campbell, Converse, et al. 1960; Stokes and Miller 1963).

A long literature echoes these doubts. The American public reputedly lacks the knowledge, interest, or even capacity to hold their representatives accountable

(Campbell, Converse, et al. 1960; Converse 1964; Delli-Carpini and Keeter 1996). Rather than choosing candidates on the basis of an informed view of the incumbents' voting record, voters, it is argued, rely primarily on the policy-free "symbols" of party identification (Stokes and Miller 1962). Politicians, it would seem, have little to fear from a public that knows little about what laws their representatives support or oppose in the legislature.

More recent research has, however, suggested that this null finding—that policy congruence matters little for constituents' assessments of their legislators—may have been due to the difficulties of measurement and the potential simultaneity between approval and perceptions of legislators' positions in surveys. Achen (1978), Erikson (1978), Weisberg (1979), and Stone (1979) point to significant measurement errors as the explanation for Miller's and Stokes's conclusions. The 1958 ANES asked legislators and constituents their attitudes on three broad issues but did not ask about specific roll-call voting behavior. It did not ask directly how people would have decided key questions before Congress; it did not ascertain how constituents thought their legislators had voted (Weissberg 1979). Goren (2004) and Ansolabehere, Rodden, and Snyder (2008) show, using repeated measures to reduce measurement error, that the American public indeed has much more structure to their belief systems than emerges from considering the typical policy question in the ANES.

Voters harbor clear beliefs about how their Members of Congress voted on important questions of the day. Several researchers have used survey questions which asked respondents directly about the roll-call positions their legislators had staked out— see, for example, Hutchings (2003) on the Clarence Thomas confirmation vote in 1991, Alvarez and Gronke (1996) on the authorization of the Persian Gulf War in early 1991, Wilson and Gronke (2000) on the vote to enact the Omnibus Crime Bill in 1994, and Clinton and Tessin (2007) on the votes to normalize trade relations with China in 2000 and to impeach President Clinton in 1997.

Groups particularly affected by a decision are especially attentive to it. Hutchings (2001), analyzing survey data from the 1992 Senate Election Study, shows that the social groups individuals belong to, as well as the political environment they live in, influence the salience of policy congruence. The vote to confirm conservative African American Clarence Thomas to the Supreme Court primed issues of race, gender, and ideology, leading members of groups who had a special interest in the nomination to perceive more accurately the votes their senators cast. These information effects were heightened by the electoral context voters were faced with. When a candidate for the Senate was female, voters were more likely to accurately perceive the votes their incumbents had cast.

A parallel set of studies find that the electoral context voters are situated in can heighten the salience of policy congruence for their decisions. Alvarez and Gronke (1996) show that in states with recent Senate elections, constituents were more likely to offer a guess as to their senators' voting records, and were more likely to be accurate in that guess. Hutchings (2001) likewise demonstrates that voters' level of information about the incumbent's policy record may be heightened by electoral factors.

This body of research has rehabilitated the idea that constituents harbor beliefs about the legislative behavior of their Members of Congress and that those beliefs have some basis in reality, and are not just party perceptions. Those with knowledge of policy are also knowledgeable about other features of their representatives, including recognition of the name, and they are most likely to vote for the incumbent (Box-Steffensmeier, Kimball, et al. 2003).

Curiously, though, none of this research has trained its sights on the big prize. *Policy* congruence never appears in the models of the vote or approval. Ansolabehere and Jones (2007, 2009) perform just such an analysis using the Cooperative Congressional Election Study. That analysis offers the first replication of the Miller and Stokes (1963) approach but using improved data and measures.

Previous studies of policy congruence have been stymied by the difficulty in measuring the degree of congruence between constituents and representatives. Matching voters' preferences with legislators' actions proved difficult since existing survey questions did not ask constituents about the same issues Members of Congress discussed, and the Likert-scale responses to issue questions were not on the same scale as up-or-down votes in the Congress (Stone 1979). One solution is to ask Members of Congress the same questions as their constituents: Miller and Stokes' (1963) classic study did just that, but the cost and difficulty means it has not been replicated since. Instead, Ansolabehere and Jones (2009) asked constituents the same questions as their Members of Congress: specifically, whether they would vote for or against a bill that the legislature was debating. The new survey items, included on the Cooperative Congressional Election Studies (CCES), allowed researchers to match constituents' preferences on policy with their perceptions of their legislators' actions and the actual votes their representatives cast.

Using these new data, Ansolabehere and Jones show that the votes incumbents cast have direct and dramatic effects on how their constituents view them. Calculating policy congruence as a percentage of bills on which constituents believe their representative voted as they would have wanted, the multivariate regression shows that approval ratings and vote choice are strongly influenced by the record of the incumbent.

Policy congruence—which ranges from 0 to 1 as the percentage of policy issues on which survey respondents agree with their legislator's position—has a strong and direct effect on job approval (coded from −1 to 1). In the 2005 survey, the OLS coefficient is .38 (SE=.01) while in the 2006 data, the coefficient was .53 (.04). The data suggest that this policy congruence is potentially as important as partisan identification. The coefficients for party congruence (coded from −1 for different parties to 1 for same party) are .29 (.03) in 2005 and .17 (.03) in 2006. These suggest that a significant part of the variance in voters' evaluations of their representatives is due to the policy representation they are afforded in Congress.

But these perceptions of where their legislator stands may be strongly influenced by constituents' prior predispositions. Party labels may interfere with constituents' perceptions of the incumbent's record: Arceneaux (2008) shows that citizens rely on partisan labels to infer their representatives' positions—inferences which may or may not be accurate (Lodge and Hamill 1986; Rahn 1993). Perhaps more significantly for studies that estimate the effect policy congruence has on voter evaluations of incumbents, those who view a member favorably are more likely to believe they have voted in congruent ways (Wilson and Gronke 2000).

To address this potential simultaneity, Ansolabehere and Jones (2009) adopt an instrumental variables approach. Using the Member of Congress' *actual* voting record as an instrument for *perceptions* of that record, the two-stage least squares regression coefficients paint a remarkably similar picture to the OLS results. Policy congruence once again has a strong and direct influence on job approval ratings (in 2005, .64 (.13); in 2006, .77 (.09)). Results of a similar magnitude are found when considering the vote choice that constituents make in addition to their assessment of the incumbent's job.

Party affiliation remains an important factor in structuring constituents' evaluations of their representative. However, it is both distinct from, and of a comparable size to the impact of policy congruence. From the constituents' point of view, the policy positions legislators cast appear equally as important as the party they stand for. Legislators who have taken positions congruent with the voter's own are evaluated more favorably; those who diverge from what the constituents' want, poorly.

Personal vote

A second aspect of dyadic representation concerns the personal connections that link constituents and Members of Congress. Representatives work hard to foster a sense of personal connection between themselves and their constituents (Fenno 1978).

Sheer familiarity with their representative underpins much of the decision to reelect the politician. A relatively low proportion of the public is able to recall the name of their representative. When given a list of potential names, however, a much larger majority can recognize who their representative is (Mann 1978). Incumbents are more recognized by their constituents than challengers—and better-liked, too (Jacobson 2004). Regression analyses predicting the Member's job approval as a function of party, issues, and other factors repeatedly find that name recognition is among the strongest predictors of support (Box-Steffensmeier, Kimball, et al. 2003; Jacobson 1978).

Although incumbents go to great lengths to cultivate a personal vote, hard evidence of the effectiveness of such activities remains elusive. Two puzzles stand out in this regard. First, Jacobson's (1980) study of money in congressional elections documented that incumbents spend substantially more, but variation in incumbent spending does not seem to matter for election outcomes. Challenger spending is negatively correlated with incumbent vote share, as one might expect, but incumbent spending is uncorrelated, or perhaps even negatively correlated, with the incumbent vote share. It has long been argued that the relationship between money and votes is simultaneous so the simple OLS regressions or correlations should not be taken at face value (Green and Krasno 1988). But attempts to solve the problem have generally failed (Jacobson 1990).

Second, survey research has been hard pressed to find large effects of casework and other constituent service activities on the vote. The 1978 American National Election Studies' Congressional Survey provides the most extensive resource for study of these questions. Analyses of that study have found weak effects of casework on approval of the Member of Congress or on electoral support (Johannes and McAdams 1985). Those findings, however, have been criticized for measurement errors and simultaneity problems. But even reevaluation of those data find mixed effects that are swamped by the effects of party and policy representation (see Cain, Ferejohn, and Fiorina 1988).

Frustrated with the weak findings in this particular domain, the American National Election Study eventually dropped its congressional component in the late 1990s and early 2000s. We suspect that important aspects of the personal vote were missed, but innovation in this area of survey research is needed in order to tease out the effects of casework. As matters stand today, policy representation appears to be a much more substantial component of the vote than casework.

Personal characteristics

Dyadic representation may extend beyond how politicians act once in office to personal characteristics of who they are. Voters may choose a person because they are of the same social group, such as a religious affiliation or ethnic group. Pitkin (1967) recognized this form of representation, terming it symbolic representation. Racial characteristics have become especially controversial in the continuing fight over the constitutionality of the Voting Rights Act, which provides for institutions to facilitate black and hispanic representation. Some have speculated that symbolic representation actually weakens policy representation as it removes the incentives for those who are buoyed by gender, race, or other group affinities to perform well in office (Mansbridge 1999).

Symbolic representation, however, actually has considerable substance. Personal characteristics identify subconstituencies that shape the representative's policy activities in Congress. Female legislators are more likely to promote gender- or family-related issues than their male colleagues (Swers 2002; Thomas 1991); black representatives are more likely to prioritize civil rights issues than whites (Cameron, Epstein, and O'Halloran 1996; Epstein and O'Halloran 1999; Lublin 1997, 1999; Whitby 1997); and openly gay politicians are more likely to support domestic partnership policies than heterosexual or closeted officials (Haider-Markel, Joslyn, and Kniss 2000). For a more thorough overview, see Swers and Rouse (this volume).

The defense of this form of representation is that it fosters participation for groups who otherwise feel alienated from politics and who need representation to correct for social discrimination. A connection based on personal characteristics also has consequences for citizens' views of the political world. Being represented by someone of the same race or gender may increase attentiveness to, and engagement with, politics (Banducci, Donovan, and Carp 2004; Bobo and Gilliam 1990; Brunell, Anderson and Cremona 2008; Rosenthal 1995).

Several scholars investigate how the race of the representative can influence turnout levels. Barreto, Segura, and Woods (2004) show that Latinos who live in areas represented by multiple Latino officials (in the U.S. House, the California state assembly, and the state Senate) are more likely to show up at the polls than similar voters in other areas. Analyzing participation in municipal elections, Bobo and Gilliam (1990) show that black turnout is higher in cities with black mayors than in cities with white mayors. Gay (2001) finds a less consistent pattern amongst African Americans represented by blacks in the U.S. House. Although there is evidence that some blacks are more likely to vote when descriptively represented, the effect varies across districts, leading Gay to conclude that descriptive representation only occasionally increases black participation.

However, one fear is that a dyadic representation based on descriptive characteristics may lead constituents to overlook or ignore the ways in which they are being substantively misrepresented (Fenno 2003; Mansbridge 1999; Tate 2001). That is, the dyadic connection between representative and represented may be tempered by the descriptive ties between them. By emphasizing the descriptive aspect of the dyadic relationship at the expense of the substantive, policy-oriented aspect, constituents may misperceive the extent to which their interests are being represented and fail to hold their members accountable.

Few studies have actually pitted these different facets of dyadic representation against one another to assess their relative importance to voters. Gay (2002) and Box-Steffensmeier, Kimber, et al. (2003) show that *non*-policy factors such as descriptive correspondence between constituent and representative and the member's legislative activity on behalf of his or her district influence various elements of the voter–legislator relationship. Constituents who share descriptive characteristics (such as race or gender) with their MC are more likely to know their representative's name, more likely to identify a reason they like the incumbent, and are ultimately more likely to vote for them. Likewise, MCs who prolifically sponsor bills and serve on committees with jurisdiction over relevant issues are more likely to be recognized and well-liked back home.

Individual-level survey results indicate that dyadic representation rests primarily on policy congruence. Policy agreement is much stronger (at least in recent years) than constituent service or personal characteristics, and it is of a comparable magnitude to party agreement. That conclusion points us back to the classical view of representation. Voters assess whether the sitting legislator has represented their interests, and if not they turn to another person to do their bidding.

AGGREGATION

Analysis of individual level data has helped to resurrect the textbook image of representation in the United States Congress. A large share of the electorate is attentive to significant legislation and holds their Representatives and Senators accountable for the votes they cast on such bills. Representation, however, is as much about aggregates as it is about individuals. Members of Congress represent entire constituencies, typically 700,000 people for the House and several million for the Senate. One cannot have a personal, unique relationship with each one, and often a vote or position on a bill will receive the support of some voters but alienate others. In this sense, representation is not properly speaking dyadic. Rather, it is the relationship of a collective, the constituency as a whole, to the representative.

How do the policy preferences of the hundreds of thousands of constituents in any congressional district or millions of voters in the typical state aggregate? Elections and public opinion polls are the obvious mechanisms, but what sense can we make of the aggregate vote?

The spatial-valence model again provides an analytical and interpretive guide. The percentage of people who will support a legislator come election time is the percentage of people who, based on valence characteristics and policy decisions, receive higher utility from choosing the incumbent over the challenger. The formulation above helps us to describe the shares of the electorate won by the challenger and incumbent. Recall that voters' preferences depend on ideological or policy proximity and a non-policy component or valence. To determine what share of the vote the incumbent representative wins we determine who is the "indifferent voter"—the voter for whom the utility differential between x and y is zero. That voter has an ideal point $w^0 = ((x+y)/2) + v/(2(y-x))$, assuming x is not equal y, and all voters choose the candidate who has the valence advantage if the two candidates promise the same policy.[6] For simplicity assume that the candidate x is the incumbent. The fraction of the electorate who vote for the incumbent representative is $F(w^0)$, where F is the cumulative distribution of voter ideal points.

Under the standard spatial model, which lacks the non-policy valence term, the cut point would be the simple mean between x and y. The valence term alters the electoral outcome. The second term in the formula for w^0 is positive if the incumbent has the net valence advantage. That would move the cut point to the right of where it would be without a valence advantage (assuming divergence), increasing the incumbent's share of the vote. That result is, fortunately, not surprising. More subtle, though, is the interaction between policy and non-policy considerations. The less distinct the candidates on policy, the more valence matters to the aggregate election outcomes.

Importantly, non-policy considerations completely change the electoral equilibrium on policy. Under the standard spatial model, two competing candidates will converge to a single point, the ideal point of the median voter, and the election is a tie. However, non-policy considerations create an opening for the candidate with the advantage. Ansolabehere and Snyder (2002) show that the incumbent may locate anywhere within an interval around the median and win with certainty, but the challenger has no winning strategy.

---

[6] See Ansolabehere and Snyder (2000) for a derivation.

The spatial model without a valence term has recently been used by Jessee (2009) to estimate the responsiveness of members of the Senate to their states. He estimates the implicit ideal points of the states' median voters from state-level survey data on hypothetical roll-call votes posed to respondents, and he uses roll-call votes from the Senate to calculate the positions of the senators. He then regressed the roll-call votes of the Senators on the ideal points of the median voters in the constituencies and finds a very strong relationship between the policy position of the median voters across the states and the ideal points of the legislators. The basic conclusion of this work is consistent with earlier studies that examined exit polls and mapped the ideological and partisan leanings of states (Erikson, Wright, and McIver 1999). Jessee's analysis improves in that these are studies of the entire constituency, not just voters, and the mapping of the data in the terms of the theoretical model of interest.

This analysis is a huge improvement over what was possible even ten years ago. Innovations in survey research methodology and the increasingly large scale of surveys permits measurement of the quantities of interest at the aggregate level. And there have been important breakthroughs in the methodology for scaling survey responses and roll-call votes in order to estimate ideal points.

The frontier in this vein of research is to incorporate the non-policy components of constituents' preferences. Specifically, we lack measures at the scale of constituencies of the magnitude of the valence advantage or of the specific activities that foster non-policy dyadic representation. Empirical analysis of the responsiveness of Members of Congress to their constituencies with both policy and non-policy components remains an important avenue for further inquiry. We do not have constituency-level indicators of many features of legislators that may be important to voters, quite apart from policy. For example, political science surveys typically do not ascertain much how citizens perceive candidates' or representatives' qualities, such as religion, age, veteran status, or marital status. Surveys such as the American National Election Study do ask respondents whether they think the representative is "honest" or "competent", but these have not been aggregated up to the district level. To estimate the relative importance of candidates' characteristics or traits on policy position-taking and election outcomes requires aggregation of such survey data to the constituency.

In addition, the spatial framework does not adequately incorporate party as a concept. This owes, in part, to the complexity of party identification. Party identification is certainly rooted in personal, psychological identity as the authors of *The American Voter* argued (Campbell, Converse, et al. 1960). Party identification, however, also reflects policy agreement with individual members and with the parties and past non-policy assessments of candidates and parties (e.g. Fiorina 1978). This has made it very difficult to sort out party and other forms of collective representation from policy and non-policy dyadic representation both in theoretical terms and empirical analysis. That challenge lies at the forefront in the continuing effort to understand the nature of representation in the United States.

REFERENCES

ACHEN, C. H. 1978. Measuring Representation. *American Journal of Political Science*, 22: 475–510.

ALESINA, A., LONDREGAN, J., and ROSENTHAL, H. 1993. A Model of the Political Economy of the United States. *American Political Science Review*, 87: 12–33.

ALVAREZ, R. M., and GRONKE, P. 1996. Constituents and Legislators: Learning about the Persian Gulf War Resolution. *Legislative Studies Quarterly*, 21(1): 105–27.

ANSOLABEHERE, S., and JONES, P. E. 2010. Constituents' Response to Congressional Roll Call Voting. *American Journal of Political Science*, 54: 589–97.

——RODDEN, J., and SNYDER, J. M. 2008. The Strength of Issues: Using Multiple Measures to Gauge Preference Stability, Ideological Constraint, and Issue Voting. *American Political Science Review*, 102: 215–32.

——SNYDER, J. M. 2000. Valence Politics and Equilibrium in Spatial Election Models. *Public Choice*, 74: 207–19.

————2002. The Incumbency Advantage in U.S. Elections: An Analysis of State and Federal Offices, 1942–2000. *Election Law Journal*, 1: 315–38.

————and STEWART, C. 2000. Old Voters, New Voters, and the Personal Vote: Using Redistricting to Measure the Incumbency Advantage. *American Journal of Political Science*, 44: 17–34.

——————2001a. The Effects of Party and Preferences on Congressional Roll Call Voting. *Legislative Studies Quarterly*, 26: 533–72.

——————2001b. Candidate Positioning in U.S. House Elections. *American Journal of Political Science*, 45: 136–59.

ARCENEAUX, K. 2008. Can Partisan Cues Diminish Democratic Accountability? *Political Behavior*, 30: 139–60.

BANDUCCI, S. A., DONOVAN, T., and KARP, J. A. 2004. Minority Representation, Empowerment, and Participation. *Journal of Politics*, 66: 534–56.

BARRETO, M. A., SEGURA, G. M., and WOODS, N. D. 2004. The Mobilizing Effect of Majority-Minority Districts on Latino Turnout. *American Political Science Review*, 98: 65–75.

BOBO, L., and GILLIAM, F. D. 1990. Race, Sociopolitical Participation, and Black Empowerment. *American Political Science Review*, 84(2): 377–93.

BOX-STEFFENSMEIER, J. M., KIMBALL, D. C., MEINKE, S. R., and TATE, K. 2003. The Effects of Political Representation on the Electoral Advantages of Incumbents. *Political Research Quarterly*, 56: 259–70.

BRUNELL, T. L., ANDERSON, C. J., and CREMONA, R. K. 2008. District Representation, District Demography, and Attitudes toward Congress Among African Americans. *Legislative Studies Quarterly*, 33(2): 223–44.

BURNHAM, W. D. 1965. The Changing Shape of the American Political Universe. *American Political Science Review*, 59: 7–28.

CAIN, B., FEREJOHN, J., and FIORINA, M. 1990. *The Personal Vote: Constituency Service and Electoral Independence.* Cambridge, MA: Harvard University Press.

CAMERON, C., EPSTEIN, D., and O'HALLORAN, S. 1996. Do Majority-Minority Districts Maximize Substantive Black Representation in Congress? *American Political Science Review*, 90(4): 794–812.

CAMPBELL, A., and MILLER W. E. 1957. The Motivational Basis of Straight and Split-Ticket Voting. *American Political Science Review*, 51: 293–312.

——CONVERSE, P. E., MILLER, W. E., and STOKES, D. E. 1960. *The American Voter.* Chicago: University of Chicago Press.

CANES-WRONE, B., BRADY, D. W., and COGAN, J. F. 2002. Out of Step, Out of Office: Electoral Accountability and House Members' Voting. *American Political Science Review*, 96: 127–40.

CANON, D. T. 1990. *Actors, Athletes, and Astronauts: Political Amateurs in the United States Congress*. Chicago: University of Chicago Press.

CLINTON, J. D., and TESSIN, J. 2007. Broken Fire Alarms: Exploring Constituency Knowledge of Roll Calls. Unpublished manuscript. Princeton University, Princeton NJ.

CONVERSE, P. E. 1964. The Nature of Belief Systems in Mass Publics, pp. 206–61 in *Ideology and Discontent*, ed. D. Apter. New York: Free Press.

DELLI-CARPINI, M. X., and KEETER, S. 1996. *What Americans Know About Politics and Why it Matters*. New Haven: Yale University Press.

EPSTEIN, D., and O'HALLORAN, S. 1999. A Social Science Approach to Race, Redistricting, and Representation. *American Political Science Review*, 93(1): 187–91.

ERIKSON, R. S. 1971. The Electoral Impact of Congressional Roll Call Voting. *American Political Science Review*, 65(4): 1018–32.

—— 1978. Constituency Opinion and Congressional Behavior: A Reexamination of the Miller-Stokes Representation Data. *American Journal of Political Science*, 22: 511–35.

—— and WRIGHT, G. C. 1980. Policy Representation of Constituency Interests. *Political Behavior*, 2: 91–106.

—— —— and McIVER, J. P. 1993. *Statehouse Democracy: Public Opinion and Policy in the American States*. Cambridge: Cambridge University Press.

EULAU, H., WAHLKE, J. C., BUCHANAN, W., and FERGUSON, L. C. 1959. The Role of the Representative: Some Empirical Observations on the Theory of Edmund Burke. *American Political Science Review*, 53: 742–56.

FENNO, R. F. 1978. *Home Style: House Members in their Districts*. Boston: Little, Brown.

—— 2003. *Going Home: Black Representatives and Their Constituents*. Chicago: University of Chicago Press.

FIORINA, M. P. 1974. *Representatives, Roll Calls, and Constituencies*. Lexington, MA: Lexington Books.

—— 1981. *Retrospective Voting in American National Elections*. New Haven: Yale University Press.

GAY, C. 2001. The Effect of Black Congressional Representation on Political Participation. *American Political Science Review*, 95: 589–602.

—— 2002. Spirals of Trust. *American Journal of Political Science*, 46 (October): 717–33.

GELMAN, A., and KING, G. 1990. Estimating Incumbency Advantage without Bias. *American Journal of Political Science*, 34: 1142–64.

GOREN, P. 2004. Political Sophistication and Policy Reasoning: A Reconsideration. *American Journal of Political Science*, 48: 462–278.

GREEN, D. P., and KRASNO, J. S. 1988. Salvation for the Spendthrift Incumbent: Reestimating the Effects of Campaign Spending in House Elections. *American Journal of Political Science*, 32: 884–907.

GROSECLOSE, T. 2001. A Model of Candidate Location When One Candidate Has a Valence Advantage. *American Journal of Political Science*, 45: 862–86.

HAIDER-MARKEL, D. P., JOSLYN, M. R., and KNISS, C. J. 2000. Minority Group Interests and Political Representation: Gay Elected Officials in the Policy Process. *Journal of Politics*, 62(2): 568–77.

HUTCHINGS, V. L. 2001. Political Context, Issue Salience, and Selective Attentiveness: Constituent Knowledge of the Clarence Thomas Confirmation Vote. *Journal of Politics*, 63: 846–68.

—— 2003. *Public Opinion and Democratic Accountability: How Citizens Learn About Politics.* Princeton: Princeton University Press.

JACOBSON, G. C. 1978. The Effects of Campaign Spending in Congressional Elections. *American Political Science Review,* 72: 469–91.

—— 1980. *Money in Congressional Elections.* New Haven: Yale University Press.

—— 1990. The Effects of Campaign Spending in House Elections: New Evidence for Old Arguments. *American Journal of Political Science,* 34: 334–62.

—— 2004. *The Politics of Congressional Elections.* New York: Pearson Longman.

JESSEE, S. 2009. Spatial Voting in the 2004 Presidential Election. *American Political Science Review,* 103: 59–81.

JOHANNES, J. R., and McADAMS, J. C. 1985. Constituency Attentiveness in the House: 1977–1982. *Journal of Politics,* 47: 1108–39.

KING, A. 1997. *Running Scared: Why America's Politicians Campaign Too Much and Govern Too Little.* New York: Simon & Shuster.

LEVITT, S. D., and WOLFRAM, C. D. 1997. Decomposing the Sources of Incumbency Advantage in the U.S. House. *Legislative Studies Quarterly,* 22: 45–60.

LODGE, M., and HAMILL, R. 1986. A Partisan Schema for Political Information Processing. *American Political Science Review,* 80: 505–19.

LUBLIN, D. 1997. *The Paradox of Representation: Racial Gerrymandering and Minority Interests in Congress.* Princeton: Princeton University Press.

—— 1999. Racial Redistricting and African-American Representation: A Critique of "Do Majority-Minority Districts Maximize Substantive Black Representation in Congress?" *American Political Science Review,* 93(1): 183–6.

MANN, T. E. 1978. *Unsafe at any Margin: Interpreting Congressional Elections.* Washington DC: AEI Press.

MANSBRIDGE, J. 1999. Should Blacks Represent Blacks and Women Represent Women? A Contingent "Yes". *Journal of Politics,* 61: 628–57.

MAYHEW, D. R. 1974. *Congress: The Electoral Connection.* New Haven: Yale University Press.

MILLER, W. E., and STOKES, D. E. 1963. Constituency Influence in Congress. *American Political Science Review,* 57: 45–56.

MOOS, M. 1952. *Politics, Presidents, and Coattails.* Baltimore: Johns Hopkins University Press.

PITKIN, H. F. 1967. *The Concept of Representation.* Berkeley: University of California Press.

RAHN, W. M. 1993. The Role of Partisan Stereotypes in Information Processing about Political Candidates. *American Journal of Political Science,* 37(2): 472–96.

ROSENTHAL, C. S. 1995. The Role of Gender in Descriptive Representation. *Political Research Quarterly,* 48(3): 599–611.

STOKES, D. E. 1966. Party Loyalty and the Likelihood of Deviating Elections, pp. 125–35 in *Elections and the Political Order.* New York: Wiley.

—— and MILLER, W. E. 1962. Party Government and the Saliency of Congress. *Public Opinion Quarterly,* 26: 531–46.

STONE, W. J. 1979. Measuring Constituency-Representative Linkages: Problems and Prospects. *Legislative Studies Quarterly,* 4: 623–39.

SULLIVAN, J. L., and USLANER, E. M. 1978. Congressional Behavior and Electoral Marginality. *American Journal of Political Science,* 22: 536–53.

SWERS, M. L. 2002. *The Difference Women Make: The Policy Impact of Women in Congress.* University of Chicago Press.

TATE, K. 2001. The Political Representation of Blacks in Congress: Does Race Matter? *Legislative Studies Quarterly,* 26(4): 623–38.

THOMAS, S. 1991. The Impact of Women on State Legislative Policies. *Journal of Politics*, 53(4): 958–76.

WEISSBERG, R. 1979. Assessing Legislator-Constituency Policy Agreement. *Legislative Studies Quarterly*, 4: 605–22.

WHITBY, K. J. 1997. *The Color of Representation: Congressional Behavior and Black Interests.* Ann Arbor, MI: University of Michigan Press.

WILSON, J. M., and GRONKE, P. 2000. Concordance and Projection in Citizen Perceptions of Congressional Roll-Call Voting. *Legislative Studies Quarterly*, 25: 445–67.

CHAPTER 14

PORK BARREL POLITICS

DIANA EVANS

PORK barrel politics is an integral part of congressional political life and the legislative process, a fact recognized by practical politicians and scholars alike. Tip O'Neill's well-known aphorism that "all politics is local" as well as David Mayhew's (1974) elegant exposition of the central role of particularized benefits in the electoral connection between members of Congress and their constituents both demonstrate a longstanding recognition that the drive to advance constituents' material interests is a fundamental fact of congressional life. Over the past several decades, a sophisticated body of research has advanced both our theoretical and empirical understanding of distributive politics in Congress.

This chapter assesses that scholarship and indicates possible directions for future research. The discussion is organized as follows. The first two sections define pork barrel benefits and their link to the reelection goal. The next section discusses the literature's implicit focus on two types of motives for supplying pork: individual-benefit and collective-benefit motives. The remainder of the chapter addresses the scholarship on strategies for supplying pork and assesses the contribution of that research to a broad understanding of pork barrel politics. That discussion begins with the central role of congressional committees in formal theories of distributive politics. Next is a consideration of the commonly used empirical measures of legislators' demand for pork and measures pork barrel benefits themselves. Following that is a discussion of the research on the patterns by which pork barrel benefits are awarded by Congress; central to that discussion is a consideration of individual-benefit and collective-benefit motivations for supplying pork; that section concludes with a consideration of the size of distributive coalitions. This review of both the theoretical and empirical literature is necessarily selective. Other chapters in this volume deal more comprehensively with formal models of policymaking, including rational choice approaches to distributive politics. This chapter touches on that important body of theory but focuses on the empirical scholarship, much of which is deeply informed by rational choice theory.

DEFINITION OF PORK BARREL AND DISTRIBUTIVE BENEFITS

Pork barrel projects, also known as distributive benefits, are discrete, highly divisible benefits targeted to specific populations such as states and congressional districts; the cost is spread across the general population through taxation. Such benefits have little policy connection to one another (Shepsle and Weingast 1981, 96), and, according to Theodore Lowi, "are characterized by the ease with which they can be disaggregated and dispensed unit by small unit more or less in isolation from other units and from any general rule" (Lowi 1964, 690).

Rational choice theorists distinguish between pork barrel and distributive benefits; they define pork barrel benefits as a subset of distributive policy consisting of inefficient policies, in the sense that the cost of a pork barrel project exceeds its benefits (Ferejohn 1974, 235; Shepsle and Weingast 1981; Baron 1991). For the purposes of this chapter, this distinction is of little practical effect, as the inefficiency of such policies most likely exerts little restraint on members of Congress. This is partly because the money spent on such projects is interpreted politically as a benefit to the district (Shepsle and Weingast 1981, 101; Weingast, Shepsle, and Johnsen 1981) and partly because the collective costs of such inefficiencies are normally invisible to constituents because those costs are dispersed.

THE REELECTION ASSUMPTION AND THE DEMAND FOR PORK BARREL BENEFITS

The reelection goal is fundamental to all of the theoretical and empirical literature on pork barrel politics. Mayhew offers perhaps the best-known and surely the most elegant formulation of the linkage between legislators' desire for reelection and particularized benefits, a category that includes pork barrel projects (Mayhew 1974, 54–5). Specifically, members of Congress have a strong incentive to devote time and energy to gaining particularized benefits, because it is for those benefits that they believably can claim credit. By contrast, very few members can make such credible claims with respect to broad-based, general interest policy. As a consequence, in this area members are likely to simply take pleasing positions, leaving the real legislative work to other, more powerfully placed legislators. Thus, members are likely to be rewarded by their constituents for efforts to make the district better off with particularized benefits and for giving nominal support for other, broad-based policies that their constituents favor. Note that Mayhew does not completely ignore broad, general-interest policymaking, but he does highlight the critical importance of particularized benefits for members' electoral well-being. It is worth noting that Mayhew focuses on the House of Representatives. As later scholarship shows, the Senate faces slightly different incentives with regard to pork-seeking, a question considered below.

MOTIVES FOR SUPPLYING PORK

While members' motives for seeking pork are clear (the demand side), we can infer from the literature two categories of reasons for supplying such benefits. First, members supply pork to themselves because they can use it to satisfy district demand. This is essentially the perspective of much of the early rational choice literature on distributive politics, which focuses largely on omnibus bills consisting of nothing but distributive benefits intended to boost the recipients' chances of reelection.[1] Theories that take this approach can be thought of as individual-benefit theories. Especially in second-generation rational choice theories (Shepsle and Weingast 1995), committees play the dominant institutional role: they have control over the legislation in their jurisdiction and are composed of members with constituency-based high demand for the benefits within that jurisdiction. They broker omnibus pork barrel bills to meet that demand by forming majority coalitions of benefit-seekers (see, for example, Weingast and Marshall 1988; Shepsle and Weingast 1995). The predicted size of such coalitions has been a matter of considerable scholarly debate in the rational choice literature (Collie, 1988, offers a detailed analysis of the formative stages of that scholarship).

A second theoretical perspective on why pork is provided is less radically individualistic: pork barrel benefits are offered by key political actors in order to achieve certain collective benefits. The suppliers of such benefits may be policy coalition leaders in Congress seeking support for their favored general interest legislation (Evans 1994, 2004; Lee 2003), or majority party leaders in Congress (or the president) seeking to protect their party's majority (Balla, Lawrence, et al. 2002; Cox and McCubbins 1993), or bureaucrats seeking congressional support for their agencies and programs

---

[1] See Shepsle and Weingast (1995) for an analysis of several generations of scholarship on distributive politics.

(Arnold 1979). Although not expressed as formal theories, this scholarship usefully can be thought of as articulating collective-benefit theories of pork barrel politics.

Regardless of the impetus behind the provision of pork barrel benefits (individual or collective benefit) and the locus of control over its distribution (e.g. committee chairs acting on their own or as agents of the majority party), rank and file members are motivated by reelection in seeking and trading votes for pork. The biases in the allocation of pork, discussed below, will be considered, where possible, in light of the motives driving the process of distribution, as will the discussion of the size of the coalition that receives benefits.

WHO GETS PORK BARREL BENEFITS?

This section starts with the central role reserved for congressional committees in most individual-benefit distributive theories, focusing on whether such committees are, as early distributive theories argue, composed of members with a high demand for the policies within the committee's jurisdiction. Next, I assess the ways in which scholars have measured the key concepts of demand for pork barrel benefits and the benefits themselves. The findings of the empirical literature are then considered in light of those measures and the reasons, individual benefit or collective benefit, for awarding pork barrel projects. The chapter ends with the literature on the size of distributive coalitions.

The committee benefit hypothesis

In individual-benefit rational choice theories of distributive politics, the role of congressional committees looms large. There are two major reasons for this. First, committees supply a structure-induced equilibrium that prevents majorities from cycling endlessly (Shepsle 1979). Second, committees can enforce logrolling bargains across distributive policy areas due to their jurisdictional monopolies and procedural floor protections (e.g. restrictive rules). Such factors enable committees to engage in interjurisdictional logrolls, using their control over their own policy areas to enforce bargains with other committees over time (Weingast and Marshall 1988). As a consequence, committee members are well positioned to extract from those bills a disproportionate share of the pork barrel benefits therein; committees thus are thought to attract members with a high demand for benefits within their respective jurisdictions. Indeed, Shepsle (1978) finds that the process of appointing members to committees in the House is structured to place high demanders on committees by means of an "interest-advocacy-accommodation syndrome" in which members request and receive appointments to committees in which their districts have a particular interest. This political structural feature of congressional organization is the basis for the prediction that committees will be composed of members who demand and receive more distributive benefits than the median member of the body.

On the other hand, some collective benefit theories of the organization of Congress do not predict high-demanding committees to the same extent. Partisan theories suggest that to the extent that the majority party pursues collective party goals (in particular, the protection and enhancement of its majority) through committee appointments, the party's concern for its collective reputation confines any impulse toward self-selection to committees with narrow jurisdictions, as the party's reputation is damaged by rampant pork barreling on committees with a broad national impact, that is, "uniform externalities" committees (Cox and McCubbins 1993, 203–6). Instead of the self-selection model prominent in early distributive theory, Cox and McCubbins propose a partisan selection model. In this model, parties use committee appointments to accomplish two goals: to help members get reelected by giving them pork and to unite the party behind broad national-impact legislation. They can afford to do the first when a committee has a narrow jurisdiction affecting few districts, as there likely will be little effect on the party's reputation. But for committees dealing in national policy, members must be more representative of the party's views (Cox and McCubbins 1993, 189–90). Thus, while the self-selection of high demanders is expected, it is limited to a few narrowly focused committees.

The informational theory of congressional organization is also concerned with a collective benefit: reliable information on the impact of policy proposals. Such information is provided in the service of floor majorities, not the majority party (Gilligan and Krehbiel 1990; Krehbiel 1992); to that end, committees are expected not to be composed of high demanders of distributive benefits but rather to be representative of the floor majority. Yet some high demanders will be allowed on committees that will satisfy their demands in return for the specialized knowledge that these members bring; restrictive legislative rules limit such gains (Krehbiel 1992, 95–9). Those limited cases lead to some extra benefits for committee members, although not to the degree predicted by distributive theories.

When the collective benefit being sought through pork distribution consists of a majority coalition for general benefit legislation, committee members are expected to benefit. This is because policy coalition leaders most often come from the ranks of powerful legislators: committee chairs, party leaders in Congress, or the president (Arnold 1990, 7). When the coalition leader is a committee chair, as is usually the case, committee members are likely to benefit disproportionately because committee leaders want, if at all possible, to see their committees solidly behind them on the floor, providing consistently supportive cues to other members (Evans 2004).[2]

Most of the theoretical literature implicitly assumes that Congress directly supplies distributive benefits; however, for reasons discussed below, many recent empirical tests of the propositions of that literature employ data on federal discretionary

---

[2] For a formal model of vote-buying that includes but is not restricted to the use of distributive benefits, see Groseclose and Snyder (1996).

spending distributed by bureaucratic agencies. To be sure, the authorizations and appropriations that supply those funds are written by Congress, but the bureaucratic discretion built into some of these programs introduces bureaucratic actors with their own goals and strategies into the distributive process.

Bureaucrats also distribute pork in order to buy support for collective benefits. Arnold (1979) argues that federal agencies allocate benefits strategically to cultivate their supporting coalitions in Congress. Consequently, members of the committees with jurisdiction over an agency can be expected to get a disproportionate share of such benefits.

This discussion shows that the expectation that members of the committees with jurisdiction in a particular policy area will disproportionately benefit from pork barrel policies (the committee benefit hypothesis), while not universal, dominates theories of distributive politics, although more uniformly for individual-benefit than collective-benefit theories.

Measuring committee demand for distributive benefits

What does the empirical research show about the prevalence of high demanders on committees? There is conflict among the results of numerous studies. A full treatment of the literature on this subject can be found in the chapter by C. Lawrence Evans in this volume. This section focuses to a limited extent on the research on the different approaches to measuring demand for pork and the conclusions reached by a number of studies on the degree to which committees are composed of high demanders.

Three measures of committee demand are commonly used. First, there are voting scores that purport to measure ideology or member preferences on one or more broad issue dimensions. The types of scores most commonly used are ADA (liberalism) and ACU (conservatism) scores, which are based on a number of different issue types, and Poole–Rosenthal NOMINATE scores, based on all non-unanimous roll-call votes cast by individual members of Congress. The second type of measure consists of ratings calculated by interest groups concerned with a particular committee's jurisdiction, such as COPE scores calculated by the AFL-CIO. The third consists of measures of likely constituent demand as inferred from appropriate district demographics. The first two types of measures are based on members' actual roll-call votes, while the third type is an attempt to measure district demand independently of members' expressed preferences. Although each is useful for measuring some types of preference outliers, they are not all equally appropriate measures of members' inclination to demand high levels of distributive benefits.

Broad voting scores are frequently used. Kiewiet and McCubbins compare the NOMINATE scores of party contingents on committees with their respective party caucuses. They find that Democrats and, to a lesser extent, Republicans on the House Appropriations committee and its subcommittees represent their party caucuses fairly closely (Kiewiet and McCubbins 1991, 110, 129). Cox and McCubbins use ADA scores to test their partisan selection hypothesis for committee appointments.

They find that a few committees, especially those with narrow jurisdictions (most of them constituency-oriented, such as the Agriculture Committee), are dominated by ideological preference outliers. However, most committees are not composed in this way, especially House control committees (which they consider to be "uniform externalities" committees). On these committees—Appropriations, Rules and Ways and Means—loyalty to the party is especially important. The authors argue that this is due to the centrality of those committees to the collective interests of the party (Cox and McCubbins 1993, 78–9).

Interest group ratings are also used. For example, Krehbiel (1990, 1992) tests informational theory's prediction that committees are representative of the floor majority and not composed of preference outliers, or high demanders. He examines nine House committees, including Appropriations, using interest group ratings appropriate to the committee's jurisdiction. He finds evidence that one committee, Armed Services, is composed of homogeneous high demanders. Otherwise, he finds only "spotty" evidence of preference outliers or of homogenous preferences (Krehbiel 1990, 1992, 130–4).

All of these studies find that high-demanding committees are relatively rare. In particular, they find little evidence of self-selection of high demanders to the House Appropriations Committee, which distributes most of the pork barrel projects awarded by Congress.

Although broad measures such as NOMINATE scores are appropriate for determining whether committees are generally representative of the chamber or whether a party's contingent on a committee resembles the House party caucuses, such measures are less well suited to determining whether members of a committee are high demanders of any distributive benefits that the committee's jurisdiction might make it possible to obtain. This is especially true when that jurisdiction is multidimensional, going well beyond distributive issues. The appropriations committee is an example, as it deals with the discretionary budget of the federal government and thus most policy areas. Members of this committee may be faithful agents of the party caucus on the policy issues that divide the two parties, but there may be particular distributive needs within members' districts that attract otherwise loyal party members to this committee and lead them to demand high levels of distributive benefits. If such benefits help to buy those members' loyalty on larger partisan issues, they may be granted them. Indeed, Maltzman and Smith (1995) find, for the House Appropriations Committee, a distributive dimension along which the committee is not representative of the chamber; yet on most issue dimensions, the committee's preferences reflect those of the chamber quite well. Broad measures of preferences, measures that may include no or relatively few district-relevant questions, are unlikely to detect high demanders of distributive benefits.

Interest group ratings pose other problems. For example, they may include issues that are extraneous to the policy areas with which they purport to be concerned. Indeed, Hall and Grofman (1990) challenge Krehbiel's (1990, 158) results, based on interest-group ratings, for the Senate Agriculture Committee and related subcommittees. They show that the relevant interest group rating scores (in this case, the

National Farmers Union) include extraneous issues; given that those scores are calculated from relatively few votes (typically a dozen or less), such extraneous issues can have a large effect. When Hall and Grofman recalculated NFU scores, purging them of such votes, the agriculture committees proved to be composed of high demanders, contrary to Krehbiel's results.[3]

All these measures are based on members' roll-call votes. The most common alternative employs district characteristics relevant to the policy jurisdiction of the committee. This approach is intended to measure demand for benefits in a way that is exogenous to members' preferences; for example, district demand for agricultural earmarks might be based on the percentage of the population engaged in farming. Hurwitz, Moiles, and Rohde (2001) use such measures; they find that members of the House Agriculture Committee and the agriculture subcommittee of the Appropriations Committee indeed tend to be high demanders. Although those members are outliers on distributive issues they vote in a partisan manner on other policy dimensions. Likewise, Hall and Grofman (1990) measure Senate committee-floor differences with constituency characteristics and find, as they do with purged interest group ratings, that the agriculture committees are composed of high demanders.

In the most extensive use of district-based measures of demand, Adler and Lapinski (1997) examine a broad range of House committees, devising a unique demand measure for each of thirteen committees. Their comparison of the differences in medians between the committees and the chamber for the years 1943–1994 shows that the "private goods" committees, including committees whose narrow jurisdictions are conducive to pork barreling, are disproportionately high-demanding (those committees are Agriculture, Interior, and Merchant Marine and Fisheries), as are other more policy-oriented committees, including Armed Services, Banking, and Education and Labor.

Sprague (2008) demonstrates (like Hall and Grofman, 1990) that the measure of demand influences the findings. Using interest group ratings, the most appropriate alternative to district characteristics, she replicates Adler and Lapinski's test for the same committees in the same years. She finds that Adler and Lapinski's constituency-based measures indeed identify more high-demanding committees than do interest group voting scores.

The level at which preferences are measured—committee or subcommittee—also has consequences for the conclusions, especially for the appropriations committees. These subcommittees are specialized by policy area, thus allowing high demanders to focus on their area of interest, and relatively autonomous (Savage 1991). As the major purveyors of earmarks in Congress, they are attractive to members who seek

---

[3] Two additional studies offer alternative measures. Londregan and Snyder (1994) devise an alternate measure designed to distinguish between preference heterogeneity and measurement error. They find that, contrary to the conclusions of the studies cited above, one-third of House committees are composed of preference outliers. On the other hand, Groseclose (1994) critiques several assumptions in this literature and develops an alternative technique that corrects the flaws he identifies. Applied to the data, he finds some mixed evidence for preference outliers, but on balance concludes that the random-selection hypothesis cannot be rejected.

high levels of distributive benefits for their districts. Thus, if there is any basis in fact to theories predicting self-selection of high demanders of pork to particular committees, we should see evidence of it on appropriations subcommittees. Kiewiet and McCubbins (1991), using NOMINATE scores (appropriately, for their purposes), test and reject the hypothesis that these subcommittees are composed of ideological preference outliers, but such measures are not the most appropriate for measuring demand for distributive benefits. Instead, the subcommittees must be examined using specific measures of demand. It is at this level that we should expect to see a full committee membership that may be generally representative of the House divide into high-demanding subcommittees.

Adler (2000) addresses this question when he applies the same methodology employed by Adler and Lapinski (1997) (district demand as measured by constituency characteristics) to ten of the thirteen House Appropriations Committee subcommittees. For the majority of those subcommittees, the median member's district exhibits a higher level of demand for spending in its jurisdiction than the chamber as a whole. Thus, an otherwise representative House Appropriations Committee (Cox and McCubbins 1993) accommodates distributive high demanders within its specialized subcommittees.

To summarize, it is clear that some committees are not composed of high demanders. Overall, it is likely that the variance is related to the type and number of issue dimensions in a committee's jurisdiction. Crucially, there is disagreement over whether the House Appropriations Committee, which has the greatest ability to engage in earmarking, is composed of high demanders. (There is far less research on the Senate Appropriations Committee.) Studies that analyze the representativeness of the committee as a whole using broad-based preference measures tend to conclude that it is not composed of preference outliers; however, the results for appropriations subcommittees depend on the measure used. Nevertheless, given that studies using district-based measures of demand for pork barrel benefits show that a number of committees, including most notably at least half of the appropriations subcommittees, are populated by members with high demand for district-level distributive benefits, we should expect to see extra shares of pork being given to members of panels with jurisdiction over bills that offer such benefits.

Before turning to an examination of the scholarly findings on the question of which groups of legislators actually are favored in the distribution of pork barrel benefits, it is necessary to consider an additional measurement issue. The next section assesses the two major ways in which scholars have operationalized the concept of pork barrel benefits.

Approaches to measuring pork barrel benefits

Scholars have measured pork barrel benefits using one of two types of data: congressionally designated earmarks for recipients in specific states and districts, attached to spending legislation (normally in committee reports) by Congress itself, and federal spending administered by the bureaucracy. When bureaucratically administered federal spending is measured as discretionary grants to members' districts, it conforms to the classic definition of distributive benefits. Such grants are, in general, highly disaggregable: a grant to a particular district can be altered or eliminated without affecting any other district's benefits. Of course, some grants impact more than one district as do some earmarks, but grants (and earmarks) are more likely to meet this definitional requirement than other types of federal spending. However, some caveats are necessary when bureaucratic spending is used to test certain theoretical propositions of the distributive literature; these issues are discussed here.

The early theoretical literature on coalition formation in Congress addresses the construction of bills consisting of pork barrel projects for individual districts by Congress. The closest real-world manifestation of such benefits is appropriations earmarks, although highway reauthorization bills have also been a rich, if less frequent, source of earmarks. Until recently, comprehensive earmark data at the level of congressional districts have been hard to come by. Indeed, extraordinary efforts were often required to connect an earmark with a congressional district, as published descriptions of earmarks themselves typically did not specify the exact districts to which they were directed.[4] Even the bureaucratic agency which was required to disburse the money was sometimes not sure where or how the money was to be spent (Savage 2009). Although there is considerable early research on water projects (Maass 1950, 1951; Ferejohn 1974), a type of earmark that, unlike most, spans much of the history of the country, in this area as well, connecting projects with individual districts, while more feasible than with many other types of earmarks, has been laborious (Wilson 1986).

This problem was ameliorated by new rules passed by both the House and Senate in 2007; the rules required that the name of the member requesting each earmark (called the earmark "sponsor") be publicly disclosed. Several independent watchdog groups have made those data available in spreadsheet format, including Taxpayers for Common Sense (TCS), (http://www.taxpayers.org), Legistorm (http://www.legistorm.com), which uses TCS data, and Citizens Against Government Waste (http://www.cagw.org). The Office of Management and Budget also provides data on all "disclosed" earmarks (http://earmarks.omb.gov). However, these data sets are not identical. Most obviously, the total value of earmarks reported by TCS, CAGW, and OMB varies: for example, for Fiscal Year 2008, the difference between the value of earmarks reported by TCS and OMB was approximately $1.7 billion, or 10 percent of the OMB total. The discrepancy in the number of earmarks reported by these organizations is lower, amounting to no more than 3.3 percent, or fewer than 400 of more than 11,000 projects granted that year. Nevertheless, these new data will enable scholars to test distributive theories far more exhaustively than has previously been possible, as earmark data for the first time are available for every policy area at

---

[4] Such data were collected either from inside congressional sources (Evans 1994, 2004), by the scholar's own labor-intensive efforts (Lee 2003; Frisch 1998), or by interested outside observers (Balla, Lawrence, et al. 2002).

the level of the congressional district. Researchers can now determine whether results previously obtained for specific kinds of earmarks (discussed below) are generalizable to all policy areas.

In contrast to the previous scarcity of earmark data at the congressional district level, data on earmarks awarded to states have been available since 1991 from Citizens Against Government Waste. Prior to Fiscal Year 2008, due to the absence of the sponsor's name and the vagueness of the descriptions of these projects, earmarks are connected only with states, although some are not coded even at this level and remain entirely obscure. Nevertheless, it is possible to use these data for research on Senate earmarking over a relatively long time span, one that includes a nearly 10-fold growth in earmarking from 1,429 projects in Fiscal Year 1995 to a peak of 13,997 in FY 2005, according to CAGW data.

As noted above, many studies use an alternative measure: the distribution of pork barrel benefits by bureaucratic agencies (for an important example, see Arnold 1979). Prior to the early 1990s, due to the difficulty of collecting wide-ranging bureaucratic data, studies of the politics of bureaucratic grants consisted of case studies that typically examined no more than a handful of federal agencies at a time. Comprehensive data were provided in 1991 by Kenneth Bickers and Robert Stein, who transformed for scholarly use the most complete source of data on spending for federal domestic assistance from the *Catalogue of Federal Domestic Assistance* and the *Federal Assistance Awards Data System* (Bickers and Stein 1991). FAADS data makes analysis possible at many levels of aggregation of federal-aid program spending in congressional districts from 1983 on. These data have been widely used in studies of distributive politics, not only in Stein and Bickers' own book, *Perpetuating the Pork Barrel: Policy Subsystems and American Democracy* (1995), but also in other important studies. This rich and flexible data-set has allowed scholars to test a wide range of hypotheses about distributive politics and federal spending more broadly.

What difference does the measure of pork barrel benefits make? Each measure, bureaucratic grants or earmarks, is best though not exclusively suited to test one type of theory of distribution. Because earmarks are particularized benefits requested and awarded within Congress, they are appropriately used to test the propositions of most distributive theories. With respect discretionary bureaucratic grants, the effect of purely congressional goals and strategies is likely to be diminished by bureaucrats' own goals as well as the requirements that members of Congress themselves often impose on the agencies. Stein and Bickers (1994a, 1995), while assuming that agencies have an incentive to allocate grants strategically to retain the favor of members of Congress, acknowledge that members' individual impact on grant allocations is limited. Frisch (1998, 18–19) critiques the use of bureaucratic grants as measures of pork barrel benefits on similar grounds, particularly focusing on the constraints on bureaucrats' discretion, such as objective program requirements (many of them specified by Congress) and peer review of grant applications (Frisch 1998, 18–22).[5]

---

[5] Frisch criticizes earlier scholarship for several flaws: incorporating non-distributive data such as formula and redistributive programs, making unwarranted conversions of state-level data to the level of

Congressional influence is indeed a step removed from the actual designation of specific projects, yet members of Congress influence the shape of the programs under which grants are awarded (especially eligibility requirements), solicit grant applications, and assist grant applicants. Moreover, bureaucrats have incentives to curry favor with legislators through their awards. These data are most appropriate for testing hypotheses about bureaucrats' allocation strategies, as Arnold (1979) does. Nevertheless, with the proper caveats, much can be learned about distributive politics from the study of the allocation of discretionary bureaucratic grants. For example, such data have allowed tests of distributive theories for time periods predating comprehensive data on earmarks. Indeed, before the modern-day explosion of earmarking, Arnold (1979, 6) noted that Congress did not, in fact, distribute individual pork barrel projects; thus, bureaucratic pork was virtually the only thing to study. It should also be noted that grants offer legislators the chance to claim credit; a look at almost any member's website will reveal multiple grant announcements in which, at a minimum, the member strongly implies that he or she helped to get the award.

Patterns of allocation of pork barrel benefits: the committee benefit hypothesis

The literature has, as discussed above, long debated the question of the self-selection of high demanders to committees and the distributional consequences of any resulting committee bias. Scholars have hypothesized that members of the committees with jurisdiction over a bill that offers distributive benefits will receive a disproportionately large share of those benefits. This proposition is especially prominent in individual-benefit distributive theory. As the discussion above indicates, the predictions of collective-benefit approaches vary.

If equal benefits do not go to all members (an extreme version of the universalism hypothesis), and there is evidence that they do not (Stein and Bickers 1994b, 1995), we are left with two potential distributional biases: committee members benefit disproportionately or members of the majority party are favored. These alternatives depend on the structure that induces a voting equilibrium—committees that serve as agents of floor majorities or as agents of the majority party.[6]

While early research found mixed results for the committee benefit hypothesis,[7] numerous recent studies have found that members of the relevant authorizing and appropriations committees receive disproportionate distributive benefits. To the extent that high demanders serve on these committees, this consequence is not unexpected, particularly in the House, where committees are more powerful than in the

congressional districts, and including awards that offer little opportunity for credit claiming by legislators (Frisch 1998, 18–19). He concedes that FAADS data remedies many of these problems.

[6] There are other possibilities: for example, a coalition leader might assemble the group of the cheapest benefits (Fiorina 1981; Lee 1998). However, less attention has been given to this hypothesis to date.

[7] See, for example, Plott (1968); Ferejohn (1974); Arnold (1979); Goss (1972); Rundquist and Griffith (1976); Ray (1980a, 1980b).

Senate. However, there is considerable variation among studies in the extent of this advantage as well as the types of benefits most subject to committee influence. For example, Evans (1994, 2004) and Lee (2003) find that members of the House Public Works Committee were advantaged in the distribution of highway demonstration projects attached to the 1987, 1991, and 1998 reauthorizations of the federal-aid highway program. In these cases, the chairs sought to use projects to secure the votes of their own committee members (of both parties) to facilitate a united front for the committee bill on the House floor. Similarly, Frisch (1998) found clear evidence in all policy areas that members of House appropriations subcommittees obtained significantly more earmarks from their own committees' bills than other members.

In one of the first articles in what will surely be a wave of important studies using the new data on earmark sponsorship by individual members of Congress, Lazarus, and Steigerwalt (2009) find that in Fiscal Year 2008 appropriations bills, members of both the House and to a lesser extent the Senate appropriations committees received disproportionate numbers of awards. The dependent variable in this study is the total number of earmarks awarded by all subcommittees; given the autonomy of the subcommittees, future analyses should disaggregate the data to determine whether subcommittees especially favor their own members or practice universalism among subcommittees as a form of inter-subcommittee logrolling.[8]

Research on Senate earmarking using state-level data shows mixed results by appropriations subcommittee. Crespin and Finocchiaro (2008) find that for most subcommittees, states represented by senators on the full committee or the relevant subcommittee receive more earmarked monies than other senators. However, the effect varies; it is greatest for four subcommittees: transportation, defense, military construction, and VA/HUD, all of which have great potential to locate benefits in members' districts. Some of the subcommittees on which no committee benefit was found—Legislative Operations, Foreign Operations, and Treasury—have little or no opportunity for district-level earmarking.

Similarly, in an examination of Senate appropriations bills from four subcommittees across three Congresses, an examination that focuses on the use of pork to buy votes, Evans (2004) found that in nearly every case, members of the relevant subcommittee benefited, but to varying degrees; such benefits were less likely to go to other members of the Appropriations Committee.

Disproportionate committee benefits are not always found. Balla, Lawrence, et al. (2002) use data on academic earmarks to test competing hypotheses concerning the allocation of pork. This research is discussed more fully below, but it should be noted here that in their joint test of benefits to members of the House and Senate appropriations committees, they found an overall benefit only for the Senate. However, they did not include membership in the relevant subcommittees in the model; the possibility of such an advantage cannot be ruled out.

Another type of committee benefit is possible. Given the considerable power and autonomy of the "cardinals," as chairs of the appropriations subcommittees are

---

[8] Using the 2008 data, Lazarus (2010) analyzes earmark allocation in seventeen federal agency budgets and finds an earmark advantage for members of the associated House authorizing committees in seven cases.

known, we might expect that they, and (depending on the subcommittee's traditions) ranking minority members grant larger shares of pork to their own states and districts. Indeed, some of the studies cited above include this variable and often find such an advantage. Crespin and Finocchiaro (2008) find this for all Senate earmarks; Balla, Lawrence, et al. (2002) find that House cardinals benefit; Senate cardinals do not. Similarly, for earmarks in highway reauthorization bills, Lee (2003) finds that House Transportation and Infrastructure Committee leaders, minority and majority, gain extra benefits. On the other hand, Lazarus and Steigerwalt (2009), in their examination of fiscal 2008 earmarks, find no extra benefit for cardinals in the House. However, the House studies all use different data, which may explain the different results. Different subcommittees and different chairs apparently award earmarks in distinctive ways.

We now turn to studies of the bureaucratic allocation of pork, focusing primarily on the type of benefit that meets the classic definition of the pork barrel: discretionary grants-in-aid to states and districts. Here the findings are mixed. For example, in the empirical portion of his ground-breaking study of the strategic allocation of grants by bureaucrats, Arnold (1979) examines model cities and water and sewer grants, along with military base closures. He finds that bureaucrats favor members of House authorizing committees and appropriations subcommittees with the most direct jurisdiction over their programs and funding; moreover, those allocations tended to be bipartisan. Rich's (1989) findings are similar for the House, but he uncovers no such effect in the Senate.

Heitshusen (2001) finds bureaucratic bias toward the jurisdictionally-narrow House Agriculture Committee and the agriculture appropriations subcommittee but not toward the more diverse Education and Labor Committee and its corresponding appropriations subcommittee. This finding is consistent with the argument that committees with fewer jurisdictional dimensions are more likely to be composed of high demanders than those with broader jurisdictions (Maltzman and Smith 1994).

Thus, the committee benefit hypothesis is not supported by the results of every study considered here, and in those that find such a benefit, the magnitude of the effect varies. However, the weight of recent evidence on this question favors this hypothesis, regardless of whether the pork barrel benefit is allocated by Congress or the bureaucracy. The key question for future research is to determine the conditions under which committees benefit. The most promising avenue concerns the breadth of committee jurisdictions, as several studies have shown that this variable conditions the tendency of committees both to attract high demanders and to favor their own members. This question is especially relevant to the study of appropriations subcommittees, which distribute most legislative earmarks.

Partisanship in the distribution of pork

For years, the common wisdom was that pork barrel benefits were allocated in a bipartisan manner. This conclusion was based on both the traditions of House and

Senate appropriations committees (Fenno 1966, 547–9) as well as other committees that deal in distributive benefits (e.g. the House Interior Committee: Fenno 1973, 58; the House Transportation and Infrastructure Committee: Evans 2004). Mayhew (1974) implicitly connects this bipartisanship to the classic rationale for the universal distribution of benefits—members want to ensure that they will get benefits (Weingast 1979); therefore, they have an incentive to agree to broad, bipartisan distribution (Mayhew 1974, 89–90). Indeed, studies that analyzed data from years prior to the mid-1990s, when they estimated the impact of party at all, tended to find a bipartisan distribution of pork.

Bureaucrats also have incentives to be evenhanded in the distribution of grants; Arnold (1979) describes those incentives and finds a pattern of bipartisan distribution in his case studies. On the other hand, Anagnoson (1982) found some evidence of partisan bias in the executive branch, but that bias affected only the timing of grant announcements rather than the awards themselves. He concluded that "the agencies seem to be at least partially successful in insulating their decisions from the political process" (Anagnoson 1982, 560). In a much broader examination of new discretionary grants in the 1980s, Stein and Bickers (1994a, 390, 1995) found no partisan bias.

In the era of amorphous party lines, there were good reasons for bureaucrats to follow a bipartisan strategy in awarding grants. However, partisan polarization in Congress increased in the years subsequent to much of the research on which conclusions about bipartisanship are based. Inconveniently for scholarship, this increase occurred at approximately the same time that data on congressional earmarking became available. McCarty, Poole, and Rosenthal (2008) show that post-war polarization in Congress began in the late 1970s, rose sharply in the 1980s and accelerated in the 1990s. This change raises the question as to whether growing congressional partisanship altered political actors' pork barrel allocation strategies. Especially in the House, as the conditions for party government (Rohde 1991) were increasingly met in the 1990s and the new Republican majority of the 104th Congress adopted a strategy of using the Appropriations Committee to further its policy goals (Aldrich and Rohde 2000), there is some indication that norms of bipartisanship in the distribution of pork barrel benefits began to break down.

The question is how a partisan distributive process might work. Partisan theories of congressional organization (Cox and McCubbins 1993; Rohde 1991) suggest a collective-benefit rationale for partisanship in allocational decisions over which Congress has full control: majority party leaders might use such benefits to secure their majority, while refining their strategies to limit damage to the party's reputation. Also, to the extent that party leaders seek to use earmarks to build majority coalitions for their general-interest policy goals, they might buy more of those votes from their own party members, given the declining chances of attracting the other party's members.

Moreover, if the politics of distribution has become more partisan, bureaucrats could face conflict among incentives to favor the majority party, on the one hand, and to avoid alienating a minority that could soon become the majority party, on the other. In scholarship that ranges over the years of increased partisanship in Congress, there is indeed somewhat more, if still mixed, evidence that partisan impulses affect bureaucratic allocation. Three studies find evidence of partisan influences on federal spending. Levitt and Snyder (1995), using FAADS data for the years 1984–90, examine the impact of partisanship on formula-based spending programs (excluding most entitlements) with programs where bureaucrats have more discretion. They find that partisanship has a significant impact on discretionary spending and an even greater influence on programs governed by formula. These results differ from Stein and Bickers's (1995) findings, but Levitt and Snyder do not as clearly restrict their measure of discretionary spending to discretionary grants as do Stein and Bickers; therefore, their results may not be directly comparable.

For military procurement contracts awarded by the Department of Defense, there is evidence of extra benefits for the majority party in both the Senate and the House. That bias was longstanding, encompassing the years 1963–95, although in the Senate it went only to conservative Democrats on defense committees. In the House, contracts went disproportionately to all committee Democrats. Thus, in the House, partisan bias in the distribution of military pork is mediated by committee membership; in the Senate, it is mediated by both committee membership and ideology (Carsey and Rundquist 1999; Rundquist and Carsey 2002, 86–97).

Finally, Carroll and Kim (2010) find that between 1983 and 1996, members of the House majority whose policy preferences were most often overridden by the party majority were compensated most generously in the form of bureaucratic grants for casting procedural votes that helped the party to maintain its agenda control.

With respect to congressional earmarks, where restraints on partisanship may be weaker than in the bureaucracy, there is evidence of evolving partisanship in the distribution of highway earmarks in highway reauthorizations. Evans (2004, 77–84) found no partisanship in the House Public Works and Transportation Committee's distribution of highway demonstration projects in the 1987 and 1991 reauthorizations of federal transportation programs. Instead, committee leaders used those projects to build bipartisan coalitions in support of the leaders' preferences on those bills. Yet despite the longstanding tradition of bipartisanship on that committee, skyrocketing congressional partisanship in the 1990s left its mark on project distribution. By the next program reauthorization in 1998, partisan effects on the earmarked projects in the bill were strong, with majority Republicans enjoying an advantage, along with committee members (Lee 2003).

However, vote-buying may not have been committee leaders' only collective-benefit motive for giving such projects in the 1998 highway bill. There is also evidence of an electoral strategy in earmark distribution in 1998. Lee (2003) found that while some earmarks went to all members electorally at risk regardless of party, vulnerable majority party members got greater numbers of, and more valuable, earmarks. Lazarus (2009) obtains a similar result using other data.

Balla, Lawrence, et al. (2002) found evidence of a similar partisan electoral strategy in the House, but not in the Senate, on academic earmarks in the 1990s. Members of the minority were as likely as the majority to be awarded at least one such earmark, but majority party members received earmarks of significantly greater dollar value.

They label this pattern "partisan blame avoidance," a strategy designed to give the majority an edge while restraining the minority from accusing the majority of wasteful spending. Unlike Lee, they did not find an effect for electoral margin, but they did not interact that variable with the member's party, making it unclear whether the majority pursued a blanket strategy of helping incumbents or targeted the most generous benefits to its vulnerable members. They explain their null findings for the Senate thus: "This result is consistent with the common claim that parties are less influential in the Senate than in the House" (Balla, Lawrence, et al. 2002, 523).

Senate bipartisanship in earmarking is not the case across the board, however. Evans (2004) found mixed results for earmarks awarded by four Senate appropriations subcommittees in three congresses in the 1990s; in some years on each of the subcommittees majority party members received more; in other years, they did not (Evans 2004, 198–202). Nevertheless, as growing partisanship would suggest, a study of all earmarks awarded to House and Senate members in Fiscal Year 2008 found a majority-party advantage in both House and Senate (Lazarus and Steigerwalt 2009).

In their examination of appropriations earmarks awarded over a longer period, 1996–2005, Crespin and Finocchiaro found that overall, states represented by two senators from the majority party received significantly more earmarks; but like the committee benefit they found, that effect was significant only for the subcommittees that tend to offer high levels of pork. Whether this is an explicit electoral strategy is unclear, as partisan effects were not mediated by a senator's next reelection date.

If unlimited data on pork barrel awards were available over the long term, it would be instructive to determine whether partisanship in pork barreling developed with the overall growth in partisan polarization or whether, given incentives favoring universal distribution, partisan pork barreling lagged overall partisanship. Unfortunately, such long-term overall data are truncated, but the policy-specific data that are available suggest growing partisanship in earmarking. Although the CAGW data on state-level earmarks span mostly the period of high partisan polarization in Congress, it is the only broad data set with which to test the hypothesis that partisanship in earmarking varies with the level of partisanship in the Senate.

The bicameral perspective

The discussion of the empirical research on the allocation of pork barrel benefits has focused on committee and partisan biases. That research has found indications of House–Senate differences; specifically, there appears to be less bias of both types in the Senate. There is another important difference between the House and Senate in the allocation of pork; a collective-benefit perspective provides the rationale. In particular, in the Senate small states enjoy an advantage in the use of federal funding to buy votes. Each state has equal representation, but policy coalition leaders can buy the votes of senators from small states more cheaply than those from large states (Lee 1998; Lee and Oppenheimer 1999). Indeed, they can assemble a majority coalition with small-state votes, a strategy that Lee (1998) and Lee and Oppenheimer (1999) found in formula program spending. In the House, of course, such extreme variation in district size does not exist, so a small-state strategy is pointless there. However, distributional patterns differ for formula and pork barrel spending, so more research is needed on whether small states enjoy an advantage in the distribution of pork. When pork is used for vote-buying, one would expect it, but to the extent that the distribution of pork has become more partisan, considerations of state size might be overwhelmed by partisan factors.

Indeed, the findings for earmarks are mixed. Balla, Lawrence, et al. (2002) found an advantage for small states in the selection of states to receive at least one academic earmark, but Evans (2004) found state size to be significant in only five of the twelve subcommittee-year models for Senate appropriations earmarks. Crespin and Finocchiaro's findings for all earmarks, 1996–2005, are similarly mixed.

Other effects of bicameralism are beginning to emerge. Shepsle, Van Houweling, et al. (2009) argue that the difference in House and Senate electoral cycles leads to strategic inter-chamber behavior: the Senate "back-loads" earmarks toward the end of senators' terms, but the House counters this tendency by ramping up earmarks to states with a senator up for reelection in a given cycle. This study is based on state-level CAGW data. Newly available district-level data for the House will allow assessments of strategic inter-chamber behavior which takes into account individual-level strategies as well. For example, such data could consider the vulnerability of House members in states with senators up for reelection, testing the hypothesis that those House districts are penalized less than others when a state's senator is up for reelection.

Summary: biases in the distribution of pork

Overall, while findings are mixed, there is evidence that committees with control over earmarks (appropriations committees and their subcommittees and highway authorization committees) extract extra benefits for themselves. Future research should be devoted to more clearly identifying the conditions under which they do so and the degree to which they display a partisan bias in the distribution of pork. Promising avenues include the degree to which a particular committee or subcommittee attracts high demanders for pork, which is likely dependent on the breadth and complexity of that committee's jurisdiction and its opportunities for distributing pork. Moreover, future research should give more consideration to the purposes for which earmarks are provided. Different collective benefit purposes can produce different patterns of earmark distribution: for example, vote buyers may be bipartisan, while party leaders may adopt a partisan electoral strategy in the distribution of pork.

The size of pork barrel coalitions

This section briefly discusses the theoretical literature on the size of distributive coalitions and considers empirical tests of its predictions. For a more in-depth consideration of the early theory on coalition size, see Collie (1988); Volden and Wiseman's contribution to this volume examines more recent theoretical developments.

Early rational choice theories assume that the distribution of benefits to members' own constituents is the major goal of public policymaking; legislation is modeled as large omnibus bills consisting of nothing but distributive benefits. Theorists have debated the equilibrium size of such pure distributive policy coalitions. On one hand, it is argued that the victorious coalition for distributive benefits is likely to be minimal winning, in which only a bare majority of members gets projects (Buchanan and Tullock 1962; Riker 1962; Riker and Ordeshook 1973; Snyder 1991). The advantage of such a coalition to its members is that total benefits are divided into fewer shares, leaving more for each member.

Others argue that universalistic coalitions form to pass omnibus pork barrel bills (Ferejohn 1974; Weingast 1979; Shepsle and Weingast 1981; Niou and Ordeshook 1985). A norm of universalism develops out of members' uncertainty as to whether they will be included in any given minimal winning coalition; a universalistic coalition eliminates that uncertainty and its attendant electoral risk (Weingast 1979; Shepsle and Weingast 1987; Weingast and Marshall 1988).

Melissa Collie noted, as of 1988, that empirical research had only minimally grappled with the testable propositions of the rational choice literature (Collie 1988, 447). While the minimal-winning and universal coalition hypotheses have rarely been tested for the House over the past twenty years; we can consider a few studies that have done so. As usual, the results are mixed. Stein and Bickers (1994b) examined federal outlays for financial assistance to congressional districts using FAADS data from the 1980s. Not only did they not find evidence of universalism, they failed to find that even a minimal majority of members received benefits within particular program areas or within broader policy subsystems, regardless of the type of spending.

With respect to Appropriations Committee earmarks for House members, there is similarly scant evidence of universalistic or even majority distribution of benefits apart from a very few policy areas, at least in the 1990s. Frisch (1998) finds that with the exception of Army Corps of Engineers water projects, which consistently benefited more than 90 percent of districts, other subcommittees' earmarks benefited a minority of districts. These results are no doubt partly explained by the fact that most districts are not eligible for many programs, such as agricultural research and National Park Service construction earmarks; as Weingast (1994) points out, universalism is not possible in such areas. But all districts are presumably eligible for transportation earmarks, yet a majority of districts got them in only one out of the six years that Frisch considered.

In the Senate, the expectation of universalism presents a much lower empirical bar. In the extreme, the receipt of benefits by as few as fifty House districts would result in universal distribution for states if those House districts were distributed among the fifty states. Not surprisingly, Frisch (1998) finds that in each of the six years he examines, all 100 senators claimed credit for earmarks. Yet even in the Senate, the expectation of universalism is not met for discretionary bureaucratic grants. Lee (1998) and Lee and Oppenheimer (1999), using FAADS data, found that the median discretionary grant program allocated money to as few as twenty-two states and as many as twenty-seven states from the 98th to 101st Congresses. Such results might be explained by the argument that senators have reason to value pork barrel benefits less than House members because, in states with more than one House district, each earmark benefits a smaller proportion of senator's constituents than formula programs; therefore, senators focus far more on gaining advantage in the latter, a more efficient strategy. However, it is also the case that when earmarks are available, senators seek them energetically.

To the extent that earmarks are added to legislation for collective-benefit reasons—for example, to buy votes for bills with a broad national impact—there is somewhat less reason to expect that all, or even a majority of members, will receive them. When policy coalition leaders add pork to a general-benefit bill to win the votes of members who have not yet committed to the bill, there is likely already a substantial base of support on the merits of the bill. Therefore, there is no need to give projects to more than a minority of members to build a majority to support the underlying bill. In fact, in the 1987 reauthorization of the federal highway program the leaders of the House Public Works and Transportation Committee gave highway earmarks to only seventy-six members, approximately 17 percent of the House. However, this less-than-majority strategy is not stable over time. Once it dawns on members that they can realize gains from trading their votes, they have an incentive to conceal their true preferences from coalition leaders in order to extract pork barrel benefits. There is indeed evidence of that effect for highway bills. At the next reauthorization, earmarks went to 60 percent of the House, more than three times as many members as in the previous reauthorization (Evans, 2004). By the 1998 reauthorization, 86 percent of House districts received earmarks Lee (2003). These results suggest that once a particular distributor of earmarks reveals a willingness to use them to buy votes, there is movement over time toward universal distribution.

On the other hand, if the relevant collective benefit is not vote-buying but the protection of a party's congressional majority, every majority party member who wants such a benefit may with certainty expect to be a member of a successful minimal winning coalition (Shepsle and Weingast 1981, 109). However, that benefit may not be exclusive; Balla, Lawrence, et al. (2002) argue that while the majority party has an incentive to favor its own party members, it also has an incentive to give less valuable projects to the minority, opening the possibility of universal distribution, albeit with systematic partisan variation in the value of those benefits. Balla, Lawrence et al. do not explicitly test the universalism hypothesis and indeed find that only a minority of districts received academic earmarks (2002, 517); however, to meaningfully test the universalism hypothesis, it would be necessary to know how many districts actually were eligible for such earmarks (Weingast 1994).

The obvious question is whether these findings are general or apply to just a few policy areas, such as public works. Unfortunately, a broad test of the hypothesis that earmarking starts with less than a majority of districts and rapidly grows to near universal proportions may be difficult to devise. Widespread earmarking in Congress has been well underway for nearly two decades, yet comprehensive data on which House districts receive earmarks have only recently become available.

Although it may not be possible to test hypotheses about the growth in earmarking over time, better tests of coalition size in the House are now possible. Research in this area had been sparse, owing primarily to the difficulty of attributing earmarks to House districts. New district-level data now make it possible to test competing hypotheses concerning coalition size in the total number of earmarks across all appropriations bills and in individual subcommittee bills, year by year.

CONCLUSION

This chapter has assessed important recent scholarship on pork barrel politics in Congress, with a particular focus on patterns of distribution and a secondary focus on measurement issues. It has also, where possible, framed the discussion in terms of the purposes for which pork is distributed and the resulting patterns of distribution. Directions for future research are suggested throughout, with an emphasis on the considerable research opportunities offered by newly available data, which now associate earmarks with their individual congressional districts. These data will allow more refined tests of the propositions of rational choice models as well as better testing and further development of collective-benefit theories of the distribution of pork barrel benefits. Moreover, the availability of comparable individual-level data for the House and the Senate will allow a fuller comparison of House and Senate allocation strategies and a more thorough consideration of the impact of bicameralism on the distribution of pork barrel benefits than has been possible to date.

How important is the study of distributive politics? It is well-established that pork barrel benefits in the form of both discretionary bureaucratic grants and congressional earmarks consume a relatively small proportion of the federal budget (Lee 2003; Stein and Bickers 1995). At the peak of congressional earmarking, in Fiscal Year 2005, earmarks accounted for 1.1 percent of total federal outlays. Perhaps due partly to the ensuing public outcry, earmarking in appropriations bills declined somewhat thereafter in numbers, value, and as a percentage of outlays. For 2009, earmarks consumed .6 percent of estimated federal outlays, a considerable decline; moreover, the dollar value was also lower, amounting to 70 percent of the unadjusted value of earmarks in 2005.[9] Clearly, the omnibus pork barrel bills envisioned by early rational choice theory are virtually non-existent. The value of studying pork barrel politics lies elsewhere. First, the study of pork barrel politics provides a window into Congress members' electoral calculations, especially as they are linked to constituents'

[9] Total federal outlays are taken from "Historical Tables, Budget of the United States Government, Fiscal Year 2009," U.S. Government Printing Office, Washington DC, 2008, accessed online at http://www.whitehouse.gov/omb/budget/fy2009/pdf/hist.pdf (accessed September 16, 2009). Figures for earmarks are taken from Citizens Against Government Waste, accessed at http://www.cagw.org (accessed September 16, 2009).

perceived demand (or, at a minimum, gratitude) for particularized benefits. Second, it has become clear that pork barrel benefits are distributed strategically by key political actors for collective-benefit purposes. As a consequence, the effects of pork barrel politics go beyond the individual-level electoral connection. Pork barrel benefits help policy coalition leaders build majority coalitions for general-interest legislation. Moreover, the strategic partisan distribution of pork demonstrates that majority party leaders use it as part of a strategy to protect their majority.

All of the literature on pork barrel politics frames the provision of pork in terms of members' reelection interests. This is equally true for scholarship that takes the individual-benefit and collective-benefit approaches. In the latter case, those who provide pork to further a collective goal do so by exploiting members' desire to use those benefits to bolster their reelection chances.

Indeed, despite the opprobrium heaped upon pork barreling, until very recently, most members of Congress stoutly defended the practice as an essential form of representation of their constituents' needs; moreover, they energetically resisted attempts to end the practice. Given such defenses, diatribes against pork barreling served mainly as an electoral positioning device for the few members who did not seek such benefits. However, in the wake of the 2010 elections that restored Republicans to the majority in the House partly on the basis of a campaign against alleged fiscal profligacy, Republicans in both houses succumbed to pressure from their most conservative members to ban earmarks for their members (this decision followed a temporary ban by House Republicans earlier in the year). As this book goes to press, it remains to be seen whether any potential collective benefit to the party that might result from such a ban can trump the perceived electoral benefits to individual members of bringing home the bacon, as the survival of the ban will depend upon it.

REFERENCES

ADLER, E. S. 2000. Constituency Characteristics and the Guardian Model of Appropriations Subcommittees. *American Journal of Political Science*, 44: 104–14.

—— and LAPINSKI, J. S. 1997. Demand-side Theory and Congressional Committee Composition: A Constituency Characteristics Approach. *American Journal of Political Science*, 41 (3): 895–918.

ALDRICH, J. H., and ROHDE, D. W. 2000. The Republican Revolution and the House Appropriations Committee. *Journal of Politics*, 62(1):1–33.

ANAGNOSON, J. T. 1982. Federal Grant Agencies and Congressional Election Campaigns. *American Journal of Political Science*, 26: 547–61.

ARNOLD, R. D. 1979. *Congress and the Bureaucracy: A Theory of Influence*. New Haven: Yale University Press.

—— 1990. *The Logic of Congressional Action*. New Haven: Yale University Press.

BALLA, S. J., LAWRENCE, E., MALTZMAN, F., and SIGELMAN, L. 2002. Partisanship, Blame Avoidance, and the Distribution of Legislative Pork. *American Journal of Political Science*, 46: 515–25.

BARON, D. P. 1991. Majoritarian Incentives, Pork Barrel Programs, and Procedural Control. *American Journal of Political Science*, 35(1): 57–90.

BICKERS, K. N., and STEIN, R. M. 1991. *Federal Domestic Outlays, 1983–1990: A Data Book.* Armonk, NY: M.E. Sharpe.

BUCHANAN, J. M., and TULLOCK, G. 1962. *The Calculus of Consent.* Ann Arbor: University of Michigan Press.

—— and YOON, Y. J. 2002. Universalism through Common Access: An Alternative Model of Distributive Majoritarian Politics. *Political Research Quarterly*, 55(3): 503–19.

CARROLL, ROYCE, and KIM, HENRY A. 2010. Party Government and the "Cohesive Power of Public Plunder." *American Journal of Political Science*, 54: 34–44.

CARSEY, T. M., and RUNDQUIST, B. 1999. Party and Committee in Distributive Politics: Evidence from Defense Spending. *Journal of Politics*, 61: 1156–69.

COLLIE, M. P. 1988. The Legislature and Distributive Policy Making in Formal Perspective. *Legislative Studies Quarterly*, 13(4): 427–58.

COX, G. W., and MCCUBBINS, M. D. 1993. *Legislative Leviathan: Party Government in the House.* Berkeley: University of California Press.

CRESPIN, M. H., and FINOCCHIARO, C. J. 2008. Distributive and Partisan Politics in the U.S. Senate: An Exploration of Earmarks, pp. 229–51 in *Why Not Parties? Party Effects in the United States Senate*, ed. N. W. Monroe, J. M. Roberts, and D. W. Rohde. Chicago: University of Chicago Press.

EVANS, D. 1994. Policy and Pork: The Use of Pork Barrel Projects to Build Policy Coalitions in the House of Representatives. *American Journal of Political Science*, 38: 894–917.

—— 2004. *Greasing the Wheels: The Use of Pork Barrel Projects to Build Majority Coalitions in Congress.* New York: Cambridge University Press.

FENNO, R. F. 1973. *Congressmen in Committees.* Boston: Little, Brown.

FENNO, R. F. 1996. *The Power of the Purse: Appropriations Politics in Congress.* Boston: Little, Brown.

FEREJOHN, J. A. 1974. *Pork Barrel Politics.* Stanford: Stanford University Press.

FIORINA, M. P. 1981. Universalism, Reciprocity, and Distributive Policymaking in Majority Rule Institutions. *Research in Public Policy Analysis and Management*, 1: 197–222.

FORGETTE, R. G., and SATURNO, J. V. 1994. 302(b) Or Not 302(b): Congressional Floor Procedures and House Appropriators. *Legislative Studies Quarterly*, 19(3): 385–96.

FREEMAN, P. K., and RICHARDSON, JR., L. E. 1996. Explaining Variation in Casework among State Legislators. *Legislative Studies Quarterly*, 21(1): 41–56.

FRISCH, S. A. 1998. *The Politics of Pork: A Study of Congressional Appropriation Earmarks.* New York: Garland.

—— and KELLY, S. Q. 2004. Self-selection Reconsidered: House Committee Assignment Requests and Constituency Characteristics. *Political Research Quarterly*, 57(2): 325–36.

GILLIGAN, T. W., and KREHBIEL, K. 1990. Organization of Informative Committees by a Rational Legislature. *American Journal of Political Science*, 3: 531–64.

GOSS, CAROL. 1972. "Military Committee Membership and Defense Related Benefits in the House of Representatives." *Western Political Quarterly*, 25: 215–33.

GROSECLOSE, T. 1994. Testing Committee Composition Hypotheses for the U.S. Congress. *Journal of Politics*, 56(2): 440–58.

—— and SNYDER, JR., J. M. 1996. Buying Supermajorities. *American Political Science Review*, 90: 303–15.

HALL, R. L., and GROFMAN, B. 1990. The Committee Assignment Process and the Conditional Nature of Committee Bias. *American Political Science Review*, 84: 1149–66.

HEITSHUSEN, V. 2001. The Allocation of Federal Money to House Committee Members. *American Politics Research*, 21: 79–97.

HURWITZ, M. S., MOILES, R. J., and ROHDE, D. W. 2001. Distributive and Partisan Issues in Agriculture Policy in the 104th House. *American Political Science Review*, 95: 911–22.

KIEWIET, D. R., and McCUBBINS, M. D. 1991. *The Logic of Delegation: Congressional Parties and the Appropriations Process*. Chicago: University of Chicago Press.

KREHBIEL, K. 1990. Are Congressional Committees Composed of Preference Outliers? *American Political Science Review*, 84(1): 149–63.

—— 1992. *Information and Legislative Organization*. Ann Arbor: University of Michigan Press.

LAZARUS, J. 2009. Party, Electoral Vulnerability, and Earmarks in the U.S. House of Representatives. *Journal of Politics*, 71: 1050–61.

—— 2010. Giving the People What They Want? The Distribution of Earmarks in the U.S. House of Representatives. *American Journal of Political Science*, 54: 338–53.

—— and STEIGERWALT, A. 2009. Different Houses: The Distribution of Earmarks in the U.S. House and Senate. *Legislative Studies Quarterly*, 34(3): 347–98.

LEE, F. E. 1998. Representation and Public Policy: The Consequences of Senate Apportionment for the Geographic Distribution of Federal Funds. *Journal of Politics*, 60(1): 34–62.

—— 2000. Senate Representation and Coalition Building in Distributive Politics. *American Political Science Review*, 94: 50–72.

—— 2003. Geographic Politics in the U.S. House of Representatives: Coalition Building and Distribution of Benefits. *American Journal of Political Science*, 47(4): 714–28.

—— 2004. Bicameralism and Geographic Politics: Allocating Funds in the House and Senate. *Legislative Studies Quarterly*, 29(2): 185.

—— and OPPENHEIMER, B. I. 1999. *Sizing Up the Senate: the Unequal Consequences of Equal Representation*. Chicago: University of Chicago Press.

LEVITT, S. D., and SNYDER, JR., J. M. 1995. Political Parties and the Distribution of Federal Outlays. *American Journal of Political Science*, 39: 958–80.

LONDREGAN, J., and SNYDER, J. M. 1994. Comparing Committee and Floor Preferences. *Legislative Studies Quarterly*, 19(2): 233–66.

LOWI, T. J. 1964. American Business, Public Policy, Case-studies, and Political Theory. *World Politics*, 16: 677–715.

MAASS, A. A. 1950. Congress and Water Resources. *American Political Science Review*, 44 (3): 576–93.

—— 1951. *Muddy Waters: The Army's Engineers and the Nation's Rivers*. Cambridge: Harvard University Press.

McCARTY, N., POOLE, K. T., and ROSENTHAL, H. 2008. *Polarized America: The Dance of Ideology and Unequal Riches*. Cambridge, MA: MIT Press.

MALTZMAN, F., and SMITH, S. S. 1994. Principals, Goals, Dimensionality, and Congressional Committees. *Legislative Studies Quarterly*, 19(4): 457–76.

—— —— 1995. Principals, Goals, Dimensionality, and Congressional Committees, pp. 253–72 in *Positive Theories of Congressional Institutions*, ed. K. A. Shepsle and B. R. Weingast. Ann Arbor: University of Michigan Press.

MAYHEW, D. R. 1974. *Congress: The Electoral Connection*. New Haven: Yale University Press.

NIOU, E. M. S., and ORDESHOOK, P. C. 1985. Universalism in Congress. *American Journal of Political Science*, 29: 246–58.

PLOTT, C. 1968. Some Organizational Influences on Urban Renewal Decisions. *American Economic Review*, 58: 306–11.

RAY, BRUCE A. 1980a. Congressional Losers in the U.S. Federal Spending Process. *Legislative Studies Quarterly*, 3: 359–72.

—— 1980b. Congressional Promotion of District Interests: Does Power on the Hill Really Make a Difference? In *Political Benefits*, ed. Barry S. Rundquist. Lexington, MA: Lexington Books.

RICH, M. J. 1989. Distributive Politics and the Allocation of Federal Grants. *American Political Science Review*, 83: 193–213.

RIKER, W. H. 1962. *The Theory of Political Coalitions.* New Haven: Yale University Press.

—— and ORDESHOOK, P. C. 1973. *An Introduction to Positive Political Theory.* Englewood Cliffs, NJ: Prentice-Hall.

ROHDE, D. W. 1991. *Parties and Leaders in the Postreform House.* Chicago: University of Chicago Press.

RUNDQUIST, B. S., and GRIFFITH, D. 1976. An Interrupted Time-series Test of the Distributive Theory of Military Policy-making. *Western Political Quarterly,* 24: 620–6.

—— and CARSEY, T. M. 2002. *Congress and Defense Spending: The Distributive Politics of Military Procurement.* Norman: University of Oklahoma Press.

SAVAGE, J. D. 1991. Saints and Cardinals in Appropriations Committees and the Fight Against Distributive Politics. *Legislative Studies Quarterly,* 16(3): 329–47.

—— 2009. The Administrative Costs of Congressional Earmarking: The Case of the Office of Naval Research. *Public Administration Review,* 69: 448–59.

SHEPSLE, K. A. 1978. *The Giant Jigsaw Puzzle.* Chicago: University of Chicago Press.

—— 1979. Institutional Arrangements and Equilibrium in Multidimensional Voting Models. *American Journal of Political Science,* 23(1): 27–59.

—— and WEINGAST, B. R. 1981. Political Preferences for the Pork Barrel. *American Journal of Political Science,* 25: 96–111.

—— —— 1987. The Institutional Foundations of Committee Power. *American Political Science Review,* 81(1): 85–104.

—— —— 1995. Positive Theories of Congressional Institutions, pp. 5–36 in *Positive Theories of Congressional Institutions,* ed. K. A. Shepsle and B. R. Weingast. Ann Arbor: University of Michigan Press.

—— VAN HOUWELING, R. P., ABRAMS, S. J., and HANSON, P. C. 2009. The Senate Electoral Cycle and Bicameral Appropriations Politics. *American Journal of Political Science,* 53(2): 343.

SNYDER, J. M. 1991. On Buying Legislatures. *Economics and Politics,* 3: 93–109.

SPRAGUE, M. 2008. The Effects of Measurement and Methods and Decisions on Committee Preference Outlier Results. *Political Research Quarterly,* 61(2): 309–18.

STEIN, R. M., and BICKERS, K. N. 1994a. Congressional Elections and the Pork Barrel. *Journal of Politics,* 56(2): 377–99.

—— —— 1994b. Universalism and the Electoral Connection: A Test and some Doubts. *Political Research Quarterly,* 47(2): 295–317.

—— —— 1995. *Perpetuating the Pork Barrel: Policy Subsystems and American Democracy.* New York: Cambridge University Press.

WEINGAST, B. R. 1979. A Rational Choice Perspective on Congressional Norms. *American Journal of Political Science* 23: 245–63.

WEINGAST, B. R. 1994. Reflections on Distributive Politics and Universalism. *Political Research Quarterly,* 47: 319–27.

—— SHEPSLE, K. A., and JOHNSEN, C. 1981. The Political Economy of Benefits and Costs: A Neoclassical Approach to Distributive Politics. *Journal of Political Economy,* 89(4): 642–64.

—— and MARSHALL, W. J. 1988. The Industrial Organization of Congress; Or, Why Legislatures, Like Firms, are Not Organized as Markets. *Journal of Political Economy,* 96(1): 132–63.

WILSON, R. K. 1986. An Empirical Test of Preferences for the Pork Barrel: District-Level Appropriations for Rivers and Harbors Legislation, 1889–1913. *American Journal of Political Science,* 30: 729–54.

CHAPTER 15

....

PUBLIC OPINION AND CONGRESSIONAL POLICY

....

DAVID W. BRADY

THE relationship between public opinion and public policy in the United States is important and much studied. It is both important and studied because in democracies public policy should roughly correspond to what the public desires. There are, however, several problems affecting the nature and extent of our profession's knowledge in this area. One significant problem is how to measure public opinion on specific policy issues. Over the course of the recent healthcare debate in the United States, one could uncover numerous polls claiming that the public favors President Obama's healthcare policy or that the public did not favor the president's healthcare policy. Certainly, question wording and other technical issues can shift public opinion toward or away from a policy. Likewise, how researchers describe the policy in question can affect the results. Clearly, there can be and are measurement problems involved in ascertaining the relationship between public opinion and public policy. A more difficult problem is that there are a number of intervening variables between public opinion and policy results. Interest groups represent business, labor, and various issue publics to the policymakers and political parties aggregate over these interest groups to collect funds, sort preferences, arrange elections, and nominate candidates who run for office on issues concerning public policy as well as perhaps making public policy. Moreover, the very form of American elections, with gerrymandered districts and primaries, structure and shape the relationship between opinion and policy. Many political scientists, as we shall see, have asserted that there is a general relationship between mass opinion and public policy. However, the presence of so many intervening institutions has led many others to question the nature of the relationship. Page and Shapiro (1983), Domhoff (1998) and Burstein and Linton (2002) all raise basic issues regarding the nature of the relationship between opinion and policy. Essentially, the problem is that even if there is a strong correlation between opinion and policy, effective power may lie elsewhere, thus diminishing the democratic connection between opinion and policy.

The nature of the relationship between public opinion and public policy as made by the U.S. Congress is a subset of this important question. How does public opinion affect policymaking by the U.S. Congress? How much does it affect policy and what policies under which conditions? In this chapter I shall try to summarize the profession's understanding of these relationships and conclude that, due to new technologies, the immediate future promises an expansion of our knowledge about opinion and congressional policy. Before beginning this task, it is necessary to deal with the issue of using Congress to study the relationship between opinion and policy.

In the general field of opinion and policy, many believe that political elites within institutions such as interest groups and political parties control the process such that "public" opinion may be correlated with policy results but is relatively unimportant in defining policy. Congress, which is an important maker of public policy, is affected by each of the aforementioned elites within the institutions mentioned above. The question becomes: can we study the relationship between opinion and policy in the Congress or should we focus on political elites elsewhere in the system? I believe Congress is an ideal place to study the relationship, not only because the Congress makes policy but, more importantly, we normally think of Congress as responding to national opinion on policy; thus, the influence relationship is more unidirectional— from opinion to the Congress. Presidents, interest groups through advertising and organizing opinion, and elites à la Zaller (1992) including governing elites, Kernell (1997) and Canes-Wrone, Herrron, et al. (2001), each speak with one voice and have been observed to shift public opinion toward their policy alternative. Congress, in contrast, is most often viewed as a responder to opinion, where members most often seek to earn slack with their constituents so that they might occasionally vote against their wishes. Members are normally seen as explainers of their policy votes, not as public opinion shifters. Thus, in this sense, Congress is a good beginning point for the study of the nature of the relationship between opinion and policy because opinion moves through 435 districts and fifty states and their representatives before policy is made.

It is worth noting that there are cases where individual members have shifted public opinion, for example Joseph McCarthy and Martin Dies on the "communist threat"; however, such cases would appear to be rare. More commonly, Congress affects public opinion on a district by district, state-by-state basis. Howell and Pevehouse (2005) see congressional debate and dissent as shaping public understandings, and Sellers (1965) shows how congressional parties shape media coverage of policy debates. Note, however, in cases where Congress affects opinion, it does so on a district-by-district basis with different voices and in the case of congressional parties, they speak with two voices, often with opposing views. These differ from the case made by the President who normally speaks with a single voice. Yet another way Congress affects public opinion is by its actions, as the recent healthcare policy reform shows. Namely, over the long-drawn-out process, the different cost estimates and the special deals for members like Senator Ben Nelson (Democrat, Nebraska) and pro-life Democrats on federal funding helped turn opinion against reform.

This chapter begins by assessing the general relationship between opinion and policy via the important studies of Stimson and then Erikson, MacKuen, and Wright and their followers. It then turns to the problems associated with determining the effect of intervening elites and institutions on the relationship between opinion and public policy. The final section of the chapter black-boxes the intervening variables and tries to assess the relationship between opinion and policy, citing studies using technical changes in polling and ideal point estimation which show great promise for progress in this area.

Political scientists have asserted that there is a general relationship between mass opinion and public policy. Notably, the work of James Stimson (1999, 2004) on public moods shows that, over time, public opinion shifts between liberal and conservative and that, in general, political party fortunes and presidential elections follow these mood swings—Democrats in liberal moods and Republicans in conservative moods. This approach uses numerous polls and varied questions to ascertain overall left and right responses, foregoing policy specificity for aggregate results. Stimson holds that public opinion is the prime mover of American policy and public opinion is moved by the "scorekeepers" not the "passionate." Scorekeepers are citizens who pay some attention to politics and when they shift their view, policy follows. Public attitudes are global toward government activity, not area specific. Thus, opinions toward race, education welfare, and education policy move together over time. Stimson argues that shifts in congressional voting and presidential position-taking generally follow public moods. In the same vein, Erikson, McIver, and Wright (1993, 2006) and Stimson, MacKuen, and Erikson (1995) among others have also argued that public opinion moves policy in either a liberal or conservative direction through elections and dynamically.

The most common mechanism through which public opinion moves policies is elections, in which there is a large turnover in congressional seats. The turnover in congressional and Senate seats when associated with a change in the governing party has, in the past, generated sweeping policy changes. The Civil War, the 1890s, and the New Deal eras are all examples of large seat shifts, government change, and major policy shifts. Brady (1988) shows how such seat shifts change the congressional preference distribution so as to allow new policy results. However, our records of the polls during these historical eras are not accurate enough to measure public opinion; thus, the direct ties to policy change have to be inferred. The one case where we have opinion data and major change was the 1964 election, which gave one party control of government with majorities sufficient to pass pathbreaking legislation on civil rights and Medicare, among other legislation. Moreover, the decisive votes for those policies came from the new members (Brady and Sinclair 1984). No election since 1964 has given either party sufficient control to guarantee the ability to dramatically change policy. The result is that significant legislation is passed not in clusters but in a more staccato fashion, as is found in Mayhew (1991). Overall responsiveness to opinion varies by institution and by state. Moreover, the analysis of "government as a whole" shows that policy responds dynamically to public opinion change. The work by Stimson, Erikson, et al. is largely responsible for the profession's generally held view that public opinion and public policy are, in fact, related.

One reason the profession has come to see these studies as determinative is because they have, over time, solved a series of causal issues. In regard to causality, the original Miller and Stokes (1963) study of representation was causally ambiguous— were citizens influencing Congress or vice versa? Erikson (1978) made progress on this issue by using district demographic data to simulate citizen policy preferences, thus lowering the probability that the influence from policy to opinion was confounding the estimates. Wright, Erikson, and McIver (1987) and Erikson, Wright, and McIver (1993) used public opinion in the states to reduce the possibility of redistricting as a determinative variable in confounding the opinion–policy relationship. Finally, Stimson, MacKuen, and Erikson (1995) and Stimson (1999, 2004) use time series analysis to determine the causal order of the relationship, essentially showing that shifts in citizen preferences toward government yield governmental responses aligned roughly with citizen preferences. The partial resolution of the causal issue over time is an important reason why this set of scholars' work dominates our profession's views of the relationship between public opinion and public policy.

While these approaches have the advantage of a large number of survey responses and can ascertain general opinion over a sixty-year-plus time period, they can for some scholars only point to a general association between opinion and policy. There is in this research the use of a left–right continuum based on answers to questions indicating whether citizens prefer liberal or conservative policies, and the overall results confirm a general relationship between public opinion, elections, and policy results. Over the last few decades, there have been attempts to extract poll questions from congressional votes on policy and to convert the votes to questions administered to a random sample of citizens. These studies gain in specificity what the "mood" studies have in the aggregate; however, due to several issues, notably different policy spaces, the generalizability of the results across policy areas is at question. We will return to these studies in the final section of the chapter.

Most political scientists would agree that the previously cited work of Stimson, Erikson, McIver, and Wright clearly shows a connection between public opinion and the direction of policy. The over-time nature of these studies and the sheer number of respondents are their strength because it allows them to evaluate opinion switches from left to right or vice versa with general policy shifts over time, for example during 1963–68, a liberal period, or 1978–90, a conservative period in elections and policy. The work does not allow us to say much about the connection between specific policies and/or broad policies, such as healthcare coverage or American defense spending. In order to explain healthcare or defense spending policy, we must be clear on what polling studies of those issues mean. Polling is a strange mixture of the science of sampling theory and the art of asking questions to objectively gain knowledge of American opinion. It is well established that question wording and placement can dramatically affect respondents' choices. Moreover, the same public opinion polls can reveal different truths to different scholars. Two examples of this problem follow.

The first is the differences between polls showing support for or opposition to the Obama healthcare proposals and their differing interpretation of which groups supported reform. Across a set of polls, the following claims were made: "sixty-seven percent of those under 30 favor the plan while 56 percent of those over 65 are opposed" (Rasmussen, Aug. 11, 2009). "Apart from Democrats, support for healthcare reform is highest among women, lower income Americans, those with post-graduate degrees, and residents of the East" (Gallup, Sept. 8, 2009). Political party, age, education, gender, income, and several other characteristics were said to drive opinion on healthcare policy. However carefully done, such polls suffer from three limitations. First, polls are often not clear on what reform is being considered. More importantly, few polls estimate the cost of reform, and third, most report bivariate statistics to ascertain group support. Since variables like age and income and gender and political party are correlated, such comparisons do not reveal which characteristics are most determinative of their opinion. Scholars studying the relation between opinion and policy need to ascertain results which avoid these three problems. Otherwise, which poll one reads can affect the overall assessment of how opinion and policy are related.

Hacker and Pierson (2006), regarded public opinion on the Bush 2001 tax cuts as a prime example of how the Republican party, the Republican Congress, and the president had used institutional arrangements to thwart majority opinion. Craig Volden and I (2006) concluded that the Senate median voters, Mac Baucus (Democrat, Montana) and Charles Grassley (Rebublican, Iowa), had read the public opinion tea-leaves quite well and shifted the president's proposed tax cut policy to the left by reducing the amount of the tax cut, delaying the timing of the cuts and, after a decade, eliminating them. Regardless of who is correct, the point is that the relationships between poll results and institutions drove us to two very different conclusions regarding the relation between public opinion and policy in the case of the Bush 2001 tax cuts. Which of us is correct? The answer to who is correct lies in the nature of the variables intervening between opinion and policy and in the nature of the causal connection between opinion and policy. These are broad and important questions to which we now turn.

While it seems clear that public opinion influences policy in the ways asserted by Stimson, Erikson, et al. (1995, 2006) and others, what this means for democratic theory is still undecided. Stimson, MacKuen, and Erickson (1995) argue that democracy works as was intended—translated in the case of Congress to mean members of Congress consistently measure and evaluate public opinion and just as consistently respond to public opinion. In their studies of American states, Erikson, Wright, and McIver's (1993) impressive results lead them to claim that the relationship between opinion and policy in the states is "awesome." Wlezien (1996), Page (1994), and

Ringquist, Hill, et al. (1997) all state similar claims about the strong relationship between opinion and policy direction.

When the policy under consideration is important to the public, that is, citizens care, there is evidence that officials, including members of Congress, are held accountable for their views. Canes-Wrone, Brady, and Cogan (2002), Canes-Wrone, Brady, et al. (2004), Arnold (1990), and Lindaman and Haider-Markel (2002) all demonstrate the strength of this relationship. Thus, there is evidence that issue salience is related to officials' policy responsiveness. How strong is this relationship, how many issues are salient and has the relationship changed over time are all questions without clear answers. Hansen (1991) and Clemens (1997) argue that due to improvements in communication and information, the connection between citizen opinion and elected officials has improved. Geer (1991) argues that polls increase politicians' knowledge of citizens' preferences. By contrast, Markoff (1996) argues that the public's views are quite often ignored, and Jacobs (2000) argues that the influence of public opinion on policy has declined over time because politicians have learned how to skirt accountability. They date this decline to the early 1970s and Haskell (2001) claims that television and new political strategy led to the decline in American trust in their government. Fiorina (2009) makes a strong case that centrist public opinion is not represented in Congress and its policies. In sum, there is agreement that Congress is responsive to public opinion in that there is at least a correlation between opinion and policy and that salience seems to matter. However, on the magnitude and direction of the relationship, there is not agreement, as is the case for ascertaining the strength of the relationship over time.

The complicated nature of the relationship between public opinion and policy results, with elections, interest groups, parties, and primaries intervening can best be shown via a median voter analysis. Implicitly, the median voter's opinion ought to be where public policy is located given democratic theory because the public opinion median is the true pivotal voter. Figure 15.1 shows an example where the median voter representing public opinion and public policy through Congress and congressional parties are perfectly matched.

In this case the Republican district elects a slightly rightist candidate (10), the Democratic district a slightly leftist candidate (2) while District 2 elects the median

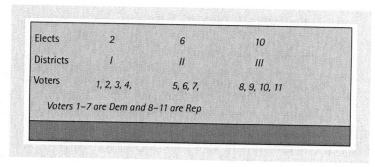

Fig. 15.1. Median legislator matches public

in its district (6). The three person legislature thus is composed of members with preferences for 2, 6, and 10 over, say, the number of private healthcare insurers to be allowed. Under median voter theory in the legislature the policy is thus 6 private insurers.

What institutional factors intervening between public opinion and policy could give us policy results in this case different from 6? There could be a strong gate-keeping committee system when the healthcare committee has 2 and 6 on it, thus resulting in a policy proposal of, say, 4.5 and suppose the Rule Committee is also composed of 2 and 6 which reports out a rule which requires voting on a 4.5 proposal either up or down. In this case, even though the median voter in the populace and the median in the legislature is a 6, the policy result would be 4.5, depending on the status quo policy (i.e. if the status quo is 7.5 or greater). (See Weingast and Marshall 1988.) Similarly, imagine that the parties in Figure 15.1 are now 1 through 6 Democrat and 7 through 11 Republican. If stronger parties à la Rohde (1991), Aldrich and Rohde (2000), Aldrich (1995), and Cox and McCubbins (2006) exist, then the policy result varies somewhat depending on the theory but all are left of the true median in the populace and the floor median due to party effects. In short, party leaders have sufficient power to move centrist party members to accept either the party median or something shifted toward the party median.

Figure 15.2 shows how parties can also use electoral districting to yield a legislative median different from the public opinion median.

Voters 1–6 are Democrats and 8 through 10 are Republicans and District I elects either 2 or 5 and District III elects either 9 or 10. In this case the median legislator is a 4 while the public opinion median is still 6 private insurers. Moreover, one can easily see how if the relevant committee is composed of 2 and 4, the policy result is a 3 while opinion favors 6. That congressional districts are drawn to advantage political parties is not in question; however, it is not clear that over the fifty states, there are systematic disadvantages to one party (Brady and Grofman 1991). But even if one party is not generically favored by redistricting across the fifty states, the tendency towards election of more extreme legislators may result. When such factors as primary vote turnout are added to the equation, electoral results may further exacerbate the election of left and right of center legislators. Thus, a political institution, partisan districting, combines with motivated voters in primaries to elect candidates out of line with citizen views.

Elects	2	4	10
District	I	II	III
Public Opinion	(1, 2, 5, 6)	(3, 4, 7)	(8, 9, 10, 11)

Fig. 15.2. Median voter not represented due to redistricting

Another issue is voter intensity. Imagine that an interest group favoring more private insurers organizes its voters to attend to business and get out the vote. Here, even with the districts drawn to favor Democrats, if only voters favoring 6 or more bother to vote, then District I elects 6, District II elects 7, and District III elects a representative favoring 8 or above, yielding a new legislative median of 7, right of the public opinion median of 6.

These examples could be elaborated on but suffice it for our purposes to show that even when we *know* the exact public opinion median, electoral, partisan, and commitment variables can yield results that differ from the public opinion choice. While the examples used above all show institutional and salience variables moving policy away from median opinion, surely there are cases where these institutions combine to yield median opinion policies. One can even imagine cases where public opinion favors 6, the committee system favors 4, but either the Rules Committee or a House–Senate conference restore 6 as the policy. In short, the institutions and elites can distort public policy toward as well as away from the public. Before the question of what is the effect of institutional arrangements as interveners between opinion and congressional policy can be fully answered, congressional scholars will have to resolve a whole series of problems. Among the most important are: are congressional parties simply composed of members with preferences or are parties as organizations endogenous actors who affect policy results? The argument between Krehbiel (1991, 1998), Aldrich and Rohde (2000), and Cox and McCubbins (2006) seems far from resolved. Do "special" interests dominate the electoral and lobbying process so as to sufficiently move policy in their direction regardless of which party is in power? And, again, sometimes special interests may move policy toward the public median for whatever reason. Do House and Senate procedures and rules, such as House Rules Committee restricted rules or the Senate's filibuster rule XXII, consistently distort policy results away from the public opinion median? Are committees in the Congress comprised of preference outliers à la Weingast and Marshall (1988) or are the important committees representative of the body as a whole, à la Krehbiel (1991)? Again, definitive answers to these questions do not seem to be forthcoming (Sprague 2008), thus hampering our ability to either confirm or put to rest the questions raised by Page and Shapiro (1983) and others.

If we are not at this point capable of solving these intervening institutional distortion issues, it does not mean that no progress is possible. Congressional scholars are working on all the issues raised above and as they make progress, the nature of the relationship between opinion, institutions, and policy will become clearer. However, for the moment let us simply black-box the institutions intervening between public median opinion and policy and turn to the question of the nature of public opinion and policy results. Here the concern is to begin by accurately measuring public opinion in relation to the policy under consideration.

Even without the institutional variables intervening in the relationship between opinion polls and policy results, there are considerable problems to be overcome. It is critical for the study of mass opinion and policy that public opinion must be measured as precisely as possible and designed for the specified policy area. The approach taken herein is to begin with an example of a careful study of public opinion in one clearly defined policy area and then to move to other approaches such as those starting with the policy area in government and then polling, using questions generated by the policy.

Bartels' (1991) study of public opinion and defense spending during the Reagan era is exemplary in that he carefully measures public opinion on the defense build-up in the Reagan 1981 budget and matches that by using a Krehbiel and Rivers (1988) technique to estimate representatives' positions on an underlying defense spending policy dimension. He uses three related votes: first, an amendment to reduce defense appropriations, then the appropriations bill itself, and, finally, the conference report reconciling House–Senate differences. Then, using the 1980 National Election Study question on defense spending, Bartels proceeds to show the effect of public opinion in the dyadic relation for the 100 plus districts in the sample and the aggregate effects over all representatives. Bartels estimates that every one point increase or decrease in mean constituency opinion results in a $13 billion defense preference for the representative. The analysis is also able to show that strong *aggregate* constituency demand for increased defense spending added an increase of $17 billion (about a 10 percent increase) to defense appropriations. Moreover, the effect was largely independent of specific political circumstances.

In this piece, we have a very clear statement that public opinion affects public policy in a specific policy area by a specified amount. Why, then, don't we have this study extended across many different areas, such as taxes, healthcare, welfare, agricultural assistance and so forth? The answer is that in these other areas the data on both the public opinion side and the representatives' voting side of the problem are not as available and clear. Public opinion favoring defense spending went from highly negative in the early and mid-1970s to 40 to 50 points positive within three years and then by 1983 back down to negative numbers—the peaking effect does not exist for many policy areas. Public opinion favoring healthcare reform or opinion estimating satisfaction with personal healthcare moves very slowly over time (Jacobs 1993) and in 1993–94, there were no votes on the Clinton healthcare plan since no legislation made it out of committee. That is, in 1994 since there was no healthcare policy voted on, one could not directly show the correspondence between opinion and policy using roll-call votes. Similar problems emerge in other policy areas, making it difficult to duplicate Bartels' excellent study. This unique combination of the 1980 NES question and the voting segments in the Congress on defense matters under Bartels' sure hand generated a first-rate study hard to duplicate because survey questions and congressional votes sufficient to analyze the connection between opinion and policy are often not present.

Bartels' work set a standard for evaluating the relationship between public opinion and public policy. Scholars have used two distinct methods to ascertain relationships between opinion and policy. The first follows Bartels and utilizes extant public surveys and carefully, à la Bartels, controls for faults in the data to adequately measure opinion on policy issues. The second method is to look at policy issues before the Congress, the president, and the courts and translate those issues into questions that can be asked of a random sample of the American public. These studies have been aided by internet surveys which allow the researcher to dramatically increase the numbers in the sample. Expanded numbers of respondents more accurately assess mass opinion trends and aid research trying to ascertain the dyadic relationship between members and opinion in their district or state by increasing the number of respondents in congressional districts and states. The use of polls with increased numbers across districts have made contributions to the study of mass opinion and public policy and, in my view, will be largely responsible for the progress made in this area in the next decade.

Careful analysis of what the public thinks is crucial to understanding congressional responsiveness. One aspect of such measurement not often mentioned in the existing literature is that much of public policy is about providing public goods, such as cleaner air, better healthcare, more or less defense, clean water, and so on. Such goods carry a cost, which is either ignored in the polling or it is treated as an afterthought. Respondents, for example, will overwhelmingly favor cleaner air, or water, or more people being covered for healthcare if such goods are seen as freely provided. Introducing cost reduces the percentage favoring the good; however, a researcher can still affect the percentages by stipulating a lower or higher cost. Economists working in the environmental area developed the contingent valuation technique to more accurately measure public opinion on these complicated issues (Mitchell and Carson 1989). Recently, the technique has been expanded to cover areas such as healthcare. Roughly speaking, the technique validates the claim that as the cost of the policy increases, the support for it declines (Carson and Hanemann 2005). This seems to be directly related to how Congress itself perceives the issue.

This technique is important because one could interpret the failure of the 1993–94 Clinton plan for healthcare reform as the result of lobbying by vested interests or mismanagement of the issue by the Clintons, or clever advertising by insurance companies. These claims all hinge, in some sense, on the polls showing that Americans initially favored reform; thus, the lack of reform is surely attributable to some reason other than that the public was not willing to pay. But Jacobs, Shapiro, and Shulman (1993) show how public opinion on healthcare can be affected by asking respondents about tradeoffs. When asked in 1990, 1991, and 1992 if they would rather pay less for medical care but wait longer to get it, or pay more and get it right away, about 80 percent said pay more (Jacobs, Shapiro, and Shulman 1993, 424). Moreover, a 1991 Gallup poll reported 88 percent of respondents were very or somewhat satisfied with the quality of healthcare they received. An Associated Press poll in 1993 found that only 26 percent of respondents were willing to pay $250 or less in increased taxes to support universal coverage. Surely these results need to be accounted for before making blanket statements about the failure of health reform reflecting a failure of responsiveness to public opinion. Bundorf and Fuchs (2007) and Blendon and Benson (2001) have argued that healthcare has failed because voters do not wish to pay for it, and Kessler and Brady (2009), using contingent valuation, show that mass opinion does not favor major reform even when priced at 50 percent of real baseline cost. Such results suggest that mass opinion may, in fact, correspond to no change from the status quo. And as legislation moves through Congress, members' votes shift depending upon various factors. Anyone following the recent healthcare debate could clearly see how representatives' and Senators' support for healthcare waxed and waned, given, among other things, cost estimates. Democrats from conservative districts and states could not support the public option because it was seen as too liberal for the district or state. Those from liberal districts or states had no problem supporting the option. And as is often the case, the House passes more extreme legislation—eight of ten of Gingrich's Contract with America and the public option in 2009—while Senators representing a more diverse set of interests vote more moderately—rejected most of the Contract with America and the public option. Such over-time variation in both public opinion and yes/no votes can be tracked given new technology in polling and estimating congressional votes.

The rise of internet polling due to the high cost of individual surveys and the high turndown rate of telephone surveys has allowed researchers to significantly increase the number of respondents, at reasonable prices. With the creation of the Cooperative Congressional Election Studies project (CCES), most congressional scholars have access to internet surveys with 33,000 respondents, and this increased size allows for better studies of representative-constituent relationships in dyads and in overall correspondence between citizen opinion and policy. In a 2007 study, Joseph Bafumi and Michael Herron use Bayesian estimation techniques in the tradition of Clinton, Jackman, and Rivers (2004) and Bafumi, Gelman, et al. (2005) to estimate ideal points for legislators. They then estimate ideal points for voters in constituencies. They carefully use data to construct a common policy space for the president, Senators, representatives and a representative sample of voters.[1] They ask the CCES sample to take positions on roll-call votes as if they were members of Congress. The survey included questions based on actual roll calls in the 109th and 110th Congresses. Having located voters in the same policy space with Senators, House members, and the president, they show that the median American voter was well represented by House and Senate chamber medians after the 2006 congressional elections. Prior to the elections of 2006, the median American voter was not well represented. This important study not only shows how elections adjust the relationship between voters and congressional preferences but they also establish a paradigm for such studies. This same study analyzes median voters across all states, shows how they are represented in Congress, and shows how congressional districts aggregate preferences. The study finds distortions in representation associated with party politics at both state and district levels. Konisky, Milyo, and Richardson (2008) used the CCES to compare public attitudes across twelve environmental issues and the results show differences in support for government intervention across issues and geographic scale.

The next step would be to carefully assess the relation of these public preferences to congressional voting and ultimately policy. In a similar vein, Ansolabehere and Jones (2006) utilize a specific internet survey to deal with the question of whether

[1] These new estimation techniques allowing analysis in a common policy space are, with increased sample size, the two phenomena which yield progress in the opinion–policy arena.

perceived citizen agreement with their representatives voting record translate into support for the member of Congress. They establish that voters have preferences over questions before the legislature and have beliefs about how their representatives voted and evaluate based on the level of perceived agreement. The most important finding is that political party matters for representation of issues because the content of party brand labels indicate representatives' party positions. In sum, the creation of CCES gives us a vehicle to set the relevant actors—Representatives, Senators, and voters—in the same policy space, allowing much more precise answers to questions of how policy results and voter opinion are related and to the disparity between overall representation—median voter to chamber or party median—and the relationship between representatives and voters in the dyadic district case. While these new surveys make it more feasible to accurately assess aggregate and district opinion toward issues, there is also a need to use consistent measure over time. Without such consistency, it will be difficult to determine whether policy moves follow or lead opinion moves. The hope is that CCES will continue over time and ask consistent questions sufficient to determine over-time patterns.

Accurate measures of public opinion combined with policy-specific questions generated from actual congressional policy options will take us a long way toward answers to the question of the nature of the relationship between opinion and policy. Having all the actors in the same policy space does not totally resolve the issue of how intervening variables, such as interest groups, parties, and salience and voter turnout, affect the relationship between public opinion and congressional policymaking. However, knowing the median opinion and the House and Senate floor, party and committee medians gives us the broad picture. With such measures reasonably accurately derived (much improved over the past), the effect of elections, parties, committees, and interest groups on the relationship between public opinion and congressional policy-making will be more tractable. The person selected to write this chapter in the next Oxford series will have, fortuitously, a more certain knowledge base from which to draw.

References

ALDRICH, J. 1995. Why Parties? The Origin and Transformation of Political Parties in America. Chicago, IL: University of Chicago Press.

ALDRICH, J. H., and ROHDE, D. W. 2000. The Republican Revolution and the House Appropriations Committee. Journal of Politics, 62 (1) (Feb.): 1–33.

ANSOLABEHERE, S., and JONES, P. 2006. Constituents' Policy Perceptions and Approval of Members of Congress. CCES Working Paper 06-01 (.pdf 205KB).

ARNOLD, R. D. 1990. The Logic of Congressional Action. New Haven, CT: Yale University Press.

BAFUMI, J., and HERRON, M. C. 2007. Preference Aggregation, Representation, and Elected American Political Institutions. CCES Working Paper 07-10 (.pdf 1MB).

——GELMAN, A., PARK, D. K., and KAPLAN, N. 2005. Practical Issues in Implementing and Understanding Bayesian Ideal Point Estimation. Political Analysis, 13: 171–87.

BARTELS, L. M. 1991. Constituency Opinion and Congressional Policy Making: The Reagan Defense Buildup. *American Political Science Review*, 85: 457–74.

BLENDON, R. J., and BENSON, J. M. 2001. Americans' Views on Health Policy: A Fifty-Year Historical Perspective. *Health Affairs*, 20(2): 33–46.

BRADY, D. 1988. *Critical Elections and Congressional Policy Making*. Stanford: Stanford University Press.

——and SINCLAIR, B. 1984. Building Majorities for Policy Change in the House of Representatives. *Journal of Politics*, 46(4): 1033–60.

——and GROFMAN, B. 1991. Sectional Differences in Partisan Bias and Electoral Responsiveness in US House Elections, 1850–1980. *British Journal of Political Science*, 1(2) (April): 247–56.

——and VOLDEN, C. 2006. *Revolving Gridlock: Politics and Policy from Jimmy Carter to George W. Bush*. Boulder, CO: Westview Press.

BUNDORF, M. K., and FUCHS, V. R. 2007. Public Support for National Health Insurance: The Roles of Attitudes and Beliefs. *Frontiers in Health Policy Research*, 10(1).

BURSTEIN, P., and LINTON, A. 2002. The Impact of Political Parties, Interest Groups, and Social Movement Organizations on Public Policy. *Social Forces*, 81: 380–408.

CANES-WRONE, B., HERRON, M. C., and SHOTTS, K. W. 2001. Leadership and Pandering: A Theory of Executive Policy Making. *American Journal of Political Science*, 45(3): 532–50.

——BRADY, D. W., and COGAN, J. F. 2002. Out of Step, Out of Office: Electoral Accountability and House Members' Voting. *American Political Science Review*, 96(1): 127–40.

——and SHOTTS, K. W. 2004. The Conditional Nature of Presidential Responsiveness to Public Opinion. *American Journal of Political Science*, 48(4): 690–706.

CARSON, R. T., and HANEMANN, W. M. 2005. Contingent Valuation. Ch. 7, p. 897 in *Handbook of Environmental Economics*, ed. K. G. Maler and J. R. Vincent. Amsterdam: Elsevier.

CLEMENS, E. S. 1997. *The People's Lobby: Organizational Innovation and the Rise of Interest Group Politics in the United States, 1890–1925*. Chicago: University of Chicago Press.

CLINTON, J., JACKMAN, S., and RIVERS, D. 2004. The Statistical Analysis of Roll Call Data. *American Political Science Review*, 98(2): 355–70.

COX, G. W., and McCUBBINS, M. D. 1993, 2006. *Legislative Leviathan: Party Government in the House*, 2nd edn. Cambridge: Cambridge University Press.

DOMHOFF, G. W. 1998. *Who Rules America: Power and Politics in the Year 2000*. Mountain View, CA: Mayfield.

ERIKSON, R. 1978. Constituency Opinion and Congressional Behavior: A Reexamination of the Miller–Stokes Representation Data. *American Journal of Political Science*, 22(3): 511–35.

——WRIGHT, JR., G. C., and McIVER, J. P. 1993. *Statehouse Democracy: Public Opinion and Policy in the American States*. New York: Cambridge University Press.

——MacKUEN, M. B., and STIMSON, J. A. 2006. Public Opinion and Congressional Policy: A Macro-Level Perspective, pp. 79–95 in *The Macropolitics of Congress*, ed. S. Adler and J. Lapinski. Chicago: University of Chicago Press.

——WRIGHT, G. C., and McIVER, J. P. 2006. Public Opinion in the States: A Quarter Century of Change and Stability. Ch. 9, pp. 209–24 in *Public Opinion in State Politics*, ed. J. Cohen. Stanford: Stanford University Press.

FIORINA, M., with ABRAMS, S. 2009. *Disconnect: The Breakdown of Representation in American Politics*. Norman, Oklahoma: University of Oklahoma Press.

GEER, J. G. 1991. Critical Realignments and the Public Opinion Poll. *Journal of Politics*, 53: 434–53.

HACKER, J. S., and PIERSON, P. 2006. *Off Center: The Republican Revolution and the Erosion of American Democracy*. New Haven, CT: Yale University Press.

HANSEN, J. M. 1991. *Gaining Access: Congress and the Farm Lobby, 1919–1981*. Chicago: University of Chicago Press.

HASKELL, J. 2001. *Direct Democracy or Representative Government?* Boulder, CO: Westview Press.

HAYS, S. P., ESLER, M., and HAYS, C. E. 1996. Environmental Commitment Among the States. *Publius: The Journal of Federalism*, 26: 41–58.

HILLYGUS, D. S., and SHIELDS, T. G. 2008. *The Persuadable Voter: Wedge Issues in Presidential Campaigns*. Princeton, NJ: Princeton University Press.

HOWELL, W., and PEVEHOUSE, J. 2005. Presidents, Congress and the Use of Force. *International Organization*, 59(1): 209–32.

JACOBS, L. R. 1993. *The Health of Nations: Public Opinion and the Making of American and British Health Policy*. Ithaca, NY: Cornell University Press.

—— 2000. *Politicians Don't Pander: Political Manipulation and the Loss of Democratic Responsiveness*. Chicago: University of Chicago Press.

—— SHAPIRO, R.Y., and SHULMAN, E.C. 1993. The Polls—Poll Trends—Medical Card in the United State—An Update. *Public Opinion Quarterly*, 57(3): 394–427.

—— and SHAPIRO, R. Y. 1997. Debunking the Pandering Politician Myth. *Public Perspective*, 8 (April/May): 3–5.

JONES, B. D. 1994. *Reconceiving Decision-making in Democratic Politics*. Chicago: University of Chicago Press.

KERNELL, S. 1997 [2006]. *Going Public: New Strategies for Presidential Leadership*. Congressional Quarterly Press.

KESSLER, D., and BRADY, D. 2009. Putting the Public's Money Where Its Mouth Is. *Health Affairs*, August 2009: 917–25.

KITSCHELT, HERBERT. 1994. *The Transformation of European Social Democracy*. Cambridge: Cambridge University Press.

KONISKY, D. M., MILYO, J., and RICHARDSON, L. E. 2008. Environmental Policy Attitudes: Issues, Geographical Scale, and Political Trust. *Social Science Quarterly*, 89(5): 1066–85.

KREHBIEL, K. 1990. Are Congressional Committees Composed of Preference Outliers? *American Political Science Review*, 84: 149–63.

—— 1991. *Information and Legislative Organization*. University of Michigan Press.

—— 1998. *Pivotal Politics: A Theory of U.S. Lawmaking*. Chicago: University of Chicago Press.

—— and RIVERS, D. 1988. The Analysis of Committee Power: An Application to Senate Voting on the Minimum Wage. *American Journal of Political Science*, 32(4) (November): 1151–74.

LINDAMAN, K., and HAIDER-MARKEL, D. P. 2002. Issue Evolution, Political Parties, and the Culture Wars. *Political Research Quarterly*, 55: 91–110.

MARKOFF, J. 1996. *Waves of Democracy: Social Movements and Political Change*. Thousand Oaks, CA: Pine Forge Press.

MAYHEW, D. 1991. *Divided We Govern: Party Control, Lawmaking and Investigation 1946–1990*. New Haven, CT: Yale University Press.

MILLER, W., and STOKES, D. 1963. Constituency Influence in Congress. *American Political Science Review*, 57(1): 45–56.

MITCHELL, R., and CARSON, R. 1989. Using Surveys to Value Public Goods: The Contingent Valuation Method, pp. 117–18 in *Resources for the Future*.

PAGE, B. I. 1994. Democratic Responsiveness? Untangling the Links Between Public Opinion and Policy. *PS: Political Science and Politics*, 27: 25–9.

—— and SHAPIRO, R. Y. 1983. Effects of Public Opinion on Policy. *American Political Science Review*, 77: 175–90.

RINGQUIST, E. J., HILL, K. Q., LEIGHLEY, J. E., and HINTON-ANDERSSON, A. 1997. Lower-class Mobilization and Policy Linkage in the U.S. States: A Correction. *American Journal of Political Science*, 41: 339–44.

ROHDE, D. 1991. *Parties and Leaders in the Postreform House*. Chicago: University of Chicago Press.

——1995. *Why Parties? The Origin and Transformation of Political Parties in America*. Chicago: University of Chicago Press.

RUSSETT, B. 1990–1. Doves, Hawks and U.S. Public Opinion. *Political Science Quarterly*, 105(4): 515–38.

SELLERS, C. 1965. The Equilibrium Cycle in Two Party Politics. *Public Opinion Quarterly*, 29(1): 16–38.

SPRAGUE, M. 2008. The Effects of Measurement and Methods Decisions on Committee Preference Outlier Results. *Political Research Quarterly*, 61(2): 309–18.

STIMSON, J A. 1999. *Public Opinion in America: Moods, Cycles, and Swings*, 2nd edn. Boulder, CO: Westview Press.

——2004. *Tides of Consent: How Public Opinion Shapes American Politics*. New York: Cambridge University Press.

——MACKUEN, M. B., and ERIKSON, R. S. 1995. Dynamic Representation. *American Political Science Review*, 89: 543–65.

TOLBERT, C. J., BOWEN, D. C., and DONOVAN, T. 2009. Initiative Campaigns: Direct Democracy and Voter Mobilization. *American Politics Research*, 37(1): 155–92.

WEINGAST, B., and MARSHALL. 1988. The Industrial Organization of Congress: or, Why Legislatures, Like Firms, Are Not Organized as Markets. *Journal of Political Economy*, 96(February): 132–68.

WRIGHT, G., ERIKSON, R. S., and McIVER, J. P. 1987. Public Opinion and Policy Liberalism in the American States. *American Journal of Political Science*, 31: 980–1001.

WLEZIAN, C. 1996. Dynamics of Representation: The Case of US Spending on Defence. *British Journal of Political Science*, 26: 81–103.

ZALLER, J. R. 1992. *The Nature and Origins of Mass Opinion*. New York: Cambridge University Press.

CHAPTER 16

....

PUBLIC
EVALUATIONS
OF CONGRESS

....

JOHN D. GRIFFIN

INTRODUCTION

....

IN July 2008, only one in seven Americans (14 percent) approved of the job Congress was doing, the lowest congressional job approval rating in the thirty-four years that the Gallup Organization has asked Americans this question. The most recent Gallup figures, for February 2010, were not much better (18 percent approving). Charged with the task of explaining this, it is tempting to point to short-term factors such as high unemployment, the mortgage crisis, concerns about healthcare reform, and congressional scandals. Undoubtedly, these idiosyncratic factors played a role in driving down congressional approval, but there are likely longer-term, systemic factors at work as well.

This chapter first discusses how evaluations of Congress as an institution and individual Members of Congress have changed over time. Then, it compares Americans' approval of Congress and their approval of other national governmental institutions to assess the degree to which congressional approval is unique. It then compares Americans' evaluations of Congress to evaluations of other legislatures in the United States and in other countries. The chapter then discusses the consequences of congressional evaluations, both for political elites and average citizens. Finally, the chapter explores several potential reforms affecting congressional approval.

CHANGE IN CONGRESSIONAL EVALUATIONS OVER TIME

Given the low current level of congressional approval, coupled with other widely held impressions about Americans' declining interest and trust in governing institutions, it is tempting to assume that congressional approval has declined over time. However, looking at the trend in congressional approval over time, what is most striking is not the existence of a linear trend, but, rather, the considerable *volatility* in congressional approval. The earliest approval data come from Harris Polling, but other surveys revealing similar patterns have been conducted by the American National Election Studies and the Gallup Organization. The Harris series, which began in 1963, found that at that point in time congressional approval was in the low 30s (on a 0–100 scale). Approval rose above 60 percent after the 1964 election, then fell steadily until 1979, when it bottomed out at 13 percent. Thereafter, it rose to more than 30 percent in the early 1980s, and more than 50 percent in the mid-1980s before eroding to 28 percent in 1992 just before the Democrats lost control of Congress. Approval rose to more than 50 percent in 2000 and over 60 percent in 2002 after the events of September 11; before falling into the 40s in 2004. According to various polling sources, congressional approval had fallen into the mid to high 20s when the Republicans lost control of both chambers of Congress in November 2006. In 2008, approval fell into the teens, where it remained through 2009 and 2010. So, it would be incorrect, or at least premature, to conclude that the currently low levels of congressional approval indicate that we have reached the end of a long downward trend in approval. Instead, congressional approval over the past half century has risen and fallen, often rather dramatically and often very quickly.

What drives congressional approval? When scholars seek to identify the factors that affect change in aggregate congressional approval over time, they tend to focus on economic conditions, the country's involvement in military conflict, and presidential approval (Stimson 2004). For example, James Stimson argues that public approval of Congress is a byproduct of the public's evaluation of how well things in the country are going (2004). For example when the economy is growing, Stimson argues, the public forms a generically positive orientation toward government institutions, including Congress. When the economy reverses, so does generic approval, including congressional approval. Two other studies build on this basic claim. After accounting for presidential popularity, divided government, and various types of congressional media coverage, one study found that the unemployment rate strongly affects public confidence in Congress, but not Congress' job approval (Patterson and Caldeira 1990). Consumer sentiment matters little for either of these. It explains these seemingly incongruous results as follows: "Americans do not think of Congress as the place where economic fates are decided" (Patterson and Caldeira 1990, 39). Finally, an analysis of the effect of the economy on congressional approval by Rudolph (2002) observed that citizens' evaluations of Congress are affected much more by "egocentric," or personal, financial factors, than by "sociotropic," or global, assessments of the health of the economy.

Congress has limited influence over the state of the economy and the country's involvement in foreign conflicts, even as these factors evidently have a major impact on congressional approval. Emphasizing that there are factors within Congress' control that also affect its approval, Durr, Gilmour, and Wolbrecht (1997) show that congressional approval declines when it passes major legislation, when it attempts veto overrides, and when it bickers. At the aggregate level, there is also evidence that these non-policy factors influence attitudes toward Congress. These authors, among others, show an effect of certain scandals on public approval of Congress, while Herrick (2003) shows that *New York Times* coverage of congressional ethics investigations depresses support for Congress. Finally, recent work from Ramirez (2009) finds an effect of partisan conflict on congressional approval. Specifically, it shows that during the period 1974 to 2000, and accounting for many other factors, congressional approval decreased the more often that 75 percent of Democrats opposed 75 percent of Republicans on the average roll-call vote.

Another significant factor affecting congressional approval only emerges when we seek to understand individual citizens' approval of Congress. Namely, one of the most striking factors affecting approval is sharing the party affiliation of the congressional majority (Citrin 1974; Patterson, Ripley, and Quinlan 1992). According to the ANES data, 40 percent of Democratic identifiers (including leaners) approved of Congress just before the 1980 election (when the Democrats controlled both the House and Senate), while just 29 percent of Republican identifiers approved. After two years of Republican Senate control, approval among Republicans rose to 39 percent while approval among Democrats fell to 34 percent. Just before the 1988 election, two years after the Democrats regained Senate control, 58 percent of Democratic identifiers approved of Congress' performance, while just 47 percent of Republicans approved. Democrats still enjoyed majorities in both chambers leading up to the 1994 election, when 40 percent of Democrats but just 24 percent of Republicans approved of Congress' performance. Two years after the 1994 Republican sweep, the proportion of Republicans approving of Congress had more than doubled, to 55 percent, while the share of Democratic identifiers approving of Congress held steady at 40 percent. From 1996 to 2004 the Republican Party's identifiers responded to the party's control of Congress with greater approval of the institution, compared to Democrats. However, the gap in identifier approval was twice as large in 1998 and 2004 (sixteen points), when the party's Senate majority was secure, than it was in 2000 and 2002 (eight points) when the party's majority status was more tenuous.

In 2008, this pattern was broken, leading to the lowest congressional approval rating on record. Although approval among Democrats surged after the party regained a majority of seats in the House and Senate in the 2006 elections, it steadily eroded such that by autumn 2008 fewer Democrats than Republicans approved of the Democratic Congress (11 percent to 18 percent respectively). So, the record-low approval of Congress in 2008 is attributable to generally low approval ratings by both Democrats and Republicans, but particularly to surprisingly low ratings among Democrats. Why so many Democrats disapproved of Congress in 2008 relative to what we would expect is a question for future research.

Individual-level factors affecting congressional approval extend beyond partisanship. Hibbing and Theiss-Morse (1995), for example, find that people with more education and political sophistication tend to have an even more dim view of Congress than the politically unsophisticated. Holding these considerations (and party identification) fixed, an analysis by the author of pooled (1980–2004) American National Election Studies data shows that women, Latinos, and young people are somewhat more likely to approve of Congress than men, non-Latino whites, and older people.

APPROVAL OF INDIVIDUAL MEMBERS OF CONGRESS

Noticeably absent from the above discussion was the importance of citizens' attitudes about their specific Member of Congress (MC). It seems reasonable to expect that citizens' assessments of the performance of their own Member of Congress will affect how they assess the performance of Congress as a whole. However, according to "Fenno's paradox," though many Americans may disapprove of Congress as a whole, they tend to approve of their own Member of Congress. This divergence in opinion may be explained by underlying disparate criteria upon which the public judges the performance of Congressmen (constituency service and personal attributes) versus Congress as a whole (domestic and foreign policy and discontent with the perceived slow pace of legislation) (Parker and Davidson 1979). Thus, while the general opinion of Congress would seem to predict otherwise, incumbents continue to enjoy a distinct advantage in elections (Cook 1979).

The facility of voters to be cognitively dissonant when evaluating both their own Members and Congress as a whole is well illustrated in the House bank scandal of 1992 (Dimock and Jacobson 1995). In 1991, many Congressmen were implicated in writing overdrafts on their House checking accounts. In the November 1992 elections, public disapproval of this practice resulted in a serious liability for incumbents, reducing the vote for incumbents as a group by 5 percentage points on average. According to Dimock and Jacobson, the voters who were most sensitive to the overdraft behavior and were least likely to assume that their incumbent had not engaged in the practice were most affected by it in the polling booth.

What are the systemic factors affecting whether citizens approve of their own congressional incumbent? If we focus on constituent characteristics, there is consistently higher approval of incumbents among partisans and among citizens who are older and more educated. Differences by race, gender, and other politically relevant characteristics were smaller. For instance, in 2004, fully 62 and 63 percent of Democratic and Republican identifiers approved of their incumbent, compared with just 49 percent of Independents. Nearly three in four (71 percent) citizens born before 1926 approved of their incumbent, while about half (47 percent) of those born after 1975 did so. This is not owing to a cohort effect; instead, congressional approval improves with age. Among those born between 1943 and 1958, just 49 percent approved of Congress in 1980 when this group was aged 22 to 37. In 2004, when this same age cohort was 46 to 61 years old, 68 percent approved of Congress. Among those who completed college, 66 percent approved of their incumbent, compared with 59 percent of high school graduates and 48 percent of elementary school completers.

There are also differences in the salience of congressional elections for citizens. The salience of congressional elections is generally greater among more educated, wealthy, older, and more partisan citizens. For instance, 76 percent of those who had a college degree said they cared who won their congressional election in 2004, compared to just 36 percent of those with just a primary school diploma. Almost 3 in 4 (73 percent) of those in the 96–100th income percentile said they cared who won in 2004, while just 57 percent of those in the 0–16th income percentile did so. Over time, though, the salience of congressional elections has increased most among women (54 percent in 1966 to 65 percent in 2004), Democrats (55 percent to 67 percent), union households (55 percent to 70 percent), the poor (42 percent to 57 percent), and African Americans (48 percent to 65 percent). So, advantaged members of society have historically tended to care more about who won their district's congressional election, while disadvantaged members of society have come some way toward closing the gap.

DIFFERENCES ACROSS INSTITUTIONS

Even if we accept that congressional approval is derivative of the public's generic approval of the country's direction a la Stimson, this cannot explain why Americans are consistently and considerably less likely to approve of Congress compared to other institutions of government. In other words, presidential approval may be highly predictive of change over time in congressional approval, but cannot explain why, at any single point in time, citizens reliably approve of other institutions at rates exceeding approval of Congress.

If we average congressional approval over the lifetime of the Gallup poll (1974–2009), congressional approval has a mean of 35 percent. In contrast, over the lifetime of the Gallup presidential approval question (1945–2009), presidential approval has averaged about 54 percent. If we limit the data to the same period as the congressional approval data (post-1974), presidential approval averages about 52 percent. Notably, every president's highest approval rating over their term of service exceeds Congress' highest ever approval rating, and by a substantial margin. Richard Nixon's highest approval rating was 67 percent, the lowest high among modern presidents but still 11 percentage points higher than Americans have ever approved of Congress (56 percent) over this period. Harry Truman's 22 percent approval rating in February 1952 is the lowest of the modern presidents but is still well above the 14 percent approval rating Congress received in October 1998.

The Supreme Court is also an institution Americans tend to approve of much more than Congress. In 2000, 62 percent of Americans approved of the job the Court was doing, compared to 40 percent for Congress. In 2008, Court approval had slipped to 48 percent, which was still well above the level of congressional approval, which was in the teens.

There are some exceptions to this general pattern. For instance, using data from Harris polls, Dennis (1981) shows that congressional approval was as high as or higher than presidential approval during Lyndon Johnson's full term (1965 to 1968) and Nixon's second term (1973 to 1974). However, in each case, it was primarily a decline in presidential approval (presumably owing to the Vietnam War and Watergate), rather than an increase in congressional approval, that allowed congressional approval to catch up. Americans only approve of Congress more than the president when they think particularly poorly of the president.

Why do Americans disapprove of Congress more than other national institutions of government? The leading explanation appears to be that the process of lawmaking in Congress is inherently conflictual, and citizens dislike conflict in government, therefore citizens tend not to approve of Congress. The leading proponents of this view, John Hibbing and Elizabeth Theiss-Morse, argue in their book *Stealth Democracy* that public disapproval of Congress is not due to partisanship, policy, or scandal, but instead due to the nature of the congressional decision-making process, which is inherently messy, slow, and confrontational. The public wants democratic government, but also wants that government to be efficient and orderly, not riddled with "uncertainty, conflicting options, long debate, competing interests, confusion, bargaining and compromised, imperfect solutions" (Hibbing and Theiss-Morse 1995, 147; see also Wawro and Schickler 2007). Congress puts all of these ugly aspects of democracy in the public eye, essentially creating its unpopularity by performing its role in the policy process. Americans have a great appreciation for the theoretical government institutions outlined by the constitution, but perceive a separation between those theoretical institutions and the "Washington system" which "seduces members away from fulfilling their responsibility to the public" (Hibbing and Theiss-Morse 1995, 62). They identify concerns about self-interested politicians and the role of special interests as citizens' key "process concerns." In an earlier treatment, *Congress as Public Enemy*, Hibbing and Theiss-Morse show that concerns over representational fairness (e.g. concerns about the role of special interests or that MCs are detached from ordinary people) are a strong predictor of individual-level support for Congress, even with controls for ideology and partisanship. Finally, this thesis receives support in a study by Carolyn Funk, who showed experimentally that public support for Congress is affected by partisan conflict.

In an alternative account, David Brady and Sean Theriault (2001) contend that the strategic behavior of MCs may influence public dissatisfaction with Congress. They point to four practices in particular: 1) avoiding difficult votes by adopting questionable legislative procedures; 2) hyperbolic rhetoric; 3) Members bad-mouth the institution for electoral gain; and 4) ideological extremists get the most media attention.

Finally, it is noteworthy that dissatisfaction with Congress does not seem to be grounded in any sense that Congress is more ideologically out of step with the public than other institutions of government (Hibbing and Theiss-Morse 1995). Indeed, one reason that study concludes that process concerns are so central to public opinion about Congress is that unhappiness with the policies Congress adopts does not seem to be particularly important.

COMPARED WITH OTHER LEGISLATURES

We might be less concerned about low congressional approval ratings if this is a general phenomenon in other countries or within the various states of the United States. Cross-sectional comparisons of legislative approval also offer a test of one of the key theories of congressional approval. If there is some generally negative characteristic associated with the role legislatures play in a democracy, as Hibbing and Theiss-Morse contend, we would expect to observe that across a wide range of democracies, citizens approve of their legislative institutions less than they approve of the executive and/or judiciary.

At the state legislative level, it is instructive that at the same time that congressional approval has hit an historic low, public approval of state legislatures seems to have bottomed out as well. A few examples are instructive. In Pennsylvania, a Quinnipiac University poll released on March 3, 2010 reported that just 29 percent of Pennsylvania voters said they approved of the job the state legislature is doing in Harrisburg, a slippage of thirteen points since May 2009. In neighboring New York, a recent Marist College Poll indicates that just 16 percent of voters believed the state Senate is doing an excellent or good job, while 82 percent rated it as fair or poor. The numbers for approval of the state Assembly were similar. In Connecticut, according to a mid-January Quinnipiac poll, the approval rating of the state legislature was at 30 percent—just one point above the body's 2003 standing, the lowest ever recorded by the poll—compared with 58 percent who disapprove. In California, 71 percent said they disapproved of the legislature as a whole. It is difficult to fully know how widespread the dislike of state legislatures is, since many states do not have publicly available survey data on state legislative approval ratings. But in the places where it is measured—typically larger states with more professionalized legislatures—the numbers are bleak.

How do public evaluations of Congress in the U.S. compare with public evaluations of legislatures in other democratic countries? Using data on seventeen democracies from two rounds of the World Values Survey, Newton and Norris (2000) show that citizen confidence in their parliament/legislature is among the lowest of all public institutions, only higher than confidence in the civil service and, on average, thirty points below the armed forces, the next lowest ranked institution. Citizens' dissatisfaction with legislatures is widely held. Whether democracies are presidential or parliamentarian, or the countries are developed or undeveloped, the elected body in charge of designing and voting on laws does not rank among the most popular institutions. So, there is somewhat reassuring evidence that compared with other national institutions, legislatures are less liked in many democracies around the world. Americans' dislike of the U.S. Congress relative to other governing institutions is not unique.

However, Americans' disapproval of Congress runs deeper than the disapproval of other nations' legislatures. According to data from the World Values Survey collected between 2004 and 2007, only 20.6 percent of Americans expressed a great deal or quite a lot of confidence in Congress. By comparison, over the same period legislative approval was 36.2 percent in England, 35.5 percent in France, 38.2 percent in Canada, 50.8 percent in Spain, and 54 percent in Switzerland. Even in developing economies like Russia and Brazil, approval of the legislature was higher (29.9 percent and 24.9 percent) than in the U.S. The only legislature with less support than the U.S. Congress was Taiwan's Legislative Yuan, approval of which stood at just 14.1 percent after a brawl erupted on the floor of the chamber.[1]

This is disconcerting on its face but also because there are reasons to expect that public approval of Congress should be higher than approval of legislatures in many other countries. Pippa Norris (2001) argues that some features of the electoral system (specifically single-member districts) promote strong voter–member of parliament linkages and as a consequence generate greater satisfaction with the political system. Because Members of Congress have, since 1842, been elected in single-member districts, we would expect that all else being equal, congressional approval would be higher than approval of legislatures to which members are elected in multi-member districts. It is not.

CONSEQUENCES OF CONGRESSIONAL EVALUATIONS

The considerable attention that is paid to congressional approval by scholars and the media alike presupposes that congressional approval matters. Approval of Congress might matter because it affects elected officials' careers and campaign strategies, and it might matter based on its consequences for voters. I will discuss these in turn.

At the elite level, Lipinski (2004) presents a survey of more than twenty MCs that finds members are concerned that low levels of institutional approval will affect their

---

[1] "Taiwan Legislature Dissolves into Chaos." *Washington Post*, January, 19, 2007. http://www.washingtonpost.com/wp-dyn/content/article/2007/01/19/AR2007011900480.html.

reelection prospects. At least for members of the majority party, this concern appears to be well founded. Recent work by Jones and McDermott (2009) shows that low levels of approval leads to higher levels of electoral defeat for the majority party. This is true for both majority party incumbents and for challengers affiliated with the majority party. This provides the majority party with the incentive to work to increase congressional approval and the minority party with the incentive to drive down congressional approval.

Fenno's (1978) original work highlighted the frequency and benefits of "running against Congress." Lipinski, Bianco, and Work (2003) build on Fenno's foundation. They examine the 1994 and 1998 mid-term elections and specifically whether members of Congress ran with or against Congress as an institution by measuring their loyalty to the institution in their constituent newsletters. They uncovered significant variation in Member loyalty, and also observed that Democrats who were loyal to Congress in 1994 were sometimes less successful (specifically when their constituents were favorably disposed toward Ross Perot).

Low levels of congressional approval may also have troubling consequences for individual citizens. Since legislatures are "in many countries [...] the most salient and dramatic symbol of the representative character of the political system" (Clarke, Kornberg, and Stewart 1984, 452), a poor opinion of elected representatives can lead to a poor popular perception of democracy. Indeed, a study of the Canadian Parliament found that the "support for Parliament has the strongest direct and total effects on regime support of any variable in the model" (Clarke, Kornberg, and Stewart 1984, 461). This suggests a link between congressional approval and citizen participation. That is, if citizens do not have a sense that government processes and outcomes are responsive to their concerns (as reflected in their assessments of Congress), this demonstrates a lack of "external political efficacy" on the part of citizens. Many have shown that political efficacy is a strong predictor of voting in elections and other forms of political participation (e.g. Finkel 1985). So, sustained poor assessments of Congress may lead to even lower electoral turnout in the U.S., which already lags behind the record of most democratic countries. A final but potentially significant concern is that citizens who do not approve of the institution that "makes the laws" may be less prone to adhere to the institutions' decisions. For instance, work by psychologist Tom Tyler (1990) shows that people who deem laws legitimate are more likely to follow those laws.

REFORM

Above, we saw that many elite actors—especially the members of the congressional majority party—have a strategic incentive to increase the level of congressional approval. We also saw that there are normative reasons to improve congressional approval—it may affect the future involvement of citizens in the political process and their compliance with federal laws.

Assuming that we wish to raise the level of Congressional approval, how might this be accomplished? One possibility that flows from the Hibbing and Theiss-Morse hypothesis is to decrease the transparency of the lawmaking process. That is, if citizens do not like what they observe when they see Congress engaged in lawmaking, perhaps citizens will think better of the institution if they are less able to see laws being made. Of course, any suggestion that C-SPAN stop broadcasting or that committee meetings be closed would probably meet with instant and vigorous public disapproval.

Alternatively, congressional procedures could remain mostly transparent if some of the tools that permit legislative minorities to obstruct legislation were curtailed. The Senate's filibuster is the most obvious example of a rule that produces the kind of wrangling that Hibbing and Theiss-Morse contend Americans so dislike. Moreover, minority obstruction in the Senate may lead to disapproval of the entire Congress if, as seems likely, the public may not know whom to blame precisely. Hibbing and Larimer (2008) suggest as much when they contend that "[a]ttempts to obtain separate assessments even of the House and the Senate are likely to produce non-attitudes rather than substantively meaningful responses" (10). If the public does not disaggregate the chambers of Congress when it attributes blame, then reforming Senate procedures or practices may have institution-wide benefits.

A third possibility to improve congressional approval is to pursue strategies to reign in the polarization of the political parties. Polarized parties lead directly to the kind of wrangling that Hibbing and Theiss-Morse contend Americans detest. If the parties were somewhat less polarized, perhaps their wrangling would not be as fierce. How to reverse party polarization is a complex question, a full treatment of which is beyond the scope of this chapter.

In the end, it is probably the case that reforms are unlikely to have any substantial positive effect on congressional approval. For instance, previous lobbying, campaign finance, and ethics reforms that Congress has adopted have not appeared to result in any sustained, positive effect on congressional approval. Furthermore, the Hibbing–Theiss-Morse findings suggest that increasing public understanding and knowledge of Congress is also unlikely to improve public attitudes toward the institution.

CONCLUSION

We have seen that congressional approval has fluctuated considerably over the last half century; that it moves in tandem with presidential approval; that it is typically much lower than presidential approval; that in many countries the national legislature is less popular than the President or Prime Minister but that Americans' dislike of Congress runs much deeper than elsewhere; and that there are some significant, potential consequences for elected officials and voters if congressional approval remains severely low.

Although we have learned a good deal about the origins and implications of congressional approval, other interesting and important research questions remain unanswered. For instance, future work might investigate why more Republicans than Democrats approved of the Democratic-controlled Congress in 2008, when historically outpartisans have registered lower levels of approval.

More broadly, it may be fruitful to investigate whether and how Americans' expectations of Congress differ from their expectations of other national, or state and local, institutions. What functions of government and what policy areas are perceived to be the responsibility of Congress, and what is the responsibility of the President or state and local governments? Do Americans look to Congress to provide a safe and clean environment, to regulate immigration, to maintain the nation's infrastructure, and to provide an economic safety net? Improving our understanding of Americans' expectations of Congress will help us to evaluate whether Americans' evaluations of Congress are affected by their assessments of its performance in these domains. Stated another way, asking Americans to "approve" or "disapprove" of the job Congress is doing may lead one to ask—what is the job of Congress?

Even more broadly, a comparative analysis of the U.S. Congress and other national legislatures would be a worthwhile contribution. Are the factors driving congressional approval the same as those driving approval of other national legislatures, and to the same degree? Why are some national legislatures so much more popular than is our Congress?

REFERENCES

BIANCO, W. T. 1994. *Trust: Representatives and Constituents.* Ann Arbor: University of Michigan Press.

BRADY, D. W., and THERIAULT, S. M. 2001. A Reassessment of Who's to Blame: A Positive Case for the Public Evaluation of Congress, pp. 175–92 in *What Is It About Government That Americans Dislike?*, ed. J. R. Hibbing and E. Theiss-Morse. Cambridge: Cambridge University Press.

BRATTON, M., and MATTES, R. 2001. Support for Democracy in Africa: Intrinsic or Instrumental. *British Journal of Political Science,* 31(3): 447–74.

CAREY, J. 2009. *Legislative Voting and Accountability.* New York: Cambridge University Press.

CARMINES, E. G., GERRITY, J. C., and WAGNER, M. W. 2005. How the American Public Views Congress: A Report Based on the Center on Congress at Indiana University's 2004 Public Opinion Survey. (http://www.centeroncongress.org/pdf/Public%20Views%20of%20Congress.pdf) (accessed August 17, 2010).

CATTERBERG, G., and MORENO, A. 2005. The Individual Bases of Political Trust: Trends in New and Established Democracies. *International Journal of Public Opinion Research,* 18(1): 31–48.

CITRIN, J. 1974. Comment: The Political Relevance of Trust in Government. *The American Political Science Review,* 68(3): 973–88.

CLARKE, H., KRONBERG, A., and STEWART, M. C. 1984. Parliament and Political Support in Canada. *American Political Science Review*, 78(2): 452–69.

COOK, T. E. 1979. Legislature vs. Legislator: A Note on the Paradox of Congressional Support. *Legislative Studies Quarterly*, 4(1): 43–52.

CORRAL, M. 2009. Not Happy? Blame your Legislature. *Americas Barometer Insights* No. 26.

DENNIS, J. 1981. Public Support for Congress. *Political Behavior*, 3(4): 319–50.

DIMOCK, M. A., and JACOBSON, G. C. 1995. Checks and Choices: The House Bank Scandal's Impact on Voters in 1992. *Journal of Politics*, 57(3): 1143–59.

DURR, R. H., GILMOUR, J. B., and WOLBRECHT, C. 1997. Explaining Congressional Approval. *American Journal of Political Science*, 41(1): 175–207.

FENNO, JR., R. F. 1975. If, as Ralph Nader Says, Congress is the "Broken Branch," How Come We Love Our Congressmen So Much?, pp. 275–87 in *Congress in Change: Evolution and Reform*, ed. N. J. Ornstein. New York: Praeger.

——1978. *Home Style: Representatives in Their Districts*. Boston: Little, Brown.

FINKEL, S. E. 1985. Reciprocal Effects of Participation and Political Efficacy: A Panel Analysis. *American Journal of Political Science*, 29(4): 891–913.

HERRICK, R. 2003. *Fashioning the More Ethical Representative: The Impact of Ethics Reforms in the U.S. House of Representatives*. Westport, CT: Praeger Publishing.

HIBBING, J. R., and THEISS-MORSE, E. 1995. *Congress as Public Enemy: Public Attitudes Towards American Political Institutions*. Cambridge: Cambridge University Press.

——and THEISS-MORSE, E. (eds.) 2001. *What Is It About Government That Americans Dislike?* Cambridge: Cambridge University Press.

——and THEISS-MORSE, E. 2002. *Stealth Democracy: Americans' Beliefs About How Government Should Work*. Cambridge: Cambridge University Press.

HIBBING, J. R., and C. W. LARIMER. 2008. The American Public's View of Congress. *The Forum*, 6(3): Article 6.

JONES, D. R., and McDERMOTT, M. L. 2009. *Americans, Congress, and Democratic Responsiveness: Public Evaluations of Congress and Electoral Consequences*. Ann Arbor: University of Michigan Press.

LIPINSKI, D. 2004. *Congressional Communication: Content and Consequences*. Ann Arbor: University of Michigan Press.

——BIANCO, W. T., and WORK, R. 2003. What Happens When House Members "Run with Congress"? The Electoral Consequences of Institutional Loyalty. *Legislative Studies Quarterly*, 28(3): 413–29.

McDERMOTT, M., and JONES, D. 2003. Do Public Evaluations of Congress Matter? *American Politics Research*, 31(2): 155–77.

MONDAK, J. J., CARMINES, E. G., HUCKFELDT, R., MITCHELL, D.-G., and SCHRAUFNAGEL, S. 2007. Does Familiarity Breed Contempt? The Impact of Information on Mass Attitudes toward Congress. *American Journal of Political Science*, 51(1): 34–48.

NEWTON, K., and P. NORRIS. 2000. Confidence in Political Institutions: Faith, Culture, or Performance?, pp. 52–73 in *Disaffected Democracies: What's Troubling the Trilateral Countries?* ed. Susan Pharr and Robert Putnam. Princeton: Princeton University Press.

NORRIS, P. 2001. The Twilight of Westminster? Electoral Reform and its Consequences. *Political Studies*, 49(5): 877–900.

ORCES, D. 2009. Popular Support for a Government without Legislatures. *Americas Barometer Insights*. No. 25.

PARKER, G. R., and DAVIDSON, R. H. 1979. Why Do Americans Love Their Congressmen So Much More Than Their Congress? *Legislative Studies Quarterly*, 4(1): 53–61.

PARKER, S. L., and PARKER, G. R. 1993. Why Do We Trust Our Congressman? *Journal of Politics*, 55(2): 442–53.

PATTERSON, S. C., and CALDEIRA, G. A. 1990. Standing Up for Congress: Variations in Public Esteem Since the 1960s. *Legislative Studies Quarterly*, 15: 25–47.

PATTERSON, S. C., RIPLEY, R. B., and QUINLAN, S. V. 1992. Citizens' Orientations Toward Legislatures: Congress and the State Legislature. *Western Political Quarterly*, 45(2): 315–38.

RAMIREZ, M. D. 2009. The Dynamics of Partisan Conflict on Congressional Approval. *American Journal of Political Science*, 53(3): 681–94.

RUDOLPH, T. J. 2002. The Economic Sources of Congressional Approval. *Legislative Studies Quarterly*, 27(4): 577–99.

STIMSON, J. A. 2004. *Tides of Consent: How Public Opinion Shapes American Politics*. New York: Cambridge University Press.

STUDLAR, D. T., and MCALLISTER, I. 1996. Constituency Activity and Representational Roles among Australian Legislators. *Journal of Politics*, 58(1): 69–90.

TYLER, T. R. 1990. *Why People Obey the Law*. New Haven: Yale University Press.

WAWRO, G., and SCHICKLER, E. 2007. *Filibuster: Obstruction and Lawmaking in the U.S. Senate*. Princeton, NJ: Princeton University Press.

PART V

....

CONGRESSIONAL INSTITUTIONS AND PROCEDURES

....

CHAPTER 17

....

PARTY LEADERSHIP

....

RANDALL W. STRAHAN*

DURING the 1990s and early 2000s, as the power of party leaders in the U.S. House of Representatives approached levels not seen in a century, one of the most prominent debates among political scientists who study American politics has been over whether political parties and party leaders matter for understanding what happens in Congress. While thoughtful observers of congressional politics continue to counsel close attention to the varieties and limits of party influence (see Cooper and Young 2002; Jones 2005; Mayhew 2008), this curious controversy among political scientists over whether parties and party leaders are important in Congress is now mostly settled in favor of the affirmative view. Alongside this debate about party influence, and at times intersecting with it, has been a stream of scholarship on the politics of congressional party leadership that reaches back to the 1960s. If most congressional scholars now accept the view that understanding parties and party leadership is important for understanding congressional politics, there remain disagreements and important unanswered questions about how party leadership institutions work, and about the extent of party leaders' influence and the conditions under which it can be consequential.

The main goal of this chapter is to offer a critical assessment of recent scholarship on congressional party leadership. This chapter will pay particular attention to the contributions of the influential rational choice institutionalist school, along with those of alternative approaches that place less emphasis on parsimony in theoretical explanations and more on fidelity to the politics and causal processes we observe in the political world. Attention will also be devoted to the scholarly debate over party

* The author gratefully acknowledges helpful comments and advice from the editors of this volume, Eric Schickler and Frances Lee, and from Clifford Carrubba, Joseph Cooper, Micheal Giles, and Byron Shafer.

influence in Congress and what has been learned from that debate that may help in understanding party leadership. Finally, the chapter will consider some persistent methodological problems that arise in the study of congressional leadership and suggest promising areas for future research.

EXPLAINING PARTY LEADERSHIP IN CONGRESS

The scholarship on congressional party leadership of the past two decades has its foundations in studies by Charles O. Jones (1968), and Joseph Cooper and David Brady (1981), which emphasize the importance of institutional context for understanding party leadership. As the question of whether parties matter for explaining outcomes in Congress was being debated in the 1990s and early 2000s, work on party leadership continued apace and new theories of party government were proposed. If the importance of institutional context for understanding party leadership in Congress is now well established, questions remain about how party leadership institutions actually work. One set of issues concerns the extent to which party leadership is conditional, and the means party leaders use to influence outcomes. A second set of issues involves whether leaders are best understood as narrowly constrained agents of their party followers or whether the independent agency of party leaders needs to be incorporated in explanations of congressional parties. Finally, party leadership in the Senate has received much less attention than in the House, and continues to pose some interesting puzzles for students of congressional politics.

As is true of recent congressional scholarship generally, rational choice institutionalist approaches have been highly influential in recent work on parties and party leadership, with spatial models and principal-agent theories supplying the most widely employed explanatory motifs. The basic logic of principal-agent theory—in which principals delegate authority to an agent, then seek to control the agent through incentives tied to institutional arrangements such as periodic elections—has been understood in political science for a very long time, certainly back to the political science of the American founders (Strahan 2003). However, the principal-agent and spatial theory frameworks employed by political scientists more recently, have primarily been imports from economics. Few would contest the idea that principal-agent and spatial theory approaches can illuminate aspects of the politics of party leadership in Congress. But among the issues being raised in recent work on this subject are questions about whether party leadership can be fully understood within spatial theory frameworks that view legislators' policy preferences as fixed, or by principal-agent approaches in which leaders are understood to be agents whose actions always reflect party followers' expectations and interests. Because most of the scholarly work on party leadership has focused on the House of Representatives, the primary focus in this first section of the chapter will also be on the House. Work on party leadership in the Senate will be the focus of a section that follows.

Foundational works on congressional leadership

In one of the earliest attempts to develop a general explanation of the politics of congressional leadership, Charles O. Jones (1968) emphasized the "limits of leadership" in the House of Representatives. Drawing on evidence from the cases of early twentieth-century Speaker Joseph Cannon and mid-century Rules Committee chair Howard W. Smith, Jones argues that leaders in the House will encounter limits because of the need to maintain a "procedural majority" that will support the rules and organizational arrangements on which the leader's authority is based. Speaker Cannon and Rules Committee chair Smith both provoked changes in House rules, Jones (1968, 619) concludes, by engaging in "excessive leadership." According to Jones, attempts by leaders to shape legislative outcomes in Congress are always limited by the majoritarian foundations of authority within the legislature; leaders must work within those limits or risk action by a chamber majority to alter rules to reduce the leader's authority.[1] Note that Jones did *not* conclude, as have the more recent studies by Keith Krehbiel (see especially 1991) that the majoritarian foundations of House rules imply that party leaders are of negligible importance. While calling attention to limits to leadership defined by procedural majorities, Jones (1968, 645) observes that "all House leaders have considerable latitude."

Political scientists who followed Jones in developing explanations of congressional leadership were drawn to the puzzle of why the House of Representatives has witnessed such different "styles" of party leadership throughout its history. The most important of these studies was Joseph Cooper and David W. Brady's, "Institutional Context and Leadership Style: The House from Cannon to Rayburn" (1981). Seeking to explain why the centralized, "czar-rule" of turn-of-the-century speakers was displaced by the decentralized, brokerage-type leadership exemplified by Texan Sam Rayburn in the 1940s and 1950s, they conclude: "institutional context rather than personal skill is the primary determinant of leadership power in the House." And: "To be sure, style is affected by personal traits. Nonetheless, style must be responsive to and congruent with both the inducements available to leaders and member expectations regarding proper behavior" (Cooper and Brady 1981, 423).

Cooper and Brady define institutional context broadly to include House rules as well as ideas members share about party loyalty. But in their view the most important condition that determines how leaders operate within a given institutional context is party strength, which is determined primarily by electoral politics *outside* the House—specifically the degree of similarity in the constituencies represented within

---

[1] For more recent research that confirms Jones' proposition with data from a much larger group of observations, see Schickler and Rich 1997, and Schickler 2000.

and across parties. Rules that concentrated power in the hands of leaders and strong norms of party loyalty are part of their explanation for the powerful leaders and hierarchical leadership styles that emerged in the late nineteenth- and early twentieth-century House. But the most important cause that explains leadership politics in this period, according to Cooper and Brady, is the high level of party unity that arose from polarization of the Democratic and Republican members' electoral constituencies along agricultural–industrial lines. The decentralized, brokerage leadership style of Sam Rayburn and the House leaders who followed him up through the late 1970s, was in turn primarily the product of the greater heterogeneity of constituency interests represented in the majority party during the more recent period.[2]

Rational choice institutionalism on party leadership: leaders as agents

Partly in response to the emergence of more activist House leaders in the 1980s, a new wave of congressional leadership studies began to appear in the 1990s. The most influential of these works were in the rational choice institutionalist vein. These studies built on work that emphasized institutional context but incorporated some new elements, including principal-agent frameworks to conceptualize leader–follower interactions and spatial models to conceptualize how parties and party leaders influence legislative outcomes.

David W. Rohde's *Parties and Leaders in the Postreform House* (1991) examined party organization and leadership in the aftermath of the 1970s reform era and introduced conditional party government theory to explain some of these developments. Rohde attributed the more active and centralized House leadership of the 1980s, most notably that of Democratic Speaker Jim Wright of Texas, primarily to greater unity (or preference homogeneity) over policy within the Democratic party, which had occurred as a consequence of the declining electoral fortunes of the party's southern conservative wing. Rohde's explanation was based on the Cooper–Brady contextual theory, stressing the level of agreement on policy within the party as a key variable that explains leadership power and behavior (Rohde 1991, 35–7). Synthesizing the contextual perspective with principal-agent theory, Rohde proposes: "[Contemporary leaders] are strong because (and when) they are agents of their memberships, who want them to be strong" (Rohde 1991, 172).

In a series of studies focused primarily on developments in the House, Rohde and co-author John Aldrich presented a wide array of both quantitative and qualitative evidence to show that under conditions of preference homogeneity in the majority party and conflict with the minority, first House Democrats (Rohde 1991), and later

---

[2] It is sometimes overlooked that Cooper and Brady acknowledge the importance of leaders' personal traits and skills as an influence on leadership power and style in the House. Their conclusion was *not* that leaders are unimportant in explaining leadership politics, but that the influence of personal characteristics of leaders occurs within parameters defined by the institutional context (Cooper and Brady 1981, 423–4).

House Republicans (Aldrich and Rohde 1997–8, 2000a, 2000b), delegated additional powers to the majority party organization and leadership, with the result that the capacity of the majority party to influence organizational and legislative outcomes was greatly augmented. Drawing on a spatial theory framework, Aldrich and Rohde proposed that efforts by the majority party leadership could result in legislative outcomes being pushed away from the preferences of the median House member toward those of the median member of the majority party, and they cited a number of cases of important legislative outcomes in the 1980s and 1990s in which this appeared to have occurred (2000a, 49–52, 70–1).

Conditional party government theory also incorporated some refinements to contextual leadership theory. Rohde (1991, 37) states that the contextual explanation of the reemergence of strong leadership in the contemporary House, "while basically correct, is not quite complete."

When conditions won't support strong leadership activity, then leaders who want to exercise power and those who do not will probably yield roughly the same results. When the membership is permissive or demanding of strong leadership, however, leaders who are aggressive and enthusiastic will likely exhibit substantially more activist behavior than will leaders who are reluctant about the exercise of their powers.   (Rohde 1991, 172)

Elaborating on conditional party government theory in an essay on the leadership of Republican Speaker Newt Gingrich in the 1990s, Rohde (2000, 5) adds: "the personality and skills of leaders play a significant role, and Gingrich epitomized this aspect of the theory. Just as Democratic Speaker Tom Foley's reluctance to use the institutional powers available to him made him a weaker Speaker than he had to be, Gingrich's approach enhanced his power and facilitated its exercise." Conditional party government theory does not address *why* some leaders might seek to exercise power more aggressively than others. This is an important problem to which we will return.

In a series of books and articles Barbara Sinclair also documented the reemergence of stronger majority party leadership in the post-reform House of Representatives and the strategies employed by party leaders over this period (Sinclair 1992, 1995, 1999, 2006). Sinclair characterizes her theory of leadership as "a principal-agent approach" as well (1995, 8). "Within this framework," she explains, "congressional party leaders are seen as agents of the members who select them and charge them with advancing members' goals, especially (though not exclusively) by facilitating the production of collective goods" (Sinclair 1995, 9). Along with Rohde, Sinclair contends that increased unity within the majority party was a key factor in the reemergence of stronger House leadership in the 1980s and 1990s. Sinclair identifies a number of additional contextual variables that can also influence leadership behavior by affecting members' expectations of leaders: the predictability of the lawmaking process; opposition party control of the White House; availability of opportunities for individual member entrepreneurship; interpretations of electoral outcomes; and confidence in leaders' strategic judgment (Sinclair 1990, 101–5; 1995, chs 1–4; 1999, 422–5, 434, 441–2).

However, in contrast to Rohde, Sinclair explicitly rejects the idea that characteristics of leaders or the independent agency of leaders should be taken into account in explanations of party leadership in Congress. She contends that explanations of leadership should "omit personality" and that both the emergence of stronger House leadership under Democratic majorities in the 1980s, and the strong, centralized leadership under Republican majorities that followed, are fully explained by changes in the political context (Sinclair 1999, 423). As Sinclair (1990, 99–100) puts it: "Predicting behavior requires some simplifying assumptions... it is reasonable to assume that retaining their leadership position is a major goal for party leaders. Since leaders are chosen by their party members, satisfying their members' expectations should be a top priority. Member expectations should be a critical determinant of leadership behavior."

In Sinclair's view, party leaders may be granted considerable latitude to choose the means to advance goals on which their partisan followers agree, but leaders cannot act independently in deciding what goals to pursue if followers are not already in agreement on those goals (Sinclair 1999, 423, 446–7). From this perspective parties matter because their leaders influence how issues get framed and which alternatives get voted on (Sinclair 2002); but the agency of party leaders is not a significant factor because the key determinant of how leaders wield this influence is what party followers want.

A third recent body of influential work on congressional leadership has been produced by Mathew D. McCubbins in collaboration with D. Roderick Kiewiet (Kiewiet and McCubbins 1991) and Gary W. Cox (Cox and McCubbins 1993, 2005). McCubbins and his co-authors have focused not so much on explaining variations in leadership style or power, as on how congressional institutions create incentives for party leaders to look out for the collective electoral interests of their fellow party members. Principal-agent theory provides the framework for explaining leadership politics in these studies as well (Kiewiet and McCubbins 1991, chs 2 and 3; Cox and McCubbins 1993, chs 4 and 5). Leaders are said to be motivated by "a desire for internal advancement" within the legislature (Cox and McCubbins 1993, 126; see also 2005, 23). The personal interest of the leader in retaining the power and prestige that come with a leadership position—especially a leadership position in the majority party—is said to provide the motive for carrying out the central task for which the agent has been delegated authority by fellow partisans: protecting the party's collective reputation with the voters. As Cox and McCubbins put it, "[B]y creating a leadership post that is both attractive and elective, a party can induce its leaders to internalize the collective electoral fate of the party" (Cox and McCubbins 1993, 132–3). As a result, the majority party in the House operates as a procedural cartel that works to protect the electoral interests of its members.

Cox and McCubbins (2005) also draw on spatial theory to conceptualize the influence of parties and party leaders. They emphasize that party influence primarily involves *negative* agenda power—that is the capacity of majority party leaders to keep issues opposed by a majority of the majority party off the legislative agenda even when (or especially when) those same measures are favored by a majority of the legislature—that is, by the median member of the chamber. When the majority party is unified over policy it may delegate more authority to leaders to enforce party discipline and advance new legislation, but the exercise of this *positive* agenda power is the "superstructure" of party government, not its "bedrock." Efforts at enforcing party discipline are said to be limited to "corralling a few votes on the margin" and are of secondary importance to controlling which issues get voted on (Cox and McCubbins 2005, 4–5). The empirical work inspired by cartel theory pays relatively little attention to the behavior or actions of actual party leaders, focusing instead on evidence that the majority party uses chamber rules to exert influence over key committees and succeeds in controlling the legislative agenda, as evidenced by rarely losing important floor votes (Cox and McCubbins 1993, 2005).

Here, at the level of theories proposed in the rational choice institutionalist studies we find one important reason why little attention has been paid to the influence or agency of individual party leaders in some of the most influential recent scholarship on Congress. At first glance this seems paradoxical given that these studies contend that parties matter in Congress and that party leaders are such important actors. Leaders are said to have primary responsibility for identifying and advancing the collective interests of the majority party. Congressional rules confer significant authority on party leaders to influence both organizational decisions (who gets appointed to what standing committee, for example) as well as the course of legislation. Choices made by party leaders have serious consequences for their followers' political careers; for determining what legislation gets advanced or blocked; and for the reputation and electoral success of the legislative party.

But within most of the leadership theories based on principal-agent models nothing of real significance occurs when one leader replaces another. Elected party leaders such as the speaker of the House are understood to be more or less interchangeable agents who respond in like manner to institutional incentives and contextual conditions, the most important of which is the degree of unity over policy among their party followers.[3] Because leaders in these theories are explicitly or implicitly assumed to be motivated primarily by the same self-interested goal—office-holding ambition—what matters for explaining the politics of congressional leadership is not who the leader is, or what goals or interests or skills he or she brings to the position, but what party followers want and how congressional institutions create incentives and tools for leaders to advance followers' interests. If principal-agent theory as applied in these studies in fact captures the most important features of the politics of party leadership, students of Congress would be ill-advised to focus much energy on closer study of party leaders, because knowing more about leaders will explain little of importance about what happens in Congress.

Remaining for a moment at the level of theory, why *should* we expect the independent agency of party leaders to matter in Congress? First, even within economic

---

[3] As we have seen, Rohde's treatment of House leadership (1991, 2000) is an exception within this mode of theorizing because he employs a principal-agent framework, yet also incorporates personal characteristics of leaders as an important cause of leadership behavior under certain conditions.

principal-agent theories, principals can never completely control their agents. The problem of incomplete control of agents (termed agency loss) arises partly because there are almost always conflicts of interest between principals and agents, and because agents can be difficult to monitor and may exploit asymmetries in the information to which they and their principals have access. Even if one is persuaded that party leadership is best understood from the perspective of principal-agent theory, such an approach does not foreclose the possibility that party leaders may have sufficient autonomy to be consequential for outcomes in Congress. In fact, principal-agent theory supplies some vital insights about why legislative leaders almost always enjoy a certain degree of autonomy from their followers. Collective principals can have even more difficulty controlling agents because agents can play groups of principals off against one another, because replacing the agent in this setting can be difficult and costly, and because the agent may have important strategic advantages over his or her principals in terms of access to information and control over decision-making processes (see Kiewiet and McCubbins 1991, 24–7, 48–55). Regarding this last possibility, one of the founders of the rational choice institutionalist school in political science, the late William Riker, emphasized that leaders can manipulate the instability of majority coalitions in collective choice settings to produce outcomes the leader favors (1980, 1986).

One new direction in recent work on congressional party leadership has been the development of new explanatory frameworks that incorporate this kind of causal agency by leaders. However, before turning to these new developments it will be helpful first to consider the congressional party influence debate that emerged in the 1990s. This debate continued for almost two decades, during which it became one of the most visible scholarly controversies in the American politics field and engaged many congressional scholars, including the proponents of the party theories just discussed. This debate and its outcome are of more than minor interest for the subject of this chapter: for party leaders to matter in congressional politics, parties have to matter.

The party influence debate: theory-induced disequilibrium

Political scientists from Woodrow Wilson to E. E. Schattschneider to David Mayhew have noted the weakness of congressional parties in comparison to parties in other democratic legislatures. But during the 1990s, as congressional parties appeared to most other scholars to be in the midst of a resurgence, Keith Krehbiel set off a major debate by pushing well beyond this generally accepted view of the relative weakness of congressional parties. Deftly wielding the theoretical tools supplied by the rational choice institutionalist school, Krehbiel proposed that parties and party leaders are of little importance for understanding either major organizational features of the House (1991) or why Congress passes or fails to pass laws (1998). The result was an extended period of what might be termed theory-induced disequilibrium in the congressional politics field. By setting forth compelling theoretical accounts of why parties would not matter in a stylized legislature whose members act as posited by the spatial theories that had gained many adherents in the legislative politics field, and marshaling a continuing stream of plausible evidence in support of his theoretical arguments, Krehbiel achieved the modern academic equivalent of King Leonidas' stand at Thermoplyae: taking on a very large subfield of American political science and keeping it engaged for the better part of two decades.

In essence, Krehbiel's argument about congressional parties and party leaders is that they are of little significance because outcomes in Congress are determined by the preferences of pivotal legislators. Congressional action is explained in terms of a spatial model in which legislators make choices on the basis of the proximity of alternatives to their preferences in a one-dimensional policy space; legislators' preferences are assumed to be determined by causes outside (exogenous to) the legislature, and consequently party leaders are considered mostly irrelevant in explaining those choices or the outcomes that result from them. What appears to be party voting or party loyalty in Congress, Krehbiel contends, is simply partisans having sufficiently similar policy preferences to vote together on the basis of those preferences.

Krehbiel did not go so far as to claim that the increased partisan activity his colleagues were finding in Congress was entirely inconsequential, arguing instead that "competing party organizations bidding for pivotal votes may roughly counterbalance one another, so final outcomes are not much different from what a simpler but completely nonpartisan theory predicts" (1998, 171). Krehbiel's approach to congressional parties reflects a strong "instrumentalist" view of scientific explanation, in which logical consistency and prediction of outcomes are the standards for evaluating explanations rather than fidelity of assumptions or causal processes posited by theory to observation or to the understandings of the actors involved. "In other words," as Krehbiel put it regarding parties and explanations of congressional politics, "parties may be important, but it does not follow that omission of parties from theories is important" (1999b, 839; see also 1991, 102, 261; 1998, 26–8).

On its own terms, the most direct test of non-partisan theory would have been evidence that "final outcomes" in Congress correspond to the policy preferences of pivotal legislators—in the terminology of spatial theory, to those legislators' "ideal points." Although techniques have been developed to estimate legislators' ideal points (the most widely used being NOMINATE), one reason the debate over party influence persisted as long as it did is that there was—and still is—no precise way independently to determine the "location" of legislative outcomes within an ideological space or dimension.[4] A second reason the party influence debate continued for so long was the ingenuity and tenacity Krehbiel demonstrated in finding evidence to support different implications of his theories. This evidence ranged from patterns in standing and conference committee assignments; to the choice of rules for debating and

---

[4] Although the NOMINATE technique has been widely used as a measure of legislators' ideology or preferences over policy, the validity of this measure is itself questionable because, being based on roll-call votes, it would include any party effects resulting from agenda control or other forms of party influence. See Rohde 1995, 124; Aldrich, Berger and Rohde 2002, 20–1; Cooper and Young 2002, 66–8; Lee 2009, 42–4, 53.

discharging legislation; to data on members' activity in co-sponsoring legislation and signing discharge petitions; to votes on restrictive rules, cloture, and veto overrides; to measures of legislative productivity and coalition size.

Krehbiel also challenged proponents of partisan explanations to identify party influence that operates independently of legislators' policy preferences (1993; 1999a). The result was a major wave of scholarship devoted to addressing Krehbiel's evidence and his challenge; some ninety-odd articles, book chapters, and books were produced by political scientists between 1993 and 2006 addressing the question of whether parties have any influence in Congress over and above legislators' preferences (Smith 2007, 100–1). In keeping with the focus on party leadership, only two of the numerous responses to Krehbiel will be discussed here—those by Cox and McCubbins in their work on cartel theory, and Aldrich and Rhode in their work on the theory of conditional party government.[5]

Although cartel theory rejects Krehbiel's view of the lack of party effects in outcomes in Congress, it rests on similar theoretical foundations. With cartel theory, as with Krehbiel's non-partisan theories, legislators' actions are understood from the perspective of spatial theory, with outcomes resulting from legislators choosing alternatives closest to their preferences in a policy space. Because cartel theory shares with non-partisan theory the assumption that legislators have fixed preferences over policy, party influence cannot involve shaping or influencing legislators' preferences over legislation. As noted above, party influence in cartel theory operates primarily in the form of negative agenda control—that is, by limiting the alternatives from which legislators choose. Cox and McCubbins express skepticism that theories positing a regular capacity of party leaders to influence members' preferences over policy or their votes on legislation can withstand Krehbiel's critique; hence their theory with its emphasis on agenda control, "sidesteps critiques that focus on the debility of party influence over floor votes" (Cox and McCubbins 2005, 4).

Where Cox and McCubbins depart from Krehbiel's theoretical approach—and these departures are crucial for sidestepping the problems Krehbiel identifies with finding party influence within this spatial theory framework—is in arguing that transaction costs and non-policy benefits enjoyed by majority party members hinder the formation of cross-partisan floor majorities that would otherwise undermine the control of a majority party cartel (2005, 3, 46–8).[6] Cox and McCubbins also grant that party leaders occasionally change votes and outcomes through the use of side payments (2005, 214–18). Given that legislators are said to delegate authority to party leaders primarily to protect their shared electoral interests, from this perspective legislators presumably would also sometimes grant priority to the party's electoral goals over their individual policy preferences when persuaded by leaders to do so. Precisely how these political interests that can influence legislators' choices on legislation mesh

---

[5] Readers interested in a more detailed account of the party influence debate and why the non-partisan approach ultimately proved unsatisfactory are advised to consult Steven Smith's (2007) book-length critical treatment.

[6] On the frequency with which cross-party coalitions have actually appeared on House rules changes, see Schickler and Rich 1997.

with the fixed policy preferences that explain choice in a spatial theory framework has not been adequately addressed in cartel theory (see Cooper and Young 2002, 103–4).

In their theory of conditional party government, Aldrich and Rohde propose that the majority party in Congress can influence congressional organization and outcomes under certain conditions—specifically those of unity (or preference homogeneity) among majority party members and polarization between the majority and minority parties. In their work developing this account of party government, Aldrich and Rohde took up Krehbiel's challenge to demonstrate party effects head-on. Regarding evidence of members acting with their party against their individual policy preferences, Aldrich and Rohde cite cases in which members voted for party-sponsored procedures that resulted in outcomes other than the ones the members personally favored (2000b, 21–4; for additional evidence of this type see Sinclair 2002, 56–60, and Young and Wilkins 2007). Aldrich and Rohde also identified a series of legislative measures during the 1980s and 1990s in which the majority party leadership almost certainly succeeded in moving the outcome away from the preferences of the pivotal (median) member of the House toward the outcome favored by most members of the majority party. These cases were not inconsequential, as they included a number of major budget and appropriations measures as well as the decision by the House in 1998 to impeach President Clinton (2000a, 49–52, 70–1).

Aldrich and Rohde also leveled a powerful, empirically grounded critique at some of the conceptual and methodological underpinnings of Krehbiel's non-partisan approach. One problem they raise concerns the assumption that measures considered in Congress involve only a single ideological or spatial dimension. Recall that Krehbiel's theories hold that outcomes in Congress are explained by the preferences of pivotal legislators; in the abstract world of spatial theory, unidimensionality is almost always required for a single legislator to be pivotal in deciding outcomes. Whether this unidimensionality assumption comports sufficiently with what we already know about congressional politics is the question Aldrich and Rohde pose and answer in the negative. They observe, for example—and surely few congressional scholars would disagree—that omnibus measures such as budget reconciliation bills "are unquestionably multidimensional" (Aldrich and Rohde 2000a, 55–6).

Of course, that a theory simplifies reality is not in itself a flaw. Aldrich and Rohde argue that the problem with this assumption is not only that it oversimplifies what we know about congressional politics, but in doing so obscures our understanding of important sources of leverage for party leaders. The first problem with the unidimensionality assumption is that it leads to the implication that there is only one possible majority in the legislature. "There may be, and at least in theory there usually are, very many majorities" (Aldrich and Rohde 1997–8, 544; see also Aldrich 1995, 207–8). One way parties exert influence in Congress is by providing the capacity to organize majorities along partisan lines rather than on the basis of other potential majorities that are almost always present. Second, party leaders often assemble legislative packages in which individual legislators are presented with tradeoffs across issues (or dimensions), with the result that legislators end up voting for provisions they might not otherwise support in order to get those they do (Aldrich and Rohde

2000a, 55–6, 59; 2000b 4–5).[7] Steven Smith (2007, 98) likewise notes the blind spots for understanding congressional parties that result from building theories of legislative politics on the assumption of unidimensionality: "The consequence of this theoretical move is to rule out important party strategies—controlling the issues and policy alternatives over which coalitions form on the floor and offering side payments to win support."

A second element of Krehbiel's non-partisan approach that comes under criticism from Aldrich and Rohde is the assumption—common to spatial theories of legislative politics—that legislators' choices are determined by the proximity of alternatives to legislators' policy preferences, with those preferences determined by causes outside (exogenous to) the legislature. As Rohde puts it: "If preferences were purely exogenous, nothing that happened within the legislature would have an effect on the induced preferences of members regarding a piece of legislation. No promise, no threat, no inducement, other than those related to the policy alternative on the bill at hand, would have an effect on preferences" (Rohde 1995, 120–1). Citing evidence such as the successful use of the "Contract with America" by Republican leaders to influence floor votes of House Republicans in 1995, Aldrich and Rohde state unequivocally, "such a view is untenable" (1997–8, 557).

Building on empirical work by Richard Fenno (1973) and others who have shown the importance of multiple goals in legislators' actions, Aldrich and Rohde argue that the multiplicity of legislators' goals creates opportunities for party leaders to influence members' choices over policies. For example, party leaders can use their influence over committee appointments or the content of legislation to induce some members to vote for measures those members might not otherwise support, because those members care about maintaining or gaining influence in the institution, or about their party's electoral success, along with their individual preferences over policy (2000a, 33, 35, 58–9; 2000b, 3–4). As do Cox and McCubbins, Aldrich and Rohde also note that party influence need not take the form of changing votes, but may also involve members' willingness, for reasons other than their policy preferences, to accept agenda control exercised by the majority party leadership (1997–8, 558; 2000b, 37–8, 54–9). Thus, theories such as Krehbiel's that are grounded on the assumption that legislators' choices are determined by exogenously determined policy preferences assume away yet another important avenue for party influence.

Finally, Aldrich and Rohde advanced a more fundamental critique of non-partisan theory based on standards that should apply to tests of theoretical explanations. Krehbiel, to his credit, is clear in stating that his work is based on the instrumentalist view that a theory should be judged on the basis of its logical consistency and the accuracy of the predictions it generates. If accurate predictions about outcomes or important features of congressional politics can be generated from theories that lack parties, Krehbiel contends, these theories are useful regardless of whether we observe

---

[7] Cox and McCubbins (2005, 2, 38–9) also reject the assumption of unidimensionality in non-partisan theories and share the view that party influence arises from party leaders allowing some voting coalitions, but not others, to form.

members of Congress devoting serious time and attention to partisan organization and activity (1999b, 839–40; 1991, 101–3, 260–1).

Aldrich and Rohde call for a higher standard of realism in the assumptions and causal processes posited by theory, and make the case that verification of an explanatory theory involves "the necessity of making sense of both behavior and outcomes" (2000a, 49; see also 1997–8, 557; 2000a, 71–2; Rohde 1995, 127–9). For example, in their careful empirical studies of the development of party organization in the contemporary House (Aldrich and Rohde 1997–8, 2000, 2000b), Aldrich and Rohde show that a crucial causal process posited by Krehbiel (1998, 171; 1999b, 839–40)—that the majority and minority parties have comparable influence over the development of legislation and therefore always cancel out one another's influence—is demonstrably incorrect. Aldrich and Rohde (2000a, 72) argue that when this type of empirical evidence is found—that is, patterns in behavior inconsistent with what a theory implies—"the theory must be regarded as falsified regardless of the aggregate results it achieves."[8]

Over the course of the party influence debate, theories of party government came in for criticism as well, and not only from Krehbiel for confusing party influence with underlying preferences. Important questions remain about whether either cartel theory or conditional party government theory provides a satisfactory account of party influence in Congress. First, by incorporating some of the same assumptions as non-partisan theory, cartel theory likewise misses important avenues by which parties and party leaders influence what happens in Congress. Second, research by Eric Schickler and his co-authors has uncovered numerous cases in which the majority party in the House was "rolled" on rules changes affecting procedural rights as well as measures on which no recorded votes were taken—especially in the post-New Deal conservative coalition era (Schickler 2001, 166–8; Schickler and Pearson 2009; Schickler and Rich 1997). This evidence suggests that the negative agenda control of the House majority party may be more conditional than Cox and McCubbins contend, and demonstrates that research on party influence needs to go beyond congressional roll-call votes (see also Smith 2007, 142–3). Finally, the absence of many of the institutional features that underlie the ability of the House majority leadership to control that chamber's agenda raises serious questions about how much cartel theory can contribute to understanding party influence and party leadership in the Senate (see Campbell, Cox, and McCubbins 2002; Cox and McCubbins 2005, 94–6; Smith 2007, 143–5).

Conditional party government theory has come in for criticism as well. Krehbiel contends that the conditions of unity within, and polarization between, parties also describe the conditions in which underlying preferences alone would result in party unity (1993, 1999a). Other criticism of conditional party government theory has focused on the lack of more systematic evidence of party influence in legislative

---

[8] For an illuminating treatment of the realist and instrumentalist positions on scientific explanation articulated by Aldrich and Rohde, and by Krehbiel, respectively, in this debate, see MacDonald 2003. For a thoughtful statement of the realist position in relation to theories of congressional politics, see Hall 1995.

outcomes and the uneven or weak support for the theory's predictions found in developments in party organization in the House prior to the 1980s, and in the Senate (see Schickler 2001; Smith 2007, 123–7).

Ultimately, neither side in the party influence debate was able to provide conclusive evidence about whether outcomes in Congress correspond to the preferences of pivotal legislators as predicted by Krehbiel's non-partisan theory, or fall closer to what most members of the majority party want, as predicted (under certain conditions) by the partisan theories. The fact that the congressional studies field is moving on to questions other than debating whether congressional parties matter, suggests that the overwhelming evidence regarding the importance of partisanship in other aspects of congressional politics, along with the lack of empirical grounding for some key assumptions of non-partisan theory, were what actually determined the outcome in favor of the view that scholars should continue to incorporate parties in explanations of congressional politics. Whatever appeal a purely non-partisan explanation of congressional politics might retain as an abstract theoretical exercise, the congressional studies field is returning to the earlier equilibrium of viewing parties and party leaders as having significant, if variable, influence, and the attention of scholars has turned from this debate about whether parties matter back to longstanding questions about how and when parties and party leaders matter.[9]

What lessons were learned from the party influence debate for understanding congressional party leadership? Two points are most important. First, analysts of congressional politics need to be careful to avoid confusing party unity arising from underlying policy agreement among partisans with party unity that results from the influence of party organization and leadership. Second, while spatial theories can help illuminate certain aspects of party influence and its limits in Congress, these theories can also create serious blind spots for understanding the influence of parties and party leaders. We turn now to more recent research on party leadership, some of which is now moving beyond earlier rational choice institutionalist work based on principal-agent theories and spatial models.

New perspectives on party leadership: leaders as causal agents

While dissents from approaches that view party leaders as narrowly constrained agents of their legislative parties have been heard in congressional scholarship for some time (see, for example, Arnold 1990; Palazzolo 1992; Bader 1996; Peters 1996; Owens 1997), one new direction in recent work in this area has been the development of explanatory frameworks that view leaders as causal agents as well as agents of their followers. One direction this new work has taken involves moving beyond the conventional assumption in many rational choice institutionalist theories that

---

[9] Krehbiel, it should be noted, remains unbowed to the claims of partisan theory on either empirical or methodological grounds. See Krehbiel 2004.

legislative decisions are the product of fixed policy preferences, and approaching the formation of legislators' preferences—and the possibility that leaders shape those preferences—as an empirical question. A second new direction involves moving beyond stylized assumptions about leaders' motivations and exploring the effects of multiple goals and interests on the activity and agency of congressional party leaders.

In one of the best books yet to appear on policymaking in the post-reform Congress, R. Kent Weaver (2000) argues that conceptualizing legislators as having a "zone of acceptable outcomes" that can shift over time and be influenced by leaders and other political factors is more useful for explaining the enactment of path-breaking welfare reform legislation in the 1990s than is the concept of ideal points based on fixed policy preferences. In a study of the role of party leaders in telecommunications and health policy legislation in the 1990s, C. Lawrence Evans and Walter Oleszek (1999) found that party leaders were not only responding to, but shaping, their followers' preferences on these measures. More recently, Evans and his co-authors are developing an important body of work that uses archival records of party whip operations to document the influence of party leaders on the formation of legislators' preferences (see Bradbury, Davidson, and Evans 2008; Evans and Grandy 2009). "Party leaders," Evans and Grandy propose, "are more than passive responders to the predetermined views and positions of legislators, and under the right conditions they can exert significant influence over the coalition building process" (Evans and Grandy 2009, 210). Regarding those conditions, Evans also challenges the view that congressional party leadership is consequential only in situations where party members are in agreement over policy, proposing instead that the independent influence of leadership "may be greatest when there is a core of support for the party positions but also significant pockets of disagreement among followers" (Evans and Grandy 2009, 197). My book, *Leading Representatives* (Strahan 2007) takes a similar approach, viewing legislators' preferences over both organization and policy as subject to persuasion by leaders, and documents a number of cases in the modern House and in earlier periods in which party leaders have shaped followers' preferences with important consequences for institutional and legislative outcomes.[10] Still other studies have found evidence that congressional leaders shaped members' policy preferences by raising the visibility of issues or taking advantage of opportunities to shape public opinion on issues being considered in Congress (Jacobs et al. 1998; Schickler 2001, 166–71). More broadly, David Mayhew has proposed that actions by leaders, as well as other members of Congress, can shape both elite and mass opinion in a public sphere, where "society's preference formation, politics, and policymaking all substantially take place" (Mayhew 2000, x).

In party leadership theories based on principal-agent models, leaders are usually assumed either explicitly or implicitly to be motivated by narrow self-interest of a

---

[10] An important earlier treatment of the importance of persuasion and deliberation in the formation of legislators' policy positions on which my work builds, is Bessette 1994.

particular type—ambition to retain a leadership office. Notes Steven Smith (2007, 39), "the complications of theorizing about leaders and their motivations are many. For this reason, if no other, theorists of congressional parties leave leaders' motivations unexamined and merely assume parties have the resources to motivate someone to perform leadership functions." Consequently, how the politics of leadership might be influenced by leaders' motivations or goals, other than ambition to retain a leadership position, has not been given serious attention in the rational choice institutionalist literature on party leadership.

A number of congressional scholars are now taking up this problem and have begun to develop explanations of party leadership that explicitly incorporate leaders' multiple goals and interests and examine new evidence about how these goals may help explain leaders' actions. In *Leading Representatives*, I argue that a number of goals beyond retaining a leadership position in Congress can motivate independent action by party leaders. These include intensely held concerns about good public policy; about how Congress should be organized; about holding higher office; or even about their own historical reputations. A series of legislative case studies from the speakerships of Henry Clay, Thomas Reed, and Newt Gingrich are used to illustrate the usefulness of this "conditional agency" framework for explaining the independent contributions party leaders can make to organizational and legislative outcomes (Strahan 2007).

In a recent study of House speakers from Sam Rayburn through Dennis Hastert, Matthew Green (2010) also argues that leaders have multiple goals that can cause them to be responsive to interests beyond simply advancing the interests of the legislative party in order to win reelection as speaker. These goals include the speaker's own reelection to the House and personal policy goals, as well as a number of goals that arise from duties that have become associated with the office of speaker—supporting the interests of the presidential party, supporting the institutional presidency (especially in the area of foreign affairs), and protecting House-wide interests. Based on examination of the most extensive body of evidence (both quantitative and qualitative) yet assembled on leadership activities of modern House speakers, Green finds that a multiple-goal framework better explains this activity than does the proposition that the speaker's leadership is always explained by the interests or preferences of the legislative party.

It is important to note that all of these studies that incorporate the causal agency of party leaders also find party followers' preferences and expectations to be important influences on the actions of leaders; none proposes that leaders are unconstrained by their party followers. However, these studies do show that explanatory theories that incorporate assumptions of fixed policy preferences for legislators, or highly stylized assumptions about leaders' motivations, miss important sources of the independent agency that can occur with party leaders, and therefore provide incomplete explanations of how party leadership in Congress works. Another respect in which explanations of congressional party leadership remain incomplete is in the relatively limited attention that has been devoted to party leadership in the Senate.

What about the Senate?

Since the 1960s, political science scholarship on Congress has been consistently House-centric. In a wonderful little essay entitled, "Looking for the Senate," Richard Fenno (2002, 12) describes this situation as "the great imbalance."[11] Scholarship on party leadership is no exception to this pattern. The more individualistic and idiosyncratic Senate probably supplies fewer of the types of behavioral regularities political scientists seek to explain, and the rules of the Senate certainly provide fewer resources for party leaders to influence organizational and legislative outcomes. Among the challenges faced by the Senate majority leadership is the supermajority requirement to end debate and the leverage this rule provides to the minority party as well as to dissident members of the majority. It is not accidental that scholarly work on party leadership has tended to focus on the House side of the Capitol with an occasional glance toward the other wing; party leaders just wield more power in the House.

Still, there has been a revival of late in scholarship on the Senate, including work on party leadership. This work has focused on two main questions, both of which involve comparisons with the House. First, how and why did the party organization and leadership offices of the modern Senate emerge and, second, how is it that partisanship in Senate voting has increased in recent decades in a pattern that resembles the House, despite the weaker agenda control and limited organizational resources in the hands of Senate party leaders?

Drawing on newspaper accounts, records of debate, and other sources reaching back into the nineteenth century, Gerald Gamm and Steven Smith (2002a, 2002b) have reconstructed parts of the sequence by which modern party organization and leadership offices emerged in the Senate, and are examining the fit between this sequence and explanations for organizational change in Congress. Among their findings is that the development of Senate party leadership institutions does not fit conditional party government theory. According to Gamm and Smith, these organizational developments have not been driven by party unity and polarization, nor has polarization tended to produce highly centralized party leadership in the Senate as it has in the contemporary House. Instead, "Senate parties elaborated party organization or created new leadership posts in periods of majority weakness, internal division, and close partisan divisions within the chamber" (Gamm and Smith 2002a, 236; see also Smith and Gamm 2009).

A second question that has been addressed in recent scholarship on Senate parties is how leaders use the limited resources they do control to advance party goals. Drawing on evidence from interviews, participant observation, and documentary sources, Patrick Sellers (2002) has shown how Senate leaders work to coordinate communications activity and to focus media coverage on issues on which their party is unified, the public supportive, and the opposition divided. Kathryn Pearson's research on sources of party discipline in the contemporary Congress has found that the partisan polarization of recent years has brought some modest increases in the

---

[11] For two recent collections intended to address this imbalance, see Oppenheimer 2002, and Monroe, Roberts, and Rohde 2008.

resources Senate leaders can use to encourage party loyalty, mostly in the form of enhanced influence over committee assignments (Pearson 2008). Den Hartog and Monroe (2008) propose that even the modest procedural advantages available to the Senate majority party make it less costly for issues favored by the majority to reach the agenda and therefore tilt policy outcomes in the Senate toward those favored by the majority.

The broadest-ranging and most theoretically ambitious recent study of Senate partisanship is Frances Lee's *Beyond Ideology* (2009). Based on an analysis of partisanship in roll-call voting on different types of issues during the period 1981–2004, as well as senators' accounts of their own actions in floor debates, Lee makes a strong case for the view that ideological polarization provides an incomplete explanation for the high levels of partisan voting in the contemporary Senate. Party unity, in her view, results from willing cooperation among senators in pursuit of their shared electoral and power interests, as well as their shared policy views. Rather than enforcing party discipline or using formal institutions to control the agenda, Senate party leadership "functions as a central channel for the intraparty communication and negotiation necessary for party members to formulate a consensus policy agenda" (Lee 2009, 165). Lee's perspective finds additional support in C. Lawrence Evans and colleagues' (Bradbury, Davidson, and Evans 2008) exploration of newly collected archival evidence on the Senate whip system, which likewise emphasizes the importance of communication networks in Senate politics, and proposes that the ability to gather information and communicate with party members through the whip system provides party leaders with tactical advantages in shaping legislation.

Lee shares the skepticism of some of the recent work on the House regarding the possibility of developing satisfactory explanations of congressional parties or party leadership within spatial theory frameworks that assume legislators have fixed ideological views or preferences over policy (Lee 2009, 45–6, 190–1). One of the most important contributions of this study lies in its appeal for scholars to recover earlier, more *political* understandings of legislative parties in which parties and their leaders discuss, deliberate, and negotiate to develop collective positions on public policy issues, rather than simply reflecting individual legislators' fixed ideological positions or preferences.

The challenge for work on party leadership in the Senate remains fitting the politics of the upper house into some broader explanatory framework. At this point, neither of the leading explanations of party organization and leadership that have been most influential in scholarship on the House of Representatives—cartel theory and conditional party government—appear to take us very far in explaining how party leadership works in the Senate. Lee's (2009) study of party politics in the Senate provides a promising beginning in developing alternative approaches that can account for the high levels of partisanship in the contemporary Senate, within an institutional context in which party leaders possess fewer procedural and organizational powers than their House counterparts. Senate parties and party leadership will undoubtedly continue to be of interest and a focus of new research in the future. Before concluding with some thoughts on other promising avenues for future research, two persistent methodological challenges that arise in studying congressional leadership merit discussion.

Finding and generalizing about leadership effects in Congress

Stated very broadly, there are two basic strategies for testing and developing theories in political science, whether these theories seek to explain congressional party leadership or some other phenomenon in politics. One involves examining specific cases of the phenomenon—say, outcomes on particular legislative measures—and determining whether the posited cause is present and was a significant cause of the outcome or effect of interest *in those particular cases*. The second involves looking at large numbers of cases of the phenomenon—say, a large sample of legislative measures, or the roll-call votes of all legislators over multiple Congresses—and determining whether the cause posited by the theory is *on average* a significant cause of the effect of interest across a large population of observations. Methodologists James Mahoney and Gary Goertz (2006) describe these strategies as the "causes of effects" and the "effects of causes" approaches, respectively, and note that the former tends to be favored by qualitative researchers in the social sciences and the latter by quantitative researchers. As Mahoney and Goertz emphasize, both of these approaches have strengths and weaknesses for establishing causal inferences (and this is not the place to rehearse that debate).

For the purposes of developing and testing theories about the influence of party leadership in Congress, it is important that scholars continue to employ both approaches. Partly because of the large and benevolent influence of Richard Fenno, the congressional politics subfield has been distinctive in the American politics field for its methodological pluralism (see Fenno 1990). This pluralism should continue to be a major strength of the subfield, and one of particular importance for understanding the politics of party leadership. Party leadership efforts—and effects—are likely to be unevenly distributed across members of the House or Senate, and across legislative measures. Methods that test for average causal effects across all members of a legislative chamber, or across large numbers of measures, may therefore have difficulty finding and accurately assessing the importance of those effects. Such methods may find weak party or leader effects, when those effects are in fact highly consequential on specific organizational or legislative outcomes. As Smith (2007, 107) has put it: "My guess is that, as a general rule, party leaders do not care about generating statistically significant influence; they would rather win legislative battles." The larger methodological point is that to establish and understand the effects of party leadership, scholars need to continue to explore the causal processes through which party influence operates in particular legislative battles—i.e. through careful case studies—as well as through quantitative research designs that consider average causal effects across large numbers of observations.

A second persistent methodological issue that arises in studying party leadership is how to generalize about leadership effects and the agency of leaders. Even if it is demonstrably true that the agency of leaders is consequential in legislative politics, for some there remain doubts about whether these effects are of importance for political science. While it might seem only common sense that political scientists should focus on leaders' influence in congressional politics if leaders' actions are consequential, this is a not a trivial objection if we accept that the goal of political science is to develop generalizations or causal explanations about regularities in politics, rather than simply describe individual actions or outcomes. The study of political leaders presents a challenging problem, especially for political scientists who seek to develop highly parsimonious and deterministic theories of politics. Tradeoffs party leaders have to manage among multiple goals—both their own and their followers'—will inevitably introduce indeterminacy in the actions and strategies leaders undertake (see Cooper and Young 2002, 102–4; Smith 2007, 35–43).

If leaders have some autonomy in the choices they make in reconciling these goals, and their choices can result in things happening in Congress that would not otherwise have occurred as a result of more general causes present in the political or institutional context, how can we generalize about when the agency of leaders will matter for influencing outcomes in Congress, or how much these leader effects will matter? One answer is that we probably cannot succeed in doing this. Brady and McCubbins (2002, 11) have argued: "The desire for parsimony almost unavoidably means that we construct theories that cannot explain some of the variance in which we are interested." In this view, rather than attempt to incorporate the agency of leaders in explanations of congressional politics, these effects are probably best treated as "idiosyncratic" because they cannot be reliably predicted by (or deduced from) a parsimonious theory (Brady and McCubbins 2002, 11).

The alternative view on which some of the newer work on party leadership is premised is that the "variance" that can result from the agency of party leaders is of sufficient importance that we need to take it into account in developing explanations of congressional politics, even if those explanations cannot take the form of highly parsimonious theories. As Schickler (2001, 15) argues in his influential study of the politics of institutional change in Congress, "The challenge . . . becomes incorporating leadership into a broader theoretical perspective." We should take up this challenge, in Schickler's view, because "leadership is not an idiosyncratic residual that defies systematic analysis. Strategic innovation by would-be leaders is endemic to legislative politics and rooted in the pluralism of member interests" (2001, 15). To which can be added that the agency of leaders may also be rooted in the pluralism of leaders' goals and interests and opportunities leaders encounter to shape their followers' preferences under certain conditions. But theories that incorporate the agency of leaders will necessarily be more conditional in the sense of proposing conditions under which leaders are likely to influence outcomes, and identifying the causal mechanisms by which this occurs, rather than seeking to offer predictions about precisely when leadership effects should always be found. Some will undoubtedly find these more complex and conditional explanatory theories unsatisfactory. As was the case in the earlier party influence debate, the ongoing debate about explaining congressional party leadership will also be in part a dialogue about different modes of explanation in political science.

FUTURE RESEARCH ON PARTY LEADERSHIP

I conclude with some thoughts on promising areas for future work on party leadership in Congress. At the level of theory, understanding legislative leadership has in some respects been hindered by thinking of legislators as having fixed preferences. To develop better explanations of legislative leadership, more work is needed on conceptualizing legislators' policy positions or preferences in ways that can incorporate the dynamism and variation in intensity that can be present in legislators' positions, and that provide opportunities for leaders to shape legislative outcomes. Lee's (2009) recent argument to the effect that advances in explaining congressional parties may come from building on modes of explanation in political science that preceded rational choice institutionalism merits serious consideration here. The challenges involved in developing and refining theories that can incorporate the agency of party leaders against the backdrop of the institutional limits on leadership in congressional politics also deserve continued attention.

Turning to promising areas for new empirical research on party leadership, it is important to note that all of these suggestions apply to the Senate as well as the House. First, more work is needed on the range of political conditions under which party leaders are active and consequential. The most influential theories of party leadership propose that leaders are most active and consequential when party members are in agreement. But more and more research is finding that leaders are active and consequential on issues where party unity *cannot* be taken for granted, or when party margins are narrow. Second, more close empirical work is needed on the variety of forms party leadership can take, and why leaders choose one approach over another. Smith's (2007, ch. 3) typology of positive/negative and direct/indirect forms of influence may provide a useful organizing framework here. Third, building on work by Jones (2005), Lee (2009), and Green (2010), more work is necessary on the interplay between party leaders in Congress and the White House. Different combinations of partisan control of the two institutions encourage different leadership strategies in Congress, including varieties of partisanship, such as bipartisanship and cross-partisanship, that remain important in an era of partisan polarization but are not well understood (Cooper and Young 1997, 2002). Fourth, although recent studies of party leadership in both the House and Senate emphasize the linkages between electoral politics and party leadership, there has been surprisingly little recent research on how party leaders actually develop and implement electoral strategies (Kolodny 1998 being one important exception). More broadly, building on Peters and Rosenthal's recent account of Speaker Nancy Pelosi and the "New American Politics" (2010), more work is required on how congressional leaders work with party organization outside of Congress, the dense networks of lobbyists and interest groups that now populate Washington, and old and new communications media. Finally, future research on party leadership needs to take up where Connelly and Pitney (1994) left off, and bring the minority party back in.

Party leadership matters in Congress. Much remains to be learned about precisely when and how.

REFERENCES

ALDRICH, J. H. 1995. *Why Parties? The Origin and Transformation of Political Parties in America.* Chicago: University of Chicago Press.

—— and ROHDE, D. W. 1997–8. The Transition to Republican Rule in the House: Implications for Theories of Congressional Politics. *Political Science Quarterly*, 112: 541–69.

—— and ROHDE, D. W. 2000a. The Consequences of Party Organization in the House: The Roles of the Majority and Minority Parties in Conditional Party Government, pp. 37–72 in *Polarized Politics: Congress and the President in a Partisan Era*, ed. J. R. Bond and R. Fleisher. Washington: CQ Press.

—— and ROHDE, D. W. 2000b. The Republican Revolution and the House Appropriations Committee. *Journal of Politics*, 62: 1–33.

—— BERGER, M. M., and ROHDE, D. W. 2002. The Historical Variability in Conditional Party Government, pp. 17–35 in *Party, Process, and Political Change in Congress: New Perspectives on the History of Congress*, ed. D. W. Brady and M. D. McCubbins. Stanford, CA: Stanford University Press.

ARNOLD, R. D. 1990. *The Logic of Congressional Action.* New Haven: Yale University Press.

BADER, J. B. 1996. *Taking the Initiative: Leadership Agendas in the Congress and the "Contract with America."* Washington DC: Georgetown University Press.

BESSETTE, J. M. 1994. *The Mild Voice of Reason: Deliberative Democracy and American National Government.* Chicago: University of Chicago Press.

BRADBURY, E. M., DAVIDSON, R. A., and EVANS, C. L. 2008. The Senate Whip System: An Exploration, pp. 73–99 in *Why Not Parties? Party Effects in the United States Senate*, ed. N. W. Monroe, J. M. Roberts, and D. W. Rohde. Chicago: University of Chicago Press.

BRADY, D. W., and MCCUBBINS, M. D. 2002. Introduction: Party, Process and Political Change: New Perspectives on the History of Congress, pp. 1–14 in *Party Process and Political Change: New Perspectives on the History of Congress*, ed. D. W. Brady and M. D. McCubbins. Stanford, CA: Stanford University Press.

CAMPBELL, A. C., COX, G. W., and MCCUBBINS, M. 2002. Agenda Power in the U.S. Senate, 1877–1986, pp. 146–65 in *Party, Process, and Political Change in Congress: New Perspectives on the History of Congress*, ed. D. W. Brady and M. D. McCubbins. Stanford, CA: Stanford University Press, 2002.

CONNELLY, JR., W. F., and PITNEY, J. J. 1994. *Congress' Permanent Minority? Republicans in the U.S. House.* Lanham, MD: Rowman & Littlefield.

COOPER, J., and BRADY, D. W. 1981. Institutional Context and Leadership Style: The House from Cannon to Rayburn. *American Political Science Review*, 75: 411–26.

——and Young, G. 1997. Partisanship, Bipartisanship, and Crosspartisanship in Congress Since the New Deal, pp. 246–73 in *Congress Reconsidered*, 6th edn, ed. B. I. Oppenheimer and L. C. Dodd. Washington DC: CQ Press.

——and Young, G. 2002. Party and Preference in Congressional Decision-making: Roll-call Voting in the House of Representatives, 1889–1999, pp. 64–106 in *Party, Process, and Political Change in Congress: New Perspectives on the History of Congress*, ed. D. W. Brady and M. D. McCubbins. Stanford, CA: Stanford University Press.

Cox, G. W., and McCubbins, M. D. 1993. *Legislative Leviathan: Party Government in the House*. Berkeley, CA: University of California Press.

——2005. *Setting the Agenda: Responsible Party Government in the U.S. House of Representatives*. New York: Cambridge University Press.

Den Hartog, C., and Monroe, N. W. 2008. Agenda Influence and Tabling Motions in the U.S. Senate, pp. 142–158 in *Why Not Parties? Party Effects in the United States Senate*, ed. N. W. Monroe, J. M. Roberts, and D. W. Rohde. Chicago: University of Chicago Press.

Evans, C. L., and Oleszek, W. J. 1999. The Strategic Context of Congressional Party Leadership. *Congress & the Presidency*, 26: 1–20.

——and Grandy, C. E. 2009. The Whip Systems of Congress, pp. 189–215 in *Congress Reconsidered*, 9th edn, ed. B. I. Oppenheimer and L. C. Dodd. Washington DC: CQ Press.

Fenno, Jr., R. F. 1973. *Congressmen in Committees*. Boston: Little, Brown.

——1990. *Watching Politicians: Essays on Participant Observation*. Berkeley, CA: IGS Press.

——2002. Looking for the Senate: Reminiscences and Residuals, pp. 12–27 in *U.S. Senate Exceptionalism*, ed. B. I. Oppenheimer. Columbus, OH: Ohio State University Press.

Gamm, G., and Smith, S. S. 2002a. Emergence of Senate Party Leadership, pp. 212–38 in *U.S. Senate Exceptionalism*, ed. B. I. Oppenheimer. Columbus, OH: Ohio State University Press.

——2002b. Policy Leadership and the Development of the Modern Senate, pp. 287–311 in *Party, Process, and Political Change in Congress: New Perspectives on the History of Congress*, ed. D. W. Brady and M. D. McCubbins. Stanford, CA: Stanford University Press.

Green, M. N. 2010. *The Speaker of the House: A Study of Leadership*. New Haven: Yale University Press.

Hall, R. L. 1995. Empiricism and Progress in Positive Theories of Legislative Institutions, pp. 273–302 in *Positive Theories of Legislative Institutions*, ed. K. A. Shepsle and B. R. Weingast. Ann Arbor: University of Michigan Press.

Jacobs, L. R., Lawrence, E. D., Shapiro, R. Y., and Smith, S. S. 1998. Congressional Leadership of Public Opinion. *Political Science Quarterly*, 113: 21–41.

Jones, C. O. 1968. Joseph G. Cannon and Howard W. Smith: An Essay on the Limits of Leadership in the House of Representatives. *Journal of Politics*, 30: 617–46.

——2005. *The Presidency in a Separated System*. 2nd edn. Washington DC: Brookings Institution.

Kiewiet, D. R., and McCubbins, M. D. 1991. *The Logic of Delegation*. Chicago: University of Chicago Press.

Kolodny, R. 1998. *Pursuing Majorities: Congressional Campaign Committees in American Politics*. Norman, OK: University of Oklahoma Press.

Krehbiel, K. 1991. *Information and Legislative Organization*. Ann Arbor, MI: University of Michigan Press.

——1993. Where's the Party? *British Journal of Political Science*, 23: 235–66.

——1998. *Pivotal Politics: A Theory of U.S. Lawmaking*. Chicago: University of Chicago Press.

——1999a. Paradoxes of Parties in Congress. *Legislative Studies Quarterly*, 24: 31–64.

——1999b. The Party Effect from A to Z and Beyond. *Journal of Politics*, 61: 832–40.

——2004. Legislative Organization. *Journal of Economic Perspectives*, 18 : 113–28.

Lee, F. E. 2009. *Beyond Ideology: Politics, Principles, and Partisanship in the U.S. Senate*. Chicago: University of Chicago Press.

MacDonald, P. K. 2003. Useful Fiction or Miracle Maker: The Competing Epistemological Foundations of Rational Choice Theory. *American Political Science Review*, 97: 551–65.

Mahoney, J., and Goertz, G. 2006. A Tale of Two Cultures: Contrasting Quantitative and Qualitative Research. *Political Analysis*, 14: 227–49.

Mayhew, D. R. 2000. *America's Congress: Actions in the Public Sphere, James Madison through Newt Gingrich*. New Haven, CT: Yale University Press.

——2008. *Parties and Policies: How the American Government Works*. New Haven: Yale University Press.

Monroe, N. W., Roberts, J. M., and Rohde, D. W. (eds.) 2008. *Why Not Parties? Party Effects in the United States Senate*. Chicago: University of Chicago Press.

Oppenheimer, B. I. (ed.) 2002. *U.S. Senate Exceptionalism*. Columbus, OH: Ohio State University Press.

Owens, J. E. 1997. The Return of Party Government in the US House of Representatives: Central Leadership-Committee Relations in the 104th Congress. *British Journal of Political Science*, 27: 247–72.

Palazzolo, D. J. 1992. *The Speaker and the Budget: Leadership in the Post-Reform House of Representatives*. Pittsburgh: University of Pittsburgh Press.

Pearson, K. 2008. Party Loyalty and Discipline in the Individualistic Senate, pp. 100–20 in *Why Not Parties? Party Effects in the United States Senate*, ed. N. W. Monroe, J. M. Roberts, and D. W. Rohde. Chicago: University of Chicago Press.

Peters, Jr., R. M. 1996. *The American Speakership: The Office in Historical Perspective*, 2nd edn. Baltimore: Johns Hopkins University Press.

——and Rosenthal, C. S. 2010. *Speaker Nancy Pelosi and the New American Politics*. New York: Oxford University Press.

Riker, W. H. 1980. Implications from the Disequilibrium of Majority Rule for the Study of Institutions. *American Political Science Review*, 74: 432–46.

——1986. *The Art of Political Manipulation*. New Haven: Yale University Press.

Rohde, D. W. 1991. *Parties and Leaders in the Postreform House*. Chicago: University of Chicago Press.

——1995. Parties and Committees in the House: Members' Motivations, Issues, and Institutional Arrangements, pp. 119–37 in *Positive Theories of Legislative Institutions*, ed. K. A. Shepsle and B. R. Weingast. Ann Arbor: University of Michigan Press.

——2000. The Gingrich Speakership in Context: Majority Leadership in the House in the Late Twentieth Century. *Extensions: A Journal of the Carl Albert Congressional Research and Studies Center* (Fall): 4–7.

——and Shepsle, K. A. 1987. Leaders and Followers in the House of Representatives: Reflections on Woodrow Wilson's *Congressional Government*. *Congress & the Presidency*, 14: 111–33.

Schickler, E. 2000. Institutional Changes in the House of Representatives, 1867–1998: A Test of Partisan and Ideological Power Balance Models. *American Political Science Review*, 94: 267–88.

——2001. *Disjointed Pluralism: Institutional Innovation and the Development of the U.S. Congress*. Princeton, NJ: Princeton University Press.

——and Rich, A. 1997. Controlling the Floor: Parties as Procedural Coalitions in the House. *American Journal of Political Science*, 41: 1340–75.

——and Pearson, K. 2009. Agenda Control, Majority Party Power, and the House Committee on Rules, 1937–52. *Legislative Studies Quarterly*, 34: 455–91.

Sellers, P. 2002. Winning Media Coverage in the U.S. Congress, pp. 132–53 in *U.S. Senate Exceptionalism*, ed. B. I. Oppenheimer. Columbus, OH: Ohio State University Press.

SINCLAIR, B. 1990. Congressional Leadership: A Review Essay and a Research Agenda, pp. 97–162 in *Leading Congress: New Styles, New Strategies*, ed. J. J. Kornacki. Washington DC: CQ Press.

——1992. The Emergence of Strong Leadership in the 1980s House of Representatives. *Journal of Politics*, 54 (August): 658–84.

——1995. *Legislators, Leaders, and Lawmaking: The House of Representatives in the Post-reform Era*. Baltimore: Johns Hopkins University Press.

——1999. Transformational Leader or Faithful Agent? Principal-agent Theory and House Majority Party Leadership. *Legislative Studies Quarterly*, 24 (August): 421–49.

——2002. Do Parties Matter? pp. 36–63 in *Party Process and Political Change: New Perspectives on the History of Congress*, ed. D. W. Brady and M. D. McCubbins. Stanford, CA: Stanford University Press.

——2006. *Party Wars: Polarization and the Politics of National Policymaking*. Norman, OK: University of Oklahoma Press.

SMITH, S. S. 2007. *Party Influence in Congress*. New York: Cambridge University Press.

——and GAMM, G. 2009. The Dynamics of Party Government in Congress, pp. 141–64 in *Congress Reconsidered*, 9th edn, ed. B. I. Oppenheimer and L. C. Dodd. Washington DC: CQ Press.

STRAHAN, R. 2003. Personal Motives, Constitutional Forms, and the Public Good: Madison on Political Leadership, pp. 63–91 in *James Madison: The Theory and Practice of Republican Government*, ed. S. Kernell. Stanford, CA: Stanford University Press.

——2007. *Leading Representatives: The Agency of Leaders in the Politics of the U.S. House*. Baltimore: Johns Hopkins University Press.

WEAVER, R. K. 2000. *Ending Welfare as We Know It*. Washington DC: Brookings Institution Press.

YOUNG, G., and WILKINS, V. 2007. Vote Switchers and Party Influence in the U.S. House. *Legislative Studies Quarterly*, 32: 59–77.

CHAPTER 18

CONGRESSIONAL COMMITTEES

C. LAWRENCE EVANS

Prior to the mid-1970s much of the most prominent scholarship about Congress concerned the internal operations and policy impact of its standing committees. Richard Fenno's classic, *Congressmen in Committees*, was the most influential of the landmark committee studies of the period. Other examples include studies of the House Agriculture Committee by Charles O. Jones, the Ways and Means and Finance Committees by John Manley, and David Price's book-length study of legislative innovation in three Senate committees. Foundational research about the history of the committee system also appeared in the 1960s and early 1970s, with Nelson Polsby producing influential articles about the importance of seniority in the selection of committee chairs, and Joseph Cooper illuminating the early origins and development of House committees. It is not much of an exaggeration to assert that political scientists of the era primarily viewed the Congress through the lens of its standing committees.

Now fast-forward forty years. Since then, the elaboration of rational choice theories of congressional behavior and institutions; the development of sophisticated new techniques for analyzing the roll-call record; a renewed interest in congressional history; and other achievements, have fundamentally altered and mostly improved the scholarly literature about Congress. Yet, the attention paid by political scientists to the internal operations of House and Senate committees has declined markedly, as have studies that consider the different ways that individual panels relate to outside constituencies or the parent chamber. Instead, contemporary scholars tend to focus more on party control of committees and whether key features of the House and Senate committee systems are consistent with competing rational choice models of congressional organization writ large. For the most part, congressional scholarship is no longer committee-centric.

This chapter reviews the important changes that have occurred in congressional scholarship as it relates to committees. The main argument is that the transformation of committee research reflects the rise of rational choice modeling and increased methodological sophistication within the discipline of political science. Indeed, congressional scholars often have led the way in formulating and testing formal models of politics. But the transformation of committee scholarship also arises from significant changes that have occurred within Congress since the 1960s, especially the growing importance of party cleavages on the major issues of the day. These changes have made the institution even more amenable to rational choice analysis. The reduced scholarly attention now devoted to internal committee operations and decision-making, however, also creates opportunities for significant new research. Even within a Congress polarized along party lines, most important legislative decisions still occur during the committee stage of the process, and most of the questions raised about congressional committees by previous generations of scholars are still relevant in the contemporary Congress. Indeed, a close examination of how and why scholarship about congressional committees has been transformed highlights important empirical and normative questions that have been under-explored in recent years, providing useful guidance for future work.

FOUNDATIONAL STUDIES

Although committee scholarship dates to Woodrow Wilson's (1885) book-length argument that "Congress in session is Congress on public exhibition, whilst Congress in its committee rooms is Congress at work," the systematic analysis of committees first emerged as a centerpiece of congressional research during the 1960s. Richard F. Fenno, Jr. (1962a, 1965), Charles O. Jones (1961, 1962), and John Manley (1969, 1970) produced the foundational studies.[1] The 1960s, it should be emphasized, were characterized by low levels of partisan polarization relative to most other periods in congressional history. According to the best measures, the two political parties in Congress were unified internally, and sharply differentiated from one another from the late 1870s until the New Deal, at which point party polarization declined. Polarization continued to be muted until the early 1970s, and then rose steadily during the 1980s and 1990s, eventually reaching historic highs during the administrations of George W. Bush and Barack Obama. The early committee studies of Fenno, Jones,

---

[1] These scholars in turn emphasized their own intellectual debt to Huitt's (1954) case study of the House Banking Committee. See also Matthews (1960), especially ch. 7.

and their contemporaries, in other words, were conducted during an unusual period on Capitol Hill when cross-partisan coalitions were commonplace.

This matters because there is evidence that the importance and operating autonomy of standing committees are inversely related to the extent of partisan polarization within the parent chamber (Cooper and Brady 1981; Rohde 1991; Maltzman 1997). As the majority party becomes more unified internally about the major issues of the day, and the gulf between the policy preferences of majority and minority party members widens, party leaders become more central to the legislative process and the influence and autonomy of committees tends to decline. Conversely, lower levels of partisan polarization are associated with stronger committees and relatively weak party leaders. Internal disagreements within the majority party tend to make rank-and-file members less willing to delegate significant control over the agenda to their leaders because the leadership might use these powers to advance a policy program contrary to their views and the interests of their constituents. Instead, the preference of rank-and-file members is that power be centered more within the committee system, where the interests that stand to gain or lose the most in a policy area are disproportionately represented. In short, research about the internal operations of standing committees was at the center of congressional scholarship during the 1960s, in part because the regular presence of cross-partisan coalitions meant that committees played an especially important role in congressional decision-making.

The catalyst for the first wave of committee scholarship was Fenno's (1962a, 1965) research about the two Appropriations Committees, which have jurisdiction over discretionary federal spending, "the historic bulwark of legislative authority [1965, xiii]." How, Fenno asked, were the two Appropriations Committees able to reconcile, or "integrate," the divergent interests, coalitions, and roles that were apparent among members and the outside constituencies affected by the panels' work? As part of the study, he conducted personal interviews with more than 170 members and staff, examined hearings transcripts and other committee documents, and compiled extensive data about spending requests, committee recommendations, and outcomes at the agency level. Over four decades later, his book about appropriations politics, *The Power of the Purse*, remains the most comprehensive and substantively rich analysis ever conducted about a congressional committee.

Among other findings, Fenno discovered that the House panel, and to a lesser extent its Senate counterpart, was able to achieve high levels of integration through shared norms that emphasized budgetary austerity and the promotion of committee prestige and autonomy. The committee's ability to minimize internal conflict was enhanced by the stability of its membership from Congress to Congress, and the nature of the Appropriations jurisdiction. Appropriations makes decisions about dollars and cents, program by program, rather than questions that inherently are ideologically divisive, facilitating compromise. Within the Appropriations Committees, thirteen semi-autonomous subcommittees made most of the decisions. Fenno argued that norms of legislative specialization and reciprocity undergirded the remarkable deference of the full panel toward the recommendations of its subcommittees, and also of the full House and Senate to the legislation reported by the two committees.

The concepts that structured Fenno's groundbreaking study of the Appropriations Committees—integration, member roles, and norms for resolving conflict and promoting specialization—mostly derived from the literature about structural functionalism that was influential at the time among sociologists. Precisely because the Appropriations Committees did appear to operate as relatively autonomous "subsystems" of the parent House and Senate, with stable patterns of decision-making and shared expectations about member behavior, the functionalist concepts helped Fenno describe and explain the work of the two panels.

Other scholars attempted to apply and extend Fenno's conceptual framework to other committees and jurisdictions. Jones (1961, 1962), for example, produced two important articles about the House Agriculture Committee that were strongly influenced by Fenno's appropriations research. His substantive focus was on how members used the Agriculture panel to promote the interests of farmers and the broader agricultural community. Like Fenno, he relied heavily on personal interviews with members and staff. Jones found that members of the Agriculture Committee disproportionately came from districts that depended economically on farming, and that the internal structure of the panel reflected the salient commodity interests and agricultural problems of the day. Separate subcommittees dealt with cotton, dairy products, livestock, and feed grains, for example, while other subcommittees were granted jurisdiction over soil conservation, crop insurance, and agricultural trade. Jones also found that the norms that fostered integration within the Appropriations panel were apparent in the internal operations of the Agriculture Committee. Compared to Appropriations, however, there was significantly less "integration" and more partisanship within Agriculture because the constituency interests of Democrats and Republicans over farming differed substantially. Members from both parties joined the committee to promote the commodity interests of their districts, but Democrats were especially likely to represent areas that produced cotton, rice, and tobacco, while Republicans mostly came from districts heavy in wheat, corn, and small grains. Divergent commodity interests produced partisan conflict, undermining committee integration. To some extent, committee leaders were able to dampen this conflict by combining commodity-specific policies into larger "omnibus" packages of importance to both Democratic and GOP farm districts, but overall the panel was less integrated and autonomous (relative to the full chamber) than was the Appropriations Committee as described by Fenno.

Manley's (1969, 1970) study of the House Committee on Ways and Means, which considered tax issues, major entitlement programs, and trade, was likewise shaped by Fenno's appropriations research. And he also relied heavily on field research and participant-observation for evidence. As was the case with Agriculture, the Ways and Means jurisdiction generated regular disagreements between Democrats and Republicans, but the potential for partisanship was more firmly rooted in ideological differences between the political parties, rather than the geographic incidence of commodity interests. As a result, the functionalist concepts that Fenno used were less helpful and he turned instead to the sociological literature on small groups, which emphasized exchange relationships, especially the balance between the rewards and benefits of committee service, on the one hand, and the expectations and costs of that service, on the other. But "norms" also were an important conceptual ingredient of Manley's research. He claimed that the Ways and Means Committee was characterized by norms of restrained partisanship, which in turn were maintained via inducements like the electoral value, prestige, and intra-chamber influence associated with service on the panel.

Manley's most significant contribution to congressional scholarship, however, was his memorable analysis of the leadership style and influence of Ways and Means Chair Wilbur Mills, then widely viewed as the most powerful committee leader on Capitol Hill. In a significant departure from most existing treatments of legislative leadership, Manley emphasized the importance of context over personal traits and skills. Mills' influence, he argued, derived from his sensitivity to the expectations and preferences of other committee members and the mood of the full House. Rather than rely on formal powers or prerogatives, in other words, his policymaking role was based on persuasion and the discretion that other lawmakers extended to him because of his responsiveness to their needs, reputation for fairness and diligence, and ability to build winning coalition on the floor. Mills' stature was further enhanced by his pivotal position on the panel between voting blocs. Often he was the swing vote on major committee legislation. Manley's conceptualization of legislative leadership, especially the impact of context on leadership style, quickly became a classic in the field and influenced a generation of scholarship about congressional leadership.

Other important studies of committee politics were conducted during this period. Masters (1961) and Bullock (1970, 1972), for example, produced the first major articles about the process through which members are assigned to committees. As mentioned, Cooper (1970) provided the first systematic description of the early development of House committees. Polsby (1968, and with Gallaher and Rundquist, 1969) shed significant new light on the emergence of seniority as a norm for selecting committee leaders (see Schickler in this volume). Prior to the 1911 revolt against Speaker Joseph Cannon, Polsby and his colleagues discovered, uncompensated violations of seniority were fairly common. After the Cannon revolt, power in the House devolved from party leaders to the standing committee system and such violations became less frequent. Following adoption of the Legislative Reorganization Act of 1946, the blueprint of the modern committee system, seniority became the nearly automatic criterion for selecting chairs, and remained so until the recentralization of power in the speakership during the 1980s and 1990s. Interestingly, the committee research of this period often featured extensive analysis of the contents of legislation. For instance, in his book, *Who Makes the Laws*, Price (1972) examined the legislative work of three Senate committees during 1965–6, arguably the most productive Congress since World War II. Price found that the ability of the Senate to compete for power with activist President Lyndon Johnson depended on the legislative creativity that occurred within its standing committees. The bottom line? As the decade of the 1960s came to a close, by most accounts committees were the central organizational feature of Congress, and scholarship about the House and Senate committee systems was at the heart of legislative studies as a sub-field.[2]

THE TURN TO RATIONAL CHOICE

Legislative scholarship changed markedly during the 1970s. Building on the pioneering work of Riker (1958), Mayhew (1974), and Fiorina (1974), scholars increasingly applied rational choice theory to the study of Congress, producing a research agenda that often was characterized as "the new institutionalism" (Shepsle 1986). In contrast to the sociologically grounded work prevalent during the 1960s, the rational choice perspective emphasized the goals of individual members and the purposive, rational pursuit of these goals subject to opportunities and constraints in the legislative arena and the broader political environment, especially member constituencies. The turn to rational choice theory resulted in part from intellectual efforts to devise more rigorously deductive theories of political behavior patterned on the economics discipline and game theory. But rational choice theory also resonated with developments in congressional politics underway at the time. As a result of the enfranchisement of African Americans following passage of the Voting Rights Act of 1965, the majority Democratic caucus became more internally unified in both the House and Senate. Energized party liberals dramatically scaled back the formal powers of committee chairs and broke the back of the Conservative Coalition. Power shifted from the chairs toward rank-and-file members, and also to centralized party leaders (Rohde 1991). Congressional campaigns also became more candidate-centered during the late 1960s. Especially after the Watergate scandal of 1973–4, there was an influx of new, highly independent, members. The expansion of government programs that accompanied Lyndon Johnson's "Great Society" also produced a larger and more active interest group environment for the legislative branch (Sinclair 1989, 1995). For all of these reasons, the Congress of the 1970s was far more individualistic and permeable toward outside interests than had been the more stable and insular institution of the 1960s. With its focus on the purposive behavior of individual political actors, rational choice theory was more useful for understanding these changes than were the sociological perspectives that had structured prior research about Congress.

In the turn to rational choice theory, Richard Fenno once again produced the pivotal committee study, *Congressmen in Committees* (1973), one of the most influential scholarly books written about the national legislature. In contrast to his appropriations study, in *Congressmen in Committees* Fenno embraced the more individualistic,

[2] Other important committee-related scholarship conducted during the 1960s includes Peabody (1963), Robinson (1963), Goodwin (1970), and Murphy (1969, 1974).

goal-oriented, perspective of rational choice theory (see also Fiorina in this volume). In part, his intellectual shift reflected the practical exigencies of comparing multiple committees. As Fenno wrote, "What struck me most forcefully in observing the House Appropriations Committee was the degree to which it was a self-contained social system, [but in] comparative perspective, the member contribution seems both large and distinctive [1973, xvii]." His conceptual transition towards individual behavior also reflected the intellectual climate within which he worked—the political science department at the University of Rochester. Under the leadership of William Riker and Fenno, that department had emerged as the early hub of rational choice modeling within the discipline of political science.

In *Congressmen in Committees*, Fenno famously asserted that members were primarily motivated in their committee work and other activities by three main goals: getting reelected, making good public policy, and securing influence within the chamber. His observations derived from hundreds of semi-structured interviews with members and staff conducted by Fenno himself, and also by John Manley, who served as his research assistant for the project. Fenno relied on his previous research for evidence about Appropriations and Manley shared with him his own data about the House Ways and Means and Senate Finance Committees. In the early 1960s, Fenno (1962b) had gathered extensive evidence about the Committee on Education and Labor as part of collaborative research on federal aid to education. Together, he and Manley conducted dozens of additional interviews in Washington with members of the Committees on Interior, Post Office and Civil Service, and Foreign Affairs, producing a sample of six House committees and their Senate counterparts for comparative study. Members were drawn to the Interior and Post Office committees, Fenno observed, primarily to help their constituents and secure reelection. In contrast, lawmakers joined the Education and Labor and Foreign Affairs panels mostly to promote their view of good public policy. Members of Appropriations and Ways and Means joined those panels to enhance their influence within the full chamber. Fenno's claims about the tri-part motivational psychology of lawmakers quickly became a staple of congressional scholarship and a central feature of textbooks about the legislative process.

Within the standing committees of Congress, Fenno maintained, members pursue their goals subject to certain environmental constraints, or clusters of interested outsiders, which vary systematically by panel and jurisdiction. Here, his conceptual framework reflected the standard language of constrained optimization featured in rational choice theories. Members of Interior, for example, pursued their reelection goals subject to opportunities and constraints created by important clientele groups, such as environmental organizations and the Forestry Association. For Ways and Means, in contrast, the executive branch and the two political parties dominated the committee environment. Fenno argued that the goal-oriented behavior of members, conditioned by elements of the relevant committee environment, shaped the internal structural operations of a panel, especially the role of subcommittees and the leadership styles of the chair and ranking minority members, and ultimately the content of committee-reported legislation.

Between member goals and environmental constraints, on the one hand, and a committee's internal structure and policy outputs, on the other, was an intermediate conceptual step that reflects both the subtlety of Fenno's understanding and the transitional nature of his comparative committee study. Committee members, he argued, share certain "strategic premises" that are shaped by the goals of members and the panel's environment, and which in turn influence decisions about committee structure and legislative recommendations to the floor. The concept of "strategic premise" was crucial to his analytic framework, Fenno reasoned, because it enabled him to analyze committees "less as an aggregation of individuals and more as a working group" (1973, 46). Strategic premises are similar conceptually to the norms that he and Manley had claimed shape committee decision-making in their earlier research. Fenno asserted that members of the Appropriations Committee shared two strategic premises in their committee work—reducing executive budget requests, and providing adequate funding for executive programs. The strategic premises held by Ways and Means members, in contrast, included writing legislation that could prevail on the floor, and promoting the relevant party agenda. Conceptually, then, the notion of "strategic premise" enabled Fenno to make the transition from the individual level (member goals) to the aggregate level (committee legislation). Empirically, the concept also allowed him to link his rational choice analysis in *Congressmen in Committees* back to the more functionalist perspective featured in his case study of the Appropriations panels. In contrast to his treatment of committee norms in his appropriations research, however, the strategic premises that Fenno described in his comparative study of committees derived from the goals of individual members. The book was firmly grounded in the emergent rational choice perspective on Congress.

Congressmen in Committees strongly influenced future scholarship about the operations of House and Senate committees. Interestingly, the book appeared at the beginning of a major wave of committee reform in the House. In 1973, for example, the year that the volume was published, the House Democratic Caucus opened up the process for selecting chairs and adopted the "subcommittee bill of rights," which further constrained the operating autonomy of full committee leaders (Davidson 1981). The following year, the power to appoint Democratic members to committees was shifted from the party's contingent on Ways and Means to the Steering and Policy Committee, a Democratic Party organ. The Speaker also was given effective control over the Committee on Rules and enhanced discretion over referring bills to committee (Oppenheimer 1977). And as 1974 came to a close, the Democratic Caucus ousted three senior committee chairs that were viewed as out of step with the liberal agenda. Many scholars maintained that the reforms devolved power from the full to the subcommittee level, creating policymaking practices that some called "subcommittee government." Indeed, using records of committee markups (bill writing sessions) from the post-reform period, Hall and Evans (1989) show that committee bills were primarily drafted by members of the relevant subcommittee; the amendments added to subcommittee legislation in full committee were mostly offered by members of the subcommittee; and subcommittees were seldom on the losing side of votes in full committee. In the decade or so following the 1970s reforms, then, subcommittees did become more institutionalized and active (see also Fiorina 1977; Haeberle 1978).

Although certain aspects of committee politics that had been richly described by Fenno were altered by the reforms of the 1970s, particularly the role of subcommittees and committee leadership styles, his main concepts and analytic framework retained their explanatory power. For instance, Price (1978) extended Fenno's concept of "environmental constraints" to better capture issue-specific factors, especially conflict between interested groups and the degree of public salience, that often vary across the different policy areas within an individual panel's jurisdiction. A decade after Fenno's study appeared, Smith and Deering (1984) produced a book-length analysis of the committee system, *Committees in Congress*, intended to capture the major changes that had occurred since the appearance of his work. Their important treatise, which has been revised and updated through two succeeding editions (1990, 1997), encompasses all House and Senate committees and includes extensive new data about diverse aspects of the committee process, ranging from assignment requests and bill referral patterns to subcommittee activity levels and floor amendments to committee legislation. Although a major, independent, contribution to the committees literature, the three editions of Smith and Deering's book closely track the analytic framework from *Congressmen in Committees*, especially Fenno's central chapter about member goals.

Perhaps the most rigorous early application of rational choice theory to congressional evidence dealt with the process through which individual lawmakers are assigned to committees. The assignment process matters substantively because it determines the distribution of policy preferences within a panel, and thus shapes committee politics. But committee assignments are also a superb topic for testing rational choice theories because the assignment process is so clearly characterized by individual "actors in pursuit of personal goals, constrained only by scarcity and institutional procedures [Rohde and Shepsle 1973]." As part of his 1960s research on Ways and Means, Manley had gathered data about Democratic committee requests. Prior to the 1970s reforms, the placement of Democratic House members on panels had been the responsibility of their fellow partisans on the Ways and Means Committee. Ways and Means Democrats, in other words, served as the "committee on committees" (CC) for their party in the chamber. Freshmen lawmakers seeking initial assignments and returning members desiring transfers to new committees submit letters to the relevant CC (there is one for all four chamber/party contingents), listing their requests in order of preference. When there is competition for an opening, which is typical for the more popular and influential panels, the CC members weigh the strengths and weakness of competing applicants and make a choice. Manley shared the assignment request notebooks for 1961–8 with Fenno, who in turn shared them with two of his graduate students at the University of Rochester, David Rohde and Kenneth Shepsle. Prior research on the committee assignment process conducted by Masters and Bullock had relied on data about the *results* of the process. Missing was analysis of the factors that shaped member *submissions* to the CC and whether or not these requests were met. The assignment request data made such an analysis feasible for the first time. And these data are especially valuable for testing rational choice theories of congressional behavior because they can serve as direct indicators of member preferences, a key component of such theories.

Together, Rohde and Shepsle (1973) published a well-regarded article demonstrating that member assignment requests were shaped by district characteristics and that the CC considered a range of factors, including constituency interests, party loyalty, and seniority, when making choices between members competing for the same opening. The most comprehensive and authoritative application of rational choice theory to the committee assignment process, however, was Shepsle's 1978 book, *The Giant Jigsaw Puzzle*. Interestingly, Shepsle's book received only mixed reviews upon publication (e.g. Hinckley 1979), but in the years that followed it set the standard for empirically testing rational choice models of congressional organization.

Conceptually and empirically, Shepsle's book was a significant elaboration of his article with Rohde. For one, he developed a formal model of member assignment requests in which the probability that a member asks for a particular panel is a function of that legislator's valuation of the slot and the likelihood that the CC will grant the request. Committee valuations are influenced by the relevance of a panel to a member's constituents, the lawmaker's policy priorities, and the overall importance of the jurisdiction. Shepsle's treatment of the motivational psychology of members, then, was similar to Fenno's observations about member goals. The probability that a request was granted by the CC, Shepsle maintained, depended on whether there was a vacancy from the member's state on the committee, the degree of in-state competition for the opening, and so on. Thus, a freshman might value an assignment on Ways and Means for electoral and policy reasons, but if her state was already represented on the panel and there was significant competition for the opening (likely, given committee's power and prestige), then the lawmaker might instead request a less desirable but more attainable committee like Banking or Public Works. Nonfreshmen seeking to transfer to a new committee followed a similar calculus, Shepsle argued, except they also considered the opportunities forgone by (possibly) giving up an existing assignment.

In the *Giant Jigsaw Puzzle*, Shepsle also modeled the responsiveness of the leadership, both in terms of negotiating committee sizes and in granting the assignment requests of individual legislators. In setting committee sizes, the leadership balanced the demand for additional slots against the desire of existing members on a panel not to "devalue" their positions by excessively expanding the committee's size. Once committee sizes, and thus the number of available openings, are set, Shepsle conceptualized the assignment choices of the CC as an optimization process in which the leadership attempts to maximize the total number of "satisfied" legislators subject to the structure of assignment opportunities. The signature strength of Shepsle's study, however, was the dozens of substantively interesting hypotheses derived from his models and put to rigorous empirical tests. It is not feasible to do full justice to these findings in a few short paragraphs, but among other results he found that the pattern of member requests was indeed consistent with the expected utility model and, especially for panels with relatively homogenous interests, these requests were closely associated with district characteristics and a lawmaker's personal background (e.g. past occupational associations with teaching or the union movement for Education and Labor). Interestingly, for nonfreshmen seeking transfers, the likelihood of success did not have a statistically significant relationship with the past party loyalty of the requester on roll calls.

In addition to these statistical tests using Democratic assignment data from 1958 to 1974, Shepsle also conducted dozens of interviews with members and staff. Indeed, one of the contributions of the study is a chapter in which he used this interview evidence to apply Fenno's (1973) analytic framework to decision-making on the CC. Overall, Shepsle's research provides ample evidence that the assignment process does not produce panels that are representative samples of the chamber, especially for committees with homogeneous jurisdictions. Instead, such committees tend to be populated with members that have strong constituency and personal ties to the issues that they consider. For the most prestigious committees such as Appropriations, however, the high level of competition for slots dwarfs the impact of parochialism. Shepsle's committee assignment study, in other words, strongly suggests that important features of congressional organization are shaped by multiple factors, not just constituency interests or the personal policy priorities of members, and that there is substantial variation in these causal relationships across jurisdictions and policy areas.[3]

MODELS OF CONGRESSIONAL ORGANIZATION

By the mid- to late 1980s, rational choice models essentially dominated scholarly attempts to theorize about the U.S. Congress, with significant implications for the study of committees. For the most part, these theories took the form of spatial models in which the preferences of legislators between competing policy alternatives are conceptualized as points along one or more underlying dimensions of evaluation, with members choosing the proposal that is spatially most proximate to their most preferred outcome, or ideal point. Committees are a central feature of all three leadings spatial theories of congressional organization—the distributive, informational, and partisan perspectives—but their role differs substantially across models.

The *distributive* theory is rooted in Mayhew (1974) and Fiorina (1977), but the most precise statements are probably Shepsle (1979, 1986) and Weingast and Marshall (1988). The internal procedures and structural arrangements in Congress, distributive theory posits, are intended to promote stable policy outcomes and the electoral interests of members. Committee jurisdictions are designed to reflect electorally

---

[3] Ray (1980, 1982) also produced several noteworthy studies of the committee assignment process around the time that *The Giant Jigsaw Puzzle* appeared.

relevant interests and the committee assignment process ensures that members generally will be placed on panels with turf important to the folks back home. The seniority system and a general deference to existing assignments combine to make committee positions a form of property right. As a result, the committees of Congress are comprised of "preference outliers," or "high demand" legislators, who report bills aimed at promoting the constituency interests most affected by the jurisdiction. On the floor, other members defer to the recommendations of the committee as part of a generalized logroll across panels, and a disproportionate share of the policy benefits in the issue area are allocated to the districts of committee members. Legislative outcomes, in other words, do not reflect centrist viewpoints within the chamber as a whole, but instead the more parochial interests of high-demand constituencies.

For scholars, the basic distributive story was the most generally accepted portrait of the committee system during the 1970s and 1980s, and for good reason—it was fairly consistent with many major studies of the era. Still, there also was significant evidence that the explanatory power of the theory was somewhat limited. Fenno, for example, had emphasized that members were motivated by policy concerns and the pursuit of power, and not just by reelection. Cooper's study of the early committee system demonstrated that committees were initially intended to enhance the legislative capability of the full House and Senate, not to promote the parochial interests of high-demand constituencies. Arnold (1981) pointed out a critical feature of the federal budget that was generally understood but nonetheless under-acknowledged in the literature: most federal expenditures do not take the form of overtly distributive policies that can be targeted toward particular districts and states, and thus most expenditures are not especially conducive to the distributive politics game. In addition, a central tenet of distributive theory is that committees wield significant power within the full House and Senate. But, some scholars asked, why would most members of the House and Senate systematically defer to committee recommendations that do not benefit their constituents? The question produced an interesting exchange in the journals that foreshadowed the spirited debate over legislative organization that would emerge within a few years.

Shepsle and Weingast (1987a, 1987b) attempted to answer the question about committee power by formulating a model in which members of the committee of jurisdiction also dominate the conference delegation responsible for ironing out differences between the House- and Senate-passed versions of a measure. In their model, a committee's control over the conference stage provides it with an "*ex post* veto" over modifications to a bill made on the House or Senate floor. Members know that if floor amendments result in a bill that the committee likes less than current law, then the committee can systematically change or even block the legislation in conference. As a result, in anticipation of the conference stage, there may be incentives for lawmakers to defer somewhat to committee recommendations on the floor. Krehbiel (1987), however, responded that conference procedures do not generally provide committees with anything like an *ex post* veto over the work of floor majorities. For example, either chamber can avoid the conference stage by playing "ping pong" and directly reporting amended legislation to the other house, or by simply accepting the other chamber's version. House rules also stipulate that the Speaker appoint a majority of conferees that support the House-passed version of the measure. Moreover, conference procedures are only used for a small fraction of bills passed by Congress. The evidence, then, is mixed that the conference procedure can translate into systematic committee power on the floor.

In another attempt to capture the institutional sources of committee power, Weingast (1989, 1992) developed a model of floor decision-making in which all members can offer amendments to a committee's bill (the functional equivalent of an open rule), but the committee is allowed a first response by offering a second-degree amendment. Indeed, in the House, the chair of the committee of jurisdiction usually does have the ability to offer second-degree amendments to floor revisions aimed at unraveling committee legislation. Using data from 1983–4, Weingast found that most amendments offered by opponents to committee bills on the floor fail, and that the unfriendly alterations that pass usually have been modified by the committee via second-degree amendments. The adoption of unfriendly floor adjustments to committee bills is rare, in other words, and when such proposals do pass, the chair is usually able to "fight fire with fire" and reduce the damage. However, as Smith (1989) shows, successful amendments to committee bills increased significantly from the 1950s to the 1980s, suggesting that committee power in the full House and Senate was in decline. Moreover, Weingast's evidence does not capture the substantive importance of opposing amendments or of the second-degree counters from committee members. Rather than fighting fire with fire, these second-degrees could be mostly face-saving devices. We simply cannot know, based on amendment counts alone. Still, in the 1970s and 1980s, when scholars generalized about the committee system, they typically reverted to the language of distributive theory and committee power, in large part because there was no precise alternative.

Beginning with a series of influential articles co-authored with Gilligan (Gilligan and Krehbiel, 1987, 1989, 1990), and then with the appearance of his 1991 book, *Information and Legislative Organization*, Keith Krehbiel provided such an alternative. The internal organization of Congress, Krehbiel argued, was not primarily designed to facilitate distributive politics and logrolling between powerful constituency groups, but instead to provide the full House and Senate with the expertise and information necessary to legislate. Krehbiel's two main assumptions were that (1) the procedural and policy choices of a legislature must be acceptable to a majority of its members, and (2) these members often are uncertain about the implications and effects of the policy options from which they must choose. In addition to promoting the parochial interests of powerful constituencies à la distributive theory, Krehbiel reasoned, committees can influence legislative outcomes by using their specialized expertise to provide the full chamber with information about the consequences of policy alternatives. The committees of the House and Senate, then, are properly conceptualized as instruments of the legislature. And the composition of their memberships, the procedures that guide the consideration of committee bills on the floor, and the eventual fate of legislation, are all determined by the full chamber.

Krehbiel's *informational* model had a profound impact on legislative scholarship, in part because it generated a number of substantively interesting hypotheses that could be tested with available evidence. For example, if chambers rely on committees as a source of information, the panels that they construct should not be systematically tilted toward narrow interests or constituencies, and instead should be relatively representative of policy preferences in the chamber as a whole. In contrast to distributive theory, then, Krehbiel argued that committees should not be generally composed of "preference outliers." Indeed, such "outlier" committees should only be tolerated if their expertise is so great that it countervails the disadvantages from their skewed policy preferences. According to distributive theory, the policy recommendations of outlier committees should receive significant procedural protections on the floor, such as restrictions on the amendments that other members can offer to committee bills, in order to ensure that the logroll between different interests will be maintained. The informational model, in contrast, predicts that all committees will not be granted the same procedural advantages in the full chamber. Instead, the higher the level of expertise within a committee, and the more representative it is of the chamber as a whole, the more likely that the full membership will be willing to protect the panel's handiwork on the floor. Krehbiel's informational theory, in other words, has implications for all major features of the committee process, from assignments and the distribution of preferences within panels, to the representativeness of committee bills and the procedures that affect the fate of these bills on the floor.

In the second half of *Information and Legislative Organization*, Krehbiel reported the results of a number of empirical tests that he claimed support the informational perspective and are inconsistent with the distributive model. His analysis of the committee outlier hypothesis has received the most attention from scholars. For indicators of "preferences," Krehbiel relied on the ratings of member roll-call votes devised by fourteen major interest groups. Two of the rating schemes tap liberal-conservative ideology, while the rest are more relevant to particular issue areas (e.g. American Security Council ratings for defense matters) and thus are potentially useful for jurisdiction-specific analysis. First, Krehbiel used the general indicators of member liberalism/conservatism to examine whether the mean and median values within standing committees diverged from the chamber mean and median during 1985–6.[4] Most committees, he found, did not have mean or median ideological scores that differed significantly from the full House. Next, he analyzed the relative representativeness of nine panels for which jurisdictionally relevant groups scores were available. The best evidence for outlier status was the House Armed Services Committee, which was significantly more pro-defense than the full chamber. Otherwise, there was little evidence that committees are high-demand preference outliers à la distributive theory. Certain panels, such as Education and Labor, had mean or median scores that diverged from the chamber statistic, but for the most part these differences

---

[4] In a related article, Krehbiel (1990) incorporated interest group ratings from 1979 to 1986, including ratings for both the House and Senate, producing results analogous to those summarized here.

were not statistically significant. In succeeding chapters, he also analyzed whether the full House or Senate provided committees with the parliamentary protections necessary for them to exert distributive power. Based on evidence about the content of House amendment rules and the use and makeup of conference committees, he concluded that there was little systematic evidence of such protections. Indeed, the use of restrictive amendment rules appeared to be negatively, rather than positively, associated with the distributive content of committee legislation.

In addition to the distributive and informational theories, legislative scholars advanced a third approach to explain congressional organization: the *partisan* perspective. Here, the majority party leadership (on behalf of the party rank and file) makes the important decisions about committee composition and structure. Of course, scholars had long argued that key institutional features of the House and Senate are influenced by party politics (see Smith 2007, for an overview). However, as the ideological differences between Democrats and Republicans increased on Capitol Hill during the 1980s and 1990s, scholarly interest in the influence of party grew substantially.

First, David Rohde (1991) devised the theory of "conditional party government," which maintains that power shifts from the committee rooms of Congress toward majority party leaders as policy preferences within each party become more homogeneous and the gulf between them widens.[5] Although Rohde's 1991 book includes an array of formal and informal tests of his theory, the most cited applications concern the transition to Republican rule following the 1994 mid-term elections and party management of committees during the years that followed. In collaboration with John Aldrich, Rohde argued that the high preference homogeneity of the new Republican majority led incoming Speaker Newt Gingrich, R-Ga., to reduce the power of committees and committee chairs through rule changes and informal practices, such as adopting term limits for committee chairs and setting aside the seniority norm to personally pick committee chairs who were especially supportive of the GOP program. Indeed, many of the committee reforms implemented by the Republicans after the 1994 elections are mostly consistent with the conditional party government argument. Moreover, the House majority party's direct involvement during committee deliberations and its strategic management of committee bills on the floor stepped up markedly during the late 1990s, as predicted by the theory (Aldrich and Rohde 1997, 2000a, Sinclair 2007). The Republican leadership's remarkable influence over committee decision-making encompassed panels as jurisdictionally diverse as Appropriations (Aldrich and Rohde 2000a) and Agriculture (Hurwitz, Moiles, and Rohde, 2001). And, when the first wave of Republican committee chairs was replaced in 2000 because of the new term limits, party loyalty and fundraising prowess superseded seniority as the main criterion for choosing replacements (Deering and Wahlbeck 2006; Cann 2009).

---

[5] Although mostly focused on the emergence of strong party leadership over time, Sinclair (1995) applies a "principal-agent" framework to party–committee relations that mostly jibes with conditional party government.

In a series of studies, Gary Cox and Mathew McCubbins formulated a related party theory, the cartel model (see especially 1993 and 2005).[6] Mostly compatible with the conditional party government approach, the cartel theory emphasizes that the name brands of the two political parties matter to voters, and, as a result, members of each party share a common electoral interest that leads them to grant to their leaders in Congress the prerogatives necessary to promote the party's agenda. In contrast to conditional party government, though, cartel theory holds that leadership power over the agenda has been a stable and long-standing feature of the House, rather than con-ditional on the distribution of preferences. In the first articulation of their theory, Cox and McCubbins (1993) conceptualized party power as both negative (blocking items from the agenda opposed by most majority party members) and positive (advancing through the chamber legislation endorsed by most majority party members), while their 2005 refinement of the theory mainly emphasizes negative power. But both articulations have implications for committee politics, and the evidence they marshal meshes well with the empirical studies of Aldrich and Rohde, Sinclair (1995), and other scholars of the congressional parties.

For one, Cox and McCubbins also evaluate and find wanting the standard distrib-utive view that committees are distinct in their memberships and autonomous vis-à-vis the full House. They use committee assignment evidence to reassess Shepsle's finding that the assignment process is mostly one of self-selection. Over 40 percent of freshmen requests are denied, they note, which seems contrary to simple self-selection. Moreover, using a more extensive data set than Shepsle, they find that members with higher levels of party loyalty on roll calls are significantly more likely to receive a committee assignment transfer from the leadership than are less loyal lawmakers. Cox and McCubbins also waded into the committee outlier debate. For indicators of member preferences, they relied on interest group ratings, as well as the Poole–Rosenthal NOMINATE scores discussed elsewhere in this volume. Examining Congresses from 1947 to 1988, they find most committees to be representative of the ideological and geographic makeup of the two party caucuses. But they did uncover more cases of biased panels than did Krehbiel.

To explain the variance, Cox and McCubbins developed an interesting typol-ogy of committees based on whether (a) the effects of a jurisdiction on commit-tee non-members are uniform or targeted, and (b) the affected constituencies are homogeneous or heterogeneous in their interests. Committees that create fairly uni-form external effects across members (e.g. Appropriations, Public Works) should have party contingents that are representative of the relevant party caucus. For these panels, they claimed, the consequences of committee action are of concern to the entire caucus, and the leadership will ensure that the party's contingent on the committee reflects this broader interest. Jurisdictions that have a more targeted, or lopsided, distribution of effects (e.g. Agriculture, Interior) are more likely to have

---

[6] Aspects of the cartel theory were also apparent in Kiewiet and McCubbins (1991), which in contrast to Fenno's research argued that the Appropriations Committees are best viewed as agents of the congressional parties.

party contingents that are unrepresentative of the relevant caucus in important ways. Here, the consequences for the party rank and file from an outlier committee are less significant because of the targeted impact of the jurisdiction. Committees that produce a mixture of uniform and targeted effects (e.g. Armed Services, Education and Labor) are less easy to predict. And within each category, the more homogeneous the interests of the affected clientele groups, the greater the likelihood of committee bias. Using NOMINATE scores and the various interest group ratings, Cox and McCubbins find that the uniform externality panels were mostly representative of the two party caucuses, while the targeted effects committees were the most likely to be unrepresentative. The mixed externality committees fell somewhere in the middle. And overall, homogeneity of interests in a committee's environment was associated with outlier status. As a result, the authors claimed that the jurisdictional characteristics of unrepresentative committees are consistent with party control over the assignment process.

As mentioned, Cox and McCubbins' (2005) refinement of cartel theory emphasized the negative agenda power of majority party leaders and, not surprisingly, most of the empirical tests in that study relate to floor decision-making. However, they do claim that when preferences within the majority party grow more heterogeneous, the role of agenda-setter becomes more decentralized within the majority party, with chairs using their own procedural powers to block divisive proposals in committee. Using data about the incidence of minority party dissents on committee reports and committee roll calls, they demonstrate that the majority party contingent in committee is seldom rolled on the motion to report.[7] Moreover, minority party members are far more likely to file dissents to committee reports, even controlling for ideology. Overall, then, the studies of Cox and McCubbins, Aldrich and Rohde, and other scholars have uncovered fairly compelling evidence for party effects within the committee rooms of Congress, thus challenging arguments that distributive or informational models alone are sufficient to understand committee politics in Congress.

Adjudicating between models

The competing models of congressional organization produced a flurry of empirical research by legislative scholars aimed at adjudicating between the models, and many of these studies dealt with committees. For one, there was a large quantity of research that attempted to sort out the divergent results about preference outliers. Literally dozens of published articles touched on the topic, but here are a few highlights.[8] Hall and Grofman (1990) questioned whether roll-call indicators could proxy for

---

[7] A majority party "roll" in committee occurs when the position taken by most majority party members within the panel on a motion to report legislation to the floor does not prevail.

[8] In the addition to the studies cited in the text, other noteworthy articles that address the committee outlier hypothesis include: Frisch and Kelly (2004); Krehbiel (1994); Londregan and Snyder (1994); Maltzman and Smith (1994); Overby and Kazee (2000); Parker, Copa, et al. (2004); Sprague (2008); and Young and Heitshusen (2003).

member preferences.[9] And even if the standard distributive story is accurate, they point out, because of cross-jurisdictional logrolling we would expect that committee proposals would be deferred to on the floor, and thus that the votes cast by panel members and non-members should be similar. Vote-based indicators of member preferences, in other words, cannot distinguish between competing models. Instead, Hall and Grofman maintain that relevant economic characteristics of a lawmaker's constituency can provide better measures. Using data about agriculture interests at the state level, they show that members of Senate panels with jurisdiction over agriculture tend to be more pro-farmer than the chamber as a whole. Adler and Lapinski (1997) and Adler (2000) likewise used economic, social and geographic characteristics of districts to test for committee outliers from 1943 to 1998, finding ample evidence of unrepresentative panels. Adler (2002) conducted a similar analysis with analogous results for Appropriations subcommittees. Groseclose (1994) questioned the statistical criteria used by Krehbiel and others to identify outlier panels. Relying on interest group ratings as preference indicators, he employed Monte Carlo techniques that avoided these methodological limitations and found little evidence in support of any of the competing theories. Groseclose concludes that it is difficult to find sufficient statistical evidence to reject the null hypothesis that members are assigned randomly to committees.

Clearly, the matter of committee representativeness is controversial in the literature. Still, considering the full range of studies, a fair assessment would be that the identification of outliers becomes more likely when one shifts from broad ideological proxies like NOMINATE to more specialized interest group ratings to jurisdictionally relevant constituency characteristics. The more tailored the preference indicator is to the programs and issues that a panel considers, the more likely that it will produce evidence that a committee is biased. And such findings are especially associated with panels that have jurisdiction over programs with strong constituency linkages or that target benefits to a limited subset of districts or states. Committee representativeness of the full chamber or the two party caucuses, in other words, varies in predictable ways by jurisdiction.

The preference outlier debate is the most prominent example of committee research aimed at adjudicating between the competing theories, but other studies that appeared during the 1990s and since then also addressed whether features of committee politics resonate with these models. For example, King (1994, 1997) examined how the jurisdictions of committees change over time, as chairs seek to expand their turf into neighboring policy areas. Mostly relying on evidence from the House Committee on Energy and Commerce, he found that formal rule changes are less important as a source of jurisdictional change than are informal adjustments resulting from the referral decisions of the parliamentarian. Moreover, the criteria used in making these

---

[9] Like Cox and McCubbins (1993), Hall and Grofman (1990) also argued that committee bias should be conditional, and more likely when the policies considered by a panel affect a relatively small portion of the membership.

decisions appear to reflect the informational needs of the floor median rather than the programmatic agenda of the majority party or some distributive coalition.

Along those lines, Cox and McCubbins (1993) claimed that decisions to create and destroy committees typically are made to enhance the interests of the majority party. Schickler and Rich (1997), however, identified every House rules change during 1919–93 that altered committee jurisdictional boundaries and found that only two of the twenty-six changes were made by party-line vote, suggesting that jurisdictions are not set to advantage the majority party relative to the minority. Similarly, Evans and Oleszek's (1997) analysis of House Republican efforts to realign jurisdictions after the 1994 mid-term elections indicates that the interests of powerful constituency groups and the personal power agendas of individual members mostly stymied efforts by Newt Gingrich and his colleagues to remake jurisdictions around the Republican agenda. Still other scholars, such as Baumgartner, Jones, and MacLeod (2000); Hardin (1998); Sheingate (2006); and Adler and Wilkerson (2008), find that rule changes can be a significant source of jurisdictional change, and that adjustments in committee turf tend to occur for myriad reasons.

Indeed, when the debate over congressional organization is considered in its entirety, the bottom line appears to be that no single theory or causal factor is adequate for understanding committees and their role. In a sense, momentum in the field is toward revisiting the central message and opening sentences of Fenno's (1973) classic volume: "This book rests on a single assumption and conveys a simple theme. The assumption is that congressional committees matter. The theme is that congressional committees differ [xiii]." In a careful study that incorporates extensive data about committee assignments, the content of amendment rules, and chamber support for committee proposals from the 1950s to the 1990s, Maltzman (1997) argues persuasively that committees are responsive to multiple "principals," including outside constituencies, the party caucuses, and the full chamber, depending on the strength of the majority party and the salience of the relevant panel's agenda. As scholars continue to refine and test theoretical models of legislative institutions, like Fenno and Maltzman they need to focus on how committees differ from one another and over time.

They also should consider whether the motivational psychology of members might matter more than the institutional arrangements so central to the debate about legislative organization. Richard Hall's 1996 book, *Participation in Congress*, explores a critical feature of committee decision-making: the choices made by members about whether and how much to participate during committees' deliberations over legislation. Hall uses records of committee sessions to construct a bill-specific indicator of member participation that taps involvement in the drafting stage, attendance at markups, the casting of roll calls in committee, the offering of amendments during markups, and so on. The documentary evidence is buttressed by more than 100 interviews with members and staff to three House committees: Agriculture, Education and Labor, and Energy and Commerce. Based on these interviews, he constructed indicators of the extent to which the dozens of bills for which he had participation data evoked the goals of individual committee members. Included among the motivational factors he tapped were the reelection, policy, and influence goals emphasized by Fenno, as well as promoting the agenda of the president.

Hall's book is chock full of insights, but especially important is his finding that on most bills, the goals of only a small subset of a committee's membership are evoked, and participation during committee deliberations is usually narrow. As a result, the distribution of NOMINATE scores or of constituency characteristics within a panel may not tell us very much about the content of a bill because only a small subset of the relevant committee is actually paying attention and participating. Most often, the active subset includes committee leaders and members of the relevant subcommittee. In Hall's view, participation at the committee stage captures the "revealed intensity" of member preferences, and intensities can matter more than direction. He finds that the biases introduced into decision-making by selective participation vary by bill and the mix of goals that are evoked. For constituency-oriented legislation, such as the items considered by the Agriculture Committee, the subset of participants hails from districts that are far more dependent on the farm economy than is typical for other members. For bills and issues that engage other goals, such as making good policy, the biases that occur because of selective participation are less pronounced. The gist of Hall's study, however, is *not* that committees are or are not composed of "preference outliers," but that the conceptual debate about legislative organization may not have been asking the right questions. The division of labor that exists within Congress is not wholly a structural manifestation based on jurisdictional boundaries, committee assignments, and procedural protections on the floor. Rather, in Hall's words, it "bubbles up from the day-to-day decisions of individual members as they decide how to best allocate the time, energy, and other resources of their enterprise on the numerous issues that arise within and beyond the panels to which they are assigned" (1996, 239). Perhaps scholars should focus less on institutional features of the committee system and more on the calculations of individual lawmakers about when and how to involve themselves in the legislative process.

FUTURE RESEARCH

Since the 1960s, the scholarly literature about Congress and its committees has been transformed from the rich descriptive treatments of Fenno, Jones, and their contemporaries, to the more rigorous, model-driven, research that characterizes ongoing debates about the foundations of legislative organization. Over time, the substantive focus has shifted from describing and comparing the internal operations of individual panels to testing hypotheses about the relative importance of distributive coalitions, party pressures, and the informational needs of the full chamber for understanding general features of the committee system. Conceptually, congressional scholars have mostly discarded elements of sociological theories, such as "integration" and member "roles," and turned instead to the more individualistic, purposive approach of rational choice theory, especially the spatial model of legislative choice. Empirically, they have reduced their reliance on interviews, the personal observation of legislators at work, and case analysis, and made greater use of systematic quantitative data, especially vote-based measures of member preferences. Most important, the study of how committees operate internally and how they differ from one another is no longer at the center of legislative studies as a sub-field. Instead, features of the committee system serve as test implications for gaging the explanatory power of general theories of legislative organization. Congressional research is no longer committee-centric and the focus is more on floor politics and the role of parties. By any measure, this scholarly transformation is remarkable.

In part, the transformation of committee scholarship reflects conceptual changes within the discipline of political science, especially the emergence of rational choice theory as the leading intellectual paradigm for studying American political institutions. But the transformation also reflects real substantive changes that have occurred in Washington politics, such as the demise of the Conservative Coalition and the concomitant rise of member individualism and party polarization. Indeed, the post-1960s changes that have taken place in congressional politics, including the role of committees, have made the institution especially conducive to applications of rational choice theory, which is one reason why congressional scholars have been at the vanguard of the rational choice project within political science. The transformation has also produced an enormous amount of new knowledge about congressional procedure; the basic structure of the roll-call record; the ideological representativeness of committees vis-à-vis the full chamber; the determinants of special rules and other procedural protections for committee bills; and so on. Still, viewing the literature from the perspective of this longer-term transformation provides considerable guidance about trajectories for future research about congressional committees.

One byproduct of the field's current fascination with floor roll calls and party influence is a paucity of research about other significant topics of traditional interest to congressional scholars. Even in an era of polarized parties and strong party leaders, most legislative decisions still are made within the committee rooms of Congress. Perhaps the best evidence of the enduring importance of committees is simply the disproportionate attention that interest groups and lobbyists continue to allocate to members of the panels with jurisdiction over their programs. Group leaders, whose professional livelihoods depend on their personal understanding of who actually matters on Capitol Hill, continue to pour campaign donations and the lion's share of their lobbying efforts on members of the House and Senate panels that consider their issues.

Yet, since the appearance of *The Giant Jigsaw Puzzle* in 1978, no study of the committee assignment process has been conducted that is as comprehensive, theoretically grounded, and methodologically sophisticated as Shepsle's landmark work. This is particularly unfortunate because Frisch and Kelly (2006) have amassed an enormous amount of new data and fascinating descriptive evidence about the committee assignment process. Thanks to their efforts, we now have assignment request data from 1947 to 1994 for House Democrats (except for 1957–8) and for House

Republicans from 1950 to 1992. The personal papers of recent congressional leaders include records of committee assignment requests into the late 1990s and 2000s. And the papers of former Senate leaders, archived in libraries around the country, include analogous, although less comprehensive, evidence about committee assignment requests for that chamber. Bullock's (1985) finding about the limited impact of constituency characteristics on Senate assignment requests is an intriguing signal of the significant bicameral differences that scholars might uncover in the assignment process. Moreover, the methodological techniques available for analyzing these data also have advanced in important ways since Shepsle conducted his research. There is a significant opportunity for further research on the committee assignment process in both chambers and over time that builds on Shepsle's theoretical and empirical accomplishments.

Another research opportunity relates to the study of member participation in committee. Hall aside, this topic is also of long-standing interest to congressional scholars because it informs so many questions about influence and policymaking. Indeed, "participation-specialization" was one of the three main features of committee decision-making analyzed in Fenno (1973), and Manley (1970) cited participation data culled from private transcripts of executive sessions dealing with Medicare and excise tax reduction in 1965. Unfortunately, the committee scholars of the 1960s lacked systematic access to data about what transpired during formal markup sessions, which for the most part were closed to the public. The Legislative Reorganization Act of 1970, however, stipulated for the first time that committees must make certain markup records publicly accessible. As a result, Hall was able to review verbatim transcripts of committee markups during the 1980s to construct the central dependent variable in his research about participation in committee. Such participation, we have seen, is critical for understanding the content of committee bills and has implications for theories of congressional organization. Yet, Hall's book mostly focuses on participation data from just three committees for a single Congress.[10] There is analogous evidence available for most other panels in the relevant committee offices in both the House and Senate. Gamble (2007) employed such data from the committees on Education and Labor, Financial Services, and Judiciary for 2001–2 to analyze the relative participation of African-American and Caucasian lawmakers, finding that black members participated more extensively than their white counterparts on bills that touched on black interests and on non-racial matters as well. Evans (1991a) is a study of member participation in three Senate committees during 1985–6. He shows that committee participation is also selective in that chamber, and that subcommittee positions in the Senate are strongly associated with legislative activism. But other than these two studies, no scholar has built on Hall's pathbreaking research about committee participation and the consequences for representation, or otherwise exploited the extensive documentary record now available for committee markup sessions.

---

[10] Hall also considered participation data for a sample of legislation from 1993–4, as well as selected evidence for an earlier Congress and for the Senate, but most of his analysis derives from evidence from just three House panels during a single Congress in the early 1980s.

Still another opening for additional committee research concerns the roll-call votes that members cast during markup sessions. These data also were made generally available for the first time by the Legislative Reorganization Act of 1970, and two books about voting in committee quickly appeared, mostly exploring the factions and voting blocs that surfaced in House committees during the 1970s (Parker and Parker 1985; Unekis and Rieselbach 1984). Similar records of roll calls cast in committee in both the House and Senate are now available in the relevant committee rooms for most panels and for more recent Congresses. Given the importance of the committee stage and the huge quantity of scholarly effort that has been allocated to scaling and analyzing the floor roll-call record, it is surprising that voting in committee has received so little scholarly attention. Indeed, recent advances in roll-call analysis using Bayesian and other techniques are particularly appropriate for analyzing votes taken in small legislatures such as committees (e.g. Peress 2009).

Like participation data, committee roll calls are potentially important for conceptual reasons. As mentioned, Cox and McCubbins (2005) use the committee votes gathered two decades ago by Parker and Parker (1985) to show that the majority party is seldom rolled in committee on motions to report, which suggests that the majority contingent exerts a degree of agenda control in committee. Along those lines, the conditional party government argument implies that party leaders influence outcomes in part by convincing members to evaluate issues on the floor in ideological, left–right terms, rather than along alternative dimensions that may tap the more parochial interests of their constituents. If leaders indeed shape the decision-making process, one indicator might be reduced roll-call dimensionality as bills move from committee to the floor to final passage. In addition, Krehbiel (1998) used repeated votes on the same questions to conduct "switcher analyses" aimed at discovering which members are subject to lobbying by party leaders and other actors seeking to influence the legislative process. The questions subject to roll calls in committee often are also the subject of votes on the floor, enabling scholars to use inconsistencies in member positions across the two stages to shed light on the dynamics of coalition building.

There is also potential for theoretically informed scholarship about legislative leadership, using committees as a laboratory and important source of contextual variation. Over the past two decades, ample research has been conducted on the role of party leaders in Congress (see Sinclair 1995 for an overview and example). But there are significant conceptual and empirical advantages to studying leadership within committees. For one, the leading theories emphasize that leadership styles and behavior are highly responsive to the decision-making context, especially the distribution of preferences among the relevant rank and file, and the availability of formal prerogatives such control over the agenda (Cooper and Brady 1981; Rohde 1991; Cox and McCubbins 2005). At any point in time, however, there is only one House Speaker and only one Senate majority leader, complicating efforts at generalization. The committee rooms of Congress, in contrast, feature dozens of chairs and ranking minority members operating within strikingly different contexts.

It is well established that the distribution of preferences on highly partisan panels such as the Ways and Means Committee differs substantially from the leadership contexts on more distributive committees such as Transportation and Infrastructure, and chairs should operate very differently across the two panels. Manley's (1970) description of the leadership of Wilbur Mills is a staple of the literature, and Fenno (1973) contrasted the styles of the chairs on his sample of committees. Strahan (1990) is a study of committee leadership on Ways and Means during the chairmanship of Dan Rostenkowski, D-Ill., in the 1980s. And Evans (1991b) compared the strategies and tactics employed by full committee leaders on four Senate panels during the 1980s, emphasizing the importance of the distribution of preferences and the internal structure of the committees for understanding important features of leadership behavior. However, as congressional scholarship turned away from the internal operations of committees and the important differences that exist between them, the analysis of leadership in committee has all but atrophied. As a result, there are significant opportunities to use the chairs and ranking minority members of current committees to shed important new light on the nature of legislative leadership.

A renewed scholarly emphasis on committees would also help address major conceptual and empirical difficulties in the controversy over legislative organization. For one, the different theories appear to be somewhat jurisdiction-specific in their explanatory power. Partisan theories seem especially appropriate for understanding member decision-making within jurisdictions that divide Democrats from Republicans, while the distributive perspective is particularly useful for understanding policies and programs that target particularistic benefits to specific geographic areas. If member decision-making—and the way that congressional structures shape decision-making—indeed varies in systematic ways by issue area, then careful analysis of how and why congressional committees differ from each other should inform scholarship about the domains in which the different theories are likely to be relevant.

In addition, a number of scholars (e.g. Katznelson and Lapinski 2006) have called for increased attention to policy and the content of legislation. The quality of representation, these scholars observe, can only be fully assessed by relating the substance of legislative outcomes to the preferences and interests of constituents. Committees are a useful vehicle for analyzing the determinants of legislative outcomes because most policy decisions occur during that stage of the legislative process, and because committee jurisdictions differ substantially in the types of policies that they contain. Indeed, the committee studies of the 1960s and 1970s typically addressed the linkages between member goals, committee structure, and the content of committee bills (e.g. Price 1972; Fenno 1973, ch. 7). Yet, recent empirical tests of the competing theories of legislative organization focus almost exclusively on behavior rather than policy, even though the most substantively consequential test implications of these theories concern the content of legislation. The main reason is the lack of systematic data about the relationship between member preferences and policy outcomes across a diversity of issue areas. Gathering such evidence should be more straightforward the narrower the policy domain. Thus, a focus on committees as arenas for policymaking could facilitate efforts to incorporate policy content into empirical studies of Congress.

Finally, stepped-up research about decision-making in committee would help scholars understand the process through which the policy preferences of legislators are formed, which is a critical conceptual and empirical gap in recent research about Congress. Four decades of descriptive research indicates that the preferences that individual lawmakers develop between competing legislative alternatives are endogenous to the lawmaking process. Certainly members have core beliefs about what constitutes good public policy, and they are loath to take positions that are inconsistent with their prior records. But as Krehbiel (1991), Arnold (1990), and other scholars emphasize, there is considerable uncertainty about the relationship that exists between policy alternatives (the legislative options on the table) and policy outcomes (the impact of these options on people's lives). As a result, members may have clear views about the ultimate impact that they seek, but still lack fully developed preferences over alternatives. Indeed, member viewpoints about legislative options are best conceptualized as *induced* preferences. As major decisions loom, they face some mix of alternatives over which the constituencies they care about (clientele groups, party leaders, and so on) may have divergent priorities and views. Members form their preferences by weighing and balancing these competing preferences emanating from the decision-making environment. It simply is not feasible to evaluate the relative importance of distributive coalitions, party pressures, or the informational needs of the full chamber, without considering the impact of these and other factors on the process through which lawmakers form preferences and make up their minds. This is why prominent scholars of American institutions, such as Smith (2007) and Fiorina (2009), maintain that spatial theories need to be refined by unpacking the concept of member preferences, which in these models typically are treated as fixed and exogenous.[11]

Committees are a great vehicle for studying preference formation. Undecided legislators on the floor often look to members of the committee of jurisdiction for cues in making up their minds about how to vote. The positions and preferences of these committee members, in turn, are generally formed during the committee stage of the process. As a result, efforts to extend leading spatial theories of congressional organization to better incorporate the process of preference formation—a critical next conceptual step, many scholars believe—would be informed by more systematic research about coalition building and decision-making within the committee rooms of Congress.

References

ADLER, E. S. 2000. Constituency Characteristics and the "Guardian Model" of Appropriations Subcommittees, 1959–1998. *American Journal of Political Science*, 44: 104–14.
—— 2002. *Why Congressional Reforms Fail: Re-election and the House Committee System.* Chicago, IL: University of Chicago Press.

---

[11] Obviously, Krehbiel (1991) is an exception and provides useful guidance about how preference formation can be integrated into spatial models of legislatures.

——and Lapinski, J. S. 1997. Demand-side Theory and Congressional Committee Composition: A Constituency Characteristics Approach. *American Journal of Political Science*, 41: 895–918.

——and Wilkerson, J. D. 2008. Intended Consequences: Jurisdictional Reform and Issue Control in the U.S. House of Representatives. *Legislative Studies Quarterly*, 33: 85–112.

Aldrich, J. H., and Rohde, D. W. 1997. The Transition to Republican Rule in the House: Implications for Theories of Congressional Politics. *Political Science Quarterly*, 112: 541–67.

——and Rohde, D. W. 2000a. The Consequences of Party Organization in the House: The Role of the Majority and Minority Parties in Conditional Party Government, pp. 31–72 in *Polarized Politics: Congress and the President in a Partisan Era*, ed. J. R. Bond and R. Fleisher. Washington, DC: Congressional Quarterly.

————2000b. The Republican Revolution and the House Appropriations Committee. *Journal of Politics*, 62: 1–33.

Arnold, R. D. 1981. The Local Roots of Domestic Policy, pp. 250–87 in *The New Congress*, ed. T. E. Mann and N. J. Ornstein. Washington, DC: American Enterprise Institute.

——1990. *The Logic of Congressional Action*. New Haven, CT: Yale University Press.

Baumgartner, F. R., Jones, B. D., and MacLeod, M. C. 2000. The Evolution of Legislative Jurisdictions. *Journal of Politics*, 62: 321–49.

Bullock, C. S. 1970. Apprenticeship and Committee Assignments in the House of Representatives. *Journal of Politics*, 32: 717–20.

——1972. Freshman Committee Assignments and Re-election in the United States House of Representatives. *American Political Science Review*, 66: 996–1007.

——1985. U.S. Senate Committee Assignments: Preferences, Motivations, and Success. *American Journal of Political Science*, 29: 789–808.

Cann, D. M. 2009. Modeling Committee Chair Selection in the U.S. House of Representatives. *Political Analysis*, 16: 274–89.

Cooper, J. 1970. *The Origins of the Standing Committees and the Development of the Modern House*. Houston: Rice University Studies.

——and Brady, D. 1981. Institutional Context and Leadership Style: The House from Cannon to Rayburn. *American Political Science Review*, 75: 411–25.

Cox, G. W., and McCubbins, M. D. 1993. *Legislative Leviathan*: Party Government in the House. Berkeley: University of California Press.

————2005. *Setting the Agenda: Responsible Party Government in the U.S. House of Representatives*. Cambridge: Cambridge University Press.

Davidson, R. 1981. Subcommittee Government: New Channels for Policy Making, pp. 99–133 in *The New Congress*, ed. T. Mann and N. J. Ornstein. Washington, DC: American Enterprise Institute.

Deering, C. J., and Smith, S. S. 1997. *Committees in Congress*, 3rd edn. Washington, DC: Congressional Quarterly.

——and Wahlbeck, P. J. 2006. U.S. House Committee Chair Selection: Republicans Play Musical Chairs in the 107th Congress. *American Politics Research*, 34: 223–42.

Evans, C. L. 1991a. Participation and Policy Making in U.S. Senate Committees. *Political Science Quarterly*, 106: 479–98.

——1991b. *Leadership in Committee: A Comparative Analysis of Leadership Behavior in the U.S. Senate*. Ann Arbor, MI: University of Michigan Press.

——and Oleszek, W. O. 1997. *Congress Under Fire: Reform Politics and the Republican Majority*. Boston, MA: Houghton, Mifflin.

Fenno, Jr., R. F. 1962a. The House Appropriations Committee as a Political System: The Problem of Integration. *American Political Science Review*, 56: 310–24.

FENNO, Jr., R. F. 1962b. The House of Representatives and Federal Aid to Education, pp. 195–236 in *New Perspectives on the House of Representatives*, ed. R. L. Peabody and N. W. Polsby. Chicago, IL: Rand McNally.

—— 1965. *The Power of the Purse: Appropriations Politics in Congress*. Boston, MA: Little, Brown.

—— 1973. *Congressmen in Committees*. Boston, MA: Little, Brown.

FEREJOHN, J. A. 1974. *Pork Barrel Politics*. Stanford, CA: Stanford University Press.

FIORINA, M. P. 1974. *Representatives, Roll Calls, and Constituencies*. Lexington, MA: Lexington Books.

—— 1977. *Congress: Keystone of the Washington Establishment*. New Haven, CT: Yale University Press.

—— 2009. *Disconnect: The Breakdown of Representation in American Politics*. Norman, OK: University of Oklahoma Press.

FRISCH, D. A., and KELLY, S. Q. 2004. Self-selection Reconsidered: House Committee Assignment Requests and Constituency Characteristics. *Political Research Quarterly*, 57: 325–36.

—— —— 2006. *Committee Assignment Politics in the U.S. House of Representatives*. Norman, OK: University of Oklahoma Press.

GAMBLE, K. L. 2007. Black Political Representation: An Examination of Legislative Activity within U.S. House Committees. *Legislative Studies Quarterly*, 32: 421–48.

GILLIGAN, T. W., and KREHBIEL, K. 1987. Collective Decision-making and Standing Committees: An Information Rationale for Restrictive Amendment Procedures. *Journal of Law, Economics, and Organization*, 3: 287–335.

—— —— 1989. Asymmetric Information and Legislative Rules with a Heterogeneous Committee. *American Journal of Political Science*, 33: 459–90.

—— —— 1990. Organization of Informative Committees by a Rational Legislature. *American Journal of Political Science*, 34: 531–64.

GOODWIN, G. 1970. *The Little Legislatures: Committees of Congress*. Amherst, MA: University of Massachusetts Press.

GROSECLOSE, T. 1994. Testing Committee Composition Hypotheses for the U.S. Congress. *Journal of Politics*, 56: 440–58.

HAEBERLE, S. H. 1978. The Institutionalization of the Subcommittee in the House of Representatives. *Journal of Politics*, 40: 1054–65.

HALL, R. L. 1996. *Participation in Congress*. New Haven, CT: Yale University Press.

—— and GROFMAN, B. 1990. The Committee Assignment Process and the Conditional Nature of Committee Bias. *American Political Science Review*, 84: 1149–66.

—— and EVANS, C. L. 1989. The Power of Subcommittees. *Journal of Politics*, 52: 335–54.

HARDIN, J. W. 1998. Advocacy versus Certainty: The Dynamics of Committee Jurisdiction Concentration. *Journal of Politics*, 60: 374–97.

HINCKLEY, B. 1972. *The Seniority System in Congress*. Bloomington, IN: Indiana University Press.

—— 1979. Review of *The Giant Jigsaw Puzzle*: Democratic Committee Assignments in the Modern House. *American Political Science Review*, 73: 886–7.

HUITT, R. K. 1954. The Congressional Committee: A Case Study. *American Political Science Review*, 48: 340–65.

HURWITZ, M. S., MOILES, R. J., and ROHDE, D. W. 2001. Distributive and Partisan Issues in Agriculture Policy in the 104th Congress. *American Political Science Review*, 95: 911–22.

JONES, C. O. 1961. Representation in Congress: The Case of the House Agriculture Committee. *American Political Science Review*, 55: 358–67.

——1962. The Role of the Congressional Subcommittee. *Midwest Journal of Political Science,* 6: 327–44.

KATZNELSON, I., and LAPINSKI, J. 2006. The Substance of Representation: Studying Policy Content and Legislative Behavior, pp. 96–128 in *The Macropolitics of Congress,* ed. E. S. Adler and J. Lapinski. Princeton, NJ: Princeton University Press.

KIEWIET, R., and MCCUBBINS, M. D. 1991. *The Logic of Delegation.* Chicago, IL: University of Chicago Press.

KING, D. C. 1994. The Nature of Congressional Committee Jurisdictions. *American Political Science Review,* 88: 48–62.

——1997. *Turf Wars: How Congressional Committees Claim Jurisdiction.* Chicago, IL: University of Chicago Press.

KREHBIEL, K. 1987. Why are Congressional Committees Powerful? *American Political Science Review,* 81: 929–35.

——1990. Are Congressional Committees Composed of Preference Outliers? *American Political Science Review,* 84: 149–63.

——1991. *Information and Legislative Organization.* Ann Arbor, MI: University of Michigan Press.

——1994. Deference, Extremism, and Interest Group Ratings. *Legislative Studies Quarterly,* 19: 61–77.

——1998. *Pivotal Politics: A Theory of U.S. Lawmaking.* Chicago, IL: University of Chicago Press.

LONDREGAN, J., and SNYDER, J. M. 1994. Comparing Committee and Floor Preferences. *Legislative Studies Quarterly,* 19: 233–66.

MALTZMAN, F. 1997. *Competing Principals: Committees, Parties, and the Organization of Congress.* Ann Arbor, MI: University of Michigan Press.

——and SMITH, S. S. 1994. Principals, Goals, Dimensionality, and Congressional Committees. *Legislative Studies Quarterly,* 19: 457–76.

MANLEY, J. F. 1969. Wilbur Mills: A Study of Congressional Leadership. *American Political Science Review,* 63: 442–64.

——1970. *The Politics of Finance: The House Committee on Ways and Means.* Boston, MA: Little, Brown.

MASTERS, N. A. 1961. Committee Assignments. *American Political Science Review,* 55: 345–57.

MATTHEWS, D. R. 1960. *U.S. Senators and Their World.* New York, NY: Random House.

MAYHEW, D. 1974. *Congress: The Electoral Connection.* New Haven, CT: Yale University Press.

MURPHY, J. T. 1969. *The House Public Works Committee: Determinants and Consequences of Committee Behavior.* PhD dissertation, University of Rochester.

——1974. Political Parties and the Pork Barrel: Party Conflict and Cooperation in House Public Works Committee Decision Making. *American Political Science Review,* 68: 169–85.

OPPENHEIMER, B. I. 1977. The Rules Committee: New Arm of Leadership in a Decentralized House, pp. 96–116 in *Congress Reconsidered,* ed. L. C. Dodd and B. I. Oppenheimer. New York, NY: Praeger.

OVERBY, L. M., and KAZEE, T. A. 2000. Outlying Committees in the Statehouse: An Examination of the Prevalence of Committee Outliers in State Legislatures. *Journal of Politics,* 62: 701–28.

PARKER, G. R., and PARKER, S. L. 1985. *Factions in House Committees.* Knoxville, TN: University of Tennessee Press.

——————COPA, J. C., and LAWHORM, M. D. 2004. The Question of Committee Bias Revisited. *Political Research Quarterly,* 57: 331–40.

PEABODY, R. L. 1963. The Enlarged Rules Committee, pp. 129–64 in *New Perspectives on the House of Representatives*, ed. R. L. Peabody and N. W. Polsby. Chicago, IL: Rand McNally & Co.

PERESS, M. 2009. Small Chamber Ideal Point Estimation. *Political Analysis*, 17: 276–90.

POLSBY, N. W. 1968. The Institutionalization of the U.S. House of Representatives. *American Political Science Review*, 62: 148–68.

——GALLAHER, M., and RUNDQUIST, B. S. 1969. The Growth of the Seniority System in the U.S. House of Representatives. *American Political Science Review*, 63: 787–807.

POOLE, K. T., and ROSENTHAL, H. 1997. *Congress: A Political-Economic History of Roll Call Voting*. New York, NY: Oxford University Press.

PRICE, D. E. 1972. *Who Makes the Laws? Creativity and Power in Senate Committees*. Cambridge, MA: Schenkman.

——1978. Policy Making in Congressional Committees: The Impact of Environmental Factors. *American Political Science Review*, 72: 548–74.

RAY, B. A. 1980. Federal Spending and the Selection of Committee Assignments in the U.S. House of Representatives. *American Journal of Political Science*, 24: 494–510.

——1982. Committee Attractiveness in the U.S. House 1963–81. *American Journal of Political Science*, 26: 609–13.

RIKER, W. H. 1958. The Paradox of Voting and Congressional Rules for Voting on Amendments. *American Political Science Review*, 52: 349–66.

ROBINSON, J. A. 1963. *The House Rules Committee*. New York, NY: Bobbs-Merrill.

ROHDE, D. W. 1991. *Parties and Leaders in the Postreform House*. Chicago, IL: University of Chicago Press.

—— and SHEPSLE, K. A. 1973. Democratic Committee Assignments in the House of Representatives: Strategic Aspects of a Social Choice Process. *American Political Science Review*, 67: 889–905.

SCHICKLER, E., and RICH, A. 1997. Controlling the Floor: Parties as Procedural Coalitions in the House. *American Journal of Political Science*, 41: 1340–75.

SHEINGATE, A. D. 2006. Structure and Opportunity: Committee Jurisdiction and Issue Attention in Congress. *American Journal of Political Science*, 50: 844–59.

SHEPSLE, K. A. 1978. *The Giant Jigsaw Puzzle: Democratic Committee Assignments in the Modern House*. Chicago, IL: University of Chicago Press.

——1979. Institutional Arrangements and Equilibrium in Multidimensional Voting Models. *American Journal of Political Science*, 23: 27–60.

——1986. Institutional Equilibrium and Equilibrium Institutions, pp. 51–81 in *Political Science: The Science of Politics*, ed. H. Weisberg. New York, NY: Agathon.

—— and WEINGAST, B. R. 1987a. The Institutional Foundations of Committee Power. *American Political Science Review*, 81: 85–105.

————1987b. Why are Congressional Committees Powerful? *American Political Science Review*, 81: 935–45.

Sinclair, B. 1989. *The Transformation of the U.S. Senate*. Baltimore, MD: Johns Hopkins University Press.

——1995. *Legislators, Leaders, and Lawmaking: The U.S. House of Representatives in the Postreform Era*. Baltimore, MD: Johns Hopkins University Press.

——2007. *Unorthodox Lawmaking: New Legislative Processes in the U.S. Congress*, 3rd edn. Washington, DC: Congressional Quarterly.

SMITH, S. S. 1989. *Call to Order: Floor Politics in the House and Senate*. Washington, DC: Brookings Institution Press.

——2007. *Party Influence in Congress*. New York, NY: Cambridge University Press.

——and DEERING, C. J. 1984. *Committees in Congress.* Washington, DC: Congressional Quarterly.

————1990. *Committees in Congress*, 2nd edn. Washington, DC: Congressional Quarterly.

SPRAGUE, M. 2008. The Effects of Measurement and Methods Decisions on Committee Preference Outlier Results. *Political Research Quarterly*, 61: 309–18.

STRAHAN, R. 1990. *New Ways and Means.* Chapel Hill, NC: University of North Carolina Press.

UNEKIS, J. K., and RIESELBACH, L. N. 1984. *Congressional Committee Politics.* New York, NY: Praeger.

WEINGAST, B. R. 1989. Floor Behavior in the U.S. Congress: Committee Power Under the Open Rule. *American Political Science Review*, 83: 795–815.

——1992. Fighting Fire with Fire: Amending Activity and Institutional Change in the Postreform Congress, pp. 142–68 in *The Postreform Congress*, ed. R. H. Davidson. New York, NY: St. Martin's Press.

——and MARSHALL, W. 1988. The Industrial Organization of Congress. *Journal of Political Economy*, 96: 123–63.

WILSON, W. 1885. *Congressional Government.* New York, NY: Meridan Books.

YOUNG, G., and HEITSHUSEN, V. 2003. Party and the Dynamics of Congressional Committee Composition in the U.S. House, 1947–1996. *British Journal of Political Science*, 33: 659–79.

CHAPTER 19

THE SUPERMAJORITY SENATE

GREGORY J. WAWRO[*]

INTRODUCTION

IMMEDIATELY upon the announcement of the nomination of Sonia Sotomayor to the Supreme Court in May of 2009, speculation in the media began as to whether she would garner the sixty votes necessary to overcome a filibuster in the Senate.[1] With Democrats at least nominally holding fifty-nine seats in the Senate at that time and then picking up one more with the resolution of the Minnesota Senate race in June of that year, it seemed likely that a three-fifths majority in support of Sotomayor would form without much difficulty. But what is perhaps more interesting about the initial discussion of her nomination was that thoughts immediately ran to concerns that the nomination would be filibustered and therefore require supermajority support to reach an up-or-down vote. This is a striking indication that the Senate has indeed become and—perhaps more importantly—is widely accepted as a supermajority institution.

[*] Kate Krimmel and Lucas Leeman provided invaluable research assistance and discussions with Richard Beth, Valerie Heitshusen, Betsy Palmer, and Elizabeth Rybicki were especially helpful during the writing of this chapter.

[1] For example, see P. Baker and J. Zeleny, "Obama Hails Judge as 'Inspiring'," *New York Times*, May 27, 2009, A1.

Another indication is the frequency with which the sixty-seat threshold is mentioned in media coverage of Senate election outcomes.[2] When discussing predictions of seat shares in the Senate, it is standard for journalists and pundits to speak not solely in terms of who will win the majority, but whether or not the winning party will win at least sixty seats in the chamber. The general perception has taken hold that it is difficult for the winning party to change policy in a meaningful way unless they can secure a supermajority in the Senate.

The supermajoritarian nature of the Senate raises several profound empirical and normative questions. We have good answers to some of these questions, while others remain elusive and under-explored. This chapter will address some of these questions, discussing the answers that political scientists have uncovered, as well as questions that demand further exploration. The key issues this chapter will discuss include institutional evolution, the interplay between supermajority procedures and advice and consent responsibilities, public opinion, and procedural innovations in response to inherited rules and changing political context. Since the Senate has not always been a supermajority institution in the sense that it is today, this chapter will focus on the historical development of supermajority rule in the chamber. A historical perspective is essential if we are to begin to understand the consequences of having one of the co-equal institutions at the top of the governing hierarchy in the United States operate by supermajoritarian procedures. Fortunately, after years of neglect by congressional scholars, the Senate has become the locus of cutting edge research, which promises to increase our understanding of the chamber to a level that matches that of the more thoroughly studied House of Representatives. While a great deal of work remains to be done, the recent trajectory of the literature on the Senate is enormously promising, instilling much confidence that significant advances will continue to be made in our understanding of this truly unique institution.

THE SUPERMAJORITY SENATE IN HISTORICAL PERSPECTIVE

The contemporary perception of the Senate as a supermajoritarian institution is unusual when placed in historical perspective. Empirically, it is only in the past three to four decades that supermajorities have been consistently required to enact legislation or confirm nominations. The Senate has traditionally operated as a con-sensual legislative body, less dependent on formal rules of procedure than the House,

---

[2] For examples, see N. Anderson and R. Simon, "New Energy in Congress Over Homeland Security Bill," *Los Angeles Times*, Nov. 11, 2002, A13; S. G. Stolberg, "On Capitol Hill, the Majority Doesn't Always Rule," *New York Times*, Nov. 7, 2004, 4; A. Nagourney, "For Buoyant Democrats, Even a Big Gain May Feel Like a Failure," *New York Times*, Nov. 7, 2006, A18; A. Roth, C. Dade, and B. McKay, "In Crucial South, Democrats Edge Closer to Republican Incumbents," *Wall Street Journal*, Nov. 1, 2008, A.4.

all the while granting its members unparalleled rights to participate in the legislative process. The Senate's current requirement of a three-fifths majority to invoke cloture—that is, to end debate and bring legislation or nominations to an up-or-down vote—provides the institutional foundation for its current supermajoritarian character. From 1806 to 1917, the Senate had no formal procedural mechanism for moving the previous question, which created opportunities for Senate action to be blocked by obstruction. But senators rarely availed themselves of these opportunities (Binder and Smith 1997). When viewed from the perspective of today's Senate, this is puzzling. A single senator had the power, in theory, to bring the institution to a halt and commit legislative extortion on a grand scale—a tremendous temptation to any self-interested, ambitious politician. And even though the Senate did (and still does) conduct an overwhelming proportion of its daily business via unanimous consent, senators typically did not exploit their prerogatives in a manner that forced the construction of unanimous coalitions. In fact, supermajority coalitions did not even appear to be generally necessary, as many of the most important and contentious questions of the day were addressed by legislation that passed with narrow majorities (Mayhew 2003; Wawro and Schickler 2006). Even after the adoption of Rule 22 in 1917, which established a procedure for cloture and set the threshold for invoking it at two-thirds of senators present and voting, the Senate rarely resorted to it. In many cases, it appeared unnecessary as coalitions in support of significant legislation and nominations regularly exceeded the two-thirds requirement.[3] In other cases, significant legislation still passed with less than supermajority support and no filibusters materialized. A few high-profile filibuster battles over civil rights legislation aside, the Senate conducted much of its business without its members exploiting their considerable prerogatives to the extent that would have made the Senate either dysfunctional or heavily reliant on the cloture procedure. This is not to say that the threat of cloture did not play an important role in the quotidian activities of the chamber. But individual senators certainly did not exercise their ability to obstruct in ways that would have forced Senate leaders and legislative entrepreneurs to suffer through the somewhat cumbersome mechanics of the cloture procedure on a regular basis.

That is, until the 1970s.

In the wake of the epic—and ultimately unsuccessful—filibusters of civil rights and voting rights legislation in the 1960s, there was an explosion in the use of obstruction in the Senate. While between 1917 and 1972, the average number of filibusters per session was 1.4, this number shot up to 9 per session between 1973 and 1996 (Binder, Lawrence, and Smith 2002). While there is some question as to how exactly one determines what is and what is not a filibuster (Beth 1995), these numbers are so striking that it is clear that something changed in the use of parliamentary obstruction. The change has been qualitative as well as quantitative. Gone are the days when

---

[3] The cloture rule was changed in 1949 to require two-thirds of the chamber, but was then lowered to the original threshold in 1959.

obstructive senators must seize control of the floor and hold it through interminable (and famously vacuous) speeches and parliamentary sabotage, when the Senate is held in continuous session, forcing senators to bed down in the Capitol building or be brought back to the chamber in the wee hours by the Sergeant at Arms. Today, senators need only announce an intent to filibuster legislation or a nomination for the chamber to resort to supermajority procedures. Thus, a great irony of contemporary American politics is that filibusters appear to have become much more common, but we actually see far less of the activity traditionally required to conduct them, since senators rarely take and hold the floor to engage in obstruction. The so-called "silent filibuster" has become the norm in the Senate, and even though obstruction has become less theatrical, it has become more central to the operation of the institution.[4]

Cloture votes have become routine and are viewed as essential for any item of business that is the least bit controversial. Legislative entrepreneurs build coalitions focusing on the three-fifths threshold, and the procedure for invoking cloture is often begun before legislation even reaches the floor. Indeed, it is unlikely that a significant bill or a nomination will even sniff the floor if it does not have a chance of receiving supermajority support. If sought-after legislation will have difficulty attracting sixty votes, supporters have the limited option of including it in a budget reconciliation bill, which requires only a simple majority for passage and is immune from filibusters. This option has been pursued for top agenda items, but is not available for all legislation (more on this below).

This is the standard narrative for *how* the Senate has become a supermajoritarian body. *Why* the Senate has become a supermajoritarian body and what this has meant for American politics are much less settled questions.

The seeds for a supermajoritarian—or at least a non-majoritarian—body were planted with the abolition of the previous question motion in 1806, which at the time was often used to delay or kill legislation rather than moving it toward final disposition (Binder 1997; Cooper 1962). When combined with senators' nearly limitless rights of recognition and no germaneness rule in the Senate, the absence of a motion to close off debate and force a vote created tremendous opportunities for minorities to obstruct. While the nineteenth century saw a handful of knock-down, drag-out battles involving obstruction that led to attempts to restrict this behavior, senators did not adopt a procedure for ending filibusters until 1917. The two-thirds vote requirement built into the cloture rule established an explicit institutional foundation for the Senate to conduct its business as a supermajoritarian body, even though over a half century would pass before legislating via supermajority coalitions would become virtually mandatory.

Wawro and Schickler (2006) argue that the reason that the Senate moved to adopt cloture at this time was that norms of restraint and threats to eliminate or substantially curtail minority rights, which helped to keep obstruction from becoming

---

[4] More extensive use of a tracking system has promoted the prevalence of the silent filibuster. Obstructed bills are placed on a separate legislative "track" for later consideration, enabling the Senate to move quickly and smoothly to other matters (Binder and Smith 1997; Ornstein 2003).

too burdensome, had become less effective. Significant increases in the size of the Senate due to the admission of new states to the Union inhibited the institution's ability to rely on informal relations and punishment strategies among senators to keep obstruction in check. The cloture rule codified a mechanism that could be used to combat minority obstruction, even without invoking it, by explicitly establishing a clear threshold that majorities would have to exceed in order to guarantee success.

There is some disagreement over the effectiveness of the cloture rule as adopted in 1917. Wawro and Schickler (2006) contend that the 1917 rule constituted meaningful reform, and present evidence on the variance of coalition sizes and increased efficiency in the appropriations process as empirical support for this contention. This stands in contrast to numerous authors who have claimed that the cloture rule was for the most part ineffective and merely a symbolic response to a pronounced flare-up of anti-filibuster public opinion (Byrd 1988, 124; Baker 1995, 46; White 1968, 60–64; Rogers 1926, 177; Dion 1997). More recently, Koger (2007) has argued that the two-thirds threshold essentially codified existing coalitional dynamics in the Senate, claiming that at least one third of the chamber was required to sustain an effective filibuster even before the 1917 rule.

But it seems relatively uncontroversial to say that the 1917 reform was the first step toward elite and popular acceptance of the Senate as a supermajoritarian body. It would take additional incremental developments that would occur over several decades before the supermajoritarian nature of the Senate would become entrenched—that the Senate would consistently and explicitly rely on supermajorities to conduct its business. A number of factors seem to be related to this change. Sinclair (1989) argues that qualitative changes in the membership of the Senate along with changes in the political environment led to fundamental changes in Senate behavior that fueled the increase in filibusters. An influx of (mostly liberal) activist senators, whose reelection strategies required them to participate visibly and vocally in the day-to-day activities of the institution, transformed the Senate from an inward-looking, "clubby" institution where senators served long apprenticeships out of the limelight, to an outward-looking and media-centric legislature whose members courted the attention of the ever-expanding number and variety of interest groups on the Washington scene. Increasing partisanship and polarization strained the institution's capacity to forge compromises and operate by unanimous consent, as it had done traditionally, fomenting the use of confrontational tactics (Binder and Smith 1997; Binder, Lawerence, and Smith 2002; Sinclair 2002). All of these changes have occurred within the context of increasing time constraints. Demands on floor time have become so substantial and senators' obligations so extraordinary, that even small delays and disruptions have become intolerable (Oppenheimer 1985; Koger 2010). This considerably increases the incentives that senators have to use their prerogatives to obstruct in an attempt to extort policy outcomes more to their liking. As it has become more likely that a given bill will experience obstruction, Senate leaders and legislative entrepreneurs have altered their strategies by attempting to preempt the disruption that filibusters can cause.

AGENDA-SETTING WORK AND NEW PATHS FORWARD

We have thus achieved a new institutional equilibrium—the 60-vote Senate—where supermajority coalitions are the norm. This is the case for legislation and more recently for judicial nominations. As this institutional equilibrium has congealed, political scientists have begun to deploy the most sophisticated research tools in the discipline to understand the myriad questions associated with the topic of the supermajoritarian Senate. Two books, Binder and Smith's *Politics or Principle?* (1997) and Krehbiel's *Pivotal Politics* (1998), marked the beginning of a new phase in research on the filibuster and to a large degree set the agenda for research on the supermajority Senate at the beginning of the millennium. The Binder and Smith book constituted the first book-length treatment of the filibuster in over fifty years and the first study to use quantitative modeling on a rich array of data relevant to the filibuster. While works such as Burdette (1940) and Rogers (1926) are important early contributions to the literature that provide valuable insight into the contours of the historical development of filibusters and the introduction of supermajority procedures to address them, they do not involve the kind of systematic analysis grounded in theory that is essential for scientific explanation. More recently, Oppenheimer (1985) and Sinclair (1989) began to shift scholars' attention to the filibuster with their analyses of contemporary changes in practice, and Beth (1994, 1995) undertook the first comprehensive effort to overcome the difficulties inherent in measuring filibusters. But Binder and Smith offered the first theoretically rooted, systematic empirical analysis of the operation of supermajority rule in the Senate.[5]

While the filibuster is one of the best-known features of the Senate, it has also been one of the least understood. Binder and Smith take aim at several aspects of the conventional wisdom surrounding the filibuster and supermajority requirements, including 1) whether the framers and early members of the Senate perceived supermajority requirements and the filibuster as a central part of the institution, 2) whether the filibuster has become trivialized, 3) whether the filibuster has killed important legislation that would have passed if not for supermajority requirements (the "little harm thesis"), 4) whether supermajority requirements induce policy moderation, and 5) whether majorities have always been opposed to reforms that would eliminate or weaken supermajority requirements, and whether such opposition is driven by adherence to principles of extended debate and deliberation. Methodically and systematically, employing a mixture of historical narrative and quantitative analysis involving innovative measures related to filibustering, the authors address each one of

---

[5] Binder (1997) is another important work that studies legislative obstruction and involves an impressive data collection effort and quantitative analysis. However, the subject is addressed from the angle of the expansion and contraction of minority rights and focuses primarily on the U.S. House. Dion (1997) employs formal and quantitative modeling in an historical analysis of minority rights and procedural reform, but also focuses on the House. Both of these works devote a chapter to the Senate.

these issues. The conclusions that emerge reveal a very different—and less favorable—picture than that depicted by the conventional wisdom and invoked by supporters of supermajority requirements. Such requirements and the absence of limits on debate associated with them were explicitly rejected by the framers and not endorsed by the members of the nascent Senate. A majority of iconic senators in the nineteenth century favored changing the rules to impose more limits on debate, although such efforts were thwarted to an extent by inherited rules that protected extended debate in the first place. Throughout the Senate's history, filibusters have been waged on mundane matters as well as the most important issues of the day, and numerous filibusters have been successful at killing legislation supported by majorities, undercutting the "little harm thesis." Supermajority requirements are not theoretically linked to the production of moderate policy outcomes, and positions on the filibuster and votes on cloture have more to do with short-term political and partisan interests than with deeply ingrained principles. Binder and Smith conclude that the filibuster is far less benign than many have portrayed it and close their book by proposing a reform that would balance senators' demands for extended debate and interests in preserving aspects of supermajority rule with the ability to reach final passage votes on legislation. Under this reform, the size of the coalition required to end debate on a measure or nomination would decrease with each sequential cloture vote, until eventually cloture could be imposed by a simple majority. The prospects for such reform are not great, according to Binder and Smith, because any such attempt to change the rules regarding debate is subject to a filibuster and therefore needs to garner the support of a two-thirds supermajority under current Senate rules. Thus, even though a majority might want to change the rules in this regard, it has an imposing hurdle to surmount.

Supermajority requirements are a central component of Krehbiel's book, even though it is not a study of the filibuster per se. Krehbiel develops a formal spatial model of institutional interaction to explain why policy change does or does not occur in the separation of powers system.[6] He argues that we can understand a tremendous amount about policy movement and legislative gridlock by focusing on the ideological positions of a few pivotal actors. These actors are pivotal not because of their political skills or prominence in national politics, but because of the influence granted to them by the institutional rules of the separation of powers system. The pivotal actors or "pivots" include the president (whose signature is required to enact legislation into law, except when his veto is overridden), the median members of the House and Senate (whose votes are needed to achieve the threshold of a simple majority for passage), the veto pivot (the member of the House or Senate whose vote is needed to achieve the two-thirds threshold for a veto override), and the filibuster pivot in the Senate (whose vote is needed to achieve the supermajority threshold required by the cloture procedure). Krehbiel assumes that for legislation to pass, the supporting coalition must be large enough to invoke cloture, even if they do not have to resort to the procedure itself. Even though final passage of legislation requires

---

[6] See also Brady and Volden (1998).

a simple majority of the Senate, the assumption is that the final passage vote will not happen unless cloture can be invoked. In essence, cloture votes are equated with final passage votes, leading to the assumption that the Senate is a supermajoritarian institution. The empirical analysis in the book demonstrates the explanatory power of focusing on pivots, and in particular, on how much of American politics is driven by the location of the filibuster pivot. Krehbiel identifies the "gridlock interval," which is bounded by the location of the two most extreme pivots and contains status quos that cannot be changed by passing legislation because the relevant pivots are better off with the laws currently on the books than they would be with new statutes. Empirically, the filibuster pivot typically demarcates one end of the gridlock interval, which would not be the case in the absence of supermajority requirements for cloture. Thus, the supermajority requirements of the cloture procedure can have profound effects on lawmaking in the United States, since legislating via sixty-vote majorities means that certain policies will not be enacted that could be enacted with smaller coalitions and the support of other pivotal players in the separation of powers system.

Krehbiel's focus on the filibuster pivot has had a tremendous influence on the way that political scientists think about the Senate, both in the contemporary period and historically. As mentioned previously, Wawro and Schickler (2006) sought to explain lawmaking in the Senate before it adopted a cloture rule, trying to determine where the filibuster pivot in the Senate was located before it was explicitly established in 1917. Their answer was that, except for the very end of a congressional session, the pivot was the median voter in the Senate, implying that senate lawmaking was largely majoritarian.

Arguments regarding the "pivotocity" of the filibuster pivot have led others to consider the impact of political parties on legislative productivity and gridlock. Binder (2003) focuses more directly on the impact of the filibuster and supermajority requirements vis à vis partisan factors and finds that the filibuster threats do not affect the percentage of agenda items that fail to pass by the conclusion of a Congress. However, a "filibuster problem," defined as either a filibuster occurring on the bill or the anticipation by Senate leaders that one would occur, detracts somewhat from legislative success generally and is strongly associated with the defeat of legislation on the Senate floor. Chiou and Rothenberg (2003) extend the pivotal politics model to incorporate parties and a filibuster pivot proximal to the president and find a role for parties in addition to supermajority requirements in explaining gridlock.

The filibuster pivot has also been a central concept in recent studies that have attempted to model formally the confirmation of presidential nominees. Models of the nomination and confirmation process have sought to extend the Romer–Rosenthal (1978) agenda-setter model by incorporating the feature that those doing the nominating and the confirming do not ultimately get to choose policy outcomes. The nominators and confirmers must consider how the appointment of an individual to a collective choice body, which they have limited to no control over, will affect the decisions produced by that body. Moraski and Shipan (1999) model explicitly the nomination and confirmation process for the Supreme Court, examining how the preferences of the Senate constrain the ability of the president to shape judicial policy through appointments. Their model and empirical analysis focus on the median as the pivotal player in the Senate, although they acknowledge that future work might consider the filibuster pivot as the key Senate player in the nomination game. Johnson and Roberts (2005) and Rohde and Shepsle (2007) do just that. The former authors derive a model that focuses on the filibuster pivot, but they also incorporate presidential capital in their model and argue that presidents can overcome constraints implied by the pivotal politics model by nominating more highly qualified candidates. Rohde and Shepsle frame their discussion in terms of how political polarization might lead to gridlock over nominations, which motivates them to focus on the reversion policy that would result if the vacancy could not be filled and the Court proceeded to operate with only eight members. The results that they obtain from their model indicate "the serious prospect for gridlock (exacerbated by polarization in the Senate)", although they also indicate hope for extreme nominees to win confirmation (p. 671). Krehbiel (2007) derives a "move the median" game that is much simpler than the Rohde–Shepsle model (and previous models) and predicts that both gridlock over appointments and immediate policy change resulting from a nomination are less likely. These results seem to be driven by different assumptions—mainly concerning the reversion point if a nomination is not made and the degree to which the nominator is gridlock-averse.

Primo et al. (2008) employ the pivotal politics framework to study nominations to the lower federal courts. Their formal model considers a large number of alternative pivots in the Senate, including the median of the judiciary committee and the median of the majority party, as well as "home-state" senators who can negatively influence a nomination through the "blue slip" process. Primo et al. conduct a horse-race of various spatial models and find that models that incorporate the filibuster pivot and the median of the majority party do best in explaining confirmation of nominees to federal trial and appellate courts. In a more exhaustive study, Binder and Maltzman (2009) uncover a periodicity to the blue slip process, finding that their status went from advisory to absolute vetoes to more recently becoming dependent on the political context and effective only when backed by a filibuster.

A worthwhile extension of this recent work would involve research on popular perceptions about the impact supermajority requirements have on advice and consent duties. Despite evidence that the filibuster pivot has long been important in confirmation decisions for the lower courts, the filibuster controversy over several of George W. Bush's nominees in 2005 seems to have marked a change in how judicial nominees and the supermajority Senate are perceived by the media. During that controversy, the Democratic minority filibustered to prevent the confirmation of several Bush nominees. The Republican leadership in the Senate threatened to eliminate filibusters of judicial nominees by using a parliamentary maneuver that required only a simple majority to establish a binding precedent that would have declared such filibusters unconstitutional. This approach, which became known popularly as the "nuclear option" (or less pejoratively as the "constitutional option"), had been contemplated and employed on numerous occasions throughout the Senate's history to limit obstructionist tactics, although it had never been used successfully to the extent that the Republican leadership was considering. The controversy was eventually defused when a bipartisan group of senators—dubbed the "Gang of Fourteen"—reached a compromise whereby the Democrats in the group would provide the cloture votes that would allow some of the nominations to come to a final vote and its Republican members would not support their leadership if it attempted the nuclear option (this maneuver is discussed in more detail below).

This very high-profile battle seems to have solidified the perception that supermajority support is now required to confirm judicial nominees. Judicial nominees offer one index for measuring how the Senate has transformed into a supermajoritarian body and the degree to which strategies in confirmation battles have been adjusted because such battles are expected to involve filibusters. I conducted a search of articles regarding Supreme Court appointments in the *New York Times* in the post-World War II era, looking for mentions of filibusters and supermajority requirements, to determine whether or not the initial discussion surrounding the Sotomayor nomination was unusual. It is important to keep in mind that filibusters of Supreme Court nominees are rare historically. Although the Senate made it clear by 1829 that Supreme Court nominations were not guaranteed an up-or-down vote (Beth and Palmer 2009), it is unusual for them not to receive one. Of the 158 nominations made between 1789 and 2006, only 25 (16 percent) did not reach a final vote and only one of these appears to have directly been the target of obstruction.[7] The first filibuster of a nominee to the high court—that was widely accepted as such—did not occur until 1968, when Lyndon Johnson attempted to elevate Abe Fortas to the position of chief justice. A cloture motion to proceed to consider the nomination failed 45–43, at which point Johnson withdrew the nomination. Three other filibusters followed quickly on the heels of this one, as the nominations of Clement Haynsworth and G. Harold Carswell went down to defeat in 1969 and 1970, and William Rehnquist's nomination to associate justice was filibustered briefly but unsuccessfully in 1971. Yet Haynsworth and Carswell were not defeated by a minority that prevented an up-or-down vote on them: both nominations came to a final vote and neither was able to secure the support of a simple majority.[8] Although a cloture vote on Rehnquist failed by eleven votes, Birch Bayh (D-IN), Rehnquist's chief antagonist, relented, allowing Rehnquist to be confirmed without the invocation of cloture (see W. Edwards, "How Rehnquist Filibuster Failed," *Chicago Tribune*, Dec. 14, 1971; J. P. MacKenzie, "Confirmation of Rehnquist Voted, 68–26," *Washington Post*, Dec. 11, 1971).

Subsequent to these three cases and prior to the showdown over lower court judges in 2005, there were essentially no filibusters of Supreme Court nominees. Although the Senate did hold a cloture vote on the nomination of Rehnquist for chief justice after five days of contentious debate in 1986, the opposition claimed their strategy to defeat Rehnquist involved filibustering only if the cloture vote failed, which it did not

---

[7] These figures are taken from Beth and Palmer (2009), which is an excellent and exhaustive history of Senate consideration of Supreme Court nominees.

[8] Beth and Palmer (2009, 29) cite the Fortas nomination as "the only time since 1873 when the Senate has terminated floor action on a Supreme Court nomination short of an up-or-down vote."

(L. Greenhouse, "Senate, 65 to 33, Votes to Confirm Rehnquist as 16th Chief Justice," *New York Times*, Sept. 18, 1986, A1). In the post-World War II era then, there do not appear to be any clear cases where a Supreme Court nomination had the support of a simple majority but failed for lack of supermajority support.[9]

Media discussion of Supreme Court nominees reflects their lack of association with filibusters. Of the thirty-six nominations to the high court that were made between 1945 and 2005, concerns about filibusters entered the discussion in only thirteen of those cases, and in all but four of those cases the discussion did not occur simultaneously with the announcement of the nomination. A bloc of Republicans threatened to filibuster the elevation of Fortas and the nomination of Homer Thornberry in 1968 on the day the nominations were made (see M. Hunter, "19 in the Senate Study Filibuster," *New York Times*, June 27, 1968, 30). The other two cases did not occur until 2005, when the nominations of John Roberts and Samuel Alito were announced.[10] When put in historical perspective, it is quite unusual that Sonia Sotomayor's nomination was immediately met with concern about a filibuster.

Arguably, this is due to the increasing occurrence of cloture votes during consideration of lower court nominees and other presidential appointees since 1968 and the new prominence that filibusters of nominees attained during the showdown over Bush nominees in 2003–05. From the time that cloture was applied to nominations in 1949 until 1967, it was moved exactly zero times. From 1968 to 2004, cloture motions were filed for twenty-five lower court nominations and for twenty-four executive branch nominations (Beth and Palmer 2005). While this does not necessarily mean that these nominations were all filibustered, it does demonstrate that cloture motions have become a much more standard way of dealing with nominations. At the same time, there has been a marked downward trend in the confirmation rates for lower court nominees (Binder and Maltzman 2009).

Despite this perception, data on coalition sizes do not indicate that Supreme Court nominations have changed all that much in the era of the supermajoritarian Senate. Throughout history, average coalition sizes for final votes on nominations have generally exceeded two-thirds. Of the 153 nominations that the president has sent to the Senate, 127 reached a final vote, and 53 percent of those were confirmed by voice vote. Of the 58 nominations that received roll calls, the average coalition size in support of the nominations was 73 percent of those present and voting; since cloture was applied to nominations in 1949, this number has been only slightly higher at 74 percent. There have been two cases since 1949 when nominees were confirmed with fewer votes than would have been needed to invoke cloture at the time of consideration: Clarence Thomas was confirmed with only fifty-two yeas and Alito was confirmed with fifty-eight yeas, just shy of the sixty-vote threshold. A filibuster of the Alito nomination did

---

[9] It is possible that simple majorities failed to coalesce around doomed nominations once it became clear they would not receive supermajority support, but an examination of existing cases does not reveal evidence of this.

[10] For example, see D. Balz and C. Lane, "A Move To the Right, An Eye to Confirmation," *The Washington Post*, July 20, 2005, A1; D. D. Kirkpatrick, "Parties Set Stage For a Showdown On Court Choice," *New York Times*, Oct 31, 2005, A1.

materialize briefly, but it was soundly defeated when cloture was invoked by a vote of 72–25. Whether or not filibusters and cloture votes on Supreme Court nominees will become the norm remains to be seen. The cloture vote on the Alito nomination was only the fourth time cloture had been attempted on a nominee to the high court; Sotomayor did not face a cloture vote and was confirmed 68–31. Interestingly, the Alito case indicates that senators do not necessarily equate cloture votes with final votes for such nominees. Why this is the case, and whether this constitutes a pattern of behavior that will be sustained into the future is a central question worthy of further systematic investigation.[11]

Another topic that is relevant to the discussion of the advice and consent power of the supermajority Senate and deserves more scholarly attention concerns "holds." A senator can place a hold on a nominee or a piece of legislation to demonstrate a particular concern about the nomination or legislation moving forward. Understanding the impact of holds has been hampered by the fact that they are not defined or prescribed in the Senate's rules or precedents and are anonymous. Some have portrayed holds as unilateral vetoes that grant tremendous power to individual senators (e.g. see Gold 2004, 84–5; Sinclair 1989, 130; "Yes, Holds Barred," *Pittsburgh Post-Gazette*, March 11, 1999, A18). Others view them as signals to the Senate leadership of a possible threat to object to a unanimous consent agreement (UCA) and to filibuster, which can lead to bargaining to appease the senators placing the holds (Tiefer 1989, 563–6).

The secrecy and vague institutional standing of holds renders them difficult to study, but the obstacles to inquiry are not insurmountable. Evans and Lipinski (2005) have shown that archives of former Senate majority leaders can be fruitful for empirical analysis of holds. Although it is difficult to assess the causal impact of holds with existing data, their systematic investigation of records kept by Howard Baker (R-TN) indicates that legislation that was targeted by holds still managed to pass, enabling us to reject the hypotheses that holds doom legislation. Jacobi (2005) demonstrates how a model based on the pivotal politics framework can bolster the theory on holds and senatorial courtesy. Apart from the need to provide insight into the question of why a majority would grant so much power to an individual senator, further scientific investigation of holds is made more urgent by news reports that depict them as a highly undemocratic feature of a broken institution. Systematic analysis can provide an assessment of whether such alarmist portrayals are accurate and reveal whether reform proposals to eliminate or curtail holds should be given more serious consideration.

---

[11] This raises a related question that is underexplored: to what extent do constituents care whether a senator expresses a preference through a cloture vote as opposed to an up-or-down vote on passage? Senators appear to make distinctions between the two kinds of votes, although it is not entirely clear why. Although their investigation is still in its preliminary stages at this time, Butler and Sempolinski (n.d.) find that differences between the way a senator votes on cloture and on final passage on a given piece of legislation can be explained systematically and appear to be related to electoral factors and to the procedural concerns of the majority party in getting to a final vote.

MAINTENANCE OF THE SUPERMAJORITY SENATE

Although reform of the Senate rules that grant tremendous influence to individual senators is a perennial topic of discussion, there seems to be broad consensus that the supermajority Senate is here to stay for the foreseeable future. However, there is far less consensus regarding why that is the case, as two distinct camps have emerged on this question. One camp argues that the supermajority Senate is the result of strong path dependency. Once the Senate deleted its provision for moving the previous question in 1806, its members set the chamber on a path where it would be extremely difficult, bordering on impossible, to change the rules in a way that would eliminate obstruction and reestablish the Senate as a majoritarian institution (Binder 1997; Binder and Smith 1997; Binder, Madonna, and Smith 2007). The lack of rules for limiting debate meant that minorities could simply use the tools of obstruction to prevent subsequent rule changes. Thus, this perspective contends that the Senate that currently exists is not necessarily the one that a majority of senators wants.

The other camp argues that a truly committed majority could use parliamentary means to eliminate the filibuster. This would involve the use of rulings by the Senate presiding officer to establish binding precedents declaring that a simple majority could bring legislation or nominations to a final vote without having to invoke cloture (Wawro and Schickler 2006; Koger 2002; Gold and Gupta 2004). There are several forms that this approach can take, but the basic idea is as follows. Suppose that during the obstruction of a nominee for the federal bench, a senator makes a point of order that, given the Senate's constitutional advise and consent responsibilities, it would be in order to decide by a majority vote to close debate and bring the nomination to an up-or-down vote. The presiding officer would rule in favor of the point of order, but the minority could appeal this decision. A senator sympathetic to the ruling could then make a motion to table the appeal. The motion to table is—crucially—not debatable, which means that the minority cannot use extended debate on the motion to prevent a decision. If a simple majority votes to table the appeal, then the ruling is upheld and establishes a precedent that is as binding as any rule that the Senate would adopt by passing a resolution.[12]

Wawro and Schickler (2006) contend that this option helped to curtail minority obstruction in the pre-cloture era, as senators limited the exercise of their broad prerogatives out of fear that they would be taken away. They point to several instances where rulings by the chair were used to curtail minority obstruction when it was deemed to be getting excessive, although these rulings fell short of the establishment of majority cloture.[13] Binder, Madonna, and Smith (2007) claim that rulings by the

---

[12] A binding precedent is established if the minority does not appeal the ruling in the first place.

[13] This "majoritarian view" allows for a role for path dependency in the evolution of supermajoritarian rules. Indeed, it argues that the use of precedents to limit minority obstruction was a mechanism that developed incrementally along a particular path during the nineteenth century. The key

chair were not and are not an ever-present, credible threat because the minority has too much leverage to stymie the majority and bring the institution to a complete halt, thus making it impossible to find a majority that would support pulling this procedural trigger.

A good deal of work remains if this debate is to be settled. The absence of data on senators' true preferences regarding alternative institutional rules makes resolving this debate particularly difficult. Even if we had an actual roll-call vote on a ruling from the chair to impose majority cloture, the nays could be interpreted in multiple ways. A nay does not necessarily mean that the senator opposes a move to majority cloture, and instead could be the result of the senators' opposition to the measure or nomination associated with the attempt to change the rules.

Better theory regarding the institutional choice of legislating by supermajorities is vital to move the debate forward. Supermajority procedures would seem to violate Krehbiel's (1991, 16) majoritarian postulate, which holds that "objects of legislative choice in both the procedural and policy domains must be chosen by a majority of the legislature." Although basic parliamentary rules and procedure establish the median voter in the chamber as the decisive figure, the rules of the Senate now effectively make the filibuster pivot the decisive figure, producing potentially off-median legislative outcomes. Why would the median voter ever go along with this if she was endowed by institutional rules to improve her situation on both procedural and policy levels? The path-dependency argument claims that the median voter essentially has no choice. The alternative view has a more difficult time justifying this, largely because a convincing theory has yet to be developed that would explain why median voters would prefer to let supermajority pivots usurp their "pivotocity." This would require a model of endogenous institutional selection that could produce off-median pivots as an equilibrium outcome in the absence of the threat of obstruction by the minority.

Formal work does exist that demonstrates the benefits of forming supermajority coalitions. Groseclose and Snyder's (1996) model of vote-buying indicates that a strategy of building supermajority coalitions can be less costly than one of building minimal winning coalitions. Caplin and Nalebuff (1988) show that problems related to cycling and the maintenance of legislative bargains can be solved by forming majorities in upwards of 64 percent of the decision-making body. Henry (2008) derives a formal model that demonstrates that it can be optimal for agenda-setters to propose supermajority coalitions because the revelation of private information held by legislators who join such coalitions can make up for the loss experienced by distributing benefits more widely beyond a simple majority coalition. Even though this formal work does not model the institutionalization of supermajority requirements as a collective choice, it does offer ways to think about how to proceed on this front in a more systematic and disciplined fashion.

---

difference between the majoritarian and the Binder–Smith perspectives is that the former claims that the problem that reformers face today is not that they are completely hand-cuffed by a procedural decision made in 1806, but that a majority of the senators believe they are better off under the current system and are thus unwilling to use the parliamentary tools at their disposal to change the rules.

A second question that is crucial to this debate and for which we do not have a satisfying answer is who would the electorate blame if the nuclear button was pushed and the Senate came to a halt? Would it hold the minority accountable for obstinate obstruction and violation of majority rule? Or would it hold the majority accountable for trying to run roughshod over the minority and for failing to legislate its agenda? Or would it not care enough to punish either the majority or the minority at the polls?

A gaping hole in our understanding of the supermajority Senate pertains to public opinion. Almost no systematic research has been conducted on voters' knowledge and views of the supermajoritarian nature of the institution. Yet extensive searches on iPoll, *National Journal's* Hotline, and pollingreport.com revealed that public opinion polls exist going back to the 1930s that could potentially shed some light on these questions. The Gallup Organization included questions related to knowledge and support for the filibuster and supermajority requirements on several surveys in the post-World War II period (in 1947, 1949, 1950, 1963, and 1964). The question wording is consistent across these years, making it feasible to conduct longitudinal analysis and uncover possible patterns in movement of opinion during a period when the filibuster became a more salient feature of the Senate, as battles over civil rights legislation came to the fore and several attempts were made to reduce the cloture threshold. The raw data for the surveys includes individual-level variables that are plausibly related to knowledge and opinion formation about supermajority requirements, opening up the possibility for quantitative modeling. Basic demographic variables, including race and education, as well as partisan/ideological measures and regional indicators are available from the surveys, and could be weighted according to methods advocated by Berinsky (2006) and Berinsky and Schickler (2006) to improve the quality of inferences drawn from the data covering this critical period of the Senate's history.

Unfortunately, searches of the aforementioned sources indicate the absence of non-partisan surveys during the 1970s, when measures of filibusters indicate that they increased dramatically in number. In fact, it is not until 2005, during the controversy over Bush's judicial nominees, that questions of the kind asked by Gallup in the 1940s–1960s appear on non-partisan polls.[14] Numerous surveys asked questions about respondents' knowledge of filibusters, whether or not they supported the filibusters of judicial nominations, and whether or not they favored efforts to prevent such filibusters. Measures are available from these surveys that could be used to model individual opinion formation. It is also possible to merge this data with contextual variables—such as the ideological positions of respondents' senators—to get a better sense of how the larger political environment might be related to opinions.

A brief look at these various surveys reveals two interesting features in aggregate opinion from the end of World War II to the beginning of the twenty-first century. The first is that knowledge of the filibuster is at about the same level as other levels of knowledge regarding basic facts of American politics and the Senate, such as how many senators represent each state (cf. Delli Carpini and Keeter 1996). That said, filibusters and supermajority requirements appear to be of low salience to the public

[14] Surveys by partisan polling organizations were conducted in 1994, 2003, and 2004.

as a general matter. The second feature suggested by the data is that there has been significant change over time in the support for the maintenance of supermajority cloture. In the 1940s–1960s, more respondents favored reducing the cloture threshold to a simple majority than did keeping it at a two-thirds majority. In the Gallup surveys conducted in 2005, more respondents than not opposed the efforts to allow simple majorities to invoke cloture on judicial appointments. While this is interesting variation, we cannot definitively conclude that opinion has changed generally. Filibusters in the earlier period were tied largely to civil rights legislation, and since positions on the filibuster tend to be based more on politics than principle, the apparent shift may have more to do with the issues at hand than it does with support for supermajority requirements in general. A much closer look at this data is warranted, and—if motivated with theoretical development that draws from existing work on opinion formation regarding recondite issues and on the behavior of elites that could provide cues for the masses—would provide a much-needed foundation for moving forward on the question of how the electorate views the supermajority Senate, with all of its complexities.[15] This kind of analysis should inform more sophisticated studies that involve designing survey questions that could elicit possibly elusive aspects of the public's knowledge of, and positions on, filibusters and supermajority requirements.

PROCEDURAL INNOVATIONS IN THE SUPERMAJORITY SENATE

The cursory inspection of public opinion data discussed in the previous section did not reveal widespread and vocal support for eliminating supermajority requirements in the contemporary Senate, which might explain in part why the Senate has maintained such requirements. Perhaps another reason why the Senate has maintained its supermajoritarian quality is that it has a safety valve in the form of "fast-track" procedures that pertain to specific pieces of legislation. These procedures are statute-specific and aim to expedite the consideration and passage of legislation by limiting or prohibiting amendments and establishing time limits for committee and floor deliberation and debate. Binder and Smith (1997, 185–95) note over thirty cases where such procedures were employed covering a wide range of domestic and foreign policy areas. Technically, these procedures require only majority approval, although there is typically widespread support for adopting them. Systematic study of fast-track procedures has the potential to grant insight into beliefs about and commitment to the supermajority Senate.

---

[15] Additional light might be shed on how the public would respond to an attempt to bring the Senate to a standstill by looking at opinion polls regarding the shutdown of the federal government in 1995–96.

Budget reconciliation bills which are covered by fast-track procedures have been used in a few instances by majorities as vehicles to pass legislative items that arguably would not have passed if they had been subject to normal supermajoritarian requirements. The Budget and Impoundment Control Act of 1974 (BICA) provides statutory filibuster "protection" to reconciliation bills—with the intent of expediting deficit-reducing legislation—by limiting debate on them to twenty hours, imposing germaneness requirements for amendments, and requiring only a simple majority for passage. As a result, reconciliation bills have become attractive vehicles for high priority, controversial legislation that would not garner sixty votes. However, senators do not have carte blanche to use reconciliation for passing substantive legislation because of constraints imposed by "the Byrd Rule." The Byrd Rule, which bears the name of its primary sponsor, Senator Robert Byrd (D-WV), is actually a set of rules that are intended to prevent provisions in reconciliation bills that have little to do with implementing budget resolution policies. The rule was adopted on a temporary basis initially in 1985, but has since become permanent as Section 313 of the BICA. Generally, the Byrd Rule enables senators to raise points of order against provisions in legislation that are inconsistent or unrelated to the goals of the reconciliation instructions—namely deficit reduction and the improvement of the federal government's fiscal posture. The Byrd Rule defines what kinds of provisions are extraneous, and senators invoke these definitions when raising points of order against provisions in reconciliation bills that they hope to eliminate. The chair rules on the points of order, aided by the parliamentarian and guided by a list of potentially extraneous provisions compiled by the Senate Budget Committee (Keith 2008). Three-fifths of the Senate are required to sustain an appeal of the ruling of the chair, and a motion to waive the Byrd Rule also requires a three-fifths vote. The general perception is that the decision as to what is extraneous is essentially the parliamentarian's to make, thrusting him into the middle of major legislative battles and granting him direct influence over policy outcomes.

The Byrd Rule was intended to limit the ability of senators to use reconciliation bills to circumvent supermajority requirements as a routine way to legislate. When introducing the initial amendment that would become the Byrd Rule, Byrd emphasized that the absence of restrictions on reconciliation provisions was threatening the unique deliberative nature of the Senate and noted how much more restrictive reconciliation procedures were when compared with how the Senate operates after cloture has been invoked (*Congressional Record*, Oct. 24, 1985, S14032). The vote to adopt the amendment was 96–0, indicating that senators broadly thought that something needed to be done with regard to limiting the usage of reconciliation. Subsequent refinements to the Byrd Rule have closed various loopholes, helping to maintain the supermajoritarian nature of the Senate. The adoption and reinforcement of the Byrd Rule is evidence that most senators favor three-fifths as a threshold for lawmaking. It is striking that senators have broadly supported imposing these kinds of restrictions that preclude the use of reconciliation to routinely circumvent the filibuster. In this regard, the Byrd Rule is somewhat unusual in Senate history because it involves broad coalitions of senators taking *positive* action to reinforce the integrity of supermajoritarian procedures, rather than more narrow coalitions using their prerogatives as a form of negative power to preserve such procedures.

This is not to say that there have been no efforts to exploit reconciliation for short-term policy gains. Even with these restrictions, policymakers have used reconciliation bills as vehicles to pass—with fewer than sixty votes—substantive legislation that is only remotely (if at all) related to the goal of deficit reduction. Reconciliation became particularly attractive in the 1990s and early years of the twenty-first century in a Senate that was evenly divided between two highly polarized parties. During this period, the Senate passed several pieces of major tax cut legislation via reconciliation, although they would arguably decrease revenues and thereby increase the deficit. The Byrd Rule has played a role in limiting the reach of the tax cuts, however, as senators have used it to force the inclusion of sunset provisions that would revoke the cuts after a period of several years. The sunset provisions meant that the legislation did not change tax law permanently and ensured that the revenue effects would be contained within the multi-year budget framework to which the reconciliation instructions were applicable (Keith 2008, 18). Other major education, health, and social welfare policy changes have been enacted using reconciliation bills, enabling both parties to achieve victories on key agenda items without securing supermajorities.

That said, only nine out of twenty-two reconciliation measures that passed between 1980 and 2007 did so with fewer than sixty votes, and three of those nine did not become law because of successful vetoes. This suggests that senators have not always availed themselves of the opportunity to legislate with simple majorities that reconciliation affords. Given the complaints about the difficulties of invoking cloture and recent increases in polarization in the Senate, it is somewhat puzzling that senators have generally still worked to build coalitions of the size that could withstand filibusters. Perhaps the gains are more from the expedited procedures that reconciliation bills enjoy than from the reduction in the threshold for passage.

The debate over the use of rulings from the chair to circumvent supermajority requirements is relevant here as well. In 1996, Senate Republicans pushed a budget resolution that called for three separate reconciliation bills—one that would slow Medicare spending, one that would overhaul welfare, and one that would cut taxes. Then-Minority Leader Tom Daschle (D-SD) raised a point of order that the latter violated the Byrd rule because it would not reduce the deficit. Daschle and other Democrats were concerned that the maneuver would establish a precedent that would undermine the minority's ability to filibuster tax cut legislation. Following a decision by the parliamentarian Robert Dove, the chair ruled against the point of order, and after Daschle appealed the ruling, it was upheld on a strict party-line vote of 53–47. Thus, the Senate established a binding precedent by a slim majority that appeared to undercut the Byrd rule. Bill Dauster, Democratic chief of staff and chief counsel of the Senate Budget Committee, declared the death of the supermajority Senate, claiming that, "From now on, the majority party can create as many reconciliation bills as it wants... From now on, the majority can use the reconciliation process to move its entire legislative agenda through the Senate with simple majority votes and few distractions" ("The Day the Senate Died: Budget Measure Weakens Minority," *Roll Call*, May 30, 1996). While Dauster's predictions have not come to pass, there is evidence that the minority has been cowed by this action. When Senate Republicans included reconciliation instructions for President George W. Bush's signature tax cut initiative in the 2001 budget resolution, minority Democrats did not oppose it. Despite its apparent violation of the Byrd Rule and despite a change of heart by parliamentarian Dove that led him to repudiate his 1996 ruling to give tax cut bills reconciliation protection, Democrats feared that disputing the move by raising a point of order would produce the same result as Daschle's earlier challenge, establishing an additional anti-supermajoritarian precedent (A. Taylor, "Law Designed for Curbing Deficits Becomes GOP Tool for Cutting Taxes," *CQ Weekly*, April 7, 2001, 770). Dove's about-face on the use of reconciliation for pure tax-cutting legislation contributed to his ouster as parliamentarian, raising concerns about the politicization of the office (A. Taylor, "Senate's Agenda to Rest on Rulings of Referee Schooled by Democrats," *CQ Weekly*, May 12, 2001, 1063). The Economic Growth and Tax Relief Reconciliation Act of 2001 (P.L. 107–16) would eventually pass 58–33, with a majority just shy of the sixty-vote threshold. Bush's second major tax cut, The Jobs and Growth Tax Relief Reconciliation Act of 2003 (P.L. 108–27) also received reconciliation protection and passed with an even slimmer majority, 51–50, with Vice President Dick Cheney casting the tie-breaking vote.

The use of reconciliation, coupled with the issue of establishing relevant precedents by simple majorities, is of profound importance for understanding the supermajority Senate. Yet, there has been little to no systematic research on this topic. Some questions worthy of investigation include: why doesn't the Senate rely *more* on reconciliation for filibuster protection? What are the limits to using it? What drives the broad commitment that seems to currently exist among senators for the Byrd Rule? What explains why this commitment sometimes falters, permitting the passage of legislation in ways that seem to violate the Byrd Rule in letter and spirit? To what extent has the Byrd Rule worked to prevent reconciliation from becoming much of a loophole? When and why are Byrd Rule challenges successful? What implications does politicization of the parliamentarian and his decisions have for theories of institutional commitment? Does reconciliation lead to the production of policy outcomes that are significantly different from what we would see if supermajority requirements were not circumvented? Fortunately, the importance of this topic means that potentially useful data has already been collected (e.g. see Keith 2008), and awaits the application of theoretical and empirical modeling.

Senators' general commitment to the Byrd Rule is not the only recent piece of evidence that they have accepted that the Senate is a supermajoritarian institution. Another indication concerns the procedural innovation of adopting UCAs that require sixty votes rather than a simple majority for the passage of legislation or amendments. Lynch (2008) points out several advantages of proceeding in this manner. First, UCAs of this variety have the advantage of still requiring supermajority support without requiring senators to follow the time-consuming steps that the cloture procedure involves.[16] Second, they enable senators to vote directly on the substance of legislation, rather than voting indirectly on the issue through a cloture motion that may or may not succeed in producing an up-or-down vote. Third, since almost all of the UCAs in this class have been used for pairs or groups of amendments that constitute competing alternatives for addressing the same issues, it provides an efficient and orderly way for senators to stake out positions and express preferences.

This procedural innovation takes the silent filibuster one step further. Not only do obstructionists no longer need to take and hold the floor to force the formation of supermajority coalitions to move legislation forward, now bill supporters no longer have to get those supermajorities to actually vote for cloture to approve items. When a sixty-vote UCA is agreed to, all senators are accepting restrictions on their prerogatives to obstruct for assurances that the approving coalition will have to be of the size that (at least in theory) could invoke cloture. Although this innovation has existed since the 1990s, there has been an upward trend in using sixty-vote UCAs in the first decade of the twenty-first century. As the use of this class of UCAs becomes more and more routinized, the status of the Senate as a supermajoritarian institution becomes more and more explicit and entrenched. Since sixty-vote UCAs have the potential to address one of the most important problems facing the Senate—time constraints—it is important to study the dynamics behind them and to determine what their overall impact might be on policy-making in the Senate.

The procedural innovations discussed in this section offer opportunities along several dimensions for theorizing about legislative institutions in general. The first dimension concerns path dependence. Procedures such as the Byrd Rule and sixty-vote UCAs are path-dependent responses to context-specific intertwining of structure and agency. Institutional designers would probably not include these kinds of procedures as part of an initial blueprint for a legislature. Yet the procedures grant insight into how legislators attempt to reconcile existing rules of the game and long-standing traditions with the need to achieve their goals and meet the demands placed on the institution by the polity. Another dimension concerns "remote majoritarianism" (Krehbiel 1991, 19), since in the case of reconciliation, there is the tension between the temptation for narrow majorities to exploit the process for short-term policy gain and the desire to maintain the long-term integrity of institutional rules adopted to protect a specific class of legislation and thereby promote the collective goal of deficit reduction. Understanding how this tension plays out provides leverage for understanding how and when majorities are willing and able to flex their muscles in the face of an institutional context that has long-empowered minorities. A related tension concerns the frustration that the electorate often expresses with a perceived inefficiency in the meeting of congressional responsibilities, juxtaposed with the apparent gradual popular acceptance of the filibuster as a legitimate and explicit feature of the Senate. There is an element of path dependence here as well, since the potential public relations

---

[16] For example, after a cloture motion has been presented, the Senate must wait two days for the cloture petition to "ripen" before it can act on it. If cloture is invoked, thirty hours of debate are allowed, which can further delay a final vote.

costs of eliminating the filibuster seem to be much higher today than they were in the nineteenth century prior to the legitimation of parliamentary obstruction through the tremendous expansion of its use in the twentieth century. The maintenance of the status quo is path-dependent—not in the sense that a majority is handcuffed by inherited institutions from changing the rules—but majorities have gradually come to perceive that it is not in their political interest to either take a public relations hit for eliminating the filibuster or to relinquish future opportunities to appeal to constituents by filibustering themselves.

Conclusion

The Senate has come a long way since the nineteenth century, when filibusters were viewed as less than legitimate and simple majorities legislated regularly and effectively. Filibusters, silent or clamorous, and the use of supermajorities to overcome them have become deeply embedded in the fabric of the institution. Many issues involving the supermajority Senate demand more investigation and debate, including its overall impact on policy-making in the U.S. as well as general normative concerns. Although there have been many calls for reforming the Senate's supermajority requirements, any such reform attempts should be based on a firm understanding of the causes and consequences of the current institutional equilibrium. In the abstract, arguments exist for and against legislating by supermajorities.[17] But such arguments need to be placed in the political and institutional context that surrounds the Senate. The polarization that has emerged in the Senate over the past four decades and the narrow majorities that have resulted from early twenty-first century elections make concerns about supermajority thresholds more pressing. With narrow partisan majorities and little to no ideological overlap between the parties, minorities have greater incentives to push their prerogatives regarding obstruction in order to force changes in legislation that will garner their support. It is important to keep in mind that the current level of polarization—and dominance of the liberal-conservative economic dimension—justifies discussing majority and minority coalitions in partisan terms. This has not generally been the case historically, since many important battles involving filibusters were not fought along party lines. Narrow majorities help to accentuate the impact of the filibuster on lawmaking. Still, any time a party holds the presidency and sixty seats in the Senate, as Democrats did as a result of the 2008 elections, it will no doubt face intense criticism regarding its ability to govern if the party fails to enact key agenda items.

It is difficult, if not impossible, to separate the normative question about whether the Senate should operate as a supermajoritarian institution from one's opinions of

---

[17] See McGann (2004) for a review of these arguments.

the policy outcomes produced by the Senate. In the short term, if we favor a given policy that could be enacted by a simple majority but would fail if a supermajority is required, then we would be tempted to favor reform to eliminate the filibuster. But there are long-term considerations as well, since changes in Senate membership mean that there will likely be measures considered in the future that we would prefer to be blocked if at least 41 opposing votes can be mustered.

The framers provide at best equivocal guidance on the question. Madison was no fan of supermajority requirements, but he did make the case in *Federalist* 63 that the Senate was "an institution that may be sometimes necessary as a defense to the people against their own temporary error and delusions." Supermajority requirements can help the Senate fulfill this role. If it was as easy to pass legislation in the Senate as it is in the House, one could argue that the framers' vision of the role that bicameralism would play in the federal system would be compromised (see Lee, this volume on bicameralism dynamics more generally). Indirect election of senators, which the framers included in the Constitution only to be eliminated by the 17th amendment, can no longer serve to insulate the Senate from the same potentially capricious electorate that chooses House members (indeed, it is not clear that indirect election ever did much in this regard). Thus, internal distinctions between the two chambers have become more important in keeping bicameralism meaningful. Minorities in the House consistently complain about being cut out of the decision-making process. If one worries about minorities having some say in policymaking, then perhaps one should be pleased that the Senate has institutionalized a greater role for them.

A staunch belief that the majority should rule does not necessarily imply opposition to supermajority requirements. Equal apportionment of senators among the states complicates the math of majority representation in the chamber. If Democratic senators are elected from the most populous states, but Republicans hold a majority of seats in the Senate, then it is possible that a minority of the membership represents a majority of the country. Supermajority requirements, then, can in some circumstances indirectly serve majority rule.[18] A systematic study of the degree to which supermajority requirements in a malapportioned legislature promote outcomes favored by macro-electoral majorities would be a worthwhile undertaking.[19]

Satisfying answers to normative questions cannot be obtained without rigorous positive political science. As this chapter has attempted to demonstrate, the trajectory of the literature on the Senate is steeply upward and hence immensely favorable to achieving the kind of understanding of the unique features of the institution that is essential for informed debates about what kind of Senate we should have. Continued investigation into the historical and contemporary Senate, using innovative methods and models, will help to ensure that we can have reasoned discourse regarding the status and place of supermajority requirements in what many have claimed to be the greatest deliberative body in the world.

[18] This appears to have been the case with the filibuster of the nomination of Josh Bolton for the position of ambassador to the United Nations (cf. Levinson 2006, 111–12).

[19] See Lee and Oppenheimer (1999) for a study of the distributive consequences of malapportionment in the Senate.

REFERENCES

BAKER, R. K. 1995. *House and Senate.* 2nd ed. New York: W. W. Norton.

BERINSKY, A. J. 2006. American Public Opinion in the 1930s and 1940s: The Analysis of Quota-Controlled Sample Survey Data. *Public Opinion Quarterly,* 70(4): 499–529.

—— and SCHICKLER, E. 2006. The American Mass Public in the 1930s and 1940s. National Science Foundation, Collaborative Research Grant. http://web.mit.edu/berinsky/www/nsf.pdf. (accessed Nov. 9, 2009).

BETH, R. S. 1994. Filibusters in the Senate, 1789–1993. Congressional Research Service Memorandum.

BETH, R. S. 1995. What We Don't Know about Filibusters. Paper presented at the Annual Meeting of the Western Political Science Association.

BETH, R. S., and PALMER, B. 2005. Cloture Attempts on Nominations. Congressional Research Service Report.

BETH, R. S., and PALMER, B. 2009. Supreme Court Nominations: Senate Floor Procedure and Practice, 1789–2009. Congressional Research Service Report.

Binder, S. A. 1997. *Minority Rights, Majority Rule.* New York: Cambridge University Press.

BINDER, S. A. 2003. *Stalemate: Causes and Consequences of Legislative Gridlock.* Washington, DC: Brookings Institution.

BINDER, S. A., LAWRENCE, E. D., and SMITH, S. S. 2002. Tracking the Filibuster, 1917 to 1996. *American Politics Research,* 30(4): 406–22.

BINDER, S. A., MADONNA, A. J., and SMITH, S. S. 2007. Going Nuclear, Senate Style. *Perspectives on Politics,* 5(4): 729–40.

BINDER, S. A., and MALTZMAN, F. 2009. *Advice and Dissent: The Struggle to Shape the Federal Judiciary.* Washington, DC: Brookings Institution Press.

BINDER, S. A., and SMITH, S. S. 1997. *Politics or Principle? Filibustering in the United States Senate.* Washington, DC: Brookings Institution.

BRADY, D. W., and VOLDEN, C. 1998. *Revolving Gridlock: Politics and Policy from Carter to Clinton.* Boulder, CO: Westview Press.

BURDETTE, F. L. 1940. *Filibustering in the Senate.* Princeton: Princeton University Press.

BUTLER, D. M., and SEMPOLINSKI, J. N.D. Ending the Debate: Examining the Determinants of Voting for Cloture. Working Paper.

BYRD, R. C. 1988. *The Senate, 1789–1989: Addresses on the History of the United States Senate.* Washington, DC: U.S. G.P.O.

CAPLIN, A., and NALEBUFF, B. 1988. On 64%-Majority Rule. *Econometrica,* 56(4): 787–814.

CHIOU, F. Y., and ROTHENBERG, L. S. 2003. When Pivotal Politics Meets Partisan Politics. *American Journal of Political Science,* 47(3): 503–22.

COOPER, J. 1962. *The Previous Question: Its Standing as a Precedent for Cloture in the United States Senate.* Senate Document 87–104. Washington, DC: G.P.O.

DELLI CARPINI, M. X., and KEETER, S. 1996. *What Americans Know About Politics and Why It Matters.* New Haven: Yale University Press.

DION, D. 1997. *Turning the Legislative Thumbscrew.* Ann Arbor: University of Michigan Press.

EVANS, C. L., and LIPINSKI, D. 2005. Obstruction and Leadership in the U.S. Senate. In *Congress Reconsidered* 8th edition, ed. L. C. Dodd and B. I. Oppenheimer. Washington, DC: Congressional Quarterly Press, pp. 227–48.

GOLD, M. 2004. *Senate Procedure and Practice.* Lanham, MD: Rowman & Littlefield.

GOLD, M. B., and GUPTA, D. 2004. The Constitutional Option to Change Senate Rules and Procedures: A Majoritarian Means to Overcome the Filibuster. *Harvard Journal of Law and Public Policy*, 28(1): 205–72.

GROSECLOSE, T., and SNYDER, J. M. 1996. Buying Supermajorities. *American Political Science Review*, 90(2): 303–15.

HENRY, E. 2008. The Informational Role of Supermajorities. *Journal of Public Economics*, 92 (10–11): 2225–39.

JACOBI, T. 2005. The Senatorial Courtesy Game: Explaining the Norm of Informal Vetoes in Advice and Consent Nominations. *Legislative Studies Quarterly*, 30(2): 193–217.

JOHNSON, T. R., and ROBERTS, J. M. 2005. Pivotal Politics, Presidential Capital, and Supreme Court Nominations. *Congress and the Presidency*, 32(1): 31–48.

KEITH, R. 2008. Budget Reconciliation Procedures: The Senate's Byrd Rule. Congressional Research Service Report RL30862.

KOGER, G. 2002. Obstruction in the House and Senate. Ph.D. thesis UCLA.

—— 2007. Filibuster Reform in the Senate, 1913–1917. pp. 215–25 in *Party, Process, and Political change in Congress*, vol. 2: *Further New Perspectives on the history of Congress*, ed. D. W. Brady and M. D. McCubbins. Stanford, CA: Stanford University Press.

—— 2010. Filibustering: A Political History of Obstruction in the House and Senate. Chicago: University of Chicago Press.

KREHBIEL, K. 1991. *Information and Legislative Organization*. Ann Arbor: University of Michigan Press.

—— 1998. *Pivotal Politics: A Theory of U.S. Lawmaking*. Chicago: University of Chicago Press.

—— 2007. Supreme Court Appointments as a Move-the-Median Game. *American Journal of Political Science*, 51(2): 231–40.

LEE, F. E., and OPPENHEIMER, B. I. 1999. *Sizing Up the Senate: The Unequal Consequences of Equal Representation*. Chicago: University of Chicago Press.

LEVINSON, S. 2006. *Our Undemocratic Constitution: Where the Constitution Goes Wrong (And How We the People Can Correct It)*. New York: Oxford University Press.

LYNCH, M. S. 2008. Unanimous Consent Agreements Establishing a 60-Vote Threshold for Passage of Legislation in the Senate. Congressional Research Service Report RL34491.

MAYHEW, D. R. 2003. Supermajority Rule in the U.S. Senate. *PS: Political Science and Politics*, 36(1): 31–6.

MCGANN, A. J. 2004. The Tyranny of the Supermajority: How Majority Rule Protects Minorities. *Journal of Theoretical Politics*, 16(1): 53–77.

MORASKI, B. J., and SHIPAN, C. R. 1999. The Politics of Supreme Court Nominations: A Theory of Institutional Constraints and Choices. *American Journal of Political Science*, 43(4): 1069–95.

OPPENHEIMER, B. I. 1985. Changing Time Constraints on Congress: Historical Perspectives on the Use of Cloture, pp. 393–413 in L. C. Dodd and B. I. Oppenheimer, editors, *Congress Reconsidered*, Washington, DC: Congressional Quarterly Press. 3rd edition.

ORNSTEIN, N. J. 2003. Reform Is Needed, but Tread Carefully. *Roll Call* (May 21).

PRIMO, D. M., BINDER, S. A., and MALTZMAN, F. 2008. Who Consents? Competing Pivots in Federal Judicial Selection. *American Journal of Political Science*, 52(3): 471–89.

ROGERS, L. 1926. *The American Senate*. New York: Alfred A. Knopf.

ROHDE, D. W., and SHEPSLE, K. A. 2007. Advising and Consenting in the 60-Vote Senate: Strategic Appointments to the Supreme Court. *Journal of Politics*, 69(3): 664–77.

ROMER, T., and ROSENTHAL, H. 1978. Political Resource Allocation, Controlled Agendas, and The Status Quo. *Public Choice*, 33(4): 27–43.

SINCLAIR, B. 1989. *The Transformation of the U.S. Senate.* Baltimore, MD: Johns Hopkins University Press.

—— 2002. The '60-Vote Senate', pp. 241–61 in *U.S. Senate Exceptionalism*, ed. B.I. Oppenheimer. Columbus: Ohio State University Press.

TIEFER, C. 1989. *Congressional Practice and Procedure: A Reference, Research, and Legislative Guide.* New York: Greenwood Press.

WAWRO, G. J., and SCHICKLER, E. 2006. *Filibuster: Obstruction and Lawmaking in the U.S. Senate.* Princeton: Princeton University Press.

WHITE, W. S. 1968. *Citadel: The Story of the U.S. Senate.* Boston: Houghton Mifflin.

C H A P T E R   2 0

....

MANAGING PLENARY TIME: THE U.S. CONGRESS IN COMPARATIVE CONTEXT*

....

GARY W. COX
MATHEW D. McCUBBINS

> Always remember that time is money.
> Benjamin Franklin

In this chapter, we argue that the ability to gain or prevent access to plenary time is the central source of power in democratic legislatures; and we highlight two strong regularities in the way busy assemblies regulate access to plenary time. First, just as there are no "open skies" at busy airports, so there are no "open skies" in busy legislatures. That is, just as aircraft are not provided landing time on a "first come, first served" basis at busy airports, so bills are not provided plenary time on a "first come, first served" basis in busy assemblies. Instead, all busy assemblies restrict access

* An earlier draft of this paper was presented at the annual meeting of the International Political Science Association, Fukuoka, Japan, July 10, 2006. Comments may be directed to gwcox@stanford.edu and mmccubbins@marshall.usc.edu. We thank Ellen Moule, Lexi Shankster, Colin McCubbins, Adriana Prata, and Royce Carroll for research assistance.

in multiple ways. Second, within the category of busy assemblies that restrict access to plenary time, majority governing coalitions always have the ability to prevent bills from claiming enough plenary time to reach a final passage vote. In some cases, the opposition coalition also has the ability to block bills, in which case the plenary agenda is set by consensus. More often, however, the opposition coalition has inferior parliamentary rights (to go along with its inferior numbers), leading to what we call cartel agenda-setting (cf. Cox and McCubbins 1993, 1994, 2005).

More specifically, we examine how restrictions on access to the legislative agenda differ across the two chambers of the U.S. Congress, the House of Representatives and the Senate. While neither chamber exhibits "open skies," the two chambers differ significantly in the distribution of parliamentary rights and privileges. In the House, the power to block the consideration of proposed bills is distributed asymmetrically. Indeed, it is a power monopolized by the majority party, allowing it to make significant policy gains at the expense of the minority party. In the Senate, however, both parties enjoy broad blocking authority, which helps explain why the minority party exhibits a greater degree of success in preventing the policies it opposes from becoming law in the Senate than it does in the House.

Several other chapters in this volume focus on the development and current configuration of congressional rules, committees, and party leadership (see, e.g., the chapters by Evans, Wawro, Jenkins, Strahan, Dion, Adler, and Schickler), each of which plays some role in shaping the allocation of plenary time. We argue, however, that a more general focus on the concept of managing plenary time allows important insights into the nature of congressional policymaking. We place our study of the U.S. Congress in broad comparative context by examining the standing orders in fourteen national (thirteen different countries) and twenty-two state assemblies in the U.S. Overall, we find broad support for the hypotheses that busy legislatures limit access to the legislative agenda to avoid the plenary bottleneck. While the U.S. House approximates an ideal-type majoritarian regime, where the governing party possesses broad tools to block access to the agenda at almost every juncture in the legislative process, the Senate is similar to more consensual bodies, where the government shares control over the legislative agenda with the opposition. This presents unique challenges to efforts by the majority party to ensure that the policies emerging from the legislative process are consistent with its preferences, though our analysis suggests that the majority largely succeeds in overcoming these challenges in the Senate.

THE PLENARY BOTTLENECK[1]

Although the details of legislative procedure differ widely across the world's democratic legislatures, one generalization holds universally: important bills can only pass

[1] This section is based on Cox (2006) and further details can be found there.

pursuant to motions formally stated and voted upon in the plenary session. This legal requirement gives rise to the typical format of a legislative journal, which reads as a sequence of motions and votes on those motions, one after the other.

The necessity of acting pursuant to formally stated motions means that every bill must consume at least some plenary time, if it is to have a chance at enactment. Thus, plenary time is the *sine qua non* of legislation. Yet, there are only twenty-four hours in a day and, hence, plenary time is scarce.

In principle, one could get around the necessity of transacting bills in the plenary by delegating law-making authority—either to committees (e.g. *leggine*), or to chief executives (e.g. decree authority), or to bureaucratic agencies (e.g. rule-making authority), or to subsidiary legislatures (e.g. Stormont).[2] In practice, however, democratic legislatures retain an important core of legislative authority that is inalienable, in the sense that the plenary retains (and cannot foreswear) the ability to rescind any delegations it may choose to make.

As soon as the aggregate demand for bills, hence plenary time, rises above a minimum threshold, a plenary bottleneck emerges. All bills must go through the plenary bottleneck in order to be enacted but only a subset can do so, leading to a coordination or bargaining problem to decide which subset it will be.

PLENARY TIME AND AIRSTRIP TIME

The plenary bottleneck in legislatures is analogous to the airstrip bottleneck at airports: bills can be passed only if they gain access to sufficient time in the plenary session, just as aircraft can be landed only if they gain access to sufficient time on the airstrip. Indeed, we believe there are important similarities between the history of how airstrip time has been managed in the U.S. and the history of how plenary time has been managed around the world.

In the early days of U.S. aviation, airstrip time was not a scarce resource and airports operated under an "open skies" policy, meaning that aircraft were served in the order of their arrival. With the spread of jets into civilian aviation after World War II, the number of aircraft increased markedly and long queues developed, with planes circling over O'Hare, La Guardia, and other major airports in the 1960s.

The inability of the open skies policy to cope with the number of aircraft converging on major American airports led to the creation of "scheduling committees" in 1968. These committees were empowered to allocate time slots to airlines

---

[2] In Italy, *leggine* (little laws) can be passed directly by committees, without consideration in the plenary session. On executive decree authority, see Carey and Shugart (1998). On delegated rule-making authority in bureaucracies, see Kiewiet and McCubbins (1991), Epstein and O'Halloran (1999), Huber and Shipan (2002), and McNollGast (2007). On the Stormont assembly, see Green (1979).

but required *unanimous agreement* among all carriers operating at a given airport. While one might have expected such committees to bicker endlessly, in practice they worked smoothly—for two reasons. First, the Civil Aeronautics Board helped to cartelize the airline industry, so that only a limited number of players had to negotiate the allocation of slots. Second, without unanimous agreement, the Federal Aviation Administration (FAA) would impose a solution. While it was not clear whether the imposed solution would be open skies, lotteries, auctions, or something else, none of the imposed solutions looked better than the scheduling committees to the carriers and some (e.g. lotteries, open skies) could lead to disastrous results. Thus, the airlines had substantial incentives to agree amongst themselves, rather than risk the imposition of one of the more costly solutions (Grether, Isaac, and Plott 1981).

After the deregulation of the airline industry in 1978, the number of players in the airline industry increased. This led eventually to a breakdown of the scheduling committee system: unanimous agreement could not be reached and the FAA began to impose solutions. Shortly thereafter, a full market in slots was introduced: slots became property that could be bought and sold (cf. Riker and Sened 1991).

The history of regulating access to plenary time in assemblies is similar to the history just sketched of regulating access to airstrip time in U.S. airports. Assemblies that are not busy, such as unprofessionalized state legislatures or the early U.S. House of Representatives, often have "open skies," with a "first come, first served" policy for bills that have been reported out of committee. As an assembly becomes busier, however, a policy that mandates bringing bills to the plenary in the order that they are reported from committee produces longer and longer queues. The earliest solutions to this problem amounted to either unanimous or supermajority consent (e.g. suspension of the rules in the U.S. House) to accelerate the progress of certain bills. This stage of legislative history corresponds to the "scheduling committee" stage of airline history.

As some assemblies became busier still, unanimous (and supermajority) consent became harder to obtain, and majority coalitions looked for ways to weaken or annul the veto of opposition forces. The erosion of opposition rights has taken many different forms and has typically been gradual and fitful, although occasionally there are dramatic revisions (as with Reed's rules in the U.S. or Debré's rules in France). In most national assemblies today, however, the government has at least some procedural advantages over the opposition, over and above its numerical advantage (recall that we focus on majority governments). In some cases, the scheduling committees in assemblies have been stacked. For example, the majority party in the U.S. House gives itself a disproportionate share of seats on its scheduling committee; and the majority coalition in Chile does as well. In other cases, de facto slots have been allocated as a species of private property—to committee chairs or ministers, for example—with the government then taking a disproportionate share of the favored posts. Either way, consensual agenda-setting often gives way to cartel agenda-setting.

How plenary time is allocated:
theoretical possibilities

In the previous section, we suggested that the natural history of plenary time follows a sequence similar to the natural history of airstrip time: first there are open skies, then scheduling committees operating under unanimity (or near-unanimity) rule, then either property rights in time slots or a cartelization of the scheduling committee or both. In this section, we consider the argument for this sequence in greater detail.

There are many theoretical perspectives on how plenary agendas are determined. We divide these perspectives into two families, those positing *free access* and those positing *restricted access*. In free-access (or open skies) models, all members of a stipulated subset of actors can introduce a bill to the plenary session at any time (and get a vote on the merits), without that bill having to pass through any pre-floor stages (e.g. consideration by a committee). Restricted-access models, in contrast, posit that any bill introduced to the chamber must pass through one or more pre-floor "veto gates"—subcommittees, committees, directing boards. A partial list of the models falling under these two headings follows.

(1a) **Free access for all.** In this family of models, any member can make a proposal at any time. Cox (1987) describes how free access to plenary time in the U.K. House of Commons in the 1830s led to over-exploitation of the common-pool resource— plenary time—and consequent difficulties in getting anything done. A number of models in this family posit unidimensional policy spaces and zero transaction costs, leading to centripetal policy outcomes, as in Krehbiel's (1998) analysis of the U.S. Congress. Others posit multidimensional policy spaces, leading to chaotic agendas and outcomes, as in Andrews' (2002) analysis of the Russian Duma.

(1b) **Free access for some.** In this family of models, only stipulated agents have the right to make proposals to the plenary. In Laver and Shepsle's (1996) model of parliamentary regimes, *ministers* have the right to propose. In one version of Shepsle's (1979) model of the U.S. Congress, *committees* have the right to propose. Other committee government models include Weingast and Marshall (1988) and Gilligan and Krehbiel (1989). Den Hartog (2004) describes one consequence of committee proposal rights in the ante- and post-bellum U.S. House: the long "first come, first served" bill queues that developed; and the inability of the majority party to ensure that its bills made it to the front of the queue.

(2) **Restricted access.** In this family of models, one or more agents can veto the placement of proposals on the plenary agenda. In the procedural cartel model of Cox and McCubbins (1993, 2005), the majority party in the post-1890 U.S. House of Representatives is able to block the advancement of bills to the floor, via its control of the committee chairs, Rules Committee, and Speakership. In Ferretti's (2005) model of the Argentine Chamber of Deputies, and Cox and McCubbins' (2005) depictions of the pre-1890 U.S. House of Representatives, both the majority and minority parties are able to block bills.

Real-world legislatures, of course, exhibit more complex combinations of rules regulating access to plenary time than the pure models outlined above would permit. Indeed, agenda-setting rules are as complex and varied as electoral rules. Just as scholars have found it useful to analyze electoral systems in terms of a few broad features, such as proportionality, we argue that agenda-setting rules are best mapped out along two dimensions.

The first dimension measures the ability of the governing coalition to block bills from reaching the plenary agenda. At one end of this dimension are cases in which governing coalitions have no special powers to block *and* lack the discipline to reliably marshal a majority of assembly votes to block; an example that approximates this pole is the U.K. House of Commons in the 1830s (Cox 1987). At the other end of this dimension are cases in which governing majorities either have special agenda-setting powers, so that they can block a bill even if they would not be able to marshal a majority on the floor against it, *or* are sufficiently disciplined to marshal a majority on the floor, *or* both. An example of a majority that has strong blocking power more by virtue of special privileges given to the government arises in the French National Assembly of the Fifth Republic (Huber 1996). An example of a majority that has strong blocking power more by virtue of iron discipline arises in the Netherlands in the twentieth century.

The second dimension measures the ability of the opposition coalition to block bills from reaching the plenary agenda. At one end of this dimension are cases in which oppositions have no special powers to block (note that they always lack the ability to reliably marshal a majority of assembly votes to block, as this would entail convincing a portion of the majority governing coalition to defect). An example that approximates this pole is the German Bundestag from 1980 to 2002 (Chandler, Cox, and McCubbins 2006). At the other end of this dimension are cases in which opposition coalitions do have entrenched special powers that help them block access to the floor, such as the Argentine Chamber of Deputies after 1963 (Ferretti 2005). The modern Senate falls squarely in this second camp.

Although in principle one might find legislatures located at any point in the two-dimensional space just suggested (delineating the amount of government blocking power and the amount of opposition blocking power), both in theory and in practice there are some important regularities.

No open skies

Our primary theoretical prediction is that busy legislatures will not allow free access to the plenary agenda. Just as large carriers operating at busy airports dislike the long "first come, first served" queues of aircraft associated with an open skies policy, so too majority parties operating in busy assemblies dislike the long "first come, first served" queues of bills associated with a free access policy. Free access for all members leads to an over-exploitation of plenary time (Cox 1987), an inability to make credible vote trades (Weingast and Marshall 1988), and an inability to reward specialization of labor within the assembly (Gilligan and Krehbiel 1989). These problems motivate majority coalitions to change the rules, introducing restrictions on members' access to plenary time.[3]

To clarify this claim, we need to define free (and restricted) access operationally; and we need to define what a busy assembly is. We consider an assembly to offer free access to the plenary agenda only if someone besides the government has free access to plenary time at any time. Cases in which someone besides the government has free access to a *small* portion of plenary time, such as private members' time or opposition time, do not count.

Consider some examples. In Colorado, after passage by initiative of the "Give A Vote to Every Legislator" Amendment, every bill introduced has been guaranteed a committee vote, and, if it passes committee, consideration on the floor (Cox, Kousser, and McCubbins 2005). In Virginia's House of Delegates during the period of one-party (Democratic) dominance, any committee could report any bill in its jurisdiction to the calendar, and bills would reach the floor in the order that they were reported (Kim 2006). These are examples of assemblies in which free access to the plenary is extensive enough that we code them as exhibiting free access.

As regards the second definitional issue, we view a legislature as busy when there are more bills that could command majority support on final passage in the assembly than are actually passed. To operationally define "busy," we take two approaches. The simplest—albeit indirect—approach is to define a high threshold and take all cases clearing the threshold to be "busy," while leaving open the question of how many of the cases not clearing the threshold are also "busy." In particular, our "high threshold" is defined as follows: we qualify as busy all lower chambers of national assemblies (not upper chambers or provincial assemblies) that satisfy three criteria—a population exceeding 300,000; a post-agricultural economy; and multi-party competition. This is obviously a very crude measure, requiring one to believe that all nations that are big enough, have complex enough economies, and have competitive party systems will probably have busy lower chambers. In support of this measure, we would note that dilatory tactics are widely used in the qualifying national chambers (Bücker 1989).

A more demanding approach is to define as *not* busy all those assemblies in which trivial votes (e.g. on commemorative bills) are handled in the same plenary-time-consuming fashion as important votes. The notion here is that, if the assembly really is busy, then it will have adopted one of the many available expedients to deal with trivial bills invented in the obviously busy assemblies. We have yet to perfect and

---

[3] Our first proposition has a functionalist cast to it. The argument is that free access will lead to a variety of problems in busy legislatures and, thus, one expects *some* restrictions on access in order to solve those problems. Because we do not specify any particular restrictions, however, we avoid the canonical logical criticism of functionalist explanations (that they cannot identify unique solutions; cf. Hempel 1968).

operationally code this second definition of "busy." Thus, in what follows, we use the first and cruder definition.

To provide evidence for our proposition that busy legislatures restrict access to the legislative agenda, we simply list, for a sample of busy assemblies, the restrictions that each imposes on two non-governmental actors (private members, opposition parties) at three pre-floor legislative stages (introduction, committee report, plenary scheduling) and at three on-floor stages (recognition, amendment, time allocation). The sample is a set of fourteen national and twenty-two state assemblies.

The logic of considering both pre-floor and on-floor restrictions is as follows. First, every assembly has pre-floor processes regulating how bills get onto the *official pre-announced* plenary agenda. These processes involve at least introduction, committee report, and scheduling decisions (e.g. by a presiding officer). Our survey of pre-floor restrictions thus looks for rules that prevent free access of bills to the official pre-announced plenary agenda. Second, it may be possible to amend the official pre-announced agenda, or to otherwise bring bills directly to the plenary. Our survey of on-floor restrictions thus looks for rules that prevent free access of bills to the plenary that by-pass the official pre-announced agenda. Tables 20.1–20.4 provide the results of our survey.

The main point to note from the tables is that *every* national and state assembly we examine imposes restrictions at *some* point on both of the non-governmental actors we investigate. Often, these restrictions are enforced at *many* points in the legislative

Table 20.1 Restrictions on private members' access to plenary time in 14 national assemblies

Country	Private members' bills can be blocked at the following pre-floor stages:			Private members' bills can be blocked at the following floor stages:		
	Introduction	Committee report	Plenary scheduling	Recognition	Amendment	Time
Brazil	No		Yes			
Czech Republic	No	No	Yes	?	Yes	No
Denmark	No	Yes	Yes	?	No	Yes
France	No	Yes	Yes	Yes	Yes	Yes
Germany	Yes	Yes	Yes	Yes	?	Yes
Italy	No	Yes	Yes	Yes	Yes	Yes
Japan	Yes	Yes	Yes	?	?	?
Netherlands	No	No	Yes	No	Yes	No
New Zealand	No	?	Yes	?	Yes	Yes
Norway	No	?	Yes	Yes	?	No
Sweden	No	No	Yes	?	?	?
U.K.	No	No	No	Yes	Yes	Yes
U.S. House	No	Yes	Yes	Yes	Yes	No
U.S. Senate	No	Yes	Yes	Yes	No	No

Table 20.2 Restrictions on opposition parties' access to plenary time in fourteen national assemblies

Country	Opposition parties' bills can be blocked at the following pre-floor stages:			Opposition parties' bills can be blocked at the following floor stages:		
	Introduction	Committee report	Plenary scheduling	Recognition	Amendment	Time
Brazil	No		Yes			
Czech Republic	No	No	Yes	?	Yes	No
Denmark	No	No	No	?	No	No
France	No	Yes	Yes	Yes	Yes	Yes
Germany	No	No	Yes	Yes	?	Yes
Italy	No	No	Yes	Yes	Yes	Yes
Japan	No	Yes	Yes	?	?	?
Netherlands	No	No	Yes	No	Yes	No
New Zealand	No	?	Yes	?	Yes	Yes
Norway	No	?	Yes	Yes	?	No
Sweden	No	No	Yes	?	?	?
U.K.	No	No	No	No	Yes	Yes
U.S. House	No	Yes	Yes	Yes	Yes	No
U.S. Senate	No	Yes	Yes	Yes	No	No

process, and in a smaller subset of assemblies, these restrictions are present at *almost every* juncture in the process. These results are consistent with our expectations that busy assemblies will not allow free access to the legislative agenda.

Restrictions on private members' access to plenary time

To provide a flavor of the results, consider first the restrictions faced by private members. Most assemblies in our sample allow free introduction of bills by private members. Germany restricts private members even at this stage: Rule 75 of the Bundestag states that "Items of business submitted by Members of the Bundestag shall be signed by a parliamentary group or five percent of the Members of the Bundestag." Thus, individual members cannot act on their own (as parliamentary groups must have at least 5 percent of the Bundestag).

A few assemblies ensure that bills (including those introduced by private members) will be reported from committee. For example, New Zealand's Rule 291(1) requires that committees "must finally report to the House on a bill within six months of the bill being referred to it," while Rule 291(3) mandates that "If the committee has not reported within the time for report, the bill is discharged from further consideration by the committee and set down for its next stage in the House on the third sitting day following." Most assemblies in our sample, however, do not require

Table 20.3 Restrictions on private members' access to plenary time in twenty-two state assemblies

Country	Private members' bills can be blocked at the following pre-floor stages:			Private members' bills can be blocked at the following floor stages:		
	Introduction	Committee report	Plenary scheduling	Recognition	Amendment	Time
Alabama	No	Yes	Yes	Yes	Yes	No
Alaska	No	No	Yes	Yes	Yes	No
Arizona	No	No	Yes	Yes	Yes	No
California	No	No	?	Yes	Yes	No
Colorado	No	Yes	?	Yes	Yes	No
Connecticut	No	Yes	Yes	No	Yes	No
Delaware	No	Yes	Yes	Yes	No	No
Florida	No	Yes	Yes	Yes	Yes	No
Georgia	No	Yes	Yes	Yes	Yes	No
Hawaii	No	Yes	No	Yes	No	No
Idaho	No	Yes	Yes	Yes	Yes	No
Illinois	No	Yes	Yes	Yes	Yes	No
Indiana	No	Yes	Yes	Yes	Yes	No
Kansas	No	Yes	?	Yes	Yes	No
Kentucky	No	Yes	Yes	Yes	Yes	No
Louisiana	No	Yes	No	?	Yes	No
Minnesota	No	No	Yes	Yes	Yes	No
Mississippi	No	Yes	No	Yes	Yes	No
Missouri	No	Yes	Yes	Yes	Yes	No
Texas	No	Yes	Yes	Yes	Yes	No
Virginia	No	Yes	No	No	?	No
Washington	No	Yes	Yes	Yes	Yes	No

that committees report on all the bills referred to them. In Italy, Article 72 of the Constitution and Rule 92 of the chamber's procedures allow either the government, or one-tenth of the members of the chamber, or one fifth of the committee members to discharge a bill from committee. While this means that opposition parties can typically discharge bills if they wish, individual private members require assistance: they cannot discharge bills on their own; in other words, their bills can be blocked in committee.

Private members' bills, even if reported from committee, are typically not guaranteed to receive consideration in the plenary session. In the U.S. House, for example, reported bills can languish and die on a calendar, unless rescued by the Rules Committee.

Even if private members were blocked at one or more of the pre-floor stages just discussed (introduction, committee report, plenary scheduling), thereby preventing their getting onto the official pre-announced plenary agenda, one might wonder whether they could somehow bring their bills directly to the attention of the plenary.

Table 20.4 Restrictions on opposition parties' access to plenary time in twenty-two state assemblies

Country	Opposition parties' bills can be blocked at the following pre-floor stages:			Opposition parties' bills can be blocked at the following floor stages:		
	Introduction	Committee report	Plenary scheduling	Recognition	Amendment	Time
Alabama	No	Yes	Yes	Yes	Yes	No
Alaska	No	No	Yes	Yes	Yes	No
Arizona	No	No	Yes	Yes	Yes	No
California	No	No	?	Yes	Yes	No
Colorado	No	Yes	?	Yes	Yes	No
Connecticut	No	Yes	Yes	No	Yes	No
Delaware	No	Yes	Yes	Yes	No	No
Florida	No	Yes	Yes	Yes	Yes	No
Georgia	No	Yes	Yes	Yes	Yes	No
Hawaii	No	Yes	No	Yes	No	No
Idaho	No	Yes	Yes	Yes	Yes	No
Illinois	No	Yes	Yes	Yes	Yes	No
Indiana	No	Yes	Yes	Yes	Yes	No
Kansas	No	Yes		Yes	Yes	No
Kentucky	No	Yes	Yes	Yes	Yes	No
Louisiana	No	Yes	No	?	Yes	No
Minnesota	No	No	Yes	Yes	Yes	No
Mississippi	No	Yes	No	Yes	Yes	No
Missouri	No		Yes	Yes	Yes	No
Texas	No	Yes	Yes	Yes	Yes	No
Virginia	No	Yes	No	No	?	No
Washington	No	Yes	Yes	Yes	Yes	No

We break this question into three separate issues: Can private members add bills to the official agenda by motions made on the floor (or is this blocked)? Can private members hijack bills that are on the official agenda by making non-germane amendments (or is this blocked)? Can private members, after having either introduced a new bill on the floor or hijacked a bill, command sufficient time to push their bill through (or is this blocked)?

Bringing up new bills (e.g. by amending the orders of the day) is never something that a single private member can do in our sample of assemblies. In some assemblies such actions are blocked by rules that explicitly require a majority (or supermajority) to amend the orders of the day, as in New Zealand. In other assemblies, introducing new bills is also made difficult by the Speaker's general power of recognition. In both the U.S. House and the Texas House, for example, the Speaker may ask for what purpose a member seeks recognition and deny or grant the request depending on the response.

Hijacking bills is also typically infeasible. Many assemblies explicitly require amendments to be germane—e.g. Italy, New Zealand, and the U.S House. Others are less explicit but appear to require germaneness in practice.

Finally, some assemblies explicitly allocate portions of plenary time to private members—e.g. the U.K. and New Zealand—yet also ensure that the amount allocated is completely inadequate to debate and pass any major bill. We view five of the assemblies we study as having set up what we call a "time ghetto" for private members, typically representing the last vestiges of ancient rights (cf. Cox 1987 for the case of England).

Restrictions on opposition parties' access to plenary time

Restrictions on opposition parties' access to plenary time are never stronger than those imposed on private members and sometimes weaker. This is because usually parliamentary rules have, or can be put in, the abstract form "Any group of members with at least X members may take action Y." Opposition parties with more than one member thus enjoy any right offered to private members and, in addition, enjoy rights conferred at higher thresholds as well. In coding whether opposition parties can be blocked, we have assumed the largest possible opposition that a majority government might face. That is, in an assembly with an odd number n of members, we have assumed an opposition with $(n-1)/2$ members.

All the assemblies we investigate allow opposition parties to introduce bills. Most allow them to ensure that their bills are not killed in committee (the exceptions are the U.S. and Japan). At the scheduling stage, however, most assemblies do not allow even large oppositions to ensure that their bills are put on the plenary agenda. For example, the Czech Republic's Chamber of Deputies has two rules that can potentially be used to block opposition bills before they reach a substantive debate in the plenary session. First, Rule 88 gives the Chairperson of the Chamber the ultimate authority to set the agenda, after considering the advice of the Organizing Committee. Second, Rule 63(1)2 makes any bill that is put on the plenary agenda immediately susceptible to a motion to put the bill aside, avoiding both the debate and the vote. An opposition party thus needs the support of the Chairperson of the Chamber to ensure placement on the agenda and of enough members of the government to ensure a debate and vote on one of their bills.

Once the plenary agenda has been set, even large opposition parties typically cannot add bills to that agenda. Adding bills to the agenda, for example, requires a majority to support it in Norway (Section 26 of the Riksdag Act) and unanimity in Germany (Rule 20). Non-germane amendments (which might be used to "hijack" another bill that is on the agenda) is clearly forbidden in several assemblies—e.g. by Rule 119 in New Zealand and Rule 63(1) in the Czech Republic. Finally, in some cases, opposition bills are restricted to a specific and exiguous portion of plenary time—as in the U.K. and New Zealand.

Majority governing coalitions wield agenda vetoes

Our first prediction is that no busy legislature should have a policy of dealing with bills in the plenary session in the order they are reported from committee, any more than a busy airport should have a policy of dealing with airplanes in the order they arrive. More generally, we argue that busy legislatures will not guarantee that any bill that is introduced or reported will receive a floor debate and vote (just as a busy airport will not guarantee to land any plane that shows up). Necessarily the denial of universal access to plenary time implies that *someone* must have the power to block access to the plenary agenda. Our theory simply specifies one particular agent that must have the power to block—a majority government. Specifically, we predict that in all busy assemblies, governing coalitions that hold a majority of seats can block or fatally restrict any bill's access to plenary time—either by virtue of their ability to marshal floor voting majorities, or by virtue of their possession of specially delegated agenda-setting powers, or both.

Suppose that majority governments did not have the power to block. Then some minorities would necessarily have the ability to push any bills they wished onto the plenary agenda and thence to a debate and vote. An example would be the once-popular committee government model of the U.S. House of Representatives (reviewed in Cox and McCubbins 1993). Our argument is that the external costs of the proposals generated by those with unfettered proposal power, both in the form of overexploiting the common-pool resource (Cox 1987) and in the form of forcing votes on issues that many do not wish to vote on (Cox and McCubbins 2005), are sufficiently high that busy assemblies are very careful in handing out privileged access to plenary time; and always ensure that majority governments can block bills from making significant claims on plenary time.

We examine our second proposition by observing roll rates for governing and opposition parties. To explain how, we first need to define rolls and introduce some additional assumptions.

A party is rolled on a final passage vote when the party votes against the bill yet the bill passes. Note that this is different from a disappointment (which occurs when the party votes for a bill that is rejected). A party's roll rate is simply the number of times that it is rolled on a final passage vote, divided by the total number of final passage votes in which it participates.[4] We shall denote the average roll rate for governing parties in country j at time t by $GovRoll_{jt}$; and the average roll rate for opposition parties in country j at time t by $OppRoll_{jt}$. (In presidential systems, we define the governing coalition to be that holding a majority of assembly seats, whether or not it is allied with the president.)

---

[4] If the party itself is split on a vote, we say that it is rolled when a majority of the party's members vote against a bill that nonetheless passes.

Four additional assumptions help us derive an operational prediction about roll rates from the theory: (A1) parties can accurately predict the final passage vote that would result, were any particular bill allowed on the plenary agenda; (A2) parties know all legislators' preferences; (A3) legislators vote sincerely on all final passage votes; and (A4) governing parties never "trade rolls." Assumption (A1) means, for example, that if a bill is allowed onto the plenary agenda, parties know what amendments will be offered, which if any will pass, and thus what the amended version of the bill will be that is pitted against the status quo in the final passage vote. Given (A1)-(A3), parties will always know which bills would result in their being rolled on the ultimate final passage vote. If the theory is correct, then each governing party will have the ability to block any bill that would lead to its being rolled. Finally, given (A4), governing parties never trade rolls (we'll allow bill A, which we know will roll us, if you allow bill B, which you know will roll you). Thus, our theory combined with (A1)-(A4) yields the prediction that the average roll rate for governing parties will be nil ($GovRoll_{jt} = 0$).[5]

Assumption (A1) may of course be violated. When it is, a governing party may be rolled "by mistake." The party may allow a bill onto the plenary agenda, only to find that the bill can be amended in ways that it failed to anticipate—and that result in its being rolled. Thus, although the idealized model predicts a nil roll rate for governing parties, the more general model in which only (A2)-(A4) are satisfied predicts that the roll rate for governing parties will equal the rate at which such parties fail to anticipate the consequences of allowing bills onto the agenda.

When there is more than one party in government, assumption (A4) may also be violated. That is, governing party 1 may propose a bill that will roll governing party 2, while 2 proposes a bill that will roll 1. Rather than 1 vetoing 2's bill and 2 vetoing 1's, they may agree to allow both bills, resulting in each party being rolled on one bill but each also passing a bill that it could not otherwise have passed.[6] Thus, if we assume only (A2)-(A3), the overall roll rate for governing parties can be positive and will reflect (a) the rate at which governing parties fail to correctly anticipate how bills will be amended on the floor; and (b) the rate at which governing parties find it profitable to trade rolls.

We assume that governing parties are very good but not perfect at anticipating amendments (and they can often restrict the allowable amendments to simplify their task); and that, if they wish to arrange a logroll, they will often prefer to put the two parts of the logroll into an omnibus vehicle (which will hide the rolls from the analyst's view), rather than have separate votes. For these reasons, we expect governing parties to have *small* but not necessarily *nil* roll rates. As an admittedly arbitrary

---

[5] There are two different types of final passage vote in the world's assemblies but our proposition works for either. One type is that used in the U.S. House, where the last vote is that which pits the bill (as-amended, if amended) against the status quo. Another type is that used in Argentina, in which the vote for a bill against the status quo occurs first, followed by a number of votes on amendments. Given (A1)–(A4), these two different sequences yield identical predictions about government roll rates.

[6] The overall utility to party j of having both bills passed need not, but certainly can, exceed the overall utility of having neither bill.

rule of thumb, we use 5 percent as a threshold: roll rates below this level are deemed increasingly consistent with the theory, those above it increasingly inconsistent.

Having established that governing parties' roll rates should be small (less than 5 percent), we note that the theory places no restriction on opposition roll rates. They might be nil, if the opposition too can block bills from reaching the plenary agenda. Or they might be high, if the opposition has no blocking power at all and happens to disagree with the government's proposals. Of course, oppositions can have intermediate powers: the ability to delay can vary and, at the upper end of the scale, delay powers merge seamlessly into blocking powers—especially in a busy legislature.

All told, then, if we plot the average roll rate of governing parties on the vertical axis and the average roll rate of opposition parties on the horizontal axis, we expect all the data points to lie near to the horizontal axis (reflecting a low government roll rate) and to be ordered along the horizontal axis in reverse order of the opposition's power to block. We present the relevant data for twelve national assemblies in Figure 20.1 (having to drop two of our cases from Tables 1a and 1b due to missing data) and for twenty-two state assemblies in Figure 20.2.

The first feature to note about Figure 20.1 is that the data points are all "near" zero on the vertical axis, indicating roll rates for governing parties below 5 percent in each case except the U.S. Senate (which is roughly 7 percent). This supports the theory. Simply put, governing parties almost never have unwanted policy changes forced upon them. Their only defeats come in the form of disappointments (bills that they wish enacted nonetheless defeated).

The second feature to note about Figure 20.1 is that the data points are spread widely on the horizontal axis, ranging from Japan's 11 percent to Brazil's 88 percent. In future, we hope to explain the wide variation in opposition parties' roll rates in terms of measurable variations in how much delaying power they each have. We already know, from studies of the lower chambers in the U.S. (Cox and McCubbins 2005), Japan (Cox, Masuyama, and McCubbins 2000), and Germany (Chandler, Cox, and

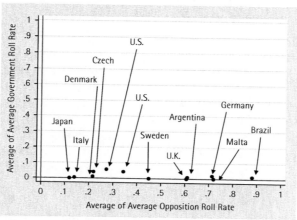

Fig. 20.1. Average country roll rates

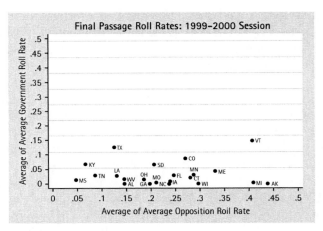

Fig. 20.2. Average state roll rates

McCubbins 2006), that opposition roll rates within a given polity decline substantially when that party holds a majority in the upper chamber, or a committee chair in the lower chamber, or the presidency. Each of these forms of "divided government" provides the opposition with better delaying or veto power, allowing them to extract concessions from the lower-chamber majority. We anticipate that cross-national variation will relate to variations across assemblies in how much the opposition can delay.

First, the opposition clearly has very poor blocking powers in each of the assemblies that exhibit the highest opposition roll rates—Brazil, Germany, and the U.K. In Brazil, the governing coalition has two potent weapons to force legislative action: first, the assembly majority itself can deploy powerful urgency motions to push a bill onto the plenary agenda quickly; second, the president (a member of the governing coalition) has even more potent urgency powers (Amorim Neto, Cox, and McCubbins 2003). In Germany, party discipline and the ability to appeal scheduling decisions to the floor for majority decision combine to mean that the opposition cannot block the government's agenda (Chandler, Cox, and McCubbins 2006). In the U.K., the bulk of plenary time is reserved for government use and a variety of rules (e.g. the guillotine) allow it to circumvent the opposition's dilatory tactics (Dion 1997). Second, the opposition plausibly has superior delaying powers in the three assemblies exhibiting the lowest opposition roll rates—Japan, Italy, and the U.S. Senate. Mochizuki (1982) and Krauss (1984) have both emphasized the strength of minority rights and norms of consultation in the Japanese legislative process—for example, sessions in Japan are quite short and bills die at the end of each session, making the opposition's delay tactics more effective than in other assemblies. Many scholars have noted that the Italian Chamber's Rule 23—which required unanimity before 1997 and a 3/4 super-majority thereafter to put a bill onto the plenary agenda—gave every significant party a veto in the legislative process (e.g. Capano and Giuliani 2006). The filibuster in the U.S. Senate is perhaps the world's most famous opposition blocking tool (Wawro and Schickler 2006).

Data on roll rates from twenty-two state lower chambers in 1999–2000 are displayed in Figure 20.2. The basic pattern is similar to that observed in the national assemblies, with essentially all the data falling below the 45 degree line: majority parties never have larger and typically have significantly smaller roll rates. Although more states exhibit majority roll rates above the 5 percent threshold, no majority party is ever rolled more than 15 percent of the time. By contrast, more than two-thirds of minority parties are rolled at above that rate in the states.

THE U.S. HOUSE AND SENATE: DIFFERENT PATHS TOWARD SIMILAR ENDS

In the broad sample of legislatures considered in this chapter, the U.S. Senate represents an important anomaly in the degree to which its rules preclude majority control over the agenda and endow the minority with blocking powers. Indeed, the rules in the Senate differ strikingly from those of the U.S. House, in ways that we argue help explain the relative weakness of the majority party's ability to block bills it opposes and the relative success of the minority party to do the same. This section briefly surveys these differences. Our contention is that, despite the unusual symmetry in parliamentary privileges woven into the institutional structure in the Senate, the majority party remains a surprisingly powerful force in shaping the chamber's legislative agenda.

In the U.S. House, which approaches the ideal-type majoritarian body described earlier in this chapter, the governing party can block access to the legislative agenda at almost every juncture of the legislative process. The majority wields these powers primarily through its control of three key organs in the House: the selection of the Speaker; the appointment of standing committees and committee chairs; and its control over the Rules Committee.

Historically, the Speaker has served as the leader of the majority party, and since the late 1890s, the office has enjoyed broad powers and privileges in the chamber. Most importantly, the Speaker plays a key role in assigning both members and bills to legislative committees. To reach the plenary agenda, bills must be voted out of the committees, which are firmly controlled by, and made accountable to, the majority party caucus (Kiewiet and McCubbins 1991; Cox and McCubbins 1993). In addition, bills voted out of committee languish at the end of a long queue unless a supermajority of the House votes to suspend its rules or the bill receives a "special rule" from the House Rules committee. These rules, which must be adopted by a simple majority vote of the House, often limit debate on the bill to specific lengths of time and expressly specify which amendments, if any, may be entertained by the floor. While the distribution of committee seats is generally proportional to each party's share of the House seats, the majority party assigns itself an overwhelming share of the Rules Committee posts and uses special rules to strictly limit access to the plenary agenda.

In the Senate, by contrast, the same three majority-controlled legislative veto gates are significantly weaker. For example, the Senate lacks a powerful presiding officer found in the House. While Senate majority party leaders, by precedent, takes charge of scheduling votes, in practice they exercise this power by conferring with the minority party leaders. Similarly, Senate committees are generally far weaker than in the House, and Rule XIV permits senators to bypass the committee system altogether and have their bill placed directly on the calendar if they fear that the relevant committee will be unsympathetic to their cause. This rule also provides that, if a committee fails to act on a referred bill, the sponsoring senator may reintroduce a new bill with exactly the same provisions and get it directly on the calendar.

Finally, individual senators can expand the agenda at the floor stage by offering non-germane amendments to existing bills. Lacking restrictions to the content of amendments, individual senators can hijack bills that *do* make it to the floor to resurrect proposals that may have been buried earlier in the legislative process.

Even as chamber rules give party leaders few formal powers to limit access to the agenda in the pre-floor stage, the power to veto legislation is shared broadly between the two parties on the floor. The filibuster allows a minority of senators to block efforts to end debate, thus precluding a floor vote. Indeed, the minority party can grind almost all Senate business to a halt by withholding its unanimous consent for trivial legislative activities. As one leading scholar of the Senate has argued, this tradition of open access and broad minority power means that "[c]ontrol of the Senate agenda...has never been structured to reflect the interests of a partisan majority" (Binder 1997, 168). This suggests that we should expect rough parity in the roll rates of the majority and minority parties in the Senate, and a clearly positive roll rate for the majority.

Results presented in Figure 20.1 and Figure 20.2, however, indicate that this is not the case. Though the majority party's roll rate is larger in the Senate than in many other legislatures, the majority's roll rate is still only about 7 percent. Elsewhere, Gailmard and Jenkins (2007) have shown that the majority's ability to block Senate-originated bills is equal in strength to the negative agenda control exercised by the majority in the House. And while the minority party's roll rate is lower than that of the opposition parties' in many other legislatures, it remains significantly above the majority party's roll rate and that of opposition parties in many state legislatures.

How is the majority party able to deliver responsible party government in the Senate given its inherently weak authority under the institutional rules? Recent scholarship has pointed to several important procedural advantages that help the majority and its leaders: the right of first recognition on the floor and the chairman's mark in committee (Den Hartog and Monroe 2010); the immunity to filibusters and non-germane amendments of budget-related legislation (Den Hartog and Monroe 2010, a rule used by President Barack Obama and the Democrats in Congress to pass the 2010 healthcare reform bill over the united opposition of the Republican Party; the ability to table non-germane amendments (Campbell, Cox, and McCubbins 2002);[7] and the ability to make a motion to recommit, which can be used to strip all amendments from a bill. The general picture, argued most comprehensively by Den Hartog and Monroe (2010), is that the majority leadership in the Senate, in comparison with their counterparts in the House, has smaller and less obvious advantages throughout the legislative procedure which it can with persistence leverage into consistently better outcomes.

In addition, the process for selecting senators also opens the door for strategic logrolling by the majority party. Because the constitution provides each state with two senators, small states are greatly overrepresented in the upper chamber of Congress. This allows the majority party to strike bargains with a sufficient number of rural representatives from the minority, trading pork for concessions on substantive policy, perhaps explaining why most budget earmarks emerge from the Senate.[8]

Despite the existence of strategies, it is important to recognize that majority party power in the Senate takes a markedly different form than in the House. In the lower chamber, the majority party can generally limit access to the legislative agenda by using long-established procedural rules and veto gates, even when it might otherwise lack the discipline to present a unified front on the floor. In the Senate, by contrast, many exercises of majority party power require the party leadership to induce discipline in the party caucus. The majority's low roll rate suggests that they are largely successful.

CONCLUSION

In this chapter, we have articulated two general theoretical claims about how plenary time is managed. First, there are no open skies in busy legislatures—meaning that such assemblies do not guarantee a debate and vote on every bill that is reported from committee. Second, a majority government in a busy legislature always has the ability to block bills from making significant claims on plenary time and reaching a final passage vote.

We provide evidence for the first proposition by examining the rules of a number of assemblies, documenting the multiple restrictions that they place on access to plenary time by non-governmental actors. We provide evidence for the second proposition by examining the roll rates of parties in majority governments and minority oppositions, respectively, in eight national and three state assemblies. We find that governing parties' roll rates are uniformly low, with the sole exception of the California Assembly

---

[7] Under Senate rules, the motion to table takes precedence over proposed amendments, allowing the majority party to exercise an ex-post veto over bills that it may mistakenly allow to reach the floor stage.

[8] In state legislatures, Gamm and Kousser (2010) do not find that representatives from small districts sponsor significantly more particularistic policies, however.

in 1995 when the majority party failed to elect its candidate as Speaker. In contrast, opposition parties' roll rates vary widely—responding, we believe, to variations in opposition powers of delay.

References

AKIRAV, O., COX, G. W., and McCUBBINS, M. D. 2010. Agenda Control in the Israeli Knesset during Ariel Sharon's Second Government. *Journal of Legislative Studies*, 16(4): 251–67.

AMORIM NETO, O., COX, G. W., and McCUBBINS, M. D. 2003. Agenda Power in Brazil's Câmara dos Deputados, 1989 to 1998. *World Politics*, 55: 550–78.

ANDREWS, J. 2002. *When Majorities Fail: The Russian Legislature, 1990-1993*. Cambridge: Cambridge University Press.

BÜCKER, J. 1989. Obstruction of Parliamentary Proceedings. *Constitutional and Parliamentary Information*, 1st series No. 158. Geneva: Inter-Parliamentary Union.

BINDER, SARAH. A. 1997. *Minority Rights, Majority Rule: Partisanship and The Development of Congress*, New York: Cambridge University Press.

CAMPBELL, C., COX G. W., and McCUBBINS M. D. 2002. Agenda Power in the U.S. Senate, 1877 to 1986, pp. 107–45 in *Party, Process, and Political Change in Congress: New Perspectives on the History of Congress*, ed. D. Brady and M. D. McCubbins. Palo Alto: Stanford University Press.

CAPANO, G., and GIULIANI, M. 2006. The Italian Parliament in Search of a New Role? Unpublished typescript. University of Bologna.

CAREY, J., and SHUGART, M. (eds.) 1998. *Executive Decree Authority*. Cambridge: Cambridge University Press.

CHANDLER, W., COX, G. W., and McCUBBINS, M. D. [*sic*] 2006. Agenda Control in the Bundestag, 1980–2002. *German Politics*, 15(1): 27–48.

COOPER, J. 1970. *The Origins of the Standing Committees and the Development of the Modern House*. Houston: Rice University.

COX, G. W. 1987. *The Efficient Secret: The Cabinet and the Development of Political Parties in Victorian England*. Cambridge: Cambridge University Press.

—— 2006. The Organization of Democratic Legislatures, pp. 141–61 in *The Oxford Handbook of Political Economy*, ed. B. Weingast and D. Wittman. Oxford: Oxford University Press.

—— HELLER, W. B., and McCUBBINS, M. D. 2008. Agenda Power in the Italian Chamber of Deputies 1988–2000. *Legislative Studies Quarterly*, 33: 171-98.

—— MASUYAMA, M., and McCUBBINS, M. D. 2000. Agenda Power in the Japanese House of Representatives. *Japanese Journal of Political Science*, 1: 1–22.

—— and McCUBBINS, M. D. 1993. *Legislative Leviathan: Party Government in the House*. Berkeley: University of California Press.

—— —— 1994. Bonding, Structure, and the Stability of Political Parties: Party Government in the House. *Legislative Studies Quarterly*, 19: 215–31.

—— —— 2002. Agenda Power in the U.S. House of Representatives, 1877 to 1986, pp. 107–45 in *Parties, Procedure and Policy: Essays on the History of Congress*, eds. D. W. Brady and M. D. McCubbins. Stanford: Stanford University Press.

—— —— 2005. *Setting the Agenda*. Cambridge: Cambridge University Press.

———— 2007. *Legislative Leviathan: Party Government in the House*, 2nd edn. Cambridge: Cambridge University Press.

——Kousser, T., and McCubbins, M. D. 2005. Party Power or Preferences?: Quasi-Experimental Evidence from the American States. *Journal of Politics 2010*, 72(3): 1–13.

Den Hartog, C. F. 2004. Limited Party Government and the Majority Party Revolution in the Nineteenth-century House. Unpublished Ph.D. dissertation. University of California, San Diego.

——and Monroe, N. W. 2010. Costly Consideration: Agenda Setting and the Majority Party Advantage in the U.S. Senate. Unpublished manuscript.

Dion, D. 1997. *Turning the Legislative Thumbscrew*. Ann Arbor: University of Michigan Press.

Epstein, D., and O'Halloran, S. 1999. *A Transaction Cost Politics to Policy Making Under Separate Powers*. New York: Cambridge University Press.

Ferretti, N. 2005. Majority Dominance or Power-Sharing? Scheduling Rules and Competitive Dynamics in the Argentine Legislature. Unpublished paper. University of California, Berkeley.

Gailmard, S., and Jenkins, J. A. 2007. Negative Agenda Control in the Senate and House: Fingerprints of Majority Party Power. *Journal of Politics*, 69(3): 689–700.

Gamm, G., and Kousser, T. 2010. Broad Bills or Particularistic Policy? Historical Patterns in American State Legislatures. *American Political Science Review*, 104: 151–70.

Gilligan, T. W., and Krehbiel, K. 1989. Asymmetric Information and Legislative Rules With a Heterogeneous Committee. *American Journal of Political Science*, 33: 459–90.

Green, A. 1979. *Devolution and Public Finance: Stormont from 1921 to 1972*. Glasgow: Centre for the Study of Public Policy, University of Strathclyde.

Grether, D. R., Isaac, M., and Plott, C. 1981. The Allocation of Landing Rights Among Competitors. *American Economic Association Papers and Proceedings*, 71(2): 166–71.

Hempel, C. 1968. The Logic of Functional Analysis, pp. 349–76 in *Readings in the Philosophy of the Social Sciences*, ed. M. Brodbeck. New York: Macmillan.

Huber, J. D. 1996. *Rationalizing Parliament: Legislative Institutions and Party Politics in France*. New York: Cambridge University Press.

Huber, J., and Shipan, C. 2002. *Deliberate Discretion?* Cambridge: Cambridge University Press.

Kiewiet, D. R., and McCubbins, M. D. 1991. *The Logic of Delegation: Congressional Parties and the Appropriations Process*. Chicago: University of Chicago Press.

Kim, H. 2006. Essays in Legislative Study. Unpublished PhD dissertation. University of California, San Diego.

Krauss, E. 1984. Conflict in the Diet: Toward Conflict Management in Parliamentary Politics, pp. 1–37 in *Conflict in Japan*, ed. E. Krauss, T. Rohlen, and P. Steinhoff. Honolulu: University of Hawaii Press.

Krehbiel, K. 1998. *Pivotal Politics: A Theory of U.S. Lawmaking*. Chicago: University of Chicago Press.

Laver, M., and Shepsle, K. A. 1996. *Making and Breaking Governments: Cabinets and Legislatures in Parliamentary Democracies*. Cambridge, New York: Cambridge University Press.

McNollgast. 2007. The Political Economy of Law: Decision Making by Judiciary, Legislative, Executive and Administrative Agencies, pp. 1651–738 in *The Handbook of Law and Economics*, ed. A. M. Polinsky and S. Shavell. Oxford: Elsevier.

Mochizuki, M. 1982. Managing and Influencing the Japanese Legislative Process: The Role of the Parties and the National Diet. Unpublished doctoral dissertation. Harvard University.

RIKER, W. H., and SENED, I. 1991. A Political Theory of the Origin of Property Rights: Airport Slots. *American Journal of Political Science*, 35(4): 951–69.

SHEPSLE, K. A. 1979. Institutional Arrangements and Equilibrium in Multidimensional Voting Models. *American Journal of Political Science*, 23: 27–59.

WAWRO, G., and SCHICKLER, E. 2006. *Filibuster: Obstruction and Lawmaking in the U.S. Senate.* Princeton: Princeton University Press.

WEINGAST, B. R., and MARSHALL, W. 1988. The Industrial Organization of Congress. *Journal of Political Economy*, 96: 132–63.

CHAPTER 21

··

CONGRESSIONAL REFORMS

··

E. SCOTT ADLER[*]

The roots of reform are to be found in how the members look at themselves
and their perceptions of how others look at them.

Charles Jones 1977a

Charles Jones was referring to the underlying motivations of lawmakers in Congress
regarding structural innovations in the chapter epigraph, though this sentiment could
also apply to how scholars of Congress view their orientation to the topic of congressional reforms. Scholarly research on changes and restructuring of congressional
institutions has developed and advanced considerably over the years, but is itself still
in need of reform. The reforms I suggest—a sustained effort to examine Congress's
structure and prospects for change, as well as greater engagement in dialog with
members of Congress to provide input on pressing institutional questions—is only
possible if scholars view themselves as having a part to play in lending lawmakers
informed insights regarding legislative organization.

In this chapter, I provide a wide-ranging review of the political science literature
on congressional reforms going back to its earliest incarnations as part of a broader
academic discipline that was just getting off the ground. The chapter recounts the
historical development of the literature and highlights the most notable milestones in
its scholarly advances. Of note, I track the transformation to large-N data collection
and hypothesis testing in reform research, and the eventual adoption of rational

  [*] The chapter benefited from the helpful comments and suggestions of Frances Lee and
Eric Schickler. The author particularly wishes to acknowledge Roger Davidson for his thorough reading
of the manuscript and a career of thoughtful insights on congressional reforms.

choice models of legislative organization that have come to guide and dominate much of the contemporary work in the field.

Along the way I emphasize the long-standing interplay between the scholarship and practice of congressional restructuring. I recount the important role that congressional scholars have played in defining the reform agenda during its various movements over the twentieth century. Ultimately I conclude that our institutional understanding of Congress is better now than it has ever been, but the deficiency in reform scholarship has been a lack of engagement between research predicated on sophisticated tests of well-developed models of legislative organization and the struggles of lawmakers to cure the institutional problems that ail the legislative body. I argue that researchers, using an ever-growing set of outlets to publicize the work and insights of congressional scholars, should make a concerted effort to expand their thinking about the rules and structures of Congress to include explicit recommendations for structural improvements based upon the knowledge gained from their research. The topic of congressional reform is one prominent area of public discourse surrounding politics that academics are uniquely equipped to provide research-based contributions for the betterment of governing institutions.

DEFINING "REFORM"

There are numerous questions fundamental to our understanding of the topic of congressional reform: why do reforms occur, what consequence do they have for the institution and its performance, why do some reform efforts fail, and so on? Though I will address the ways in which scholars have treated these questions over the last century or more, it is perhaps most critical to begin by defining our boundaries—what are reforms? By specifying exactly what scholars are studying we can determine what constitutes this portion of the congressional literature and where the advances have been made.

Perhaps more than almost any other single term associated with Congress, there is no word more loaded with ambiguity than "reform" (Evans and Oleszek 1997, 3). Oleszek refers to this ambiguity as the "iron law," that "congressional reform means many things to different people" (1977, 3). A corollary to that law is that what some see as an improvement in congressional structure may to others look like a new impediment. Stated more succinctly: "one person's reform is another's stumbling block" (Davidson and Oleszek 1977, 2). Not surprisingly, this sentiment is quite frequently repeated when scholars seek to define the topic of reform (see, for example, Rieselbach 1994; Schickler 2001).

Surprising or not, scholars working in the field of congressional reforms have never settled on a clear definition of what should and should not be considered a reform.

Moreover, the term is quite often applied to changes in a wide range of institutional and party rules, statutes, ethical codes, and norms of behavior. As the reform literature was reaching maturity in the 1970s, some scholars began theorizing about how we should view reforms and their likely effect on the institution. For instance, Oleszek (1977) constructed a systematic categorization of reform by subject, intent, and cause. Similarly, Jones (1977b) tackled the question of how reforms change various aspects of Congress with a multi-layered classification of reforms: what was the immediate target of reform (what is meant to be changed), what changes were accomplished, what functions were served as a result of the changes (here Jones refers to Davidson and Oleszek's 1976 "adaptation and consolidation" concepts), and finally what were the longer run institutional effects. Rieselbach (1977) reflected upon the extent to which the reforms improved the "responsibility, responsiveness, and accountability" of the legislative body.

Though this contemplation on the meaning of reform has helped to frame the literature, it still leaves us wanting for a simple set of boundaries to get our review of the reform literature off the ground. Therefore, I will keep it simple: a reform proposal is a plan to transform aspects of congressional operations in such a way as someone believes the change is for the better (Oleszek 1977; Evans 2005). The focus will be on changes internal to the operations of the body as a lawmaking institution. So, for example, this would include literature on institutional changes codified in the rules of the chambers or the party caucuses or those written into statute, like budgetary reforms in the 1970s and 1980s that revamped how Congress goes about writing spending and tax legislation.

What will not be considered is research that explores changes to Congress that are explicitly outward looking. For example, changes to campaign finance laws or the rules of congressional elections will not fall under my purview (see Kolodny, Chapter 10, this volume, on campaign finance, and McDonald, Chapter 9, on redistricting). Additionally, I will not touch on the sizable literature on reforms in other legislatures (state, local, or foreign legislatures). Though this is a somewhat arbitrary limitation, and their will be plenty of rules changes that are ambiguous given my restrictions (for example, the adoption of sunshine provisions in the early 1970s that ensured public access to congressional deliberations were changes in the internal rules but were explicitly aimed at an external constituency), this limitation certainly does not overly restrict the review to a small set of literature. The research on changes to the internal rules of Congress is vast.

REFORM RESEARCH IN ITS INFANCY

Scholarship exploring the causes and consequences of congressional reforms has a long, rich history dating back to the beginnings of academic work on the U.S.

Congress. Many of the works of early scholars commonly cited for their insights on the organization and operations of Congress, were, at least in part, prescribing changes to the structure of the legislative body (Polsby and Schickler 2002). For instance, prior to the turn of the century, McConachie (1898) details much of the history and operations of Congress, well beyond the observations regarding committees for which he is frequently cited. Based on little more than his personal reflections of specific events and occurrences, and little systematic evidence, McConachie offered recommendations for changes to the body's structure and rules. To some degree, attention to the structure of Congress and, more importantly, alterations in that structure was propelled by the progressive era reform movement that not only advocated for changes to election laws but also increased pressure on lawmakers to clean their own house.

Thus, as the field of political science developed in the early twentieth century, interest in the internal organization of Congress expanded as well, into a broad set of studies of various aspects of congressional rules and structures. Scholarly focus on legislative structures was often placed within longer considerations of the legislative activities and accomplishment of a given congressional term (see, for example, Rogers 1921). Alternatively, scholars would occasionally turn their attention to specific alterations in Congress to consider their effects on the legislature's operations and output. These included ruminations on the growth of staff (Rogers 1941), the creation of the legislative reference service (Putnam 1915), and the adoption of the 17th Amendment (Haynes 1914). Some reflections and observations on congressional structure published in political science journals came from members of Congress and addressed matters like the use of sub-committees (French 1915) or the removal of the legislature's responsibility over private bills and claims (Luce 1932). But the most common consideration of congressional reforms were imbedded in matter-of-fact reflections on the state of affairs and operations of Congress by leading congressional scholars of the day (Alexander 1916; Luce 1926, 1935; Rogers 1926;[1] Hasbrouck 1927; Willoughby 1934; and Haynes 1938).

In many ways the works of this period provided useful insight into the details of organization and organizational change in Congress and serve as a foundation for later research that gathers large data sets and test theories of institutional organization. Contemporary congressional researchers owe much to this early era of scholarship for their fine-grained depiction of Congress in the late nineteenth and early twentieth centuries. However, it is precisely this lack of theoretical direction and meaningful context that Aldrich and Shepsle (2000) note about most political science of this pre-World War II era. In reviewing early congressional scholarship, they disparage this form of political science as "thick description," where the details of events offer explanation but little understanding of, or insight into, their meaning. As they describe it, the primary deficiency is selection of facts with no real "selection principle."

---

[1] Rogers would subsequently update and revise many of his views on changes in the Senate toward the end of his career Rogers (1968).

Reform scholarship and legislative reorganization in the 1940s

The first real wave of both political and academic interest in broad-scale restructuring of congressional operations began during World War II. Vigorous consideration of congressional restructuring was an outgrowth of heightened public sensitivities during the war to the perquisites of legislators and the weakened policy position of Congress vis-à-vis the president (Young 1943). Numerous major magazine and academic articles and books were published recounting the failings of Congress and largely placing blame for its inadequacies on an obsolete committee structure and outmoded leadership arrangements. Millett and Rogers (1941), for instance, consider the deficiencies of governmental structure that surrounded the Reorganization Act of 1939 and the use of the recently created legislative veto on presidential initiatives to rearrange institutions in the executive branch.

Lawmakers were again a big part of the public debate over reforms (see, for example, Gore 1943; La Follette 1943). Like much of the reform research in the first few decades of the twentieth century, the discussion of congressional reforms amongst scholars (Perkins 1944) was indistinguishable from the same discussion engaged by other observers of Congress (journalists, interest groups, etc.) or members of Congress themselves. Although, the debate regarding reforms had been ongoing during the war, any serious consideration of radical restructuring in Congress had been put on hold until the war's end.

Perhaps no scholarly treatment of the topic of congressional reforms shaped the public debate in this period more than that undertaken by the American Political Science Association (APSA) in a report that had been in the works for many years (American Political Science Association 1945). In 1941, the APSA appointed a "Committee on Congress," chaired by a leading scholar of congressional procedure and structure, George Galloway. Formerly Assistant Research Director of the Twentieth Century Fund, Galloway had earned a Ph.D. in Political Science from the short-lived Brookings graduate program, where he focused his studies on Congress (Baker 2001). The committee was not only charged with the responsibility of gathering information to make recommendations for changes to congressional structure—much of which was accomplished through a series of in-depth interviews with lawmakers—but also acted as the "chief analytic agent of congressional reform" (Galloway 1946). Accordingly, the committee fanned a widespread public debate on the issue of congressional restructuring. It encouraged public forums, newspaper editorials, magazine articles, scholarly work, and at least one other major report on the subject by the National Planning Association (Heller 1945; see also Byrd 1988).

Late in 1944 Congress approved a resolution creating a joint committee to identify the major problems facing Congress and to draw up a list of reform proposals. Thanks to his clear mastery of the issues, Galloway was appointed as the sole staff member of the Joint Committee on the Organization of Congress. As the committee was finishing up its work and issuing its proposals, Galloway hastily put together *Congress at the Crossroads* (Galloway 1946). Largely drawn from his experiences on the Joint Committee, this broad account of the problems facing Congress and the numerous proposed solutions contained within the legislation was meant to add further scholarly legitimacy to the reform effort and build momentum in favor of the restructuring package (Baker 2001). The work of reformers elicited significant reflection within the scholarly community regarding the details of the recommendations under consideration (Chamberlain 1945; Outland 1945; Harris 1946).

When the dust settled, the version of the Legislative Reorganization Act adopted in 1946 was somewhat less ambitious than reformers had hoped. It did rein in the unbridled growth of House committees—consolidating dozens of panels into a smaller number of considerably larger and more powerful panels (see Schickler, Chapter 31, this volume). The act also increased the size of staff associated with lawmaking tasks, particularly committee staff. As well, it removed congressional responsibility over a number of different private claims. However, other aspects of the statute fell flat, such as provisions that constructed a budgetary process that were never properly implemented. Additionally, other alterations to committee policy authority advocated by reform proponents—such as party policy committees and committee "docket days"—were rejected outright.

Ultimately, the reform movement of the 1940s—of which scholars would count themselves a major part—demonstrated that broad-scale changes in such a powerful and entrenched body were possible. However, what was also unmistakable was that no matter how widespread the movement or strong the arguments in favor of change, there are great obstacles and inertia to overcome to move lawmakers from the certainty of existing rules to the uncertainty of proposed reforms.

REFORM RESEARCH EBBS, THEN FLOWS

It did not take long after the adoption of the 1946 Legislative Reorganization Act for Congress to shift its attention toward individual rules changes that had not been part of the package of changes considered at the end of the war. These changes included enactment of the 21-day rule in 1949–50 and again in 1965,[2] enlargement of the Rules Committee—temporarily in 1961, and permanently in 1963—attempts at changes in the Senate cloture threshold in 1949 and 1959, and a small number of rules changes in the Senate in 1963. Rather than expend its efforts and resources on large-scale institutional restructuring, Zelizer (2004) asserts that lawmakers focused more on pressing policy matters during the 1950s and early 1960s, particularly civil rights.

As the second tide of congressional reform momentum grew, we saw again a small number of lawmakers with an introspective, almost academic, interest in the structure of congressional rules, promote a number of internal changes. Such works included

---

[2] This change made it easier to bypass gatekeeping by the House Rules Committee.

books by Senator Joseph Clark (D-PA ; Clark 1964, 1965) and Congressman Richard Bolling (D-MO; Bolling 1965, 1968). By the mid-1960s a renewed movement for consideration of changes to legislative rules had developed to the point where proponents of change—some, like Senator Mike Monoroney (D-OK), had been involved in the reform effort two decades earlier—were able to form a second Joint Committee on the Organization of Congress.

As before, a simultaneous academic interest in the topic of congressional reorganization had manifested itself, some of which was grounded in the established approach of exploring Congress's operations from a historical and largely atheoretical perspective (Harris 1963; Berman 1964; Bailey 1966). At the same time, however, a new crop of legislative scholars was emerging—as has been recounted elsewhere in this volume—whose research was more theoretically driven and empirically supported through systematic collection of quantitative and qualitative evidence (see Oppenheimer, Chapter 2, this volume). A number of these works had the aim of putting the structure of Congress and proposed reforms in perspective with the goals and actions of lawmakers and the legislature as a whole. These included research in a volume by de Grazia 1966 (see de Grazia 1966; Wildavsky 1966), as well as an edited book by leading congressional scholar, David Truman (1965; specifically pieces by Fenno 1965; Huntington 1965; Truman 1965).

More profoundly, however, the work of congressional scholars was transforming the way researchers approached questions regarding legislative change. Two developments were key to the transformation. The first emerged out of earlier meetings between a small group of congressional scholars and reformist members of Congress (Chet Holifield D-CA and Thomas Curtis R-MO). Subsequent to those meetings the Carnegie Corporation in 1964 awarded the APSA $230,000 to study congressional organization and operations. The Study of Congress project, led by Ralph Huitt, fostered work by a new generation of congressional scholars to conduct more systematic research on legislative organization. These young scholars were adopting emerging advances in the social sciences—like sophisticated statistical techniques and models of organizational design and actor behavior (Polsby and Schickler 2002; Zelizer 2004)—and, in part, applying their expertise to vital questions about structural changes. For example, Lewis Froman's treatment of strategy and rules in Congress ends with an assessment of what recent changes had been achieved and what additional reforms should be considered (Froman 1967).

Also among the work supported by the Study of Congress project was that of Robert Peabody, a Stanford-trained political scientist who had already undertaken several studies of the decision to enlarge the Rules Committee. Particularly important in Peabody's research was the application of functionalist theory, which had been gaining traction in various fields of social science (see also Fiellin 1962). While generally aimed at understanding the purpose or function of an actor or system and deriving predictions from that understanding (Hempel 1959), Peabody's application to Congress was effectively an early version of principal-agent theory. Peabody asked which principal this agent (the members of the Rules Committee) serves—the chamber majority, the majority party, the nation as whole, or the committee members' own constituents (Peabody 1963). His data consisted of a set of intensive interviews with majority and minority party leadership, the fifteen members of the committee, and several other lawmakers and staff involved in the rules expansion fight. In addition, Peabody conducted a detailed analysis of the initial contentious vote, looking at the voting patterns by region, ideology (using liberalism scores compiled based on roll calls selected by Americans for Democratic Action), and constituency characteristics (Cummings and Peabody 1963). The findings with regard to Rules Committee enlargement are unsurprising; the addition of three members to the committee helped solidify the majority party's influence over the actions of this critical legislative traffic cop. But more importantly, Peabody—along with many of his peers in the Study of Congress project—nudged scholars to begin thinking in a broader manner about the different coalitions who influence the structure and operations of Congress.

At around the same time another profound development in the study of congressional reforms was led by a young, Columbia-trained scholar, Roger Davidson. In his book *Congress in Crisis*, co-authored with Kovenock, and O'Leary, we see one of the best early examples of scholarship that combines the guidance of well-constructed theoretical models with a carefully collected and large data set analyzing changes to congressional structure (Davidson, Kovenock, and O'Leary 1966). A number of things made this book a real turning point: First, it took the issue of congressional reforms as its sole focus. Davidson and colleagues use three theories to guide their research on reforms—a literary theory, an executive-force theory, and a party-government theory (1966, 17). Second, a major part of their analysis was the collection of significant survey information from a large number of sitting members of Congress on their attitudes regarding the institutional problems facing Congress and their sentiments about potential structural solutions in legislative rules and procedures. Like a fair number of studies at the time, interviews with lawmakers were the central source of data, but in this case the authors converted the information into explicit data to be analyzed statistically. Third, and most importantly, Davidson, Kovenock, and O'Leary seem to be conscious that their work (and that of some of their peers) was part of a turning point in the literature. That is, in undertaking a systematically guided exploration of legislative organization and the opportunities and directions for change, the authors note that they "are not insensitive to the implications that our findings may have for innovative behavior. We presume that this study will serve as an antidote for much of the previous reformist literature, in which the authors accept little or no responsibility for the political implications of their arguments" (1966, 5).

Ultimately, the efforts of the mid-1960s Joint Committee did not bear fruit for many years. But during this time the constituency of lawmakers eager for overturning the existing power arrangements in Congress had grown considerably, resulting in a significantly watered-down Legislative Reorganization Act of 1970. The act mainly sought to loosen the reins of control that committee chairs possessed over the operations of their panels and to open up committee deliberations to public scrutiny. The statute included provisions that granted both backbenchers and minority party law-makers the right to more fully participate in committee activities by calling witnesses and bringing legislation to the floor over the objection of intransigent chairs. It also made it easier to obtain a recorded vote on floor amendments. Sustained attention to the issue of legislative structure served to capture the interest and imagination of more and more young congressional scholars of the time. Scholars now had new approaches—pioneered by the work of individuals like Peabody and Davidson—to look at the topic of institutional changes in Congress in a different way.

THE REFORM PERIOD OF THE 1970S

By the mid-1970s the debate around congressional structure had built a full head of steam. Like the reform era that had emerged three decades earlier, the movement for an overhaul of congressional rules and operations did not exist in a policy vacuum. Much of the underlying motivation for revamping party and chamber rules was aimed at allowing more liberal backbenchers to pursue their policy goals in the face of reluctant and often obstructionist senior colleagues and eventually an antagonistic president. Accordingly the literature on congressional reforms at this time reflects this agenda by focusing on whether proposed or enacted changes have the effect of elevating the influence of junior lawmakers or the legislative branch vis-à-vis the executive.

By the early 1970s lawmakers in Congress were fully in reform mode, with the creation in the House of a Select Committee on Committees, under the control of one of its most learned critics of congressional operations—Representative Richard Bolling (D-MO). Among its many superb staff members, Bolling and Vice-chair Representative David Martin (R-NE) brought on board two congressional scholars—Roger Davidson and Walter Oleszek (a Congressional Research Service [hereafter CRS] staff member with a Ph.D. in Political Science from SUNY Albany). Moreover, the panel received extensive input and insights from nearly all the major legislative scholars of the time (Select Committee on Committees 1973): Fenno, Polsby, Goodwin, Cooper, Brady, Peabody, Ripley, Bibby, Jones, Saloma, Maass, Schneier, Rosenthal, Jewell, just to name a few. And, like previous reform eras, advocates of reform within Congress used academic outlets to make their case for changes, such as reform proponent, Representative Donald Fraser (DFL-MN) (Fraser and Nathanson 1975).

As had previously been the case, the ramp up to this sizable reform effort served as an impetus for a very sizable expansion of academic work on the topic of congressional structure and change. The earliest of this new wave of work was mainly focused on the reforms that had taken place in the initial surge of restructuring in the prior half-decade, and mainly focused on the attempts of junior lawmakers to chip away at the seniority system and the unwavering control of committees by senior colleagues. Among these was Rohde's assessment of the effects of the Democratic caucus's "Subcommittee Bill of Rights" (Rohde 1974)—rules adopted by the House majority in 1973 that granted policy property rights to subcommittees and democratized the process of subcommittee chair selection. As well, Norman Ornstein (who would eventually become an important analyst and advocate for reforms, but then was an assistant professor at Catholic University) produced his own account of the events that led up to, and the effects of, the Subcommittee of Bill of Rights, and their immediate impact on the operations of the body (Ornstein 1975b).

The ensuing battle over reforms during 1973–4 was perhaps the most bitter in the modern era. Ultimately Bolling was only able to get a portion of the jurisdictional changes he sought, as more cautious elements in the Democratic caucus supported a severely diluted reform plan offered by Representative Julia Butler Hansen (Democrat, D-WA). Rather than making major jurisdictional changes, the Hansen reforms authorized multiple referrals, allowing the Speaker to refer one bill to multiple committees for consideration prior to floor deliberation. Even in the midst of Congress's deliberations, scholars were offering frank assessments of the work of the Bolling Committee, as in David Price's review of the proposals being batted around on Capitol Hill (Price 1974).

It was the immediate aftermath of the Bolling–Martin reform effort, however, that induced a virtual explosion of research on reforms. As with other attempts at structural changes in Congress, there were a number of scholars who gave their accounting of the events, often with some limited perspective on their effects and long-term prospects. Among the more notable of these were Davidson and Oleszek's (1977) insider account of the history of the events leading up to and during the Bolling Committee effort, including a fine assessment of the historical and theoretical context. In addition were a number of studies exploring the alterations in individual committee rules, composition, and powers (Price 1978; Kaiser 1978; Rudder 1978; Ornstein and Rohde 1977; Ellwood and Thurber 1977). A topic that captured the attention of numerous scholars was the budgetary reforms that served as Congress's reaction to heavy-handedness by the president—particularly Nixon's impoundment of funds for programs he did not support (Schick 1973; Fisher 1977; Thurber 1976, 1978; Munselle 1978). Sundquist (1981), who focused in part on the budgetary reforms, gave a more detailed account of the ebb and flow in power relations between Congress and the president (see Gilmour, Chapter 22, this volume).

But more was occurring in the reform literature than just reflections on what led up to and transpired during the restructuring effort in Congress over the previous decade. As the 1960s had ushered in a new era of theorizing about the causes and consequences of reforms, the aftermath of the Bolling–Martin effort saw a blossoming of this work in several new directions. One set of theoretical works explores the factors affecting institutional reforms (or preventing them). Simultaneous to their work chronicling the House reform effort, Davidson and Oleszek were using their intimate knowledge of the reform process to hypothesize that the impetus for "adaptation and consolidation" in legislative structures arises from stress in the organization's external environment or internal dynamics and asks how reforms affect the policy-related elements contained within (Davidson and Oleszek 1976). Davidson (1977) also asserts that the existing clientele relationship between congressional committees and the groups they regulate is a major hindrance to the success of reform efforts. Several years later Sheppard (1985) takes a similar perspective in his detailed view of the entire reform period of the 1970s. Dodd (1986) proposes a theory of congressional cycles—both in terms of the resources and skills of lawmakers and the structure of Congress itself—which suggests that efforts to reorganize rules, as well as innovations in existing public policies, will recur in patterns over time.

Moreover, at about the same time, we saw an expansion in innovative hypothesis testing geared around reforms affecting committee composition and leadership—a topic that would become central to later innovations in congressional research. Stanga and Farnsworth's (1978) large N tests analyze whether or not reforms that democratized the selection of committee chairs actually brought about changes in the use of the seniority system in committees, even though it was probably too soon after the changes to have observed much upheaval in standard procedures. Similarly, Berg (1978) explored how the Democratic caucus changes that allowed for the removal of recalcitrant committee chairs altered the leadership characteristics and committee performance of the three panels in which this action was used in the mid-1970s. As well, in the epilogue to his book *The Giant Jigsaw Puzzle*, Shepsle (1978) explores how recent reforms in the committee assignment process in the Democratic caucus altered the ability of members to get their requested panels and the composition of those committees.

The picture that emerges from the 1970s reform literature is of scholars taking stock of the degree to which revamping of congressional and party rules advanced the goals of reform proponents. The goals were to a large degree aimed at internal democratization—dismantling institutional and normative obstacles to the decision-making influence of backbenchers—and external potency—reinvigorating Congress as an equal governing partner with the president. Scholars at the time were not in complete agreement as to the effectiveness of the structural changes in achieving these objectives (see, for example, Davidson 1977 and Berg 1978 for skeptical viewpoints, and Rudder 1978 and Thurber 1978 for more optimistic perspectives). But in part, this uncertainty may have been the result of assessments made with only short-run evidence.

Interestingly, one of the more unique attempts to understand reforms came as a purely theoretical exercise from David Rohde and Ken Shepsle—two young scholars trained at Rochester by William Riker and Richard Fenno. Employing the combination of formal modeling skills and a keen interest in the structure of governing bodies, particularly Congress, they used a constrained maximization model to pose the question of whether reforms in legislatures are necessary, at least from a theoretical perspective, to experience policy innovation (Rohde and Shepsle 1978). Their theoretical finding is an important one in light of the prior decade of efforts at procedural changes in Congress largely aimed at pursuing a liberal legislative agenda: membership and institutional changes are neither necessary nor sufficient conditions to ensure policy changes.

SUSTAINED INTEREST IN REFORMS

Armed with fresh data on structural changes from the prolonged effort of congressional reforms in the 1970s and a new, more deductive approach to questions of institutional organization, congressional scholars in the 1980s and early 1990s sustained and diversified their interest in the effects reforms were having on the operations and output of the legislative body. On the one hand were studies with a narrow focus on a limited set of changes or the effect of reforms for one aspect of the legislature's performance. Among the more popular topics for analysis was the impact that multiple referrals had on congressional deliberations and legislative outcomes (Davidson 1988, 1989; Davidson, Oleszek, and Kephart 1988; Bach and Smith 1988; Sinclair 1989, 1992; Strahan 1990; Davidson and Oleszek 1992; Young and Cooper 1993). Additionally, scholars returned to the topic of budgetary reforms as balloning budget deficits caused this to be the only area of significant institutional tinkering during the 1980s—the Gramm–Rudman–Hollings deficit reduction act in 1985, and adoption of the Byrd Rule. Accordingly, the impact of changes to Congress's spending procedures was seen as a ripe area for analysis (Fisher 1985; Leloup, Graham, and Barwick 1987; Thurber 1992).

Given that scholars had several waves of institutional change through which to view the organizational evolution of the body, the post-reform period also generated broader perspectives on congressional "eras" and transitions. Davidson (1986), for example, catalogs the evolution of three eras of modern congressional organization— classic, reform, and post-reform—noting the 1960s and 1970s as the important period of transition to fundamentally different lawmaker goals and ways in which they see the institution's purpose. Shepsle (1989) took a similar perspective on the transformation of Congress away from what he viewed as its "textbook" equilibrium (see Huntington 1965 for an earlier incarnation of this kind of work).

The most significant shift in work on congressional reform that occurred in this post-reform period was a development that mirrored the larger changeover in congressional scholarship. Theorizing and the creation of general models regarding congressional structure began to subsume the research on Congress. As described elsewhere in this volume, debates over congressional organization by the mid-1980s were more and more centered on the foundational assumptions behind basic structures. Based on models of lawmakers as rational goal-maximizers, scholars began to develop theoretical lenses through which to understand the rationale and effect of particular aspects of legislative rules—the purpose of the committee system, the aims of specific rules within the legislature, and so on. Theorizing quickly evolved into empirical tests of hypotheses derived from these models, and initially many were testing their notion of congressional organization on the powers and composition of congressional committees (see Chapters 3, 14, and 37 by Volden and Wiseman, Evans, and Fiorina respectively, this volume). However, one set of scholars began to look for fertile untilled areas of congressional history to examine these theoretical questions. Congressional reforms seemed ideal as a source of data to test notions of congressional organization. If theories of organization explain why certain rules and structures exist, they should also explain the motivations behind changes to congressional rules (Binder 1997; Adler 2002).

In many ways, the new breed of reform scholars were melding styles of political science research that were already well established: general theoretical models of legislative organization, traditional large-N data collection, with a hint of earlier work theorizing about the motivations for congressional reforms. What made this research different is that the interest in the cause (and to some extent the effects) of reforms or explicit changes to institutional rules was coequal to theoretical questions about purpose of congressional organization.

Possibly the most important early work in this respect was Charles Stewart's research on budgetary reforms. Stewart saw the topic of budgetary politics in Congress as not only fertile ground for understanding congressional reforms but also for exploring theories of congressional behavior. His early research (Stewart 1987, 1988), including the eventual publication of his dissertation (Stewart 1989), highlights the transition to more positivist and rational choice-oriented research on congressional reforms. Stewart develops a theory of institutional preferences, in which lawmakers' constituency interests and institutional position induce their preferences and behavior on congressional budgetary reforms. He then explores the utility of his theoretical framework as a means of understanding budgetary reforms pursued between the creation of the House Appropriations Committee in 1865 and the Budget and Accounting Act in 1921, which instituted the modern-day budgetary relationship between Congress and the president (for a somewhat similar constituency-motivated argument regarding budgetary reforms written about the same time, see Brady and Morgan 1987; see Schickler Chapter 31, this volume, for additional consideration of Stewart's work).

Other works joined Stewart's in setting a new direction for research on congressional reforms. Smith's involvement in two books was important for reinvigorating an interest in the development and changes in floor procedures in Congress (Bach and Smith 1988; Smith 1989). For example, Smith (1989) explores the effects of reforms of the 1970s on the operations of Congress, particularly how changes to rules made legislating on the floor more attractive. Smith argues that these changes weakened the powers of committees—long the locus of legislative authority in Congress. In another important work, Rohde (1991) explores the electoral changes and demands that led to many of the reforms in the 1970s and 1980s, which achieved greater policy authority for party leaders. More to the point, in the context of studying reforms, Rohde outlined what would become a central theory through which to understand legislative organization—"conditional party government" (see Strahan, Chapter 17, this volume).

THE REPUBLICAN REVOLUTION AN A NEW REFORM RESEARCH AGENDA

Spurred by a number of high profile scandals in Congress, including one that consumed the Speaker of the House (Jim Wright, D-TX), a new citizen movement emerged to redirect "business as usual" in Washington. This eventually bolstered the presidential candidacy of Ross Perot in 1992 and the creation of his Reform Party. Concurrently, the early 1990s saw a renewed interest in reforms in Congress, sparking the creation of another joint committee to debate and propose changes in the legislature's committee system and deliberative process. Though ultimately not successful in passing a package of reforms, the ensuing election of a Republican majority in 1994 did result in the adoption of substantial changes to House and Senate rules by the new leadership. The changes were the most significant restructuring of the operations of Congress since the mid-1970s.

As with previous periods of reform, the momentum for changes to congressional structure, in part, built on the work of supportive scholars. Lawmakers worked hand in hand with scholars in constructing a reform agenda. In 1992 reform proponents in Congress met with congressional specialists from the American Enterprise Institute and Brookings Institution—Norman Ornstein and Thomas Mann, respectively—to request that the two think-tanks build a scholarly constituency for a renewed reform effort. Eventually this led to two important reports that outlined a number of potential changes in congressional procedures and operations (Ornstein and Mann 1992, 1993), which built on the contributions and input of numerous congressional experts, such as Davidson, Jones, Fenno, Polsby, Rudder, and Smith (Mann 1995).

Additionally, like its predecessors, the new incarnation of the Joint Committee on the Organization of Congress again not only utilized the input of congressional scholars, both formally and informally (Dreier 1995), but also took advantage of the work of veteran CRS staffer and reform expert, Walter Oleszek, and emerging congressional scholar, Larry Evans. Ramped-up scholarly interest in the topic resulted in a number of important projects placing the reform effort in context. Among them were Rieselbach's (1994) broad examination of the political struggles that led to the reform period of the 1970s, their subsequent effects on congressional operations, and the new reform agenda in the first few years of the 1990s. A conference hosted by

Jim Thurber at American University just prior to the upheaval of the 1994 elections, brought together many leading reform scholars to reflect on the unfulfilled efforts of the Joint Committee and assess what lay before lawmakers during the coming term. By the time the edited volume from Thurber's conference was published (Thurber and Davidson 1995), the Republicans had swept into control of Congress and instituted a number of changes, including severe cuts in committee staff, disbanding three standing committees, banning proxy voting in committees, and alterations to the rules governing multiple referrals. Evans and Oleszek (1997) wrote the most definitive chronicle of the events surrounding the reform efforts of the Joint Committee and the subsequent changes implemented by the new Republican majority after the 1994 elections, in a vein similar to the earlier Davidson and Oleszek book recounting the reform proceedings in the 1970s (Davidson and Oleszek 1977). Evans and Oleszek cast a critical eye on the process and changes brought about by this restructuring, but were again constrained by the limitations of time in taking full account of the effect of revamping congressional and party rules. Nevertheless, Evans and Oleszek projected that increasing party polarization is unlikely to derail the direction that reforms took during this period. Admirably, they did not shy away from contemplating where problems still lay—hindrances to minority involvement in deliberations, excessive obstruction in the Senate, and so on.

The late 1990s is when we see scholarship on congressional reforms taking a distinctive flavor, dominated by the confluence of previous advancements in the study of political institutions—superior statistical methods, tightly constructed deductive theories of legislative organization and behavior, and the mining of congressional history to create sizable and comprehensive data sets on institutional development. The result was a number of studies of congressional change that were clearly based in the contemporary scholarly debates over the underlying motives of legislative organization; questions such as what is the role of parties in a legislature? Do parties use the rules to control the legislative agenda? Do reelection motivations bleed into other behaviors beyond policymaking? And how much of the organization of Congress is influenced by established procedures and norms?

Among these studies were several for whom partisan influences was the motivating question. Binder (1997) contends that changes in the rules governing the powers and privileges of minority parties have been conditioned by the state of interparty political divisions and the existence of cross-party cleavages. In particular, she contends that two factors—partisan need and party capacity—are central to the historical trends in the imposition or relaxation of minority rights in Congress. Similarly, Dion finds that "small majorities are more cohesive, cohesive majorities lead to minority obstruction, minority obstruction leads to procedural changes on the part of the majority to limit obstruction" (Dion 1997, 245; see also Dion, Chapter 32, this volume). In the best tradition of scholarship, Binder and Dion working almost simultaneously reach very different conclusions as to restrictions on minority rights in legislatures: Dion asserts that small majorities will put the "thumbscrews" to the minority opposition, while Binder sees the return to large, cohesive majorities as leading to tightening of minority privileges.

Conversely, Schickler and Rich's (1997) study of House rules changes from 1919 to 1994 calls into serious question the ability of the majority party to control the extent or direction of structural modifications in the policy process until the more recent period, when the majority party became more homogenous and unified. Even then the majority caucus has been constrained in what types of structural arrangements it can implement. Schickler (2001; see also Schickler 2000) further argues that no one theory of legislative organization can explain the institutional development of Congress. Rather there exists a "disjointed pluralism" in which numerous different interests influence the process of change in legislative arrangements during different periods.

Other studies explored reforms, but focused on different theoretical perspectives. King's (1997) examination of changes in committee jurisdictions argues that important transformations in issue property rights do not happen as a result of formal efforts to alter the structure of committee arrangements written into the chamber rules, but rather as informal encroachments by committees on other panels' turf or adoption of emerging policy arenas. In many ways King's analysis tackles the role of path dependence in determining institutional changes and developments. That is, King sees the slow, evolutionary efforts of lawmakers to build on existing issue jurisdictions as more transformative in altering committee policy influence than the occasional, high-profile reform events. From a different angle, Adler's (2002) examination of committee restructuring in the House since World War II makes the case that the reelection imperative of lawmakers drives their preferences on congressional structure and has thus been the largest impediment to profound reforms in Congress. He contends that the deep-seeded constituency interest that influences lawmakers' committee assignments often makes them resistant to restructuring efforts that threaten to up-end their ability to provide for constituents through policy control. Examining roll call, co-sponsorship, and survey data on a number of different reforms in the 1970s Schickler, McGhee, and Sides (2003) also find that partisanship is not a good predictor of support for congressional restructuring in that period.

Among the recent wave of work that considers the structure and change in Congress have been a number of reflective works by preeminent congressional scholars on the state of Congress and the prospects for reform. Polsby's (2004) memoir-like study of congressional change in the last half-century makes the case that the seeds of institutional change are sewn in the demographic and electoral changes that shape the institution's membership. Mostly through an examination of the House, Polsby shows that specific developments over time—institutionalization (Polsby 1968), technological changes, social and political movements, and political innovations—beget institutional changes in Congress. Mann and Ornstein (2006) revisit the topic of congressional reform in a book-length indictment of congressional proceedings. They offer a number of proposals to improve legislative operations running the gamut from full workweeks and more conservative use of restrictive rules, to lobbying and ethics reforms (see also Mayhew 2009; Shepsle 2009; and Sinclair 2004, 2009 for reflections on the contemporary state of affairs in Congress and the outlook for reform).

The discipline of History has also seen a resurgence of interest in congressional reforms, propelled almost single-handedly by the work of Julian Zelizer. Perhaps no more comprehensive history of the modern reform efforts exists than Zelizer's (2004) account (see Evans (2005) for a similar review of modern reform efforts). Zelizer takes a historian's perspective—with a partial political scientist's eye—and weaves together the social and political events and influences that shaped the reform sentiments and institutional changes (and failures) of the last half of the twentieth century. He highlights how institutional entrepreneurs interweave their objectives with the goals of advocates for policy change to achieve their organizational aims. Zelizer's work is not only comprehensive, but offers a wealth of sources that future generations of reform scholars will no doubt seize upon as data opportunities.

Other innovative historical accounts of reforms in recent years have come from current and former Senate Historians, Donald Ritchie and Richard Baker. Ritchie (2001) culls through oral histories of former Senate staffers—from insights of the former parliamentarian to observations of cloakroom attendants—to glean their reflections of how reforms in the Senate altered the body, its members, and particularly its staff. Baker (2001) focuses specifically on the contributions of three scholars of Congress from a bygone era—Lindsay Rogers, George Haynes, and George Galloway. Baker, not only recounts their observations, analysis, and recommendations for Senate changes, but he particularly highlights the ways in which each scholar was influential in shaping both the scholarly and public debate regarding its institutional development.

Since the year 2000, we have also seen an increase in the number of studies examining a narrow set of rules and structures in Congress, similar to what Smith was doing in the late 1980s. This has taken the form of interest in changes in agenda control procedures such as special rules in the House or unanimous consent agreements in the Senate (Roberts and Smith 2007), the filibuster and changes in rules regarding cloture (Wawro and Schickler 2006; Wawro and Schickler 2007; Koger 2007), motions to recommit (Cox, Den Hartog, and McCubbins 2007; Kiewiet and Roust 2007; Wolfensberger 2007), and the dynamics of congressional committee jurisdictions (Adler and Wilkerson 2008)

DISCUSSION: GETTING BACK IN THE GAME

The literature on congressional reform dates back to the earliest works in political science and is vast. For many decades attention paid to the subject of congressional reforms by scholars ebbed and flowed as the matter came up for consideration and movement stirred in and around Congress to alter its rules and operations. Though a small number of scholars have maintained longer-term interest in the topic regardless of public and political attention (Roger Davidson and Leroy Rieselbach, to name two), it was often the case that the field of congressional scholars only had sporadic interest in studying and analyzing reforms as such efforts gathered steam in Congress. Consistent attention, however, seems to have improved in the last decade or two with a more sustained focus of study on the causes and consequences of reforms as a means of leveraging broader questions about institutional structure.

Additionally, the continuous study of reforms and expanded interest in mining the history of reform events and structural changes has also helped to address another persistent complication in this literature: no matter how good the intentions of reform scholars, often the research was conducted directly in the wake of the actual structural changes (or attempts at structural changes), thus giving researchers little time to gather data and, more importantly, little perspective with which to assess the true effects of the changes. Throughout the 1970s, scholars, anxious to use new theoretical and statistical tools, were evaluating the impact of reforms that had occurred only a few years earlier. Fortunately, we now have the benefit of distance from many of the most significant changes and an inclination to collect relevant data on earlier eras thus allowing for studies of the effect reforms have had on the operations of Congress and the actions of lawmakers.

But more than anything else, there is one primary aspect of this literature that has still not fulfilled its potential: the inclination of skilled and experienced scholars to go beyond merely answering theoretical questions and adapting their research in ways that contributes to the public and elite discourse on structural improvements in congressional organization. To some extent this is a throwback to earlier eras of congressional scholarship. As highlighted throughout this account, scholars have almost always played an important role in shaping the debate that has surrounded movements for restructuring and reorganization in Congress. One feature lost in the transition to theoretically motivated research on congressional reform was an interest in making recommendations regarding more effective structural arrangements and rules. Generally the contemporary works of scholars studying reforms from a new institutional perspective have done a superb job assessing the theoretical implications of their findings, but fall flat when it comes to steering lawmakers on the topic of reforms. At best, we find scholars burying recommendations regarding institutional arrangements at the end of books that are largely unseen by congressional insiders.

The suggestion that theoretically grounded and empirically sophisticated social science should strive for greater relevance in its application to real world events is certainly not a new one. On occasion we have even seen researchers utilize insights gleaned from their studies of the organization of Congress to provide recommendations for specific and concrete changes. For example, Cooper's (1975) exploration of congressional structure—the role of the body vis-à-vis other policymaking entities, the organizational goals and constraints, and so on—ends with a very explicit set of institutional recommendations motivated by one scholar's profound understanding of the body and the effects of its rules. Cooper utilizes his analytical framework regarding Congress's policymaking responsibilities to both review reform events and offer insights on future recommendations for change. More recently, Binder and Smith's (1996) exhaustive exploration of filibusters in the Senate, offers a number of recommendations regarding changes to Senate's Rule 22 regarding the invocation of cloture, based on their reading of the history and empirical evidence.

It is through this type of prescriptive orientation that research on congressional reforms could add significantly to the public debate about the effectiveness of governing institutions, not to mention the public recognition of political science as an academic field. Today we know more than ever about the organization of Congress and the effect of different structures on the powers and influence of legislative actors and policy outcomes. Among the many areas of strength, we understand better the role of congressional committees and parties in controlling institutional performance, we have a fairly good handle on the factors that influence the legislative behaviors of lawmakers, and we have a superb sense of the institution's structural development over its life. It is this mastery that is unquestionably our greatest asset. The entire field of congressional studies, not just those toiling in questions of structural change in Congress, could benefit by redirecting some of its energy toward using this knowledge to help shape debates about future reform. Much insight could be gained if scholars of Congress were able to marshal their collective knowledge of the history, development, institutional successes and failures, and legislative performance more directly toward rigorous academic work that also provides insights for institutional problem-solvers.

In the last decade there have been positive steps in this direction with the expansion of outlets for political scientists to enter into the public discourse on matters that we can offer very useful commentary and guidance. Online news and political publications have expanded considerably, many of which seek the input of political scientists. As well, more academically oriented blogs help us to do a better job publicizing the work and findings of scholars. In addition, along with existing journals, such as *Political Science Quarterly*, we see an expansion of scholarly outlets specifically seeking work that illuminates the applied aspects of serious scholarship (see, for example *The Forum*). Nevertheless, there is plenty of room for improvement. In part, this can be accomplished by encouraging our best graduate students to think about the application of their research and findings for political actors.

REFERENCES

ADLER, E. S. 2002. *Why Congressional Reforms Fail: Reelection and the House Committee System.* Chicago: University of Chicago Press.

—— and WILKERSON, J. D. 2008. Intended Consequences: Jurisdictional Reform and Issue Control in the U.S. House of Representatives. *Legislative Studies Quarterly*, 33: 85–112.

ALDRICH, J. H., and SHEPSLE, K. A. 2000. Explaining Institutional Change: Soaking, Poking, and Modeling the U.S. Congress, pp. 23–45 in *Congress on Display, Congress at Work*, ed. W. T. Bianco. University of Michigan Press.

ALEXANDER, D. S. 1916. *History and Procedure of the House of Representatives.* Boston: Houghton Mifflin Company.

AMERICAN POLITICAL SCIENCE ASSOCIATION. 1945. *The Reorganization of Congress, A Report of the Committee on Congress of the American Political Science Association.* Washington, DC: Public Affairs Press.

BACH, S., and SMITH, S. S. 1988. *Managing Uncertainty in the House of Representatives: Adaptation and Innovation in Special Rules*. Washington, DC: Brookings Institution Press.

BAILEY, S. K. 1966. *The New Congress*. New York: St. Martin's.

BAKER, R. A. 2001. Twentieth-century Senate Reform: Three Views from the Outside, pp. 147–66 in *The Contentious Senate*, eds. C. C. Campbell and N. C. Rae. Lanham, MD: Rowman and Littlefield.

BERG, J. 1978. The Effect of Seniority Reform on Three House Committees in the 94th Congress, pp. 9–22 in *Legislative Reform: The Policy Impact*, ed. L. N. Rieselbach. Lexington, MA: Lexington Books.

BERMAN, D. M. 1964. *In Congress Assembled: The Legislative Process in the National Government*. New York: Macmillan.

BINDER, S. A. 1997. *Minority Rights, Majority Rule: Partisanship and the Development of Congress*. New York: Cambridge University Press.

BINDER, S. A., and SMITH, S. S. 1996. *Politics or Principle?: Filibustering in the United States Senate*. Washington, DC: Brookings Institution Press.

BOLLING, R. 1965. *House Out of Order*. New York: Dutton.

——1968. *Power in the House*. New York: E. P. Dutton & Co.

BRADY, D., and MORGAN, M. A. 1987. Reforming the Structure of the House Appropriations Process: The Effects of the 1885 and 1919–20 Reforms on Money Decisions, pp. 207–34 in *Congress: Structure and Policy*, ed. M. D. McCubbins and T. Sullivan. Cambridge: Cambridge University Press.

BULLOCK, C. S. 1978. Congress in the Sunshine, pp. 209–21 in *Legislative Reform: The Policy Impact*, ed. L. N. Rieselbach. Lexington, MA: Lexington Books.

BYRD, R. C. 1988. Congressional Reform: The Legislative Reorganization Act of 1946, pp. 537–50 in *The Senate, 1789–1989: Addresses on the History of the United States Senate*. Washington, DC: U.S. Government Printing Office.

CHAMBERLAIN, L. H. 1945. Congress–Diagnosis and Prescription. *Political Science Quarterly*, 60(3): 437–45.

CLARK, J. S. 1964. *Congress: The Sapless Branch*. New York: Harper and Row.

——1965. *Congressional Reform: Problems and Prospects*. New York: Thomas Y. Crowell.

COOPER, J. 1975. Strengthening The Congress: An Organizational Analysis. *Harvard Journal on Legislation*, 12(3): 307–68.

COX, G. W., DEN HARTOG, C., and MCCUBBINS, M. D. 2007. The Motion to Recommit in the U.S. House of Representatives, pp. 296–300 in *Party, Process, and Political Change in Congress: Further New Perspectives on the History of Congress*, ed. D. Brady and M. D. McCubbins. Stanford, CA: Stanford University Press.

CUMMINGS, Jr., M. C., and PEABODY, R. 1963. The Decision to Enlarge the Committee on Rules: An Analysis of the 1961 Vote, pp. 167–94 in *New Perspectives on the House of Representatives*, ed. R. Peabody and N. W. Polsby. Chicago: Rand McNally.

DAVIDSON, R. H. 1977. Breaking Up Those 'Cozy Triangles': An Impossible Dream, pp. 30–53 in *Legislative Reform and Public Policy*, ed. S. Welch and J. Peters. New York: Praeger.

——1981. Congressional Leaders As Agents Of Change, pp. 135–56 in *Understanding Congressional Leadership*, Washington, DC: Congressional Quarterly Press.

——1986. Congressional Committees As Moving Targets. *Legislative Studies Quarterly*, 11: 19–33.

——1988. The New Centralization on Capitol Hill. *The Review of Politics*, 50(3): 345–64.

——1989. Multiple Referral of Legislation in the U.S. Senate. *Legislative Studies Quarterly*, 14(3): 375–92.

——1990. The Legislative Reorganization Act of 1946. *Legislative Studies Quarterly*, 15: 357–73.

—— Kovenock, D. M., and O'Leary, M. K. 1966. *Congress In Crisis: Politics and Congressional Reform*. Belmont, CA: Wadsworth Publishing.

—— and Oleszek, W. J. 1976. Adaptation and Consolidation: Structural Innovation in the U.S. House of Representatives. *Legislative Studies Quarterly*, 1(1): 37–65.

—— —— 1977. *Congress Against Itself*. Bloomington: Indiana University Press.

—— —— 1992. From Monopoly to Management: Changing Patterns of Committee Deliberation, pp. 129–41 in *The Postreform Congress*, ed. R. H. Davidson. New York: St. Martin's Press.

—— —— and Kephart, T. 1988. One Bill, Many Committees: Multiple Referrals in the U.S. House of Representatives. *Legislative Studies Quarterly*, 13: 3–28.

Dion, D. 1997. *Turning the Legislative Thumbscrews: Minority Rights and Procedural Change in Legislative Politics*. Ann Arbor, MI: University of Michigan Press.

Dodd, L. C. 1986. A Theory of Congressional Cycles: Solving the Puzzle of Change, pp. 3–44 in *Congress and Policy Change*, ed. G. C. Wright, L. N. Rieselbach, and L. C. Dodd. New York: Agathon.

Dreier, D. 1995. Forward, pp. ix–xi, in *Remaking Congress: Change and Stability in the 1990s*, ed. J. A. Thurber and R. H. Davidson. Washington, DC: Congressional Quarterly.

Ellwood, J. W., and Thurber, J. A. 1977. The New Congressional Budget Process: It's Causes, Consequences, and Possible Success, pp. 82–97 in *Legislative Reform and Public Policy*, ed. S. Welch and J. G. Peters. New York: Praeger.

Evans, C. L. 2005. Politics of Congressional Reform, pp. 492–522 in *The Legislative Branch*, New York: Oxford University Press.

—— and Oleszek, W. J. 1997. *Congress Under Fire: Reform Politics and the Republican Majority*. Boston: Houghton Mifflin Company.

Fenno, R. F. 1965. The Internal Distribution of Influence: The House, pp. 52–76 in *The Congress and America's Future*, ed. D. B. Truman. Englewood Cliffs, NJ: Prentice-Hall.

Fiellin, A. 1962. The Functions of Informal Groups in Legislative Institutions. *The Journal of Politics*, 24(1): 72–91.

Fisher, L. 1977. Congressional Budget Reform: The First Two Years. *Harvard Journal of Legislation*, 14: 413–57.

—— 1985. Ten Years of the Budget Act: Still Searching for Controls. *Public Budgeting & Finance*, 5(3): 3–28.

Fraser, D. A., and Nathanson, I. 1975. Rebuilding the House of Representatives, pp. 288–94 in *Congress In Change: Evolution and Reform*, ed. N. J. Ornstein. New York: Praeger Publishers.

French, B. L. 1915. Sub-Committees of Congress. *American Political Science Review*, 9(1): 68–92.

Froman, L. A. 1967. *The Congressional Process: Strategies, Rules, and Procedures*. Boston: Little, Brown and Co.

Galloway, G. B. 1946. *Congress at the Crossroads*. New York: Thomas Y. Crowell.

Gore, A. 1943. Congress Can Save Itself. *Collier's Magazine*, 13: 32–3.

de Grazia, A., ed. 1966. *Congress: The First Branch*. Washington, DC: American Enterprise Institute.

—— 1966. Toward a New Model of Congress, pp. 1–22 in *Congress: The First Branch*, ed. A. de Grazia. Washington, DC: American Enterprise Institute.

Grumm, J. G. 1971. The Effects of Legislative Structure on Legislative Performance, pp. 298–322 in *State and Urban Politics*, ed. R. I. Hofferbert and I. Sharkansky. Boston: Little, Brown and Co.

Harris, J. P. 1946. The Reorganization of Congress. *Public Administration Review*, 6: 267–82.

—— 1963. *Congress and the Legislative Process*. New York: McGraw-Hill.

HASBROUCK, P. D. 1927. *Party Government in the House of Representatives*. New York: Macmillan.

HAYNES, G. H. 1914. The Changing Senate. *North American Review*, 200: 222–34.

—— 1938. *The Senate of the United States*. Boston: Houghton Mifflin.

HELLER, R. 1945. *Strengthening the Congress*. Washington, DC: National Planning Association.

HEMPEL, C. G. 1959. The Logic of Functional Analysis, pp. 271–301 in *Symposium on Sociological Theory*, ed. L. Gross. New York: Harper & Row.

HUNTINGTON, S. P. 1965. Congressional Responses to the Twentieth Century, pp. 5–31 in *The Congress and America's Future*, ed. D. B. Truman. Englewood Cliffs, NJ: Prentice-Hall.

JONES, C. O. 1977a. Will Reform Change Congress? pp. 247–60 in *Congress Reconsidered*, ed. L. C. Dodd and B. I. Oppenheimer. New York: Praeger.

—— 1977b. How Reform Changes Congress, pp. 11–29 in *Legislative Reform and Public Policy*, ed. S. Welch and J. G. Peters. New York: Praeger.

KAISER, F. M. 1978. Congressional Change and Foreign Policy: The House Committee on International Relations, pp. 61–72 in *Legislative Reform: The Policy Impact*, ed. L. Rieselbach. Lexington, MA: Lexington Books.

KIEWIET, D. R., and ROUST, K. 2007. The Motion to Recommit: More Than an Amendment? pp. 301–8 in *Party, Process, and Political Change in Congress: Further New Perspectives on the History of Congress*, ed. D. Brady and M. D. McCubbins. Stanford, CA: Stanford University Press.

KING, D. C. 1997. *Turf Wars: How Congressional Committees Claim Jurisdictions*. Chicago: University of Chicago Press.

KOGER, G. 2007. Filibuster Reform in the Senate, 1913–17, pp. 205–25 in *Party, Process, and Political Change in Congress: Further New Perspectives on the History of Congress*, ed. D. Brady and M. D. McCubbins. Stanford, CA: Stanford University Press.

LA FOLLETTE, JR., R. M. 1943. A Senator Looks at Congress. *The Atlantic Monthly*, 174 (July), 91–6.

LELOUP, L. T., GRAHAM, B. L., and BARWICK, S. 1987. Deficit Politics and Constitutional Government: The Impact of Gramm-Rudman-Hollings. *Public Budgeting & Finance*, 7(1): 83–103.

LUCE, R. 1926. *Congress: An Explanation*. Cambridge, MA: Harvard University Press.

—— 1932. Petty Business in Congress. *American Political Science Review*, 26: 815–28.

—— 1935. *Legislative Problems: Development, Status, and Trend of the Treatment and Exercise of Lawmaking Powers*. Boston: Houghton Mifflin.

MANN, T. E. 1995. Renewing Congress: A Report from the Front Lines, pp. 174–85 in *Remaking Congress: Change and Stability in the 1990s*, ed. J. A. Thurber and R. H. Davidson. Washington, DC: Congressional Quarterly.

—— and ORNSTEIN, N. J. 2006. *The Broken Branch: How Congress is Failing America and How To Get It Back On Track*. New York: Oxford University Press.

MAYHEW, D. R. 2009. Is Congress 'The Broken Branch'? *Boston University Law Review*, 89: 357–69.

McCONACHIE, L. G. 1898. *Congressional Committees: A Study of the Origins and Development of our National and Local Legislative Methods*. New York: Crowell.

MILLETT, J. D., and ROGERS, L. 1941. The Legislative Veto and the Reorganization Act of 1939. *Public Administration Review*, 1(2): 176–89.

MUNSELLE, W. G. 1978. Presidential Impoundment and Congressional Reform, pp. 9–22 in *Legislative Reform: The Policy Impact*, ed. L. N. Rieselbach. Lexington, MA: Lexington Books.

OLESZEK, W. J. 1977. A Perspective on Congressional Reform, pp. 3–10 in *Legislative Reform and Public Policy*, ed. S. Welch and J. G. Peters. New York: Praeger.

ORNSTEIN, N. J. 1975b. Causes and Consequences of Congressional Change: Subcommittee Reforms in the House of Representatives, 1970–73, pp. 88–114 in *Congress In Change: Evolution and Reform*, ed. N. J. Ornstein. New York: Praeger Publishers.

——and MANN, T. E. 1992. *Renewing Congress: A First Report*. Washington, DC: Brookings Institution Press.

————1993. *Renewing Congress: A Second Report*. Washington, DC: Brookings Institution Press.

——and ROHDE, D. W. 1977. Revolt From Within: Congressional Change, Legislative Policy, and the House Commerce Committee, pp. 54–72 in *Legislative Reform and Public Policy*, ed. S. Welch and J. G. Peters. New York: Praeger.

OUTLAND, G. E. 1945. We Must Modernize Congress. *Reader's Digest*.

PARRIS, J. H. 1979. The Senate Reorganizes Its Committees, 1977. *Political Science Quarterly*, 94: 319–37.

PEABODY, R. L. 1963b. The Enlarged Rules Committee, pp. 129–64 in *New Perspectives on the House of Representatives*, ed. R. L. Peabody and N. W. Polsby. Chicago: Rand McNally.

——1969. Research on Congress: A Coming of Age, pp. 3–73 in *Congress: Two Decades of Analysis*, ed. R. L. Peabody and R. K. Huitt. New York: Harper & Row.

PERKINS, J. 1944. Congressional Self-Improvement. *American Political Science Review*, 38: 499–511.

POLSBY, N. W. 1968. The Institutionalization of the House of Representatives. *American Political Science Review*, 63: 144–68.

——2004. *How Congress Evolves: Social Bases of Institutional Change*. New York: Oxford University Press.

POLSBY, N. W., and SCHICKLER, E. 2002. Landmarks in the Study of Congress Since 1945. *Annual Review of Political Science*, 5(1): 333–67.

PRICE, D. E. 1974. Review: The Ambivalence of Congressional Reform. *Public Administration Review*, 34(6): 601–08.

——1978. The Impact of Reform: The House Commerce Subcommittee on Oversight and Investigations, pp. 133–58 in *Legislative Reform: The Policy Impact*, ed. L. N. Rieselbach. Lexington, MA: Lexington Books.

PUTNAM, H. 1915. Legislative Reference for Congress. *The American Political Science Review*, 9(3): 542–9.

QUIRK, P. J. 1992. Structures and Performance: An Evaluation, pp. 303–24 in *The Postreform Congress*, ed. R. H. Davidson. New York: St. Martin's Press.

RIESELBACH, L. N. 1977. *Congressional Reform in the Seventies*. Morristown, NJ: General Learning Press.

——1994. *Congressional Reform: The Changing Modern Congress*. Washington, DC: Congressional Quarterly.

RITCHIE, D. A. 2001. Twentieth-century Senate Reform: The View from the Inside, pp. 13–46 in *The Contentious Senate*, ed. C. C. Campbell and N. C. Rae. Lanham, MD: Rowman and Littlefield.

ROBERTS, J. M., and SMITH, S. S. 2007. The Evolution of Agenda-Setting Institutions in Congress: Path Dependency in House and Senate Institutional Development, pp. 182–204 in *Party, Process, and Political Change in Congress: Further New Perspectives on the History of Congress*, ed. D. Brady and M. D. McCubbins. Stanford, CA: Stanford University Press.

ROGERS, L. 1921. Notes on Procedure. *The American Political Science Review*, 15(3): 372–9.

——1926. *The American Senate*. New York: Alfred A. Knopf.

——1941. The Staffing of Congress. *Political Science Quarterly*, 56(1): 1–22.

——1968. *The American Senate*. New York: Johnson Reprints.

ROHDE, D. W. 1991. *Parties and Leaders in the Postreform House*. Chicago: University of Chicago.

—— and SHEPSLE, K. A. 1978. Thinking About Legislative Reform, pp. 9–22 in *Legislative Reform: The Policy Impact*, ed. L. N. Rieselbach. Lexington, MA: Lexington Books.

ROHDE, D. W. 1974. Committee Reform in the House of Representatives and the Subcommittee Bill of Rights. *The ANNALS of the American Academy of Political and Social Science*, 411(1): 39–47.

RUDDER, C. 1978. The Policy Impact of Reform of the Committee on Ways and Means, pp. 73–90 in *Legislative Reform: The Policy Impact*, ed. L. Rieselbach. Lexington, MA: Lexington Books.

SCHICK, A. 1973. Budget Reform Legislation: Reorganizing Congressional Centers of Fiscal Power. *Harvard Journal of Legislation*, 11: 303–50.

SCHICKLER, E. 2000. Institutional Change in the House of Representatives, 1867–1998: A Test of Partisan and Ideological Power Balance Models. *American Political Science Review*, 94: 269–88.

—— 2001. *Disjointed Pluralism: Institutional Innovation and the Development of the U.S. Congress*. Princeton: Princeton University Press.

—— 2005. Institutional Development of Congress, pp. 35–62 in *The Legislative Branch*, New York: Oxford University Press.

—— McGHEE, E., and SIDES, J. 2003. Remaking the House and Senate: Personal Power, Ideology, and the 1970s Reforms. *Legislative Studies Quarterly*, 28(3): 297–331.

—— and RICH, A. 1997. Controlling the Floor: Parties as Procedural Coalitions in the House. *American Journal of Political Science*, 41: 1340–75.

—— and SIDES, J. 2000. Intergenerational Warfare: The Senate Decentralizes Appropriations. *Legislative Studies Quarterly*, 25(4): 551–75.

SELECT COMMITTEE ON COMMITTEES. 1973. *Committee Organization in the House: Panel Discussions Before the Select Committee on Committees*. Washington, DC: U.S. Government Printing Office.

SHAW, M. 1981. Congress in the 1970s: A Decade of Reform. *Parliamentary Affairs*, 34: 253–90.

SHEPPARD, B. D. 1985. *Rethinking Congressional Reform: The Reform Roots of the Special Interest Congress*. Cambridge, MA: Schenkman Books.

SHEPSLE, K. A. 1978. *The Giant Jigsaw Puzzle*. Chicago: University of Chicago Press.

—— 1989. The Changing Textbook Congress, pp. 238–66 in *Can The Government Govern?*, ed. J. Chubb and P. Peterson. Washington, DC: Brookings Institution.

—— 2009. Dysfunctional Congress. *Boston University Law Review*, 89: 371.

SINCLAIR, B. 1989. *The Transformation of the U.S. Senate*. Baltimore, MD: Johns Hopkins University Press.

—— 1992. The Emergence of Strong Leadership in the 1980s House of Representatives. *The Journal of Politics*, 54(3): 657–84.

—— 2004. Congressional Reform, pp. 625–37 in *The American Congress: The Building of Democracy*, ed. J. E. Zelizer. New York: Houghton Mifflin.

—— 2009. Question: What's Wrong with Congress—Answer: It's a Democratic Legislature. *Boston University Law Review*, 89: 387.

SMITH, S. S. 1989. *Call to Order: Floor Politics in the House and Senate*. Illustrated edition. Washington, DC: Brookings Institution Press.

STANGA, J. E., and FARNSWORTH, D. N. 1978. Seniority and Democratic Reforms in the House of Representatives: Committees and Subcommittees, pp. 9–22 in *Legislative Reform: The Policy Impact*, ed. L. N. Rieselbach. Lexington, MA: Lexington Books.

STEWART, C. H. 1987. Does Structure Matter? The Effects of Structural Change on Spending Decisions in the House, 1871 to 1922. *American Journal of Political Science*, 31: 584–605.

—— 1988. Budget Reform as Strategic Legislative Action: An Exploration. *Journal of Politics*, 50: 292–321.

—— 1989. *Budget Reform Politics: The Design of Appropriations Process in the House of Representatives, 1865–1921.* New York: Cambridge University Press.

STRAHAN, R. 1990. *New Ways and Means: Reform and Change in a Congressional Committee.* Chapel Hill, NC: University of North Carolina Press.

SUNDQUIST, J. L. 1981. *The Decline and Resurgence of Congress.* Washington, DC: Brookings Institution.

THURBER, J. A. 1976. Congressional Budget Reform and New Demands for Policy Analysis. *Policy Analysis,* 2: 198–214.

—— 1978. New Powers of the Purse: An Assessment of Congressional Budget Reform, pp. 9–22 in *Legislative Reform: The Policy Impact,* ed. L. N. Rieselbach. Lexington, MA: Lexington Books.

—— 1992. New Rules for an Old Game: Zero-Sum Budgeting in the Postreform Congress, pp. 257–78 in *The Postreform Congress,* ed. R. H. Davidson. New York: St. Martin's Press.

THURBER, J. A., and DAVIDSON, R. H. (eds.) 1995. *Remaking Congress: Change and Stability in the 1990s.* Washington, DC: Congressional Quarterly.

TRUMAN, D. B., ed. 1965. *The Congress and America's Future.* Englewood Cliffs, NJ: Prentice-Hall.

—— 1965. The Prospects for Change, pp. 52–76 in *The Congress and America's Future,* ed. D. B. Truman. Englewood Cliffs, NJ: Prentice-Hall.

WAWRO, G. J., and SCHICKLER, E. 2006. *Filibuster: Obstruction and Lawmaking in the U.S. Senate.* Princeton, NJ: Princeton University Press.

—— —— 2007. Cloture Reform Reconsidered, pp. 226–48 in *Party, Process, and Political Change in Congress: Further New Perspectives on the History of Congress,* ed. D. Brady and M. D. McCubbins. Stanford, CA: Stanford University Press.

WILDAVSKY, A. 1966. Toward a Radical Incrementalism, pp. 115–65 in *Congress: The First Branch,* ed. A. de Grazia. Washington, DC: American Enterprise Institute.

WILLOUGHBY, W. F. 1934. *Principles of Legislative Organization and Administration.* Washington, DC: Brookings Institution.

WOLFENSBERGER, D. R. 2007. The Motion to Recommit in the House: The Creation, Evisceration, and Restoration of a Minority Right, pp. 271–95 in *Party, Process, and Political Change in Congress: Further New Perspectives on the History of Congress,* ed. D. W. Brady and M. D. McCubbins. Stanford, CA: Stanford University Press.

YOUNG, G., and COOPER, J. 1993. Multiple Referral and the Transformation of House Decision Making, pp. 211–34 in *Congress Reconsidered.* Washington, DC: Congressional Quarterly.

YOUNG, R. 1943. *This is Congress.* New York: A. A. Knopf.

ZELIZER, J. E. 2004. *On Capitol Hill: The Struggle to Reform Congress and its Consequences, 1948–2000.* New York: Cambridge University Press.

....

CHAPTER 22

THE CONGRESSIONAL BUDGET PROCESS

....

JOHN B. GILMOUR

THE congressional budget process is the set of formal procedures and rules, as well as informal practices, that structure action by the United States Congress on budgetary issues. There are at least two important senses in which people use the term: one sense relates to the entirety of congressional process relative to the budget; another may refer more restrictively to the formal congressional budget process centering on the adoption of a budget resolution that was created in 1974 by the enactment of the Congressional Budget and Impoundment Control Act. This chapter will have two somewhat distinct purposes: first, to explain what the congressional budget process is, how it works and how it developed, and, second, to explore the scholarship of the budget process and the crucial intellectual debates that have formed around the study of congressional budgeting. The congressional budget process is extraordinarily complicated and confusing, especially compared with the streamlined legislative budget adoptions found in parliamentary political systems. In Great Britain, the executive branch of the government proposes the budget, which is adopted unchanged the same day by the House of Commons (Rogers, Walters, and Walters 2006). By contrast, congressional adoption of the budget stretches over nine months—sometimes more—and involves literally hundreds of separate decisions in committee and on the floor in the House and Senate. The United States Congress always makes important changes to the budget proposed by the president. Furthermore, the congressional budget process (the reconciliation process in particular) is the means by which many of the most important laws of the past thirty years have been enacted. President Ronald

Reagan's tax and spending cuts in 1981, massive deficit reduction bills in 1990 and 1993, President George W. Bush's tax cuts in 2001 and 2003, and President Barack Obama's healthcare reform in 2010 were adopted by means of the reconciliation procedure, a key element of the congressional budget process. Understanding the congressional budget process is thus important in understanding the legislative process more generally.

Explaining what constitutes the federal budget is a more complicated question than it might appear on the surface. In the language of Washington, DC, when people speak of "the budget" they are often referring to the president's budget, a massive document issued annually, in early February, that lays out the president's comprehensive recommendation for federal budget policy. The president's budget lays out recommended funding levels for every federal program, and also details a plan for funding government activities. It also incorporates nearly all policy changes the president wants Congress to pass (and assumes that Congress will pass all of them) and thus represents the clearest statement of presidential priorities. An irony of the president's budget is that, although producing it is a mammoth effort, it is only a recommendation; its impact is the influence it has on Congress as Congress makes decisions on the budget.[1]

References to the budget can also mean the Congressional Budget Resolution, a document that should be adopted each year by both chambers of Congress, and which constitutes a comprehensive statement of what Congress wants spending and tax policy to be in a fiscal year, although it is vastly less detailed than the president's budget.

Finally, when people speak of the budget, they may be referring to the entire complex of budget policies that emerge from the enactment of appropriations bills, tax bills, and entitlement changes—that is, the overall budget policy of the U.S. government. It is important to bear in mind that this latter notion of the budget is one that is never acted upon or adopted by Congress. Rather, it is the sum of numerous other actions that have an impact on spending and revenue.

The process of adopting a budget by Congress never unfolds in the same way twice, and in some years key features of the process are often ignored. Sometimes supposedly required elements of the process are adopted absurdly late or not at all. Sometimes appropriations are adopted in twelve or thirteen separate bills, and sometimes they are adopted in a single omnibus. Sometimes (rarely) appropriations are adopted on time, before a new fiscal year begins, but more commonly they are adopted late. On occasion, appropriations bills have not been passed until more than half of a fiscal year has gone by. Charles Tiefer (1989) wondered if, given the frequency with which congressional procedure more generally is violated or ignored, we can really say that there is such a thing as "congressional procedure." The same can be asked of congressional budget procedure. If a process is ignored or violated as much or more than it is adhered to, perhaps there really is no congressional budget process. Irene Rubin (2007) suggests that since 2001 the budget process has "unraveled" as deadlines

---

[1] Robert Keith (2008b) provides a valuable, brief summary of the entire congressional budget process.

and requirements have been ignored, and appropriations have been adopted woefully late. If one demands of a "process" that it be highly standardized and similar from year to year, then clearly there is no congressional budget process. A more useful way of thinking about the congressional budget process may be to see it as a collection of tools that can be employed by majorities in the House and the Senate when useful. Elements of the congressional budget process that are not helpful can be and are ignored until the day comes when they can help to solve a problem.

This suggests a way of thinking about the congressional budget process that will guide much of this chapter. The budget process was created by members of Congress to help solve problems with budget policy. It does not exist as a freestanding, self-enforcing entity, independent of congressional wishes.[2] It is a servant of the congressional majority. When the process does not serve interests of the congressional majority, it will not be used, but when the procedures that comprise the congressional budget process are useful to the majority, they will be used, sometimes with far-reaching impact. Furthermore, they will be used in ways unanticipated by their designers and creators, as the current generation of senators and representatives seeks ways of bending existing rules to their purposes.

The budget is controversial in the United States and probably in every other democratic government because it is governed by a peculiar politically charged math. Deficits are unpopular because they are associated with excessive government and fiscal mismanagement (Savage 1990). But the only way to reduce or eliminate a deficit is to cut spending or to increase taxes. Spending is popular and wins friends among voters, and tax increases are unpopular while tax cuts are favored by voters. Unfortunately for politicians, it is impossible to reduce deficits without invoking anger among some voters. Conversely, the actions that politicians undertake to ingratiate themselves with voters typically make the deficit worse. There is no simple solution to this dilemma.

In states in the U.S. and in other nations, the budget is normally adopted as a single measure. The U.S. Congress, by contrast, adopts its budget piecemeal, and never adopts the president's budget as submitted. Perhaps the single most important thing to know about the congressional budget process is that instead of adopting a single measure that implements the budget, Congress instead adopts the budget through a series of individual appropriations bills and separate bills to make changes in tax law and other bills to make changes in entitlement programs. The sum of these separately adopted measures is the actual budget of the United States. The budget of the U.S. government consists of three distinct components, each of which requires fundamentally different tools to control. The three are: appropriations, which are twelve bills passed each year to fund government operations; entitlements, which are programs that mostly provide government payments to individuals; and revenue, which means mostly taxes, but other sources as well. The complexity of budget policy

---

[2] Exceptions to this generalization include Gramm-Rudman-Hollings (GRH) and the Budget Enforcement Act (BEA), both of which sought to create external enforcement devices. GRH was a failure, but the BEA had some success, although there were always ways around it.

is part of why the congressional budget process is so complex (Schick and LoStracco 2007).

Passing the budget in multiple pieces reflects the decentralized structure of Congress (Schick and LoStracco 2007). A fractured budget apportions power to multiple committees, and keeps any one committee from becoming overly powerful with centralized control over budget policy. In 1950, the House Appropriations Committee experimented with passing all appropriations in a single measure, but House members were displeased with the result because it gave the Appropriations Committee too much power, and quickly abandoned the practice (Nelson 1953).

Micro- and macro-budgeting

Micro-budgeting, also known as bottom-up budgeting, is a way of making budgets that focuses attention on the details and the parts of the budget. It is a kind of budgeting that forms a budget based on preferences about spending levels on individual programs. The spending total is the function of choices on the parts. Macro-budgeting, also known as top-down budgeting, is a budgeting style that focuses attention on budgetary aggregates such as the total amount of spending, the total amount of revenue, and the size of the deficit or surplus. Spending on individual programs must be trimmed to fit within a pre-determined total. Both macro- and micro-budgeting perspectives make sense to a degree and are important, but individual preferences on micro-budgeting and macro-budgeting are likely to be in conflict. That is, many or perhaps most members of Congress will seek to increase spending on individual programs, especially spending that lands in their state or district, but they will also want to keep overall spending low, taxes low, and deficits small. While it is sensible for an individual to have these preferences, it is impossible for any budget to satisfy them all simultaneously. The committees of Congress, both authorizing committees and the appropriations committees, have jurisdictions defined in micro-budgeting terms. That is, they look at programs and their funding needs, and only the Budget Committees have macro-budgetary issues as part of their jurisdiction. (LeLoup 2005).

Congress's decentralized structure makes it better equipped to engage in micro-budgeting than macro-budgeting. The practice of dividing power over budgetary issues among multiple committees is a product of the dispersed power in the U.S. Congress, which in turn reflects the larger U.S. political system, in which individual members of Congress are largely responsible for their own reelection (Schick and LoStracco 2007). Members of Congress are concerned with national policy issues but they must also be very local in their orientation. In addition, the electoral incentives of Congress incline its members far more toward micro-budgeting. Members of Congress can claim credit for benefits they gain for their constituents in the form of spending or tax breaks, but it is difficult to claim credit for a public good such as a balanced budget (Mayhew 1974). It is similarly difficult for an electoral opponent to pin responsibility for a budget deficit on a single member of Congress.

The history of congressional budgeting since 1974 has been a series of efforts to graft onto the fragmented, micro-oriented congressional budgeting system a set of procedures that allow members of Congress to have a greater ability to control the macro aspects of budgeting. This is difficult because at any time, members want to be able to spend money on their constituents and popular programs, cut taxes, and avoid deficits. Satisfying all these goals simultaneously is impossible under normal circumstances. A purpose of any budget process must be to manage these conflicting desires and produce a balance among them that members find acceptable.

The challenge of congressional budgeting is to give "proper" weight simultaneously to members' preferences over the parts of the budget and their preferences over the total. This is closely related to the problem of Ulysses and the sirens as discussed by Elster (1985), and the problem of "self-command" as discussed by Schelling (1984), wherein individuals struggle to give weight to one set of preferences over another, and find that in order to succeed they must adopt some form of artificial or external restraint on their choices. A long-standing, decentralized, congressional process focused entirely on appropriations and tax legislation managed to achieve a reasonable balance among competing preferences for many decades, until it began to fail in the late 1960s (see discussion below). Following the failure of the established process, Congress entered a period of experimentation with budget process that lasted from 1974, with the passage of the Congressional Budget Act in 1974 through the multiple enactments of the Budget Enforcement Act in the 1990s. All of these were efforts, of varying success, to manage preferences and give higher priority to macro-budgetary goals.

An increased emphasis on macro-budgeting is the result of a number of problems. One was the recognition that government budgets in the United States and elsewhere were growing significantly faster than the economy, and that this trend could not continue forever. Another was the increased importance of the budget as a part of economic management. The increased attention to the macro-budget has occurred not just in the United States, but also across nearly all the wealthy nations of North America and Europe (Schick 2003). An emphasis on macro-budgeting tends to shift power from Congress to the White House since the fragmentation of Congress makes it more proficient at micro-budgeting (Schick 1994, 105).

THE GEOLOGY OF THE CONGRESSIONAL BUDGET PROCESS

The budget process of Congress consists of an accretion of procedures that have built up over time, one over another. When a problem arises in congressional budgeting such that the existing procedures consistently deliver a product senators and representatives dislike, Congress reacts in a somewhat volcanic way, shooting up new procedures that settle atop the old procedures without removing them. The collection of new and old process resemble geologic strata, with older parts of the congressional process remaining substantially intact and unchanged by the addition of newer layers of process. In examining the addition of new budget procedures over time, it is important to pay attention to the stresses in Congress that led to the eruption of each new procedural wrinkle. Each new layer exists because it helped members of Congress solve a problem that existing procedures dealt with inadequately.

The two oldest strata of the congressional budgeting system are the appropriations process and the tax process. The power to appropriate, which derives directly from the Constitution, is the core congressional power and arguably the one upon which much other congressional power rests.[3] Congressional handling of appropriations has varied considerably over time. The House Ways and Means Committee was created as a standing committee in 1801, and was given jurisdiction over both appropriations and revenue legislation. This broad power continued until 1865 when a separate Appropriations Committee was created, thus splitting control over spending and taxing. For a time in the late nineteenth century, the appropriations power was in part stripped away from the House Appropriations Committee, and jurisdiction over authorizations and appropriations were merged in several committees (Stewart 1989). Then the appropriations power was subsequently unified again in the Appropriations Committee (see Schickler, Chapter 31, this volume).

Appropriations are laws passed each year that allocate funding to programs, agencies, and departments in the executive branch, as well as to fund Congress and the judiciary. Appropriations bills when passed and signed create *budget authority*, which gives agencies the authority to spend money (Fisher 1979; Rubin 1988; Streeter 2008). When the money is actually spent or obligated, it becomes an *outlay*. There are currently twelve appropriations bills, although the number varies. Appropriations generally fund the purchase of goods and services through the use of *obligations*, which are contracts or other financial commitments to pay for goods or services. Practically all normal government operations are funded out of appropriations, such as salaries of government employees, office supplies, defense weapons systems, NIH grants, lighting the White House Christmas tree, and so on (Stith 1988).

Appropriations allocate money, but do not create or design programs, which is the purpose of a separate process called "authorizations." Before a program or agency can receive an appropriation, it must first be authorized. Authorizations are the province of the other standing committees of Congress, such as Agriculture, Interior, Financial Services, and so on. The rules of the House prohibit "legislating on an appropriations

---

[3] *U.S. Constitution*, Article 1, Section 9 reads: "No Money shall be drawn from the Treasury, but in Consequence of Appropriations made by Law." Arguably, congressional power over war now rests more on the appropriations power than on the "declare war" provision of Article 1. In *Campbell v. Clinton*, the circuit court declared that members of Congress lacked standing to enforce the declare war provision, unless Congress' power had been "totally negated." This has been understood to mean that Congress must use its power of the purse if it wants to stop a war (Fisher 2004).

bill," a restriction designed to prevent the appropriations committees from taking over the entire legislative business of Congress (Fisher 1979; Rubin 1988; Streeter 2008).

Nearly all appropriations have a fixed duration of a few years at most, a restriction that has important ramifications for budget politics. The overwhelming majority of appropriations are spent (and become outlays) in the year in which they are passed. Some budget authority from one fiscal year will carry over into a second year, or even further into the future, although defense appropriations are constitutionally limited to no more than two years. When appropriations lapse at the end of a fiscal year, agencies are not allowed to spend any more until new appropriations are passed. This is implied by the Constitution and explicitly required by the Anti-Deficiency Act,[4] which dates from the nineteenth century. If appropriations are not passed, agencies must shut down until the appropriations bill or a continuing resolution is passed. A key feature of the politics of appropriations is that government shutdowns result when appropriations do not pass on time. Memorable shutdowns occurred in 1990, the result of a showdown between a Democratic Congress and President George H. W. Bush, and in 1995–96, the result of a titanic battle between the Republican Congress and President Clinton (Stith 1988; Streeter 2008).

Membership on the House Appropriations Committee is one of the most sought-after committee assignments in the House. Members of the committee exercise power because they have the power to decide spending levels of federal programs. They are able to promote their reelection by directing spending toward their districts. Furthermore, they have the power to do favors for colleagues in the House by directing projects toward their districts. Because there is so much demand for Appropriations appointments, freshmen representatives are seldom appointed to the committee (Fenno 1973; Savage 1991).

The appropriations process has long been characterized as a quasi-adversarial process with "claimants" and "guardians" (Wildavsky 1964; Fenno 1966). The claimants include the agencies and programs themselves, who naturally always believe they can use more money effectively. Within Congress, the principal claimants are the authorizing committees, which tend to be well stocked with representatives and senators from states and districts that have an important constituency interest in the business of the committee. They often, although certainly not always, support increasing spending on programs in their committee jurisdictions. The principal guardians of the Treasury are the Office of Management and Budget (Berman 1979; Mosher 1986; Schick and LoStracco 2007; Tomkin 1998), which has an institutional mission of pushing back against demands for more spending by agencies, and the appropriations committees in Congress.

The revenue process bears an important resemblance to the spending process in that much of its work consists of enacting special tax provisions that exempt particular categories of income from taxation. The distribution of these provisions is a variant of pork barrel politics that should be logically seen as a kind of spending.

---

[4] (31 U.S. Code 1341).

Hence, special tax provisions are known as "tax expenditures" (Surrey 1980; Witte 1986; Howard 1999). The power to tax also derives from the Constitution. The Ways and Means Committee in the House and its Senate counterpart, the Finance Committee, have long been among the most powerful committees in Congress, and consequently positions on these committees have been keenly sought by members (Manley 1970; Strahan 1990).

The next stage in the development of the congressional budget process actually occurred in the executive branch, with the creation of the executive budget process by means of the Budget and Accounting Act of 1921. This law created a unified executive budget and an executive budget agency, the Bureau of the Budget (later the Office of Management and Budget). Previously, executive agencies submitted budget requests directly to Congress. The submission of the president's budget each year has had a great influence on Congress since it puts all of the pieces of the budget together in a coherent whole. The appropriations committees use the president's budget as a starting point for their deliberations, and always compare their spending levels to those in the president's budget. Between 1921 and 1974, the president's budget was the chief unifying force in an otherwise highly fragmented process. Despite its influence, Congress was in no way obliged to follow or in any way respect the totals or the items in the president's budget. A detailed examination of the executive budget process is unnecessary here, but it is useful to point out that in general the agencies and department submit requests to OMB, which tends to reduce them. OMB is responsible for assembling a complete budget request consistent with the president's overall budget and policy guidelines. Budget requests by the agencies are mediated by OMB, so Congress never sees the original budget requests from agencies, only the final amount in the president's budget. Agency officials are required to defend before Congress whatever level of spending OMB has recommended for it, even when it is less than the agency has requested. The creation of the executive budget reduced congressional power to some extent by depriving it of some information. It increased the president's power over the budget, but added no complexity to the congressional process.

THE CONGRESSIONAL BUDGET ACT

Until the enactment of the Congressional Budget Process in 1974 there was no formal coordination between the separate revenue and appropriations processes. Each of these processes proceeded independently on its own track and timetable, and there was no mechanism to ensure that the plans of the taxing committees were consistent with the plans of the spending committees.

From 1921 to 1974 the structure of the congressional budget process consisted of the appropriating and taxing committees, and was remarkably stable. The system succeeded by a couple of measures. First, even though deficits were common through this era, the magnitude of deficits remained moderate and politically acceptable. Second, the system managed conflict and kept the budget from becoming overly contentious. By the mid-1960s forces were at work that would undermine these long-standing arrangements. Budget deficits grew to unacceptable levels, and conflict increased.

The rise of entitlement spending, beginning with the passage of the Social Security Act in 1935 (Witte 1962), contributed importantly to the decline of the traditional, appropriations-centered budget process. Like other developments in budgetary process, entitlements did not replace any existing process; they only added a new geological wrinkle. Entitlement programs represent an alternative to appropriations as a means of spending money. Entitlements are different from appropriations in that they are usually open-ended with respect to the total amount of spending, and usually remain as is until changed by a new law. They are called entitlements because individuals are entitled to benefits under law. The total amount of spending is determined by the number of people who qualify for benefits and the level of benefits to which they are entitled. No one either in Congress or the executive branch decides how much money will be spent on entitlements—they are the opposite of budgeting in that the level of spending is determined by conditions such as the economy and health costs that are beyond the control of the government. Entitlements grow in cost as the number of participants grows, as cost of living adjustments raise benefits, or as healthcare costs rise.

Costs of entitlement programs rose steadily but not rapidly until 1965, when costs began to rise more quickly with the enactment of Medicare and Medicaid (Weaver 1989; White 1999; Marmor 2000). Figure 22.1 shows the growth of payments to individuals since 1952. Following the enactment of Medicare and Medicaid, a seemingly inexorable increase began.

A key feature of the politics of entitlements is that they continue unchanged, and often becoming ever more expensive, until a new law is passed making changes.[5] With appropriations, the overall bias of the political system toward slowness and inaction works to stop spending, since with no new legislation there is no more spending, but it is just the opposite with entitlements. The difficulty of passing legislation means entitlement programs will continue as before, often increasing in cost (Weaver 1989).

The next major seismic event in the accumulation of congressional budgeting procedures was the enactment of the Congressional Budget and Impoundment Control Act of 1974. This landmark law did not seek to supplant any previously existing process: its purpose was to create a structure for coordinating actions that had previously been carried on as distinct processes. The immediate impetus for the adoption of the Congressional Budget Act was the failure of Congress in the preceding years

---

[5] An important exception to many generalizations about entitlements is the State Children's Health Insurance Program (S-CHIP), which was first enacted in 1997. It was limited in the amount of money that could be spent on it, and it sunset after ten years. It was subsequently reauthorized.

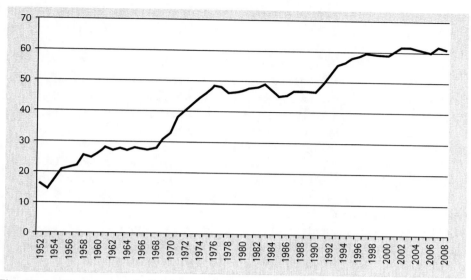

Fig. 22.1. Payments to individuals as a percentage of total outlays, 1952–2008

to exercise effective control over the budget. Schick (1980) calls this the "seven year budget war." The deficit rose higher than Congress believed proper, yet Congress found itself incapable of fixing the problem. For several years in the Johnson Administration, Congress passed laws giving Johnson the power to cut spending to reduce deficits, even though Johnson did not seek this power. This abdication of power was an extraordinary recognition by Congress that it was not managing the power of the purse. After the inauguration of Nixon in 1969, the Democratic Congress could no longer trust the president, a Republican, to cut budgets, but Congress did not step up and reduce deficits. So Nixon embarked on a campaign of impoundments, refusing to allow departments to spend money appropriated by Congress. (Fisher 1975, 2000; Pfiffner 1979; Schick 1980)

Why did the decentralized process that had worked well for decades begin to fail in the mid- and late 1960s? The most important cause of the failure of the old decentralized process was the rise of entitlement programs. With the enactment of Medicare and Medicaid in 1965, entitlements spending comprised an ever-rising portion of total federal spending, and the Appropriations Committees had no control over their spending levels. Many of the entitlements were given automatic inflation adjustments, which tended to increase their rate of increase (Weaver 1989; White 1999). Appropriations constituted a shrinking share of total spending, which meant that restraining appropriations, formerly a good means of controlling deficits, had less impact than before. Schick (1994) documents the gradual dispersion of spending authority in Congress over the course of the twentieth century, a trend that left the Appropriations Committees with a severely diminished jurisdiction, and similarly limited ability to control overall spending levels.

The challenge for Congress in devising the Congressional Budget Act was to come up with a new process that would allow some degree of coordination of separate processes that had formerly been entirely separate.

The Congressional Budget Act was a complex piece of legislation that had a number of important elements. It created new Budget Committees in the House and Senate. These committees had jurisdiction only over budget process issues, but no legislative jurisdiction. The Act created the Congressional Budget Office, giving Congress for the first time a professional budget staff, thus reducing its reliance on the executive branch for budget information (Ippolito 1981).

The centerpiece of the congressional budget process is the adoption of a budget resolution. The budget resolution allowed Congress for the first time ever to adopt a comprehensive statement of what the overall shape of the budget should be. A budget resolution is passed in the form of a concurrent resolution, meaning that it is passed by the House and Senate in identical version, but not submitted to the president for a signature. In short, it is not a law. It is a purely congressional document, intended to provide guidance and structure congressional action on the budget.

A decision that the deficit will be a certain amount in a given fiscal year means nothing unless there is some means of translating macro goals into specific spending and taxing policies that are consistent with the overall targets (Primo 2007). Thus the process also contains specific means of translating macro-targets into the decisions at the level of appropriations bills, entitlement legislation, and tax legislation. The key test of the budget process would be the ability to ensure that the macro targets were not merely aspirational goals that had no impact on the specifics of actual budget policy.

In its essence, a budget resolution is a simple document. It states what the desired levels of spending, revenue, deficit, and debt are for a period of up to ten years. It also contains a breakdown of the total amount of spending into functions such as health, national defense, international affairs, agriculture, transportation, and so on. The purpose of budget functions is to allow political decision-makers the opportunity to compare and prioritize the broad programmatic operations of the government, rather than simply examine programs and budgets on a lint-item basis. The functions correspond to OMB accounts, not congressional committee juris-dictions. The budget resolution can also contain a variety of additional provisions concerning enforcement, and they often contain extraneous "sense of the Senate language" that can be longer than the rest of the budget resolution. The spending on the different functions cannot add up to more than the total amount of spending in the resolution. And the deficit must equal the difference between revenue and spending. Thus the budget resolution involves difficult choices and complex tradeoffs between competing values in budgeting. This makes budget resolutions controversial and difficult to pass. Often resolutions pass late. There have been several years in which the intractability of the problem led Congress not to pass a budget resolu-tion at all. This is an indication that budget resolutions are seen as consequential documents.

Successful implementation of the guidelines in the resolution requires that subsequent congressional action on budget-related legislation be consistent with the plan. "Coordination" of action in Congress is never easy to achieve because it means subordinating the aspirations of committees and individual members to a plan endorsed by the majority. Enforcement is crucial to make the budget process meaningful, but everything about the decentralized structure of Congress makes enforcement difficult. The key to successful enforcement is having means tailored to the unique circumstances of appropriations, entitlements, and revenue.

Initially, the budget process contained better means of controlling appropriations than entitlements. When the budget resolution passes, the Appropriations Committees in the House and Senate receive a sum that they are allowed to spend. They divide this very large amount of money among their subcommittees, a process known as a 302(b) allocation. Once adopted, the 302(b) for each Appropriations subcommittee acts as a ceiling for each of the bills. A bill exceeding its 302(b) can be blocked on the floor by a point of order (Saturno 2008). On many occasions, the ceiling is inconvenient and discarded by adopting a waiver through a special rule from the Rules Committee. But if Congress disregards the 302(b) and "breaks the budget," it does so knowing what it is doing. Prior to the Budget Act, Congress had trouble knowing the impact of spending decisions on the overall budget. Hixon and Marshall (2002) have shown that waivers of Budget Act rules are a large part of the total number of rules waivers granted in the House of Representatives. Examining four congresses in the 1980s and 1990s, they find that Budget Act waivers constitute between 38 percent and 18 percent of all waivers granted on bills and substitute amendments. Having a process that allows members to enforce macro budgetary decisions at the level of appropriations bills does not mean they will choose to use it.

Much of the force of the budget process is informational: when members of Congress vote on appropriations, they will know whether the specific measure before them fits within the adopted budget and its impact on the deficit. They can vote for "budget-busting" measures, but at least they will know that is what they are doing. Prior to the Budget Act, there was no way of knowing with certainty how individual bills related to an overall budget policy. Knowing that a bill will increase the deficit beyond the target in the budget resolution is not a strong reed on which to rest the budget process.

The first several years of the congressional budget process were inauspicious. Although the exact purpose of the Budget Act was ambiguous, with conservatives asserting that it was to reduce spending and deficits, and liberals claiming it was to stop presidential impoundments, it was largely a failure in its first years by any measure. It did not reduce deficits. Some critics believed that it actually resulted in increased rather than decreased spending and a diminished ability to pass appropriations on time. It did not control entitlement spending, which was a more important source of spending growth (Schick 1980; Fisher 1985). However, Geiger (1994) and Jones, Baumgartner, and True (1998) show that spending growth actually slowed somewhat following the passage of the Budget Act.

RECONCILIATION

Despite a slow start, the congressional budget process was rescued from possible futility by the next stage in the geologic growth of congressional budgeting: the rise of the reconciliation process. Reconciliation has emerged in the years since 1980 as by far the most important element of the budget process, one with the power to transform budget policy. "Reconciliation" is a procedure for "reconciling" entitlement and tax legislation with the overall targets in the budget resolution. It is an important part of an overall package of tools to enforce a budget resolution; without it there are only tools for enforcing the budget resolution against new legislation. Enforcement against entitlements is vital since spending on these programs can grow from year to year, causing the deficit to rise, without any action by Congress. Reconciliation was first used in 1980, the last year of the Carter administration, in a small way. The next year, under Reagan, the reconciliation process became the primary vehicle for driving Reagan's budget legislation through Congress. It has since been the vehicle for numerous deficit reduction bills—in 1981, 1982, 1990, 1993, 1997, to list only some (Schick 1990; White and Wildavsky 1989; Gilmour 1990). Reconciliation is a flexible tool. It has been used to require cuts in entitlements, increases in taxes, cuts in taxes, and cuts in the authorized levels of programs. In 1996 Republicans used the reconciliation process to pass welfare reform, and in 2010 Democrats used the process to pass parts of their healthcare reform package.

Reconciliation works as a two-stage process that greatly compresses the legislative process. First, reconciliation instructions are included in and passed as part of the budget resolution. The instructions tell different committees to produce legislation reducing deficits by specific amounts, and to send that legislation to the budget committee in their chamber. Second, the two budget committees package all the individual committee-produced bills into a single, sometimes massive, reconciliation bill that then goes to the chamber floor for consideration. Reconciliation is a means by which the congressional majority can pry loose from committees legislation to cut spending on entitlements that the committees would, under normal circumstances, be very reluctant to endorse.

By means of the reconciliation process, President Reagan and his energetic OMB Director, David Stockman, were able to get Congress to endorse and enact Reagan's budget policy, including tax cuts and spending reductions, nearly intact, even though the House was controlled by Democrats. Without the reconciliation process, passing the same package of dozens of spending cuts, spread across nearly all standing committees, would have required Republican victories in hundreds of votes in subcommittee, full committee, and on the floor. In the House in 1981 a coalition of conservative Democrats plus nearly all Republicans effectively gained control of the chamber despite nominal Democratic party control.

Reconciliation bills—like budget resolutions—are protected in the Senate against filibusters by a statutory limit on the time of debate. Thus, even controversial bills can pass by a bare majority vote, without the necessity of gathering sixty votes on a cloture vote to overcome a filibuster. Reconciliation serves as a legislative expressway. The normal veto points of the legislative process are enormously reduced in number and power if a bill is a reconciliation bill. Reconciliation thus serves not only as a means of passing deficit reductions, but also as a means of getting around obstruction in the Senate.

Because of the procedural compression it permits, reconciliation alters the balance of power in Congress. The winners include party leaders and the White House. The primary losers include committees and committee chairs. A fear at the beginning of the reconciliation process was that the Budget Committee would become very powerful at the expense of the other committees, but that has not occurred. The reconciliation process empowers who or whatever can mobilize congressional majorities behind packages of tax and spending changes. Mostly, reconciliation has served as a means of adopting a package of deficit reductions that have been agreed to at a summit negotiation between congressional party and committee leaders and representatives of the White House. These inter-branch negotiations became a prominent feature of politics in the 1980s and 1990s as Congress and the president struggled to deal with large deficits. Without the reconciliation process to help speed the agreements reached in these negotiations through Congress, there would have been little point even in having the negotiation. Committees must write the legislation that actually forms the reconciliation bill, but they serve more as agents of the summit negotiation than as principals (Gilmour 1990; White and Wildavsky 1989; Schick 1990).

Reconciliation does not necessarily serve the purpose of reducing deficits. The Byrd rule requires that all provisions of reconciliation bills be related to the budget (Keith 2008a), but there is no requirement that reconciliation bills cut spending or increase taxes. In 1981, 2001, and 2003, Congress used the reconciliation process to pass bills cutting taxes and increasing deficits.

The congressional budget process and reconciliation are procedural reforms that give a congressional majority the ability to do nearly anything they want to with the budget, including balancing it. However, there must be a majority ready to use these powerful tools. Through the 1980s there were unprecedentedly large budget deficits (given peacetime conditions), but there was no congressional majority in this period with the will to cut spending enough or raise taxes enough to balance the budget. This led to frustration with the purely procedural nature of the congressional budget process, and Congress began experimenting with outcome-oriented reforms.

OUTCOME-ORIENTED REFORMS

The first experiment with outcome-oriented budget reform was the enactment in 1985 of the Gramm-Rudman-Hollings (GRH) law that mandated a balanced budget in seven years. GRH established a binding schedule of equal annual deficit reductions that would lead to a balanced budget after seven years. If the annual target was not met, the General Accounting Office was to issue an order implementing proportional spending cuts (called sequesters) across the executive branch, large enough to satisfy the deficit reduction target. The purported goal behind GRH was to raise the specter of large, automatic cuts as a means of forcing Congress and the president to pass legislation satisfying the target. The automatic cuts would, it was hoped, be too damaging to valued programs to leave in place, encouraging negotiations to reduce deficits to meet the targets. Presumably, the reconciliation process would be used to implement the product of the negotiations (Stith 1988b; Gilmour 1990; White and Wildavsky 1989; Schier 1992). Hahm, Kamlet, and Mowery (1992) find that GRH tended to reduce defense spending to below what it would have been, according to their model, in the absence of the budget balancing law.

GRH never worked as intended and disappeared after several tumultuous years. The first problem to emerge was a successful legal challenge. The Supreme Court declared in *Synar v. Bowsher* 478 U.S. 714 (1986) that lodging the trigger for automatic cuts in the relatively apolitical General Accounting Office(GAO) was unconstitutional.[6] Without automatic cuts to drive negotiations, GRH was pointless. But GRH was soon revived with a constitutionally sound trigger lodged with the far more political Director of the Office of Management and Budget. Thereafter, automatic sequestration was avoided by one of two means. Either the OMB Director claimed that the GRH target was satisfied, even when it was clearly not, as happened in 1989, or Congress passed legislation changing deadlines and deficit targets. Budgets were not cut, deficits did not decline, and automatic cuts did not occur. Faced with the "train wreck" of sequestration, both legislative and executive branches preferred to change the rules rather than negotiate to reduce deficits (Gilmour 1990). Much of the dissatisfaction with GRH stemmed from its mindlessness. Sequestration was to occur even when conditions beyond the control of Congress (such as the economy) caused the deficit target to be exceeded. Furthermore, across the board sequestration would have the effect of punishing all programs, not just the ones that caused an excess deficit.

Faced with the failure of GRH, Congress in 1990 adopted a new outcome-oriented approach to budget procedure called the Budget Enforcement Act (BEA). Congress passed a major reconciliation bill in 1990, the product of intense negotiations between the White House and congressional leaders; as part of that effort it repealed GRH and substituted the Budget Enforcement Act, which sought to preserve the idea of sequestration while avoiding the defects of GRH. The BEA had two important components. First, instead of having a deficit ceiling, it created "discretionary spending caps" for several categories of spending. If these were breached, the result would be automatic spending cuts—but the cuts would be limited to the category of discretionary spending that went over its cap. Second, BEA adopted "pay as you go" rules (PAYGO) for entitlement and tax legislation. Points of order in the House and Senate would prevent floor consideration of tax and entitlement legislation that caused an

---

[6] Renamed the Government Accountability Office in 2004.

increased budget deficit, unless the bill offset those increases with entitlement or revenue changes (Schick and LoStracco 2007; White and Wildavsky 1989; Ippolito 2004; LeLoup 2005).

The Budget Enforcement Act was an important, if qualified, success. The limits on discretionary spending were somewhat effective and limited spending. PAYGO rules were similarly successful in blocking tax cuts or entitlement increases. A confluence of factors, including the BEA, produced a surprising outcome in the late 1990s—the emergence of budget surpluses for the first time in decades. Other factors were two important reconciliation bills in 1990 and 1993, a strong economy in the Clinton years, and a stalemate after 1995 between a Republican Congress and a Democratic president that prevented Republicans from passing tax cuts and Democrats from passing spending increases, and, finally, a 1997 deal between President Clinton and the Republican Congress to balance the budget (Fenno 1997; Palazzolo 1999).

BEA rules were violated frequently, although generally not flagrantly (General Accounting Office 1998). The discretionary spending caps were often alleged to be unduly restrictive, and Congress regularly got around the caps by passing "emergency" supplemental appropriations (Congressional Budget Office 2001). The 2000 United States Census was paid for with an emergency supplemental, even though no category of spending is more foreseeable than the decennial Census. Despite the evasions, discretionary appropriations rose at a reduced rate between 1990 and 2000. The massive budget deficits of the 1980s and first half of the 1990s turned into the first budget surpluses since FY 1969.

In the George W. Bush Administration, PAYGO rules no longer served the interests of the Republican president and majorities in Congress intent on cutting taxes, and so in 2002 the BEA expired and was not renewed. When Democrats regained control of Congress in 2007 they reinstated the BEA, seeking to distinguish themselves from the spendthrift Republicans. The result was to complicate and partly frustrate their own legislative desires after Barack Obama was elected president in 2008.

The 1974 through 1990 period was an era of extraordinary creativity and innovation in congressional budget procedure. This was motivated by historically large budget deficits and the inadequacy of conventional congressional procedures to give members of Congress the ability to deal with them. Members of Congress of both parties were deeply concerned about the size of the deficit and its possible impact on the economy and their own elections. The experimentation ended with the BEA in 1990, which along with the budget process and reconciliation, gave Congress reasonably effective tools for controlling the budget and deficits. Concern with the congressional budget process declined in the later 1990s as large persistent deficits were replaced by a few years of surpluses. In addition, members of Congress appear to have become less concerned with the budget deficit as an issue, after the deficits of the 1980s did not seem to have the dire economic consequences that many politicians had long assumed. In addition, the public did not appear to punish members of Congress for deficits. When budget deficits reemerged after 2001, concern with the budget process did not come back with them, largely, it appears, because the Republican majority in Congress was less concerned with the deficit than with reducing taxes.

When Democrats regained control of Congress in 2007 they reinstated some of the lapsed budget controls of the BEA, but deficits did not decline. Rather, the onset of a financial and economic crisis in 2008 led to expensive legislation that produced extremely large deficits. Congress had at its disposal tools that would have facilitated the enactment of deficit reducing legislation, but members of Congress were not as interested in reducing deficits as they were in pursuing other policy goals.

Over time Congress has adopted a series of budget process reforms and innovations that are largely layered one upon another. These include the appropriations and tax process, the executive budget process, the congressional budget process, reconciliation, and the Budget Enforcement Act. These processes give Congress tools for allocating spending and writing tax law, and they also give Congress power to control both appropriations and entitlements, as well as taxation. Budget process innovations since 1974 have increased Congress' capacity to control the macro-budget, but do not compel action against deficits. Indeed, the reconciliation process, a key weapon in the macro-budgetary arsenal, can be and has been used to cut taxes and thus increases deficits.

PROCEDURE AND CHOICE

A question that has guided much research on congressional budgeting is: can procedures change the decisions of Congress, or do the choices made by Congress represent the underlying preferences of members? One of the greatest challenges for Congress as an institution is to act with consistency on the aggregate features of the budget. Coherent action on the budget as a whole is made difficult by the nature of Congress as a body each of whose members represents a distinct geographic area. For representatives and senators to represent their state or district adequately requires them (at least according to certain notions of representation) to maximize the flow of federal benefits to their constituents. Yet these individually rational actions will undermine efforts to act on the whole of the budget. Do the procedures of Congress help its members overcome the particularistic tendencies that derive from its representational basis?

Since the 1860s the traditional budget process in Congress has reflected the general tendency in Congress to be decentralized and committee-centered. Appropriations and taxation have long been housed in separate committees, which means that there is an institutional divide between power over spending and power over revenue. This structure tends to focus attention more on specific details in the budget, in the form of special tax provisions and items in appropriations bills, but does not give Congress tools for dealing with or even discussing the total amount of spending, taxes, or deficit. Within the Appropriations committees, responsibility is fragmented further by dealing with appropriations in twelve separate subcommittees that operate largely independently of each other. Individual members of Congress who sought new or increased spending on particular programs knew who to contact. The same was true for individual members who wanted to obtain tax relief for a particular individual or industry.

The fragmentation and geographic pull of districts is manifested in the tendency of Congress to pass bills distributing geographically targeted benefits. Congressional efforts to restrain members' desire to spend began with arrangements within the House Appropriations Committee. Fenno (1966) contends that George Mahon, a long-time Chairman of the House Appropriations Committee (1964–79), sought to counter pro-spending tendencies within the committee by appointing members to subcommittees with jurisdictions that do not bear closely on the interests of their districts. The idea was that by serving on a committee unrelated to their immediate reelection concerns, they could better serve the public interest. This strategy apparently was also followed by earlier chairmen. Even as early as 1943, Arthur MacMahon (1943, 176–82) expressed reservations about the efficacy of this strategy. "Given time," he contended, "men will achieve the subcommittee they especially desire" (178). By 1981, Schick reported that the appropriations committees were "subdued guardians," which is what they appear to remain at present. Geiger (1994) analyzed House Appropriations Committee decisions in the period 1963–82 and found that the committee became more of a spending advocate over this time. Recent research by Adler (2000) supports MacMahon's conclusion. Adler found that several of the House Appropriations subcommittees have been composed disproportionately of members whose districts needed benefits provided by the subcommittee. He also found a shift to a greater "advocacy" rather than guardian tendency in the early 1960s, but this has remained fairly stable since then.

Savage (1991) details another means by which procedure can help to restrain spending tendencies in the House Appropriations Committee. In an examination of academic earmarks from 1980 to 1990, Savage found dramatic differences across appropriations subcommittees in the number of earmarks included in the bills. Savage's explanation rests on differences in the policy and procedural preferences of the subcommittee chairmen, some of whom on policy grounds strongly opposed allocating spending in this way. He shows how the dominance of the chairman's mark in appropriations subcommittee deliberations limited the ability of subcommittee members to insert amendments favoring specific interests.

Similar arguments are made about the use of procedure in the House Ways and Means Committee under chairman Wilbur Mills. Mills sought to control members of his committee by having no established subcommittees, thus preventing members from working their way onto subcommittees from which they could maximally benefit their districts (Manley 1970). The "subcommittee bill of rights" adopted in 1973, however, required that all committees have subcommittees with fixed jurisdictions and chairmanships determined by seniority, thus eliminating the use of this tactic and creating opportunities for members to work their way onto subcommittees from which they could best serve their districts and states by enacting favorable tax provisions (Davidson and Oleszek 1979).

Another strand of research examines the effectiveness of the 1974 Congressional Budget Act in changing behavior. Gilmour (1990) contends that reconciliation, because it often aggregates many separate provisions reducing spending into a single measure, made it easier to pass legislation cutting spending than under the normal congressional process of passing one change at a time. The aggregation of numerous cuts into a single bill focuses attention on the deficit cutting aspect of the bill and away from the adverse impact of the individual spending cuts themselves. Similarly, Ellwood (1984) contends that "by grouping a series of reductions into a single bill, [the reconciliation process] gives greater power to the aggregates. The political debate can be shifted from the parts to the whole" (Ellwood 1984). According to this logic, Congress needs no procedural help in increasing spending and deficits, but a procedural fix such as reconciliation can create circumstances in which representatives and senators will be better able to vote to cut spending and reduce deficits.

Ferejohn and Krehbiel (1987) disagree with this logic and argue that the aggregation of the budget process can lead to a higher level of spending, and not just to reduced spending. They simplify the budget process as a two-stage process of first deciding on a level of spending and then on an allocation among programs. The conventional understanding of the budget process, they argue, is that if members are to decide on a level of spending first, they will pick a lower level than if they decide on individual appropriations bills first. They contend instead that sophisticated members of Congress will understand the implications of a restrictive spending level, and will vote for a ceiling that will accommodate their spending desires. The use of the reconciliation process in the early George W. Bush Administration to pass tax cuts that later contributed to large deficits may in some measure support Ferejohn and Krehbiel's contentions.

A fundamental problem with any effort to constrain congressional behavior through rules is that Congress at a particular time cannot constrain itself at a later time. It can adopt a budget target in April, but cannot establish rules that will keep it from changing its mind later. Any rule that Congress adopts it can change, and the Congress that exists at the present moment is always supreme over any previous Congress. Meyers (1996) does an admirable job of explaining the myriad dodges and tricks available to Congress to evade budget rules.

Since Congress can undo or evade any rule it creates for itself, another option is to create an external enforcement, a *deus ex machina* that will enforce budget rules on Congress even when Congress is unwilling to do it for itself. Congress tried this with Gramm-Rudman, but even a GRH style of external enforcement is of limited effectiveness since Congress can repeal it with new legislation anytime its consequences are undesirable. In the successor to GRH, the Budget Enforcement Act, sequestration was retained, but Congress left itself with a way around the rules in the form of emergency spending. The only truly external enforcement available would be a constitutional amendment. But constitutional requirements are not themselves self-enforcing. The often-made analogy between state balanced budget requirements and a federal balanced budget requirement are flawed, and state budgets are often not actually balanced because of capital borrowing and various tricks (Briffault 1996).

Primo (2007) explores the question of using rules to limit behavior and concludes that the fundamental problem with budget reform is the problem of enforcement. Any rules that Congress creates to limit its ability to spend, Congress can also waive or eliminate. The only real enforcement would have to be external. Congress will seldom, if ever, commit itself to a truly binding external enforcement.

THE INCREMENTALISM DEBATE

In addition to scholarship on congressional procedure, there has long been interest in the policy outcomes generated by the budget process. The first important study in this genre was by V. O. Key, one of the leading political scientists of the twentieth century, who noted in an influential article "the lack of a budgetary theory" (1940). By this he meant a theory to answer the question: "On what basis shall it be decided to allocate *x* dollars to activity A instead of activity B?" Key asserted that this was a problem of great importance, but in the end he had little to say about how such a theory might be devised. Wildavsky (1961) provided a convincing explanation as to why no such theory had been or could be found. He argued: "A theory which contains criteria for determining what ought to be in the budget is nothing less than a theory stating what the government ought to do." No such theory is possible in a democracy, he argued.

Wildavsky effectively established the modern field of budgetary research by shifting the focus from a normative concern with how budgets should be made to how they are actually made. His landmark book *The Politics of the Budgetary Process*, first published in 1964 and re-issued in several subsequent editions, made several related assertions about congressional budgeting. The most important was an empirical claim that budgetary decision-making is incremental. "The beginning of wisdom about an agency budget," he wrote, "is that it is almost never actively reviewed as a whole each year.... Instead it is based on last year's budget with special attention given to a narrow range of increases or decreases" (1964, 15). He further asserted more normatively that changes in the budget are incremental because more comprehensive alternative approaches to budgets overwhelm the human capacity for what he termed "calculations." People cannot collect enough information about programs and their merits to make truly rational calculations about correct funding levels. Instead, they make small changes at the margins, and then wait to see if anything good or bad ensues. Finally, Wildavsky asserted that reforms seeking to implement comprehensive budget analysis will fail because of inherent limits to calculations.

Soon after the publication of *The Politics of the Budgetary Process*, Wildavsky undertook empirical tests of the incrementalism hypothesis with coauthors. The result of this work was a substantial confirmation of the core insights of Wildavsky's book: they found that simple decision rules could describe budget decisions. In particular, they found that the budgetary base—last year's spending level—had a powerful impact on the next year's level (Davis, Dempster, and Wildavsky 1966). A provocative thesis in a field with ample data is sure to attract attention, and the claims of Wildavsky and his co-authors have spawned a large scholarly literature devoted to the empirical investigation of how budget decisions are made.

Empirical investigations of the incrementalism hypothesis have left it largely in tatters. Meyers (1996) effectively summarizes the first twenty-five years of this large literature. Researchers picking up from Wildavsky found that changes in spending levels from year to year vary far more than Wildavsky allowed. Many non-incremental changes were found. Questions arose as to how large a change could still be described as incremental. Was a change of more than 10 percent non-incremental (Bailey and O'Connor 1975)? There is no good answer to this (Dempster and Wildavsky 1979). Questions also arose as to the correct unit of analysis. Should analysis be conducted at the level of the agency or bureau, as Wildavsky and his colleagues did, or at the level of the program? Program allocations were found to be more volatile than agency budgets, since money could be shifted around among programs within an agency in non-incremental ways, but if the agency budget remains fairly stable, it would tend to mask non-incremental change within the agency (Natchez and Bupp 1973). Subsequent research found that appropriations are far more volatile than Wildavsky had alleged. Even the concept of incrementalism came under close examination; Berry (1990) identified 12 distinct meanings of the term "incrementalism" that he found in the literature, many of them inconsistent with each other. In the interests of clarity, he proposed banishing the term from future discourse. His wish was not granted, but subsequent research has been more fastidious about specifying what is meant by the term incrementalism.

Recent research in the incrementalism thread tends to focus on when and under what circumstances budget decision-making is incremental or not. Jones, Baumgartner, and True (1998) show that changes in allocations of federal budget authority are characterized by periods of stasis, when year-to-year changes are modest, and periods of "policy punctuation" when the changes are far larger. Dezhbakhsh, Tohamy, and Aranson (2003) show that periods of incremental change are followed by periods of non-incremental changes. Causes of non-incremental change are changes in party control of government and presidential elections.

What remains of incrementalism is its explanation of what budgeting is not and cannot be. Allen Schick writes that the incremental theory "asserts that budget makers cannot reexamine every item in the budget every year. They cannot pit all programs against one another in a competition for scarce funds. They cannot canvas all options that might merit consideration. ... To do all these things would overload the budget process, require more data and calculations than can be handled in the time available for preparing the budget, and would open intractable conflicts over money" (Schick 1983).

Incrementalism thus remains influential as a prescriptive theory. Wildavsky argued that participants in budgetary processes adopt incremental strategies because they are a helpful or necessary means of dealing with the overwhelming complexity of governmental budgets. Wildavsky proposed incrementalism as an alternative to comprehensive or synoptic approaches to budgeting. The advantage of incrementalism is that it imposes lower informational requirements on participants than comprehensive approaches. Wildavsky's perspective remain fresh to this day because budgetary reforms are almost always rooted in a comprehensive approach. Program budgeting (Schick 1966), zero-base budgeting, management by objective, and, most recently, performance budgeting, are all based on the idea that with more information, more systematic comparisons among government programs will be possible, leading to a more rational allocation. The incrementalist reply to all of these is that they require more information than people can handle and manage. The incrementalist approach was influential in OMB as it developed President George W. Bush's signature budget reform, the Program Assessment Rating Tool (PART). To avoid the overload characteristic of other budget reforms, PART assessed only one-fifth of all programs each year (Gilmour 2006).

Conclusion

Interest in budget research tends to rise and fall with the budget deficit. The 1970s and 1980s were a heyday of budget process research because budget deficits were larger than most politicians were comfortable with, and thus the deficit was an issue of great concern in Congress. Congress adopted a major reform of its budgeting process in 1974 and tinkered with it on a regular basis over the next fifteen years. Budget reform activity was accompanied by a corresponding surge in scholarly attention to the budget. In the late 1990s a combination of fiscal restraint and rapidly rising revenues produced the first large federal budget surpluses since the 1920s, and this led to a lack of interest in the budget process both among politicians and scholars.

The close connection between deficits and scholarly interest seems to have declined in the twenty-first century. In 2001 and 2003 Congress passed tax cuts at the behest of President Bush that consumed the future surplus and, along with expenses of the wars in Iraq and Afghanistan led once again to the emergence of budget deficits. These deficits did not lead to the same level of concern, or the same kind of experimentation with budget process, as the deficits of the Jimmy Carter, Ronald Reagan, and George H. W. Bush years.

An important characteristic of pre-2000 deficit anxiety was that it led members of Congress and the president to compromise on their most cherished political goals in order to achieve deficit reduction. That is, President Reagan and congressional Republicans agreed to certain "revenue enhancements" as part of reconciliation bills in 1982 and 1984 in order to reduce deficits, and at the same time Democrats in Congress agreed to cuts in Medicare and other entitlements. Republicans hated the tax increases and Democrats were reluctant to cut entitlements, but both sides recognized that a balanced compromise that required concessions from both parties was the only means of reducing deficits in a time of divided government. Similar compromises by both parties on issues of high importance to their political bases led to enactment of another reconciliation bill in 1990. Since approximately 1990 both parties, but especially the Republican party, have become less willing to agree to such compromise agreements, and thus the usefulness of the budget process as a tool to reduce deficits has dwindled.

At the close of the first decade of the twenty-first century, circumstances may conspire to increase public, congressional, and scholarly interest in deficits and tools to control them. The onset of a major recession in 2008 and the subsequent adoption of counter-cyclical stimulus legislation and financial rescues sent budget deficits in 2008 and 2009 to the highest levels since World War II—almost 10 percent of gross domestic product (GDP). Deficits are likely to remain high by historical standards for years to come, pushing federal debt to 66 percent of GDP by 2012, about double the level in 2003 and the highest it has been since the 1950s (Congressional Budget Office 2010). Anticipated growth in healthcare costs and pension programs will make already difficult budgetary choices even more intractable in the next decade. These trends will create a challenging environment for budgeting, and likely will increase interest among members of Congress in budget issues and tools for controlling deficits.

References

ADLER, E. S. 2000. Constituency Characteristics and the "Guardian" Model of Appropriations Subcommittees, 1959–1998. *American Journal of Political Science*, 44(1): 104–14.

BAILEY, J. J., and O'CONNOR, R. J. 1975. Operationalizing Incrementalism: Measuring the Muddles. *Public Administration Review*, 35: 60–6.

BERMAN, L. 1979. *The Office of Management and Budget and the Presidency, 1921–1979*. Princeton: Princeton University Press.

BERRY, W. D. 1990. The Confusing Case of Budgetary Incrementalism: Too Many Meanings for a Single Concept. *Journal of Politics*, 52: 167–96.

BRIFFAULT, R. 1996. *Balancing Acts: The Reality Behind State Balanced Budget Requirements*. New York: Century Foundation.

CONGRESSIONAL BUDGET OFFICE. 2001. *Supplemental Appropriations in the 1990s*. Washington, DC: Congressional Budget Office.

—— 2010. *The Budget and Economic Outlook: Fiscal Years 2010 to 2020*. Washington, DC: Congressional Budget Office.

DAVIDSON, R., and OLESZEK, W. 1979. *Congress Against Itself*. Bloomington: Indiana University Press.

DAVIS, O. A., DEMPSTER, M. A. H., and WILDAVSKY, A. 1966. A Theory of the Budgetary Process. *American Political Science Review*, 60: 529–47.

DEMPSTER, M. A. H., and WILDAVSKY, A. 1979. On Change: Or, There is No Magic Size for an Increment. *Political Studies*, 27: 371–89.

DEZHBAKHSH, H., TOHAMY, S. M., and ARANSON, P. H. 2003. A New Approach for Testing Budgetary Incrementalism. *Journal of Politics*, 65(2): 532–58.

ELLWOOD, J. 1984. Comments on Shepsle and Weingast's "Legislative Politics and Budget Outcomes," pp. 366–71 in *Federal Budget Policy in the 1980s*, ed. G. B. Mills and J. L. Palmer. Washington, DC: Urban Institute.

ELSTER, J. 1985. *Ulysses and the Syrens*. Cambridge: Cambridge University Press.

FENNO, R. 1966. *The Power of the Purse*. Boston: Little, Brown.

—— 1973. *Congressmen in Committee*. Boston: Little, Brown.

—— 1997. *Learning to Govern: An Institutional View of the 104th Congress*. Washington, DC: Brookings.

FEREJOHN, J., and KREHBIEL, K. 1987. The Budget Process and the Size of the Budget. *American Journal of Political Science*, 31(2): 296–320.

FISHER, L. 1975. *Presidential Spending Power*. Princeton: Princeton University Press.

—— 1979. The Authorization-Appropriation Process in Congress: Formal Rules and Informal Practices, *Catholic University Law Review*, 29(1): 51–105.

—— 1985. Ten Years of the Budget Act: Still Searching for Controls. *Public Budgeting and Finance*, 5(3): 3–28.

—— 2000. *Congressional Abdication on War and Spending*. College Station: Texas A&M University Press.

—— 2004. Litigating the War Power with Campbell v. Clinton. *Presidential Studies Quarterly*, 30: 564–74.

GEIGER, S. M. 1994. The House Appropriations Committee, FY 1963–82: A Micro-Budgetary Perspective. *Legislative Studies Quarterly*, 19(3): 397–416.

GENERAL ACCOUNTING OFFICE. 1998. *Budget Issues: Budget Enforcement Compliance Report*. Washington, DC: General Accounting Office.

GILMOUR, J. B. 1990. *Reconcilable Differences? Congress and Its Budget Process*. Berkeley: University of California Press.

—— 2006. *Implementing OMB's Program Assessment Rating Tool (PART): Meeting the Challenges of Integrating Budget and Performance*. Washington, DC: IBM Center for the Business of Government.

HAHM, S. D., KAMLET, M. S., and MOWERY, D. C. 1992. U.S. Defense Spending under the Gramm-Rudman-Hollings Act, 1986–1989. *Public Administration Review*, 52(1): 8–15.

HIXON, W., and MARSHALL, B. W. 2002. Examining Claims about Procedural Choice: The Use of Floor Waivers in the U.S. House. *Political Research Quarterly*, 55(4): 923–38.

HOWARD, C. 1999. *The Hidden Welfare State*. Princeton: Princeton University Press.

IPPOLITO, D. S. 1981. *Congressional Spending*. Ithaca: Cornell University Press.

—— 2004. *Why Budgets Matter: Budget Policy and American Politics*. University Park: Penn State University Press.

JONES, B. D., BAUMGARTNER, F. R., and TRUE, J. L. 1998. Policy Punctuations: U.S. Budget Authority, 1947–1995. *Journal of Politics*, 60(1): 1–33.

KEITH, R. 2008a. The Budget Reconciliation Process: The Senate's Byrd Rule. Washington, DC: Congressional Research Service. Available online at: http://budget.house.gov/crs-reports/RL30862.pdf (accessed August 31, 2010).

—— 2008b. Introduction to the Federal Budget Process. CRS Report 98–721. Washington, DC: Congressional Research Service. Available at: budget.house.gov/crs-reports/98–721.pdf (accessed August 31, 2010).

KEY, V. O. 1940. The Lack of a Budgetary Theory. *American Political Science Review*, 34: 1137–44.

KING, R. 2000. *Budgeting Entitlements: The Politics of Food Stamps*. Washington, DC: Georgetown University Press.

LELOUP, L. 2005. *Parties, Rules, and the Evolution of Congressional Budgeting*. Columbus: Ohio State University Press.

MACMAHON, A. W. 1943. Congressional Oversight of Administration. *Political Science Quarterly*, 58(3): 380–414.

MANLEY, J. 1970. *The Politics of Finance*. Boston: Little, Brown.

MARMOR, T. R. 2000. *The Politics of Medicare*. Hawthorne, NY: Aldine de Gruyter.

MAYHEW, D. 1974. *Congress: The Electoral Connection*. New Haven: Yale University Press.

MEYERS, R. 1996. *Strategic Budgeting*. Ann Arbor: University of Michigan Press.

MOSHER, F. C. 1986. *A Tale of Two Agencies*. Baton Rouge: LSU Press.

NATCHEZ, P. B., and BUPP, I. C. 1973. Policy and Priority in the Budgetary Process. *American Political Science Review*, 67: 951–63.

NELSON, D. H. 1953. The Omnibus Appropriations Act of 1950. *The Journal of Politics*, 15(2): 274–88.

OBERLANDER, J. 2003. *The Political Life of Medicare*. Chapel Hill: University of North Carolina Press.

PALAZZOLO, D. J. 1999. *Done Deal?: The Politics of the 1997 Budget Agreement*. Chatham, NJ: Chatham House.

PFIFFNER, J. 1979. *The President, the Budget, and Congress: Impoundment and the 1974 Budget Act*. Boulder, CO: Westview Press.

PRIMO, D. 2007. *Rules and Restraint: Government Spending and the Design of Institutions*. Chicago: University of Chicago Press.

ROGERS, R., WALTERS, R., and WALTERS, R. H. 2006. *How Parliament Works*. 6th edn. London: Pearson.

RUBIN, I. 1988. The Authorization Process: Implications for Budget Theory, pp. 124–47 in *New Directions in Budget Theory*, ed. I. Rubin. Albany: SUNY Press.

—— 2007. The Great Unraveling: Federal Budgeting, 1998–2006. *Public Administration Review*, 67(4): 608–17.

SATURNO, J. V. 2008. *Points of Order in the Congressional Budget Process*. CRS Report 97–865. Washington, DC: Congressional Research Service. Available online at: http://www. senate.gov/CRSReports/crs-publish.cfm?pid=%26*2%404RLC%3E%0A (accessed August 26, 2010).

SAVAGE, J. D. 1990. *Balanced Budgets and American Politics*. Ithaca: Cornell University Press.

—— 1991. Saints and Cardinals in Appropriations Committees and the Fight against Distributive Politics. *Legislative Studies Quarterly*, 16: 329–47.

—— 2008. *Making the EMU: The Politics of Budgetary Surveillance and the Enforcement of Maastricht*. Oxford: Oxford University Press.

SCHELLING, T. 1984. Self-Command in Practice, in Policy and in a Theory of Rational Choice. *American Economic Review*, 74: 1–11.

SCHICK, A. 1966. The Road to PPB: The Stages of Budget Reform. *Public Administration Review*, 26: 243–58.

SCHICK, A. 1980. *Congress and Money*. Washington, DC: Urban Institute.

—— 1983. Incremental Budgeting in a Decremental Age. *Policy Sciences*, 16: 1–25.

—— 1990. *The Capacity to Budget*. Washington, DC: Urban Institute.

—— 1994. The Study of Microbudgeting, pp. 104–20 in *The Budget Puzzle*, ed. J. F. Cogan, T. J. Muris, and A. Schick. Stanford, CA: Stanford University Press.

—— 2003. Does Budgeting Have a Future. *OECD Journal on Budgeting*, 2: 7–48.

—— and LOSTRACCO, F. 2007. *The Federal Budget: Politics, Policy, Process*. 3rd edn. Washington, DC: Brookings.

SCHIER, S. 1992. *A Decade of Deficits: Congressional Thought and Fiscal Action*. Albany, NY: SUNY Press.

STEWART, C. 1989. *Budget Reform Politics*. Cambridge: Cambridge University Press.

STITH, K. 1988. Congress' Power of the Purse. *Yale Law Journal*, 97: 1343–96.

—— 1988b. Rewriting the Fiscal Constitution: The Case of Gramm-Rudman-Hollings *California Law Review*, 76: 593–668.

STRAHAN, R. 1990. *New Ways and Means.* Chapel Hill: University of North Carolina Press.

STREETER, S. 2008. *The Congressional Appropriations Process: An Introduction.* CRS Report 97–684. Washington, DC: Congressional Research Service. Available at: http://assets. opencrs.com/rpts/97–684_20081202.pdf (accessed August 26, 2010).

SURREY, S. 1980. *Tax Expenditures.* Cambridge: Harvard University Press.

TANNER, D. 2003. Politics of the Labour Movement, 1900–1939, pp. 38–55 in *A Companion to Early Twentieth-Century Britain*, ed. C. Wrigley. London: Wiley.

TIEFER, C. 1989. *Congressional Practice and Procedure: A Reference, Research, and Legislative Guide.* Westport, CT: Greenwood Press.

TOMKIN, S. L. 1998. *Inside OMB: Politics and Process in the President's Budget Office.* Armonk, N.Y.: M. E. Sharpe.

WEAVER, K. 1989. *Automatic Government: The Politics of Indexation.* Washington, DC: Brookings.

WHITE, J. 1999. Budgeting for Entitlements, pp. 678–98 in *Handbook of Government Budgeting*, ed. Roy Meyers. Jossey-Bass.

WHITE, J., and WILDAVSKY, A. 1989. *The Deficit and the Public Interest.* Berkeley: University of California Press.

WILDAVSKY, A. 1961. Political Implications of Budgetary Reform. *Public Administration Review*, 21(4): 183–90.

—— 1964. *The Politics of the Budgetary Process.* Boston: Little, Brown.

WITTE, E. 1962. *Development of the Social Security Act.* Madison: University of Wisconsin Press.

WITTE, J. 1986. *The Politics and Development Federal Income Tax.* Madison: University of Wisconsin Press.

PART VI

....

POLITICS AND POLICYMAKING

....

CHAPTER 23

....

PARTY POLARIZATION

....

BRIAN F. SCHAFFNER

THERE are few threads in the field of American politics that have woven through as many disparate topics in recent years as that of partisan polarization. Polarization has been documented and analyzed by scholars studying voting behavior, public opinion, state politics, the courts, the presidency, and, especially, the research on Congress. Indeed, the U.S. Congress served as one of the leading indicators of partisan polarization in America and it has remained a popular venue for studying the causes and (to a lesser extent) the consequences of this trend. In fact, it almost seems like a prerequisite for a contemporary study of Congress to have something to say about polarization.

In this chapter, I review the extensive body of work that examines the causes of congressional polarization and the somewhat more limited research into the consequences of this polarization. I argue that, while scholars have developed a fairly complete understanding of the former, there is far more to be done in understanding the latter. In general, scholars seeking to conduct research in this area should focus their sights on how polarization has affected the way that Congress operates internally, but also how it interacts with other aspects of the political system. The best research in this area will take advantage of new methods to build extensive data sources that document polarization in other congressional arenas and it will also look to the historical record to compare the present period of polarization with earlier ones. However, before describing the existing work on congressional polarization or the avenues for future research, I begin with the basic task of describing the increasing polarization in Congress.

DOCUMENTING POLARIZATION IN CONGRESS

In most congressional research, partisan polarization is defined by the large (and growing) ideological differences between the Democratic and Republican Parties. The role of parties in defining congressional polarization is important because, as Marc Hetherington notes, "The 1960s and 1970s witnessed plenty of polarized rhetoric and behavior about divisive issues like Vietnam and Civil Rights. But differences did not break down along party lines" (2009, 417). To say that Congress has become more polarized is to claim that the parties in Congress have become more ideologically distinct from each other. Most studies capture polarization by measuring the difference in roll-call voting behavior between the average Democrat and the average Republican.

Figure 23.1 uses the NOMINATE scores developed by Keith Poole and Howard Rosenthal to present two plots that help set the terms for our understanding of congressional polarization. First, Panel A shows the difference between the average Democrat and average Republican in each Congress from 1879 to 2008. Remarkably, the data indicate that the 109th Congress witnessed the highest levels of polarization, at least since Reconstruction. The NOMINATE data also help us determine when this trend began. In the House, a sharp trend toward polarization appeared to begin in the late 1970s and has continued for three decades. In the Senate, this trend appeared to begin as early as the 1950s. The ability to pinpoint the timing of these trends has been crucial to scholars attempting to sort out why this polarization occurred and what the effects of this polarization may have been.

The other important pattern to take note of in Panel A is the fact that polarization in the Senate has tracked very closely with polarization in the House; indeed, the contemporary Senate is nearly as polarized as the House. This point is important because, as I will note in the following section, it has helped scholars largely rule out explanations for polarization that could not apply to both chambers. While it is certainly possible that the Senate and House polarized at the same time and by roughly similar amounts for entirely different reasons, it is far more likely that the same factors have driven polarization in both chambers.

Panel B in Figure 23.1 plots the average NOMINATE scores of the parties in the House over time, but also plots northern and southern Democrats separately. As I will discuss in more depth in the following section, partisan realignment in the South was one of the first and most convincing explanations for a polarizing Congress (Rohde 1991; Abramowitz and Saunders 1998; Jacobson 2000; Black and Black 2002; Roberts and Smith 2003). To be sure, Panel B shows that southern Democrats have become significantly more liberal during the past several decades, providing some evidence for the claim. However, northern Democrats have also become more liberal during this period, indicating that partisan change in the South cannot fully explain congressional polarization. It is also noteworthy that this figure does not account for another change occurring during this period: a significantly greater proportion of the Democratic caucus became comprised of northern Democrats.

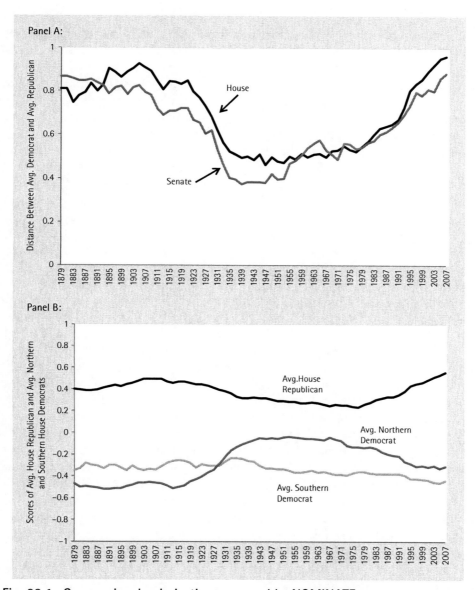

Fig. 23.1. Congressional polarization measured by NOMINATE scores, 1879–2008

Source: Keith T. Poole, University of California at San Diego, http://voteview.com.

Limitations

While trends in members' voting behavior have played a crucial role in allowing scholars to document and study congressional polarization, relying solely on roll-call data may limit our understanding of this phenomenon in at least two ways. First, using roll-call votes to construct measures of ideology in Congress confounds our ability to understand the causes of polarization. As I will document in the following section, scholars have debated the extent to which polarization is driven by external factors—such as increasing polarization among constituents and/or activists—versus internal factors—such as the extent to which party leaders are structuring choices in ways that make legislators appear more partisan than they may actually be. Since roll-call votes are used to construct measures of legislator ideology, it is very difficult to distinguish between these two causes. Ideally, we would have a measure of ideology that was exogenous to the legislative behavior we were attempting to explain (e.g. Ansolabehere, Snyder, and Stewart 2001; Jenkins, Schickler, and Carson 2004). Unfortunately, there appear to be few alternatives for constructing such an exogenous measure, particularly over the extended period during which polarization has increased in Congress.

A second limitation of relying on measures based on roll-call votes to study polarization is that it limits the scope with which the field has studied this change. Despite their significance in the legislative process, roll-call votes are just one aspect of legislative behavior. While the polarization of roll-call voting has been described and explained in detail, far less attention has been given to those aspects of legislative behavior that are not as easy to document. To be sure, some work documents increasing polarization in other legislative activities. For example, Jamieson and Falk (2000) demonstrate that floor speeches have become increasingly uncivil in the House, and Zhang et al. (2007) use network analysis to show that cosponsorship activity has also become increasingly polarized. But the research documenting polarization in other aspects of legislative behavior could benefit from much greater development. Consider that congressional scholars have demonstrated that the factors that determine how a member votes on legislation can be quite different from the dynamics that structure their behavior in other activities (Hall 1996). If scholars produce measures of polarization in these other arenas, it will not be surprising to find that patterns of polarization differ significantly from one activity to the next and that polarization dynamics are even more complicated than roll-call data alone suggest.

Despite the limitations inherent in using roll-call votes to study polarization, these data are central in documenting and understanding congressional polarization. Such measures clearly show that polarization occurred, that the magnitude of the polarization is historically significant, and that no single simple explanation for it will suffice. As a result, a cottage industry of research surfaced that focused on solving the origins of congressional polarization. Collectively, this work reached a conclusion that is, in hindsight, not entirely surprising. In short, the answer is complicated.

WHAT CAUSED THE CONTEMPORARY CONGRESSIONAL POLARIZATION?

The most significant body of work on contemporary congressional polarization has focused on understanding why Congress has become polarized. Scholars have put forward a litany of explanations for the phenomenon, but they ultimately fall into one of two broad perspectives. The first focuses on how changes external to Congress have led to polarization within the chamber. This perspective looks to changes in the electorate and the nature of legislators' constituencies to explain why members' ideologies have changed. The second perspective focuses on changes internal to the institution, such as the increasing influence of party leaders or the evolving nature of the congressional agenda.

Before reviewing this literature, it is important to place these perspectives within the broader debate about the extent of party influence on legislative behavior. This debate, which is ably described in Chapter 17, pits scholars who question whether parties influence legislative behavior (e.g. Krehbiel) against those who emphasize the role of party leaders in affecting legislative outcomes (e.g. Aldrich and Rohde; Cox and McCubbins). The research on the causes of partisan polarization simply adds a dynamic component to this question of party influence. If the limited party outlook is accurate, then congressional polarization should be driven entirely by exogenous forces that serve to alter legislators' ideologies. In other words, legislators' ideologies changed, most likely because the nature of their constituencies changed, and these changes were reflected in the increasingly divisive nature of roll-call voting in recent decades.

On the other hand, the Conditional Party Government perspective sees polarization as driven by both internal and external factors (Aldrich and Rohde 2001). In this view, party caucuses initially become more polarized and cohesive due to exogenous (electoral) forces. However, once these changes are initiated, legislators then delegate more power to their party leaders, who structure choices in a way that further increases polarization. In this view, external and internal factors are mutually reinforcing and polarization begets increasing polarization.

In the following discussion, I will describe both the external and internal dynamics that have been linked to congressional polarization. Ultimately, integrating these two perspectives appears to provide the best explanation for the rise in congressional polarization over the past several decades.

External causes

If congressional scholars have settled anything with certainty, it is that a significant proportion of what a member of Congress does in office is aimed at pleasing his or her constituents in order to win reelection (Mayhew 1974). It is hardly surprising, then, that congressional scholars would have considered mass partisan change as a likely suspect in the search for answers to the changing patterns of partisanship in Congress. Indeed, on many measures, the American public seems more polarized than it has been in the past. This seemingly straightforward relationship belies the fact, however, that the external causes of polarization are quite varied and include partisan realignment in the South, partisan sorting throughout the country, the increasing homogeneity of states and congressional districts, and the rising importance of party activists.

One of the simplest explanations for the increased polarization in Congress focuses on the role of realignment in the South (Rohde 1991; Abramowitz and Saunders 1998; Jacobson 2000; Black and Black 2002; Roberts and Smith 2003). For much of the twentieth century, the South was dominated by the Democratic Party despite the fact that many Democrats held ideologically conservative views. However, by the 1970s, conservatives in the South began disassociating with the Democratic Party and Republican politicians reaped the benefits. This change in the nature of the southern electorate was ultimately reflected in Congress. Following the 1994 election, more than half of the southern congressional delegation was comprised of Republicans. In most cases, these Republicans had replaced conservative Democrats, which led to an increasingly liberal Democratic Party and a more conservative Republican Party.

Two factors make the southern realignment explanation for polarization particularly compelling. First, the timing works out nicely. The share of southern House seats held by Republicans more than doubled from the mid-1970s through the mid-1990s, the same period during which polarization in Congress was rapidly increasing. Second, there is a clear link between changes that occurred in the South and the ideological makeup of the party caucuses in Congress. Every time a conservative southern Democrat lost an election to a more conservative southern Republican, the Republican caucus became more conservative and the Democratic caucus became increasingly liberal.

However, while southern realignment has clearly played a role in driving congressional polarization, it has also become clear that it is only part of the story (Jacobson 2000; McCarty, Poole, and Rosenthal 2006). First, the share of southern seats held by Republicans leveled off during the 1990s; yet, polarization has continued to increase through the 110th Congress. Southern partisan change cannot account for this continuing trend. Of course, Republicans lost seats outside the South following the 1994 elections, so the share of the Republican caucus made up by southerners continued to increase. Indeed, following the 2006 elections, southerners made up more than 40 percent of all Republicans in both chambers indicating that partisan change in the South has contributed at least partly to the polarization phenomenon.

Second, as noted earlier, southern members of Congress are not the only group that polarized during this period. Indeed, even northern Democrats and Republicans became more ideologically extreme at the same time (Jacobson 2000; Brewer, Mariani, and Stonecash 2002; McCarty, Poole, and Rosenthal 2006). Indeed, some scholars have pointed out the broader context of partisan change nationwide. During the period of low-levels of polarization experienced from the 1930s until the 1970s, the Democratic Party's coalition included rural voters in the South and Midwest along with urban voters in the Midwest and Northeast (Sundquist 1983; Cooper and Brady 1981). However, recent decades have witnessed a more homogeneous Democratic base that eschews rural southerners and relies more heavily on urban voters while Republicans have turned to a coalition of rural and exurban voters (Stonecash, Brewer, and Mariani 2003). Mass partisan change in the South has been dramatic, to be sure, but partisan change has not been confined to that region of the country.

While realignment in the South was easy to detect, scholars have debated whether the American public has become increasingly ideologically polarized. It is clear that Americans have become far more consistent with regard to their partisan and ideological preferences (Hetherington 2001) and this has carried into their voting behavior as well (Jacobson 2000). While some scholars have pointed to these changes as evidence of a more polarized public, the point has been famously disputed by Fiorina, Abrams, and Pope (2006). In many respects, the debate appears to hinge more on a difference in terminology than on fundamentally dissimilar views of the changes that took place in the electorate (though see Abramowitz and Saunders 2005; Jacobson 2007). Indeed, Fiorina concedes that partisan sorting has occurred: "Those who affiliate with a party today are more likely to affiliate with the ideologically 'correct' party than they were in earlier periods" (2006, 61). This sorting explains why citizens' issue positions are increasingly correlated with their partisanship and vote choices, and split-ticket voting has become less common (Jacobson 2000). It would also cause the average Democratic citizen to appear more liberal over time (as conservatives left the Democratic Party) and the average Republican more conservative (as liberals left the Republican Party) even if the distribution of citizens' ideologies has not actually changed. Thus, as Hetherington notes,

Those who argue that polarization exists on the mass level are, for the most part, conceptualizing polarization differently from Fiorina. They most often highlight increasing distances between the average Republican and average Democrat in the electorate irrespective of whether those opinions are clustering near the ideological poles. (2009, 436)

In short, Americans appear to have sorted themselves into the parties that best match their ideologies, but they have not necessarily become more ideologically disparate from each other.

Fiorina argues that the American public may seem more extreme than it actually is because voters are forced to make choices between more polarized candidates from increasingly polarized parties (2006). Indeed, most accounts indicate that polarization among candidates and elected officials preceded ideological sorting at the mass level (Jacobson 2000). The elite-led explanation is particularly central to understanding sorting in the South as this sorting only occurred after Republican and Democratic elites began taking clear and differentiated positions on civil rights issues (Carmines and Stimson 1989). Of course, even on this front, the answer is not entirely obvious; indeed, it is muddled enough that Gary Jacobson refers to it as a "chicken or egg" problem (2000, 25). He points out that while elite decisions to sort themselves on civil right issues may have been critical in sparking partisan sorting in the American public, these decisions were based on (and constrained by) the political opportunities that the parties thought they could take advantage of at the mass level.

While elites acted strategically to take advantage of electoral opportunities, those decisions may also have been guided by the influence of party activists. Indeed, several studies have documented the fact that party activists have become increasingly polarized over the past several decades, particularly when compared to the general public (Saunders and Abramowitz 2004; Layman et al. 2006; Fiorina 2006). At the same time, party activists may have gained more influence over the electoral process (Layman, Carsey, and Horowitz 2006). Thus, as Layman, Carsey, and Horowitz note,

Policy-oriented activists have grown more prevalent in recent years and several factors have increased their influence in party politics. This has probably increased the incentives for party candidates and elected officials to take ideologically extreme positions on multiple policy agendas, which in turn has pushed the parties' coalitions toward more polarized positions on various issues.   (2006, 104)

Party activists may have played a significant role, both directly and indirectly, in driving the increased polarization witnessed in Congress and the public over the past several decades.

The role of increasingly homogenous constituencies may also be important in exacerbating the influence of activists. Some research demonstrates that citizens are increasingly choosing to live in more ideologically homogenous areas (Gimpel and Schuknect 2001; Oppenheimer 2005). This geographic sorting leads to more homogenous electoral districts at both the House and Senate level. Such districts may reduce incentives for members of Congress to take moderate positions in order to attract supporters from the opposing party. In fact, when incumbents represent more homogenous constituencies, they may need to become more responsive to primary constituencies and therefore more ideologically extreme, particularly if they face a challenger in the primary election (Burden 2004).

While geographic sorting may be partially to blame for the more homogenous constituencies represented by members of Congress, some have argued that redistricting is also to blame for this pattern. Carson et al. (2007) show that polarization in the House is in some measure due to the increasingly partisan ways in which congressional districts are drawn. However, the authors also rightly note that the effect they uncover is substantively small. Indeed, Sean Theriault's (2008) analysis (which differs from the approach taken by Carson et al.) indicates that redistricting likely accounts for only 10 to 20 percent of the polarization that has occurred in the House of Representatives since the 1970s. Brunell and Grofman (2008) show that members from safer districts are no more polarized than those from competitive districts, which leads them to the conclusion that redistricting is not to blame for polarization in the House. It is also important to note that redistricting cannot explain any of the polarization that occurred in the Senate, further limiting its usefulness in understanding the larger process that has driven congressional polarization (McCarty, Poole, and Rosenthal 2006). Unfortunately, this fact has not kept political scientists or journalists from placing far more emphasis on the role of redistricting in causing polarization than evidence warrants (see Theriault 2008 and Brunell 2008 for a discussion).

Overall, the literature points to several notable candidates that explain the increase in congressional polarization. In particular, political elites and party activists sparked a substantial realignment in the South which, along with significant partisan sorting elsewhere, created an electorate that now holds more ideologically consistent partisan attachments. This partisan sorting also happened in the context of geographical sorting, with Americans becoming more likely to live in ideologically homogenous communities than they were in the past. Members of Congress now represent more homogenous constituencies, which reduces the electoral incentives for engaging in bipartisan compromise and makes them more beholden to the polarizing forces of party activists. Overall, these changes in the electorate not only produced the proper conditions to allow for congressional polarization, but they also appear to be responsible for a significant amount of that polarization.

Internal causes

While external changes in the nature of congressional constituencies appear to have played a role in driving polarization in Congress, internal changes may also be responsible for much of this change. Several scholars have identified such internal causes for polarization, which range from changes in the way that votes are recorded in the House to the evolving nature of the congressional agenda.

Jason Roberts and Steven Smith (2003) note that beginning in 1971, the House began to allow recorded voting when it met in Committee of the Whole (COW); by 1973, these votes were recorded electronically. The authors argue that this change in process fundamentally altered the composition of the roll-call record in the House, as members could now force votes on amendments that would compel their colleagues to take public positions on controversial issues. In other words, these votes became an ideal forum for recording differences on particularly polarizing issues. While Roberts and Smith do not claim that these procedural changes caused polarization in the House, they do suggest that it may influence the historical timing:

COW votes are responsible for most of the modest net increase in party voting during the 1970s and early 1980s. While counterfactuals are not always strong inferential tools, the data ... suggest that without the inclusion of COW votes, party voting is likely to have shown little upward trend until the late 1980s. (2003, 310)

The caution included in their conclusion is appropriate since we cannot rule out the possibility that the introduction of COW votes simply happened to coincide with the occurrence of polarization. It may be the case that the chamber was polarizing anyway during this period and that COW votes were simply the first venue in which this polarization was observable. Without these votes, polarization may have still been evident, just on roll calls held during other legislative stages. Furthermore, Roberts and Smith do not offer an explanation for why the Senate would also be polarizing during this time.

Frances Lee (2008) also offers an internal explanation for polarization, though the Senate is the locus of her study. Lee examines the Senate roll-call record from 1981 to 2004, dividing votes into different issue categories. She finds that economic issues tend to be the most polarizing in the Senate during this period and that these issues have taken up a larger share of the Senate agenda over time. Lee's finding about the polarizing nature of economic issues is consistent with other work on polarization. Despite popular accounts that blame morality or cultural issues on contemporary polarization, political scientists have consistently found that economic issues are much more polarizing (Bartels 2006; McCarty, Poole, and Rosenthal 2006).

Although Lee shows that over one-third of the Senate polarization that occurred during this period can be explained by the increasing prominence of economic issues on the Senate agenda, she also concedes that "the policy issues before Congress are neither 'given' nor entirely exogenous to the institution" (2008, 216). While Lee attempts to include controls for the polarized nature of the Senate's membership (or specifically, their constituencies), this measure is, at best, a rough one. In short, the causality of the process is not entirely clear. Has the agenda come to focus on more polarizing issues because the membership has become more polarized? If so, then can the legislative agenda also serve as an explanation for the growing polarization in the Senate?

Theriault (2008) offers his own account for how internal congressional dynamics influenced the pattern of increasing polarization in Congress. He argues that particular types of votes, namely procedural votes, may provide members with more leeway to support their parties compared to substantive votes on amendments or final passage. In fact, he demonstrates that a member's constituency is a less important predictor than party for how members vote on procedural issues while the opposite is true on substantive votes. He also shows that the proportion of procedural votes has increased markedly during the past three decades. Thus, he concludes that a substantial proportion of the increase in congressional polarization has been driven by an increase in the number of procedural votes, and that polarization on procedural votes cannot be fully linked to changes in members' constituencies.

I will discuss Theriault's work in greater detail below, but two points warrant mention here. First, it is important to note that none of the internal explanations for party polarization purport to rule out external causes. In fact, these studies essentially presuppose that part of polarization is being driven in part by changes at the mass level. Second, one of the major contributions of these studies is to unpack NOMINATE scores to gain a more nuanced understanding of what is changing in Congress. Indeed, while NOMINATE scores provide a useful way of tracking polarization over time, they are ultimately calculated using all non-unanimous votes that are recorded in each Congress. Roberts and Smith, Lee, and Theriault each show that the nature agenda of roll-call votes has changed significantly over the past several decades, a fact that appears to have enhanced the amount of polarization witnessed in both chambers.

A unified explanation

Theriault's book *Party Polarization in Congress* (2008) is the most complete investigation into the causes of congressional polarization. Theriault begins by summarizing the existing work on polarization:

The primary problem with the extant studies of these explanations is that scholars do not, for the most part, rigorously test any explanation other than the one they proffer. At the end of the day, we have sufficient evidence that each causes party polarization, but we do not know the relative importance of each, nor do we know how they affect one another. (2008, 54)

Theriault sets out to address this weakness in the literature by testing the most prominent explanations against one another to determine the role each has played in causing polarization in Congress. More importantly, he develops an understanding of polarization that incorporates both external and internal dynamics. Ultimately, he shows that congressional polarization was caused first by the polarization of members' constituencies and then exacerbated by the increased willingness of members to cede power to party leaders to structure the legislative process in an even more partisan way.

This explanation for congressional polarization is attractive on a number of fronts. First, it is presented with convincing empirical evidence that, in most instances, is robust to alternative specifications. Indeed, the single major limitation on Theriault's empirical investigation is that it only extends back to the early 1970s, thereby missing a significant portion of the de-polarized era as a comparative baseline. Second, Theriault's study accounts for both chambers of Congress, a trait lacking in too many other examinations of congressional polarization. In fact, not only does Theriault examine the dynamics of polarization in each chamber, but he also shows how polarization in the House has had a spillover effect in fueling polarization in the Senate. This happened when a significant number of Republicans moved from the House to the Senate, bringing a more polarizing style of lawmaking with them into the chamber. Third, Theriault's explanation comports well with the Conditional Party Government thesis, to which many congressional scholars subscribe. Indeed, at a more general level, one could argue that there is little that is theoretically novel about Theriault's claim; it is largely an application of the conditional party government thesis to explain the case of congressional polarization. Overall, Theriault's book provides a compelling account of how polarization took hold of Congress. In fact, between this book and the litany of studies that preceded it, one might reasonably conclude that congressional scholars have sufficiently addressed the question of why Congress has become polarized over the past several decades. Indeed, it is difficult to imagine an entirely novel account of this phenomenon, particularly given the accumulated evidence demonstrating that no single factor can be tied to the emergence of a polarized Congress. Scholars may continue to look for novel explanations for polarization and if they look hard enough, they may just uncover small pieces (like redistricting) that played a substantively marginal, though statistically significant, role. But to what extent will such studies truly enrich our understanding of the causes of congressional polarization? At best, these studies might add only marginally to our understanding of polarization; at worst, they could result in a flurry of work that attempts to repackage what we already seem to know.

I do not mean to argue that all work in this area should cease. But scholars should be mindful of what has been done and proceed accordingly. On one hand, unless one thinks Theriault's account is wrong (and those who question the influence of party leaders may have their doubts), then work in this area will only lead to incremental advances in what we know about the recent polarization of Congress. On the other hand, the congressional subfield still has much work to do in understanding the more general phenomenon of polarization in Congress. After all, the historical record suggests that the de-polarized Congress of the 1930s–60s may have been the exception in congressional history and that a polarized Congress has been the standard. Despite this fact, few scholars have investigated historical periods of polarization to generate broader theories of the phenomenon that are not bound to the current era (see Jenkins, Schickler, and Carson 2004 and McCarty, Poole, and Rosenthal 2006 for notable exceptions). McCarty, Poole, and Rosenthal's (2006) work is perhaps the finest illustration of how congressional scholars can take a longer view at understanding congressional polarization. The authors argue that the ebb and flow of polarization during the twentieth century was largely driven by levels of income inequality among the American public. The reason that their book *Polarized America* makes such a significant contribution is because the theory and empirical evidence both encompass a much longer timeframe than most studies on polarization. Future work that also approaches the topic from a more historically complete perspective is likely to make the greatest impact on our understanding of congressional polarization.

CONSEQUENCES OF POLARIZATION

While a great deal of scholarship has focused on understanding the causes of congressional polarization, much less work has been devoted to understanding the consequences. In other words, polarization has been a dependent variable in a large number of studies, but it has acted as an independent variable much less frequently. In this section I describe the work examining the consequences of polarization in Congress and highlight ways in which this work can and should be expanded.

Policymaking

In 1950, the American Political Science Association (APSA) issued a report that advocated reforms that would increase the level of party unity in Congress as a way of clarifying party platforms and offering a meaningful choice in policies to the electorate. The notion was that such a system would improve the quality of policymaking in the United States. A cohesive party elected into power could enact its policy platform and then be held responsible for the success or failure of those policies in the next election.

Revisiting Figure 23.1 reveals that the APSA report was released during one of the most de-polarized eras in American history. During this period, political scientists were concerned with the lack of clarity between the two political parties rather than the ideological distance between them. In the committee's view, the path to avoiding policy gridlock was not through compromise between the two parties, but by having a single cohesive party controlling government at one time. In stark contrast to this view of policymaking, contemporary scholars and pundits largely blame polarization for policy gridlock—the inability to pass important legislation into law. This conclusion is based on the notion that successful policymaking generally requires bipartisan cooperation.

Given that congressional polarization is defined by the changing preferences of elected officials, it seems reasonable to expect that increasing polarization in Congress has affected the nature of policymaking in some manner. Thus, not surprisingly, several studies have examined the relationship between congressional polarization and the presence (or absence) of policy gridlock. Sarah Binder conducts a comprehensive analysis of legislative gridlock from 1947 to 1996 (Binder 1999). Analyzing *New York Times* editorials to determine which issues were on the policy agenda during each congress, Binder then examines legislative measures designed to address these issues. Binder finds that the percentage of members of Congress who are ideological moderates has a negative relationship with policy gridlock. When there are fewer moderates in Congress, the proportion of issues that suffer from gridlock increases.

David Jones also examines the effect of polarization on legislative gridlock (2001). However, his analysis accounts for the supermajoritarian nature of congressional institutions; in particular, his model incorporates the need for sixty votes for a filibuster-proof majority in the Senate and the need for a three-fifths majority in both chambers to overcome a presidential veto. He finds that the effect of polarization on gridlock is contingent on the share of seats held by the parties in Congress. Polarization has a strong effect on increasing legislative gridlock when the president's party holds a minority of seats or even just a bare majority of seats. However, Jones' model predicts that when the president's party holds over 60 percent of the seats in Congress, the effect of polarization on gridlock will be greatly reduced.

Jones' analysis illuminates an important point about the claims made by responsible party government advocates. Until the 111th Congress, high levels of polarization in Congress occurred in tandem with a comparatively close division of seats in both chambers (especially the Senate). Thus, even when the Republican Party controlled the presidency and both chambers of Congress from 2003 through 2006, Democrats still held enough seats in the Senate to sustain a filibuster. Under these conditions—where some bipartisan cooperation is still necessary to pass legislation—it should not be surprising that polarized parties would lead to increased legislative gridlock (Krehbiel 1998). After all, a more polarized (and, therefore, unified) Democratic Party would find it easier to sustain a filibuster than one that had more moderate members willing to compromise with Republicans.

While Democrats did not begin the 111th Congress with enough seats to invoke cloture in the Senate, they did achieve this figure midway through the first year of that term. This benchmark provides congressional scholars with a unique opportunity to study the policy process under polarized conditions when one party controls both branches of government and holds a filibuster-proof majority in the Senate. According to the responsible party government perspective, the Democratic Party should be able to pass a programmatic agenda through Congress and then be held accountable for that agenda in subsequent elections. While the practicality of fully capitalizing on supermajority status has been tempered by health issues suffered by members of the Democratic caucus, future research should attempt to leverage this period to gain important insights into the possibly contingent effect of congressional polarization on the policymaking process.

In addition to using the recent increase in Democratic strength in the Senate to gain leverage over the problem of the way supermajoritarian procedures condition the effects of polarization on the policymaking process, scholars should also consider unpacking the policy process to gain a better understanding of how polarization influences lawmaking. Barbara Sinclair's book Party Wars, probably includes the most comprehensive discussion of many of the possible consequences of congressional polarization to date (2006). Sinclair examines the influence of polarization on a number of congressional processes. For example, she shows that committee hearings in both chambers have increasingly become fora for partisan debates rather than serving their traditional role as venues for reaching bipartisan compromise. This pattern is even evident within conference committees, which are now frequently stacked strategically by party leaders to ensure the party's favored outcome. In fact, polarization may also have contributed to the fact that the use of conference committees has become increasingly rare over the last couple of decades since it has become harder to get conferees appointed in the Senate and party leaders may prefer a less transparent process in a polarized environment (Oleszek 2008). Sinclair also outlines how majority party leaders in the House have increasingly used restrictive rules when debating legislation and how the Rules Committee's votes on establishing those rules have also become consistently split along party lines. In the Senate, the use of filibusters and the prevalence of cloture votes has steadily increased, signaling the increasing willingness of the minority party to take advantage of any procedural tools at their disposal.

While Sinclair's treatment of the influence of polarization on policymaking in Congress is extensive, it is really more of a beginning than an end to this line of inquiry. In many cases, her data are more suggestive than definitive in demonstrating a causal link between polarization and the changing nature of congressional institutions and procedures. For example, one such extension of Sinclair's work might question why committees have also grown more partisan in their activities during this period of polarization. Is it an inevitable out-growth from the change in membership or a concerted strategy by party leaders to stack committee leadership positions with the most loyal members of the caucus? Lawrence Becker and Vincent Moscardelli suggest that the former explanation is the most accurate. They note that seniority is still the most common path to becoming a committee chair, but that the most senior members also tend to be those from the most liberal and conservative constituencies. They explain that the consequences of this pattern are significant since, "If seniority remains the primary route to committee leadership, and electorally-secure senior members represent increasingly deep red and deep blue constituencies, then the prospects for cooperation would seem slim" (2008, 82).

Another promising line of inquiry addressed by Sinclair is the influence of polarization on the relationship between Congress and other branches of government. Sinclair shows that polarization has led to a significant change in how presidents deal with Congress, noting in particular that presidents are now more likely to make use of veto threats and to develop elaborate ways of "going public" to put pressure on Congress (Kernell 2006).

Richard Fleisher and Jon Bond also examine the changing dynamics in the relationship between congress and the president during the period of polarization. They note that increasing polarization means that fewer members of Congress are cross-pressured and fewer cross-pressured members means fewer members of the opposing party are realistic targets for presidential persuasion. Their analysis also indicates that increased polarization has not necessarily led to more presidential support form a president's own party in Congress. As a result, "presidents often find it more difficult to attract support from the opposition party without a corresponding increase in the certainty of support from their own partisans. Consequently, increased partisanship has made the president's job of governing more difficult rather than less" (2000, 182).

Fleisher and Bond's analysis of presidential support in Congress extends only through 1996; as a result, their findings should be interpreted with caution. Indeed, their study misses the second Clinton term and both terms of George W. Bush, a president who enjoyed unusually high levels of support from Republican legislators through most of his presidency. It may be the case that presidential support from co-partisans in Congress is a function both of polarization and majority status in the chamber. Ten of the twelve years that Fleisher and Bond classify as the "more partisan periods" witnessed divided party government (2000, 177). Yet, much of the Bush and (so far) Obama presidencies occurred under unified party control. Given theories of conditional party government, it would not be surprising to find that presidents would have an easier time attracting support from co-partisans in Congress under conditions of polarization when their party held a majority of seats. Thus, research that extends this line of inquiry into and beyond the Bush presidency will undoubtedly provide a more complete understanding of how polarization has affected the relationship between the president and Congress.

Increasing levels of congressional polarization also appear to have affected the confirmation process. Confirmation hearings have become more contentious, as evidenced by the nature of the questions senators ask of contemporary nominees (Williams and Baum 2003). However, at least as notable is the finding that nominees are far less likely to be even considered by the Senate than they once were (Goldman 2003; Binder and Maltzman 2005). An increasing number of nominations are delayed or obstructed by the Senate, and many of those whose hearings are delayed ultimately fail to win confirmation. In fact, Bond, Fleisher, and Krutz (2009) argue that delay has become the favored strategy for senators seeking to derail presidential nominations. This strategy is appealing to partisans in the Senate since it allows them to defeat objectionable nominees while also avoiding the public scrutiny that confirmation hearings invite. The authors show that, prior to congressional polarization, very few nominations failed due to Senate inaction; however, in recent decades, Senate inaction became the dominant source of such failure.

Of course, the research examining the effects of polarization on the confirmation process may suffer from the same limitations as studies on legislative gridlock. That is, polarization may serve to slow or hamper the president's ability to place judges on the bench (or political appointees in the executive branch) as long as the president's party does not have enough votes to invoke cloture. But once the filibuster-proof benchmark is reached, we might expect presidents to enjoy even greater success with their nominees than would traditionally be the case under less polarized circumstances. As with the research on policy gridlock, scholars should take advantage of the Democratic supermajority in the Senate to learn more about the contingent effects of polarization on presidential influence in Congress.

Polarization and policy debates

Studies of policy gridlock and presidential influence have been the most common arenas for studying the consequences of congressional polarization. Monroe, Colaresi, and Quinn suggest one reason for this focus, "Efforts to systematically analyze political conflict, especially in the American context, have previously focused on behaviors that are easily quantified but obscure substance (e.g. votes)" (2008, 399). Indeed, there has been far too little attention paid to how polarization has affected the content of policy debates, particularly the way in which these debates play out in the public sphere. After all, members of Congress spend significant time and effort attempting to influence public opinion to help advance their issue agendas in Congress. Furthermore, increasing polarization in Congress would likely enhance the extent to which these public relations strategies would be orchestrated by party leaders (Harris 2009; Sellers 2009).

Thus, one important extension of the literature seeking to understand the consequences of polarization will examine the extent to which polarization has influenced the public relations strategies pursued by members of Congress and their party leaders. Party leaders work hard to set particular issues on the public agenda and then frame those issues in a way that favors their party's position. During periods of low polarization, these leaders may have found it difficult to convince their caucus to engage in a concerted public relations effort along these lines. However, as polarization has driven members of Congress to vote along with their parties much more frequently, it also stands to reason that they would be similarly loyal to party efforts to frame issues in particular ways.

Despite the obvious importance of these party-led efforts to frame issues, we know much less about the factors that affect how caucus members are promoting their party's issue frames in the public sphere. We might expect to find even greater polarization when it comes to the words that members of Congress use compared to the votes they cast. After all, votes are more traceable than words and members of Congress are far more likely to be held accountable to their constituents for the way they voted on an issue than they are for the way they framed that issue. Thus, even a moderate Democrat who must break with her party on whether to repeal the inheritance tax can still support her party leaders by using the Democratic framing of "estate tax" rather than the Republican framing of "death tax."

Work in this area has traditionally been limited by the challenges involved in quantifying the way in which legislators talk about issues. Fortunately, automated textual analysis methods being developed by political scientists hold the promise of making this pursuit easier (Monroe et al. 2009). Monroe, Colaresi, and Quinn describe how these methods can help illuminate the effect of polarization on the content of policy debates. Two examples from their article deserve particular mention. First, when analyzing all floor speeches on the topic of taxation from the 106th Congress they uncover significant differences between the types of words used by Democrats and Republicans. In fact, their methods allow them to determine that speech on this issue was far more partisan than it was for debates on abortion (providing further evidence that polarization is fueled more by economic issues than by cultural ones). Furthermore, once they identify the words used most frequently by each party they can then search for these words in other arenas. In the case of the tax debate, they are able to show that the *New York Times* was more likely to use Democratic frames than the *Washington Times*. This finding may not be surprising on its own, but what is notable is the ability to easily automate the collection and analysis of this information. Indeed, one can imagine using this technique to determine a new kind of party support score, one that measures how frequently Democratic and Republican members of Congress use their own party's frames compared to those of the other party.

A second example from the work of Monroe, Colaresi, and Quinn shows the potential of automated textual analysis for measuring the dynamics of polarization in speech over time. Tracking congressional speeches from 1998 through 2005, they show the ebb and flow of polarization on several issues over time. For example, they demonstrate that speech on national defense issues was devoid of polarization for a brief period following 9/11. In other words, Republican and Democratic members of Congress used the same types of words when discussing the issue. However, speech on defense became increasingly polarized in the months and years afterward, particularly following the invasion and occupation of Iraq. They also show that speeches on education issues were quite polarized during the debate over No Child Left Behind, but subsided following passage of the legislation.

Advances in automated textual analysis should enable congressional scholars to gain new insight into polarization by allowing one to measure not just the positions legislators take on issues, but also how they talk about those issues. As noted above, there are good reasons to think that the dynamics may be different for polarization in speech compared to polarization in votes, and exploring these differences (or similarities) will help the field develop a more complete story of the causes and consequences of congressional polarization.

Polarization and congressional representation

One of the most important and well-developed areas of congressional research examines the extent to which members of Congress represent their constituents. As described in detail earlier in this chapter, representation plays a key role in theories that aim to explain the increasing levels of polarization in Congress. Many scholars argue that a significant portion of the increased polarization in Congress has been driven by the determination of legislators to represent their more polarized (but ideologically homogenous) constituents. However, if, as many scholars argue, much polarization is also caused by factors internal to Congress, then the increasing polarization may have significant consequences for representation as well.

Political scientists have often viewed representation either at the macro level (e.g. Erikson, Mackuen, and Stimson 2002) or dyadic level (e.g. Miller and Stokes 1963). At a dyadic level, increasing polarization may provide evidence that constituents are receiving better representation. Brunell (2008) argues that more ideologically homogenous districts almost certainly provide citizens with greater levels of representation because they reduce the number of constituents that are not represented by their House member's views. For example, a district where 50 percent of the constituents are conservatives and 50 percent are liberals will see very competitive elections and might produce a more moderate incumbent. However, the winning candidate will ultimately only represent the views of half of her constituents. A district that is 80 percent conservative may never see a competitive election; yet, a Republican incumbent from this district would likely represent the views of all but 20 percent of her constituents. Thus, at least at a dyadic level, it is possible that increasing levels of polarization may have coincided with increasing levels of representation. However, few studies have directly examined the consequences of congressional polarization for dyadic representation.

Studies of dyadic representation go beyond simply accounting for policy congruence between members and their constituents. Understanding how members of Congress interact with constituents is also significant. It appears that little research has examined the effect of congressional polarization on the nature of members' home styles (Fenno 1978). Do members make the same efforts to reach out to voters who opposed them in previous elections as they once did? Can these efforts be as successful as they were under less polarized conditions? Unfortunately, we do not have a strong view of how polarization has affected this dynamic, though there is some evidence that the relationship may have changed. Wagner (2007) finds that as polarization in Congress has increased, constituents have been less likely to seek casework from their representatives and have expressed less satisfaction with their casework experiences. This decreasing satisfaction exists both for members of the incumbent's party and those from the opposing party. Thus, the rise in polarization appears to be influencing the relationship between citizens and their House members and more research is needed to understand the precise nature of these changes.

At least as important as dyadic representation is the extent to which Congress represents the American public in the aggregate (Weissberg 1978; Erikson, Mackuen, and Stimson 2002). In general, studies typically show that Congress is responsive to changes in public opinion, both through forces of electoral replacement and rational anticipation. However, it is not clear whether congressional polarization has influenced the level of dynamic responsiveness from Congress. Indeed, one might expect that polarization would serve to place ideological constraints on members of Congress that would limit the extent to which they could respond dynamically to public opinion. As a result, under conditions of polarization, dynamic representation may come to work more through electoral replacement than rational anticipation. There may be some anecdotal support for such a hypothesis. After all, the Republican-controlled congress did not appear to adjust their legislative outputs to account for the shift in public opinion that occurred following the 2004 election as rational anticipators might have done. Instead, electoral replacement in 2006 and 2008 was the mechanism that brought Congress more into line with public sentiment.

Polarization and public views of Congress

Related to the question of how well Congress represents the American public is that of how Americans evaluate Congress. It is not entirely clear how one might expect congressional approval to be influenced by polarization. On one hand, John Hibbing and Elizabeth Theiss-Morse (2002) note that much of the American public is averse to conflict and that this aversion is to blame for levels of dissatisfaction in how government operates. Elite-level conflict has certainly become more public in the era of congressional polarization, which might lead to decreased satisfaction with Congress. On the other hand, Hibbing and Theiss-Morse also find that the public tends to dislike political compromise, an activity that may have become less common under polarized conditions.

When one examines Gallup data on congressional approval, it is difficult to uncover a trend that tracks in any discernible way with the rise in polarization. Approval of Congress actually increased through the mid-1990s, spiked following 9/11, and then has declined steadily to record-low levels ever since. Polarization has risen consistently throughout this entire period. Thus, the question of whether (and how) polarization affects the public's view of Congress remains an open one, and certainly deserving of attention. As the discussion in this section has conveyed, this is just one of many fertile areas where scholars might focus more attention in developing a better understanding of the consequences of congressional polarization.

CONCLUSION

This examination of the literature on congressional polarization has pointed both to questions that scholars have addressed repeatedly (why polarization occurred) as well as some that have largely escaped attention (how polarization has affected congressional representation). It is clear that there is a strong impulse for scholars to conduct research in this area. The impulse is understandable, particularly given the dramatic nature of the changes attributed to polarization. However, given the intense interest that this topic has attracted from political scientists, it is especially important to be mindful of the areas where more work is needed and resist the impulse to keep asking and answering the same questions.

I have argued that scholars should focus more attention on the consequences of polarization and less on further attempts to explain its origins. Research in this area is likely to expand our view of polarization beyond votes and legislative outcomes to gain more insight into the nature of the policymaking process itself. Scholars should also pay greater heed to fundamental questions of representation. There are good reasons to believe that polarization may have substantially changed the way incumbents represent their constituents (and Congress represents its public), but there is precious little research examining this dynamic.

Finally, congressional scholars should strive to place the recent era of polarization into the proper context. As noted earlier, the historical record suggests that the de-polarized Congress of the 1930s–60s may have been the exception in congressional history, and that partisan polarization is a far more common occurrence. Yet, most congressional research has focused exclusively on understanding the most recent instance of polarization (see Jenkins, Schickler, and Carson 2004 and McCarty, Poole, and Rosenthal 2006 for notable exceptions). For example, Smith (2007) observes that the Conditional Party Government thesis was largely crafted to explain changes that occurred in Congress as it became increasingly polarized in the 1980s and 1990s. Yet, he notes that this theory does not fare nearly as well at explaining congressional dynamics during earlier polarized periods. While this critique is best evaluated in another venue, the point does underscore the care that scholars should take in seeking to understand congressional polarization. Crafting theories and analyses to explain this particular instance of polarization may undermine the ability to say something about polarization more generally, and achieving the latter will leave us with a richer understanding of Congress than settling for the former.

REFERENCES

Abramowitz, A., and Saunders, K. L. 1998. Ideological Realignment in the U.S. Electorate. *Journal of Politics*, 60(3): 634–52.
—— 2005. Why Can't We All Just Get Along? The Reality of a Polarized America. *The Forum*, 3(2): 1–21.

ALDRICH, J. H., and ROHDE, D. 2001. The Logic of Conditional Party Government: Revisiting the Electoral Connection, pp. 269–92 in *Congress Reconsidered*, 7th edn, ed. L. C. Dodd and B. I. Oppenheimer. Washington, DC: Congressional Quarterly Press.

ANSOLABEHERE, S., SNYDER, J. M., and STEWART, III, C. 2001. Candidate Positioning in US House Elections. *American Journal of Political Science*, 45(1): 136–59.

BARTELS, L. M. 2006. What's the Matter with What's the Matter with Kansas? *Quantitative Journal of Political Science*, 1(2): 201–26.

BECKER, L., and MOSCARDELLI, V. G. 2008. Congressional Leadership on the Front Lines: Committee Chairs, Electoral Security, and Ideology. *PS: Political Science & Politics*, 41(1): 77–82.

BINDER, S. A. 1999. The Dynamics of Legislative Gridlock, 1947–96. *American Political Science Review*, 93(3): 519–33.

—— and MALTZMAN, F. 2005. Congress and the Politics of Judicial Appointments, pp. 297–317 in Congress Reconsidered, 8th edn, ed. L. C. Dodd and B. I. Oppenheimer. Washington, DC: Congressional Quarterly Press.

BLACK, E., and BLACK, M. 2002. *Rise of the Southern Republicans*. Cambridge, MA: Harvard University Press.

BOND, J. R., FLEISHER, R., and KRUTZ, G. S. 2009. Malign Neglect: Evidence that Delay Has Become the Primary Method of Defeating Presidential Appointments. *Congress & the Presidency*, 36(3): 226–43.

BREWER, M. D., MARIANI, M. D., and STONECASH, J. M. 2002. Northern Democrats and Party Polarization in the U.S. House. *Legislative Studies Quarterly*, 27(3): 423–44.

BRUNELL, T. L. 2008. *Redistricting and Representation: Why Competitive Elections are Bad for America*. New York, NY: Routledge.

—— and GROFMAN, B. 2008. Evaluating the Impact of Redistricting on District Homogeneity, Political Competition, and Political Extremism in the U.S. House of Representatives, 1962–2006, pp. 117–40 in *Designing Democratic Government: Making Institutions Work*, ed. M. Levi, J. Johnson, J. Knight, and S. Stokes. New York: Russell Sage Press.

BURDEN, B. C. 2004. Candidate Positioning in US Congressional Elections. *British Journal of Political Science*, 34: 211–27.

CARMINES, E. G., and STIMSON, J. A. 1989. *Issue Evolution: Race and the Transformation of American Politics*. Princeton, NJ: Princeton University Press.

CARSON, J., CRESPIN, M. H., FINOCCHIARO, C. J., and ROHDE. D. W. 2007. Redistricting and Party Polarization in the U.S. House of Representatives. *American Politics Research*, 35(4): 878–904.

COOPER, JOSEPH, and BRADY, DAVID W. 1981. Institutional Context and Leadership Style: The House from Cannon to Rayburn. *American Political Science Review* 75(2): 411–25.

COX, G. W., and MCCUBBINS, M. D. 2005. *Setting the Agenda: Responsible Party Government in the U.S. House of Representatives*. New York, NY: Cambridge University Press.

ERIKSON, R. S., MACKUEN, M. B., and STIMSON, J. A. 2002. *The Macro Polity*. New York, NY: Cambridge University Press.

FENNO, R. F. 1978. *Home Style: House Members in their Districts*. Boston: Little, Brown.

FIORINA, M. P., ABRAMS, S. J., and POPE, J. C. 2006. *Culture War? The Myth of a Polarized America*. New York, NY: Pearson Longman.

FLEISHER, R., and BOND, J. R. 2000. Partisanship and the President's Quest for Votes on the Floor of Congress, pp. 154–85 in *Polarized Politics: Congress and the President in a Partisan Era*, ed. J. R. Bond and R. Fleisher. Washington, DC: Congressional Quarterly Press.

GIMPEL, J. G., and SCHUKNECHT, J. E. 2001. Interstate Migration and Electoral Politics. *Journal of Politics*, 63(1): 207–31.

GOLDMAN, S. 2003. Assessing the Senate Judicial Confirmation Process: The Index of Obstruction and Delay. *Judicature*, 86: 251–7.

HALL, R. L. 1996. *Participation in Congress*. New Haven, CT: Yale University Press.

HARRIS, D. B. 2009. Partisan Framing in Legislative Debates, pp. 41–59 in *Winning With Words*, ed. B. F. Schaffner and P. J. Sellers. New York, NY: Routledge.

HETHERINGTON, M. J. 2001. Resurgent Mass Partisanship: The Role of Elite Polarization. *American Political Science Review*, 95(3): 619–31.

—— 2009. Review Article: Putting Polarization in Perspective. *British Journal of Political Science*, 39: 413–48.

HIBBING, J. R., and THEISS-MORSE, E. 2002. *Stealth Democracy: Americans' Beliefs about How Government Should Work*. New York, NY: Cambridge University Press.

JACOBSON, G. C. 2000. Party Polarization in National Politics: The Electoral Connection, pp. 9–30 in *Polarized Politics: Congress and the President in a Partisan Era*, ed. J. R. Bond and R. Fleisher. Washington, DC: Congressional Quarterly Press.

—— 2007. *A Divider, Not a Uniter: George W. Bush and the American People, the 2006 Election and Beyond*. New York, NY: Pearson Longman.

JAMIESON, K. H., and FALK, E. 2000. Continuity and Change in Civility in the House, pp. 96–108 in *Polarized Politics: Congress and the President in a Partisan Era*, ed. J. R. Bond and R. Fleisher. Washington, DC: Congressional Quarterly Press.

JENKINS, J. A., SCHICKLER, E., and CARSON, J. L. 2004. Constituency Cleavages and Congressional Parties: Measuring Homogeneity and Polarization. *Social Science History*, 28(4): 537–73.

JONES, D. R. 2001. Party Polarization and Legislative Gridlock. *Political Research Quarterly*, 54(1): 125–41.

KERNELL, S. 2006. *Going Public: New Strategies of Presidential Leadership*. 4th edn. Washington, DC: Congressional Quarterly Press.

KREHBIEL, K. 1998. *Pivotal Politics*. Chicago, IL: University of Chicago Press.

LAYMAN, G. C., CARSEY, T. M., and HOROWITZE, J. M. 2006. Party Polarization in American Politics: Characteristics, Causes and Consequences. *Annual Review of Political Science*, 9: 83–110.

LEE, F. 2008. Agreeing to Disagree: Agenda Content and Senate Partisanship, 1981–2004. *Legislative Studies Quarterly*, 32(2): 199–222.

MAYHEW, D. R. 1974. *Congress: The Electoral Connection*. New Haven, CT: Yale University Press.

MCCARTY, N., POOLE, K., and ROSENTHAL, H. 2006. *Polarized America: The Dance of Ideology and Unequal Riches*. Cambridge, MA: Massachusetts Institute of Technology Press.

MILLER, W. E., and STOKES, D. E. 1963. Constituency Influence in Congress. *American Political Science Review*, 57(1): 45–56.

MONROE, B. L., COLARESI, M. P., and QUINN, K. M. 2008. Fightin' Words: Lexical Feature Selection and Evaluation for Identifying the Content of Political Conflict. *Political Analysis*, 16(4): 372–403.

OLESZEK, W. 2008. *Whither the Role of Conference Committees: An Analysis*. Washington, DC: Congressional Research Service.

OPPENHEIMER, B. I. 2005. Deep Red and Blue Congressional Districts, pp. 135–57 in *Congress Reconsidered*, 8th edn, ed. L. C. Dodd and B. I. Oppenheimer. Washington, DC: Congressional Quarterly Press.

ROBERTS, J. M., and SMITH, S. S. 2003. Procedural Contexts, Party Strategy, and Conditional Party Voting in the U.S. House of Representatives, 1971–2000. *American Journal of Political Science*, 47(2): 305–17.

ROHDE, D. W. 1991. *Parties and Leaders in the Postreform House*. Chicago, IL: The University of Chicago Press.

SAUNDERS, KYLE L., and ABRAMOWITZ, ALAN I. 2004. "Ideological Realignment and Active Partisans in the American Electorate." *American Politics Research*, 32(3): 285–309.

SELLERS, P. 2009. *Cycles of Spin: Strategic Communication in the U.S. Congress*. New York: Cambridge University Press.

SINCLAIR, B. 2006. *Party Wars: Polarization and the Politics of National Policy Making*. Norman, OK: University of Oklahoma Press.

SMITH, S. S. 2007. *Party Influence in Congress*. New York, NY: Cambridge University Press.

STONECASH, J. M., BREWER, M. D., and MARIANI, M. D. 2003. *Diverging Parties: Social Change, Realignment, and Party Polarization*. Boulder, CO: Westview Press.

SUNDQUIST, JAMES L. 1983. *Dynamics of the Party System: Alignment and Realignment of Political Parties in the United States*. Washington, DC: Brookings Institution.

THERIAULT, S. M. 2008. *Party Polarization in Congress*. New York, NY: Cambridge University Press.

Toward a More Responsible Two-Party System: A Report of the Committee on Political Parties. 1950. *American Political Science Review*, 44(3) Part 2, Supplement.

WAGNER, M. W. 2007. Beyond Policy Representation in the U.S. House: Partisanship, Polarization, and Citizens' Attitudes About Casework. *American Politics Research*, 35(6): 771–89.

WEISSBERG, R. 1978. Collective vs. Dyadic Representation in Congress. *American Political Science Review*, 72(2): 535–47.

WILLIAMS, M., and BAUM, L. 2006. Questioning Judges About Their Decisions: Supreme Court Nominees Before the Senate Judiciary Committee. *Judicature*, 90: 73–80.

ZHANG, Y., FRIEND, A. J., TRAUD, A. L., PORTER, M. A., FOWLER, J. H., and MUCHA, P. J. 2007. Community Structure in Congressional Cosponsorship Networks. *Physica A: Statistical Mechanics and its Applications*, 387(7): 1705–12.

CHAPTER 24

DELIBERATION IN CONGRESS

PAUL J. QUIRK

WILLIAM BENDIX

POLITICAL scientists like to say that politics is about "who wins and who loses." Winning and losing is certainly a prominent feature of politics in Congress—an institution that makes decisions by counting votes. But politics, especially in Congress, is also about a different question: put crudely, are policies smart or dumb? The issue, more precisely, is whether decisions are *intelligent* in view of the circumstances of policy and the goals and interests relevant to a decision. Such intelligence depends on Congress's use of information and reasoning in making decisions—or, in our terms, on the quality or effectiveness of *deliberation*. Research on Congress has focused almost entirely, however, on influence, coalitions, and other issues about winning and losing. It has largely overlooked deliberation and the intelligence of decisions.

The neglect is unfortunate. Making intelligent decisions is often difficult for Congress, and the stakes are sometimes huge. In 2008 and 2009, for example, Congress undertook several exceptionally important ventures in policymaking. Working with the Bush administration to prevent a threatened economic collapse, it passed a rescue package of US$700 billion to shore up the financial sector. Early in the Obama administration, it passed a financial stimulus package of US$787 billion. Although the measures moderated the economic downturn, their benefits were compromised by serious flaws. The financial rescue package failed to ensure that public funds were used to restore liquidity to credit markets. Vast amounts ended up paying bonuses to executives of rescued firms. In what was probably the outstanding case of deliberative failure in recent years, Congress in 2002 authorized a disastrous preemptive war in Iraq on the basis of unsubstantiated Bush administration claims that Iraq possessed weapons of mass destruction (Priest and Pincus 2004; Commission 2005).

There are a number of likely causes of Congress's failing to obtain available information or to weigh it intelligently in a particular case (Quirk 2005). Among others, the members may ignore unresolved uncertainties when acting in response to crisis or political pressure. They may lack patience for considerations that will be lost on their constituencies. Advocates may use false or misleading claims to promote their positions. Congress may give scarce attention to provisions that are added to a bill in the late stages of the legislative process or that are buried in a massively complex omnibus measure.

But rather than seeking to understand the deliberative function and the challenges to effective performance, scholars of Congress have generally proceeded as if preferences about public policies were unproblematic—and all participants in the legislative process know at every stage what policies they want (and should want) Congress to adopt. The only issue for analysis, therefore, has been who succeeds in getting it to do so.

Increasingly, however, political scientists have turned their attention to the processes and problems of deliberation in Congress, producing a modest stream of books and articles. The trend has originated partly among scholars of Congress, prompted by their own efforts to understand the institution (Cooper 1970; Maass 1983; Bessette 1994). But it also has been motivated by distinct scholarly agendas, associated with independent developments in rational-choice analysis (Krehbiel 1991; Bianco 1997) and normative political theory (Steiner, Bächtiger, et al. 2004). To an important extent, it has been led by scholars seeking to understand public policy-making (Kingdon 1984; Derthick and Quirk 1985; Landy, Roberts, and Thomas 1990; Mucciaroni and Quirk 2006).

Research in this area faces considerable challenges. Even though the literature is small, it is highly diverse. It ranges from formal modeling, to qualitative interpretation of rhetoric, to quantitative content analysis, to narrative accounts of policy-making processes and institutional change, among other approaches. Researchers use different definitions of deliberation and concepts of deliberative performance. In any case, they face the challenges of studying a process that turns on the beliefs and judgments of members of Congress.

In an article in the mid-1990s about the prospects for empirical research on legislative deliberation, Lascher offered what he called a "blunt" assessment of what had been achieved to date: "We are presently ill-prepared to assess legislative deliberation in practice, let alone to make recommendations for institutional reform" (1996, 502). The intervening years have seen growth in the literature and genuine progress. Nevertheless, we are still in the early stages of learning how to deal with this difficult subject.

In this chapter, we review the development of the literature, with attention to conflicts and ambiguities, as well as advances. We then offer some suggestions about promising directions for future work.

DEVELOPMENTS AND APPROACHES

Attention to the matter of deliberation in Congress has had ups and downs. Deliberation was a central preoccupation of the Framers of the Constitution and has always been a frequent concern of members of Congress. It was scrupulously ignored, however, in the early stages of behavioral political science. More recently, legislative deliberation has emerged as a significant focus of research, partly because of developments in rational-choice analysis and normative political theory.

Practitioners: from the framers to contemporary members

The framers sought to ensure that the government would make carefully considered decisions (Bessette 1994; Granstaff 1999). They believed that elected officials, both legislative and executive, too often acted on reckless or unjust demands of the citizenry. They thus sought to design processes for policy deliberation that would protect rights and liberty and ensure that government served the common interests of the citizens.

As Joseph Bessette (1980, 1994) points out, the framers' design for deliberation had several elements. The large expanse of the country—the "extended republic" of Madison's *Federalist* 10 (1987)—would help to prevent "majority faction" by making cohesive majorities of any kind unlikely. The separation of powers and checks and balances would help to block unwise or unjust actions that might arise from the ambitions of the executive or from legislative pandering to a popular majority. The differences in lengths of terms and geographic constituencies between the president, the House, and the Senate would ensure that a variety of perspectives were brought to bear. And indirect election of the president and senators, with lengthy terms and large constituencies, would promote the selection of accomplished individuals who would take a broad perspective and serve the common interests of the citizenry. In what became a common feature of academic literature on deliberation, the framers associated intelligence and careful thought with efforts to serve broad interests.

Members of Congress have carried forward the framers' concern with the deliberative function. As Cooper (1970) demonstrated in a pathbreaking historical study, early nineteenth-century House members debated how establishing a committee system would affect the chamber's ability to reason carefully about decisions. Maass (1983) showed that deliberation has been an ongoing concern in modern debates about procedural issues. From 1995 to 2006, congressional Democrats roundly criticized the Republican Congress for undermining deliberative processes (Mann and Ornstein 2006). Former Republican House staff member Donald Wolfensberger (2000), influential former Democratic Representative Lee Hamilton (2009), and senior Democratic Representative Henry Waxman (2009) have all made deliberation a central concern in thoughtful books about improving Congress.

Principled neglect: from pluralism to rational choice

In the early stages of behavioral political research, in the 1950s and early 1960s, this enduring real-world concern with deliberation did not register at all with scholars. Developing a "pluralist" or interest-group interpretation of American politics, scholars generally ignored the phenomenon of deliberation, and sometimes virtually denied its existence. In his influential study of the 1946 Full Employment Act, Stephen K. Bailey (1950) explained congressional decision-making as the product of members' responses to pressures from external constituencies, especially interest groups. He assigned no explanatory role to members' judgments or preferences about policy.

In several works, especially *The Intelligence of Democracy* (1965; see also Braybrooke and Lindblom 1963; Lindblom 1968, 1979), Charles E. Lindblom developed a pluralist analysis of how policymakers use information. Lindblom (1965) discounted the notion of policymakers deliberating from the perspective of general interests. He argued that policymakers who attempted such a "synoptic" approach would fail to comprehend the complexity of those interests and end up making mistakes. Workable outcomes result from "partisan mutual adjustment," in which competing groups use "partisan analysis" to defend their demands and come to an efficient resolution through bargaining. Lindblom's analysis implied that for legislators to deliberate about common interests was usually a bad idea.[1]

With the emergence of rational-choice literature on Congress in the 1970s, the rejection of deliberation was elevated to the status of an impossibility theorem. Depending on their focus, rational-choice scholars in this period modeled legislators either as seekers of reelection (Fiorina 1974; Mayhew 1974) or as maximizers of policy preferences taken as given (for a review, see Strom 1990).[2] Neither approach had room for deliberation. As other scholars began to explore the role of ideas in the late 1970s, rational-choice theorist Kenneth Shepsle (1980) dismissed their work on the grounds that policymakers used ideas only as "weapons," not as grounds for decision.[3]

By contrast, research on other policymaking institutions has long dealt with deliberation and related processes. Scholars of the presidency have studied how presidents organize their advisory processes, and how they use information and advice in making decisions (Burke and Greenstein 1989; Neustadt 1990; Burke 2000). Research on executive agencies has examined the effects on these processes of hierarchy, organizational cultures, and other influences (Downs 1967; Wilensky 1967; Kaufman 1973).

---

[1] Lindblom avoided blanket judgments about the most effective methods of making decisions. He recognized that synoptic decision-making would have superior results in some circumstances.

[2] The fixed preferences in the latter models were assumed to be determined outside the models, for example, on the basis of constituency demands.

[3] Shepsle did not consider why ideas would be useful as weapons if no one used them as grounds for decision. In an extreme manifestation of the self-interest approach, Morris Fiorina (1977) turned the denial of deliberation upside down. He argued that Congress intentionally designed programs to work inefficiently and produce complaints in order to generate requests for politically profitable constituency service. Ironically, to do so would require deliberation. He thus took for granted that Congress could accurately predict the effects of program designs, resist constituency preferences (for workable programs), and act on behalf of a collective interest (in improved prospects for reelection)—essentially all the capabilities that deliberation skeptics denied.

A modest literature assesses the ability of courts to deal with the complexities of public policy (Horowitz 1977; Melnick 1983; Derthick 2001; Dunn 2008). There is no rationale for addressing issues of deliberation in one policymaking institution and not another. If the president, for example, can act intelligently or not, and make mistakes or not, then so can Congress.

Rediscovering legislative deliberation

The first modern scholars of Congress who insisted on the importance of legislative deliberation were disciplinary traditionalists, critical of mainstream behavioral political science, who labored in obscurity for long periods before gaining recognition for their contributions. Arthur Maass, a professor of government at Harvard University from 1948 to 1984, rarely published but for many years taught a course on legislative–executive relations in which he developed an idiosyncratic, semi-normative, and mostly enthusiastic account of national policymaking institutions.[4] His first significant publication about deliberation in Congress came near the end of his career, when he used his course lectures as the basis for a book, *Congress and the Common Good* (1983).

The central notion of what Maass called his "discussion model," or alternatively "deliberation model," of American government was that the political system comprised a hierarchy of forums for discussion of the standards and desires of the political community. Congress and the committees were at the center of a larger process of discussion. Maass analyzed the effects of various structures and practices on Congress's ability to discuss issues thoroughly and take account of relevant information. But his main concern was whether institutions that defined broad interests (the community, the whole House and Senate) controlled those that tended to over-represent narrower interests (standing committees), and thus whether decision processes focused sufficiently on common interests. As with the framers, Maass' concern was largely about the substantive objectives, rather than the intelligence or thoroughness, of deliberation.[5]

The other early proponent of research on legislative deliberation, Joseph Bessette, influenced by Straussian training at the University of Chicago, wrote a dissertation on deliberation in Congress in the late 1970s, but then worked outside of academe for most of a decade. His unpublished convention paper comprising the entire dissertation (Bessette 1979) was one of the main citations on congressional deliberation (see,

---

[4] As a matter of full disclosure, we mention that Quirk was a graduate student at Harvard in the early 1970s but did not study with Maass.

[5] Maass wrote in a manner that appears methodologically or epistemologically unsophisticated to contemporary political scientists. He made little effort to distinguish normative and empirical claims, and described congressional activities in a manner that was normatively loaded. He recognized that Congress sometimes failed to meet the requirements of his normative model, but his account was mostly one of an elaborate design working well. In *Information and Legislative Organization* (1991), Keith Krehbiel credited Maass with initiating the contemporary study of congressional deliberation.

for example, Mansbridge 1988; see also Bessette 1980) until he returned to academe and published a revised and expanded study as *The Mild Voice of Reason* (1994).

More sophisticated than Maass' work, the book also received more attention in the discipline. Much of the book merely demonstrated through case studies that Congress did indeed deliberate. The cases showed that some members of Congress invested prodigious efforts in understanding the substance of issues, with no prospect of significant electoral rewards for doing so; and that large numbers of them some-times changed their minds, reversing outcomes, as a result of receiving new infor-mation. Bessette also evaluated recent changes in congressional rules and struc-tures, often echoing the framers' concern about excessive influence of public opinion (1980, ch.5).

Although discussing numerous specific institutional issues, neither Maass nor Bes-sette offered general theories of the depth or quality of legislative deliberation. Nor did they propose systematic methods of assessing deliberation. Their main contribu-tion was to establish the reality and importance of the phenomenon.

Converging agendas

By the time Bessette's book was published, two independent developments in the discipline—respectively, in rational-choice analysis and normative political theory—were already aiding and abetting efforts to study deliberation in any context. They swept away skepticism about the validity of the subject and helped make deliberation a high-profile concern of the discipline. They also led research on legislative deliber-ation in new directions, with both costs and benefits.

Rational choice and games of incomplete information

The first such development, in rational-choice theory, was the introduction of games of incomplete information and their use in addressing issues of information trans-mission, lobbying, deliberation, and legislative organization (Austen-Smith 1990; Gilligan and Krehbiel 1990; Krehbiel 1991; Lupia and McCubbins 1994). Rational-choice analysis requires attributing well-defined preferences over a set of out-comes to the relevant actors. The early political applications assumed that actors had fixed preferences over some object of direct political decision—policies, elec-tion results, budget allocations, or the like (Ordeshook 1986; Shepsle and Bonchek 1997). With preferences precisely stipulated, the models allowed no possible role for deliberation.

In the 1980s, however, rational-choice scholars of legislative politics began to explore a new type of game, based on conditions of incomplete information (Gilligan and Krehbiel 1990; Krehbiel 1991; Austen-Smith 1992). The games incorpo-rated several assumptions: 1) Legislators do not have fixed preferences over policies. Rather, they have preferences over the social, economic, or other outcomes that the policies will produce. Legislators' preferences over policies are induced by their beliefs about where the actual outcomes will fall. 2) The exact outcome of a given policy is initially uncertain—predictable only within some range. 3) Certain actors have opportunity to learn the outcome that a policy will produce by investing in costly information (as a committee may obtain information, for example, by holding hearings). Finally, 4) if an actor does obtain the information, she may have a choice of whether to reveal it to other actors, and whether to do so accurately.

The means of revelation are of two major types. In some models, the informed actor can make a statement about the outcome. These are called models of "cheap talk," because the statements have no costs or consequences other than those of communication (for accessible reviews, see Austen-Smith 1992; Austen-Smith and Feddersen 2009). In other models, the informed actor signals the information through an action that also has other consequences—for example, by proposing a bill (Gilligan and Krehbiel 1990; Krehbiel 1991). If the informed actor's preferences over outcomes are general knowledge, the bill she proposes signals the information she has obtained about actual outcomes. In either sort of game (although especially the cheap-talk variety), the informed actor may provide misleading information to improve the prospects for her preferred outcome. The other legislators, however, will recognize the incentive for distortion and attempt to adjust their beliefs to account for it. The situation leads to an intricate game of mutual anticipation and—much as with bluffing in poker—mixed strategies and variable results.

The principal work employing games of incomplete information with direct reference to Congress is Keith Krehbiel's imposing book *Information and Legislative Organization* (1991), along with an article co-authored with Thomas Gilligan (1990). The article develops the massively complex model and solutions that provide the analytic foundation of the book (which omits most of the technical material).

Krehbiel does not model legislative deliberation itself. Rather, using a signaling approach, he models a majority-rule legislature's decisions in designing institutions for deliberation—specifically, a committee system (1991, ch. 3). The model has three stages. In the first stage, a majority-rule legislature makes decisions to set up a committee. It chooses members of a certain type and a procedure for floor consideration of the committee's bills. Although these decisions about the committee are the focus of the investigation, the model assumes that the legislators in this institutional-design stage look ahead to a second stage, in which the committee, as constituted, decides whether to expend resources to obtain information about a bill. In making that decision, the committee in turn looks ahead to the third and last stage: The committee proposes a bill. The floor interprets the proposal as a signal of the committee's beliefs. It may amend the bill, if the rules established in the first stage permit amendments. Finally, it votes to pass or defeat the resulting measure. The actual outcome of the resulting policy—known by the floor or not—determines the payoffs for all the actors.

The complexity of the strategic calculations—with legislators thinking about poker-type strategic games two stages ahead—is stupendous (accounting for the profuse mathematics in the article). But the main considerations that drive the analysis are fairly straightforward. The legislature can appoint committee members whose policy preferences on the committee's issues are either representative of the whole body or else relatively extreme (as with members from rural areas appointed to the Agriculture Committees). Of the two types, members with representative preferences offer the advantage that they will not send misleading signals; but they also will have less incentive to obtain information and are more likely not to do so. Conversely, members with extreme preferences, "preference outliers," have strong incentives to obtain information, but they are more likely to send misleading signals about what they learn. Floor procedures may permit floor amendments or prohibit them. If floor amendments are permitted, the floor can protect itself against biased committee bills; but if committee bills are likely to be amended, the committee has less incentive to obtain information. In making its decisions about the committee, the floor balances these conflicting considerations.

Krehbiel's most important hypothesis—supported by his empirical evidence—is that contrary to disciplinary and political lore, committee members will generally have policy preferences close to those of the whole chamber. Another is that the full chamber provides protections against floor amendment mainly for committees that have representative preferences. It requires unrepresentative committees to face the discipline of floor amendment.

Scholars have tested Krehbiel's empirical claims, especially with respect to the representativeness of committees, with mixed results (Parker et al. 2004). In fact, the concrete findings resulting from his remarkable effort have been fairly modest to date. Krehbiel offered only a few hypotheses that can be tested using congressional data. And there have been few further applications of signaling games to issues of deliberation or institutional design in Congress (Bianco 1997). On the other hand, his conception of committees as providers of information, rather than vehicles for logrolling, has become commonplace in the discipline.

Scholars who have studied models of political talk, in contrast with Krehbiel's signaling approach, generally have not engaged directly with the literature on Congress, or addressed specific features of the institution. The most pertinent models deal with decision-making by a majority-rule committee, and focus on the incentives of committee members or other actors, such as lobbyists, to reveal their private information accurately (Austen-Smith 1992; Austen-Smith and Feddersen 2009). Because the actors in these models reveal their information by making statements, independent of any otherwise consequential action, these analyses provide a sharp focus on the conditions for full and accurate communication.

As Austen-Smith and Feddersen have observed, the political-talk models have yielded some findings that comport with intuition or observation (2009, 766–7). They find that larger differences in actors' preferences lead to less accurate communication; that an ability of one actor to expend resources to verify another actor's statement induces more accurate communication; and that conditions that provide direct rewards for accuracy or punishments for inaccuracy—for example, through reputation—also induce accuracy. Austen-Smith and Feddersen comment that although these findings are generally intuitive, the results that occur under particular conditions are often not apparent prior to analysis. If particular conditions matter, however, such results will be difficult to extrapolate to any real-world legislature because the legislature will only approximately fit any set of experimental conditions. These models—motivated by more general theoretical interests—may make only a limited contribution to developing useful hypotheses about deliberation in Congress.

Whatever the concrete payoffs for the study of Congress, the rational-choice work demonstrated that deliberation can be conceptualized precisely, has important consequences for decision-making, and can be subjected to rigorous analysis.

Normative political theory: deliberative democracy

The second independent development that promoted work on legislative deliberation came, so to speak, from the opposite corner of the political science discipline—a generally left-leaning branch of normative political theory. In a body of work inspired largely by critical theorist Jürgen Habermas (1984, 1990, 1994), theorists of deliberative democracy (Benhabib 1996; Gutmann and Thompson, 1996, 2004; Warren 1999; Mansbridge 2003) have explored possibilities for enhanced forms of democratic citizenship. These theorists call for new forums that would permit ordinary citizens to deliberate and decide policy issues directly. And they propose demanding norms for the conduct of those deliberations—that is, a "discourse ethics."

More specifically, the prescriptions of discourse ethics are designed to ensure that political decisions are reached by consensus through open discussions among citizens. To define the norms, Habermas identifies requirements of what he calls an "ideal speech situation" (1990, 88). Participants must have full and equal opportunity to express their views; they must treat each other with respect; they must avoid distortions and portray their positions honestly; and they must use rational arguments, addressing common interests, among other requirements (Flyvbjerg 1998, 213). In his view, such deliberation accomplishes several objectives: it expands participation among citizens; it leads to agreement on the basis of the best available arguments and evidence, eliminating other forms of power; thus it both promotes good decisions and enhances the legitimacy of those decisions (Edgar 2006, 65). Importantly, the deliberative theorists have not advocated these norms primarily, if at all, for application to the proceedings of a representative legislature. Even if one grants the claims of Habermasian democratic theory, the implications for legislative deliberations do not follow straightforwardly.

Nevertheless, deliberative democratic theory has influenced research on legislative deliberation in two ways. First, it has promoted the establishment of a multitude of special forums for citizen deliberation, in various settings, and researchers have undertaken numerous empirical studies of their outcomes (Thompson 2008). The theorists' expectation of cognitive and attitudinal benefits for participants has not received much support. But the flood of systematic, sometimes experimental research has helped close the book on disciplinary skepticism toward the subject of deliberation.

Second, and more directly relevant, one major study has used measures based on Habermas' norms to evaluate deliberation in legislatures. In *Deliberative Politics in Action*, Steiner, Bächtiger, et al. (2004) undertake an ambitious comparative assessment of fifty-two legislative debates, from the 1970s to the 1990s, in four national legislatures—three European parliaments and the U.S. Congress. It is certainly the most ambitious empirical study of legislative deliberation.

Steiner, Bächtiger, et al. select apparently representative debates about major policy issues (such as crime and abortion) in each country and then perform systematic content analysis of each debate. Basing the analysis on Habermas' requirements for an ideal speech situation, they code each speech for a number of features, using rigorous tests to ensure the reliability of the measures. Are speakers able to make their statements without interruption? Do they provide justifications for their positions? If so, do the justifications appeal to common interests, and spell out how the policies will advance those interests. Do speakers avoid *ad hominem* arguments and express respect for opponents, their positions, and the groups or interests they represent? And do they demonstrate a willingness to compromise and seek common ground (2004, 107–8, 171–9)? They then aggregate the measures to assess the quality of each debate.

The findings generally comport with the authors' expectations, derived from comparative politics literature on consensualist versus majoritarian institutions (Lijphart 1984). Steiner, Bächtiger, et al. find that institutional conditions that require a consensus for action, rather than facilitating majority rule, tend to produce superior debates. However, the findings on Congress largely do not fit their expectations. Steiner, Bächtiger, et al. had expected to see a relatively high quality of discourse in Congress, because members can easily cross party lines, increasing the need for broad support. In fact, the performance of Congress is significantly inferior to that of the German and British parliaments (2004, 122–5). Beyond institutional conditions, these authors find that debates are inferior when the issues are characterized by polarized partisan conflict and when they are highly salient to the general public.

With its careful methods and comparative design, the study by Steiner, Bächtiger, et al. is a major development in the literature on legislative deliberation. Nevertheless, the value of the study is compromised, in our view, by measures that are not designed for debate among political elites and do not focus on substantive content. The measures deal instead with what we might call debate comportment (absence of interruption, mutual respect, openness to compromise) and formal attributes of arguments (fully articulated justifications, appeal to common interests).

The norms associated with these measures are in our view problematic in two respects. First, the norms calling for mutual respect, compromise and cooperation, and appeals to common interests are sometimes incompatible with the requirements of a competitive democracy. Intense partisan competition may almost inevitably produce hard-ball rhetorical methods: disparaging the opposition's positions; questioning their motives; expressing determination to defeat them; and using appeals to fear and anger, among others. Such methods are often important in getting citizens to pay attention to politics, a central challenge for representative democracy (Marcus, Neuman, and MacKuen 2000; Geer 2006). To be sure, the contemporary Congress arguably has become excessively partisan and conflictual (Quirk 2005; Mann and Ornstein 2006; Hamilton 2009). Nevertheless, a set of norms that seeks to minimize tough rhetoric is in our view inappropriate to the congressional context.

Second, the Steiner, Bächtiger, et al. measures do not deal with the accuracy of factual claims, the validity of causal arguments, attention to relevant considerations, or other staple topics in substantive criticism of policy arguments. In their nearest approach to substantive assessment of arguments, the measures attribute superior quality to justifications that spell out how a policy will lead to achieving a goal. But such justifications are not in fact necessarily superior. Indeed, one reason a speaker may not spell out a justification is that the audience can fill in the missing steps. More-over, the measures give full credit to all factual and causal premises of justifications. Other things equal, for example, a justification premised on acknowledging human-induced climate change would score no higher, by Steiner, Bächtiger, et al.'s measures, than one premised on denying it.

Importantly, even though the measures in this study do not directly address the intelligence or substantive merits of deliberations, it is possible that they provide a serviceable proxy for those attributes. Debates that comply with norms of Haber-masian discourse ethics may generally use informed, intelligent substantive argu-ments. Debates that violate those norms may also use uninformed or misleading arguments. But whether this convenient situation actually exists is by no means self-evident.

******

The impressive and important work motivated respectively by the rational-choice and deliberative democratic-theory agendas, more than any other influences, have made research on deliberation in Congress an entirely respectable enterprise in the discipline. For reasons we have discussed, their substantive payoffs with respect to Congress have been limited. Additional work, however, has derived from research on the institutional politics of Congress or the politics of policymaking.

Deliberation and the politics of institutional structure

Scholars have extensively investigated the development of congressional institutions (see Part V, this volume). Although much of the work has bearing on how Congress performs its deliberative function, very little of it explicitly discusses it. C. Lawrence Evans's (1999) review of literature on legislative structures and procedures did not use the word *deliberation*. Only a few modest works, all published since that review, have dealt directly with the development of Congress's deliberative capability.

A central theme in the literature is the conflict between facilitating control by the majority and enabling minorities to block or delay action. The never-ending struggle between majorities and minorities figures prominently in work on party leadership, floor procedure, the committee system, the Senate filibuster, and many other topics (Cox and McCubbins 1993, 2005; Sinclair 1997, 2005; Binder and Smith 1997; Smith

2005; Wawro and Schickler 2006). In work on conditional party government, Rohde (1991), Aldrich (1995), Sinclair (2005, 2006), and others (see also Jacobson 2003) have traced variations in the resulting choices largely to changes in the ideological composition of the congressional parties. Wawro and Schickler (2006) focus on interactions between ideological distributions, legislative workloads, and other factors to explain variation in the Senate rules and practices regarding the filibuster.

In part, the bearing of majority-versus-minority institutional conflict on deliberation is straightforward. Any rule or procedure that enables a minority to block or delay action will create additional opportunity for information-gathering and debate. In Schattschneider's (1960) terms, it may expand "the scope of conflict," engaging more participants in discussion. At the same time, however, it may increase opportunity for sheer obstructionism—just saying *no*—by the minority.

A wide range of other literature on congressional institutions also bears on deliberation. Research on committees, the committee system, and committee power investigates Congress's central mechanism for deliberation and policy development (Maltzman 1997; Rohde 2005; Baughman 2006). Much of this research concerns tradeoffs between committee autonomy and whole-chamber or party control. It addresses the role of specialization and expertise, the influence of broadly based versus narrowly based interests, and other aspects of deliberation. Other relevant topics include leadership (Strahan 2007), legislative careers and professionalization (Sinclair 2009), the growth of staff and staff agencies (Bimber 1996), the several generations of budget reform (Patashnik 2000, 2005), pork barrel spending (Lee 2005), omnibus legislation (Krutz 2001), and congressional access to executive branch information (Johannes 1976, 1977), among others. Much of the relevant literature does not emphasize the concept of deliberation, or even use the term (see, however, Smith 1989; Sinclair 2005; Baughman 2006; Strahan 2007). But research and theory on deliberation needs to incorporate relevant findings of the institutional literature even if they are not explicitly presented in those terms.

A few works analyze the development of congressional institutions with respect specifically to their impact on deliberation (Maass 1983; Krehbiel 1991; Bessette 1994). In a largely speculative essay, Quirk (1993) assesses the significance for deliberation of institutional developments in the reform and post-reform Congresses from the mid-1970s to the early 1990s. These works often indicate tradeoffs between deliberation and other institutional values (Quirk 1993). For example, rules that make the legislative process transparent—such as televised floor debate and recorded votes—make it easier for members to resist pressure from narrowly based political forces but harder to resist those from mass constituencies. Rules that strengthen the majority party leadership will enhance Congress's ability to deliberate about collective goods, for example, in setting fiscal policy, but they will also shut the minority party and even majority-party moderates out of deliberations (Fiorina 1980; Cox and McCubbins 2005). Baughman (2006) finds that referral of bills to multiple committees in the House promotes consideration of competing interests and perspectives but also reduces opportunity for collective deliberation within the committee.

Several scholars have used easily observed manifestations of deliberation to make developmental comparisons. Wirls (2007) compared House and Senate debates in the pre-Civil War Congress, using data on the numbers and length of speeches, the breadth of members' participation, the educational backgrounds of participants, and the degree of news coverage to challenge notions of a "Golden Age of the Senate." On some major issues, House debates were superior to the Senate's in these terms. Conner and Oppenheimer (1993) measured Congress's deliberative activities in three Congresses from 1923 to 1980, demonstrating the effects of increasing workload. From 1923–4 to 1955–6, the House dealt with rising legislative demands by devoting more days and hours to legislative work. By 1979–80, however, that option had been exhausted and the House could only respond to the growing workload by cutting back on deliberation. It conducted business with few members in attendance and disposed of lesser bills after very brief consideration. Krutz (2001) describes the recent tendency for Congress to fold enormous amounts of policymaking into omnibus bills, with decisions dominated by party leaders and their staff. We need research to evaluate empirically the effects of time and attention in debate on the substantive quality of deliberation. A reasonable presumption, however, is that the expanding volume of policymaking that Congress undertakes has major costs in the quality of deliberation.

In two books (1993, 2006), Mann and Ornstein have tracked a decline in the quality of congressional deliberations over the last two decades. In their 1993 study, they attributed the decline to a jump in committee assignments and an obstructionist Senate, among other factors. Committee chairs were often left alone to question witnesses at hearings. Individual senators were holding the chamber "hostage" by threatening to filibuster on both major and minor bills (1993, 49; compare Wawro and Schickler 2006). In *The Broken Branch* (2006), Mann and Ornstein argue that since the late 1990s there has been "a virtual collapse of genuine deliberation in the House" (106) and an unabated use of capricious filibusters in the Senate (108). They attribute this collapse primarily to almost "tribal" levels of partisanship since the 1994 Republican takeover of Congress (x).

In a recent essay, Quirk (2005) suggests a general theoretical perspective for understanding why Congress adopts or fails to adopt structures that support deliberation. He identifies three distinct processes that shape these structures. First, in the initial establishment and early development of the institution, members choose structures largely for long-term consequences. They will readily adopt whatever structures— for example, rules of order, a committee system, and provisions for amendment and debate—appear essential for effective deliberation.

Second, at all subsequent stages, Congress continues to amend institutional structures; but members invest nearly all of their energy in a constantly changing competition for influence (Schickler 2001; Evans 2005; compare Davidson and Oleszek 1977). Some of the resulting institutional changes—especially those sponsored by centrist factions or the minority party—strengthen deliberative capability. Others weaken it. And many have no effect. In any case, most changes in deliberative capability are byproducts of conflicts over other interests.

Third, even in later stages, Congress has a residual ability to make institutional changes for the purpose of improving deliberation. To be feasible, such changes must correct major defects in deliberative practices, have no major costs or politically invidious effects, or both. In 1974, Congress was able to transform the budget process, despite profoundly diminishing the power and prestige of the appropriations committees, because the Nixon administration was exploiting Congress's manifest incompetence in managing fiscal policy to challenge its authority. On the other hand, Congress has been able to adopt pay-as-you-go budget rules in certain periods largely because they constrained liberal and conservative proposals in the same way (Patashnik 2005).

Bimber's (1996) study of the birth, growth, and eventual death of a congressional staff agency, the Office of Technology Assessment (OTA), in the 1970s and 1980s, demonstrates the stringency of the partisan neutrality that may be required. To avoid getting enmeshed in partisan conflict, the OTA avoided either endorsing or opposing specific policies in its reports. Even so, congressional Republicans eventually concluded that OTA was disproportionately supporting Democratic positions, and succeeded in killing it in 1995.[6]

Even after the initial phase of development, therefore, Congress has some ability to adopt rules and structures for the express purpose of improving deliberation, but it is contingent upon special circumstances.

Deliberation and policymaking

Finally, a few scholars have begun to examine the content of debate, and sometimes the resulting decisions, to assess and explain the character of deliberations in Congress. We have already discussed one such study, Steiner, Bächtiger, et al. (2004), inspired by deliberative democratic theory. Much of the additional work has been done by scholars with prior interests in public policy.

Studies of policymaking for decades have occasionally explored what policymakers know or believe about policy decisions, and the sources and quality of their information.[7] However, the first work we know that used case studies of congressional policymaking specifically to assess the deliberation is a study by Landy, Roberts, and Thomas (1990) on environmental policymaking in the 1970s and early 1980s. Although mainly concerned with decisions and leadership by the Environmental Protection Agency (EPA), Landy, Roberts, and Thomas present a chapter-length analysis of the development of one major piece of environmental legislation, the 1980 Superfund law (ch. 5). The landmark legislation established a massive program to clean up hazardous waste sites, while requiring firms and industries responsible for the waste to pay the costs.

---

[6] Another agency designed to enhance deliberation, the Congressional Research Service, has managed to survive despite facing increased partisan pressures.

[7] See, for example, Moynihan (1973), Steiner (1971), Derthick (1979), Stein (1984), Derthick and Quirk (1985), Weatherford (1987).

Landy, Roberts, and Thomas set forth an elaborate normative framework, defining several requirements for satisfactory deliberation. But their procedure for assessing the deliberation is simple. Drawing on their own expertise in environmental policy, they examine the content of media coverage, EPA statements, and congressional debates in an unstructured, open-ended manner to evaluate their usefulness in clarifying issues and informing decision-making. The question is whether Congress was given an adequate understanding of the substantive issues, in relation to the information available at the time.

Landy, Roberts, and Thomas argue that Congress's consideration of the hazardous waste problem was distorted by a hysterical national reaction to the discovery of contamination of a residential neighborhood from a mismanaged waste disposal facility at Love Canal, New York. Both EPA and media rhetoric greatly exaggerated the evidence of a threat and led to a virtual panic in Congress. The inability to conduct a calm discussion precluded development of rational criteria for assessing the risks of abandoned hazardous waste sites. It also led Congress to ignore alternatives to clean-up, such as moving people away from a contaminated area, that would sometimes be safer and less costly.

Using these open-ended methods, therefore, Landy, Roberts, and Thomas are able to connect defects of deliberation to problems of the policies adopted—directly explaining policy failure. The disadvantage of their approach, however, is that it lacks any specific criteria or procedures for evaluation. In principle, it is vulnerable to ideological bias or other subjective judgments, and is essentially not replicable.

An intriguing, though problematic study by Granstaff (1999) assessed congressional deliberation on three major foreign-policy issues, primarily on the basis of the logical validity of advocates' arguments. He identifies a list of ten logical fallacies that he suggests can be identified relatively clearly in reviewing a debate—*ad hominem* appeals, inferring causality from mere sequence, and eight others. He then assesses each sentence in a speech to determine whether it contains or contributes to any of the fallacies and computes the percentage of such fallacious sentences. In a qualitative component of the assessment, Granstaff explores whether speakers adequately addressed certain generic issues. Thus, for example, he finds the congressional debate on the 1982 intervention in Lebanon unsatisfactory because participants argued about various outcomes without explaining the national interest in Lebanon. In our view, Granstaff's methods overlook the fact that real-world persuasive rhetoric rarely makes fully explicit, logically complete arguments. We are skeptical that an approach focusing on logical fallacies and omissions can produce useful measures of the effectiveness of deliberation.

At around the same time, Lascher (1999) undertook a comparative case study of legislative deliberation on automobile insurance reform in two American states and two Canadian provinces. Although the research does not focus on Congress, one aspect of his approach is noteworthy. Lascher took advantage of a special feature of automobile insurance reform, namely, that popular discontent with rising premium rates was prompting demands for certain policies—mandatory rate cuts and rate controls—that were almost certainly not workable according to any reputable economic analysis. He was able to show that the legislatures that had superior resources (with respect to staffing, professionalization, and length of sessions) conducted better informed discussion and managed to avoid the dubious policies. The study illustrates the analytic advantages for research on deliberation of studying policy issues that elicit a high degree of expert consensus.

Esterling (2004; see also Esterling 2007) looks at similar issues in a study that focuses specifically on the influence of experts in congressional decision-making. Esterling examines three cases in which Congress considered major market-based reforms to existing regulatory or administrative programs. In each case, economic analysis promised that the reforms would produce sizable gains in social efficiency. Esterling examines the exchanges between hearing witnesses and committee members, using the members' questions to identify the issues and information they attended to. He then traces the legislative process and the policy outcome. He seeks to discover whether and under what conditions Congress learns from expert advice.

Esterling argues that interest groups are central to Congress's ability to learn from experts. If opposing interest groups make conflicting claims about a policy, he suggests, Congress has no way to assess their validity. Even if the best analysis supports the policy, Congress will be unable to act. In the 1972 debate over reforming Medicare payment practices, Esterling argues, the American Medical Association and other healthcare interest groups created a fog of unsupported objections to the reforms. The resulting uncertainties forced Congress to abandon them (2004, ch. 8).

We doubt that Congress relies on inferences from interest-group positions to discern what experts conclude about a policy. A congressional committee should have little difficulty finding out about the reputable policy analysis on a legislative issue, if it wants to do so. Interest groups may play a larger role in learning by Congress members who do not serve on the relevant committees and devote minimal time to an issue (Mucciaroni and Quirk 2006). But in general we see merit in the conventional assumption that policy analysis and interest-group demands are independent, often competing influences on policymaking, operating largely through separate paths.

In a recent book-length study, Mucciaroni and Quirk (2006) present an approach for analyzing congressional deliberation that deals with the substantive content of debate—that is, the information it conveys about the policy issue—and yet is relatively systematic and replicable. In their theoretical discussion, Mucciaroni and Quirk argue that the information value or intelligence of legislative debate turns on the tradeoffs that opposing advocates make between two, often conflicting attributes of their possible claims. They can select claims either for persuasive *force* (the magnitude of a claim's effect on an audience's policy preferences, given their acceptance of it) or else for credibility (a claim's ability to sustain such acceptance, given exposure to criticism and scrutiny). The authors develop theoretical expectations about the conditions under which advocates will favor more credible claims and thus provide more reliable information for decision-making.

In assessing floor debate, Mucciaroni and Quirk focus on the opposing sides' empirical claims that bear on the effects of policies. Analyzing three major legislative issues of the mid-1990s (welfare reform, estate tax repeal, and telecommunications deregulation), they begin by identifying the most prominent effect issues in each debate. They next identify the opposing sides' principal claims about each effect issue. In the most distinctive feature of their analysis, they compare the respective claims with the available evidence—in published policy research, government reports, or other sources—and assign scores for the claims' accuracy in representing the evidence (ch. 2). For example, they note that advocates of the 1996 Republican welfare reform bill persistently alleged—despite extensive contrary empirical evidence—that the welfare program had caused an increase in births to unmarried mothers (69–72). Finally, Mucciaroni and Quirk aggregate these scores to measure the information value of the debates on each effect issue and for each of the three policies.

In general, Mucciaroni and Quirk find a fairly low level of information value and high levels of distortion and inaccuracy. They find tendencies toward superior deliberation, however, on issues where debate is less ideologically polarized, where interest groups are actively engaged on both sides of the policy issue, and in the Senate as opposed to the House, among other conditions.

By contrast with the open-ended substantive assessment used by Landy, Roberts, and Thomas, Mucciaroni and Quirk's more structured approach reduces the risk of ideological or political bias on the researchers' part. The measures are still subject to potentially biased interpretation. But the most critical interpretive task requires the researchers to do something that researchers in any area are required to do, namely, to summarize and assess a body of prior evidence. The main disadvantage of the approach is that it requires a sizable investment of skilled effort for each legislative case. Unlike the Steiner, Bächtiger, et al. (2004) coding methods, it is not suitable for a large-N or even medium-N comparative study.

CHALLENGES AND DIRECTIONS

The study of deliberation in Congress is by now a going concern. It has made significant strides since Maass and Bessette had to work hard just to establish the validity of the subject (Austen-Smith and Riker 1987; Landy, Roberts, and Thomas 1990; Krehbiel 1991), and has gained momentum in the last several years (Esterling 2004; Steiner, Bächtiger, et al. 2004; Mucciaroni and Quirk 2006). It has begun to replace the mere aspirations that Lascher described in 1996 with actual achievements. Theory and evidence from a handful of studies have converged on some findings about broad conditions affecting the quality of deliberation—indicating negative effects of partisan polarization and positive effects of structures that require broad support for action (Landy, Roberts, and Thomas 1990; Granstaff 1999; Steiner, Bächtiger, et al. 2004; Mann and Ornstein 2006; Mucciaroni and Quirk 2006; Austen-Smith 2009). The research has supported some additional common expectations—for example, the superiority of Senate over House debate and the adverse effects of brevity and crowded agendas (Mucciaroni and Quirk 2006). On the other hand, it has produced complex or inconsistent findings on other issues, such as the effects of public salience and of interest-group activity (Landy, Roberts, and Thomas 1990; Esterling 2004; Steiner, Bächtiger, et al. 2004; Mucciaroni and Quirk 2006), indicating the need for further work.

The work, in fact, is just beginning. Taken together, the literature is based on a very small body of observations on congressional deliberation. The findings from systematic research alone are far from sufficient, for example, to provide usable guidance for decisions about institutional structures or management of deliberative processes. At this point, however, they at least add value to analyses and recommendations by informed commentators (Hamilton 2009).

To continue making progress, scholars of deliberation in Congress must deal with four kinds of challenges. First, the field needs to overcome confusion about basic issues of concepts and criteria of performance. The difficulties begin with the definition of *deliberation* itself. Scholars influenced by theories of deliberative democracy are inclined to think of deliberation as a special event—centered on discussion in a large group, such as an assembly of ordinary citizens, and established through an institutional innovation or experiment.[8] Others scholars, such as Bessette (1994, 46–54), incorporate normative elements in their definition, such that deliberation requires legislators to engage extensively with other legislators, to assess policies from the standpoint of common interests, and to weigh new evidence and arguments seriously with a real possibility of changing their minds.

We believe that the field will be better served by a barebone, dictionary definition of deliberation, adjusted for application to a collective entity.[9] We would define legislative deliberation as the cognitive or intellectual process—which can be embedded in any of a variety of social and institutional processes—in which the legislature uses information and reasoning to make policy decisions. It thus occurs in committee hearings, members' meetings with lobbyists, floor debate, and many other occasions for communication, learning, and reflection. It aims to serve common interests, parochial ones, or both. Defining deliberation broadly in this way enables other features to enter the analysis, appropriately, as variables: deliberation can be thorough or superficial; focus on common interests or conflicting ones; have broad or narrow participation; exhibit mutual respect and cooperation or a lack of them; observe constitutional and institutional norms or fail to do so, and so on. The definition permits comparison between radically different alternative processes of deliberation.

Studies of legislative deliberation have addressed diverse notions of results and performance. We do not dismiss the potential benefits of certain forms of citizen

[8] Even Maass, who did not cite Habermas, sometimes wrote as if *deliberation* and *discussion* were synonyms.

[9] The following is a typical dictionary entry for the definition of *deliberate*: Verb, intransitive: 1. To think carefully and often slowly, as about a choice to be made. 2. To consult with another or others in a process of reaching a decision. Verb, transitive: To consider (a matter) carefully and often slowly, as by weighing alternatives. *The American Heritage Dictionary of the English Language*, 4th edn (Boston: Houghton Mifflin, 2009).

deliberation and participatory democracy (Fishkin and Laslett 2003; Sturgis 2003; Warren and Pearse 2008). Nevertheless, we believe that research on deliberation in Congress should address primarily the requirements of representative democracy and the American constitutional system. The central question for such research, following the framers, is whether Congress makes informed, well-reasoned decisions, resulting in intelligent policies. The main motivation is that citizens have to live with the decisions that Congress makes. Further issues include whether, in its deliberations, Congress follows its own established norms and practices (such as "regular order") and whether it maintains a significant degree of independence of the executive branch (Cooper 2009). From this perspective, it is not very relevant whether Congress meets expectations of discourse ethics that arise from a fundamentally distinct reform program and that conflict, in some degree, with the requirements of vigorous electoral competition.

Second, research on deliberation needs a great deal of creative work on strategies of observation and measurement. As we have seen, approaches to assessing deliberation vary enormously—from open-ended critical analysis, using whatever speeches, news reports, research studies, and other documents are available (Landy, Roberts, and Thomas 1990) to systematic content analysis of well-defined samples of speeches (Steiner, Bächtiger, et al. 2004). The wide range of approaches reflects the apparently severe tradeoffs that exist between incorporating substantive information about policy issues in assessments of deliberation, on the one hand, and both economizing on research resources (permitting larger numbers of observations) and minimizing the potential for political bias or other subjective influences, on the other. (The Mucciaroni and Quirk [2006] study occupies a middle ground on these tradeoffs, but does not escape them.) In our view, studies that deal in depth with one or a few policy decisions, permitting close attention to substantive issues, will remain central to assessing legislative deliberations (see Bendix and Quirk 2009). But scholars should also seek methods of content analysis that produce workable proxies for the substantive intelligence of deliberation.[10] Such a strategy would require that certain features of rhetoric itself serve as markers of the relation between that rhetoric and the realities of policy. The Steiner, Bächtiger, et al. measures, especially the quality of justifications, should be evaluated from this standpoint. In any case, scholars should also entertain new measures specifically designed for the proxy strategy. For example, the magnitude of the discrepancies between opposing sides' factual claims might indicate a debate's degree of factual accuracy. In the end, however, it may be impossible to judge whether deliberations are informed and intelligent without bringing to bear significant, independent knowledge of the issues.

Ultimately, research should link the quality of deliberations to their most relevant results—the actual consequences of policy decisions. In both large- and small-N studies, scholars should seek indicators of the intelligence (efficiency, workability,

---

[10] Although considerable caution is warranted in using automated methods that merely, for example, count words to study the subtle phenomenon of deliberation, these efforts may benefit from the expanding availability of digitized congressional documents. See Monroe, Colaresi, and Quinn 2007.

justice, and so on) of the resulting decisions. With appropriate controls for partisan and ideological change, for example, they might look at the frequency or magnitude of subsequent amendments as an indicator of the intelligence of legislative decisions.

Third, the field needs much more theoretical work that focuses directly on the conditions and processes for informed, intelligent deliberation. It is not sufficient to treat the capacity for deliberation as equivalent to the procedural rights of the minority party or to the opportunities for small groups of legislators to block action. Majorities may deliberate intelligently, or not; and obstruction may enhance deliberation, or not. A variety of unrelated factors shape the quality of deliberation. To deal with the full range of relevant factors, theoretical efforts should seek to integrate findings from rational-choice formal models, the psychology of decision-making, and the existing theoretical and empirical work on Congress. A central theme of such theorizing is a kind of bootstrapping: how does Congress, with all its conflicting goals and interests, decide about deliberative practices in ways that lead to deciding other matters more intelligently?

Finally, research on deliberation needs to keep up—or more accurately, catch up—with developments in Congress. For two decades, the trend in Congress has been toward increasing partisan conflict and majority-party control of the legislative process, especially in the House of Representatives. To a great extent, party leaders and party organs have taken over policy formulation, relegating the standing committees to subordinate roles (Sinclair 1997, 2005). Commentators (Mann and Ornstein 2006), former members (Hamilton 2009), and others lament the loss of deliberation. But we need to recognize that party control of policy formulation does not simply abolish deliberation, as we define it; it accomplishes deliberation, however well or poorly, by other means. Deliberations in closed, like-minded groups are vulnerable to severe bias and error (Sunstein 2000). But in the absence of grounds for expecting any substantial return to bipartisanship in the foreseeable future, we need to come to grips with deliberation in the partisan Congress.[11]

References

ALDRICH, J. H. 1995. *Why Parties? The Origin and Transformation of Political Parties in America.* Chicago: University of Chicago Press.

AUSTEN-SMITH, D. 1990. Information Transmission in Debate. *American Journal of Political Science,* 34(1): 124–52.

AUSTEN-SMITH, D. 1992. Strategic Models of Talk in Political Decision Making. *International Political Science Review,* 13(1): 45–58.

——and FEDDERSEN, T. J. 2009. Review: Information Aggregation and Communication in Committees. *Philosophical Transactions of the Royal Society B,* 364(1518): 763–9.

——and RIKER, W. H. 1987. Asymmetric Information and the Coherence of Legislation. *American Political Science Review,* 81(3): 897–918.

[11] William Bendix's dissertation, in progress at the University of British Columbia, examines the processes of deliberation in the partisan Congress.

BAILEY, S. K. 1950. *Congress Makes a Law: The Story behind the Employment Act of 1946*. New York: Columbia University Press.

BAUGHMAN, J. 2006. *Common Ground: Committee Politics in the U.S. House of Representatives*. Stanford, CA: Stanford University Press.

BENDIX, W., and QUIRK, P. J. 2009. Deliberating Security and Democracy: The Patriot Act and Surveillance Policy, 2001–2008. Paper presented at the annual meeting of the Midwest Political Science Association 67th Annual National Conference, The Palmer House Hilton, Chicago, IL.

BENHABIB, S. 1996. Toward a Deliberative Model of Democratic Legitimacy, pp. 67–94 in *Democracy and Difference: Contesting the Boundaries of the Political*, ed. S. Benhabib. Princeton, NJ: Princeton University Press.

BESSETTE, J. 1979. Deliberation in Congress. Paper presented at the 1979 Annual Meeting of the American Political Science Association.

——1980. Deliberative Democracy: The Majority Principle in American Government, pp. 102–16 in *How Democratic Is the Constitution?*, ed. R. A. Goldwin and W. A. Schambra. Washington, DC: AEI Press.

——1994. *The Mild Voice of Reason*. Chicago: University of Chicago Press.

BIANCO, W. T. 1997. Reliable Sources or Usual Suspects? Cue-taking, Information Transmission, and Legislative Committees. *The Journal of Politics*, 59(3): 913–24.

BIMBER, B. 1996. *The Politics of Expertise in Congress: The Rise and Fall of the Office of Technology Assessment*. Albany, NY: New York State University Press.

BINDER, S. A. 1997. *Minority Rights, Majority Rule: Partisanship and the Development of Congress*. New York: Cambridge University Press.

——2005. Elections, Parties, and Governance, pp. 148–70 in *The Legislative Branch*, ed. P. J. Quirk and S. Binder. New York: Oxford University Press.

——and SMITH, S. S. 1997. *Politics or Principle? Filibustering in the United States Senate*. Washington, DC: Brookings Institution.

BRAYBROOKE, D., and LINDBLOM, C. 1963. *A Strategy of Decision*. New York: Free Press.

BURKE, J. P. 2000. *The Institutional Presidency: Organizing and Managing the White House from FDR to Clinton*. 2nd edn. Baltimore: Johns Hopkins University Press.

——and GREENSTEIN, F. 1989. *How Presidents Test Reality: Decisions on Vietnam, 1954 and 1965*. New York: Russell Sage Foundation.

COMMISSION ON THE INTELLIGENCE CAPABILITIES OF THE UNITED STATES REGARDING WEAPONS OF MASS DESTRUCTION. 2005. Report to the President of the United States (May 31), available at http://www.gpoaccess.gov/wmd/pdf/full_wmd_report.pdf (accessed September 3, 2010).

CONNOR, G. E., and OPPENHEIMER, B. I. 1993. Deliberation: An Untimed Value in a Timed Game, pp. 315–20 in *Congress Reconsidered*, 5th edn, ed. L. C. Dodd and B. I. Oppenheimer. Washington, DC: CQ Press.

COOPER, J. 1970. *The Origins of the Standing Committees and the Development of the Modern House*. Houston: William Marsh Rice University.

——2009. From Congressional to Presidential Preeminence: Power and Politics in Late Nineteenth-century America and Today, pp. 361–91 in *Congress Reconsidered*, 9th edn, ed. L. C. Dodd and B. I. Oppenheimer. Washington, DC: CQ Press.

COX, G. W., and MCCUBBINS, M. D. 1993. *Legislative Leviathan: Party Government in the House*. Berkley, CA: University of California Press.

————2005. *Setting the Agenda: Responsible Party Government in the U.S. House of Representatives*. New York: Cambridge University Press.

DAVIDSON R. H., and OLESZEK, W. J. 1977. *Congress Against Itself.* Bloomington, IN: Indiana University Press.

DERTHICK, M. 1979. *Policymaking for Social Security.* Washington, DC: Brookings Institution.

——2001. *Up in Smoke: From Legislation to Litigation in Tobacco Politics.* Washington, DC: CQ Press.

——and QUIRK, P. J. 1985. *The Politics of Deregulation.* Washington, DC: Brookings Institution.

DOWNS, A. 1967. *Inside Bureaucracy.* Boston: Little, Brown.

DUNN, J. M. 2008. *Complex Justice: The Case of Missouri v. Jenkins.* Chapel Hill, NC: University of North Carolina Press.

EDGAR, A. 2006. *Habermas: The Key Concepts.* London: Routledge.

ESTERLING, K. M. 2004. *The Political Economy of Expertise: Information and Efficiency in American National Politics.* Ann Arbor, MI: University of Michigan.

——2007. Buying Expertise: Campaign Contributions and Attention to Policy Analysis in Congressional Committees. *American Political Science Review,* 101(1): 93–109.

EVANS, C. L. 1999. Legislative Structure: Rules, Precedents, and Jurisdictions. *Legislative Studies Quarterly,* 24(4): 605–42.

——2005. Politics of Congressional Reform, pp. 490–524 in *The Legislative Branch,* ed. P. J. Quirk and S. Binder. New York: Oxford University Press.

FIORINA, M. P. 1974. *Representatives, Roll Calls, and Constituents.* Lexington, VA: Lexington Books.

——1977. *Congress: Keystone of the Washington Establishment.* New Haven: Yale University Press.

——1980. The Decline of Collective Responsibility in American Politics. *Daedalus,* 109: 25–45.

FISHKIN, J. S., and LASLETT, P., ed. 2003. *Debating Deliberative Democracy.* Oxford: Blackwell Publishing.

FLYVBJERG, B. 1998. Habermas and Foucault: Thinkers for Civil Society? *The British Journal of Sociology,* 49(2): 210–33.

GEER, J. G. 2006. *In Defense of Negativity: Attack Ads in Presidential Campaigns.* Chicago: University of Chicago.

GILLIGAN, T., and KREHBIEL, K. 1990. Organization of Informative Committees by a Rational Legislature. *American Journal of Political Science,* 34(2): 531–65.

GRANSTAFF, B. 1999. *Losing Our Democratic Spirit: Congressional Deliberation and the Dictatorship of Propaganda.* Westport, CT: Praeger.

GUTMANN, A., and THOMPSON, D. 1996. *Democracy and Disagreement.* Cambridge, MA: Harvard University Press.

——2004. *Why Deliberative Democracy?* Princeton, NJ: Princeton University Press.

HABERMAS, J. 1984. *The Theory of Communicative Action,* translated by T. McCarthy. Boston: Beacon Press.

——1990. *Moral Consciousness and Communicative Action,* translated by C. Lenhart and S. Weber Nicholson. Cambridge, MA: MIT Press.

——1994. Three Normative Models of Democracy: Liberal, Republican, Procedural. *Constellations,* 1(1): 1–10.

HAMILTON, L. H. 2009. *Strengthening Congress.* Bloomington, IN: Indiana University Press.

HOROWITZ, D. L. 1977. *The Courts and Social Policy.* Washington, DC: Brookings Institution.

JACOBSON, G. 2003. Partisan Polarization in Presidential Support: The Electoral Connection. *Congress & The Presidency* 30: 1–37.

JANIS, I. L. 1982. *Groupthink: Psychological Studies of Policy Decisions and Fiascoes*. 2nd edn. Boston: Houghton Mifflin.

JOHANNES, J. R. 1976. Study and Recommend: Statutory Reporting Requirements as a Technique of Legislative Initiation. *Western Political Quarterly*, 24: 589–96.

——1977. Statutory Reporting Requirements: Information and Influence for Congress, pp. 33–60 in *Comparative Legislative Reforms and Innovations*, ed. A. Baaklini. Albany, NY: State University of New York Press.

KAUFMAN, H. 1973. *Administrative Feedback: Monitoring Subordinates Behavior*. Washington, DC: Brookings Institution.

KREHBIEL, K. 1991. *Information and Legislative Organization*. Ann Arbor, MI: University of Michigan.

KRUTZ, G. S. 2001. *Hitching a Ride: Omnibus Legislating in the U.S. Congress*. Columbus, OH: The Ohio State University Press.

LANDY, M. K., ROBERTS, M. J., and THOMAS, S. R. 1990. *The Environmental Protection Agency: Asking the Wrong Questions*. New York: Oxford University Press.

LASCHER, Jr., E. L. 1996. Assessing Legislative Deliberation: A Preface to Empirical Analysis. *Legislative Studies Quarterly*, 21(4): 501–19.

——1999. *The Politics of Automobile Insurance Reform: Ideas, Institutions, and Public Policy in North America*. Washington, DC: Georgetown University Press.

LEE, F. E. 2005. Interests, Constituents, and Policy Making, pp. 281–313 in *The Legislative Branch*, ed. P. J. Quirk and S. Binder. New York: Oxford University Press.

LINDBLOM, C. E. 1965. *The Intelligence of Democracy: Decision Making Through Mutual Adjustment*. New York: The Free Press.

——1968. The Policy-Making Process. Englewood, NJ: Prentice-Hall.

——1979. Still Middling, Not Yet Through. *Public Administration Review*, 39(6): 517–26.

LIJPHART, A. 1984. *Democracies: Patterns of Majoritarian and Consensus Government in Twenty-one Countries*. New Haven, CT: Yale University Press.

LUPIA, A., and McCUBBINS, M. D. 1994. Who Controls? Information and the Structure of Legislative Decision Making. *Legislative Studies Quarterly*, 19: 361–84.

MAASS, A. 1951. *Muddy Waters: The Army Engineers and the Nation's Rivers*, Cambridge, MA: Harvard University Press.

——1983. *Congress and the Common Good*. New York: Basic Books.

MADISON, J., HAMILTON, A., and JAY, J. 1987 (1788). *Federalist Papers*, ed. I. Kramnick. Harmondsworth: Penguin.

MALTZMAN, F. 1997. *Competing Principals: Committees, Parties, and the Organization of Congress*. Ann Arbor, MI: University of Michigan Press.

MANN, T. E., and ORNSTEIN, N. J. 1993. *A Second Report of the Renewing Congress Project*. Washington, DC: American Enterprise Institute and the Brookings Institution.

————2006. *The Broken Branch: How Congress Is Failing America and How to Get It Back on Track*. New York: Oxford University Press.

MANSBRIDGE, J. 1988. Motivating Deliberation in Congress, pp. 59–86 in *Constitutionalism in America*, vol. 2, ed. S. Baumgartner Thurow. Lanham, MD: University Press of America.

——2003. Rethinking Representation. *American Political Science Review*, 97(4): 515–28.

MARCUS, G. E., NEUMAN, W. N., and MacKUEN, M. 2000. *Affective Intelligence and Political Judgment*. Chicago: University of Chicago Press.

MAYHEW, D. R. 1974. *Congress: The Electoral Connection*. New Haven, CT: Yale University Press.

MELNICK, R. S. 1983. *Regulation and the Courts: The Case of the Clean Air Act*. Washington, DC: Brookings Institution.

MONROE, B. L., COLARESI, M. P., and QUINN, K. M. 2008. Fightin' Words: Lexical Feature Selection and Evaluation for Identifying the Content of Political Conflict. *Political Analysis*, 16: 372–403.

MOYNIHAN, D. P. 1973. *The Politics of a Guaranteed Income: The Nixon Administration and the Family Assistance Plan*. New York: Random House.

MUCCIARONI, G., and QUIRK, P. J. 2006. *Deliberative Choices: Debating Public Policy in Congress*. Chicago: University of Chicago Press.

NEUSTADT, R. 1990. *Presidential Power and the Modern Presidents*. New York: Free Press.

ORDESHOOK, P. C. 1986. *Game Theory and Political Theory: An Introduction*. New York: Cambridge University Press.

PARKER, G. R., PARKER, S. L., COPA, J. C., and LAWHORN, M. D. 2004. The Question of Committee Bias Revisited. *Political Research Quarterly*, 57(3): 431–40.

PATASHNIK, E. 2000. *Putting Trust in the U.S. Budget: Federal Trust Funds and the Politics of Commitment*. New York: Cambridge University Press.

—— 2005. Budgets and Fiscal Policy, pp. 382–406 in *The Legislative Branch*, ed. P. J. Quirk and S. Binder. New York: Oxford University Press.

PRIEST, D., and PINCUS, W. 2004. U.S. 'Almost All Wrong' on Weapons; Report on Iraq Contradicts Bush Administration Claims. *Washington Post*, October 7, A01.

QUIRK, P. J. 1993. Structures and Performance: An Evaluation, pp. 303–24 in *The Post-Reform Congress*, ed. R. Davidson. New York: St. Martin's Press.

—— 2005. Deliberation and Decision Making, pp. 314–48 in *The Legislative Branch*, ed. P. J. Quirk and S. Binder. New York: Oxford University Press.

ROHDE, D. W. 1991. *Parties and Leaders in the Postreform House*. Chicago: University of Chicago.

—— 2005. Committees and Policy Formulation, pp. 201–23 in *The Legislative Branch*, ed. P. J. Quirk and S. Binder. New York: Oxford University Press.

SCHATTSCHNEIDER, E. E. 1960. *The Semi-Sovereign People: A Realist's View of Democracy in America*. New York: Holt, Rinehart, and Winston.

SCHICKLER, E. 2001. *Disjointed Pluralism: Institutional Innovation and the Development of the U.S. Congress*. Princeton, NJ: Princeton University Press.

SHEPSLE, K. A. 1980. The Private Use of the Public Interest, *Society*, 17: 35–42.

—— and BONCHEK, M. S. 1997. *Analyzing Politics: Rationality, Behavior, and Institutions*. New York: W.W. Norton.

SINCLAIR, B. 1997. *Unorthodox Lawmaking: New Legislative Processes in the U.S. Congress*. Washington, DC: CQ Press.

—— 2005. Parties and Leadership in the House, pp. 224–54 in *The Legislative Branch*, ed. P. J. Quirk and S. Binder. New York: Oxford University Press.

—— 2006. *Party Wars: Polarization and the Politics of National Policy Making*. Norman, OK: University of Oklahoma Press.

—— 2009. The New World of U.S. Senators, pp. 1–22 in *Congress Reconsidered*, 9th edn, ed. L. C. Dodd and B. I. Oppenheimer. Washington, DC: CQ Press.

SMITH, S. S. 1989. *Call to Order: Floor Politics in the House and Senate*. Washington, DC: Brookings Institution.

—— 2005. Parties and Leadership in the Senate, pp. 255–78 in *The Legislative Branch*, ed. P. J. Quirk and S. Binder. New York: Oxford University Press.

STEIN, HERBERT. 1984. *Presidential Economics: The Making of Economic Policy from Roosevelt to Reagan and Beyond*. New York: Simon and Schuster.

STEINER, G. Y. 1971. *The State of Welfare*. Washington, DC: Brookings Institution.

STEINER, J., BÄCHTIGER, A., SPÖRNDLI, M., and STEENBERGEN, M. R. 2004. *Deliberative Politics in Action: Analyzing Parliamentary Discourse*. Cambridge: Cambridge University Press.

STRAHAN, R. 2007. *Leading Representatives: The Agency of Leaders in the Politics of the U.S. House*. Baltimore: Johns Hopkins University Press.

STROM, G. S. 1990. *The Logic of Lawmaking: A Spatial Theory Approach*. Baltimore: Johns Hopkins University Press.

STURGIS, P. 2003. Knowledge and Collective Preferences: A Comparison of Two Approaches to Estimating the Opinions of a Better Informed Public. *Sociological Methods Research*, 31(4): 453–85.

SUNSTEIN, C. R. 2000. Deliberative Trouble? Why Groups Go To Extremes. *The Yale Law Journal*, 110: 71–119.

THOMPSON, D. F. 2008. Deliberative Democratic Theory and Empirical Political Science. *American Review of Political Science*, 11: 497–520.

WARREN, M., ed. 1999. *Democracy and Trust*. New York: Cambridge University Press.

——and PEARSE, H., eds. 2008. *Designing Deliberative Democracy: The British Columbia Citizens' Assembly*. New York: Cambridge University Press.

WAWRO, G. J., and SCHICKLER, E. 2006. *Filibuster: Obstruction and Lawmaking in the U.S. Senate*. Princeton, NJ: Princeton University Press.

WAXMAN, H. 2009. *The Waxman Report: How Congress Really Works*. New York: Grand Central Publishing.

WEATHERFORD, M. S. 1987. The Interplay of Ideology and Advice in Economic Policy-Making: The Case of Political Business Cycle. *The Journal of Politics*, 49(4): 925–52.

WILENSKY, H. 1967. *Organizational Intelligence: Knowledge and Policy in Government and Industry*. New York: Basic Books.

WIRLS, D. 2007. The 'Golden Age' Senate and Floor Debate in the Antebellum Congress. *Legislative Studies Quarterly*, 32(2): 193–222.

WOLFENSBERGER, D. R. 2000. *Congress and the People: Deliberative Democracy on Trial*. Washington, DC: The Woodrow Wilson Center Press.

CHAPTER 25

....

ROLL-CALL VOTES

....

SEAN THERIAULT
PATRICK HICKEY
ABBY BLASS

VOTING is the most visible and potentially vulnerable act that members of Congress perform. Roll-call votes take place in the open and are recorded for posterity in the public record. Party leaders, presidents, interest groups, donors, and constituents, who all pay varying degrees of attention to members' votes, can and will withdraw their political, financial, and electoral support if they do not approve. Such punishment may not take place at the time of the vote, but months or even years later. Members cannot duck their responsibility to vote because missed votes can hurt members as much as, or more, than potentially "wrong" votes. Indeed, members must step carefully through the minefield of roll-call votes that they cast.

Given their frequency, availability, and importance, congressional roll-call votes are, perhaps, the most studied decisions in the whole of political science. Too often, though, political observers and scholars treat them as exogenous situations in which members have little control over either their creation or how they are structured. A roll-call vote occurs because someone in the process wants members to go on the official record, and only sometimes is that person's motivation to change public policy. Nonetheless, the series of yeas and nays can reveal a member's preferences, which are remarkably consistent across issues, vote types, and over time (Poole and Rosenthal 1997).

In the classic representation set-up, members employ one of two strategies when they vote (Burke 1774). They can act as "delegates" and vote their constituency's preferences, or they can act as "trustees" and rely upon their own preferences. A world in which they act as delegates could be very different from a world where they act as trustees.[1] Neither the delegate nor the trustee model is observed, however, in its pure form because members face both constitutional and institutional constraints throughout the legislative process.

Constitutional constraints include term lengths, constituencies, and the other branches of government.[2] The difference in term lengths between the House and the Senate can sometimes cause senators to act more like trustees and House members to act more like delegates. Constituencies ensure that no member will act too much as a trustee if doing so significantly impairs their electoral chances. The executive and judicial branches influence the items on the legislative agenda and sometimes even the disposition of legislation in Congress.

Institutional arrangements, including the committee system, rules, procedures, and opportunities for strategic voting, constrain members' votes as well. Committees determine the policy areas that members get to vote on by acting as a filter, whether in gathering information and selecting what committee members see as the best policy options (Krehbiel 1991) or in reporting legislation that the majority party prefers (Cox and McCubbins 2005). Rules and procedures constrain decisions by controlling whether members get to offer amendments, vote orally or on record, or even vote at all. At times committee outputs, rules, and procedures combine to offer members opportunities for strategic voting behavior. In such situations members may decide to vote against their own preferences at one stage in the legislative process in order to achieve what they see as the optimal outcome at a later stage.

These constitutional and institutional constraints influence not only how members vote, but also, and perhaps more profoundly, what they vote on. In this chapter, we outline the influences on members' votes, discuss what we see as resolved debates in the literature, and identify fertile ground for future research. Members' votes are shaped by their constituents, political parties, presidents, interest groups, and their own preferences. The existing congressional literature does a particularly good job explaining the influences behind roll-call votes and the effect of party control on the legislative agenda. Future research should examine more closely how variation in types of roll-call votes (e.g. procedural, amendment, final passage) affect member decision-making, along with how roll-call decisions compare to member decisions about other forms of legislative participation (e.g. cosponsorship and floor speeches), the effect of external stimuli—such as big exogenous shocks—on member decision-making, the consequences of negative agenda power, and natural experiments rooted in the institutional design of Congress.

[1] Members could also act as "politicos," a style of representation that combines the delegate and trustee models. "Politicos" act as delegates on salient or controversial issues and act as trustees on all other issues (Wahlke, Eulau, and Buchanan 1962 and Davidson 1969). This simplification belies recent literature that has expanded the classic representation typology. Mansbridge (2003) names four types of representatives based on which constituency actually gets represented, whereas Rehfeld (2009) develops eight types based on members' aims, judgment, and responsiveness.

[2] The Constitution originally provided each chamber with different methods of election, but the 17th Amendment made all representatives subject to direct elections.

Roll-call voting influences

In this section, we explore the influences upon members' roll-call votes. In turn, we discuss how the people, political parties, presidents, interest groups, and the members' own preferences affect members' roll-call votes.

The people

The framers designed frequent elections to ensure that legislators would be responsive to their constituents' interests and preferences (*Federalist* 52). The health of representative democracy in the United States depends upon the success of this mechanism. Electoral incentives ensure that members will, at least at times, act like delegates. The literature on congressional accountability finds a correlation between representatives' votes and their constituents' preferences, identifies a causal mechanism to explain that correlation (including but not limited to campaigns), specifies the conditions that give particular constituent interests greater influence, assesses the varying influence of constituent opinion across particular issues, and debates how to measure the indirect influence of constituent opinion on member behavior.

Scholars first evaluated the linkage between constituent opinion and member behavior by comparing public opinion polls to members' roll-call votes. These correlations, now more than forty years old, revealed varying levels of policy agreement between representatives and their constituents depending upon the salience of the issue and the unity of the constituents' preferences (Miller and Stokes 1963). In continuing this issue-based explanation, Kingdon (1973) finds that members, in roll-call voting, attempt to avoid controversy by choosing the path of least resistance. Nonetheless, Miller and Stokes' (1963, 56) modest conclusion persists: "The conditions of constituency influence...are met well enough to give the local constituency a measure of control over the actions of its Representatives."

Yet—as the adage goes—correlation does not imply causation. High correlation between constituent opinion and member voting may reflect a variety of indistinguishable influences, and simple correlations cannot isolate and evaluate a member's degree of responsiveness. Moreover, measures of correlation are theoretically vacuous and can be misleading: they do not offer measures of representation that can be interpreted in terms of democratic theory, and "leaders' opinions can correlate strongly with those of constituents even though the representatives are distant from electors and they can correlate weakly when the representatives are close" (Achen 1977; and Achen 1978, 476). Indeed, when Achen (1978) applied three theoretically informed statistical measures of representation—proximity, centrism, and responsiveness—to Miller and Stokes' data he found evidence that winning members were *less* representative than losers for two of the measures (proximity and centrism) though they were more responsive to differences in mean opinion across districts. On the other hand, when Erikson (1978) corrected for the sampling error in measures of constituent opinion, he found a stronger relationship between member voting and constituent opinion. These aggregated results do not resolve the nature of the constituent–member relationship, but they do point to the difficulty of appropriately testing it.

No paradigm has been more influential for the study of member behavior than Mayhew's (1974, 5) axiom that members of Congress are "single-minded seekers of reelection." Because reelection requires the support of district opinion leaders as well as the primary and November electorates, members provide each group with "particularized benefits" (1974, 40–5). Subsequent research complements and builds on Mayhew's descriptive analysis to produce a more systematic and nuanced conception of electoral forces on legislative behavior. Fiorina (1974, 1975) finds that constituent opinion is not a single force, but rather the sum of diverse forces that together shape members' reelection prospects. Furthermore, Fenno (1977, 1978) argues that members perceive their districts as four concentric circles—their personal, primary, reelection and geographic constituencies—and pursue distinct strategies tailored to win the trust and support of each. During this process, members develop a "home style" because trust and support at home can empower a member in Washington to pursue their policy goals and maintain power. Even constituents who are not politically attuned affect the process when members consider the "potential preferences" of "inattentive publics" (Arnold 1990).

The power of the "attentive publics" speaks to reelection-minded members' desire to avoid "wrong votes," whether they amount to a string of questionable votes (Kingdon 1973) or one vote that is counter to a member's "home style" (Fenno 1977, 1978). When members have to start explaining their votes to their constituents, electoral danger usually follows. Congressional history contains enough stories of wrong votes costing members their seats to keep the rest of the members scared of being "audited" (Arnold 1990). Senator Albert Gore Sr.'s vote for the Voting Rights Act of 1965 and Representative Marjorie Margolies-Mezvinsky's vote for the Clinton Budget in 1993 are two examples that have now become part of congressional folklore.

Political scientists have used these examples and others to motivate more generalized and systematic studies. Focusing more on members' overall voting records—typically operationalized as some sort of voting score (Poole and Rosenthal 1997; and Groseclose, Levitt, and Snyder 1999)—and their constituencies' ideologies—typically operationalized as either a summary of their voting patterns (Ansolabehere, Snyder, and Stewart 2001; Hirsch 2003; Theriault 2008) or aggregated survey results (McIver, Erikson, and Wright 1994; Wright, Erikson, and McIver 1994)—sufficient evidence exists that members generally abide by their constituents' desires even if constituents have not yet developed a fine-tuned instrument to weed out and systematically punish these members (Jacobson 1987; and Canes-Wrone, Brady, and Cogan 2002).

Bartels (1991) finds that constituent influence is less blunt than imagined. He shows that even the safest members are quite responsive to constituent opinion. When public opinion changes, members are quick to change their position to avoid electoral jeopardy. Indeed, members deviate from the delegate model at their own risk. Theriault (2001, 2005), too, offers evidence of constituent influence. He examines issues that divide representatives' personal desires from constituent opinion to isolate the public's influence. Under normal conditions representatives behave according to their own desires, but in times of heightened political awareness they do respond to organized and united constituencies. In such times, members—particularly those in vulnerable seats—typically vote their constituents' preferences ahead of their own else they suffer an electoral consequence.

While members face scrutiny on important votes that ultimately determine major public policies, they can use the legislative process to hide or skirt more explosive votes. When members have to start explaining the minutiae of the legislative process to a disinterested public (Hibbing and Theiss-Morse 1995, 2002), they must tread carefully. As the party wars have escalated, though, members have increasingly devoted time not to the public policy consequences of their votes, but rather to how the vote could be portrayed to their constituents by current or future political opponents (Sinclair 2006; Mann and Ornstein 2006).[3]

As more than forty years of research attests, constituents constrain member voting. Such a conclusion, though, is more complex than it may seem. Members can and do act like delegates, but only under certain conditions. Different issues, differently informed constituencies, and different stages in the legislative and electoral processes make the relationship more contingent, but also more interesting to study.

The political parties

If, as Mayhew (1974) argues, reelection is the proximate goal—the member's goal that must be achieved first—an increasing number of members are achieving that goal through their political party. As the voters have sorted themselves ideologically (Fiorina 2006) and, with a bit of help from those redrawing district lines, geographically (Bishop 2008), fewer members have faced the dilemma of siding with their constituents over their party or vice versa (Theriault 2008). Increasingly, members' constituencies and their party leaders hold the same view, which entices members to act more as delegates. When members' constituents and party leaders hold opposite views, though, members face a trickier dilemma. In charting their course in these difficult situations, members cannot easily ignore some important advantages of siding with their parties. As Strahan documents in his chapter in this volume (see Chapter 17), party leaders maintain the power to appoint members to committees (and as committee chairs) and increasingly use these powers to reward party loyalty. Furthermore, party leaders can provide particular electoral or campaign support to their vulnerable members.

Building on the earlier work of Froman and Ripley (1965); and Sinclair (1994); Cox and McCubbins (2005) show how the legislative process helps members serve two masters simultaneously. On the procedural votes that often stack the deck in favor of a particular policy, constituents tend not to be particularly attentive, which allows

---

[3] Elections remain the clearest exercise of constituent influence, but accountability would be limited if public influence ended with them. Constituencies have other indirect ways of affecting members' behavior. See Sulkin, Chapter 8, this volume, on how campaigns shape member behavior.

members to vote with their party at minimal electoral risk (Den Hartog and Monroe 2008). If the party does its job at the first stage, the member can vote consistently with their constituency's preferences at the more visible final passage stage if there is tension between their party's position and their constituents' preferences.

The considerations above suggest that members will vote with their parties unless they confront a strong countervailing force. The best reason to buck the party is still to please the constituency. As fewer members face conflict between siding with their constituents or their parties, they increasingly act as delegates. This trend helps explain the increasing polarization between the political parties in Congress.

Presidents

The American system is famously described as a system of "separate institutions sharing power" (Neustadt 1960). Though they share lawmaking power, Congress and the president have their own distinct set of constitutional, formal, and informal powers. Additionally, they are responsive to different constituencies, which can create conflict between them; on other occasions, the will of the people can keep members of Congress and the president on the same page. Nonetheless, because of his impressive powers, the president is a major actor in the legislative process.

Members' voting decisions are at times influenced by the president's formal powers. The veto is the president's only constitutionally conferred power in the legislative arena, though the president can also strategically employ a veto threat to modify a bill's content (Kiewiet and McCubbins 1988; Cameron 2000). The president's "power to persuade" (Neustadt 1960), either through behind-the-scenes bargaining or public pressure, is perhaps even more important than his veto power. Presidents from Teddy Roosevelt onward have used "the bully pulpit" to push their legislative agenda and attempt to compel a reticent Congress to support the president's preferred policy (Tulis 1987). When presidents go public in primetime speeches, press conferences, and other high-profile appearances, they hope to garner public support for their programs and use this support as leverage to encourage members to vote with the president or face the public's wrath (Kernell 1986). While some presidential appeals may fall "on deaf ears" (Edwards 2003), others help persuade members to support the president's agenda.

Conventional wisdom holds that members will respond to the president's informal powers in accordance with his popularity, but some political scientists doubt this proposition. A number of studies find no relationship between presidential popularity and presidential success in passing legislation (Edwards 1989; Bond and Fleisher 1990; Jones 1994; Collier and Sullivan 1995) while others find a positive relationship (Edwards 1980; Ostrom and Simon 1985; Rivers and Rose 1985; Brace and Hinckley 1992). These conflicting conclusions compel us to determine what type of presidential popularity matters and under what circumstances.

It is likely that the mass presidential appeals have differentiated effects on members, who are more likely to respond to the president's popularity within their districts than his overall numbers in the country. Members from districts where the president won a higher vote share tend to support the president more often than their party alone would suggest (Edwards 1978). If a member's support for the president deviates too much from the president's popularity in her district, she risks losing her seat in the next election (Gronke, Koch, and Wilson 2003). Members ignore their constituency's opinion of the president at their own peril.

Presidential popularity plays a particularly large role in members' vote choices in policy domains where citizens are relatively uninformed, issues are salient, and the debates involved are complex (Canes-Wrone and de Marchi 2002). In these domains citizens may look to the president for direction. Foreign policy is one such area (Miller and Stokes 1963; Wildavsky 1966). The public tends to give popular presidents the benefit of the doubt in these policy domains and members are hesitant to vote against popular presidents on complex, salient issues.

Finally, member voting decisions may be swayed by other informal presidential tools such as bargaining and arm-twisting. Systematic evidence of members basing their voting decisions on direct presidential persuasion and bargaining is in part difficult to come by due to the small number of members involved. For example, Olympia Snowe played a crucial role in reducing George Bush's tax cuts in 2001 as well as in passing President Obama's economic stimulus package in 2009. While these legislative actions could be explained by Snowe's ideology, they are as accurately understood by how the president was viewed among her constituents. Krehbiel's (1998) pivotal politics model gives us leverage on which members are most likely to be targets of presidential persuasion and how their participation will affect the bill's outcome, but it does not offer much insight into how exactly the president shapes these critical voting decisions. While systematic evidence of the mechanics of presidential persuasion is difficult to come by, there is no doubt that these tactics do take place behind closed doors. Perhaps no better example of such arm twisting exists than Lyndon Johnson's physically and mentally intimidating "treatment" of undecided members.

Ultimately, members' response to presidential power is always contingent. Formal tools such as the veto power depend on the partisan composition of Congress, the relevant legislative coalitions supporting the bill in question, and the president's own reputation. Informal powers depend on the issues involved, the composition of the member's constituency, and the president's standing with the public.

Interest groups

The relationship between members of Congress and interest groups is complex. Regrettably for Congress's reputation among the public, the popular conception is that interest groups bribe members of Congress to vote a particular way. Unfortunately, enough cases of such bribery exist to give the promoters of this popular conception ammunition to make their charges stick. Little systematic evidence, however, exists to show that bribing makes even an infrequent appearance in either chamber.

Instead, most systematic evidence suggests that money flows from a good voting record and not vice versa (see Wawro 2001; Brunell 2005; Jacobson 2009). That is, groups donate to members who already have a proven record of voting in accord with their priorities. Nonetheless, a superficial reading of the political science literature can lead to the adoption of the conventional wisdom. A series of important rational choice studies from the 1990s suggest that interest groups would be using their resources most efficiently if they "bought off" the indifferent or nearly indifferent legislators (Snyder 1991; Groseclose 1996; Groseclose and Snyder 1996; see also Wiseman 2004 for a test of this argument). These findings and the language that the scholars use give credence to the conventional wisdom, though a careful review of the studies suggests only that interest groups would be *most efficient* if they followed this practice. The disjoint between these findings and the observed behavior of interest groups suggests one of two propositions. First, interest groups' top priority may not be efficiency. Second, members recognize the impropriety of being "bought off" and avoid situations that may be characterized in such a light.

What is clear from a long list of studies on the influence of interest groups on voting in Congress is that interest groups support their friends, like to have access to decision-makers, and provide information to members of Congress (Jacobson 2009; see also Smith 1995 for a good review of this literature). Members of Congress, on the other hand, are dependent upon interest groups for campaign contributions. That there is a relationship between the two is not in dispute—the nature of the relationship, however, is probably less dramatic than the conventional wisdom would suggest. The biggest influence of interest groups is probably not in changing members' votes as much as it is in altering the legislative agenda. Interest group activity likely keeps some issues off the agenda and pushes other issues to the top of the agenda (see Wayman 1985 and Hall 1996 for two good studies in this line of research).

Members' personal preferences

While it would help shed light on the extent to which members behave like delegates or trustees, isolating the influence of personal ideology is an enduring challenge for scholars of legislative behavior. Personal ideology, according to Converse (1964), is a set of values that organize political attitudes. Isolating and estimating the effect of member's personal ideologies remains elusive because the ideologies themselves defy both direct observation and simple operationalization. Accordingly, they must either be deduced or carefully estimated.

Rohde (1991) suggests a distinction between a legislator's *personal* and *operative* preferences. Personal preferences are free from external influence by constituents, parties, and interest groups, while operative preferences depend—sometimes critically—on these factors. Burden (2007) shows how influential the former are in predicting members' votes. Many scholars, though, consider the latter measure preferable to capture member's preferences because legislators unconstrained by their constituents, party, and powerful interests—in short, those unresponsive to electoral incentives—do not last long in Congress (Mayhew 1974; Bender and Lott 1996; Canes-Wrone, Brady, and Cogan 2002; Theriault 2005).

Scholars have attempted to estimate member's personal ideology both directly (using interviews and surveys) and indirectly (via constituents' preferences or roll-call votes). Empirical evidence suggests that personal ideology does affect legislative behavior (Kau and Rubin 1979, 1993), even if its influence is diminished after taking the constituency's preferences into account (Peltzman 1984). When members are caught consistently voting outside the mainstream of their constituencies' preferences, they are quickly punished by the voters (Kau and Rubin 1993). Numerous scholars find that this behavior is relatively rare and usually inconsequential to the final vote outcome (Kau and Rubin 1993; Bender and Lott 1996; and Lott and Davis 1992). Interestingly, once the electoral connection has been severed—when members are unconstrained by electoral or other incentives due to voluntary retirement—members do not engage in ideological shirking, though they do exert less effort, or engage in what has been called "participatory shirking" (Rothenberg and Sanders 2000). Such a finding suggests that members of Congress authentically represent their constituents' views, which, under this condition, would ultimately lead to similar behavior for representatives invoking either the trustee or delegate role. Conceptually separating members' personal beliefs from those of their constituents, parties, presidents, and interest groups is an arduous task. Doing so statistically is even more difficult. Members' personal beliefs remain empirically amorphous. Resisting the temptation to call everything not explained by the aforementioned systematic factors "members' personal preferences" is likely to yield better theory and empirical work.

AREAS OF SETTLED RESEARCH

We do not think it too much of a stretch to say that no set of political decisions has received more time, attention, and analysis from political scientists than congressional roll-call votes. As typically happens, when the studies mount, the unresolved questions only proliferate. Nonetheless, we think that two areas are unlikely to yield important new advances in our understanding of member behavior or the legislative process. From the outset, though, let us be clear: we do not think these areas are unimportant; quite the contrary, we think that they involve some of the most important questions in congressional research. Nevertheless, long debates in congressional studies have made it exceedingly difficult to break interesting new ground in these areas.

The aggregated influences on roll-call voting

Members balance the interests of their constituents, their party leaders, presidents, interest groups, and their own preferences in casting their votes. We think the marginal contribution of the next study that verifies that one of these variables matters is relatively small. Congressional scholars should shift their focus away from these generic roll-call voting analyses.

We offer this assessment with two qualifications. First, we have much to learn about when certain factors do or do not influence member roll-call voting behavior. In other words, a slight transformation of the research question from "do constituencies influence member behavior?" to "when do constituencies influence member behavior?" would greatly enhance our understanding of the legislative process. We can learn much from a study that begins to systematize our results in lieu of breaking new ground on a new vote taken in the House or Senate (Schickler 2001 provides one good example of this line of research). We know that constituents, party leaders, presidents, interest groups, and member's own preferences generally matter; we have much to learn about when one influence is irrelevant or dominates the others.

Second, studies that add to the universe of influences on member voting can still greatly contribute to the literature. Finding new variables or new ways to operationalize old variables could still significantly advance the field of roll-call voting. Consider two recent examples. When examining the president's influence on roll-call voting, a first set of researchers examined votes when the president had a publicly stated position on the issue (see, for example, Bond and Fleisher 1980; Edwards 1980; Edwards 1989; Bond and Fleisher 1990; and Borrelli and Simmons 1993). Pritchard (1985), however, points out that presidential support scores do not necessarily measure presidential influence because members may vote with the president's position for a number of reasons other than presidential influence. Accordingly, Canes-Wrone (2001, 2006) refined that measure to include items the president discussed in major speeches. This refinement led us to learn that presidents involve the public in the legislative process when majority opinion can move legislative outcomes closer to both the president's and the public's preferred policy. Under certain circumstances, going public enables the president and the people to work together to influence congressional vote choices.

Another example of where new operationalizations of variables could still contribute to roll-call analyses comes from the dyadic relationship between members and their constituents. Although Miller and Stokes (1963); Mayhew (1974); and Fenno (1978) demonstrate that constituent opinion is translated—if imperfectly—into members' votes, we could uncover significant findings by measuring preferences in new ways. For example, Bailey (2007), in a study about the relationship among legislators, judges, and the president, generates comparable preference estimates by examining survey responses rather than roll-call votes. At the other end of the relationship, Jessee (2009), in a study that examines voters' views and candidate choice, estimates voters' preferences on the same scale as candidates by asking voters to "vote on" the same set of issues that competing candidates have faced in the legislative arena. Though little work has been done in applying these innovations to measure the degree of representation in roll-call voting, these two innovations may give more precise estimates for the underlying preferences of the representatives and the represented.

The role of political parties in the legislative process

No subfield of congressional scholarship has been more interesting and vibrant over the last twenty years than examining the role of political parties in the legislative process. Thanks to the arguments of Rohde (1991), Cox and McCubbins (1993, 2005), Aldrich (1995), Sinclair (2006), and Smith (2007) we know why parties exist, how party members conspire to control the legislative agenda, and under what conditions party leaders will have the most power. Although some tensions exist among their specific arguments and conclusions, these scholars, collectively, have established that parties shape and constrain member voting decisions. Krehbiel (1993, 1998), who may disagree with these aggregated results, has pushed these scholars to be explicit in their assumptions, thoughtful in their tests, and careful in their conclusions.

Nonetheless, some questions remain unsettled. For example, more so than in the past, the decisions that members make on roll-call votes are increasingly structured by the majority party leadership. While it has always been the case that members vote on the matters that are raised by their leadership, as open rules and the regular order have become less common, the majority party leadership increasingly decides which roll-call votes are to be taken. As power over the legislative process becomes increasingly concentrated in the leadership of the majority party, the set of roll-call votes reveals more about members' commitments to their political party and less about their underlying personal preferences. This description, of course, is more accurate in the House, though even the Senate has become a less open and free-wheeling legislature.

Consider the following analogy from our classrooms. If one teacher composes a test for a student, we can observe the student's knowledge in light of that one teacher. If multiple teachers contribute to the development of the test, we will have a broader understanding of the student's knowledge. If many teachers with different interests, backgrounds, and abilities compose the test, we will observe the student's general base of knowledge. For members of Congress, the authors of the tests have changed over time. In the Textbook Congress era, amendments were relatively infrequent. With the advent of electronic voting and the continuation of open rules, many different authors were offering test questions. As rules became more restrictive, the majority party leadership has been writing an increasing proportion of test questions. This evolution suggests that our roll-call summary scores—everything from DW-NOMINATE to ADA and ACU scores—have varied across these different periods, though congressional scholars have not considered the consequences among these different roll-call generating procedures.

In short, we know the influences of members' voting decisions, but we also know that these voting decisions do not necessarily reflect the member's true policy preferences. Indeed, we should not be surprised that members' voting scores since the mid-1970s, are becoming increasingly polarized as the tests are increasingly written by the majority party leadership. We need to use this party influence literature to further theorize about what voting scores, however measured, actually mean.

FERTILE GROUND FOR FUTURE RESEARCH

While the last fifty years of congressional research has convinced us that parties, constituencies, presidents, and interest groups influence roll-call voting and that parties have an important role in structuring the legislative process, other areas are less developed and ripe for additional study. In this section, we outline research paths along which we encourage more exploration.

Not all roll-call votes are the same

While we think that analyses of yeas and nays offer one of the least interesting paths to discover new information about the legislative process, roll-call votes, nonetheless, can still yield new findings. We encourage researchers to abandon the fiction that all roll-call votes are the same. We think important distinctions between roll-call votes can be leveraged to gain additional insight into the legislative process.

To revert back to the analogy of roll-call votes as test questions, we think there are some roll calls that would be legitimate questions on any test of general intelligence. Other roll calls, though, are written by very particular teachers to reveal very particular knowledge. We think there is a fundamental difference in what a member's answers to these two types of questions reveal. If members rely upon different influences in answering those two types of questions, we would know, at a minimum, that the members perceive a difference in these types of votes.

Congressional scholars have only begun to analyze the *type* of roll-call votes members face. We encourage more of this type of research. Until now, two kinds of analyses have been suggested, though we could imagine more. The first examines the underlying issue being decided. For example, Frances Lee (2009) does an exemplary job understanding how the underlying partisan dynamic changes in accord with the substantive issues being decided. The differences in how a member acts on these different issues revealed new interesting aspects of the legislative process. She finds that the increase in party polarization in the Senate is partly a consequence of the kinds of issues that are being debated on the Senate floor. Scholars largely gave up the promising research agenda of Clausen (1973) and Kingdon (1973), who divided roll-call votes into policy specific areas, when Poole and Rosenthal (1997) demonstrated the consistency with which members voted across issue areas. But Lee's work shows that this move may have been a mistake (Lapinski 2008 also shows the advantages of disaggregating into issue areas).

The second set of analyses examines when in the process the vote is taken. Theriault (2008) differentiates procedural, amendment, and final passage votes from one another. Again, his analysis reveals that members act very differently on these different sets of votes. In the 1970s, members were similarly influenced by their party and their constituents on procedural and final passage votes. Over time, members' procedural votes were cast without concern for their constituencies, whereas final passage votes remained a mix of both constituent and party influence. The differences in member behavior on the two types of votes reveals important aspects of the legislative process that would have remained uncovered had he treated all roll calls alike. This distinction comes about because of the relative invisibility of procedural votes (Froman and Ripley 1965; Den Hartog and Monroe 2008).

The most obvious extension of this type of research is a combination of the two. What scholars are now analyzing in one dimension (kind of issue or type of vote), can be analyzed in two dimensions (both kind of issue and type of vote). Furthermore, additional leverage could be ascertained by examining the author of the vote or, if you will, the test question. Questions written by minority party members should reveal very different information than questions written by the majority party. Additionally, questions written by party leaders should elicit a very different response than test questions written by back benchers.

Along the same line of thinking, Snyder and Groseclose (2000) and Cox and Poole (2002) started us down a fruitful path that could still produce noteworthy findings. Rather than using all votes to derive an ideology measure, they use lopsided votes because it is unlikely that members were not rigorously lobbied by party leaders on these votes. We think more can be made of the differences between all votes, close votes, and lopsided votes, though the McCarty, Poole, and Rosenthal (2001) admonition to go slowly seems prudent. Nonetheless, we think the different pressures that are borne out on each are likely to reveal interesting windows into how members decide to cast their roll-call votes.

Policy decisions made without roll-call votes

Changes in public policy frequently happen without a roll-call vote ever being taken (Clinton and Lapinski 2008). Just because the yeas and nays cannot be assigned to particular members does not mean that major policy decisions were not reached on the chambers' floors. Indeed, it is only the anonymity that comes with voice, teller, and standing votes that have, at times, resulted in policy change. Nonetheless, the congressional literature largely ignores changes in public policy except inasmuch as they align with the yeas and nays of a member's record.

In analyzing the long history of roll-call votes, scholars rarely recognize that the underlying dynamics of what has come up for a roll-call vote has changed over time. Perhaps no change has been greater than the House's first electronic roll-call vote on

January 23, 1973. What had taken up to an hour prior to this innovation could now be accomplished in as little as five minutes. Bach and Smith (1988) highlight some of the changes brought about by this technological advance.

While electronic voting may provide the sharpest break in the roll-call dataset, it is not the only change. As the House has transformed from an institution dominated by its committees to one dominated by parties, the matters subject to roll-call votes likely changed. So too when the Senate went from an institution dominated by Nelson Aldrich's (R-RI) gang of four at the turn of the twentieth century to one where gangs of six or fourteen at the turn of the twenty-first century are needed to bridge the divide between the parties on health care or judicial nominations. Senators increasing use of holds is another important change that affects the issues decided by roll-call votes (Sinclair 2007). More work can clearly be done in analyzing what comes up for a roll-call vote and why.

Members' other decisions

A perusal of the congressional literature would suggest that members, day in and day out, face only one type of decision: whether to vote yea or nay on roll-call votes. Although several good studies have been done on lawmakers' other decisions (e.g. Hall 1996), they are swamped in volume by the good studies done on how members vote. We think the proportion of research on member decisions should be more in line with the proportion of decisions that members make in conducting their legislative duties.

Roll calls are good decisions to analyze for a number of reasons. First, members take many roll-call votes every session and have done so since Frederick Muhlenberg was elected the first Speaker. Second, roll-call votes contain variance that can be leveraged by exploring the diversity of members casting them. Third, roll-call voting is done in the light of day, recorded in the *Congressional Record* (or its precursors), and, now, widely available within seconds on the Internet. Fourth, we know roll-call voting correlates nicely with member ideology, party affiliation, and members' constituencies, which suggests that underlying systematic explanations can be uncovered.

The other decisions that members make do not match roll-call votes on all of these dimensions. Nonetheless, we think the marginal contribution that can be made by studying other decisions, even if they are not as systematic or widely available, would be much greater than the information learned by doing additional roll-call studies.

We highlight two kinds of decisions that members regularly face that are prime for additional study. The first set of decisions speaks to the intensity or extremity of members' preferences rather than simply the direction of those preferences. The roll-call yeas and nays tell us on which side of the divide a member falls, but it does not tell us how close the member was to the divide. A yea for the first member may be a "strong yea" whereas for a second member it may be just "barely a yea." Throughout the legislative process, members can indicate the intensity underlying their position through cosponsorship, taking a leading role in committee, speaking on the floor, or signing a discharge petition. Pearson and Schickler's (2009) recent work on the discharge petitions, Rocca's (2007) work on 1-minute speeches and special order addresses, and Fowler's (2006) and Koger's (2003) work on cosponsorships are all steps in the right direction. While members are not forced to do these things, we can learn from the members who do. In fact, it is precisely because members must choose to do these things that we can make inferences about intensity.

The second set of decisions involves the connection between interest groups and members. While interest groups affect both elections and legislation, we know little about the micro-level activity between members and interest groups. Such research was unimaginable in the past, but the confluence of openness and technology has given researchers—not to mention constituents, colleagues, and reporters—access to members' daily activities. Members' webpages, blogs, and "tweets" may uncover the relationship that individual members have to interest groups. Beneath these data certainly lurks either legislative causes or effects.

While no decision is as easily accessible and systemic as roll-call votes, we encourage researchers to use "sloppier" data to examine other parts of the legislative process. After all, the steps before the actual roll-call votes set the stage for the ultimate, and often least surprising or interesting, decision.

Negative power

While Cox and McCubbins' (1993, 2005) "party cartel theory" lays out the purposes underlying the use of negative agenda power, the substantive consequences of negative agenda power are an avenue for future research. After all, "the definition of alternatives is the supreme instrument of power" (Schattschneider 1960). Thus, analyzing the issues members are not allowed to vote on is a worthy enterprise.

The political consequences of positive agenda power are clear, but the political consequences of negative agenda power are murky. First, we need to determine which policy areas Congress declines to address and why members of Congress decide to ignore these areas. Baumgartner and Jones' (1993) list of ignored issues—drug abuse, alcohol abuse, and child abuse—offers a good starting point. Stokes (1963) defines "valence issues" as policy debates where one side is either universally approved or universally disapproved by the electorate. Uncovering other, less sensational "valence issues" where only one side is perceived to be legitimate and the policy consequences of such a lopsided debate is a worthy research objective. Second, we must understand why these issues fail to reach the legislative agenda. Is there a lack of member intensity and so the issue just drifts around without a true patron? Are members actively discouraging the issue from receiving congressional attention? Do these factors change over time? Why? How? A third potential avenue for future research is outlining the circumstances under which issues that divide the majority party get on the agenda despite the majority party's negative agenda power. Immigration reform is a good example. These and other questions will illuminate the policy implications of negative agenda power.

Constitutional experiments

In addition to prescribing a government that has endured for more than 200 years, the Framers of the Constitution also provided the structures for some thoughtful social scientific inquiries. Political scientists have not used these structures to their fullest advantage. We encourage congressional scholars to examine more frequently and more closely experiments based in the structure of the House and Senate. For illustrative purposes, we offer two examples.

The House and Senate have the same ultimate purpose—to write the laws of the land. Although they have the same purpose, they are structured very differently. They have different entrance requirements, lengths of term, leadership structures, rules, legislative procedures, and norms. The first natural experiment congressional scholars should more closely examine are the similarities and differences between the House and the Senate. While we applaud the increasing number of studies that examine both chambers, we think more studies can gain insight into the legislative process by utilizing the bicameral set-up established by the Constitution. We are not only encouraging the often heard "study the Senate more" complaint, but also actually using the differences within the chambers to leverage explanations of the bills that each pass.

We offer two specific examples of how differences and similarities between the House and the Senate can advance our understanding of each. The Senate floor is much more open than the House. Individual senators retain the right to debate whatever topic they desire on the Senate floor. With few restrictions, they can offer amendments and force votes in a way that House members cannot. As such, contrasting the set of votes coming up in the Senate versus the House can speak to important differences in the floor procedures of each. A second example involves the party polarization in each. Although the parties in the Senate have polarized almost as much as the House, the explanations offered by scholars for polarization, such as floor practices, redistricting, and geographic sorting, are much more tailored to the House (Theriault 2008). Why, then, has the Senate polarized almost as much as the House?

Second, the Constitution assigns two senators to represent the exact same constituency. Because this key factor is constant across the two senators, we can examine the differences in their characteristics to explain differences in their behavior. Wendy Schiller (2000) started us down this path with her insightful book *Partners and Rivals*. We think more scholars should continue the journey down this path. Researchers can add those states that have only one House member into the mix. This twist in research would not only illuminate the different behaviors exhibited by members of Congress with the same constituency, but it would also reveal important distinctions between the chambers.

The dynamics of extraordinary politics

Finally, it is important to study the legislative process under not only "normal politics," but also extraordinary circumstances. Exogenous shocks to the political system—such as the attacks of September 11, natural disasters, domestic or global economic depressions, and pandemics—may significantly alter the legislative process.

Much current research suggests that crises empower and embolden the president. By virtue of his unitary office, his command of the armed forces and the executive branch's hierarchical organization relative to Congress's decentralized, deliberative structure, the president can respond to crises with vigor and dispatch (*Federalist 70*). Conversely, the Supreme Court traditionally assumes a more deferential posture in times of crisis, preferring to leave overtly political questions to the elected branches and voting along with the dominant ruling coalition (Dahl 1957; and Powe 2009). We do not yet have a systematic account of legislative behavior in these circumstances.

While the tendency of Congress to "rally around the flag"—and implicitly, the president—in a foreign crisis is well documented (Brody 1991), the consequences of that "rally" effect are not. Recent research has begun to uncover the role of constituent opinion in the "rally" process. Baum (2002) finds that individuals respond to crises differently, and these disparate responses are a function of partisanship and political sophistication. We suspect that this line of research will implicate legislative responsiveness in the post-9/11 world. Recent scholarship on the effect of congressional checks on the president's war power suggests that Congress does systematically influence presidential use of military force (Howell and Pevehouse 2007). Presidents are less likely to use force abroad when Congress is controlled by the opposite party, and congressional influence is frequently achieved through public appeals to constituents and increased media attention. The ongoing War on Terror has altered the balance of power between Congress and the president. Future research might illuminate with greater specificity the effect of a "crisis valence" on member voting of all types, including but not limited to votes on foreign policy.

We can imagine several possible consequences for member behavior of governing under extraordinary political circumstances; the implications for responsiveness are ambiguous. Voting to authorize or not authorize a war is a potent political weapon for those who seek to unseat incumbents (witness the 2006 and 2008 elections). Conversely, members might feel compelled to authorize the use of military force despite constituent opinion for fear of stifling the president's ability to defend U.S. interests and lives. Because the link between constituent opinion and member voting is strong and because the public is no more immune to the "rally phenomenon" than members of Congress, this dynamic is unlikely to be mitigated by public opinion; indeed, it may be amplified (Mueller 1970). Both members' trustee and delegate roles may lead them to empower the president in the midst of crisis.

Crises might alter member behavior in subtler ways, too. War, natural disaster, and economic hardship might reasonably saturate media coverage of the legislative agenda, overwhelming less visible votes or debates. Because issue salience increases the probability that constituent opinion will be a decisive determinant of member vote choice, voting during periods of crisis might privilege some votes at the expense of others in discoverable ways. These "shocks" to the system—whether exogenous or endogenous—can affect member behavior in important ways and deserve greater attention and systematic analysis.

CONCLUSION

The influences on members' votes cataloged by scholars and outlined here cause members to act more or less like delegates and trustees at different stages and on different issues in the legislative process. A volume of literature shows that the people, the parties, the president, interest groups, and members' personal preferences all shape their votes. Excellent research into roll-call voting behavior and party agenda control demonstrate that the above actors all influence member voting behavior. Work still remains to be done in a number of areas. We have a rather good map showing the general lay of the land and many important features, but many details remain murky and require further explication.

Roll-call analyses show us that the final outcome of a member's decision is generally some sort of equilibrium that balances delegate behavior driven by electoral incentives with trustee behavior driven by personal preferences and information gleaned from other political actors. Scholars can now work to determine the exact points in the process that outside actors affect member voting decisions and thus when members act like delegates or like trustees. Moreover, scholars can use new constituency and member ideology measurement techniques to determine the extent to which members behave as delegates and vote in line with their constituents.

Beyond roll-call voting, other decisions of individual members also have implications for representation, democratic accountability, and policymaking. Examples include the collective decisions of individual members via party caucuses, reactions to national crises, individual-level variation in members' commitment to a bill's passage, systematic behavioral differences between representatives and senators, and different vote choices by senators from the same state. These decisions offer political scientists new avenues to formulate positive theories of member voting decisions and normative theories of their consequences.

Members' roll-call votes have afforded political scientists a fertile ground in which the most important questions have been asked with the most innovative technology available providing satisfying—though preliminary—answers. The extent of democratic accountability and representativeness has been analyzed by tools utilizing the historical record, introduced by the behavioral revolution, and proffered by positive political theory. Congressional scholars need to continue asking the big questions and developing the methodologies to answer them. There is no doubt that members' votes will remain an important source of data, but the importance of our questions and the sophistication of our tools must be matched by the originality of our data sources for congressional scholarship to remain as vibrant in the future as it has been in the past.

REFERENCES

ACHEN, C. H. 1977. Measuring Representation: The Perils of the Correlation Coefficient. *American Journal of Political Science*, 21(4): 805–15.

ACHEN, C. H. 1978. Measuring Representation. *American Journal of Political Science*, 22(3): 475–510.

ALDRICH, J. H. 1995. *Why Parties?: The Origin and Transformation of Political Parties in America*. Chicago: University of Chicago Press.

——and ROHDE, D. W. 2001. The Logic of Conditional Party Government: Revisiting the Electoral Connection, pp. 269–92 in *Congress Reconsidered*, 7th edn, eds. L. C. Dodd and B. I. Oppenheimer. Washington, DC: CQ Press.

ANSOLABEHERE, S., SNYDER, Jr., J. M, and STEWART, III, C. 2001. The Effects of Party and Preferences on Congressional Roll-Call Voting. *Legislative Studies Quarterly*, 26(4): 533–72.

ARNOLD, R. D. 1990. *The Logic of Congressional Action*. New Haven, CT: Yale University Press.

BACH, S., and SMITH, S. S. 1988. *Managing Uncertainty in the House of Representatives: Adaptation and Innovation in Special Rules*. Washington, DC: Brookings.

BAILEY, M. A. 2007. Comparable Preference Estimates across Time and Institutions for the Court, Congress, and Presidency. *American Journal of Political Science*, 51(3): 433–48.

BARTELS, L. 1991. Constituency Opinion and Congressional Policymaking: The Reagan Defense Buildup. *American Political Science Review*, 85: 457–74.

BAUM, M. A. 2002. The Constituent Foundations of the Rally-Round-the-Flag Phenomenon. *International Studies Quarterly*, 46(2): 263–98.

BAUMGARTNER, F. R., and JONES, B. D. 1993. *Agendas and Instability in American Politics*. Chicago: University of Chicago Press.

BENDER, B., and LOTT, JR., J. R. 1996. Legislator Voting and Shirking: A Critical Review of the Literature. *Public Choice*, 87: 67–100.

BINDER, S. 1997. *Minority Rights, Majority Rule: Partisanship and the Development of Congress*. New York: Cambridge University Press.

BISHOP, B. 2008. *The Big Sort: Why the Clustering of Like-Minded America is Tearing Us Apart*. Boston: Houghton Mifflin Company.

BOND, J. R., and FLEISHER, R. 1980. The Limits of Presidential Popularity as a Source of Influence in the U.S. House. *Legislative Studies Quarterly*, 5(1): 69–78.

————1990. *The President in the Legislative Arena*. Chicago: University of Chicago Press.

————and NORTHUP, M. 1988. Public Opinion and Presidential Support. *Annals*, 499(1): 47–63.

BORRELLI, S. A., and SIMMONS, G. 1993. Congressional Responsiveness to Presidential Popularity: The Electoral Context. *Political Behavior*, 15(2): 93–112.

BRACE, P., and HINCKLEY, B. 1992. *Follow the Leader: Opinion Polls and the Modern Presidents*. New York, NY: Basic Books.

BRODY, R. A. 1991. *Assessing the President*. Stanford, CA: Stanford University Press.

BRUNELL, T. L. 2005. The Relationship between Political Parties and Interest Groups: Explaining Patterns of PAC Contributions. *Political Research Quarterly*, 58(4): 681–8.

BURDEN, B. C., CALDEIRA, G. A., and GROSECLOSE, T. 2000. Measuring the Ideologies of U.S. Senators: The Song Remains the Same. *Legislative Studies Quarterly*, 25: 237–58.

BURDEN, B. C. 2007. *The Personal Roots of Representation*. Princeton: Princeton University Press.

BURKE, E. 1774. *The Works of the Right Honorable Edmund Burke*. London: Henry G. Bohn.

CAMERON, C. M. 2000. *Veto Bargaining: Presidents and the Politics of Negative Power*. New York: Cambridge University Press.

CANES-WRONE, B. 2001. The President's Influence from Legislative Appeals. *American Journal of Political Science*, 45(2): 313–29.

——2006. *Who Leads Whom?: Presidents, Policy and the Public*. Chicago: University of Chicago Press.

CANES-WRONE, B., and DE MARCHI, S. 2002. Presidential Approval and Legislative Success. *American Journal of Political Science*, 64(2): 491–509.

—— BRADY, D. W., and COGAN, J. F. 2002. Out of Step, Out of Office: Electoral Accountability and House Members' Voting. *The American Political Science Review*, 96(1): 127–40.

CLAUSEN, A. R. 1973. *How Congressmen Decide: A Policy Focus*. New York: St. Martin's Press.

CLINTON, J. D., and LAPINSKI, J. 2008. Laws and Roll Calls in the U.S. Congress, 1891–1994. *Legislative Studies Quarterly*, 33(4): 511–41.

COLLIER, K., and SULLIVAN, T. 1995. New Evidence Undercutting the Linkage of Approval with Presidential Support and Influence. *The Journal of Politics*, 57(1): 197–209.

CONVERSE, P. E. 1964. The Nature of Belief Systems in Mass Publics, pp. 206–61 in *Ideology and Discontent*, ed. D. Apter. New York: Free Press.

COX, G. W., and MCCUBBINS, M. 1993. *Legislative Leviathan: Party Government in the House*. Berkeley: University of California Press.

—— —— 2005. *Setting the Agenda: Responsible Party Government in the House Of Representatives*. Cambridge, NY: Cambridge University Press.

—— and POOLE, K. T. 2002. On Measuring Partisanship in Roll-Call Voting: The U.S. House of Representatives, 1877–1999. *American Journal of Political Science*, 46(3): 477–89.

DAHL, R. A. 1957. Decision-Making in a Democracy: The Supreme Court as a National Policy-Maker. *Journal of Public Law*, 6: 279–95.

DAVIDSON, R. H. 1969. *The Role of Congressman*. New York: Pegasus.

DEN HARTOG, C., and MONROE, N. W. 2008. Agenda Influence and Tabling Motions in the U.S. Senate, pp. 142–58 in *Why Not Parties? Party Effects in the U.S. Senate,* ed. N. W. Monroe, J. R. Roberts, and D. W. Rohde. Chicago, IL.: University of Chicago Press.

EDWARDS, III, G. C. 1978. Presidential Electoral Performance as a Source of Presidential Power. *American Journal of Political Science*, 22(1): 152–68.

—— 1980. *Presidential Influence in Congress*. San Francisco: W.H. Freeman & Company.

—— 1989. *At The Margins: Presidential Leadership of Congress*. New Haven, CT: Yale University Press.

—— 2003. *On Deaf Ears: The Limits of the Bully Pulpit*. New Haven, CT: Yale University Press.

ERIKSON, R. S. 1978. Constituency Opinion and Congressional Behavior: A Reexamination of the Miller-Stokes Representation Data. *American Journal of Political Science*, 22(3): 511–35.

FENNO, R. 1977. U.S. House Members in Their Constituencies: An Exploration. *American Political Science Review*, 71(3): 883–917.

—— 1978. *Home Style: House Members in Their Districts*. Boston: Little, Brown.

FIORINA, M. P. 1974. *Representatives, Roll Calls, and Constituencies*. Lexington, MA: Heath.

—— 1975. Constituency Influence: A Generalized Model and its Implications for Statistical Studies of Roll Call Behavior. *Political Methodology*, 2: 249–66.

—— 2006. *Culture War? The Myth of a Polarized America*. 2nd ed. New York: Pearson Longman.

FOWLER, JAMES H. 2006. Connecting the Congress: A Study of Cosponsorship Networks. *Political Analysis*, 14: 456–87.

FROMAN, L. A., and RIPLEY, R. B. 1965. Conditions for Party Leadership: The Case of the House Democrats. *American Political Science Review*, 59: 52–63.

GRONKE, P., KOCH, J., and WILSON, J. M. 2003. Follow the Leader? Presidential Approval, Presidential Support, and Representatives' Electoral Fortunes. *The Journal of Politics*, 65(3): 785–808.

GROSECLOSE, T. 1996. An Examination of the Market for Favors and Votes in Congress. *Economic Inquiry*, 34(2): 320–40.

—— Levitt, S. D., and Snyder, Jr., J. M. 1999. Comparing Interest Group Scores across Time and Chambers: Adjusted ADA Scores for the U.S. Congress. *The American Political Science Review*, 93(1): 33–50.

—— and Snyder, Jr., J. M. 1996. Buying Supermajorities. *American Political Science Review*, 90(2): 303–15.

Hall, R. L. 1996. *Participation in Congress*. New Haven, CT: Yale University Press.

Hibbing, J. R., and Theiss-Morse, E. 1995. *Congress as Public Enemy: Public Attitudes toward American Political Institutions*. Cambridge: Cambridge University Press.

—— —— 2002. *Stealth Democracy: Americans' Beliefs about How Government Should Work*. Cambridge: Cambridge University Press.

Hirsch, S. 2003. The United States of Unrepresentatives: What Went Wrong in the Latest Round of Congressional Redistricting. *Election Law Journal*, 2: 179–216.

Howell, W. G., and Pevehouse, J. C. 2007. *While Dangers Gather Congressional Checks on Presidential War Powers*. Princeton, NJ: Princeton University Press.

Jacobson, G. C. 1987. The Marginals Never Vanished: Incumbency and Competition in Elections to the U.S. House of Representatives, 1952–82. *American Journal of Political Science*, 31(1): 126–41.

—— 1997. *The Politics of Congressional Elections*. 4th edn. New York: Pearson Longman.

—— 2009. *The Politics of Congressional Elections*. 7th edn. New York: Pearson Longman.

Jessee, S. 2009. Spatial Voting in the 2004 Presidential Election. *American Political Science Review*, 103(1): 59–81.

Jones, C. O. 1994. *The Presidency in a Separated System*. Washington, DC: The Brookings Institution.

Jones, D. R., and McDermott, M. L. 2009. *Americans, Congress, and Democratic Responsiveness*. Ann Arbor: University of Michigan Press.

Kau, J. B., and Rubin, P. H. 1979. Self Interest, Ideology, and Logrolling in Congressional Voting. *Journal of Law and Economics*, 22: 365–84.

—— —— 1993. Ideology, Voting and Shirking. *Public Choice*, 76: 151–72.

Kernell, S. 1986. *Going Public: New Strategies of Presidential Leadership*. Washington, DC: Congressional Quarterly Press.

Kiewiet, D. R., and McCubbins, M. D. 1988. Presidential Influence on Congressional Appropriations Decisions. *American Journal of Political Science*, 32(3): 713–36.

Kingdon, J. W. 1973. *Congressmen's Voting Decisions*. New York: Harper and Row.

—— 1977. Models of Legislative Voting. *Journal of Politics*, 39: 563–95.

Koger, Gregory. 2003. Position Taking and Cosponsorship in the U.S. House. *Legislative Studies Quarterly*, 28(2): 225–46.

Krehbiel, K. 1991. *Information and Legislative Organization*. Ann Arbor: University of Michigan Press.

—— 1993. Constituency Characteristics and Legislative Preferences. *Public Choice*, 76: 21–37.

—— 1998. *Pivotal Politics: A Theory of U.S. Lawmaking*. Chicago: University of Chicago Press.

Lapinski, J. S. 2008. Policy Substance and Performancce in American Lawmaking, 1877–1994. *American Journal of Political Science*, 52(2): 235–51.

Lee, F. 2009. *Beyond Ideology: Politics, Principles, and Partisanship in the U.S. Senate*. Chicago: University of Chicago Press.

Lott, J. R., and Davis, M. L. 1992. A Critical Review and an Extension of the Political Shirking Literature. *Public Choice*, 74(4): 461–84.

McCarty, N., Poole, K., and Rosenthal, H. 2001. The Hunt for Party Discipline. *American Political Science Review*, 95(3): 673–87.

McIver, J. P., Erikson, R. S., and Wright, G. C. 1994. Public Opinion and Public Policy: A View From the States, pp. 249–66 in *New Perspectives in American Politics*, ed. L. C. Dodd and C. Jillson. Washington, DC: Congressional Quarterly Press.

Mann, T. E., and Ornstein, N. J. 2006. *The Broken Branch: How Congress Is Failing America and How to Get It Back on Track*. New York: Oxford University Press.

Mansbridge, J. 2003. Rethinking Representation. *American Political Science Review*, 97(4): 515–28.

Mayhew, D. R. 1974. *Congress: The Electoral Connection*. New Haven: Yale University Press.

Miller, W. E., and Stokes, D. E. 1963. Constituency Influence in Congress. *American Political Science Review*, 57(1): 45–56.

Mueller, J. 1970. Presidential Popularity from Truman to Johnson. *American Political Science Review*, 64: 18–34.

Neustadt, R. 1960. *Presidential Power: The Politics of Leadership*. New York: John Wiley & Sons, Inc.

Ostrom, Jr., C. W., and Simon, D. M. 1985. Promise and Performance: A Dynamic Model of Presidential Popularity. *The American Political Science Review*, 79(2): 334–58.

Pearson, K., and Schickler, E. 2009. Discharge Petitions, Agenda Control, and the Congressional Committee System, 1929–76. *The Journal of Politics*, 71(4): 1238–56.

Peltzman, S. 1984. Constituent Interest and Congressional Voting. *Journal of Law and Economics*, 27(1): 181–210.

Poole, K. T., and Rosenthal, H. 1997. *Congress: A Political-Economic History of Roll-call voting*. New York: Oxford University Press.

Powe, Jr., L. A. 2009. *The Supreme Court and The American Elite, 1789–2008*. Cambridge, MA: Harvard University Press.

Pritchard, A. 1985. An Evaluation of CQ Presidential Support Scores: The Relationship between Presidential Election Results and Congressional Voting Decisions. *American Journal of Political Science*, 30(2): 480–95.

Rehfeld, A. 2009. Representation Rethought: On Trustees, Delegates, and Gyroscopes in the Study of Political Representation and Democracy. *American Political Science Review*, 103(2): 214–30.

Rivers, D., and Rose, N. L. 1985. Passing the President's Program: Public Opinion and Presidential Influence in Congress. *American Journal of Political Science*, 29(2): 183–96.

Rocca, Michael S. 2007. Non Legislative Debate in the U.S. House of Representatives. *American Politics Review*, 35(4): 489–505.

Rohde, D. W. 1991. *Parties and Leaders in the Postreform House*. Chicago: University of Chicago Press.

Rossiter, C., ed. 2003. *The Federalist Papers*. New York: Signet Classic.

Rothenberg, L. S., and Sanders, M. S. 2000. Severing the Electoral Connection: Shirking in the Contemporary Congress. *American Journal of Political Science*, 44: 316–25.

Schattschneider, E. E. 1960. *The Semi-Sovereign People: A Realist's View of Democracy in America*. New York: Holt, Rinehart and Winston.

Schickler, E. 2001. *Disjointed Pluralism: Institutional Innovation and the Development of the U.S. Congress*. Princeton, NJ: Princeton University Press.

Schiller, W. J. 2000. *Partners and Rivals: Representation in U.S. Senate Delegations*. Princeton, NJ: Princeton University Press.

Shepsle, K. A. 1974. *The Giant Jigsaw Puzzle: Democratic Committee Assignments in the Modern House*. Chicago: University of Chicago Press.

Sinclair, B. 1994. Special Rules and the Institutional Design Controversy. *Legislative Studies Quarterly*, 19: 477–94.

—— 2006. *Party Wars: Polarization and the Politics of National Policy Making.* Norman: The University of Oklahoma Press.

—— 2007. *Unorthodox Lawmaking: New Legislative Processes in the U.S. Congress.* 3rd edn. Washington, DC: CQ Press.

SMITH, R. A. 1995. Interest Group Influence in the U. S. Congress. *Legislative Studies Quarterly,* 20(1): 89–139.

SMITH, S. S. 2007. *Party Influence in Congress.* New York: Cambridge University Press.

SNYDER, J. 1991. On Buying Legislatures. *Economics and Politics,* 3: 93–109.

—— and GROSECLOSE, T. 2000. Estimating Party Influence on Congressional Roll-Call Voting. *American Journal of Political Science,* 44: 187–205.

STOKES, D. E. 1963. Spatial Models of Party Competition. *American Political Science Review,* 57(2): 368–77.

SULKIN, T. 2005. *Issue Politics in Congress.* New York: Cambridge University Press.

THERIAULT, S. M. 2001. Patronage, the Pendleton Act, and the Power of the People. *The Journal of Politics,* 65(1): 50–68.

—— 2005. *The Power of the People: Congressional Competition, Public Attention, and Voter Retribution.* Columbus: Ohio State University Press.

—— 2008. *Party Polarization in Congress.* New York: Cambridge University Press.

TULIS, J. K. 1987. *The Rhetorical Presidency.* Princeton, NJ: Princeton University Press.

WAHLKE, J. C., EULAU, H., and BUCHANAN, W. 1962. *The Legislative System: Explorations in Legislative Behavior.* New York: Wiley.

WAWRO, G. 2001. A Panel Probit Analysis of Campaign Contributions and Roll-Call Votes. *American Journal of Political Science,* 45(3): 563–79.

WAYMAN, F. W. 1985. Arms Control and Strategic Arms Voting in the U.S. Senate: Patterns of Change, 1967–1983. *The Journal of Conflict Resolution,* 29: 225–51.

WILDAVSKY, A. 1966. The Two Presidencies. *Trans-Action,* 4: 7–14.

WISEMAN, A. E. 2004. Test of Vote-Buyer Theories of Coalition Formation in Legislatures. *Political Research Quarterly,* 57(3): 441–50.

WRIGHT, G. C., ERIKSON, R. S., and McIVER, J. P. 1994. The Impact of State Party Elite Ideology. *Annual Review of Politics,* 15(3): 315–27.

CHAPTER 26

....

LOBBYING AND INTEREST GROUP ADVOCACY

....

BETH L. LEECH

IN the mid-twentieth century, political scientists who studied the role of lobbyists often described a political process with "pressure groups" at its core. It was the heyday of the group approach to politics, and not only were such groups at the center of how policymaking was understood—consider, for example, David Truman's book about interest groups, which he called *The Governmental Process* (1951)—they were usually assumed to be quite influential. Popular books about Washington had names like *The Pressure Boys* and *American Democracy under Pressure* (Crawford 1939; Blaisdell 1957). Lobbyists were described as twisting arms and "pressuring" members of Congress to do their bidding.

By the 1960s, however, a new view of lobbying was taking hold, at least among the political scientists who studied the topic systematically rather than anecdotally. A multi-method, multi-year project by Bauer, Pool, and Dexter, while still using the old term, found to the researchers' surprise that the groups were not as coercive as was often assumed: "All in all," they wrote, "the staff members of pressure groups, hard-working though they were, could scarcely be characterized as crusaders anxious to engage the enemy in open combat. Their major contacts, both in frequency and effectiveness, were with friends of their cause" (Bauer, Pool, and Dexter 1963, 357). Surveys of lobbyists and legislators by Milbrath (1963) and Scott and Hunt (1966) provided similar findings, and the pressure term seemed outdated and ill-conceived. New terminology joined the new view: lobbyists now represented "interest" groups.

The change in terminology has for the most part endured, but outside the relatively narrow world of interest group scholars, there has been a constant slippage back to the old view of the lobbyist as arm-twister. In the popular media, in the speeches of politicians, and even in the assumptions of many political scientists, the power of "special interests" is great indeed. Lobbyists make a useful scapegoat in Washington for anything that goes contrary to plan, whether one is a mere observer or a political participant. An interest group becomes a "special interest" whenever one disagrees with the policy position that the group is advocating. This all-powerful view of lobbyists is curious, especially since the work of interest group scholars over the past few decades has documented again and again that the relationships between lobbyists and legislators are symbiotic, more often involving cooperation than anything that looks like pressure.

Today the term *pressure group* has faded from use. Most scholars talk about *interest groups* or *organized interests*, terms that encompass any type of organization that attempts to influence public policy, with the exception of political parties and government institutions (see Baumgartner and Leech 1998, ch. 2, for a discussion of the variety of definitions for the term *interest group*). The use of the word "lobby" to mean advocacy for public policy developed in the nineteenth century, and quite literally referred to a person who would stand in the lobby of the Capitol, waiting to plead his case with a member of Congress. It is no wonder, then, that one definition of lobbying is restricted to the act of speaking to a legislator in an effort to influence public policy. Most interest-group scholars, however, use a broader definition of "lobbying" as describing policy advocacy more generally, including such things as filing lawsuits, contacting agency officials, producing policy-related research reports, mounting grassroots campaigns, undertaking public relations or mass media campaigns, and even simply engaging in monitoring what policymakers are doing. Any actions that are taken with the goal of influencing policy would be included under this broader usage of the term. Some interest group scholars would prefer to avoid the words "lobbying" and "lobbyist" altogether because of the negative connotations and narrow meaning the words often have in general usage. Heinz, Laumann, et al. (1993) spoke of "Washington representatives" rather than lobbyists and Schlozman and Tierney (1986) referred to "techniques of influence" rather than "lobbying tactics." Likewise, Baumgartner, Berry, et al. (2009) often spoke of "policy advocacy" rather than "lobbying," since this allowed them to include the study of advocacy by government officials together with advocacy by private interests. Problematic or not, the word lobbying is so ingrained in everyday usage that we can hardly avoid it altogether, and so I will use the term "lobbying" interchangeably with "advocacy," when speaking about interest group efforts to affect policymaking. These struggles with definitions are indicative of the conceptual struggles as well. In this chapter I will survey the literature on lobbying and interest group influence in Congress, showing along the way that research has not supported many of the popular beliefs about lobbying and interest groups. A more collaborative view of advocacy is a better fit with the evidence.

THE PROBLEM OF ASSESSING INFLUENCE

....

While stories in the mainstream media may be certain of the power of interest groups and their lobbyists, political scientists have had a much harder time pinning down that influence. Smith (1995) reviewed thirty-seven studies of contributions by political action committees (PACs) and subsequent roll-call votes in the House and Senate and discovered that fewer than half of the studies found evidence that campaign contributions affected how members of Congress voted. Baumgartner and Leech (1998) examined fifteen quantitative studies of lobbying influence and thirty-three studies of PAC influence and also found that most studies found either marginal or no observable effects on congressional voting. More recent empirical work has either failed to find a relationship or found relationships that were statistically significant but substantively small (e.g. Wawro 2001, for an alternate view that finds PACs have an impact on outcomes under some circumstances, see Witko 2006).

Baumgartner, Berry, et al. (2009) studied more than 1,000 organizations active on a random sample of ninety-eight issues and analyzed the effect of more than a dozen different measures of monetary resources on outcomes. None of them was correlated with wished-for outcomes for the groups studied. PAC contributions, in fact, were *negatively* correlated with success (although the result was not statistically significant). More lobbying or more campaign donations did not equal more influence. When Burstein and Linton (2002) conducted their meta analysis of all studies of interest group influence published in major political science and sociology journals from 1990 to 2000, they found that more than half of the fifty-three articles analyzed showed no impact on congressional voting decisions resulting from campaign contributions. Burstein and Linton pointed out that given that the studies virtually never controlled for public opinion and given that most journals have a publication bias against null findings, the actual effects of interest group influence were likely even weaker. Throughout the studies, any interest group influence over members of Congress was strongly limited by other variables such as constituency, ideology, and the visibility of the issue (see Leech 2010 for a review of the literature on influence by interest groups).

While the effects of campaign expenditures on votes in Congress is hard to see, there are some indications that contributions may affect earlier stages of the process. While floor votes are very public, activities in committee are less so and are less likely to come to the attention of mass constituencies. It is often expected, therefore, that interest groups with the ability to donate money—but without strong links to a member's constituency interests—may have greater influence in committee. In addition, while floor votes are dichotomous and thus have less variance to predict (Baumgartner and Leech 1998), measuring participation in committee hearings can give researchers greater methodological traction (Hall and Wayman 1990; Hall and Miler 2008). It also is in committee where policy proposals are shaped, and this offers enormous potential opportunities for influence (Hojnacki and Kimball 1998, 1999).

Despite strong theoretical reasons why we might expect to see interest group influence most strongly in these early stages, there are relatively few empirical examinations of interest group activities in committee, at least compared to analyses of floor votes. Why? Data availability. It is much easier to try to correlate a floor vote with campaign contribution data—one never needs to leave the office. Analyses of lobbying activity have traditionally necessitated surveys or in-person interviews with interest group leaders and/or members of Congress. Although the Lobbying Disclosure Act of 1995 has lessened this problem to a great degree, providing data on the issues on which interest groups lobbied and how much they spent, if researchers hope to link this information to particular members of Congress, interviews are still necessary. And so there are but a handful of very good studies of lobbying in committee.

Even in this small group of studies focusing on lobbying in committee, the levels of influence observed are attenuated, and it is not clear that campaign contributions are what matters. Wright (1990), for example, examined interest group voting in committee and found that PAC donations seemed to contribute to success only because they were paired with lobbying contacts. The number of lobbying contacts on each side did help to predict votes (although those contacts tended to be directed more at allied members of Congress than at those opposing the interest group's perspective). Hojnacki and Kimball (2001) also found that PAC donations were correlated with more contacts of committee members, but they conclude that these greater contacts resulted from overall greater resources and stronger district ties. Hall and Wayman (1990) found that PAC donations increased the amount that allied members of Congress (but not opposing members) participated in committee hearings, although the effect was relatively small. Here, as in studies of floor votes, most variance in congressional behavior is explained by ideological considerations, constituency preferences, and other such variables, with interest groups' relative influence either not measurable or marginal.

Many scholars have suggested that PAC donations may "buy" access, although evidence on this point is much more scarce than assertions about it. While Langbein (1986) found some evidence of such a link, Chin, Bond, and Geva (2000) and Hojnacki and Kimball (2001) did not. A related finding from Miler (2007) indicates that donations may increase attention from congressional offices, helping ensure that certain groups are remembered by congressional staff as having a stake in the issue. Given that about two-thirds of the organizations active in Washington do not have an affiliated PAC, however, the money-buys-access hypothesis fails to address why and how it is that many of those organizations without PACs often have the ears of members of Congress and are often viewed as enjoying policy success, despite never offering a campaign contribution. One possibility that has been suggested in the literature is the importance of constituency linkages. Interest group influence is often seen as being limited by constituent concerns (e.g. Denzau and Munger 1986), but constituency concerns also can enhance interest group influence. Hansen (1990) found that farm groups historically got better access to Congress when they were electorally important than during periods when they were not. One problem, of course, is that mass publics are known to be inattentive to most issues, so their influence may depend on whether the issue is expected to become salient and whether they are expected to vote (Arnold 1990; Goldstein 1999).

The approach taken in most of the efforts to assess the impact of PAC donations on policy outcomes derives from what Lowery and Gray (2004) call the "transactions" model of interest group influence. In this model, legislative votes are traded for the benefits lobbyists can provide. Lowery and Gray contrast this approach with the more current "neopluralist view" (see also McFarland 2004), which pays greater attention to the role of policy preferences and the representational role that interest groups can potentially play, while recognizing that organizational biases mean that not all interests are equally represented. Scholars in the neopluralist tradition suggest that one reason why there have been so many null and conflicting findings in studies of PAC and lobbying influence is that the relationship between interest groups and legislators has been misspecified.

To better understand what that relationship is, it is helpful to take a step back to look at what research tells us about what interest groups actually do and whom they contact.

LOBBYING TACTICS: LOOKING AT WHAT GROUPS DO

If lobbying consists of attempts to influence policy—however influential or non-influential those attempts may be—what do those attempts consist of? If we consider just the most narrow definition of lobbying—contacting government officials to directly present a point of view—research based on surveys and elite interviews indicate that such activities are engaged in by almost every interest group active in Washington (Schlozman and Tierney 1983, 1986; Heinz, Laumann, et al. 1993; Baumgartner, Berry, et al. 2009). But such direct contacts are hardly the only tactic used by interest groups in their attempts at advocacy. Schlozman and Tierney's survey of interest groups active in Washington asked about twenty-seven different tactics of influence, ranging from testifying at hearings to engaging in litigation to engaging in protest. The top tactic was indeed contacting officials directly—98 percent of the groups reported using this tactic and it also was the tactic with the greatest percentage of groups (36 percent) naming it as one of the top three tactics on which they spent substantial time. And yet, that percentage means that for at least two-thirds of the groups in Washington, other types of advocacy activities were more important. These other activities included presenting research results (92 percent did it; 27 percent said it was one of the top three tactics in terms of importance) and consulting with government officials to plan legislative strategy (85 percent of the organizations did it and 19 percent picked it as one of the top three tactics).

Other studies have come to similar or at least complementary conclusions. Heinz, Laumann, et al. (1993) interviewed representatives from more than 300 interest groups that were among the most active in Washington during the 1980s. Among the advocacy activities described as being especially important by more than half the respondents were maintaining relations with officials, providing information to officials, and simply monitoring changes in rules, regulations, or laws (Heinz, Laumann, et al. 1993, 99). The picture painted is one of consultation, not pressure, a world in which interest groups need to be aware of what government is doing so that they can react to it and express their viewpoints on it. On the other hand, raising money for PAC donations was an important activity for only 19 percent of those who were surveyed.

The ninety-eight case studies in Baumgartner, Berry, et al. (2009) support this view of lobbying as well. The most commonly mentioned tactic among the 155 lobbyists interviewed was, unsurprisingly, direct contacts of members of Congress and their staffs. But the second most commonly mentioned tactic was working with legislative allies, with challengers of the status quo even more likely than those defending the status quo to make use of this tactic (77 percent versus 57 percent). As in the other studies, the respondents in Baumgartner, Berry, et al. also reported that disseminating in-house research was one of the most commonly used tactics, while more public tactics such as testifying at congressional hearings and mobilizing mass memberships for a grassroots lobbying campaign were somewhat less common (35 percent and 48 percent, respectively). Challengers of the status quo were more likely to undertake public relations or educational campaigns about their issues (22 percent versus 8 percent) and to work to mobilize a mass public to speak out about the issue (22 percent versus 11 percent). This points to the importance of signaling momentum and general public support for the issue in order to move it onto the voting agenda.

Of course, a long series of studies of policy subsystems—what once were called "iron triangles"—had shown close relationships between interest groups and the agency and congressional committee involved in a given policy area (e.g. Freeman 1955; Fritschler 1975; Bosso 1987; Browne 1990). Actors in such policy areas often have shared policy goals or at least a shared interest in preserving the status quo. Although such subsystems are occasionally rocked by—or broken up by—conflict from within, they also may function cooperatively for years. In these subsystems information and ideas are shared and the work of all is made somewhat easier as a result.

Cooperative interactions exist among legislators and lobbyists outside such subsystems as well, however. Ainsworth (1997) describes these small, informal groups of interest group lobbyists and members of Congress as "lobbying enterprises," which arise whenever a sympathetic legislator is willing to work with interest groups to advance some policy goal. He notes that the patterns of association described by Heinz, Laumann, et al. (1993, 194) showed that most lobbyists maintain regular contacts with about five government officials. While each lobbyist in the study by Heinz and colleagues contacted a mean of about twenty officials, the lobbyists met regularly with just a subset of those officials, and it is with those officials that it would be possible to plan legislative strategy, draft legislation, and work together toward passage of a bill. Sympathetic lawmakers are sometimes identified by the use of voting scorecards compiled by interest groups (see Fowler 1982). While a handful of interest groups have maintained formal scorecard ratings of legislators for decades (including Americans for Democratic Action, the American Conservative Union, and the AFL-CIO), what is more common is informal tracking of a few key votes that are then reported in newsletters to members and other interested parties. Up to 44 percent of interest groups engage in this type of informal vote tracking and publication, according to Schlozman and Tierney (1983, 1986). The more formal scorecards are much less common and are more important in the world of political science as a proxy for legislator ideology than they are in the world of lobbyists as an advocacy tool.[1]

Providing information

In one way or another, provision of information arises as an important tactic in most interest group studies, and information is at the heart of most modern theories of influence. DeGregorio (1997) interviewed lobbyists and congressional staffers to track the interactions of interest groups and their congressional champions on six issues. Her respondents attested to the critical importance of information as an interest group resource. As one lobbyist told her: "Information is always valuable to the members. It's amazing sometimes the things you can tell them that they are not familiar with. Outsiders provide a different perspective and a useful perspective." (1997, 107).

Legislators do care about good public policy in addition to reelection, but the probable effectiveness and potential side-effects of any proposed policy are always a question. Esterling (2004) argues that legislators thus turn to interest groups for their policy expertise.

Despite the importance of information in both theory and practice, Burstein and Hirsh (2007) point out that most studies of interest group influence fail to measure the content of lobbying messages. These authors analyzed the content of hearing testimony in Congress on twenty-seven policy proposals and found that the type of information presented did have an impact on the outcomes. Information about the expected effectiveness of a proposal substantially increased its probability of passage while information about why the proposal would not work decreased its chances. On the other hand, information about importance and attempts to reframe the issue did not have much effect. While such information may matter at earlier stages of the policy process, it seems not to have much impact by the hearing stage.

Electoral concerns were for the most part unmentioned in the hearings analyzed by Burstein and Hirsh, despite members' motivations for reelection and despite

---

[1] The use of these scorecards as a proxy for ideology is problematic, however. Not only is the researcher, in the words of Jackson and Kingdon (1992, 809), "explaining votes with votes," but the results may exaggerate congressional polarization (Snyder 1992) and reflect a selection of issues of that does not necessarily reflect policymaking more broadly (Fowler 1982).

theory that suggests that interest groups are important providers of such information. Likewise, Baumgartner, Berry, et al. (2009) found that in their ninety-eight issues, arguments containing electoral content were rarely featured in lobbying messages at any stage. Only 3 percent of the cases in both Baumgartner, Berry, et al. and in Burstein and Hirsh contained electoral lobbying arguments. Even though electoral arguments and the provision of electoral information by lobbyists are rare, that does not mean that electoral concerns do not matter. Members of Congress may well know this information already from other sources, or the information may be transmitted implicitly (signaled), for instance through grassroots mobilization (Kollman 1998; Goldstein 1999), rather than transmitted explicitly through words. Hansen (1990) considered lobbying on farm hearings over seven decades and found that variation in the relative electoral *importance* of farm groups affected the access those groups received in Congress. So there is some evidence that the actual electoral importance may matter, while explicit electoral information may not.

Friends versus foes

While in theory information could be used to persuade undecided or opposing legislators, in practice lobbyists more often inform members of Congress who have similar preferences, according to social network analyses done by Carpenter, Esterling, and Lazar (2004). Who knows whom matters a great deal as well, as the study found that connections through social networks were even more important than shared policy preferences—that, is, lobbyists and legislators consulted people they knew and the contacts of those people. It is possible that PAC contributions serve a purpose here in helping to create the social connections necessary to be thought of as a trusted information source. As Hall and Deardorff (2006) have proposed, the campaign contributions may serve primarily as one way to signal to a legislator that the organization shares his or her policy preferences. The work of Robert Salisbury and Ken Shepsle (1981) suggests that these interactions may also be eased by the revolving-door nature of many congressional staff jobs. Most congressional staffers are young, turnover is high, and many end up in better-paying jobs in the lobbying community. Salisbury and Shepsle call these "once-removed" members of congressional enterprises: "Though no longer involved exclusively in legislative machinations, he may nevertheless serve his former boss as a source of information and occasional assistance," they write (1981, 562).

The idea that interest groups spend more time contacting members of Congress who agree with them has sometimes been seen as illogical (Austen-Smith and Wright 1994) because lobbying people who already support one's preferred policy seems redundant and wasteful. Spending time with legislative allies makes sense, however, if we take a broader view of lobbying as more than just a message that says "vote with me." As Baumgartner and Leech (1996) have argued, allied officials are the most likely to introduce legislation, to work to amend a bill in committee, or to help gather together the congressional support needed for the bill to move forward and get the opportunity for a floor vote. Interest groups also may lobby their allies because those officials in turn may lobby other officials on behalf of the group (Leech and Baumgartner 1998). These legislators may also serve as a kind of elite lobbyist on behalf of the issue an interest group supports, since Kingdon's work (1973) suggests that members of Congress often rely on other members for cues on how to vote.

Hojnacki and Kimball (1998) argue that working with allies may be most common at the committee stage of the process: "In our view, much of the strategic activity in committee involves passing along draft legislation, statistics, talking points, and other information to friendly legislators so they can rebut amendments, dilatory tactics, and arguments made by legislative opponents" (1998, 785).

These activities are best conducted with members of Congress who already agree with the policy positions of the lobbyists—it is hard to imagine pressure great enough to convince an opponent of an idea to introduce a bill to enact it. But as Hojnacki and Kimball also note, it also is useful for lobbyists to be able to *expand* their coalitions of support, both in committee and beyond. Here persuasion enters in again as lobbyists work to show both those who are undecided and those who are opposed enough evidence and enough reasons to consider voting the way the interest group prefers. Hojnacki and Kimball do find that interest groups with greater resources are able to make greater use of these attempts to persuade—but the resources that matter are not the usual ones we see in political scandals. Instead, interest groups who reported having district support among a member of Congress's constituency were more likely to lobby that member, even if the member was undecided. Having access to a PAC and having a large lobbying staff (a proxy measure for amount spent on lobbying) were not significantly related to more lobbying contacts of any kind.

Kollman (1997) argues that interest groups may lobby their allies in committee in part because that's who is there. The self-selecting biases inherent in much committee assignment as well as in interest group formation means that members of a committee and the interest groups who tend to lobby there are likely to share preferences. And indeed, Kollman found a correlation between the ideologies of interest groups that lobby a committee and the ideologies of members of that committee. This is most likely to be the case on committees that are primarily faced with issues that are valence issues for the committee, such as is the case with the Agriculture Committee. Committees without a great deal of internal conflict may also find that the interests present are fairly homogenous, while committees facing internal divides may find that their lobbyists are divided as well.

Of course, if lobbying were nothing but cooperation—if the information and pressure were never used to persuade rather than provide service, then lobbyists would never contact any members of Congress who did not already agree with them. Research clearly shows that this is not the case. A survey I conducted in 1996 of nearly 800 interest groups asked them to characterize the nature of their lobbying efforts on the issue they had worked on most recently, in terms of whom they lobbied— allies, undecideds, or opponents (Leech and Baumgartner 1998). The respondents could agree with any or all of the statements: 76 percent said that trying to persuade undecided officials was a good description of their lobbying campaign, 63 percent said that working with allied officials was a good description of what they had done, and 58 percent said that trying to persuade officials who disagreed with the group's point of view was a good description of their efforts. Working with allies is central, but clearly other methods of advancing a group's policy goals are also important.

For grassroots mobilizations, for example, the logic changes somewhat. Rather than being more likely to lobby members of Congress who agree with the interest group, as is the case with direct lobbying, interest groups are more likely to wage grassroots campaigns in districts where they already have support. Hojnacki and Kimball (1999) found that grassroots lobbying in committee was usually combined with direct lobbying and focused primarily on raising support in districts where there was moderate to high support for the interest group. The support of the districts is thus being mobilized to put pressure on opposing members of Congress and to provide additional support for sympathetic members of Congress. Goldstein (1999) has complementary conclusions, finding that television issue advertising by interest groups is targeted in the districts of members of committees with jurisdiction on the issue, and especially in the districts of undecided committee members.

LOBBYING AS A SYMBIOTIC PROCESS

Lobbyists and legislators often work together, but why do they do so? A transactions model that considers only material exchange and leaves out policy preferences and information is clearly not well supported by the evidence. A better starting point is provided by Hojnacki and Kimball's (1998) theoretical expectations about interest group strategic activity in committee—interest groups there spend the most time lobbying allies because it is allies who are best able to perform the tasks that must be done in committee, including the formation of a policy proposal that is in line with the interest group's preferences. The flip side of these strategic considerations on the part of groups arises in Hall and Deardorff's (2006) theory of lobbying subsidy, which provides the rationale for why legislators would listen to those lobbying messages. While Bauer, Pool, and Dexter (1963) had suggested that interest groups primarily contacted their allies because they, like most people, wanted to avoid conflict and uncomfortable situations, Hall and Deardorff suggest a rationale that is a better fit with what we know about the highly professionalized world of Washington lobbyists. Their formal model indicates that it is the organization best able to provide what politicians need—information, facts, supporters, media coverage, or strategic expertise—that will be the most influential interest group. Every member of Congress has many different causes and issues that he or she supports, and each has numerous possible venues in which to become involved. One way that interest groups can be influential is by lowering the cost to government officials of working on the issue that the interest group cares about, by making it easier to take up that cause rather than another. Thus interest groups lobby their allies in order to provide the information, arguments, and attention to the issue that will be needed if the issue is to succeed.

Hall and Miler (2008) provide a test of some of the hypotheses derived from Hall and Deardorff. They examine efforts by the House Commerce Committee to oversee efforts by the Environmental Protection Agency in 1997 to strengthen air quality standards for smog and soot. They analyzed transcripts of five oversight hearings to measure participation in committee, as Hall (1996) and Hall and Wayman (1990) had done previously. They found that lobbying by allied groups increased legislative participation in these hearings: essentially the interest groups subsidized the interventions of congressional overseers. The findings suggest that not only do interest groups sound the alarm, warning members of Congress that oversight is needed (McCubbins and Schwartz 1984), but they help to make those follow-up investigations possible. Esterling (2007) provides additional evidence from the point of view of the lobbyists themselves. He finds that interest groups are most likely to contribute PAC donations (one form of subsidy) to the legislators who are most able to serve as a "workhorse" on an issue and to develop effective policy. The subsidies are given to those most able and most useful politically.

Information (and other resources) in the subsidy model work not to change legislators' opinions about an issue (as was so often modeled in the transaction theories of interest group influence) but rather to change those legislators' *priorities* regarding an issue. Influence via interest group subsidy is a form of agenda-setting. It is the legislators' agendas and their decisions about how much time and effort to expend on a particular issue that are changed in the process. It is a process that displays symbiotic mutualism—both sides benefit from the relationship. Legislators receive information and other support, helping to further all three of their central goals as identified by Fenno (1973): reelection, good public policy, and enhanced reputations in Washington. The lobbyists get chances to shape policies in the ways they prefer and chances to encourage legislators to spend time on the issues their groups prefer rather than on some other issues.

Legislative entrepreneurship is costly and difficult (DeGregorio 1997; Wawro 2000). Even for congressional leadership, "mustering the support needed to pass legislation of any consequence is not easy," argues DeGregorio (1997, 2), whose research shows that lobbyists help them to do this: "The facts are indisputable. Legislators are assisted by a vast array of individuals when they promulgate major policy. ... The data reveal a highly permeable institution in which officeholders welcome and initiate contacts with hundreds of advocates who work on behalf of widely diverse organizational interests" (1997, 139–40).

The work of Heaney (2006) suggests that interest groups act as "brokers" throughout this process, providing the personal linkages that connect other interest groups and legislators of opposing parties.

Not only the personnel of policymaking but also the topics of the proposed legislation itself may come from interest groups. Browne and Paik (1993) found that members of Congress who had introduced legislation related to agricultural concerns reported that organized interests were of central importance for their decisions about which issues to work on. Interest groups were second only to constituents as the most common source of issues to champion—and that is despite a certain undercount of interest groups, since interest groups that were based in the home district were coded as constituents.

Conceptualizing lobbying as subsidy does not mean, however, that the interest group system is "fair" or accurately represents all interests. Some types of interests find it easier than others to organize and then to be represented before Congress, for reasons that have their basis in collective action theory (Olson 1971). Surveys and other counts of the interest group system have consistently found that businesses, trade associations, and professional associations dominate, accounting for up to 80 percent of the interests active in Washington (Schlozman and Tierney 1986; Walker 1991; Baumgartner and Leech 2001). Interests that are not organized or present in Washington obviously cannot subsidize legislative efforts, and so some segments of society may lack strong representation in part because there is no outside effort to promote their interests. Citizen membership organizations and nonprofits that represent non-occupational interests do, however, seem to have an impact on policy-making that belies their relatively low numbers (Berry 1999; Baumgartner, Berry, et al. 2009), and certainly under some circumstances organized efforts are not necessary for representation (Denzau and Munger 1986).

Lobbying as subsidy provides a good description of what most lobbying looks like and conceptualizing lobbying in this way helps to explain much of what would otherwise seem to be peculiar behavior by lobbyists—spending so much time with their friends, for example. But even subsidy is far from a magic bullet for lobbyists. While Hall and Wayman (1990) found a slight increase in participation in committee among allies who received PAC contributions, and Hall and Miler (2008) likewise found that legislators who had received lobbying support participated more in oversight committees, Wawro (2000) found no effects of campaign contributions on legislative entrepreneurship.

Economic theories of lobbying, including rent-seeking approaches, of course also posit that the lobbyist-legislator relationship is mutually beneficial (e.g. Tullock 1967; Buchanan, Tollison, and Tullock 1980; Parker 1996; for a review of economic approaches to interest groups see Mitchell and Munger 1991). The primary difference between these perspectives and the subsidy perspective is in the hypothesized motivations for that symbiotic relationship. In the rent-seeking perspective, the interest group influence stems solely from the material benefits that accrue to the legislator. It is a transactions or exchange model. In the subsidy perspective, those material benefits are viewed as secondary. The interest group and the legislator are assumed to have existing shared policy goals that predate any material subsidy. Subsidies reduce the cost to the legislator (and increase the legislator's chance of policy success and reputation enhancement), but the subsidies are not large enough to overcome pre-existing ideological positions and "buy" public policy. If they were, the relationship would shift from subsidy to bribery. In the world of public policy, this is certainly possible but thankfully seems to be rare both because dollar amounts of campaign contributions are limited by law and because it is rare for a single member to be able to act alone—a majority of the Congress would need to be bought. But there are aspects of what legislators do that are less public and that face fewer checks on potentially improper influence. It is there that our concern should focus.

Public and private lobbying

The interest group activities that I (and most of the scholars cited so far) have been describing involve lobbying for collective goods, that is, public policies. While changes in public policy will affect constituents and industry generally, interest groups also may lobby for private goods such as line-items, earmarks, and other governmental actions that benefit a single individual or single corporation. Godwin and Seldon (2002, see also Godwin, Lopez, and Seldon 2008) have developed this idea most clearly. They give an example from a defense contractor lobbyist who was asked what was the most important vote she had influenced. The lobbyist replied, "Do you mean the most important vote, or the most important thing I did for the firm?" The lobbyist once succeeded in getting a 25 percent increase in the price of a missile her firm made. But a recorded vote never took place. The price increase occurred during committee markup of an omnibus defense bill. Although this outcome boosted the firm's profits by $50 million over five years, no legislator voted directly on the price increase (Godwin and Seldon, 2002, 206).

As a result of potential private benefits like the change in the missile, firms that are highly regulated by the federal government are likely to spend the most on lobbying, Godwin and Seldon predict, because the regulatory relationship means that there are opportunities to receive private goods from the government. Godwin and Seldon examined firms in three industries—airlines, rubber resin, and publishing—making use of the varying degrees of government regulation in these areas from airlines with the most to publishing with the least. Airlines, which face regulations by the Federal Aviation Administration on everything from employee work hours to routes they can fly, did indeed lobby more often than the firms of equivalent size in other industries and they were more likely to lobby alone rather than in coalitions. Coalitions, of course, are critical in lobbying for collective goods, where many voices are needed to push a bill forward, but not important in lobbying for private goods, where less attention is actually an advantage.

There are important differences to be found in the theory and evidence regarding lobbying for collective goods and lobbying for private goods. Lobbying for public policy often looks more like collaboration than a transaction for three reasons. First, the activities are public, or at least have a greater chance of becoming so. Second, the friction of the public policy process (Jones and Baumgartner 2005) and the need to get so many political actors on one's side if a bill is actually going to become a law, means that the cost of outright vote buying increases exorbitantly. And finally, and most importantly, the friction of the public policy process means that it is all but impossible for a single actor to "deliver" a policy. I will discuss each of these points in turn.

The process of creating public policy—a law, in the case of congressional policymaking—actually provides some safeguards against corruption in a democratic society where constituents are at least retrospectively attentive. The process from policy idea to law involves several public steps: introduction of a bill, possibly a hearing, committee votes, and floor votes. At many stages of the process, from signing on as a co-sponsor to the final vote, there is documentation of where lawmakers stand and what they are doing. The possibility that a challenger or organized interest might make a campaign issue out of one of these stands is something that remains at the back of candidate's minds and makes it less likely that they would act or vote contrary to ideology or the interests of constituents (Arnold 1990). On the other hand, many instances of private goods can be completed relatively clandestinely. A line item may be inserted with the knowledge of only a handful of people. A call to a regulatory agency on behalf of a business may go unremarked. It is not a coincidence that many of the most famous bribery scandals involve lobbying for private benefits, not for public policy. The case of lobbyist Jack Abramoff in 2005, for example, involved aid promised to Native American casino owners. The Keating Five scandal involved five members of Congress accused of intervening with an agency concerning regulatory issues affecting a financial institution. The Abscam scandal of the 1970s, in which a U.S. senator and six members of the House were convicted, involved a sting operation in which "Arab sheiks" offered bribes in return for help in gaining U.S. asylum and setting up financial investments. In all these cases, private goods were promised or supplied to individuals or individual companies—the focus was not on legislation or regulation that would affect a wide swath of individuals or corporations. The efforts for the most part took place behind the scenes; improper influence seeks to avoid documentation.

The friction of the policymaking process also provides a safeguard against the potential for money to buy public policy. Even for members of Congress and even for leadership within Congress, gathering together adequate support to pass a public policy is difficult (DeGregorio 1997; Wawro 2000). Members of Congress and lobbyists need each other in order to build coalitions and attract enough attention to their issue that it does not end up as one of the thousands of bills introduced each session that never make it beyond being referred to committee. DeGregorio notes that party leaders "must cajole rather than command their way to a following" (1997, 90). Collective goods, because they affect a wide swath of people, are also more like to attract competing or conflictual groups, although that is certainly not always the case. Baumgartner and Leech (2001), for example, found that the median issue in Congress in which interest groups are involved attracted fewer than fifteen interest organizations. Attention to most policy issues is low. Some studies, especially those that have considered agency policymaking (e.g. Browne 1990), have suggested that interest groups are more influential on low-salience issues that attract little public attention. This may be true, but for any issue that requires passage of an entire bill, this low attention can be a double-edged sword. Baumgartner, Berry, et al. 2009 found that one of those most-cited obstacles that challengers of existing policy faced was that few people were taking their issue seriously enough to act on it. Gaining co-sponsors, scheduling mark-ups, scheduling votes, all are time-consuming processes that only the minority of bills ever experience. For private goods, lack of attention increases the chances of success. But in the case of most collective goods, inattention means the issue isn't going anywhere.

Finally, the relative inability of any single member of Congress to affect the outcome of a public policy decision diminishes the effectiveness of any attempt at improper influence. The principal-agent problem is central to many economic analyses of lobbying (see, for example, Dixit, Grossman, and Helpman 1997). If the principals are the lobbyists and the agent is the legislator, the possibilities for shirking are enormous in the lobbying-for-public-policy case, because the opportunities for the bill to fail are almost endless. While the legislator may indeed vote for the bill (should the bill ever reach that stage), there still are myriad reasons why a bill may fail to become a law, and most of them cannot be blamed on a single individual. Of course, on votes that are extremely close, it may indeed be the case that only a few votes would need to be "bought" for the interest group to succeed. Fleisher (1993) shows some evidence that campaign contributions seem to have more of an impact on the voting behavior of "fence-sitting" moderate legislators than on others, for example. But in general, the process of public policymaking is a group effort, requiring many individuals to come together, and so the tempting of just one (or a handful) of legislators to act improperly is unlikely to have much impact on the outcome.

These observations, taken together, suggest that three elements are important to interest group success in Congress: 1) the resources to lobby, 2) at least one allied member of Congress who shares the interest group's policy preferences for either substantive or constituency reasons, and 3) the ability of that/those member(s) of Congress to act successfully on behalf of the group. In many policymaking situations—in particular in policymaking situations in which Congress must act collectively if change is to occur—a solitary member of Congress may not have the capacity to provide what the interest group seeks. A collective action is needed within the Congress. This is both one of the reasons why interest group power may be limited and one of the reasons why it is so hard to measure. An interest group may succeed in influencing a given member of Congress, but if that member lacks the capacity to act unilaterally or to force collective congressional action, the influence of the interest group will have little observable result on outcomes.

Although lobbying for private goods does not face the same roadblocks to influence as lobbying for public goods faces, even influence on private issues is not unlimited. De Figueredo and Silverman (2006) looked at attempts by universities to lobby for earmarked funds, which are a private good, since those earmarks go only to the university that lobbied for them, not to universities in general. De Figueredo and Silverman found that if the university was in the district (or state) of a member of the House (or Senate) Appropriations Committee, then lobbying contacts increased the probability that the university would receive the earmark that it sought. For those universities without such representation, there was no measurable effect from lobbying.

CONCLUSION

Interest group scholars often quote Madison in Federalist 10, noting that the tendency toward "faction" or groups each arguing their own interest, "is sown in the nature of man." Interest groups and lobbying are ever present in Washington because interests are ever present. And while, as Madison noted, we cannot get rid of the lobbyists without getting rid of the freedom to petition government, we can work to understand them and to temper their potential negative and unrepresentative effects. Limiting the ability of members of Congress to distribute private goods (earmarks) and requiring greater transparency for those earmarks that are awarded would go a long way toward minimizing the worst tendencies. There is little incentive to attempt to bribe someone who cannot deliver the goods, and documented awards are less likely to be improper. The Lobbying Disclosure Act of 1995 and the Honest Leadership and Open Government Act of 2007 both have helped move the congressional-lobbyist relationship in this direction. Members of Congress and their staffs may not accept gifts, meals, or travel from lobbyists. Lobbying organizations must register with the government and disclose what bills they lobbied on and how much they spent. Earmarks must be disclosed by the member that authored them (although follow-through on this requirement is uneven and information about those earmarks is still difficult to compile since there is no central repository for reporting). Even with full disclosure we may never prevent all improper exchanges and such cases are indeed troubling and potentially costly to taxpayers. But these private transactions are minor parts of the overall budget (by most counts only a fraction of a percent) and minor parts of citizens' daily lives compared with the issues decided in the more public realm of policymaking. Unlike earmarks and other private political goods, changes in public policy have the potential to do far more than just inflate the budget. And so it is of critical importance that we understand the role of faction in these debates.

In the popular media—and still too often in scholarly work—a transactions model of interest group lobbying still predominates. The problem with this view of interest groups as "pressure groups" or "special interests" that almost always get their way is that not only is it not well supported empirically, but as a model of lobbyist-legislator relations it is likely to distract us from the areas where influence does actually take place. It wrongly encourages us to focus on roll-call votes and to look for evidence that members of Congress have "changed their minds" in the face of interest group pressure. In so doing we may miss the collaborative efforts of interest groups and legislators, which is where the real power lies.

The symbiotic view of interest group–legislative relationships does not mean that improper influence is no longer a concern. Bias still exists in the system: there are more of some types of groups than others and some groups are better able to subsidize their issues than others. The symbiotic view of interest group–legislative relations means that it is more important than ever to consider which groups and which interests are represented in Washington and whether those groups are all able to make use of the same variety of tactics. It means that we must look more closely at informal interactions and at agenda-setting processes, and not only at votes and policy outcomes. By looking at the points where interest groups and members of Congress work together, we are more likely to identify the ways in which interest groups really do influence policy.

References

Ainsworth, S. H. 1997. The Role of Legislators in the Determination of Interest Group Influence. *Legislative Studies Quarterly*, 22(4): 517–33.

Arnold, R. D. 1990. *The Logic of Congressional Action*. New Haven: Yale University Press.

Austen-Smith, D., and Wright, J. R. 1994. Counteractive Lobbying. *American Journal of Political Science*, 38: 25–44.

Bauer, R. A., de Sola Pool, I., and Dexter, L.A. 1963. *American Business and Public Policy: The Politics of Foreign Trade*. New York: Atherton Press.

Baumgartner, F. R., and Leech, B. L. 1996. The Multiple Ambiguities of 'Counteractive Lobbying.' *American Journal of Political Science*, 40: 521–42.

———— 1998. *Basic Interests: The Importance of Groups in Politics and in Political Science*. Princeton: Princeton University Press.

———— 2001. Issue Niches and Policy Bandwagons: Patterns of Interest Group Involvement in National Politics. *Journal of Politics*, 63: 1191–213.

—— Berry, J. M., Hojnacki, M., Kimball, D. C., and Leech, B. L. 2009. *Lobbying and Policy Change: Who Wins, Who Loses, and Why*. Chicago: University of Chicago Press.

Berry, J. M. 1999. *The New Liberalism: The Rising Power of Citizen Groups*. Washington, DC: Brookings.

Blaisdell, D. C. 1957. *American Democracy Under Pressure*. New York: The Ronald Press.

Bosso, C. J. 1987. *Pesticides and Politics: The Life Cycle of a Public Issue*. Pittsburgh: University of Pittsburgh Press.

Browne, W. P. 1990. Organized Interests and their Issue Niches: A Search for Pluralism in a Policy Domain. *Journal of Politics*, 52: 477–509.

—— and Paik, W. K. 1993. Beyond the Domain: Recasting Network Politics in the Postreform Congress. *American Journal of Political Science*, 37: 1054–78.

Buchanan, J. M., Tollison, R. D., and Tullock, G., eds. 1980. *Toward a Theory of the Rent-Seeking Society*. College Station: Texas A&M Press.

Burstein, P., and Linton, A. 2002. The Impact of Political Parties, Interest Groups, and Social Movement Organizations on Public Policy: Some Recent Evidence and Theoretical Concerns. *Social Forces*, 81(2): 381–408.

—— and Hirsh, C. E. 2007. Interest Organizations, Information, and Policy Innovation in the U.S. Congress. *Sociological Forum*, 22(2): 174–99.

CARPENTER, D. P., ESTERLING, K. M., and LAZAR, D. M. J. 2004. Friends, Brokers, and Transitivity: Who Informs Whom in Washington Politics? *Journal of Politics*, 66(1): 224–46.

CHIN, M. L., BOND, J. R., and GEVA, N. 2000. A Foot in the Door: An Experimental Study of PAC and Constituency Effects on Access. *Journal of Politics*, 62: 534–49.

CRAWFORD, K. G. 1939. *The Pressure Boys: The Inside Story of Lobbying in America*. New York: J. Messner.

DE FIGUEIREDO, J. M., and SILVERMAN, B. S. 2006. "The Returns to Lobbying: University Lobbying Efforts and the Allocation of 'Earmarked' Academic Grants." *Journal of Law and Economics*, 49(2): 597–626.

DEGREGORIO, C. A. 1997. *Networks of Champions: Leadership, Access, and Advocacy in the U.S. House of Representatives*. Ann Arbor: University of Michigan Press.

DENZAU, A. T., and MUNGER, M. C. 1986. Legislators and Interest Groups: How Unorganized Interests Get Represented. *American Political Science Review*, 80: 89–106.

DIXIT, A., GROSSMAN, G. M., and HELPMAN, E. 1997. Common Agency and Coordination: General Theory and Application to Government Policy Making. *Journal of Political Economy*, 105(4): 752–69.

ESTERLING, K. 2004. *The Political Economy of Expertise*. Ann Arbor: University of Michigan Press.

—— 2007. Buying Expertise: Campaign Contributions and Attention to Policy Analysis in Congressional Committees. *American Political Science Review*, 101: 93–109.

FENNO, JR., R. F. 1973. *Congressmen in Committees*. Boston: Little, Brown.

FLEISHER, R. 1993. PAC Contributions and Congressional Voting on National Defense. *Legislative Studies Quarterly*, 18: 391–409.

FOWLER, L. L. 1982. How Interest Groups Select Issues for Rating Voting Records of Members of the U. S. Congress. *Legislative Studies Quarterly*, 7(3): 401–13.

FREEMAN, J. L. 1955. *The Political Process*. Garden City, NJ: Doubleday.

FRITSCHLER, A. L. 1975. *Smoking and Politics*. 2nd edn. Englewood Cliffs, NJ: Prentice-Hall.

GODWIN, R. K., LOPEZ, E. J., and SELDON, B. J. 2008. Allocating Lobbying Resources between Collective and Private Rents. *Political Research Quarterly*, 61(2): 345–59.

—— and SELDON, B. J. 2002. What Corporations Really Want from Government, pp. 205–24 in *Interest Group Politics*, 6th edn, ed. A. Cigler and B. Loomis. Washington: Congressional Quarterly Press.

GOLDSTEIN, K. M. 1999. *Interest Groups, Lobbying, and Participation in America*. Cambridge: Cambridge University Press.

GRAY, V., and LOWERY, D. 1996. *The Population Ecology of Interest Representation: Lobbying Communities in the American States*. Ann Arbor: University of Michigan Press.

HALL, R. L. 1996. *Participation in Congress*. New Haven: Yale University Press.

—— and DEARDORFF, A. V. 2006. Lobbying as Legislative Subsidy. *American Political Science Review*, 100: 69–84.

—— and WAYMAN, F. W. 1990. Buying Time: Moneyed Interests and the Mobilization of Bias in Congressional Committees. *American Political Science Review*, 84: 797–820.

—— and MILER, K. C. 2008. What Happens After the Alarm? Interest Group Subsidies to Legislative Overseers. *Journal of Politics*, 70(4): 990–1005.

HANSEN, J. M. 1990. *Gaining Access: Congress and the Farm Lobby, 1919–1981*. Chicago: The University of Chicago Press.

HEANEY, M. T. 2006. Brokering Health Policy: Coalitions, Parties, and Interest Group Influence. *Journal of Health Politics, Policy & Law*, 31(5): 887–44.

HEINZ, J. P., LAUMANN, E. O., NELSON, R. L., and SALISBURY, R. H. 1993. *The Hollow Core: Private Interests in National Policymaking*. Cambridge, MA: Harvard University Press.

HOJNACKI, M., and KIMBALL, D. C. 1998. Organized Interests and the Decision of Whom to Lobby in Congress. *American Political Science Review*, 92: 775–90.

————1999. The Who and How of Organizations' Lobbying Strategies in Committee. *Journal of Politics*, 61(4): 999–1024.

————2001. PAC Contributions and Lobbying Contacts in Congressional Committees. *Political Research Quarterly*, 54: 161–80.

JACKSON, J. E., and KINGDON, J. W. 1992. Ideology, Interest Group Scores, and Legislative Votes. *American Journal of Political Science*, 36(3): 805–23.

JONES, B. D., and BAUMGARTNER, F. R. 2005. *The Politics of Attention: How Government Prioritizes Problems*. Chicago: University of Chicago Press.

KINGDON, J. W. 1973. Congressmen's Voting Decisions. New York: Harper & Row.

KOLLMAN, K. 1997. Inviting Friends to Lobby: Interest Groups, Ideological Bias, and Congressional Committees. *American Journal of Political Science*, 41(2): 519–44.

————1998. *Outside Lobbying: Public Opinion and Interest Group Strategies*. Princeton: Princeton University Press.

LANGBEIN, L. I. 1986. Money and Access: Some Empirical Evidence. *Journal of Politics*, 48(4): 1052–62.

LEECH, B. L. 2010. Lobbying Influence, pp. 533–51 in *The Oxford Handbook of Political Organizations*, ed. J. M. Berry and S. Maisel. Oxford: Oxford University Press.

————and BAUMGARTNER, F. R. 1998. Lobbying Friends and Foes in Washington, pp. 217–33 in *Interest Group Politics*, 5th edn, ed. A. J. Cigler and A. L. Burdett. Washington, DC: Congressional Quarterly Press.

————LA PIRA, T. M., and SEMANKO, N. A. 2005. Drawing Lobbyists to Washington: Government Activity and the Demand for Advocacy. *Political Research Quarterly*, 58: 19–30.

LOWERY, D. 2007. Why Do Organized Interests Lobby? A Multi-Goal, Multi-Context Theory of Lobbying. *Polity*, 39(1): 29–54.

————and GRAY, V. 2004. A Neopluralist Perspective on Research on Organized Interests. *Political Research Quarterly*, 57: 163–75.

McCUBBINS, M. D., and SCHWARTZ, T. 1984. Congressional Oversight Overlooked: Police Patrols Versus Fire Alarms. *American Journal of Political Science*, 28(1): 165–79.

McFARLAND, A. S. 2004. *Neopluralism: The Evolution of Political Process Theory*. Lawrence: University of Kansas Press.

MILBRATH, L. W. 1963. *The Washington Lobbyists*. Chicago: Rand McNally.

MILER, K.C. 2007. The View from the Hill: Legislative Perceptions of the District. *Legislative Studies Quarterly*, 32(4): 597–628.

MITCHELL, W., and MUNGER, M. C. 1991. Economic Models of Interest Groups: An Introductory Survey. *American Journal of Political Science*, 35: 512–46.

OLSON, M. 1971. *The Logic of Collective Action*. 2nd edn. Cambridge, MA: Harvard University Press.

PARKER, G. R. 1996. *Congress and the Rent-Seeking Society*. Ann Arbor: University of Michigan Press.

SALISBURY, R. H., and SHEPSLE, K. A. 1981. Congressional Staff Turnover and the Ties-that-Bind. *American Political Science Review*, 75(2): 381–96.

SCHLOZMAN, K. L. 1984. What Accent the Heavenly Chorus?: Political Equality and the American Pressure System. *Journal of Politics*, 46: 1006–32.

————and TIERNEY, J. T. 1983. More of the Same: Washington Pressure Group Activity in a Decade of Change. *Journal of Politics*, 45: 351–77.

————1986. *Organized Interests and American Democracy*. New York: Harper and Row.

SCOTT, A. M., and HUNT, M. A. 1966. *Congress and Lobbies: Image and Reality*. Chapel Hill: University of North Carolina Press.

SMITH, R. A. 1995. Interest Group Influence in the U.S. Congress. *Legislative Studies Quarterly*, 20: 89–139.

SNYDER, JR., J. M. 1992. Artificial Extremism in Interest Group Ratings. *Legislative Studies Quarterly*, 17(3): 319–45.

TRUMAN, D. B. 1993 [1951]. *The Governmental Process: Political Interests and Public Opinion*. 2nd edition. Berkeley: Institute of Governmental Studies.

TULLOCK, G. 1967. The Welfare Costs of Tariffs, Monopolies, and Theft. *Western Economic Journal*, 5: 224–32.

WALKER, JR., JACK L. 1991. *Mobilizing Interest Groups in America*. Ann Arbor, MI: University of Michigan Press.

WAWRO, G. 2000. Legislative Entrepreneurship in the U.S. House of Representatives. Ann Arbor, MI: University of Michigan Press.

WAWRO, G. 2001. A Panel Probit Analysis of Campaign Contributions and Roll Call Votes. *American Journal of Political Science*, 45: 563–79.

WITKO, C. 2006. PACs, Issue Context, and Congressional Decision Making. *Political Research Quarterly*, 59: 283–95.

WRIGHT, J. R. 1990. Contributions, Lobbying, and Committee Voting in the U.S. House of Representatives. *American Political Science Review*, 84: 417–38.

....

CHAPTER 27

THE TIES THAT BIND: COALITIONS IN CONGRESS

....

JOHN D. WILKERSON[*]
BARRY PUMP

"Then again all is seemingly confusion, and the crossed lines of different groups seem too tangled to be followed."

Arthur F. Bentley (1908, 204)

INTRODUCTION

....

THE term "coalition" is widely yet imprecisely used in congressional studies. Most generally, a coalition exists when two or more individuals or groups—sometimes with completely different aims—join forces to achieve something that each could not otherwise achieve alone. Naturally, the study of coalitions in Congress is ripe territory for both theoretical and empirical work, often with the empirical work discovering contingencies which theory did not anticipate. In this chapter, by reviewing the extant literature, we address what coalitions are and how they differ. In the process, we shed

[*] The author would like to thank the editors, Peter J. May, Kevin M. Esterling, Ashley E. Jochim, and Asaph Glosser for their valuable comments and advice.

light on some unanswered questions and propose directions for future research that speak to why coalitions are analytically interesting.

Coalitions in Congress take various forms: geographic, distributive, programmatic, ideological, and partisan, to name just a few. They are the result of political interests at national and local levels as well as the policy preferences of legislators, which are often consubstantial with other interests. Every issue that gains a spot on the legislative agenda is put there by some form of coalition, and every law that is passed by Congress is a result of a coalition voting for its passage. Accordingly, coalitions are ubiquitous in legislatures. Indeed, because of their omnipresence, one could rightly ask why "coalition" is an analytically useful concept at all, especially if the term merely denotes a group of legislators voting one way rather than another (Humphneys 2008, 352).

"Coalition building," Riker (1962, 103) notes, "begins when a leader, who is defined simply and circularly as a member who manages the growth of a coalition, undertakes to form one on a particular issue for decision. In order to form a coalition, a leader must attract followers who are also defined simply and circularly as those members of the body who join the association the leader forms." In Congress, coalition building begins with the recognition that important actions, such as passing a law or setting the legislative agenda, require collective action (see Olson 1971). These shared interests can be transitory and specific, as in the case of a logroll, or enduring and general, as in the case of a political party or policy subsystem.

As a noun, "coalition" is uninteresting in itself; after all, it is a group formed of other groups or members. Football teams are largely uninteresting until they are competing on the field. Similarly, what is interesting about coalitions is the action. How do coalitions form? What do coalitions do after they are formed? Why do some coalitions persist while others vanish quickly? What binds members to coalitions? How large must coalitions be to form a winning majority? While a few of these questions have received a great deal of scholarly ink, many interestingly have not.

Understanding how electoral and policy goals influence member behavior is a central objective of legislative studies. A central goal of coalitional studies is to understand why legislators engage in collective action. In the simplest scenario, knowing something about legislators' preferences and the available policy alternatives may be sufficient to explain the coalitions that form. In other situations, however, explaining the coalitions that form can be considerably more challenging. Legislators with similar preferences may hold different beliefs about the policy and electoral consequences of a given set of alternatives (Arnold 1990). Outside observers may also have difficulty discerning which provisions of a policy carry the most weight in a legislator's decision calculus, or how legislators will behave when the political benefits of a policy are in conflict with its policy benefits. Small incentives or promises may also tip the balance between support and opposition to a proposal (Riker 1962).

Even when lawmakers' policy preferences are known, there are reasons to expect errors in behavioral predictions. Vote trades are possible because legislators care more intensely about some issues than others. This intensity can lead a lawmaker to exchange her support today for another legislator's support on a more important issue another day. Another reason is strategic. Majority party members may support leadership agenda control even though it means that policy alternatives they prefer will never make it to the floor (Cox and McCubbins 2005).

By definition, the members of a coalition share common interests that they do not share with other legislators. Put another way, barriers to entry may make the costs of defecting (leaving the coalition) prohibitively high. In Congress, these barriers may take many forms: beliefs or ideology, electoral incentives, agenda control, information, or side payments to name a few (Smith 2007; Lee 2009). The significance of these barriers varies across issues, over time, across members, and across decision-making contexts. Two legislators may share policy views on some issues but not on others; longer-serving legislators may be in positions of greater influence (and therefore obligation) within their parties; some legislators are team players while others are more opportunistic or pragmatic; how a choice is framed (ideology? reelection?) can influence which considerations carry the most weight in a legislator's decision calculus (Arnold 1990).

Existing research on coalitions frequently centers on explaining a particular type of coalition, such as party coalitions or distributive coalitions, to the exclusion of others. In this chapter, our goal is to provide a broader perspective on coalitions in Congress. With the complications noted above in mind, we propose a typology that differentiates coalitions in Congress by their *issue* and *temporal* attributes (Table 27.1). The purpose of the typology is to help clarify an amorphous subject rather than to provide a definitive classification system for a subject that clearly defies simple classification. Despite its limitations, we hope to show that the two dimensions (issues and time) are helpful for making sense of the questions posed earlier.

The ties that bind a coalition may originate in an effort to advance a particular issue at a particular point in time, what we term entrepreneurial politics. Sometimes, the focus of a coalition building effort is to promote a particular proposal by merging disparate issue concerns, as in the case of logroll politics. Coalitions may also revolve around sustained shared interest in a single issue, as in policy subsystems and advocacy coalitions. Finally, some of the most important coalitions in Congress reflect sustained, shared interests across multiple issues, as in the case of political parties or cross-party ideological coalitions.

The remainder of this chapter proceeds as follows. We begin by considering the coalitions that have received the greatest scholarly attention in the literature: enduring multi-issue coalitions. Political parties are the prima facie example followed by the Conservative Coalition. We then turn to multi-issue transitory coalitions, focusing in particular on coalitions constructed around distributive considerations. Next we

Table 27.1 A typology of coalitions

	Single Issue	Multi-Issue
Enduring	Policy Subsystems	Political Parties
Transitory	Entrepreneurial Politics	Logroll Politics

turn to research on what we term entrepreneur-led coalitions, where the focus is understanding the role of the policy entrepreneur in advancing a particular policy, before concluding with research on enduring coalitions that revolve around particular issues, as epitomized by policy subsystems and advocacy coalitions.

A leading question of much of the research on enduring coalitions is why they endure. Research on transitory coalitions, in contrast, has been centrally concerned with understanding how such coalitions form. For both sets of inquiry, there has been an interesting interplay between theory and empirics. Theoretical findings motivated much of the early research on coalitions in Congress. However, subsequent empirical research has on occasion raised doubts about the relevance of the theories, or at least demonstrated their limitations. We conclude, perhaps unsatisfactorily, with unanswered questions and directions for future research.

ENDURING, MULTI-ISSUE COALITIONS

Party cartels

Political parties are a natural starting point for a study of coalitions in Congress. Despite Madison's exhortation against faction in *Federalist* 10, parties are formed in Congress and control critical decisions about organization and legislative priorities. When the House of Representatives first convenes every second January, the Clerk of the House recognizes the party caucus or conference chairs to nominate candidates for Speaker. In the Senate, the presiding officer recognizes the Majority Leader before other senators during legislative proceedings. In both chambers, committee seats are allocated according to the number of legislative seats held by each party (though not in exact proportion), and party steering committees determine members' committee assignments.

Shared policy and electoral interests are the primary ties that bind members to parties in Congress. Candidates generally associate with the national party that most closely reflects their own political views because party "brand" is a meaningful policy signal for voters. When elected, these candidates (now legislators) have more in common with the members of their own party than with members of the opposing party. But because of the nature of American politics and the personal vote, legislators are beholden to their constituencies first and foremost (Mayhew 1974; Carey and Shugart 1995; Brady and Buckley 2002). Party members support their leaders as far as their preferences and constituencies allow (Cooper and Brady 1981).

Some of the over-time variation in partisan behavior within Congress can be explained by changes in the constituencies that legislators represent (Aldrich and Rohde 2001; Theriault 2008). Redistricting and population shifts produced more homogeneous legislative districts, but the impact on partisan behavior in Congress (i.e. the frequency of roll-call votes where a majority of Democrats vote in opposition to a majority of Republicans) is equivocal (Theriault 2008). Indeed, much of the observed increase in partisanship in the last 40 years remains to be explained.

One of the more contentious questions in contemporary congressional studies has been whether "partisanship" is observably distinct from "preferenceship" (Krehbiel 1993): would legislative outcomes be any different without party organization? This question gets to the nature of party coalitions. There is evidence that members toe the party line more often than broad indicators of their policy preferences predict (Smith 2007; Jenkins, Crespin, and Carson 2005; see also Strahan, this volume). However, the most compelling evidence of party influence is often anecdotal. In 1993, Representative Marjorie Margolies-Mezvinsky stated her opposition to a tax hike deemed essential to President Bill Clinton's economic program. After considerable party lobbying and a promise of a presidential visit to her district, Margolies-Mezvinsky changed her position and voted with the president. A year later, she lost her reelection bid (Theriault 2008, 142).

It seems hard to imagine that party leaders could compel party members to fall on their swords, as seems to have been the case for Margolies-Mezvinsky. But how do we explain the fact that lawmakers are sometimes more supportive of their party than prior indicators of their preferences would seem to predict? Another perspective on partisan effects is offered by Karol (2009), who portrays politicians as managers of coalitions of intense interests. Keeping coalition members in the tent is a central preoccupation of parties. As a result, legislators' preferences do not exist in a vacuum. As electoral conditions change, their positions on issues should correspondingly change. Business groups originally allied with the Republican Party in the nineteenth century. In the 1930s, the party adopted an anti-union stance in order to preserve this long-standing source of political support. In contemporary contexts we might similarly expect lawmakers to support party positions because they understand that certain issues are critical to preserving the party's core bases of support (health care reform comes to mind). In some cases this may entail taking positions that have electoral risks (although party leaders should work to minimize the traceability of such actions as discussed below).

Parties as procedural coalitions also deserve additional attention (Jenkins, Crespin, and Carson 2005). Lawmakers who share common policy interests also have incentives to leverage procedure to their advantage. Schattschneider (1942, 37) argues that "majority rule is an invitation to party organization" in commenting:

Possession of the vast resources of a modern government, its authority, its organization, administrative establishment, and so on, will provide something for nearly everyone willing to join hands in the political enterprise. The winners get so much more than the losers that the difference is worth the struggle.

Partisan theory (Cox and McCubbins 2007) proposes that majority party members exercise party discipline on procedural matters. Important policy decisions are made in caucus, where the party median is pivotal. Where partisan theory assumes that party members will vote the party line on the floor, cartel theory proposes a more limited role for parties—preventing proposals the party median opposes from reaching the floor (Cox and McCubbins 2005).

Neither theory fully explains why the chamber median (also a member of the majority party) consents to a process that favors the majority party median. Cox (2008) proposes that agenda scarcity is a central consideration. A primary benefit (for all members of the majority party) is control over how limited floor time and resources are allocated. However, the agenda-setting power that comes with partisan control of legislative offices does not by itself explain why the policy agenda should be biased in favor of the party median. Cox and McCubbins (2005, ch. 1) devote considerable attention to this subject. They argue that party leaders can compensate the chamber median for policy losses incurred as a result of supporting the party on procedural matters. Yet, as the pivotal voter, the chamber median is in a position to play both parties. To advance a partisan policy agenda (i.e. the party median's agenda), it would seem that party leaders would need to fully compensate the chamber median for all policy losses. In our view, this is a far cry from party government.

The classic party cartel commonly featured in the literature (where the party median decides the policy) might be expected if the chamber median's ideal point lies close to the party median (Wiseman and Wright 2008). It might also be expected if the chamber median's ability to negotiate with the minority party is somehow constrained. In this respect, the advantage majority party leaders possess on matters of procedural control appears to be rooted in elections. In particular, if the chamber median cannot credibly threaten to switch parties, then the majority party leadership may be able to exercise negative agenda control to prevent alternatives the chamber median favors (but the party median opposes) from coming to a vote (Cox and McCubbins 2005). In other words, the majority party has greater ability to punish the median for defecting on procedural matters, if she cannot credibly threaten to switch parties. However, there is much less reason to expect that party leaders can exercise positive agenda control to shape policy outcomes once issues reach the floor.

Finally, extant research gives us little reason to think carefully about the role of the minority party as a significant coalition. Given the advantages of majority party membership, it could appear puzzling that members persist in belonging to the minority. There are electorally induced reasons to belong to one party over another, and there are ideological reasons as well. Regardless, minority party leaders are able to hold members together across a range of votes—both procedural and substantive— even when a member's electoral chances may be jeopardized as a result. Minority leaders can also be instrumental in creating winning majorities on certain issues which cross-cut ideological divisions. In one of the few studies of congressional minorities, Charles O. Jones describes an array of potentially successful strategies for the minority, from complete obstruction of the majority's agenda to "responsible" cooperation. He concludes that "it is possible for the minority party to employ a wide range of strategies successfully even when the party is at a considerable numerical disadvantage" (Jones 1970, 193).

Scholars have yet to fully understand the causes and consequences of party polarization. Additional research on sources of party influence is also warranted. Finally, partisan theory appears to predict policy outcomes somewhere between the majority party and chamber medians, depending on the importance of partisan cues in elections (and perhaps assymetries in the electoral resources available to majority and minority party leaders). For all these reasons, appreciating the extent to which partisan coalitions are indicative of party influence, ideological correspondence or something in between remains an important goal of future coalitions research.

Ideological coalitions

Party coalitions are sustained in large part by the fact that party members share electoral interests across a range of issues. Coalitions may also form around sustained electoral interests in issues that transcend party lines. Besides parties, the Conservative Coalition has been the most visible and enduring crossparty ideological coalition of recent decades. The informal nature of the alliance makes it particularly noteworthy (Schickler 2001; Nye 1993; Brady and Bullock 1980). Conservative southern Democrats and northern Republicans first banded together to oppose New Deal pro-union policies in the 1930s. They remained an important force in congressional politics until the end of the twentieth century.

Why did southern legislators, who often had more in common ideologically with their Republican counterparts, remain members of the Democratic Party for so long? What led to the realignment of the South in the late twentieth century? The ties that bound southern legislators to the Democratic Party throughout the twentieth century were likely a combination of prohibitively high electoral costs of switching parties, and agenda-setting opportunities embedded in long-standing Democratic procedures (specifically the seniority rule). Path dependence played an important role. The legacy of the "war of northern aggression" meant that there was no viable Republican Party in the South to benefit when the national Democratic Party moved to the left under President Franklin D. Roosevelt. Instead of joining the Republican Party, conservative southern legislators, such as Strom Thurmond, abandoned the Democratic Party and formed third parties (e.g. the Dixiecrats) that reflected the unique sentiments of many white southerners at the time. But switching parties in this way came with costs. Thurmond had an up-and-down electoral career until he settled in with the Republican Party in 1964.

Cox and McCubbins (2007) argue that the Democratic leadership held the party coalition together by appointing conservative southerners to important offices. Schickler (2001) disputes this, arguing instead that southern Democrats benefited from long-standing caucus procedures. One-party Democratic control in the South also meant greater electoral security for southern legislators, who by virtue of the seniority rule chaired the most important congressional committees. Southern Democrats and their Republican colleagues thus put policy victories ahead of political victories.

Nye (1993) notes considerable variation in the votes of the Conservative Coalition over time. What changed? The decline of the Conservative Coalition can be partly attributed to a gradual electoral realignment at the local level. Redistricting and the enfranchisement of new voters forced Democratic candidates in the South to the left, initially encouraging third-party candidates and eventually creating opportunities for Republican candidates. As the urban South elected ideologically liberal Democrats and the rural and suburban South became more receptive to Republicans (such as Ronald Reagan), the national parties became more ideologically cohesive. Eventually, conservative southern Democrats all but disappeared from the majority party. Following the Democratic landslide election of 1932, all but two members of the southern congressional delegation were Democrats during the 73rd Congress (98.7 percent). Republicans gradually made inroads so that by 1975, they made up 26 percent of the southern delegation. By 2010, Republicans held almost 60 percent of the South's seats.

Less emphasized in existing realignment research is the role of internal Democratic caucus reforms. The importance of the Conservative Coalition is often assessed by how frequently (majorities of) southern Democrats and Republicans oppose northern Democrats on the floor. Figure 27.1 plots the proportion of all recorded votes in the House where this division among Democrats was present since the 1950s (data for earlier periods are more difficult to obtain). The presence of House floor coalitions dividing the Democratic Party peaked in the 1960s and 1970s—a time when the "new issues" of civil rights, environmentalism, and Vietnam created major rifts within the party (Deering and Smith 1997; Baumgartner and Jones 1993).

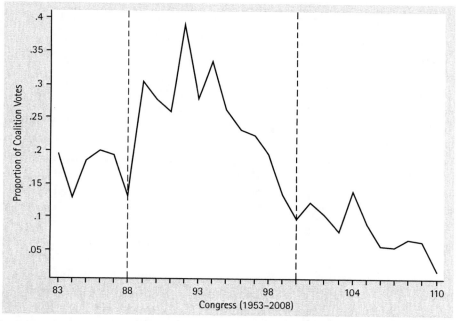

Fig. 27.1. The proportion of all votes where the Conservative Coalition appeared over time. The bars indicate the rise and fall of the Conservative Coalition's influence, from the 88th Congress to the 100th Congress

Source: David W. Rohde, Political Institutions and Public Choice House Roll-Call Database. Duke University, Durham, NC. 2010.

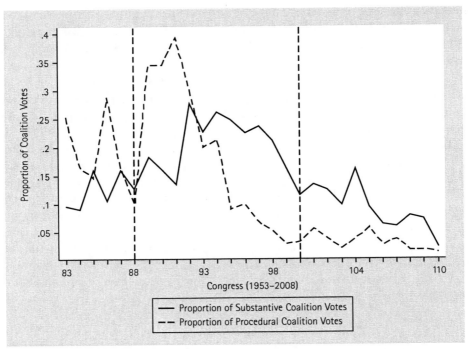

Fig. 27.2. The proportions of substantive and procedural Conservative Coalition votes over time

Source: David W. Rohde, Political Institutions and Public Choice House Roll-Call Database. Duke University, Durham, NC. 2010.

Figure 27.2 differentiates the same votes by procedural versus policy decisions. There is a marked shift in activity. Earlier in the period, the divisions centered on procedural matters. In the 91st Congress, for example, the Conservative Coalition was present on nearly 40 percent of all procedural decisions, compared to just 12 percent of all policy decisions. By the 94th Congress, it was present more often on policy decisions than procedural decisions. This shift in emphasis coincided with important House reforms. In the early 1970s, liberal Democrats spearheaded an effort to weaken the grip of southern Democratic chairmen, particularly on the Rules Committee (Adler 2002; Schickler, McGhee, and Sides 2003).

Initially, southern Democrats responded to challenges within their party by coalescing with Republicans to block liberal initiatives from the floor (Schickler and Pearson 2009). The shift in emphasis beginning in the 93rd Congress likely reflected the fact that southern Democrats had lost much of their ability to block liberal bills due to the reforms (Bach and Smith 1988). Thus, caucus reforms eroded longstanding procedural advantages around the same time that the southern electoral environment was becoming more conducive to Republican candidacies (third-party candidacies also declined around the same time).

In summary, the answer to the question of what caused the decline of the Conservative Coalition is multi-faceted. Southern legislators had little reason to complain about a system that provided them with extraordinary procedural influence. However, this alone probably does not explain why Republicans were unable to bring southern legislators into their party. Switching parties was not a viable electoral strategy for most southern legislators for most of the twentieth century. This changed beginning in the 1960s as the Democratic Party median shifted leftward with the rise of new issues and the election of growing numbers of liberal members in the early 1970s. The realignment probably would have occurred regardless of whether Democrats reformed the committee system, but the reforms probably did accelerate the shift.

Finally, it is worth noting that the Conservative Coalition is only one example of a long-lasting ideological coalition that is not attached to a party label. In a highly polarized political environment such as what we see today, it is more difficult to recall that at one point common ground was often found between the parties on major issues. There were, for example, silver and gold "bugs" in the House and Senate from both parties that had strongly held views about monetary and other policies (Ritter 1997). On the flip side of the Conservative Coalition, there was a strong, bipartisan group of members who focused on civil rights issues. Indeed, the Civil Rights Act of 1964 would not have passed the Senate but for liberal Republicans' support for ending the conservative filibuster. Cross-partisan ideological coalitions have been important throughout congressional history and will likely be again in the future.

TRANSITORY, MULTI-ISSUE COALITIONS

The logroll and distributive politics

Distributive policies are distinguished by their geographically concentrated benefits and broadly distributed costs (Lowi 1964). Weingast (1994, 321) sets three criteria for a policy to be "distributive" in nature. First, projects must be divisible in that they can "be varied in size, scope, and dollar amount independently of one another"; second, the policy is a collection of many divisible projects "within a policy area"; and third, the legislation must be an expenditure: "its main task is to allocate a given amount of funds." Although many policies have geographic implications, the best examples of distributive policies involve allocations of federal dollars at the local level (e.g. public works authorizations or appropriations earmarks). Research on distributive politics has moved in two distinct directions relevant to the study of coalitions in Congress. One direction examines distributive policymaking as an end goal and central organizing objective (Mayhew 1974; Shepsle 1978; Shepsle and Weingast 1987). The second considers the role that distributive benefits (i.e. pork) play in building support for other types of policies (Ellwood and Patashnik 1993).

A good starting point for research on distributive coalition building is Riker's *The Theory of Political Coalitions* (1962), which portrays politics as a zero-sum contest between rival coalition leaders. Riker's size principle—that leaders maximize their own policy gains by building coalitions no larger than the minimum required for passage—constituted an important starting point for the study of voting coalitions on distributive issues in Congress, but it has not withstood empirical scrutiny (Hinckley 1972). Subsequent research has therefore tried to explain why coalitions tend to be substantially larger than what is needed to ensure passage. Mayhew's response took issue with Riker's zero sum assumption, arguing that where particularized benefits are concerned, "to reward one congressman is not obviously to deprive others" (1974, 88; see also Hardin 1976). Shepsle and Weingast (1981) proposed that uncertainty motivates coalition leaders to build larger than minimum winning coalitions. Balla, Lawrence, et al. (2002), in contrast, argue that "blame avoiding" is behind majority party decisions to allocate distributive benefits in bipartisan fashion. Minority party members are less likely to criticize pork spending by the majority party if they are also beneficiaries.

However, spatial theories of voting that portray congressional decision-making as a multidimensional bargaining game have gained the most leverage in explaining why distributive coalitions tend to be greater than minimum winning. When "Congress must decide how to divide the federal budget pie among members districts . . . *there simply is no median legislator*" (Cox and McCubbins 2005, 46 at note 13, emphasis in original). In such an environment, minimum winning coalitions are less stable than larger, "universalistic" coalitions (Weingast 1994, 322). Related research proposes that "norms of reciprocity" also help to promote policy stability. Specifically, legislators enter into a "gains from trade" arrangement where each agrees to defer in policy areas not critical to reelection, as long as others agree to do the same (Ferejohn 1974; Weingast and Marshall 1988; Shepsle and Weingast 1987). Such an arrangement reduces transaction costs while advancing the goal that lawmakers value most— "bringing home the bacon."

An important limitation of many distributive politics studies is that they focus on voting outcomes, based on the (typically untested) assumption that legislators' support for a program depends on whether it includes something for them. Bickers and Stein carefully documented who benefited from a range of distributive programs and "reluctantly concluded that [they] could not confirm the proposition that most distributive programs, viewed individually or bundled by agency portfolios, provide awards to a majority of districts" (1994, 329). The fact that most distributive programs do not benefit even a majority of legislators, much less a supermajority or universalistic majority, is troubling for approaches that portray distributive benefits as the primary consideration shaping support for such programs.

A second, more recent direction in distributive politics research emphasizes the benefits of pork as a coalition-building tool for other policies. Mayhew (1974) famously observed that lawmakers have little electoral incentive to invest in activities that enhance the collective performance of Congress. A growing literature argues that coalition leaders leverage lawmakers' innate desire for pork to help Congress advance other collective goals. Ellwood and Patashnik (1993) go so far as to "praise" pork. Without it, Congress would have difficulty passing unpopular but necessary legislation, such as the federal budget. Evans (1994, 17) emphasizes that the benefits of pork as a coalition-building tool extend beyond tax and spending legislation to include a broad range of policy areas: "Policymakers turn the distributive impulse to the task of making general interest legislation, using the particularized benefits that damage the institutional reputation of Congress to save it." Pork is also distinctive as a bipartisan currency that coalition leaders (e.g. committee chairs) employ to build support across party lines. Furthermore, and in sharp contrast to models portraying pork as the be-all and end-all of legislative politics, a little bit of pork goes a long way. Ellwood and Patashnik (1993, 26) point out that pork makes up less than 1 percent of the annual budget. Lee (2003) finds that relatively inexpensive earmarks better predict legislative support for highway legislation than total district or state spending. If, by "greasing the wheels," pork enables Congress to do the right thing at a lower cost, then the widespread public criticism of pork seems misplaced.

In summary, the role of distributive considerations in congressional coalition building is far from settled. There is a substantial disjuncture between research suggesting that legislative coalitions are frequently assembled around distributive goals, and research suggesting that pork plays a supporting role in the coalition building process. It is quite possible that each perspective helps to explain coalition building in particular contexts, but current research offers limited guidance in terms of appreciating which perspective is most applicable when.

TRANSITORY, SINGLE-ISSUE COALITIONS

Entrepreneurial politics

Entrepreneur-led coalitions can be distinguished from other types of coalitions by the fact that they are more likely to be coalitions of convenience. If environmentalists and tourism interests will back a proposal to limit offshore oil-drilling legislation, then whether such an alliance is detrimental to environmental policymaking, or to party organization over the longer term, is of limited concern (Brady and Buckley 2002). Bills often fail not because they lack merit, but because legislative time and resources are limited: "Many potential agenda items are perfectly worthy of serious consideration, yet they do not rise high on the governmental policy agenda because they simply get crowded aside in the press of business" (Kingdon 2003, 184). An entrepreneur advancing a particular issue is at a decided disadvantage in the competition for limited agenda space. She must be an opportunist.

It is well known that only a small percentage of introduced bills pass their respective chambers and that an even smaller number become law. Less appreciated is the fact that the vast majority of successful bills (about 80 percent) originate in the committee of jurisdiction (Adler and Wilkerson 2005; Cox and Terry 2008). These patterns underscore the fact that access to the legislative agenda is far from random.

The agenda is consumed by issues that must be addressed, from program renewals to budget cycles to presidential priorities to focusing events (Walker 1977). A legislative entrepreneur can work to attach her solution to salient problems, and she can work to make her proposal more politically attractive. But her ability to influence whether an issue is taken up is limited. It is not surprising, then, that a disproportionate number of the successful bills sponsored by non-committee members address minor issues, such as the naming of post offices. Important successful legislation, in contrast, almost always originates in committee (Adler and Wilkerson 2008).

Persistent and/or fortunate entrepreneurs do occasionally succeed, however, and it is worth considering what research says about this success. Entrepreneurial coalition building has been the focus of considerable theoretical attention. Wawro (2000, 2) defines legislative entrepreneurs as members who "invest time, staff, and other resources to acquire knowledge of particular policy areas, draft legislation addressing issues in those areas, and shepherd their proposals through the legislative process by building and maintaining coalitions." Arnold (1990, 88), concerned with coalition leaders more generally and not just policy entrepreneurs, argues that they "define the problems, shape the alternatives, initiate action, mobilize support, arrange compromises, and work to see that Congress passes specific bills."

Kingdon (2003, 181) argues that persistence is the most important attribute of a policy entrepreneur. In an environment where legislative opportunities are limited and often difficult to anticipate, successful entrepreneurs must be prepared to "surf the wave" when it comes along (Kingdon 2003, 183). The best possess social acuity, are good team builders, and lead by example (Mintrom and Norman 2009, 651). However, given the unpredictability of the policy process, "dumb luck" can also account for the difference between success and failure. (Kingdon 2003, 183).

In terms of strategy, Riker (1962) portrays coalition building as a zero sum game, where a coalition leader's objective is to build a minimum winning coalition in order to maximize her own gains. Given the difficulty of constructing winning coalitions in a world where policy windows open and close quickly, it seems likely that legislative entrepreneurs would err on the side of caution. As noted earlier, most policies pass with larger than minimum winning support (Hinckley 1972). Riker (1962) and other formal theorists additionally place responsibility for outcomes squarely in the hands of agenda-setters rather than the median voter (because choice spaces are multidimensional). Coalition leaders practice "heresthetics," or the art of "structuring the world so you can win" (Riker 1986, ix; see also Schattschneider 1960; Baumgartner and Jones 1993). At the height of the Vietnam War, Washington Senator Warren Magnuson wanted to prevent nerve gas from being shipped through the port of Seattle. Magnuson had little success persuading his Senate colleagues that the issue should be a priority for them until he reframed the debate from one about routine military weapons handling to one about whether the executive branch had overstepped its authority (Riker 1986).

In some cases, eliminating rather than shifting dimensions may be required. In the 1930s, Senator Robert Wagner, a Democrat from New York, worked tirelessly over two Congresses to bring about the National Labor Relations Act of 1935, also known as the Wagner Act (Katznelson 2005). Wagner initially sought to grant union protections to all manual laborers, including farm and domestic workers. His first bill, which included protections for (largely African-American and Latino) farm and domestic laborers failed to emerge from Alabama Senator Hugo Black's committee. His second attempt excluded farm and domestic workers and passed the full Senate with the support of many southern conservatives.

In other cases, adding provisions may be effective: "In an attempt to broaden the coalition, a member may draft a bill that addresses a range of issues that many members care about so that they will become interested in the legislation" (Wawro 2000, 33). A controversial water project in North Dakota earned the antipathy of fiscal conservatives for being too expensive and of environmentalists for being a threat to wetlands. Representative George Miller, a California Democrat, ultimately won the support of both groups by adding a trust fund for wetland preservation and by reducing the cost and size of the project (Wawro 2000).

Arnold (1990) classifies floor coalition building strategies into three categories. As the examples above illustrate, coalition leaders can modify proposals to increase (or decrease) support (strategies of modification). Through debate, they can also try to shape lawmakers' perceptions of a proposal's policy and political consequences (strategies of persuasion). The nerve gas case illustrates how entrepreneurs can use argument or attention to shape which dimensions or considerations are primary in a legislator's calculus. Information can also be a valuable commodity (Krehbiel 1991).

Finally, coalition leaders can leverage procedures to help lawmakers avoid blame for unpopular decisions (procedural strategies). The more visible the decision, the more likely it is that interest groups, potential political challengers, and constituents will be paying attention (Weaver 1986; Wilkerson 1999; Becker 2005; Theriault 2008). The result is that members are concerned about what Arnold calls "traceability," which occurs when "a citizen can plausibly trace an observed effect first back to a governmental action and then back to a representative's individual contribution" (1990, 47). This line of argument is similar to Hedrick Smith's ninth rule of coalition politics: "make votes politically easy" (1988, 479). Coalition leaders want their members to avoid blame for unpopular decisions and take credit for popular ones.

Research suggests additional coalition-building strategies. Party leaders' ability to promise side payments and arrange vote trades can be an important source of party influence (Groseclose and Snyder 2000; Sinclair 1983). Riker (1962) suggests the same tactics are used by other coalition leaders. However, *The Theory of Political Coalitions* describes not only tangible selective incentives such as side payments, but less tangible ones as well, such as personal charisma. Lyndon Johnson's "treatment" comes to mind, or perhaps a desire to see the nation's first black president succeed. Sophisticated voting was once widely considered to be an important component of coalition building (Riker 1986; Enelow and Koehler 1980), but more recent systematic empirical research finds little (perhaps no) evidence that such efforts succeed (Krehbiel and Rivers 1990; Wilkerson 1999; Finocchiaro and Jenkins 2008; Groseclose and Milyo 2010). Some entrepreneurs are also better positioned to win support (e.g. presidents through their ability to affect public opinion, or committee leaders through their ability to set the agenda or provide earmarks). Yet other research warns us not to attribute too much influence to position. Kingdon (2003) cites numerous instances where relatively obscure entrepreneurs made a difference through their persistence and creativity.

In summary, entrepreneur-led coalitions have received considerable attention in the congressional literature, and are the archetype of many textbook descriptions of the legislative process. The existing literature, however, places too much emphasis on the importance of entrepreneurs in shaping the legislative agenda. Congress is often preoccupied with issues that it must address, from program renewals to appropriations to external shocks (Walker 1977). Whether the existing policy is unsatisfactory to a majority of legislators (or, lies outside of the gridlock interval) is relevant, but it is only one of the considerations influencing how scarce legislative agenda space is allocated (Krehbiel 1998). Effective entrepreneurs recognize this and work to "couple" their preferred policy solutions to the problems, constraints, and political opportunities of the day (Kingdon 2003).

Enduring, single-issue coalitions

Policy subsystems and advocacy coalitions

Richard Fenno's classic 1973 study, *Congressmen in Committees*, asked a simple question: "Which outside groups have the greatest capacity for affecting my ability to make public policy contributions?" He answers it: "Whatever groups dominate the policy coalitions confronting the committee" (Fenno 1973, 26). The political context of policymaking is an important component of coalition building. Often legislative coalition building revolves around "policy subsystems," which surround different policy areas and are made up of interested legislators from particular committees or subcommittees, executive agency personnel, and well-organized interest groups. Unlike the conscious choice members make to join a coalition, participants do not explicitly choose to join a subsystem. They become part of one by virtue of volitional choices they make about what committees to serve on and on what policy topics to specialize. Regardless, the dynamics and norms of the policymaking process within each subsystem shape opportunities for enduring single-issue coalitions, because the subsystem notion highlights how the roots of policymaking are deeper than partisan battles or even the individual members themselves.

Griffith (1939, 182) first developed the idea of policy "whirlpools": "It is my opinion that ordinarily the relationship among these men—legislators, administrators, lobbyists, scholars—who are interested in a common problem is a much more real relationship than the relationship between congressmen generally or between administrators generally." Freeman (1965, 11) defines subsystem as "the pattern of interactions of participants, or actors, involved in making decisions in a special area of public policy" with particular focus on an "executive bureau and congressional committees, with special interest groups intimately attached." Alas, the concept is not settled, and McCool (1998) rightly critiques it for its lack of precision and the concept's wide use in the policy literature.

Issues are the glue that holds subsystems together. While pluralists identified the players and the competition in the political process, they neglected the disaggregated nature of decision-making (Lowi 1964). Others responded by focusing on the institutional contexts and the development of "issue niches" (Browne 1990). Subsystems develop around each niche, and there is a vocabulary and *modus operandi* for each subsystem. "Policies with publics," such as those around crime, drugs, or health care, have well-developed coalitions of interest groups and their own relationships with members of Congress. "Policies without publics," such as those around technological hazards, by contrast, are more limited to technical or scientific communities (May 1991, 192). There is also considerable competition within and across subsystems at both the committee and interest group levels: turf wars over which issues fall in the domain of which subsystems, for example (King 1997). There are often new participants. Conversely, some members may "peel off" to form their own subsystem or join another (Worsham 1998).

If we take subsystems at their most general, however, we can easily see the connection to coalitions. Their members are heavily invested in a particular set of policy issues. To gain such an expertise, a member must research the issue considerably; develop relationships with important interest group representatives and executive agency officials, as well as relationships with other like-minded legislators. They must also invest in staff that can specialize in the issue. A member who sits on the House Subcommittee on Horticulture and Organic Agriculture would develop strong relationships with the Senate Subcommittee on Domestic and Foreign Marketing, Inspection, and Plant and Animal Health, as well as the USDA and FDA, not to mention the Farm Bureau and the Organic Consumers Association. These relationships would constitute a coalition in a broad sense, particularly when the group would want to move an issue to the wider legislative agenda. Participants in a subsystem, however, do not always share the same policy goals, even if they are interested in seeing an issue reach the light of the chamber floor.

Fenno distinguishes between executive-led, party-led, clientele-led, and mixed coalitions (Fenno 1973, 22). Mixed coalitions feature some attributes of more than one of the primary three types. These coalitions are also intimately related to the primary goals of members: reelection, influence within the chamber, and "good" public policy.

The Appropriations Committee, for example, features executive-led coalitions because of the necessary relationship between it and the administration's budget duties. Party-led coalitions, which are groups led by the Speaker, Majority Leader and other party officers, are found on the Ways and Means and Education and Labor Committees. This aligns with the notion of those committees relating to a member's sense of "good" public policy, and the relationship of the party to a member's policy preferences. Ways and Means also has some attributes of an executive-led committee because of its jurisdiction over taxation. The Committee on Natural Resources (Interior in Fenno's volume) is an example of a clientele-led committee because of the relationship between committee members and the interest groups that are related to forestry, parks, oil, and similar issues. These groups can also be influential to a member's reelection goal.

Fenno's typology is related to a subset of the subsystem literature: the Advocacy Coalition Framework (ACF), developed by Paul Sabatier, Hank Jenkins-Smith, and Christopher Weible. ACF defines coalition participants as actors who "(a) share policy core beliefs and (b) engage in a nontrivial degree of coordinated action in order to translate those beliefs into public policy" (Weible and Sabatier 2005, 183). ACF takes the coalition notion a step further to include shared beliefs, which is not a necessary condition for most of the studies of legislative coalitions, such as logrolls.

Continuing the example from above, hypothetically, we could say an advocacy coalition forms when a subcommittee member from Northern California with a large number of organic farms in her district allies with the Organic Consumers Association to push for an organic foods program for public school lunches. While a member from Western Iowa, with many traditional or factory farms, would ally with the Farm Bureau to alter or kill the program. Depending on the political control of the executive, the USDA or FDA may side with either member, providing supporting research or help in implementation. All the organizations participate in the same subsystem, but each would belong to a particular advocacy coalition within the subsystem.

What does all this say about coalitions in Congress? First, it says that context matters for single-issue coalitions. Entrepreneurs and other coalition leaders cannot enter into a closed system of policymaking decisions and expect immediate returns, despite the fact that limited networks of actors characterize American politics (Baumgartner and Jones 1993; Worsham 1998). Instead, these leaders must work within already established channels or create their own.

Second, subsystem studies show the interconnected nature of congressional coalitions. Coalitions are not simply assemblies of members voting one way rather than another on a question before the House or Senate. They are involved at every stage of the governing process. Subsystem research describes the single-issue coalition process beyond the observable roll calls (the institutions) and details the ideas, issues, and interests as well.

Third, the roots of congressional coalitions are far deeper than the members of Congress themselves. Coalitions are the result of the administration, party, and special interests as well as the base desire of members to be reelected. All of these players have common interests in issues and policy specialization, and they form a mutually reinforcing network around those issues that results in closed arenas of decision-making with regard to those issues.

FUTURE RESEARCH DIRECTIONS

Our goal in this chapter has been to offer a broad perspective on coalitions in Congress rather than providing a comprehensive treatment of any particular perspective. A coalition exists when two or more individuals or groups—sometimes with completely different aims—join forces to achieve something that each could not otherwise achieve alone. We proposed a typology that categorizes coalitions by whether the common interests that lead to their formation are essentially transitory or enduring, and whether those common interests center on a particular issue or involve multiple issues. At the expense of a complete discussion of any one type of coalition, we then discussed important areas of research that helped to illustrate a range of perspectives and questions about coalition-building in Congress.

What can we learn from this review? We highlight two limitations of existing research in this concluding section. First, existing congressional scholarship devotes limited attention to the dynamics of coalition formation. As mentioned in the section on party coalitions, much of the research to date focuses on providing indirect evidence that parties matter while saying little (beyond anecdotes) about the specific things that bind members to parties. Our discussion of the rise and fall of the Conservative Coalition noted the potential value of additional research into its decline, or why the South realigned when it did. Our discussion of entrepreneur-led coalitions drew attention to public policy research that emphasizes that an entrepreneur's success and strategy are strongly influenced by context.

Second, other fields offer valuable insights into coalition-building in Congress. Public policy research in particular emphasizes issues as central to understanding coalition formation and stability. Moreover, this literature highlights the role that interests, actors, and events outside of Congress play in shaping priorities and influencing behavior within Congress.

With respect to dynamics, Riker (1962) observes that coalition building is a competitive process. Arnold (1990) additionally notes that some issues are more likely to attract coalition leaders than others, and coalition leaders may be more likely to emerge on one side of an issue depending on the political incentives. How the presence or absence of an opposing coalition leader plays into the mix, and how coalition leaders compete for the support of lawmakers has received little attention other than in the realm of sophisticated voting. Instead, existing approaches treat coalition leaders as if they act in isolation. Party leaders promise side payments and induce party members to switch their positions. Why that pivotal voter fails to attract competing offers (or declines to accept them) is not explicitly considered.

Another aspect of the dynamics of coalition-building that deserves additional consideration relates to the promises coalition leaders make to gain support. What, specifically, are the mechanisms that induce members to join different types of coalition? What types of incentive (positive and negative) do different coalition leaders offer? Are some promises more credible than others, and if so why? How do norms, structure and sequence play into these calculations?

We also hope that our typology encourages congressional scholars to revisit long-standing perspectives that in recent years have been dominated by a focus on party coalitions. In particular, the public policy literature highlights issues as central to understanding coalition formation in Congress. This research raises important questions about theories that highlight preference shifts, party agendas, or the "special skills" of effective legislators as central to understanding when policy change occurs (Anderson, Box-Steffensmeier, and Chapman 2003).

Legislative agenda space is a scarce commodity. When agenda space is scarce, decisions about which issues to take up are as important as decisions about which alternative is preferred. A policy perspective on coalition-building emphasizes that there are things legislatures must do (regardless of which party is in power). These non-discretionary demands constrain the ability of legislatures to do other things. Cartel theory assumes that the party members share a common interest in promoting the party's reputation. We would suggest that this reputation depends in part on whether the party in power manages existing programs, the budget, and external crises to the satisfaction of voters. Such issues can always be set aside in favor of partisan priorities. But our understanding of coalition-building in Congress changes to the extent that agenda space is scarce and lawmakers feel compelled to address those partisan priorities.

Existing research suggests that party coalition leaders (or policy entrepreneurs) play important roles in building winning coalitions around policy alternatives, whereas policy subsystem actors may play more important roles where the selection of issues is concerned (Kingdon 2003, 186). Decisions about program renewals, for example, will have less to do with electoral shifts or partisan agendas, and more to do with governing obligations. How such considerations affect legislative agendas and coalition formation is deserving of more attention.

Bickers and Stein (1994, 331) similarly argue that the "the more fruitful direction for future (distributive politics) research is to focus on how the different political actors that are involved in the policy subsystems that develop in particular areas operate to build political support in the legislature for distributive programs." And indeed, recent distributive politics research portrays distributive benefits as another means for building policy support, which may help to explain the puzzle of why proposals that do not distribute benefits in universal fashion often pass by large majorities. Along these lines, the size of coalitions (voting coalitions in particular) remains a puzzle. Bipartisan voting coalitions have always been the norm rather than the exception in Congress. In our view, existing theories, including theories incorporating bicameralism (Brady and Volden 2005; Krehbiel 1998), do not provide satisfactory explanations for this pattern.

In summary, existing research on coalitions in Congress offers valuable insights into the role of preferences and procedural control in shaping legislative organization and outcomes. However, many questions remain unanswered including some that we have not been able to address here. We hope that we have at least demonstrated that coalition formation in Congress belies sweeping generalizations, and that many research opportunities remain in this important subject area.

REFERENCES

ADLER, E. S. 2002. *Why Congressional Reforms Fail: Reelection and the House Committee System.* Chicago: The University of Chicago Press.

—— and WILKERSON, J. D., 2005. The Scope and Urgency of Legislation: Reconsidering Bill Success in the House of Representatives. Paper presented at the American Political Science Association Annual Meeting in Washington, DC.

—— —— 2008. Intended Consequences: Jurisdictional Reform and Issue Control in the U.S. House of Representatives. *Legislative Studies Quarterly,* 33(1): 85–112.

ALDRICH, J. H., and ROHDE, D. W. 2001. The Logic of Congressional Party Government: Revisiting the Electoral Connection, pp. 269–92 in *Congress Reconsidered,* ed. Lawrence C. Dodd and Bruce I. Oppenheimer. 7th edn. Washington: CQ Press.

ANDERSON, W. D., BOX-STEFFENSMEIER, J. M., and SINCLAIR CHAPMAN, V. 2003. The Keys to Legislative Success in the U.S. House of Representatives. *Legislative Studies Quarterly,* 28(3): 57–86.

ARNOLD, R. 1990. *The Logic of Congressional Action.* New York: Yale University Press.

BACH, S., and SMITH S. S. 1988. *Managing Uncertainty in the House of Representatives: Adaptation and Innovation in Special Rules.* Washington: The Brookings Institution.

BALLA, S. J., LAWRENCE, E. D., MALTZMAN, F., and SIGELMAN, L. 2002. Partisanship, Blame Avoidance, and the Distribution of Legislative Pork. *American Journal of Political Science,* 46(3): 15–25.

BAUMGARTNER, F. R., and JONES, B. D. 1993. *Agendas and Instability in American Politics.* Chicago: The University of Chicago Press.

BECKER, L. 2005. *Doing the Right Thing: Collective Action and Procedural Choice in the New Legislative Process.* Columbus: The Ohio State University Press.

BENTLEY, A. F. 1908. *The Process of Government: A Study of Social Pressures.* Evanston, IL.: The Principia Press of Illinois.

BICKERS, K. N., and STEIN, R. M. 1994. Response to Barry Weingast's Reflections. *Political Research Quarterly,* 47(2): 329–33.

BRADY, D. W., and BULLOCK, C. S. 1980. Is There a Conservative Coalition in the House? *The Journal of Politics,* 42(2): 549–59.

BRADY, D. W., and VOLDEN, C. 2005. *Revolving Gridlock: Politics and Policy from Jimmy Carter to George W. Bush.* Boulder, CO: Westview Press.

BRADY, D. W., and BUCKLEY, K. Z. 2002. Governing by Coalition: Policymaking in the U.S. Congress, pp. 231–66 in *The Parties Respond: Changes in American Parties and Campaigns,* ed. L. Sandy Maisel. 4th ed. Cambridge, MA.: Westview Press.

BROWNE, W. P. 1990. Organized Interests and Their Issue Niches: A Search for Pluralism in a Policy Domain. *The Journal of Politics,* 52(2): 477–509.

CAREY, J. M., and SHUGART, M. S. 1995. Incentives to Cultivate a Personal Vote: A rank ordering of electoral formulas. *Electoral Studies,* 14(4): 417–39.

COOPER, J., and BRADY, D. W. 1981. Institutional Context and Leadership Style: The House from Cannon to Rayburn. *The American Political Science Review,* 75(2): 411–25.

COX, G. W. 2008. The Organization of Democratic Legislatures, pp. 141–61 in *The Oxford Handbook of Political Economy,* ed. Barry R. Weingast and Donald A. Wittman. New York: Oxford University Press.

—— and MCCUBBINS, M. D. 2005. *Setting the Agenda: Responsible Party Government in the U.S. House of Representatives.* New York: Cambridge University Press.

—— —— 2007. *Legislative Leviathan: Party Government in the House.* 2nd ed. New York: Cambridge University Press.

Cox, G. W., and Terry, W. C. 2008. Legislative Productivity in the 93d-110th Congresses. *Legislative Studies Quarterly*, 33(4): 603–18.

Deering, C. J., and Smith, S. S. 1997. *Committees in Congress*. 3rd ed. Washington: CQ Press.

Ellwood, J. W., and Patashnik, E. M. 1993. In Praise of Pork. *The Public Interest*, pp. 19–33.

Enelow, J. M., and Koehler, D. H. 1980. The Amendment in Legislative Strategy: Sophisticated Voting in the U.S. Congress. *The Journal of Politics*, 42(2): 396–413.

Evans, D. 1994. Policy and Pork: The Use of Pork Barrel Projects to Build Policy Coalitions in the House of Representatives. *American Journal of Political Science*, 38(4): 894–917.

Fenno, R. F. 1973. *Congressmen in Committees*. Boston: Little, Brown and Company.

Ferejohn, J. A. 1974. *Pork Barrel Politics: Rivers and Harbors Legislation, 1947–1968*. Palo Alto, Calif.: Stanford University Press.

Finocchiaro, C. J., and Jenkins, J. A. 2008. In Search of Killer Amendments in the Modern U.S. House. *Legislative Studies Quarterly*, 33(2): 263–94.

Freeman, J. L. 1965. *The Political Process*. rev. ed. New York: Random House.

Griffith, E. S. 1939. *The Impasse of Democracy*. New York: Harrison-Hilton Books.

Groseclose, T., and Snyder, J. M. 2000. Vote Buying, Supermajorities, and Flooded Coalitions. *The American Political Science Review*, 94(3): 683–4.

Groseclose, T., and Milyo, J. 2010. Sincere Versus Sophisticated Voting in Congress: Theory and Evidence. *The Journal of Politics* 72(1): 60–73.

Hardin, R. 1976. Hollow Victory: The Minimum Winning Coalition. *The American Political Science Review*, 70(4): 1202–14.

Hinckley, B. 1972. Coalitions in Congress: Size and Ideological Distance. *Midwest Journal of Political Science* 16(2): 197–207.

Humphreys, M. 2008. Coalitions. *Annual Review of Political Science*, 11: 351–86.

Jenkins, J. A., Crespin, M. H., and Carson, J. L. 2005. Parties as Procedural Coalitions in Congress: An Examination of Differing Career Tracks. *Legislative Studies Quarterly*, 30(3): 365–90.

Jones, B. D. 2001. *Politics and the Architecture of Choice: Bounded Rationality and Governance*. Chicago: The University of Chicago Press.

Jones, B. D., and Baumgartner, F. R. 2005. *The Politics of Attention: How Government Prioritizes Problems*. Chicago: The University of Chicago Press.

Jones, B. D., Baumgartner, F. R., and Talbert, J. C. 1993. The Destruction of Issue Monopolies in Congress. *The American Political Science Review*, 87(3): 673–87.

Karol, D. 2009. *Party Position Change in American Politics: Coalition Management*. New York: Cambridge University Press.

Katznelson, I. 2005. *When Affirmative Action Was White: An Untold History of Racial Inequality*. New York: W. W. Norton and Company.

King, D. C. 1997. *Turf Wars: How Congressional Committees Claim Jurisdiction*. Chicago: The University of Chicago Press.

Kingdon, J. W. 2003. *Agendas, Alternatives, and Public Policies*. 2nd ed. New York: Longman.

Krehbiel, K. 1991. *Information and Legislative Organization*. Ann Arbor: University of Michigan Press.

—— 1993. Where's the Party? *British Journal of Political Science*, 23(2): 235–66.

—— 1998. *Pivotal Politics: A Theory of U.S. Lawmaking*. Chicago: The University of Chicago Press.

—— and Rivers, D. 1990. Sophisticated Voting in Congress: A Reconsideration. *The Journal of Politics*, 52(2): 548–78.

LEE, F. E. 2000. Senate Representation and Coalition Building in Distributive Politics. *The American Political Science Review*, 94(1): 59–72.

——2003. Geographic Politics in the U.S. House of Representatives: Coalition Building and Distribution of Benefts. *American Journal of Political Science*, 47(4): 714–28.

——2009. *Beyond Ideology: Politics, Principles, and Partisanship in the U.S. Senate*. Chicago: The University of Chicago Press.

LOWI, T. J. 1964. American Business, Public Policy, Case Studies and Political Theory. *World Politics*, 16: 677–93.

MCCOOL, D. 1998. The Subsystem Family of Concepts: A Critique and a Proposal. *Political Research Quarterly* 51(2): 551–70.

MAY, P. J. 1991. Reconsidering Policy Design: Policies and Publics. *Journal of Public Policy*, 11(2): 187–206.

MAYHEW, D. 1974. *Congress: The Electoral Connection*. New Haven, CT: Yale University Press.

MINTROM, M., and NORMAN, P. 2009. Policy Entrepreneurship and Policy Change. *Policy Studies Journal*, 37(4): 649–68.

NYE, M. A. 1993. Conservative Coalition Support in the House of Representatives, 1963-1988. *Legislative Studies Quarterly*, 18(2): 255–70.

OLSON, M. 1971. *The Logic of Collective Action: Public Goods and The Theory of Groups*. Boston: Harvard University Press.

RIKER, W. H. 1962. *A Theory of Political Coalitions*. New Haven, CT: Yale University Press.

——1986. *The Art of Political Manipulation*. New Haven, CT: Yale University Press.

RITTER, G. 1997. Goldbugs and Greenbacks: The Anti-Monopoly Tradition and the Politics of Finance in America, 1865–1896. NY: Cambridge.

SCHATTSCHNEIDER, E. E. 1942. *Party Government*. New York: Farrar and Rinehart, Inc.

——1960. *The Semisovereign People: A Realist's View of Democracy in America*. New York: Wadsworth Thomson Learning.

SCHICKLER, E. 2001. *Disjointed Pluralism: Institutional Innovation and the Development of the U.S. Congress*. Princeton, NJ: Princeton University Press.

——MCGHEE, E., and SIDES, J. 2003. Remaking the House and Senate: Personal Power, Ideology and the 1970s Reforms. *Legislative Studies Quarterly*, 28(3): 297–331.

——and PEARSON, K. 2009. Agenda Control, Majority Party Power, and the House Committee on Rules, 1937–52. *Legislative Studies Quarterly*, 34(4): 455–91.

SHEPSLE, K. A. 1978. *The Giant Jigsaw Puzzle: Democratic Committee Assignments in the Modern House*. Chicago: The University of Chicago Press.

——and WEINGAST, B. R. 1981. Political Preferences for the Pork Barrel: A Generalization. *American Journal of Political Science*, 25(1): 96–111.

SHEPSLE, K. A., and WEINGAST, B. R. 1987. The Institutional Foundations of Committee Power. *The American Political Science Review*, 81(1): 85–104.

SINCLAIR, B. 1983. *Majority Leadership in the U.S. House*. Baltimore: The Johns Hopkins University Press.

SMITH, H. 1988. *The Power Game: How Washington Works*. New York: Ballantine Books.

SMITH, S. S. 2007. *Party Influence in Congress*. New York: Cambridge University Press.

THERIAULT, S. M. 2008. *Party Polarization in Congress*. New York: Cambridge University Press.

WALKER, J. L. 1977. Setting the Agenda in the U.S. Senate: A Theory of Problem Selection. *British Journal of Political Science*, 7(4): 423–45.

WAWRO, G. J. 2000. *Legislative Entrepreneurship in the U.S. House of Representatives*. Ann Arbor: University of Michigan Press.

WEAVER, R. K. 1986. The Politics of Blame Avoidance. *Journal of Public Policy*, 6(4): 371–98.

WEIBLE, C. M., and SABATIER, P. A. 2005. Comparing Policy Networks: Marine Protected Areas in California. *Policy Studies Journal*, 33(2): 181–201.

WEINGAST, B. R. 1994. Reflections on Distributive Politics and Universalism. *Political Research Quarterly*, 47(2): 319–27.

WEINGAST, B. R., and MARSHALL, W. J. 1988. The Industrial Organization of Congress; or, Why Legislators, Like Firms, Are Not Organized as Markets. *The Journal of Political Economy*, 96(1): 132–63.

WILKERSON, J. D. 1999. Killer Amendments in Congress. *The American Political Science Review*, 93(3): 535–52.

WISEMAN, A. E., and WRIGHT, J. R. 2008. The Legislative Median and Partisan Policy. *Journal of Theoretical Politics*, 20(1): 5–29.

WORSHAM, J. 1998. Wavering Equilibriums: Subsystem Dynamics and Agenda Control. *American Politics Quarterly*, 26(4): 485–512.

CHAPTER 28

....

LEGISLATIVE PRODUCTIVITY AND GRIDLOCK

....

SARAH BINDER

APPROXIMATELY twenty-five years ago, legislative students of the U.S. Congress took stock of the state of the literature, producing the thick volume *The Handbook of Legislative Research* (Loewenberg, Patterson, and Jewell 1985). Remarkably, as Charles Jones (1995) pointed out a decade later, none of the sixteen chapters of that otherwise comprehensive volume studied lawmaking. Many of the chapters were "relevant to an understanding of lawmaking ... But the volume indicates that scholars are more interested in elections, voting, committees, and leadership than in lawmaking" (1995, 9n1). In this new effort to survey legislative scholarship, macro-level questions about Congress as a lawmaking body finally earn their day in the sun. To be sure, the field's traditional focus on elections, voting, and institutional features of Congress still casts a long shadow over such questions. But chapters addressing legislative capacity, constitutional matters and other systemic level issues reflect changes in congressional scholarship that have emerged over the past two decades. In this chapter, I reflect on the turn to studies of legislative performance, review recent developments in the literature, and offer some guidance about the future direction of scholarship in this area.

PATTERNS IN THE STUDY OF CONGRESS

....

The study of congressional performance has deep roots within political science. We might even say that political science as a discipline had its origins partially in the study of American national institutions—their legal contours, institutional details, and broader function or performance in the American political system. Attention to Congress's lawmaking performance would not have been considered unusual to Lindsay Rogers, Henry James Ford, Frank Goodnow, or any of the discipline's first political scientists. Indeed, before the American Political Science Association was launched in 1906, Goodnow and other Columbia professors contemplated creating an American Society for the Study of Comparative Legislation (Gunnell 2006). Although today we often tag this early work as descriptive and normative, such studies collectively sought to bring social science to bear on questions about politics and policy— to create "a practical role for social science." Those scholars naturally turned to analyses of the separation of powers, asking whether congressional, presidential, and administrative bodies were sufficiently accountable to the broader needs of the country. Certainly Woodrow Wilson's many times revised *Congressional Government* fits this vein—outing congressional committees as venues for "specially commissioned minorities" (Wilson 1885).

By World War II, the field's focus on institutional performance had taken a back seat to new questions and methods brought to legislative studies by the behavioral revolution of mid-century. Not only did many political scientists of this era have little interest in institutional performance, few had interest in institutions. Turning to the fields of psychology and sociology, political scientists came to consider individuals, their roles and their behaviors as central building blocks in the study of politics. Political action in turn stemmed from the aggregation of individual behavior. In a world in which individuals followed roles and rules and learned by socialization, there was relatively little interest in institutions. As Kenneth Shepsle (1989, 133) has observed, institutions were "empty shells to be filled by individual roles, statuses and values...There was no need to study institutions; they were epiphenomenal." Although some legislative scholars remained dedicated to the study of institutions in this period—think Polsby (1968) on institutionalization and Cooper (1988) on the origins of the committee system—Shepsle's comment captures the behavioral focus of the era.

The turn to economics in the 1970s helped to return legislative scholars' focus to institutions. Instead of seeing institutions as unimportant in the building of theory, scholars now considered both actors' preferences and the structures and procedures of the legislative game. Influence conferred by rules and organization empowered certain individuals in the pursuit of their preferences. The host of applications—to the study of congressional committees, floor voting, coalition-building, and so on— was impressive, and offered bedrock contributions to our understanding of legislative strategy and choice. Still, the analytical focus remained at the micro level. Theory was tuned to explain how rationally motivated individuals pursued their goals, and how institutional features served to enhance or to constrain such purposive behavior.

In contrast, "macro" politics received little attention in this era. Roughly speaking, we can think of macro politics as the study of outputs—policy outcomes, lawmaking, systemic performance (whether electoral, constitutional, institutional) and so forth. To be sure, questions about Congress's legislative performance were entertained at mid-century by scholars including Lawrence Chamberlain (1948) and James Sundquist (1968). But little sustained effort to build macro-level theory occurred in this period. We gained detailed analyses of legislative performance in different eras, but were left with little in the way of generalizable explanation. Nor did other scholars take up these works to test their implications in other periods or contexts. Micro-level analyses—first advanced by sociological perspectives in the 1950s and 1960s and then followed by economics-based theory in the 1970s and 1980s—dominated legislative studies.

THE TURN TO MACRO-LEVEL STUDIES

Legislative scholars typically credit David Mayhew's 1991 *Divided We Govern* with redirecting attention to questions of macro politics. Mayhew certainly produced the landmark piece of scholarship in this generation of research, the first to directly test claims about the impact of divided government on lawmaking. Moreover, Mayhew's work (discussed in detail below) set the agenda for a series of subsequent articles and books—each aiming to build on Mayhew's signal contribution. It is important, however, to put Mayhew's contribution into perspective, as it helps to explain why, when, and how congressional scholars turned to questions of macro, rather than micro, politics.

Divided We Govern came on the heels of a series of works by presidential and legislative scholars perplexed and frustrated by the frequent periods of divided party government that prevailed after World War II. Between 1897 and 1954, divided party control of government occurred 14 percent of the time; between 1955 and 1990, two-thirds of the time. These scholars, including most prominently James Sundquist, called for a new theory of coalitional government to explain how Congress and the president could secure major policy change in the presence of divided government (Sundquist 1988–9). The assumption—untested, as even Sundquist admitted—was that major change was near impossible in the absence of the common policy and electoral interests (seemingly) ensured by strong political parties. That view of political parties, of course, had long been enshrined as the "doctrine of responsible parties"—the idea that parties were essential to democratic life. As E. E. Schattschneider put it best in 1942, "The political parties created democracy and . . . modern democracy is unthinkable save in terms of the parties" (Schattschneider 1942, 1). Only parties—by virtue of their goal of assembling majorities to win elections—could claim authority and legitimacy to rule in a democracy. And as V. O. Key made the connection in the 1960s, "Common partisan control of executive and legislature does not assure energetic government, but division of party control precludes it" (Key 1964, 688).

These scholars' concerns were often normative. But it is this line of argument—crystallized in Sundquist's call in the late 1980s to better understand how lawmaking could proceed in periods of divided government—that spurred a flood of subsequent studies of divided government's effects. Before turning to Mayhew's *Divided We Govern* study, I think it is helpful to note briefly the differences between studies of divided government and the studies of legislative productivity that followed on their heels. The former start with an independent variable—divided party control—and test for its impact on the dependent variable of patterns in lawmaking. A typical such study, say Mayhew's, asks: does the configuration of party control matter in shaping Congress's productivity? In contrast, studies of legislative performance start with the dependent variable (performance) and then seek to explain its variation as a function of several causal forces, one of which is typically divided government. In other words, it might be fair to consider the subfield's recent emphasis on macro-level questions of congressional performance as a byproduct of scholars' preoccupation in the 1980s with the persistence and impact of divided government. Many scholars cared about divided government precisely because they thought it was impeding lawmaking. Certainly the attention to "gridlock" around the time of the 1992 elections reinforced these concerns. Recall, for example, Reform Party candidate Ross Perot's declaration that if elected, he would open up the hood of government and "fix it."

I would hazard that most of the research questions that have galvanized legislative scholars' attention in recent years have not emerged from normative debates about Congress and its policymaking capacity. For example, studies of congressional committees—specifically, debates about whether or not committees were outliers—reemerged in the early 1990s as a means of testing competing theories of legislative organization (even though earlier committee studies focusing on committee representativeness may have been more normative). Nor did the debate about party effects in the late 1990s stem from normative concerns about party potential. That in part is what is different about the impact of *Divided We Govern* on the agenda of many legislative scholars. Normative concerns about the impact of divided government spurred empirical tests, which in turn generated new theoretical perspectives about the dynamics of lawmaking.

Divided we govern

This brings us to Mayhew's original contribution in 1991. *Divided We Govern* (2005a, 34) asks a simple and accessible question about Congress's performance in the postwar era: "Were many important laws passed?" Mayhew's empirical goal is to set up a simple test of the effect of divided party control on the level of lawmaking. (He studies as well the impact of divided government on oversight, asking whether party control affects the incidence of high-profile investigations; he finds that it does not.) Toward that end, he identified landmark laws in a two-stage process. In the first stage, Sweep 1, Mayhew used annual end of session wrap-up articles from the *New York Times* and *Washington Post* to survey contemporary judgments about the significance of Congress's work each session. In the second stage, Sweep 2, Mayhew relied on policy specialists' retrospective judgments about the importance of legislation. Using the results of Sweep 1 to inform his selection of laws in Sweep 2, Mayhew generated a comprehensive list of landmark laws enacted in each Congress between 1946 and 1990 (subsequently updated through 2008); either contemporary recognition (Sweep 1) or historical significance (Sweep 2) was considered sufficient to merit landmark designation. Mayhew then tested whether the presence of divided government reduced the number of major laws enacted each Congress.

The key contribution of *Divided We Govern* was the null result for the impact of divided government on lawmaking. Unified party control of Congress and the White House fails to yield significantly higher levels of lawmaking. It matters little whether a single party controls both the White House and Congress: not much more gets done than under divided party control. Having absolved divided government as a cause of legislative inaction, Mayhew disentangles several other influences on Congress's performance. Some of those forces—including legislators' electoral incentives—point towards constancy in the record of lawmaking. But other forces, Mayhew demonstrates, appear to be important alternative sources of variation in explaining congressional productivity, including shifting public moods, presidential cycles, and issue coalitions that cut across the left–right divide.

Mayhew's empirical results lead to an important set of conclusions. Most importantly, Mayhew argues, parties have been misperceived as "governing instruments," capable of delivering major policy change when they hold all reins of power. Instead, Mayhew suggests that parties are more accurately conceived of as "policy factions"— coalitions that can muster majorities for legislative change regardless of the configuration of party control. Mayhew offers a decidedly pluralist view of American politics, one that suggests that the rhythms of lawmaking are unlikely to follow partisan winds. Unified party control of government, we learn, cannot guarantee the compromise necessary for breaking deadlock in American politics.

RESPONSES TO MAYHEW

Divided We Govern opened the gates to a torrent of scholarship—not least on account of its findings that ran counter to received wisdom about unified party control. The scholarship that flowed from Mayhew's book took several tracks, spanning theoretical, empirical, and methodological grounds. Considered together, these responses and challenges grappled with definitions and measurement of legislative change, as well as with broader theories of lawmaking and legislative deadlock. Nearly two decades after Mayhew's original contribution, I would contend that we know more about the contours and causes of legislative productivity, and that we have a renewed appreciation for both the potential and the limits of party control in shaping major policy change in Washington.

Recalibrating legislative significance

Initial responses to Mayhew reconsidered his indicator of lawmaking's importance, asking for example whether both of Mayhew's sweeps should be considered necessary for determining episodes of landmark lawmaking. What if, Sean Kelly (1993) asked, a law had to be considered landmark both during and long after passage? Rather than following Mayhew's coding rule that either a Sweep 1 or 2 designation was sufficient to secure a landmark designation, Kelly recoded Mayhew's data requiring a law to appear in both Sweeps 1 and 2. With that new definition of "truly landmark" laws, Kelly found that divided government did in fact decrease Congress's productivity.

Other efforts to recalculate legislative significance followed on Kelly's heels. Howell, Adler, Cameron, and Riemann (2000) provide an alternative approach by classifying all enacted legislation in the postwar period in to four categories of significance ranging from landmark down to minor. The authors' findings are mixed, showing that landmark legislation does appear to be enacted in higher numbers in periods of unified government, but other types of legislation do not. Other scholars moved to replicate Mayhew's findings but in a different venue, with Rogers (2005) offering a state-based analysis of divided government's effects. Across state legislatures, Rogers detects an impact of divided government, showing that divided party control reduces legislative output by some 30 percent.

One of the limitations of Mayhew's measure is the difficulty of replicating it for the period before 1946, largely due to the lack of a systematic source of journalistic coverage of Congress akin to the round-up stories Mayhew relies on. The empirical limitation is also conceivably a theoretical limitation, as we lack a long enough time series to test how well contemporary lawmaking dynamics hold up over the course of the nineteenth century. Heitshusen and Young (2006) offer an alternative measure with a longer historical sweep. Instead of using external evaluators of Congress to detect legislative significance, the authors measure significance by looking at the legal footprint of each public law enacted each Congress. Summing up the number of sections within each title of the U.S. code that are changed with each new law's enactment, the authors create a measure that helps us to detect the level of significant lawmaking over a long sweep of time, stretching back to the late nineteenth century. Armed with the new measure, Heitshusen and Young find that lawmaking does not seem to ebb and flow with divided government, but it does seem to be ratcheted up after critical elections and as parties grow more durable and cohesive.

One strong value of the Heitshusen and Young approach is the historical availability of statutes, producing a systematic base from which to develop measures of lawmaking importance. One drawback, though, is that legal complexity (captured by counting up changes to the federal code) need not run in tandem with legislative importance. The most significant laws need not be the most complex. Clinton and Lapinski (2006) offer an alternative measure of statute significance, integrating a dataset on public statutes (1877–1994) with a large sample of elite evaluations of the importance of the statutes. Rather than using journalistic roundups of legislative sessions or retrospective histories by a single author, the Clinton–Lapinski method uses an item-response model to integrate the evaluations from several "raters" (adjusting for rater differences) to create a long time series measuring Congress's record. The method is striking as it generates statute-level estimates (and standard errors) of legislative significance, using information from the rated statutes to estimate significance levels for non-rated measures. (See also Grant and Kelly 2008, which similarly focuses on a time series of public law enactments.) The result is a time series of congressional "accomplishment," one that seems to be responsive to the onset of unified party control. The extremely high correlation with the levels of lawmaking in Mayhew's two sweeps (.94 for both time series) bolsters the case for using the measure to detect serious lawmaking in previous times.

Numerators and denominators

Each of these efforts to generate potentially more robust measures of legislative significance falls prey to a common dilemma. Each of them captures what Congress accomplished, but none of them detects what Congress failed to do. If our ultimate interest is in explaining Congress's productivity, then capturing both successes and failures could prove important. To be fair to Mayhew, of course, his measure was fine-tuned to answer the question he posed: "How much of importance does Congress get done?" Asking the question somewhat differently, we might prefer—as Jones (1994, 196) did—to evaluate the "success of that system in treating public problems." Any such evaluations, however, would require us to know both what Congress and the president succeeded in enacting, as well as what proposals floundered.

Mayhew certainly recognized the differences between thinking in terms of numerators (what passed) and denominators (what did not pass). As Mayhew himself defined the challenge, we are interested in "some actually-did-pass numerator over some all-that-were-possibilities-for-passage denominator." Still, as Mayhew argued, "it is very difficult to see what a denominator for a Congress—an agenda of potential enactments—might be. 'As demanded by the needs of the time,' perhaps?... That would be hopeless to administer" (1991, 35–6). Reflecting years later on the move to incorporate denominators into measures of legislative accomplishments, Mayhew defended his focus on actual policy change, arguing that "All the rest can be a kind of vapor that surrounds real legislative action without being very real itself... Such offerings are often vague, shifting, untested, infeasible, or otherwise insubstantial" (Mayhew 2006, 241–2). Moreover, picking up on Shipan's (2006) argument that agendas are larger in periods of divided government, Mayhew argues that legislative agendas may be endogenous to the politics of the time and thus tainted by "artifactuality" (Mayhew 2006, 242). Still, by excluding a numerator, we are left with what Fiorina (1996) called "an irreducible ambiguity in Mayhew's findings... Essentially, he has studied the supply of federal legislation and found that the supply is more or less the same during modern unified and divided government periods. But we have no information about the demand for legislation" (1996, 89).

Edwards, Barrett, and Peake (1997) offered the first attempt to incorporate a denominator following Mayhew's study. Their effort relied on *Congressional Quarterly* reporting to determine the most important measures that were "seriously considered" that failed to become law in the Congress in which they were considered (1997, 549). Recognizing that "significance" remains a "series of judgments rather than straightforward codifications," Edwards and colleagues locate 638 seriously considered failed measures between 1947 and 1992. They determine the president's position on each of the measures, and test for the impact of divided government. They expect and find that more measures fail in periods of divided government than in periods of unified control. Pointing to the impact of the president, they show that presidents oppose more measures during divided periods, thus increasing their odds of failure. Presidential opposition to congressional initiatives in periods of divided government seems to account for the impact of party control that they detect.

The Edwards, Barrett, and Peake study advanced scholars' thinking about how to construct measures of an elusive denominator. Two aspects of their data, however, encouraged others to experiment with new measures. Such efforts aimed to reduce the subjectivity of the coding process for determining legislative significance and to seek a single source of data for both successful and failed measures. Using a single source of data would circumvent the limitation of the Edwards' ratio that was formed by mixing Mayhew's numerator with Edwards' denominator. Without a single source of data, the resulting ratio risked mixing apples and oranges in tapping Congress's legislative accomplishments.

In my own studies of legislative gridlock (Binder 1999, 2003) I addressed both of these challenges in developing a measure of stalemate. In my studies, I used the daily (unsigned) editorials that appeared in the *New York Times* between 1947 and 2000 to recreate the political agenda for each Congress. From the editorials, I extracted the issues that plausibly constituted the political agenda, coding as well the number of editorials the *Times* wrote on each of the issues in each Congress as a measure of the public or political salience of the issue. Once the disposition of each issue was determined in each Congress, I calculated a gridlock score, consisting of the percentage of agenda items that failed to be enacted into law by the end of the Congress. Thus, in contrast to the Mayhew measure that captured actual policy change, the new measure tapped both the legislative successes and failures each Congress, and combined them into a single ratio to capture the degree of stalemate each Congress.

Not surprisingly, the two time series tell different stories about Congress's performance over the postwar period, as the denominator puts into perspective the relative activism of Congress over time. Periods like the 1950s that produced relatively few laws (looking unproductive by Mayhew's measure) look quite productive once the small legislative agendas of the decade are taken into account. Conversely, Mayhew's measure suggests that the 1970s were highly productive years, given how many landmark laws were enacted by Congress and the president. But those were also years of high policy demand, yielding high levels of gridlock once the denominator is incorporated. Of course the two measures yield similar results for the 1980s, a period in which Congress and the president produced relatively few landmark laws in face of large legislative agendas.

BEYOND DIVIDED GOVERNMENT

Armed with new measures of legislative performance, scholars also responded to Mayhew's work by tackling his central contribution—the null effect for the impact of divided government on landmark lawmaking. Some of these works—discussed in this section—proceeded by adding a new variable or two to Mayhew's basic model, and then reestimated the model with one or more of Mayhew's, Binder's, or Edwards and colleagues' dependent variables. Other works (discussed below) offered alternative theoretical approaches to modeling the dynamics of legislative productivity.

Coleman (1999) offered a prominent revision of the Mayhew model, revisiting the writings of the postwar generation of party scholars and incorporating the impact of congressional rules on what party coalitions can hope to achieve. Addressing the incentives that parties have to cooperate to build coalitions, Coleman revised Mayhew's model to capture the public mood, the diversity of policy views within the two major parties, and the closeness of Democratic and Republican majorities to filibuster-proof status. His study reaffirms the limits imposed on policymaking by supermajority rules, and points to the disparate impact of Democratic and Republican majorities on Congress's policy performance. More generally, Coleman's approach points to the conditional impact of unified party control, pointing to the institutional and partisan arrangements under which unified control is more likely to facilitate major policy change.

Other studies delve further into the ways in which institutional strategies alter the prospects for major policy change. Krutz (2000), for example, explores the impact of omnibus legislating on policy outcomes, estimating the impact of combining multiple measures from often different policy areas into a single legislative vehicle. The frequent practice of combining several federal spending bills into a single "omnibus" as the end of a session draws near is a prime example. Krutz finds, in fact, that the omnibus method does affect legislative productivity, giving legislators a tool for circumventing obstacles and securing agreement within Congress and with the president. Because omnibus legislating may be more likely in periods of divided government, Krutz argues that the constancy Mayhew detects in lawmaking may result because omnibus legislating helps reduce obstacles to passage in periods of unified control. Other pieces around this time also shed new light on the forces driving Congress's performance, including Taylor's (1998) effort to detect the influence of fiscal conditions (including the size of the national debt) on policy output.

Such efforts to address the null effect of divided government helped to flesh out the ways in which party coalitions, interacting with the rules of game, might help or harm legislative efforts to secure major policy change. Rather than thinking solely in terms of the impact of party control, these studies also encouraged the field to think about the heterogeneity that attends to legislative parties and about variation in such diversity over time. And, as important, the studies highlighted the impact of both formal rules and informal strategies in enhancing the likelihood of major policy change. Indeed, capturing these multiple ingredients—parties, preferences, rules—became central to concurrent efforts to build new theories of lawmaking, often in response to Mayhew's contributions. I turn to these new perspectives below.

Before turning to the series of spatial models that emerged after Mayhew's work, a brief detour to consider an alternative account offered by Erikson, MacKuen, and Stimson in their work *The Macro Polity* (2002). Rather than estimating policy outcomes as a function of the rules of the game, Erikson and colleagues posit that governing activity responds to the prevailing political mood across the country. Coding Mayhew's landmarks as either expanding (liberal) or contracting (conservative) government at the time they were passed, the authors devise a measure to capture the ideological imprint of significant lawmaking (subtracting conservative laws from liberal ones to craft an annual ideological bent of landmark laws). The direction of policy is then modeled as a function of the prevailing public mood and degree of party control of the House, Senate, and White House. Consistent with a theory they term "dynamic representation," Erikson and colleagues show that liberal moods push Congress towards more liberal policy choices, made easier when the majority controls Congress and the White House; the public's mood in turn is said to respond to the ideological bent of new laws. Although the authors' theoretical interests focus on the nature of policy change, rather than predicting its incidence, *The Macro Polity* results provide an alternative way to think about the impact of divided government and encourage us to consider how broader political or societal trends can affect Congress's performance.

THEORY BUILDING AFTER *DIVIDED WE GOVERN*

Theory-oriented, macro-level studies proliferated after publication of *Divided We Govern*. Most of these works built on the standard spatial model, predicting outcomes as a function of the array of preferences interacting with the rules of the legislative game. Although these studies were not the first to consider the simple spatial model in a multi-institutional setting (see, for example, Ferejohn and Shipan 1990), works such as Tsebelis (1995) placed down the marker for subsequent studies seeking to explain variation in legislative performance (whether over time or in a cross-national perspective). After noting the differences that attend to political systems that vary in institutional features (unicameral versus bicameral, presidential versus parliamentary systems, strong versus weak parties, and so on), Tsebelis notes that "without a theoretical model, it is difficult to sort out which of these differences are causally prior to others" (1995, 291).

Tsebelis' (1995, 2002) theoretical contribution spells out the concept of the "veto player," the player or players whose agreement is necessary for policy change. Most importantly, he shows how the location, number, and internal congruence of the veto players affect the likelihood for policy change in a political system. In a multi-dimensional setting, Tsebelis uses the winsets and yolks produced by the players' ideal points to show the regions of policy stability. Including both constitutionally determined veto players as well as partisan veto players (whose support, Tsebelis argues, is neither necessary nor sufficient to secure policy change), Tsebelis applies the model loosely to the U.S. He suggests that the frequency of deadlock may be a function of the often distant preferences of a partisan House majority and a moderate Senate majority. Policy stability is more likely in such a context, compared to one in which the veto players see eye to eye.

The standard spatial model has also been extended into multi-institutional settings by Krehbiel (1998) and Brady and Volden (1998). Both of these works books developed the spatial model to explain the dynamics of lawmaking in the U.S. Congress. The key insight of these studies—dubbed the "pivotal politics theory" by Krehbiel—is that constitutional and extra-constitutional institutional rules create "pivotal" players on whom collective choices depend. In the context of studying legislative productivity, that collective choice is of course the making of public law. Focusing on the presidential veto and the Senate filibuster, both Krehbiel (1998) and Brady and Volden (1998) argue that the cloture and veto pivots are the critical actors for determining whether or not changes in public policy will be adopted. Given a particular sequence of play, the model predicts an equilibrium outcome of gridlock based on the preferences of the pivotal players and the location of the status quo points. In other words, legislative stalemate will occur in spite of a legislative majority in favor of a policy change. That region of stalemate is termed the "gridlock interval," the region of policy that cannot be moved from the status quo.

The pivotal politics theory has several important implications for understanding the conditions under which Congress and the president should be able to agree to major policy change. First, policy outcomes are consistent with the views of the supermajority pivots of the legislature. Still, although the pivots are consequential, they are not in Krehbiel's terms "gatekeepers"; their power derives from their location in relation to the policy status quo. With a conservative president and a conservative majority, any effort to move policy substantially to the right would be blocked by a liberal filibuster pivot; right of center status quos would also remain unchanged, since a conservative president would veto any movement left of the policy and the veto would be sustained by the veto pivot. That gridlock interval—anchored by the filibuster pivot on the left and the veto pivot on the right—would prevent change to the policy in question. Not surprisingly then, the conditions that make policy ripe for change include elections and major exogenous shocks that might alter the location of the policy status quo, leaving it outside the existing gridlock interval.

Second, neither the Krehbiel nor the Brady and Volden model includes an analytical role for political parties. Legislators in the basic model are individual utility maximizers, rather than partisans seeking collective goals for the party. Given that parties are not considered to have pivotal players in the model, one of the model's nice features is that it helps to explain why unified party control often fails to produce major policy change. Failure to secure the support of the filibuster pivot has doomed many a new majority party, including President Clinton's push in 1993 for a large stimulus bill or President George W. Bush's 2005 push for privatizing social security. Certainly Democrats' difficulty in securing sixty votes for President Barack Obama's health care reform package in the 111th Congress (2009–10) is consistent with the model.

Gridlock in periods of divided government also follows from the model, given that a liberal congressional majority's effort to move centrally located policy to the left would be thwarted by a right-side filibuster pivot, as well as a right-side presidential veto. The veto pivot, whose vote would be necessary to override the president's veto, is also unlikely to prefer the liberal majority's bill proposal to the status quo. In short, policy gridlock results. Given the implication of the pivotal politics model that gridlock can occur under both unified and divided government, the model provides the theoretical basis for Mayhew's null effect for divided government. Mayhew, Krehbiel, and Brady and Volden all predict that major policy change is likely only in the context of large, bipartisan coalitions. Moreover, as Krehbiel argues, the model helps to account for the other empirical regularities identified by Mayhew, including the "honeymoon" effect in which new presidents secure major policy change. The pivotal politics model suggests that gridlock would indeed be broken if a new president pushes major change when he inherits extreme status quo points that are "out of equilibrium" (1998, 46) from the new array of congressional and presidential preferences.

The pivotal politics model has subsequently been challenged by party scholars seeking to build theory that predicts party influence over the shape of policy outcomes. Jones (2001), for example, highlights the potential impact of partisan polarization—conditional on a party's proximity to a filibuster-proof majority—on the likelihood of gridlock. More formally, Cox and McCubbins (2005) offer a party cartel model in which the key agenda-setter is the majority party leadership. As a pivotal agenda-setter, the majority party median is able to gatekeep access to the floor agenda, systematically keeping proposals off the floor when the party prefers the policy status quo. Such exercise of negative power forms the core of the party cartel theory, which Cox and McCubbins test with "roll rates" that capture the frequency with which the majority party loses to the minority on floor votes. Although the party cartel theory theorizes a role for the majority party's positive power—the party's ability to move policy outcomes off center towards the majority party's preferences—it takes a back seat to the work's considerable attention to the cartel's negative power. Moreover, the evidence on positive power looks at the size of the legislative agenda, as Cox and McCubbins argue that agendas get larger as the party increases in size and policy diversity (see Strahan, Chapter 17, this volume, on party leadership more generally).

Although Cox and McCubbins provide a strong theoretical alternative to Krehbiel's focus on supermajority institutions and median voters, their work speaks less directly to arguments about the politics of lawmaking. The party cartel model informs us about a majority's ability to keep things off the table, but leaves open the question of the conditions under which parties can mold policies to their advantage. To be sure, Cox and McCubbins model the incidence of left-moving policy change. Because the measure is based on the NOMINATE scores for legislators voting for proposals, however, it can be difficult to distill the location of policy from the ideological scores (unless we assume that all votes indicate legislators' sincere preferences).

Others have tried to test the pivotal politics model directly, using NOMINATE scores to anchor the relevant gridlock intervals and adding partisan and bicameral veto players as pivotal anchors. Chiou and Rothenberg (2003), for example, incorporate the preferences of the majority party median (to test a "party unity" model), and suggest that party cohesion—with or without presidential leadership—may be sufficient to enhance legislative productivity. Primo, Binder, and Maltzman (2008) also find a party effect when they use gridlock intervals to predict the likelihood of stalemate over the confirmation of new federal judges. Increases in the size of the gridlock interval lead to a higher rate of confirmation failure. Of the several competing pivotal politics models that they attempt to fit to the confirmation data, the best-fitting model incorporates the majority party median and the 60th senator as the anchoring pivots.

All told, these spatial models have improved our analytical thinking about theories of lawmaking, encouraging legislative scholars to be more explicit about the theoretical links between preferences, parties, and institutional rules. Still, this eclectic family of models has its limits (see Smith 2007 for a comprehensive treatment). First, most of these models assume a unicameral legislature. Second, the models assume that political players have but one goal—the attainment of policy outcomes as close as possible to their (single) ideal point. But if players—parties in particular—have both electoral and policy goals and if parties vary in their ideological diversity and cohesion, then their behavior may not fit the expectations derived from the model. The desire to build the majority's reputation, for example, might encourage the majority leadership to support measures that do not constitute a clear improvement over the status quo. Third, these are typically one-dimensional models for an often multi-dimensional policy world. Given that successful episodes of lawmaking typically require leaders' involvement in the crafting of coalitions across different dimensions (Sinclair 2006), assuming a single dimension may be limiting what we can learn from these competing models.

Some, but not all of these concerns about the models have been addressed in subsequent work. In my work on gridlock (Binder 1999, 2003, 2008), for example, I test for the impact of party diversity and bicameralism. First, I show that the degree of partisan polarization matters, as ideologically distant parties make harder the crafting of large bipartisan majorities necessary for durable policy change. Second, I capture the policy distance between the two chambers over time by showing that deadlock is at least in part a consequence of bicameral differences in policy views. Although methodological (Chiou and Rothenberg 2008) and theoretical (McCarty and Cutrone 2006) questions remain about the measurement and impact of bicameralism, I suggest that intra-branch and inter-chamber conflict may be equally likely to raise the bar against successful coalition building. Evidence that there are policy consequences of bicameralism (as opposed to unicameralism) is further suggestive of the potential impact of inter-chamber differences on legislative performance (Heller 1997).

FUTURE DIRECTIONS

The legislative field has reached a mile marker after a twenty-year burst of energy to distill and explain the dynamics of lawmaking in Congress. Along the way, scholars have:

- crystallized arguments about the impact of divided government;
- questioned whether party control is the key factor in explaining congressional performance over time;
- crafted measures of legislative accomplishment, capturing both supply and demand for legislated policy change;
- advanced theory to isolate the importance of policy preferences and supermajority rules in predicting likelihood of policy change;
- identified the partisan, electoral, and institutional conditions under which legislative motion is more or less likely to end in stalemate.

All told, we can count an impressive array of methodological, empirical, and theoretical gains that flowed in large part from Mayhew's contribution. We know much more about why divided government does not necessarily doom legislative efforts to stalemate, and more about the conditions under which it does. We have tackled the matter of partisan polarization and tried to understand how ideological and partisan disagreements unravel the legislative process. And we know far more about how congressional rules allocate advantages and disadvantages across Congress, endowing pivotal players with veto powers when they are content to preserve the status quo.

Where should the field go next? First, echoing Smith's (2006) concerns about the state of party theory-building, moving beyond single goal theories of parties seems appropriate. Assuming that parties seek to maximize both policy and electoral goals would encourage students of lawmaking to think about a party's incentive or disincentive to cooperate with the other party—even after controlling for the array of policy preferences. Considering electoral motivations might help to explain anomalous findings in light of the pivotal politics model—such as times when senators opt not to filibuster despite having the votes to block a measure. Incorporating electoral goals might also help to disentangle the dynamics that give rise to obstructionist "team play" (Lee 2009), even when the parties are not divided along ideological lines. In short, moving beyond the simple spatial model might prove valuable in building macro-level theory to explain patterns in legislative outcomes.

Second, despite the progress in mapping patterns in legislative outcomes over the postwar period (and more recently over the full course of congressional history), existing measures fall short in some ways. We know much about the quantity of lawmaking—both in absolute and relative terms—and we have reasonable methods for detecting the salience of such legislative efforts. But such measures fail to capture the substance of Congress's performance. Does doing a lot or a little (or a large or small portion of the agenda) matter? Is that what we seek to capture when we study macro-level outcomes? Or should we be seeking a more substantive way of evaluating

Congress's performance? Do episodes of major lawmaking make a difference? How well (or when) does Congress succeed in solving problems? The danger in pursuing such questions, of course, is that it risks veering onto normative ground—some place legislative scholars tend not to want to go.

Still, scholars' recent efforts to explain variation in the durability of laws (Maltzman and Shipan 2008), the stickiness of major policy reforms (Patashnik 2008), and the impact of policy type on legislative outcomes (Lapinski 2008) are all important movements in this direction. Lapinski (2008), for example, questions the assumption often used in testing pivotal politics models that status quo points are uniformly distributed across the ideological spectrum (see also Mayhew 2005b). Lapinski (2008) shows that legislative dynamics may vary across policy types; for instance, partisan polarization seems not to deter foreign policy lawmaking, suggesting that the array of status quo points might vary by policy area. One of the challenges for future work in this area of course is the measurement of policy preferences by policy type. Using left–right ideological scores (that is, versions of Poole and Rosenthal's 1997 NOMINATE data) to capture policy views in particular areas complicates the estimation of lawmaking models.

Third, the most prominent models of lawmaking are based on the postwar period, which features a particular constellation of presidential-congressional relations, legislative organization, and political party dynamics. Although in theory pivotal politics and party cartel type theories should be applicable in different historical contexts, there has been little progress in devising and testing alternative models for earlier times. One might wonder how numerous structural and political features of the nineteenth century might have affected the dynamics of lawmaking. How, if at all, did the lack of a cloture rule affect bicameral politics? Did Congress's assertiveness with respect to the president affect the lawmaking process? How did the booms and busts of an economy without a central bank—a situation that plunged Congress into the thicket of monetary issues until the early twentieth century—affect the formation of successful policy coalitions? How well does a pivotal politics model fit in a period in which the left–right continuum fails to capture the main movements of legislative politics? We now have measures of lawmaking that extend back to 1789 (though we lack measures of policy demand before the mid-twentieth century), but thus far they have been used to test Mayhew-type models. Whether and how such models might need to be amended to capture the political and institutional context of the nineteenth century remains unknown.

The last handbook of legislative research, appearing in the 1970s, could be forgiven for not including a chapter on legislative productivity and gridlock, given how little scholarship had been pursued on the topic. Soon thereafter, however, the persistence of divided governments and the bouts of stalemate that sometimes accompanied them put the macro-politics of Congress back on the table. Adherents of strong parties in the 1980s got to the table first, bemoaning the harm done by divided control and helping to spur Mayhew's agenda-setting contribution that questioned whether divided government really mattered after all. It is perhaps ironic then that the major formal theoretical contribution in this area in the form of the pivotal politics model posited no analytical role for parties in the dynamics of lawmaking. As many students of Congress push to reconsider the relevance of parties in lawmaking, debates about how best to measure, model, and test for the relative importance of rules, preferences, and parties will no doubt remain high on scholars' agendas.

References

BINDER, S. A. 1999. The Dynamics of Legislative Gridlock: 1947–1996. *American Political Science Review*, 93: 519–33.
—— 2003. *Stalemate: Causes and Consequences of Legislative Stalemate*. Washington, DC: Brookings Institution Press.
—— 2008. Taking the Measure of Congress: Reply to Chiou and Rothenberg. *Political Analysis*, 16(2): 213–25.
BRADY, D., and VOLDEN, C. 1998. *Revolving Gridlock*. Boulder, CO: Westview Press.
CHAMBERLAIN, L. 1946. *The President, Congress and Legislation*. New York: Columbia University Press.
CHIOU, F. Y., and ROTHENBERG, L. 2003. When Pivotal Politics Meets Party Politics. *American Journal of Political Science*, 47(3): 503–22.
—— —— 2008. Comparing Legislators and Legislatures: The Dynamics of Legislative Gridlock Reconsidered. *Political Analysis*, 16(2): 197–212.
CLINTON, J., and LAPINSKI, J. S. 2006. Measuring Legislative Accomplishment, 1877–1946. *American Journal of Political Science*, 50: 232–49.
COLEMAN, J. J. 1999. Unified Government, Divided Government, and Party Responsiveness. *American Political Science Review*, 93(4): 821–35.
COOPER, J. 1988 [1960]. *Congress and Its Committees*. New York: Garland.
COX, G., and McCUBBINS, M. 2005. *Setting the Agenda*. New York: Cambridge University Press.
EDWARDS, III, G. C., BARRETT, A., and PEAKE, J. 1997. The Legislative Impact of Divided Government. *American Journal of Political Science*, 41(2): 545–63.
ERIKSON, R. S., MACKUEN, M. B., and STIMSON, J. A. 2002. *The Macro Polity*. New York: Cambridge University Press.
FEREJOHN, J., and SHIPAN, C. 1990. Congressional Influence on the Bureaucracy. *Journal of Law, Economics, and Organization*, 6(SI): 1–20.
FIORINA, M. 1996. *Divided Government*. 2nd edition. Boston: Allyn and Bacon.
GRANT, T. J., and KELLY, N. J. 2008. Legislative Productivity of the U.S. Congress, 1789–2004. *Political Analysis*, 16: 303–23.
GUNNELL, J. G. 2006. The Founding of the American Political Science Association: Discipline, Profession, Political Theory, and Politics. *American Political Science Review*, 100(4): 479–86.
HAMMOND, T. H., and MILLER, G. J. 1987. The Core of the Constitution. *American Political Science Review*, 81(4): 1155–74.
HEITSHUSEN, V., and YOUNG, G. 2006. Macropolitics and Changes in the U.S. Code: Testing Competing Theories of Policy Production, 1874–1946, pp. 129–50 in *The Macropolitics of Congress*, ed. E. S. Adler and J. Lapinski. Princeton, NJ.: Princeton University Press.
HELLER, W. B. 1997. Bicameralism and Budget Deficits: The Effect of Parliamentary Structure on Government Spending. *Legislative Studies Quarterly*, 12(4): 485–516.
HOWELL, W., ADLER, E. S., CAMERON, C., and RIEMANN, C. 2005. Divided Government and the Legislative Productivity of Congress, 1945–1994. *Legislative Studies Quarterly*, (25): 285–312.

JONES, C. O. 1994. *The Presidency in a Separated System.* Washington, Politics. *American Journal of Political Science,* 47(3): 503–22. DC: The Brookings Institution.

—— 1995. A Way of Life and Law. *American Political Science Review,* 89(1): 1–9.

JONES, D. R. 2001. Party Polarization and Legislative Gridlock. *Political Research Quarterly,* 54(1): 125–41.

KELLY, S. Q. 1993. Divided We Govern? A Reassessment. *Polity,* 25(3): 475–84.

KEY, JR., V. O. 1964. *Politics, Parties, and Pressure Groups.* 5th edition. New York: Thomas Y. Crowell Company.

KREHBIEL, K. 1998. *Pivotal Politics.* Chicago, IL: University of Chicago Press.

KRUTZ, G. S. 2000. Getting around Gridlock: The Effect of Omnibus Utilization on Legislative Productivity. *Legislative Studies Quarterly,* 25(4): 533–49.

LAPINSKI, J. S. 2008. Policy Substance and Performance in American Lawmaking, 1877–1994. *American Journal of Political Science,* 52(2): 235–51.

LEE, F. E. 2009. *Beyond Ideology: Politics, Principles, and Partisanship in the U.S. Senate.* Chicago, IL: University of Chicago Press.

LOEWENBERG, G., PATTERSON, S. C., and JEWELL, M. E. 1985. *The Handbook of Legislative Research.* Cambridge: Harvard University Press.

MALTZMAN, F., and SHIPAN, C. R. 2008. Change, Continuity and the Evolution of the Law. *American Journal of Political Science,* 52(2): 252–67.

MAYHEW, D. 1991. *Divided We Govern.* New Haven, CT: Yale University Press.

—— 2005a. *Divided We Govern.* 2nd edition. New Haven, CT: Yale University Press.

MAYHEW, D. R. 2005b. Wars and American Politics. *Perspectives on Politics,* 3(3): 473–93.

—— 2006. Lawmaking and History, pp. 241–50 in *The Macropolitics of Congress,* ed. E. S. Adler and J. S. Lapinski. Princeton, NJ: Princeton University Press.

McCARTY, N., and CUTRONE, M. 2006. Does Bicameralism Matter? *Handbook of Political Economy,* ed. D. Wittman and B. Weingast. New York: Oxford University Press.

—— POOLE, K., and ROSENTHAL, H. 2006. *Polarized America: The Dance of Ideology and Unequal Riches.* Cambridge, MA: MIT Press.

PATASHNIK, E. 2008. *Reforms at Risk: What Happens After Major Policy Changes are Enacted.* Princeton, NJ: Princeton University Press.

PRIMO, D. M., BINDER, S. A., and MALTZMAN, F. 2008. Who Consents? Competing Pivots in Federal Judicial Selection. *American Journal of Political Science,* 52(3): 471–89.

POLSBY, N. 1968. The Institutionalization of the House of Representatives. *American Political Science Review,* 62: 144–68.

POOLE, K., and ROSENTHAL, H. 1997. *Congress: A Political-Economic History of Roll Call Voting.* New York: Oxford University Press.

ROGERS, J. R. 2005. The Impact of Divided Government on Legislative Production. *Public Choice,* 123(1–2): 217–33.

SCHATTSCHNEIDER, E. E. 1942. Party Government. New York: Farrar & Rinehart.

SHEPSLE, K. A. 1989. Studying Institutions: Some Lessons from the Rational Choice Approach. *Journal of Theoretical Politics,* 1(2): 131–47.

SHIPAN, C. R. 2006. Does Divided Government Increase the Size of the Legislative Agenda? pp. 151–70 in The Macropolitics of Congress, ed. E. S. Adler and J. S. Lapinski. Princeton, NJ: Princeton University Press.

SINCLAIR, B. 2006. *Party Wars: Polarization and the Politics of National Policy Making.* Norman, OK: University of Oklahoma Press.

SMITH, S. S. 2007. *Party Influence in Congress.* New York: Cambridge University Press.

SUNDQUIST, J. L. 1968. *Politics and Policy; the Eisenhower, Kennedy, and Johnson Years.* Washington, DC: The Brookings Institution.

——1988–89. Needed: A Political Theory for the New Era of Coalition Government in the United States. *Political Science Quarterly*, 103(4): 613–35.

TAYLOR, A. J. 1998. Explaining Government Productivity. *American Politics Research*, 26(4): 439–58.

THORSON, G. R. 1998. Divided Government and the Passage of Partisan Legislation, 1947–1990. *Political Research Quarterly*, 51(3): 751–64.

TSEBELIS, G. 1995. Decision Making in Political Systems: Veto Players in Presidentialism, Parliamentarism, Multicameralism and Multipartyism. *British Journal of Political Science*, 25(3): 289–325.

——2002. *Veto Players: How Political Institutions Work*. Princeton, NJ: Princeton University Press.

WILSON, W. 1981 [1885]. *Congressional Government*. Baltimore, MD: The Johns Hopkins University Press.

PART VII

CONGRESSIONAL DEVELOPMENT

CHAPTER 29

....

THE DEVELOPMENT
OF CONGRESSIONAL
ELECTIONS

....

WENDY J. SCHILLER

To understand what we know today about the development of congressional elections requires thinking about scholarship as a path of intended and unintended consequences. The resources available to investigate and answer important questions about democratic institutions vary over time. How scholars choose which questions to study, and how each successive generation uses existing work, will have major consequences for our comprehensive understanding of political development. What we know—and what we do not know—about the development of congressional elections is a function of these decisions. In this chapter, I focus on what our scholarly choices have revealed about the capacity for congressional elections to serve as an effective electoral mechanism in a democracy, and what additional questions should be asked and answered by future generations.

It has been well documented how and why the Founders created a bicameral legislature and instituted different mechanisms for election to the House of Representatives and the U.S. Senate (e.g. Robertson 2005 and Jillson 2002). The House was apportioned by population, with the original configuration of 1 member per 30,000 residents in a state. Members of the House were directly elected by the people, and they served two-year terms. In the Senate, each state was given two senators who represented the entire state, served six years, and were elected by a majority of the members of both chambers of the state legislature. The Founders also divided the Senate membership into classes, which meant that senators from the same state would not run for election at the same time. The division into classes theoretically gave senators from the same state independence from each other. It also ensured stability for the state's Senate representation in that any temporary political tide would not sweep both senators from that state out of office simultaneously. For each chamber, the Constitution empowered the states to regulate when and how these elections occurred, with the caveat that Congress could at any time "make or alter such regulations" (see Article 1, Section 4). Historically, the most striking change that states made was to ratify the 17th Amendment on April 13, 1913, which gave voters the right to elect their senators directly.

GOING BACKWARDS IN TIME: THE EVOLUTION OF SCHOLARSHIP ON CONGRESSIONAL ELECTIONS

Our earliest source of knowledge about congressional elections was built on biographies about prominent political actors, or autobiographies written by the politicians themselves. The systematic study of aggregate trends in congressional elections did not begin until the mid- to late 1950s. As record-keeping methods improved and computational methods became more readily available, scholars turned their attention in earnest to collecting data on levels of turnout and participation in congressional and presidential elections (e.g. Burnham 1965; Rusk 1970; Martis 1982). However, because of the time and labor costs involved in collecting historical data, the agenda-setting power of this research remained limited.

The 1970s marked a significant rise in the use of computer technology and statistical methods in political science generally, and scholars of congressional elections were at the head of the pack in analyzing modern trends. The widespread availability of survey data in the National Election Study, which was administered by the Center for Political Studies at the University of Michigan, focused attention on the amount of information voters held about candidates, and allowed hypothesis testing on which variables were included in their decision calculus. In addition, the 1971 Federal Elections Campaign Act implemented strict reporting requirements and transparency in campaign finance, which provided an entirely new set of data for scholars to analyze on the dynamics of fundraising in congressional elections and the actual impact of that money on the probability of winning an election. The availability of the NES survey opinion data, coupled with improved sources of information about voting patterns and campaign finance, created a synergy between scholars who wanted to advance the use of quantitative methods and scholars who were searching for answers to explain modern trends in congressional elections.

This emphasis on quantitative analysis of electoral returns also created a stark imbalance in the amount of active research that was conducted on the U.S.

Senate as compared with the House. The large N of the House, combined with the availability of voter survey and campaign finance data, made it a very attractive study subject. Several major works were produced that analyzed the variables that voters used to make their choice in House elections, as well as explain congressional election outcomes more generally (e.g. Mann 1978; Jacobson 1978; Mann and Wolfinger 1980), and this body of work set much of the agenda for the 1980s and 1990s. Scholars across the field of congressional studies, from graduate students to full professors, veered toward a study of the House over the Senate for very practical reasons.

Some scholars also used rational choice methods to explain candidate entry and success in congressional elections, and their techniques ranged from "soft" or descriptive rational theory to mathematical modeling. The work of Anthony Downs (1958) argued that, at the most general level, using the party affiliation of a candidate was a good predictor of future behavior in office and that voters used party affiliation as an informational shortcut. But subsequent rational choice work proposed that voters were more complex than that, and they sought to reconcile their political beliefs with the party platform offered by candidates in a specific election (Fiorina 1976). The real challenge to rational choice theorists who sought confirmation for party effects in congressional elections came from the fact that from the time Downs published his work through the 1980s, party loyalty among voters was declining (Jacobson 2004). Congressional campaigns had become highly candidate-centered throughout the 1970s and 1980s, with the candidates themselves deemphasizing their party affiliation (Wattenberg 1998, 1991). Jacobson and Kernell (1983) showed that such candidate behavior in this environment could still be rational; they argued that good quality challengers only entered congressional races when the incumbent was vulnerable, and that incumbents worked hard to maintain their own individual reputation to insulate themselves from any national trends that reflected badly on their party.

The contentious part of this approach was its assumption that both the candidate and the voter acted rationally when survey research had revealed that voters were generally uninformed about their congressperson's record. It was hard to argue that voters could be rational about their choice for Congress with so little information about the consequences of that choice. As such, the field of congressional elections remained divided as to whether voters used party identification, candidate promises, or incumbent legislative records, or some combination of all three factors, when they cast votes in House and Senate elections.

Even more challenging is the task of testing these two hypotheses on a long time series of voting behavior. Identifying these voting factors is important because the answers will either show that the nature of voting in congressional elections has fundamentally changed over the course of history, or the answers will show that voters judge Congress members much the same way as they did a century ago.

The work of Alford and Brady (1989) sheds light on the partisan versus personal incumbency advantage in congressional elections over time. They use two measures—retirement slump and sophomore surge—to describe the change in electoral margins in districts from 1846 to 1986. Retirement slump is the percentage of votes that the incumbent party loses when an incumbent retires, and the sophomore surge is the increase in percentage of votes that the winner of the open seat wins in his or her subsequent reelection campaign (1989, 160–1). Alford and Brady hypothesized that historically, if there was a personal component to incumbency advantage, the sophomore surge would be positive and the retirement slump would be negative, but they do not find consistent evidence of this pattern prior to the late 1960s. In other words, their work confirms that the personal component to incumbency advantage is a relatively new element in the history of congressional elections.

Moreover, the task of disentangling personal from partisan factors in explaining congressional electoral outcomes in the second half of the twentieth century is complicated by the fact that from 1954 to 1994, Democrats held control of the House. Even with the advent of sophisticated technical methods, with one party so dominant for so long, it is difficult to uncouple incumbency advantage from party affiliation for members of the majority party. Scholars have responded to this problem by extending the timeline for the study of congressional elections back into the late nineteenth century. The work of Ansolabehere, Snyder, and Stewart (2000) uses changes in district composition after redistricting to see how patterns of support changed for incumbent members of Congress, and they find that incumbents who were pushed into districts with less favorable partisan distributions still retained strong electoral support, regardless of challenger quality. Other scholars, notably Cox and Katz (2002), pointed to the interaction of redistricting with the quality of challengers and found that the quality of challengers had decreased notably over time, thus giving incumbents easier paths to reelection.

There is more work to be done to explain the nature of historical congressional elections. Of course, the lack of historical survey data presents a serious obstacle; without any evidence of exactly what voters were considering when they cast their ballots, the best that scholars can do is speculate as to the motivations for voters to support candidates and parties. It is distinctly possible that voters could have been making decisions on localized benefits, such as the availability of jobs and infrastructure, rather than exhibiting support for a consistent set of policy positions that comprised party platforms and holding a legislator accountable for his loyalty to that party platform on the House or Senate floor.

Unlike the study of House elections, where data had been readily available for decades, it was not until the Interuniversity Consortium for Political and Social Research (ICPSR) administered the Senate Election Study (SES) in 1988, 1990, and 1992 that scholars could attempt to study Senate elections in the same systematic way. There is an impressive body of work using this data (e.g. Westlye 1991; Abramowitz and Segal 1992; Krasno 1994; Sellers 1998; Kahn and Kenney 1999; Gronke 2001). These works pointed out that Senate elections were more competitive than House elections because the quality of challenger was typically better, senators had to win statewide without the luxury of redistricting, and there was typically more money spent on voter information than in House campaigns. Scholars found that voters were not particularly well informed about their incumbent senators; that party identification was a significant variable in predicting vote choice; and that national trends in the economy and foreign affairs affected Senate races more than House races.

Although these differences between House and Senate elections are significant, the same set of fundamental components: incumbency advantage, partisan affiliation, fundraising, and challenger quality have been shown to determine the outcome of both types of congressional elections. Although the limited duration of the SES restricted it as a resource for explaining changes in Senate electoral outcomes over time relative to the longer set of voter survey data available on House elections, this work showed that, in general, there were more similarities than differences in House and Senate election dynamics.

Fortunately for the study of congressional elections, a major upheaval occurred in 1994 when the Republicans took control of the House of Representatives as well as the U.S. Senate. Under the leadership of then Republican minority leader Newt Gingrich (Republican, GA) the Republicans mounted a two-pronged assault on Democratic control of the House by unifying the minority party against Democratic legislative proposals and constructing a single national platform (The Contract with America) for every Republican candidate to share. Gingrich took advantage of the culmination of a long trend of movement from the Democratic to Republican Party in the South, an unpopular sitting president (Bill Clinton), and the inability of Democrats to produce meaningful legislation in the preceding Congress. Gingrich also made full use of his fundraising ability to recruit qualified challengers, and support incumbent Republicans whom he perceived to be loyal to his vision of the party's platform (Herrnson 1995).

Representative Gingrich was subsequently elected Speaker of the House. Gingrich tried to maintain party loyalty in the chamber by persuading individual members that their probability of reelection would increase if the majority party accomplished its policy agenda. So long as the rank and file in the party voted together on the House floor, the majority party could claim success. In contrast, internal conflict within the party would create the perception that it was unable to govern which might reflect badly on individual members. This model kept the Republican Party electorally and institutionally dominant for the next twelve years, and during that time incumbency advantage shifted from an individualized focus to one based on a shared personal and partisan identity (Desposato and Petrocik 2003). At the same time, the shift in party allegiance in southern states from Democrat to Republican gave the Republicans a solid electoral base on which to base their majority party control (Lublin 2004).

The model of a single cohesive national governing party was emulated by the Democratic minority leader, Nancy Pelosi (D-CA) and Rahm Emanuel (D-IL), the chairman of the Democratic Congressional Campaign Committee. Together, they sought to nationalize the 2006 mid-term elections by emphasizing the Iraq War, the unpopularity of the Republican president, and several prominent scandals in the Republican Party that were characterized as an atmosphere of corruption (Jacobson 2007; Ceaser and DiSalvo 2007). Emanuel also sought out quality candidates to run in open seats or against vulnerable Republican incumbents in districts that had not previously been competitive for Democrats. These more moderate candidates were given significant resources to fund their campaigns and so long as they adhered to the three general themes of the national Democratic Party, they could tailor their messages on other issues (such as abortion, gun control, and farm policy) as they saw fit.

In the Senate, it has always been harder to coordinate all Senate candidates around a single set of issues because not all senators are up for reelection simultaneously, Senate campaigns are typically higher profile, and they involve a more complex set of local and national issues than House campaigns. Nonetheless, Minority leader Harry Reid (D-NV) and Senator Charles Schumer (D-NY) who headed the Democratic Senatorial Campaign Committee also relied on the Iraq War and the unpopularity of President Bush to reinforce Democratic incumbents and target Republican-held Senate seats. One component that was highly publicized in Senate campaigns was the importance of each individual Senate seat in granting the Democrats majority control. As it became increasingly likely that the Democrats would take control of the House, Senate Democratic leaders began emphasizing how crucial full majority control of Congress would be to slow or reverse Republican policy (Ceaser and DiSalvo 2007). The Democrats succeeded in winning back control of the House and Senate in 2006, and expanding their majority margin of control in the 2008 congressional elections. In the 2010 elections, the Republicans replicated the same party cohesion strategy as 1994 in that they ran against a unified Democratic Party majority government. Their electoral success in those elections, winning back majority control in the House and adding seats in the Senate, serves as reinforcement for the importance of party in modern congressional campaigns.

The resurgence of the national party in congressional elections and the internal workings of the House and Senate created new interest in the history of congressional behavior and elections. If it was true that voters ultimately used party as their key decision guide in congressional elections in the 1990s and 2000s, was that really any different from what they had done in the 1890s and 1900s? In other words, had the period of candidate-centered elections merely been a blip in congressional history, and the real foundation for congressional elections has always been party identification? To answer these questions requires applying modern data collection and quantitative tools to historical elections, and trying to do a better job of establishing parity in our understanding of House and Senate elections over time.

The pioneers of comprehensive systematic historical research on Congress focused primarily on institutional behavior (Polsby 1968; Kernell 1977), and modern scholars took up the mantle of this type of research in full force in the mid-1990s (Binder 1997; Schickler 2001; Wawro and Schickler 2007). It made perfect sense to build on our enhanced understanding of the path development of Congress with a comprehensive focus on congressional elections. Many of the obstacles to conducting systematic historical research have been removed or ameliorated by the digitalization of a wide range of archival data, including state and federal electoral records, local newspapers, and personal letters and diaries.

As more data is collected and disseminated, scholars have begun in earnest to test the applicability of modern theories of congressional elections on previous historical eras. In studying historical congressional elections, the overarching challenge is to conduct research that will parallel our understanding of modern congressional elections. As such, I propose the following five questions to guide this research:

- How did geographic boundaries influence congressional elections?
- What role did ballot structure and voting procedures play in electoral outcomes?
- How has party organization control of the nomination and general election process changed?
- How have congressional elections served as a mechanism of accountability over time?
- How have congressional elections served as instruments of participation and representation?

In seeking answers to these questions, scholars can construct a coherent explanation of congressional elections which pays attention to historic path development. In this effort, it is crucial to recognize that these factors influence House and Senate elections differently over time because of the different apportionment and election mechanisms for each chamber.

HOW DID GEOGRAPHIC BOUNDARIES INFLUENCE CONGRESSIONAL ELECTIONS?

The potential influence of geography has always been more obvious in the context of House elections than in Senate elections. The Constitution mandates a reapportionment of the number of congressional seats per state after every decennial census, and it does not specifically dictate that only one member may be elected from a single district. From 1789 to 1842, states could assign seats in Congress as they wished, and many states chose to draw multi-member districts, where candidates would compete in the same district for a set number of House seats (Calabrese 2000). Because multiple House seats were grouped this way, this type of system made it more likely that a single party would win most, if not all, of the congressional seats where the party was favored by the majority of voters. In single member districts, by contrast, there was only one seat at stake in each district, so parties did not have as much opportunity to convert a popular edge among voters into additional seats. In 1842, Congress passed the Apportionment Bill, which established the single member geographically bounded district as the standard unit of representation for the House. Although most states gradually adopted a single member district system, some states simply ignored this instruction, or adapted very slowly. As the number of multi-member districts declined over time, parties found it harder to sweep an entire state's House delegation.

It is after this point that gerrymandering, or rigging the boundaries of House districts, becomes very important. Even with federal instructions to assign a single member to a single district, states still retained the capacity to redraw district boundaries as they saw fit. For most of the nineteenth century, majority parties in states sought to maximize their seats by drawing House districts with as narrow partisan majorities as possible (Carson, Engstrom, and Roberts 2006). Such a system guaranteed big seat margins in years when the party was strong, both in the state and nationally, but it also left them vulnerable in years where there was a big shift in national political tides. By drawing House district lines in such a way, it appears that state legislators believed that voters responded to partisan cues when voting for members of the House.

In the Senate, there was no opportunity for gerrymandering because state boundaries were set and did not change as a result of census changes in population. However, because there are two senators representing the same geographic district, states can be considered multi-member districts and the election of a single U.S. senator is always made in the context of dual representation of the state (Schiller 2000). During indirect elections, in both the nomination and election process, state legislators considered how the candidates would match up with the other incumbent senator. From the very first Senate elections in the nation's history, the state legislature considered how they could balance the interests of the state in selecting a pair of senators. In doing so, they sought regional, political, and economic balance in constructing their Senate delegations: for example, if one senator was from the eastern part of the state, they would purposely seek to elect a senator from the western part of the state (Schiller 2006). Today, in the direct election period, voters make implicit and explicit comparisons between the sitting senators when they judge each of their performances in office (Schaffner, Schiller, and Sellers 2003).

WHAT ROLE DID BALLOT STRUCTURE AND VOTING PROCEDURES PLAY IN ELECTORAL OUTCOMES?

In addition to drawing the boundaries of House districts, states also determined ballot access as well as the type of ballot used in congressional elections. Engstrom and Kernell argue that "consolidated party ballots and efficient gerrymandering strategies" created a strong relationship between presidential voting and congressional election outcomes for most of the nineteenth century (2005, 533). They demonstrate a strong connection between House electoral outcomes and the vote for president after 1872, when Congress mandated that all House elections be held on the same day across the country every two years and be held on the same day as presidential elections every four years.

During the period 1840 to 1888, parties printed up ballots that listed all levels of elected office on them, and handed them to voters who then filled them out in plain sight. This type of ballot made it difficult to cast a split-ticket vote—that is, casting a vote for a candidate from one party for one office while voting for a candidate from another party for a different elected office. When the Australian ballot was introduced in 1888, it transferred the printing and control of ballots from parties to state governments, and provided that voters fill out the ballot in secret. Ballots came in two forms: party column where all the candidates from a single party would be listed in one column, and the office bloc, which listed each set of candidates for a specific electoral office together. In either form, these new ballots allowed voters to cross party lines, and because they could do so in private, party officials would never know for sure how they voted (Rusk 1970). Once the Australian ballot was widely introduced, voters had more freedom from straight party ticket balloting and the tight relationship between presidential vote totals and swings in congressional seats loosened (Engstrom and Kernell 2005). In combination with the introduction of the direct primary as a means of securing the party's nomination for office, local party organizations lost much of their control over House elections.

What once had been a sure bet at the ballot box for a dominant local or state party became less certain, and in order to guarantee control of House seats, state parties altered the way they gerrymandered House districts. During this era, before the policy of "one man, one vote" was instituted, state legislatures had a great deal of flexibility in terms of the size and configuration of congressional districts they created (Engstrom 2006). Prior to ballot reform, majority parties in state legislatures created as many districts as possible where they had a narrow majority of party supporters, counting on party loyalty among voters to maximize the number of congressional seats the party could win. After ballot reform, majority parties in state legislatures calculated that they needed districts with larger numbers of party supporters to ensure that they would win that district, which meant that supporters of the minority party would all be grouped together in as few districts as possible (Engstrom 2006). As such, majority parties solidified their probability of winning a certain number of House seats, while conceding as few House seats to the minority party as possible.

From 1789 to 1914, U.S. senators were chosen in state legislatures and not directly by voters, therefore the type of ballot was not a factor in electoral outcomes, and the change in ballot type had little direct impact on the electoral process in state legislatures. In contrast to the House of Representatives, state legislatures were free to set the parameters for how and when they selected their U.S. Senators. For the first seventy-seven years of the nation's history, there was no uniform procedure dictating when and how states should select their senators, and as a result, factional and regional conflict in states frequently results in deadlocks, delayed elections, and rampant corruption.

In response to the chaos that marked Senate elections in state elections, the Federal government enacted an 1866 law regulating Senate elections in all states. It required that each state legislature meet at noon on the second Tuesday after the start of their legislative year and vote for a U.S. senator. Each chamber of the state legislature would meet separately, and if a majority of each chamber selected the same candidate, the next day the entire legislature would convene in joint assembly to certify that a senator was elected. However, if no candidate had garnered a majority in the separate elections in each chamber, then the state legislature would convene in joint assembly the next day to elect a senator. If no decision was reached on that day, the state legislature would have to convene in joint session every day of their legislative year until a choice was made, or until they adjourned. If the state legislature adjourned without selecting a senator, the Governor could appoint a U.S. senator to hold the seat for the remainder of the congressional session. However, many governors were reluctant to go over the heads of the state legislators for fear of damaging their own political prospects in their state.

The structure of the indirect voting process for Senate greatly enhanced the power of the Republican Party at the national level for two key reasons. First, more state legislatures were controlled by the Republican Party than by the Democratic Party, and second, the Republican Party effectively used their power to redistrict state legislative seats in such a way as to give themselves a strong electoral advantage. Republicans tended to be much stronger in rural areas within and across states, so they carved up state legislative districts in rural areas to maximize the number of seats they could win in both the state House and state Senate (Stewart and Weingast 1992; King and Ellis 1996). Greater numerical strength in state legislatures translated into the election of Republicans to the U.S. Senate in significant numbers to give them a working majority for most of the latter nineteenth century. In addition, Republicans were dominant in the eleven western territories that became states from the 1870s to 1912, which added to their numerical strength in the U.S. Senate (Stewart and Weingast 1992). From 1871 through 1913, Republicans were the majority party in the Senate for twenty Congresses, while the Democrats held control for two Congresses. In contrast, from 1914 to 2008, Democrats controlled the Senate for thirty-two Congresses, and Republicans held control for fifteen Congresses.[1] Clearly, Republicans benefited greatly from the combination of indirect elections and disproportionate numerical strength in state legislatures.

How has party organization control of the nomination and general election process changed?

Samuel Kernell published a groundbreaking article in 1977 which argued that the decline in party competition at the district level and the disappearance of the norm of rotation facilitated the careers of ambitious politicians who saw value in winning a House seat as a means of building an individual career as a politician (Kernell

---

[1] United States Senate. Office of the Senate Historian, "Party Division in the Senate 1789-Present." http://www.senate.gov/pagelayout/history/one_item_and_teasers/partydiv.htm (accessed December 29, 2009).

1977, 690–2). Kernell tested three explanations for the longer careers in the House of Representatives: decline in party competition, local norms of rotation of congressional seats, and a rise in the personal ambition of elected officials. He found that, in fact, the number of House members who sought reelection increased before party competition began to decline. Kernell also looked at local norms of rotation, where parties would select and support House nominees with the tacit agreement that they would only serve one or two terms and then return to the district with the hopes of securing a different office or some other form of localized benefit. He showed that the norm of rotation declined nationwide, due mostly to the difficulty parties faced in controlling nominations to office. With the decline in enforced rotation, aspiring candidates to the House, as well as incumbent members, could take greater charge of their own opportunities to run for Congress.

Carson and Roberts (2006) add to Kernell's work by studying incumbency advantage and challenger quality between 1874 and 1914. They find that while the aggregate fate of each party ebbed and flowed, the impetus to run for office looked very much the same as it does in modern congressional elections. In amassing and analyzing an original data set on the quality of challengers, Carson and Roberts find that quality challengers picked races where they had a good chance to win, that is, where the incumbent's prior margin of victory was slim or where there was an open seat. The fact that there is nearly a twenty-year gap in these two articles points out the large opportunity for increased scholarship on the extent of party control over elections to the House.

To date, there is much less published work on the role of political parties in electing U.S. senators in the nineteenth century, from the candidate selection process to the actual balloting. With the exception of Mayhew's *Placing Parties in America* (1986), scholars have developed little systematic evaluation of the actual strength and cohesiveness of state party organizations in the late nineteenth century. There are stylized facts about different city machines or factions scattered across historical accounts, but we do not have a concrete measure of party strength in terms of commanding the consistent loyalty of elected officials at all levels in state government. One exception is the ongoing research by Gamm and Kousser (2010) on political and factional dynamics within state legislatures. Their work has revealed that, even within the same party, regional factions caused conflict in the distribution of what were otherwise universalistic benefits to constituents.

But we are still left with a big black hole in understanding the environment in which Senate elections occurred during the indirect election period. In fact, all we know from the existing literature is that the vast majority of U.S. senators elected during indirect elections were from the majority party in the legislature. There have been significant obstacles to studying Senate elections in state legislatures, primarily due to the resource costs associated with collecting and analyzing archival data on a wide scale. Charles Stewart III and I have begun to address this gap by constructing the *U.S. Senate Election Data Base 1871–1913* using data from state House and Senate journals, newspaper archives, and state records on all elections for U.S. Senate in state legislatures, as well as the party affiliation (where available) of all state legislators who served during this period.[2]

In all, we have confirmed that 733 elections for U.S. Senate seats were held in state legislatures for the Senate seats spanning 1871 to 1913. Any member of the state legislature in either chamber could nominate someone to run for U.S. Senate, and these nominations took place after the state legislature had convened its session. In general, these candidates were selected from the states' political and business elite, such as state legislators, business owners, and in some cases even governors (Schiller 2006). Of Senate elections held during this time period, 69 percent were settled on the first ballot and 29 percent required a joint ballot, meaning that no candidate secured a majority on the first ballot held separately in each chamber.[3]

The elections that occurred without extended conflict tended to be in states where the majority party managed to choose a nominee before the balloting started, a choice usually dictated by party bosses and wealthy economic actors in the state. However, there were a non-trivial number of cases where the majority party failed to reach a consensus before the onset of balloting. For conflictual Senate elections, the number of joint ballots ranged from 1 to 209; 27 percent of these elections were resolved on the first joint ballot, 11 percent were resolved in four or fewer joint ballots, and 62 percent were resolved in greater than four joint session ballots. On average, it took state legislatures thirty-four joint session ballots to resolve highly conflictual elections (Schiller and Stewart n.d.) In such cases, there were multiple nominees from the same party, and even an incumbent senator had to worry about being officially renominated for office; because of turnover in state legislatures, he was facing an almost entirely new set of legislators from those that had previously elected him. The fact that, in some states, parties failed to coalesce around a single nominee on a consistent basis prior to the onset of balloting is the first clue that state party organizations varied considerably in their ability to control the gateways to the U.S. Senate.

State legislators did not act alone in shifting their support during these contested Senate elections. Legislators shifted their votes in bloc, which may suggest the existence of regional coalitions, or an effort by party leaders to either secure a victory for their preferred candidate, or the success of the minority party in blocking the majority party from coalescing around a victor. There was also a level of corruption in these elections, in which candidates themselves would spread money throughout the legislature to secure votes; the problem for a candidate trying to buy a Senate election was that they would have to start over after every failed joint ballot. For example, in the Montana Senate election of 1899, William Clark, a Democrat, faced off against W. G. Conrad, a Republican, and both men vigorously spent money to secure votes on each ballot. One of Clark's targeted legislators testified before a House Select Committee investigating corruption charges that "They claimed to have bought an equal number of republicans and democrats, but they would not pay over five

---

[2] At this time, the type of resolution for 2% of these elections is still undetermined.
[3] At this time, the type of resolution for 1% of these elections is still undetermined.

thousand dollars for republicans." (*Montana House Journal*, January 8, 1899, 31). There were a total of eighteen ballots in that election, and Clark emerged the winner but he was not seated because the election was deemed corrupt.[4] In some elections, the state legislature was unable to reach a decision before they adjourned; in the period 1871–1913, there were seventeen Senate seats that went unfilled as a result of an inability to elect a candidate.

The major unanswered question here is what drove the conflict in state legislatures over the choice for U.S. Senate. Part of the explanation rests in the size of the majority and minority parties in the legislature; in states with very narrow margins of control or lopsided margins of control, conflict was more likely. In the former case, if the majority party failed to walk in the door with a preferred candidate, they would split their majority and allow the minority to offer up its own alternatives. In states with a single dominant party, especially in southern states under one party rule, regional and personal factions existed and control of Senate elections was part of a larger set of benefits afforded to a specific faction. Lastly, the effort to create extended balloting was also a purposeful strategy by minority parties to block the addition of another majority party senator to the U.S. Senate roster; for them, it was better to have no sitting senator at all. Surprisingly variables, such as state size, region, and year of entry into the Union, did not exert a significant effect on the likelihood of conflict in Senate elections.

The number and intensity of conflictual Senate elections in state legislatures declined after 1900. Much of this decline can be attributed to the introduction of a wider use of nominating conventions, direct primaries, and pseudo popular elections of senators, where Senate candidates' names would be placed on the state ballot and voters could register their preferences as a guide to the state legislatures (Lapinski 2000; Campbell, Cox, and McCubbins 2002). There was also a growing movement to adopt a Constitutional amendment to institute the direct election of U.S. senators. At the same time, the state legislature was becoming a more important stepping stone to higher office, and even a short-term career in and of itself. As the state legislatures became more professional and measures of public input into the choice for U.S. senator became more commonly used, state legislators had greater incentives to rally around specific individuals early in the Senate election process.

The transition between indirect and direct elections to the U.S. Senate that began officially in 1914 turned out to be far less traumatic than anyone might have predicted. Work examining the impact of the 17th Amendment converges on the conclusion that the behavior and responsiveness of senators was not markedly different in the two time periods (Stewart 1992; King and Ellis 1996; Brandes Crook and Hibbing 1997; Wirls 1999; Bernhard and Sala 2006; Wawro and Schickler 2007; Gailmard and Jenkins 2009). There were two visible impacts on the Senate as a result of the switch from indirect to direct elections: senators' terms in office tended to be longer, and Democrats won far more Senate seats. Surprisingly, there were few significant changes

---

[4] Mr. Clark ran for the U.S. Senate again in 1901, won that election, and was allowed to take his seat.

in the type of people elected to the Senate, their party loyalty, and their legislative portfolios.

However, it would be inaccurate to suggest that Senate campaigns themselves have not changed at all since 1914. Senators are much more vulnerable to intra-party challenge by virtue of the direct primary, and they can rely less on party machines to turn out the vote on their behalf. Senators still cultivate local party and elected officials and seek their endorsements, but they run for office as candidates distinct from the state party organization. Partisanship is still a major factor in Senate campaigns, and voters tend to judge Senate candidates in the context of their party's national issue positions, and if they are incumbents, their performance in office (Abramowitz and Segal 1992).

HOW HAVE CONGRESSIONAL ELECTIONS SERVED AS A MECHANISM OF ACCOUNTABILITY OVER TIME?

One relatively underexplored topic is the extent to which congressional elections served as a referendum on the job performance of individual members of the House and Senate. For the first century of our history, scholars generally agree that serving in the House of Representatives was a short-term occupation (Polsby 1968; Kernell 1977). Kernell writes that for most of the nineteenth century the House was merely a "temporary way-station where anonymous amateurs and professional politicians alike stopped over on their way to other careers" (Kernell 1977, 671), and Polsby adds that the average member of Congress served no more than two terms in office in the nineteenth century (Polsby 1968, 146). It can be argued that members who were serving for only a short time in the House would have been less concerned with voter reaction than those who wanted to make a career out of House service. Coupled with party dominance over congressional elections, individual members were most likely viewed as an extension of their party and not held individually accountable.

However, some scholars argue that a lack of long-term ambition in the House did not preclude responsiveness to public opinion back home in the district. Bianco, Spence, and Wilkerson (1996) use historical evidence, both anecdotal and quantitative, on the Compensation Act of 1816, which was essentially a pay raise for members of Congress, to study responsiveness. They show that members who voted for the Compensation Act of 1816 were less likely to run for reelection than members who voted against it, and that the number of these "voluntary retirements" was higher than expected due to the negative reaction that the bill engendered among constituents. Carson and Engstrom (2005) looked at the election of 1826–27 and demonstrated that members of Congress who went against their constituents' wishes in the 1824 presidential election were more likely to lose their bids for reelection than members whose vote aligned with their district. That suggests a combination of individual accountability in congressional elections and the emergence of constituents' expectations of partisan loyalty by their House members.

There were other means of addressing constituents' needs besides, or in addition to, party line voting. Wilson's (1986) analysis of the 1889–1913 demonstrated a pattern of universalism in the provision of appropriations for river and harbors across House districts. Wilson claims that even in a period not dominated by a reelection incentive, House members valued district level benefits to facilitate their prospects once they left the House and returned to their districts. Whether they sought higher or lateral electoral office back home, or merely wanted to use federal projects to cement local business connections, the House as an institution engaged in universalistic pork barrel politics before the modern reelection motive was firmly established. In the absence of good survey data from this period of history, it is not possible to know exactly how much value voters put on these projects. We do know that such behavior persists today, in an era where getting elected and reelected to the House of Representatives is viewed as a full time career, which suggests that securing local benefits always held electoral value.

With respect to the Senate, the conventional wisdom has been that state legislative elections created an electoral connection between the voters and their senators, otherwise known as the public canvass. The works of Haynes (1906), Riker (1955), and Rothman (1966) all depict an electoral world where candidates for U.S. Senate aligned publicly with state legislators as the latter were running for election, and the entire enterprise was coordinated by their state party organizations. These alliances were viewed as a type of campaign pledge by a state legislator that, if elected, he would vote for a specific Senate candidate in the legislature.

However, there is good reason to suspect that the canvass was not an effective intermediate link between voters and senators. Because Senate elections took place after the state legislatures commenced their sessions, and most members of state legislatures did not typically serve more than one term, there was little in the way of accountability for this pledge (Schiller 2006). There was no doubt that candidates for the Senate would court candidates who were running for state legislative seats, but as noted above, a campaign pledge held no guarantee once balloting for the Senate seat began in earnest. The evidence cited above points again to the precarious nature of the campaign pledge a state legislator made to support a specific candidate. Such a pledge was easy to keep if the candidate in question garnered majority support on the first or second ballot. But in many of the extended ballot elections, state legislators quickly abandoned their original vote choice when it appeared he would not carry a majority in joint assembly. Once that happened, any electoral connection between the voters, a campaign pledge, and the state legislator disappeared.

Given the unpredictability of state legislators in honoring their campaign pledges, Senate candidates and incumbents crafted a two-pronged electoral approach; they aligned with state legislators and they made direct appeals to constituents. Schiller (2006) shows that even though the canvass did not guarantee state legislators' support, it was an effective means of establishing name recognition across the state.

Once elected, senators made a point of addressing local constituent needs through private bills and appropriations to shore up their statewide reputation. In effect, senators wanted to make themselves valuable assets to their state party organization, hoping that such loyalty would be rewarded with reelection. If that strategy failed, then senators could always point to their statewide popularity as a reason for members of the legislature to reelect them. Consequently the same types of characteristics and campaign behavior could be successfully employed in both indirect and direct electoral environments, which is one reason why scholars have had difficulty showing that the adoption of the 17th Amendment dramatically increased accountability in Senate elections.

How have congressional elections served as instruments of participation and representation?

Intrinsically linked to the concept of accountability in congressional elections is the question of how such elections enhance political participation and representation. Do we see a markedly different type of House member in the modern versus historical era of Congress? Did the norm of party rotation actually succeed in bringing a diverse range of representation to a district over time? What do we know about the evolution of the demographic characteristics of members of Congress over time?

Existing literature tells us a good deal about congressional candidates over time, but the majority of our information consists of data on the candidates who actually won and entered the House. There is far less information about candidates who ran but lost their election bids for the House and Senate. It is clear that the demographic characteristics of members of the House have changed over time. For example, in 1800, only 40 percent of members of the House had any college education, but by 1900, that number had risen to 62 percent, and by 2009, nearly 94 percent of members had some college education (Bogue, Clubb, et al. 1976; Amer and Manning 2009). Professionally, a background in law has always been the dominant occupation for members who get elected to Congress; in 1800 nearly 45 percent of members had a background in law; in 2009, 38 percent of members reported being a lawyer prior to coming to Congress. What has also changed strikingly is the percentage of members who report some business background; in 1800 only 13 percent of members came from a business occupation and that percentage rose to 38 percent in 2009, which is equal to the percentage of members who report law as their occupation. The average age of members of Congress has also increased over our history; in 1900, he was 45, in 2009, he or she was 50 years old. These numbers should be placed in context because the average life expectancy was only 47 years in 1900, whereas today it averages 78, which means that current House members are young relative to their historical counterparts.[5]

Another characteristic of successful candidates for Congress that has varied considerably over our history is the percentage of members with some military service. In 1800, 54 percent of members reported some military service, in 1900, that number had fallen to 31 percent, in the 1970s it rose again to 70 percent, and in 2009, it fell to 23 percent. (Bianco 2005; Amer and Manning 2009). The actual supply of candidates for Congress in a congressional election who have served in the military is strongly influenced by the temporal proximity and size of U.S. military conflicts; and the electoral value of being a military veteran will also depend on the public view of the particular military conflict in which the candidate served. Another element of congressional membership that has changed over time is the percentage of members who had a relative who served in Congress, either before or with them; in 1800, we had a high of 34 percent of members with a relative who also served in the House, but by 1900 that percentage had dropped to 12 percent, and in 2009, only 10 percent of the members of the House reported any connection to relatives in Congress.

For most of the nation's history, legal and de facto barriers to political participation drastically limited men and women of color from serving in the House and Senate. Men of color briefly served during the period of Reconstruction, but due to Jim Crow laws in the South and widespread discrimination in the North they were effectively prevented from running and winning congressional office. The first post-Reconstruction African American elected to Congress was Oscar Stanton DePriest, a Republican elected in 1928 from Illinois who served three terms.[6] The first Hispanic Representative in Congress was Romualdo Pacheco, a Republican from California elected in 1876.[7] Although women were not granted the vote by the federal government until the 19th Amendment was ratified in 1920, the first female Representative was Jeanette Rankin, a Republican from Montana who was elected to Congress in 1917 (Montana had granted women the vote in 1914).[8] In the 111th House of Representatives (2009–2010), there were 41 (8 percent) African Americans; 27 Hispanic members (5 percent), and 76 women (17 of whom were African American).

In the Senate, the historical research is less comprehensive and the demographic history far less diverse; the vast majority of U.S. senators have been white men both in the time of indirect and direct elections. The first post-Reconstruction African-

[5] U.S. Census Bureau. *The 2003 Statistical Abstract*. Washington DC: Government Printing Office, pp. 26–7. Accessed online at http://www.census.gov/compendia/statab/hist_stats.html; U.S. Center for National Health Statistics, National Vital Statistics Report (NVSR) *Deaths: Final Data for 2006*, 57(14), April 17, 2009.

[6] U.S. House of Representatives. Office of History and Preservation, Office of the Clerk, *Black Americans in Congress, 1870–2007*. Washington, DC: U.S. Government Printing Office, 2008. Accessed online at http://baic.house.gov/member-profiles/profile.html?intID=28 (accessed June 2, 2009).

[7] U.S. House of Representatives. Office of the Clerk, U.S. House of Representatives, *House History Timeline*. Note that Joseph Marion Hernandez served as a delegate from the Florida territory in 1822. Accessed online at http://clerk.house.gov/art_history/timeline/xml/1800events.xml.

[8] U.S. House of Representatives. Office of History and Preservation, Office of the Clerk, *Women in Congress, 1917–2006*. Washington, DC: U.S. Government Printing Office, 2007. Accessed online at http://womenincongress.house.gov (accessed June 2, 2009).

American elected to the Senate was Senator Edward Brooke (R-MA) who served from 1967 to 1979. The first female elected to the Senate was Hattie Wyatt Caraway (D-AR) who served from 1931 to 1945. And the first Hispanic elected to the Senate to serve a full term was Dennis Chavez (D-NM) who served from 1935 to 1962. The 111th Congress (2009–10) included one African-American senator (appointed), two Hispanic senators, and seventeen female senators.

The study of race and gender in congressional elections is dominated by the study of House elections for the simple reason that there is still too little diversity in Senate candidates and winners to produce systematic conclusions. In fact, some scholars have argued that the apportionment of Senate seats itself is a structural barrier to enhanced minority power (Lee and Oppenheimer 2002; Griffin 2006). The study of race and gender in Congress is well documented in Chapter 11, this volume, where Michele Swers and Stella Rouse provide a comprehensive analysis of current literature in those areas.

There are several areas within this broad subset of work that can be expanded in the context of congressional elections. For example, there has been little systematic research conducted on the effect of being both a woman and a member of a minority group on the probability of winning a congressional election. There have also been too few cases, particularly in the Senate, which have involved women or men of color challenging each other in a competitive election. Until the numbers of these types of elections rise, it will be difficult for scholars to unpack the effects of minority status from the current category of "non-white" to get at the underlying differences in racial and ethnic dynamics in congressional elections.

With an increasingly diverse electorate, it seems logical for political science to broaden the study of race, gender, and ethnicity in congressional elections. Moreover, the election of the first African-American president, Democrat Barack Obama, exerted an impact in congressional elections, in both the candidate and voter arenas. As color and gender lines become more muted over time, the styles and agendas of members of the House and Senate may reflect a convergence of interests across these traditional dividing lines, or produce starker divisions between different smaller subgroups of members.

FUTURE AVENUES FOR RESEARCH

Over the next decade, there are five broad areas of study that can help produce a continuous and coherent analysis of the evolution of congressional elections. Just as the study of congressional elections has been at the forefront in methodological changes in political science, progress on these topics will keep congressional election scholarship on the cutting edge.

Political parties

Political science has focused on the role of political parties as organizations and party identification as a strong informational cue to voters. Emerging scholars might take the field forward by trying to identify the extent to which political parties coordinated efforts to win both House and Senate elections over time, despite the fact that the U.S. constitutional design works to prevent such coordination. The end of the nineteenth century witnessed a fracturing of party coordination whereas the end of the twentieth century was witness to a resurgence of party coordination. Using a case study approach, scholars could choose a sample of states and collect data on party activities, including platforms, partisan newspaper coverage, joint candidate rallies, and fundraising efforts, to draw a fuller picture of the ebb and flow of party coordination over congressional elections over time.

Candidate emergence

One of the striking similarities between the historical and modern eras of congressional elections is the upward mobility of legislators as candidates. Existing work shows that state legislators were prime candidates for the House of Representatives, and in turn, House members comprised the bulk of potential candidates for the U.S. Senate; this was true a century ago and it is still true today. How did this trajectory influence the content and strategy of the campaigns themselves? How did it affect the representational link between elections and legislative behavior? To answer these questions, researchers could compare campaigns and electoral success for candidates with legislative experience to those without such experience over different eras in history. Such a perspective could inform us as to the relative value of holding legislative office over time to voters in congressional elections.

Impact of social movements over time

How are social movements and shifting social values reflected in congressional elections? There are excellent studies of the impact of the progressive movement, women's suffragette, and even civil rights on elections in a broad sense. But scholars have yet to systematically compare the tactics that groups used to influence elections in different eras of history to the tactics employed by today's activists on the issues of same sex marriage and immigration. The scholarship on congressional elections is frequently too focused on campaign contributions as the single marker for group influence. There is a local basis for social activism and group influence that is less studied; comparing campaign positions within and across state congressional delegations might reveal variation in group influence over space and time.

Geography, population movements, and redistricting

Redistricting has remained a powerful environmental determinant for House elections but the primary focus of studies in this area has been shifts in partisan populations. Equally relevant to election outcomes are the demographic changes that have occurred across districts over time, especially over the last decade of the twentieth century and the first decade of the twenty-first century. The combination of immigration and population changes has changed the character of many House districts such that elections are being waged differently than in the past, on dimensions such as home style, issue content, and ideology. But American history has seen such changes before, especially at the end of the nineteenth century. Candidates and political parties react to such changes in concrete ways, and with the weapon of digital technology, scholars can demonstrate the variation in response across a wide range of districts.

Technological innovation in campaign communication

The twenty-first century congressional campaign employs methods of communication that nineteenth- and twentieth-century candidates might never have dreamed of using to win elective office. Most candidates have Facebook (www.facebook.com) pages, Twitter accounts, and frequently post speeches and campaign appearances on YouTube (www.youtube.com). Twenty years ago, incumbents relied on hard copy newsletters and today their constituents receive email updates from them, and in some cases, brief text messages. Incumbents and challengers in congressional campaigns for the House and the Senate are more publicly exposed on every level than ever before in history. For survey researchers, this poses a new challenge and opportunity to study how this widespread information about candidates is processed and used by voters to make their choice. For example, how does the information overload affect the use of party identification as an informational shortcut? Is it harder for candidates to distinguish themselves from each other in a world full of political noise? Given all these relatively free media outlets that are available to reach voters, how might technological innovation undermine the importance of money in buying advertising?

One of the aims of this chapter was to point out where studies of House and Senate elections could come together under one theoretical umbrella and where the construct of the rules of the elections to each chamber prohibit the development of an all-encompassing theory of elections. Scholars in this subfield have expanded our understanding of congressional elections by building on the work of past generations, and the twenty-first century has brought a welcome balance between the study of House and Senate elections. It is crucial to recognize that House and Senate elections can be studied jointly so long as researchers acknowledge that the same set of variables will likely exert differential effects. In this way we can achieve a more holistic understanding of the evolution of congressional elections.

REFERENCES

ABRAMOWITZ, A., and SEGAL, J. A. 1992. *Senate Elections*. Ann Arbor: University of Michigan Press.

ALFORD, J. R., and BRADY, D. W. 1989. Personal and Partisan Advantage in U.S. Congressional Elections, 1846–1986, pp. 141–57 in *Congress Reconsidered*, 4th edn, ed. L. C. Dodd and B. I. Oppenheimer. Washington, DC: Congressional Quarterly Inc.

AMER, M., and MANNING, J. 2009. Membership of the 111th Congress: A Profile. Washington, DC: Congressional Research Service.

ANSOLABEHERE, S., SNYDER, JR., J. M., and STEWART, III, C. 2000. Old Voters, New Voters, and the Personal Vote: Using Redistricting to Measure the Incumbency Advantage. *American Journal of Political Science*, 44(1): 17–34.

BERNHARD, W., and SALA, B. R. 2006. The Remaking of an American Senate: The 17th Amendment and Ideological Responsiveness. *Journal of Politics*, 68: 345–57.

BIANCO, W. T. 2005. Last Post for the "Greatest Generation": The Policy Implications of the Decline of Military Experience in the U.S. Congress. *Legislative Studies Quarterly*, 30: 85–102.

——Spence, D. B., and Wilkerson, J. D. 1996. The Electoral Connection in the Early Congress: The Case of the Compensation Act of 1816. *American Journal of Political Science*, 40(1): 145–71.

BINDER, S. A. 1997. *Minority Rights, Majority Rule: Partisanship and the Development of Congress*. New York: Cambridge University Press.

BOGUE, A., CLUB, J. M., McKIBBIN, C. M., and TRAUGOTT, S. A. 1976. Members of the House of Representatives and the Process of Modernization, 1789–1960. *Journal of American History*, 63: 275–302.

BRANDES CROOK, S., and HIBBING, J. R. 1997. A Not-so-distant Mirror: The 17th Amendment and Congressional Change. *American Political Science Review*, 91: 845–53.

BURNHAM, W. D. 1965. The Changing Shape of the American Political Universe. *American Political Science Review*, 59(1): 7–28.

CALABRESE, S. 2000. Multimember District Congressional Elections. *Legislative Studies Quarterly*, 25(4): 611–36.

CAMPBELL, A. C., COX, G. W., and McCUBBINS, M. D. 2002. Agenda Power in the U.S. Senate 1877–1986, pp. 146–65 in *Party, Process, and Political Change in Congress*, ed. D. W. Brady and M. D. McCubbins. Stanford: Stanford University Press.

CARSON, J. L., and ENGSTROM, E. J. 2005. Assessing the Electoral Connection: Evidence from the Early United States. *American Journal of Political Science*, 49(4): 746–57.

————and ROBERTS, J. M. 2006. Redistricting, Candidate Entry, and the Politics of Nineteenth Century U.S. House Elections. *American Journal of Political Science*, 50(2): 283–93.

——and ROBERTS, J. M. 2006. Strategic Politicians and U.S. House Elections, 1874–1914. *Journal of Politics*, 67(2): 474–96.

CEASER, J. W., and DISALVO, D. 2007. Midterm Elections, Partisan Context, and Political Leadership: The 2006 Elections and Party Alignment. *The Forum*, Berkeley, CA: The Berkeley Electronic Press.

COX, G. W., and KATZ, J. N. 2002. *Elbridge Gerry's Salamander: The Electoral Consequences of the Reapportionment Revolution*. New York: Cambridge University Press.

DESPOSATO, S. W., and PETROCIK, J. R. 2003. The Variable Incumbency Advantage: New Voters, Redistricting, and the Personal Vote. *American Journal of Political Science*, 47(1): 18–32.

DOWNS, A. M. 1958. *An Economic Theory of Democracy*. New York: Harper & Row.

ENGSTROM, E. J. 2006. Stacking the States, Stacking the House: The Partisan Consequences of Redistricting in the nineteenth century. *American Political Science Review*, 100(3): 419–27.

——and KERNELL, S. 2005. Manufactured Responsiveness: The Impact of State Electoral Laws on Unified Party Control of the Presidency and House of Representatives. *American Journal of Political Science*, 49(3): 531–49.

FIORINA, M. P. 1976. The Voting Decision: Instrumental and Expressive Aspects. *Journal of Politics*, 38(2): 390–413.

GAILMARD, S., and JENKINS, J. 2009. Agency Problems, Electoral Institutions, and the 17th Amendment. *American Journal of Political Science*, 53(2): 324–42.

GAMM, G., and KOUSSER, T. 2010. Broad Bills or Particularistic Policy? Historical Patterns in American State Legislatures. *American Political Science Review*, 104(1): 151–70.

GRIFFIN, J. 2006. Senate Apportionment as a Source of Political Inequality. *Legislative Studies Quarterly*, 31(3): 405–32.

GRONKE, P. 2001. *The Electorate, the Campaign, and the Office: A Unified Approach to Senate and House Elections*. Ann Arbor: University of Michigan Press.

HAYNES, G. H. 1906. *The Election of Senators*. New York: Henry Holt.

——1938. *The Senate of the United States*. Boston: Houghton Mifflin.

HERRNSON, P. 1995. *Congressional Elections: Campaigning at Home and in Washington*. Washington DC: Congressional Quarterly Press.

JACOBSON, G. C. 1978. The Effects of Campaign Spending on Congressional Elections. *American Political Science Review*, 72(2): 469–91.

——2004. *The Politics of Congressional Elections*. 6th edn. New York: Pearson-Longman.

——2007. Referendum: The 2006 Congressional Midterm Elections. *Political Science Quarterly*, 22(1): 1–24.

——and KERNELL, S. 1983. *Strategy and Choice in Congressional Elections*. New Haven: Yale University Press.

JILLSON, C. C. 2002. *Constitution Making: Consensus and Conflict in the Federal Convention of 1787*. New York: Algora Publishing.

KAHN, K. F., and KENNEY, P. J. 1999. *The Spectacle of U.S. Senate Campaigns*. Princeton: Princeton University Press.

KERNELL, S. 1977. Toward Understanding 19th Century Congressional Careers: Ambition, Competition, and Rotation. *American Journal of Political Science*, 21(4): 669–93.

KING, R. F., and ELLIS, S. 1996. Partisan Advantage and Constitutional Change: The Case of the Seventeenth Amendment. *Studies in American Political Development*, 10: 69–102.

KRASNO, J. 1994. *Challengers, Competition, and Reelection: Comparing Senate and House Elections*. New Haven: Yale University Press.

LAPINKSI, J. S. 2000. Representation and Reform: A Congress Centered Approach to American Political Development. Ph.D. thesis, Columbia University.

LEE, F. E., and OPPENHEIMER, B. I. 2002. *Sizing up the Senate: The Unequal Consequences of Equal Representation*. New York: Cambridge University Press.

LUBLIN, D. I. 2004 *The Republican South: Democratization and Partisan Change*. Princeton: Princeton University Press.

MANN, T. E. 1978. *Unsafe at Any Margin*. Washington, DC: American Enterprise Institute.

——and WOLFINGER, R. E. 1980. Candidates and Parties in Congressional Elections. *American Political Science Review*, 74(3): 617–32.

MARTIS, K. C. 1982. *Historical Atlas of United States Congressional Districts*. New York: Free Press.

MAYHEW, D. R. 1986. *Placing Parties in American Politics*. Princeton: Princeton University Press.

STATE OF MONTANA. 1899. *House Journal of the Sixth Session of the Legislative Assembly of the State of Montana*. Helena, MT: State Printers and Binders.

POLSBY, N. W. 1968. The Institutionalization of the U.S. House of Representatives. *American Political Science Review*, 62(1): 144–68.

RIKER, W. H. 1955. The Senate and American Federalism. *American Political Science Review*, 49: 452–69.

ROBERTSON, D. B. 2005. *The Constitution and America's Destiny*. New York: Cambridge University Press.

ROTHMAN, D. J. 1966. *Politics and Power: The United States Senate*, 1869–1901. Cambridge, MA: Harvard University Press.

RUSK, J. G. 1970. The Effect of the Australian Ballot Reform on Split-Ticket Voting 1876–1908. *American Political Science Review*, 64(4): 1220–38.

SCHAFFNER, B. F., SCHILLER, W. J., and SELLERS, P. J. 2003. Tactical and Contextual Determinants of U.S. Senators' Approval Ratings. *Legislative Studies Quarterly*, 28: 203–23.

SCHICKLER, E. 2001. *Disjointed Pluralism: Institutional Innovation and the Development of the U.S. Congress*. Princeton: Princeton University Press.

SCHILLER, W. J. 2000. *Partners and Rivals: Representation in U.S. Senate Delegations*. Princeton: Princeton University Press.

—— 2006. Building Careers and Courting Constituents: U.S. Senate Representation 1889–1924. *Studies in American Political Development*, 20: 185–97.

—— and STEWART, III, C. n.d. Challenging the Myths of nineteenth century Party Dominance: Evidence from Indirect Senate Elections 1871–1913. Unpublished manuscript.

SELLERS, P. 1998. Strategy and Background in Congressional Campaigns. *American Political Science Review*, 92(1): 159–71.

STEWART, III, C. H. 1992. Responsiveness in the Upper Chamber: The Constitution and the Institutional Development of the Senate, pp. 63–96 in *The Constitution and American Political Development*, ed. P. F. Nardulli. Urbana: University of Illinois Press.

—— and WEINGAST, B. R. 1992. Stacking the Senate, Changing the Nation: Republican Rotten Boroughs, Statehood Politics, and American Political Development. *Studies in American Political Development*, 6: 223–71.

WATTENBERG, M. P. 1998. *The Decline of Political Parties 1952–1996*. Cambridge MA: Harvard University Press.

—— 1991. *The Rise of Candidate Centered Politics*. Cambridge, MA: Harvard University Press.

WAWRO, G. J., and SCHICKLER, E. 2007. *Filibustering, Obstruction, and Lawmaking in the U.S. Senate*. Princeton: Princeton University Press.

WESTLYE, M. C. 1991. *Senate Elections and Campaign Intensity*. Baltimore: Johns Hopkins University Press.

WILSON, R. K. 1986. An Empirical Test of Preferences for the Political Pork Barrel: District Level Appropriations for River and Harbor Legislation, 1889–1913. *American Journal of Political Science*, 30(4): 729–54.

WIRLS, D. 1999. Regionalism, Rotten Boroughs, Race, and Realignment: The Seventeenth Amendment and the Politics of Representation. *Studies in American Political Development*, 13: 1–30.

CHAPTER 30

THE EVOLUTION OF PARTY LEADERSHIP

JEFFERY A. JENKINS

THE study of leadership in Congress has nearly always focused on *party* leadership as the key driving force. Party leadership has been the subject of congressional studies since George Rothwell Brown's *The Leadership of Congress* in 1922 and Paul Hasbrouck's *Party Government in The House of Representatives* in 1927.[1] Since then, party leadership has continued to elicit the interest of congressional scholars, from the era of "committee dominance"—which includes Randall Ripley's *Party Leaders in the House of Representatives* in 1967 and *Majority Party Leadership in Congress* in 1969—to the era of "party resurgence"—which includes David W. Rohde's *Parties and Leaders in the Postreform House* in 1991. Today, party leadership is at the heart of many congressional theories of behavior and organization, and the degree to which party leaders wield influence (generally in Congress, and specifically within each chamber) has been perhaps the most studied question in the Congress field over the last two decades (see Chapter 17 by Randall Strahan in this volume).

One limitation in the aforementioned studies is that they have been largely time bound, as scholars have focused mostly on examining party leadership within particular congressional eras. How party leadership has *evolved* over time, by comparison, has elicited far fewer treatments. This chapter takes up the question, by incorporating

---

[1] Identifying the earliest studies of "party leadership in Congress" is open to some interpretation. Earlier academic studies of party influence existed, such as Lowell's (1902) comparison of voting in the U.S. House of Representatives and British House of Commons, but did not focus on party leadership explicitly. A number of narrower academic studies, focusing only on the House speakership, such as Follett (1896) and Fuller (1909), preceded Brown and Hasbrouck. And, finally, journalistic accounts of party leadership, like Thompson (1906), existed, but were designed mainly as biographical compilations without a distinct theoretical overview or perspective.

studies of different eras to trace out how party leadership in Congress has evolved from the late eighteenth century through the present day. In doing so, I will describe how meaningful party leadership emerged in the early nineteenth century, how it grew slowly for a time before rising dramatically late in the century and peaking during the "strong party" period between 1890 and 1910, and then how it dropped off considerably before resurging yet again beginning in the late 1970s. Over the course of this historical tracing, I will note how party leadership in the House and Senate may have evolved similarly or differently over time. Finally, I will also indicate where significant substantive gaps exist in the literature and what the frontiers for future studies of party leadership might look like.

PARTY LEADERSHIP IN THE ANTEBELLUM ERA

Party leadership in Congress prior to the Civil War can be divided—relatively neatly—into three more or less distinct periods: 1789–1811, 1811–37, and 1837–61. These periods witnessed a fairly linear increase in party leadership.

Weak beginnings, 1789–1811

Party leadership in Congress was weak early in our federal system, in part because parties were not part of the nation's formal landscape. Indeed, as Hofstadter (1969) notes, parties were cast in an exceedingly negative light by the Founders and other enlightened citizens, often excoriated as "factions" that were driven by intrigue and selfish motives. Yet, informal party organizations in Congress emerged almost immediately to serve as solutions to collective-action problems that existed in the legislative process (Aldrich 1995). These informal party organizations—proto-caucuses, proto-whips, and so on—were not institutionalized, however, and more importantly, the formal (constitutionally designated) leadership positions in Congress—the Speaker in the House, and the Vice President and President Pro Tempore in the Senate—did not become overt partisan positions during the new nation's first two decades.

In the years preceding the War of 1812, the election of Speaker and other House officers (like the Clerk and Sergeant-at-Arms, which were created by statute) occurred in a chamber whose internal institutions were in flux. Party affiliation among the rank and file was loose, even as some polarization was evident around the personalities and policies of Thomas Jefferson and Alexander Hamilton. The general consensus in the literature, according to Jenkins and Stewart (forthcoming), is that Speakers gave little weight to party (however construed) in overseeing the House, and the basic authority given to the Speaker to control debate and appoint committees was rarely used to programmatic ends.

The only meaningful exception to this Speaker-as-non-partisan perspective occurred during John Adams's administration, during the tenures of Jonathan Dayton and Theodore Sedgwick, Federalist Speakers in the 5th and 6th Congresses (1797–1801). According to Risjord (1992), both Dayton and Sedgwick used their powers to hasten a Federalist agenda. Dayton took an active part in House debate and began the process of using committees for partisan benefit (see, also, Strahan, Gunning, and Vining 2006). Sedgwick was an especially aggressive partisan, actively stacking committees to hasten a distinctly partisan policy agenda. He was also crucial (via a tie-breaking vote) in removing from the House floor two reporters from the *National Intelligencer*, a Republican newspaper that had been critical of the Federalists and the Speaker in particular. This move produced a Republican uproar over censorship and denial of free speech that lasted for months. Both Dayton and Sedgwick left the speakership amid a good deal of partisan rancor.[2] Consequently, the two succeeding Republican Speakers, Nathaniel Macon and Joseph Varnum, were less overtly partisan.

Thus, except for a brief period in the late 1790s, the speakership was regarded as a minor prize among the rank and file and those who might rise to the office. At least four Speaker elections during the first eleven Congresses were multi-ballot affairs,[3] not because the chamber was riven with deep partisan divisions, but because politicking for the post was haphazard and personal factions and nascent party organizations were not strong enough to winnow down the field prior to the actual convening of the House. The lack of intense and lasting animosities over the choice of Speaker is evident in that none of the multi-ballot affairs were protracted. Thus, the repercussions of organizational jockeying tended to be minor.

Alexander (1916) and Harlow (1917) note that the informal position of floor leader emerged during this era, and was in fact more powerful than the Speaker. Rather than being a distinct *party* leader, the floor leader acted as lieutenant of the president, especially during Jefferson's reign.[4] Thus, the floor leader could best be viewed as channeling presidential preferences rather than broader party preferences (when these, in fact, differed).[5] Beyond these early studies, however, little is known of the floor leader's evolution during this time.

The literature on Senate party leadership during this era is much spottier than that of the House. (This will actually be a recurring theme throughout most sections of this chapter, as scholars have devoted far less time to the study of Senate party leadership.) In her book on Senate change, Swift (1996) notes that informal party organizations developed early, just as in the House, but that these organizations were

[2] As a result of their overt partisanship, Dayton and Sedgwick received divided votes of "thanks" as their tenures came to an end, 40–22 and 40–35, respectively (*Annals of Congress*, 5–3, 3/3/1799, 3054; 6–2, 3/3/1801, 1079). Such votes of thanks, prior to that time, had been unanimous.

[3] Ballot data for the first two Speaker elections do not exist.

[4] As Harlow (1917, 177) notes, during Jefferson's presidency, "[floor leaders] were presidential agents, appointed by the executive, and dismissed at his pleasure." This differed from the Federalist-dominated era, when the floor leader acted more as "an assistant to the Speaker" (176).

[5] The distinction between presidential and party preferences was not often great, as the president (and his cabinet members) often defined the party at this point.

weak and sporadically employed. Moreover, she notes that neither the Vice President nor President Pro Tempore "had much influence over the Senate's proceedings" (1996, 76), mirroring the limited Speaker-organized environment of the House. Instead, leadership in the Senate was committee-based rather than party-based, with important figures on key select committees effectively holding the reins of power. Swift's book remains the best account—and one of the very few—of leadership, and party leadership more specifically, in the pre-War of 1812 Senate.

This period also witnessed procedural decisions in each chamber that would influence the development of party leadership. As Binder (1997) notes, a previous question rule—a procedure for cutting off debate and proceeding to a vote on the underlying subject of a bill—was passed in the House in 1811, while such a rule, which had been in place in the Senate, was eliminated in 1806.[6] Thus, after 1811, a cohesive majority in the House—perhaps led by an active leadership—had a clear procedural means to work its will, while a cohesive majority in the Senate lacked a similar procedural mechanism to stifle a vocal minority.[7] This, according to Roberts and Smith (2007), created different incentives for the development of party leadership, and consequently set the two chambers on different evolutionary paths.

Emergence of party leadership, 1811–37

From a modern perspective, the House during the first eleven Congresses was underdeveloped. As the speakerships of Jonathan Dayton and Theodore Sedgwick show, however, it was possible for leadership positions to be put to partisan use. Still, in an era where a "Jeffersonian ethos" (Cooper 1970; cf. Risjord 1992) characterized the House culture, there were no loud and persistent voices who argued that the organization of the chamber should be constructed self-consciously with partisan ends in mind. The House as a formal institution was underfunded and underorganized. As a consequence, any role that the incumbent of a House office might play in policy or partisan intrigues was ad hoc and far from institutionalized.

That began to change around the time Henry Clay, a freshman House member from Kentucky, became Speaker in the 12th Congress (1811–13).[8] From Clay's first speakership until the time when the House began to ballot for its Speakers publicly

---

[6] In addition, Binder finds evidence to suggest that partisanship was a *cause* of the passage of the previous question rule in the House, despite the fact that party feelings were very much in a formative stage in Congress at this time.

[7] While Wawro and Schickler (2006, 64) agree that "[t]he absence of a previous question rule did complicate efforts to end Senate obstruction," they contend there were other rules and precedents available to floor majorities in the Senate to overcome obstructionist behavior. More generally, they argue that the Senate was fairly majoritarian during much of the nineteenth century, and that minority obstruction was a bigger problem in the House than the Senate prior to 1890 (and the advent of the Reed Rules). For a burgeoning debate on procedural development, minority power, and governing in the Senate during the nineteenth and early twentieth centuries, see Binder (1997); Binder and Smith (1997); Wawro and Schickler (2006); Binder, Madonna, and Smith (2007); Koger (2010).

[8] Much has been written about Clay and his role in the institutionalization of the House, both by augmenting the Speaker's role in guiding debate and in developing the standing committee system. See

in the 26th Congress (1839–41), the formal structure of the House became more complex, the role of political parties was transformed, and the value of House offices, including subsidiary positions like the Clerk and Printer, was much enhanced.

In the Speaker's chair, Clay showed that the office could be used to the programmatic advantage of the faction that controlled it, whether that faction be personality-driven or purely partisan. As Stewart (2007) describes, Clay's dynamic leadership in the run-up to the War of 1812 demonstrated that it was possible for the House to take an active, leading role in momentous policy decisions. Clay used relatively new parliamentary tools, such as the ability to cut off floor debate, in a skillful way—taking advantage of Republican homogeneity on war-related issues to pass a clear policy agenda. The 1810s also were the time when both chambers of Congress shifted from select to standing committees to process most legislation (Gamm and Shepsle 1989; Jenkins 1998). Although the power and capacity of these standing committees was still in the formative stages, it was the Speaker who appointed them (see Chapter 31 by Eric Schickler in this volume). Thus, the Speaker was now in possession of parliamentary tools—ruling on points of order, recognizing members in debate, and appointing committees—that could, at least in principle, make this office the most influential policy post in the nation.

Clay's leadership-led policy success unraveled after the war, as the Federalists' demise left a one-party (Republican) system in place that factionalized into regional camps around powerful presidential hopefuls (see Young 1966; Gamm and Shepsle 1989; Jenkins 1998). Yet, the leadership potential of the speakership was a lesson that all now realized. This became clear when the House balloted to replace Clay for Speaker in the second session of the 16th Congress (1819–21).[9] The contest required twenty-two ballots stretching over three days before John W. Taylor (NY) was elected. This battle had strong sectional undercurrents, as the contest took place amidst the extended proceedings on Missouri's admittance into the Union. As Jenkins and Stewart (2002) note, both supporters and opponents of Taylor based their votes largely on beliefs as to what he might do in staffing the committees, especially those that dealt with the Missouri question. Although Taylor attempted to be conciliatory in his appointment of committees and the "Missouri Compromise" was considered to be a slight victory for pro-slavery advocates, southern House members distrusted Taylor and succeeded in ousting him from the Speaker's chair in favor of one of their own in the next Congress.

By the late 1820s, a new two-party system was beginning to form around the policies and personality of President Andrew Jackson. Jackson's supporters selected Andrew Stevenson (VA) as their speakership candidate, and he served from 1826 to 1834, working closely with Jackson to further the president's policy agenda in Congress. In 1834, Stevenson accepted an ambassadorship to England, and six Jacksonians competed to replace him in the Speaker's chair. The contest required twelve ballots, and eventually reduced to a race between James K. Polk (TN) and John Bell

---

particularly Gamm and Shepsle (1989); Jenkins (1998); Strahan, Moscardelli, et al (2000); Stewart (2007); Strahan (2007).

[9] Clay retired to Kentucky temporarily because of health and financial reasons.

(TN), with Bell emerging triumphant by appealing directly to Anti-Jacksonians (soon to be called "Whigs") who were willing to join in coalition with pro-Bank Democrats (Sellers 1957). Bell, in turn, favored Anti-Jacksonians in making his committee assignments and eventually took on the Anti-Jacksonian (Whig) label himself. Bell's actions as Speaker galvanized Jackson's supporters, who rallied behind Polk at the opening of the 24th Congress (1835–7), electing him easily on the first ballot. Polk would be a loyal Jacksonian in the Speaker's chair, while Bell, now a leader of the minority in the House, would harass Polk throughout his tenure as Speaker, employing the full range of dilatory tactics at his (and the minority's) disposal. Thus, within a quarter-century of Clay's initial election, the speakership had evolved from a chamber office with partisan potential to a clearly partisan office. And the often contentious and lengthy battles over the speakership, as evidence of the strong partisanship attached to the office, would continue—and heighten—into the future.

Also during this time, as Jenkins and Stewart (2003; forthcoming) note, other House officer positions would be viewed through a partisan lens. The two most prominent were the Clerk and Printer.[10] The Clerk presided over a sizeable patronage empire, controlled the House's contingent fund (worth upwards of US$10 million in today's dollars), and was the presiding officer in the chamber at the opening of each new Congress (calling the roll of members-elect and thereby formally determining the House membership for organizational purposes). The Printer was responsible for printing and distributing House reports and other official documents, as well as disseminating such information to newspapers throughout the country (which came with funds to keep said newspapers afloat financially), and possessed considerable patronage capacities as well. As the Second Party System developed, and Democratic (formerly Jacksonian) politicians looked for ways to maintain an advantage over the newly forming Whigs, the Clerk and Printer positions would be reconfigured as party leadership positions, with their internal capabilities and sets of resources rechanneled for the benefit of the party rather than the overall chamber. Election struggles over the two positions took on a distinct partisan hue in the mid-1830s, mirroring the situation in speakership elections. And when the Democrats lost the printership at the beginning of the 26th Congress (1837–9), thanks to a cross-party intrigue, Democratic leaders began calling for a new leadership institution to coordinate nominations and elections on the floor. The new leadership institution, a party nominating caucus, will be examined in the next section.

The informal floor leader, who had been a tool of the presidency prior to 1811, increasingly became an agent of the majority party in the House during this era. As the speakership emerged as a partisan power center, other nodes of power were also needed. As Alexander (1916) and Riddick (1949) argue, the Speaker typically selected the Chairman of the Ways and Means Committee to serve as the informal floor leader in the chamber. This was often a concession to intra-party harmony, as the

---

[10] Other more minor elected Houser officer positions included the Sergeant-at-Arms, the Doorkeeper, and the Postmaster. While all had significant patronage potential, none compared in stature and influence to the Clerk and Printer.

Ways and Means Chair was often a rival of the Speaker. How the floor leader's functions and duties changed as the position became more partisan has never been examined in any detail, and the subject deserves a comprehensive examination.

On the Senate side, less is known about the evolution of party leadership between 1811 and 1837. For example, while scholars have studied the development of the major House officer positions, little attention—other than a few short overviews by Byrd (1991)—has been paid to the subsidiary positions (the Secretary and the Printer) below the Senate's presiding officer. These were positions that, at a minimum, provided the same sorts of benefits as their House counterparts. And while Smith (1977) notes that the amounts paid to Senate Printers were roughly one-third of what House Printers received, he describes Senate Printer elections as being very contentious during this time (just as in the House). This is clearly an area begging for research.

What *is* known about the evolution of Senate party leadership during this era has been provided almost exclusively by Byrd (1991), Swift (1996), and Gamm and Smith (2000; 2002). These studies show that, unlike the Speaker of the House, the Senate's presiding officer never developed as a strong party leader. This was because the Vice President, who served as the President of the Senate, was not elected by the chamber and thus not trusted by the members. The President Pro Tempore, who chaired proceedings in the Vice President's absence, was elected by the Senate, but the position itself was only temporary in nature. That is, whenever the Vice President appeared in the chamber, the current President Pro Tempore's term officially ended. The partisan ramifications of the Senate's weak presiding officer relative to the House's stronger presiding officer are put into context nicely by Roberts and Smith (2007, 184):

The Senate, which did not have a previous-question motion or a presiding officer elected from its membership, lacked the means by which a majority party could assert control over the floor agenda. Instead, it evolved mechanisms that, under most circumstances, require the consent of both majority and minority members to organize floor debate and amending activity.

As a result, as the speakership was evolving into a party leadership institution during this era, the majority party in the Senate struggled to consolidate its power. For example, from 1815–37, the Senate adopted different arrangements for staffing committees, sometimes granting the President Pro Tempore the power (if it was felt that he would be available—and could be trusted—to perform the duty) and at other times choosing instead to ballot (for a breakdown, see Table 6–1 in Gamm and Smith 2000). The ballot option would become a stronger consideration as partisanship ramped up in the 1830s. Indeed, the Anti-Jacksonian majority turned to the ballot in 1833, unwilling to allow Hugh White, the President Pro Tempore and a Jacksonian holdover from the previous Congress, to appoint the committees. As Gamm and Smith (2002, 222) note, "It was in this era, when control of the chamber was fiercely contested and often in doubt, that committee chairmanships became partisan positions." And just as partisans in the House began searching for a new party leadership mechanism to better secure positions of power, partisans in the Senate also sought such an institutional solution. Interestingly, the answer in the Senate would be the same as in the House—a party caucus.

Fits and starts, 1837–61

To better secure the formal House leadership positions, the Democratic majority pushed for two institutional changes: 1) a move from a secret to a public ballot in House officer elections and 2) the adoption of a party nominating caucus to settle intra-partisan differences and decide on partisan nominees in advance. As Jenkins and Stewart (forthcoming) explain, these choices were pushed by Martin Van Buren, the titular leader of the national Democratic Party. Van Buren came to power in New York state politics in the 1820s, where the caucus stood at the heart of an organization—the Albany Regency—built on tenets of strict party discipline and unwavering party loyalty (Wallace 1968; Hofstadter 1969).

The public ballot—or *viva voce* voting—was first adopted in a replacement election for House Clerk in 1838, and was extended to all House officer elections in 1839. The passage of *viva voce* voting would allow Van Buren and his supporters to institutionalize a party nominating caucus in the House, which would meet just prior to the start of a new Congress. Within the confines of the caucus, nominations for each of the major House officer positions would be held, after which elections would be conducted and choices made. Minority factions—those members of the party who supported unsuccessful nominees—would be placated, usually through committee assignments or promises of patronage, and in exchange their support of the caucus nominees on the House floor (or "being regular") was expected. And unlike the secret-ballot era, Democratic leaders could examine whether party members followed through and voted for the caucus nominees. Dissidents could no longer defect and escape punishment. The caucus thus had the potential to be *binding*.[11]

Wasting no time, the Democrats organized a party nominating caucus prior to the opening of the 26th Congress (1839–41). The Whigs made a half-hearted attempt to follow the Democrats' lead, before actively adopting the same caucus machinery prior to the opening in the 27th Congress (1841–3), wherein they would enjoy majority control of the House. And, as a result, a caucus-led system of House organization had begun.

The first decade of Van Buren's caucus-based nominating system produced mixed results. In 1839, the majority Democrats lost the speakership, thanks to key defections from the Calhounites, while in 1841, the majority Whigs lost the clerkship, thanks to the rejection of Henry Clay's handpicked candidate by the rank and file. The next three sets of officer elections, in the 28th through 30th Congresses (1843–9), followed the caucus dictate exactly, giving party leaders hope that Regency-level discipline and loyalty was institutionalizing. These general successes hid the fact that groups of northern and southern firebrands continued to defect from the caucus agreement,

---

[11] Caucuses themselves were not a new phenomenon on the congressional landscape. They had a long history in congressional politics, with legislative party caucuses going back to the early federalist era and the Congressional Nominating Caucus (or "King Caucus") dictating party selection of presidential nominees from 1800 through 1824. But for the first four decades of our federal system, a regular party caucus to select House officer candidates never took hold, perhaps due to the secret ballot (and resulting "enforceability issues") that ultimately determined officer selection on the House floor.

but their numbers were not large enough in these Congresses to prevent the majority party from achieving its preferred outcome.

Beginning in 1849, the tenuous caucus-based nominating system would flounder. The sectional strains that had permeated nominations and speakership elections over the past decade broke through with a vengeance. The U.S. victory in the Mexican-American War brought the slavery issue front and center, as newly acquired western land would need to be organized. Several years later, similar slavery-extension concerns would crop up in the organization of the Kansas–Nebraska territories (after the Missouri Compromise was annulled). The slavery issue would eventually tear the nation apart and lead to Civil War in 1861. But before then, House organizational politics were a spectacle.

Lengthy speakership elections would take place in 1849 (31st Congress), 1855–6 (34th Congress), and 1859–60 (36th Congress). In 1849, the plurality Democrats finally elected their caucus nominee after sixty-one ballots and three weeks, but then went on to lose the clerkship to the Whigs in a twenty-ballot affair. Officer elections went according to the caucus plan in 1851 and 1853, thanks to the Democrats' large majorities in the chamber. In 1855–6, the newly formed Republicans, comprising a plurality of the chamber, were able to elect a Speaker after 133 ballots and two months, but lost the Printer to a coalition of Americans and Democrats. In 1857, the Democrats took advantage of Republican-American electoral squabbling to elect their caucus slate. And, finally, in 1859, the Republicans were able to capture all major House offices, including the speakership, after forty-four ballots and two months, but only after dropping their initial choices for those offices.[12]

Thus, the initial attempt to bind party members to nomination choices in caucus was undermined by sectional divisions. Van Buren's dream to further party consolidation in the House by using the caucus as a leadership device did not come to fruition. At least not yet.

In the Senate, the caucus was also at the forefront of members' partisan machinations. Because the presiding officer did not develop as a partisan leader in the Senate, as the Speaker did in the House, the majority party sought to influence the composition of committees (and notably, committee chairmanships) directly. By 1845, as Gamm and Smith (2002) explain, a decision was made to assemble committees by public ballot on the floor—and thus bypass the presiding officer completely—using the caucus as the coordination mechanism. Very quickly, the Democrats and Whigs established a precedent by which committee lists (organized and ranked by party) would be assembled in caucus and adopted on the floor by unanimous consent. Soon thereafter, in 1847, the Democratic caucus created its first committee on committees, which "quickly became a powerful organ of the party" (223). The Republicans would follow suit with their own committee on committees in 1859.

---

[12] The Republicans did not make explicit caucus nominations until the 38th Congress (1863–5). Prior to that time, they adopted an informal agreement that members would be allowed to vote their true preferences on the first ballot (for a given office) and then coordinate around the top vote-getter thereafter.

Thus, the Senate parties' adoption of the caucus to deal with their chamber-specific collective-action problem (assembling committees) followed shortly after the House parties' adoption of the caucus to deal with *their* chamber-specific collective-action problem (electing officers, like the Speaker, who among other things assembled committees). This pattern of the House acting first and the Senate copying the behavior also occurred at least once before—in the conversion of the committee system from one in which select committees dominated to one in which standing committees dominated. This parallel has not been noted before in the literature, and the notion of Senate decision-makers reacting to (and following) House decision-makers probably deserves further investigation.

PARTY LEADERSHIP FROM THE CIVIL WAR THROUGH THE PRE-NEW DEAL

From the Civil War through the 1920s, party leadership in Congress went through various cycles. First, there was an early consolidation, centering around the emergence of the party caucus as a viable and influential leadership mechanism. This led to a period of party power in Congress—unrivaled until the present day—that spanned two decades around the turn of the twentieth century. Finally, a backlash against strong party leadership occurred, and power was decentralized in both chambers. A brief resurgence of traditional party leadership took place in the 1920s, but this proved to be a temporary respite from the trend toward greater decentralization.

Party consolidation, 1861–90

The difficulties that the parties faced in organizing the House seemingly vanished with the advent of the Civil War. As Jenkins and Stewart (forthcoming) describe, beginning in 1861, no speakership election would extend beyond a single ballot for more than sixty years. And no other House officer elections would ever require more than a single ballot. The party nominating caucus, which had only limited success in the antebellum era, finally took firm hold. And while sectional issues would emerge again to test the parties—see Chapter 33 by Richard Bensel in this volume—caucus decisions, however contentious, would be honored on the floor.

The importance of a caucus in advance of floor voting was underscored in the days before the speakership election of 1863. There, the House Clerk, Emerson Etheridge, planned an institutional coup by organizing Democrats and border-state Conservatives to join in coalition against the Republicans, who by themselves lacked a floor majority. Etheridge had been the Republican's Clerk candidate in 1861, but broke with the party after Lincoln's Emancipation Proclamation in 1863. As presiding officer of the new Congress, Etheridge planned to use his ability to determine the roll of members-elect to reject certain Republicans who did not have their election certificates properly in order. But, as Belz (1970) describes, Republican leaders got wind of Etheridge's plan and were able to resolve the certification issue and thereby snuff out the Clerk's coup attempt. This served as a wakeup call for the Republicans, who were slow in adopting a nominating caucus. Beginning with the 39th Congress (1865–7), *both* major parties made their officer nominations in a caucus that met shortly before the convening of a new Congress.

Notable caucus nomination battles involved the tussle between Democrats Samuel Randall (PA) and Joseph J. Blackburn (KY) in 1879 and the bruising 16-ballot affair between Republicans Frank Hiscock (NY) and J. Warren Keifer (OH) in 1881.[13] In each, and in all other cases during this era, the caucus loser was magnanimous in defeat and called for party unity on the floor. For example, Blackburn's statement upon losing the caucus nomination in 1881 is especially revealing of how far the caucus had come as a leadership institution within the party: "The edict of this caucus is to be final and conclusive, and if there be one among the 57 gentlemen whose partial friendship has given me their votes that hesitates or doubts, to him I now appeal to make the verdict of this caucus effective when to-morrow's roll is called" (*New York Times*, March 18, 1879, 1). According to Jenkins and Stewart (forthcoming), fidelity to the caucus occurred because party "losers" were compensated by the newly elected Speaker through his distribution of committee assignments. Thus, the caucus was an important institution, along with the Speaker and the committees, in maintaining cohesion within the majority party.

As the party caucuses grew in importance, the caucus chairmen, who directed their proceedings and helped determine their rules, took on positions of leadership within each party. The floor leader as a partisan position also continued to evolve during this period; for example, beginning in 1865, floor leadership responsibility often shifted from the Ways and Means Chairman to the Appropriations Chairman (Alexander 1916; Riddick 1949).[14] Finally, House officer positions under the Speaker became less influential in the postbellum era. The House Clerk receded into the background after Etheridge's failed coup attempt, while the House Printer (and its Senate counterpart) was eliminated entirely in 1860 after a series of public printing scandals were uncovered. Both positions—especially the printership—had been important sources of patronage and funds that could be used for party development. In their place, congressional campaign committees (CCCs) appeared. As Kolodny (1998) documents, the Republican Congressional Committee (RCC) was created in 1866, with the Democratic Congressional Committee (DCC) following two years

---

[13]   Perhaps the most contentious caucus nomination battle occurred just outside of the sub-era, in 1891, as Democrats Charles F. Crisp (GA) and John Q. Mills (TX) clashed for thirty ballots over two days, before Crisp was finally nominated.

[14]   This occurred after Appropriations became a stand-alone committee in 1865. Such a shift was not *complete*, however, as several Ways and Means Chairmen during the 1870s and 1880s, like William Morrison (IL), Fernando Wood (NY), William Kelley (PN), and William McKinley (IL), also doubled as floor leaders.

later in 1868. These institutions were created to direct and fund their respective party's efforts to achieve (or maintain) majority party status in the House. Beyond Kolodny's impressive study, little is known of the evolution of CCCs (see also Chapter 10 by Robin Kolodny in this volume).

On the Senate side, Gamm and Smith (2002) have culled through an older and often fragmented literature on party leadership, while also expanding our collective knowledge through intensive archival work. They observe that each party established formal caucus chairmen during this time—the Democrats in 1857 and the Republicans in 1873—and that subunits within the Democratic caucus, an ad hoc steering committee and a committee on committees, began taking responsibility for policy recommendations and committee decisions within the party. Moreover, Gamm and Smith note that Democrats in the 1870s began making officer positions, like the Secretary, the Clerk, the Doorkeepers, etc., into elected positions, thereby transforming them into distinct patronage engines. This is interesting, as Smith (1977) and others note that some Senate positions like the Printer in the antebellum period were elected—and a perusal of the *Congressional Globe* suggests that other positions, like the Doorkeeper, were also occasionally elected. Both perspectives are likely correct, as changes in methods of officer selection probably occurred from time and time. More broadly, this suggests that a more comprehensive examination of Senate officer positions during the nineteenth century is needed, so that the evolution is fully documented.

Finally, the continuing divergence in institutional evolution between the House and Senate is detailed nicely by Roberts and Smith (2007). As noted, the chambers differed because of early decisions in their histories (presiding officer differences, previous question differences), which affected subsequent decisions about setting the floor agenda. In the House, special orders first emerged in the 1880s, as a way to centralize authority in the Rules Committee (staffed by the Speaker) to dictate how business would be conducted on the floor. (The active use of such special rules would not become prevalent for another decade.) Around the same time, complex unanimous consent agreements (UCAs) emerged in the Senate, to limit debate or amendments. While special orders clearly benefitted the majority party in asserting procedural control in the House, UCAs required cross-party coalitions to work efficiently. Thus, party leadership in the two chambers continued to evolve on very different paths.

The high tide of party, 1890–1910

The two decades between 1890 and 1910 would emerge as the high tide of party government in the U.S. Congress. Powerful leaders and leadership organizations would dictate legislative proceedings and outputs in both chambers of Congress.

In the House, Republican Thomas Reed (ME) was elected Speaker in the 51st Congress (1889–91), and under his leadership the majority party would work its will in a way never before seen in chamber history. In the years prior to Reed's ascension, hints that the House majority was attempting to gain firmer control of the chamber abounded—mechanisms like special orders emerged (as already noted) to help manage House business, and, as Binder (1997) and Dion (1997) note, attempts to stifle minority dissent (through limits on procedural rights) were plentiful but only marginally successful. As a result, Cox and McCubbins (2005) consider 1880s-era House politics to have been governed by a "dual veto," wherein dilatory threats (and often behavior) by the minority along with antiquated rules for doing business on the floor (the calendar system of the time) effectively meant that each party shared agenda power. Once in the Speaker's chair, Reed set out to eliminate minority obstruction. This story is well known and has been described in detail by many scholars (see, e.g., Schickler 2001). With his Republican majority backing him on the floor in the face of Democratic challenges, Reed changed the rules by which quorums were counted, reduced the quorum requirement in the Committee of the Whole to 100 members, and provided the Speaker with discretion to rule dilatory motions out of order. In addition, Reed oversaw the transformation of special orders into special rules, which further enhanced the authority of the Rules Committee (chaired by the Speaker) and gave the majority party much more flexibility in shaping the legislative agenda.[15]

Thanks to these changes, the House majority party—when cohesive—could govern effectively and efficiently. Reed's mantle was later taken up by Republican Joseph Cannon (IL), who, beginning in the 58th Congress (1903–05), would further consolidate power in the speakership.[16] Elsewhere in the House, the floor leader position continued to evolve. Beginning in 1896, the Chair of Ways and Means largely took control of the position from the Chair of Appropriations (Riddick 1949), and in 1899, the floor leader became a formally identified position—the Majority Leader (Ripley 1967).[17] Also, in 1897, a new formal party position, the Whip, was created by the majority Republicans (with the minority Democrats following suit in 1900) to serve as an information conduit between leaders and the rank and file (Ripley 1964).

In the Senate, the lack of a Speaker-like presiding officer made it more difficult for party leadership to emerge. Instead of a single individual, a group of four powerful Republican senators—Nelson Aldrich (RI), William Allison (IA), Orville Platt (CT), and John Spooner (WI)—emerged to coordinate party activity. Key to their success, as discussed by Gamm and Smith (2002), was the expanding power of the Republican caucus. Instead of using ad hoc caucus committees, which had been the norm in the 1870s an 1880s, the Republicans instituted a regular steering committee in 1892, to organize the party's legislative agenda. Thanks to its more permanent institutional

---

[15] While a special order provided for the consideration of bills reported from committee, they did not typically alter the *procedures* by which the bills would be considered. A special rule provided for consideration *and* stipulated procedural limits, such as restrictions on debate and/or amendments.

[16] The Democrats, after taking back the House in the 52nd Congress (1891–3), would repeal the Reed Rules. But after facing dilatory behavior led by Reed himself, they would reinstate many of the Reed Rules in the 53rd Congress (1893–5). The Republicans would retake the House, and Reed would return to the Speaker's chair in the 54th and 55th Congresses (1895–9), before yielding to David Henderson (IA) in the 56th and 57th Congresses (1899–1903). Historians have generally considered Henderson to have been a weak presiding officer, but recent work by Finocchiaro and Rohde (2007) suggests that this may be an overstatement.

[17] Discrepancies exist as to when a formal Minority Leader position emerged. Ripley (1967) suggests 1881, while other sources (like Galloway (1961) and Heitshusen (2007)) suggest 1899 or 1901.

status, the new steering committee was considered more legitimate by party members, and its influence grew accordingly.[18] (The minority Democrats would adopt their own regular steering committee a year later in 1893.) And while party leadership centralization occurred in the Senate—to the point that, as Rothman (1966, 59) states, "Senators knew they had to consult the [steering] committee before attempting to raise even minor matters"—it did not approximate the level reached in the House. The process and structure of the Senate, relative to that of the House, limited what could be achieved.

As to why party leadership consolidated during this time, scholars such as Rohde and Shepsle (1987) point to the electorally induced preference distributions of the parties.[19] In the House, parties became more internally homogenous and polarized from one another, creating a context that allowed—and encouraged—members to delegate authority to leaders. In later work, Rohde (1991) would refer to this homogeneity/polarization requirement as the *condition* that is needed to produce delegation and subsequent strong party government.[20] Smith and Gamm (2009) generally agree with the Rohde and Shepsle account for the House, but note that a similar story does not hold for the Senate, as the timing between homogeneity/polarization and Republican Party consolidation is not nearly as clean. Schickler (2001) and Jenkins, Schickler, and Carson (2004) question the Rohde/Shepsle explanation more generally, however, as they find—using district-level economic data and constituency characteristics, rather than roll-call votes—that Republican districts did not become increasingly homogenous and polarized from Democratic districts until several years after the adoption of the Reed Rules. Strahan (2007) acknowledges the logic of the homogeneity/polarization argument, but contends—in a case study of Reed's speakership—that the individual skills of (would-be) leaders are important considerations that have been undervalued in the literature. Valelly (2009) makes a related point, stating that leadership is also related to political context, which in his view has largely been ignored; more specifically, he makes the claim that Reed's rise to power occurred as part of "a grand strategy of Republican party building" that centered on federally regulating southern House elections (2009, 115).

In short, questions remain regarding why (and how) party leadership consolidated during the 1890–1910 period, the high-water mark of party government in Congress. Additional studies are needed before any kind of consensus can be reached.

Insurgency, the binding policy caucus, and the resurgence of party leadership, 1910–33

Although Speaker Joe Cannon presided over a centralized party organization in the first decade of the twentieth century, disaffection was growing within the majority

---

[18] Schickler (2001), based on a survey of the secondary literature, points to 1897 as the key date in which party-leadership influence fully consolidated.

[19] See, also, Cooper and Brady (1981) on this general point.

[20] Rohde referred to this as "conditional party government."

Republican party. As Jenkins and Stewart (forthcoming) recount, young House Republicans—the so-called "progressive" Republicans—were increasingly unhappy with Cannon and the way that he used his powers to favor the interests of senior, "Old Guard" Republicans.[21] As a result, spirited calls for reform emerged in the latter part of the 60th Congress (1907–09), but fell just short of being enacted. A show of opposition against Cannon was then made in the Republican caucus elections in March 1909, in advance of the opening of the 61st Congress (1909–11). Cannon, who had received the Republican speakership nomination by acclamation three previous times, received 162 votes, with 25 votes scattering and 30 absences.

The caucus vote on Cannon would be a harbinger. In March 1910, the progressive Republicans, led by George W. Norris (NE), would combine with the Democrats in the chamber to change the House rules by removing the Speaker from the Rules Committee and expanding its membership from five to ten, with Rules Committee members elected by the House (see Holt 1967; Schickler 2001).[22] When the Democrats took control of the House in the following (62nd) Congress, they finished the job by stripping the Speaker of his ability to make *all* standing committee assignments. This famous episode in the history of the House would have lasting effects, as the decentralization of power from the Speaker to the committees would remain the institutional status quo until the latter part of the twentieth century.

A similar "revolt" against the leadership did not occur in the Senate, but the Republican-led coalition faced significant challenges to its authority during the same time.[23] Increasingly, as Smith and Gamm (2009) detail, a determined minority was able to use the filibuster and other dilatory tactics to stymie the Republican policy agenda. And there were simply more internal divisions within the Senate Republican party during the Aldrich era of Republican rule, making party consolidation extremely difficult. Inevitably, a weak organization (due to the particulars of the Senate institutional context) simply got weaker over time. And by 1911, with Aldrich's retirement from the Senate, the group of four powerful Republican senators who had coordinated Republican Senate activity were all gone.

The first six years of President Woodrow Wilson's administration (1913–19) would usher in unified Democratic control of government for the first time since 1893–5.

---

[21] Recently, a debate has emerged around Cannon's committee assignments and whether he truly acted as a majority-party "tyrant." Krehbiel and Wiseman (2001, 2005) find evidence to suggest that Cannon's committee slates often reflected a bipartisan tinge, while Lawrence, Maltzman, and Wahlbeck (2001) find that partisanship was one of several factors that helped explain Cannon's committee assignments.

[22] Progressive Republicans lost their initial skirmish with Cannon in March 1909, on the adoption of the House rules, thanks to a few Democrats who backed Cannon in exchange for a minor reform concession. Later, after winning their showdown with Cannon in 1910, the progressive Republicans stopped short of a complete "coup" by leaving him—now shorn of much of his agenda power—in the Speaker's chair. See Holt (1967) and Schickler (2001) for detailed overviews.

[23] Schickler and Sides (2000), however, do note an earlier insurgency within the Republican-controlled Senate—in 1899, a set of junior and western senators took on the Aldrich/Allison leadership and successfully decentralized appropriations away from Allison's Appropriations Committee. This was indicative of the difficulty that Republican leaders in the Senate had—relative to Republican leaders in the House—throughout the "strong party era" of 1890–1910.

Once in power, the Democrats would turn to a new organizational tool to con-solidate party power and push a party agenda: the binding policy caucus. Part of the move to caucus government in the House followed on progressive changes in the wake of the Cannon revolt.[24] For example, the caucus would now be supreme on organizational matters—choosing both the Speaker and the Majority Leader. The Majority Leader would be appointed by the caucus to chair the Ways and Means Committee, and the Democrats on Ways and Means would fill out the rest of the House's committee assignments. The Speaker thus was a bit player in the new caucus-led drama, with the Majority Leader being the most important indi-vidual leader. The caucus would be secret in its proceedings and a two-thirds vote would bind all members on subsequent floor action (see Galloway 1961). In the Senate, the Democratic takeover would usher in formal leadership changes, with the caucus chairman (John Worth Kern, IN) becoming the designated Majority Leader and a Whip position created, both in 1913. (Republicans would follow suit by designating a Minority Leader in 1913 and a Whip in 1915.) To better mimic the House's ability to centralize decision-making—and to fortify its spot in the binding caucus system—the Majority Leader made decisions directly, bypassing the former steering committees that had emerged in the late nineteenth century (Smith and Gamm 2009).

The best analysis of the binding caucus, by far, is provided by Green (2002), who examines the Democratic caucus in the House from 1911 to 1919. Green argues that the caucus was not as powerful as some historians have thought, as he finds that "the caucus bound Democrats' votes on just 15 legislative measures in four Congresses" (2002, 622). Moreover, many of these binding caucus resolutions proved to be unnec-essary, as they were linked to bills that were already supported by a sizeable majority of Democrats on pure ideological grounds. When a measure *was* ideologically divisive, a binding caucus resolution could not typically compel party allegiance on the floor, as defections were often numerous. In sum, Green's results suggest that instituting parliamentary-style rules on matters other than organizational votes is difficult, espe-cially when cross-cutting or ideologically dividing issues emerge. A similar analysis to Green's for the Senate has not been conducted.[25]

The Republicans returned to power in the 66th Congress (1919–21) and controlled both chambers of Congress through the early 1930s. While they would not continue with the Democrats' use of a binding policy caucus, a resurgence of partisanship would take place during this time, in both the House and Senate, in the face of new progressive challenges. These episodes have been recounted in detail by Schickler (2001) and Jenkins and Stewart (forthcoming).

In the House, the first multi-ballot speakership battle since before the Civil War took place in 1923, at the opening of the 68th Congress (1923–5).[26] A new generation

---

[24] One such progressive change was to eliminate much of the remaining patronage controlled by the subsidiary House officers (Clerk, Sergeant-at-Arms, Doorkeeper, Postmaster) and redirect it to a Committee on Committees within the Democratic caucus. See Jenkins and Stewart (forthcoming).

[25] The best portrait of Senate party leadership during the 1910s is provided by Oleszek (1991).

[26] This would also be the *last* multi-ballot speakership battle on the House floor.

of progressive Republicans, demanding a liberalization of House rules to free up legislation that languished in committees dominated by Republican regulars, used their pivotal numbers (roughly twenty members) to delay the reelection of Republican Speaker Frederick Gillett (MA). Nicholas Longworth (OH), the Republican Majority Leader, was enraged by the progressives' actions and tried to face them down—without success. After eight speakership ballots over two days, Longworth conceded and offered the progressives a deal, which would provide an opening for the liberalization of House rules. The progressives accepted the deal, threw their support behind Gillett on a ninth floor ballot—thereby electing him—and then used Longworth's opening to initiate several rules changes, such as developing a workable discharge rule to draw legislation out of committee and eliminating the power of the Rules Committee Chairman to perform a "pocket veto" on resolutions approved by the Rules Committee. A portion of this progressive group of Republicans would then defect from the Republican presidential ticket of Coolidge and Dawes in 1924, in favor of Robert La Follette's Progressive Party candidacy.

In the 69th Congress (1925–7), Longworth was elected Speaker, and he would have his revenge on the progressives. Thanks to "regular" Republican electoral gains in the 1924 elections, the progressive wing of the party was no longer pivotal in officer selection. Thus, Longworth, with the help of Bertrand Snell (NY), the Rules Committee Chair and Majority Leader, and the Republican Committee on Committees (RCOC), kicked 13 progressives out of the Republican caucus and announced that they would be welcomed back when they became "regular" once again on speakership votes. Longworth's hard line was intended to reestablish a strong party organization in the House and return the speakership to a position of prominence. And, once in the Speaker's chair, he proceeded to oversee the rolling back of the progressive-led rules reforms of the previous Congress. The progressive Republicans rejected Longworth's demands for a time, but being read out of the Republican caucus and losing their committee seniority was eventually too much to bear—and they returned "home" and voted for Longworth for Speaker in the 70th Congress (1927–9). Thus, Longworth had reestablished a Speaker-led system of party organization in the House, albeit one that incorporated the intra-party power sharing realities of the post-Cannon era. Moreover, as Bacon (1998) documents, Longworth ushered in procedural leadership that struck observers as a friendlier version of the Reed–Cannon years.

In general, less is known about Senate party leadership during the 1920s. Schickler (2001) does note, however, that an anti-progressive backlash occurred that mirrored the House case. In 1925, the Republican Senate conference excluded Robert La Follette (WI), Edwin Ladd (ND), Smith Brookhart (IA), and Lynn Frazier (ND) for refusing to support the Coolidge–Dawes ticket. This punishment aside, the regular Republicans often found the progressive element in their ranks—midwestern and western members, often referred to as the "Farm bloc"—too large to contain adequately. This Republican heterogeneity, as Smith and Gamm (2009) note, made it difficult for strong party leadership to develop. Indeed, Gould (2005) goes so far as to refer to Republican party leaders—formal Majority Leaders like Henry Cabot Lodge,

Sr. (MA), Charles Curtis (KS), and James E. Watson (IN), as well as informal leaders like William Borah (ID)—as "spearless" during this era.[27]

Party leadership from the New Deal through the present

Beginning in the 1930s, a period of weak party leadership emerged in both chambers, as contextual conditions led to power residing almost wholly within the committee system. Over time, conditions would evolve and create a congressional environment that was ripe for a resurgence in partisanship. In turn, a strengthening of party leadership would occur. This would be most clearly visible in the House, thanks to the passage of a host of party and chamber rules designed to strengthen the hand of leaders. In the Senate, where a similar spate of formal rules changes did not take place, leaders have had to rely upon more informal techniques to enhance their authority.

Committee ascendancy, 1933–60

After the Democrats won control of both chambers of Congress in 1932, as part of FDR's electoral tidal wave, they would maintain their status as the majority party— aside from two blips in the 80th (1947–9) and 83rd (1953–5) Congresses—until Ronald Reagan's election in 1980. Thus, majority party leadership for much of the New Deal era and beyond would be shaped by contextual conditions within the Democratic Party.

The first four years of FDR's presidency saw executive-led policymaking in Congress, as Democrats in both the House and Senate largely acquiesced to the New Deal agenda. For example, the Rules Committee in the House worked hand-in-hand with FDR to get his legislative priorities passed. Beginning in 1937, however, a transformation occurred as conservative Democrats and Republicans began cooperating to stymie FDR's momentum. This "conservative coalition" has been well documented in the literature—put simply, conservative southern Democrats, were concerned about the expansive liberal direction that FDR and northern Democrats were taking, especially in terms of how it might affect (and challenge) the Jim Crow system that had developed in the South after Reconstruction. Thus, in the House, the Rules Committee stopped being an arm of the majority party leadership and began operating as an independent bipartisan force, one that represented ideological (conservative) rather than partisan interests (Galloway 1961).

From 1937 through 1960, therefore, a very different system operated in Congress. Party leadership was weak in each chamber, thanks in part to the heterogeneity within the majority Democratic Party. With large liberal and conservative wings, located in the North and South, no consensus emerged about a "party" agenda, and thus little power was delegated to leaders. House leaders (the Speaker and Majority Leader)

[27] See Chapter 6 of Gould's (2005) history of the modern Senate, entitled "Spearless Leaders in the 1920s."

were very much like Senate leaders (the Majority Leader) during this time, operating as agents who could work to coordinate interests, but possessing little to no formal authority to dictate or compel behavior. Leadership influence thus occurred at the margins, and relied heavily upon the interpersonal skill and savvy of the leaders themselves; Speaker Sam Rayburn (TX) in the House and Majority Leader Lyndon Johnson (TX) in the Senate, for example, were noted for their ability to use communication networks and individual relationships to help achieve certain partisan goals (see, e.g., Huitt 1961; Cooper and Brady 1981; Hardeman and Bacon 1987; Caro 2002).[28] Instead, power was decentralized in the standing committees (and especially in the committee chairmen), jurisdictional control was paramount, and intercommittee reciprocity was how business got done (Sinclair 2005). Positions of power on committees were determined by seniority, and, as a result, southern Democrats—thanks to their long tenures in Congress—came to control many of the jurisdictional fiefdoms. As Shepsle (1989) notes, this portrait represents the "textbook Congress" that many scholars post-World War II came to know so well.

While this account of party leadership weakness during the conservative coalition era is widely shared, Cox and McCubbins (1993, 2005) have offered some evidence to the contrary. Simply put, they have argued that parties in the House have exerted influence continuously going back to the Reed Rules—such influence has been *procedural* in nature, as majority-party members have been expected to support caucus decisions on rules (or risk punishment, which can include being passed over for committee chairmanships and can be as severe as expulsion from the caucus) and majority-party leaders (the Speaker, committee chairs, the Rules Committee) have been expected to avoid taking actions that would harm a majority of the majority party. These works by Cox and McCubbins have been influential, and scholars have responded to their claims. The chief critiques have come from Schickler and Rich (1997a, 1997b), Schickler and Pearson (2009), and Pearson and Schickler (2009), who examine such legislative features as House rules, committee jurisdictions, seniority violations, and discharge petitions during the conservative coalition era and argue that cross-party coalitions were more important than majority-party leadership in explaining observed outcomes. Cox and McCubbins (1997, 2005) have responded to many of these critiques, and in doing so have helped foster a lively academic debate. Currently, both sides agree that the conservative coalition exerted *negative* influence in this period—blocking liberal Democratic initiatives that many Democrats favored—but they disagree about whether the conservative coalition exerted *positive* influence—pushing an agenda actively hostile to majority-party Democratic interests. Sorting out these conflicting claims in a definitive way will require new (and better) theories of positive agenda control—a phenomenon we know less about as a

---

[28] "Persuasion" seemed to be the main tool of party leaders during this era, regardless of chamber. For example, Republican Speaker Joe Martin noted, "I worked by persuasion and drew heavily on long-established personal friendships" (Martin 1960, 182), while Democratic Senate Majority Leader Lyndon B. Johnson argued, "The only real power to the [majority] leader is the power of persuasion" (quoted in Peabody 1976, 339).

scholarly community than negative agenda control—and (very likely) new and better empirical measures as well.[29]

Reform, transformation, and contemporary party leadership, 1960–2010

To understand the current state of party leadership in the contemporary Congress, scholars have typically focused on the 1958 congressional elections as an initial flash-point. In that year, a swath of new liberal Democrats were elected to the House and Senate, and they found (very quickly) that their programmatic policy demands were stymied by the conservative-based, committee-dominated system that was in place in both chambers. This tension—which escalated through the 1960s as subsequent elections brought in more liberal Democrats—led to chamber development that occurred along two separate paths: institutional reform in the House and a transformation in behavior in the Senate. A number of excellent book-length treatments exist on the development of the House and Senate during this era. Examples include Rohde (1991), Sinclair (1989, 1998, 2006, 2007), and Smith (1989). Other, shorter, accounts include Sinclair (2005), Smith (2005), and Aldrich and Rohde (2009). This section borrows heavily from these various works.

In the House, an initial change occurred in 1961, when Speaker Rayburn helped spearhead an expansion of the Rules Committee (from twelve to fifteen members), in response to concerns that President Kennedy's legislative agenda would otherwise stagnate. A significant burst of change would then occur between 1969 and 1975, as the Democratic caucus continued to move in a liberal direction, helped along by the electoral effects of the Voting Rights Act of 1965. Such changes included the elimination of the seniority system that automatically governed committee chairmanships, as a caucus rules change provided for a secret ballot for all chairmanships at the beginning of each Congress (conditional on the request of 20 percent of the caucus membership); a decentralization of authority from committees to subcommittees; an expansion of resources throughout the congressional ranks, which gave junior members more opportunities to participate; and a strengthening of the powers of the Speaker, who was granted the ability to appoint the Chair and Democratic members of the Rules Committee (making the Rules Committee once again an arm of the party leadership), given new authority to determine appointments to all other standing committees (through disproportionate influence on the new Steering and Policy

---

[29] For an overview of negative and positive agenda control, see Cox and McCubbins (2005) and Finocchiaro and Rohde (2008).

Committee), and provided with the right to refer bills to more than one committee (i.e. "multiple referral") and set deadlines for reporting.

In the early years after the reforms, decentralization of power in the House predominated, as party leaders, like the Speaker, were reluctant to exert their newfound influence. But as politics in the House became unwieldy, thanks to a proliferation of participatory efforts by members looking to make their mark and appeal to constituent sentiment, the Democratic rank and file looked to the leadership for guidance and coordination. Because the Democratic Party had become increasingly homogenous by the late 1970s, as southern conservative Democrats began disappearing, the caucus was willing to allow leaders more discretion in setting and overseeing the legislative agenda. To control proceedings, the leadership began relying on special (restrictive) rules to structure debate and floor voting—by the late 1980s, as Sinclair (2005, 231) notes, "Democratic leaders developed restrictive rules into powerful tools for advancing their members' legislative preferences." Leaders also took on a more active role at the pre-floor stage, negotiating with committees on the content and language of legislation and generally using their authority to insure that the party's agenda proceeded expeditiously. By this time, the Republican minority, increasingly homogenous as a conservative group, began adopting similar caucus-based rules in the hopes of better countering the Democrats. When the House changed partisan hands after the 1994 elections, the Republicans under Newt Gingrich (GA), and then later under Dennis Hastert (IL), further centralized decision-making authority in the Speaker, who took an ever more active role in committee selection (chairs and members) and legislative policymaking. Nancy Pelosi (CA), who became Speaker when the Democrats recaptured the House following the 2006 elections, has followed the Gingrich–Hastert plan in terms of activity and assertiveness, but has also relied more upon the expertise of committee chairmen to share in leadership decisions.

In the Senate, the decentralization of the textbook era gave way to individualism. With the influx of new, liberal members eager to make their mark, norms that had operated in the previous era—respect for seniority, deference to committees and committee chairs, etc.—quickly eroded. Much as in the House, floor participation increased, especially in regards to amendment votes and extended floor debate (Sinclair 1989). In addition, and more problematically, obstruction also increased, as members' use of filibusters and other forms of dilatory behavior (such as "holds") became more prevalent. But, unlike the House, the dominant party caucus in the Senate has not formally delegated new procedural authority to the Majority Leader to respond to these changing chamber conditions. As throughout history, the Senate's institutional path—as a smaller, more consensual body, with biases toward relatively weak leadership and unimpeded debate—have limited what chamber leaders could accomplish. If anything, the post-1960 era has made majority-party leaders rely even more upon bargaining and persuasion to direct the policymaking process in the Senate. That said, they have also sought new ways to lead effectively, especially as dilatory behavior by the minority has escalated. For example, Smith and Gamm (2009) note that Senate leaders have become more creative in managing Senate business— examples include attempting to stave off filibusters by splitting or combining bills, seeking unanimous consent agreements to require sixty-vote majorities, and bypassing the conference stage in inter-chamber proceedings and negotiating directly with House leaders.[30] In addition, Lee (2008) argues that as Senate parties have become more effective in recent years at steering the legislative agenda toward party cleavage issues—those on which there is internal party unity and wide divergence between the two parties—a strengthening of formal leadership structures in the Senate has also occurred, with party caucuses meeting more frequently and enhanced resources (both funds and staff levels) being devoted to party leadership offices.[31]

While these new leadership developments have been helpful, the minority's privileged procedural position in the Senate is a never-ending problem—as Harry Reid, the Democratic Majority Leader since January 2007, has discovered time and time again. In the end, the majority's inability (or, perhaps more accurately, *unwillingness*) to delegate broad formal authority to its leader has limited what can be accomplished in the Senate relative to the House. Instead, the majority party in the Senate has relied upon more informal channels to achieve its goals, along with a basic (and sometimes slightly naïve) "hope that its dedicated floor leader can improve efficiency and persuade the public of its program" (Smith and Gamm 2009, 161).

WHAT'S NEXT? FRONTIERS IN STUDYING THE EVOLUTION OF PARTY LEADERSHIP

While party leadership in Congress has been a central focus of study over the past two decades or more, a number of interesting and important research avenues remain. A complete list is beyond the scope of this chapter, but I will highlight several that strike me as especially ripe for study.

The turn to the historical study of Congress is still relatively new, and as I have indicated throughout this chapter, there is still much that we (as an academic community) do not know about party development in the U.S. Senate. Gamm and Smith (2000, 2002; Smith and Gamm 2009) have done a tremendous job of filling in many of the gaps in our collective knowledge, but a host of additional questions remain. Perhaps the biggest question is: how did party leadership develop, and how did it affect Senate decision-making, in the antebellum era? Moreover, the historical role of the Senate Majority leader—and how the position evolved from a more informal "floor leader" position—begs for greater explanation. This includes evolution extending into the "modern" period. For example, Smith (2007, 68) notes that the Majority Leader

---

[30] For additional evidence of majority-party effects in the Senate—which are not tied exclusively to leadership influence—see the essays in Monroe, Roberts, and Rohde (2008).

[31] More generally, Lee contends that majority-party members have *informally* delegated authority to leaders to pursue common goals, by willingly acquiescing to leaders' agenda decisions; this contrasts with the formal delegation that has occurred in the House.

achieved the "full range of modern leadership responsibilities," which included the right of first recognition, in the 1930s—yet, scholars know little about even these more recent developments. In addition, Lee's (2008) work on the rise of informal mechanisms of party power offers a fresh perspective for understanding party leadership development in the Senate—and one that is not tied to "orthodox" ideas stemming from House-based theories. In short, someone looking to make a mark in the study of party leadership in Congress would not go wrong in selecting the Senate as his/her area of focus.

Much more is known about the evolution of party leadership in the House. But this does not mean gaps in our collective knowledge do not exist. While the development of the speakership has elicited a good amount of attention (e.g. Peters 1997; Peters and Rosenthal 2010; Jenkins and Stewart, forthcoming), as has the whip system (e.g. Ripley 1964; Evans and Grandy 2009), very little is known about the development of the Majority Leader position. In general, understanding the evolution of floor leadership in *both* the House and the Senate is fertile ground for systematic inquiry.

The timing of institutional adoption across chambers has also not been studied systematically. For example, in noting that the House and Senate adopted standing committees (1810s) and caucuses (1840s) around the same time, one question to ask is: does cross-chamber "learning" go on? Do party leaders in one chamber analyze what institutional choices work (or not) in the other chamber—and copy (or not) accordingly? And are there other examples of "copying" beyond standing committees and caucuses? Relatedly, the differing membership sizes of the House and Senate over time may affect leadership choice and, more generally, how party leadership in the two chambers has evolved. While other cross-chamber choices early in congressional history have been stressed—on presiding-officer capabilities and previous-question rule decisions—the increasing size gap between the House and Senate through the early twentieth century is an institutional (structural) factor that deserves greater attention in future explanations of cross-chamber leadership development.

Examining how congressional party leaders manage relations with the president is also an area that requires greater attention. The president's role in influencing the party agenda in Congress is not often part of contemporary theoretical treatments (see Cox and McCubbins 2005 for an exception); this was not always the case, as Truman's (1959) study of the congressional party focused heavily on the intersection between party leaders and the president. Prime questions for examination would include: when do party leaders depend on presidential help, given unified party government?; to what extent are leaders' jobs dictated by a president's strategic choices rather than a simple product of what most caucus members want?; and how has the interaction between congressional leaders and the president varied by time and by chamber?

Finally, in studying the contemporary Congress, a number of topics Barbara Sinclair refers to as "unorthodox lawmaking" deserve more systematic analysis (see Sinclair 2006, 2007). First, she notes the emergence of "task forces" in both the House and Senate in recent decades; these task forces represent both complements and challenges to the chambers' committee systems. When and under what conditions do leaders turn to task forces? And is there evidence that the existence of task forces affects political outcomes in some predictable ways? Second, Sinclair describes party leaders being more active in the policymaking process in both chambers, sometimes bypassing the committee system (and their established jurisdictions). Does this happen often? And is it more likely to happen with committees that are less representative of the majority party? Third, Sinclair notes that party leadership also involves thinking beyond the particular chamber in question—House leaders and Senate leaders often have to coordinate on policy questions in order to expedite the production of laws. When do leaders bypass the traditional cross-institutional mechanisms for cooperation (i.e. conference committees) and negotiate directly with the other chamber's leaders? Is this happening more often over time? And what explains the variation—the substantive issue area under consideration, coalition size in each chamber, ideological dispersion in each chamber, divided government, or something else?

In sum, while the congressional literature on party leadership is full of important and insightful works, opportunities for new research abound. Studies that focus on the *evolution* of party leadership are especially well positioned to make a significant scholarly impact. As we, as an academic community, learn more about how party leadership operates in different eras (and sub-eras), the next logical step is to assess how, when, and why party leadership *changes* (or not) across eras (and sub-eras) in a *systematic* way. Some excellent research in this regard is being done, as I have indicated throughout this chapter, but more is needed—and will undoubtedly be produced in upcoming years. I eagerly await such work.

REFERENCES

ALDRICH, J. H. 1995. *Why Parties?: The Origin and Transformation of Party Politics in America*. Chicago: University of Chicago Press.

ALDRICH, J. H., and ROHDE, D. W. 2009. Congressional Committees in a Continuing Partisan Era, pp. 217–40 in *Congress Reconsidered*, 9th edn, ed. L. C. Dodd and B. I. Oppenheimer. Washington: CQ Press.

ALEXANDER, D. A. 1916. *History and Procedure of the House of Representatives*. Boston: Houghton Mifflin.

BACON, D. C. 1998. Nicholas Longworth: The Genial Czar, pp. 119–43 in *Masters of the House*, ed. R. H. Davidson, S. Webb Hammond, and R. M. Smock. Boulder: Westview.

BELZ, H. 1970. The Etheridge Conspiracy of 1863: A Projected Conservative Coup. *Journal of Southern History*, 36: 549–67.

BINDER, S. A. 1997. *Minority Rights, Majority Rule: Partisanship and the Development of Congress*. Cambridge: Cambridge University Press.

——MADONNA, A. J., and SMITH, S. S. 2007. Going Nuclear, Senate Style. *Perspectives on Politics*, 5: 729–40.

——and SMITH, S. S. 1997. *Politics or Principle?: Filibuster in the United States Senate*. Washington: Brookings Institution Press.

BROWN, G. R. 1922. *The Leadership of Congress.* Indianapolis: The Bobbs-Merrill Company.

BYRD, R. C. 1991. *The Senate, 1789–1989: Addresses on the History of the United States Senate,* Vol. 2. Washington: Government Printing Office.

CARO, R. A. 2002. *Master of the Senate.* New York: Knopf.

COOPER, J. 1970. *The Origins of the Standing Committees and the Development of the Modern House.* Houston: Rice University Studies.

——and BRADY, D. W. 1981. Institutional Context and Leadership Style: The House from Cannon to Rayburn. *American Political Science Review,* 75: 411–25.

COX, G. W., and McCUBBINS, M. D. 1993. *Legislative Leviathan: Party Government in the House.* Berkeley: University of California Press.

————1997. Toward a Theory of Legislative Rules Changes: Assessing Schickler and Rich's Evidence. *American Journal of Political Science,* 41: 1376–86.

————2005. *Setting the Agenda: Responsible Party Government in the U.S. House of Representatives.* Cambridge: Cambridge University Press.

DION, D. 1997. *Turning the Legislative Thumbscrew: Minority Rights and Procedural Change in Congress.* Ann Arbor: University of Michigan Press.

EVANS, C. L., and GRANDY, C. E. 2009. The Whip Systems of Congress, pp. 189–215 in *Congress Reconsidered,* 9th edn, ed. L. C. Dodd and B. I. Oppenheimer. Washington: CQ Press.

FINOCCHIARO, C. J., and ROHDE, D. W. 2007. Speaker David Henderson and the Partisan Era of the U.S. House, pp. 259–70 in *Party, Process, and Political Change in Congress,* Vol. 2, ed. D. W. Brady and M. D. McCubbins. Stanford: Stanford University Press.

————2008. War for the Floor: Partisan Theory and Agenda Control in the U.S. House of Representatives. *Legislative Studies Quarterly,* 33: 35–61.

FOLLETT, M. P. 1896. *The Speaker of the House of Representatives.* New York: Longmans, Green, and Co.

FULLER, H. B. 1909. *The Speakers of the House.* Boston: Little, Brown, and Company.

GALLOWAY, G. B. 1961. *History of the House of Representatives.* New York: Thomas Y. Crowell Company.

GAMM, G., and SHEPSLE, K. 1989. Emergence of Legislative Institutions: Standing Committees in the House and Senate, 1810–1825. *Legislative Studies Quarterly,* 14: 39–66.

——and SMITH, S. S. 2000. Last Among Equals: The Senate's Presiding Officer, pp. 105–34 in *Esteemed Colleagues: Civility and Deliberation in the U.S. Senate,* ed. B. A. Loomis. Washington: Brookings Institution Press.

————2002. Emergence of Senate Party Leadership, pp. 212–40 in *U.S. Senate Exceptionalism,* ed. B. I. Oppenheimer. Columbus: The Ohio State University Press.

GOULD, L. L. 2005. *The Most Exclusive Club: A History of the Modern United States Senate.* New York: Basic Books.

GREEN, M. N. 2002. Institutional Change, Party Discipline, and the House Democratic Caucus, 1911–1919. *Legislative Studies Quarterly,* 27: 601–33.

HARDEMAN, D. B., and BACON, D. C. 1987. *Rayburn: A Biography.* Lanham, MD: Madison Books.

HARLOW, R. V. 1917. *The History of Legislative Methods in the Period Before 1825.* New Haven: Yale University Press.

HASBROUCK, P. D. 1927. *Party Government in The House of Representatives.* New York: Macmillan.

HEITSHUSEN, V. 2007. Party Leaders in the U.S. Congress, 1789–2007. CRS Report for Congress, RL30567.

HOFSTADTER, R. 1969. *The Idea of a Party System: The Rise of Legitimate Opposition in the United States, 1789–1840.* Berkeley: University of California Press.

HOLT, J. 1967. *Congressional Insurgents and the Party System, 1909–1916*. Cambridge, MA: Harvard University Press.

HUITT, R. K. 1961. Democratic Party Leadership in the Senate. *American Political Science Review*, 55: 333–44.

JENKINS, J. A. 1998. Property Rights and the Emergence of Standing Committee Dominance in the Nineteenth–Century House. *Legislative Studies Quarterly*, 23: 493–519.

——SCHICKLER, E., and CARSON, J. L. 2004. Constituency Cleavages and Congressional Parties: Measuring Homogeneity and Polarization, 1857–1913. *Social Science History*, 28: 537–73.

——and STEWART, III, C. 2002. Order from Chaos: The Transformation of the Committee System in the House, 1816–1822, pp. 195–236 in *Party, Process, and Political Change in Congress: New Perspectives on the History of Congress*, ed. D. W. Brady and M. D. McCubbins. Stanford: Stanford University Press.

————2003. Out in the Open: The Emergence of *Viva Voce* Voting in House Speakership Elections. *Legislative Studies Quarterly*, 28: 481–508.

————Forthcoming. *Fighting for the Speakership: The House and the Rise of Party Government*. Princeton: Princeton University Press.

KOGER, G. 2010. *Filibustering: A Political History of Obstruction in the House and Senate*. Chicago: University of Chicago Press.

KOLODNY, R. 1998. *Pursuing Majorities: Congressional Campaign Committees in American Politics*. Norman: University of Oklahoma Press.

KREHBIEL, K., and WISEMAN, A. 2001. Joseph G. Cannon: Majoritarian from Illinois. *Legislative Studies Quarterly*, 26: 357–89.

————2005. Joe Cannon and the Minority Party: Tyranny or Bipartisanship? *Legislative Studies Quarterly*, 30: 497–505.

LAWRENCE, E. D., MALTZMAN, F., and WAHLBECK, P. J. 2001. The Politics of Speaker Cannon's Committee Assignments. *American Journal of Political Science*, 45: 551–62.

LEE, F. E. 2008. Agreeing to Disagree: Agenda Content and Senate Partisanship, 1981–2004. *Legislative Studies Quarterly*, 33: 199–222.

LOWELL, A. L. 1902. The Influence of Party upon Legislation in England and America. *Annual Report of the American Historical Association for 1901*, 1: 321–544.

MARTIN, J. 1960. *My First Fifty Years in Politics*. New York: McGraw-Hill.

MONROE, N. W., ROBERTS, J. M., and ROHDE, D. W. (eds). 2008. *What Not Parties?: Party Effects in the United States Senate*. Chicago: University of Chicago Press.

OLESZEK, W. J. 1991. John Worth Kern: Portrait of a Floor Leader, pp. 7–37 in *First Among Equals: Outstanding Senate Leaders of the Twentieth Century*, ed. R. A. Baker and R. H. Davidson. Washington: CQ Press.

PEABODY, R. L. 1976. *Leadership in Congress: Stability, Succession, and Change*. Boston: Little, Brown and Company.

PEARSON, K., and SCHICKLER, E. 2009. Discharge Petitions, Agenda Control, and the Congressional Committee System, 1929–76. *Journal of Politics*, 71: 1238–56.

PETERS, JR., R. M. 1997. *The American Speakership: The Office in Historical Perspective*. 2nd edn. Baltimore: Johns Hopkins University Press.

——and ROSENTHAL, C. S. 2010. *Speaker Nancy Pelosi and the New American Politics*. Norman: University of Oklahoma Press.

RIDDICK, F. M. 1949. *The United States Congress: Organization and Procedure*. Manassas, VA: National Capitol Publishers.

RIPLEY, R. B. 1964. The Party Whip Organizations in the United States House of Representatives. *American Political Science Review*, 58: 561–76.

RIPLEY, R. B. 1967. *Party Leaders in the House of Representatives*. Washington: The Brookings Institution.

—— 1969. *Majority Party Leadership in Congress*. Boston: Little, Brown and Company.

RISJORD, N. K. 1992. Partisanship and Power: House Committees and the Powers of the Speaker, 1789–1801. *William and Mary Quarterly*, 49: 628–51.

ROBERTS, J. M., and SMITH, S. S. 2007. The Evolution of Agenda-Setting Institutions in Congress: Path Dependency in House and Senate Institutional Development, pp. 182–204 in *Party, Process, and Political Change in Congress*, Vol. 2, ed. D. W. Brady and M. D. McCubbins. Stanford: Stanford University Press.

ROHDE, D. W. 1991. *Parties and Leaders in the Postreform House*. Chicago: University of Chicago Press.

—— and SHEPSLE, K. A. 1987. Leaders and Followers in the House of Representatives: Reflections on Woodrow Wilson's Congressional Government. *Congress and the Presidency*, 14: 111–33.

ROTHMAN, D. J. 1966. *Politics and Power: The United States Senate 1869–1901*. Cambridge, MA: Harvard University Press.

SCHICKLER, E. 2001. *Disjointed Pluralism: Institutional Innovation and the Development of the U.S. Congress*. Princeton: Princeton University Press.

—— and PEARSON, K. 2009. Agenda Control, Majority Party Power, and the House Committee on Rules, 1937–1952. *Legislative Studies Quarterly*, 34: 455–92.

—— and RICH, A. 1997a. Controlling the Floor: Parties as Procedural Coalitions in the House. *American Journal of Political Science*, 41: 1340–75.

—— —— 1997b. Party Government in the House Reconsidered: A Response to Cox and McCubbins. *American Journal of Political Science*, 41: 1387–94.

—— and SIDES, J. 2000. Intergenerational Warfare: The Senate Decentralizes Appropriations. *Legislative Studies Quarterly*, 25: 551–75.

SELLERS, JR., C. G. 1957. *James K. Polk: Jacksonian*. Princeton: Princeton University Press.

SHEPSLE, K. A. 1989. The Changing Textbook Congress, pp. 238–67 in *Can the Government Govern?*, ed. J. E. Chubb and P. E. Peterson. Washington: Brookings Institution.

SINCLAIR, B. 1989. *The Transformation of the U.S. Senate*. Baltimore: Johns Hopkins University Press.

—— 1998. *Legislators, Leaders, and Lawmaking: The U.S. House of Representatives in the Postreform Era*. Baltimore: Johns Hopkins University Press.

—— 2005. Parties and Leadership in the House, pp. 224–54 in *The Legislative Branch*, ed. P. J. Quirk and S. A. Binder. Oxford: Oxford University Press.

—— 2006. *Party Wars: Polarization and the Politics of National Policy Making*. Norman: University of Oklahoma Press.

—— 2007. *Unorthodox Lawmaking: New Legislative Processes in the U.S. Congress*. Washington: CQ Press.

SMITH, C. H. 1977. *The Press, Politics, and Patronage: The American Government's Use of Newspapers, 1789–1875*. Athens: The University of Georgia Press.

SMITH, S. S. 1989. *Call to Order: Floor Politics in the House and Senate*. Washington: Brookings Institution.

—— 2005. Parties and Leadership in the Senate, pp. 255–78 in *The Legislative Branch*, ed. P. J. Quirk and S. A. Binder. Oxford: Oxford University Press.

—— 2007. *Party Influence in Congress*. Cambridge: Cambridge University Press.

—— and GAMM, G. 2009. The Dynamics of Party Government in Congress, pp. 141–64 in *Congress Reconsidered*, 9th edn, ed. L. C. Dodd and B. I. Oppenheimer. Washington: CQ Press.

STEWART, III, C. 2007. Architect or Tactician? Henry Clay and the Institutional Development of the U.S. House of Representatives, pp. 133–56 in *Party, Process, and Political Change in Congress*, Vol. 2, ed. D. W. Brady and M. D. McCubbins. Stanford: Stanford University Press.

STRAHAN, R. 2007. *Leading Representatives: The Agency of Leaders in the Politics of the U.S. House*. Baltimore: The Johns Hopkins University Press.

—— GUNNING, M., and VINING, JR., R. L. 2006. From Moderator to Leader: Floor Participation by U.S. House Speakers, 1789–1841. *Social Science History*, 30: 51–74.

—— MOSCARDELLI, V., HASPEL, M., and R. WIKE. 2000. The Clay Speakership Revisited. *Polity* 32: 561–93.

SWIFT, E. K. 1996. *The Making of an American Senate: Reconstitutive Change in Congress, 1787–1841*. Ann Arbor: University of Michigan Press.

THOMPSON, C. W. 1906. *Party Leaders of the Time*. New York: G. W. Dillingham Co.

TRUMAN, D. B. 1959. *The Congressional Party: A Case Study*. New York: Wiley.

VALELLY, R. M. 2009. The Reed Rules and Republican Party Building: A New Look. *Studies in American Political Development*, 23: 115–42.

WALLACE, M. 1968. Changing Concepts of Party in the United States: New York, 1815–1828. *American Historical Review*, 74: 453–91.

WAWRO, G. J., and SCHICKLER, E. 2006. *Filibuster: Obstruction and Lawmaking in the U.S. Senate*. Princeton: Princeton University Press.

YOUNG, J. S. 1966. *The Washington Community, 1800–1828*. New York: Columbia University Press.

CHAPTER 31

....

THE DEVELOPMENT OF THE CONGRESSIONAL COMMITTEE SYSTEM

....

ERIC SCHICKLER[*]

CONGRESSIONAL committees have been a core preoccupation of Congress scholars for generations. Woodrow Wilson's landmark *Congressional Government* (1885) highlighted the standing committee system as the most important locus of power in Congress. Lauros McConachie's *Congressional Committees*, a detailed history tracing legislative committees' origins back to British practice, was published in 1898. Classic works of the 1950s and 1960s, such as Polsby's (1968) study of the institutionalization of the House and Fenno's *Power of the Purse* (1966), put the operations of the committee system front and center. Contemporary theories of legislative organization—such as the distributive, informational, and partisan models—hone in on the committee system as a key site for understanding the motivations behind decisions about congressional organization (see Chapter 18, this volume, by C. Lawrence Evans). Committees also play a critical role in shaping policy outcomes and in defining Congress's relationship to the executive branch.

* I thank Ruth Bloch Rubin for her excellent research assistance and for her helpful comments on the manuscript. The valuable comments of Joseph Cooper and Frances Lee are also gratefully acknowledged.

Nonetheless, the *development* of the committee system has arguably received less attention than other key features of the congressional landscape. This chapter traces the literature on committee development, starting with studies of the origins of the committee system, and moving from there to research on the expansion of the system in the nineteenth century and the consolidation that took place in the middle decades of the twentieth century. The chapter concludes with a briefer discussion of more recent changes, such as the reforms of the 1970s and mid-1990s (see Diana Evans, Chapter 14, this volume, and E. Scott Adler, Chapter 21, this volume, for more detailed reviews of these reforms). In assessing the development of the modern committee system, I consider the changing roles played by committees in congressional politics, highlighting the rise of investigations as a crucial, understudied aspect of committee development.

The development of the committee system provides considerable cross-sectional and over-time variation that could be used to evaluate and refine contemporary theories of legislative politics. Much of this promise has not yet been realized, but recent data collection efforts concerning committee creation and composition could provide a firmer empirical basis for a new generation of studies of committee development.

Understanding the development of the committee system is crucial because it speaks to both Congress's place in the political system and the internal distribution of power in the legislative branch. The existence of a committee system that allows for division of labor and specialization is arguably the single internal institutional feature that most clearly differentiates legislatures that retain their influence from those that cede their power to the executive branch (Polsby 1975). The story of Congress's development of legislative capacity is to a substantial extent the story of committee development. Given committees' centrality to lawmaking, it should not be a surprise that the question of "who governs" in Congress has depended heavily on the kinds of coalitions and legislative actors in control of the committee system. Eras of party government are marked by effective mechanisms of majority party control over the committee system, just as eras of weak parties feature cross-party coalitions directing key committees. As a result, changes in the committee system serve as a window into broader changes in who governs the legislative branch.

THE ORIGINS OF STANDING COMMITTEES

Several decades after its publication, the most influential study of committee development continues to be Joseph Cooper's *Congress and Its Committees* (1960 [1988]), along with Cooper's related monograph, *The Origins of the Standing Committees and the Development of the Modern House* (1970). Cooper sought to understand one of the most important transformations in congressional history: the creation in the early nineteenth century of a system of specialized standing committees.

Contemporary observers take the existence of a standing committee system for granted. Yet it is by no means the norm when one considers legislatures from a cross-national perspective (see Polsby 1975), and members of Congress were initially hostile to the creation of a specialized committee system. As Cooper highlights, representatives in the first several congresses distrusted concentrations of power over legislating, which they believed threatened the equality of the members. Jeffersonian thought, which Cooper demonstrates was widely accepted by rank-and-file legislators, held that the full chamber should make all important decisions about legislation. Consistent with this outlook, legislative proposals were initially considered by the full membership in the 1790s. The chamber as a whole would decide whether action was warranted and, if so, refer the proposal to a temporary select committee for detailed drafting. The select committee would then report back to the floor for further debate, possible amendments, and approval. Select committees initially existed to draft only a single piece of legislation and thus generally did not develop expertise or influence. The House created 220 select committees in the First Congress alone. In the first fourteen Congresses (1789–1817), the House and Senate each appointed over two thousand select committees (Canon and Stewart 2001).

The centrality of temporary committees gradually gave way in the House from the 1790s through the 1820s (Skladony 1985). By 1809, which coincided with the end of Thomas Jefferson's administration, the House had created nine standing committees. Seven new standing committees were formed in 1816, including six committees tasked with overseeing spending in various executive departments. Three additional standing committees were created in 1822. During this same period, changes in practice—codified in the rules by the early 1820s—strengthened standing committees' jurisdictional claims. In the past, legislation could be referred to a select committee even when a standing committee already existed that evidently had jurisdiction over that topic. By 1822 House rules and practice circumscribed this process. In addition, the House made important changes in who could initiate legislation. As Cooper describes, under Jeffersonian theory, legislation must originate in the full chamber. The House gradually departed from this understanding over the first two decades of the nineteenth century, so that by the early 1820s it was clearly understood that committees could propose legislation on their own initiative. Finally, the House adopted a strict germaneness rule that blocked floor amendments that were unrelated to the text of the bill under consideration. Together, these innovations began to establish standing committees' jurisdictional claims.

Cooper identifies two major sources for this broad transformation in the committee system. First, conflict with the executive branch gave members a strong incentive to enhance their institution's access to independent expertise. In the absence of standing committees, members of Congress had to rely upon the executive departments for information about pending legislative proposals. Treasury Secretary Alexander Hamilton capitalized upon his informational advantage when Congress debated his ambitious economic development program in the 1790s. The House gave the Committee on Ways and Means standing status in the Fourth Congress (1795–7), evidently to counterbalance Hamilton's advantage (Cooper 1960). Second, Cooper (1970, 49) highlights the role of the increased size and workload of the House during these years, which made it far more difficult to rely upon select committees as a mechanism to process legislation.[1] However, Cooper emphasizes that size and workload alone are insufficient to explain the *form* of the change. While it was no longer feasible to debate each topic of legislation on the floor prior to reference to a committee, it would have been possible to delegate to the executive branch or some other body to scrutinize proposals and filter out which bills warrant floor consideration. However, such delegation was viewed as anathema in the context of members' understanding that the legislative branch itself—and its rank-and-file members—ought to control the writing of legislation in order for it to be legitimate. As a result, standing committees emerged as a solution to members' desire to simultaneously satisfy their informational needs and personal power goals, while creating a process that would be viewed as legitimate in light of widely accepted republican norms (see Swift 1996 as well on situating congressional development with respect to democratic norms).

While Cooper acknowledges that party leaders and partisan interests contributed to these developments—for example, by exacerbating conflicts in the policy and political interests of the two branches—his emphasis is on separation of powers (see Hammond and Monroe 2005). Several more recent studies have assessed the role of party leaders in generating committee development. Most notably, Gamm and Shepsle (1989) argue that Speaker of the House Henry Clay played a key role in converting the system of select and "semi-standing" committees into permanent standing committees.[2] Specifically, as Clay's coalition began to fray in the aftermath of the War of 1812, the Speaker saw the potential benefits of decentralizing power to standing committees. In the absence of a unified platform that his members could agree upon, Clay doled out turf to various factions in order to keep each reasonably satisfied—and thus, to maintain their support for his election to the speakership and for his presidential aspirations. Jenkins (1998) similarly emphasizes Clay's role in spearheading the committee system's creation, arguing that Clay distributed committee property rights to bolster support for his presidential aspirations.

While the Gamm and Shepsle and Jenkins accounts make a strong circumstantial case that Clay's ambitions played an important role, subsequent research has called into question accounts that emphasize individual leadership. For example, Randall Strahan's (2007) detailed study of the Clay speakership indicates that the Kentuckian orchestrated the creation of a single standing committee, the Committee on Manufacturers, in 1819. Clay sought the new committee in order to promote his high tariff agenda in the face of resistance from the Ways and Means and Commerce Committees, each of which had a jurisdictional claim to the policy. But Strahan's

---

[1] Along these lines, it is worth noting that many of the earliest standing committees were created to process the onslaught of private claims and other types of minor legislation. With a few notable exceptions—such as Ways and Means and Judiciary—the first standing committees dealt with the high volume of minor, constituency-oriented legislation that members confronted.

[2] Semi-standing committees were select committees that were regularly reappointed across multiple sessions, reflecting an intermediate stage between select and permanent standing committees (Skladony 1985).

careful search of Clay's papers and other primary sources found no evidence that Clay directed any of the other committee system innovations while he was Speaker. Similarly, Stewart (2007) challenges accounts that place Clay at the center of the committee system's development, noting that the gradual rise of standing committees continued both during congresses in which Clay served as Speaker *and* Congresses in which Clay was not even a member.

Even more importantly, Stewart (2007) points out that the Senate actually experienced a more sudden increase in the number of standing committees than the House, while Clay was serving in the lower chamber. The Senate did not establish its first standing committee until 1807, and that committee dealt only with internal housekeeping responsibilities. But the Senate caught up with the House in 1816, when it created twelve new standing committees, including the Finance, Judiciary, and Foreign Relations Committees. Following this change, the number of select committees in the upper chamber fell dramatically and referral to the appropriate standing committee became the norm.[3] The parallel Senate and House developments suggest that broader contextual forces likely generated the demand for a standing committee system.

Stewart's (2007) analysis suggests that there may be good reason to reframe the question when it comes to committee development. Instead of asking why the House developed a standing committee system in the early nineteenth century, a more fruitful line of inquiry may be to ask why the House and Senate created standing committee systems during these years, which coincided on some dimensions while differing along other dimensions. The similarity in timing across the two chambers suggests that underlying common demands—such as legislative-executive tensions and new policy challenges—likely had an important impact (see also Swift 1996). Yet it is also worth noting that the Senate provided committees with less extensive prerogatives than in the House. It never adopted a strict germaneness rule and continued to allow bills to be referred to the floor without going to committee, thus providing individual senators with greater leverage in relation to the committees. These differences may well reflect the smaller size of the upper chamber.

More generally, greater explanatory leverage likely can be obtained by systematic comparisons of the committee system's development in the two chambers. Canon and Stewart (2001) begin to take up this challenge, while developing a promising dataset that should put studies of committee development on a firmer empirical footing. Canon and Stewart pored through the House and Senate Journals, along with compilations of congressional debates, with the goal of documenting the creation of each select and standing committee in both chambers from 1789 to 1879. They also attempted to track all assignments to each committee and to track whether select committees were created to consider a specific bill or a more general subject area,

---

[3] Even the Senate change may have been more gradual than it appears at first glance: Robinson (1955) shows that several of the standing committees nominally created in 1816 had been treated as semi-standing committees for nearly a decade. Similarly, Gould (1959) argues that the Senate Foreign Relations Committee had gradually become a long-term fixture before it formally gained standing status in 1816.

and when the committees reported to the floor. Canon and Stewart present several intriguing findings based on this new data. First, they show that select committees faded away more gradually in the House than the Senate, but that Senate select committees were more likely to focus on a single piece of legislation, while House select committees were more likely to be granted wider latitude. Second, they find very high turnover on standing committees during this era, even after one accounts for the high level of electoral turnover in both chambers. This goes against the notion that committees built up high levels of specialized expertise early on. They also find suggestive support for distributive models of committees: when a select committee was created to deal with a locally based claim or petition, members from that state were especially likely to be appointed. While Canon and Stewart steer clear of broad claims about what their data tell us about the sources of the transformation in the two chambers' committee systems, their impressive data collection efforts provide the basis for further systematic tests.

New research by Jenkins and Stewart (forthcoming) also points the way towards how novel data sources, combined with contemporary theoretical approaches, can enrich our understanding of committee development. Jenkins and Stewart explore the changes in House rules and practices, which as described above, provided committees with clearer jurisdictional claims over legislation. Jenkins and Stewart argue that the changes were, in part, a response to the chaos engulfing the chamber as party lines gave way to a more amorphous factionalism. With parties largely absent, speakership elections turned into protracted battles. Jenkins and Stewart show that these battles were repeatedly resolved through compromises involving the Speaker's use of committee assignments to put together a broad coalition. They hypothesize that the changes solidifying committee jurisdictions were essential to enforce these compromises; otherwise, rewarding potential opponents with valuable committee assignments would not necessarily be a credible concession. As the committee system became more institutionalized, committee assignments became an effective coalition-building currency. Drawing upon a combination of qualitative evidence and data on committee composition and roll-call voting, Jenkins and Stewart provide considerable evidence for their account. The Jenkins–Stewart hypothesis is also consistent with the Senate's decision not to provide similar protections for its committees. Since the Constitution named the vice president as the Senate's presiding officer, the chamber did not have organizing battles analogous to speakership elections. Instead, the Senate continued to operate more on the basis of informal rules that left considerable latitude for individual members. The relatively small size of the Senate also likely contributed to its ability to rely upon informal constraints rather than formal rules to provide a modicum of order and organizational stability (Wawro and Schickler 2006).

These chamber differences continued to grow over the course of the nineteenth century. In the 1820s, while House standing committee jurisdictions enjoyed several protections, they still lacked firm property rights over legislation. For example, Cooper and Young (1989) find that it was still relatively common for bill referrals to include detailed resolutions of instruction in the 1820s. Committee jurisdictions were also sparsely specified, and referrals to the appropriate committee, while expected, were not mandatory. Furthermore, motions to discharge committees were a viable option during this period (Cooper and Young 1989). A series of new precedents and rules adopted over the course of the nineteenth century—culminating in a major revision in 1880—made it much harder to extract bills from committee and made referrals mandatory. The Senate, by contrast, retained greater flexibility in terms of its referral process and accorded members greater leeway to bypass committees (e.g. through non-germane amendments).

In sum, the literature on the early development and consolidation of the committee system has made considerable advances since Joseph Cooper's landmark account. While the causal factors identified by Cooper evidently remain the most plausible general sources for the change—that is, competition with the executive branch and the onset of a more diverse and demanding legislative workload—recent data collection efforts have begun to enhance our understanding of precisely which mechanisms account for the creation of standing committees and what explains the partially divergent choices by the House and Senate on how to structure their committee systems.

THE EXPANSION OF THE COMMITTEE SYSTEM, 1820S–1910S

Two major themes emerge when one considers committee system development from the 1820s through the first decades of the twentieth century. First, the committee system expanded over time, as new committees were created to deal with new policy challenges and as control over spending was parceled out to more committees. Second, the relationship of committees to the party system was tightened in both chambers. This involved both changes in committee assignments and the development of the House Rules Committee as an agenda-setting tool.

The literature on the expansion of the committee system is surprisingly thin, given the subject's relevance for informational, distributive, and partisan theories of legislative organization. The sheer number of standing committees in both chambers increased dramatically during these years. The House, which had nineteen standing committees in 1817, added new committees at a steady pace over the ensuing decades, and had thirty-seven standing committees on the eve of the Civil War and nearly sixty standing committees by 1918 (see Canon and Stewart 2001; Cooper and Young 1989). The Senate added committees more gradually in the 1820s–50s; it had twenty-six standing committees as the Civil War began (Canon and Stewart 2001). But the upper chamber then surpassed the House in creating many new standing committees, so that by 1918 there were seventy-four Senate standing committees (Deering and

Smith 1997, 27–8). Yet this dramatic growth does not mean that these committees were all active participants in the legislative process; indeed, Robinson (1955) argues that many Senate committees never met and instead were primarily used to justify granting office space, a clerk, and printing allowance to their chairmen. Indeed, by the early twentieth century, all majority party senators could typically count on being able to chair a committee, and the inactive committees even provided sinecures for senior minority party members, who shared in the chairmanship appointments (Kravitz 1974).

While scholars have documented the year in which each standing committee was created (see, e.g., Canon and Stewart 2001; Robinson 1955; Kravitz 1974), there has been little research into explaining why the House and Senate created standing committees at particular times and to address particular subjects. At a broad level, it seems clear that the expanded agenda of the federal government played an important role, but this still leaves important questions unanswered. Potential research questions include whether standing committees tend to be created after there is a noticeable increase in relevant legislation in their jurisdictional area. Are particular types of policy issues—for example, distributive, regulatory, or redistributive—more likely to generate new standing committees, as opposed to having the policies absorbed by existing committees? What factors predict whether an existing select committee is turned into a standing committee, as opposed to continuing its temporary status or being dropped? Are new standing committees more likely to be created when the existing committees with "close" jurisdiction have preferences that are out of alignment with the majority party or chamber as a whole? What explains whether an existing committee becomes inactive over time? Is it simply a matter of its subject area losing relevance amid changing conditions or is its jurisdiction encroached upon by other committees (see King 1997)? Finally, how did the development of the committee system influence the balance of power with other institutions, such as the president and burgeoning bureaucracy? These and other potential questions with important theoretical implications could be answered through systematic study of committee creation and activities in this period. It would be necessary to bring to bear other data sources—such as information on bill introductions and the legislative agenda more generally—but the result could enrich our understanding of the purposes served by committees over time.

There have been scholarly studies of a handful of specific committee changes in this period, particularly with regard to appropriations. In 1865, the House took the power to report spending bills from the Ways and Means Committee and gave it to the newly created Appropriations Committee. The Senate followed suit in the next Congress, creating an Appropriations Committee to take over the spending duties of its Finance Committee. Wander (1982, 27) provides one of the few analyses of the 1865–7 changes, arguing that the "pressures spawned by economic burdens produced by the long years of war" motivated members. Indeed, Wander shows that the workload of Ways and Means and Finance had increased dramatically during the Civil War, and that this excessive workload led even key members of the two committees to support taking away some of their jurisdiction. Wander adds that long-simmering resentment against the disproportionate power of the committees also played some role, but concludes that the difficulty of formulating a response to the budgetary challenges brought about by the war constituted the main "occasion for innovation" (1982, 28). Stewart (1989) agrees with Wander that widely shared concerns about workload were the impetus for the 1865–7 reforms, but suggests a potentially important refinement to this argument: while the Civil War made the existing Ways and Means Committee's duties excessive, legislators could have adopted a range of solutions to this problem. For example, it would have been feasible to expand the committee and develop further the nascent subcommittee system to provide both division of labor and coordination. Stewart conjectures that members chose instead to create a new Appropriations Committee (along with a new Banking and Currency Committee, taking Ways and Means' control over the financial system), because expanding Ways and Means would have created a power center so formidable that it threatened the influence of both the Speaker and of the remaining members who did not serve on the Committee. Since the change itself passed on a voice vote with little debate and scant press coverage, Stewart is unable to put this hypothesis to a test. But it suggests a possible frame for studying committee creation more generally: that is, members are more likely to create a new committee to handle an issue when the existing committee with the strongest claim to jurisdiction is viewed as a rival for power to the Speaker or, alternatively, is viewed as particularly privileged by rank-and-file members.

The absence of roll-call votes surrounding the creation of the House Appropriations Committee (HAC) and the Senate Appropriations Committee (SAC) make systematic analysis difficult. However, the presence of a full roll-call record has allowed several important works to investigate the diffusion of control over House appropriations that began in 1878 and culminated in 1885. During that period, the House voted to distribute the power over reporting spending bills in their substantive area to seven authorizing committees, leaving the Appropriations Committee with control over just a handful of spending measures. Wander (1982) and Brady and Morgan (1987) claim that these reforms stemmed from representatives' discontent with the Appropriations Committee's stingy allocations to popular programs. Members thus decentralized appropriations to increase spending. Kiewiet and McCubbins (1991) offer an alternative, party-based account. Majority party Democrats targeted the Appropriations Committee because it was chaired by Samuel Randall (D-PA), a dissident Democrat who had repeatedly used his influence to fight Democratic leaders' efforts to reduce tariffs.

Stewart (1989) offers the most detailed and nuanced treatment of the House appropriations changes. He argues that individual members' electoral goals generated recurring pressure to decentralize appropriations, particularly when it came to pork-barrel programs. Those seeking increased spending won a series of skirmishes in 1878–80, which shifted jurisdiction over appropriations for rivers and harbors and agriculture to the Commerce and Agriculture Committees, respectively. But this did not ease the pressure to decentralize. In 1885, discontent with Appropriations' stinginess intersected with Democratic leaders' desire to limit Randall's influence to produce a large-scale decentralization. In contrast to Kiewiet and McCubbins, Stewart downplays partisan concerns. His regression analyses suggest that party membership did not affect support for the change, controlling for region and membership on Appropriations. Interestingly, while Appropriations Committee members naturally opposed decentralization, those members whose committees stood to gain jurisdiction were not more likely to vote for decentralization than were members who served on unaffected committees. Concerns about jurisdictional losses appear more salient than the potential for jursidictional gains.

The trend towards spreading power in the committee system continued in 1899, when the Senate voted to decentralize control of its appropriations bills. While the 1899 change was approved without a roll-call vote, it was highly controversial. Party leaders had fought off a similar effort in 1896, which was subject to roll-call votes. The 1899 reform succeeded after supporters circulated a petition urging action that was signed by a majority of senators. This show of strength forced party leaders to the negotiating table and eventually resulted in an agreement to bring the measure to the floor. Schickler and Sides (2000) analyze the 1896 roll calls and the decision to sign the 1899 petition. They find junior senators and members from the West and South were more likely to support the reform. Appropriations Committee members opposed the change disproportionately; members who stood to gain jurisdiction were somewhat more supportive than other senators, though the estimates for this variable were generally not statistically significant.

Taken together, these studies indicate that the spread of power to more committees and the creation of new committees in the mid- to late nineteenth century were rooted in a combination of workload pressures, rank-and-file discontent with concentrations of power in the hands of existing committees, and perhaps, the desire for increased spending and programmatic innovation. Whether these findings generalize to other policy areas beyond appropriations is worth exploration in future work.

Committees and the party system: tightening the relationship

Beyond the sheer expansion in the scope of the committee system, a second major theme in the committee system's development during the mid- to late nineteenth century was a tightening of relationships between the committee and party systems. A major aspect of this change in both chambers was enhanced partisan structuring of committee assignments. A second aspect, unique to the House, was the Rules Committee's emergent role as a central agenda-setting body in the chamber.

From 1790 through 1911, the House rules specified that the Speaker would appoint committees, except in cases otherwise specifically directed by the House. Starting in 1911, appointments were made by party committees, subject to confirmation of the committee slates on the House floor. Canon and Stewart (2002, 166) report that the House majority party had difficulty dominating committee memberships up through the 1820s, but that greater influence "began to take hold" in the decades leading up to the Civil War. By the 1860s, the majority party had cemented its control of committees, so that committees routinely had a majority of majority party members and were chaired by a majority party member.

A handful of recent studies have examined which majority party members received the best committee appointments when the Speaker handed out appointments. Canon and Stewart (2009) find little evidence that loyal majority party members received particularly good assignments early in the era of Speaker assignments.[4] They argue that it was only in the middle-to-late nineteenth century that the ability to dole out good assignments became a key resource for party leaders. Even then, Den Hartog and Goodman (2007) show that only Republicans rewarded loyal party members with good assignments when they were in the majority; by contrast, Democratic Speakers—facing a more internally factionalized party—evidently did not favor members with a record of party loyalty.

A major question raised by the Canon–Stewart and Den Hartog–Goodman studies is how minority party assignments were handled in the era before 1911. Observers at the time claimed that Speaker Joseph Cannon (R-IL) allowed the minority leader, John Sharp Williams (D-MS), to make his party's assignments from 1903 to 1908 (Thompson 1906; Ripley 1967). Krehbiel and Wiseman's (2001) study of committee assignments during the Cannon era finds that minority party members seem to have received assignments that were, on average, as good as those for majority members, and finds scant evidence that Cannon used his control of assignments to reward supporters.[5] But beyond this one study, we do not have a strong evidence base for understanding how minority party assignments were doled out in the nineteenth and early twentieth centuries, and whether these assignments were generally used strategically by the Speaker to build broader coalitions for his policy or political goals.

The Senate experienced a good deal more churning in its committee appointment process than the House in the nineteenth century. The Constitution's provision that an outsider—the Vice President—would preside over the Senate meant that delegating control of assignments to an officer like the Speaker was less palatable to senators. The Senate experimented with selecting committees by ballot (that is, vote of the full membership) and by the vice president or president pro tem of the Senate,[6] in the 1790s–1830s. But selection by ballot proved cumbersome, and delegation to the vice president was highly problematic, since that officer did not owe his position to the Senate and could differ from most senators' partisan and policy allegiances.[7] Party caucuses gained the dominant role in committee assignments in 1846, and soon delegated this authority to a party committee on committees. Canon and Stewart (2002, 161) describe the deliberations surrounding the 1846 move: after being stymied

---

[4] Den Hartog and Goodman (2007) do find evidence that loyal majority party members were more likely to gain assignments on Ways and Means during the 1827–61 period.

[5] See Lawrence, Malzman, and Wahlbeck (2001) for an assessment of Cannon's assignments to majority party Republicans.

[6] The president pro tem is a senator selected to preside over the chamber when the vice president is absent.

[7] Delegation to the president pro tem was also problematic because, in the nineteenth century, it was understood that the president pro tem's term would end whenever the vice president returned (see Smith and Gamm 2001).

for days due to endless balloting over committee assignments, Senators Ambrose Sevier (D-AR) and Jesse Speight (D-NC) proposed that the remaining twenty-one committee slates be adopted by unanimous consent from lists provided by the two parties (see also Kravitz 1974). This practice quickly became (almost) routine.[8] After the shift to party control of assignments, the majority party enjoyed a majority on nearly all of the major committees, in contrast to the more uneven record when committees were selected by ballot or by the presiding officer (Canon and Stewart 2002). Minority party members were still allocated a share of chairmanships, but these were of generally inactive, minor committees.

Canon and Stewart also provide suggestive evidence that seniority became an important predictor of member assignments in the mid- to late nineteenth century. Similarly, Kravitz (1974) argues that the seniority practices began to emerge once the Senate parties took control of assignments. The assignments dataset put together by Canon and Stewart holds the promise to provide a more nuanced account of when the seniority system took hold and under what conditions seniority was violated in the nineteenth and early twentieth centuries (see Katz and Sala 1996 on the House).

The Rules Committee and House agenda-setting

A key difference in committee system development across the chambers is that the House Rules Committee emerged as an agenda-setting body in the lower chamber by the end of the nineteenth century. This arguably undercut the influence of most other legislative committees, which increasingly had to turn to the Rules Committee in order to have their bills reach the floor.[9] The Rules Committee initially had a narrow jurisdiction: its duties focused on proposing changes in the permanent rules governing the House. But its role expanded dramatically in the 1880s-90s in ways that promoted a fusion of majority party power and the committee system. Starting in 1883, the committee began to use "special" (that is, temporary) rules to allow the House to bring matters to the floor out of their regular order by just a majority vote (see Bach 1981; Peters 1997). This move was initiated by Rules member (and future Speaker) Thomas Reed (R-ME), in order to help Republicans pass a controversial tariff bill as adjournment loomed.

Over the ensuing decade, the Committee gradually experimented with greater use of special rules. In 1892, Democrats on the Rules Committee proposed successful

---

[8] The main complication arose when third-party senators, such as Free Soilers, objected to the allocation of slots to their members. Still, as Canon and Stewart (2002, 163) conclude, the parties had "for the most part, taken control of the assignment process."

[9] Several committees had "privileged" status under the House rules, and thus could report at any time on matters in their jurisdiction. This provided an outlet for some committees, allowing them to reach the floor without the help of the Rules Committee. There has been scant work concerning which committees were granted privileged status and why (see Alexander 1916). More generally, we do not have a firm understanding of how bills typically reached the floor prior to the Rules Committee's rise: that is, we do not know what share of bills were reached through privilege, unanimous consent, suspension of the rules, and so on, in each Congress.

rules changes granting the committee the privilege of immediate consideration of its reports, with no dilatory motions allowed. This protected bills carrying the Rules Committee's endorsement from many filibuster tactics (Schickler 2001). After 1892, the Rules Committee increasingly became a key traffic cop for the House, with a greater share of major legislation passing through the panel en route to the floor (Cooper 1960; Roberts 2010). Schickler (2001) argues broadly based bipartisan concern about the House's capacity to legislate contributed to the development of centralized agenda control in the hands of the Rules Committee in the late nineteenth century, even as the majority party's more immediate legislative goals were likely the impetus for reform. In a recent empirical analysis of rule selection from 1883 to 1937, Roberts (2010) shows that the Rules Committee was more likely to grant a special rule when it was closer to the majority party median and when the majority party was relatively unified, suggesting support for the hypothesis that the early Rules Committee acted in part as a majority party agent.

The Rules Committee's role in linking the committee system and party leadership came under fire in 1910, when a coalition of dissident, mostly-progressive Republicans joined with Democrats to remove Speaker Cannon from his role as chair of the Committee, and to enlarge the panel and make it subject to election by the full House. The Cannon revolt was fueled by internal ideological splits within the Republican coalition, along with a widespread member desire for secure access to individual power bases in the committee system (Schickler 2001). This 1910 revolt presaged a decision the following year to take away the Speaker's power to appoint all standing committees. Together, these changes contributed to a trend of separation in the committee leadership and party leadership systems. However, it is worth noting that party committees ended up with the responsibility for proposing committee assignments, subject to ratification by the full caucus and by the floor. Therefore, while the Cannon revolt weakened the Speaker's personal influence over the committee system, it did not necessarily lead to an immediate loss of party-based influence. Instead, the change in committee assignments practices created the conditions for future battles between cross-party and majority party-based coalitions over control of the committee system.

AFTER THE CANNON REVOLT: AN ERA OF CONSOLIDATION AND SENIORITY

Changes in the committee system during the twentieth century have been subject to far more extensive social scientific studies than in earlier periods. Three major developments that took hold in the decades following the revolt against Speaker Cannon stand out as particularly important. The first is the consolidation in the committee system, as both the House and the Senate eliminated many committees, recentralized control of appropriations, and attempted to systematize jurisdictions. The second is an increased reliance on seniority in selecting committee leaders. Together, these developments helped give shape to what some scholars have called the "textbook Congress," a system in which committees were the central agenda-setting actors in both chambers. According to the textbook view, these committees often operated on a relatively bipartisan basis, in which senior Republicans and Democrats cooperated with one another and acted with substantial independence from party leaders. A third key development is the rise of committees as aggressive investigative units, which highlight both executive misdeeds and societal problems.

Committee consolidation

After a prolonged period of committee system expansion, both chambers shifted gears soon after World War I. The first move was Senate approval of a May 1920 rules change eliminating forty minor committees and reducing the size of the remaining committees. The proposed change was reported unanimously by the Senate Rules Committee and gained floor approval on a voice vote without objection. In some ways, this change was more symbolic than substantive: the committees that were eliminated rarely met, and the lack of any visible opposition suggests that the stakes were understood to be quite low. When the Senate office building opened in 1909, the main rationale for many of the committees—providing an office for their chairmen—evaporated (Haynes 1938, 284). Yet when Senator Elmer Burkett (R-NE) proposed that senators do away with thirty-six committees shortly after the building opened, his colleagues rebuffed him and instead created a handful of new committees (Congressional Quarterly 1982, 253; Robinson 1955). There is suggestive evidence that World War I sparked the change, both by demonstrating the need to streamline congressional organization in order to compete with the executive and by generating immense budget deficits that directed public attention to waste and inefficiency. Indeed, it appears that Republican and Democratic leaders competed to gain political credit for the reform (Schickler 2001).[10]

While the absence of roll-call votes and extensive floor debate have limited analysis of the 1920 Senate consolidation, scholars have been able to analyze in depth the more substantively important—and controversial—1920 decision by the House to recentralize control of Appropriations, along with the Senate's 1922 decision to follow suit. The House change poses the puzzle of why the chamber voted to reduce the jurisdiction of committees with 146 members, while strengthening the jurisdiction of a single committee? Stewart (1989) points out that the appropriations changes were part of a broader effort to create a new budget process in the wake of the World War I deficits. The Budget and Accounting Act of 1921—which was initially approved in the House shortly before passage of the appropriations recentralization—created the Bureau of the Budget to provide greater executive coordination of budgeting,

---

[10] The House eliminated eleven minor committees in 1927, also with little controversy.

and the "logic of the national budget system required Congress to match the president in institutional centralization" (Stewart 1989, 184). That is, if the president was now going to submit a single coherent budget, it made little institutional sense to have eight House committees separately take up its components. But beyond this general institutional interest, Stewart also shows that partisan, regional, and committee ties each predicted support for the change. Minority party Democrats, southerners, westerners, and members of committees losing jurisdiction were more likely to vote against the change, while Republicans, northeasterners, Midwesterners, and Appropriations Committee members disproportionately supported the reform. Stewart argues that Republicans were more likely to support the change both due to their fiscal conservatism and due to their shared interest in generating a party reputation for efficient governance (see also Kiewiet and McCubbins 1991, 172). At the same time, key Democratic leaders also backed the change; furthermore, 52 of 145 Democrats voted for the special rule to consider the recentralization and a majority of party members voted for its passage (Schickler 2001). Thus, the 1920 recentralization can be viewed as a case in which broadly-based concerns about congressional capacity combined with partisan and policy-based considerations to overcome individual members' commitment to preserving their existing committee power bases.

Opposition to recentralization was stronger in the Senate, where a majority of the chamber—sixty-six members—stood to lose influence. Still, once the House had given jurisdiction over appropriations to a single committee, senators experienced considerable pressure to follow suit. Indeed, the newly empowered House Appropriations Committee changed the titles and contents of its spending bills, rendering Senate jurisdiction over several bills ambiguous and potentially leaving the Senate Appropriations Committee with almost no jurisdiction (Schickler 2001). The Senate responded to these competing imperatives by adopting a reform plan that included significant concessions to the recentralization opponents: when appropriations for programs within a particular legislative committee's jurisdiction came under consideration, that committee (if it formerly had the power to report appropriations) could choose three of its members to act as *ex officio* members of the Senate Appropriations Committee; when the bill went to conference, the legislative committee could place one representative on the conference committee (Fenno 1966, 518).[11] The resulting package drew the strong support of Democratic leaders Oscar Underwood (D-AL) and Joseph Robinson (D-AK), as well as leading progressive Republicans such as George Norris (R-NE), and passed with relative ease. The *ex officio* membership rule gave the Senate's appropriations process an important element of decentralization, which endured for decades. Fenno (1966, 518) notes that House leaders had gained support for recentralization in part by enlarging HAC and appointing a few members of legislative committees to these new slots, while the Senate provided the legislative committees with permanent representation on SAC. This difference

---

[11] The Senate also restricted the ability of SAC to add legislation to spending bills, mandating that an entire bill would be subject to a point of order if the Appropriations Committee had added any amendments that contained new or general legislation.

had long-term implications, as noted by Fenno: "the House solution made possible an exclusive, differentiated Appropriations Committee, whereas the Senate solution perpetuated a direct substantive committee influence in the appropriations process" (1966, 518).

While the appropriations recentralization and elimination of minor committees represented a partial reversal of the nineteenth century trend towards a more fragmented committee system, there still were forty-eight House standing committees and thirty-three Senate standing committees, often with vague and overlapping jurisdictions. The Legislative Reorganization Act of 1946 pushed much further in attempting to create a more streamlined and systematic organization. For the first time, the Act defined committee jurisdictions in specific terms and made these jurisdictions more systematic and comprehensive.[12] It also combined committees with related responsibilities, leaving the House with nineteen standing committees and the Senate with fifteen committees. The act also provided committees with professional staff so that they would have the expertise to frame their own legislative initiatives independently of the executive branch.

Several studies have examined the forces that spurred Congress to enact the Reorganization Act and have evaluated the Act's legacy for the modern committee system. Most accounts emphasize that the Act represented a response to broadly-based member concerns about executive aggrandizement during the New Deal and World War II (see Davidson and Oleszek 1977; Cooper 1960; King 1997). Davidson (1990) highlights the role of procedural entrepreneurs—such as Robert La Follette (I-WI), Mike Monroney (D-OK), and Everett Dirksen (R-IL)—who crafted proposals to overcome the opposition of members who would lose personal power due to the elimination of so many committees. These entrepreneurs deliberately included such features as a congressional pay raise and pension system in order to make the jurisdictional losses more palatable (Schickler 2001). Interestingly, there is little evidence that partisan dynamics shaped the committee streamlining. The plan that served as the basis for the changes in House jurisdictions was crafted by a minority party member, James Wadsworth of New York (Davidson and Oleszek 1977, 8). It is difficult to imagine a member of the minority taking on such a role in more recent decades, given increased party polarization. This suggests that the dynamics of committee jurisdictions have changed considerably over time.

It should be emphasized that while the committee consolidation eliminated many committees, there also was considerable continuity in the decisions made. King (1994, 1997) shows that the committees that were merged generally had closely related jurisdictions and shared several members in common. Moreover, many of the eliminated committees reemerged soon thereafter as subcommittees. Adler (2002) offers a broad critique of the notion that the LRA represented a dramatic break with previous committee structure, concluding that Congress "crafted a package of changes that would help to perpetuate the distributive and electoral status quo" (109). Adler argues that the House never seriously contemplated the sort of fundamental rethinking of

---

[12] The Senate's rules had not specified jurisdictions at all prior to 1946.

committee jurisdictions or prerogatives that would threaten the provision of distributive benefits or members' electoral concerns. The case thus fits into Adler's broader argument that efforts to reform congressional politics in general—and the committee system in particular—run aground in the face of members' narrow electoral incentives.

While the LRA clearly fell short of reformers' aspirations, it nonetheless had an important impact on congressional operations. First, by creating a smaller set of committees with wider jurisdictions, the Act bolstered the influence of committee chairmen, helping "to guarantee that committee chairs would dominate congressional policy making for the foreseeable future" (Smith and Deering 1990, 39; see also Kravitz 1974; Davidson 1990). The many new subcommittees that emerged after the Act enhanced the influence of the chairmen because prior to the 1970s, the full committee chairs generally appointed subcommittee leaders, controlled the subcommittee staff, and shaped subcommittee jurisdictions. In addition, prior to the Reorganization Act, the large number of committees had afforded party leaders with more flexibility in handing out committee assignments, and the overlapping and ambiguous committee jurisdictions had provided leaders with more opportunities to affect bill referrals (Goodwin 1970, 38; Davidson 1990, 367; Adler 2002). If the goals of the Reorganization Act were to provide greater centralized party control or a set of committee jurisdictions that are not tied to constituency interests, then it is appropriate to judge the measure as a failure (Adler 2002). However, an alternative assessment is that the primary goal of reform was to strengthen the policymaking capacity of committees as a rival to the executive branch. Achieving that goal required accommodating members' personal power and electoral goals, but the resulting package left an important legacy for congressional operations: the Act strengthened committee chairs—by bolstering their jurisdictions and providing them with the staff to help formulate policy—making them central actors in the policy process. The executive branch would have to deal with these chairmen as co-equal competitors and partners over the next several decades.

The seniority system

A second major development in the committee system in the decades following the Cannon revolt was the full emergence of the seniority system, which was a key feature of the "textbook Congress" from the 1910s until the 1970s reform era. While seniority—typically understood to mean the length of continuous service on a committee—had long been among the factors considered in committee leadership appointments, most scholars agree that it only became the dominant factor after 1910. Several studies have shown that seniority violations fell in the House soon after the committee assignment power was taken away from the Speaker. In one of the earliest studies, Polsby, Gallagher, and Rundquist (1969) gather data on committee chairmanships from 1881 to 1965. Their data clearly show a sharp trend towards reliance on seniority in selecting chairmen, with 1911 as a key break point.

Specifically, "uncompensated" seniority violations (in which the person entitled to the chairmanship by seniority is not given some other benefit that may be better than the chairmanship, such as an assignment on a much better committee) drop after 1911 and are reduced to zero in most Congresses by 1919. Similarly, in a key early study, Abram and Cooper (1968) show that seniority violations fell dramatically during this same period.

Polsby and colleagues, along with Abram and Cooper, emphasize that the rise of seniority was partly a response to the Speaker's loss of control over assignments: once the caucus or a party committee gained control of assignments, seniority became a way to sidestep personal and factional conflicts. Both accounts also hint at what would become the "conditional party government" understanding of the seniority system: an internally divided party will have greater incentive to rely on "neutral" criteria than will a more cohesive party. These neutral criteria, in turn, afford committee leaders with a degree of independence from party leaders (see Rohde 1991). Polsby and colleagues (1969), however, link the claim about party strength to a broader argument about the "institutionalization" of the House, as impersonal, automatic criteria replace discretionary methods for allocating positions (see also Polsby 1968).

The development of the seniority system in the Senate appears to have started earlier than in the House, though it only became clearly institutionalized in the twentieth century. Canon and Stewart (2001) argue that by the late 1850s, it had become extremely unusual for a senator to be removed from a committee without his consent and there was a strong norm of committee rankings being determined by seniority. Kravitz (1974) notes, however, that the criterion for measuring seniority was less clear-cut in the Senate. Prior to 1920, seniority was often based on the length of a member's service in the chamber, rather than his tenure on a specific committee. After the elimination of many minor committees in 1920, Kravitz claims that "length of service on a particular committee, rather than in the Senate, became the invariable usage" in appointing chairmen (Kravitz 1974, 35). This shift would presumably have strengthened incentives for individual specialization.

The seniority system afforded committee leaders with a measure of independence because it made it unlikely that their position would be challenged due to disloyalty or idiosyncratic behavior. The prevalence of one-party rule in the South meant that many of the chairmen were conservative southern Democrats who had a seemingly permanent hold on their seats. As southern and northern Democrats became more distinctive in their policy views in the late 1930s and 1940s, the overrepresentation of southerners among the chairmen became a source of considerable liberal dissatisfaction with the seniority system. Indeed, many key committees were evidently run cooperatively by their conservative southern chairman and ranking Republican, with liberal northerners at times left complaining about their lack of influence (Schickler 2001). Where the committee system was largely seen as a tool of House party leaders in the late nineteenth century, it was often a tool of cross-party majorities in the era of the so-called conservative coalition, which started in the late 1930s and lasted into the 1960s.

The development of committees as investigative units

A third important feature of committee development during the 1910s–40s was the dramatic increase in the role of committees as investigative units. While investigations by special committees can be traced back to the 1790s, committee-based oversight was limited, in practice, for much of American history.[13] For example, Harris (1964, 264) shows that Congress conducted just 185 investigations from 1789–1918. But a handful of high-profile investigations during the Progressive Era, such as the House Banking Committee investigation of the "Money Trust" during 1912–13 (popularly known as the Pujo Hearings), suggested the potential for investigations to gather favorable publicity and exert substantial political pressure on opponents (Taylor 1954). During the 1920s, notwithstanding unified Republican control of the White House and Congress, Senate investigators played a lead role in uncovering the Teapot Dome scandal. Following the market crash of 1929, the Senate Banking Committee investigation of Wall Street—referred to as the Pecora Investigation—offered a further example of the potential to use investigations to expose alleged wrongdoing. But the share of attention and resources devoted to oversight was still relatively low in the 1930s. As late as 1940, the Senate spent just US$170,000 on all of its investigations.

Starting in the late 1930s, however, committee oversight became a more routine part of political combat, with the executive branch and various left-leaning societal groups the primary targets. Created in 1938, the Dies Committee on Un-American Activities set the stage, garnering immense press attention for its efforts to expose communist subversion in government agencies, labor unions, and throughout society. Conservatives quickly followed Dies' lead and hatched investigations of the National Labor Relations Board and Works Progress Administration that helped undermine support for both agencies in 1939–40. The conservative majority on the House Rules Committee routinely green-lighted investigations that promised to embarrass the Roosevelt administration and to tarnish liberal interest groups (Schickler 2007).

The volume, scope, and diversity of investigations accelerated once the United States entered World War II. Schickler (2007) finds that the House voted to authorize seventy-three investigations from 1941 to 1946, while the Senate authorized an additional fifty-four inquiries. Both chambers frequently relied upon special committees to conduct these investigations. While these investigations often provided searching scrutiny of executive branch activities, critics within Congress charged that reliance

---

[13]   There were a handful of noteworthy exceptions, such as the Joint Committee on the Conduct of the War, which played an important role in overseeing the Civil War effort, and the investigation of the Crédit Mobilier scandal in the 1870s (Taylor 1954). It is important to emphasize that investigations were regarded as something unusual—and thus required two separate House resolutions (first to authorize the probe and then to fund it). They were generally called "special" investigations—even when conducted by a standing committee—because they were not viewed as something ordinarily done by legislatures (see McGeary 1940).

on ad hoc special committees resulted in duplication and inefficiency.[14] With the Legislative Reorganization Act, both chambers sought to shift oversight from special committees to the existing standing committee system. Each committee was charged with exercising "continuous watchfulness" over the agencies in their jurisdiction. This new charge signaled a shift from viewing investigations as justified by special circumstances to understanding oversight as part of the routine responsibilities of the committee system. The Senate granted each standing committee subpoena power to conduct investigations; House Speaker Sam Rayburn (D-TX) and GOP leader Joe Martin (R-MA) agreed, however, to limit subpoena power to just three committees, Appropriations, Expenditures in the Executive Departments, and Un-American Activities. In other cases, standing committees would require floor approval before conducting probes that require the use of subpoenas. The remaining committees were finally granted subpoena power as part of a committee reorganization proposal approved by the House in 1974 (known as the Hansen reforms).

Following the Reorganization Act, both chambers continued to devote increased resources to committee-based oversight. By 1952, the Senate was spending US$1.63 million annually on investigations. Spending continued to increase rapidly in the 1950s, topping US$5 million annually by the end of the decade (Harris 1964, 265). A similar increase occurred in the House. David Mayhew's (2002) study of "significant" member actions depicts a similar pattern: he finds that investigative actions became a substantially greater share of historically significant member activity starting in the 1940s and accelerating into the 1950s. By this time, it had become accepted that one of the central responsibilities of standing committees was to oversee the executive branch and, more controversially, to expose wrongdoing by societal actors, such as alleged communists, labor racketeers, and Wall Street financiers. More recently, as parties have gained greater control of the committee system, investigations seem to have become less common under unified party government and instead are used more as a partisan tool rather than as an instrument of defending congressional power (Schickler 2007; Kriner and Schwarz 2008).

The rise of committee-based oversight is crucial for understanding the committee system because it is a domain of action that is consequential for the political system yet largely separate from the more well-understood legislative tasks of committees. Where legislative success ultimately depends upon chamber (and typically, presidential) approval of committee products, investigations are different. Members can use investigations to shape public perceptions and the terms of debate with a degree of independence from the chamber as a whole; this was especially the case in the post-1946 Senate, in which committees did not require floor approval to issue subpoenas.

Yet there has been surprisingly little scholarly work on the development of investigations as a committee tool. Aberbach (1990) provides the most detailed account of the factors shaping committee oversight in the 1960s–80s. Mayhew (1993) finds that

[14] It is worth noting that some investigations actually defended executive branch actions. For example, the investigations of Pearl Harbor and of President Truman's decision to fire General Douglas MacArthur during the Korean War both ended up shoring up the president's standing.

high-profile investigations in the post-World War II era were about as likely under unified government as under divided government (see Kriner and Schwarz 2008 for a different assessment). But there are more general questions about the development of committee-based oversight that have not been explored. For example, how have changes in committee resources affected their ability to undertake oversight? What kinds of problems and actors are more likely to be targeted by congressional investigations, and how have these targets changed over time? What leads some committees to be more active investigative units than others, both over-time and cross-sectionally? To what extent have committee investigative units acted as agents of either the majority party or the chamber as a whole, and under what conditions are committee investigators able to carve out independent influence? Finally, under what conditions are committee overseers genuine adversaries to executive agencies as opposed to their allies or enablers?

COMMITTEE DEVELOPMENT SINCE 1946

The twenty-five years following the adoption of the Reorganization Act are often seen as the heyday of committee government. The stylized portrait of the "textbook Congress" in which relatively autonomous committees, often operating on a bipartisan basis, shaped legislation has been a staple of both behavioral and early rational choice accounts of Congress (see Goodwin 1970; Shepsle 1989). Yet elements of that portrait—such as the notion that floor deference to committees meant that there was little meaningful amending activity—are based on a remarkably thin empirical record. As Bach and Smith (1988) and Smith (1989) document, the lack of recorded votes on most floor amendments in the House made it less likely that foes of a committee bill would be able to pressure members into voting for politically popular amendments opposed by committee and party leaders. But given that the vast majority of bills came to the floor under open amending rules, there nonetheless were many opportunities to change committee products. Case study evidence suggests that non-recorded floor amendments were used to change committee products in dramatic fashion in the late 1930s–50s (Schickler and Pearson 2009), but systematic data gathering on the extent to which legislation approved on the floor reflected committee, as opposed to floor, dynamics has generally been absent. Thus, while there is no doubt that committees were central agenda-setting actors in the textbook era, we do not have a clear sense of the conditions under which the floor deferred to committee expertise as opposed to challenging committee products.[15]

---

[15] Pearson and Schickler (2009) draw upon discharge petition data to suggest deference to committee prerogatives varied based on members' stake in the committee system: members with good committee assignments and senior committee leadership posts were more likely to defer to committees than were junior members lacking good assignments.

As Evans documents in his chapter on the contemporary committee system (see Chapter 18), members of Congress transformed key elements of the committee system starting in the 1970s. Most famously, the House seniority system came under severe challenge in the 1970s—when Democrats subjected chairmen to secret ballot votes and overthrew three long-standing southern chairmen—and in 1995, when a new Republican majority violated seniority in selecting several chairs and imposed term limits on committee leaders. As a result of these changes, all House committee chairs have been on notice since the mid-1970s that seniority would no longer necessarily be respected. Many scholars in the conditional party government tradition have traced this decline in seniority to the increased cohesion of the majority party and polarization of the two parties (see Rohde 1991; Aldrich and Rohde 2005). It is striking, however, that even though Senate parties now have formal mechanisms for weighing in on committee leadership appointments, seniority violations have not been used as a tool of discipline in the upper chamber. Even in cases where senators angry at disloyalty have raised the specter of punishment, thus far senators have defied their party without losing their committee seniority. This difference from the House—which has endured for three decades, though it is uncertain how much longer it will endure in the face of intense party polarization—may warrant examination of the sufficiency of conditional party government accounts of the seniority system. In other words, it appears that polarized, unified parties are not a sufficient condition for overriding seniority, even in the face of instances of defiance by senior committee leaders. One element of the calculus appears to be that Senate leaders fear that a seniority violation risks alienating a senator whose vote will be needed on many other occasions; in the smaller Senate, this "revenge" or alienation factor may loom larger than in the House.[16]

Additional committee changes in the 1970s–90s have reinforced party leverage over the committee system, particularly in the House. The Speaker regained control of the Rules Committee in 1975, when Democrats granted the Speaker the power to select the majority party's members on the Committee. Since then, the Committee has become a key agenda-setting tool for party leaders, often using creative special rules to structure floor consideration of bills (see Evans, Chapter 18, this volume; Strahan, Chapter 17, this volume). The Speaker was also granted the power to refer bills to multiple committees in 1974, which provided a tool for coordinating committee consideration of complex legislation. Party leaders have also experimented with the use of task forces to formulate major bills that crosscut the jurisdiction of multiple committees (see Sinclair 2000, more generally, on the growth in "unorthodox lawmaking"). Finally, the use of term limits for committee leaders by House and Senate Republicans has weakened the ability of senior members to build up their own power bases in the committee system.

---

[16] Minority party Republicans evidently have shown greater willingness to threaten individual senators. For example, Olympia Snowe (R-ME) reportedly came under considerable pressure—including threats regarding a potential committee leadership position—when she voted for the Democratic health care bill in the Senate Finance Committee in 2009. She eventually voted against the bill on the floor.

In sum, the balance of leverage between party and committee leaders has changed dramatically over the past three decades. Committee leaders increasingly see themselves as members of partisan teams competing for power and policy (Lee 2009), with a marked reduction in cooperation between committee chairmen and ranking minority members (Rohde 1991). The more centralized budget process brought about by the 1974 Budget Act—along with the related rise in omnibus legislating—has reduced the independence of the appropriations committees and provided party leaders with greater tools to influence major spending and tax decisions (see Gilmour, this volume). With the increased salience of partisanship, many observers have worried that committees have lost their commitment to both oversight and legislative craftsmanship (see Mann and Ornstein 2006). The strength of the committee system that took shape in the 1920s–60s was its ability to subject the individual pieces of legislative and executive programs to searching, specialized scrutiny, at the potential cost of failing to provide the sort of overarching, coordinated product sought by advocates of responsible party government. Amid challenges to committee leader seniority and efforts to strengthen partisan control of committee deliberations, there is more in the way of party coordination, but potentially at the cost of sacrificing the specialized expertise and legislative craftsmanship that were the strengths of the textbook Congress committee system. Indeed, as "message politics"—in which partisan teams compete to win public relations battles over legislative proposals—has become a central element of congressional politics, the importance of policy "substance" has arguably been displaced by the contest to score political points (Evans 2001).

These recent changes are strong evidence that the congressional committee system has not developed towards a single institutionalized end state. In the 1960s, it seemed plausible to suppose that the specialized, decentralized, seniority-based committee system represented *the* solution to maintaining Congress's power as a coequal branch amid modern policymaking challenges. Yet the displacement of key elements of that settlement over the past three decades—even as the basic structure of formal committee jurisdictions has remained largely intact—reinforces Roger Davidson's (1986) conclusion that "congressional committees are moving targets." Congressional committees are designed by members to serve a range of potentially incompatible goals and the relative salience of these goals changes over time as the larger political system is transformed by new electoral dynamics, technologies, and policy challenges. The development of the committee system— through the adoption and refinement of committee property rights in the early nineteenth century, the creation and elimination of committees over time, changes in assignment practices and seniority, and changes in committee behavior, such as the rise of investigations—constitutes a rich data source for understanding the forces driving congressional organization and for appreciating the sources of both Congress's strengths and vulnerabilities in America's separation of powers system.

References

ABERBACH, J. 1990. *Keeping a Watchful Eye: The Politics of Congressional Oversight*. Washington, DC: Brookings Institution.

ABRAM, M., and COOPER, J. 1968. The Rise of Seniority in the House of Representatives. *Polity*, 1: 52–85.

ADLER, E. S. 2002. *Why Congressional Reforms Fail: Reelection and the House Committee System*. Chicago: University of Chicago Press.

ALDRICH, J. H., and ROHDE, D. W. 2005. Congressional Committees in a Partisan Era, pp. 249–69 in *Congress Reconsidered*, 8th edn, ed. L. Dodd and B. Oppenheimer. Washington, DC: CQ Press.

ALEXANDER, D. A. 1916. *History and Procedure of the House of Representatives*. Boston and New York: Houghton Mifflin.

BACH, S. 1981. Special Rules in the House of Representatives: Themes and Contemporary Variations. *Congressional Studies*, 8: 37–58.

——and SMITH, S. S. 1988. *Managing Uncertainty in the House*. Washington, DC: Brookings Institution.

BRADY, D. W., and MORGAN, M. A. 1987. Reforming the Structure of the House Appropriations Process, pp. 207–34 in *Congress: Structure and Policy*, ed. M. McCubbins and T. Sullivan, New York: Cambridge University Press.

CANON, D. T., and STEWART, C. H. 2001. The Evolution of the Committee System in Congress, pp. 163–89 in *Congress Reconsidered*, 7th edn, ed. L. Dodd and B. I. Oppenheimer. Washington: CQ Press.

————2002. The Evolution of the Committee System in the Senate, pp. 157–81 in *Senate Exceptionalism*, ed. B. Oppenheimer. Columbus: Ohio State University Press.

————2009. Committee Hierarchy and Assignments in the U.S. Congress: Testing Theories of Legislative Organization, 1789–1946. Paper presented at the Duke University Conference on Bicameralism.

Congressional Quarterly. 1982. *Origins and Development of Congress*, 2nd edn. Washington, DC: Congressional Quarterly.

COOPER, J. 1970. *The Origins of the Standing Committees and the Development of the Modern House*. Houston, TX: Rice University Studies.

——[1960]. *Congress and Its Committees*. New York: Garland.

——and YOUNG, C. D. 1989. Bill Introduction in the Nineteenth Century: A Study of Institutional Change. *Legislative Studies Quarterly*, 14: 67–105.

——1986. Congressional Committees as Moving Targets. *Legislative Studies Quarterly*, 11: 19–33.

——1990. The Legislative Reorganization Act of 1946 and the Advent of the Modern Congress. *Legislative Studies Quarterly*, 15: 357–73.

——and OLESZEK, W. J. 1977. *Congress against Itself*. Bloomington: Indiana University Press.

DEERING, C. J., and SMITH, S. S. 1997. *Committees in Congress*, 3rd edn. Washington, DC: Congressional Quarterly.

EVANS, C. L. 2001. "Committees, Leaders, and Message Politics," pp 217–43 in *Congress Reconsidered*, 7th edn, ed. L. Dodd and B. I. Oppenheimer. Washington: CQ Press.

FENNO, R. F. 1966. *Power of the Purse*. Boston: Little, Brown.

GAMM, G., and SHEPSLE, K. 1989. Emergence of Legislative Institutions: Standing Committees in the House and Senate, 1810–1825. *Legislative Studies Quarterly*, 14: 39–66.

GOODWIN, JR., G. 1970. *The Little Legislatures*. Amherst: University of Massachusetts.

GOULD, J. W. 1959. The Origins of the Senate Committee on Foreign Relations. *Political Research Quarterly*, 12: 670–81.

HAMMOND, T. H., and MONROE, N. W. 2005. A Multi-Institutional Explanation for the Emergence of Standing Committees in the U.S. House, 1789–1829. Paper presented at the Annual Meeting of the American Political Science Association, Washington, DC, 1–4 September 2005.

HARRIS, J. P. 1964. *Congressional Control of Administration*. Washington, DC: Brookings Institution.

HARTOG, C. D., and GOODMAN, C. 2007. "Committee Composition in the Absence of a Strong Speaker," pp. 157–64 in *Party, Process, and Political Change in Congress*, vol. 2, ed. D. W. Brady and M. D. McCubbins. Stanford: Stanford University Press.

HAYNES, G. H. 1938. *The Senate of the United States*. Boston: Houghton-Mifflin.

JENKINS, J. A. 1998. Property Rights and the Emergence of Standing Committee Dominance in the Nineteenth-century House. *Legislative Studies Quarterly*, 23: 493–519.

JENKINS, J. A., and STEWART, III, C. Forthcoming. *Fighting for the Speakership: The House and the Rise of Party Government*. Princeton: Princeton University Press.

KATZ, J. N., and SALA, B. R. 1996. Careerism, Committee Assignments, and the Electoral Connection. *American Political Science Review*, 90: 21–33.

KIEWIET, R. D., and McCUBBINS, M. D. 1991. *The Logic of Delegation*. Chicago: University of Chicago Press.

KING, D. C. 1994. The Nature of Congressional Committee Jurisdictions. *American Political Science Review*, 88(1): 48–62.

——— *Turf Wars: How Congressional Committees Claim Jurisdiction*. Chicago: University of Chicago Press.

KRAVITZ, W. 1974. Evolution of the Senate's Committee System. *Annals of the American Academy of Political and Social Science*, 411: 27–38.

KREHBIEL, K., and WISEMAN, A. 2001. Joseph G. Cannon: Majoritarian From Illinois. *Legislative Studies Quarterly*, 26(3): 357–89.

KRINER, D., and SCHWARTZ, L. 2008. Divided Government and Congressional Investigations. *Legislative Studies Quarterly*, 33: 295–321.

LAWRENCE, E. D., MALTZMAN, F., and WAHLBECK, P. J. 2001. The Politics of Speaker Cannon's Committee Assignments. *American Journal of Political Science*, 45(3): 551–62.

LEE, F. 2009. *Beyond Ideology: Politics, Principles, and Partisanship in the U.S. Senate*. Chicago: University of Chicago Press.

McCONACHIE, L. 1898. *Congressional Committees*. New York: T.Y. Crowell.

McGEARY, N. M. 1940. *The Development of Congressional Investigative Power*. New York: Columbia University Press.

MANN, T. E., and ORNSTEIN, N. 2006. *The Broken Branch: How Congress is Failing America and How to Get it Back on Track*. Oxford and New York: Oxford University Press.

MAYHEW, D. R. 1993. *Divided We Govern: Party Control, Lawmaking, and Investigations, 1946–1990*. New Haven: Yale University Press.

MAYHEW, D. R. 2002. *America's Congress: Actions in the Public Sphere, James Madison through Newt Gingrich*. New Haven: Yale University Press.

PEARSON, K., and SCHICKLER, E. 2009. Discharge Petitions, Agenda Control, and the Congressional Committee System, 1929–1976. *Journal of Politics*, 71: 1238–56.

PETERS, R. 1997. *The American Speakership: The Office in Historical Perspective*, 2nd edn. Baltimore and London: Johns Hopkins University Press.

POLSBY, N. W. 1968. The Institutionalization of the House of Representatives. *American Political Science Review*, 62: 144–68.

—— 1975. Legislatures, pp. 257–319 in *Handbook of Political Science*, ed. F. I. Greenstein and N. W. Polsby. Reading, MA: Addison-Wesley.

—— GALLAGHER, M., and RUNDQUIST, B. S. 1969. The Growth of the Seniority System in the U.S. House of Representatives. *American Political Science Review*, 63: 787–807.

RIPLEY, R. B. 1967. *Party Leaders in the House of Representatives*. Washington, DC: Brookings Institution.

ROBERTS, J. 2010. The Development of Special Orders and Special Rules in the U.S. House, 1881–1937. *Legislative Studies Quarterly* 30: 307–36.

ROBINSON, G. L. 1955. The Development of the Senate Committee System. Ph.D. dissertation, New York University.

ROHDE, D. W. 1991. *Parties and Leaders in the Postreform House*. Chicago and London: University of Chicago Press.

SCHICKLER, E. 2001. *Disjointed Pluralism: Institutional Innovation and the Development of the U.S. Congress*. Princeton: Princeton University Press.

—— 2007. Entrepreneurial Defenses of Congressional Power, pp. 293–315 in *Formative Acts: Reckoning with Agency in American Politics*, ed. S. Skowronek and M. Glassman, Philadelphia: University of Pennsylvania Press.

—— and PEARSON, K. 2009. Agenda Control, Majority Party Power, and the House Committee on Rules, 1939–1952. *Legislative Studies Quarterly* 34: 455–91.

—— and SIDES, J. 2000. Intergenerational Warfare: The Senate Decentralizes Appropriations. *Legislative Studies Quarterly*, 25: 551–75.

SHEPSLE, K. A. 1989. The Changing Textbook Congress, pp. 238–66 in *Can the Government Govern?*, J. E. Chubb and P. E. Peterson, Washington, DC: Brookings Institution.

SINCLAIR, B. 2001. *Unorthodox Lawmaking: New Legislative Processes in the U.S. Congress*, 2*nd* edn. Washington, DC: CQ Press.

SKLADONY, T. W. 1985. The House Goes to Work: Select and Standing Committees in the U.S. House of Representatives, 1789–1828. *Congress & The Presidency*, 12: 165–87.

SMITH, S. S. 1989. *Call to Order*. Washington, DC: Brookings Institution.

—— and DEERING, C. J. 1990. *Committees in Congress*, 2nd edn. Washington, DC: Congressional Quarterly.

—— and GAMM, G. 2001. The Dynamics of Party Government in Congress, pp. 245–67 in *Congress Reconsidered*, 7th edn, ed. L. Dodd and B. I. Oppenheimer. Washington: CQ Press.

STEWART, C. H. 1989. *Budget Reform Politics*. Cambridge: Cambridge University Press.

—— 2007. Architect or Tactician? Henry Clay and the Institutional Development of the U.S. House of Representatives, pp. 133–56 in *Party, Process, and Political Change in Congress*, vol. 2, ed. D. W. Brady and M. D. McCubbins. Stanford: Stanford University Press.

STRAHAN, R. 2007. *Leading Representatives: The Agency of Leaders in the Politics of the U.S. House*. Baltimore: Johns Hopkins University Press.

SWIFT, E. K. 1996. *The Making of an American Senate: Reconstitutive Change in Congress, 1787–1841*. Ann Arbor: University of Michigan Press.

TAYLOR, T. 1954. *Grand Inquest: The Story of Congressional Investigations*. New York: Simon and Schuster.

THOMPSON, C. W. 1906. *Party Leaders of the Time*. New York: G. W. Dillingham.

WANDER, W. T. 1982. Patterns of Change in the Congressional Budget Process, 1865–1974. *Congress and the Presidency*, 9: 23–49.

WAWRO, G., and E. SCHICKLER. *Filibuster: Obstruction and Lawmaking in the United States Senate*. Princeton University Press, 2006.

WILSON, W. 1885. *Congressional Government*. Boston: Houghton-Mifflin.

CHAPTER 32

MAJORITY RULE AND MINORITY RIGHTS

DOUGLAS DION[*]

INTRODUCTION

As Robert Dahl (1956) wrote, the topic of majority rule and minority rights runs like a red thread through democratic theory. Typically, concerns about minority rights have centered on issues relevant to the general public—the right of individuals to free speech, assembly, political representation, and so on. As important as these issues are, one difficulty with studying any of them is the multiplicity of causal relationships at play in such broad societal arenas. Getting even a rough handle on how a society defines the notion of a minority, much less how it determines the allocation of rights to the same, presents an intimidating intellectual challenge.

One way to approach these complicated issues is to concentrate on the exercise of majority rule and minority rights within the context of legislative bodies. In many ways, legislatures provide an ideal setting for studying these issues. First, majorities and minorities can be tracked along party lines, thus helping to limit the set of potential cleavages that can be considered. At the same

 * I would like to thank Sarah Binder, Frances Lee, Eric Schickler, and Jason Roberts for helpful suggestions.

time, party is often not completely determinative of legislative behavior, and so there is room for understanding complex issues, for example why I might decide to adopt minority rights even though I am a member of a majority party. Second, institutional commitments to majoritarian decision-making help sharpen the issues at stake. How the rights of any minority in the larger society are determined is a subtle combination of decisions by various structures and agencies; within a legislature, things are much simpler. Third, professionalized legislatures typically characterize the rights of members in standing procedures and precedents, thus providing a useful codification of accepted practices (although accepted practices can of course differ from statutory guidelines, see King 1997).

The ideal study would of course be to determine why individual legislatures across the globe arrive at particular constructions of minority rights at particular moments in time. Such a project seems especially daunting, since ideas about minority rights within legislatures will inevitably be shaped by ideas about minority rights in general, which can be expected to differ across political cultures and historical eras.

Consequently, it is not surprising that most of the work in this area has focused on explaining the historical record within a single case, typically the American national legislature. While it may be difficult to explain why any legislature happens to settle on a particular set of minority rights, it is much easier to determine the factors that might lead a legislature to enhance or diminish minority rights at particular times rather than others. It may, after all, be impossible to determine precisely why a river crests at a particular height; understanding why it happened to rise in the first place is much easier.

This chapter therefore follows the literature in concentrating on the theoretical and empirical attempts to explain the changes that have taken place with respect to minority rights in legislatures over time. With apologies to those left out, I will concentrate on four sets of explanations: the informational account of Gilligan and Krehbiel (1987), the majority size account of Dion (1991, 1997), the supply/demand analysis of Binder (1997), and the ideological power balance view of Schickler (2000). I will then suggest some more recent work that bears on the questions raised in this literature. Finally, I present a few topics that future research might take.

Three caveats are in order. First, since the problem of filibustering will be treated elsewhere in this volume, the analysis here focuses on the U.S. House more than is otherwise warranted or desirable. Second, those looking for the nitty-gritty procedural details are urged to turn to the cited works. My concern here is more on the theoretical explanations that have been advanced for understanding minority rights than the ins and outs of the procedural technicalities. Third, as one of the individuals involved in this literature, much of what I write reflects one particular viewpoint on a broad topic.

Rogue's gallery

Gilligan and Krehbiel

The modern treatment of the problem of majority rule and minority rights in legislatures can be traced to the seminal article by Thomas Gilligan and Keith Krehbiel (Krehbiel and Gilligan 1987; see also Krehbiel 1992).[1] The key question in that article was why a majority would willingly limit its right to amend legislation proposed to it by a minority of its members. The answer was the protection of the minority's incentive to acquire costly information beneficial to the majority. Without such protections, minorities open themselves up to the possibility that the information they acquire at cost will be used in a way contrary to their interests. A bill from the Agriculture Committee suggesting a small increase in corn subsidies, for example, might be taken as a signal that in fact the case for corn subsidies is weaker than had previously seemed the case, and so could in fact invite *decreases* that would work contrary to the interests of members of the committee. Anticipating this use, the committee will be reluctant to make the investment necessary to gather the information. By committing to a straight up or down vote on the committee proposal, the majority provides the minority (the committee) with the assurance that its ability to alter the proposal will be limited. The committee is therefore more willing to invest, and the resulting information makes the majority and the minority, both risk-averse actors, better off.

At this point, the phrase "informational advantage" has acquired a patina of excess previously held only by Wilson's "dim dungeons of silence" and Mayhew's "single-minded seekers of reelection." All three represent deep truths about legislatures that in a sense have suffered overexposure. It is important to take a step back, however, and recognize how important the idea is. In a sense, Gilligan and Krehbiel provide a formal underpinning to John Stuart Mill's claims about tolerating dissent. One reason majorities may tolerate minority positions, after all, is because the minority may know something that the majority does not. How many of us, for example, even knowing the Condorcet Jury Theorem, would be willing to let a decision on surgery be determined by a majority vote of 100 friends rather than a single doctor? Information clearly provides an explanation for the extension of minority rights.

As important a perspective as informational theory provides, however, it cannot be the last word on the issue of minority rights, for a number of reasons. First, formal-theoretic underpinning of the informational model is far from clear. Krishna and Morgan (2001) raise questions about the equilibrium selected by Gilligan and Krehbiel under the open rule (for a response see Krehbiel 2001). Kim and Rothenberg (2008) have placed a spotlight on the treatment of the status quo in the Gilligan and Krehbiel model, in particular the assumption that the outcome from the status quo

---

[1] More properly, if one describes a committee as a minority, one can trace the earliest efforts at least as far back as Black (1958), and if minority rights are instantiated in supermajority voting rules, then at least as far as Buchanan and Tullock (1962).

policy is just as uncertain as the outcome from policy innovation. Most interestingly, Dessein (2002) has argued that in the presence of informational asymmetries, the best response of a majoritarian legislature would be complete deferral to the committee, rather than an *ex post* veto in the form of a closed rule. Second, the structure of decision-making assumed in the original Gilligan and Krehbiel piece in fact contradicts the structure in the U.S. House (see Krehbiel 1997; Dion and Huber 1997).[2] Finally, however powerful their theoretical logic, the historical analysis presented by Gilligan and Krehbiel has some difficulties. For their account to work, Gilligan and Krehbiel must explain why informational needs acquired enhanced force at the end of the nineteenth century (when many of the procedural changes they reference took place). Their argument hinges on the forces of industrialization and the associated uncertainties of legislation, but the Gilded Age certainly had no monopoly on a lack of certainty about adopted policies. In fact, one could argue that the Gilded Age represented a much more certain policymaking environment than, say, the Jacksonian era or the period of the Civil War.

Your humble narrator

If I recall correctly, I read Gilligan and Krehbiel's piece shortly after I decided to do a dissertation on majority rule and minority rights in legislative politics. Prior to this time, I had been attempting to fill out my limited historical knowledge of the U.S. House, and particularly of the eras of major rules reforms.[3] This research suggested a few points that, upon reflection, seemed at odds with the Gilligan and Krehbiel account. First, much of the conflict over procedures in the nineteenth century, reaching a crescendo with the adoption of the Reed Rules in 1890, revolved around the question of minority obstruction rather than majority amendment. This seemed to be at odds with the informational story, since even the obstructionists themselves seemed somewhat lackadaisical about the informational value of their filibustering. Second, concentrating on the end of the nineteenth century ignored many rules changes that had taken place earlier in the century. Indeed, the record of rules changes seemed to be episodic, according to the best evidence at the time: major changes taking place, followed by periods of inaction (Galloway 1969). It was not clear precisely how an industrialization (or informational) argument could explain the timing of these procedural changes. An adequate account should not only provide an explanation of the timing of these changes, but also their content.

It was here that John Aldrich's work on the majority party caucus in the legislature was critical (eventually published as Aldrich 1994). Using cooperative game theory,

---

[2] In the original Gilligan and Krehbiel model, the floor was able to commit to a closed rule in advance of action by the substantive committee, while actual House procedures have the Rules Committee acting after the reporting committee.

[3] The entire literature on procedural change owes a huge debt to Kenneth Shepsle, whose work on institutional structure led elegantly to the question of why institutions remained stable, and why they changed.

Aldrich built upon a formal result from Greenberg (1979) to show that a majority party caucus mechanism induced stability in a legislative setting when the majority was small. This was similar to Riker's (1962) size principle (that small majorities are more cohesive in majoritiarian settings than large majorities), but pointed towards an important mechanism missing in Riker, the caucus. In essence, the game posited that an alternative was the proposal of the caucus unless some other alternative could defeat it by a floor majority composed only of votes from the majority party (hence the caucus). When the majority party consists of all seats, this essentially requires a majority rule winner, which is a rarity in multidimensional policy spaces. When the majority is small, the voting rule is essentially unanimity, there will always be an equilibrium at the caucus stage, and hence in the legislative game. In between, whether the majority party is cohesive (that is, whether the majority party caucus holds) depends on both the size of the party as well as the number of dimensions under consideration.

The argument at that point was straightforward. Small majorities were more likely to be cohesive. Being cohesive, minorities would be unable to adopt a "divide and conquer" policy of successful amendments. The minority is therefore left with one strategy, that of obstruction. The majority, however, anticipating obstruction, and being cohesive, is in a position to enact procedural changes to limit minority rights. As a result, periods of procedural change to limit minority rights to obstruct legislation should occur when the majority party is small.

This argument was presented in a 1991 dissertation, which also set out the evidence for the case of the House of Representatives during the partisan era (for my purposes, 1836 to 1896). The empirical evidence was then expanded in a book published in 1997 to include the case of the nineteenth-century House of Commons, the U.S. Senate, and an entertaining incident of minority obstruction and procedural change in the Austro-Hungarian parliament witnessed by Mark Twain.[4]

While the book is still useful and entertaining, there are limits that should be noted. For one, the theory developed in the book relies too heavily on the then-current and about-to-be-phased-out technology of cooperative game theory.[5] Individuals within the majority party agree to the party position when there is no alternative floor majority within the party caucus. But why should a member who disagrees with the party position agree to gather votes only from the majority party? Why not renege on any agreement to support the caucus, and instead open up the issue on the floor? (For a much more successful effort, see Patty 2008.) Second, minority party strategy was not explicitly modeled—at least not as explicitly modeled as one would expect nowadays. In essence, obstruction was simply the only reaction possible to the success of a majority caucus—something that may be empirically valid but fails to be theoretically insightful.

---

[4] In a playful conversation Gerald Gamm once accused me of using a fictional account as empirical evidence. Ignoring the question of whether this is in fact unusual in the social sciences, for the record almost everything Twain said was true.

[5] The book does a less than successful attempt to adapt the theory into a non-cooperative framework.

Binder

These results were presented at various locales, including the University of Minnesota, where they happily engaged the attention of Sarah Binder. With an enviable attention to empirical detail and context, she scoured the records of the House and the Senate for procedural changes regarding minority rights, including those that had not received discussion in historical accounts of legislative proceedings. In particular, her work looks at the entire history of the House and the Senate, from 1789 on, uncovering new procedural changes, including expansions in minority rights.

If this was all she did, her work would still be an impressive contribution to our understanding of minority rights. But she also added to this her own theory. This theory consists of two parts, a demand part, and a supply part. The demand part of the theory points to the use of minority tactics. The more a minority obstructs, for example, the more likely a majority is to attempt to limit obstruction. While this may miss some element of anticipated reactions (something I stressed in my own analysis), I think a good case could be made that there is no reason to alter the rules unless the minority is able to credibly show that it is willing to obstruct.

The supply element of the theory, however, is probably the most innovative and compelling part of the enterprise. In essence, Binder is interested in determining the probability that a member will find him or herself on the floor in the majority. She approximates this probability by a "Party Strength" measure. This measure consists of two terms, a majority term and a minority term. The majority term is the product of the size and the Rice cohesion score of the majority party. The minority term is the product of the same terms calculated for the minority party Rice cohesion score and the size of the minority. The second term is subtracted from the first to arrive at the Party Strength variable. Binder shows, against a much richer dataset than that employed in the rest of the literature, that Party Strength has a significant effect on the adoption of procedural changes limiting minority rights.

One quibble with the Party Strength measure is that it lacks a (formal) theoretical foundation. A more important question is why we would expect Party Strength to be related to procedural change. Party Strength is maximized when the majority party holds all the seats, and votes identically. In such a case, the argument goes, the majority will attempt to alter the rules to limit minority rights. But why should a majority fear a non-existent minority? Similarly, the use of the Rice cohesion scores, which look at cohesion *within* parties rather than across parties, can miss important differences. There is certainly a difference between a majority and a minority that always agree, and a minority and majority that never agree, yet both would have the same Rice cohesion score, and thus (assuming size doesn't change) would have the same Party Strength score. Yet the case where the majority and minority disagree would seem to be much more likely to lead to limits in minority rights than the case where both agree.

My main objection to Party Strength, however, has to do with endogeneity. If party size was unrelated to party cohesion, or if majority party size and majority party cohesion varied in the same way, then the meaning of the interaction term would be clearer. The problem, however, is that there are strong theoretical reasons for believing that smaller majorities are more cohesive. The Party Strength measure hides this effect. It is impossible to know, for example, whether restrictions in minority rights are adopted primarily because the increases in cohesion for the majority outbalance the decreases in party size, or if in fact larger majorities are more cohesive.

Still, Binder has provided the standard work for understanding majority rule and minority rights in legislative politics.

Schickler

A different take on the politics of institutional change with respect to minority rights is provided by the ideological power balance theory of Eric Schickler. Schickler departs from the multidimensional setting, returning to the unidimensional case explored by Gilligan and Krehbiel. The difference, besides the lack of an explicit formal model, is that there is no informational asymmetry in Schickler's work. Instead, he compares the location of the median member of the majority party and the median member of the minority party. His explanation of procedural change is compellingly simple: when the floor median moves closer to the median of the majority party, the legislature will restrict minority rights, while movement of the floor median away from the majority party enhances minority rights. In a sense, Schickler's theory builds on the conditional party government ideas that underlie much of this literature (Rohde and Ornstein 1978; Cooper and Brady 1981; Aldrich and Rohde 2000). The primary insight of this literature is that majority party power is increased when there is intraparty homogeneity and interparty difference. The idea of interparty difference is echoed in the Gilligan and Krehbiel theory, where too great a distance between the committee and the floor eliminates the possibility of informative signaling. While homogeneity is not that central, interparty difference plays a large role in the non-cooperative version of the theory presented in Dion (1997). Binder's Party Strength measure can be thought of as an attempt to capture party homogeneity through the Rice cohesion measures, with the subtraction in a sense substituting for interparty differences.

Schickler's adoption of the unidimensional perspective enables him to capitalize on the extraordinary data on spatial locations assembled by Poole and Rosenthal (1997). Much more than the other authors (with the exception of Krehbiel's later work), this provides Schickler with a concrete grasp on party preferences. His explicit incorporation of time-series elements (in the form of lags) also represents an advance in the literature.

As in Binder, there is no explicit model of choice in Schickler's account. It would be easy, however, to construct one. Only two elements are required. The first would be some cost to institutional change, making the majority unwilling to simply adopt limits on minority rights at every single legislative sitting. The second would be some recognition that the bargaining outcome produced between the majority and minority party are a function of existing minority rights (representing, perhaps, bargaining impasses in a Rubinstein bargaining model), with infringements in minority rights leading to bargaining outcomes closer to the ideal point of the majority party. In such a case, I would conjecture that a given shift in the bargaining outcome will have a great impact on utility for the majority party when the majority and minority are far apart than when they are closer. *Ceteris paribus*, then, procedural changes to limit minority rights should be more likely to take place when the majority and minority party are further apart.

What is more troubling, and harder to dismiss, is the relevance of the majority and minority medians in a unidimensional setting. Why, in such a setting, wouldn't the median voter always wish for unconstrained majority rule? There is no uncertainty to the model, so there is no informational advantage to be had from deferring to the minority. And in the unidimensional setting, there are no chaos problems to worry about. To put it differently, in a unidimensional world, why would legislators want to play the game Schickler envisions?

SOME SPECIFIC MINORITY RIGHTS

The work set out above takes a general look at minority rights. That is, it generalizes the notion of minority rights and then attempts to figure out a general mechanism covering the various instantiations. Other work has concentrated on particular procedures guaranteeing minority rights, attempting to work out the theory within a particular context.

Motion to recommit

Prior to the final consideration of a bill in the House of Representatives, members of the minority party have traditionally had the right to offer a motion to recommit. This motion, in essence, sends the bill back to the committee. There are three basic types of motion to recommit: a motion to recommit without instructions, a motion to recommit with instructions to the committee to report back "promptly," and finally a motion to recommit with specific instructions (which is in essence an amendment of the original bill, the parliamentary fiction being adopted that the committee has referred the amended bill back to the House "forthwith"). The conventional wisdom is that the motion to recommit provides an important right to the minority, a "last shot" at proposed legislation.

The motion to recommit gained a far greater public profile in the late 1980s and early 1990s, when the continued use of special rules to preclude the motion to recommit aroused the ire of then minority Republicans. Once in the majority, the Republicans carried through on their procedural stance by guaranteeing the motion to recommit. Since that time, the motion has had an interesting career, some seeing it as an important element in the minority arsenal, while others seeing it as essentially a meaningless tactic that succeeds only in placing the majority members in a difficult voting position.

Motivated more by the debates in the literature on party influence than the substantive squabble over procedure, Krehbiel and Meirowitz (2002) studied the use of the motion to recommit in the context of a multidimensional, three-player game. Two agents in the game were members of the majority, while the remaining member was a member of the minority. Each made a social choice involving the replacement of a status quo point (this point assumed to lie in the Pareto set of the three legislators).[6] The game proceeds as follows: a majority member proposes a bill, which is then subject to a motion to recommit with instructions (formally, an amendment), which is then voted on.

Using this setup, Krehbiel and Meirowitz show that the incorporation of the motion to recommit raises serious questions about the validity of the "conditional party government thesis," which suggests increasing majority party power with increasing interparty difference and intraparty homogeneity. More relevant for this study is the theoretical finding that the motion to recommit does in fact limit majority power, essentially resulting in bipartisan voting outcomes.

Roberts (2005), however, has suggested limitations to Krehbiel and Meirowitz's study. One prong of his argument highlights the differences in actual procedure governing the motion to recommit and the theoretical model the latter employ in their formal model. Most important is the ability of the majority party to "fight fire with fire" via an amendment of the motion to recommit. Roberts also notes, however, that the Krehbiel and Meirowitz model implies (a) that the minority always makes a motion to recommit with instructions, and (b) this motion always passes. In fact, using evidence from 1909 to 2002, only 31 percent of bills had such motions, and of these only 10 percent of the motions to recommit (with instructions) actually succeeded in gathering a majority.

Even if we grant that the motion to recommit is not as powerful as it might seem, its mere presence in House and Senate procedure does raise an interesting question, especially in light of the previous studies, namely why the majority in fact gives the minority the ability to offer such a motion at all. A historical perspective on this question is offered by Donald Wolfensberger (2003), chief of staff for the House Rules Committee during the 1995–6 session. Wolfensberger notes that one of the earliest rationales for the motion to recommit was to give the majority a chance to "clean up" bills, for example in cases where contradictory amendments had both been approved.

---

[6] A policy is Pareto-dominated if there is some other policy leaving every individual at least as well off as the original policy, and some individuals strictly better off. The Pareto set is simply the set of policies that are not Pareto dominated. If the players have the circular indifference curves, then the Pareto set consists of the points lying on and within the triangle formed by the ideal points of the three players.

The motion to recommit was also included in a series of reforms in 1909 intended to forestall the emerging revolt against Speaker Cannon. Indeed, Wolfensberger notes that a limitation of the minority right to recommit was made as early as 1934 by Speaker Rainey. This information suggests that the motion to recommit has, at least historically, not always acted as a tool of the minority.

At bottom, however, we are still left with the puzzle of why a minority right might be allowed to exist at all. Krehbiel and Meirowitz take up this issue at the close of their piece, offering three potential arguments.

The first rationale for minority rights, a rationale embraced by Wolfensberger, is that members of the majority actually hold "principled views on fairness of procedures" (2003, 13). The authors argue that this view may "seem improbable," and point to Binder and Smith's (1997) book on the filibuster as providing evidence against this hypothesis. I shall take up this issue later in the chapter.

The second rationale points to the possibility of risk aversion and repeat play. The possibility that repeat play explains the extension or reduction of minority rights is addressed in Dion (1997), and, just to recap, the evidence is not very strong. Analytically, it is difficult to figure out the implications of either risk aversion or repeat play: should I worry about the risks of being in the minority and being overridden by the majority, or the risks of being in the majority and being stymied by the minority? Answering this question requires a much more detailed model of either risk aversion or repeat play than the authors are able to provide.

The third rationale is in some ways the most interesting of all. This points to the potential heterogeneity within the majority party. While extremist members of the majority leadership would prefer restrictive rules that promote non-centrist outcomes, they will be opposed in this by the moderate members of their own party, who will wish to retain procedures such as the motion to recommit. I refer to this argument as interesting mostly because it seems to reproduce the very conditional party government argument that the paper aims at demolishing.

At the same time, it pays to remember that minority rights are far from stable in a majoritarian world. In January of 2009, the Democrats under Speaker Nancy Pelosi placed limits on the right of the minority to recommit "promptly." This was done after repeated use of the motion to recommit by the Republican minority to score political points during the previous Congress, at least according to one account.[7]

Gatekeeping

Whether gatekeeping can be considered a minority right or not depends on the position of committees within a legislature. If committees are essentially the creatures of majority parties, then the ability to prevent the introduction of legislature counts

[7] See http://www.majorityleader.gov/docUploads/MTRFactSheet010509.pdf, available at Majority Leader Steny Hoyer's web page (accessed September 13, 2010).

as an arm of majority party strength, while if committees are isolated baronies of individual influence (as the pre-reform caricature goes), then gatekeeping could well qualify as a minority right.

Epstein (1997) expands the original Gilligan and Krehbiel model by adding an opportunity for the committee to unilaterally prevent policy changes. He is able to show that gatekeeping will occur in equilibrium: for certain values of private information, the committee will simply not propose a bill. Furthermore, Epstein shows that allowing gatekeeping on the part of a committee typically improves the welfare of the majority: the informational advantages from gatekeeping outweigh the distributional losses from delegation.

Epstein's results are especially interesting since he conceptualizes gatekeeping as obstruction. Since obstruction is not isolated to committees, but is a part of minority party strategy, Epstein's work can also be seen as providing an informational rationale for filibustering. The key, of course, is that the obstructionist must be better informed than the legislature. Oddly, this may suggest an explanation for senatorial tolerance of civil rights filibusters over much of the twentieth century. As long as southern members could credibly claim greater knowledge of the "unique culture" of the South, the possibility of informational obstruction remains. When that claim becomes harder to sustain, due to the work of social scientists and historians such as C. Vann Woodward, Gunnar Myrdal, and numerous others, the informational advantage is erased, and the toleration of obstruction fails. Epstein thus provides an important non-cooperative perspective on the politics of obstruction studied by Dion and Binder.

Epstein's approach strongly contrasts with the complete information model studied in Crombez, Groseclose, and Krehbiel (2006). Here, it would be preferable to offer the committee an *ex post* veto over majority proposals rather than an *ex ante* veto over change (i.e. gatekeeping). This argument is used to advance the empirical premise that gatekeeping is a rare element in legislative design. While some elements of the argument could be sharpened (the Constitution, after all, does give Congress the right *not* to propose legislation, which can be considered a type of gatekeeping right, something that is not clear in their discussion), the paper makes an important contribution to the discussion here by introducing a distinction between *rights* and *power*, with procedural rights being a necessary condition for the exercise of power. Of course, power can often be blithely uninterested in procedure, so that claiming a necessary condition may seem empirically rather strong, but the difference between offering a right and having that right exercised is one that has been missing in the analysis of procedural changes regarding minorities addressed above. Quite simply, we know much more about how minority rights changed in the nineteenth and twentieth centuries than we do about how those minorities took advantage of those rights (with the notable exception of the filibuster, of course: see Binder and Smith 1997; and especially Wawro and Schickler 2006).

Work that needs to be done (within the paradigm)

A review of a topic, particularly one of such importance as majority rule and minority rights, would be remiss if it did not suggest topics for future research, areas that seem to be crying out for monograph-length treatments. I divide up my suggestions into two parts. First, I suggest avenues for analysis that seem in the main consistent with the rational choice framework that loosely characterizes the work in this area. Second, I suggest some approaches that are intended to broaden the intellectual vista, no doubt in what will be considered a heretical direction. My apologies to any whose work I have inadvertently overlooked in this section.

Disentangling party strength

One analysis that would be quite straightforward to perform would be disentangling the various effects conjoined in Binder's Party Strength variable. As Bambor, Clark, and Golder (2006) argue, interpretation of interactive terms without inclusion of their constituent effects is problematic (but see Kam and Franzese 2007, 99f). The Party Strength variable, representing the difference between two interaction terms, compounds the difficulty. This is a straightforward, but important exercise.

I also think that we need to think more carefully about our theories and measures of party cohesion. No one thinks that party votes are an ideal measure of party cohesion. This is especially the case if, as seems plausible, procedural changes to limit minority rights have the causal effect of increasing party voting. One suggestion would be to replace the party cohesion variables with other measures, such as actual constituency differences (see Jenkins, Schickler, and Carson 2004 for excellent measures based on census data).

Finally, I have to raise what is probably the holy grail of procedural change studies. We know that constituency characteristics influence institutional structure, which influences rules, which then influence constituency characteristics. Passing the Reed Rules, I would argue, did not simply enable the Republican Party to represent its existing constituency, but also to some extent crafted what was its constituency over the subsequent decades. That is, the passage of the procedural changes enabled the Republicans to drop some constituent groups while attracting others, thus altering bases of the parties. Richard Vallely (2009), for example, has recently presented a fascinating argument that the desire for electoral reform (which by definition would have changed the party constituencies) is the central motivation of the Reed Rules changes. We all know that there is a deep simultaneity problem between measures based on votes and institutional structures and change, and yet typically attempt to avoid it. My own narrow interest on majority party size, for example, was an attempt to sidestep this very problem. Much time has since passed, and the solution of this problem is more than overdue.

Minority party strategy

The minority party in many ways receives the short end of the scholarly stick in legislative studies. It is always much more interesting to pursue majorities, which are assumed to be the engine of policy change, than minorities. And even among the studies of majority rule and minority rights, the strategic elements of minority party strategy remain, to my mind, underexplored.

Consider, for example, the argument in Wawro and Schickler (2006) that antebellum southerners would be more likely to obstruct as the number of individuals within their minority decreased (2006, 162). The logic seems to rest on the premise that as the northern delegation increased in size, the potential for changes in slavery policy increased. This assumes, of course, that larger majorities are not less cohesive than smaller majorities. Clearly, the idea of a large majority will be threatening to a small majority, but so would a cohesive majority, and which is relevant is something that existing theory is far from clear on.

Rather than cursing the darkness, let me propose at least one toy model of obstruction that I think would be interesting for studying obstruction. Let's start with a very simple model, say three individuals facing a set of m issues. We can assume that the preferences over these issues are separable for each legislator (that is, total utility of any legislative session is simply the sum of the individual utilities from passage or rejection of each of the individual bills). Without loss of generality, we can let the payoff to each player from the status quo be 0. A positive payoff for the passage of a bill, then, indicates support, while a negative payoff indicates opposition. The consideration of each issue consumes 1 unit of time. In addition, each of the individuals can expend an extra unit of time in "filibustering." We can define a calendar, then, as a sequence of issues that could potentially be addressed within some finite available amount T. Since time is finite, employing time in filibustering means altering the set of achievable policy change. The general model here is similar to that employed by Patty and Penn (2008), although the addition of obstruction is my own.

Such a model raises two questions. First, given any particular calendar, what happens? When do individuals obstruct? How significant will that obstruction be? This problem is actually more involved than one might think. While the problem easily lends itself to backwards induction, it seems to have substantial strategic complexity. My own attempts at obstruction, for example, may make it possible for you to engage in an obstructive enterprise of your own that would have been impossible without my earlier attempts. Even harder to deal with is the existence of indifference over various outcomes: who does the filibustering and who doesn't is not automatically clear. It seems frustrating that the literature (myself included) talks so easily of the exercise of obstruction, and yet how it would be practiced in even a simple model such as this one seems much more complicated than one would be led to believe.

The second question raises a fundamental issue for studying the strategic interaction of majorities and minorities. Given the potential for obstruction, what is the optimal scheduling of legislation? Is it possible to deter obstruction through the clever positioning of agenda items, leaving the candy for the minority until they have eaten their vegetables? Consider, for example, the scheduling issue presented to Democrats in the 89th Congress (1965–7). As J. David Greenstone noted, voices within the labor camp urged scheduling the repeal of Taft-Hartley prior to consideration of the bulk of Great Society policies, precisely in order to deter a possible filibuster (Greenstone 1969, 332–3). Others, however, feared that such debate over such a contentious policy might in fact sour political support for the larger package. The final decision, scheduling the repeal towards the end of the session, may well explain its failure. More recently, the House leadership has decided to schedule debate on the estate tax, a key issue for Republicans, until after consideration of health care, a key target of Republican opposition.

Comparative legislatures

As Kiewiet, Loewenberg, and Squire (2002) note, when it comes to comparative work the field of legislative politics is sharply unbalanced. Our knowledge of the U.S. House (and, increasingly, the Senate) has yet to be balanced by the study of non-American legislatures (not to mention American state legislatures).

This is especially true when it comes to majority rule and minority rights. For those looking for easy targets, my own work on the British Parliament might serve as a suitable scapegoat. An Americanist by training and avocation, my turn to the British Parliament was due solely to a fear that the relationship between minority rights and majority party size was simply an American aberration. A lack of modern language skills drove me to the British case. While I attempted to do a serviceable job, I am confident that anyone looking at the British Parliament, or any other non-American legislature, for that matter, in a historical perspective could uncover much more than I was able to.

Among the exceptions, let me point to an interesting essay by Mark Williams on the European Parliament (EP). The EP has a number of features of interest to legislative scholars, including ideological parties that cross national boundaries. Williams notes that minority rights within the EP have changed over time, citing an increase in such rights in 1981 and a limitation in 1993. Straightforward application of the models from American politics are difficult in such situations due to the lack of a two-party system. At the same time, the fact that minority rights were limited suggests multiple parties are no guarantee against the diminution of minority rights.

This last point is especially relevant to the study of minority rights. One of the constant explanations for the preservation of minority rights is that individuals are uncertain about whether they will be within the majority or the minority. The idea, then, seems to be that the less likely a majority party is to form, the safer minority rights are. But the existence of a majority party seems not to be a necessary component for limiting the rights of the minority. How individuals make calculations within such complicated environments promises to help us understand the politics of majority rule at a deeper level.

The European Parliament is an important topic for modern politics, but we should not neglect the comparative historical angle. How have legislative rules changed over time in non-American legislatures is an important topic that needs a great deal more work. One especially intriguing case crying out for analysis is the French legislature under the Constitution of the Year VIII.[8] This legislature was in fact tricameral, with a Conservative Senate of elders, a Tribunate of 100 members who debated and proposed laws, and a Legislative Body (Corps législatif) of 300 who were constitutionally barred from participating in debate, their decision-making parsed down to a secret-ballot vote on proposals from the Tribunate and the government (controlled by First Consul Napoleon Bonaparte). Minority rights within the Legislative Body are therefore limited to the right to vote no. My assumption would be that such a body would act as a rubber stamp, but if the study of legislative processes has taught us anything, it is that even apparently trivial rubber stamps can have unexpected policy influences.

WORK THAT NEEDS TO BE DONE
(OFF THE BEATEN PATH)

One of the most frustrating elements of the study of legislative politics (since I am speaking among friends) is a certain staid nature to much of what we do. On the one hand, this can be considered a testament to our collective abilities to generate new and interesting insights using a common approach with a well-defined series of topics and questions. On the other hand, one sometimes longs for something more exotic in the field.

Let's face it: if you were throwing a party, how many experts in legislative procedure would you invite?

Since one goal of this Handbook is to suggest alternative perspectives on legislative politics, I offer some suggestions of literatures that have seemed to me to have some relevance for legislative politics, but which, as far as I am aware, rarely if ever seem to capture the attention of scholars working in the area. If much of this chapter seems idiosyncratic, this section especially will be so.

---

[8] For the actual text of the Constitution of Year VIII, see http://www.napoleon-series.org/research/government/legislation/c_constitution8.html#title3 (accessed September 13, 2010).

Have we killed minority rights?

In his fascinating book (1992), Jack Knight made a subtle but important point: too many of our models of collective choice downplay the distributive implications of politics. Explanations of institutions that rely on (Pareto) optimality properties offer an easy way out: who could argue with an institution that makes everyone at least as well off and at least one individual strictly better off?

In real politics, however, decisions are often made over the objections of an opposition. This is especially true of attempts to alter minority rights, which are typically (although, even I would admit, not always) the subject of serious contention among legislators. People tend to get very upset when minority rights are changed in a way that seems inconsistent with the assumption that welfare-improving changes are being made.

This has a great deal of relevance for the informational approach to minority rights. Without downplaying the intellectual importance of these contributions, they tend to follow a common format: something that we consider a benefit for the minority turns out, once correctly modeled, to be something that in fact improves the welfare of the majority.

There is nothing wrong with this view, of course, but it does raise the question of whether we haven't simply proved that there is no such thing as a minority right in a legislature. If all minority rights are justified simply by the welfare calculations of the majority, then how precisely is the minority afforded any actual protection? One is reminded of the Federalist argument against the Bill of Rights—that it was pointless since the government would really have no incentive to abrogate the rights being spelled out.

This criticism is of course not unique to the study of minority rights—political science is often quite silent on what would seem to be a central issue, namely why some individuals decide at certain points to simply eviscerate others, and why they sometimes do not.

It would be interesting to see an explanation of why a majority would in fact retain or eliminate minority rights, despite calculations of self-interest. This of course means jettisoning the rational choice approach. I certainly will not plan on following anyone on that path, nor do I propose great benefits to those who do. But I think we need to recognize that the rational choice revolution in legislative politics has made two important but ultimately separable methodological advances. The first is concentrating attention on the idea of goals and maximizing behavior. The second, however, is to make us much more careful in setting out and testing theories. Talking about norms does not have to involve a regress into a quagmire of bad 1950s sociology about norms. Instead, it can give us some idea about precisely how individuals conceptualize the notion of minority rights as a normative commitment rather than a technique to further utility maximization.

To take an example, consider the Ultimatum Game (Güth, Schmittberger, and Schwarze 1982). The game is by this point well known: one individual proposes a division of some good, and the second player is given the choice of either accepting or rejecting the offer. Game theoretic models predict that the individual will propose giving nothing to the second player, who will then accept it. This prediction has been disconfirmed in numerous experiments since that time.

What is most troubling about the Ultimatum game is that the basic Romer–Rosenthal model with a closed rule, the model that underlies a large proportion of our formal results in legislative politics, in fact shares important elements with the ultimatum game (see Romer and Rosenthal 1978). Committees under a closed rule propose policies that give them their best outcome, consistent to the floor being at least indifferent between the proposal and the status quo. In certain cases, then, the committee will take all the "surplus," leaving the floor indifferent between the status quo and the committee proposal.

At first this seems disturbing: could our results be built on sand? But there are two responses to make. First, as Riker (1962) argued, maximization behavior is often more likely in cases where agents work for others than in cases where an individual decides for themselves. Since legislatures typically involve elected representatives, the plausibility of maximizing behavior increases. I may feel that cutting a little slack on a health care bill is perfectly called for, but my constituents may feel otherwise.

Second, what the work on the ultimatum game has done is to think through much more rigorously the explanations for such apparently irrational behavior. There is an important difference between offering a positive amount because you think it is the correct thing to do, and offering a positive amount because you think that the other player is irrationally vengeful to unfair offers. By thinking through these issues and constructing experiments capable of distinguishing the various explanations, we can arrive at a more nuanced view of why minority rights might be extended even in cases where equilibrium behavior would predict otherwise.

Rudeness, ordinary and extraordinary

Much of the work on minority rights looks at procedural guarantees. But individual rights need not be limited to procedural guarantees. I have a right, let's say, not to be splattered with pig's blood on my way to a lecture. We could file this under some sort of right to be free from assault, but in a way this simply misses the point, which is that individuals within a community are often expected as a matter of right to extend certain courtesies to others. We can evaluate the structure of minority rights, then, by comparing the way individuals behave within a legislature to the way those same individuals would behave outside. Doing so has the advantage of enabling us to get an idea of the way in which societal views about decency and comity translate (or fail to translate) into legislative behavior (for the still-untapped classic exposition, see Uslaner 1993).

One minimal element of decency is the right to speak uninterrupted by others. Interruption rates were an important part of Lyn Kathlene's (1994) study of the impact of gender on committee hearings. Whether minority members are interrupted more than majority members offers a similar way to get at the problem. This could theoretically be compared to the interactions of the same members with the greater public, thus controlling for societal norms. The existence of committee hearing transcripts offers a clear data source for analyzing this, as does the coverage of floor debates.

Looking at this issue, I predict, will not only help us understand minority rights considered from the partisan perspective common in this literature, but also minority rights more broadly conceived (based on race, class, gender, etc.) Suppose, for example, that we find that African-American legislators are interrupted at higher rates than white legislators. In some cases, we might find that interruption rates for African-American legislators within a majority party are below the interruption rates for whites in the minority, thus suggesting that African Americans are "second-class citizens" in their party but are treated better than the minority party. If, however, the interruption rates are even higher than those for minority party whites, it suggests an even more troubling view for the issue of race in legislatures.

Interruption rates are of course only one element of rudeness. There are millions of other ways in which individuals (partisan minorities as well as demographic minorities) might be systematically excluded from influence—situations in which rights are in essence trampled. Perhaps the most extreme would be the use of violence. I am inspired here by Eugene Wolfe's fascinating study of violence in legislatures, a portion of which was finally published in 2004. Wolfe has assembled a history of the use of physical violence in legislative politics. Because this behavior does not fit into the usual model of legislatures, however, such an important topic has been widely understudied, and even normally open scholars can have odd reactions (for example, believing that physical violence has no place in legislative politics, which is, first, palpably false, and second, ontologically questionable). But the use of violence ultimately brings us to the final guarantee of majority control—the final thing the majority can do, after all else has been eliminated, is to dispose of minority opposition by force.

Freedom from interruptions and from violence constitute only two topics that are fit for a study of minority rights. Bringing in particular cultural sensibilities would easily expand this list. What, for example, about throwing shoes at legislators in the legislatures of the Middle East?

Remember psychology?

At least since the 1970s switch to purposive models, legislative studies has with relatively few exceptions (prime among them Donald D. Searing, see, e.g., Searing 1994) abandoned the psychological approach. This of course stands in quite strong contrast to our subfield confederates in voting and elections, as well as other fields. Most of our advances in the field have come through the application of rational choice models and techniques more familiar in economics.

Recently, however, even economists have started to attempt to reintegrate the study of market behavior with more realistic psychological models (for reviews, see Rabin

1998, 2002). I am neither expert in psychological work, nor especially well positioned to suggest the most promising leads for legislative research. In fact, I generally find psychological approaches either woefully undertheorized or painfully obvious. In the interest of broader approaches, let me suggest two avenues of research that might be advantageous.

The first relies on the psychological notion of "reference groups," but within a game-theoretic context. A model of identity as developed by Moses Shayo (2009) (see also Penn 2008) posits agents as deciding upon identity based upon utility calculations. An individual in those models either identifies with the nation or with their own group. Within the legislative context, this would be, I think, equivalent to identifying with the median voter, or with the median of the party. What drives the decision to identify with the group is the possibility of gains from making social and political comparisons with the other group(s). Identifying with the median means forgoing the pleasure of seeing the minority party crushed underfoot. These models are fully as formal as any in legislative politics, yet include an element of malice that is sorely lacking in most of our theories (which more typically are characterized by the adoption of institutional features that make everyone better off).

For those who disdain halfway measures, a second avenue might be more preferable. Most political scientists are familiar with the conformity studies of Solomon Asch and Stanley Milgram. Asch, for example, established that individuals will go against the evidence of their own senses in the face of group consensus, while Milgram demonstrated the lengths to which ordinary individuals would go in following the commands of authority.

Less well known (at least to me) is the work of Serge Moscovici. (To provide an ironic link, Moscovici's son Pierre is a prominent Socialist member of the French National Assembly.) Moscovici studied the possibility of "minority influence." His main contribution is to emphasize the role of consistency in explaining minority influence (see Moscovici, Lage, and Naffrechoux 1969 for an early statement). Minorities which bounce around tend to be ignored.

Such a perspective, I think, sidesteps the problem of "majority interest." It also can provide an alternative perspective on existing theories of minority rights. For example, Binder's Party Strength measure increases as the cohesion of the minority party diminishes. Does this lack of cohesion among the minority eliminate minority influence, and thus pave the way for procedural changes enhancing majority rule, or does it essentially make the minority irrelevant to majority calculations? What other influences from psychology might we find to explain steps taken to limit (or enhance) minority rights?

Your computer is a legislature, and other thoughts

I will now offer a few off-the-wall suggestions (comparatively speaking), for what they are worth. The first has to do with computing. It turns out that an important issue in that field has to do with the problem of faulty sub-units. As Danezis and Anderson (2004) note, systems with a single node are highly vulnerable to attack. By distributing tasks across nodes (with some redundancy), security is enhanced. At the same time, however, doing so requires some system for reconciling conflicts, which brings us closer to legislatures. Andrei Sejantov and Ross Anderson (2004, 1), for example, observe that "peer-to-peer systems are often vulnerable to disruption by minorities," language that could come directly out of the legislative literature, and apply social choice theory to their attempt to understand how to deal with adversaries "fairly." I suggest that this literature might offer some new perspectives on legislatures—we can think of these processors as a sort of legislature, where conceivably there might be committees of sub-units that report to higher units, just as committees report to the floor. (For a more traditional model along similar lines, see Sah and Stiglitz 1988.)

A second potential approach has to do with models of dominance. It is a commonplace of the U.S. Congress that it resembles your basic high school, and I am sure many other legislatures are similar in possessing the same brew of popularity, maneuvering, and dominance. It might be interesting, for example, to compare the revolt against Speaker Joseph Cannon with the leadership revolt so powerfully described by Frans de Waal (2007). One approach for linking this more biologically based material with the traditional approaches in legislative politics might be the use of evolutionary game models. Dominance games would be an excellent starting point (see Maynard Smith 1982 for the classic exposition of the evolutionary game approach, as well as important points on dominance contests). Perhaps one day, if my colleagues are correct, we will be stealing combs and chewing gum from Congressional garbage bins to run DNA tests to identify the genetic components responsible for minority tolerance.

Conclusion

Few areas of legislative politics hold as much promise for enhancing our understanding of workings of democratic politics than the study of majority rule and minority rights. Thanks to a number of researchers in this area, we have definitely made some important strides in this direction, gaining a much better grasp of the ways in which institutional structures are altered. It is, however, still true, even if a cliché, that much can still be done.

References

ALDRICH, J. H. 1994. A Model of a Legislature with Two Parties and a Committee System. *Legislative Studies Quarterly*, 19(3): 313–39.

——and ROHDE, D. 2000. The Logic of Conditional Party Government: Revisiting the Electoral Connection, pp. 269–92 in *Congress Reconsidered*, ed. L. Dodd and B. Oppenheimer, 7th edn. Washington, DC: CQ Press.

BAMBOR, T., ROBERTS CLARK, W., and GOLDER, M. 2006. Understanding Interaction Models: Improving Empirical Analyses. *Political Analysis*, 14: 63–82.

BINDER, S. A. 1995. Partisanship and Procedural Change in the Early Congress, 1789–1823. *Journal of Politics*, 57: 1093–117.

—— 1996. The Partisan Basis of Procedural Choice: Allocating Parliamentary Rights in the House, 1789–1990. *American Political Science Review*, 90: 8–20.

—— 1997. *Minority Rights, Majority Rule*. NY: Cambridge University Press.

—— and SMITH, S. S. 1997. *Politics or Principle: Filibustering in the United States Senate*. Washington, DC: Brookings Institution.

BLACK, D. 1958. *The Theory of Committees and Elections*. Cambridge: Cambridge University Press.

BUCHANAN, J. M., and TULLOCK, G. 1962. *The Calculus of Consent*. Ann Arbor: University of Michigan Press.

COOPER, J., and BRADY, D. 1981. Institutional Context and Leadership Style. *American Political Science Review*, 75: 411–25.

CROMBEZ, C., GROSECLOSE, T., and KREHBIEL, KEITH. 2006. Gatekeeping. *Journal of Politics*, 68(2): 322–34.

DAHL, R. A. 1956. *A Preface to Democratic Theory*. Chicago: University of Chicago Press.

DANEZIS, G., and ANDERSON, R. 2004. The Economics of Censorship Resistance. Workshop on Economics and Information Security. In Proceedings of the Third Annual Workshop on the Economics of Information Security, May 2004. Available at http://citeseerx.ist.psu.edu/viewdoc/download?doi=10.1.1.4.7003&rep=rep1&type=pdf (accessed September 13, 2010).

DESSEIN, W. 2002. Authority and Communication in Organizations. *Review of Economic Studies*, 69(4): 811–38.

DION, D. 1991. Removing the Obstructions: Minority Rights and the Politics of Procedural Change in the Nineteenth Century House of Representatives. Ph.D. diss., University of Michigan, Ann Arbor.

—— 1997. *Turning the Legislative Thumbscrew: Minority Rights and Procedural Change in Legislative Politics*. Ann Arbor: University of Michigan Press.

—— and HUBER, J. D. 1996. Party Leadership and Procedural Choice in Legislatures. *Journal of Politics*, 58(1): 25–53.

—— and HUBER, J. D. 1997. Sense and Sensibility: The Role of Rules (A Response to Keith Krehbiel). *American Journal of Political Science*, 41(3): 945–57.

EPSTEIN, D. 1997. An Informational Rationale for Committee Gatekeeping Power. *Public Choice*, 91: 271–99.

GALLOWAY, G. 1969. *History of the House of Representatives*. New York: Thomas Y. Crowell Co.

GILLIGAN, T. W., and KREHBIEL, K. 1987. Collective Decisionmaking and Standing Committees: An Informational Rationale for Restrictive Amendment Procedures. *Journal of Law, Economics, & Organization*, 3(3): 287–335.

GREENBERG, J. 1979. Consistent Majority Rules over Compact Sets of Alternatives. *Econometrica*, 47(3): 627–36.

GREENSTONE, J. D. 1969. *Labor in American Politics*. NY: Alfred A. Knopf.

GÜTH, W., SCHMITTBERGER, R., and SCHWARZE, B. 1982. An Experimental Analysis of Ultimatum Bargaining. *Journal of Economic Behavior and Organization*, 3(4): 367–88.

JENKINS, J. A., SCHICKLER, E., and CARSON, J. L. 2004. Constituency Cleavages and Congressional Parties: Measuring Homogeneity and Polarization, 1857–1913. *Social Science History*, 28(4): 537–73.

KAM, C. D., and FRANZESE, JR., R. J. 2007. *Modeling and Interpreting Interactive Hypotheses in Regression Analysis*. Ann Arbor: University of Michigan Press.

KATHLENE, L. 1994. Power and Influence in State Legislative Policymaking: The Interaction of Gender and Position in Committee Hearing Debates. *American Political Science Review*, 88(3): 560–76.

KIEWIET, D. R., LOEWENBERG, G., and SQUIRE, P. 2002. The Implications of the Study of the U.S. Congress for Comparative Legislative Research, pp. 3–22 in *Legislatures: Comparative Perspectives on Representative Assemblies*, ed. G. Loewenberg, P. Squire, and D. R. Kiewiet. Ann Arbor: University of Michigan Press.

KIM, J., and ROTHENBERG, L. S. 2008. Foundations of Legislative Organization and Committee Influence. *Journal of Theoretical Politics*, 20: 339–74.

KING, D. C. 1997. *Turf Wars: How Congressional Committees Claim Jurisdiction*. Chicago: University of Chicago Press.

KNIGHT, J. 1992. *Institutions and Social Conflict*. NY: Cambridge University Press.

KREHBIEL, K. 1992. *Information and Legislative Organization*. Ann Arbor MI: University of Michigan Press.

——1997. Restrictive Rules Reconsidered. *American Journal of Political Science*, 41(3): 919–44.

——2001. Plausibility of Signals by a Heterogeneous Committee. *American Political Science Review*, 95(2): 453–7.

——and MEIROWITZ, A. 2002. Minority Rights and Majority Power: Theoretical Consequences of the Motion to Recommit. *Legislative Studies Quarterly*, 27(2): 191–217.

KRISHNA, V., and MORGAN, J. 2001. Asymmetric Information and Legislative Rules: Some Amendments. *American Political Science Review*, 95(2): 435–52.

MAYNARD SMITH, J. 1982. *Evolution and the Theory of Games*. New York: Cambridge University Press.

MOSCOVICI, S., LAGE, E., and NAFFRECHOUX, M. 1969. Influence of a Consistent Minority on the Responses of a Majority in a Color Perception Task. *Sociometry*, 32(4): 365–80.

PATTY, J. 2008. Equilibrium Party Government. *American Journal of Political Science*, 52(3): 636–55.

——and PENN, E. M. 2008. The Legislative Calendar. *Mathematical and Computer Modelling*, 48: 1590–1601.

PENN, E. M. 2008. Citizenship versus Ethnicity: The Role of Institutions in Shaping Identity Choice. *Journal of Politics*, 70(4): 956–73.

POOLE, K., and ROSENTHAL, H. 1997. *Congress: A Political-Economic History of Roll-call Voting*. New York: Oxford University Press.

RABIN, M. 1998. Psychology and Economics. *Journal of Economic Literature*, 36(1): 11–46.

——2002. A Perspective on Psychology and Economics. *European Economic Review*, 46(4–5): 657–85.

RIKER, W. H. 1962. *The Theory of Political Coalitions*. New Haven, CT: Yale University Press.

ROBERTS, J. M. 2005. Minority Rights and Majority Power: Conditional Party Government and the Motion to Recommit in the House. *Legislative Studies Quarterly*, 30(2): 219–34.

ROHDE, D. W., and ORNSTEIN, N. J. 1978. Political Parties and Congressional Reform, pp. 280–94 in *Parties and Elections in an Anti-Party Age*, ed. J. Fishel. Bloomington: Indiana University Press.

ROMER, T., and ROSENTHAL, H. 1978. Political Resource Allocation, Controlled Agendas, and the Status Quo. *Public Choice*, 33(3): 27–43.

SAH, R. K. S., and STIGLITZ, J. E. 1988. Committees, Hierarchies and Polyarchies. *Economic Journal*, 98: 451–70.

SCHICKLER, E. 2000. Institutional Change in the House of Representatives, 1967–1998: A Test of Partisan and Ideological Power Balance Models. *American Political Science Review*, 94: 269–88.

SEARING, D. D. 1994. *Westminster's World*. Cambridge, MA: Harvard University Press.

SERJANTOV, A., and ANDERSON, R. 2004. On Dealing with Adversaries Fairly. In *The Third Annual Workshop on Economics and Information Security* (WEIS04), Minnesota, US, 13–14 May 2004. Available at http://citeseerx.ist.psu.edu/viewdoc/download? doi=10.1.1.5.1705&rep=rep1&type=pdf (accessed September 13, 2010).

SHAYO, M. 2009. A Model of Social Identity with an Application to Political Economy: Nation, Class, and Redistribution. *American Political Science Review*, 103(2): 147–74.

USLANER, E. M. 1993. *The Decline of Comity in Congress*. Ann Arbor: University of Michigan Press.

VALLELY, R. M. 2009. The Reed Rules and Republican Party Building: A New Look. *Studies in American Political Development*, 23: 115–42.

WAAL, F. DE. 2007. *Chimpanzee Politics: Power and Sex among Apes*, 25th anniversary edn. Baltimore, MD: Johns Hopkins University Press.

WAWRO, G. J., and SCHICKLER, E. 2006. *Filibuster: Obstruction and Lawmaking in the U.S. Senate*. Princeton, NJ: Princeton University Press.

WILLIAMS, M. The European Parliament: Political Groups, Minority Rights and the "Rationalisation" of Parliamentary Organisation. A Research Note, pp. 391–404 in *Parliaments and Majority Rule in Western Europe*, ed. H. Döring. Frankfurt: Campus Verlag.

WOLFE, E. L. 2004. Creating Democracy's Good Losers: The Rise, Fall, and Return of Parliamentary Disorder in Post-war Japan. *Government and Opposition*, 39(1): 55–79.

WOLFENSBERGER, D. R. 2003. The Motion to Recommit in the House: The Creation, Evisceration, and Restoration of a Minority Right. Paper presented at Conference on the History of Congress, University of California, San Diego, 5–6 December.

CHAPTER 33

....

SECTIONALISM AND CONGRESSIONAL DEVELOPMENT

....

RICHARD BENSEL

UNLIKE the presidency, which unites the entire nation into a single constituency, members of Congress represent geographically distinct districts and states. Given the large and diverse political economy of the United States, the way in which members of Congress and senators represent their districts and states has necessarily produced conflict between them. Attempts to weld durable national majorities out of this diversity and conflict have, in turn, produced alternative relationships between the national party system, the organization of the legislative process, and the nature of sectional alignments in federal policymaking. One result of these attempts to weld durable majorities has been that changes in the sectional alignment of the national party system have driven much of the oscillation in Congress between centralized party control of the legislative process and decentralized domination by an autonomous committee system. And, as will be shown, the connection runs in the opposite direction as well in that the institutional organization of the legislative process has also had a profound impact on the sectional alignment of the national party system. By integrating these dimensions of American political development into a single interpretive narrative, a sectional perspective embeds institutional transformations in Congress within a larger, national perspective in a way that most of the traditional literature on Congress does not do. In constructing this interpretive narrative, this chapter integrates the literature on sectionalism within a historical interpretation of its influence on congressional development.

Sectionalism arises out of public policy disputes that become political contests between geographically defined communities. That contestation, in turn, produces regional identities that then become one of the frames through which members of Congress interpret the interests of their constituencies. These interpretations subsequently constitute an important and sometimes the dominant way through which members represent themselves and their legislative record in elections. As interpretive frames, sections create a "commonality of interest" between localities that otherwise, on the basis of their individual characteristics, might be opposed to one another. For example, because of their agricultural economies, congressional districts in upstate New York have particular interests (such as government regulation of the price and supply of milk) that are often at odds with those of metropolitan New York City. And party divisions within New York have often reflected that divergence, with Republicans historically much stronger upstate and Democrats dominating New York City.[1]

But their interdependency within the national political economy (e.g. when city consumers prosper, they are able to pay a higher price for milk) has produced a partial convergence of interest in Congress in such a way that Republicans from upstate New York have tended to align much more often with New York City Democrats than Republicans from otherwise similar districts in the rest of the country. And it is this convergence of interest, spanning and thus uniting individual districts into a common community of interest, that has made sectionalism an important influence in congressional development. Because sectionalism postulates entire communities as interest-bearing actors in national politics, the sectional construction of politics tends to supplant alternative frames of conflict within regions. Sectional constructions of political interests, for example, tend to displace alternative forms that might otherwise arise out of social and economic classes, urban and rural policy demands, and ethnic and racial identities (Bensel 1984, 3–5). In fact, because these cleavages might otherwise internally divide the interests of sectional communities, they are often explicitly suppressed.

Compared with other nations, class and ethnic cleavages have been weak on the national stage during most of American political development. Instead, the large continental expanse that became the United States produced regionally distinct and often competing political economies that have, in turn, given rise to a particularly materialist construction of competing sectional policy demands. At the most general level, these demands have sorted out the nation into, on the one hand, a relatively advanced core in which a wealthy, capital-rich economy encouraged the emergence and development of technologically complex industrial sectors and, on the other, a largely rural periphery in which the production of export agricultural commodities provided the economic base of the region. In the early nineteenth century, this bipolar sectional competition was supplemented by the often cross-cutting demands of a

[1] This convergence of interest within the national political economy would not necessarily occur within New York state, because policymaking within the state legislature would be much more likely to produce zero-sum outcomes as rural and urban areas divided up the costs and benefits of policy decisions (e.g. over the price of milk). For that reason, we should expect state politics (e.g. alignments with the state legislature) to reflect the competing interests of localities within the state in a more contentious manner than they would at the national level.

relatively large frontier sector that favored internal improvements and other policies encouraging settlement.

Sectional competition has influenced congressional development in at least three important ways. First, the sectional construction of political conflict has been an important factor in the evolution of the party system and the internal structure of national political parties (Bensel 1984, 368–88). When competition within the national party system aligned with the major sections, for example, the membership of the two parties has become sectionally polarized with each of the two parties dominating either the core or the periphery. Party discipline and programmatic cohesion have tended to be relatively high in such periods. When competition within the national party system has straddled the major sections, party discipline and programmatic cohesion have been impaired by cross-cutting sectional cleavages.

Second, sectionalism has frequently affected the content and outcome of congressional politics. The selection of the Speaker of the House of Representatives and the major officers of the two dominant parties has, for example, been directly influenced by both sectionally framed policy demands and the need to balance the leadership positions between the party's regional factions. In addition, many of the factions that have operated outside formal party organizations have represented interests associated with one or another of the nation's sections. Finally, sectional political competition has shaped the development of the legislative structure and parliamentary rules. The ability of members to conduct filibusters in the United States Senate, for example, became almost exclusively identified with southern Democrats during the twentieth century as they attempted to forestall civil rights legislation. The power and influence of the Committee on Rules in the House of Representatives waxed and waned over the same period depending on whether or not southern Democrats were able to fend off the demands of their northern colleagues for a more open political process. The prominence of individual legislative committees likewise has often turned on how important its policy jurisdiction was to the programmatic basis of sectional competition. The Committee on Territories, for example, became the legislative focal point for the western expansion of slavery. The Committee on Coinage was similarly implicated in the late nineteenth century struggle over the gold standard. The Ways and Means Committee has served as the primary legislative field of battle for advocates and opponents of a protective tariff. In each of these and other cases, the policy basis of sectional competition was written into the very structure of Congress.

SECTIONALISM, CONGRESS, AND AMERICAN POLITICAL DEVELOPMENT

One of the distinctive features of sectional competition is that it often carries separatist implications. By dividing a nation into regional communities with different policy demands, sectionalism simultaneously reinforces the political identities of regions while weakening their commitment to an overarching national framework (Key 1964, 233). Throughout most of American history, politically dominant sections have been nationalist, favoring a stronger central government and repression of separatist claims. Subordinate sections have correspondingly favored the devolution of state authority to the individual states.

During the young republic's first years, Alexander Hamilton's proposals to assume the indebtedness of the individual states, to charter a national bank, and related fiscal policies ultimately divided members of Congress into two new political parties: the Federalists and the Republicans. Although the sections were also internally divided, the Federalists dominated the northern commercial centers while the Republicans were stronger in the South and along the western frontier. The emergence of these political parties politicized control over the legislative process while structuring perceptions of common and antithetical political interest. Only a few years later, Thomas Jefferson's trade embargo during the Napoleonic Wars, combined with American hostilities with Great Britain in the War of 1812, both increased sectional stress within the young nation (leading, for example, to the Hartford Convention 1815) and further strengthened party allegiances and organizations in Congress. Andrew Jackson's victory in New Orleans, along with the Treaty of Ghent, effectively destroyed the Federalists as a formal political party (Aldrich 1995, 98).

By this point, the primary sectional alignment in American politics had been set down as competition between the North and the South with the political economy of slavery as the major flashpoint in national politics. The Missouri Compromise in 1820, with the dual admission of Maine (as a free state) and Missouri (as a slave state), implicitly recognized both the significance of slavery and its vulnerability by making the United States Senate the legislative forum in which future sectional compromises would be constructed. The House of Representatives was already dominated by members from the more rapidly growing northern states and would henceforth be regarded as unfriendly to slavery. But the Senate, with its equal apportionment of senators (two to each state), was much more susceptible as a vehicle for reconciling sectional tension between the North and the South, as long as there were an equal number of slave and free states in the Union. From this point until the outbreak of the Civil War, the United States Senate flourished as its prominence attracted and retained the best political talent in the nation. Never before or since has vivid political oratory and high statesmanship been so prominent in either chamber of Congress (Mayhew 2000, 181–2, 213–14).

But the major party organizations were not aligned along this sectional divide during the three decades following the Missouri Compromise. Instead, they spanned the North and South, taking the form of the Democratic and Whig parties until the next crisis occurred over slavery. During this period, thousands of petitions were sent to Congress asking for the abolition of slavery and abolition of the slave trade in Washington, DC. In 1836, the House of Representatives adopted a "gag rule" that automatically "tabled" all such petitions without any other formal action being taken on them. This "gag rule" was readopted in every Congress from 1836 until December,

1844, when increasing opposition by northern Democrats enabled rescission. By this time, the prospective annexation of Texas had once more provoked a political crisis over slavery. However, the national party system was now unable to confine the sectional implications. In 1845, Texas was annexed in votes that split both the Whig and Democratic parties along sectional lines (Silbey 2009). This act brought on a war with Mexico that, in turn, led to the annexation of vast new territories in what became the American Southwest.

In complex negotiations attending the treatment of slavery in these new territories, including the admission of California as a free state, Congress hammered out what became the Compromise of 1850 (Holt 2005). Although the compromise temporarily calmed the conflict over the issues surrounding the war, the Whig Party was torn apart by the sectional tension. In the South, the Whig Party was absorbed by the Democrats as the region increasingly became a one-party bastion and the Democrats posed as the protectors of slavery in national politics. In the North, the Whigs simply disappeared as the rise of the new Know-Nothing (nativist) and Republican parties absorbed their voters. In a very few years, the Know-Nothing Party also disappeared as the Republican Party increasingly became the vehicle of free state interests in the North. A small band of northern Democrats, internally divided over slavery, nonetheless prevented the Republicans from exercising the same degree of hegemony that the Democrats exercised in the South.

In the decade before the Civil War, members of Congress operated in the midst of constitutional crisis in which the very conception of their roles as congressmen and senators was at stake. On the one hand, southerners more or less saw themselves as ambassadors to a loosely organized federal republic in which the continuing membership of their states in the Union was contingent upon the protection of their sovereign "rights." Northerners, on the other hand, were evolving an increasingly strident nationalist stance in which their commitments as members of Congress were, first and foremost, to that national Union and only secondarily to the individual state from which they hailed. While both parties were becoming increasingly cohesive, the Democrats were internally divided over whether or not secession was and should be a viable option. Since the states would necessarily secede one at a time, the problem on the Democratic side of the aisle was how to coordinate that action because, even if they chose to remain in the Union, the threat of secession had become their most important card in inter-sectional negotiations. In order to credibly play that card, they had to present a unified front behind what was an inherently fragmented constitutional claim. Although nationalism gave them a common set of symbols and institutions behind which to rally, Republicans had their own problems. One of these was that they were still a young party under whose tent had gathered the remnants of the now defunct Whig, Know-Nothing, and Liberty parties, along with emigres from the anti-slavery northern wing of the Democratic Party. They were united only in their unqualified support for the Union and their opposition to slavery's expansion into the western territories. On most other issues, they were not much more than pragmatic politicians in search of a viable party vehicle for their personal ambitions.

The most important occasion for inter-sectional negotiations was often the election of a Speaker in the House of Representatives. One of these contests resulted in the election of Nathaniel Banks of Massachusetts in 1856 after 133 recorded votes cast over almost two months. Although elected as a member of the Know-Nothing Party, Banks' anti-slavery sentiments rapidly moved him to associate with the then very young Republican Party (Jenkins and Sala 1998; Jenkins and Nokken 2000). Another contest consumed several months and 44 ballots in the winter of 1859–60 before William Pennington of New Jersey, the last surviving Whig in the House of Representatives, was elected. Pennington, too, affiliated with the Republicans (Bensel 1990, 47–57). In both instances, the inter-sectional bargaining that finally elevated these men to the speakership involved many issues in addition to slavery, particularly the tariff and nativism. The power of the Speaker in this period was limited but he did have the ability to appoint standing committees in the House and, by promising appointments to the various factions on these issues, a successful candidate usually cobbled together a majority just durable enough to gain election. But the primary conflict was nonetheless over the present and future prospects of slavery. And compromise on this issue was no longer feasible in anything but the most fleeting of political contexts (Bensel 1990, 18–93).

The Republican Party, Civil War, and Industrialization

Lincoln's election was followed by secession of the southern states, which then founded the Confederate States of America. The Confederate Congress was almost a carbon copy of its northern counterpart and many of the southern representatives and senators who did not accept commissions in the Confederate Army served in either upper or lower chamber in Richmond. In Washington, secession radically shifted the balance of power to the Republicans even before members of the new Congress took their seats. In effect, control of the American state had been transferred from the Democratic to the Republican parties, from the South to the North, and from ambivalent federationists to fervent nationalists. This conflation of partisan commitment, sectionalism, and nationalism produced the Republican party-state, a regime characterized by: "1) a political system in which a single party dominates all other contenders for power; 2) the dominant party coalition excludes important groups and classes in the national political economy from almost all participation in government decision making; and 3) membership in the dominant party is the most important single qualification for office holding within the state bureaucracy (Bensel 1990, 4)." For the next decade and a half, until the southern states were readmitted into the Union, the Republican Party ruled without significant challenge.

The Republican party-state pursued three national projects. The first was military defeat of the Confederacy and the resumption of Union authority throughout the South. Although military operations were controlled by the executive branch, prosecution of the war depended upon favorable northern public opinion. Forming what became a vital link between the Lincoln administration's mobilization of men and materiel and the northern citizenry, Congressional Republicans constructed nationalist sentiment in the North by both sanctifying the survival of the Union and castigating the Democratic opposition as southern sympathizers and traitors. Republican Party organizations throughout the North effectively, if not explicitly, constructed the central pillar of the American state as a northern, rural, white, Protestant, native born, Union soldier. After the war ended, the massive organization of Union war veterans known as the Grand Army of the Republic (the G.A.R.) became so identified with the Republican Party that detractors termed the movement "Generally All Republicans."

The second national project pursued by the Republican party-state was the reconstruction of the southern political economy. In the years immediately following the end of the Civil War, the primary purpose of that reconstruction was the political suppression of southern separatism. To that end, military governments in the South sponsored the emergence of the black freedman as a major element in the construction of a regional Republican Party that, it was hoped, would successfully compete with the white plantation elite for political supremacy in the region. When these indigenous Republican parties could not sustain themselves at the polls, northern Republicans used their power to seat representatives from the South and overturned southern elections in which fraud and violence had been used to produce Democratic victories. By reviewing, in Washington, the results of elections conducted in the South, the Republicans shifted the goal of reconstruction from a permanent transformation of the southern political economy to a tactical preservation of their party's national power. After prolonged negotiations in and out of Congress accompanying the counting of contested electoral votes, the Compromise of 1876 resulted in the election of Republican Rutherford B. Hayes. Ending all hope of permanently reshaping the southern political economy, Hayes subsequently removed federal military support for the last remaining Republican state governments in the South.

The third national project was the promotion of northern industrial expansion. Only two days before Lincoln was inaugurated, congressional Republicans passed the Morrill Tariff. Although the customs duties set down in this act were only a pale shadow of what was to come, this tariff initiated more than half a century of protectionist barriers to foreign competition for northern industry. Behind these barriers American manufacturing first expanded to fill national markets, then consolidated into giant corporations (many of them becoming quasi-monopolies), and finally reemerged in the international economy as the most technologically advanced industrial producers in the world. In terms of its economic effects, the protective tariff, however, may have been the least important of the tripod of policies that promoted northern industrial expansion. The most important policy was probably the commitment of the American state to the international gold standard. That commitment effectively pegged the American dollar to the British pound and, by eliminating fluctuations in the exchange rate, enabled the consolidation of the New York and London capital markets. That consolidation, in turn, encouraged the retention of industrial and commercial profits in the United States where they were reinvested in what became a self-sustaining economic expansion within an unregulated market of continental dimensions. The third leg of the developmental tripod constructed the free market for goods and services as the United States Supreme Court struck down attempts by the individual states, many of them in the South, to regulate interstate commerce (Bensel 2000, 6–11).

Congress was implicated in each of the legs of industrial expansion but in varying ways. Aside from Senate ratification of nominees to the United States Supreme Court, for example, Congress did very little to construct an unregulated national market for industrial products and commercial goods. The leading role of the Supreme Court as an arbiter between the regulatory claims of the nation and the individual states insulated this leg from electoral politics. Adopting a passive role, Congress merely acquiesced by declining to regulate interstate commerce (Bensel 2000, 289–354). Congress was much more aggressive with respect to the gold standard. Maintenance of the gold standard required both a long-term balance between income and revenue (so that adequate reserves of gold could be retained in Treasury vaults) and short-term operations in the nation's money markets in order to accommodate shifts in international and domestic trade. Through management of the United States Treasury, especially the New York Subtreasury, the executive branch was primarily responsible for monetary operations and, because every president elected after the Civil War was committed to defense of the gold standard, these operations supported gold. But Congress was much less supportive. At times, one of the chambers even contained a majority that would have preferred abandonment of the gold standard in favor of silver payments. In the decades following resumption of the gold standard in 1879, congressional ambivalence toward gold and favorable sentiment toward silver, along with a vast expansion of pension benefits to Union Civil War veterans, threatened to push the nation off gold by producing almost insurmountable deficits in the national budget. Presidential action in the nation's money markets (just barely) countered these deficits until the return of large Republican majorities in Congress following the 1896 Battle of the Standards between William McKinley and William Jennings Bryan. Along with Republican victory in that election came revenue surpluses and, for the first time, a clear congressional commitment to maintenance of gold payments.

Congress clearly dominated construction of the protective tariff. In deliberations that routinely transformed tariff schedules into a distributive saturnalia for northern industrial interests, congressional committees festooned tariff legislation with benefits tailored to each of the major and minor constituencies comprising the Republican Party coalition. With the exception of a few duties (sugar, for example, produced much of the revenue brought in by the tariff and iron and steel were so central to industrial expansion that they were protected as a matter of high party policy), tariffs were built from the "bottom up" with little guidance from the executive branch. The tariff became the quintessential political policy that, in election after election, produced an electoral surplus that could be used, both metaphorically and explicitly, to subsidize the much less popular gold standard and unregulated national market. Congress thus mediated between the electoral demands of a democratic public and the economic imperatives of industrial expansion but this mediation was affected by the institutional location of these expansionary policies.

Because industrialization was largely confined to the Northeast and the shoreline of the Great Lakes, the benefits of these developmental policies were regionally concentrated. The costs, in terms of the higher prices of commercial goods imposed by the tariff and the deflationary impact of the gold standard on the prices of agricultural commodities, were largely born by the southern and western periphery (Ritter 1997). The highly sectional distribution of these costs and benefits followed, for the most part, the regional pattern of slavery, secession, and the Civil War: the northern states that had remained in the Union drew most of the benefits from these developmental policies while the former slave states bore a disproportional share of the costs. The continuity of divisions over the Civil War and industrial development were reflected in congressional recruitment. In the 46th Congress (1879–81), for example, former Confederate officers and government officials held over 80 percent of all southern seats in the United States House of Representatives and every single one of them joined the Democratic Party caucus. Union officers were less prominent in the Republican Party but, even so, former Confederate and Union officers comprised between 40 and 50 percent of all members between 1877 and 1891 (Bensel 1990, 405–13). And these officers, the greater part of them former brigadier generals, voted just as they had fought.

Both the "bloody shirt" and the "full dinner pail" (the latter symbolizing the interests of the industrial worker in the protective tariff) produced a highly polarized party system during the late nineteenth and early twentieth centuries. National party competition rested in the South upon the cotton complex, including plantation cultivation, transportation and processing, the financial arrangements underpinning the crop's domestic marketing and export, and the commercial sector that supplied consumer goods, fertilizer, and agricultural equipment. In the North, the base of the Republican Party was similarly composed of industrial and commercial producers, the financiers that serviced the capital needs of these firms, farmers who produced food that fed industrial workers, and Union veterans who drew their pensions from revenue thrown off by the protective tariff.

As a result, almost everyone in the southern white elite affiliated with the Democratic Party while most of the northern elite supported the Republicans. But the lower classes in both regions more or less divided in the opposite direction. While most industrial workers in the North supported the Republican Party, particularly when developmental policies were threatened, immigrant workers, Catholics, and poorer farmers tended to back the Democrats. In the South, black sharecroppers, tenant farmers, and poor mountain whites supported the Republican Party. These intraregional divisions meant that the national party system encompassed a "sectionally inverted class alignment" in that the upper class in the South and the lower class in the North supported the Democratic Party while the upper class in the North and the lower class in the South backed the Republicans (Bensel 2000, 523). At the national level, the class alignments of the two parties were incoherent in that policies that might have redistributed wealth between the upper and lower classes could not be pursued by either party without alienating one or the other of their regional wings. However, the Republicans could more easily ignore their southern base because the freedmen had nowhere else to go; if they shifted their support to the Democratic Party they would have had to vote for their former masters.

The Democrats, on the other hand, required at least some northern electoral votes (usually drawn from New York state) in order to be competitive in presidential elections. For them, the inverted class alignment created an imperative to somehow distinguish the class implications of their national platform so as to attract elite votes in the South and lower class votes in the North. In the last decade of the nineteenth century, the Democrats imposed a more or less durable solution to this problem by disfranchising almost all blacks and most poor whites in the South. For the next seventy years or so, the class base of the party in the South made its primary priority in national politics the preservation of the sectional political autonomy that allowed the region to maintain its racially segregated and elite-friendly class arrangements. Disfranchisement also meant that the Republicans had to attract large majorities in its northern bastion to counter the almost hegemonic grip the Democrats had on the somewhat smaller South. Everything considered, it is difficult (and perhaps pointless) to determine whether sectional elites simply transformed congressional parties into vehicles for their interests *or* congressional parties designed public policies so that they created safe constituencies for party incumbents in their respective sections (for maps of party strength in this period, see Martis 1989). The symbiosis between sections and parties was almost perfect.

However, the very success of the developmental policies producing rapid industrial expansion in the North undercut harmony between the eastern and midwestern wings of the Republican Party. By 1900, the giant industrial corporations that arose within the unregulated national market became so technologically advanced and efficient that many of them no longer benefited from tariff protection. And the hundreds of thousands of Union veterans that had made the Grand Army of the Republic a charter member of the Republican Party began to die off. Their deaths eliminated the primary way in which the Republicans had brought the benefits of tariff protection into homes and communities in the rural western plains, far from the steel mills and iron foundries of the East.

As both the economic rationale and the electoral underpinning of the tariff complex deteriorated, the Republican Party began to split between a regular faction that still supported traditional party commitments and a small band of midwestern "progressives" who were willing to ally with congressional Democrats on a legislative program that would regulate the giant trusts, address the social problems of the mushrooming industrial cities, and, by reducing customs duties, redistribute income from the comparatively wealthy core regions of the nation to impoverished rural areas in the periphery (Sanders 1999). In Congress, the fracturing of the Republican Party produced a revolt in 1910 against the autocratic rule of Speaker Joseph Cannon of Illinois (Schickler 2001, 78–83; Robinson 1914). Although the immediate effect of this revolt was fairly limited, the removal of the power to appoint committees from the Speaker set in motion a long-term process that ultimately produced a radically decentralized and autonomous committee system. The hierarchically controlled and programmatically cohesive congressional parties of the late nineteenth and early twentieth centuries were fatally weakened by this and other progressive procedural reforms. We thus see, once again, how congressional organization has been closely tied to the sectional basis of the party system. When party and section are closely aligned, control over the legislative process has been centralized in the hands of the party leaders. When party and section are not aligned, control over the legislative process tends to decentralize into the committee system.

Congress and the New Deal Coalition in the Democratic Party

In the 1930s inter-sectional relations within the Democratic Party also became much more complicated (Turner 1951, ch. 6). Industrialization had by then created a vast working class within equally vast urban conglomerations throughout the northern manufacturing belt. The New Deal promised these workers massive relief programs, a nationally-protected right to organize into labor unions, and social welfare programs for the elderly and disabled. These measures turned party competition in the North into something akin to class warfare as Democrats colored the Republican opposition as the agents of "class privilege" and the Republicans called New Deal Democrats "reds." In the South, a much milder form of class insurgency erupted within the Democratic Party but the shrunken electorate and the hegemonic dominance of the party in the region made this threat more apparent than real. The problem facing the national Democratic Party, however, was very real: how could the New Deal meet the insistent demands of northern workers for a sweeping reorganization of the industrial political economy without also undermining the elite-dominated class and racial order in the South?

The solution was the emergence of what became the New Deal Democratic coalition, an uneasy marriage of convenience between white elite southerners and northern workers. This coalition differed from its cross-sectional Democratic antecedents in several ways. For one thing, the northern wing of the party was now an almost equal partner. Prior to the New Deal, northern Democrats were usually no more than a rump faction, largely confined to New York City and a few other districts but otherwise vastly outnumbered by their southern brethren. From 1930 forward, however, the northern wing often outnumbered the southern branch in Congress and controlled sizable delegate majorities in the quadrennial national conventions. In those national conventions, presidential nominees were pledged to platforms that reflected northern policy demands and thus addressed the competitive nature of contests in the northern states. Because the demands the northern wing placed before the party required a national policy response, regional détente could no longer be the near-automatic response of a radical devolution of policy responsibility to the individual states with northern states going in one direction and southern states in another.

The divergent needs of the northern and southern wings of the New Deal coalition produced a distinctive political economy that accommodated the class contradictions within the Democratic Party (Katznelson, Geiger, and Kryder 1993). One element in that political economy was the design of national policies in such a way that the insurgent class implications were largely confined to the North. Because the South was still predominantly rural with a largely agricultural workforce, one of the primary elements in this design simply distinguished between agricultural and non-agricultural workers. By writing legislation in such a way that only the latter were extended federal protection, for example, the South was exempted from most of the class implications of labor regulation. Another strategy simply left discretion over the implementation of federal programs to administration officials who usually accommodated federal policy to local political contexts.

Both policy design and bureaucratic discretion were, in turn, the product of the most distinctive contributor to the New Deal coalition: the congressional committee system. The committee system had been becoming increasingly autonomous from party control for decades. One of the factors strengthening committee independence was the growing career orientation of congressmen and senators. Many of them now measured their congressional service in decades, accumulating experience and expertise over particular policy areas and the departments and agencies that implemented legislation. At the same time, both chambers had been gradually reinforcing committee jurisdictions so that most of these policy areas were now the jurisdiction of a single committee. In addition, both political parties had adopted practices that permitted most members to select their committee assignments and most committees were now staffed by members who wanted to work on the legislation that was referred to it (Bensel 1984, 317–67).

Once assigned to a committee, these members accumulated seniority, automatically rising up the committee ladder as other members above them left the panel through death, retirement, or defeat at the polls (Polsby, Gallaher, and Rundquist 1969). The seniority system thus provided a career ladder for ambitious congressmen and senators that was largely outside party influence and control. In fact, the autonomous committee system transformed electoral competition for congressional seats by allowing individual members to adapt their legislative record to the particular needs and desires of their districts and states. As a result, the autonomous committee system gradually weakened party cohesion by encouraging the election and reelection of deviant members who could tailor their platforms in ways that matched their districts. Once in Congress, such members owed their political survival to the autonomy of the committee system and thus became its strongest advocates.

Thus, the autonomous committee system both encouraged and accommodated intra-party diversity and dissent in ways that may even have widened the policy contradictions underlying the New Deal coalition. The southern wing of the Democratic Party harbored many members whose political views could fairly be described as reactionary while the northern wing sheltered many members whose policy inclinations might be seen as just short of socialist. If these two factions were to share power, they needed an institutional framework that minimized friction by more or less automatically arbitrating between their clearly incompatible policy preferences. By attracting members through a voluntary, self-selection process, the individual committees in effect absorbed those members who most wanted to legislate on policies within their respective jurisdictions. Given the preeminence of the agricultural economy in the South, for example, southern members willingly gravitated toward the Committee on Agriculture where, along with Republicans from the Farm Belt, they presided over commodity price supports and rural development (Bensel 1984, 191–222). After the establishment of military bases throughout the South, members from the region became increasingly attracted to the Committee on Armed Services as well.

Northern members from urban districts, on the other hand, gravitated toward the Committees on Banking and Education and Labor where they controlled legislation on international finance, investment, and federal regulation of labor relations. The committee system thus automatically distributed members in such a way that the southern and northern wings came to dominate those parts of the national political economy that were most important to their respective sections. In effect, the committee system divided up the federal government between the two great wings of the Democratic Party in such a way that decentralized committee control of legislation absorbed most of the stress that would have otherwise arisen had the Democrats had to work out their differences in a party caucus. And, in fact, the caucus rarely met; there was, literally, almost nothing for it to do.

The autonomous committee system was the product of long-term trends and developments that had, for the most part, unfolded under Democratic control of Congress. Although the Republicans had their own serious divisions (divisions that had, as previously noted, led up to the Cannon revolt), internal cleavages within that party were nothing like the chasm that separated the Democrats. And that chasm had opened up somewhat suddenly with the onset of the Great Depression. As the Roosevelt administration attempted to put together what became the New Deal, congressional Democrats were at first quite united because most emergency programs were just that, emergency programs. They distributed relief through temporary agencies with few federal regulations that might intrude into the southern political economy in a way that might upset the region's traditional class structure and racial order. But, as the depression persisted, an increasing number of permanent bureaus, agencies, and programs began to penetrate the South and their destabilizing implications for that traditional order became unmistakable. When the southern wing began to balk at policy demands made by the northern wing, the autonomous committee system was, in a sense, ready to mediate and adjust inter-sectional tension within the party. Party leaders had only to perfect its design.

As an institutional structure for accommodating contradictions within the New Deal coalition, the congressional committee system tended to produce distributive benefits, such as water projects and highways, while devolving policy decisions over such things as welfare eligibility to the individual states. The divisibility of benefits enabled credit-claiming by the member in whose district the water project or highway was constructed, further individualizing the electoral identity of congressmen and senators. And the devolution of policy implementation allowed the same program to be implemented in very different ways, depending on the political complexion of the community (Bensel 1984, 147–73). The entire edifice rested upon two of the most long-standing of these devolutions: the determination of suffrage qualifications and the regulation of race relations. From the very beginning, the adhesion of the southern wing to the New Deal coalition was contingent upon northern Democratic tolerance of the region's white supremacist political and social order.

Many northern Democrats at least nominally challenged this détente (Feinstein and Schickler 2008; Schickler, Pearson, and Feinstein 2010. When added to Republicans who were only too happy to create mischief in the opponent party's ranks, there were enough northern Democrats to make defense of the status quo time-consuming. But the committee system absorbed the vast majority of these challenges by burying in committee proposals to prevent lynching, expand voting rights in the South, and desegregate public facilities. Those bills that did manage to reach the floor of the House of Representatives always passed the chamber. But these were either entombed in a Senate committee or filibustered to death on the Senate floor (Wawro and Schickler 2007). As long as this détente endured, however frayed and tattered it might be, the South remained loyal to the Democratic Party (Bensel 1984, 222–51).

The institutional order created and sustained by the autonomous committee system was described as the "textbook Congress" by political scientists and was interpreted as the culmination of a linear, upward trend in institutional modernization (Polsby 1968; Shepsle 1989). The apparent stability of this institutional order was attributed to its emphasis on distributive benefits and reciprocity between committees (Weingast and Marshall 1988). The nation routinely validated this institutional order by returning Democratic majorities to Congress. In the House of Representatives, Speaker Sam Rayburn presided over the Democratic Party by assuaging the egos of committee barons and the anxieties of freshmen members. And after every election southern segregationists and northern liberals renewed their fellowship by once again elevating Rayburn to the speaker's chair. After that ritual was concluded, however, southern Democrats and Republicans often coalesced in opposition to northern Democrats. Although these coalitions occurred frequently, they never elected leaders or became formalized as caucuses. They nonetheless became known as the "Conservative Coalition" and the *Congressional Quarterly* began in 1959 to calculate scores for individual members with respect to how frequently they voted with one or the other faction when a majority of southern Democrats and a majority of Republicans lined up on one side of an issue with a majority of northern Democrats on the other side. These scores conflated section (no member representing a southern district could cast a liberal vote if the chamber were perfectly aligned ideologically on a roll call), party (no Republican could cast a liberal vote), and sectional faction (no Northern Democrat could cast a conservative vote). Although there was certainly a policy basis for such alignments in roll-call voting (e.g. agricultural subsidies, military procurement), the "Conservative Coalition" index instantiated party and section as the foundation of ideological competition in Congress.

Outside Washington, however, there were trends that slowly but surely ate away at the foundations of the New Deal coalition. The most important development was the migration of southern blacks to northern cities in search of higher incomes and an escape from segregation (Lemann 1992). World War II had started the migration North by creating jobs for the production of military equipment and supplies. The beachheads in northern communities that had been established then became the destination for those that followed. As they rode the trains and buses North, southern blacks became eligible to vote and their residential concentration in cities such as Chicago, Detroit, Philadelphia, and New York both carved out districts from which a black man might be elected to Congress and made them a pivotal bloc in presidential and senate elections as well. Unlike northern whites who had little or no connection with the South, black migrants retained close kinship and friendship connections within the region. For these migrants, civil rights was not an idle principle that could be pragmatically abandoned but a vital imperative that overrode any other rationale for politics. As a result, an increasing number of northern Democrats in Congress could no longer tolerate southern segregation as a precondition for national party unity.

And the South was also changing. Although southern Democrats attempted to insulate the region's racial order from the effects of economic development, particularly urbanization and industrial expansion, segregation and modernization were fundamentally incompatible. As charter members of the New Deal coalition, southern Democrats sought their share of distributive benefits, including improvements in the region's economic infrastructure, subsidies for commodity production (including oil and gas), and developmental aid for impoverished areas in Appalachia and the Tennessee Valley (Schulman 1991). The development of the air conditioner as a residential appliance also encouraged migration of northern whites into booming southern cities such as Atlanta, Jacksonville, Miami, Houston, and Charlotte (Polsby 2004). In many cases, these northerners were Republicans and their movement into the South enabled (albeit limited) party competition in general elections. These migrants also expected, as a matter of course, to participate in elections, thus expanding the electorate in the region's cities and, as a reaction, encouraging people to register to vote in rural areas as well. Although northern migrants were rarely in the civil rights vanguard, they also were not committed to the defense of racial segregation. As northern migrants leavened the demographic composition of southern cities, blacks found it easier to navigate the intricacies and, sometimes, sheer brutality of what had previously been insurmountable barriers to electoral participation. The fundamental choice that had been placed before the South was between continued economic development and the maintenance of segregationist institutions. And there were enough southerners leaning in the former direction to make it clear that segregation's days were numbered (Johnson 2010).

CIVIL RIGHTS AND THE DEMISE OF THE AUTONOMOUS COMMITTEE SYSTEM

These two migrations, southern blacks into northern cities and northern whites into southern cities, were spontaneous movements in response to economic opportunity that no one could have prevented. They also occurred over the course of decades and, although their political consequences were perceptible to astute observers, they unfolded so slowly that there was never a moment that could be identified as the "turning point" that spelled the doom of the New Deal coalition. In the end, both these processes came together as civil rights protests in the South brought federal intervention from the North. In Congress, the civil rights movement ultimately destroyed the autonomous committee system. The opening salvo was the packing of the Rules Committee membership in 1961. For decades, the Democratic majority on the Rules Committee had used its authority to block legislation in order to prevent floor consideration of bills that threatened to split the party. Under Howard Smith of Virginia, the chairman of the committee, this responsibility had been primarily interpreted as an injunction to block legislation that southern Democrats did not want to see enacted. With the election of John F. Kennedy of Massachusetts, a new Democratic administration would be occupying the White House and there was widespread concern that Smith would use the committee to block administration proposals. The remedy, crafted by Speaker Rayburn, was to add two administration loyalists to the Democratic side of the committee and one Republican (certain to be opposed to the administration) on the other side. This "packing" of the committee would tilt Rules towards the administration. Without the additions on the Democratic side, the committee would have often been evenly divided.

This very mild reform could have been interpreted as a mere house-keeping measure. The size of some committees changed in every Congress, usually in response to increases or decreases in the demand for assignment by individual members, and was, in this sense, consistent with the maintenance of the prerogatives of the committee system. But the size of the Rules Committee had traditionally been set at 12 members and the intent of the change was publicly acknowledged to be to undercut chairman Smith's authority. Although Rayburn was able to persuade the chamber to adopt the reform (Republicans generally opposed the change because it would upset their working relationship with southern Democrats and Smith in particular), the vote was very close (217 Yea, 212 Nay; Democrats: 195–64; Republicans: 22–148). Despite this victory, the Kennedy administration did not push very hard for federal civil rights legislation.

Kennedy's assassination in 1963 brought Lyndon Johnson of Texas into the White House. Civil rights protests in the South, particularly those in Birmingham and Selma, prompted Johnson to move much more aggressively for a federal response. Passage of the 1964 Civil Rights Act in turn provoked an open revolt by white southerners who left the Democratic Party in droves in the ensuing presidential election. But even more white northerners left the Republican Party because they did not approve Barry Goldwater's extreme conservatism, including opposition to federal intervention in the South. In Congress, the net result of the 1964 election was minor Republican gains in the Deep South but massive losses throughout the North and West. The lop-sided Democratic majorities in the subsequent 89th Congress, tilted heavily toward the northern industrial and commercial core, lost no time in passing the 1965 Voting Rights Act, a measure that sharply accelerated what had already been a steady increase in the size of the black electorate in the South. This measure, along with other legislation that passed under the rubric "the Great Society," overturned traditional political alignments in the South. Blacks entered the electorate in large numbers for the first time since the end of Reconstruction. For obvious reasons, almost all of them registered as Democrats and, because they were much poorer than southern whites, the party now came to represent the region's lower classes. Most southern whites eventually switched their allegiance to the Republican Party, making that party a viable alternative in southern politics and, at the same time, committing it to the defense of white, usually upper-class, interests. Put another way, the party alignment of whites and blacks was now the inverse of what it had been during Reconstruction and, because the class alignment remained unchanged in the North, both national parties now had consistent class alignments throughout the nation: the Republicans represented upper-class segments of the electorate in both the North and the South and the Democrats, conversely, represented lower-class interests in both sections. The stage was now set for the emergence of class competition in party appeals to the national electorate.

While the New Deal coalition was now defunct in presidential elections, Congress lagged far behind. Southern Democratic members, many of them with enough seniority to preside over legislative committees, sought a middle path between the leftward-leaning predilections of their northern colleagues and the rightward-leaning preferences of the Republicans who increasingly challenged them in southern elections. In 1975, northern Democrats in the House removed three southern chairmen from their posts, replacing them with northern colleagues. This was the first serious violation of the vested "rights" of senior members in many years. All Democratic members, not just southerners, soon understood that they served at the pleasure of their colleagues in the party caucus. The committee system was no longer autonomous of the party. However, there was just enough leeway for moderate southern Democrats to hold on to their seats, as long as they could satisfy the minimal expectations of their northern colleagues and could bring home benefits to their districts. These southern Democrats survived, some of them for several decades, as a remnant artifact of the New Deal coalition and autonomous committee system. As they retired, they were ever more frequently replaced by new Republican members.

As a result, party lines in the South eventually came to resemble those in the North. That process was accelerated by judicial rulings that mandated the construction of "majority-minority" districts so that southern blacks would be elected to the House of Representatives despite massive white opposition.

The convergence of party alignments in the two sections made policy dispositions within the respective party caucuses much more homogenous than they had been during the heyday of the New Deal coalition (Mellow 2008, 31). This increasing homogeneity, combined with the lingering influence of high-seniority southern Democrats, produced a tendency to shift authority in the House of Representatives away from committee chairs toward, in the first instance, the party caucus and subcommittee chairs and, later and more durably, toward the party leadership, particularly the Speaker (Schickler 2001, 189–217; Dodd and Oppenheimer 2001; Aldrich and Rohde 2005; Zelizer 2006, 256–7). In the beginning, Democratic Speakers were reluctant to use their new authority because their ability to collegially accommodate the various elements of the party had been the original reason that they had been elected to a leadership position. But Jim Wright of Texas broke that mold through his forceful use of the new office's power during his short (and otherwise ill-fated) tenure as Speaker (1987–89).

Although the Republicans had been the minority party in the House for decades, developments in that party had silently paralleled those in the Democratic caucus (Bensel 2000). When the Republicans won a landslide victory in the 1994 congressional elections, they promoted Newt Gingrich of Georgia to the speaker's chair and Gingrich subsequently became the most powerful presiding officer since Joseph Cannon. Among other things, Gingrich personally appointed committee chairmen through his domination of the Republican Committee on Committees, imposed term limits on committee chairmen, promoted freshmen loyalists to prestigious committees, named the chair of the Republican Congressional Campaign Committee, and frequently bypassed legislative committees altogether as he moved the provisions of his Contract with America through the House of Representatives (Aldrich and Rohde 2005; Sinclair 2005). Joining Gingrich as Republican leaders in the House were Texans Dick Armey (majority leader) and Tom DeLay (majority whip). Together they formed a southern triumvirate that both confirmed the region's dominant influence in the Republican caucus and indicated the direction that further consolidation of party and section would take.

When the Democrats returned to power in the House in 2006, Nancy Pelosi of California became Speaker and immediately demonstrated that the Democrats could also elect presiding officers who were not afraid to exercise the authority that had been steadily accumulating in the speaker's office. The consolidation of authority in the majority and minority leaderships has encouraged even more cohesion within the respective parties as the party leaderships have come to be held responsible for the party's legislative achievements. This pressure to conform to the party program has become so intense that Republican members have found winning elections in the Northeast increasingly difficult because they cannot differentiate their individual records from their party's relatively unpopular positions. On the

Democratic side, the South has similarly become increasingly hostile territory for party candidates.

Over the last six decades, in fact, the major parties have switched sectional bases (Mellow 2008, 34–7). The four Congresses selected for analysis in Table 33.1 had almost identical party divisions in the House of Representatives with around a 60 percent majority for the Democrats in each case. But the Democrats put together that majority in very different ways over the years. In 1949, for example, 43.7 percent of House Democrats came from periphery states (the eleven states of the former Confederacy plus Arizona, New Mexico, and Oklahoma). In 2009, that percentage had almost been halved (26.5 percent). On the Republican side, only two members came from the periphery in 1949 but, in 2009, members from that section composed almost half (44.4 percent) of the Republican caucus. And the trends that made the periphery the contemporary sectional base of the Republican Party were reversed in the core states. That section had produced over three-quarters of all Republicans in the House in 1949 but only a little over a third (34.8 percent) in 2009. The growing importance of the core states to the making of Democratic Party majorities is equally dramatic. The mixed states, almost all of them situated between the core and periphery, showed little or no trend over the last sixty years. Before leaving this table, we should also note that reapportionment has added 30 members to periphery delegations since 1949 and

Table 33.1 Sectional party strength in the U.S. House of Representatives: 1849–2010

Section	81st Congress (1949–50)		87th Congress (1961–62)		103rd Congress (1993–94)		111th Congress (2009–10)	
	R	D	R	D	R	D	R	D
Core	134	95 (1)	121	114	91	131 (1)	62	154
	(58.3)	(41.3)	(51.5)	(48.5)	(40.8)	(58.7)	(28.7)	(71.3)
Periphery	2	115	9	107	55	85	79	68
	(1.7)	(98.3)	(7.8)	(92.2)	(39.3)	(60.7)	(53.7)	(46.3)
Mixed	35	53	44	42	30	42	37	35
	(39.8)	(60.2)	(51.2)	(48.8)	(41.7)	(58.3)	(51.4)	(48.6)
Nation	171	263 (1)	174	263	176	258 (1)	178	257
	(39.3)	(60.5)	(39.8)	(60.2)	(40.5)	(59.3)	(40.9)	(59.1)

Note: Percentages of party strength are in parentheses. In the 81st Congress, one member belonged with the American Labor Party; in the 103rd Congress, one member belonged to the Socialist Party. Core states include California, Connecticut, Delaware, Hawaii, Illinois, Iowa, Maine, Maryland, Massachusetts, Michigan, Minnesota, New Hampshire, New Jersey, New York, Oregon, Pennsylvania, Rhode Island, Vermont, Washington, and Wisconsin. Periphery states include Alabama, Arizona, Arkansas, Florida, Georgia, Louisiana, Mississippi, New Mexico, North Carolina, Oklahoma, South Carolina, Tennessee, Texas, and Virginia. Mixed states include Alaska, Colorado, Idaho, Indiana, Kansas, Kentucky, Missouri, Montana, Nebraska, Nevada, North Dakota, Ohio, South Dakota, Utah, West Virginia, and Wyoming.
Source: Sectional categories adapted from (Bensel 1984, 54).

reduced the number of core districts by 14 (if California is excluded, the reduction is 43 seats).

This massive realignment of the party system has no precedent in American political development (on the continuity of the party system in the nineteenth century, see Silbey 1991). The proximate cause, as many analysts have noted, was the civil rights revolution in the South that brought millions of black voters into the electorate for the first time since Reconstruction. Their entry provoked southern whites to switch allegiance to the Republican Party, first in presidential elections and more gradually in congressional races. And the increasing ambivalence of the national Republican Party toward civil rights issues estranged those northern whites that had traditionally aligned with the party of Lincoln. So they moved in the opposite direction, ultimately making the Democrats the dominant party in the core. This interpretation of the sectional realignment in the party system accounts for the acceleration of what had been a weak long-term trend in the 1960s and, in combination with the somewhat slower dismantling of the autonomous committee system in Congress, can explain why party strength within Congress did not respond as rapidly as voting in presidential elections.

However, as important as race has been in southern politics and in the nation at large, the contemporary sectional alignment of the party system appears to be grounded in a much wider array of issues. Many of these have been described as cultural (e.g. church and state relations, the institution of marriage, the preservation of the family). Others are related to differences in the sectional political economies. The periphery states are still, for example, a low-wage region in which labor unions are weak. They also have more than their share of military installations and military retirees. Housing costs in the periphery are relatively low and urban population densities are often a fraction of those in northeastern cities (which means, for one thing, that mass transit systems are much less viable). All of these have combined to produce strong differences in the ways in which the core and periphery view federal public policy decisions. So much so that the former have come to be known as the "blue states" and the latter the "red states" with, it is said, an almost unbridgeable chasm between them (Gelman 2008).

If race were the primary ground which constructs this chasm, then the realignment process would now be more or less complete in that the trends outlined in Table 33.1 would now stabilize. In fact, with a relaxation of racial tension, they might even reverse a bit so as to produce a nationalized party system in which both parties competed on more or less equal terms in every section. That nationalization was once, in fact, the expectation of those who believed that the Democratic Party could both enact civil rights legislation and remain the majority party in national politics (Bensel 1984, 253–5; Mellow 2008, 3). Whatever role we assign to race in the historical sectional alignment of congressional parties, the inversion of the sectional bases of the two parties (with the Republicans exchanging North for South and the Democrats travelling in the opposite direction) would not have occurred without the aid of the autonomous committee system and other institutional mechanics enabling the New Deal coalition. These both insulated the South from the class implications of the growth of the Democratic Party in the North and empowered northern Democrats in their competition with Republicans in that region. In a sense, the autonomous committee system and the New Deal coalition incubated the northern wing of the party until it was strong enough to take over the national party. This outcome, to be sure, had not been intended by those southern Democrats that had subscribed to the Democratic inter-sectional détente. And this raises the question of the future of sectionalism, both in the nation at large and as a continuing influence in congressional development.

THE FUTURE OF SECTIONALISM

Some of the most technologically advanced sectors of the American economy are now more or less aligned with the Democratic Party. Although there are internal divisions on particular issues, most of the health sector supports government intervention in the form of medical benefits, socialized health insurance, and government subsidization of research. Education, too, is solidly aligned with the Democratic Party all the way from the earliest pre-kindergarten caretakers to those who train doctoral candidates. Much of the high technology sector, including cybernetic development and alternative energy sources, is also now associated with the Democratic Party, along with advanced sectors that dominate international finance and trade. And that other highly skilled handmaiden of corporate capitalism, the legal profession, also tilts towards the Democrats. These are all growth industries and, taken together, account for much of the increasing Democratic strength along the northeastern and Pacific coasts.

The Republicans, on the other hand, are still the favorite party for heavy industry, the proprietors of small businesses, commercial distribution, the manufacturers of military equipment, and most agricultural producers. These are, for the most part, not high-growth sectors. The Republicans, however, are the strongest party in the most rapidly growing regions of the nation. That implies that, on the one hand, Democratic strength in the core states should continue to consolidate until, perhaps, the core begins to resemble the one-party South of the early and mid-twentieth century. And the periphery states should continue to be dominated by the Republican Party but, because of counter trends within those states produced by high growth sectors, stabilize at something like the present party division.

But this would be mere idle speculation without some description of the policy differences upon which this sectional system might rest. The most enduring of these differences might arise out of the way the two major parties are oriented toward the role of the United States in the world economy and international affairs. Dramatically simplifying contemporary American politics, there are two orientations toward the rest of the world. One of these we could call the "Globalization" complex in that it combines free trade, diplomatic negotiation, participation in international organizations, comparatively relaxed restrictions on immigration, and fairly open policies toward the international flow of capital. All of these tend to exploit the relative advantages of the United States as a capital-rich, technologically-advanced economy that can, among other things, offer access to a vast domestic market in return for a relaxation of trade and capital restrictions on American goods and investment. All of these policies tend to integrate the United States in the world economy by increasing the porosity of national borders. And that means that one of the ideational glues that holds these policies together is a comparatively weak commitment to nationalism.

That weak commitment to nationalism is the potential Achilles heel of the Democratic Party because it is one of the primary staples of Republican rhetoric. In fact, nationalism is so important as an orientation toward the rest of the world that we could call the combination of policies that make up that orientation the "Nationalism" complex. The policies in this complex combine trade protection, restrictions on immigration, a heavier reliance on the unilateral use of military force in international affairs, a reluctance to participate in international organizations, and a more skeptical attitude toward the relaxation of national controls on the movement of capital. All of these policies tend to enhance the ability of the United States to "stand alone" within the international community, a stance that clearly enhances the importance of national borders and national identity. One of the most visible symbols of this policy complex is the massive fence that now marks out the border between the United States and Mexico. Nationalism is not only a complex of policies, it is also a cultural and ideational attitude, an attitude very compatible with the Republican Party's positions on social policies.

By marking out these "Globalization" and "Nationalism" perspectives, we can identify some of the factors that have caused a radical shift in the regional bases of the two parties over the last half century. The emergence of the New Deal coalition introduced potentially wide policy contradictions into the heart of the Democratic Party but reconciled them through institutional brokering, administrative discretion, and a devolution of authority to the individual states. The recentralization of congressional party organizations has weakened the influence of all these arrangements in such a way that the national parties are now compelled, primarily through attrition of dissident members, to eliminate policy inconsistencies within their respective coalitions. Many of the workers in the automobile industry, for example, are strongly protectionist in the hope that trade restrictions on auto imports will help their companies survive and thus save their jobs. Fifty years ago the American auto industry was a leading economic sector, more than competitive in the world economy and a charter member of the post-World War II "Globalization" coalition. But times have changed. The traditional commitment of the Democratic Party to industrial labor unions means that the party still pays some attention to their pleas but their policy demands are no longer among the central elements in party doctrine. Instead, these protectionist demands constitute stresses with the party coalition, stresses that in the long run will probably become weaker as the sector becomes increasingly unimportant in American politics.

Stresses within the Republican Party are also evident but run in the opposite direction. For decades, the Republicans have practiced a kind of nationalist protection, denying trade privileges to nations that oppose American interests abroad. These denials, not incidentally, protect domestic economic sectors in the United States that, in part for that reason, have adhered to the "Nationalism" policy coalition. But the Republicans are at least nominally and, often, substantively committed to open markets for trade and capital. And those commitments prevent the party from openly advocating trade protection or backing broad regulations on the international movement of capital. As a result, both parties tilt toward free trade in goods and capital and these will continue to be more or less consensual policies in American politics. If one of the parties does move toward trade protection, it would probably be the Republicans, using nationalist arguments as their justification (for a competing interpretation, see Mellow 2008, 47–81).

But the key differences between the parties will be over American involvement in international organizations and choices between a reliance on diplomacy or on the unilateral use of military force. Historical trends favor the "Globalization" coalition on these issues and, for that reason, the Democratic Party. But, in predicting institutional change in Congress, the key factor is not which party is dominant but whether or not the coalitions within parties are coherent and, thus, cohesive (Binder 1997). From that perspective, the major parties appear to be progressively weeding out dissident elements. That bodes well for the preservation of what has become a very centralized, party-centered institutional design, particularly on the Democratic side of the aisle. And, because the two parties have traveled parallel paths with respect to institutional design, the Republicans may likewise favor centralization when they return to power. Thus, both the autonomous committee system and the New Deal coalition increasingly appear to have been historical anomalies. Resurrecting the autonomous committee system as the dominant element in the legislative process, for example, would require so many changes in institutional design (e.g. practices for referring legislation to committees, a reinstitution of the seniority system, a drastic reduction in the authority of party leaders over committee assignment, etc.) that only a major political upheaval could carry it out. In the twentieth century, that upheaval occurred first in the dominant Republican Party, subsequently setting in motion an institutional dynamic that produced the key features of the autonomous committee system, and, finally, providing for its inhabitation and perfection by the New Deal coalition. There are at present no signs that history will repeat itself.

Sectionalism has clearly been an important force driving the institutional development of the United States House of Representatives. In fact, it would be difficult to describe the internal and external factors shaping institutional change without reference to regionally based factions such as southern Democrats, Progressive Republicans, and the northern-liberal dominated Democratic Study Group. And this makes the study of sectionalism essential to the study of institutional development, particularly the connection between social and political change outside Congress and changes in the design of the legislative process within the institution. Major institutional reforms, such as the adoption of Reed's Rules in 1890, the Cannon Revolt in 1910, the Legislative Reorganization Act of 1946, the revision of Democratic Party procedures in the early 1970s, and the Republican consolidation of the authority of the Speaker in 1995, have never closely coincided with major realigning elections that introduced a new framework for major party competition. Instead, these reforms have almost always been the culmination of long-term, incremental changes in the internal distribution of power and level of cohesion within the congressional parties. And while there is an obvious connection between factional strength within congressional parties and electoral competition in the nation at large, how and when members shift from, on the one hand, trying to accommodate pursuit of their party's collective interests within a particular institutional design to desiring, on the other hand, major reforms in that institutional design is not at all clear. Because it has been the major force behind the rise and decline of party factions, the study of sectionalism will thus be essential to our understanding of institutional development in Congress, building on work already done on the relationship between institutional change and short-term changes in party strength and cohesion (Binder 1997; Dion 2001).

From that perspective, the most important area of study should be the relationship between institutional design, the role of the party leadership, and the durability of the New Deal coalition. In particular, we need to know how much of the suppression of party-splitting issues, such as those involving racial questions, was due to conscious control of the legislative agenda by party leaders and how much was the automatic product of the autonomous committee system, particularly the discretionary authority of southern committee chairmen (on agendas and party leaders generally, see Cox and McCubbins 2005). This, too, will be part of a larger field of research in which the general legislative impact of alternative institutional designs should be studied. For example, the autonomous committee system lodged vast budgetary responsibility in the Appropriations and Ways and Means Committees and distributed authorization authority throughout the institution and, yet, managed to balance income and expenditures for the federal government much better than the centralized, party-centered Congresses of recent decades (Stewart 1989; Fenno 1966; Zelizer 2000). Why this should be the case is also not at all clear.

Finally, the policy basis of sectionalism itself needs much more study. For example, the two most important factors that historically produced, in the first instance, a separatist South and, then, a congressional faction so distinct as to almost resemble a third party in national politics were the cotton complex in the southern political economy and troubled relations between the races (e.g. white supremacy). Cotton has now vanished in most of the South and the quality of race relations in the region is now comparable to those in the North. In addition, no section in contemporary American politics has the kind of vulnerability that the South had after it had erected segregation and created shrunken electorates in the late nineteenth century. Much of the structure of inter-sectional politics in the twentieth century revolved around the desperate southern defense of what were clearly anomalous and thus highly vulnerable political and social arrangements in the region. There is nothing comparable in contemporary American politics that might so reinforce regional identity and cohesion. Furthermore, the once very striking differences between the southern and northern political economies have dissipated to a large extent as the South has rapidly urbanized and income levels have risen faster than in the North. The question that arises, then, is why sectionalism continues to be so influential in American politics. And there is no obvious answer to that question.

References

ALDRICH, J. H. 1995. *Why Parties? The Origin and Transformation of Party Politics in America.* Chicago: University of Chicago Press.

—— and ROHDE, D. W. 2005. Congressional Committees in a Partisan Era, pp. 269–92 in *Congress Reconsidered,* ed. L. C. Dodd and B. I. Oppenheimer, 8th edn. Washington: Congressional Quarterly Press.

BENSEL, R. 1984. *Sectionalism and American Political Development, 1880–1980.* Madison: University of Wisconsin Press.

—— 1990. *Yankee Leviathan: The Origins of Central State Authority in America, 1859–1877.* New York: Cambridge University Press.

—— 2000. *The Political Economy of American Industrialization, 1877–1900.* New York: Cambridge University Press.

—— 2000. Of Rules and Speakers: Towards a Theory of Institutional Change for the U.S. House of Representatives. *Social Science History,* 24(Summer): 349–66.

BINDER, S. A. 1997. *Minority Rights, Majority Rule: Partisanship and the Development of Congress.* New York: Cambridge University Press.

COX, G. W., and MCCUBBINS, M. D. 2005. *Setting the Agenda: Responsible Party Government in the U.S. House of Representatives.* New York: Cambridge University Press.

DION, G. D. 2001. *Turning the Legislative Thumbscrew: Minority Rights and Procedural Change in Legislative Politics.* Ann Arbor: University of Michigan Press.

DODD, L. C., and OPPENHEIMER, B. I. 2001. A House Divided: The Struggle for Partisan Control, 1994–2000, pp. 21–44 in *Congress Reconsidered,* ed. L. C. Dodd and B. I. Oppenheimer, 7th edn. Washington: Congressional Quarterly Press.

FEINSTEIN, B. D., and SCHICKLER, E. 2008. Platforms and Partners: The Civil Rights Realignment Reconsidered. *Studies in American Political Development,* 22(1): 1–31.

FENNO, JR., R. F. 1966. *The Power of the Purse: Appropriations Politics in Congress.* Boston: Little, Brown.

GELMAN, A. 2008. *Red State, Blue State, Rich State, Poor State: Why Americans Vote the Way They Do.* Princeton, NJ: Princeton University Press.

HOLT, M. F. 2005. *The Fate of their Country: Politicians, Slavery Extension, and the Coming of the Civil War.* New York: Hill and Wang.

JENKINS, J. A., and SALA, B. R. 1998. The Spatial Theory of Voting and the Presidential Election of 1824. *American Journal of Political Science,* 42: 1157–79.

—— and NOKKEN, T. P. 2000. The Institutional Origins of the Republican Party: Spatial Voting and the House Speakership Election of 1855–56. *Legislative Studies Quarterly,* 25: 101–30.

JOHNSON, K. 2010. *Reforming Jim Crow: Southern Politics and Society in the Age before Brown.* New York: Oxford University Press.

KATZNELSON, I., GEIGER, K., and KRYDER, D. 1993. Limiting Liberalism: The Southern Veto in Congress, 1933–1950. *Political Science Quarterly,* 108(2): 283–306.

KEY, V. O. 1964. *Politics, Parties, and Pressure Groups.* New York: Thomas Y. Crowell.

LEMANN, N. 1992. *The Promised Land: The Great Black Migration and How It Changed America.* New York: Vintage Books.

MARTIS, K. C. 1989. *The Historical Atlas of Political Parties in the United States Congress, 1789–1989.* New York: Macmillan.

MAYHEW, D. R. 2000. *America's Congress: Actions in the Public Sphere.* New Haven, CT: Yale University Press.

MELLOW, N. 2008. *The State of Disunion: Regional Sources of Modern American Partisanship.* Baltimore: Johns Hopkins University Press.

POLSBY, N. 2004. *How Congress Evolves: Social Bases of Institutional Change.* New York: Oxford University Press.

——1968. The Institutionalization of the House of Representatives. *American Political Science Review*, 62(1): 144–68.

——GALLAHER, M., and RUNDQUIST, B. S. 1969. The Growth of the Seniority System in the House of Representatives. *American Political Science Review*, 63: 787–807.

RITTER, G. 1997. *Goldbugs and Greenbacks: The Antimonopoly Tradition and the Politics of Finance in America, 1865–1896.* New York: Cambridge University Press.

ROBINSON, E. E. 1914. Recent Manifestations of Sectionalism. *American Journal of Sociology*, 19(4): 446–67.

SANDERS, E. 1999. *Roots of Reform: Farmers, Workers, and the American State, 1877–1917.* Chicago: University of Chicago Press.

SCHICKLER, E. 2001. *Disjointed Pluralism: Institutional Innovation and the Development of the U.S. Congress.* Princeton, NJ: Princeton University Press.

——PEARSON, K., and FEINSTEIN, B. D. 2010. Congressional Parties and Civil Rights Politics from 1933 to 1972. *Journal of Politics*, 72: 672–89.

SCHULMAN, B. 1991. *From Cotton Belt to Sunbelt: Federal Policy, Economic Development, and the Transformation of the South, 1938–1980.* New York: Oxford University Press.

SHEPSLE, K. 1989. The Changing Textbook Congress, pp. 19–44 in ed. J. Chubb and P. Peterson. Washington, DC: Brookings Institution.

SILBEY, J. 1991. *The American Political Nation, 1838–1893.* Stanford, CA: Stanford University Press.

——2009. *Party over Section: The Rough and Ready Presidential Election of 1848.* Lawrence: University Press of Kansas.

SINCLAIR, B. 2005. Parties and Leadership in the House, pp. 224–54 in *The Legislative Branch*, ed. P. J. Quirk and S. A. Binder. New York: Oxford University Press.

STEWART, III, C. 1989. *Budget Reform Politics: The Design of the Appropriations Process in the House of Representatives, 1865–1921.* New York: Cambridge University Press.

TURNER, J. 1951. *Party and Constituency: Pressures on Congress.* Baltimore: Johns Hopkins University Studies in Historical and Political Science.

WAWRO, G. J., and SCHICKLER, E. 2007. *Filibuster: Obstruction and Lawmaking in the U.S. Senate.* Princeton, NJ: Princeton University Press.

WEINGAST, B., and MARSHALL, W. 1988. The Industrial Organization of Congress. *Journal of Political Economy*, 96: 132–63.

ZELIZER, J. E. 2000. *Taxing America: Wilbur D. Mills, Congress, and the State, 1945–1975.* New York: Cambridge University Press.

——2006. *On Capitol Hill: The Struggle to Reform Congress and Its Consequences, 1948–2000.* New York: Cambridge University Press.

PART VIII

CONGRESS AND THE CONSTITUTIONAL SYSTEM

CHAPTER 34

CONGRESS AND THE EXECUTIVE BRANCH: DELEGATION AND PRESIDENTIAL DOMINANCE

B. DAN WOOD

IN many respects, the presidency envisioned by the founders was to be a passive *agent* of Congress. Americans' experience with monarchy resulted in great suspicion of executive power. As a result, a deliberate attempt was made to limit executive power through institutional design. Article I of the Constitution states "ALL legislative powers, herein granted, shall be vested in a Congress of the United States" (emphasis in the original). Congress was granted specific enumerated powers enabling it to make policy broadly. In contrast, the Constitution granted the Chief Executive no explicit policymaking powers.

The president was given a limited veto to potentially negate what it considered unwise policy. However, early presidents rarely used the veto, considering it an illicit intrusion into the legislative domain. The president was to report to Congress on the "State of the Union" and recommend "necessary and expedient" measures. The president was also given specific tasks and responsibilities to facilitate executive power, such as making nominations, receiving ambassadors, negotiating treaties, and commanding the military.

However, presidents were not intended to be policymakers. Rather, the Chief Executive was to "take care that the laws be *faithfully* executed" (emphasis added). In executing the will of Congress, there is no indication that the founders intended presidents to interpret or alter congressional intent. This early view of presidents as clerks who simply carried out the will of Congress persisted through the eighteenth and nineteenth centuries. Accordingly, Woodrow Wilson (1901) labeled this mode of governing "congressional government."

Yet, modern American government could hardly be called "congressional government." The modern presidency is now widely viewed as the centerpiece of the American political system. The spectacle of presidential election and inauguration creates far more symbolic presence than would ever be available to Congress or the Court. As a result, new presidencies typically enjoy an aura of democratic legitimacy beyond that of any other political institution. The continuing high status of the presidency through time makes it a constant focus of media and public attention.

The modern presidency is also important legislatively. Presidents typically achieve from Congress a substantial part of what they promise (Fishel 1985). They have long been recognized as the most important legislative agenda-setters (Huntington 1973; Baumgartner and Jones 1993, 241; Kingdon 1995, 23; Edwards and Barrett 2000). Indeed, presidentially initiated legislation is far more successful in Congress than that originating within the two chambers (Edwards and Barrett 2000, 127–32).

After legislative action, modern presidents are also important through their role as Chief Executive. They independently exercise policy control over the bureaucracy, formulate budgets, make personnel assignments, issue directives, promulgate executive orders, act as a policy clearing house, and can unilaterally affect agency structure. With increasing congressional deference to the executive, presidents have developed an institutional apparatus within the Executive Office of the President (EOP) for exercising administrative authority. Moreover, modern presidents not only execute policy, but also make policy through various powers and institutions that have accrued to the presidency through time.

What changed to produce a much more dominant presidency than was envisioned by the founders? Why did Congress cede power to the Executive? What were the consequences of congressional delegation for power relations between Congress and the Executive? This chapter addresses these questions through the theoretical lenses of agency theory and transaction cost politics.

Of course, a large political science literature has developed which explores the causes and consequences of congressional delegation to the Executive. Much of that literature implies that Congress increasingly delegated policymaking authority to the Chief Executive because it is ill-equipped to deal with many of the issues facing modern society. More generally, I will argue that delegation of authority by Congress to the Executive is a natural outgrowth of the founders' vision of the Chief Executive as an agent of Congress. Modern presidents face high expectations, and have strong incentives to lower their own transaction costs for policymaking and administration. When presidents exerted power to reduce their transaction costs in these areas,

Congress consistently deferred to the Executive. Such delegations and deference of policymaking authority were nowhere foreseen by the founders. Yet, modern presidents are now the dominant actors for the plethora of policies emanating from both the legislative and administrative policy processes.

AGENCY THEORY AND CONGRESSIONAL DELEGATION TO THE EXECUTIVE

Congressional delegation of policymaking authority has been a major mechanism whereby modern presidents have become much more powerful through time. Delegation is the assignment of authority and responsibility by one entity to another entity to carry out specific activities. Delegation usually allows the receiving entity to make decisions necessary to implement the specific activities. However, the delegating entity remains responsible for the activities and has a continuing interest in seeing them performed well.

It is widely understood by the scholarly community that the politics of delegation can be understood through the theoretical lens of agency theory (e.g. see Bendor, Glazer, and Hammond 2001; see also Krause 2010). Wood (2010) provides a detailed discussion of agency theory as it applies to political control of the bureaucracy. This chapter discusses insights that flow from looking at congressional delegation as an application of agency theory coupled with transaction cost politics.

Of course, the very nature of the *originally intended* relationship between Congress and the Executive is one of agency. Congress makes policy and the Constitution gives authority to the Executive to implement that policy on its behalf. Congressional and executive interests often diverge. As a result, presidents do not always agree with all aspects of congressional policy. So, Congress faces a possible shirking problem by the Executive. However, it retains control over the manner in which presidents execute policy through various checks on executive power. In the unitary principal version of agency theory, the institutions through which policy is administered are designed and created purely by the legislature. Political appointees who are responsible for administration must often be approved by the Senate. Congress oversees executive activities and ultimately holds the power of the purse, which is often required for policy execution. Congress can also overturn executive actions through new legislation. However, presidents are ultimately independent actors who have interests of their own and tools that can be used to counteract legislative power in each of these areas.

It is important to understand that congressional delegation and the problems of agency are intrinsic to the American system. Unlike parliamentary systems where the legislative and executive functions are integrated, the American system involves separate institutional control of the legislative and executive functions. Within our separation of powers system, Congress is a deliberative body, not an administrative body. It is neither equipped nor authorized to execute policy. It must *always* rely on others to do its designated work. Hence, there is *always* a problem of agency for any policy constructed by Congress to be executed by others.

The agency theoretic relationship is also fundamental to understanding the evolution of congressional delegation of policymaking authority through time. The founders did not foresee an increasingly complex era in which Congress would be ill-equipped to construct policy in such a way as to provide all of the details of implementation. The modern Congress lacks the expertise and/or predictive ability to write comprehensive legislation in many areas. Adaptability may also be required for effective administration. These are attributes of bureaucracies, many of which are executive agencies. Thus, congressional delegation has occurred to enable more specialized decision-making about increasingly technical policy problems. Of course, this scenario is similar to the classical application of agency theory where a business owner assigns work to a manager with more specialized skills, but who may also have divergent interests (e.g. see Wood 2010).

Congress also deals with some issues that are "too hot to handle" in the political arena. As a fragmented institution characterized by diverse preferences, policy solutions are often compromises. Those favoring a policy want effective solutions, while those opposing a policy may actually seek to cripple efforts at problem solving. Under this circumstance, legislation often results in a compromise that is not designed to be effective (Moe 1989). Legislative policy becomes little more than a guideline for future action. The policy is given life, but little more. Congress yields policymaking authority to a bureaucracy that presumably operates in an environment that is less politically charged.

Thus, delegation of policymaking authority occurs because Congress is an imperfect policymaking institution. It is often either too ill-informed, uncertain, or politically charged to make effective policies. It passes this authority to others with the hope and expectation that they will produce policy consistent with congressional intentions. Of course, those hopes are largely pinned to whether the bureaucracy, often under Executive control, shares the preferences of the winning legislative coalition. Thus, like the business owner who wants work optimized by a business manager (Wood 2010), Congress always faces uncertainties about shirking by the Executive and sub-optimality of the resulting work product.

Agency theory and the congressional dominance perspective

While Congress is an imperfect policymaking institution, many have argued that it can make informed choices about the institutions through which implementation occurs. From this standpoint, various scholars have advocated a theory of "congressional dominance" under which legislative design is used to mold and shape policy administration. As with the business owner who designs a contract to optimize work performed on its behalf, Congress is viewed as generally able to design institutions that will produce results consistent with legislative preferences.

For example, Weingast and Moran (1983; see also Weingast 1981, 1984) argued that Congress can ensure faithful execution by engaging in *ex post* efforts at political control using tools that were embedded in legislation *ex ante*. It can increase administrative accountability by including provisions for regular oversight hearings and reporting requirements. Budget reauthorization requirements and potential new legislation can be used as threats or sanctions to assure administrative compliance. In support of their argument for *ex post* legislative control, Weingast and Moran (1983) showed that Federal Trade Commission enforcements tend to covary with the composition of congressional oversight committees.

McCubbins (1984) emphasized the importance of administrative procedures. He argued that procedural arrangements can solve problems of shirking and drift by constraining the discretion of administrative actors and by channeling decision-making to alternatives that are consistent with legislative intent. Following from this perspective, a seminal article by McCubbins, Noll, and Weingast (1987; see also McCubbins, Noll, and Weingast 1989) laid out in great detail how procedural constraints can be used by Congress to control subsequent policy implementation. Specifically, legislators can design institutions for compliance with administrative procedures that "stack the deck" in favor of the legislature by making administrative policymaking subject to the Administrative Procedure Act (APA). Under this law administrative policymakers must announce beforehand their intentions to change policy in the *Federal Register*. The APA also requires that they solicit comments from interested parties prior to making policy changes. Of course, this provides feedback both to legislators and their constituencies. The sequence of decision-making under the APA provides multiple opportunities for legislative principals to intervene in administrative policymaking.

Other methods of legislative "deck stacking" include enfranchising legislative constituents (e.g. giving explicit standing to sue to interest groups), subsidized representation (e.g. the intervenor process such as exists at multiple agencies), agenda control (e.g. enabling groups or other agencies to influence administrative agendas), assigning the burden of proof (e.g. drug companies must prove drugs safe before FDA certification), and setting administrative processes on "autopilot" so that the agency has sufficient flexibility to protect future constituent interests without the need for new legislative struggles.

Congress may also attempt to control policy execution through the design of structural arrangements (Moe 1989, 1990; Moe and Wilson 1994). If it mistrusts the Executive it can try to make legislation self-enforcing through the legal system, rather than creating an administrative agency. For example, a business-friendly Republican Congress, fearful of the Executive, but facing strong public demand passed the Sherman Antitrust Act of 1890 to be enforced through the legal system and courts. Of course, this did not prevent Republican President Theodore Roosevelt from initiating antitrust litigation in 1902 on behalf of the public against J. P. Morgan's Northern

Securities Company, which had attempted to monopolize the railroad industry. However, it was not until the Federal Trade Commission Act of 1914 that Congress delegated authority to an administrative agency responsible for consistently regulating antitrust activities. In these regards, Fiorina (1982, 1986) studied the determinants of congressional choices of execution through the legal system versus delegating to a bureaucracy. Presidents played no role in Fiorina's decision-theoretic model. Consistent with this omission, his model suggested that self-enforcing legislation diminishes the executive role in policy execution.

Execution through the legal system presumably diminishes the executive role, but this is not always possible or the most beneficial approach. Thus, Congress also sometimes chooses a middle ground of delegating authority to an independent agency or commission that is relatively insulated from the Executive. In many of these cases presidents still retain some influence over administrative activities through appointments and/or budgets. However, most of these implementing entities are designed in such a way as to remove policymaking from the Executive. Lewis (2003) examined questions of why some administrative agencies are designed for political insulation. He showed that members of Congress seek to remove agencies from political control when future presidents are likely to exert influence over an agency in a way that is inconsistent with their preferences. Similarly, Wood and Bohte (2004) studied the politics of administrative insulation using a framework emphasizing potential mistrust between Congress and the president, as well as the possibility that future congressional coalitions might seek to alter policy.

Alternatively, Congress can charge the president to implement policy through an executive agency. Here the president's role is greater, because the Chief Executive is charged with supervising executive branch activities. If presidents favor the legislature's policy, the potential payoff to Congress and its constituents is greatest. Presidents can push and defend the policy more effectively than implementation through the legal system or an independent agency. Friendly executive control can also be more effective from the standpoint of adaptive implementation. Presidents can direct an agency to make changes to enhance implementation. However, because the executive role is greater when Congress lodges implementation in the Executive, the danger of executive subversion is also greater. All the assets of flexible and adaptive implementation become liabilities under a presidency that is hostile to the policy.

POLITICAL TRANSACTION COSTS AND CONGRESSIONAL DELEGATION TO THE EXECUTIVE

Given the various options available to Congress in the politics of institutional design, why does it sometimes delegate greater policy control to the Executive versus using the legal system or administrative insulation? Furthermore, why does it mandate administrative procedures and controls that limit executive (and future legislative) discretion versus making future control easy? I argue that the answer to these questions lies in considering the political transaction costs facing legislators considering different administrative designs (Williamson 1975, 1996; Dixit 1996; Epstein and O'Halloran 1999; Wood and Bohte 2004).

Political principals want to optimize future benefits for themselves and their constituents, while at the same time optimizing political transaction costs facing future coalitions. In a general context, *political transaction costs are those costs incurred due to political exchange.* They are usually non-monetary. In the more specific agency theory context, political transaction costs are the costs to the principal of monitoring and maintaining the principal-agent contract. Such costs include the difficulty of obtaining information about implementation, the difficulty of redirecting the implementation process, and the difficulty of exercising institutional prerogatives. Political transaction costs affect the efficiency with which future political actors can mold and shape implementation.

Political principals always prefer institutional designs which yield the highest expected benefits while optimizing political transaction costs. For example, legislators may hard-wire a policy using greater legislative specificity. Tightly written self-enforcing legislation would be the extreme case of hard-wiring. With self-enforcing legislation there is no need for Congress to interact with either the Executive or a bureaucracy. Implementation occurs automatically through the courts and legal system. Policies designed in such a way can provide greater certainty of execution.

However, such designs may not provide maximum benefits, and can also raise future political transaction costs. Using the legal system there is no unified entity pushing the policy. Presidents are unable to alter policy on behalf of Congress to mold benefits for legislators and constituents. With self-enforcing legislation it also becomes more costly and difficult for legislators to alter policy implementation. This is because law must be changed to affect policy. Congress also has less flexibility to change policy through informal means, such as would be available through a bureaucracy subject to strong congressional control. Thus, legislators often face a tradeoff between achieving certainty of execution versus preserving ongoing policy control and institutional prerogatives. Of course, reelection-seeking legislators commonly prefer to retain future control over benefits to constituents. They may also seek to preserve institutional prerogatives to promote future institutional interests.

Clearly, the role that political transaction costs play in the institutional design process is strongly determined by political goals. For example, one possible goal involves making effective public policy. Political actors may simply want to promote a public policy because they believe in the policy. If the Chief Executive also supports the policy, then embedding it in an executive agency is often best for assuring effective implementation. Such policies are easier to change at a future date. Executive branch implementation also enables a friendly Executive to have greater adaptability, which will in turn optimize policy benefits for constituents.

However, there is also the possibility that some future Chief Executive will oppose the policy. In this case, legislators must assess the probability of "political holdup" by a future Executive, and design administrative arrangements accordingly (e.g. see Epstein and O'Halloran 1999, 47–8). If the probability of political holdup is high, then they may choose to hard-wire the policy by writing more specific legislation or by insulating it structurally. If the probability of political holdup is low, then they may prefer to leave legislation vague to enable greater executive flexibility for effective implementation.

Again, the politics of delegation to the Executive involves political principals seeking to maximize expected benefits, while also optimizing future transaction costs. While political principals may want to accomplish these ends, the hitch is in knowing how to do it. Decision-makers at the time of institutional design are only boundedly rational, with limited information and knowledge of the implications of particular institutional choices (Simon 1947). In other words, they do not know what institutional design will provide the highest payoff, either in terms of policy outcomes or institutional prerogatives. Therefore, they make their best forecast of *expected* benefits from different institutional designs. These forecasts involve making a best guess about the *potential* benefits from a particular design, as well as the *probability that the potential benefit will actually occur*. Because decision-makers are only boundedly rational, these assessments virtually always involve uncertainty.

Thus, enacting coalitions attempt to forecast expected benefits based on rough calculations of potential benefits and the probability of political holdup. Of course, the potential benefits of a design depend on whether the holdup problem actually occurs. Therefore, the calculation for institutional design L is performed as follows.

$$E(L) = p_L Benefit_{HL} + (1 - p_L) Benefit_{\overline{H}L} \tag{1}$$

Here, $E(L)$ is the expected benefit from institutional design L, p_L is the probability of political holdup for design L, $Benefit_{HL}$ is the potential benefit from design L given that the holdup problem occurs, and $Benefit_{\overline{H}L}$ is the potential benefit from design L if the holdup problem does not occur.

In choosing an institutional design, decision-makers weigh the expected benefit from competing designs, and choose the design that gives the highest payoff. For example, consider the choice between two designs, L and H, representing respectively low and high political transaction cost designs.

$$E(L) = p_L Benefit_{HL} + (1 - p_L) Benefit_{\overline{H}L} \tag{2}$$

$$E(H) = p_H Benefit_{HH} + (1 - p_H) Benefit_{\overline{H}H} \tag{3}$$

In choosing between the two designs the enacting coalition makes the following assumptions. First, the potential benefit for both designs is always higher when the political holdup problem does not occur. Second, when the political holdup problem does not occur, the potential benefit from the low transaction cost design is always larger. Third, when the political holdup problem does occur, the potential benefit from the high transaction cost design is always larger. Fourth, the probability of political holdup is always larger under the low transaction cost design relative to the high transaction cost design. Using these assumptions, the enacting coalition bases its choice between designs on the expected benefit calculations in equations 2 and 3.

$$Choice(L/H) = \begin{cases} L & \text{if } E(L) - E(H) \geq 0 \\ H & \text{if } E(L) - E(H) \geq 0 \end{cases} \tag{4}$$

The enacting coalition chooses design L if the expected benefit from design L is greater than or equal to the expected benefit from design H. The enacting coalition chooses design H if the expected benefit for design H is larger than for design L. Note here that we can assume a small bias toward low transaction cost designs when there is no difference in expected benefits.

By substitution from equations 2 and 3 and with some further simplification, $E(L) - E(H)$ in equation 4 can be expressed as follows.

$$E(L) - E(H) = p_H(Benefit_{\overline{H}H} - Benefit_{HH}) - p_L(Benefit_{\overline{H}L} - Benefit_{HL}) +$$
$$(Benefit_{\overline{H}L} - Benefit_{\overline{H}H}) \tag{5}$$

Evaluating equation 5, it becomes clear that the choice of institutional design depends on three factors. First, the choice depends on the difference in potential losses for the two designs if the political holdup problem occurs (i.e. $Benefit_{\overline{H}H} - Benefit_{HH}$ and $Benefit_{\overline{H}L} - Benefit_{HL}$). From the second and third assumptions above the potential losses are always greater for the low transaction cost design. However, this fact alone does not weigh the decision toward the high transaction cost design. The choice of institutional design rides on the relative magnitudes of these differences. A large disparity in benefits for the high transaction cost design or one that is not much different from the low transaction cost design weighs the decision toward the low transaction cost design. A large disparity in benefits for the low transaction cost design or one where the difference is much larger than for the high transaction cost design weighs the decision toward a low transaction cost design.

Second, the choice of institutional design depends on the perceived probability of political holdup for the two designs (p_L and p_H). By assumption four above, we know $p_L > p_H$. However, it is again the relative disparity in the probabilities of holdup for the two designs that is more important. A large probability of holdup for low transaction cost designs weights the decision toward choosing a high transaction cost design. However, if the probability of holdup is also large for the high transaction cost design, then this weighs the decision toward the low transaction cost design.

Of course, the probabilities of holdup and potential losses must be considered together. Both the probability of political holdup and potential losses are greater for the low transaction cost design. So why would an enacting coalition ever choose the low transaction cost design? It is because the potential benefits of the low transaction cost design are always greater when there is little prospect of political holdup (i.e. $Benefit_{\overline{H}L} - Benefit_{\overline{H}H} > 0$). Thus, the third factor affecting institutional design is the difference in the maximum potential benefit from the low and high transaction cost designs. If this difference is sufficiently large, then decision-makers may be willing to risk experiencing losses in order to gain the potential benefits when no political holdup occurs.

These results imply that the choice of institutional design during the politics of delegation requires decision-makers to weigh the potential benefits of competing institutional designs against the potential losses conditional on perceived probabilities of political holdup. For example, a design delegating substantial power to the Chief Executive provides a higher potential benefit than a design that is highly insulated. A friendly Chief Executive can always adapt policy execution to achieve higher benefits for legislators and their constituents. However, delegation to the Executive also has a higher probability of political holdup and larger potential losses if the holdup occurs.

Thus, the politics of delegation involves assessing a tradeoff between larger potential benefits and a smaller, more certain package of benefits with less risk of political holdup. The calculations required to assess this tradeoff are necessarily coarse. Political decision-makers seldom know the potential benefit from a particular institutional design beforehand, and the probability of political holdup is also uncertain. Therefore, decision-makers attempt to forecast the future by relying on cues from the past and current political environment (e.g. see Wood and Bohte 2004).

The presidential dominance perspective

If the politics of delegation functioned in the manner *intended* by the founders, then the tradeoff decision faced by legislators in the politics of delegation would be easy. They would always lodge implementation with the Executive in anticipation of the highest potential benefits and lowest political transaction costs. The Chief Executive would always execute the law *faithfully*, as expressed by the Constitution. Recognizing a very remote potential for political holdup, Congress might independently design institutions to control executive behavior through procedural safeguards, easy monitoring, feedback, sanctions, and corrections to unwanted behaviors. However, these checks should be unnecessary, because the probability of political holdup would be very low. Under the founders' intentions, the Chief Executive would be an agent of Congress and implement policy to maximize benefits for legislators and their constituents.

Presidential dominance and the *ex ante* politics of delegation

However, the modern Chief Executive is not a passive agent of Congress. Rather, the president is now a co-principal in the legislative process. Congress does not independently design the institutional arrangements of delegation. Presidents propose and participate in the design of many policies. They are savvy actors in the legislative process through which policy develops and implementing institutions evolve. Presidents are also major agenda-setters for Congress and strongly affect the end products of deliberation (Huntington 1973; Baumgartner and Jones 1993, 241; Kingdon 1995, 23; Cameron 2000; Edwards and Barrett 2000). For policy to succeed in the legislature, presidents must approve the design of implementing institutions. Therefore, the politics of legislative delegation is systematically biased toward presidential dominance.

More theoretically, a simple model of agency is not strictly applicable to Congress and the Executive in the modern politics of delegation. The principal-agent contract is not designed by a singular principal (i.e. the Congress), as assumed by some scholars. Rather, the contract is a matter for plural negotiation (i.e. Congress and the Executive) with the presumed agent (i.e. the Executive) who also happens to be a principal during the institutional design process. In other words, the agent strongly affects the institutions whereby the agent is to be controlled. What is the nature of the contract that is likely to emerge from such a process? The answer to this question suggests the appropriateness of the fox/ henhouse analogy. What happens when the farmer allows the fox into the henhouse? The fox eats the farmer's chickens. Similarly, the politics of delegation is systematically biased in favor of the presidency due to the Executive being integral to the design of implementing institutions.

In designing the institutions of delegation, the Chief Executive consistently seeks to lower its own transaction costs for interacting with the bureaucracy. Obviously, presidents have more difficulty shaping implementation when it occurs through the legal system or independent agencies. Therefore, they strongly prefer implementation through executive agencies with few procedural constraints imposed by Congress. More generally, presidents prefer freedom to mold policy toward their own ends with as little interference from Congress as possible.

Presidents face high expectations for policy success, and are also held accountable for policy failures. Thus, as suggested by Moe (1985b), they seek an institutional system that is responsive to their needs as political leaders. A primary means through which presidents seek this end is centralization of power and the politicization of administration. Presidents are compelled by political incentives toward actively pursuing structures and procedures friendly to executive control during the politics of institutional design.

Of course, some scholars have suggested that presidents are less successful at achieving their goal of executive control during periods of divided government. According to Epstein and O'Halloran (1994, 1996, 1999), legislatures delegate more discretion to independent agencies/commissions under divided government. Under unified government more discretion is granted to the Executive. Huber, Shipan, and Pfahler (2001) also find that divided government and presidential opposition are important in devising statutory controls for Medicaid programs. Consistent with this argument, using the political transaction costs theory outlined above, under divided government the legislature should grant less discretion to the Executive because of the higher probability of political holdup.

However, Volden (2002) develops a model in which executives can retain previously delegated power when government moves from unified to divided control. This is especially true if the Chief Executive's preferences align with the bureaucracy. According to Volden's analysis, it is not just the alignment of congressional and executive preferences that matter in the politics of delegation. Rather, it is preferences relative to the status quo and the possibility of an executive veto. When the Executive prefers the status quo over the legislature's preferred new position, the executive veto can prevent reductions in executive discretion. When the Chief Executive prefers change in the status quo under divided government the Chief Executive will be less successful, but can still retain previously granted discretion. Thus, executive discretion increases during periods of unified government, but may not change during periods of divided government.

The overall trajectory of executive discretion emerging from Volden's (2002) analysis is one of increasing presidential dominance. Most delegation to the Executive occurs during periods of unified government. However, delegation does not reverse itself under periods of divided control. Presidents have tools to prevent such reversals, and they are willing to use them. They can use veto bargaining (Cameron 2000) to block efforts to curtail their authority and will generally prevail with support from their fellow partisans in Congress.

Furthermore, Congress has difficulty mobilizing to reverse delegation to the Executive under either unified or divided government. Congress is a fragmented institution without a strong central coordinating mechanism. Most interactions with executive agencies occur at the committee or subcommittee level. Yet committees have few resources that can be used to counter executive discretion. They can make recommendations to other committees about appropriations or suggest legal restrictions. However, such proposals require cooperation from many others and approval by the entire body. There are, of course, occasional counter examples to this general trend (Katznelson and Pietrykowski 1991; Schickler 2007; Schickler and Pearson forthcoming). Notwithstanding, presidents generally prevail against Congress in a struggle for control over delegated authority.

Additionally, presidents are *unilateral* participants in the institutional design process associated with delegation (Moe and Wilson 1994; Moe and Howell 1999a, 1999b; Howell 2003; Lewis 2003; Wood and Bohte 2004). As such, they can often counter past legislative successes through their powers as Chief Executive. Modern presidents have often employed such actions as a way to impose their own procedures and structures on bureaucracies.

For example, modern presidents have increasingly used signing statements to alter new legislation (Cooper 2002). "Presidential signing statements are official pronouncements issued by the President contemporaneously to the signing of a bill into law that . . . forward the President's interpretation of the statutory language; to assert constitutional objections to the provisions contained therein; and, concordantly, to announce that the provisions of the law will be administered in a manner that comports with the Administration's conception of the President's constitutional prerogatives." (Halstead 2007, 1). Many signing statements are focused on the constitutional principle that presidents have unitary supervisory control of the executive branch. In other words, Congress cannot tell the Executive how to use its discretion.

Other signing statements claim a unilateral presidential authority to interpret law so as to guide executive agencies during implementation. Presidents have increasingly exercised signing statements of both types to guide policy in directions contrary to legislative intent. For example, Presidents Reagan, George H. W. Bush, and Clinton issued 247 such signing statements. By way of comparison, George W. Bush issued 161 such signing statements, challenging over 1,100 provisions of federal law (compiled by Greene (2009) from *Weekly Compilation of Presidential Documents*).

Another example of how unilateral executive authority has been used to alter relationships after legislative delegation relates to the expansion of the EOP. The Bureau of the Budget (BOB) was created as a result of the Budget and Accounting Act of 1921 to assist the president in preparing an annual budget for presentation to Congress. The BOB was originally located in the Treasury Department, which is responsible to the president, but which may also develop autonomous tendencies (e.g. see Heclo 1977; Kaufman 1981). Thus, President Roosevelt issued Reorganization Plan I in 1939 which transferred the BOB to the EOP. There it was coordinated by White House staff, rather than more remotely in the Treasury Department.

Then, President Nixon in 1970 again used reorganization authority to transfer the functions of the BOB to a new organization within EOP, the Office of Management and Budget (OMB). While the BOB was focused more on budgetary efficiency and audits, the OMB became a political arm of the White House. Thus, over a period of fifty years through unilateral action, presidents created an institutional apparatus that reduced transaction costs for the presidency, raised them for Congress, and afforded the presidency greater policy control over the executive branch (see Wiseman forthcoming for why Congress might voluntarily cede such authority to the Executive).

The chief responsibilities and functions of the OMB remain the development of the president's annual budget. In this regard, all funding requests by executive agencies are cleared and adjusted by the OMB. Additionally, the Legislative Reference Division (LRD) exercises central clearance authority over bureaucratically initiated legislative proposals to assure consistency with administration policies. It also prepares statements of administration positions on legislation pending before Congress that does not originate within executive agencies. The LRD also makes veto recommendations to the president concerning bills that have passed both houses of Congress and are awaiting presidential signature. Thus, the LRD enables central coordination by the Executive of policymaking with respect to Congress and executive agencies.

The OMB also exercises policy control over various regulatory processes. For example, Executive Order 12291, issued by President Reagan in 1981, significantly altered the procedures used for bureaucratic policymaking (Mayer 1999, 2001; Cooper 2002; Howell 2003). It required that all major rules promulgated by executive agencies be subject to cost-benefit analysis. Reports from these analyses are submitted to the Office of Information and Regulatory Affairs (OIRA) within OMB. This created what is effectively a "central clearance" process for administrative rulemaking. Subsequent presidents significantly expanded this process (Clinton's Executive Order 12866; George W. Bush's Executive Order 13422), even requiring that new regulations be consistent with administration policy. Generally, Republican presidents have used the central clearance process to stem the flow of regulations that might adversely affect their business constituents, while Democratic presidents have used the process to favor more liberal interests.

Using unilateral power, presidents have also preempted Congress by creating new administrative agencies prior to congressional action. Executive orders, executive reorganization plans, and orders by cabinet secretaries working for the president have been used to create a large number of federal agencies with lines in the federal budget and without legislative approval. Indeed, almost 60 percent of all new agencies created since 1946 have been through executive means, not through Congress (Howell 2003; Lewis 2003). Agencies created by the Executive are typically designed for greater responsiveness to the president, located in the president's direct chain of command and with fewer qualifying restrictions on political appointments (Lewis and Howell 2002). Presidentially created agencies include many of the most important in the federal government (e.g. the previous Department of Health, Education, and Welfare, Environmental Protection Agency, Occupational Safety and Health Administration, the Bureau of Alcohol, Tobacco, and Firearms, Drug Enforcement Agency, Federal Emergency Management Agency, Defense Intelligence Agency, National Security Agency, Peace Corps, etc.)

Furthermore, when presidents do act unilaterally to preempt Congress, there is little chance that their actions will be overturned. Again, the political transaction costs of mounting legislation to overturn presidential actions are high, and usually insurmountable. Multiple veto points exist within Congress, and in the end presidents only need to garner support from one-third plus one member of a single chamber of Congress to prevail. This is why fewer than 3 percent of all unilateral actions by presidents ever receive serious legislative scrutiny, and the vast majority of legislative proposals to overturn direct presidential actions fail (Howell 2003, 113).

In summary, presidents have strong incentives to favor institutions that reduce their own transaction costs. They face high expectations for performance in an increasingly difficult political environment. As a result of these expectations, presidents use their formidable legislative powers to bias the politics of delegation toward the Executive. Most new agencies are situated within the executive branch under institutional arrangements friendly to executive control. Presidential discretion has increased through time during periods of unified government, and that discretion has not decreased during periods of divided government. Under either regime, presidents have significant ability to block congressional action. Also, the fragmentation and lack of a central coordinating mechanism by Congress means that presidents have a continuing advantage in the politics of delegation. Presidents have also employed their unilateral powers to increase their control over executive policymaking. In response to increased expectations for presidential performance, they have created new institutions and procedures that better suit their political needs. When presidential discretion has increased, either through legislative delegation or unilateral action, Congress has essentially deferred to new executive institutions. Thus, the image that emerges from the president's role in the *ex ante* politics of delegation is one of presidential dominance.

Presidential dominance in the *ex post* politics of delegation

Presidents mostly succeed in securing institutional arrangements friendly to the Executive in the *ex ante* politics of delegation. For example, using data compiled by Lewis (2003), roughly 85 percent of all new agencies created since 1946 have been located within the direct chain of command of the president. Because they are generally successful in this endeavor, the *ex post* politics of delegation also favors the Chief Executive. Presidents can use their various administrative tools to shape policies and procedures within the bureaucracy. They can also use executive institutions such as the various offices within OMB to reinforce adherence to Executive preferences. Presidents also use political appointments, personnel authority, budgeting, directives, executive orders, and informal incentives to induce bureaucratic compliance.

Past research suggests that political appointments are a very important tool of presidential control of executive agencies (Nathan 1983; Waterman 1989; Wood and Waterman 1991, 1993a, 1994). Presidents since Ronald Reagan have selected political appointees through a systematic process emphasizing a set of ideas, rather than simple loyalty to the president, policy, or agency. They have also taken full advantage of changes in the civil service system instituted through the Civil Service Reform Act of 1980. This legislation enabled presidents to move loyalists to the upper levels of bureaucracy for areas of major policy concern (Aberbach and Peterson 2006, 529). As a result of these changes, political appointees now establish the administration's policy intentions within the bureaucracy and are an important tool for projecting presidential influence.

Presidential appointees affect all aspects of the administrative process, including planning, organizing, staffing, development, coordinating, reporting, and budgeting. They direct bureaucratic activities and provide a face for the president's policies before Congress and administrative policymakers. They shape virtually all bureaucratic activities by standing at the top of the administrative hierarchy of most executive agencies. In a fairly strict sense, then, it can be argued that modern executive appointees are the president's agents contracted to pursue presidential goals (e.g. see Wood and Marchbanks 2007).

The penetration of presidential appointees into the bureaucracy has also increased significantly over time. The number of presidential appointees has grown as part of the Executive's effort to increase the number of management layers for promoting presidential leadership, bureaucratic responsiveness, and accountability (Aberbach and Peterson 2006, 533). As observed by Light (1995), the executive branch is now "thickened" with presidential appointees. This process has increased sharply in recent times. For example, the 2004 edition of the "Plum Book" (*United States Government Policy and Supporting Positions*) shows that federal jobs available to political appointees increased by about 15 percent from the 2000 edition. The largest growth was in jobs that do not require Senate confirmation, suggesting more loyalty to the president. These increased by almost one-quarter between 2000 and 2004. Of course, this process reflects continuing presidential efforts to centralize and politicize executive agencies toward greater responsiveness to administration policies.

Of course, many presidential appointees are subject to Senate confirmation, suggesting joint presidential and congressional control. However, presidents usually have more ability to control Senate-confirmed appointees than Congress. Presidents are given wide latitude by the Senate in their selection of political appointees. Fewer than 5 percent of all presidential nominations fail the Senate confirmation process (Krutz, Fleisher, and Bond 1998). This could, of course, be considered evidence that presidents do a good job of selecting nominees who will be acceptable to the Senate. However, most nominees are approved *en masse*, implying that the Senate pays little attention to each individual nominee. Most observers of the appointments process believe that there is a presumption of accepting the president's choice if a nominee is competent and not widely perceived as too ideologically extreme (e.g. see Moe 1987, 489).

Furthermore, only about half of all executive branch appointees are subject to Senate confirmation. The remainder serve purely at the pleasure of the president. Most officials within the EOP are appointed independently by the president, enabling an expectation of even greater loyalty. Additionally, since 1980 federal personnel rules have allowed the president to designate a large number of Schedule C appointees who can extend presidential influence deeper within administrative hierarchies. Schedule C appointees are top-level career personnel who are deemed reliable and useful for achieving presidential goals. Thus, presidents are in a far better position than Congress to claim the loyalty of many top officials within the bureaucracy.

Another mechanism for *ex post* presidential control of the bureaucracy is the budget. Since the Budget and Accounting Act of 1921 presidents have had the first move in budgeting. This legislation made presidents the agenda-setters for budgets with respect to Congress and the entire federal bureaucracy (e.g. see Wood 2009). The intended purpose of this legislation was to bring greater rationality to budgeting, since a fragmented Congress is less able to achieve a coherent outcome than a unitary Executive.

An important result of giving presidents the first move in budgeting has been a process that is strongly influenced by the Executive. Beginning with Wildavsky (1964), various studies have shown that final appropriations by Congress are heavily influenced by the president's budget proposals (see also Kiewiet and McCubbins 1991, 197). As discussed earlier, presidentially initiated reforms in 1970 which created the OMB have further enhanced the president's ability to politicize budgeting. The OMB now exercises central clearance over budget requests flowing from federal bureaucracies. This provides an added layer of presidential control, since most agencies are headed by presidential appointees. Budgets are not only absolute incentives and constraints to enforce bureaucratic compliance, but also send powerful signals to the bureaucracy of presidential intentions (Carpenter 1996).

As discussed earlier, the OMB also vets all policy proposals flowing from the bureaucracy toward Congress through the LRD. The OMB also evaluates all major new regulations flowing from the bureaucracy through the OIRA. The result is that policymaking authority over the bureaucracy has been increasingly centralized to the presidency.

Presidents also affect administrative policymaking *ex post* through the unilateral powers of issuing directives, executive orders, and proclamations (Mayer 2001; Cooper 2002; Howell 2003). Executive orders are typically directed at government officials. They are "directives issued to officers of the executive branch, requiring them to take an action, stop a certain type of activity, alter policy, change management practices, or accept a delegation of authority under which they will be responsible for implementation of law" (Cooper 2002, 16–17). For example, new presidents routinely issue memoranda in their first week to halt rulemaking across the entire executive branch, until the new administration has the opportunity to consider the policy implications of the previous administration's proposed rules (Copeland 2008). Executive orders have been used by various presidents to alter abortion policy, civil rights, civil liberties, use of federal lands, environmental compliance, worker safety, wage and price freezes, and a plethora of other important issues.

An advantage of using executive orders to shape public policy is that presidents obtain a first move advantage with respect to Congress (Howell 2003, 14–16). Executive orders have the force of law, except to the extent they conflict with existing law or the Constitution. This places Congress in the position of either accepting the president's policy or attempting to overturn it. Given the high transaction costs for Congress in overturning presidential actions, as discussed earlier most executive orders go unchallenged (Howell 2003, 112–20).

Another advantage of using executive orders to shape administrative policy is their low political transaction costs for the president. Presidents do not need to engage in coalition building, negotiation, or to overcome the obstacles associated with obtaining legislation. Rather, presidents deal only with loyal staff in the EOP for writing and promulgating executive orders. Furthermore, they face little probability of political holdup by Congress, given the high transaction costs for overturning executive orders.

However, a disadvantage of executive orders is that transaction costs are also low for future presidents wanting to overturn them. An executive order can easily be changed with another executive order. Therefore, presidents must consider the possibility of political holdup by future presidents in precisely the same way as described in equation 5 above. For this reason, they face choices about whether to attempt altering administrative policy unilaterally, or through the higher transaction cost approach of obtaining new legislation.

Finally, presidents are in a better position than Congress to employ monitoring and sanctions to affect administrative behavior. Political appointees, whose authority flows mainly from the president, can also be viewed as monitoring mechanisms. The OMB provides a separate layer of presidential monitoring. Since political appointees also help formulate and approve agency budgets and their distribution within bureaucracies, these agents of the president can also be seen as tools of the president for disciplining those who might disagree with the administration. The complementary nature of the appointment and budgeting processes means that presidents can enforce a coherent agenda both within individual bureaucracies, as well as across government generally.

In contrast, Congress is poorly situated to engage in monitoring and sanctions to shape administrative activities. Institutional fragmentation, multiple committee jurisdictions, and cross-cutting interests mean that it is ill-equipped for this purpose. Legislative incentives generally lie in achieving reelection, making new public policy, and problem solving (Mayhew 1974; Kingdon 1989). Thus, monitoring the bureaucracy generally has a low political payoff for legislators (Ogul 1978; Aberbach 1990).

Of course, congressional dominance advocates might counter that legislators can rely on "fire alarms" to alert them when bureaucratic activities run adrift from original intentions (McCubbins and Schwarz 1984). Furthermore, under divided government legislators may have incentives to use investigations to embarrass and pressure the current administration. The example of the Bush administration's arbitrary firing of U.S. attorneys, which led to Attorney General Gonzales' resignation, suggests the ability under some circumstances to use oversight hearings to make presidents pay a political price for unilateral actions. One could also argue that a decentralized committee system, with each standing committee required to designate an oversight subcommittee, provides the opportunity for legislators to specialize in and use oversight to promote own careers even as they fight the executive branch (e.g. see Schickler 2007; Kriner and Schwartz 2008). However, legislative coalitions also drift through time (Shepsle 1992), meaning that there may be weakened or even adverse incentives to acting when presidents drift from initial legislative intentions.

Consistent with these arguments, substantial empirical evidence has accumulated that presidents are very important actors in the *ex post* politics of delegation. Moe (1982) showed that presidents systematically achieve a measure of direction and control over independent regulatory commissions. Later, Moe (1985a) focused intently on the National Labor Relations Board to find that presidents, congressional committees, the courts, agency staff, and constituents have important influence on bureaucratic decisions.

Various other studies have considered the presidency as an actor embedded in a multi-institutional system of political control. For example, Chubb (1985) showed that constituency oriented demands made through the White House have important effects on the allocation of intergovernmental education grants. Scholz and Wei (1986) demonstrated the importance of presidents to the allocation and type of enforcements by the Occupational Safety and Health Administration. Wood and Waterman (1991, 1993a, 1993b, 1994) explored the scope of political control of federal bureaucracies, and the most important mechanisms of that control. They found that presidents are important actors in changing outputs from at least eight different bureaucracies. They also found that the most important mechanism through which presidential control occurs is political appointments. While budgeting, legislation, congressional signals, and administrative reorganizations are sometimes important, they are less systematically important than the president's ability to shape bureaucratic behavior by installing their appointed agents at the top of an administrative hierarchy.

CONCLUSIONS

The founders were fearful of executive power and did not expect presidents to be major policymakers in the U.S. system. Nonetheless, Article II of the Constitution left the definition of executive power vague so as to enable the evolution of the presidency through time. Accordingly, the modern politics of delegation has enabled presidents to significantly expand their policymaking role relative to Congress. This expansion has occurred for a variety of reasons.

Presidents are co-principals in designing the institutions of delegation. As such, they have a strategic advantage over Congress. Through veto bargaining, presidents can block arrangements which impose high transaction costs on the Executive. Because presidents help design policies which they are themselves often responsible for implementing, most newly created agencies are situated in the executive branch, with few constraints, and subject to the president's authority as Chief Executive. Modern presidents have also created many new agencies through executive orders, reorganization authority, or Department heads to effectively preempt Congress in designing the institutions of delegation.

The expansion of presidential power in the politics of delegation has also been enabled by Congress's inferiority as a policymaker in technical areas, areas of adaptive uncertainty, and when issues are too controversial to handle in a charged political environment. Presidents and the bureaucracies they administer have a natural advantage under all of these conditions. Free from the constraints of an electoral cycle, executive bureaucracies are commonly endowed with greater expertise, longer time horizons, fewer political constraints, and an ability to alter policy when conditions or technologies change. Thus, it is natural that presidents and the bureaucracies they administer should become important policymakers.

Presidential power has also increased through time because of structural advantages that presidents have relative to Congress after delegation. As Chief Executives, presidents strongly influence the leadership of administrative agencies, their personnel, budgets, organization, and procedures for policymaking. They can also unilaterally create their own special institutions to help shape policy implementation. Through time, presidents have centralized power over administrative policymaking to the EOP. The OMB now exercises central clearance over budgets, legislative proposals, and administrative rulemaking. Presidents also commonly issue directives and executive orders to ensure that administrative policymaking is consistent with their intentions. The end result of these changes is presidential dominance in the politics of delegation.

I have argued that presidents have significant advantages over Congress in the politics of delegation. However, there are many remaining research questions that might be addressed to better understand these relations. Here are a few areas for potential future research.

Why has Congress ceded greater control of the politics of delegation to the Executive? It seems natural that Congress would seek more, not less control. Yet, it has yielded significant authority over budgeting, allowed greater centralization of administrative policymaking, enabled the thickening of presidential appointments within bureaucracies, and tolerated executive reinterpretation of legislative intent. Why?

Under what conditions might Congress's *ex post* oversight and investigative tools have an impact on executive decision-making? Congressional dominance advocates assume too easily that these controls make a difference. Yet this chapter suggests they generally do not. Thus, we need studies of when and how congressional oversight makes a difference to executive behavior (jettisoning the *assumption* of some that it does work).

How do rising party polarization and party government affect incentives for Congress to fight for control of bureaucracy? Much of the work in this area is from an era of weak parties. But under divided party control, one could argue that party government in Congress could make a difference. Yet we lack good empirical work showing it does make a difference.

More normatively, it is unclear whether the founders would approve of the modern Chief Executive as a major policymaker. Alexander Hamilton, in *Federalist 70*, argued that a strong Executive is essential to avoiding bad government. In contrast, Thomas Jefferson was suspicious of the Executive and placed more faith in the "body politic" manifest through the legislature. He lamented the Federalist presidency as having "raised up an Executive power which is too strong for the legislature" (Jefferson 1797). Both arguments have obvious merit. Without a strong executive policymaking role, it would not be possible to effectively address many of the technical and contentious issues facing the nation. However, we might also want to be cautious of executive power when presidents substitute their will for that of the "body politic." This seems clearly the case for some presidential policymaking. Nevertheless, a discussion of the normative implications of presidential dominance in the politics of delegation must also be left to future work.

REFERENCES

ABERBACH, J. D. 1990. *Keeping a Watchful Eye: The Politics of Congressional Oversight.* Washington, DC: The Brookings Institution.

——and PETERSON, M. A. 2006. Control and Accountability: Dilemmas of the Executive Branch, pp. 525–54 in *The Executive Branch*, ed. J. D. Aberbach and M. A. Peterson. New York: Oxford University Press.

BAUMGARTNER, F. R., and JONES, B. D. 1993. *Agendas and Instability in American Politics.* Chicago: University of Chicago Press.

BENDOR, J., GLAZER, A., and HAMMOND, T. 2001. Theories of Delegation. *Annual Review of Political Science*, 4: 235–69.

CAMERON, C. M. 2000. *Veto Bargaining: Presidents and the Politics of Negative Power.* New York: Cambridge University Press.

CARPENTER, D. P. 1996. Adaptive Signal Processing, Hierarchy, and Budgetary Control in Federal Regulation. *American Political Science Review*, 90(2): 283–302.

CHUBB, J. 1985. The Political Economy of Federalism. *American Political Science Review*, 79(4): 994–1015.

COOPER, P. J. 2002. *By Order of the President: The Use and Abuse of Executive Direct Action.* Lawrence, KS: University of Kansas Press.

COPELAND, C. W. 2008. Midnight Rulemaking: Considerations for Congress and a New Administration. ed. C. R. Service. Washington, DC: US Government Printing Office.

DIXIT, A. K. 1996. *The Making of Economic Policy: A Transaction-Cost Politics Perspective.* Cambridge, MA: MIT Press.

EDWARDS, III, G. C., and BARRETT, A. 2000. Presidential Agenda Setting in Congress, pp. 109–33 in *Polarized Politics: Congress and the President in a Partisan Era*, ed. J. R. Bond and R. Fleisher. Washington, DC: Congressional Quarterly Press.

EPSTEIN, D., and O'HALLORAN, S. 1994. Administrative Procedures, Information, and Agency Discretion. *American Journal of Political Science*, 38(3): 697–722.

————1996. Divided Government and the Design of Administrative Procedures. *Journal of Politics*, 58(2): 373–97.

————1999. *Delegating Powers: A Transaction Cost Politics Approach to Policy Making Under Separate Powers.* New York: Cambridge University Press.

FIORINA, M. 1982. Legislative Choice of Regulatory Forms: Legal Process or Administrative Process. *Public Choice*, 39(1): 33–66.

————1986. Legislator Uncertainty, Legislator Control, and Delegation of Legislative Power. *Journal of Law, Economics, and Organization*, 2(1): 33–51.

FISHEL, J. 1985. *Presidents and Promises.* Washington, DC: Congressional Quarterly Press.

GREENE, J. A. 2009. *Presidential Signing Statements.* 2009 [cited 2009]. Available at: http://www.coherentbabble.com/faqs.htm (accessed September 8, 2010).

HALSTEAD, T. J. 2007. *Presidential Signing Statements: Constitutional and Institutional Implications.* ed. C. R. Service. Washington: U.S. Government Printing Office.

HECLO, H. 1977. *A Government of Strangers.* Washington, DC: Brookings Institution.

HOWELL, W. G. 2003. *Power Without Persuasion: The Politics of Direct Presidential Action.* Princeton, NJ: Princeton University Press.

HUBER, J. D., SHIPAN, C. R., and PFAHLER, M. 2001. Legislatures and Statutory Control of Bureaucracy. *American Journal of Political Science*, 45(2): 330–45.

HUNTINGTON, S. P. 1973. Congressional Response to the Twentieth Century, pp. 5–31 in *Congress and America's Future*, ed. D. P. Truman. Englewood Cliffs, NJ: Prentice-Hall.

JEFFERSON, T. 1797. Letter from Thomas Jefferson to Arthur Campbell, September 1, 1797. in *The Works of Thomas Jefferson in Twelve Volumes, Federal Edition*, ed. P. L. Ford. New York: G. P. Putnam's Sons. Available at: http://oll.libertyfund.org/title/805/87108 (accessed September 8, 2010).

KATZNELSON, I., and PIETRYKOWSKI, B. 1991. Rebuilding the American State: Evidence from the 1940s. *Studies in American Political Development*, 5: 301–9.

KAUFMAN, H. 1981. *The Administrative Behavior of Federal Bureau Chiefs.* Washington, DC: Brookings Institution.

KIEWIET, D. R., and MCCUBBINS, M. D. 1991. *The Logic of Delegation: Congressional Parties and the Appropriations Process.* Vol. 32. Chicago: University of Chicago Press.

KINGDON, J. W. 1989. *Congressmen's Voting Decisions.* 3rd edition. Ann Arbor: University of Michigan Press.

————1995. *Agendas, Alternatives, and Public Policies.* New York: Harper Collins.

KRAUSE, G. Forthcoming. Congressional Delegation of Authority to Bureaucratic Agencies, in *Oxford Handbook of American Bureaucracy*, ed. R. F. Durant. New York: Oxford University Press.

KRINER, D. L., and SCHWARTZ, L. 2008. Divided Government and Congressional Investigations. *Legislative Studies Quarterly*, 32: 507–30.

KRUTZ, G. S., FLEISHER, R., and BOND, J. R. 1998. From Abe Fortas to Zoe Baird: Why Some Nominations Fail in the Senate. *American Political Science Review*, 92(4): 871–81.

LEWIS, D. E. 2003. *Presidents and the Politics of Agency Design*. Palo Alto, CA: Stanford University Press.

——and HOWELL, W. G. 2002. Agencies by Presidential Design. *Journal of Politics*, 64(4): 1095–114.

LIGHT, P. C. 1995. *Thickening Government: Federal Hierarchy and the Diffusion of Accountability*. Washington, DC: Brookings Institution.

MAYER, K. R. 1999. Executive Orders and Presidential Power. *Journal of Politics*, 61: 445–66.

——2001. *With the Stroke of a Pen: Executive Orders and Presidential Power*. Princeton, NJ: Princeton University Press.

MAYHEW, D. R. 1974. *Congress: The Electoral Connection*. New Haven: Yale University Press.

MCCUBBINS, M. D. 1984. The Legislative Design of Regulatory Structure. *American Journal of Political Science*, 29(4): 721–48.

——Noll, R. G., and Weingast, B. R. 1987. Administrative Procedures as Instruments of Political Control. *Journal of Law, Economics, and Organization*, 3: 243–77.

————————1989. Structure and Process, Politics, and Policy: Administrative Arrangements and the Political Control of Agencies. *Virginia Law Review*, 75(2): 431–82.

——and SCHWARZ, T. 1984. Congressional Oversight Overlooked: Police Patrols and Fire Alarms. *American Journal of Political Science*, 28(1): 165–79.

MOE, T. M. 1982. Regulatory Performance and Presidential Administration. *American Journal of Political Science*, 26(May): 197–224.

——1985a. Control and Feedback in Economic Regulation. *American Political Science Review*, 79(Dec): 1094–116.

——1985b. The Politicized Presidency, pp. 235–72 in *The New Direction in American Politics*, ed. J. Chubb and P. Peterson. Washington, DC: Brookings Institution.

——1987. An Assessment of the Positive Theory of Congressional Dominance. *Legislative Studies Quarterly*, 12(2): 475–520.

——1989. The Politics of Bureaucratic Structure, pp. 267–330 in *Can the Government Govern?*, ed. J. E. Chubb and P. E. Peterson. Washington, DC: The Brookings Institution.

——1990. The Politics of Structural Choice: Toward a Theory of Public Bureaucracy, pp. 116–53 in *Organization Theory: From Chester Barnard to the Present and Beyond*, ed. O. E. Williamson. New York: Oxford University Press.

——and HOWELL, W. G. 1999a. The Presidential Power of Unilateral Action. *Journal of Law, Economics, and Organization*, 15(1): 132–79.

——1999b. Unilateral Action and Presidential Power: A Theory. *Presidential Studies Quarterly*, 29(4): 850–73.

——and WILSON, S. A. 1994. Presidents and the Politics of Structure. *Law and Contemporary Problems*, 57(1): 1–44.

NATHAN, R. P. 1983. *The Administrative Presidency*. New York: Wiley.

OGUL, M. 1978. *Congress Oversees the Bureaucracy*. Pittsburgh, PA: University of Pittsburgh Press.

SCHICKLER, E. 2007. Entrepreneurial Defenses of Congressional Power, pp. 293–315 in *Formative Acts: American Politics in the Making*, ed. S. Skowronek and M. Glassman. Philadelphia, Penn: University of Pennsylvania Press.

——and PEARSON, K. Forthcoming. Agenda Control, Majority Party Power, and the House Committee on Rules, 1937–1952. *Legislative Studies Quarterly*.

Scholz, J. T., and Wei, F. H. 1986. Regulatory Enforcement in a Federalist System. *American Political Science Review*, 80(4): 1249–70.

Shepsle, K. A. 1992. Bureaucratic Drift, Coalitional Drift, and Time Inconsistency: A Comment on Macey. *Journal of Law, Economics, and Organization*, 8(1): 111–8.

Simon, H. A. 1947. *Administrative Behavior*. New York: Free Press.

Volden, C. 2002. A Formal Model of the Politics of Delegation in a Separation of Powers System. *American Journal of Political Science*, 46(1): 113–33.

Waterman, R. W. 1989. *Presidential Influence and the Administrative State*. Knoxville: University of Tennessee Press.

Weingast, B. R. 1981. Regulation, Reregulation, and Deregulation: The Political Foundations of Agency Clientele Relationships. *Law and Contemporary Problems*, 44(1): 147–77.

—— 1984. The Congressional-Bureaucratic System: A Principal Agent Perspective (with Applications to the SEC). *Public Choice*, 44(1): 147–91.

—— and Moran, M. J. 1983. Bureaucratic Discretion or Congressional Control? Regulatory Policymaking by the Federal Trade Commission. *The Journal of Political Economy*, 91(Oct): 765–800.

Wildavsky, A. 1964. *The Politics of the Budgetary Process*. Boston: Little, Brown.

Williamson, O. E. 1975. *Markets and Hierarchies: Analysis and Antitrust Implications*. New York: Free Press.

—— 1996. *The Mechanisms of Governance*. New York: Oxford University Press.

Wilson, W. 1901. *Congressional Government: A Study in American Politics*. Boston: Houghton, Mifflin and Company.

Wiseman, A. E. Forthcoming. Delegation and Positive-Sum Bureaucracies. *Journal of Politics*.

Wood, B. D. 2009. The President and the Political Agenda, pp. 108–34 in *Oxford Handbook of the American Presidency*, ed. I. G. C. Edwards. New York: Oxford University Press.

—— Forthcoming. Agency Theory and the Bureaucracy, in *Oxford Handbook of American Bureaucracy*, ed. R. F. Durant. New York: Oxford University Press.

—— and Bohte, J. 2004. Political Transaction Costs and the Politics of Administrative Design. *Journal of Politics*, 66(1): 176–202.

—— and Marchbanks, M. P. 2007. What Determines How Long Political Appointees Serve. *Journal of Public Administration Research and Theory*, doi: 10.1093/jopart/mum019 (August).

—— and Waterman, R. W. 1991. The Dynamics of Political Control of the Bureaucracy. *American Political Science Review*, 85(3): 801–28.

—— —— 1993a. The Dynamics of Political-Bureaucratic Adaptation. *American Journal of Political Science*, 37(2): 497–528.

—— —— 1993b. Policy Monitoring and Policy Analysis. *Journal of Policy Analysis and Management*, 12: 685–99.

—— —— 1994. *Bureaucratic Dynamics: The Role of Bureaucracy in a Democracy*. Boulder, CO: Westview Press.

CHAPTER 35

CONGRESSIONAL WAR POWERS

LINDA L. FOWLER

INTRODUCTION

ANYONE familiar with standard texts or previous handbooks on the U.S. Congress will recognize that the editors of this volume have taken the unusual step of including a chapter on "Congressional War Powers," a phrase that to contemporary eyes appears to be an oxymoron. Since World War II, presidents have dominated international affairs, while legislators have used their war powers reactively and infrequently. Lawmakers appear to have diminished capacity for responding to executive initiatives and seem to put party loyalty ahead of institutional loyalty in overseeing foreign and defense policy. Nevertheless, the Constitution remains in force, conferring formidable powers on the House and Senate that are a *potential* source of constraint on the executive.

Like members of Congress, legislative specialists tend to shy away from national security policy. They concentrate instead on patterns of behavior within the domestic arena, including representation, elections, procedures, parties, and committees. Such neglect is regrettable because war has always had a profound effect on American political development (Jacobson and Kernell 2004; Mayhew 2005). Moreover, globalization of the economy and ubiquitous terrorist networks have made the line between domestic and international politics increasingly unclear (Fisher 2008; Whittington and Carpenter 2003).

Among scholars who investigate congressional war powers, several approaches predominate. Most numerous are studies of the constitutional prerogatives of Congress and the president and the historical evolution of each branch's influence. Together these literatures have proved inconclusive: the constitutional case for an assertive Congress is very strong, but the historical record of legislative delegation to the president and deference to executive energy and secrecy is even more powerful.

Scholars' second line of inquiry entails analysis of specific cases of legislative influence on foreign and defense policy. Sometimes they look for *direct* constraint over specific military actions, while at other times they focus on *indirect* limits on presidential calculations about the costs and benefits of using force. Efforts to uncover direct influence of Congress have yielded modest effects at best, which Hinckley (1994) aptly summarized as "less than meets the eye." Yet emerging work on indirect outcomes suggests that the latent power of Congress continues to limit executive action. Individual members influence elite discourse and public opinion regarding presidential decisions, while party competition within the institution impacts the initiation or duration of military conflicts. As a whole, the literature implies that Congress remains relevant to decisions regarding war and peace, although individual members lack sufficient political incentives and organizational mechanisms to fully discharge their constitutional responsibilities.

The question of congressional war powers has consequences for literatures in international relations with respect to domestic effects on negotiation and conflict. For decades, the dominant realist paradigm pushed internal politics to the analytic sidelines because of preoccupation with state rivalries in an anarchic international system. Theories that incorporate domestic constraints, however, challenge the realist orientation in two ways: first, they predict increased credibility of commitments when societies have open decision processes (Clark and Nordstrom 2005; Lipson 2003; Martin 2000); and second, they incorporate audience costs that inhibit leaders from initiating conflicts with a low probability of success (Fearon 1994; Gelpi, Feaver, and Reifler 2005; Schultz 1998, 2001; Wolford 2007). Related lines of inquiry have stressed the role of internal politics through such diverse questions as the democratic peace [the empirical phenomenon that democracies do not war with each other (Doyle 2005; Huth and Allee 2002; Kinsella 2005; Rohde 2005; Rosato 2003; Slantchev et al., Alexandrova, and Gartzke 2005); the duration of conflicts (Kriner 2010; Stam 1996); the use of war as a diversion from domestic problems (Moore and Lanoe 2003; Ostrom and Job 1986); and the success of democracies in war (Reiter and Stam 2002). Nevertheless, domestic politics remains a "stepchild" of international relations (Bueno de Mesquita and Lalman 1992).

The issue of congressional war powers has normative implications for constitutional governance and democratic accountability, as well. Executive responsibility for the use of force has been a perennial issue in American politics since Washington's fruitless meeting with the Senate to discuss hostilities with border tribes (Flexner 1970). The Cold War aroused fears of an imperial presidency, which subsided with the fall of the Berlin Wall, but reemerged with the Bush Administration's "war on terror" (Fisher 2006; Rudalevige 2006). Bush's claims of executive prerogative both at home and abroad not only exposed the institutional weaknesses of Congress, but also stimulated movement for reform (National War Powers Commission 2008;

War Powers Initiative 2005). Equally important, Bush's departure from office under a cloud of public disapproval, like Truman's and Johnson's before him, provided a stark reminder that presidents pay a heavy price for assuming sole responsibility for prolonged military conflict.

Despite the significance of congressional war powers, several factors inhibit the development of a research agenda. First, congressional scholars are most interested in the internal workings of the institution, although public disapproval of the war in Iraq sparked criticism of congressional conduct during the Bush years (Fisher 2006, 2008; Irons 2005; Mann and Ornstein 2006; Ornstein and Mann 2006). Second, researchers typically evaluate inter-branch relations through the lens of executive success in passing laws or shaping congressional roll-call votes. This approach not only privileges the presidency, but overlooks activities most applicable to national security, such as oversight, investigations, and informal consultation (Lindsay 1992–3, 1994). Third, subfield biases permeate the literature on congressional war powers with legislative specialists—including this author—embracing a more expansive view of their institution's powers than is the case for other researchers. Louis Fisher's extensive corpus of work typifies the Congress-centered approach toward institutional responsibilities in national security affairs, while resurgent scholarship regarding the "two presidencies," reinforces a view of executive predominance (Canes-Wrone, Howell, and Lewis 2008). Fourth, the infrequent or unobtrusive exercise of congressional constraint raises vexing questions over what counts as influence and how to measure it (Howell and Pevehouse 2005).

In evaluating the literature on congressional war powers, this chapter first considers how extra-constitutional developments in both the legislative and executive branches have produced the relatively weak institution of today. The discussion then compares direct and indirect pathways for lawmakers to affect executive decision-making and suggests that less visible forms of constraint are quite potent, albeit difficult to measure. Finally, the focus turns to future directions for research, particularly the role of parties in shaping the balance between the legislative and executive branches and indirect forms of influence on the use of force.

SACRED TEXTS AND EXTRA-CONSTITUTIONAL DEVELOPMENTS

The U.S. system of separate and shared powers leads to perpetual debate about the boundaries of congressional and presidential responsibilities in the use of military force. As noted constitutional scholar Edward S. Corwin asserted in an oft-quoted statement: the Constitution sets up "an invitation to struggle for the privilege of directing American foreign policy" (Crabb and Holt 1992). Scholars generally agree that Congress enjoys formidable powers with respect to war, but is ill-suited to manage emergencies. Thus, presidents have acted independently in accordance with the doctrine of *salus populi*, while seeking approval for their decisions after the fact. An uneasy balance between the branches persisted for most of American history, but finally collapsed under the weight of the near permanent state of alert in the U.S. since World War II, when presidents began to claim *inherent* powers to initiate and prosecute war on their own. Despite efforts among conservatives to promote a broad reading of presidential powers, the prerogatives of the presidency today rest on congressional delegation and deference rather than constitutional principles.

The multiple meanings of the Constitution

The Constitution is a paradoxical mix of clearly defined war powers for Congress and implied prerogatives for the president. The framers addressed legislative capabilities in Article I, thus symbolizing their understanding that in a republic the legislature is the most powerful branch (Hamilton, Jay, and Madison 1962, 338). Section 8 reflects the eighteenth-century view of warfare as a formal relationship among nation states, and it confers both general and specific powers on the legislature necessary for conducting hostilities. Briefly, these include: the authorization of conflict; the authorization and appropriation of funds for weapons and personnel; the management of military personnel through establishment of rules of conduct; the creation and oversight of executive capabilities for intelligence-gathering, diplomacy, and military operations; and the termination of hostilities through ratification of treaties.[1] The president's powers in Article II, in contrast, include the short and vaguely worded presidential oath in Section 1 "to faithfully execute the Office .... and to preserve, protect and defend the Constitution;" the position of commander in chief; and the charge in Section 3 to "take care that the Laws be faithfully executed."

The contrasting language in the two articles raises challenges and opportunities for the two institutions. Most legislative and constitutional scholars see the specificity of congressional powers as a signal from the framers that Congress would be actively engaged in shaping decisions about the initiation and conduct of war (Deering 2005; Fisher 2000, 2006, 2008; Hendrickson 2002; Irons 2005; Koh 1990; Silverstein 1997). Indeed, the extensive debate over standing armies articulated in the *Federalist* papers (numbers 26, 27, and 28) indicates that Congress would serve as a bulwark against an executive tempted toward military adventures or domestic conquest.[2] The Constitution's brevity regarding formal presidential powers, as well as the minimal discussion about military matters at the Philadelphia convention, imply further that the framers intended the president to carry out the directives of Congress (Fisher 1997).

The historical record provides considerable evidence for a robust interpretation of congressional war powers. During the nineteenth century, presidents deferred

---

[1] Significantly, the privateers, who received letters of marque and reprisal and served as critical extensions of the nation's military capabilities at the time of the nation's founding, came under the jurisdiction of the Congress rather than the president.

[2] The constitutional limits on any appropriation to fund U.S. troops for no more than two years drive home the idea of legislative restraint of the president.

to Congress, with Jackson, Lincoln, and Polk as notable exceptions (Fisher 1997; Silverstein 1997). When executives did make decisions without consultation, as in Jefferson's dealings with the Barbary pirates or Louisiana Purchase, they sought congressional approval afterward. Moreover, the period of extraordinary executive powers during the Civil War quickly gave way to the conventional pattern of weak presidents. "By 1875," one scholar noted, "you would not know there had been a war or a Lincoln" (quoted in James 2005). Even during the twentieth century, presidents leading up to and including FDR sought congressional approval of military actions, and their subsequent claims of inherent powers did not firmly take root until the 1960s (Silverstein 1997).

National emergencies pose a challenge, however, to advocates of extensive war powers for Congress. Although the Constitution gives Congress the power to "declare" war, earlier drafts had authorized the legislature to "make" war. From the limited discussion in the *Notes on the Convention* (Madison 1987) it appears that the framers were concerned about crises, particularly when Congress was out of session: a real threat with France, Britain, and Spain all occupying territory on U.S. borders. Thus, the shift in verbs strongly suggests presidential authority to respond to sudden attacks, while requiring congressional approval to engage in full-scale warfare.

Political theorists in the last decade have revisited the doctrine of *salus populi* in the writings of Locke and Blackstone as the basis for presidential dominance in matters of war. Locke recognized a fundamental dilemma for constitutional government when the "welfare of the people" required the executive to exercise discretion in order to attain "the publick[sic] good, without the prescription of the Law, and sometimes even against it" (quoted in James 2005, 6). In the absence of clear legal authority, executives had the prerogative to act, but the legitimacy of their decisions depended upon approval of the results after the fact (James 2005; Kleinerman 2007; Rudalevige 2006). In effect, the executive's duty required his discretion, but subjected him to the risk that the citizenry would react negatively to poor results.

The emergency prerogative power is a significant loophole in Lockean constitutionalism, although it does not rule out a congressional role. The trouble arises from the fact that citizens lack both information and incentive to punish leaders who have misused their discretion (Kleinerman 2007). Moreover, during crises, liberal democracies tend to put aside their foundational premises of rational deliberation to bestow "godlike" qualities on leaders (Fatovic 2008). Given the limitations of the *populi*, then, institutional actors are critical for the public's protection. As Madison noted: "Those who are to conduct a war cannot in the nature of things be proper or safe judges whether a war ought to be commenced, continued or concluded" (quoted in MacKenzie 2008). Lawmakers have greater capacity and stronger motivation than the public to question executive actions, but the doctrine of *salus populi* is vague about whether they should prevent executives from exercising discretion.

Presidents gain license to use force, as well, from vagueness of Article II. Given the care with which the framers enumerated legislative powers, their silence with respect to the executive suggests to some scholars that anything not denied to the president is permissible. Similarly, the many implied powers in the Constitution for the legislature and judiciary generate a reasonable expectation that the authority of commander in chief and the executive function also confers latitude. Foreign policy realists have been the most committed champions of a powerful national security president on pragmatic rather than constitutional grounds. But the internationalist heirs of Woodrow Wilson joined in the broad reading of Article II after World War II as a natural extension of their conviction that presidents serve as the engine of progressive change both at home and abroad. Historical accounts of FDR's presidency reinforced the idea of an heroic executive figure who should not be pinned down by Lilliputian lawmakers (Lowi 1985).

Advocates for broad grants of executive authority have emerged among conservatives since the Reagan administration. The argument for presidential autonomy began as a Republican political project (Bacevich 2005; Cheney 1990; Crovitz and Rabkin 1989), but found defenders among conservative legal scholars affiliated with the Federalist Society. Following the precepts of limited government and "originalist" jurisprudence to examine constitutional language as it was understood at the time, they invoke a strict interpretation of the separation of powers, known as the theory of the unitary executive, and apply British constitutional doctrine regarding the monarch's prerogatives to the president.

Proponents of the theory of the unitary executive have been primarily concerned with domestic policy, particularly the president's prerogative to appoint or remove federal officials (Yoo, Calabresi, and Colangelo 2005; Calabresi and Yoo 2008; Bailey 2008). Nevertheless, the theory's interpretation of the logic of separation implies that the powers of commander in chief are solely the president's and therefore insulated from congressional intrusion. Such a reading of the Constitution's language and history seems strained, at best, and contradicts the most fundamental principle of Madisonian democracy articulated in *Federalist 51* that for "ambition to counteract ambition" each branch requires both a "will of its own" and the "means of keeping each other in their proper places" (Hamilton et al. 1962, 336). The Bush Administration cited the theory of the unitary executive in its brief regarding the president's powers as commander in chief with respect to the detention of enemy combatants at Guantanamo, but the Supreme Court's ruling in *Hamdan v. Rumsfeld* (2006) rejected the premise of the unitary executive. Moreover, the theory's most visible proponent, Justice Antonin Scalia, joined in the majority opinion.

John Yoo (2005) has provided the most comprehensive contemporary effort to ground executive prerogative in the British monarchy, although his reputation is now tainted by his co-authorship in the Bush Administration of the so-called "torture memos." Yoo argued the framers were so imbued with the British tradition of parliamentary deference to the monarch in war and diplomacy that they saw no need to write specific language into the Constitution and simply assumed equivalent powers for the two executives.[3] The equation of presidential and monarchical pre-

---

[3] In some respects, this interpretation is a revised version of Justice Sutherland's "sole organ" theory of the presidency in *Curtiss v. Wright* (1936), which asserted that the powers of the Crown simply transferred to the federal executive, because the states had no sovereignty over international affairs prior to the formation of the republic.

rogatives distorts the historical record in several respects, however. First, the states under the Articles of Confederation had autonomy to engage in external affairs, so that sovereignty did not pass directly from the Crown to the president. Second, Hamilton's powerful arguments in *Federalist 70, 71*, and *72* about unity and energy in the executive aim at the anti-Federalists, not the Congress, in order to assert a vigorous *national* government and refute demands for a *plural executive*. Third, Jay's famous passage regarding "energy, secrecy and dispatch" in *Federalist 64*, so often used to justify executive prerogative, occurred in a discussion of diplomacy, not war, and focused on reassuring the states that the Senate would not ride roughshod over their interests (Deering 2005). Fourth, the framers, especially Hamilton, held that the nation's greatest safety lay in developing its economy and trade and required only a limited military force to discourage opportunistic behavior by European powers. Finally, recent scholarship indicates that British economic development and empire were possible only because Parliament constrained the king at home and abroad (Katznelson and Lapinski 2006).

The constitutional debates also contained numerous examples of the founders' fear that the presidency was the "foetus of monarchy" (Madison 1987). Most telling perhaps is *Federalist 69*, a lengthy treatise that scholars typically overlook, in which Hamilton assures his readers that he is not advocating a king. He notes that "[the power] of the British king extends to the *declaring* of war and to the *raising* and *regulating* of fleets and armies—all of which, by the Constitution under considera-tion, would appertain to the legislature" (1962, 448; italics in the original). He further contends that New York, and perhaps New Hampshire and Massachusetts, confer "larger powers upon their respective governors"(1962, 449), and he ends the essay with a lengthy list of the many ways in which the powers of the president are inferior to those of the king such that "there is no pretence for the parallel which has been attempted" (1962, 453).

A deeper problem for conservatives, though, is the risk that expansive interpre-tations of presidential power abroad breed executive over-reaching at home (Fisher 2008; Rudalevige 2006). As Silverstein (1997) notes, only one Constitution governs in the U.S., and it makes no distinction between domestic and foreign affairs. The dilemma is visible in the discomfort Federalist Society members, including co-founder Steven Calabresi, expressed in a recent law review article (Yoo, Calabresi, and Colangelo 2005). The theory of the unitary executive, the authors assert, "does not necessarily require supporting the broad claims of inherent executive authority advanced by the Bush Administration," [which had] "pushed an overly vigorous view of presidential power that expanded far beyond the logical boundaries of the unitary executive" (2005, x).

The Supreme Court has provided relatively little guidance in resolving the issue of congressional war powers. The contemporary Court frequently is deferential to claims of executive prerogative (Silverstein 1997), as in the *Korematsu* (1944) case regarding the detention of Japanese Americans during World War II. Challenges to presidential power typically originate with individuals under the Bill of Rights, rather than lawmakers, and the occasional suits initiated by both Democratic and

Republican members in recent years have not progressed beyond the District Courts. The Court also has taken a generous view of the executive powers delegated by Congress (Silverstein 1997). In *Dames & Moore v. Regan* (1981), for example, The Court upheld the president's executive orders dealing with financial claims on the Iranian government because Congress had conferred broad discretion via statute to manage economic disputes with foreign governments.

Nevertheless, explicit congressional support is often necessary to legitimize executive decisions. The famous opinion by Justice Jackson in the *Youngstown Sheet and Tube* case overturning Truman's seizure of the steel mills in 1952 asserts that the president is at the height of his powers when Congress specifically approves an action; operates in a "zone of twilight" when he acts in the absence of congressional authorization; and has least discretion when Congress has expressly forbidden a particular action. In this spirit, the justices struck down the executive's creation of military commissions in the *Hamdan v. Rumsfeld* (2006) case to try prisoners held at Guantanamo Bay because Congress had established the Military Code of Justice and had not authorized separate procedures for detainees.

Overall, a fair reading of the Constitution and the *Federalist* papers suggests that the framers did not intend either branch to dominate; nor did they equate a strong national government with presidential rule. Noted theorist Robert Dahl (2001) reminds us that the framers were engaged in an intense political struggle and that they made a series of pragmatic compromises, some of which Madison and Jefferson later acknowledged were mistakes. The *Federalist* papers, too, reflected the point and counter-point of heated argument, and despite their brilliance, did not add up to a coherent political philosophy (Dahl 2001). In sum, only Congress and the president, acting within a particular time and context, can resolve debates over institutional prerogatives.

Extra-constitutional and historical developments

Whatever interpretation one adopts of America's sacred texts, the historical evolution of the legislative and executive branches indicates that the ambition of Congress has not matched the ambition of the president. The executive has gained vast resources to coordinate policy implementation, to propose a legislative agenda and to manage national security, while the legislature has relinquished important functions and neglected its institutional capacities. Scholars writing in the tradition of American political development have produced an ample literature on the rise of the presidency, which fits nicely with their interests in state building and party systems (Whittington and Carpenter 2003). Nothing comparable exists in the congressional literature, despite the fact that the legislature was instrumental in creating the administrative state and operates within the same party framework as the presidency (Katznelson and Lapinski 2006). Historically minded congressional scholars have been most interested in the distribution of power *within* the legislature rather than *across* the branches, using past events as evidence to test micro-theories regarding rules and procedures. Nevertheless, recent literature on committees and parties suggests that efforts within Congress to form cohesive majorities in order to enact statutes may have undermined the institution's capacity to exercise its war powers or oversee the authority it has delegated to the president.

Congress's diminished role in national security stems in part from inattention to its own capabilities. For generations, strong, autonomous committees served as the legislature's chief bulwark against executive encroachment (Fenno 1973; Sundquist 1981), a feature that progressives operating within the Wilsonian tradition frequently found frustrating as summarized in the famous American Political Science Association's report on party government (Ranney 1950). Committees also provided continuity and institutional memory, attributes critical to Hamilton's view of energetic government, but often deficient in the executive branch which has been plagued first by patronage politics and subsequently by a revolving door of political appointees (Bailey 2008).

Until the 1970s, committees with jurisdiction over foreign and defense policy enjoyed particular prestige inside and outside of Congress. The Senate Foreign Relations Committee had been the most preferred committee for over a century (Canon and Stewart 2002), and its chairs were often highly visible in the press. Foreign Relations took an active role, creating the international order after World War II, challenged presidents, such as Lyndon Johnson over the Vietnam War (Mayhew 2000), and spearheaded reform of U.S. intelligence activities under Senator Frank Church in the 1970s. The Armed Services committees, while less visible nationally, variously tackled difficult problems that stumped the executive branch, such as military procurement reform and base consolidation in the 1980s and protection of vulnerable nuclear weapons after the collapse of the Soviet Union in the 1990s. Today, these once mighty Senate committees have less status (Deering 2001, 2005). Foreign Relations began experiencing difficulty attracting new members in the 1980s (Stewart and Groseclose 1999) and has suffered a dramatic decline in prestige ever since, particularly among Republicans (Fowler and Law 2008b). Armed Services, while experiencing less dramatic change, experienced an overall diminution in senators' interest in military affairs relative to taxation and appropriations.[4] Press attention to Congress has dropped steadily in the post-World War II era, but the two committees' coverage declined even more dramatically, shrinking from more than 9 percent of all *New York Times* mentions of the Congress to just 2 percent today (Fowler and Law 2008b, 364–5).

The ability of committees to act as a counter-weight to the executive branch ultimately depends upon their interaction with the congressional parties. Yet scholars have viewed parties as a solution to internal problems of coordination (Aldrich 1995) while neglecting how they affect the balance of power across branches. Early calls for reform of Congress stressed the importance of offsetting the fragmentation and lack of accountability of the committee system by strengthening the majority

---

[4] The hierarchy of the Senate committee system has flattened partly because members have increased their average number of assignments from a little over one per member to well over three per member. Thus, the difference between top-ranked and bottom-ranked committees has shrunk over time along with the changes in the rank ordering (Fowler and Law 2008a).

party (Ranney 1950). Most recently, the literature on committees has been concerned primarily with two issues: 1) the extent to which members use their informational advantages and gate-keeping authority to thwart or reflect the preferences of the median legislator or the majority party; and 2) their role as agents of the party leadership in keeping votes that divide the majority off the floor. Both perspectives on committees, as either obstacles to majority rule or facilitators of party control of the agenda, are extremely important issues in understanding the internal workings of Congress, its rules, procedures and policy choices (Aldrich and Rhode 2005). But some recent critics of Congress have depicted the weakening of the committee system as the source of many of the problems plaguing the institution today (Mann and Ornstein 2006; Rohde 2005).

As head of their party, presidents are well positioned to exploit the weakened capacity of the national security committees. Some scholars have argued that political parties have operated as a constraint on presidential power and that presidents bent on asserting their prerogatives relied primarily on the administrative state rather than legislative parties (Milkis 1993). Nevertheless, party leadership from the White House has coincided with eras of presidential dominance of Congress (James 2005; Skowronek 1993), and in recent years, presidents have endeavored to strengthen legislative party organizations (Milkis and Rhodes 2007). Increased executive engagement has exacerbated conflict within Congress generally and has had an especially divisive effect in military policy, increasing polarization of senators' voting records by fully 10 percent (Lee 2008, 923).

The link between congressional prerogatives and party strength is variable, however, because presidential *power* and presidential *authority* differ. Skowronek (1993) makes this distinction in his study of the transformative potential of the American presidency. He bases his argument on the fact that all presidents draw on the same constitutional powers, although their organizational and political resources have grown over time. Skowronek contends that political circumstances constrain or enhance their leadership efforts and asserts that the "political order" in which each president exerts leadership reflects the ideological coherence and the strength of the prevailing party system. Thus, Jimmy Carter and Ronald Reagan assumed roughly equivalent powers, but enjoyed vastly different leeway to utilize the assets of the office. From Skowronek's account, members of Congress lack the capacity to "make politics," unless the party system breaks up.

The most problematic aspect of congressional war powers, however, is the extent to which lawmakers have delegated their prerogatives to the president. The literature on delegation generally refutes the idea that delegation produces institutional weakness because lawmakers can write statutes in ways that hold executive principals accountable to their legislative agents (see, for example, Epstein and O'Halloran 1999). Whittington and Carpenter are skeptical about Congress's ability to retain control over delegated authority, noting that: "Within the narrative of congressional dominance, foreign policy is rarely considered" (2003, 504). In addition, they worry that the national security state, which "stands astride the artificial boundaries between the domestic and foreign affairs," threatens all types of principal-agent relations (2003, 504).

Congress has endeavored to exercise greater control over executive discretion by attaching procedural constraints to the authorities it has conferred on the executive. Lawmakers have employed reporting requirements in the realm of foreign aid and arms sales, and they have also attempted to monitor the use of executive agreements by requiring more information from the president (Howell 2003). Few observers judge these restraints a success (Hinckley 1994), and some find them counterproductive. The courts tend to emphasize the granting of authority and ignore the procedural strings (Silverstein 1997), although the *Hamdan* (2006) ruling was notable for its pointed statement that in authorizing warfare, Congress had not issued the president "a blank check." Moreover, procedural remedies to the problem of delegation have an ambiguous legal status. In *Immigration and Naturalization Service v. Chadha* (1983), for example, the Court struck down the legislative veto on the grounds that it violated separation of powers, ruling that: "Congress must abide by its delegation of authority until that delegation is legislatively altered or revoked" (quoted in O'Brien 1995, 394).

The obvious example of congressional attempts to constrain delegated authority is the War Powers Resolution enacted in 1973. The legislation epitomizes all of the pitfalls Congress confronts in balancing executive leeway to manage crises while retaining a role for itself. No president has recognized the Resolution's constitutionality; only one president has started the sixty-day "clock" that permits commitment of military forces without explicit congressional approval and determines the time when they must be withdrawn; and no president has been compelled by Congress to remove military forces in compliance with its provisions (Hinckley 1994). Critics of the War Powers Resolution contend that Congress expressly granted the president authority that previously was only implied, thus perversely weakening the hand of the legislature. They further charge that procedural constraints are not sufficient to rein in a president who is bent on military action (Hess 2006; Malbin 1989). Yet, some have argued that the very existence of the Act has deterred presidents from military adventures and that things might have been a good deal worse without it (Auerswald and Cowhey 1997). Nevertheless, many public officials, including two independent commissions, have called for repeal of the War Powers Act (National War Powers Commission 2008; War Powers Initiative 2005), and reformers broached the idea to President-elect Obama before he took office (*New York Times*, December 12, 2008).

The primary lever Congress can use to assert its war powers is through the appropriation of funds. Even an aggressive advocate of executive power, such as John Yoo (2005), concedes that the power of the purse is the legislature's ultimate weapon against the executive. Yet, the record is decidedly mixed. During intense battles with the Reagan Administration over strategic responses to communist insurgencies in Central America, lawmakers twice limited the use of funds for military aid to the Contras in Nicaragua, an action that ultimately led to a constitutional crisis. Similarly, lawmakers tied the authorization of force to expel Iraq from Kuwait in 1991 to the UN Resolution to limit the scope of the conflict, and they used the appropriation process to restrict presidential discretion in dealing with the use of military forces in Bosnia during the mid-1990s (Henderson 1998). Generally, the president's strategic advantage as the "first mover" tends to diminish the power of the purse when U.S. troops are in harm's way, for Congress's reluctance to cut off funds is a matter of political will rather than constitutional prerogative.

In sum, the language and interpretation of the Constitution confer major responsibilities on Congress, but extra-constitutional developments have tilted the balance in favor of the president, especially in recent years. The committee and party systems appear to be factors in the interaction between the two branches, although scholars have not developed a clear connection. Delegation of power to the executive is the most problematic aspect of congressional war powers, and the failure of procedural constraints has prompted some observers to note that Congress should change the way it does business rather than try to change the behavior of the executive (Silverstein 1997; Irons 2005; Whittington and Carpenter 2003; Fisher 2000; Mann and Ornstein 2006).

DIRECT AND INDIRECT CONGRESSIONAL INFLUENCE

The history of the post-World War II era contains many examples of congressional challenges to presidential power in the conduct of war. Systematic analyses of legislative influence are relatively scarce, but the existing literature suggests that Congress rarely imposes its will on the president. The Cold War observation that the U.S. system operates with two presidencies (Wildavsky 1966), seems far from obsolete today. Yet the hunt for indirect constraints on presidential decision-making has begun to provide interesting results that suggest a far more nuanced view of congressional war powers.

The political reaction to Vietnam and Watergate sparked a burst of scholarly studies of individual foreign policy decisions. On the one hand, the Cold War consensus that broke down over the Vietnam War witnessed more conflict than many commentators have recognized (Meernik 1993). On the other hand, aggressive legislative actions under both Democratic and Republican majorities after Vietnam masked a great deal of deference to the executive (Hendrickson 2002; Hinckley 1994; Scott and Carter 2002; Vanderbush and Haney 2002).

An additional area of potential congressional influence lies in legislators' response to presidential spending initiatives in foreign and defense policy. Roll-call votes on spending for defense and foreign aid are not a major source of institutional strain compared to commitment of troops by the president, but they are relevant to

Congress's key power of the purse and the president's inherent advantages of influencing public opinion, moving first, and controlling vital information. Statistical analyses confirm that presidents behave differently in their efforts to influence Congress on appropriations for defense and foreign aid programs compared to domestic spending, although the results convey a mixed picture. Presidents not only make relatively few public appeals regarding defense and foreign policy program, but they also tend to call for support on matters that are unpopular with citizens (Canes-Wrone 2006). Moreover, their success rate on foreign affairs budget legislation, when they do go over the heads of members of Congress, is notably lower than on domestic policy appeals, amounting to about 2 percent increase in the probability of passage (Canes-Wrone 2006). Nevertheless, presidents receive budget requests in foreign affairs that are closer to their original proposal than is the case for domestic programs; and, they are more successful in influencing the characteristics of new agencies that deal with foreign affairs than with domestic affairs (Canes-Wrone, Howell and Lewis 2008). In sum, Congress gives greater weight to presidential preferences in legislating appropriations in the realm of foreign affairs, but it has not relinquished control.

In addition, Congress can challenge presidential prerogatives in war by using its investigative powers.[5] The need for such activity increased greatly with the creation of the national security state after World War II. Few observers give the institution high marks for oversight, but dramatic examples have occurred that have had a powerful effect. Investigation of military procurement during World War II, for example, exposed profiteering and reputedly saved the nation millions of dollars, suggesting that Congress can play a constructive role even at the height of military engagement. Senate hearings in 1965–6 revealed the extent to which the president and the Pentagon had misled the public regarding the goals and efficacy of the nation's involvement in Vietnam, undermining public support for the war's continuation. Hearings in the 1970s uncovered intelligence operations that violated U.S. laws and norms, sparking major reforms. Mindful of this experience, observers of Congress during the George W. Bush Administration lamented the lack of oversight under Republican majorities in Congress and applauded the increase when the Democrats took over in 2007 (Ornstein and Mann 2006; Ornstein and Mann 2009).

Scholars know relatively little about the determinants of congressional oversight activity and what they do know derives from analyzing the frequency of hearings. A dramatic increase occurred between 1969 and 1983, although less in the Senate and for redistributive programs (Aberbach 1990, ch. 3). Part of the increase resulted from the high incidence of divided government, with the remainder a product of increased staff and the number of days in session (Aberbach 1990). Since peaking in the

---

[5] Executive oversight is an extra-constitutional prerogative of the legislature that is implied under the "necessary and proper" clause in Article I (see O'Brien 1995, 445–9) and includes powers of subpoena and citation for contempt. Congress officially declared its responsibility for oversight in the 1947 Legislative Reorganization Act.

mid-1980s, oversight declined steadily through 1997 (Aberbach 2002). In addition, major investigations of executive wrongdoing became more frequent in recent years with divided government again a major factor (Kriner and Schwarz 2008; Mayhew 2006; Parker and Dull 2009).

None of these analyses of oversight distinguishes between foreign and domestic affairs, however. Kriner's recent analysis of the frequency of oversight hearings regarding the war in Iraq from March 2003 to April 2008 indicates that the number of days in session and divided government played a significant role, but the big driver of congressional attention was casualties, both monthly totals and cumulative deaths (Kriner 2009). So far, scholars have yet to link oversight to party variables other than divided government. As noted earlier, shifts away from committee government toward stronger majority party control and increased presidential engagement with party building are potential candidates for further investigation.

The limited evidence regarding direct control of presidential action in war suggests that Congress exercises some constraint, but the more complicated question is whether Congress exerts its war powers indirectly. Scholars have pursued two lines of inquiry: 1) how the size of the president's party coalition affects the president's decision to employ military force; and 2) how members influence elite discourse and public opinion. Again, the literature is very incomplete, but highly suggestive of avenues for future research.

The great obstacle in assessing congressional war powers is measurement of legislative influence. Scholars have hypothesized that congressional independence from the president would be at its maximum under divided government when rivalry over party reputations pushes the branches in opposite directions. Initial findings indicated, however, that Congress appeared to have little impact on the executive's decision to initiate military action (Gowa 1998). Subsequent research did report positive results for divided government, but uncovered a much stronger relationship with the size of the president's party coalition (Howell and Pevehouse 2005). Similarly, the strength of the president's majority in Congress relates positively to the length of time that hostilities last (Kriner 2010). In other words, presidents were more likely to initiate hostilities and to prolong conflicts as their party's majority grew larger.

More perplexing issues arise with non-events in which presidents anticipate a possible congressional reaction and alter their behavior accordingly. The literature has examples for both military conflicts and diplomatic treaties. With respect to the use of force, a key question is whether the president considered commitment of U.S. troops, but refrained from such action (Howell and Pevehouse 2007). In an ingenious research design, Howell and Pevehouse (2007) collected data on all international crises with a potential impact on U.S. interests from 1945 to 2000, thus, capturing the situations when presidents weigh strategic choices against their potential costs. Their results are impressive, showing that presidents will deploy military forces if they have a large majority in Congress. In contrast, presidents are less likely to initiate the use of force as the size of the party coalition shrinks.

With respect to diplomacy, scholars assume that Congress follows the president unquestioningly because the legislature so seldom rejects a treaty. Again, the evidence pattern is unclear because presidents anticipate the issues that are likely to inspire a hostile reaction in the Senate, often preclearing provisions with interested senators (Auerswald and Maltzman 2003). Moreover, senators attach reservations or conditions to about 20 percent of all the treaties they consider, and are most likely to constrain the president when matters of "high politics" involving national security and sovereignty are involved (2003, 1105).

Congress has the potential to influence the executive's use of force, as well, through participation in elite discourse. For years, scholars assumed that Congress takes a back seat to the White House in mobilizing public opinion, but recent studies cast doubt on the ability of the president to shape public attitudes (Edwards 2003; Edwards and Wood 1999; Groeling and Baum 2008). Moreover, analysis of Congress over time indicates that the institution has played a major role in defining the nation's "public sphere" (Mayhew 2000). Although scholars have not explored this issue in depth with respect to national security, several factors appear to matter: the sensitivity of voters to conflict among elites (Zaller 1994); the propensity of the press to "index" its coverage of events to authoritative actors (Bennett 1990); and the professional norms that elevate conflict among prominent political actors as newsworthy (Groeling and Baum 2008).

Members of Congress, by speaking against a conflict, shape public perceptions of whether armed conflict is justifiable or not. The risks to the president of congressional criticism emerge even during so-called "rally events," because the press tends to focus on negative criticism from members of Congress, both in the president's party and the opposition (Groeling and Baum 2008, 1075). The effects are particularly pronounced among citizens who do not share the president's party label, precisely the group the president needs to reach. Finally, legislators appear to play a role in the public's sensitivity to casualties. Citizens tolerate loss of life in a "good war," but turn against those they decide are not worth the costs (Gelpi, Feaver, and Feifler 2007; Voeten and Brewer 2006).

Recent analyses of the Iraq War highlight the importance of congressional criticism in shaping public support for the conflict. First, the press coverage of the decision to go to war tracked congressional debate over the authorization of force (Howell and Pevehouse 2007). Moreover, members' criticism in the local press of Bush's handling of the war eroded district-level support for his policies (Howell and Pevehouse 2007). Similarly, oversight hearings in Congress decreased popular support for military involvement; for every three days of hearings, national approval of the war in Iraq declined in national polls by 1.5 percent (Kriner 2009, 790).

In sum, Congress can constrain presidential decisions with respect to military conflict, despite its weakened state. The scholarly findings noted above are robust in establishing that direct influence is possible. More important, the threat of opposition on Capitol Hill can deter the use of force or de-legitimize the commitment of troops already in the field. These results do not establish *when* Congress will choose to exercise its powers, but they suggest that the question is well worth asking.

IMPLICATIONS FOR REFORM AND FUTURE RESEARCH

The literature holds several lessons for the future of Congress and those who study it. First, congressional war powers remain a contestable proposition for lawmakers, presidents, and scholars, because of the ill-defined boundaries between the legislature and executive. Second, the extra-constitutional development of the two branches has occurred unevenly to the detriment of Congress, but it is neither an inevitable nor irreversible pattern. Third, the extent of lawmakers' influence over the use of force occurs at the margins and seldom involves head-on battles between institutions. Overall, the elusive quality of congressional engagement in war not only makes prediction about lawmakers' behavior difficult, but also raises the stakes for getting it right—for both presidents and political scientists.

The nation is in the midst of intense debate about how best to safeguard its security while defending its political freedoms. The arguments, whether theoretical, legal, or political, have focused heavily on what the framers' intended and how to apply their eighteenth-century doctrine and language to the twenty-first-century dilemma of protecting against large-scale violence by non-state actors. In revisiting basic questions of legislative and executive prerogative, this chapter calls attention to the lack of clear answers in America's sacred texts. The Constitution may be the law of the land and confer formidable powers on Congress, but legal reasoning will not suffice when the legislature lacks political will. The *Federalist* papers may be brilliant commentary on the framework of the new government, but they are also political propaganda. Centuries later, advocates use them to score points, taking phrases out of context, ignoring contradictions, or overlooking relevant but obscure passages. The excessive legalism of today's debate regarding institutional power reflects a deep-seated discomfort with political conflict in the U.S. Yet much contemporary scholarship demonstrates that such an approach is unlikely to yield answers to America's current security dilemma. Indeed, the procedural constraints Congress has imposed on the president do little to constrain the office and establish precedents that further undermine the legislature's authority over the use of force.

The historical record of extra-constitutional development is equally unsatisfying in terms of defining an appropriate sphere for Congress to exercise its war powers. The literature makes clear that the relative strength of the legislative and executive branches is highly contingent on time and political party systems. Scholars appear to be in agreement that Congress has not been the victim of a presidential coup, but has willingly conceded authority to the executive. The uncertainty arises from assessing whether the institution's position of deference is necessary and permanent. Congressional scholars have not been as attentive as students of the presidency to state building and institutional capacity. Moreover, they have been most interested in the internal dynamics of rules and structures, such as committees and parties, rather than the consequences for relationships between the branches. In addition, when researchers have examined legislative–executive interaction through the lens of delegation, their focus has been on the domestic arena rather than international affairs. David Mayhew challenges the assumption that the behavior of lawmakers in one domain is separate from its influence in the other, however. After tracing the rise of legislative powers in Britain and the U.S., he observed: "To hold its own at the level of the nation state, its members have needed to assert a role in foreign policymaking" (2000, 128).

Viewed more broadly, the matter of congressional war powers has become a collective action problem of major proportions for lawmakers. Congressional scholars typically think of political parties as necessary mechanisms of coordination and coalition building, but the downside of more cohesive majorities may be a loss of institutional autonomy. The decline in prestige and visibility of the national security committees means that Congress has less capacity to challenge an aggressive president. Similarly, the increased influence of the White House within the legislative parties weakens lawmakers' resolve to defend their institutional prerogatives when party reputations are at stake. Ultimately, the individual power of members depends upon the clout of the institution, so failure to address the unbalanced relationship with the executive in international affairs will eventually undermine the legislature's position with respect to domestic matters. In the past, political scientists have considered presidential leadership in the legislature to be a positive development, but they may want to reconsider such views in light of developments after 9/11. At the very least, the status of congressional war powers serves as a reminder that dysfunction in the Congress does not necessarily produce constructive reform and that reform itself may yield perverse consequences (Schickler 2001).

Congressional war powers further challenge scholars to rethink theories of causation and measures of influence. The burgeoning scholarship in international relations clearly indicates that domestic constraints are important in understanding military disputes, but the processes involved are obscure. The legislature is not the only player, but it certainly is a factor in the transparency, credibility, and public support of threats and commitments. The era of modern warfare places the executive at the center of strategic calculations about a nation's intentions and capabilities, but if Congress has indirect avenues for exerting restraint, then causal chains will be more complicated than the conventional format of $\Delta X => \Delta Y$. Moreover, scholars will need to pay heed to unobtrusive measures of legislative behavior and focus their attention on non-events. Analysis of counterfactuals, a thriving enterprise in international relations, may have a role to play in future research on the exercise of congressional war powers.

Finally, students of the Congress will have to become less insular in the way that they think about their institution. Like it or not, the combination of heightened partisanship and national security concerns, means that congressional scholars can no longer confine their attention to the internal workings of the institution. Such a shift has important implications for the modeling of legislative behavior on two counts because analysts can no longer assume that members' goals are fixed and exogenous to the institution. In addition, they may find it useful to redirect historical inquiries to capture the interdependence of the legislative and executive branches in their institutional development. This review suggests that the search for evidence of congressional war powers can yield large dividends for those scholars who take up the hunt.

REFERENCES

ABERBACH, J. D. 1990. *Keeping a Watchful Eye: The Politics of Congressional Oversight.* Washington, DC: Brookings Institution.

—— 2002. What's Happened to the Watchful Eye? *Congress and the Presidency,* 29(1): 3–24.

ALDRICH, J. J. 1995. *Why Parties? The Origin and Transformation of Political Parties in America.* Ann Arbor: University of Michigan.

—— and RHODE, D. W. 2005. Congressional Committees in a Partisan Era, pp. 249–70 in *Congress Reconsidered,* ed. L. C. Dodd and B. I. Oppenheimer. Washington, DC: CQ Press.

AUERSWALD, D., and COWHEY, P. 1997. Ballotbox Diplomacy: The War Powers Resolution and the Use of Force. *International Studies Quarterly,* 85(2): 508–28.

—— and FORREST MALTZMAN. 2003. Policymaking through Advice and Consent: Treaty Consideration by the United States Senate *Journal of Politics,* 65(4): 1097–110.

BACEVICH, A. J. 2005. *The New American Imperialism: How Americans are Seduced by War.* New York: Oxford University Press.

BAILEY, J. D. 2008. The New Unitary Executive and Democratic Theory: The Problem of Alexander Hamilton. *American Political Science Review,* 102(4): 453–65.

BENNETT, W. L. 1990. Toward a Theory of Press–State Relations in the United States. *Journal of Communication,* 40: 103–25.

BUENO DE MESQUITA, B., and LALMAN, D. 1992. *War and Reason: Domestic and International Imperatives.* New Haven: Yale University Press.

CALABRESI, S. G., and YOO, C. S. 2008. *The Unitary Executive: Presidential Power from Washington to Bush.* New Haven: Yale University Press.

CANES-WRONE, B. 2006. *Who Leads Whom? Presidents, Policy, and the Public.* Chicago: University of Chicago Press.

—— HOWELL, W. D., and LEWIS, D. 2008. Toward a Broader Understanding of Presidential Power: A Reevaluation of the Two Presidencies Thesis. *Journal of Politics,* 70(1): 1–16.

CANON, D. T., and STEWART, III, C. 2002. Parties and Hierarchies in Senate Committees, 1789–1946, pp. 157–81 in *U.S. Senate Exceptionalism,* ed. B. I. Oppenheimer. Columbus: Ohio State University Press.

CHENEY, D. 1990. Congressional Overreaching in Foreign Policy, pp. 101–21 in *Foreign Policy and the Constitution,* ed. R. G. A. Goldwin and R. A. Licht. Washington, DC: American Enterprise Institute.

CLARK, D. H., and NORDSTROM, T. 2005. Democratic Variants and Democratic Variance: How Domestic Constraints Shape Interstate Conflict. *Journal of Politics,* 67(1): 250–70.

CRABB, C. V., and HOLT, P. M. 1992. *Invitation to Struggle: Congress, the President and Foreign Policy,* 4th edn. Washington, DC: CQ Press.

CROVITZ, L. G., and RABKIN, J. A. eds. 1989. *The Fettered Presidency: Legal Constraints on the Executive Branch.* Washington, DC: American Enterprise Institute.

DAHL, R. A. 2001. *How Democratic is the American Constitution?* New Haven: Yale University Press.

DEERING, C. J. 2001. Principle or Party? Foreign and National Security Policymaking in the Senate, pp. 43–64 in *The Contentious Senate,* ed. C. C. Campbell and N. Rae. Lanham: Rowman and Littlefield.

—— 2005. Foreign Affairs and War, pp. 348–81 in *The Legislative Branch and American Democracy: Institutions and Performance*, ed. P. Quirk and S. Binder. New York: Oxford University Press.

Doyle, M. 2005. Three Pillars of the Liberal Peace. *American Political Science Review*, 99(3): 463–6.

Edwards, III, G. C. 2003. *On Deaf Ears: The Limits of the Bully Pulpit*. New Haven: Yale University Press.

—— and Wood, B. D. 1999. Who Influences Whom? The President, Congress and the Media. *American Political Science Review*, 93(2): 327–44.

Epstein, D., and O'Halloran, S. 1999. *Delegating Powers: A Transaction Cost Politics Approach to Policy Making Under Separate Powers*. New York: Cambridge University Press.

Fatovic, C. 2008. The Political Theology of Prerogative: The Jurisprudential Miracle in Liberal Constitutional Thought. *Perspectives*, 6(3): 487–502.

Fearon, J. D. 1994. Domestic Political Audiences and the Escalation of International Disputes. *American Political Science Review*, 88(3): 577–92.

Fenno, Jr., R. F. 1973. *Congressmen in Committees*. Boston: Little, Brown and Company.

Fisher, L. A. 1997. *Constitutional Conflicts between Congress and the President*, 4th rev. edn. Lawrence, KA: University Press of Kansas.

—— 2000. *Congressional Abdication on War and Spending*. College Station, TX: Texas A&M University Press.

—— 2006. *In the Name of National Security: Unchecked Presidential Power and the Reynolds Case*. Lawrence, KA: University of Kansas Press.

—— 2008. *The Constitution and 9/11: Recurring Threats to America's Freedoms*. Lawrence, KA: University of Kansas Press.

Flexner, J. T. 1970. *George Washington and the New Nation, 1783–1793*. Boston: Little, Brown.

Fowler, L. L., and Law, R. B. 2008a. Make Way for the Party: The Rise and Fall of the Senate National Security Committees, 1947–2006, pp. 121–41 in *Why Not Parties? Party Effects in the United States Senate*, ed. N. W. Monroe, J. M. Roberts, and D. W. Rohde. Chicago: University of Chicago Press.

—— 2008b. Seen but Not Heard: Committee Visibility and Institutional Change in the Senate National Security Committees, 1947–2006. *Legislative Studies Quarterly*, 33(3): 357–86.

Gelpi, C., Feaver, P. D., and Reifler, J. 2005. Success Matters: Casualty Sensitivity and the War in Iraq. *International Security*, 30(3): 7–46.

—— 2007. Iraq the Vote: Retrospective and Prospective Foreign Policy Judgments on Candidate Choice and Casualty Tolerance. *Political Behavior*, 29: 151–74.

Gowa, J. 1998. Politics at the Water's Edge: Parties, Voters and the Use of Force Abroad. *International Organization*, 52(2): 307–24.

Groeling, T., and Baum, M. 2008. Crossing the Water's Edge: Elite Rhetoric, Media Coverage, and the Rally-Round-the-Flag Phenomenon. *Journal of Politics*, 70: 1065–85.

Hamilton, A., Jay, J., and Madison, J. 1962. *The Federalist: A Commentary on the Constitution of the United States*. New York: Modern Library.

Henderson, R. C. 1998. War Powers, Bosnia and the 104th Congress. *Political Science Quarterly*, 113(2): 241–58.

Hendrickson, R. C. 2002. *The Clinton Wars: The Constitution, Congress, and War Powers*. Nashville: Vanderbilt University Press.

Hess, G. R. 2006. Presidents and Congressional War Resolutions in 1991 and 2002. *Political Science Quarterly*, 121(1): 93–118.

Hinckley, B. 1994. *Less Than Meets the Eye. Foreign Policy and the Myth of the Assertive Congress*. Chicago: University of Chicago Press.

HOWELL, W. G. 2003. *Power Without Persuasion: The Politics of Direct Presidential Action.* Princeton, NJ: Princeton University Press.

HOWELL, W. G., and PEVEHOUSE, J. C. 2005. Presidents, Congress, and the Use of Force. *International Organization,* 59: 209–32.

—— 2007. *While Dangers Gather: Congressional Checks on Presidential War Powers.* Princeton, NJ: Princeton University Press.

HUTH, P. K., and ALLEE, T. L. 2002. *The Democratic Peace and Territorial Conflict in the Twentieth Century.* New York: Cambridge University Press.

IRONS, P. H. 2005. *War Powers: How the Imperial Presidency Hijacked the Constitution.* New York: Metropolitan Books.

JACOBSON, G. C., and KERNELL, S. 2004. The Logic of American Politics in Wartime, pp. 1–49 in *The Logic of American Politics,* 2nd ed. S. Kernell and G. C. Jacobson. Washington, DC: Congressional Quarterly Press.

JAMES, S. C. 2005. The Evolution of the Presidency: Between the Promise and the Fear, pp. 3–40 in *The Executive Branch,* ed. J. D. Aberbach and M. A. Peterson. New York: Oxford University Press.

KATZNELSON, I., and LAPINSKI, J. S. 2006. At the Crossroads: Congress and American Political Development. *Perspectives,* 4(2): 243–60.

KINSELLA, D. 2005. No Rest for the Democratic Peace. *American Political Science Review,* 99(3): 453–7.

KLEINERMAN, B. A. 2007. Can the Prince Really be Tamed? Executive Prerogative, Popular Apathy, and the Constitutional Frame in Locke's *Second Treatise. American Political Science Review,* 101(2): 209–22.

KOH, H. H. 1990. *The National Security Constitution: Sharing Power after the Iran-Contra Affair.* New Haven: Yale University Press.

KRINER, D. 2009. Can Enhanced Oversight Repair "The Broken Branch"? *Boston University Law Review,* 89: 765–80.

—— and SCHWARZ, L. 2008. Divided Government and Congressional Investigations. *Legislative Studies Quarterly,* 33(2): 295–321.

KRINER, D. L. 2010. *After the Rubicon: Congress, Presidents and the Politics of Waging War.* Chicago: University of Chicago Press.

LEE, F. S. Dividers Not Uniters: Presidential Leadership and Senate Partisanship, 1981–2004. *Journal of Politics,* 70(4): 914–28.

LINDSAY, J. 1994. *Congress and the Politics of U.S. Foreign Policy.* Baltimore: Johns Hopkins University Press.

LINDSAY, J. M. 1992–3. Congress and Foreign Policy: Why the Hill Matters. *Political Science Quarterly,* 107(4): 607–28.

LIPSON, C. 2003. *Reliable Partners: How Democracies Have a Separate Peace.* Princeton, NJ: Princeton University Press.

LOWI, T. J. 1985. *The Personal President: Power Invested, Promise Unfulfilled.* Ithaca, NY: Cornell University Press.

MacKENZIE, J. P. 2008. *Absolute Power: How the Unitary Executive Theory is Undermining the Constitution.* New York: Century Foundation Press.

MADISON, J. 1987. *Notes on Debates in the Federal Convention of 1787.* New York: W.W. Norton.

MALBIN, M. J. 1989. Legalism versus Political Checks and Balances: Legislative-Executive Relations in the Wake of Iran-Contra, pp. 273–90 in *The Fettered Presidency: Legal Constraints on the Executive Branch,* ed. L. G. Crovitz and J. A. Rabkin. Washington, DC: American Enterprise Institute.

MANN, T. E., and ORNSTEIN, N. J. 2006. *The Broken Branch: How Congress is Failing America and How to Get It Back on Track.* New York: Oxford University Press.

MARTIN, L. L. 2000. *Democratic Commitments: Legislatures and International Cooperation.* Princeton, NJ: Princeton University Press.

MAYHEW, D. M. 2000. *America's Congress.* New Haven: Yale University Press.

MAYHEW, D. R. 2005. Wars and American Politics. *Perspectives,* 3(3): 473–93.

—— 2006. *Divided We Govern: Party Control, Lawmaking, and Investigations, 1946–2002,* 2nd edn. New Haven: Yale University Press.

MEERNIK, J. 1993. Presidential Support in Congress: Conflict and Consensus on Foreign and Defense Policy. *Journal of Politics,* 55(3): 569–87.

MILKIS, S. 1993. *The President and the Parties: The Transformation of the American Party System since the New Deal.* New York: Oxford University Press.

—— and RHODES, J. H. 2007. George W. Bush, the Republican Party, and the "New" American Party System. *Perspectives,* 5(3): 461–88.

MOORE, W. H., and LANOE, D. J. 2003. Domestic Politics and U.S. Foreign Policy: A Study of Cold War Conflict Behavior. *Journal of Politics,* 65(2): 376–96.

National War Powers Commission. 2008. The National War Powers Commission Report. Miller Center, University of Virginia. http://millercenter.org/policy/commissions/warpowers/index 7/08/08 (accessed March 20, 2009).

O'BRIEN, D. M. 1995. *Constitutional Law and Politics: Struggles for Power and Government Accountability.* New York: W.W. Norton & Company.

ORNSTEIN, N. J., and MANN, T. E. 2009. The Hill is Alive With the Sound of Hearings. *Foreign Affairs* http://www.foreignaffairs.com/articles/64245/norman-j-ornstein-and-thomas-e-mann/the-hill-is-alive-with-the-sound-of-hearings (accessed March 31, 2009).

—— 2006. When Congress Checks Out. *Foreign Affairs:* http://www.foreignaffairs.com/articles/62091/norman-j-ornstein-and-thomas-e-mann/when-congress-checks-out (accessed August 15, 2007).

OSTROM, C., and JOB, B. 1986. The President and the Political Use of Force. *American Political Science Review,* 80(2): 541–66.

PARKER, D. C. W., and DULL, M. 2009. Divided We Quarrel: The Politics of Congressional Investigations, 1947–2004. *Legislative Studies Quarterly,* 34(3): 319–46.

RANNEY, A. 1950. Toward a More Responsible Two-party System: A Report on the Committee on Political Parties. *American Political Science Review,* 44(3): 488–99.

REITER, D., and STAM, A. C. 2002. *Democracies at War.* Princeton, NJ: Princeton University Press.

ROHDE, D. W. 2005. Committees and Policy Formulation, pp. 221–4 in *The Legislative Branch,* ed. P. J. Quirk and S. Binder. New York: Oxford University Press.

ROSATO, S. 2003. The Flawed Logic of the Democratic Peace. *American Political Science Review,* 97(4): 585–602.

RUDALEVIGE, A. 2006. *The New Imperial Presidency: Renewing Presidential Power after Watergate.* Ann Arbor, MI: University of Michigan Press.

SCHICKLER, E. 2001. *Disjointed Pluralism: Institutional Innovation and the Development of the U.S. Congress.* Princeton, NJ: Princeton University Press.

SCHULTZ, K. A. 1998. Domestic Opposition and Signaling in International Crises. *American Political Science Review,* 92(4): 829–44.

—— 2001. *Democracy and Coercive Diplomacy.* Cambridge: Cambridge University Press.

SCOTT, J. M., and CARTER, R. G. 2002. Acting on the Hill: Congressional Assertiveness in U.S. Foreign Policy. *Congress & the Presidency,* 29(2): 151–69.

SILVERSTEIN, G. 1997. *Imbalance of Powers: Constitutional Interpretation and the Making of American Foreign Policy.* New York: Oxford University Press.

SKOWRONEK, S. 1993. *The Politics Presidents Make: Leadership from John Adams to George Bush.* Cambridge, MA: Harvard University Press.

SLANTCHEV, B., ALEXANDROVA, A., and GARTZKE, E. 2005. Probabilistic Causality, Selection Bias, and the Logic of the Democratic Peace. *American Political Science Review*, 99(3): 459–66.

STAM, A. C. 1996. *Win, Lose or Draw: Domestic Politics and the Crucible of War*. Ann Arbor, MI: University of Michigan Press.

STEWART, III, C., and GROSECLOSE, T. 1999. The Value of Committee Seats in the United States Senate, 1947–1991. *American Journal of Political Science*, 43: 963–73.

SUNDQUIST, J. 1981. *The Decline and Resurgence of Congress*. Washington, DC: Brookings Institution.

VANDERBUSH, W., and HANEY, P. J. 2002. Clinton, Congress and Cuba Policy Between Two Codifications: The Changing Executive–Legislative Relationship in Foreign Policy Making. *Congress & the Presidency*, 29(2): 171–94.

VOETEN, E., and BREWER, P. R. 2006. Public Opinion, the War in Iraq and Presidential Accountability. *Journal of Conflict Resolution*, 50(6): 809–30.

War Powers Initiative. 2005. Deciding to Use Force Abroad: War Powers in a System of Checks and Balances. The Constitution Project. http://www.constitutionproject. org/article.cfm?messageID=69 (accessed January 16, 2009).

WHITTINGTON, K. E., and CARPENTER, D. P. 2003. Executive Power in American Institutional Development. *Perspectives on Politics*, 1(3): 495–514.

WILDAVSKY, A. 1966. The Two Presidencies. *Trans-Action*, 4: 7–14.

WOLFORD, S. 2007. The Turnover Trap: New Leaders, Reputations and International Conflict. *American Journal of Political Science*, 51(4): 772–88.

YOO, C. S., CALABRESI, S. G., and COLANGELO, A. J. 2005. The Unitary Executive during the Modern Era, 1945–2004. *Iowa Law Review*, 90.

YOO, J. 2005. *The Powers of War and Peace: The Constitution and Foreign Affairs after 9/11*. Chicago: University of Chicago Press.

ZALLER, J. R. 1994. Elite Leadership of Mass Opinion: New Evidence from the Gulf War, pp. 186–209 in *Taken by Storm: The Media, Public Opinion, and U.S. Foreign Policy in the Gulf War*, ed. L. Bennett and D. Paletz. Chicago: University of Chicago Press.

CHAPTER 36

....

THE AMORPHOUS RELATIONSHIP BETWEEN CONGRESS AND THE COURTS

....

MICHAEL A. BAILEY

FORREST MALTZMAN

CHARLES R. SHIPAN

THE relationship between the judiciary and Congress is a complex relationship that is poorly defined or understood. Some have argued that the Constitution safeguards the independence of the judicial branch from political pressures by guaranteeing life tenure and by precluding downward adjustment of judicial salaries. Nevertheless, Congress retains important power over the court system. The Constitution grants Congress the power to make regulations and exceptions to the appellate jurisdiction of the Supreme Court, although the Constitution sets the outer limits of the jurisdiction of the federal courts. The Constitution also vests Congress with the power "to constitute Tribunals inferior to the Supreme Court." The lower federal courts—what Article III terms "inferior courts"—are created by statute, a result of the so-called "Madisonian Compromise." From the Judiciary Act of 1789 through contemporary disputes over, for example, breaking up the liberal Ninth Circuit, Congress has played a key role in designing, organizing, and defining the role of the inferior courts in the federal system. Likewise, the Constitution does not articulate what legal doctrines must shape judicial decision-making or even if judiciary has the authority to strike acts of Congress down.

The result of the ambiguity that exists is an ill-defined relationship between Congress and the courts. Whereas Congress's relationship with the executive is spelled out in detail in the Constitution, the relationship between Congress and the judiciary was left by the founders to be defined by history. Since history is rarely tidy or consistent, the relationship that exists between the courts and Congress is as messy as the Constitution itself.

The murkiness of the relationship that exists stems from several factors. First, the relationship has clearly changed over time. Second, modern accounts of the relationship have produced a set of theoretical claims that have been empirically difficult to validate. Third, the multiple dimensions of the interdependence of the two institutions makes it hard to ascertain whether Congress is constrained by the law and whether the Court is constrained by Congress.

THE EVOLUTION OF CONSTITUTIONAL INTERPRETATION

Today, debates about the relationship largely focus on the ability or likelihood of Congress to constrain the judiciary and the judiciary's willingness to limit the actions of the elected branches. These debates have become central, thanks in part to two important historical patterns. First, Congress has largely, albeit not completely, abandoned its role as an interpreter of the Constitution. Second, the federal judiciary has become a venue for policymaking.

Who interprets?

In contemporary American government textbooks, the respective roles of Congress and the Supreme Court are agreed upon and seem relatively clear: the former legislates within the boundaries of the Constitution, while the latter interprets the Constitution and decides where these boundaries lie, with the ability to invalidate acts of Congress it deems unconstitutional through judicial review.

This textbook view was not always held, and is not necessarily the inevitable result of the logic of the Constitution. Contemporary constitutional scholars, most notably Keith Whittington, argue that constitutional interpretation has not always been the exclusive purview of the courts, and that it may not be even today (see also Devins and Fisher 2004; Fisher 1988; Ackerman 1991). According to Whittington, this power was gradually ceded to the courts by the elected branches of government through distinctly political (as opposed to legal or constitutional) processes, and the elected branches retain the ability to exercise or reclaim some of this power in certain circumstances (Whittington 2007, 2009).

In the early years of the republic, according to Whittington, there were two competing theories of constitutional power: judicial supremacy and departmentalism. Judicial supremacy, as the name implies, holds that the judicial branch is the ultimate constitutional authority, while departmentalism (favored by Thomas Jefferson, among others) envisions each branch of government playing a role in constitutional interpretation (Whittington 2007, xi). While conventional wisdom holds that judicial review and judicial supremacy sprang suddenly into being through the legal maneuverings of the Marshall Court in the *Marbury v. Madison* decision, Whittington argues that these concepts developed gradually throughout the nineteenth century (2007, 2009). "[B]y the 1850s," according to Whittington, "the federal courts had become a forum within which constitutional objections to federal legislation could be raised and resolved" (2009, 1259). By the mid-twentieth century, the time of the Warren Court, the doctrine of judicial supremacy had clearly won out, to the point where the Court explicitly stated in *Baker v. Carr* (1962) that it was the "ultimate interpreter of the Constitution" (cited in Whittington 2007, 3).

According to Whittington, however, this state of affairs was not merely the result of the actions of the Court itself. The elected branches of government played a role in transferring supreme constitutional authority to the judicial branch because it was in their political interests to do so. Whittington offers a number of scenarios in which judicial supremacy could be advantageous to elected leaders. For example, the leaders of an embattled governing coalition can avoid making unpopular decisions by deferring to the judgment of the Court, as President Buchanan did on the question of slavery in the 1850s and President Carter did on the question of abortion in the 1970s (Whittington 2007, 66–9). In other words, judicial supremacy offers a way for elected leaders to attempt to depoliticize controversial issues that threaten their governing coalitions. Similarly, judicial supremacy may offer elected leaders the opportunity to attain desirable policy outcomes without incurring the transaction costs of organizing coalitions in the elected branches. Graber (1993, 36) articulates this argument:

Historically, the justices have most often exercised their power to declare state and federal practices unconstitutional only when the dominant national coalition is unable or unwilling to settle some public dispute. The justices in these circumstances do not merely fill a void created by the legislative failure to choose between competing political proposals. On the contrary, prominent elected officials consciously invite the judiciary to resolve political controversies that they cannot or would rather not address.

Of course, elected officials have frequently resisted judicial supremacy. Whittington cites several important "reconstructive" presidents (e.g. Jackson, Lincoln, Franklin Roosevelt, and others) who were successful in wresting some measure of constitutional power from the Supreme Court. According to Whittington, only a president (and a rare president at that) is able to muster the type of political force necessary for this kind of high-profile challenge. Nonetheless, he argues that Congress is still capable of challenging and criticizing the Court over specific issues (2007, 15–16). Furthermore, a head-on challenge to the Court is not the only way that Congress can play a role in constitutional interpretation. Gant (1997) offers the example of a section in the 1965 Voting Rights Act in which Congress prohibited states from denying the vote to people educated in Spanish-language schools in Puerto Rico on the basis of their inability to speak English. Congress acted in this instance based on its own interpretation of the enforcement clause of the Fourteenth Amendment, an interpretation that was more expansive than that laid out in previous Supreme Court decisions, and the Court ruled that it was appropriate for Congress to do so in *Katzenbach v. Morgan* (Gant 1997, 374–5). In another study, Whittington finds that a surprising range of congressional committees discuss constitutional issues in their public hearings, implying that members of Congress see some role for themselves in constitutional interpretation (Whittington 2005), even as there is evidence that congressional invocations of constitutionality are largely instrumental (Pickerill 2004, 8).

The larger point to be taken from this literature is that constitutional authority is structured by politics, and as such it is dynamic. While Congress may not be in the position to launch a full-scale assault on the interpretive authority of the Supreme Court, it still plays a real and arguably legitimate role in constitutional interpretation.

Having said this, the Court's dominant role in the interpretation of the Constitution has helped to cement the legitimacy of judicial review. This review is critical to ensuring the Court a role in the policymaking process.

Who makes policy?

The second important element in shaping judicial-legislative relations in the twenty-first century is the politicization of the law (Ferejohn 2002; Kagan 2001; Lovell 2003; Burke 2004; Barnes 2004; Silverstein 2009). Rather than viewing the courts as merely a mechanism for clarifying legal ambiguities and for enforcing the law, legal venues are increasingly being used as a mechanism for pursuing one's policy goals. There are several reasons for this. First, as Congress itself has carved out a more active role for the federal government, they inevitably created the opportunity for a more aggressive use of the courts. Laws such as the 1964 Civil Rights Act and the Clean Water Act invited increased litigation. Congress itself realized that by incentivizing private parties to utilize the courts it could simultaneously incentivize private actors to regulate market behavior through adjudication and to ensure compliance with congressional preferences (Farhang 2009). Second, organized interests have found that the judiciary itself is a viable (and frequently less costly) alternative to congressional incapacity. Evidence of the law's politicization is clear. Perhaps the most important indicators are that more disputes are taken to the legal system. For example, in 1961 approximately 13,500 statutory claims were filed in Federal District Courts. In 1970, close to 40,000 statutory claims were filed; in 1980 more than 75,000 claims; in 1990 over 125,000; and by 1998 close to 160,000 claims (Barnes 2004; United States 2000).[1] These disputes are also drawing in more actors. Between 1958 and 1961, an average of 4.75 Supreme Court *amicus* briefs were filed each year by public interest groups or law firms. Between 1978 and 1981, interests groups filed an average of 45.5 briefs each term. Between 1986 and 1990, an average of 103 Supreme Court briefs were filed each year (Epstein, Segal, et al. 2003, 689). Once again, the pattern is clear. Organized interests are increasingly using the courts as a vehicle for pursuing and protecting their policy agendas.

It is not surprising that gun control groups, property right groups, anti-smoking groups, pro-choice groups, organized labor, and environmentalists utilize the legal process to pursue agendas that might not be implemented by elected officials (Silverstein 2009). While Congress and the courts expanded the definition of "public law" through both statute and legal precedent, organized interests further pushed the aggressive use of the judiciary to accomplish policy goals. When legislators seem unable and unwilling to definitively resolve controversial policy questions, adversaries not surprisingly turn to the courts to pursue their agenda (Lovell 2003).

Through both congressional intent and congressional neglect and with legal precedent providing less and less resistance, the definition of public law has expanded. It is this phenomenon that recently led Justice Antonin Scalia to question "the propriety, indeed the sanity, of having value-laden decisions such as these [capital punishment, abortion, and physician-assisted suicide] made for the entire society...by judges" (Belkin 2004). Although lawmakers seem incapable of erecting barriers between the judiciary and the policy arena, it is also fair to note that as the courts have become increasingly controversial and accessible policymakers, rather than merely interpreters of legal facts and cases, the Congress and the President have tried to block each other's attempt to influence the judiciary. Given the stakes of Court decisions, neither is willing to allow another branch unfettered influence over the judiciary and its pivotal legal choices.

The congressional response to the Court

As the judiciary has become more active in the policy arena, members of Congress have spent more time shaping and responding to the Federal bench. Political scientists have argued that this response is manifested in three different ways. First, Congress adopts legislation with an eye to impending judicial review. Second, Congress utilizes its power to retaliate against a judiciary that ignores its interests. Third, Congress plays a more assertive role in the nomination process.

---

[1] Although we are reporting on Federal trends, since Congress has a direct impact on federal law and the federal judiciary, there has inevitably been a politicization in state courts too.

Legislative anticipation of judicial review

Although there is a great deal of empirical and theoretical exploration to be done, congressional anticipation of judicial review has altered the legislative process and legislation. Until the end of the twentieth century, the anticipation effect of judicial review was mainly described in terms of congressional attempts to shape the legislative histories upon which the Court would rely in its review and interpretation of statutes. For example, Katzmann (1997) calls for Congress to improve legislative drafting; have committee members sign committee reports; and have floor managers designate specific floor colloquies as authoritative.

Over the past two decades, scholars interested in the relationship between the courts and Congress have tried to explore when and why Congress systematically attempts to shape the judicial review and interpretation process. It is clear, that in the area of administrative law, Congress has the capacity to establish the parameters of judicial review. In particular, Congress has used the legislative process to structure judicial review so that policy outcomes are closer to its preferences. It can do this by specifying what agency provisions can be reviewed; expanding standing; and by specifying the venue where review will take place (Baum 2011). All of these tactics are crafted by Congress to ensure an outcome consistent with its preferences (Shipan 2000; Eskridge 1991; Eskridge and Ferejohn 1992; McNollgast 1995; Spiller and Gely 1992).

The most sophisticated of the studies have tried to identify when various policy alignments have produced specific review alignments. Although a great deal of theoretical firepower has been directed at dissecting congressional manipulation of judicial review, theoretical and empirical limitations abound. On the theoretical front, most of the work has been restricted to preference-based models. Accordingly, Congress defers to the Court when judicial preferences will produce a favorable outcome. Such models are based upon the assumption that the judiciary itself bases its decisions upon policy preferences. Although some judicial scholars accept this (most notably Segal and Spaeth 2002), there is also solid empirical evidence that legal rules structure the decisions made by judges (Bailey and Maltzman 2008; Richards and Kritzer 2002; Friedman 2006). Indeed, there is a great deal of evidence that precedents of the Court (such as *Chevron*) have discouraged the judiciary from actively engaging in the review of administrative decisions (Richard, Smith, and Kritzer 2006).

A number of studies have begun to provide empirical examples and descriptions of the political design of judicial review. One of the most thorough discussions of the political battles over the specification of review can be found in Light's (1992) analysis of Congress's decision to change the law that for decades had precluded judicial review of decisions about veterans' medical benefits. Cass (1989) and Shipan (1997a, 1997b) provide detailed analyses of legislative battles over review provisions during the writing of the Communications Act of 1934. Smith (1997, 1998) demonstrates that members of Congress battled over the extent to which courts should be allowed to review the actions of the Environmental Protection Agency during each of the attempts to amend the Clean Air Act during the past thirty years. Spiller and Tiller

(1997) also show how Congress attempted to use decision costs to affect judicial review in the Comprehensive Regulatory Reform Act of 1995 and the 1975 Bumpers Amendment.[2]

While much of this empirical evidence is persuasive about specific instances, it has largely taken the form of case studies rather than large-N analyses. This stems from the difficulty associated with collecting the data needed. In particular, scholars have been hindered by the lack of good cross-institution preference measures and the expense associated with systematically coding review provisions, although this is changing (Bailey 2007). The problem is further exacerbated by the fact that neither the courts nor Congress is a unitary actor. Thus, identifying what Congress (or the judiciary) want is complicated. Do the House median, the Senate median, the Senate majority party median, the House majority party median, the filibuster pivots, or the enacting legislature's preferences reflect what the Congress wants? Likewise, what judge or justice represents judicial preferences?

Congressional reaction to hostile Court activity

Despite the fact that judges are involved in the policymaking process and that Congress tries to shape judicial decision-making, there is no widespread tendency of Congress to override the courts. Decisions of the federal judiciary produce frequent criticism by members of Congress (Eskridge 1991; Barnes 2004) and rarely successful overrides. As we explain below, political scientists normally portray the courts adopting policies that fall within a range defined by the House, Senate, and the president as acceptable (often referred to as the Pareto set as a move from any point within this range will make at least one actor worse off). The Court's ability to do this stems from the fact that political scientists have typically assumed that each branch of government can understand the others' intentions and capabilities.

For example, in classic separation of power models, justices do not craft opinions they know will be overridden by Congress, and Congress does not pass laws likely to be struck down or interpreted in a manner hostile to Congress's interests (e.g. Ferejohn and Shipan 1990). In other words, they know how others will react, and alter their actions accordingly. In many respects, then, political scientists who explore inter-institutional relations downplay the sorts of interactions that occur across and between institutions. In reality, of course, the assumption of complete information and unitary actors within institutions is tenuous: the transmission of information between the branches is less than perfect and multiple players matter within each branch. Members of Congress lack the capacity to perfectly anticipate future judicial decisions, and judges cannot anticipate how institutions composed of elected officials will respond.[3] Hence, the courts regularly thwart congressional goals, and Congress on occasion overrules judicial attempts at policymaking. For example, according to

---

[2] The 1975 Bumpers amendment to the Administrative Procedures Act was designed to encourage courts to be less deferential toward federal agencies. For a discussion of the act, see Levin 1983.

[3] It is possible that Congress occasionally adopts legislation that it knows is unconstitutional, but that will enable it to make a political statement.

Hettinger and Zorn, Congress overrides 12 percent of the Court's labor and antitrust decisions. Similarly, Hausegger and Baum (1999) inform us that Congress attempts to override the Court approximately 6 percent of the time.[4]

Recently, political scientists have tried to move beyond a debate as to whether Congress attempts to override the Court. In particular, political scientists have started to develop a more sophisticated portrait of the relationship that exists between Congress and the courts. This portrait has been elaborated upon in two ways. First, scholars have started to build models that take into account the Court's recognition that Congress is not a unitary actor. For example, Ferejohn and Shipan (1990) develop a model that incorporates both the preferences of the Court and Congress, but also of key legislative leaders who hold formal positions via the committee system. Second, scholars have started to recognize the branches are imperfect at anticipating the actions of each other (Barnes 2004; Katzmann 1988). Instead of clearly articulating the law, Congress routinely obscures its true preferences in vague language. Likewise, judicial outcomes are difficult to predict when Congress frequently does not know what context in and with what judge a case will appear in and who will be on the federal bench.

In Barnes (2004), the author asks a question that students of American politics have ignored for too long: what happens when Congress adopts legislation that undoes the judiciary's interpretation of a federal statute? Barnes demonstrates that when Congress passes legislation to override a decision of the bench that involved statutory interpretation, the Court tends to be more deferential to Congress on subsequent rulings involving the same law. Even though meaningful dialogues between the Court and Congress are rare, when they do occur they tend to result in a resolution of conflict.

Congressional assertiveness in the nomination process

The increased involvement of judges in the policymaking process has led both members of Congress and legislative scholars to focus on the Senate's role in the confirmation process. There has also been more coverage of the Court in the press and, especially since the failed Bork nomination of 1987, more attention to the process from interest groups. The situation becomes all the more intense in light of the limited opportunities to shape the judiciary via the confirmation process. On the federal trial and appellate benches, the turnover rate is approximately 4 percent each year (Carp, Manning, and Stidham 2004). In the Supreme Court, the turnover rate throughout our nation's history has been approximately one justice every two-year period.

The Senate and Lower Court confirmations

When it comes to district and circuit appointments, individual senators often have the incentive and power to restrict the president's choices.[5] Senators' influence arises

[4] For a discussion of this distinction and its significance, see Brenner and Whitmeyer (2009, 118–19).

[5] For a comprehensive overview of the nomination and confirmation process, see Goldman 1997, Epstein and Segal 2005, and Binder and Maltzman 2009.

from several corners. First, the geographic design of the federal courts strongly shapes the nature of Senate involvement in selecting federal judges. Because federal trial and appellate level courts are territorially defined, each federal judgeship is associated with a home state, and new judges are typically drawn from that state. As a result, senators attempt to influence the president's choice of appointees to federal courts in their states.

Second, Senate procedures that empower individual senators curtail a president's power. Although the Constitution prescribes Senate "advice" as well as "consent," nothing in the Constitution requires the president to respect the views of interested senators from the state. In practice, however, judicial nominees must pass muster with the entire chamber. Senate procedures that enable a minority of Senators to block a nominee with a filibuster make Senate leaders reluctant to consider nominees who do not have broad support.

These issues came to a head in 2005 when Senate Majority Leader, Bill Frist (R-Tennessee) attempted to eliminate filibusters of judicial nominees through an approach that became known as the "the nuclear option" (Klotz 2004; Wawro and Schickler 2007; Koger 2010). Under this approach, a simple majority of the Senate would seek, through parliamentary appeals, to establish the precedent that filibusters against nominations were unconstitutional (see Wawro, Chapter 19, this volume).[6]

Such procedural roadblocks lead presidents to anticipate objections from home-state and other pivotal senators in making appointments. In the past, federal judge-ships rarely elicited the interest of senators outside the nominee's home state, so the views of the home-state senators from the president's party were typically sufficient to determine whether or not nominees would be confirmed. Other senators would typically defer to the views of the home-state senator from the president's party, thus establishing the norm of *senatorial courtesy*. Moreover, the Senate Judiciary Committee in the early twentieth century established the "blue slip," a process in which the views of home-state senators—regardless of whether they hailed from the president's party—were solicited before the committee passed judgment on the nom-inees (Binder and Maltzman 2004; Binder and Maltzman 2009). By granting home-state senators a role in the confirmation process, individual senators could threaten to block a nominee during confirmation and thus encourage the president to consider senators' views before making appointments. In other words, the blue slip and *sena-torial courtesy* provided individual senators with some leverage over the president.

Third, the Senate rarely considers nominations that lack the support of the Senate Judiciary Committee. For example, Orrin Hatch (R-UT) used his leverage as chair of the Judiciary panel to force President Bill Clinton to nominate Hatch's friend Ted Stewart to a Utah district court seat. Although Clinton was reluctant to nominate Stewart because of his perceived anti-environmental record as the head of Utah's

---

[6] The approach was dubbed the nuclear option because of the anticipated consequences if the attempt were to succeed: Democrats would exploit their remaining procedural advantages and shut down most Senate business. Frist was forced to abandon adoption of this tactic when a bipartisan coalition refused to support such a procedure.

Department of Natural Resources during the 1980s, Hatch held as hostage forty-two other judicial nominations until Clinton made the nomination (Ring 2004).

Fourth, divided party control of the Senate and White House also limits the president's ability to stack the judiciary as he sees fit. In such periods, the opposition party controlling the Senate is unwilling to give the president much leeway to reshape the federal bench. Instead, the opposition will allow home-state senators and the Judiciary Committee chair to block nominees they oppose (Binder and Maltzman 2002, 2004, 2009).

Likewise, the fact that the Senate calendar is set by the majority party empowers those opposing the president during periods of divided government (Binder and Maltzman 2002, 2004, 2009). During periods when the Senate is controlled by the president's party, the Senate is more likely to ignore the will of home-state Senators and Judiciary Committee chairs are more likely to envision their role as one of shepherding through presidential nominations.

Ideological and partisan considerations clearly play a role in what is an increasingly congressional-dominated process. Although some have argued that the confirmation process has not changed (Epstein and Segal 2005), numerous scholars have suggested that at all levels the Senate has played a more aggressive role in the nomination process. Likewise, whereas at one time the Senate's treatment was determined exclusively by its Judiciary Committee and home-state senators, the role of the Court in the policymaking process has led to more widespread senatorial involvement in both the confirmation and nomination process (Goldman 1997; Binder and Maltzman 2009; Nemachek 2008).[7]

Although members of Congress have always been involved in attempting to shape the federal judiciary in their home state, in recent years the nature of the legislative involvement has changed. Whereas at one time, senatorial courtesy was largely a vehicle for ensuring judgeship pork, the fact that the judiciary has begun to play a more active policymaking role has changed the nature of congressional involvement. In recent years, it has not been uncommon for a senator to attempt to block the confirmation of a judicial nominee who resides in a different state. The widespread congressional involvement stems in large part from the more prominent role the judiciary plays in the policymaking process (Binder and Maltzman 2009).

Even though it is clear that the capacity of the president to utilize their nomination powers to shape judicial outcomes is constrained by Congress, it is also clear that within the Senate there are numerous potential pivots who have the capacity to exercise the veto (Primo, Binder, and Maltzman 2008).[8] The ability of individual members to block Senate consideration of nominees who do not have the support of a supermajority, the Judiciary Committee's use of the blue slip, the Judiciary Committee's role in getting nominations to the floor, and the majority party's role in setting the Senate's calendar all create veto players who can block a nominee.

[7] Similarly, Shipan (2008) demonstrates that the increasing divisiveness of Supreme Court confirmations stems at least in part from the growing partisanship and increased polarization in Congress.

[8] For a similar discussion focused on Supreme Court nominations, see Rohde and Shepsle 2007.

Isolating a single senator or senate institution as being determinative is complicated because of three facts. First, the preferred nominee of a senator and of the
president is going to inevitably be shaped by the status quo of each Court. If a Court
is more conservative than a particular senator prefers, the senator might support
a nominee who was more liberal than the senator's preferred outcome. Given the
court as a collegial body with multiple members, a senator might strategically prefer
a more extreme nominee so as to produce an outcome near his or her true preferred
point. Second, measurement of both nominees and the status quo has been imprecise.
Third, frequently the exercise of a veto by a pivotal player is observationally equivalent
to the veto expressed by a different pivotal player (Primo, Binder, and Maltzman
2008). If a nominee is not confirmed, this could be a result of opposition by any
one of numerous pivotal players. All of these factors discouraged intensive analytical
study of confirmation politics until relatively recently.

Recent work has used length-to-confirmation data to assess what conditions facilitate confirmation of judges (Binder and Maltzman 2002, 2009; Martinek, Kemper,
and VanWinkle 2002; Shipan and Shannon 2003; Nixon and Goss 2001; Scherer,
Bartels, and Steigerwalt 2008). These studies make clear that the time needed to
confirm a nominee depends upon partisan and institutional forces. In particular, the
confirmation process itself takes longer when the president's party does not control
the Senate, when the Senate Judiciary Committee and the president have distinct
policy preferences, and in the case of lower federal courts when home-state senators
oppose the nominee. They also show that when a seat on the bench is most likely to
affect the ideological balance of a court, the confirmation process is more contentious
(see Binder and Maltzman 2009; Moraski and Shipan 1999; Lemieux and Stewart 1988;
Ruckman 1993).

The Senate and Supreme Court confirmations

The Supreme Court nomination and confirmation process is even more politicized.
Having politicized nominations is not novel (Abraham 1999; Maltese 1995; Yalof
1999), but the current period is likely among the most politicized. Most point to
the Bork nomination as a point-of-no-return as interest groups learned to enter
the debate with full force and now feel they cannot do otherwise lest the other side
dominate the story.

Political scientists have developed a set of tools to structure how we think about the
influence of the Senate on Court nominations. Moraski and Shipan (1999) develop
a model in which the president moves first to choose a nominee with a known
ideal point in one-dimensional liberal–conservative space. The Senate then decides
whether to accept or reject the nominee. The model provides different predictions
for nominees for three distinct configurations of presidential and Senate preferences
relative to the status quo or reversion point, which is defined as the median of
the returning eight-person court. There is *deadlock* when the president and Senate
want to move policy in opposite directions. In this case the predicted outcome is a
nominee with an ideology at the status quo. The president is *unconstrained* when the
president is closer to the status quo than the Senate, or when the Senate is closer

to the status quo but even closer to the president. In these situations, the predicted nominee ideology is the same as the president's ideal point. The president is *partially constrained* when the president and Senate want to move policy in the same direction, but the Senate is closer to the status quo than to the president. In this case, the Senate's indifference point is the predicted outcome.

The Moraski and Shipan model helps us understand many aspects of the nomination process. One is that not all nominations are equally contentious. The Senate confirmed Justice Scalia with no votes against and a year later Robert Bork, a nominee with similar background and views as Scalia, was blocked in an epochal battle. What accounted for the difference? Scalia was (effectively) replacing Chief Justice Burger (as Justice Rehnquist was moved to Chief Justice and Scalia took the open seat), a conservative justice. In the Moraski and Shipan model, we see that replacing a conservative with a conservative would have no impact and liberals would have little to gain by blocking Scalia. Bork, however, was nominated to replace a moderate, Justice Powell; replacing him with a conservative would move the median decisively, giving liberals strong reason to block Bork.

At the same time, the Moraski and Shipan model omits several factors that enter into the confirmation process. For starters, there is uncertainty about what any given nominee will do once on the court. For example, President Truman noted "packing the court simply can't be done...I've tried and it won't work...Whenever you put a man on the Supreme Court, he ceases to be your friend" (quoted in Tribe 1985, 51; for additional examples, see Segal, Timpone, and Howard 2000, 559). Bailey and Chang (2003) argue that this uncertainty gives presidents incentives to nominate more extreme individuals to the court, which in part may contribute to periods of polarization within the Court. Furthermore, actors other than the president, Senate median, and Court median may influence the process. As Johnson and Roberts (2005) have argued, for example, the filibuster pivot may play an important role (see also Rohde and Shepsle 2007). The previous median on the Court, rather than the median of the Court during a vacancy, might provide a more appropriate baseline (Krehbiel 2007; Zigerell 2010). The ideology of the departing justice may influence confirmation votes (Zigerell 2010), as may public opinion (Kastellec, Lax, and Phillips 2010). And both ideology and partisanship seem to be increasing in importance in recent years (Epstein et al. 2006; Shipan 2008). These and other studies provide numerous suggestions of the ways in which additional political factors can influence both the nomination and the confirmation process.

JUDICIAL ANTICIPATION OF CONGRESSIONAL REVIEW

It is also possible that Congress may be able to influence judicial decision-making in an ongoing manner. Judges may be so worried about congressional retaliation that they are reluctant to pursue policies that are unacceptable to elected officials. This view suggests that justices are constrained because the Court is embedded in a separation-of-powers game (Murphy 1964; Eskridge 1991; Ferejohn and Shipan 1990; Ferejohn and Weingast 1992; Ferejohn 1999; Gely and Spiller 1990; Spiller and Gely 1992; Eskridge, Ferejohn, and Gandhi 2002).[9] Rather than viewing justices as independent, separation-of-powers models suggest that the Supreme Court will anticipate the reactions of Congress and craft its statutory interpretation decisions so that they will not be overturned. According to Baum, when Justices understand that their interpretation would provoke a congressional override,

justices modify their interpretations to avoid that result. By making implicit this compromise with Congress, the justices could get the possible result under the circumstances: not the interpretation of a statute that they favor most, but one that is closer to their preferences than the new statute that Congress would enact to override the Court's decision. (Baum 2007, 147).

Baum's view is consistent with Murphy's claim that justices pursue a "broad range of strategic or at least tactical advantages" in "situation[s] in which [their] objections would be threatened by programs currently being considered seriously in the legislative or executive branches of government" (Murphy 1964, 156).

Separation-of-powers models contradict Segal and Spaeth's attitudinal model that has figured extremely prominently in the Court literature (Maltzman, Spriggs, and Wahlbeck 1999; Brenner and Whitmeyer 2009). Whereas the attitudinal model is based upon the premise that constitutional safeguards such as lifetime appointments and a guaranteed salary enable judges to pursue their personal policy preferences, separation-of-powers models are based upon the assumptions that judges realize the limits of the constitutional protections.

Separation-of-powers models are built on two pillars. One pillar is the notion that justices fear the sanctions that the elected branches can impose on the Court and its justices. Elected branches can overturn the Court's rulings through statutory revisions or constitutional amendment, and they can sanction the Court by engaging in "Court-curbing" actions, such as curtailing its jurisdiction, limiting its budget, manipulating the size of the bench, or even impeaching justices (Murphy 1964; Cross and Nelson 2001; Rosenberg 1991; Toma 1991; McNollgast 1995; Friedman 1990, 1998; Ferejohn 1999; Peretti 1999; Epstein, Knight, and Martin 2004; Barnes 2004; Clark 2009).

The other pillar is the notion of anticipated reaction. According to this view, fear of potential sanctions induces justices to take into account legislative and executive preferences when making their decisions. Justices, like all strategic actors, are forward-looking individuals who base their decisions in part upon expectations about how others will respond to their choices. As a result, the rarity of formal sanctions is not seen as an indication that the Court has no need to fear the elected branches. As

---

[9] Ironically, the separation-of-powers model is rooted in the notion of checks and balances, rather than the separation of powers.

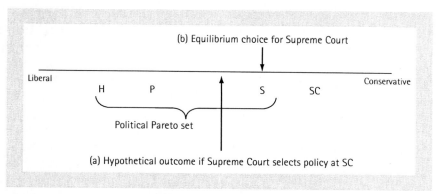

Fig. 36.1. Judicial outcomes under separation–of–powers model

Paretti explains, "The 'rule of anticipated reactions' is the typical manner in which political checks operate" (1999, 145).[10]

Figure 36.1 presents the logic of separation of powers models (Epstein and Knight 1998; Gely and Spiller 1990; Ferejohn and Shipan 1990). In the basic version of these models, actors have preferences that fall on a single dimension with the Court, House and Senate each represented by their median member. The Court (SC) in this example is outside of the elected branch "Pareto set" defined by the preferences of the House (H), Senate (S), and President (P).[11] If the Court were to rule in a manner that set policy at their ideal point, SC, all three elected players would be united in wanting to push policy to the left. If it were a statutory case, Congress and the President could simply pass legislation that would produce a policy at some other point.[12] In the figure, the location is at (a), a point relatively far from the desired policy of the Supreme Court median. Hence, a strategic Court selects the equilibrium outcome. In the figure, this is at the Senate's most preferred point. The exact location of the resulting policy would depend on the location of the status quo and the relative power of the elected branches, but it could be quite far from the Court's preferred policy. Thus, the strategic court identifies.

Skeptics of separation-of-powers models have raised questions about both pillars. In particular, they have argued that the Court has little ability to anticipate congressional reaction and little to fear from Congress (Segal 1997; Segal and Spaeth

---

[10] Although separation-of-powers models are based upon the notion that justices defer to Congress out of fear of congressional response, justices might also defer because of the value that they place on judicial restraint. Bailey and Maltzman (2010) demonstrate that legal doctrines are a constraint on Supreme Court decision-making.

[11] While Figure 36.1 is a simple version of the separation-of-powers model, more sophisticated versions take in legislative and constitutional features that empower specific members. For example, rather than assuming the Senate and House medians and the President define the Pareto set, one could alter the model by recognizing the pivotal role of those Senators whose support is needed to invoke cloture. Alternatively, one could take into account members of Congress who hold key leadership or committee positions. To simplify the presentation, we highlight the role of the median senator.

[12] If it were a constitutional case, elected officials could either punish the judiciary or if a supermajority of the House and Senate disagreed with the Court, they could begin the process of amending the Constitution.

2002; Brenner and Whitmeyer 2009). Therefore, they argue that the Court has no reason to allow congressional preferences to structure its decision-making. According to skeptics of the separation-of-powers models, judicial independence is protected because there are so many pivotal players (see note 7) that the set of Pareto optimal outcomes is likely to encompass the median justice (Krehbiel 1998; Ferejohn and Shipan 1990; Tsebelis 2002).[13] Judicial independence is further protected because building a winning coalition to overturn the Court is deemed to be too costly.

The costs that Congress incurs in overriding the court can take several forms (Segal and Spaeth 2002, 207). One cost is derived from the regular and frequent interactions between Congress and the Court. As Segal (1997) has put it, the assumption that Congress has "last licks" is simply false. If Congress attempts to sanction or override the Court, it has no idea if the Court will back down or if the Court will "go nuclear" via judicial review. A second cost stems from the idea that a large part (albeit not necessarily a majority) of the public values the concept of judicial independence. Given legislators' uncertainty about the public's views about judicial independence and about when the elected branches should intervene, members of Congress who might challenge court decisions may be uncertain about whether such intervention will cost them at the polls.[14] Likewise, many members of Congress understand the inherent risks associated with infringing upon judicial independence. If Congress does overturn the Court on a routine basis, future winning coalitions with different policy priorities may feel entitled to use the Court as a vehicle for undermining previously-enacted programs and policies. Such a dynamic would clearly limit legislators' abilities to lock-in policies over time.

Perhaps the most important costs pertain to the transaction costs associated with building a winning legislative coalition. These costs can be significant and can hinder Congress's capacity to curtail the court (Segal 1997). As Segal has noted, "even if the committee-gatekeeping or party-caucus model is a more accurate representation of the lawmaking process, and justices are often outside the set of Pareto optimals, sincere voting by justices may still be rational if there are high opportunity and/or transaction costs to passing legislation..." (1997, 42).

Even if Congress could efficiently overturn the Court and if the Court realized when this was likely, the extent of the constraint is limited by the fact that the Supreme Court is usually within the Pareto set of the elected branches. This is particularly true if one characterizes the legislative process as involving numerous pivotal actors

---

[13] The fact that justices are selected by the executive and legislative branches enhances the probability that judicial preferences will be acceptable to a pivotal player (Dahl 1957).

[14] Polls that were conducted immediately after Congress passed a bill that tried to circumvent judicial decisions that permitted Terry Schiavo's husband to disconnect the feeding tube from his wife who was in a vegetative state, illustrates the electoral hazards politicians encounter when they challenge the judiciary. According to a *Time* magazine poll (www.pollingreport.com) conducted March 22–24, 2005, 75 percent of the American public responded "not right" to the following poll question: "Regardless of your opinion on the Schiavo case, do you think it was right for Congress to intervene in this matter, or not?" The same poll had 54 percent of respondents select "less likely" when asked: "If your congressman voted to move the Schiavo case to the federal courts, would this make you more likely to vote for him or less likely?"

who effectively possess the ability to block legislative action. These would include chamber medians, committee chairs and medians and, in the case of the Senate, filibuster pivots (see, for example, Brady and Volden 1998; Krehbiel 1998; Ferejohn and Shipan 1990; Tsebelis 2002). Not surprisingly, studies of Congressional overrides of Supreme Court decisions suggest a weak relationship between the ideological congruence of the Court and Congress and congressional overrides (Hettinger and Zorn 2005). This suggests that preference-based models should not hold a monopoly in explaining the relationship between the courts and Congress (Ignagni, Meernik, and King 1998).

Empirical analysis of separation of powers models comes in two forms. The first is from case studies of instances in which the Supreme Court appeared to respond to political pressure, cases that include *Marbury v. Madison* (Knight and Epstein 1996; O'Brien 2000), *Ex parte Milligan* (Epstein and Knight 1998), and *West Coast Hotel Co. v. Parrish* (Leuchtenburg 1995; Oren 1995; Carson and Kleinerman 2002; but see White 2005). The last case is famously known as the "switch in time that saved nine" as the change of heart by the Court that led it to be more permissive toward Roosevelt's New Deal agenda may well have saved the court from Roosevelt's court-packing plan. Rosenberg (1992) examines periods of congressional hostility toward the Court and found that in six of nine periods the Court clearly moved in the direction desired by Congress.

The second type of empirical analysis has been quantitative. Here there have been two waves of research. The early wave put the theory to test using the measurement tools available at that time. While Spiller and Tiller (1992) found evidence consistent with congressional constraint on the court, Segal (1997) found none. Segal examined the voting record of each justice on an annual basis between 1947–1992 and assessed whether justices' voting on statutory civil liberties changed when their preferences fell outside a range that would be acceptable to pivotal players within Congress. One of the challenges is we need to know something about justices' actual preferences and then we need to compare them against observed behavior. Since we typically use observed behavior to infer preferences, this presents a bit of a quandary. Segal's key insight was to use judicial behavior on constitutional cases to measures of "true" (unconstrained) preferences and judicial behavior on statutory cases to measure possible constrained behavior. The limitation of this approach, of course, is that it assumes separation-of-powers theory only applies to statutory cases, something contested by many scholars (Harvey and Friedman 2006, 2009; Meernick and Ignagni 1997; Murphy 1964).

One of the limitations of this generation of work was that the preference measurement technology had not caught up to the demands of separation of powers theory.[15] The theory unqualifiedly requires inferences about preference differences across institutions; however, the state of measurement at the time offered no statisti-

---

[15] A related point is that, as Spriggs and Sala demonstrate, empirical work needs to be tied more closely to the underlying theoretical models.

cally defensible way to calibrate preferences across institutions, a fact well-appreciated by scholars involved in the literature (see, e.g., Segal 1997, 36).[16]

Bailey (2007) provided an approach that yielded preferences that were comparable across institutions. Building on Bailey and Chang (2001), he incorporated an extensive and substantially original data set of observations of presidents and members of Congress taking positions on Supreme Court cases. That is, by including, for example, Senators taking positions on Supreme Court cases via amicus briefs and statements on the floor, the differences across institutions could be pinned down.

The next generation of the literature used such improved preference measures to reevaluate separation-of-powers theory. Bailey and Maltzman (2010) conducted two tests. First, following Segal (1997) they assessed whether justices were constrained on statutory cases. Inter-institutional preferences based only on constitutional cases were used to generate "true" preferences needed to assess whether the Court was in or out of the political Pareto set. Their approach also was able to build on techniques from Bailey and Maltzman (2008) so as to control for individual justice level differences in how they value precedent, deference to Congress, and free speech rights. They found that twelve of the twenty-five justices from 1950 to 2008 for whom adequate data existed were significantly more likely to be more conservative when the political Pareto set was conservative and vice versa. These justices spanned the ideology spectrum from Warren, Brennan, Fortas, Douglas, Stevens, on the left to Souter, Stewart, Powell, O'Connor in the middle and Kennedy, Scalia, and Thomas on the right.

But since many believe that the ability of Congress to retaliate against the Court and its justices for its constitutional decisions could also lead to separation-of-powers constraints applying on constitutional cases. In this instance, the Segal approach to identifying the constraints will not work. Bailey and Maltzman (2010) therefore looked at all instances of major election shifts, which could lead to a change in the political Pareto set. If justices were constrained, they should become more liberal after a Democratic victory as either a conservative constraint is removed or a liberal constraint is imposed; justices should become more conservative after a Republican victory as either a liberal constraint is removed or a conservative constraint is imposed. But since justices could move in the direction of an election victory due to general changes in political views, Bailey and Maltzman look for justices to move relative to members of Congress. That is, they look for justices to shift not only to the right after Republicans win the presidency, but to jump over some Republican members of Congress. For example, before the 1980 election, Justice Rehnquist was to the left of Senator Stennis; after the election, which undid a liberal political constraint on the court, Rehnquist was to the right of Senator Stennis.

---

[16] Other concerns centered on the use of Segal–Cover scores that are fixed for each justice across their entire career. Considerable evidence exists that justices' preferences vary over time (Bailey 2007). In addition, assessing cross-time variation is difficult; Bailey (2007) shows that the widely used Martin and Quinn (2002) scores imply that the Court median was as conservative in 1973 when it decided *Roe* as it was in the heyday of the Rehnquist Court. By using cross-time bridging observations, Bailey (2007) develops scores that do not exhibit such anomalies.

Across six major shifts in the political Pareto set associated with changes in presidency, justices moved significantly in the expected direction more often than not. In some cases the pattern was extremely strong, such as 1980 when all justices moved in the expected direction. And, the movement was as strong or stronger on salient cases, which would be expected given separation of powers theory and the critiques of it with regard to congressional interest and capacity to act.

The literature has also dealt in a sophisticated manner with other inferential challenges. One is agenda bias. If justices are smart, they should shy away from taking on cases on which they should be constrained. Hence, we may not even "see" the cases on which constraint is strongest. Therefore Harvey and Friedman (2006) focus on laws passed by Congress and assess whether the Court is more likely to overturn a given law if the Court is inside or outside the Pareto set central to the separation of powers theory. They find that laws enacted by Congress between 1987 and 2000 were significantly more likely to be declared unconstitutional and argue that this was related to the degree of constraint imposed on the Court by Congress on Constitutional cases.[17] Harvey and Friedman (2009) followed up to show that the Court's docket is less likely to include cases where there are large deviations between what the Court would like to do, and what separation of powers theory predicts it can do in its final rulings.

Not only may justices be forced to do what Congress wants by political reality, they sometimes try to push things back on Congress. Hausegger and Baum (1999) show that 7 percent of majority decisions by the Supreme Court have some kind of invitation to Congress to relegislate on some point. Such invitations take the form of majority opinion language suggesting a congressional override in the form of a statutory clarification (Hausegger and Baum 1999). This behavior implies that the Court feels some constraints such that it would rather Congress dealt with a policy. It also points to an ongoing interactive relationship consistent with the coordinate construction literature we began by discussing.

THE WAY FORWARD

Scholars, like members of Congress, federal judges, and those who authored the United States Constitution, understand that it is possible for the judiciary to shape policy outcomes and for Congress to infringe upon judicial independence. But how these understandings translate into political behavior is murky at best. This murkiness stems from three central causes. First, the relationship has evolved over time. Second, the relationship is multifaceted. It involves questions of how judges make

---

[17] Although the find has a statistically significant effect, it is worth noting that the substantive effect is small.

decisions, legislators debate and write statutes, and even confirmation politics. Third, empirical analysis has been constrained by inferential challenges ranging from difficulty of working with complex theories to lack of data to lack of appropriate measures. Political scientists have made considerable progress in dealing with these challenges and can now identify with more confidence several aspects of the interaction between the courts and Congress.

However, all is not known and three other factors may make it difficult to fully understand the relationship between Congress and the courts. First, relationships are highly contextual and diverse. This is always true in any political system, but even more true with regard to the Court where life-tenure and other institutional safeguards give actors more latitude to act independently. Such independence can lead to autonomy and rejection of inappropriate political interference (as was the intent), but it can also lead to simple idiosyncrasy. Bailey and Maltzman (2010) show substantial evidence of heterogeneity across justices in whether they are bound by legal factors and, if so, which ones. They also show that not all justices are equally influenced by Congress; political prudence is not a trait that is served in equal portions to all justices.

A second, and related, point is that both Congress and the Supreme Court are collegial bodies made up of multiple members and employ procedures that do not consistently empower any particular member. Committees, party leaders, filibuster pivots, chamber medians, opinion authors, the Chief Justice, and the bench median all have power in particular instances. Likewise, the judiciary is made up of judges who occupy different levels of Court and who approach their responsibilities differently, and Congress is made up of both members of the House and Senate. Although many of the theoretical models exploring the relationship between the courts and Congress portray the institutions as unitary actors neither institution really fits this bill.

Third, efforts to understand the relationship that exists between Congress and the courts need to recognize that a bi-institution portrait is underspecified. Understanding how Congress responds to the judiciary can only be done while taking into account the relationships that exist between Congress, the courts, other government entities (such as the bureaucracy), and non-government actors. Looking at the relationship between Congress and the courts in isolation misses an important part of the story. For example, elected officials may resist overturning a court decision to avoid an unfavorable public response. Such a possibility is a reasonable concern since the courts are typically viewed favorably by the American public and congressional intervention is frequently unpopular. As a result, politicians may be reluctant to incur the electoral costs associated with overturning the Court. Likewise, looking at the relationship between Congress and the courts without considering the distribution of power within Congress might also miss a key part of the story. For example, the courts have the capacity to ensure compliance with the law and to be a healthy check on a federal agency. The value of this check might depend upon both the preferences of the agency and the executive and on the relationship between the committee that oversees the agency and Congress as a whole.

Almost thirty years ago, Gibson (1983) made a plea to be more sensitive to the microlevel links between the Court and the broader political environment. Rather than testing separation of powers by examining the Court as a whole, Gibson made a case for studying the decisions of individual justices. Rather than ignoring environmental constraints, Gibson called for an approach that recognized that individuals make decisions "within the context of group, institutional, and environmental constraints." Claims that the Court as a whole is either constrained by Congress or is purely independent potentially miss substantial and systematic justice-level and case-level variation in judicial outcomes. The bottom line is that inter-branch relations are complicated, and it is this complication that provides scholars both the greatest challenge and the greatest opportunity.

REFERENCES

ABRAHAM, H. 1999. *Justices, Presidents and Senators: A History of the U.S. Supreme Court Appointments from Washington to Clinton.* Lanham, MD: Rowman and Littlefield.

ACKERMAN, B. 1991. *We the People: Foundations.* Cambridge, MA: Harvard University Press.

BAILEY, M. A. 2007. Comparable Preference Estimates across Time and Institutions for the Court, Congress and Presidency. *American Journal of Political Science,* 51: 433–48.

——and CHANG, K. 2001. Comparing Presidents, Senators, and Justices: Inter-institutional Preference Estimation. *Journal of Law, Economics and Organization,* 17: 477–506.

——and CHANG, K. 2003. Extremists on the Court: The Inter-Institutional Politics of Supreme Court Appointments. Manuscript, Georgetown University.

——and MALTZMAN, F. 2008. Does Legal Doctrine Matter? Unpacking Law and Policy Preferences on the U.S. Supreme Court. *American Political Science Review,* 102: 369–84.

——and MALTZMAN, F. 2011. *The Constrained Court: Law, Politics, and the Decisions Justices Make.* Princeton University Press.

BARNES, J. 2004. *Overruled? Legislative Overrides, Pluralism and Contemporary Court-Congress Relations.* Stanford: Stanford University Press.

BAUM, L. 2007. *The Supreme Court,* 9th edn. Washington, DC: CQ Press.

——2011. *Specializing the Courts.* Chicago, IL: University of Chicago Press.

BELKIN, DOUGLAS. 2004. Scalia Decries Judicial Activism in Harvard Talk. *Boston Globe,* September 29.

BINDER, S. A., and SMITH, S. S. 1997. *Politics or Principle? Filibustering in the United States Senate.* Washington, DC: Brookings Institution.

——and MALTZMAN, F. 2002. Senatorial Delay in Confirming Federal Judges, 1947–1998. *American Journal of Political Science,* 46(January): 190–9.

——and MALTZMAN, F. 2004. The Limits of Senatorial Courtesy. *Legislative Studies Quarterly* 24 (February): 5–22.

——and MALTZMAN, F. 2009. *Advice and Dissent: The Struggle to Shape the Federal Judiciary.* Washington, DC: Brookings Institution.

BLAZ, D. 2005. Nomination Could be Defining Moment for Bush. *Washington Post,* 2 July.

BRADY, D. W., and VOLDEN, C. 1998. *Revolving Gridlock: Politics and Policy from Carter to Clinton.* Boulder, CO: Westview Press.

BRENNER, S., and WHITMEYER, J. M. 2009. *Strategy on the United States Supreme Court.* New York: Cambridge University Press.

BURKE, THOMAS. 2004. *Lawyers, Lawsuits, and Legal Rights: The Battle over Litigation in American Society.* Berkeley, CA: University of California Press.

CARP, R. A., MANNING, K. L., and STIDHAM, R. 2004. The Decision-making Behavior of George W. Bush's Judicial Appointees. *Judicature,* 88: 20–8.

CARSON, J. L., and KLEINERMAN, B. A. 2002. A Switch in Time Saves Nine: Institutions, Strategic Actors, and FDR's Court-Packing Plan. *Public Choice,* 113 (December): 301–24.

CASS, R. A. 1989. Review, Enforcement, and Power under the Communications Act of 1934: Choice and Change in Institutional Design, pp. 79–96 in *A Legislative History of the Communications Act of 1934,* ed. M. D. Paglin. New York: Oxford University Press.

CHASE, H. W. 1972. *Federal Judges: The Appointing Process.* Minneapolis: University of Minnesota Press.

CLARK, T. S. 2009. The Separation of Powers, Court-curbing and Judicial Legitimacy. *American Journal of Political Science,* 53: 971–89.

CROSS, F. B., and NELSON, B. J. 2001. Strategic Institutional Effects on Supreme Court Decision-making. *Northwestern University Law Review,* 95: 1437–94.

DAHL, R. 1957. Decision-making in a Democracy: The Supreme Court as National Policy Maker. *Journal of Public Law,* 6: 279–95.

DEVINS, N., and FISHER, L. 2004. *The Democratic Constitution.* New York: Oxford University Press.

EPSTEIN, L., and KNIGHT, J. 1998. *The Choices Justices Make.* Washington, DC: CQ Press.

—— KNIGHT, J., and MARTIN, A. 2004. Constitutional Interpretation from a Strategic Perspective, pp. 170–188 in *Making Policy: Making Law,* ed. M. C. Miller and J. Barnes. Washington, DC: Georgetown University Press.

—— LINDSTADT, R., SEGAL, J. A., and WESTERLAND, C. 2006. The Changing Dynamics of Senate Voting on Supreme Court Nominees. *Journal of Politics,* 68: 296–307.

—— and SEGAL, J. A. 2005. *Advice and Consent: The Politics of Judicial Appointments.* New York: Oxford University Press.

—— and SEGAL, J. A., SPAETH, H. J., and WALKER T. J. 2003. *The Supreme Court Compendium: Data, Decisions, and Developments.* Washington, DC: CQ Press.

ESKRIDGE, W. 1991. Overriding Supreme Court Statutory Interpretation Decisions. *Yale Law School Journal,* 101: 331–65.

—— and FEREJOHN, J. 1992. The Article I, Section 7 Game. *Georgetown Law Journal,* 80: 523–64.

—— FEREJOHN, J., and GANDHI, N. 2002. Strategic Voting in the Supreme Court: Civil Rights, the Court and Congress in the 1970s and 1980s. Midwest Political Science Association Meetings.

FARHANG, S. 2009. Congressional Mobilization of Private Litigants: Evidence from the Civil Rights Act of 1991. *Journal of Empirical Legal Studies,* 6 (2009): 1–34.

FEREJOHN, J. 1999. Independent Judges, Dependent Judiciary: Explaining Judicial Independence. *Southern California Law Review,* 72 (January–March): 353–84.

—— 2002. Judicializing Politics, Politicizing Law. *Law and Contemporary Problems,* 65(3): 41–68.

—— and SHIPAN, C. 1990. Congressional Influence on Bureaucracy. *Journal of Law, Economics, and Organization,* 6 (Special Issue): 1–20.

—— and WEINGAST, B. 1992. A Positive Theory of Statutory Interpretation. *International Journal of Law and Economics,* 12: 263–79.

FIORINA, M. 2006. *Culture War? The Myth of a Polarized Electorate*, 2nd edn. New York: Pearson Longman.

FISHER, L. 1988. *Constitutional Dialogues: Interpretation as a Political Process*. Princeton, NJ: Princeton University Press.

FRIEDMAN, B. 1990. A Different Dialogue: The Supreme Court, Congress and Federal Jurisdiction. *Northwestern University Law Review*, 85: 1–61.

—— 1998. The History of the Countermajoritarian Difficulty, Part One: The Road to Judicial Supremacy. *New York University Law Review*, 73: 333–433.

—— 2006. Taking Law Seriously. *Perspectives on Politics*, 4: 261–76.

GANT, S. E. 1997. Judicial Supremacy and Nonjudicial Interpretation of the Constitution. *Hastings Constitutional Law Quarterly*, 24: 359–440.

GELY, R., and SPILLER, P. 1990. A Rational Choice Theory of Supreme Court Statutory Decisions with Applications to the State Farm and Grove City Cases. *Journal of Law, Economics and Organization*, 6: 263–300.

GIBSON, J. L. 1983. From Simplicity to Complexity: The Development of Theory in the Study of Judicial Behavior. *Political Behavior*, 5(1): 7–49.

GOLDMAN, S. 1997. *Picking Federal Judges: Lower Court Selection from Roosevelt through Reagan*. New Haven, CT: Yale University Press.

GRABER, M. A. 1993. The Nonmajoritarian Difficulty: Legislative Deference to the Judiciary. *Studies in American Political Development*, 7: 35–73.

HARRIS, J. P. 1953. *The Advice and Consent of the Senate*. Berkeley: University of California Press.

HARVEY, A., and FRIEDMAN, B. 2006. Pulling Punches: Congressional Constraints on the Supreme Court's Constitutional Rulings, 1987–2000. *Legislative Studies Quarterly*, 31: 533–62.

—— 2009. Ducking Trouble: Congressionally Induced Selection Bias in the Supreme Court's Agenda. *Journal of Politics*, 71: 574–92.

HAUSEGGER, L., and BAUM, L. 1999. Inviting Congressional Action: A Study of Supreme Court Motivations in Statutory Interpretation. *American Journal of Political Science*, 43(1): 162–85.

HETTINGER, V. A., and ZORN, C. 2005. Explaining the Incidence and Timing of Congressional Responses to the U.S. Supreme Court. *Legislative Studies Quarterly*, 30(1): 5–28.

IGNAGNI, J., MEERNIK, J., and KING, K. L. 1998. Statutory Construction and Congressional Response. *American Politics Research* 26(4) 459–84.

JOHNSON, T. R., and ROBERTS, J. M. 2005. Pivotal Politics, Presidential Capital, and Supreme Court Nominations. *Congress and the Presidency*, 32(1): 31–48.

KAGAN, R. 2001. *Adversarial Legalism: The American Way of Law*. Cambridge, MA: Harvard University Press.

KASTELLEC, L., LAX, J. R., and PHILLIPS, J. 2010. Public Opinion and Senate Confirmation of Supreme Court Nominees. *Journal of Politics*, 72: 767–84.

KATZMANN, R. 1997. *Courts and Congress*. Washington, DC: Brookings Institution.

—— 1988. *Judges and Legislators: Toward Institutional Comity*. Washington, DC: Brookings Institution.

KLOTZ, R. 2004. The Nuclear Option for Stopping Filibusters. *PS: Political Science and Politics*, 37 (October): 843–5.

KNIGHT, J., and EPSTEIN, L. 1996. On the Struggle for Judicial Supremacy. *Law and Society Review*, 30: 87–120.

KOGER, G. 2010. *Filibustering: A Political History of Obstruction in the House and Senate*. Chicago, IL: University of Chicago Press.

KREHBIEL, K. 1998. *Pivotal Politics: A Theory of U.S. Lawmaking*. Chicago: University of Chicago Press.

—— 2007. Supreme Court Appointments as a Move-the-Median Game. *American Journal of Political Science*, 51(2): 231–40.

LEMIEUX, P. H., and STEWART, III, C. H. 1988. Advise? Yes. Consent? Maybe. Senate Confirmation of Supreme Court Nominations. Presented at the annual meeting of the American Political Science Association, Washington, DC.

LEUCHTENBURG, W. E. 1995. *The Supreme Court Reborn: The Constitutional Revolution in the Age of Roosevelt*. New York: Oxford University Press.

LEVIN, R. M. 1983. Review of "Jurisdictional" Issues under the Bumpers Amendment. *Duke Law Journal*, 1983(2): 355–87.

LIGHT, P. 1992. *Forging Legislation*. New York: W.W. Norton.

LOVELL, G. I. 2003. *Legislative Deferrals: Statutory Ambiguity, Judicial Power, and American Democracy*. New York: Cambridge University Press.

MALTESE, J. 1995. The Selling of Supreme Court Nominees. Baltimore, MD: Johns Hopkins University Press.

MALTZMAN, F., SPRIGGS, J. F., and WAHLBECK, P. J. 1999. "Strategy and Judicial Choice: New Institutionalist Approaches to Supreme Court Decision-making," pp. 43–64 in *Supreme Court Decision-making: New Institutionalist Approach*, ed. C.W. Clayton and H. Gillman. Chicago, IL: University of Chicago.

MARTIN, A., and QUINN, K. 2002. Dynamic Ideal Point Estimation via Markov Chain Monte Carlo for the U.S. Supreme Court, 1953–1999. *Political Analysis*, 10(2): 134–53.

MARTIN, A. D. 2006. Statutory Battles and Constitutional Wars: Congress and the Supreme Court, pp. 3–23 in *Institutional Games and the U.S. Supreme Court*, ed. J. R. Bond, R. B. Flemming, and J. R. Rogers. Charlottesville: University of Virginia Press.

MARTINEK, W. L., KEMPER. M., and VAN WINKLE, S. R. 2002. To Advise and Consent: The Senate and Lower Federal Court Nominations, 1977–1998. *Journal of Politics*, 62(2): 337–61.

McNOLLGAST. 1995. Politics and the Courts: A Positive Theory of Judicial Doctrine and the Rule of Law. *Southern California Law Review*, 68: 1631–82.

MEERNIK, J., and IGNAGNI, J. 1997. Judicial Review and Coordinate Construction of the Constitution. *American Journal of Political Science*, 41: 447–67.

MORASKI, B., and SHIPAN, C. 1999. The Politics of Supreme Court Nominations: A Theory of Institutional Constraints and Choices. *American Journal of Political Science*, 43: 1069–95.

MURPHY, W. 1964. *Elements of Judicial Strategy*. Chicago, IL: University of Chicago Press.

NEMACHEK, C. 2008. *Strategic Selection*. Charlottesville: University of Virginia Press.

NIXON, D. C., and GOSS, D. L. 2001. Confirmation Delay for Vacancies on the Circuit Courts of Appeals. *American Politics Research*, 29(3): 246–74.

O'BRIEN, D. M. 2000. *Storm Center: The Supreme Court in American Politics*, 6th edn. New York: W. W. Norton & Company.

OREN, K. 1995. The Primacy of Labor in American Constitutional Development. *American Political Science Review*, 88(2): 377–88.

PERETTI, T. J. 1999. *In Defense of a Political Court*. Princeton, NJ: Princeton University Press.

PICKERILL, J. M. 2004. *Constitutional Deliberation in Congress: The Impact of Judicial Review in a Separated System*. Durham, NC: Duke University Press.

POOLE, K. 2005. Description of NOMINATE data. http://voteview.com/page2a.htm.

—— and ROSENTHAL, H. 1997. *Congress: A Political-Economic History of Roll Call Voting*. Oxford: Oxford University Press.

PRIMO, D. M., BINDER, S. A., and MALTZMAN, F. 2008. Who Consents? Competing Pivots in Federal Judicial Selection. *American Journal of Political Science*, 52 (July): 471–89.

RICHARDS, M. J., and KRITZER, H. 2002. Jurisprudential Regimes in Supreme Court Decision Making. *American Political Science Review*, 96: 305–20.

—— SMITH, J. L., and KRITZER, H. M. 2006. Does Chevron Matter? *Law and Policy* 28: 444–69.

RING, R. 2004. Tipping the scales. *High Country News*, 16 February.

ROGERS, J. 2001. Information and Judicial Review: A Signaling Game of Legislative-Judicial Interaction. *American Journal of Political Science*, 45(January): 84–99.

ROHDE, D. W., and SHEPSLE, K. A. 2007. Advising and Consenting in the 60-Vote Senate: Strategic Appointment to the Supreme Court. *Journal of Politics*, 69(3): 664–77.

ROSENBERG, G. 1991. *The Hollow Hope: Can Courts Bring about Social Change?* Chicago: University of Chicago Press.

—— 1992. Judicial Independence and the Reality of Political Power. *Review of Politics*, 54: 369.

RUCKMAN, P. J. 1993. The Supreme Court, Critical Nominations, and the Senate Confirmation Process. *Journal of Politics*, 55: 793–805.

SCHERER, N., BARTELS, B., and STEIGERWALT, A. 2008. Sounding the Fire Alarm: The Role of Interest Groups in the Lower Federal Court Confirmation Process. *Journal of Politics*, 70(4): 1026–39.

SEGAL, J. 1997. Separation of Powers Games in the Positive Theory of Congress and Courts. *American Political Science Review*, 91: 28–44.

—— and COVER, A. 1989. Ideological Values and the Votes of U.S. Supreme Court Justices. *American Political Science Review*, 91: 28–44.

—— TIMPONE, R., and HOWARD, R. 2000. Buyer Beware? Presidential Success through Supreme Court Appointments. *Political Research Quarterly*, 53(3): 557–95.

—— and SPAETH, H. J. 2002. *The Supreme Court and the Attitudinal Model Revisited*. New York: Cambridge University Press.

—— WESTERLAND, C., and LINDQUIST, S. 2007. Congress, the Supreme Court and Judicial Review. Paper presented at Annual Meeting of Midwest Political Science Association.

SHIPAN, C. R. 1997a. *Designing Judicial Review: Interest Groups, Congress, and Communications Policy*. Ann Arbor: University of Michigan Press.

—— 1997b. Interest Groups, Judicial Review, and the Origins of Broadcast Regulation. *Administrative Law Review*, 49(3): 549–84.

—— 2000. The Legislative Design of Judicial Review: A Formal Analysis. *Journal of Theoretical Politics*, 12(3): 269–304.

—— 2008. Partisanship, Ideology, and Senate Voting on Supreme Court Nominees. *Journal of Empirical Legal Studies*, 5(1): 55–76.

—— and SHANNON, M. 2003. Delaying Justice(s): A Duration Model of Supreme Court Confirmations. *American Journal of Political Science*, 47(4): 654–68.

SILVERSTEIN, G. 2009. *Law's Allure: How Law Shapes, Constrains, Saves, and Kills Politics.* New York: Cambridge University Press.

SLOTNICK, E. 1988. Federal Judicial Recruitment and Selection Research: A Review Essay. *Judicature*, 71: 317–24.

SMITH, J. 1997. Congressional Management of Judicial Policy Making: The Case of Environmental Policy. Paper presented at the annual meeting of the Midwest Political Science Association, Chicago, IL.

—— 1998. An Emprical Test of Congressional Control of Judicial Review. Paper presented at the annual meeting of the Midwest Political Science Association, Chicago, IL.

SPILLER, P., and GELY, R. 1992. Congressional Control or Judicial Independence: The Determinants of U.S. Supreme Court Labor-Relations Decisions, 1949–1988. *RAND Journal of Economics*, 23: 463–92.

SPILLER, P. T., and TILLER, E. H. 1997. Decision Costs and the Strategic Design of Administrative Process and Judicial Review. *Journal of Legal Studies*, 26: 347–70.

TOMA, E. F. 1991. Congressional Influence and the Supreme Court: The Budget as a Signaling Device. *Journal of Legal Studies*, 20: 131–46.

TRIBE, L. 1985. *God Save This Honorable Court: How the Choice of Supreme Court Justices Shapes Our History*. New York: Random House.

TSEBELIS, G. 2002. *Veto Players: How Political Institutions Work*. Princeton, NJ: Princeton University Press.

United States, Department of Commerce. 2000. *Statistical Abstract of the United States*. Washington, DC: Government Printing Office.

WAWRO, G. J., and SCHICKLER, E. 2007. *Filibuster: Obstruction and Lawmaking in the U.S. Senate*. Princeton, NJ: Princeton University Press.

WHITE, E. G. 2005. Constitutional Change and the New Deal: The Internalist/Externalist Debate. *American Historical Review*, 110(4). http://www.historycooperative.org/journals/ahr/110.4/white.html.

WHITTINGTON, K. E. 2005. Hearing About the Constitution in Congressional Committees, pp. 87–109 in *Congress and the Constitution*, ed. N. Devins and K. E. Whittington. Durham, NC: Duke University Press.

——— 2007. *Political Foundations of Judicial Supremacy: The Presidency, the Court, and Constitutional Leadership in U.S. History*. Princeton, NJ: Princeton University Press.

——— 2009. Judicial Review of Congress before the Civil War. *Georgetown Law Journal*, 97: 1256–332.

YALOF, D. A. 1999. *Pursuit of Justices: Presidential Politics and the Selection of Supreme Court Nominees*. Chicago: University of Chicago Press.

ZIGERELL, L. J. 2010. Senator Opposition to Supreme Court Nominations: Reference Dependence on the Departing Justice. *Legislative Studies Quarterly*, 35: 393–416.

PART IX

REFLECTIONS

....

CHAPTER 37

REFLECTIONS ON THE STUDY OF CONGRESS 1969–2009

....

MORRIS P. FIORINA[*]

THE editors of this Handbook have invited two senior scholars to reflect on the study of Congress. Other than a word limit, the invitation offered no guidance about what was expected, perhaps reflecting a pessimistic belief that scholars our age tend to ignore such instructions anyway, or perhaps expressing a more optimistic hope that we might write something more interesting if unguided, than if guided. I will assume the latter more positive interpretation and hope that the editors' confidence is justified. On reflection I have decided to make no attempt at a comprehensive mulling-over of forty-odd years of work. Rather, I will write from the standpoint of one personally associated with a number of lines of research and one particular approach. This is certainly not to discount other lines of work and other approaches, but only to express my confidence that these will be adequately covered by the authors of the earlier chapters in this volume.

* I wish to thank Keith Krehbiel and Ken Shepsle for helpful comments and suggestions.

THE ROAD TO THE TEXTBOOK CONGRESS

My association with congressional studies began in the spring of 1969 when a dozen or so University of Rochester graduate students crowded into Richard Fenno's quasi-annual Congress seminar.[1] The literature was relatively sparse at the time, but growing rapidly. As Polsby and Schickler (2002) recount, political science as we know it today had only recently come to the study of Congress. Briefly summarizing their discussion, beginning in the 1950s a few empirically minded scholars with a behavioral orientation had moved into what previously had been a subfield, characterized more by evaluative and prescriptive than empirical work. Then around 1960 the fruits of the American Political Science Association Congressional Fellowship Program began to appear in the literature, and by the end of the decade the APSA Study of Congress Project was producing a rich scholarly return on its investment. Looking back it is clear to see how this first generation of research cumulated into what Shepsle (1989) later termed the "Textbook Congress," a stable, rule-bound institution inhabited by weak party leaders, strong full committee chairs, and a rank and file relatively unconstrained by constituents, parties, interest groups, and presidents, whose congressional careers advanced slowly and predictably through the inviolable operation of seniority.[2] By the time this portrait had become widely accepted it was already beginning to change, but we didn't know that at the time.[3] More on that below.

As I recall, the first two-thirds or so of Fenno's seminar was devoted to careful reading and evaluation of recently published books and articles. We discussed Bauer, Poole, and Dexter (1968) on interest groups, compared classic case studies like Stephen Bailey (1950) to the latest ones like Eidenberg and Morey (1969), learned all about norms in the Senate (Matthews 1960), the House Appropriations Committee (Fenno 1962), and the House Ways and Means Committee (Manley 1965). And we pored over historical articles by Bob Peabody, Nelson Polsby, Doug Price, and Rip Ripley. Although *Home Style* (Fenno 1978) was far in the future, Fenno had already begun thinking about representation, so we spent a session or two reading a thin and generally confusing literature on congressional and state legislative constituencies and elections, the starting point for what became my Ph.D. thesis (Fiorina 1974).

---

[1] Quasi-annual because Fenno seemed to spend a lot of time on leave, so the word among the graduate students was that whenever he offered the seminar, take it.

[2] See Chapter's 17, 18, 30, and 31, this volume. The usual qualification about the portrait applying primarily to the House and somewhat less to the Senate applies, of course.

[3] Like the oft-cited "traditional family," the textbook Congress was clearly an idealization; moreover, it may have held sway for a shorter period than we presume today. Schickler and Pearson (2009) report that in the late New Deal period intense ideological and partisan conflict and floor rejection of committee proposals were not uncommon. In retrospect the textbook Congress may have been an idealization of the Congress as it operated from the early 1950s to the late 1960s, another instance of Mayhew's (Chapter 38, this volume) "time localism."

This eclectic list of topics shows just how far the field has developed. Today scholars conduct entire seminars on several of the topics we covered in a week or two.[4]

In "The Institutionalization of the U.S. House of Representatives," Polsby (1968) advanced a sweeping evolutionary account of the House. His argument illustrates a style of thinking that was quite common in that era—a tendency to view the world in terms of (generally positive) continuous development toward some end, a progressive view of politics and society. Thus, earlier in the decade sociologists had pronounced the "end of ideology" (e.g. Bell 1960). Simplifying, in a world where the ends of foreign policy (the containment of Communism) and domestic policy (economic growth and prosperity) were consensual, the only remaining questions were ones of means. Pragmatic policymaking would replace ideological struggle. The kinds of ideological conflicts that had taken place in the advanced democracies in the first half of the twentieth century were things of the past. Later in the decade *Time* magazine noted that theologians were debating the question, "Is God Dead?" According to modernization theory, as societies developed economically and became more prosperous, and as education—especially science education—spread, the inevitable consequence was the fading away of traditional religion and the ascendance of secularization.

Polsby's argument was more specific and limited, of course. In order for democratically elected legislatures to retain legitimacy and perform the necessary functions of lawmaking and representation they must be institutionalized, where the latter term encompassed three major components. First, the legislature had to be bounded—differentiated from the rest of the political and societal environment. The chief indicator of such boundaries would be a stable membership, one characterized by low turnover and high tenure. Second, the legislature had to be internally differentiated, evidencing specialization and division of labor. The chief indicators of such differentiation in the U.S. House were the committee system, the formal party leadership structure, and the presence of staff and other support structures. Third, the legislature would operate according to automatic or universalistic procedures, rather than personal or political considerations. For example, members would advance to committee leadership positions via recognized and accepted procedures like seniority, rather than membership in one or another personal or political faction. Judged according to these criteria, the U.S. House of Representatives was clearly one of the most institutionalized legislatures in the world.

Polsby himself noted that curvilinearities in his data indicated that the process of institutionalization could reverse (and had, in the case of the Civil War era), but my sense is that there was a widespread, if unstated, view that the process of institutionalization was one of movement toward a teleological end, the textbook Congress in this case.[5] Few, if any of us, could have foreseen the "reform era" which was about to burst upon us, let alone a return to anything approaching the caucus

---

[4] And some of today's major topics were altogether missing from our reading list. For example, I don't recall that we spent any time on campaign finance.

[5] "As institutions grow, our expectations about the displacement of resources inward do give us warrant to predict that they will resist decay, but ... institutions are also continuously subject to

government days of the Woodrow Wilson Administration (Haines 1915), which the Republican Congresses of the post-reform era seemed to approach (Chapter 21, this volume).

As it turned out, developments beginning in the mid- to late 1960s were providing strong suggestions that pronouncements of the end of ideology were premature. And by the late 1970s it was clear that the same was true for pronouncements of the death of God. Similarly, within a few years of Fenno's 1969 seminar, developments in Congress provided the first indications that some aspects of institutionalization as Polsby had defined it indeed were reversing, and the textbook Congress was passing from the scene.

From inside to outside models

Among our seminar readings was a review of the legislative literature by Heinz Eulau and Katherine Hinckley (1966). Their review was organized under two major headings: the "inside model" and the "outside model," with subheads dealing with the major examples of each.[6] Studies that adopted the inside model explained features of congressional behavior and operation by reference to factors internal to the institution, especially the fellow members—not only the sticks and carrots controlled by party leaders and committee chairs, but the informal expectations of peers. Fenno's (1962) study of the norms constraining member behavior in the House Appropriations Committee at mid-century epitomized the inside model. Studies that adopted the outside model explained features of congressional behavior and operation by reference to factors outside the institution—chiefly political parties, interest groups, and constituents. Turner's (1951) detailed roll-call analyses that described, ethnic, racial, regional, and urban–rural constituency cleavages in roll-call voting epitomized the outside model.

Of course, some studies like Jones' (1961) analysis of agriculture policy in Congress did not fit neatly into one category or the other. Moreover, the object to be explained had much to do with whether a scholar took up an inside or outside model. If the goal was to account for the failure of an Appropriations Committee member to offer floor amendments to the Committee bill, inside factors obviously come first to mind. But if the goal was to explain why members from agricultural districts cast roll-call votes differently from their colleagues from urban districts, then outside factors just as obviously come primarily to mind.

---

environmental influence and their power to modify and channel that influence is bound to be less than all-encompassing." (Polsby 1968: 168).

[6] In a personal conversation decades later Eulau told me that this distinction originated with Polsby, but that a footnote crediting Polsby was edited out of the Eulau–Hinckley article during the publication process.

Still, I think that in addition to distinctions between the congressional dependent variables, a temporal trend was operating; namely, that the textbook Congress was increasingly subject to outside influences, so that over time the inside model came to explain less about congressional features of interest and the outside model more. The late 1960s and early 1970s was a time of great political upheaval. The surprising primary candidacy of George Wallace in 1964 showed the potency of the racial issue and its potential to split the New Deal Democratic Coalition. Bitter disagreement over the conduct of the Vietnam War and reaction to the rise of the counter-culture reinforced the racial split, enabling Republicans to reorient their appeal and make inroads into significant groups heretofore in the Democratic coalition—especially southern whites and northern blue-collar workers. The country saw the rise of new social movements and an "advocacy explosion" (Berry 1989). Journalists and political scientists described and decried the decomposition of the parties. Political scientists noticed the growth of an incumbency advantage (Erikson 1971; Mayhew 1974a), and more generally the rise of candidate-centered politics. This new, more fragmented, more conflictual political environment soon found a reflection in Congress. My recollection is that congressional scholars first noted unusually harsh words spoken in floor debate in the late 1960s, as well as increasing examples of declining deference to committees and declining committee cohesion (even in Appropriations!), but soon more systematic evidence began to accrue. Asher (1973) reported the erosion of some congressional norms. Less senior Democrats representing constituencies and interest groups disadvantaged in the textbook Congress forced major changes in the rules and internal power structure of Congress, changes carefully tracked by scholars such as David Brady, Joseph Cooper, Roger Davidson, Thomas Mann, Walter Oleszek, Norman Ornstein, David Rohde, and others (Chapters 30, 33, 21, this volume). By 1980 the emerging post-reform Congress looked quite different from the picture of the textbook Congress painted in the 1960s.

Shepsle argued that the textbook Congress reflected an equilibrium of geography, jurisdiction, and party. From the New Deal to the 1960s, the electoral landscape was fairly stable. With only short interruptions in 1946 and 1952, Democratic majorities controlled Congress, but the party was split between northern and southern wings, neither of which was strong enough to assert its will except to block legislation; southern Democrats and Republicans together could kill the more liberal initiatives of northern Democrats (Sundquist 1981). Most members came from safe districts. Internal processes reflected these electoral facts, and equilibrium prevailed. But this equilibrium began to give way in the 1970s, buffeted by demographic changes like the movement of African Americans from the South to the North; the growth of the Sunbelt (Polsby 2004); suburbanization (Fiorina and Abrams 2009); the reapportionment revolution (Ansolabehere and Snyder 2008); the rise of new interests (Berry 1989); and other factors, all of which changed the electoral environment. The result was a Congress whose members were less insulated from outside forces: internal processes were more open to the inspection of those forces, and internal operations were more susceptible to influence by those forces.

Thus, the increasing emphasis on the outside model was largely a reflection of the research agendas of congressional scholars, agendas that I have always felt follow what is actually transpiring in the real world to a greater degree than the agendas of many subfields of political science. When Congress appeared to be an elite men's (mostly) club whose members were, if not unworried, at least not terrified by constituents and interest groups, the language of the inside model—sociological and social-psychological concepts like role expectations, norms, and sanctions—seemed quite appropriate. But in the changed environment of the 1970s, when Congress appeared to have become an every man (still mostly) for himself collection of individual entrepreneurs, researchers soon reached for the language of economics.

FROM SOCIOLOGY TO ECONOMICS

Near the end of our seminar Fenno distributed draft chapters of what was to become *Congressmen in Committees* (1973), assigning us to read and come prepared to critically discuss the work next session. We eagerly took up the task. In forty years in the profession I have never since encountered anything approaching the level of arrogance that prevailed among Rochester graduate students of that era. After digesting the chapters the participants in our seminar collectively decided that they simply would not do. Heart-wrenching though it might be, it was our duty to save Fenno from the embarrassment of publishing the manuscript with its then-existing framework of member goals, committee goals, and policy outcomes.

On the appointed day we filed into the classroom and took our seats around the table, our mood somber in light of what must be done. Dave Rohde, one of our more senior members, took the lead. He patiently explained to Fenno that from social choice theory we knew that collectivities did not have goals, only individuals had goals.[7] Thus, the whole concept of committee goals must be excised from the manuscript. Others followed Rohde. I helpfully suggested that perhaps Fenno could reformulate committee goals as decision rules that the committee believed would maximize achievement of their individual goals in the legislative context. Someone else (Richard McKelvey?) suggested that committee goals could be viewed as coalition strategies that the committee members believed were optimal, given their environments. Showing his characteristic good humor Fenno absorbed our pious pronouncements with a bemused look on his face.

By the time *Congressmen in Committees* appeared several years later we had all left the scene, but we were elated on reading its now classic formulation

---

[7] Of course, under Arrow's (1951) theorem, a collectivity that was a dictatorship could have a well-defined preference ordering. But even in the era of strong full committees, no one believed that the chairs could be treated as dictators. As Krehbiel argued later, there is always a majoritarian "club behind the door."

of member goals/environmental constraints/strategic premises/decision-making processes/policy decisions. If the author of "The House Appropriations Committee as a Political System" could be turned to the rational choice side, the future looked bright; far brighter than we could imagine, as it turned out. A year later Mayhew (1974b) published his classic *Congress: The Electoral Connection* and the field has not been the same since. Mayhew's sweeping reformulation of the ever-accumulating literature under an informal rational choice framework, based on the single motivational assumption of reelection, took the congressional field by storm.

The behavioral movement that invaded the study of Congress in the 1950s and 1960s drew primarily on sociology and social-psychology for its core concepts. Scholars examined roles (e.g. Huitt 1961), norms and sanctions (e.g. Huitt 1957; Matthews 1960), and integration, conflict management, and socialization (e.g. Fenno 1962, 1965; Manley 1965, 1970). The explanatory frameworks in the background were those of small group and systems theories. By the late 1960s congressional scholars were beginning to find those frameworks inadequate, as illustrated by Fenno's move from an approach rooted in structural-functionalism and systems theory in his study of the House Appropriations Committee, to a more purposive goal-oriented framework in his comparative committee study.[8] Fenno's move was symptomatic of a more general move within the study of Congress. In the late 1960s rational choice ideas were virtually absent from the field; by the late 1970s a kind of informal "soft" rational choice approach had become a common, if not the most common, approach.[9]

As Polsby and Schickler note, the movement of rational choice ideas into the study of Congress reflected more general currents in political science, but it seems to me that there were two features of the move into congressional studies that were distinct. The first was the speed with which rational choice ideas took hold. The second was the peacefulness with which the intellectual transition occurred.

Anthony Downs published *An Economic Theory of Democracy* in 1957. This rational choice account of democratic politics and policymaking certainly had an impact, and was generally regarded as a provocative new take on the subject, but it did not become the most common approach to any of the subjects it addressed for nearly two decades. In contrast, within a few years Mayhew's mode of analyzing Congress had become the dominant mode. No doubt part of the explanation is simply that Downs proposed a theory of democracy, whereas Mayhew offered only a theory of Congress. Moreover, in addition to greater generality, some parts of Downs' subject, principally mass political behavior, have proved less amenable to rational choice analysis than Mayhew's subject of an institution containing a small number of professional politicians whose political lives were periodically at stake. But I think a larger part of the explanation was that the Congress that scholars were observing was clearly changing. During the "reform era" (Chapters 30 and 21, this volume) members transformed the textbook Congress in reaction to events and developments in their environment, and

---

[8] See the lengthy note 1 in his Introduction (1973, xvii).

[9] Formal rational choice models came somewhat later. Volden and Wiseman (Chapter 3, this volume) provide an excellent survey. I believe that the earliest attempt to bring some of the formal apparatus of rational choice theory to the study of Congress was Ferejohn (1974: Conclusion and Appendix 3).

the Congress that emerged in the post-reform era differed in significant ways from the pre-reform Congresses.

As is generally recognized, systems and related theories are not of much help in accounting for change. They offer mechanisms for system maintenance—socialization into patterns of norms and sanctions for those who violate them, for example. But they offer no explicit predictions for when individuals cease to follow the norms even under threat of sanction, or when individuals choose not to sanction violators and the norms change or disappear. In an era of ongoing change the frameworks used to describe the stable Congresses of the mid-century seemed less useful.

The individualistic rational choice model advanced by Mayhew filled the explanatory gap. The method fit the time. Above all, individual members desired to be reelected; hence, they would design the institution so as to maximize attainment of the reelection goal. When electoral conditions dramatically changed, as they had, one would expect members to remodel the institution. The outside world—Fenno's environmental constraints—was the engine of change. The equilibrium represented by the textbook Congress was upset and replaced by a new one when members found the old equilibrium no longer optimal for attaining their goals in a changed world.[10]

I don't have one simple hypothesis for how the transition from a sociological and social-psychological approach could happen with less intellectual conflict than in many other subfields, but there are several factors that probably contributed. One is the highly empirical orientation of those who study Congress. It has often been noted that the density of scholarly arguments about theories and approaches in a subfield is inversely related to the amount of data available (some subfields of International Relations, until recently, for example). When shown an approach that seemed to shed more explanatory light on an empirical question that intrigued them, congressional scholars did not hesitate to adopt it. Again, the method fit the time. Had Mayhew published in 1960, acceptance likely would have been slower.

A second contributing factor might be that adopting a rational choice framework did not require anyone to renounce their previous work or pull down the statues of earlier scholarly heroes. Most of the empirical findings in the subfield were susceptible to reinterpretation in rational choice terms. Shepsle's general portrayal of the textbook Congress as an equilibrium is an obvious example, but there are numerous much more specific reinterpretations as well. Weingast (1979) reformulated congressional norms like universalism and reciprocity as coalition strategies that overcame the instability of the distributive politics game. Krehbiel (1991) showed how specialization in committees could make perfect (rational) sense. Steve Smith (1989), and Gary Cox and Mat McCubbins (1993), offered a rich portrait of the role played by congressional rules and procedures.

---

[10] Brady and Epstein (1997) present an analogous explanation for the transition from the partisan Congress of the late nineteenth century to what became the textbook Congress, arguing that the revolt against central party leadership and the rise of seniority reflected rising electoral heterogeneity among members.

Still a third contributing factor is the most impressionistic and subjective, but I believe that it did play a role, and that is the stance of the senior leadership in the subfield. These senior scholars were generally open-minded to the newer approach, emphasizing that the goal was greater understanding of the Congress, not scoring academic points, and they set an example of professionalism for younger scholars. In the summer of 1974 I was fortunate to attend a large conference on Congress in Aspen, Colorado. For several days modelers, roll-call analysts, and soakers and pokers peacefully interacted with one another.[11] A lot of us left that conference with generally positive views of our fellow congressional scholars, whatever their methodological persuasions, and feeling that we would try to maintain the relationships established there. To a considerable degree I believe the research community succeeded. If one looks at the work of important senior congressional scholars today, and the students they have trained, one sees scholars who confidently use basic rational choice ideas in detailed empirical analysis of questions, some of which first arose during a more sociological era.[12]

One final point is especially important to those not familiar with the congressional literature of the past generation. The rapid spread of the rational choice approach in the study of Congress by no means came at the expense of intellectual homogenization. On the contrary, some of the most active debates in the contemporary literature have been conducted by scholars trained in the rational choice tradition. Do committees serve a distributive or informational function (Chapter 18, this, volume)? What is the nature of party influence and what is its source (Chapters 17 and 23, this volume)? Debates surrounding these and other questions do not pit rational choice scholars against scholars from other traditions; rather, they pit rational choice scholars against each other (e.g. Shepsle and Weingast 1995). The approach is sufficiently general that a variety of different, and at times conflicting, theories can be developed within it.

The normative question

Polsby and Schickler observe that pre-behavioral work on Congress was often critical of the institution. In particular, scholars bemoaned the absence of responsible parties in Congress, contrasting congressional operations unfavorably with the operation of the British House of Commons, the Mother of Parliaments. From Woodrow Wilson's *Congressional Government* (1885) to Burns' *The Deadlock of Democracy* (1963), scholars

[11] I can still remember overhearing a casual conversation between two of my senior colleagues during a break in the proceedings. They were pondering whether members of Congress were more concerned with maximizing their numerical vote or their probability of reelection. It made my head spin—the pages of Mayhew's book had barely cooled off by this time.

[12] I won't begin to try to name them all, but the *corpus* of Steve Smith and his students certainly deserves special mention, particularly since Smith himself was not trained in one of the original rational choice outposts.

decried the lack of congressional party discipline in general, and the failure of the congressional parties to follow presidential leadership in particular.

With few exceptions the behavioral generation was not critical of Congress. I think there were at least two reasons for this. One is that the first generation of behavioral scholars was very sensitive about their scientific *bona fides*. Scope and methods courses of the era discussed the fact-value dichotomy and how a genuinely scientific political science must be empirical, not normative.[13] Congressional scholars of the 1960s took pains to differentiate their enterprise from what had occupied most scholars of earlier generations. Accurate description and scientific explanation was the goal, not evaluation and prescription.

A second reason for the uncritical approach to the study of Congress is that congressional scholars of the 1960s seemed to have a genuine affection for Congress and its members. Fenno (1998) writes about "the Boys of Congress," a group of eight congressional scholars who had a grant to get together in Washington and (among other things) take Congressmen to dinner! In those days the pace of congressional life was slower and staffs were small (Clapp 1963). It was relatively easy to get an interview with a member, and my sense is that more scholars had personal acquaintances serving in Congress than is the case today. Congressional scholars of the time noted the benefits of incremental, as opposed to comprehensive, policymaking (Lindblom 1959). They viewed the willingness of members to "take half a loaf rather than none" as a positive orientation that contributed to incremental progress. And, in truth, it is arguable that with the glaring exception of racial issues, the behavioralists' stance was not unreasonable. As noted above, a post-war consensus reigned in foreign affairs, and Congressional Republicans had come to accept the fundamentals of New Deal social and economic policy. Incrementalism fit the time.

If the pre-behavioral generation of scholars criticized the failure of Congress to act decisively on major policy initiatives (developed by the president, of course), the behavioral generation noted that Congress did some things well—namely represent and respond to the diversity of interests in American democracy. An early example was Turner's (1951) critical response to the 1950 APSA report that advocated more responsible parties. Among other things Turner contended that the heterogeneity of interests in the country would lead to the demise of party competition in many areas where the national views of one party or the other were unacceptable.

But once again as times changed, scholarly views followed. The conflicts of the 1960s brought the long-suppressed racial issue to the fore and reignited socio-cultural issues that had been dormant for a generation. The environmental movement erupted. The post-war consensus on foreign and defense policy shattered in the aftermath of the Vietnam War. Stagflation and energy crises staggered the economy. And to many of us the Congress did not seem to respond well to these various challenges. Party cohesion had fallen to a level not seen since before the Civil War, and

---

[13] Many of us were taught what my colleague John Ferejohn called the "Joe Friday" approach to political science. Detective Friday was the principal character in the popular 1950s police show *Dragnet*. His mantra was "All we want are the facts, ma'am."

congressional politics seemed to have degenerated into a free-for-all of unprincipled bargaining in which participants blithely sacrificed general interests in their advocacy of particularistic constituency interests. President Jimmy Carter enjoyed large congressional majorities, but failed to deal effectively with the aforementioned problems, contributing to the view that national politics was in a sorry state.

True, the 1970s Congress was responsive, but to whom? Responsiveness to all the particularistic interests in the country did not guarantee responsiveness to the general interest; quite the contrary.[14] In many respects the congresses of the 1970s seemed to illustrate the collective action problem, an idea that rational choice scholars had imported into congressional studies. Each member doing what was individually in his or her interest produced a congressional product that did not serve the country's collective interest.

The result was a renewal of scholarly criticism of Congress. Larry Dodd (1977) propounded a cyclical theory in which congressional operations periodically deteriorated into the kind of unconstrained individual maximization that Mayhew posited, which resulted in bad public policy, popular disapproval, and finally a new majority party that would rejuvenate the institution—for a time.[15] I (Fiorina 1977) attacked the New Deal model of policymaking in which Congress would (should) pass general laws and delegate to an expert agency the task of implementing the specific policies. It seemed to me that the model had deteriorated to the point that its whole purpose had become the reelection of members who would claim credit for adopting policies while avoiding responsibility for their negative consequences, then intervene and claim credit again when the latter became apparent. The result was incoherent policy and electoral unaccountability. Even Fenno (1978, 168) struck a critical note when he concluded: "Members of Congress run for Congress by running against Congress. The strategy is ubiquitous, addictive, cost-free and foolproof. ... In the short run everybody plays and nearly everybody wins. Yet the institution bleeds from 435 separate cuts."

Evaluation and criticism of congressional procedures and policies became more common in the literature as scholars increasingly became willing to draw out the implications of their findings for representation, responsiveness, accountability, governance, efficiency, and other long-standing concerns in democratic theory. On balance, my view is that this is a good thing. In one way or another American society supports our research, so if that research has implications for improving the way society is governed, are we not professionally obligated to communicate it? In addition, there is the more practical question: if not us, whom? There are plenty of people with partisan and ideological axes to grind who do not hesitate to evaluate the Congress and prescribe "reforms." If more disinterested professionals who have

---

[14] The behavioral generation had read the concept of the public interest out of political science, of course, but however difficult it might be to define in principle, some of us in the next generation of scholars felt that it was often clear which interests were general and which were not.

[15] Arguably Dodd's prediction came true in 1994 and again in 2006.

specialized expertise refrain from joining the debate, whatever change occurs may be for the worse.[16]

I continue to believe, however, that it is critical to clearly separate partisan and ideological criticism from professional criticism that evaluates Congress against more abstract standards that transcend the partisan and ideological divisions of the time. Political theorists have been pondering the operation of representative institutions for centuries. Questions of governance v. responsiveness, distributive justice v. allocative efficiency, tradeoffs between particular and general and short and long term—these and others are fair game, and the study of Congress should include them as legitimate parts of the enterprise. In an era when even the mainstream media increasingly display identifiable partisan and ideological slants, there is a critical need for honest brokers. Given the partisan and ideological inclinations of most political scientists, it has undoubtedly been especially challenging to separate such perspectives from more general critical commentary on the operations of the Republican Congresses of the 1995–2006 years, but I believe that for the most part (but not entirely) congressional scholars have managed to maintain the separation. At the very least it should be a goal at which we aim.

* * * * * *

All in all, the study of Congress has shown impressive progress during the past half-century. The research enterprise has adapted to significant change in political conditions by making significant changes in methodological approach. The result is a significant advance in our understanding of Congress, and an improved capacity to evaluate it. Those who have been part of this enterprise can take deserved satisfaction in a job well done. And I am optimistic that rising cohorts of scholars will continue the progress that previous generations have made.

REFERENCES

ANSOLABEHERE, S., and SNYDER, JR., J. M. 2008. *The End of Inequality*. New York: Norton.

ARROW, K. J. 1951. *Social Choice and Individual Values*. New York: Wiley.

ASHER, H. B. 1973. The Learning of Legislative Norms. *American Political Science Review*, 67(2): 499–513.

BAUER, R. A., POOL, I. DE S., and DEXTER, L. A. 1968. *American Business and Public Policy*. New York: Atherton Press.

BAILEY, STEPHEN K. 1950. Congress Makes a Law. New York: Columbia.

BELL, D. 1960. *The End of Ideology*. Cambridge, MA: Harvard University Press.

BERRY, J. M. 1989. *The Interest Group Society*. Glenview, IL: Scott Foresman.

BRADY, D., and EPSTEIN, D. 1997. Intraparty Preferences, Heterogeneity, and the Origins of the Modern Congress: Progressive Reformers in the House and Senate, 1890–1920. *Journal of Law, Economics and Organization*, 13 (1997): 26–49.

[16] A case in point is the term limits movement of the 1990s. Many congressional and other legislative scholars wrote and spoke about the likely negative consequences of such a move.

BURNS, J. M. 1963. *The Deadlock of Democracy*. Englewood Cliffs, NJ: Prentice-Hall.

CLAPP, CHARLES L. 1963. The Congressman: His Work as He Sees It. New York: Doubleday.

COX, GARY W., and MCCUBBINS, MATHEW D. 1963. *Legislative Leviathan: Party Government in the House*. Berkeley: University of California Press.

DODD, L. C. 1977. Congress and the Quest for Power, pp. 269–307 in *Congress Reconsidered*, 1st edn, ed. L. C. Dodd and B. I. Oppenheimer. New York: Praeger.

DOWNS, A. 1957. *An Economic Theory of Democracy*. New York: Harper & Row.

Eidenberg, E., and Morey, R. D. 1969. *An Act of Congress*. New York: Norton.

ERIKSON, R. S. 1971. The Advantage of Incumbency in Congressional Elections. *Polity*, 3: 395–405.

EULAU, H., and HINCKLEY, K. 1966. Legislative Institutions and Processes, pp. 85–189 in *Political Science Annual*, ed. James A. Robinson. Indianapolis, IN: Bobbs-Merrill.

FENNO, JR., R. F. 1962. The House Appropriations Committee as a Political System: The Problem of Integration. *American Political Science Review*, 56: 310–24.

—— 1965. *The Power of the Purse: Appropriations Politics in Congress*. Boston, MA: Little, Brown.

—— 1973. *Congressmen in Committees*. Boston: Little, Brown.

—— 1978. *Home Style*. Boston: Little, Brown.

—— 1998. Introduction, pp. xiii–xv in *Explorations in Evolution of Congress*, ed. N. W. Polsby. Berkeley, Institute of Governmental Studies Press.

FEREJOHN, J. A. 1974. *Pork Barrel Politics*. Stanford, CA: Stanford University Press.

FIORINA, M. P. 1974. *Representatives, Roll Calls, and Constituencies*. Lexington, MA: D. C. Heath.

—— 1977. *Congress: Keystone of the Washington Establishment*. New Haven, CT: Yale University Press.

—— and ABRAMS, S. J. 2009. *Disconnect: The Breakdown of Representation in American Politics*. Norman, OK: University of Oklahoma Press.

HAINES, W. H. 1915. The Congressional Caucus of Today. *American Political Science Review*, 9 (1915): 696–706.

HUITT, R. K. 1957. The Morse Committee Assignment Controversy: A Study in Senate Norms. *American Political Science Review*, 51: 313–29.

—— 1961. The Outsider in the Senate: An Alternative Role. *American Political Science Review*, 55 (September): 566–75.

JONES, C. O. 1961. Representation in Congress: The Case of the House Agriculture Committee. *American Political Science Review*, 55: 358–67.

KREHBIEL, K. 1991. *Information and Legislative Organization*. Ann Arbor, MI: University of Michigan Press.

LINDBLOM, C. E. 1959. The Science of Muddling Through. *Public Administration Review*, 19: 79–88.

MANLEY, J. F. 1965. The House Committee on Ways and Means: Conflict Management in a Congressional Committee. *American Political Science Review*, 59: 927–39.

—— 1970. *The Politics of Finance: The House Committee on Ways and Means*. Boston, MA: Little, Brown.

MATTHEWS, D. R. 1960. *U.S. Senators and their World*. New York: Vintage Books.

MAYHEW, D. R. 1974a. Congressional Elections: The Case of the Vanishing Marginals. *Polity*, 6: 295–317.

—— 1974b. *Congress: The Electoral Connection*. New Haven and London: Yale University Press.

POLSBY, N. W. 1968. The Institutionalization of the U.S. House of Representatives. *American Political Science Review*, 62: 148–68.

POLSBY, N. W. 2004. *How Congress Evolves: Social Bases of Institutional Change.* Oxford: Oxford University Press.

—— and SCHICKLER, E. 2002. Landmarks in the Study of Congress since 1945. *Annual Review of Political Science,* 5: 333–67. Reprinted in *The Evolution of Political Knowledge: Theory and Inquiry in American Politics* ed. E. D. Mansfield and R. Sisson. Columbus: Ohio University Press (January 2004).

SCHICKLER, E., and PEARSON, K. 2009. Agenda Control, Majority Party Power, and the House Committee on Rules, 1939–1952. *Legislative Studies Quarterly,* 34: 455–91.

SHEPSLE, K. A. 1989. The Changing Textbook Congress, pp. 238–66 in *Can the Government Govern?,* ed. J. E. Chubb and P. E. Peterson. Washington, DC: Brookings Institution.

—— and WEINGAST, B. R. 1995. *Positive Theories of Congressional Institutions.* Ann: Arbor, MI: University of Michigan Press.

SMITH, S. S. 1989. *Call to Order: Floor Politics in the House and Senate.* Washington, DC: Brookings Institution Press.

SUNDQUIST, JAMES L. 1981. *The Decline and Resurgence of Congress.* Washington, DC: Brookings.

TURNER, J. 1951. *Party and Constituency.* Baltimore: Johns Hopkins University Press.

WEINGAST, B. R. 1979. A Rational Choice Perspective on Congressional Norms. *American Journal of Political Science,* 23(2): 245–62.

WILSON, W. 1885. *Congressional Government.* New York: Meridan Books.

CHAPTER 38

....

THEORIZING
ABOUT CONGRESS

....

DAVID R. MAYHEW

In the beginning was Woodrow Wilson. That was the introduction many of us got as students of Congress. In political science, Wilson's *Congressional Government* of 1885 was the founding text. It was Wilson who famously wrote: "I know not how better to describe our form of government in a single phrase than by calling it a government by the chairmen of the Standing Committees of Congress" (Wilson 1981, 82).

What kind of a claim was that? Well, it was a scientific claim, in a way. It addressed the essence of something, not just the secondary traits. It was meant to apply across time, not just at the moment. It was a simplification, but it reached for the roots: from it, considerable illumination of the American system in general was supposed to emanate. Of special importance in Wilson's view, it was a positive claim rather than a murky, conventional mixture of aspiration and constitutional rhetoric. A positive approach was in order (although Wilson had a normative side, too). Wilson was much taken by Walter Bagehot's *English Constitution* (1867), which, in a break from customary discourse, had reported in gloves-off fashion how that country's system really worked.[1] Models, it might even be said, percolated in Wilson's mind. One was of the British system motored at the top by party leaders like the eloquent William Gladstone (Wilson 1981, 57–8, 101–2, 144, 167, 209). A different model—Wilson's invention in *Congressional Government*—was of the inferior (he thought) American system marked by disorder and shrouded dealings on Capitol Hill.

How much explanatory utility does Wilson's claim, or a claim like it, offer? With hindsight—a lot of hindsight in the Wilson case, since more than a century has gone by—we might wish to apply certain boundaries to the future president's

[1] For Wilson's reliance on Bagehot, see Wilson 1981, 49, 131, 150–2, 164, 202, 205.

argument of 1885. We can see that, on the facts, it ran up against difficulties or limits. Two limits are of particular interest. The "standing committees are the game" claim was an exhibit of *highlighting* as well as, in a time sense, *localism*. The highlighting is no doubt obvious. Wilson was emphasizing, or exaggerating, or placing the standing committees in relief, to make a point. But it is as well to realize just how much reality he was intentionally ignoring, or not being aware of, or setting aside as secondary or contingent, as he wove his argument while sitting in the library at Johns Hopkins University. What about the main legislative enactment of those years—the Pendleton Act of 1883 creating the civil service? As Wilson knew, that move had little to do with the standing committees: "It was a formulated demand of public opinion made upon Congress," which eventually "Congress heeded" (Wilson 1981, 190).[2] Absent in Wilson's work is any mention of the riveting square-off between President Rutherford B. Hayes and congressional Democrats during the 46th Congress of 1879–81 over appropriations riders targeting the enforcement of Reconstruction-era civil rights laws in the South. The Republican Hayes cast a series of seven vetoes to emerge dramatically victorious.[3] Here was a recent exhibit of presidential power. One wonders if Wilson had been following the newspapers.

As for localism, in a time sense, Wilson's claim seems to have fit best the season of his writing. That was the brief era of Chester A. Arthur—a recessive lame-duck president sharing the government for nearly four years with, to boot, a recessive congressional leadership. No doubt the standing committees flourished. But earlier had loomed the stubborn Hayes.[4] Just later came the assertive Grover Cleveland (a prototype for Wilson himself as he warmed to the idea of White House leadership), as well as Speaker Thomas B. Reed, who broke molds. To pose a wider time envelope, a generation earlier offered the public leadership of, for example, Abraham Lincoln and Thaddeus Stevens, as well as Congress's striking override of its own standing committees during the Civil War and Reconstruction as ad hoc special committees decked with leading politicians and sensitive to crisis needs were crafted on the spot to handle much of the institution's major work (Mayhew 2000, 178, 180). A generation after 1885 would come the presidential leadership of Theodore Roosevelt and Wilson himself.

---

[2] Wilson's discussion is cursory. For a recent analysis of the passage of the Pendleton Act, see Theriault 2005, ch. 3. Party strategies as well as public opinion figured in the result.

[3] An account appears in White 1958, 35–8. Wilson was hostile to the intrusions of the Reconstruction era into the South's elections and jury system that brought on those Democratic riders (see Wilson 1981, 39–40, 42–3). In approaching *Congressional Government*, it helps to realize that Wilson was a typical southern Democrat of those post-Civil War times. It comes as no surprise that he was not a great admirer of either the U.S. national system or the policies that it was generating. On the policy front, besides the enforcement of the civil rights acts, he criticizes the Tenure of Office Act of 1867 (51–2); the era's internal improvements policies (40–1, 119–21, 133); tariff policy (100–1, 120, 123–4, 133); the government's extravagant spending (102) and running of surpluses (102); the Republicans' plans for federal aid to education (40–1); and, at least by implication, the Civil War pension system (132). All this was standard positioning for the southern, and indeed largely the northern, Democrats of those times.

[4] See the discussion of Hayes and Arthur in White 1958, 25.

Is this discussion a putdown of Wilson? No, it is not. Notwithstanding the complexities, he hit on a basic truth. He drew a picture of Congress, or at least the House of Representatives, as an arena of dispersed influence and deliberation. As one side-effect of this dispersion, a Gladstonian kind of crystallizing debate was not ordinarily to be found there. Peering through it all, the standing committees were fundamental units. For good reason, this was an arresting picture. It has served as an analytic template since. Among other things, it helped inject a discordant Anglophile model into the study of American institutions: "The British system is perfected party government," Wilson wrote (1981, 91). As a focused presentation, Wilson's idea of Congress as an arena of dispersed influence and deliberation was novel. We do not see it in, for example, the country's earlier theoretical text, the *Federalist*.

As a political scientist, Wilson set a powerful example. Since his time, a good deal of scholarship about Congress—or, more broadly, about the complex of U.S. national institutions into which Congress fits—has borne a scientific stamp something like his. Highlighting—the urge to simplify, to reach for the basics and bypass the rest—has been much in evidence. But so has localism. Explanatory enterprises apt for their times have ordinarily sagged or faltered somewhat, albeit not to the limit of complete non-utility, when carried outside their times. That is the way the scholarship has gone.

I will discuss certain aspects of that scholarship here in these terms. Some of it has dwelt on Congress in isolation, some on the constellation of Congress and the presidency. My choice of authors or schools is selective—not, of course, anything like exhaustive. One of the analytic schools is partly my own. I organize the discussion under six rubrics, each of which has featured, in the Wilsonian sense, a claim.

Spatial dissonance

The mid-twentieth century brought a reprise of Wilson in the "responsible parties" school of analysis. Here again the ingredients included Anglophilia; a broad brush; a theme of lamentation; a blending of the normative with the positive; a juxtaposing of Congress to the presidency; and a boundless regard for party leadership. It was a fetching mix. The analysis had its epicenter around 1950, but its life spanned from the mid-1940s through the mid-1960s. In those days, political science was not as differentiated professionally as it later became. Leading authors could double as academics and public intellectuals.[5] One author I draw on here, Congressman Richard Bolling (1965, 1968), was not an academic at all, yet his writing seems to fit into the responsible parties school more or less seamlessly. Otherwise, the main authors of the school included at least E. E. Schattschneider (1942, also a major author of *Toward*

---

[5] Also, three of the leading authors I discuss here wrote from liberal arts colleges, not research universities—James MacGregor Burns (Williams), E.E. Schattschneider (Wesleyan), and Stephen K. Bailey (Wesleyan).

a More Responsible Two-party System, 1950—henceforth *APSA Report*), Stephen K. Bailey (1950), and James MacGregor Burns (1949, 1963).

The responsible parties approach is ordinarily seen as normative, yet it was positive, too. Without a positive side, the school would likely have drawn little enthusiasm or notice. What was that positive side? As I see it, the writers were pitching an idea of spatial dissonance. I use "spatial" here in the dimensional sense that the term enjoys today. This usage is anachronistic: the authors back then did not use the term or have a developed sense of dimensions. But they did see an issue or policy space confronting American society that, looking back, with perhaps some squeezing, appears unidimensional. There was not a uniformity of labeling. A "coherent" or "nationwide" stance on policy matters as opposed to a sectional, localistic, or special-interest stance was one coding (Schattschneider 1942, 206–7; Bailey 1950, ix, 239; *APSA Report* 1950, 4, 33–4; Burns 1949, 42–3). Yet a coding of liberal versus conservative was often the formulation, too (Bailey 1950, xi, 75–7, ch. 5, ch. 7, 190–218; Burns 1963, 198, 199, 252; Bolling 1965, 71, 81, 91). It all seems to have come down to more or less the same thing, at least on domestic matters.[6]

With regard to this dimension, these authors argued that a dissonance of treatment and outcome inhered in the array of national institutions. Burns saw a "four-party system" in which the presidential Democrats operated at the liberal extreme, the congressional Republicans at the conservative extreme, and the congressional Democrats and presidential Republicans near the middle—"in general, though, both presidential parties [consider Dewey, Eisenhower] have been more liberal, and both congressional parties have been more conservative" (1963, 199). Eisenhower, like the Democratic presidents in Burns' view, often pressed a reluctant Congress from the liberal side (Burns 1963, 192).[7] In a finer judgment, the House of Representatives was sometimes seen to bound the system—except on civil rights—on the conservative side. Bolling wrote in 1968 (15–16): "The primary failures of political leadership [read: policy positioning] at the Federal level are found in the United States Congress: more particularly in the place where I serve, the House of Representatives rather than in the United States Senate, with the exception of the one critical field of civil rights."[8] Relevantly, a separate scholarship (not the responsible parties school) has asked of those post-war decades the question: why is the Senate more liberal than the House? (Koenig 1962; Froman 1963, ch. 6; Cleaveland 1969, 374; Kernell 1973;

---

[6] It is not all that hard to discern the burr under the saddle of the responsible parties school in its early, most prominent years. These writers were unhappy that too many of the domestic designs of the Roosevelt and Truman presidencies were not being realized. Schattschneider, for his part, was plainly disconsolate that FDR's "purge" of dissident Democratic members of Congress in the 1938 primaries had not worked (1942, 163–9). Bailey, in the case of the Employment Act of 1946, favored a heavier dose of government control of the economy than Congress ended up buying (1950, xi). The *APSA Report* telegraphs its stance in its second paragraph: "It is in terms of party programs that political leaders can attempt to consolidate public attitudes toward the work plans of government" (p. 1). The work plans of government? It seems a lay-down bet that those, in the minds of the *APSA Report* writers, were the brand of domestic initiatives promoted by New Dealers and Fair Dealers associated with the White House during the 1930s and 1940s.

[7] This was not Bolling's view (see 1968, 189–91).

[8] See also, for example, Bailey 1950, 126–7, 153, 182.

Grofman, Griffin, and Glazer 1991). The responsible parties writers saw the dissonance across the three institutions—presidency, Senate, and House—as a major feature of the American system. Vexatious policy deadlock, or at least a good deal of grinding, frustration, and delay could result. As instances of unfortunate congressional foot-dragging or naysaying over the years, the school's authors mention the minimum wage in 1938 and later (Burns 1949, 68–82; 1963, 163; Bolling 1965, 199, 209; 1968, 136–7); price controls during World War II (Burns 1949, 82–90); employment policy in 1946 (Bailey 1950); Truman's proposed Missouri Valley Authority (Burns 1949, 90–7); Eisenhower's plan to expand social security in 1954 (Burns 1963, 192); Kennedy's 1961 program in general (Burns 1963, 2); civil rights (Bolling 1965, 85–6, 209; 1968, 197); education (Bolling 1965, 82, 208; 1968, 197, 200, 212); housing (Bolling 1965, 93, 208); labor policy (Bolling 1965, 96–7); aid to depressed areas (Bolling 1965, 208; 1968, 198–9); and medicare (Bolling 1968, 241).[9] It is a substantial list.

Cause as well as pattern figured in the responsible parties claim. What might explain the spatial dissonance? It wasn't clear, but an industry bent to the task of explanation. Possibly the electoral college nudged the presidency in an urban direction (Burns 1963, 198, 252). Certainly the Senate filibuster dammed up civil rights. Spotlighted most often was the House of Representatives, whose parochial-minded members (Schattschneider 1942, 142–50; Bailey 1950, 159–60, 181–6; Burns 1949, ch. 1; 1963, 242–4), districts biased toward rural areas (*APSA Report* 75–6; Burns 1949, 49–54, 140–1; Bolling 1965, 25–6), and conservative committee oligarchies—notably the Rules Committee (Bailey 1950, 151–3, 164–6; Burns 1949, 54–66; 1963, 197–8, 245–9; Bolling 1965, 70–2, chs 4 and 10; 1968, 197–200, 212, 239–45)—were seen to offer explanatory leverage. Strengthening the party leaders and caucuses in the House (read: the Democratic ones) was a prime reform aim of the responsible parties school (Burns 1949, 202–7; 1963, 320; Bolling 1965, 125, ch. 11; 1968, 16, 265–71).

A certain highlighting was going on in this responsible parties presentation. Alleged features of the system were singled out and pressed. The four-parties idea was a stretch. In hindsight, at least, apparently overblown, was the idea, often stated or implied, that a House oligarchy of the time was blocking the wishes of the chamber's median member.[10] There was localism—in a time sense. The school's gestalt of pattern and explanation looked important and at least plausible as it applied to, say, the late 1930s through the mid-1960s, but a telling application of it before or after that era would be harder. Still, taken as a claim, the responsible parties presentation was probably the chief analytic offering of the American political science discipline at the midpoint of the twentieth century, and it was ambitious and engaging.

---

[9] In the employment sphere, the authors of the *APSA Report* were clearly admirers of the Employment Act of 1946—it was the sort of thing the government should be doing (32)—but they do not comment on the act's difficult congressional birth.

[10] The idea appears in, for example, Burns 1949, 56; Bolling 1965, 21. Recent analysis bearing on the question appears in Schickler and Pearson 2009; Pearson and Schickler 2009; Mayhew 2011, ch. 3.

SYSTEMS WITH NORMS AND ROLES

A decade later, judging in terms of prominence and influence, came an abrupt, indeed sometimes haughtily dismissive, break with the responsible parties school. A "great generation" of congressional scholars came along, offering serious interview work on Capitol Hill—this was new—and a dedication to professional, as opposed to armchair or "literary," social science.[11] The new school's authors included Richard F. Fenno, Jr. (1962, 1966), Ralph K. Huitt (1954, 1957, 1961), Donald R. Matthews (1960), John F. Manley (1965), Roger H. Davidson (1969), and Nelson W. Polsby (1968).[12] Writing as a kind of outrider to the school in the 1950s was the journalist William S. White (1956).

These authors lodged a trademark claim: the best way to understand Congress is to see it as a bounded "system," or a set of "subsystems," in which embedded "norms" or "roles" induce behavior. The theoretical borrowing was from sociology.[13] Abundant in the new school's writings were such terms as "function," "socialization," "adaptation," "differentiation," "integration," "autonomy," "institutionalization," "interdependence," and "system maintenance." In the Senate, Matthews (1960, ch. 5) detected a pattern of "folkways" that nurtured such behavior as specialization, courtesy, and reciprocity. White (1956, ch. 7), labeling that upper body a "citadel"—the ultimate in boundedness—found at its core an "inner club."[14] These various insights were not pointless. Aided by them, we could see better how Congress really worked. It *did* work, these authors argued. Thanks in part to the force of the system's norms and roles, goals could be achieved, problems could be solved, conflict could be managed, and duties could be performed (Fenno 1962, 310; Manley 1965, 927; Matthews 1960, 116; Polsby 1968, 144). As much as anything, the edge could be taken off partisan conflict. Fenno (1962, 317) saw in the House Appropriations Committee, for example, a norm of "minimal partisanship." Manley (1965, 929) saw in the House Ways and Means Committee a norm of "restrained partisanship."

It is no surprise that this generation's work, saturated as it was with interesting information, insights, and methodological innovations, has remained the gold standard in the study of Congress. Basic, enduring truths were laid out. Today's Senate, for example, given its encumbering rules, might come to a halt within twenty-four hours if it were not for some sense of comity shared by its members. Not to be lost in any view of Congress is that it is an organization, which means that it is laden with inner impulses and connections that need to be witnessed and parsed close up to be appreciated. In a close-up inspection, they *will* be appreciated.

---

[11] Discussions of this new school appear in Peabody 1969, especially, regarding analytic content, 14–16, 19–22, 54–7, 59–63; Polsby and Schickler 2002, 335–46.

[12] These authors seem to fit best the intellectual thrust I discuss here.

[13] See, for example, Fenno 1966, xviii; Manley 1965, 928; Polsby 1968, 166.

[14] White's analysis is more casual than that of the political scientists, but his message is similar if more edgy.

Still, there was highlighting in this school's message. For one thing, a congressional scholarship built on the experience of the late 1940s through the early 1960s, as this one was, might have emphasized other things—for example, the Senate's endless protection of the South's racial caste system through filibuster politics, or the parties' occasionally explosive drives to enact their legislative programs (the focus for the responsible parties writers).[15] Selection of what to look at was going on. Also, there was an ingredient of time localism. The school's interpretation matched the 1950s very nicely. Evolved into a crustacean perfection by then was Congress's seniority system (Polsby, Gallagher, and Rundquist 1969). The Keynesian synthesis, the waging of the Cold War, the demise of the far left around 1950, and the anesthetic calm administered by President Eisenhower, had tamped down the level of conflict that had been present in U.S. national politics previously, and would flare again in the late 1960s and 1970s. In hindsight, the 1950s was a kind of timeout. On the institutional side, certain features of Congress, given exquisite life by the systems school of the 1960s, would frazzle away in succeeding decades as partisan combat overtook Capitol Hill. By the time of Newt Gingrich and Nancy Pelosi, the House Appropriations and Ways and Means Committees, for example, would come to look different.

PURPOSIVE POLITICIANS

The 1970s brought a new theoretical claim: the best way to get a handle on Congress was to see its individual members as goal-seekers. Basically, they *were* that, it was argued. What's more, there were implications. Because the members were goal-seekers, they would organize their Capitol Hill structures and activities and generate public policy in corresponding ways.[16] Three authors, it is probably fair to say, set this scholarly course. Fenno again, reflecting an evolution in his thinking, led off a new work in 1973 with a chapter entitled "Member Goals," of which he saw three as fundamental to explanation: "reelection," "influence within the House," and "good public policy" (Fenno 1973, 1).[17] Committee processes were thus illuminated. Morris P. Fiorina and David R. Mayhew built cases for accenting a single goal—reelection. Fiorina (1977) saw a "Washington establishment" cementing itself in place in the 1970s, thanks to members of Congress who created federal programs and then curried favor with voters through "fixit" services as those programs sprang bureaucratic leaks.[18] Mayhew (1974a, 5, 49–73, 125–38) posited members of Congress

---

[15] Fenno, in a co-authored work of a different kind (Munger and Fenno 1962), did exactly address a sequence of policy drives in the area of education.

[16] For a discussion of the congressional scholarship centering on purposive politicians, see Mezey 1993.

[17] Dodd (1977) also addressed the influence-seeking goal.

[18] See also Fiorina 1974.

to be "single-minded seekers of re-election" who to that end engaged in "advertising," "credit claiming," and "position taking." Stemming from these practices, at the level of Congress as a whole, was said to be a pattern of "assembly coherence" marked by delay, particularism, servicing of the organized, and symbolism. This was a pure individualistic view of Congress that downplayed the political parties: "The fact is that no theoretical treatment of the United States Congress that posits parties as analytic units will go very far" (Mayhew 1974a, 27).

To view members of Congress as blinkered seekers of reelection was an obvious instance of theoretical highlighting. Indeed, Fenno's notion of multiple goals offered a kind of antidote to the idea. Also, in hindsight, the individualization of congressional politics in these "goals" theories—at least the reelection theories—looks like a case of time localism. Where were the parties?[19] Their faint showing had reasons. On today's evidence, the early 1970s—the juncture when these theories were being hatched—stands out in a number of century-long time series as an all-time low in party conflict in the House of Representatives. Action that flouted party lines was peaking (Aldrich, Berger, and Rohde 2002, 23, 24, 27; Brady and Han 2006, 141, 142). Also, the late 1960s had brought a unique surge in the value of personal incumbency in House elections (Erikson 1971; Mayhew 1974b). Accordingly, as possibly never before, individual exertion was looking like the name of the game in congressional politics. One realm for that exertion was a record high in government programs crying out for corrective casework.

The "goals" theories arose and thrived in this 1970s context. This is not to say that their utility has fallen to zero since. Adding traction to the reelection account, R. Douglas Arnold (1990) has written of the "traceability" of the members' activities. The sinews of a "Washington establishment" may figure in Diana Evans' recent (2004) account of congressional earmark politics. "There they go again" was one possible reaction to the House's "cap and trade" energy bill of 2009, which began as a stern blueprint to raise revenue and auction off pollution permits, yet ended as more of a distributive subsidy measure leaner in revenue and blurrier in its incentive effects as specific districts and industries, including agriculture, had to be appeased. Thrusts toward symbolism (that is, a gap between label and content), particularism, and servicing of the organized, mushroomed as the need for 218 votes loomed.[20] It was a familiar performance.

---

[19] Mayhew's downplaying of the parties has been criticized in light of later historical experience. See, for example, Aldrich 2001, 255–6. Also: "It is obvious that party leaders no longer 'leave members alone' to vote in their constituencies' interests on issues that are deemed important by the leadership" (Abramowitz 2001, 258).

[20] See "Cap and trade, with handouts and loopholes: The first climate-change bill with a chance of passing is weaker and worse than expected," *The Economist*, May 22-9, 2009, online; John M. Broder, "Adding Something for Everyone, House Leaders Won Climate Bill," *New York Times*, July 1, 2009, pp. A1, A17; Steven Pearlman, "For the Farm Lobby, Too Much Is Never Enough," *Washington Post*, June 26, 2009, online; Jim Tankersley, "House climate bill was flooded with last-minute changes: Many provisions were narrowly focused to help certain industries," *Los Angeles Times*, July 20, 2009, online.

THE COMMITTEES, THE PARTIES, THE FLOOR

In the selection of claims I have discussed so far, there is a certain pre-Socratic texture. What is basically true? The universe is made of water, said Thales. No, the answer is air, said Anaximenes. Pythagoras opted for number. And so on. Similarly, the early scholarship about Congress brought a cascade of essentialism in what I have called the spatial dissonance, norms and rules, and purposive politicians schools. This cascade continued in a burst of creativity around 1990 as a generation of formal theorists put their ideas on the boards. This school could be approached as at least three distinct schools that each offered its own influential take on what is basically true. Yet there was a trademark commonality in intellectual origin and style, as well as a good deal of interlocking discussion, and, following a custom set by the school itself, I will take it up as a whole.[21] The "claim" treated in this section is thus actually a small family of claims prominently similar in DNA and some traits.

Look to the committees was the formulation of Barry R. Weingast and William J. Marshall (1988; see also Shepsle and Weingast 1987). As with Woodrow Wilson, those are the congressional nodes that best support theorizing. The committee system is "the formal expression of a comprehensive logrolling arrangement" (Fiorina 1987, 338) whereby the members of Congress, to serve their particular policy and reelection aims, award jurisdictional monopolies and agenda-setting edges to committees made up of policy advancers, as in agriculture and urban housing, and then profit through gains from exchange as those panels defer to each other on the floor. In this sense, the committees rule. No, argued Gary W. Cox and Mathew D. McCubbins (1993, 2005): look to the House majority party, not the committees. The majority party, crystallizing itself into a "cartel," wields committee appointments and floor agenda control so as to serve the electoral interests of its membership. "The party's reputation, based on its record, is a public good for all legislators in the party" (Cox and McCubbins 1993, 123). Among other things, "The more favorable is the majority party's record of legislative accomplishment, the better its reputation or brand name will be...." (Cox and McCubbins 2005, 7). Wrong on both counts, argued Keith Krehbiel. In back of the committees and parties, exercising at least remote control, is a legislative chamber's floor majority indexed by the stance of the median member. A "majoritarian postulate" pertains (Krehbiel 1992, 15–19). The floor is sovereign. Majority parties if divided can be overridden. Committees exist to serve the informational needs of the floor, not the possibly sectoral needs of their own memberships—and, anyway, how much do those memberships really exhibit sectoral tilts?

There was plenty of highlighting in these formal presentations. That, in a sense, was their aim. An excellent guide to the various authors' possible overclaiming, so to speak, has been a stream of writing within the school itself. Vigorous criticism has been endogenous to the school.[22] Krehbiel has asked, for example (1992, 9–14,

---

[21] For an informative overview, see Shepsle and Weingast 1995.
[22] See, for example, Krehbiel 1992, ch. 2; Cox and McCubbins 2005, 243–51.

255): is it really true that the classic House Agriculture Committee could get its way by structuring proceedings on the floor? Cox and McCubbins have asked (2005, 89, 243–51): isn't our account of majority-party "rolls"—that is, instances where the bulk of the House majority party loses out in a final-passage roll call to a cross-party coalition—better than Krehbiel's? External criticism is possible, too. There are matters of emphasis. For example, as a statistical matter, Cox and McCubbins document that cross-party coalitions have not "rolled" the House majority party all that often. Yet in fact, when the publicity runs high, notably when the White House pushes its priorities, things can be different.[23] Think what the history of the last thirty years would look like, without the majority-party "rolls" on the votes listed here in Table 38.1. Veteran followers of public affairs will find all these showdowns familiar.[24] In presiding over one of them—the funding of the Iraq War by a Democratic House in 2007—Nancy Pelosi commented, "I'm the Speaker of the House. . . . I have to take into consideration something broader than the majority of the majority in the Democratic Caucus" (Davis 2007, 1).

Time localism has also figured in certain offerings of the formal school. The committee theorizing looked backward. In the 1980s, as the new politics of multiple bill referrals and caucus selection of committee chairs played out, the grip of the House committees was fading. Marching to their own drums was getting tougher. The party theorizing, on the other hand, looked forward. To crank best in previous times, Cox and McCubbins' analysis seemed to need a codicil that the congressional Democrats had amounted to two factions, not one coherent party, but the analysis fit more surefootedly the oncoming age of Gingrich and Pelosi.[25]

A signal contribution of the formal school was to offer a catechism of sharpness. There had been vagueness in congressional studies. Exactly what, here and there, was being argued for? How could we tell if it was right? The formalists brought a pioneering finesse in definition, theoretical workup, and evidence testing. Even the inconclusiveness of the school in addressing certain questions was an advance, since we could see better how to think about them. Regarding the history of the discipline, here might be an interesting class assignment for students steeped in the formalist writings: turn them loose on Wilson's *Congressional Government* with a directive to

---

[23] Cox and McCubbins (2005, 106, see generally ch. 6) do acknowledge that "intense public pressure" may alter the odds.

[24] Regrettably, not included in Table 38.1 is the House vote in 1981 approving the Reagan tax cuts. Few House decisions during the last half-century have rivaled this one in importance, and probably none has been more devastating to the policy causes of a House majority party. Widely recognized as the showdown vote on this question was the approval of a Barber Conable substitute, backed by a cross-party conservative coalition, by 238 to 195. The majority Democrats voted 48 to 194, the minority Republicans 190 to 1. This was a roll, in a sense that the position of the floor median defeated that of the majority-party caucus median. In this instance, the O'Neill-led majority party did not devise an effective procedure to ward off cross-party floor trouble, and it did not dominate the floor result. But we do not see here a final-passage roll. As a general proposition, members of Congress do not relish voting against tax cuts. The final-passage vote was 323 to 107, with Democrats voting 133 to 106, Republicans 190 to 1.

[25] A codicil addressing the northern and southern Democratic factions of earlier times appears in Cox and McCubbins 1993, 271. On House floor control during those times, see also the empirical analysis in Schickler and Pearson 2009; Pearson and Schickler 2009.

Table 38.1 Selected notable final-passage "rolls" of the House majority party since 1980[26]

Year	President	Majority party vote	Minority party vote	Measure
1981	Reagan	47 to 188	185 to 5	Reagan spending cuts (OBRA)
1991	Bush 41	86 to 179	164 to 3	Persian Gulf War resolution
1993	Clinton	102 to 156	132 to 43	North American Free Trade Agreement (NAFTA)
2002	Bush 43	41 to 176	198 to 12	Campaign finance reform (BCRA)
2007	Bush 43	86 to 140	194 to 2	Fund the Iraq War
2008	Bush 43	80 to 151	188 to 4	Fund the Iraq War
2008	Bush 43	105 to128	188 to 1	Authorize domestic surveillance procedures (the FISA fix)

sharpen it. For example, does the Wilson analysis map better onto Weingast and Marshall's committee idea, or onto Krehbiel's "information" idea? Did Wilson see the difference? Is there any sign of a "party cartel" in Wilson? What aspects of Wilson's case wouldn't be reached in such an inquiry? For one thing, his emphasis on the lack of Gladstone-quality public debate in Congress.

BRACKETING PIVOTS

Of all the theorizing about Congress, perhaps the most elegant came a few years later in Keith Krehbiel's *Pivotal Politics* (1998, ch. 2).[27] All else aside, Krehbiel argued, anyone wishing to understand congressional lawmaking needs to know about the "pivots" that bracket a central span of the policy space, stipulated to be unidimensional, that Congress operates in. At the very center is a "gridlock interval," now second nature to congressional scholars. Already existing policy located within that space cannot be changed. Key to the analysis are the presidential veto, supplying a pivot at the two-thirds mark, and the Senate cloture rule, supplying one at the sixty-vote mark. The pivots are blocking points that mirror each other. The elegance of the

[26] Except for campaign finance reform in 2001, all these instances involved White House-led legislative drives that successfully rolled the House Democratic party. Campaign finance reform brought a roll of the House Republican party by a Democratic-centered cross-party coalition enabled by favorable publicity. The Iraq war votes of 2007 and 2008 brought a peculiar, possibly unique, process wrinkle. In each case, *two* final-passage roll calls were held. Sweeteners for the core of the Democratic party unhappy with the war funding figured in the companion votes. In the case of OBRA in 1981, the final-passage vote occurred quickly after a closer 217 to 211 approval of a Gramm-Latta amendment that really decided the issue. The party break on that roll call was Democrats 29 to 209, Republicans 188 to 2.

[27] See also Brady and Volden 1998.

theory has lain in the explication of this mirroring. As a practical matter, in 1993–4, for example, a Senate Republican party numbering in the forties, wielding filibusters, could block certain initiatives of the Clinton administration and the majority Democratic parties on Capitol Hill. In 1995–6, Clinton wielding vetoes could block certain initiatives of the now Republican Congress led by Newt Gingrich and Bob Dole. So much for congressional majority rule.

As always, there was highlighting here. White House budgets and trade agreements are shielded from filibusters—a non-trivial dose of reality. Exact parallelism is missing from the veto and cloture-point analogy since congressional rules are endogenous, which means they can be changed or significantly reconstrued, and sometimes they have been, on the spot, and the senators' realization that this can happen may bear on the politics.[28] Cross-pressured senators can diversify their positioning by voting one way on cloture and another on policy, which clouds, theoretically, what they are up to. Also, shouldn't a consideration of intensity enter into this discussion (Bawn and Koger 2008)?[29]

In addition, there is a time localism to the Krehbiel presentation. The Senate filibuster of yesterday doesn't seem to have amounted to the more or less absolute veto instrument that we see it as today. Why, is another matter, but that seems to be the what (Wawro and Schickler 2006). See Table 38.2, for example, for some relevant data from the 1950s and 1960s. It lists a number of White House legislative priorities of that era that drew heated opposition from minorities numbering better than one-third of the senators—the cloture juncture at that time—but cleared the upper chamber anyway.[30] Where were the blocking coalitions? Catherine Fisk and Erwin Chemerinsky concluded in a detailed assessment in 1997 (184), "The contemporary filibuster is an entirely different—and generally more powerful—weapon than the filibuster of the past."[31]

Even so, the pivots analysis has offered a compelling analytic fit—arguably the best fit—to the congressional politics of the last two decades. That is a considerable accomplishment. Krehbiel, in writing *Pivotal Politics*, cut his teeth on the lawmaking drives of the Clinton era, but the George W. Bush era lined up for the ideas just as nicely, and the Obama era may follow. One attractive feature of the pivots analysis is that, by taking up veto politics, it has brought the presidency back into the picture. Since Burns' *Deadlock of Democracy* in 1963 and Fenno's *Power of the Purse* in 1966, which in different ways theorized the House and Senate to be parts of an overall

---

[28] See, for example, Koger 2010.

[29] A pronounced intensity gap between northern and southern senators on civil rights questions seems to have underpinned the filibuster politics in that area from 1890 into the 1960s.

[30] So far as one can tell from accounts in *Congressional Quarterly Almanac*, in only one of the seven instances listed in Table 38.2 did a losing Senate minority even contemplate filibuster obstruction. The exception was the tidelands oil bill in 1953, where an intense opposing minority contemplated and also conducted a filibuster for a while yet did not prevail. The material in Table 38.2 is from Mayhew 2011, ch. 4. It draws from a larger dataset of White House domestic legislative priorities advanced by post-war presidents from Truman through George W. Bush during their first Congresses after getting elected or reelected. For the dataset and the sources underpinning it, see
http://pantheon.yale.edu/~dmayhew/data5.html.

[31] See also Binder and Smith 1997, 6–19.

Table 38.2 White House priorities approved by the Senate in the 1950s and 1960s by margins under the cloture barrier

Congress	President	Presidential request	The vote
83rd	Eisenhower	Tidelands oil	56 to 35
83rd	Eisenhower	St Lawrence Seaway	51 to 33
87th	Kennedy	Federal aid to education	49 to 4
87th	Kennedy	Housing Act of 1961	53 to 38
89th	Johnson	Creation of HUD	57 to 33
89th	Johnson	Housing Act of 1965	54 to 30
91st	Nixon	DC crime control	54 to 33

three-ring system, the study of Congress had grown narrow to the point of positing single chambers to be theoretically isolated. It was good to have the White House back.[32]

TEMPORAL INSTABILITY

All the theorizing I have covered so far has been static. A side glance at change has occurred here and there, but that is it.[33] Yet let me resort to the pre-Socratics again. An outlier among them was Heraclitus, who saw change as exactly the essence of things. Hard as change may be to theorize, students of Congress have increasingly been addressing it. Perhaps this attention is itself a localism phenomenon. Once seemingly timeless, Congress's institutions and processes have undergone changes since the 1960s that have not been easy to ignore. The chin-scratching has taken a while, but it has brought scholarship.[34]

Narrative spiced with genetic and probabilistic explanation (Nagel 1961, 564–75)—that is, these particular events and contexts generated those results, the analytic stock-in-trade of historians—has characterized some accounts. Often that kind of approach seems like enough. James L. Sundquist contributed *The Decline and Resurgence of Congress* in 1981. Just recently, Julian E. Zelizer and Nelson W. Polsby have recounted the long-drawn-out reform of Congress during the 1950s through the 1970s in, respectively, their *On Capitol Hill* (2004) and *How Congress Evolves* (2004).[35] Working in that same historical terrain, also in a narrative frame, David Rohde in his *Parties and Leaders in the Postreform House* (1991, 31–4, ch. 6; see also Cooper and Brady 1981) has

---

[32] It is also back in, for example, McCarty and Groseclose 2000; Cameron 2000; Jones 2005.
[33] A dynamic note figures in Krehbiel 1998, ch. 3.
[34] On the increasing interest in congressional history, see Polsby and Schickler 2002, 353–6.
[35] These authors discuss their respective analytic designs in Zelizer 2004, ch. 1; Polsby 2004, 3–4, ch. 5.

added an analysis-of-variance logic: in general, this X will cause that Y. Here, Rohde's X is ideological homogeneity in a chamber's majority party. His Y is a resulting empowerment of party leadership. The X and thus the Y are said to have kicked into place in the House of Representatives a generation ago.

In 2001, Eric Schickler carried the change analysis a step further in his *Disjointed Pluralism*.[36] Generous ingredients of narrative, historical causation, and analysis of variance appear in this Schickler work, yet there is also a guiding *developmental* component. This is an additional logic. In general, over a very long period of time, what is it that has motored Congress's continuing bent toward changing its institutions and processes? In fact, those institutions and processes do not seem to stay still. Why is that? Members of Congress have a kit of "multiple interests," Schickler argues—reelection, party, policy, personal power bases, and the power and capacity of Congress as an institution—not just one goal or interest. As a result, the coalitions that the members join to create internal institutions and processes—such as the strong House Speakership of the early twentieth century—tend to produce "untidy compromises" that incorporate "tensions and contradictions" (Schickler 2001, 3). Such settlements are thus unravelable and they may indeed unravel as their ramifications are experienced and new issues, contexts, members, and itchy institutional reformers come along. Basic member interests that once were recessive can jump ahead in the line—as did, for example, the need to curb a growingly powerful White House as an upshot of the New Deal and World War II. In this case, reforms ensued (Schickler 2001, 24–5, 140–63). In general, there exists a built-in instability in the realm of congressional institutions and processes. A stable equilibrium is not to be found.[37]

Perhaps in all these accounts of change there is a certain highlighting. One of the more striking features of the American regime, after all, is the *continuity* in its basic formal processes since 1789. Samuel C. Patterson wrote in 1978 (132), "If Henry Clay were alive today, and he were to serve again in the House and Senate to which he was chosen so many times in the nineteenth century, he would find much that was very familiar." The United States enjoys "one of the world's more antique polities," Samuel P. Huntington wrote in 1968 (129, 133). "With a few exceptions, such as a handful of colleges and churches, the oldest institutions in American society are governmental institutions." That antiquity includes Congress. Tough control of revenue processes by the Ways and Means Committee dates to the 1790s. Raising the roof over the presidents' conduct of national security policy dates to the 1790s (Mayhew 2000, 103–13). Flashy impeachment moves began under Jefferson. Polarization in Congress reached one of its peaks around 1800 (Poole and Rosenthal 2007, 39). Legislative drives could offer drama back then as well as now. For example, Congress's approval of the Jay Treaty in 1795–6 (Elkins and McKitrick 1993, 425–49), was largely mirrored in its

---

[36] Analytic design is discussed in chs 1 and 6.

[37] There is a certain kinship between Schickler's account and standard "cycling" theory, which also addresses instability. But in the standard account, "cycling" occurs in principle at the instant. In Schickler's account, experience is needed with the real downstream effects of an accomplished institutional or procedural initiative before its potential unravelers warm up to unravel. In this sense, we see in Schickler a historicizing of the cycling idea.

approval of NAFTA in 1993. Both cases brought a familiar pattern of executive initiative, staunch opposition, drawn-out public debate, each side campaigning for support back in the states and districts, and final roll-call victories in which an executive-led coalition "rolled" a House majority party. There has been a lot of sameness. There is a lot to be said for the fundamental importance of Constitutional structure.

DISCUSSION

What does theorizing about Congress amount to? Novelty, breadth, bite, and credible insight need to figure in the mix—that we could all agree on—but so does simplification. Yet simplification entails "highlighting," which in turn brings on empirical vulnerability. Yet such vulnerability can be productive if it spurs a continuing conversation of empirical testing and counter-theorizing. This seems to be the way things work. Of great importance is a tradition of stern empirical testing that keeps the tires getting kicked.

There is nothing surprising in this argument. A bit more surprising, perhaps, is the case I have made for the persistence of time localism in theorizing about Congress. It is a weed that will not go away. We tend not to see it as clearly as we might because we live in the present, think in the present, and write books and articles in the present. There is nothing particularly culpable in this localism tendency. I would guess all the social sciences exhibit a pretty clear pattern of time localism in the ways they go about theorizing. Yes, it might be wise for us to step back and think a bit more than we ordinarily do before launching that new theory. Is it really as timeless as its label says? But, on the record, the grip of this advice is likely to have limits. It is an ontological matter. Time localism, to some degree anyway, is probably baked into the nature of the theoretical trade. Like highlighting, it stays with us.

Is this an argument against the possibility of progress? No, it is not. Yes, we tend to lurch from claim to claim. We tend to highlight and think local. Yet in rereading the various works addressed in this chapter, I have been impressed by the standing on earlier shoulders.[38] Concepts, arguments, and measurement have gotten continually sharper. Reference lists have become thicker as new authors take heed of earlier ones. Most important, the evolving thinking shows a large component of cumulativeness. Authors often build new ideas by bouncing themselves against earlier ones, as in the opening chapters of Krehbiel's *Pivotal Politics* and Schickler's *Disjointed Pluralism*.

With all this, is it possible for a theoretical tradition to evolve into a rut? It is a question not to lose sight of. Highlighting can build on highlighting. A good feature of the tradition of theorizing about Congress is that it offers a cupboard of variety. That cupboard is always available to be consulted. Today, for example, notwithstanding

---

[38] Agreement on a pattern of progress may be found in Fiorina 1995.

its long-term constancies, Congress has changed a good deal in certain ways since the Fenno generation of the 1960s pinned down its internal workings through on-site examination. There are troubles. These days, a composite downside image of Congress might go as follows: its members are mediocre slackers given to nastiness, pork-barreling, corruption, extremism, broken processes, lapdog behavior toward presidents of their own party, and other behaviors that vitiate policymaking and leave the public cold.[39] For the most part, political science is not targeting these widely alleged difficulties. Roll-call analysis and most existent theorizing are not much help. As in the 1960s, a new behavioral revolution steeped in on-site experience might be in order.[40] On such evidence, fresh theoretical claims might lurk out there waiting to be born.

References

ABRAMOWITZ, A. A. 2001. Mr Mayhew, Meet Mr DeLay. *PS: Political Science and Politics*, 34: 257–8.

ALDRICH, J. A. 2001. Congress: The Electoral Connection. Reflections on Its First Quarter-Century. *PS: Political Science and Politics*, 34: 259–64.

—— BERGER, M. M., and ROHDE, D. W. 2002. The Historical Variability in Conditional Party Government, 1877–1994. Ch. 2 in *Party, Process, and Political Change in Congress*, ed. D. W. Brady and M. D. McCubbins. Stanford, CA: Stanford University Press.

ARNOLD, R. D. 1990. *The Logic of Congressional Action*. New Haven, CT: Yale University Press.

BAGEHOT, W. 1867. *The English Constitution*. London: Chapman and Hall.

BAILEY, S. K. 1950. *Congress Makes a Law: The Story behind the Employment Act of 1946*. New York: Columbia University Press.

BAWN, K., and KOGER, G. 2008. Effort, Intensity and Position Taking: Reconsidering Obstruction in the Pre-Cloture Senate. *Journal of Theoretical Politics*, 20: 67–92.

BINDER, S. A., and SMITH, S. S. 1997. *Politics or Principle? Filibustering in the United States Senate*. Washington, DC: Brookings Institution Press.

BOLLING, R. 1965. *House Out of Order*. New York: E.P. Dutton.

—— 1968. *Power in the House: A History of Leadership in the House of Representatives*. New York: E. P. Dutton.

BRADY, D. W., and VOLDEN, C. 1998. *Revolving Gridlock: Politics and Policy from Carter to Clinton*. Boulder, CO: Westview.

—— and HAN, H. C. 2006. Polarization Then and Now: A Historical Perspective. Ch. 3 in *Red and Blue Nation*, vol. 1: *Characteristics and Causes of America's Polarized Politics*, ed. P. S. Nivola and D. W. Brady. Washington, DC: Brookings Institution Press.

BURNS, J. M. 1949. *Congress on Trial: The Legislative Process and the Administrative State*. New York: Harper and Brothers.

—— 1963. *The Deadlock of Democracy: Four-Party Politics in America*. Englewood Cliffs, NJ: Prentice-Hall.

CAMERON, C. 2000. *Veto Bargaining: Presidents and the Politics of Negative Power*. New York: Cambridge University Press.

[39] Ingredients of this indictment may be found in Eilperin 2006; Mann and Ornstein 2008.
[40] Works in this vein are Hall 1996; Sinclair 2000; Lee 2009.

CLEAVELAND, F. N. 1969. Legislating for Urban Areas: An Overview, pp. 350–89 in *Congress and Urban Problems*, ed. F. N. Cleaveland. Washington, DC: Brookings Institution Press.

COOPER, J., and BRADY, D. W. 1981. Institutional Context and Leadership Style: The House from Cannon to Rayburn. *American Political Science Review*, 75: 411–25.

COX, G. W., and McCUBBINS, M. D. 1993. *Legislative Leviathan: Party Government in the House*. Berkeley: University of California Press.

—— and McCUBBINS, M. D. 2005. *Setting the Agenda: Responsible Party Government in the U.S. House of Representatives*. New York: Cambridge University Press.

DAVIDSON, R. H. 1969. *The Role of the Congressman*. New York: Pegasus.

DAVIS, S. 2007. Pelosi Brings End to "Hastert Rule." *Roll Call*, 29 May.

DODD, L. C. 1977. Congress and the Quest for Power. Ch. 14 in *Congress Reconsidered*, ed. L. C. Dodd and B. I. Oppenheimer. New York: Praeger.

EILPERIN, J. 2006. *Fight Club Politics: How Partisanship Is Poisoning the House of Representatives*. Lanham, MD: Rowman and Littlefield.

ELKINS, S., and McKITRICK, E. 1993. *The Age of Federalism: The Early American Republic, 1788–1800*. New York: Oxford University Press.

ERIKSON, R. 1971. The Advantage of Incumbency in Congressional Elections. *Polity*, 3: 395–405.

EVANS, D. 2004. *Greasing the Wheels: Using Pork Barrel Projects to Build Majority Coalitions in Congress*. New York: Cambridge University Press.

FENNO, JR., R. F. 1962. The House Appropriations Committee as a Political System. *American Political Science Review*, 56: 310–24.

—— 1966. *The Power of the Purse: Appropriations Politics in Congress*. Boston: Little, Brown.

—— 1973. *Congressmen in Committees*. Boston: Little, Brown.

FIORINA, M. P. 1974. *Representatives, Roll Calls, and Constituencies*. Lexington, MA: D.C. Heath.

—— 1977. *Congress: Keystone of the Washington Establishment*. New Haven, CT: Yale University Press.

—— 1987. Alternative Rationales for Restrictive Procedures. *Journal of Law, Economics, and Organization*, 3: 337–45.

—— 1995. Afterword (But Undoubtedly Not the Last Word, pp. 303–12 in *Positive Theories of Congressional Institutions*, ed. K. A. Shepsle and B. R. Weingast. Ann Arbor: University of Michigan Press.

FISK, C., and CHEMERINSKY, E. 1997. The Filibuster. *Stanford Law Review*, 49: 181–254.

FROMAN, JR., L. A. 1963. *Congressmen and Their Constituencies*. Chicago: Rand McNally.

GROFMAN, B., GRIFFIN, R., and GLAZER, A. 1991. Is the Senate More Liberal Than the House: Another Look. *Legislative Studies Quarterly*, 16: 281–95.

HALL, R. L. 1996. *Participation in Congress*. New Haven, CT: Yale University Press.

HUITT, R. K. 1954. The Congressional Committee: A Case Study. *American Political Science Review*, 48: 340–65.

—— 1957. The Morse Committee Assignment Controversy: A Study in Senate Norms. *American Political Science Review*, 51: 313–29.

—— 1961. The Outsider in the Senate: An Alternative Role. *American Political Science Review*, 55: 565–75.

HUNTINGTON, S. P. 1968. *Political Order in Changing Societies*. New Haven, CT: Yale University Press.

JONES, C. O. 2005. *The Presidency in a Separated System*, 2nd edn. Washington, DC: Brookings Institution Press.

KERNELL, S. 1973. Is the Senate More Liberal than the House? *Journal of Politics*, 35: 332–66.

KOENIG, L. W. 1962. Kennedy and the 87th Congress, pp. 80–1 in *American Government Annual, 1962–1963*. New York: Holt, Rinehart and Winston.

KOGER, G. 2010. *Filibustering: A Political History of Obstruction in the House and Senate*. Chicago: University of Chicago Press.

KREHBIEL, K. 1992. *Information and Legislative Organization*. Ann Arbor: University of Michigan Press.

——1998. *Pivotal Politics: A Theory of U.S. Lawmaking*. Chicago: University of Chicago Press.

LEE, F. E. 2009. *Beyond Ideology: Politics, Principle, and Partisanship in the U.S. Senate*. Chicago: University of Chicago Press.

MCCARTY, N., and GROSECLOSE, T. 2000. The Politics of Blame: Bargaining Before an Audience. *American Journal of Political Science*, 45: 100–19.

MANLEY, J. R. 1965. The House Committee on Ways and Means: Conflict Management in a Congressional Committee. *American Political Science Review*, 59: 927–39.

MANN, T. E., and ORNSTEIN, N. J. 2008. *The Broken Branch: How Congress is Failing America and How to Get it Back on Track*. New York: Oxford University Press.

MATTHEWS, D. R. 1960. *U.S. Senators and Their World*. Chapel Hill: University of North Carolina Press.

MAYHEW, D. R. 1974a. *Congress: The Electoral Connection*. New Haven, CT: Yale University Press.

——1974b. Congressional Elections: The Case of the Vanishing Marginals. *Polity*, 6: 295–317.

——2000. *America's Congress: Actions in the Public Sphere, James Madison through Newt Gingrich*. New Haven, CT: Yale University Press.

——2011. *Partisan Balance: Why Political Parties Don't Kill the U.S. Constitutional System*. Princeton, NJ: Princeton University Press.

MEZEY, M. L. 1993. Legislatures: Individual Purpose and Institutional Performance. Ch. 13 in *Political Science: The State of the Discipline II*, ed. A. W. Finifter. Washington, DC: American Political Science Association.

MUNGER, F. J., and FENNO, JR., R. F. 1962. *National Politics and Federal Aid to Education*. Syracuse, NY: Syracuse University Press.

NAGEL, E. 1961. *The Structure of Science: Problems in the Logic of Scientific Explanation*. New York: Harcourt, Brace and World.

PATTERSON, S. C. 1978. The Semi-Sovereign Congress. Ch. 4 in *The New American Political System*, ed. A. King. Washington, DC: American Enterprise Institute.

PEABODY, R. L. 1969. Research on Congress: A Coming of Age. Pt I in *Congress: Two Decades of Analysis* ed. R. K. Huitt and R. L. Peabody. New York: Harper and Row.

PEARSON, K., and SCHICKLER, E. 2009. Discharge Petitions, Agenda Control, and the Congressional Committee System, 1929–1976. *Journal of Politics*, 71: 1238–56.

POLSBY, N. W. 1968. The Institutionalization of the U.S. House of Representatives. *American Political Science Review*, 62: 144–68.

——2004. *How Congress Evolves: Social Bases of Institutional Change*. New York: Oxford University Press.

——GALLAGHER, M., and RUNDQUIST, B. S. 1969. The Growth of the Seniority System in the U.S. House of Representatives. *American Political Science Review*, 63: 787–807.

——and SCHICKLER, E. 2002. Landmarks in the Study of Congress since 1945. *Annual Review of Political Science*, 5: 333–67.

POOLE, K. T., and ROSENTHAL, H. 2007. *Ideology and Congress*. New Brunswick, NJ: Transaction.

ROHDE, D. W. 1991. *Parties and Leaders in the Postreform House*. Chicago: University of Chicago Press.

SCHATTSCHNEIDER, E. E. 1942. *Party Government*. New York: Holt, Rinehart and Winston.

SCHICKLER, E. 2001. *Disjointed Pluralism: Institutional Innovation and the Development of the U.S. Congress*. Princeton, NJ: Princeton University Press.

—— and Pearson, K. 2009. Agenda Control, Majority Party Power, and the House Committee on Rules, 1937–1952. *Legislative Studies Quarterly*, 34: 455–91.

Shepsle, K. A., and Weingast, B. R. 1987. The Institutional Foundations of Committee Power. *American Political Science Review*, 81: 85–104.

—— and Weingast, B. R. 1995. Positive Theories of Congressional Institutions, pp. 5–35 in *Positive Theories of Congressional Institutions*, ed. K. A. Shepsle and B. R. Weingast. Ann Arbor: University of Michigan Press.

Sinclair, B. 2000. *Unorthodox Lawmaking: New Legislative Processes in the U.S. Congress*, 2nd edn. Washington, DC: Congressional Quarterly Press.

Sundquist, J. L. 1981. *The Decline and Resurgence of Congress*. Washington, DC: Brookings Institution Press.

Theriault, S. M. 2005. *Congressional Competition, Public Attention, and Voter Retribution*. Columbus: Ohio State University Press. *Toward a More Responsible Two-party System*. 1950. A Report of the Committee on Political Parties, American Political Science Association. New York: Rinehart.

Wawro, G. J., and Schickler, E. 2006. *Filibuster: Obstruction and Lawmaking in the U.S. Senate*. Princeton, NJ: Princeton University Press.

Weingast, B. R., and Marshall, W. J. 1988. The Industrial Organization of Congress; or, Why Legislatures, Like Firms, Are Not Organized as Markets. *Journal of Political Economy*, 96: 132–63.

White, L. D. 1958. *The Republican Era: A Study in Administrative History, 1869–1901*. New York: Macmillan.

White, W. S. 1956. *Citadel: The Story of the U.S. Senate*. New York: Harper and Brothers.

Wilson, W. 1981 [1885]. *Congressional Government: A Study in American Politics*. Baltimore, MD: Johns Hopkins University Press.

Zelizer, J. E. 2004. *On Capitol Hill: The Struggle to Reform Congress and Its Consequences, 1948–2000*. New York: Cambridge University Press.

Name Index

Subject Index

Note: All cited legal cases are indexed under Supreme Court.